MICROECONOMICS ESSENTIALS

Elasticity

The elasticity of demand is a measure of how sensitive the quantity demanded is to a change in price.

$$E_d = \frac{\text{Percentage Change in Quantity Demanded}}{\text{Percentage Change in Price}} = \frac{\%\Delta Q_{demanded}}{\%\Delta \text{Price}} = \frac{\dfrac{Q_{before} - Q_{after}}{(Q_{before} + Q_{after})/2}}{\dfrac{P_{before} - P_{after}}{(P_{before} + P_{after})/2}}$$

Inelastic Demand

$|E_d| < 1$

Quantity is not very Sensitive to Price

Revenue and price move in same direction.

$$R = P \times Q$$

Elastic Demand

$|E_d| > 1$

Quantity is very Sensitive to Price

Revenue and price move in opposite directions.

$$R = P \times Q$$

Monopoly

Marginal Revenue, MR, is the change in total revenue from selling an additional unit.

Marginal Cost, MC, is the change in total cost from producing an additional unit.

To maximize profit, a firm produces until $MR = MC$.

The more inelastic the demand, the greater the monopoly markup of P over MC.

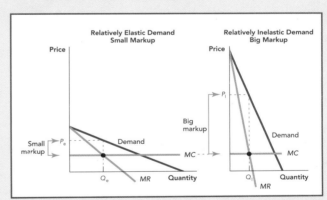

The Principles of Price Discrimination

1a. If the demand curves are different, it is more profitable to set different prices in different markets than a single price that covers all markets.

1b. To maximize profit the firm should set a higher price in markets with more inelastic demand.

2. Arbitrage makes it difficult for a firm to set different prices in different markets, thereby reducing the profit from price discrimination.

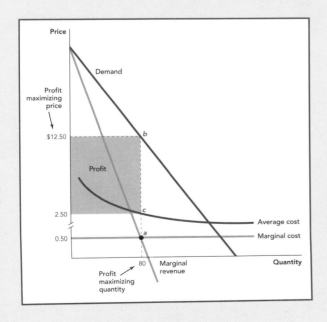

Externalities

An **external cost** is a cost paid by people other than the consumer or the producer trading in the market: for example, pollution creates an external cost. When external costs are significant, output is too high.

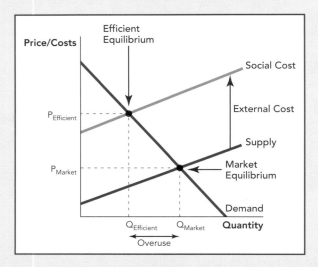

An **external benefit** is a benefit received by people other than the consumers or producers trading in the market; for example, flu shots create an external benefit. When external benefits are significant, output is too low.

Labor Markets

In a competitive market, firms will hire workers until the marginal product of labor equals the wage, $MPL = W$.

Incentives and Labor Markets

Three lessons of good incentive design:

1. You get what you pay for but what you pay for is not always what you want.
2. Tie pay to performance to reduce risk.
3. Money isn't everything.

A **compensating differential** is a difference in wages that offsets differences in working conditions.

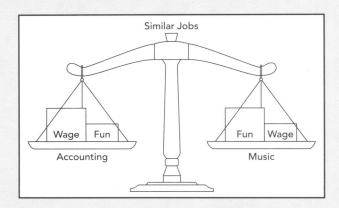

Public Goods and Tragedy of the Commons

A **good is nonexcludable** if people who don't pay cannot be easily prevented from using the good.

A **good is nonrival** if one person's use of the good does not reduce the ability of another person to use the same good.

A **free rider** enjoys the benefits of a public good without paying a share of the costs.

A **forced rider** is someone who pays a share of the costs of a public good but who does not enjoy the benefits.

The **tragedy of the commons** is the tendency of any resource that is unowned and hence nonexcludable to be overused and undermaintained.

The Four Types of Goods

	Excludable	Nonexcludable
Rival	**Private Goods**	**Common Resources**
	Jeans	Tuna in the ocean
	Hamburgers	The environment
	Contact lenses	Public roads
Nonrival	**Nonrival Private Goods**	**Public Goods**
	Cable TV	Asteroid deflection
	Wi-Fi	National defense
	Digital music	Mosquito control

MODERN PRINCIPLES:
ECONOMICS

MODERN PRINCIPLES:
ECONOMICS

Tyler Cowen
George Mason University

Alex Tabarrok
George Mason University

Worth Publishers

Senior Publisher: Craig Bleyer

Senior Acquisitions Editor: Sarah Dorger

Senior Marketing Manager: Scott Guile

Consulting Editor: Paul Shensa

Development Editor: Bruce Kaplan

Associate Media and Supplements Editor: Lorraine Klimowich

Assistant Supplements Editor: Tom Acox

Director of Market Research and Development: Steven Rigolosi

Associate Managing Editor: Tracey Kuehn

Project Editors: Dana Kasowitz
            Timothy Rodes, Pre-PressPMG

Art Director: Babs Reingold

Cover Designer: Kevin Kall

Text Designer: Lissi Sigillo

Photo Editor: Christine Buese

Photo Researcher: Julie Tesser

Production Manager: Barbara Anne Seixas

Composition: Pre-PressPMG

Printing and Binding: RR Donnelley

Cover Photo: Ralph Mercer/Getty Images

Library of Congress Cataloging-in-Publication Number: 2009925112

ISBN-13: 978-1-4292-0227-5
ISBN-10: 1-4929-0227-0

Printed in the United States of America

Second Printing

Worth Publishers
41 Madison Avenue
New York, NY 10010
www.worthpublishers.com

Economics is the study of how to get the most out of life.

Tyler and Alex

ABOUT THE AUTHORS

Tyler Cowen (left) is Holbert C. Harris Professor of Economics at George Mason University. His latest book is *Create Your Own Economy: The Path to Prosperity in a Disordered World*. With Alex Tabarrok, he writes an economics blog at www.marginalrevolution.com. He has published in the *American Economic Review, Journal of Political Economy*, and many other economics journals. He also writes regularly for the popular press, including the *New York Times, the Washington Post, Forbes, the Wilson Quarterly, Money Magazine*, and many other outlets.

Alex Tabarrok (right) is Bartley J. Madden Chair in Economics at the Mercatus Center at George Mason University and director of research for *The Independent Institute*. His recent research looks at bounty hunters, judicial incentives and elections, crime control, patent reform, methods to increase the supply of human organs for transplant, and the regulation of pharmaceuticals. He is the editor of the books *Entrepreneurial Economics: Bright Ideas from the Dismal Science* and *The Voluntary City: Choice, Community, and Civil Society* among others. His papers have appeared in the *Journal of Law and Economics, Public Choice, Economic Inquiry, the Journal of Health Economics, the Journal of Theoretical Politics, the American Law and Economics Review,* and many other journals. Popular articles have appeared in the *New York Times, the Wall Street Journal, Forbes,* and many other magazines and newspapers.

BRIEF CONTENTS

Preface xxv

CHAPTER 1 The Big Ideas 1

Part 1: Supply and Demand

CHAPTER 2 Supply and Demand...13

CHAPTER 3 Equilibrium: How Supply and Demand Determine Prices.........33

CHAPTER 4 Elasticity and Its Applications.................................51

Part 2: The Price System

CHAPTER 5 The Price System: Signals, Speculation, and Prediction 79

CHAPTER 6 Price Ceilings 97

CHAPTER 7 Price Floors, Taxes, and Subsidies 119

CHAPTER 8 International Trade 143

CHAPTER 9 Externalities: When Prices Send the Wrong Signals 169

Part 3: Firms and Factor Markets

CHAPTER 10 Profits, Prices, and Costs under Competition 187

CHAPTER 11 Monopoly 219

CHAPTER 12 Price Discrimination...243

CHAPTER 13 Cartels, Games, and Network Goods 265

CHAPTER 14 Labor Markets 289

CHAPTER 15 Getting Incentives Right: Lessons for Business, Sports, Politics, and Life 313

CHAPTER 16 Stock Markets and Personal Finance...................331

Part 4: Government

CHAPTER 17 Public Goods and the Tragedy of the Commons 347

CHAPTER 18 Economics, Ethics, and Public Policy 365

CHAPTER 19 Political Economy 381

Part 5: Economic Growth

CHAPTER 20 GDP and The Measurement of Progress 405

CHAPTER 21 The Wealth of Nations and Economic Growth 427

CHAPTER 22 Growth, Capital Accumulation and the Economics of Ideas: Catching Up vs. The Cutting Edge....................451

CHAPTER 23 Saving, Investment, and the Financial System......................483

Part 6: Business Fluctuations

CHAPTER 24 Unemployment and Labor Force Participation 513

CHAPTER 25 Inflation and the Quantity Theory of Money 537

CHAPTER 26 Business Fluctuations and the Dynamic Aggregate Demand–Aggregate Supply Model...561

CHAPTER 27 The Real Business Cycle Model: Shocks and Transmission Mechanisms 589

Part 7: Macroeconomic Policy and Institutions

CHAPTER 28 The Federal Reserve System and Open Market Operations...609

CHAPTER 29 Monetary Policy...633

CHAPTER 30 The Federal Budget: Taxes and Spending 655

CHAPTER 31 Fiscal Policy 679

Part 8: International Economics

CHAPTER 32 International Finance..701

APPENDIX A Reading Graphs and Making Graphs.....................................A-1

APPENDIX B Answers to Check Yourself Questions B-1

Glossary G–1

References R–1

Index I–0

CONTENTS

Preface   xxv

CHAPTER 1 The Big Ideas 1

Big Idea One: Incentives Matter   2

Big Idea Two: Good Institutions Align Self-Interest with the
 Social Interest   2

Big Idea Three: Trade-offs Are Everywhere   3

   Opportunity Cost   4

Big Idea Four: Thinking on the Margin   5

Big Idea Five: Tampering with the Laws of Supply and Demand
 Has Consequences   6

Big Idea Six: The Importance of Wealth and Economic Growth   6

Big Idea Seven: Institutions Matter   7

Big Idea Eight: Economic Booms and Busts Cannot Be Avoided
 but Can Be Moderated   8

Big Idea Nine: Prices Rise When the Government Prints
 Too Much Money   8

Big Idea Ten: Central Banking Is a Hard Job   9

The Biggest Idea of All: Economics Is Fun   9

Chapter Review   10

Part 1: Supply and Demand

CHAPTER 2 Supply and Demand 13

The Demand Curve for Oil   13

   Consumer Surplus   16

   What Shifts the Demand Curve?   17

   Important Demand Shifters   17

      Income   18
      Population   18
      Price of Substitutes   18
      Price of Complements   18
      Expectations   19
      Tastes   19

The Supply Curve for Oil   20

   Producer Surplus   23

   What Shifts the Supply Curve?   23

   Important Supply Shifters   23

      Technological Innovations and Changes in the Price of Inputs   24
      Taxes and Subsidies   24
      Expectations   25
      Entry or Exit of Producers   25
      Changes in Opportunity Costs   26

Takeaway   27

Chapter Review   28

CHAPTER 3 Equilibrium: How Supply and Demand Determine Prices 33

Equilibrium and the Adjustment Process 33
  Who Competes with Whom? 35

Gains from Trade Are Maximized at the Equilibrium Price and Quantity 35

Does the Model Work? Evidence from the Laboratory 38

Shifting Demand and Supply Curves 40

Terminology: Demand Compared to Quantity Demanded and Supply Compared to Quantity Supplied 42

Understanding the Price of Oil 44

Takeaway 46

Chapter Review 47

CHAPTER 4 Elasticity and Its Applications 51

The Elasticity of Demand 52
  Determinants of the Elasticity of Demand 53
  Calculating the Elasticity of Demand 54
    Using the Midpoint Method to Calculate the Elasticity of Demand 55
  Total Revenues and the Elasticity of Demand 56
  Applications of Demand Elasticity 58
    How American Farmers Have Worked Themselves Out of a Job 58
    Why the War on Drugs Is Hard to Win 59

The Elasticity of Supply 60
  Determinants of the Elasticity of Supply 61
  Calculating the Elasticity of Supply 63
    Using the Midpoint Method to Calculate the Elasticity of Supply 63
  Applications of Supply Elasticity 63
    Gun Buyback Programs 63
    The Economics of Slave Redemption 65

Using Elasticities for Quick Predictions (Optional) 68
    How Much Would the Price of Oil Fall if the Artic National Wildlife Refuge Were Opened up for Drilling? 68

Takeaway 69

Chapter Review 69

Appendix: Using Excel to Calculate Elasticities 74

Appendix: Other Types of Elasticities 76
  The Cross-Price Elasticity of Demand 76
  The Income Elasticity of Demand 76

Part 2: The Price System

CHAPTER 5 The Price System: Signals, Speculation, and Prediction 79

Markets Link the World 79

Markets Link to Each Other 80
    From Oil to Candy Bars and Brick Driveways 81

Solving the Great Economic Problem 81

A Price Is a Signal Wrapped Up in an Incentive   84

Speculation   85

Signal Watching   88

Prediction Markets   88

Takeaway   91

Chapter Review   91

CHAPTER 6 Price Ceilings 97

Price Ceilings   97

   Shortages   98

   Reductions in Quality   98

   Wasteful Lines and Other Search Costs   99

   Lost Gains from Trade   101

   Misallocation of Resources 102

      Advanced Material: The Loss from Random Allocation   104

      Misallocation and Production Chaos   104

   The End of Price Ceilings   105

Rent Controls (Optional Section)   106

   Shortages   106

   Reductions in Product Quality   108

   Wasteful Lines, Search Costs, and Lost Gains from Trade   108

   Misallocation of Resources   109

   Rent Regulation   109

Arguments for Price Controls   110

Universal Price Controls   111

Takeaway   112

Chapter Review   113

CHAPTER 7 Price Floors, Taxes, and Subsidies 119

Price Floors   119

   Surpluses   120

   Lost Gains from Trade   121

   Wasteful Increases in Quality   122

   Misallocation of Resources   124

Commodity Taxes   125

   Who Ultimately Pays the Tax Does Not Depend on Who Writes the Check   125

   Who Ultimately Pays the Tax Depends on the Relative Elasticities of Supply and Demand   127

      The Wedge Shortcut   128

   Health Insurance Mandates and Tax Analysis   130

   Who Pays the Cigarette Tax?   130

   A Commodity Tax Raises Revenue and Creates Lost Gains from Trade (Deadweight Loss)   131

Subsidies   133

   King Cotton and the Deadweight Loss of Water Subsidies   135

   Wage Subsidies   136

Takeaway   137

Chapter Review   138

CHAPTER 8 International Trade..143

Why Trade? 143
  The Division of Knowledge 143
  Economies of Scale and Creating Competition 145
  Comparative Advantage 145
  Adam Smith on Trade 149

Analyzing Trade with Supply and Demand 149
  Analyzing Tariffs with Demand and Supply 150

The Costs of Protectionism 152
  Winners and Losers from Trade 154

Arguments against International Trade 155
  Trade and Jobs 155
  Child Labor 156
  Trade and National Security 158
  Key Industries 158
  Strategic Trade Protectionism 159

Trade and Globalization 159

Takeaway 160
Chapter Review 160

CHAPTER 9 Externalities: When Prices Send the Wrong Signals 169

External Costs, External Benefits, and Efficiency 170
  External Costs 171
  External Benefits 173

Private Solutions to Externality Problems 175

Government Solutions to Externality Problems 177
  Command and Control 177
  Tradable Allowances 179
  Comparing Tradable Allowances and Pigouvian Taxes-Advanced Material 181

Takeaway 182
Chapter Review 182

Part 3: Firms and Factor Markets

CHAPTER 10 Profits, Prices, and Costs under Competition...........187

What Price to Set? 188

What Quantity to Produce ? 190

Invisible Hand Property #1: The Minimization of the Total Costs of Production 193

Profits and the Average Cost Curve 195

When to Enter and Exit an Industry 198

Entry and Exit with Uncertainty and Sunk Costs 199

Invisible Hand Property #2: The Balance of Industries 200
  Creative Destruction 201

Deriving Industry Supply Curves 202
  Constant Cost Industries 202
  Increasing Cost Industries 205
  A Special Case: The Decreasing Cost Industry 207

Takeaway   208

Chapter Review   209

Appendix: Using Excel to Graph Cost Curves   216

CHAPTER 11 Monopoly..219

Market Power   220

How a Firm Uses Market Power to Maximize Profit   220

   The Elasticity of Demand and the Monopoly Markup   223

The Costs of Monopoly: Deadweight Loss   225

The Costs of Monopoly: Corruption and Inefficiency   226

The Benefits of Monopoly: Incentives for Research
and Development   227

   Patent Buyouts-A Potential Solution?   228

Economies of Scale and the Regulation of Monopoly   229

   I Want My MTV   231

   Electric Shock   232

   California's Perfect Storm   233

Other Sources of Market Power   234

Takeaway   235

Chapter Review   235

CHAPTER 12 Price Discrimination 243

Price Discrimination   243

   Preventing Arbitrage   245

Price Discrimination is Common   246

   Universities and Perfect Price Discrimination   248

Is Price Discrimination Bad?   250

   Why Misery Loves Company and How Price Discrimination Helps to Cover
   Fixed Costs   251

Tying and Bundling   252

   Tying   252

   Bundling   253

   Bundling and Cable TV   255

Takeaway   255

Chapter Review   256

Appendix: Solving Price Discrimination Problems with Excel
(Advanced Section)   261

CHAPTER 13 Cartels, Games, and Network Goods........................265

Cartels   266

   Cheating on the OPEC Cartel   268

   New Entrants and Demand Response Break Down Cartels   272

   Sustainable Cartels in a Market Setting   273

   Government Prosecution and Regulation   274

      Government Supported Cartels   274

   Summing Up: Successful Cartels   275

Network Goods   275

   Network Goods Are Usually Sold by Monopolies or Oligopolies   276

   The "Best" Product May Not Always Win   276

   Standard Wars Are Common   278

Competition "For the Market" instead of "In the Market" 279
Music Is a Network Good 280

Takeaway 281

Chapter Review 281

CHAPTER 14 Labor Markets 289

The Demand for Labor and the Marginal Product of Labor 289

Supply of Labor 291

Labor Market Issues 293

Why Do Janitors in the United States Earn More Than Janitors in India even When They Do the Same Job? 293
Human Capital 295
Compensating Differentials 296
Do Unions Raise Wages? 299

How Bad Is Labor Market Discrimination, or Can Lakisha Catch a Break? 300

Statistical Discrimination 301
Preference-based Discrimination 301
Discrimination by Employers 302
Discrimination by Customers 303
Discrimination by Employees 304
Discrimination by Government 304
Why Discrimination Isn't Always Easy to Identify 305

Takeaway 306

Chapter Review 307

CHAPTER 15 Getting Incentives Right: Lessons for Business, Sports, Politics, and Life 313

Lesson One: You Get What You Pay For 313

Prisons for Profit? 315
Piece Rates vs. Hourly Wages 316

Lesson Two: Tie Pay to Performance to Reduce Risk 317

Tournament Theory 318
Improving Executive Compensation with Pay for Relative Performance 319
Environment Risk and Ability Risk 320
Tournaments and Grades 321

Lesson Three: Money Isn't Everything 322

Takeaway 324

Chapter Review 325

CHAPTER 16 Stock Markets and Personal Finance 331

Passive vs. Active Investing 331

Why Is It Hard to Beat the Market? 333

How to Really Pick Stocks, Seriously 335

Diversify 335
Avoid High Fees 337
Compound Returns Build Wealth 338
The No Free Lunch Principle or No Return Without Risk 339

Other Benefits and Costs of Stock Markets   341
    Bubble, Bubble, Toil, and Trouble   342
Takeaway   343
Chapter Review   344

Part 4: Government

CHAPTER 17 Public Goods and the Tragedy of the Commons.....347

Four Types of Goods   348
Private Goods and Public Goods   349
Nonrival Private Goods   351
    The Peculiar Case of Advertising   351
Common Resources and the Tragedy of the Commons   352
    Happy Solutions to the Tragedy of the Commons   354
Takeaway   355
Chapter Review 356
    Appendix: The Tragedy of the Commons: How Fast?   362

CHAPTER 18 Economics, Ethics, and Public Policy.........................365

The Case for Exporting Pollution and Importing Kidneys   366
Exploitation   367
Meddlesome Preferences   368
Fair and Equal Treatment   369
Cultural Goods and Paternalism   369
Poverty, Inequality, and the Distribution of Income   370
    Rawls's Maximin Principle   370
    Utilitarianism   371
    Robert Nozick's Entitlement Theory   372
Who Counts? Immigration   374
Economic Ethics   375
Takeaway   376
Chapter Review   376

CHAPTER 19 Political Economy..381

Voters and the Incentive to be Ignorant   382
    Why Rational Ignorance Matters   383
Special Interests and the Incentive to Be Informed   383
    One Formula for Political Success: Diffuse Costs, Concentrate Benefits   385
Voter Myopia and Political Business Cycles   387
Two Cheers for Democracy   389
    The Median Voter Theorem   390
    Democracy and Non-Democracy   392
    Democracy and Famine   393
    Democracy and Growth   395
Takeaway   396
Chapter Review   397

Part 5: Economic Growth

CHAPTER 20 GDP and The Measurement of Progress 405

What Is GDP? 406
GDP Is the Market Value . . . 407
. . . of All Final . . . 407
. . . Goods and Services . . . 407
. . . Produced . . . 408
. . . within a Country . . . 408
. . . in a Year 408

Growth Rates 409

Nominal vs. Real GDP 409
Real GDP Growth 410
Real GDP Growth per Capita 410

Cyclical and Short-Run Changes in GDP 412

The Many Ways of Splitting GDP 413
The National Spending Approach: $Y = C + I + G + NX$ 414
The Factor Income Approach: The Other Side of the Spending Coin 415
Why Split 416

Problems with GDP as a Measure of Output and Welfare 416
GDP Does not Count the Underground Economy 417
GDP Does not Count Nonmarket Production 418
GDP Does not Count Leisure 418
GDP Does not Count Bads: Environmental Costs 418
GDP Does not Measure the Distribution of Income 419

Takeaway 420
Chapter Review 421

CHAPTER 21 The Wealth of Nations and Economic Growth 427

Key Facts about the Wealth of Nations and Economic Growth 428
Fact One: GDP per Capita Today Varies Enormously among Nations 428
Fact Two: Everyone Used to Be Poor 429
Fact Three: There Are Growth Miracles and Growth Disasters 432
Summarizing the Facts: Good and Bad News 433

Understanding the Wealth of Nations 433
The Factors of Production 433

Incentives and Institutions 435
Institutions 437
Institutions of Economic Growth 437
Property Rights 437
Honest Government 438
Political Stability 439
A Dependable Legal System 439
Competitive and Open Markets 440
Institutions and Growth Miracles Revisited 441

Takeaway 442
Chapter Review 442
Appendix: The Magic of Compound Growth:
Using a Spreadsheet 447

CHAPTER 22 Growth, Capital Accumulation, and the
Economics of Ideas: Catching Up vs. The Cutting Edge..............451

The Solow Model and Catch-Up Growth 452
  Capital, Production and Diminishing Returns 453
  Capital Growth Equals Investment Minus Depreciation 455
  Why Capital Alone Cannot Be the Key to Economic Growth 456
  Better Ideas Drive Long-Run Economic Growth 458

The Solow Model—Details and Further Lessons (Optional section) 460
  The Solow Model and an Increase in the Investment Rate 461
  The Solow Model and Conditional Convergence 463
  From Catching Up to Cutting Edge 464
  Solow and the Economics of Ideas in One Diagram 464

Growing on the Cutting Edge: The Economics of Ideas 466
  Research and Development Is Investment for Profit 466
  Spillovers, and Why There Aren't Enough Good Ideas 468
  Government's Role in the Production of New Ideas 468
  Market Size and Research and Development 469

The Future of Economic Growth 470

Takeaway 472

Chapter Review 473

Appendix: Excellent Growth 478

CHAPTER 23 Saving, Investment, and the Financial System 483

The Supply of Savings 484
  Individuals Want to Smooth Consumption 484
  Individuals Are Impatient 485
  Marketing and Psychological Factors 486
  The Interest Rate 486

The Demand to Borrow 487
  Individuals Want to Smooth Consumption 487
  Borrowing Is Necessary to Finance Large Investments 488
  The Interest Rate 489

Equilibrium in the Market for Loanable Funds 489
  Shifts in Supply and Demand 490

The Role of Intermediaries: Banks, Bonds, and Stock Markets 492
  Banks 493
  The Bond Market 494
    Bond Prices and Interest Rates 496
  The Stock Market 497

What Happens When Intermediation Fails? 498
  Insecure Property Rights 498
  Controls on Interest Rates and Inflation 499
  Politicized Lending and Government-Owned Banks 501
  Bank Failures and Panics 501

Takeaway 503

Chapter Review 503

Appendix: Bond Pricing and Arbitrage...508

Part 6: Business Fluctuations

CHAPTER 24 Unemployment and Labor Force Participation.........513

Defining Unemployment 515
How Good an Indicator Is the Unemployment Rate? 515

Frictional Unemployment 516

Structural Unemployment 517
Labor Regulations and Structural Unemployment 518
Unemployment Benefits 519
Minimum Wages and Unions 520
Employment Protection Laws 521
A Tale of Two Riots 522
Labor Regulations to Reduce Structural Unemployment 523
Factors That Affect Structural Unemployment 524

Cyclical Unemployment 524
The Natural Unemployment Rate 526

Labor Force Participation 527
Lifecycle Effects and Demographics 527
Incentives 528
Taxes and Benefits 528
Incentives and the Increase in Female Labor Force Participation 529
How the Pill Increased Female Labor Force Participation 531

Takeaway 532
Chapter Review 533

CHAPTER 25 Inflation and the Quantity Theory of Money............537

Defining and Measuring Inflation 538
Price Indexes 538
Inflation in the United States and Around the World 539

The Quantity Theory of Money 542
The Cause of Inflation 543
An Inflation Parable 545

The Costs of Inflation 546
Price Confusion and Money Illusion 547
Inflation Redistributes Wealth 547
Hyperinflation and the Breakdown of Financial Intermediation 551
Inflation Interacts with Other Taxes 551
Inflation Is Painful to Stop 542

Takeaway 542
Chapter Review 543

Appendix: Get Real! An Excellent Adventure................................556

CHAPTER 26 Business Fluctuations and the Dynamic Aggregate
Demand–Aggregate Supply Model...561

A Skeleton Model 563
The Solow Growth Curve 563
Shifts in the Solow Growth Curve 564
The Dynamic Aggregate Demand Curve 564
Shifts in the Dynamic Aggregate Demand Curve 566

**The Real Business Cycle Model: Real Shocks and the Solow
Growth Curve** 567
Shocks to Aggregate Demand in the Real Business Cycle Model 569

The New Keynesian Model 570

  The Short-Run Aggregate Supply Curve 570

    Sticky Wages 571

    Shifting the SRAS Curve 571

    The Parable of the Angry Professor 572

    Sticky Prices 574

Shocks to Aggregate Demand in the New Keynesian Model 575

  An Increase in $\vec{M}$ the New Keynesian Model 575

  Shocks to the Components of Aggregate Demand 576

  A Decrease in $\vec{C}$ the New Keynesian Model 576

  Why Changes in $\vec{v}$ Tend to Be Temporary 577

  Other Factors That Shift the AD Curve 577

**Understanding the Great Depression: Aggregate Demand Shocks
and Real Shocks 579**

  Aggregate Demand Shocks and the Great Depression 579

  Real Shocks and the Great Depression 580

Takeaway 582

Chapter Review 583

CHAPTER 27 The Real Business Cycle Model: Shocks and
Transmission Mechanisms 589

Shocks 589

  Oil Shocks 590

  Shocks, Shocks, Shocks 593

How Transmission Mechanisms Amplify and Spread Shocks 593

  Intertemporal Substitution 594

  Uncertainty and Irreversible Investments 596

  Labor Adjustment Costs 597

  Time Bunching 598

  Sticky Wages and Prices 600

  Transmission Mechanisms: Summary 601

Takeaway 602

Chapter Review 603

Appendix: Business Fluctuations and the Solow Model.................606

Part 7: Macroeconomic Policy and Institutions

CHAPTER 28 The Federal Reserve System and Open Market
Operations 609

What Is the Federal Reserve System? 609

The U.S. Money Supplies 610

**Fractional Reserve Banking, the Reserve Ratio, and the Money
Multiplier 613**

How the Fed Controls the Money Supply 615

  Open Market Operations 615

    Open Market Operations and Interest Rates 616

    The Fed Controls a Real Rate Only in the Short Run 617

  Discount Rate Lending and the Term Auction Facility 617

    The Term Auction Facility 619

  Required Reserves and Payment of Interest on Reserves 620

The Federal Reserve and Systemic Risk   620

Revisiting Aggregate Demand and Monetary Policy   621

Who Controls the Fed?   623

Takeaway   624

Chapter Review   625

Appendix: The Money Multiplier Process in Detail 629

CHAPTER 29 Monetary Policy 633

Monetary Policy: The Best Case   634

Rules vs. Discretion   636

Reversing Course and Engineering a Decrease in AD   637

The Fed as Manager of Market Confidence   638

The Negative Real Shock Dilemma   639

The Problem with Positive Shocks:
The 1997–2006 Housing Boom and Bust   642

Takeaway   644

Chapter Review   644

CHAPTER 30 The Federal Budget: Taxes and Spending 655

Tax Revenues   655

The Individual Income Tax   656

Taxes on Capital Gains and Interest and Dividends   658
The Alternative Minimum Tax (AMT)   659

Social Security and Medicare Taxes   659

The Corporate Income Tax   660

The Bottom Line on the Distribution of Federal Taxes   660

Spending   662

Social Security   662

Defense   664

Medicare and Medicaid   665

Unemployment Insurance and Welfare Spending   665

Everything Else   666

The National Debt, Interest on the National Debt, and Deficits   667

Will the U.S. Government Go Bankrupt?   669

The Future Is Hard to Predict   670

Revenues and Spending Undercount the Role
of Government in the Economy   672

Takeaway   672

Chapter Review   673

CHAPTER 31 Fiscal Policy..679

Fiscal Policy: The Best Case   680

The Multiplier   681

The Limits to Fiscal Policy   682

Crowding Out   683

Selling More Bonds to Finance Fiscal Policy   683
Tax Rebates and Tax Cuts as a Tool of Fiscal Policy   684
A Special Case of Crowding Out: Ricardian Equivalence   685

A Drop in the Bucket: Can Government Spend Enough to Stimulate
Aggregate Demand? 687

A Matter of Timing 687

Automatic Stabilizers 689

Government Spending versus Tax Cuts as Expansionary Fiscal Policy 689

Fiscal Policy Does Not Work Well to Combat Real Shocks 690

When Fiscal Policy Might Make Matters Worse 692

So When Is Fiscal Policy a Good Idea? 693

Takeaway 694

Chapter Review 695

Part 8: International Economics

CHAPTER 32 International Finance 701

The U.S. Trade Deficit and Your Trade Deficit 702

The Balance of Payments 703

The Current Account 704

The Capital Account, Sometimes Called the Financial Account 704

The Official Reserves Account 705

How the Pieces Fit Together 705

Two Sides, One Coin 705

The Bottom Line on the Trade Deficit 707

What Are Exchange Rates? 707

Exchange Rate Determination in the Short Run 708

Changes in Demand for a Currency 709

Changes in the Supply of a Currency 710

Exchange Rate Determination in the Long Run 711

The Purchasing Power Parity Theorem Is only Approximately True 712

How Monetary and Fiscal Policy Affect Exchange Rates and How
Exchange Rates Affect Aggregate Demand 714

Monetary Policy 714

Fiscal Policy 716

Fixed vs. Floating Exchange Rates 716

The Problem with Pegs 717

What Are the IMF and the World Bank? 718

International Monetary Fund 718

The World Bank 719

Takeaway 720

Chapter Review 720

Appendix A Reading Graphs and Making Graphs A-1

Appendix B Answers to Check Yourself Questions B-1

Glossary G–1   References R–1   Index I–0

PREFACE: TO THE INSTRUCTOR

Economics has never seemed more relevant and more important, so welcome to the first edition of *Modern Principles: Economics.*

Make the invisible hand visible. Demonstrate the power of incentives. Present modern models and applications. Make it simpler. These were our goals in writing *Modern Principles: Economics.*

Make the Invisible Hand Visible

One of the most remarkable discoveries of economic science is that under the right conditions the pursuit of self-interest can promote the social good. Nobel laureate Vernon Smith put it this way:

> At the heart of economics is a scientific mystery . . . a scientific mystery as deep, fundamental and inspiring as that of the expanding universe or the forces that bind matter . . . How is order produced from freedom of choice?

We want students to be inspired by this mystery and by how economists have begun to solve it. Thus, we will explain how markets generate cooperation from people across the world, how prices act as signals and coordinate appropriate responses to changes in economic conditions, and how profit maximization leads to the minimization of industry costs (even though no one intends such an end). We strive to make the invisible hand visible.

In Chapter 5, for example, we show how the invisible hand links romantic American teenagers with Kenyan flower growers, Dutch clocks, British airplanes, Colombian coffee, and Finnish cell phones. We also show how prices signal information and how markets help to solve the *great economic problem* of arranging our limited resources to satisfy as many of our infinite wants as possible.

The focus on the invisible hand or the *price system* continues in Chapters 6 and 7. As in other texts, we show how a price ceiling causes a shortage. But a shortage in one market can spill over into other markets (for example, shortages of oil in the 1970s meant that oil rigs off the coast of California could not get enough oil to operate). In addition, a price ceiling reduces the incentive to move resources from low-valued uses to high-valued uses, so in the 1970s we saw long lines for gasoline in some states yet *at the same time* gas was plentiful in other states just a few hours away. Price ceilings, therefore, cause a misallocation of resources across markets as well as a shortage within a particular market. We think of Chapter 5 and especially Chapter 6 as a package: Chapter 5 illustrates the price system when it is working and Chapter 6 illustrates what happens when the price system is impeded.

Students who catch even a glimpse of the invisible hand learn something of great importance. Civilization is possible only because under some conditions the pursuit of self-interest promotes the public good.

In discussing the invisible hand, we bring more Hayekian economics into the classroom without proselytizing for Hayekian politics. That is, we want to show how prices communicate information and coordinate action while still recognizing that markets do not always communicate the right information. Thus, our chapters on the price system are rounded out with what we think is an equally interesting and compelling chapter on externalities. The subtitle of Chapter 9, When Prices Send the Wrong Signals, harkens directly back to Chapter 5. By giving examples where the price signal is right and examples where the price signal is wrong, we convey a sophisticated understanding of the role of prices.

Demonstrate the Power of Incentives

Our second goal in writing *Modern Principles: Economics* was to show—again and again—that incentives matter. In fact, incentives are the theme throughout *Modern Principles*, whether discussing the tragedy of the commons, political economy, or what economics has to say about wise investing. We also include Chapter 15, *Getting Incentives Right: Lessons for Business, Sports, Politics and Life*. In this chapter we explain topics such as the trade-offs between fixed salaries and piece rates, when tournaments work well, and how best to incentivize executives. This chapter can be read profitably by anyone with an interest in *incentive design*—by managers, teachers, even parents! Chapter 15 will be of special interest to business and MBA students (and professors).

Present Modern Models and Applications

"Modern" was our third goal in writing *Modern Principles: Economics*. For example, we include an entire chapter on price discrimination, in which we cover not just traditional models but also tying and bundling. Students today are familiar with tied goods like cell phones and minutes, or printers and ink, as well as with bundles like Microsoft Office. A modern microeconomics textbook should help students to *understand their world.*

Modern Principles is also an integrated textbook; our macroeconomics truly builds upon the microfoundations laid down in earlier chapters. In our chapter on costs (Chapter 10), we jettison some of the old and incorrect rules about when to enter and exit an industry and instead give students a more modern introduction to sunk costs, uncertainty, and the necessity of estimating lifetime expected profits. Our discussion is more modern than in other texts yet it's also simpler and more streamlined, with less focus on the menagerie of cost curves that in other texts chokes off learning.

Our modern discussion of cost curves connects with our discussion of the real business cycle in Chapter 27. In that chapter we show how uncertainty and sunk costs can cause businesses and workers to delay investment decisions during a recession. Uncertainty and sunk costs are exactly the same principles that we use to discuss entry and exit decisions in Chapter 10. Macroeconomics in *Modern Principles* is truly based upon and consistent with microeconomic intuitions.

We also present a modern perspective on the costs and benefits of market power. A significant amount of market power today is tied to innovation, patents, and high fixed costs. Understanding the trade-offs involved with pricing AIDS drugs at marginal cost, for example, is critically important to understanding pharmaceutical policy. Similar issues arise with music, movies, software, chip design, and universities.

Our material on monopoly and innovation is consistent with and provides a foundation for modern theories of economic growth and the economics of ideas that we present in Chapter 22 in the macroeconomics part of this book.

We knew that to reflect modern macroeconomics we had to cover the Solow model and the economics of ideas, real business cycles, and New Keynesian economics. While most textbooks now cover the rudiments of economic growth, the importance of ideas as a driving factor is rarely even mentioned. Other textbooks do not offer a balanced treatment of real business cycle theory and New Keynesian theory, instead favoring one theory and relegating the other to a few pages that are poorly integrated with the overall macro model. In contrast, we believe that adequately explaining business fluctuations, unemployment, and both the potential and limits of monetary and fiscal policy requires a balanced treatment of both models.

We also knew that financial crises and bubbles are very real, and that short-run fluctuations are a social and economic issue around the world. In fact, we included substantial material on banking panics, bubbles, wealth shocks, and the importance of financial intermediation in the very first draft of *Modern Principles*. Our book incorporates these topics from the ground floor rather than attempting to squeeze such material into hastily added boxes or appended paragraphs.

Make it Simpler

We knew that our efforts to reflect modern economics—macroeconomics in particular—would be wasted if we reached only a small percentage of the students. We had to make the material simpler, more compelling, and more intuitive. We also knew that we were writing for a generation that doesn't always have the patience for slow delivery.

By boiling the Solow model down to its essence and by providing multiple paths through the material, we have made it accessible to all principles students. Our modern approach to business fluctuations is also more advanced yet simpler at the same time. It is more advanced because we recognize that all recessions are not alike. The economy is buffeted by shocks stemming from different sources, amplified and spread by different transmission mechanisms. As a result, a balanced approach to real business cycles and New Keynesian economics, with both models rooted in microeconomic intuition, is necessary if students are to understand their world. By discussing both the real business cycle and New Keynesian approaches to business fluctuations, we can better explain the different types of recessions from the Great Depression to the recessions of the 1970s and the current one.

Our approach to business fluctuations is simpler because we model them as fluctuations in the growth rate of output, rather than in the level of output. That creates a natural progression from growth theory to business fluctuations. Moreover, by embedding real business cycles and the New Keynesian models within a single, unified dynamic AD-AS model, we simplify presentation and make a sophisticated account of business fluctuations accessible to principles students of all levels. Our modern approach also means that we can offer a more realistic analysis of monetary and fiscal policy in responding to the different types of shocks.

Modern Principles is designed to be accessible to college and university students, whether they are economics majors or not, whether they know advanced mathematics or not. *Modern Principles* aims to make the world intelligible to all readers and users. From this desire stems our tagline *See the Invisible Hand. Understand Your World.*

In short, we believe that no other textbook offers a more modern or more accessible treatment of economic growth and business fluctuations in macroeconomics and the price system and incentives in microeconomics.

Guiding Principles and Innovations: In a Nutshell

Modern Principles offers the following features and benefits:

1. We teach the economic way of thinking.

2. *Modern Principles* has a more intuitive development of markets and their interconnectedness than does any other textbook. More than any other textbook we teach students how the price system works.

3. *Modern Principles* helps students to see the invisible hand. We offer an intuitive proof of several "invisible hand theorems." For example, we show that through the operation of incentives and the price system, well-functioning markets will minimize the aggregate sum of the costs of production even though no one intends this result. Local knowledge creates a global benefit.

4. We offer an entire chapter on incentives and how they apply to business decisions, sports, and incentive design. When, for instance, should you reward your employees with a tournament form of compensation, and when a straight salary? Most texts are oddly silent on such practical issues, but it is precisely such issues that interest many students and show them the relevance of the economic way of thinking.

5. We offer an entire chapter on the stock market, a topic of concern to many students. We teach the basic trade-off between risk and return and explain why it is a good idea to diversify investments. We also explain the microeconomics of bubbles.

6. Why are some nations rich and other nations poor? *Modern Principles* has more material on development and growth than any other principles textbook.

7. *Modern Principles* has the most intuitive development of the Solow model of growth in any textbook.

8. The real business cycle model is developed as a natural extension of the Solow model.

9. *Modern Principles* is the only principles book with a balanced treatment of real business cycle theory and New Keynesian macroeconomics.

10. Financial panics and asset bubbles are covered—a topic of great interest in today's environment! There are separate and comprehensive chapters on financial intermediation and on the stock market. We also cover the financial crisis that began in 2007.

11. *Modern Principles* explains how fiscal and monetary policy work differently, depending on whether the shock hitting the economy is a real shock or a nominal shock.

12. Today's students live in a globalized economy. Events in China, India, Europe, and the Middle East affect their lives. *Modern Principles* features international examples and applications throughout. We cover the world from Algeria to Zimbabwe.

13. Less is more. This is a textbook of *principles*, not a survey or encyclopedia. A textbook that focuses on what is important helps the student to focus on what is important. There are fewer yet more consistent and more comprehensive models.

14. No tools without applications. Real-world applications are used to develop theory. Applications are not pushed aside into distracting boxes that students do not read.

15. Excel is used as a tool in appendices to help students develop insight, hands-on experience, and modeling ability.

Tools for Learning

Economics should come across as elegant, intuitive, and unified, falling directly out of real-world experience. Thus, we focus on core tools such as supply and demand and price elasticity. In macroeconomics we cover more content with fewer distinct models than ever before, thereby focusing on what is truly essential. That is why the book has a text length of only 725 pages, making it shorter than its major competitors, while actually covering more material.

Economics should be a practical discipline, so we embraced the principle of "No tools without applications."

1. Vivid applications

Nothing sticks with a student like a good example. *Modern Principles* is full of vivid illustrations of core economic principles. From the first sentence in our textbook, "The prisoners were dying of scurvy, typhoid fever, and smallpox, but nothing was killing them more than bad incentives," we strive to draw students into the economic way of thinking and to teach them that economics matters. Or consider the opening to our chapter on inflation:

> Robert Mugabe had a problem. The dictatorial president of Zimbabwe needed money. Unfortunately, Mugabe's policy of seizing commercial farms had driven productive farmers and entrepreneurs out of the country, frightened off foreign investors, and pushed Zimbabwe, once called the breadbasket of Africa, to the verge of mass starvation. Zimbabwe had almost nothing left to tax, but Mugabe still needed money to bribe his enemies and reward his supporters, especially the still loyal Zimbabwean army. Mugabe thus turned to the last refuge of needy governments, the printing press.

Our opening example suggests (a) the proximate cause of inflation (an increase in the supply of money), (b) why a government might print money at breakneck speed (when alternative taxes become unavailable), and (c) how economics is a practical science that can help students to understand their world.

2. Simpler graphs

Modern Principles presents microeconomics with fewer curves than you will find in other microeconomics books, yet without skimping on substantive results. This follows from our presentation of integrated and consistent models. For instance, on cost curves we strip the key ideas down to their intuitive essentials. If you look at the clunkier expositions of cost curves—which multiply the number of curves beyond reason—how many students actually learn or remember all of the distinctions presented? Moreover, as we know from the modern theory of investment under uncertainty, the old shut-down "rules" such as P<AVC are wrong, so why present them?[1]

You will also find fewer curves than in other macroeconomics books, yet without skimping on substantive results. This follows from our presentation of integrated and consistent macroeconomic models, especially for aggregate demand and aggregate supply. We don't need to shift to a new analytical apparatus for each macroeconomic topic. To the student it will feel that macroeconomics *makes sense* and that macroeconomics involves learning one integrated approach, covering both growth and business cycles. Some textbooks serve up a bewildering array of shifting curves, multiple and possibly conflicting graphs, or even overlaid transparencies to capture all of the curves and shifts. We say if the idea is intuitive—as good economics should be—the graph should be intuitive too.

Economics students *do* need to learn how to think in terms of graphs. But that's best done by making graphs manageable, not by making graphs forbidding.

3. No set-off boxes that interrupt the flow of the text

We know that students usually skip these boxes. So we've skipped them too. If the material is important enough for the student to learn, we've put it in the text. If it's not important, we've left it out. We want our pages to look attractive and easy to read. That will get students to read more of the material that really matters.

4. Extensive questions and problems sections

At the end of each chapter, we typically start with "Facts and Tools," questions designed to test knowledge of basic concepts. The next section, "Thinking and Problem Solving," tests whether the student can apply those concepts to examples and also to problems that require a definite solution. The final section, "Challenges," tests whether students understand key concepts in a deep fashion and can apply them to nontrivial examples and problems. If a student can do well in the challenges, he or she has not just memorized some material but is truly thinking like an economist. The multiple tiers for the end-of-chapter material help us teach both different skills and different levels of understanding.

5. Nuggets

The chapter margins offer captioned photos, cartoons, and short informational bits. The examples are chosen for being memorable and sometimes for being humorous. Reading a principles textbook is not always sugar but every now and then it should be fun. The students should look forward to at least some part of the reading and some part of the lesson. We have written *Modern Principles* with this philosophy.

6. Excel appendices

Modern Principles gives the instructor the option of running simulations with the students, using the common software package Excel. For instance, how does "catch-up" growth work in the Solow model and how quickly does it operate? Try a hands-on approach, using numbers taken from the model. Or how do bond prices vary inversely with interest rates? We all know that

---

[1] On the modern theory of investment under uncertainty see Dixit, Avinash. 1992. "Investment and hysteresis." *Journal of Economic Perspectives* 6, no. 1: 107–132.

quantitative magnitudes matter, so why not give the student a good sense of this? We walk the student through this material in a step-by-step manner. But notice: if you don't wish to cover or present this material, no other part of the text depends on it.

7. Notation

The book has a minimum of notational requirements. Students need to be familiar with simple one-line equations, with basic algebra, and with reading graphs. For help with reading graphs we offer a useful 14-page appendix. Overall, our notation is minimal and standard.

What's in the Chapters?
Part 1: Supply and Demand

We review the key aspects of supply and demand and the price system, done in four chapters. We present incentives as the most important idea in microeconomics. Microeconomics should be intuitive, should teach the skill of thinking like an economist, and should be drawn from examples from everyday life. Along these lines, these chapters run as follows: Chapter 1 introduces economics by providing ten big ideas, Chapter 2 covers the basics of supply and demand, Chapter 3 brings supply and demand together by focusing on equilibrium, and Chapter 4 deals with elasticity.

We take special care to illustrate how demand and supply curves can be read "horizontally" or "vertically." That is, a demand curve tells you the quantity demanded at every price and the maximum willingness to pay (per unit) for any quantity. It takes a bit more work to explain these concepts early on, but students who learn to read demand and supply curves in both ways get a deeper understanding of the curves and they find consumer and producer surplus, taxes, and the analysis of price controls much easier to understand.

Elasticity is often considered a dull topic so we begin Chapter 4 with a shocking story:

> In fall 2000, Harvard sophomore Jay Williams flew to the Sudan where a terrible civil war had resulted in many thousands of deaths. Women and children captured in raids by warring tribes were being enslaved and held for ransom. Working with Christian Solidarity International, Williams was able to pay for the release of 4,000 people. But did Williams do the right thing?

What is a discussion of modern slavery doing in a principles of economics book? We want to show students that economics is a social science, that it asks important questions and provides important answers for people who want to understand their world. We take economics seriously and in *Modern Principles* we analyze serious topics.

Part 2: The Price System

"A price is a signal wrapped up in an incentive." That's one of the most important ideas of economics, even if it takes a little work from the students. And that is an idea that we drive home. Partial equilibrium analysis can sometimes obscure the big picture of markets and how they fit together. General equilibrium analysis, either done mathematically or with an Edgeworth box, captures neither the "marvel of the market" (to use Hayek's phrase) nor the student's interest. We give a fast-paced, intuitive, general equilibrium view of markets in Chapter 5 and how they tie together. We are linked to the world economy, and goods and services are shipped from one corner of the globe to another, yet without the guidance of a central planner. We show how the price of oil is linked to the price of candy bars. We also show how markets can predict the future, even the future of a movie like *American Pie 2*! For those familiar with Leonard Read's classic essay, this chapter is "I, Pencil" for the twenty-first century.

There is no better way to understand how the price system works than to see what happens when the price system does *not* work very well. Thus in Chapters 6 and 7 we cover the economics of price controls, paying special attention to how price controls reduce the signaling role of prices and break down the integrated nature of the price system.

We also use the supply and demand framework to analyze commodity taxes and subsidies (in Chapter 7). We have all heard the phrases "Who pays?" and "Follow the money," but few people understand how to apply these ideas correctly. The economist knows that the final incidence of a tax does not necessarily depend on where it is levied, and this can be taught as yet another "invisible hand" result. Teaching the incidence of taxes and subsidies also gives yet another way of driving home the concept of elasticity, its intuitive meaning, and its real-world importance.

The basics of international trade start with the division of knowledge, economies of scale, and comparative advantage as foundations for trade. In Chapter 8, we consider the costs of protectionism, international trade and market power, trade and wages, and most of all trade and jobs. Is protectionism ever a good idea? The chapter also offers a brief history of globalization as it relates to trade. We emphasize that the principles covering trade across nations are the same as those that govern trade within nations.

Prices do not always signal the right information and incentives, most of all when external costs and benefits are present. A medical patient may use an antibiotic, for instance, without taking into account the fact that disease-causing microorganisms evolve and mutate and that antibiotic use can in the long run lead to bacteria that are antibiotic-resistant. Similarly, not enough people get flu vaccinations, because they don't take into account how other people benefit from a lower chance of catching a contagious ailment. Private markets sometimes can "internalize" these external costs and benefits by writing good contracts, and we give students the tools to understand when such contracts will be possible and when not (Chapter 9). Market contracts, tradable permits, taxes, and command and control are alternative means of treating externalities. Building upon our previous understanding of the invisible hand, we consider when these approaches will produce efficient results and when not.

Part 3: Firms and Factor Markets

Prices and costs send signals to firms and guide their production decisions, just as a price at Wal-Mart shapes the behavior of consumers. But how exactly does this work? We've all seen textbooks that serve up an overwhelming confusion of different cost curves, all plastered on the same graph and not always corresponding in a simple or direct manner to economic intuition.

We focus on the essentials in Chapter 10, combining costs and competition. A firm must make three key decisions: What price to set? What quantity to produce? When to enter and exit an industry? Building on invisible hand results, we show—using simple arguments and demonstrations—that market prices lead competitive firms to produce a given set of outputs at minimum cost. We also derive traditional results about marginal revenue, marginal cost, and market price. A simple notion of average cost suffices to cover decisions of firm entry and exit, while avoiding a tangle of excess concepts. Unlike many books, we stress the importance of "wait and see" and option value strategies. These strategies show up again in macroeconomics.

We build upon concepts such as cost curves and elasticity to flesh out the economics and also the public policy of monopoly (Chapter 11).

Modern Principles devotes an entire chapter (Chapter 12) to the topic of price discrimination, which is fun, practical, and contains lots of economics. Students, in their roles as consumers, face (or, as sellers, practice!) price discrimination all the time, and that includes from their colleges and universities—remember in-state vs. out-of-state tuition? A lot of what students already "know" can be turned into more systematic economic intuition, including the concepts of demand and elasticity, and whether marginal cost is rising or falling. The pricing of printers and ink, pharmaceuticals, and cable TV all derive naturally from this analysis. Once students understand price discrimination, their eyes will be open to a world of economics in practice every day.

In Chapter 13, we also cover network goods: a lot of us use Microsoft Word because so many other people do too. Blu-ray beat out HD-DVD to become the standard because again, for reasons of convenience, consumers want to share a common network or system. Markets like this have some unusual properties. They tend to have lots of monopoly, lots of innovation (competition "for the market" vs. competition "in the market"), and they change suddenly in fits and starts, rather than gradually.

We include two chapters (Chapters 14 and 15) on labor markets. Work touches almost all of our lives and most of the fundamental matters and conditions of work are ruled by economics: wages, working conditions, bonuses, and investments in human capital and education. The marginal product of labor has the strongest influence over the wage of a particular job. Risky jobs, like going out on dangerous fishing boats, pay more. Labor unions boost the wages of some workers but hurt the wages of others. On the controversial topic of discrimination in labor markets, we show how some kinds of discrimination may survive while others will tend to fall away, due to the pressure of market forces. All of these issues are covered in Chapter 14.

Incentives matter! That may be the key single lesson of economics but a lot of textbooks don't have a complete chapter on incentives, as we do (Chapter 15). Business applications, sports applications, and personal life all provide plenty of illustrations of economic principles. You get what you pay for, so if you can't measure quality very well a lot of incentive schemes will backfire. Piece rates make a lot of workers more productive but strong incentives can impose risk on workers and induce them to quit the job altogether. As with grading on a curve, sometimes a boss wishes to pay workers relative to the performance of other workers. A lot of the most important incentives are about pride, fun, and fame, not just money.

The stock market is the one topic that just about every student of economics cares about, and yet it is neglected in many textbooks. We view the stock market as a "teaching moment" as well as an important topic in its own right. What other economic topic commands so much attention from the popular press? Yet not every principles course gives the student the tools to understand media discussions or to dissect fallacies. We remedy that state of affairs in Chapter 16. This chapter covers passive versus active investing, the trade-off between risk and return, "how to really pick stocks," diversification, why high fees should be avoided, compound returns, and asset price bubbles. The operation of asset markets is something students need to know if they are to understand today's economy and also the financial crisis.

And, yes, we do offer students some very direct and practical investment advice. Most people should diversify and "buy and hold," and we explain why. In terms of direct, practical value, we try to make this book worth its price!

Part 4: Government

Public goods and externalities help us understand when private property rights do not always lead to good outcomes. The concepts of excludability and non-rivalry help us classify why governments have to provide national defense but why movie theaters are usually left to the private sector.

Why is it that the world is running out of so many kinds of fish? Economics has the best answer and it involves the Tragedy of the Commons. In Chapter 17, we show that economics is the single best entry point for understanding many common dilemmas of the environment, as well as public goods problems.

Unfortunately, most principles students leave the classroom still underequipped to understand real-world policy debates over economic issues. So often the debate descends into ethics: Are markets fair? Is the distribution of income just? Is it important that individual rights be respected? When is paternalism justified? We do *not* try to provide final, take-away answers to these questions, but in Chapter 18 we do give students the tools to unpack how these questions intersect with the economic issues they have been studying.

Economics has a lot to say about how politics works and the results aren't always pretty. Voters have a rational incentive to be ignorant or underinformed, and the end result is that special interests have a big say over many economic policies. Dairy farmers have a bigger say over milk subsidies than do the people who drink milk, and that is why the United States has milk price supports. In Chapter 19, we deal with these issues of political economy.

Part 5: Economic Growth

Why are some nations rich while others are mired in terrible poverty? How can growth be extended to all parts of our world? Students are eager to understand the key issues of growth and development, and economics has much of importance to teach on this vital topic. Thus, we begin the macroeconomics part of the book with economic growth.

After introducing and *motivating* the idea of GDP in Chapter 20, we start Chapter 21 by presenting the basic facts of economic growth: (1) GDP per capita varies enormously between nations, (2) everyone used to be poor, and (3) there are growth miracles and growth disasters. The key factors behind economic growth include capital, labor, and technology, but we also offer the student a deeper understanding of the importance of incentives and institutions. It is important to connect the physical factors of production with an understanding of how they got there. That means combining Solow and Romer-like models with institutional economics and an analysis of property rights.

A quick tour of the world shows why the student needs to learn different approaches to understanding economic growth.

Let's say we wish to understand why South Korea is wealthy while North Korea starves. The best approach is to consider the roles of property rights and incentives in the two countries, a topic we cover in Chapter 21. Let's say we want to understand why China had been growing at 10 percent a year for almost 30 years. Then, the student needs to learn the Solow model and the idea of "catch-up," which we cover in the first half of Chapter 22. Finally, let's say we want to understand why growth rates today are higher than in the nineteenth century, or why the future might bring a very high standard of living. We then need to turn to the Romer model and the idea of increasing returns to scale, which we cover in the second half of Chapter 22. Our approach to economic growth presents all these ideas in an integrated fashion.

Yes, the Solow model finally has come to a principles book. Maybe that sounds daunting, but we offer a super simple version of Solow, intuitive every step along the way. One reviewer for the chapter wrote:

> This chapter is by itself one of the greatest selling points of the book. The chapter is superbly written and presents a difficult concept in a way that an intro level student would not have trouble understanding. The authors . . . have done a great service to both instructors and students.

Another wrote:

> My first reaction was "no way the Solow model belongs in macro principles." However, after reading both the growth chapters, I changed my mind. These are excellent.

The Solow model stands at the foundation of modern approaches to economic growth. We cover some math but focus on the intuition behind the model, for instance how diminishing returns to capital explain why China can grow faster than the United States. We cover capital growth, investment, and depreciation as concepts relevant for economic growth. As optional material, we explain how an increase in the investment rate increases GDP per capita but in the long run does not increase the growth rate. We also cover why ever more capital cannot be the reason for long-run economic growth and the importance of ideas for economic growth. The appendix offers the quantitative relations of the Solow model in a simple spreadsheet.

Financial intermediation doesn't always receive a lot of attention from macro textbooks, but recent events have shown that the topic is critical. In Chapter 23, *Modern Principles* presents basic concepts behind intermediation, including consumption smoothing, the demand and supply of savings, equilibrium in the market for loanable funds, and the role of banks, bonds, and stock markets. We explain bank failures, panics, illiquidity, insolvency, and what happens when financial intermediation fails. The student should understand why it is bad if a country has a broken banking system and how it got that way. All of this analysis will later be integrated with aggregate demand and supply. At the end of the chapter, an appendix presents bond pricing in terms of a spreadsheet and shows economically why bond prices and interest rates vary inversely. Modern macroeconomics is very much about banking and this chapter reflects the importance of the topic.

Part 6: Business Fluctuations

In Chapter 24, we define the different kinds of unemployment: frictional, structural, and cyclical. We consider how unemployment is linked to economic growth and how so much unemployment can arise from business cycles. We cover structural unemployment in both Europe and the United States, and we also cover labor force participation rates to a greater extent than in other textbooks. Why is it, for example, that in Belgium only one-third of men ages 55–64 are working while in the United States only one-third of men this age are retired?

In Chapter 25, we introduce the quantity of money as a central concept in macroeconomics that will be used to explain inflation and, in future chapters, aggregate demand.

In Chapter 26, we introduce a skeleton model of business fluctuations that can incorporate New Keynesian and real business cycle ideas. We present the simplest real business cycle model and relate it to real-world concepts and examples. Supply-side fluctuations show up as shifts in the Solow growth curve, while a dynamic aggregate demand curve is based on the quantity theory. Using the quantity theory to derive an AD curve reduces the number of models the students must learn and allows us to proceed quickly to sophisticated analyses of monetary and fiscal policy.

Real business cycle models can be forbiddingly complex, but they are built on the simple underlying ideas of shocks and how transmission mechanisms amplify and spread shocks. We illustrate real-world shocks in Chapter 27 and we give intuitive explanations of transmission mechanisms such as intertemporal substitution, uncertainty and irreversible investments, labor adjustment costs, time bunching, and sticky wages and prices. An appendix ties together the real business cycle analysis of business fluctuations and the Solow model.

Part 7: Macroeconomic Policy and Institutions

To understand the Federal Reserve system, in Chapter 28 we introduce key concepts such as the U.S. money supplies, fractional reserve banking, the reserve ratio, the money multiplier, open market operations, and Fed influence over interest rates.

Building on the analysis of the Fed, we consider the dilemmas of monetary policy in detail in Chapter 29. The relevant cases include, among others: negative shocks to aggregate demand, rules vs. discretion, analyzing a decline in the rate of monetary growth, and responding to negative real shocks. We devote special attention to the Fed as a manager of market confidence and to how the Fed should respond to positive shocks and possible asset price bubbles, including in the housing market.

Students need to understand the institutional details of government receipts and spending. That includes tax revenues (their size and nature), the individual income tax, taxes on capital gains and interest and dividends, the alternative minimum tax, Social Security and Medicare taxes, the corporate income tax, and the question of who really pays federal taxes. We cover these ideas in Chapter 30.

What forms does fiscal policy take and when does it work best to improve macroeconomic performance? What are the limits of fiscal policy and when will a fiscal stimulus work best? In Chapter 31, we cover crowding out, bond vs. tax finance of expansionary fiscal policy, tax rebates and tax cuts, automatic stabilizers, and Ricardian equivalence. Students also learn when fiscal policy is potent enough, when timing issues get in the way of effective fiscal policy, and whether fiscal policy can address the macroeconomic problems from negative real shocks. When is government debt a problem and how can debt crises bring an economy to its knees? The overall purpose of this chapter is to teach students when fiscal policy is a good or bad idea.

Part 8: International Economics

The multiplicity of currencies sometimes makes international finance a daunting topic, but in Chapter 32 we keep it simple and show how it applies core economic principles that the student already understands. Topics include the U.S. trade deficit, the balance of payments, the current account, the capital account (the financial account), the Official Reserves account, and the two sides of accounting identity behind the balance of payments. All of these topics are explained in terms of consistent economic intuitions. We also consider what a trade deficit really means, and we relate that to the trading behavior of individuals. The chapter analyzes exchange rates and their determinants in terms of supply and demand analysis, as stems from goods markets and asset markets. Long-run exchange rates have an (imperfect) connection to purchasing power parity, due to trade and economic arbitrage. Building on aggregate demand analysis, we consider how monetary and fiscal policy affect exchange rates and so influence output and employment. In this framework we consider the relative merits of fixed vs. floating exchange rates. The chapter closes with a presentation of the nature and functions of the IMF and World Bank.

Alternative Paths through the Book

Modern Principles: Economics has been written with trade-offs in mind and it's easy to pick and choose from among the chapters when time constrains. We offer a few quick suggestions. Chapter 5 is fun to teach but more difficult to test than some of the other chapters. But don't worry, you will find plenty of testable material in other chapters, and for your best students the introduction to the price system in Chapters 5 and 6 will be an eye-opener!

We spend more time on price controls than do other books because we don't confine ourselves to the usual shortage diagram, but we also illustrate the general equilibrium effects of price controls. In Chapter 6, however, we have made it easy to skip the second application on rent controls. We have also included a short section of advanced material on the losses from random allocation that may be skipped in larger classes or if time constrains.

We have greatly simplified the presentation on cost curves and removed most of production theory, so do take the time to cover monopoly and the chapter on price discrimination. Students love the material on price discrimination because once they understand the concepts, they see the applications all around them.

Chapter 15, *Getting Incentives Right*, is fun to teach but it goes beyond the core and can be skipped. We think this chapter will be especially appropriate for management, MBA, and pre-law students.

We encourage everyone to teach Chapter 16 on stock markets but it can be taught in either the microeconomics or macroeconomics sequence. Asteroid deflection and the decline of the tuna fisheries are a must, so do cover Chapter 17 on *Public Goods and the Tragedy of the Commons*. Once again, students appreciate the focus on important, real-world applications of the economic way of thinking.

Chapters 18 and 19 on ethics and political economy are optional. If you can teach only one chapter, we think Chapter 19 on *Political Economy* has crucial material for avoiding the nirvana fallacy: we should always compare real-world markets with real-world governments when doing political economy. Chapter 18 on ethics works great in smaller classes with lots of student interaction—we think it important that the philosophy professors are not the ones who get the only say on questions of ethics!

The basics of GDP and economic growth are critical but it's easy to cover only a portion of the Solow model in Chapter 22. We sometimes do this in our larger classes so this will be a good choice for many. The chapter has been written so the most intuitive and important aspects of the model are covered in the beginning, more difficult and detailed material in the middle may be skipped, and then important material on growth and ideas is covered toward the end of the chapter. The material in the middle may be skipped without loss of continuity. Teachers with smaller and more advanced classes can easily cover the full chapter.

One important point: it is not at all necessary to teach the Solow model to cover our chapters on business fluctuations. We offer a "Solow growth curve" in these chapters, but without delving into the details of the Solow model, the curve is readily explained as a potential growth curve analogous to a potential GDP curve.

We have divided the chapters in macroeconomic policy and institutions so that a teacher can cover monetary policy without covering the details of the Federal Reserve system and open market operations, and one can cover fiscal policy without covering the details of the federal budget: taxes and spending. The details are important and these chapters place monetary and fiscal policy within an institutional context so we do not necessarily recommend this approach but when time binds, more options are better than fewer.

Finally, one could skip international finance. To us, international economics means primarily that economics can help us to understand the world, not just one country and not just one time. As a result, we have included many international examples throughout *Modern Principles: Economics*. If time constrains, the details of tariffs, exchange rates, and trade deficits may be left to another course. Alas, we live in a finite world.

Most of all we hope that *Modern Principles* helps you, the teacher, to have fun! We love economics and we have fun teaching economics. We have written this text for people not afraid to say the same. Don't hesitate to e-mail us with your questions, thoughts, and experiences, or just to say hello!

Supplements and Media
Innovative Resources for Teaching *Modern Principles: Economics*

Cowen and Tabarrok take a modern approach to economics. Worth Publishers takes an equally modern approach to instructor resources and supplementary material. In addition to providing traditional resources, which we list below, the economics team at Worth will be working constantly throughout this first edition to develop new resources that will help keep your course current, exciting to the students, and most of all, relevant to today's economic environment. Check www.worthpublishers.com/cowentabarrok for the latest developments in supplements and media.

An accompanying blog to *Modern Principles: Economics* can be found at www.seetheinvisiblehand.com. This site mirrors the authors' personal site www.MarginalRevolution.com and includes the ability for professors to tag MR posts by chapter topic, to share teaching ideas, and to foster the *Modern Principles* community.

Instructor Supplements

Instructor's Resource Manual with Solutions Manual

Prepared by John Dawson (Appalachian State University) for macroeconomics and Benjamin Powell (Suffolk University) for microeconomics. For each chapter in the textbook, the Instructor's Resource Manual provides:

> *Learning Objectives:* bulleted list of the key "takeaways" of the chapter.

> *Chapter Outline:* listing chapter heads and subheadings for quick reference.

> *Chapter Narrative:* detailed coverage of chapter material, including breakdowns of graphs, Teaching Tips, Strategies, Key Learning Points, and Potential Pitfalls.

> *Inside-* and *Outside-the-Classroom Activities:* problems and exercises relating to chapter material designed to engage students in lecture material.

> Detailed solutions to all of the end-of-chapter questions and problems from the textbook prepared by Garett Jones (George Mason University).

Printed Test Bank

The test bank provides creative and versatile questions ranging in levels of difficulty and format to assess students' comprehension, interpretation, analysis, and synthesis skills. Containing roughly 135 questions per chapter, the test bank offers a variety of multiple-choice, true/false, and short-answer questions. The macroeconomics test bank is being coordinated by David Gillette (Truman State University). Authors of test questions are Lillian Kamal (University of Hartford), Mark Wheeler (University of Western Michigan), Jim Self (Indiana University), Jim Lee (Texas A&M—Corpus Christi), and J. J. Arias (Georgia College and State University). The microeconomics test bank is being coordinated by Jennifer Platania (Elon University). Authors of test questions are Lillian Kamal (University of Hartford), David Kalist (Shippensburg University), Michael Welker (Franciscan University of Steubenville), and Sheng Yang (Black Hills State University).

Computerized Test Bank

The printed test bank will be available in CD-ROM format for both Windows and Macintosh users. With Diploma software, instructors can easily create and print tests as well as write and edit questions.

Instructor's Resource CD-ROM

Using the Instructor's Resource CD-ROM, instructors can easily build classroom presentations or enhance online courses. This CD-ROM contains all text figures (in JPEG and PPT formats), PowerPoint Lecture Presentations with animated figures and tables, and detailed solutions to all end-of-chapter questions in the textbook.

Student Supplements
Study Guide

Prepared by David Mitchell (University of South Alabama) for macroeconomics and James Swofford (University of South Alabama) for microeconomics. For each key section of each chapter, the study guide provides:

> *Brief Chapter Summary.*

> *Key Terms:* listed, with space for students to write in the definitions themselves.

> *Detailed Section Summaries with Student Tips and Concept-Related Questions:* including coverage of all applications, tips to help students with difficult concepts, and 3–5 questions per section to reinforce learning of key concepts.

> *Self-Test End-of-Chapter Questions:* 15–20 application-oriented, multiple-choice questions.

> *Worked-Out solutions:* including solutions to all study guide review questions.

Online Offerings
Companion Web Site for Students and Instructors
www.SeeTheInvisibleHand.com

The companion site is a virtual study guide for students and an excellent resource for instructors. For each chapter in the textbook, the tools on the site include:

Instructor Resources:

> **Quiz Gradebook:** The site gives instructors the ability to track students' interactions with the practice quizzes via an online gradebook. Instructors may choose to have students' results emailed directly to them.

> **PowerPoint Lecture Presentations:** These customizable PowerPoint slides, prepared by Michael Applegate (Oklahoma State University) for macroeconomics and Darrin Gulla (University of Kentucky) for microeconomics are designed to assist instructors with lecture preparation and presentation by providing learning objectives, animated figures and tables, equations from the textbook, key concepts, and bulleted lecture outlines.

> **Illustration PowerPoint Slides:** A complete set of figures and tables from the textbook in JPEG and PowerPoint formats.

> **Images from the Textbook:** Instructors have access to a complete set of figures and tables from the textbook in high-res and low-res JPEG formats.

Student Resources:

> **Self-Test Quizzes:** This quizzing engine provides 20 multiple-choice questions per chapter with immediate and appropriate feedback along with topic references for students to refer back to in the textbook for further review. The questions as well as the answer choices are randomized to give students a different quiz with every refresh of the screen.

> **Key Term Flashcards:** Students can test themselves on the key terms with these pop-up electronic flashcards.

eBook

Students who purchase the *Modern Principles* eBook have access to the interactive textbook featuring:

> Quick, intuitive navigation

> Customizable note-taking

> Highlighting

> Searchable glossary

> Self-testing

With the *Modern Principles* eBook, instructors can:

> Focus on only the chapters they want. You can assign the entire text or a custom version with only the chapters that correspond to your syllabus. Students see your customized version, with your selected chapters only.

> Annotate any page of the text. Your notes can include text, Web links, and even photos and images from the book's media or other sources. Your students can get an eBook annotated just for them, customized for your course.

> Access online quizzing. The eBook integrates the online quizzing from the book's companion Web site, provided by Timothy M. Diette (Washington and Lee University).

WebCT E-pack and Blackboard Cartridge

Text-specific, rich Web content for Cowen and Tabarrok's *Modern Principles: Economics*, with features including preprogrammed quizzes, tests pulled from the computerizes test bank, and an array of other materials, are available for users of WebCT or Blackboard in the appropriate format.

EconPortal—*AVAILABLE FOR SPRING 2011*

EconPortal is the digital gateway to *Modern Principles*, designed to enrich your course and improve your students' understanding of economics. EconPortal provides a powerful, easy-to-use, completely customizable teaching and learning management system complete with the following:

> *An Interactive eBook with Embedded Learning Resources:* The eBook's functionality will provide for highlighting, note-taking, graph and example enlargements, and a full text and glossary search. Embedded icons will link students directly to resources available to enhance their understanding of the key concepts.

> *A Personalized Study Plan for Students, Featuring Diagnostic Quizzing:* Students will be asked to take the PSP: Self-Assessment Quiz after they have read the chapter and before they come to the lecture that discusses that chapter. Once they've taken the quiz, a personalized study plan (PSP) based on the quiz results is created for them. This PSP will provide a path to the appropriate eBook materials and resources for further study and exploration, helping students learn and retain the course material.

> *A Fully Integrated Learning Management System:* EconPortal is meant to be a fully customizable and highly interactive one-stop shop for all the

resources tied to the book. The system will carefully integrate the teaching and learning resources for the book into an easy-to-use system. EconPortal will enable you to create assignments from a variety of question types to prepare self-graded homework, quizzes, or tests, saving many hours of preparation time.

> Instructors can assign and track any aspect of their students' EconPortal activities. The Gradebook will capture students' results and allow for easily exporting reports as well as importing grades from offline assignments.

Additional Offerings
i>clicker

Developed by a team of University of Illinois physicists, i>clicker is the most flexible and most reliable classroom response system available. It is the only solution created *for* educators, *by* educators—with continuous product improvements made through direct classroom testing and faculty feedback. You'll love i>clicker no matter your level of technical expertise, because the focus is on *your* teaching, *not the technology*. To learn more about packaging i>clicker with this textbook, please contact your local sales rep or visit www.iclicker.com.

***Wall Street Journal* Edition:** For adopters of the Cowen/Tabarrok textbook, Worth Publishers and the *Wall Street Journal* are offering a 15-week subscription to students at a tremendous savings. Instructors also receive their own free *Wall Street Journal* subscription plus additional instructor supplements created exclusively by the *Wall Street Journal*. Please contact your local sales rep for more information or go to the *Wall Street Journal* online at www.wsj.com.

***Financial Times* Edition:** For adopters of the Cowen/Tabarrok textbook, Worth Publishers and the *Financial Times* are offering a 15-week subscription to students at a tremendous savings. Instructors also receive their own free *Financial Times* subscription for one year. Students and instructors may access research and archived information at www.ft.com.

Dismal Scientist: A high-powered business database and analysis service comes to the classroom! Dismal Scientist offers real-time monitoring of the global economy, produced locally by economists and professionals at Economy.com's London, Sydney, and West Chester offices. Dismal Scientist is *free* when packaged with the Cowen/Tabarrok textbook. Please contact your local sales rep for more information or go to www.economy.com.

The Economist has partnered with Worth Publishers to create an exclusive offer that will enhance the classroom experience. Faculty receive a complimentary 15-week subscription when 10 or more students purchase a subscription. Students get 15 issues of *The Economist* at a huge savings.

Inside and outside the classroom, *The Economist* provides a global perspective that helps students keep abreast of what's going on in the world, and gives insight into how the world views the United States. *The Economist* ignites dialogue, encourages debate, and enables readers to form well-reasoned opinions—while providing a deeper understanding of key political, social, and business issues. Supplement your textbook with the knowledge and insight that only *The Economist* can provide.

To get 15 issues of *The Economist*, go to www.economistacademic.com/worth.

Acknowledgments

We are most indebted and grateful to the following focus group participants, reviewers, and class testers for their comments and suggestions. Every one of them has contributed to the final product, *Modern Principles.*

Rashid Al-Hmoud
Texas Tech University

Michael Applegate
Oklahoma State University

J. J. Arias
Georgia College and State University

Jim Barbour
Elon University

David Beckworth
Texas State University

Robert Beckman
University of Tampa

Ryan Bosworth
North Carolina State University

Jennifer Brown
Eastern Connecticut State University

Douglas Campbell
University of Memphis

Michael Carew
Baruch College

Shawn Carter
Jacksonville State University

Philip Coelho
Ball State University

Jim Couch
North Alabama University

Scott Cunningham
University of Georgia

Amlan Datta
Texas Tech University

John Dawson
Appalachian State University

Timothy M. Diette
Washington and Lee University

Ann Eike
University of Kentucky

Tisha Emerson
Baylor University

Molly Espey
Clemson University

William Feipel
Illinois Central University

Amanda S. Freeman
Kansas State University

Gary Galles
Pepperdine University

Neil Garston
California State University, Los Angeles

William Gibson
Unviersity of Vermont

David Gillette
Truman State University

Lynn G. Gillette
Sierra Nevada College

Stephan F. Gohmann
University of Louisville

Michael Gootzeit
University of Memphis

Carole Green
University of South Florida

Paul Grimes
Mississippi State University

Philip J. Grossman
St. Cloud State University

Darrin Gulla
University of Kentucky

Kyle Hampton
The Ohio State University

Joe Haslag
University of Missouri—Columbia

Sarah Helms
University of Alabama—Birmingham

Matthew Henry
University of Georgia

John Hsu
Contra Costa College

Jeffrey Hummel
San Jose State University

Sarah Jackson
Indiana University of Pennsylvania

Dennis Jansen
Texas A&M University

Bruce Johnson
Centre College

Veronica Kalich
Baldwin Wallace College

Lillian Kamal
University of Hartford

John Keating
University of Kansas

Logan Kelly
Bryant University

Brian Kench
University of Tampa

David Kreutzer
James Madison University

Robert Krol
California State University, Northridge

Gary Lape
Liberty University

Rodolfo Ledesma
Marian College

Jim Lee
Texas A&M University—Corpus Christi

Daniel Lin
American University

Edward Lopez
San Jose State University

Hari Luitel
St. Cloud State University

Douglas Mackenzie
State University of New York— Plattsburgh

Michael Makowsky
Towson University

John Marcis
Coastal Carolina University

Catherine Matraves
Michigan State University

Meghan Millea
Mississippi State University

Stephen Miller
University of Nevada, Las Vegas

Ida Mirzaie
The Ohio State University

David (Mitch) Mitchell
South Alabama University

Ranganath Murthy
Bucknell University

Todd Myers
Grossmont College

Andre Neveu
Skidmore College

Lydia Ortega
San Jose State University

Alexandre Padilla
Metropolitan State College of Denver

Biru Paksha Paul
State University of New York—Cortland

John Perry
Centre College

Gina C. Pieters
University of Minnesota

Dennis Placone
Clemson University

Jennifer M. Platania
Elon University

Brennan Platt
Brigham Young University

William Polley
Western Illinois University

Benjamin Powell
Suffolk University

Margaret Ray
University of Mary Washington

Dan Rickman
Oklahoma State University

Fred Ruppel
Eastern Kentucky University

Mikael Sandberg
University of Florida

Michael Scott
University of Oklahoma

James Self
Indiana University

David Shideler
Murray State University

Mark Showalter
Brigham Young University

Martin Spechler
Indiana University–Purdue University, Indianapolis

David Spencer
Brigham Young University

Richard Stahl
Louisiana State University

Dean Stansel
Florida Gulf Coast University

Liliana V. Stern
Auburn Univeristy

Kay Strong
Bowling Green State University— Firelands

Jim Swofford
University of South Alabama

Sandra Trejos
Clarion University of Pennsylvania

Marie Truesdell
Marian College

T. Norman Van Cott
Ball State University

Kristin A. Van Gaasbeck
California State University— Sacramento

Michael Visser
Sonoma State University

Yoav Wachsman
Coastal Carolina University

Doug Walker
Georgia College and State University

Christopher Waller
Notre Dame University

Robert Whaples
Wake Forest University

Mark Wheeler
Western Michigan University

Additional suggestions for improving the manuscript were given by our talented supplement authors. John Dawson, Appalachian State University, taught our Solow growth chapter in a summer class and provided invaluable comments on how to make the presentation even better. David Gillette, Truman State University, contributed useful perspectives on the introductory macro chapters. David Mitchell, University of South Alabama, gave numerous suggestions on making the macro material clearer. Jennifer Platania, Elon University, was a careful reviewer of many micro chapters and contributed an invaluable perspective on the introductory micro course. Benjamin Powell, Suffolk University, provided useful comments on how to make the presentation of micro concepts even better. James Swofford, University of South Alabama, gave numerous suggestions on making the micro material clearer. We are grateful to all of them.

We were fortunate to have several eagle-eyed readers of the proofs of the book during the production process. James L. Lapp, Lillian Kamal, University of Hartford, and Gary Lape, Liberty University, were careful readers of the page proofs. Eric P. Chiang, Florida Atlantic University, did a great job examining the revised page proofs. All of these reviewers had a remarkable focus on detail.

Our colleague Garett Jones and his expertise have been a lifesaver for the problems and questions. We were fortunate to have research assistance from Amanda Agan, Robert Warren Anderson, Eli Dourado, Yan Li, Ross Williams, and David Youngberg. Carl Close provided useful suggestions. The Mercatus Center supplied an essential work environment. Jane Perry helped us to proof many of the chapters and with Lisa Hill-Corley provided important daily assistance. Teresa Hartnett has done a great job as our agent.

Most of all we are grateful to the team at Worth. The idea for this book was conceived by Paul Shensa, who has seen it through with wise advice from day one until the end. Craig Bleyer has been a wonderful publisher and Sarah Dorger has led the editing work and been a joy to work with. Becca Hicks was a delight to work with and introduced us to the key elements of a textbook. Bruce Kaplan, our primary development editor, is the George Martin of book production; he has done a tremendous amount of nitty-gritty work on the manuscript to make every note just right and he has offered excellent counsel throughout.

We are fortunate to have had such a talented production and design group for our book. Dana Kasowitz coordinated the entire production process with the help of Timothy Rodes and Tracey Kuehn. Kevin Kall created the beautiful interior design and the cover. Christine Buese went beyond the call of duty in tracking down sometimes obscure photos. Barbara Seixas showed a deft hand with the manufacturing aspects of the book. It has been a delight to work with all of them.

The supplements were put together by several people. Matt Driskill put together the supplements team. Tom Acox ably brought the supplements package to market. Marie McHale and Lorraine Klimowich provided essential effort on the electronic Portal. And, the work of Stacey Alexander and Laura McGinn helped bring the content to print.

Two people stand out in the marketing of this book. Steven Rigolosi ran the extensive market development program that introduced this book to the market. Scott Guile has been energetic and relentless in marketing this book.

Most of all, we want to thank our families for their support and understanding. Tyler wishes to offer his personal thanks to Natasha and Yana. It is Alex's great fortune to be able to thank Monique, Connor, and Maxwell and his parents for years of support and encouragement.

Tyler Cowen
Alex Tabarrok

MODERN PRINCIPLES:
ECONOMICS

1

The Big Ideas

The prisoners were dying of scurvy, typhoid fever, and small-pox, but nothing was killing them more than bad incentives. In 1787, the British government had hired sea captains to ship convicted felons to Australia. Conditions on board the ships were monstrous; some even said the conditions were worse than on slave ships. On one voyage, more than a third of the males died and the rest arrived beaten, starved, and sick. A first mate remarked cruelly of the convicts "let them die and be damned the owners have [already] been paid for their passage."[1]

The British public had no love for the convicts, but it wasn't prepared to give them a death sentence either. Newspapers editorialized in favor of better conditions, clergy appealed to the captains' sense of humanity, and legislators passed regulations requiring better food and water, light and air, and proper medical care. Yet the death rate remained shockingly high. Nothing appeared to be working until an economist suggested something new. Can you guess what the economist suggested?

Instead of paying the captains for each prisoner placed on board ship in Great Britain, the economist suggesting paying for each prisoner that walked off the ship in Australia. In 1793, the new system was implemented and immediately the survival rate shot up to 99 percent. One astute observer explained what had happened, "economy beat sentiment and benevolence."[2]

The story of the convict ships illustrates the first big lesson that runs throughout this book and throughout economics, *incentives matter*.

By **incentives,** we mean rewards and penalties that motivate behavior. Let's take a closer look at incentives and some of the other big ideas in economics. On first reading, some of these ideas may seem surprising or difficult to understand. Don't worry: we will be explaining everything in more detail.

CHAPTER OUTLINE

Big Ideas in Economics

1. Incentives Matter
2. Good Institutions Align Self-Interest with the Social Interest
3. Trade-offs Are Everywhere
4. Thinking on the Margin
5. Tampering with the Laws of Supply and Demand Has Consequences
6. The Importance of Wealth and Economic Growth
7. Institutions Matter
8. Economic Booms and Busts Cannot Be Avoided but Can Be Moderated
9. Prices Rise When the Government Prints Too Much Money
10. Central Banking Is a Hard Job

The Biggest Idea of All: Economics Is Fun

Incentives are rewards and penalties that motivate behavior.

We see the following list as the most important and fundamental contributions of economics to human understanding; we call these contributions **Big Ideas**. Some economists might arrange this list in a different manner or order, but these are generally accepted principles among good economists everywhere.

Big Idea One: Incentives Matter

When the captains were paid for every prisoner that they took on board, they had little incentive to treat the prisoners well. In fact, the incentives were to treat the prisoners badly. Instead of feeding the prisoners, for example, some of the captains hoarded the prisoners' food, selling it in Australia for a tidy profit.

When the captains were paid for prisoners who survived the journey, however, their incentives changed. Whereas before, the captains had benefited from a prisoner's death, now the incentive system "secured to every poor man who died at least one sincere mourner."[3] The sincere mourner? The captain, who at least was sincere about mourning the money he would have earned had the poor man survived.

Incentives are everywhere. In the United States, we take it for granted that when we go to the supermarket the shelves will be stocked with kiwi fruit from New Zealand, rice from India, and wine from Chile. Every day we rely on the work of millions of other people to provide us with food, clothing, and shelter. Why do so many people work for our benefit? In his 1776 classic, *The Wealth of Nations*, Adam Smith explained:

> It is not from the benevolence of the butcher, the brewer, or the baker, that we expect our dinner, but from their regard to their own interest.

Do economists think that everyone is self-interested all the time? Of course not. We love our spouses and children just like everyone else! But economists do think that people respond in predictable ways to incentives of all kinds. Fame, power, reputation, sex, and love are all important incentives. Economists even think that benevolence responds to incentives. It's not surprising to an economist, for example, that charities publicize the names of their donors. Some people do give anonymously, but how many buildings on your campus are named Anonymous Hall?

Big Idea Two: Good Institutions Align Self-Interest with the Social Interest

The story of the convict ships hints at a second lesson that runs throughout this book: When self-interest aligns with the broader public interest, we get good outcomes, but when self-interest and the social interest are at odds, we get bad outcomes, sometimes even cruel and inhumane outcomes. Paying the ship captains for every prisoner who walked off the ship was a good payment system because it created incentives for the ship captains to do the right thing, not just for themselves but also for the prisoners and for the government that was paying them.

It's a remarkable finding of economics that under the right conditions markets align self-interest with the social interest. You can see what we mean by thinking back to the supermarket we mentioned earlier. The supermarket is stocked with products from around the world because markets channel and coordinate the self-interest of millions of people to achieve a social good. The farmer who awoke at 5 AM to tend his crops, the trucker who delivered the goods to the market, the entrepreneur who risked his or her capital to build the supermarket— each of these people acted in their own interest, but in so doing they also acted in your interest.

In a striking metaphor, Adam Smith said that when markets work well, those who pursue their own interest end up promoting the social interest, as if led to do so by an "invisible hand." The idea that the pursuit of self-interest can be in the social interest—that at least sometimes, "greed is good"—was one of the most surprising discoveries of economic science, and after several hundred years this insight is still not always appreciated. Throughout this book, we emphasize ways in which individuals acting in their self-interest produce outcomes that were not part of their intention nor design, but which nevertheless have desirable properties. The invisible hand icon, seen in the margin, will be a symbol of these ideas.

see the
invisible hand

Markets, however, do not always align self-interest with the social interest. Sometimes the invisible hand is absent, not just invisible. Market incentives, for example, can be too strong. A firm that doesn't pay for the pollution that it emits into the air has too great an incentive to emit pollution. Fishermen sometimes have too strong an incentive to catch fish, thereby driving the stock of fish into collapse. In other cases, market incentives are too weak. Did you get your flu shot this year? The flu shot prevents you from getting the flu (usually) but it also reduces the chances that other people will get the flu. When deciding whether to get a flu shot, did you take into account the social interest or just your self-interest?

When markets don't properly align self-interest with the social interest, another important lesson of economics is that government can sometime improve the situation by changing incentives with taxes, subsidies, or other regulations.

Big Idea Three: Trade-offs Are Everywhere

Vioxx users were outraged when in September 2004 Merck withdrew the arthritis drug from the market; at the time a new study showed that Vioxx could cause strokes and heart attacks. Vioxx had been on the market for 5 years and had been used by millions of people. Patients were angry at Merck and at the Food and Drug Administration (FDA). How could the FDA, which is charged with ensuring that new pharmaceuticals are safe and effective, have let Vioxx onto the market? Many people demanded more testing and safer pharmaceuticals. Economists worried that approved pharmaceuticals could become too safe.

Too safe! Is it possible to be too safe?! Yes, because trade-offs are everywhere. Researching, developing, and testing a new drug costs time and resources. On average, it takes about 12 years and $900 million dollars to bring a new drug to market. More testing means that approved drugs will have fewer side effects, but there are two important trade-offs: *drug lag* and *drug loss*.

Testing takes time so more testing means that good drugs are delayed, just like bad drugs. On average, new drugs work better than old drugs. So the longer it takes to bring new drugs to market, the more people are harmed who could have benefited if the new drugs had been approved earlier.[4] You can die because an unsafe drug is approved—you can also die because a safe drug has *not yet* been approved. This is *drug lag*.

Testing not only takes time, it is costly. The greater the costs of testing, the fewer new drugs there will be. The costs of testing are a hurdle that each potential drug must leap if it is to be developed. Higher costs mean a higher hurdle, fewer new drugs and fewer lives saved. You can die because an unsafe drug is approved—you can also die because a safe drug is *never* developed. This is *drug loss*.

Thus, society faces a trade-off. More testing means the drugs that are (eventually) approved will be safer but it also means more drug lag and drug loss. When thinking about FDA policy, we need to look at both sides of the trade-off if we are to choose wisely.

Trade-offs are closely related to another important idea in economics, opportunity cost.

Opportunity Cost

The **opportunity cost** of a choice is the value of the opportunities lost.

Every choice involves something gained and something lost. The **opportunity cost** of a choice is the value of the opportunities lost. Consider the choice to attend college. What is the cost of attending college? At first, you might calculate the cost by adding together the price of tuition, books, and room and board—that might be $15,000 a year. But that's not the opportunity cost of attending college. What opportunities are you losing when you attend college?

The main opportunity that is lost when you attend college is (probably) the opportunity to have a full-time job. Most of you reading this book could easily get a job earning $25,000 a year or maybe quite a bit more (Bill Gates was a college dropout). If you spend four years in college, that's $100,000 that you are giving up to get an education. The opportunity cost of college is probably higher than you thought. Perhaps you ought to ask more questions in class in order to get your money's worth! (But go back to the list of items we totaled earlier—tuition, books, and room and board—one of these items should *not* count as part of the opportunity cost of college. Which one? Answer: Room and board is not a cost of college if you would have to pay for it whether you go to college or not.)

The concept of opportunity cost is important for two reasons. First, if you don't understand the opportunities that you are losing when you make a choice, you won't recognize the real trade-offs that you face. Recognizing trade-offs is the first step to making wise choices. Second, most of the time people do respond to changes in opportunity costs—*even when money costs have not changed*—so if you want to understand behavior, you need to understand opportunity cost.

What would you predict, for example, would happen to college enrollment during a recession? The price of tuition, books, and room and board doesn't fall during a recession but the opportunity cost of attending college does fall. Why? During a recession, the unemployment rate increases so it's harder to get a high-paying job. That means you lose less by attending college when the unemployment rate is high. We, therefore, predict that college enrollments increase when the unemployment rate increases; in opportunity costs terms, it is cheaper to go to college. Figure 1.1 shows that this is correct—when the unemployment rate is unusually high (above trend), the college enrollment rate tends to be unusually high as well. The reverse is also true: When the economy is booming and the unemployment rate is unusually low, the college enrollment rate tends to be low as well. Of course, many other factors other than the unemployment rate influence college enrollment rates so the relationship is not

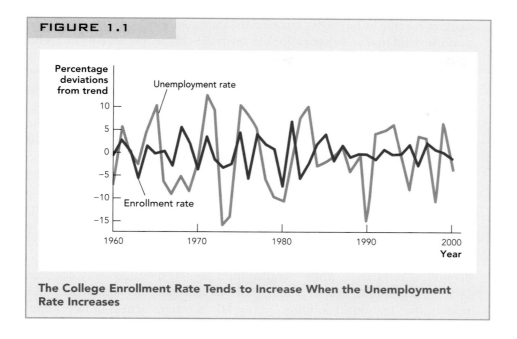

FIGURE 1.1

Percentage deviations from trend

Unemployment rate

Enrollment rate

1960   1970   1980   1990   2000

Year

The College Enrollment Rate Tends to Increase When the Unemployment Rate Increases

exact, but Figure 1.1 shows that as a general tendency the enrollment rate tends to be unusually high when the unemployment rate is unusually high.

Big Idea Four: Thinking on the Margin

People cheered when, in the 1990s, Speaker of the House Newt Gingrich advocated mandatory executions for drug dealers. But economists wondered why Gingrich wanted to *decrease* the penalty for murder. How does the death penalty for drug dealers decrease the penalty for murder? Think about it this way: Suppose that Gingrich's bill becomes law and the police bust into an apartment where three drug dealers have hidden their stash. What happens? The drug dealers know that if they give up, they will be put to death. So why not try to kill the police? If the dealers are lucky, they get away. If the dealers are unlucky, they are no worse off than if they didn't fight because when drug dealing is a capital offense, drug dealers face no *additional* penalty for murder.

Imposing the death penalty on drug dealers may decrease the number of drug dealers but increase the number of murders. Similarly, if we increase the penalties for robbery we are reducing the additional or *marginal* penalty for armed robbery. Thus, tougher penalties for robbery can increase the number of armed robberies. Is this a good trade-off?

The surprising effects of policies to "get tough on crime" illustrate the importance of what economists call *thinking on the margin*. When a drug dealer decides whether to commit the crime of murder, he or she doesn't think about the penalty for murder—the drug dealer thinks about the marginal or additional penalty for murder given what he or she is doing already. More generally, most choices are usually marginal choices—should we do a little bit more or a little bit less of some activity?

In this book, you will find lots of talk about marginal choices, which includes marginal cost (the addition to cost from producing one more unit), marginal revenue (the addition to revenue from producing one more unit), and the marginal tax rate (the tax rate on an additional dollar of income). This point about margins is really just a way of restating the importance of trade-offs. If you wish to understand human behavior, look at the trade-offs people actually face. Those trade-offs usually involve choices about a little bit more or a little bit less.

Let's give a personal example that illustrates the importance of thinking on the margin. Say you have graduated from your university and are earning a healthy salary of $64,000 a year. You are offered another job with a higher salary, but it's in a different town and you really don't want to move. Should you take the new job? A lot will depend on how much of the higher income you get to keep and how much the government will take in taxes. To figure this out, don't ask how much of your current income is taken in taxes. Ask how much tax there will be on your additional income if you take the new job. The average tax rate on income of $64,000 is about 13 percent, but the government will take 25 percent of every dollar you earn above $64,000. The new job may not look so good when you look at the relevant tax rate for your choice, namely the marginal tax rate.

The importance of thinking at the margin did not become commonplace in economics until 1871, when marginal thinking was simultaneously discovered by three economists: Stanley Jevons, Carl Menger, and Leon Walras. Economists refer to the "marginal revolution" to explain this transformation in economic thought.

Big Idea Five: Tampering with the Laws of Supply and Demand Has Consequences

Nearly two thousand years ago the Roman Emperor Diocletian made it illegal to sell beef, grain, eggs, clothing, and a thousand other goods at prices greater than he decreed. Merchants who disobeyed were sentenced to death. The historian Lactantius reported the results: "the people brought provisions no more to markets, since they could not get a reasonable price for them and this increased the dearth [shortage] so much, that at last after many had died by it, the law itself was set aside."

Markets respond in predictable ways to price controls. When President Richard Nixon imposed price controls on the U.S. economy in 1971, the results were very similar to those in Diocletian's time: shortages, long lines, lower quality goods, and waste. And, just as in Diocletian's time, the policy was eventually abandoned as a failure.

Price controls are hardly a thing of the past. Even today when the price of gasoline rises, consumers become angry and politicians will sometimes try to appease this anger by promising to make high prices illegal. But economics explains why price controls rarely work. Rather than solving the problem of low purchasing power, price controls tend to make the situation worse by reducing the incentive to supply goods.

We think that many of the most important issues in the world today cannot be understood without understanding economics. Throughout this textbook we will use the icon seen in the margin to emphasize some of the most important ways in which economics helps you to Understand Your World.

Big Idea Six: The Importance of Wealth and Economic Growth

In 2007, more than half a billion people in the world contracted malaria and about a million of them—mostly children—died from it. Today, we think of malaria as a "tropical" disease but malaria was once common in the United States. George Washington caught malaria, as did James Monroe, Andrew Jackson, Abraham Lincoln, Ulysses S. Grant, and James A. Garfield. Malaria was present in America until the late 1940s, when the last cases were wiped out by better drainage, removal of mosquito breeding sites, and the spraying of insecticides. The lesson? Wealth—the ability to pay for the prevention of malaria—ended malaria in the United States and wealth comes from economic growth, so the incidence of malaria is not just about geography—it's also about economics.

Malaria is far from the only problem that diminishes with wealth and economic growth. In the United States, one of the world's richest countries, 993 out of every 1,000 children born survive to the age of 5. In Liberia, one of the world's poorest countries, only about 765 children survive to age 5 (i.e., 235 of every 1,000 children die before seeing their fifth birthday). Overall, it's the wealthiest countries that have the highest rates of infant survival.

Indeed, if you look at most of the things that people care about, they are much easier to come by in the wealthier economies. Wealth brings us flush toilets, antibiotics, higher education, the ability to choose the career we want, fun vacations, and of course a greater ability to protect our families against catastrophes. Wealth also brings women's rights and political liberty, at least in most (but not all) countries. Wealthier economies lead to richer and more fulfilled human lives. In short, *wealth matters and understanding economic growth is one of the most important tasks of economics.*

Big Idea Seven: Institutions Matter

If wealth is so important, what makes a country rich? The most proximate cause is that wealthy countries have lots of physical and human capital per worker and they produce things in a relatively efficient manner, using the latest technological knowledge. But why do some countries have more physical and human capital and why is it organized well using the latest technological knowledge? In a word, incentives, which of course relates back to Big Idea One.

Entrepreneurs, investors, and savers need incentives to save and invest in physical capital, human capital, innovation, and efficient organization. Among the most powerful institutions for supporting good incentives are property rights, political stability, honest government, a dependable legal system, and competitive and open markets.

Consider South and North Korea. South Korea has a per capita income more than 10 times greater than its immediate neighbor, North Korea. South Korea is a modern, developed economy but in North Korea people still starve or can go for months without eating meat. And yet both countries were equally poor in 1950 and of course the two countries share the same language and cultural and historical background. What differs is their economic systems and the incentives at work.

Macroeconomists are especially interested in the incentives to produce new ideas. If the world never had any new ideas the standard of living eventually would stagnate. But in fact entrepreneurs innovate with iPhones, soil fertilizer, the Prius, and many other discoveries. Just about any device you use in daily life is based on a multitude of ideas and innovations, the lifeblood of economic growth. New ideas, of course, require incentives and that means an active scientific community and the freedom and incentive to put new ideas into action. Ideas also have peculiar properties. One apple feeds one man but one idea can feed the world. Ideas, in other words, aren't used up when they are used and that has tremendous implications for understanding the benefits of trade, the future of economic growth, and many other topics.

Big Idea Eight: Economic Booms and Busts Cannot Be Avoided but Can Be Moderated

We have seen that growth matters and that the right institutions foster growth. But no economy grows at a constant pace. It advances and recedes, rises and falls, booms and busts. In a recession, wages fall and many people are thrown into miserable unemployment. Unfortunately, we cannot avoid all recessions. Booms and busts are part of the normal response of an economy to changing economic conditions. When the weather is bad in India, for example, crops fail and the economy grows more slowly or perhaps it grows not at all. The weather doesn't much affect the economy in the United States, but the U.S. economy is buffeted by other unavoidable shocks.

Although some booms and busts are part of the normal response of an economy to changing economic conditions, not all booms and busts are normal. The Great Depression (1929–1940) was not normal, but rather it was the most catastrophic economic event in the history of the United States. National output plummeted by 30 percent, unemployment rates exceeded 20 percent, and the stock market fell to less than a third of its original value. Almost overnight the United States went from confidence to desperation. The Great Depression, however, didn't have to happen. Most economists today believe that if the government, especially the U.S. Federal Reserve, had acted more quickly and more appropriately, the Great Depression would have been shorter and less deep. At the time, however, the tools at the government's disposal—monetary and fiscal policy—were not well understood.

Today, the tools of monetary and fiscal policy are much better understood. When used appropriately, these tools can reduce swings in unemployment and GDP. Unemployment insurance can also reduce some of the misery that accompanies a recession. The tools of monetary and fiscal policy, however, are not all powerful. At one time it was thought that these tools could end all recessions, but we know now that this is not the case. Furthermore, when used poorly, monetary and fiscal policy can make recessions worse and the economy more volatile.

A significant task of macroeconomic theory is to understand both the promise and the limits of monetary and fiscal policy in smoothing out the normal booms and busts of the macroeconomy.

Big Idea Nine: Prices Rise When the Government Prints Too Much Money

Inflation is an increase in the general level of prices.

Yes, economic policy can be useful but sometimes policy goes awry, for instance when **inflation** gets out of hand. Inflation, one of the most common problems in macroeconomics, refers to an increase in the general level of prices. Inflation makes people feel poorer but, perhaps more important, rising and especially volatile prices make it harder for people to figure out the real values of goods, services, and investments. For these and other reasons, most people (and economists) dislike inflation.

But where does inflation come from? The answer is simple: Inflation comes about when there is a sustained increase in the supply of money. When people have more money, they spend it, and without an increase in the supply of goods, prices must rise. As Economics Nobel Laureate Milton Friedman once wrote: "Inflation is always and everywhere a monetary phenomenon."

The United States, like other advanced economies, has a central bank called the Federal Reserve Bank. The Federal Reserve Bank has the power and the responsibility to regulate the supply of money in the American economy. This power can be used for good, such as when the Federal Reserve holds off or minimizes a recession. But the power also can be used for great harm if the Federal Reserve encourages too much growth in the supply of money. The result will be inflation and economic disruption.

In Zimbabwe, the government has been running the printing presses at full tilt for many years and by the end of 2007 prices were rising at an astonishing rate of 150,000 percent a year. The United States has never had a problem of this scope or anything close to it but inflation remains a perennial concern.

Amazingly, the inflation rate in Zimbabwe kept rising in 2008 and is now close to the highest inflation rate ever recorded with prices rising by *billions* of percent per month!

Inflation rates of 150,000 percent a year mean that this Zimbabwean $10 million note isn't enough to buy a hamburger and fries.

Big Idea Ten: Central Banking Is a Hard Job

The U.S. central bank, the Federal Reserve Bank ("the Fed"), is often called on to combat recessions. But this is not always easy to do. Typically, there is a lag—often of many months—between when the Fed makes a decision and when the effects of that decision on the economy are known. In the meantime, economic conditions have changed so you should think of the Fed as shooting at a moving target. No one can foresee the future perfectly and so the Fed's decisions are not always the right ones.

As mentioned above, too much money in the economy means that inflation will result. But not enough money in the economy is bad as well and can lead to a recession or a slowing of economic growth. These ideas are an important and extensive topic in macroeconomics, but the key problem is that a low or falling money supply forces people to cut their prices and wages and this adjustment doesn't always go smoothly.

The Fed is always trying to get it "just right," but some of the time it fails. Sometimes the failure is a mistake the Fed could have avoided, but other times it simply isn't possible to always make the right guess about where the world is headed. Thus, in some situations the Fed must accept a certain amount of either inflation or unemployment. Central banking relies on economic tools, but in the final analysis it is as much an art as a science.

Most economists think that the Fed does more good than harm. But if you are going to understand the Fed, you have to think of it as a highly fallible institution that faces a very difficult job.

The Biggest Idea of All: Economics Is Fun

When you put all these ideas and others together, we think that economics is both exciting and important. Economics teaches us how to make the world a better place. It's about the difference between wealth and poverty, work and unemployment, happiness and squalor. Economics increases your understanding of the distant past, present events, and future possibilities.

As you will see, the basic principles of economics hold everywhere, whether it is in a rice paddy in Vietnam or a stock market in Sao Paulo, Brazil. No matter what the topic, the principles of economics apply to all countries, not just to your own. Moreover, in today's globalized world, events in China and India influence the economy in the United States, and vice versa. For this reason, you will find that our book is truly international and full of examples and applications from Algeria to Zimbabwe.

But economics is also linked to everyday life. Economics can help you think about your quest for a job, how to manage your personal finances and how to deal with debt, inflation, a recession, or a bursting stock market bubble. In short, economics is about understanding your world.

We are excited about economics and we hope that you will be too. Perhaps some of you will even become economics majors. If you are thinking about majoring, you might want to know that economics is the fastest-growing major over the last 10 years. That reflects the value of an economics degree and the world's recognition of that value. But if your passion lies elsewhere, that's okay too, a course in the principles of economics will take you a long way toward understanding your world. With a good course, a good professor, and a good textbook, you'll never look at the world the same way again. So just remember: *See the Invisible Hand. Understand Your World.*

□ CHAPTER REVIEW

KEY CONCEPTS

Incentives, p. 1

Opportunity cost, p. 4

Inflation, p. 8

FACTS AND TOOLS

1. A headline[5] in the *New York Times* read: "Study Finds Enrollment Is Up at Colleges Despite Recession." How would you rewrite this headline now that you understand the idea of opportunity cost?

2. When bad weather in India destroys the crop harvest, does this sound like a fall in the total "supply" of crops or a fall in people's "demand" for crops? Keep your answer in mind as you learn about economic booms and busts later on.

3. How much did national output fall during the Great Depression? According to the chapter, which government agency might have helped to avoid much of the Great Depression had it acted more quickly and appropriately?

4. The chapter lists four things that entrepreneurs save and invest in. Which of the four are actual objects, and which are more intangible, like concepts or ideas or plans? Feel free to use Wikipedia or some other reference source to get definitions of unfamiliar terms.

5. Who has a better incentive to work long hours in a laboratory researching new cures for diseases: a scientist who earns a percentage of the profits from any new medicine she might invent, or a scientist who will get a handshake and a thank you note from her boss if she invents a new medicine?

THINKING AND PROBLEM SOLVING

1. In recent years, Zimbabwe has had hyperinflation, with prices tripling (or more!) every month. According to what you learned in this chapter, what do you think the government can do to end this hyperinflation?

2. Some people worry that machines will take jobs away from people, making people permanently

unemployed. In the United States, only 150 years ago most people were farmers. Now, machines do almost all of the farm work and fewer than 2 percent of Americans are farmers, yet that 2 percent produces enough food to feed the entire country while still exporting food overseas.

  a. What happened to all of those people who used to work on farms? Do you think most adult males in the U.S. are unemployed nowadays, now that the farm work is gone?

  b. Some people say that it's okay for machines to take jobs, since we'll get jobs fixing the machines. Just from looking around, do you think that most working Americans are earning a living by fixing farm equipment? If not, what do you think most working people are doing instead? (We'll give a full answer later in this book.)

3. Let's connect Big Ideas Six and Nine: Do you think that people in poor countries are poor because they don't have enough money? In other words, could a country get richer by printing more pieces of paper called "money" and handing those out to its citizens?

4. Nobel Prize–winner Milton Friedman said that a bad central banker is like a "fool in the shower." In a shower, of course, when you turn the faucet right now, it won't show up in the showerhead for a few seconds. So if a "fool in the shower" is always making big changes in the temperature based on how the water feels *right now*, the water is likely to swing back and forth between too hot and too cold. How does this apply to central banking?

5. According to the United Nations, there were roughly 300 million humans on the planet a thousand years ago. Essentially all of them were poor by modern standards: They lacked antibiotics, almost all lacked indoor plumbing, and none traveled faster than a horse or a river could carry them. Today, between 1 and 3 billion humans are poor out of about 7 billion total humans. So, over the last thousand years, what has happened to the *fraction* of humans who are poor: Did it rise, fall, or stay about the same? What happened to the total *number* of people living in deep poverty: Rise, fall, or no change?

CHALLENGES

1. We claim that part of the reason the Great Depression was so destructive is because economists didn't understand how to use government policy very well in the 1930s. In your opinion, do you think that economists during the Great Depression would have agreed? In other words, if you had asked them why the Depression was so bad, would they have said, "Because the government ignored our wise advice," or would they have said, "Because we don't have any good ideas about how to fix this?" What does your answer tell you about the confidence of economists and other experts?

2. Some problems that economists try to solve are easy *as economic problems* but hard *as political problems.* Medical doctors face similar kinds of situations: Preventing most deaths from obesity or lung cancer is easy *as a medical problem* (eat less, exercise more, don't smoke) but hard *as a self-control problem.* With this in mind, how is ending hyperinflation like losing 100 pounds?

3. As Nobel prize winner and *New York Times* columnist Paul Krugman has noted, the field of economics is a lot like the field of medicine: They are fields where knowledge is limited (both are new as real scientific disciplines), and where many cures are quite painful ("opportunity cost"), but where regular people care deeply about the issues. What are some other ways that economics and medicine are alike?

4. Economics is sometimes called "the dismal science." Of the big ideas in this chapter, which sound "dismal"—like bad news?

2

Supply and Demand

CHAPTER OUTLINE

The Demand Curve for Oil

The Supply Curve for Oil

Takeaway

The world runs on oil. Every day about 82 *million* barrels of "black gold" flow from the earth and the sea to fuel the world's demand. Changes in the demand for and supply of oil can plunge one economy into recession while igniting a boom in another. In capitals from Washington to Riyadh, politicians carefully monitor the price of oil and so do ordinary consumers. Gasoline is made from oil so when world events like war in the Middle East disrupt the oil supply, prices at the corner gas station rise. The oil market is arguably the single most important market in the world.

The most important tools in economics are supply, demand, and the idea of equilibrium. Even if you understand little else, you may rightly claim yourself economically literate if you understand these tools. Fail to understand these tools and you will understand little else. In this chapter, we use the supply and demand for oil to explain the concepts of supply and demand. In the next chapter, we use supply, demand, and the idea of equilibrium to explain how prices are determined. So pay attention: this chapter and the next one are important. Really important.

The Demand Curve for Oil

How much oil would be demanded if the price of oil were $5 per barrel? What quantity would be demanded if the price were $20? What quantity would be demanded if the price were $55? A demand curve answers these questions. A **demand curve** is a function that shows the quantity demanded at different prices.

In Figure 2.1 on the next page we show a hypothetical demand curve for oil and a table illustrating how a demand curve can be constructed from information on prices and quantities demanded. The demand curve tells us, for example, that at a price of $55 per barrel buyers are willing and able to buy

A **demand curve** is a function that shows the quantity demanded at different prices.

13

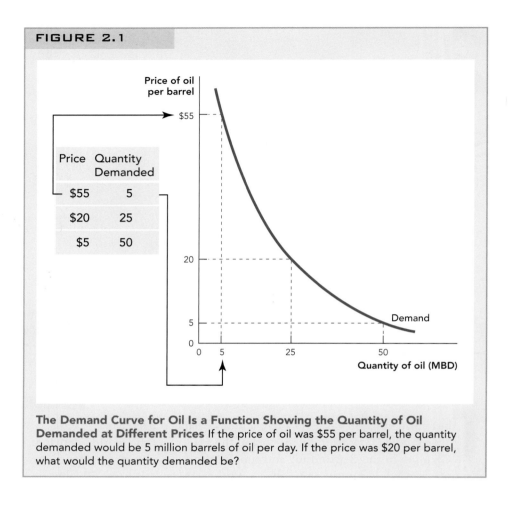

FIGURE 2.1

Price	Quantity Demanded
$55	5
$20	25
$5	50

The Demand Curve for Oil Is a Function Showing the Quantity of Oil Demanded at Different Prices If the price of oil was $55 per barrel, the quantity demanded would be 5 million barrels of oil per day. If the price was $20 per barrel, what would the quantity demanded be?

The **quantity demanded** is the quantity that buyers are willing and able to buy at a particular price.

5 million barrels of oil a day or, more simply, at a price of $55 the **quantity demanded** is 5 million barrels a day (MBD).

Demand curves can be read in two ways. Read "horizontally" we can see from Figure 2.2 that at a price of $20 per barrel demanders are willing and able to buy 25 million barrels of oil per day. Read "vertically" we can see that the maximum price that demanders are willing to pay for 25 million barrels of oil a day is $20 per barrel. Thus, demand curves tell us the quantity demanded at any price or the maximum willingness to pay (per unit) for any quantity. Some applications are easier to understand with one reading than with the other so you should be familiar with both.

Okay, a demand curve is a function that shows the quantity that demanders are willing to buy at different prices. But what does the demand curve *mean*? And why is the demand curve negatively sloped; that is, why is a greater quantity of oil demanded when the price is low?

Oil has many uses. A barrel of oil contains 42 gallons, and a little over half of that is used to produce gasoline (19.5 gallons) and jet fuel (4 gallons). The remaining 18.5 gallons are used for heating and energy generation and to make products such as lubricants, kerosene, asphalt, plastics, tires, and even rubber duckies (which are actually made not from rubber but from vinyl plastic).

Oil, however, is not equally valuable in all of its uses. Oil is more valuable for producing gasoline and jet fuel than it is for producing heating or rubber duckies. Oil is very valuable for transportation because in that use oil has few substitutes. There is

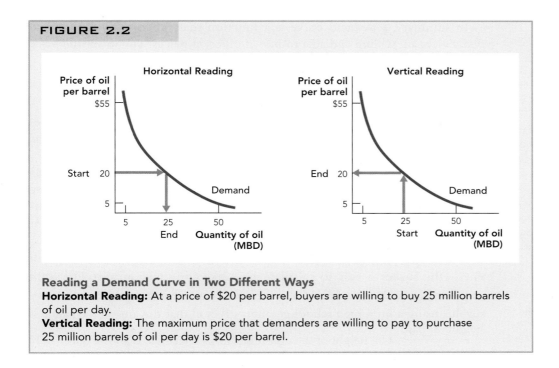

FIGURE 2.2

Reading a Demand Curve in Two Different Ways
Horizontal Reading: At a price of $20 per barrel, buyers are willing to buy 25 million barrels of oil per day.
Vertical Reading: The maximum price that demanders are willing to pay to purchase 25 million barrels of oil per day is $20 per barrel.

no reasonable substitute for oil as jet fuel, for example, and while some hybrids like the Prius are moderately successful, pure electric cars remain costly and inconvenient. There are more substitutes for oil in heating and energy generation. In these fields, oil competes directly or indirectly against natural gas, coal, and electricity. Within each of these fields are also more and less valuable uses. It's more valuable, for example, to raise the temperature in your house on a winter's day from 40 degrees to 65 degrees than it is to raise the temperature from 65 degrees to 70 degrees. Vinyl has high value as wire wrapping because it is fire retardant, but we can probably substitute wooden toy boats for rubber duckies.

The fact that oil is not equally valuable in all of its uses explains why the demand curve for oil has a negative slope. When the price of oil is high, consumers will choose to use oil *only* in its most valuable uses (e.g., gasoline and jet fuel). As the price of oil falls, consumers will choose to also use oil in its less and less valued uses (heating and rubber duckies). Thus, a demand curve summarizes how millions of consumers choose to use oil given their preferences and the possibilities for substitution. Figure 2.3 illustrates these ideas with a demand curve for oil.

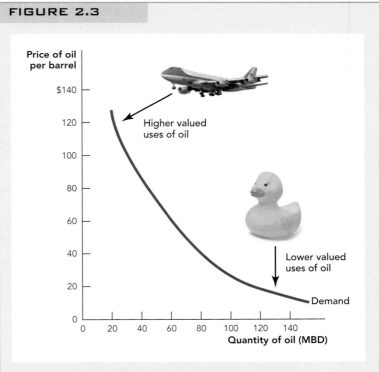

FIGURE 2.3

The Demand for Oil Depends on the Value of Oil in Different Uses When the price of oil is high, oil will only be used in its higher valued uses. As the price of oil falls, oil will also be used in lower valued uses.
(Top photo: EuroStyle Graphics/Alamy)
(Bottom: Lew Robertson/Corbis)

In summary, a demand curve is a function that shows the quantity that demanders are willing and able to buy at different prices. The lower the price the greater the quantity demanded—this is often called the "law of demand."

Consumer Surplus

If a consumer, say the President of the United States, is willing to pay $80 per barrel to fuel his jet plane but the price of oil is only $20 per barrel then the President earns a consumer surplus of $60 per barrel. If Joe is willing to pay $25 and the price of oil is $20 per barrel, then Joe earns a consumer surplus of $5 per barrel. **Consumer surplus** is the consumer's gain from exchange. Adding up consumer surplus for each consumer and for each unit, we can find **total consumer surplus.** On a graph, *total consumer surplus is the shaded area beneath the demand curve and above the price* (see Figure 2.4).

It's often convenient to approximate demand and supply curves with straight lines—this makes it easy to calculate areas like consumer surplus. The right panel of Figure 2.4 simplifies the left panel. Now we can calculate consumer surplus using a little high school geometry. Recall that the area of a triangle is $\frac{\text{height} \times \text{base}}{2}$. The height of the consumer surplus triangle is $60 = $80 - $20 and the base is 90 million barrels so consumer surplus equals $2,700 million ($60 × 90 million/2).

Consumer surplus is the consumer's gain from exchange, or the difference between the maximum price a consumer is willing to pay for a certain quantity and the market price.

Total consumer surplus is measured by the area beneath the demand curve and above the price.

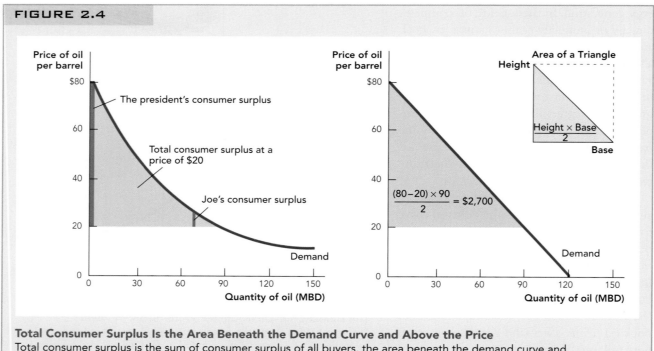

FIGURE 2.4

Total Consumer Surplus Is the Area Beneath the Demand Curve and Above the Price
Total consumer surplus is the sum of consumer surplus of all buyers, the area beneath the demand curve and above the price.
In the right panel we show that consumer surplus is easy to calculate with a linear demand curve.

What Shifts the Demand Curve?

The demand curve for oil tells us the quantity of oil that people are willing to buy at a given price. Assume for example that at a price of $25 per barrel, the world demand for oil is 70 million barrels per day. An increase in demand means that at a price of $25, the quantity demanded increases to say 80 million barrels per day. Or, equivalently, it means that the maximum willingness to pay for 70 million barrels increases to say $50 per barrel. The left panel of Figure 2.5 shows an increase in demand. *An increase in demand shifts the demand curve outward, up and to the right.*

The right panel of Figure 2.5 shows a decrease in demand. *A decrease in demand shifts the demand curve inward, down, and to the left.*

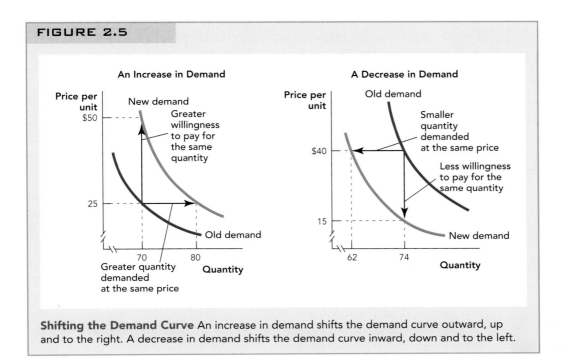

FIGURE 2.5

Shifting the Demand Curve An increase in demand shifts the demand curve outward, up and to the right. A decrease in demand shifts the demand curve inward, down and to the left.

What kinds of things will increase or decrease demand? Unfortunately for economics students, a lot of things! Here is a list of some important demand shifters:

Important Demand Shifters

> Income
> Population
> Price of substitutes
> Price of complements
> Expectations
> Tastes

If you must, memorize the list. But keep in mind the question, "What would make people willing to buy a greater quantity at the same price?" Or equivalently, "What would make people willing to pay more for the same quantity?" With these questions in mind, you should always be able to come up with a pretty good list on your own.

Here are some examples of demand shifters in action.

Income When people get richer, they buy more stuff. In the United States, people buy bigger cars when their income increases and big cars increase the demand for oil. When income increases in China or India, many people buy their first car and that too increases the demand for oil. Thus, an increase in income will increase the demand for oil exactly as shown in the left panel of Figure 2.5.

When an *increase* in income *increases* the demand for a good, we say the good is a **normal good.** Most goods are normal; for example, cars, electronics, and restaurant meals are normal goods. Can you think of some goods for which an increase in income will *decrease* the demand? When we were young economics students, we didn't have a lot of money to go to expensive restaurants. For 50 cents and some boiling water, however, we could get a nice bowl of instant ramen noodles. Ah, good times. When our income increased, however, our demand for ramen noodles decreased—we don't buy ramen noodles anymore! A good like ramen noodles for which an *increase* in income *decreases* the demand is called an **inferior good.** What goods are you consuming now that you probably wouldn't consume if you were rich? Economic growth is rapidly increasing the incomes of millions of poor people in China and India. What goods do poor people consume in these countries today that they will consume less of 20 years from now?

Population More people, more demand. That's simple enough. Things get more interesting when some subpopulations increase more than others. The United States, for example, is aging. Today the 65-year-old and older crowd makes up about 13 percent of the population. By 2030, 19.4 percent of the population will be 65 years or older. In fact, demographers estimate that by 2030 18.2 million people in the United States will be over 85 years of age![1] What sorts of goods and services will increase in demand with this increase in population? Which will decrease in demand? Entrepreneurs want to know the answers to these questions because big profits will flow to those who can anticipate new and expanded markets.

Price of Substitutes Natural gas is a substitute for oil in some uses such as heating. Suppose that the price of natural gas goes down. What will happen to the quantity of oil demanded? When the price of natural gas goes down, some people will switch from oil furnaces to natural gas, so the quantity of oil demanded will decrease—the demand curve shifts down and to the left. Figure 2.6 illustrates.

More generally, a decrease in the price of a **substitute** will decrease demand for the other good. A decrease in the price of Pepsi, for example, will decrease the demand for Coca-Cola. A decrease in the price of rental apartments will reduce the demand for condominiums. Naturally, an increase in the price of a substitute will increase demand for the other substituted good.

Price of Complements **Complements** are things that go well together: French fries and ketchup, sugar and tea, DVD movies and DVD players. More technically, good A is a complement to good B if greater consumption of A encourages greater consumption of B. Ground beef and hamburger buns are complements. Suppose the price of beef goes down. What happens to the demand for hamburger buns? If the price of beef goes down, people buy more ground beef and they also increase their demand for hamburger buns, that is, the demand curve

---

A **normal good** is a good for which demand increases when income increases.

An **inferior good** is a good for which demand decreases when income increases.

MARK HAMILTON/ZEFA/CORBIS

Demographics and Demand
The number of old people in the United States is increasing. How will this increase in the elderly population shift the demand curve for different goods?

If two goods are **substitutes** a decrease in the price of one good leads to a decrease in demand for the other good.

If two goods are **complements** a decrease in the price of one good leads to an increase in the demand for the other good.

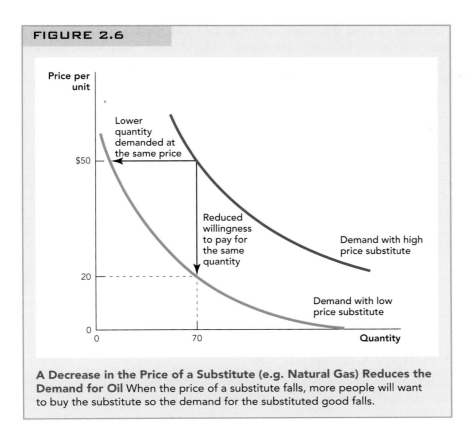

FIGURE 2.6

A Decrease in the Price of a Substitute (e.g. Natural Gas) Reduces the Demand for Oil When the price of a substitute falls, more people will want to buy the substitute so the demand for the substituted good falls.

for hamburger buns shifts up and to the right. A supermarket having a sale on ground beef, for example, will also want to stock up on hamburger buns.

A decrease in the price of a complement increases the demand for the complementary good. An increase in the price of a complement decreases the demand for the complementary good. It sounds complicated, so just remember that ground beef and hamburger buns are complements and you should be able to work out the relationship.

Expectations In July 2007, a construction worker in the oil fields of Southern Nigeria was kidnapped. On hearing the news, oil prices around the world jumped to record high levels.[2] Was a single construction worker so critical to the world supply of oil? No. What spooked the world's oil markets was the fear that the kidnapping was the beginning of large-scale disruption in the Niger Delta, Nigeria's main oil producing region and the base for many anti-government rebels. Fear of future disruptions increased the demand for oil as businesses and governments worked to increase their emergency stockpiles. In other words, *the expectation of a reduction in the future oil supply increased the demand for oil today.*

You have probably responded to expectations about future events in a similar way. When the weather forecaster predicts a big storm, many people rush to the stores to stock up on storm supplies. In the week before Hurricane Katrina hit New Orleans, for example, sales of flashlights increased by 700 percent and battery sales increased by 250 percent compared to the week before.[3]

Expectations are powerful—they can be as powerful in affecting demand (and supply) as events themselves.

Tastes In the 1990s, doctors warned that too much fat could lead to heart attacks and demand for beef decreased. The 2001 publication of *Dr. Atkins' New*

Diet Revolution, a book promising weight loss on a high-protein, low-carb diet, increased the demand for beef. Steakhouses like Outback Steakhouse and the Brazilian-inspired Fogo De Chao started to appear everywhere.

Michael Jordan's popularity and his six NBA championships with the Chicago Bulls created a huge increase in demand for Nike's innovative Air Jordans. Demand for the shoes was so high that some young boys became victims of "shoe jackings." Changes in tastes caused by fads, fashions, and advertising can all increase or decrease demand.

Can tastes change something like the demand for oil? Sure. The environmental movement has made people more aware of global climate change and how the consumption of oil adds carbon dioxide to the atmosphere. As a result, the demand for hybrid cars has increased, more people are recycling things like plastic bags, and nuclear power is once again being discussed as an alternative source of energy. All of these changes can be understood as a change in tastes or preferences.

The bottom line is that while many different factors can shape market demand, most of these factors should make intuitive sense. After all, you are, on a daily basis, part of market demand.

The Supply Curve for Oil

How much oil would oil producers supply to the world market if the price of oil were $5 per barrel? What quantity would be supplied if the price were $20? What quantity if the price were $55? A supply curve for oil answers these questions.

The **supply curve** for oil is a function showing the quantity of oil that suppliers would be willing and able to sell at different prices or more simply the supply curve shows the **quantity supplied** at different prices. Figure 2.7 shows a hypothetical supply curve for oil. The price is on the vertical axis and the quantity of oil is on the horizontal axis. The table beside the graph shows how a supply curve can be constructed from a table of prices and quantities supplied.

The supply curve tells us, for example, that at a price of $20 the quantity supplied is 30 million barrels of oil a day.

As with demand curves, supply curves can be read in two ways. Read "horizontally" Figure 2.8 shows that at a price of $20 per barrel suppliers are willing to sell 30 million barrels of oil per day. Read "vertically" the supply curve tells us that to produce 30 million barrels of oil a day suppliers must be paid at least $20 per barrel. Thus, the supply curve tells us the maximum quantity that suppliers will supply at different prices or the minimum price at which suppliers will sell different quantities. The two ways of reading a supply curve are equivalent, but some applications are easier to understand with one reading than with the other so you should be familiar with both.

Our hypothetical supply curve is not realistic because we just made up the numbers. But now that we know the technical meaning of a supply curve— *a function that shows the quantity that suppliers would be willing to sell at different prices*—we can easily explain its economic meaning.

Saudi Arabia, the world's largest oil producer, produces about 10 million barrels of oil per day. Surprisingly, the United States is not far behind, producing nearly 9 million barrels per day. But there is one big difference between Saudi oil and U.S. oil: U.S. oil costs much more to produce. The United States has been producing major quantities of oil since early 1901 when, after drilling to

CHECK YOURSELF

> Economic growth in India is raising the income of Indian workers. What do you predict will happen to the demand for automobiles? What about the demand for charcoal bricks for home heating?

> As the price of oil rises, what do you predict will happen to the demand for mopeds?

The **supply curve** is a function that shows the quantity supplied at different prices.

The **quantity supplied** is the amount of a good that sellers are willing and able to sell at a particular price.

FIGURE 2.7

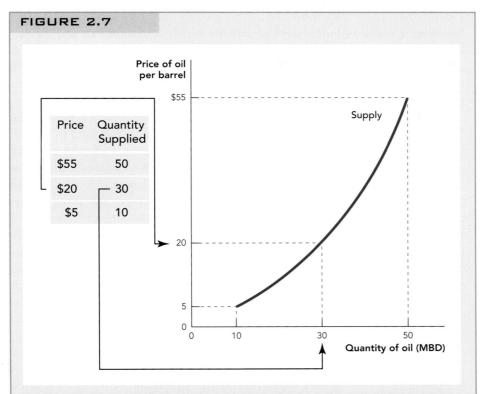

Price	Quantity Supplied
$55	50
$20	30
$5	10

The Supply Curve for Oil Is a Function Showing the Quantity of Oil Supplied at Different Prices If the price of oil was $20 per barrel, the quantity of oil supplied would be 30 million barrels of oil per day. How much oil would suppliers be willing and able to sell at $55?

FIGURE 2.8

Reading a Supply Curve in Two Different Ways Horizontal Reading: At a price of $20 per barrel, suppliers are willing to sell 30 million barrels of oil per day.
Vertical Reading: To produce 30 million barrels of oil a day, suppliers must be paid at least $20 per barrel.

a depth of 1,020 feet, mud started to bubble out of an oil well dug in Spindletop, Texas. Minutes later the drill bit exploded into the air and a fountain of oil leapt 150 feet into the sky. It took nine days to cap the well, and in the process a million barrels of oil were spilt. No one had ever seen so much oil. Within months the price of oil dropped from $2 per barrel to just 3 cents per barrel.[4]

It's safe to say that the United States will never see another gusher like Spindletop. Today the typical new well in the United States is drilled to a depth of more than two miles. Instead of gushing, most of the wells must be pumped or flooded with water in order to push the oil to the surface.[5] All of this makes oil production in the United States much more expensive than it used to be and much more expensive than in Saudi Arabia, where oil is more plentiful than anywhere else in the world.

In Saudi Arabia, lifting a barrel of oil to the surface costs about $2. Costs in Iran and Iraq are only slightly higher. Nigerian and Russian oil can be extracted at a cost of around $5 and $7 per barrel, respectively. Alaskan oil costs around $10 to extract. Oil from Britain's North Sea costs about $12 to extract. There is more oil in Canada's tar sands than in all of Iran, but it costs about $22.50 per barrel to get the oil out of the sand.[6] In the continental United States, one of the oldest and most developed oil regions in the world, lifting costs are about $27.50. At a price of $40 per barrel, it becomes profitable to "sweat" oil out of Oklahoma oil shale.

Putting all of this together, we can construct a simple supply curve for oil. At a price of $2 per barrel, the only oil that would be profitable to produce would be oil from the lowest cost wells in places like Saudi Arabia. As the price of oil rises, oil from Iran and Iraq become profitable. When the price reaches $5, Nigerian and then Russian producers begin to just break even. As the price rises yet further toward $10, Alaskan oil starts to break even and then become profitable. North Sea, Canadian, and then Texan oil fields come online and increase production as the price rises further. At higher prices, it becomes profitable to extract oil using even more exotic technologies or deeper wells in more inhospitable parts of the world. Figure 2.9 illustrates.

What's important to understand about Figure 2.9 is that as the price of oil rises, it becomes profitable to produce oil using methods and from regions of the world with higher costs of production. The higher the price of oil, the deeper the wells.

In summary, a supply curve is a function that shows the quantity that suppliers would be willing to sell at different prices. The higher the price, the greater the quantity supplied—this is often called the "law of supply."

FIGURE 2.9

The Supply Curve for Oil As the price of oil rises, it becomes profitable to extract oil from more costly sources. Thus, as the price of oil rises the quantity of oil supplied increases.

(Top photo: Dan Lamont/Corbis)

(Bottom: Bettmann/Corbis)

Producer Surplus

Figure 2.9 suggests two other concepts of importance. If the price of oil is $40 per barrel and Saudi Arabia can produce oil at $2 per barrel, then we say that Saudi Arabia earns a **producer surplus** of $38 per barrel. Similarly, if the price of oil is $40 per barrel and Nigeria can produce at $5 a barrel, Nigeria earns a producer surplus of $35 per barrel. Adding the producer surplus for each producer for each unit, we can find total producer surplus. Fortunately, this is easy to do on a diagram. *Total producer surplus is the shaded area above the supply curve and below the price* (see Figure 2.10).

Producer surplus is the producer's gain from exchange, or the difference between the market price and the minimum price at which a producer would be willing to sell a particular quantity.

Total producer surplus is measured by the area above the supply curve and below the price.

What Shifts the Supply Curve?

The second important concept suggested by Figure 2.9 is the connection between the supply curve and costs. What happens to the supply curve when the cost of producing oil falls? Suppose, for example, that a technological innovation in oil drilling such as sidewise drilling allows more oil to be produced at the same cost. What happens to the supply curve? The supply curve tells us how much suppliers are willing to sell at a particular price. The new technology makes some oil fields profitable that were previously unprofitable, so *at any price* suppliers are now willing to supply a greater quantity. Equivalently, the new technology lowers costs, so suppliers will be willing to sell any given quantity at a lower price. Either way economists say that a decrease in costs increases supply. In terms of the diagram, *a decrease in costs mean that the supply curve shifts down and to the right.* The left panel of Figure 2.11 on the next page illustrates. Of course, *higher costs mean that the supply curve shifts in the opposite direction, up and to the left* as illustrated in the right panel of Figure 2.11.

FIGURE 2.10

Total Producer Surplus Is the Area Above the Supply Curve and Below the Price Total producer surplus is the sum of the producer surplus of each seller, the area above the supply curve and below the price.

Once you know that a decrease in costs shifts the supply curve down and to the right and an increase in costs shifts the supply curve up and to the left, then you really know everything there is to know about supply shifts. It can take a little practice, however, to identify the many factors that can change costs. Here are some important supply shifters:

Important Supply Shifters

> Technological innovations and changes in the price of inputs

> Taxes and subsidies

> Expectations

> Entry or exit of producers

> Changes in opportunity costs

It can also help in analyzing supply shifters to know that sometimes it's easier to think of cost changes as shifting the supply curve right or left, and sometimes it's a little easier to think of cost changes as shifting the supply curve up or down. These two methods of thinking about supply shifts are equivalent and correspond to the two methods of reading a supply curve, the horizontal and

FIGURE 2.11

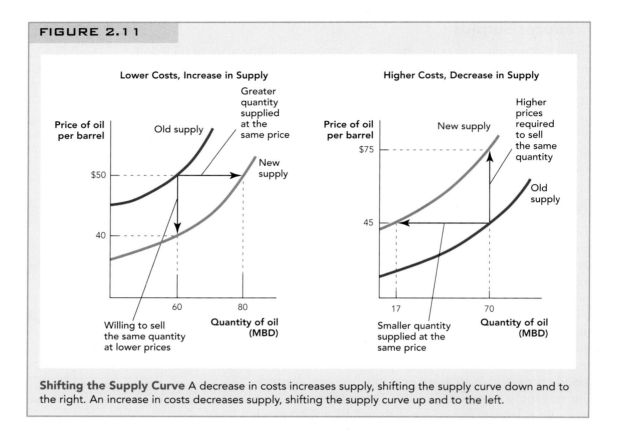

Shifting the Supply Curve A decrease in costs increases supply, shifting the supply curve down and to the right. An increase in costs decreases supply, shifting the supply curve up and to the left.

vertical readings respectively. We will give examples of each method as we examine some cost shifters in action.

Technological Innovations and Changes in the Price of Inputs
We have already given an example of how improvements in technology can reduce costs, thus increasing supply. A reduction in input prices also reduces costs and thus has a similar effect. A fall in the wages of oil rig workers, for example, will reduce the cost of producing oil, shifting the supply curve down and to the right as in the left panel of Figure 2.11. Alternatively, an increase in the wages of oil rig workers will increase the cost of producing oil, shifting the supply curve up and to the left as in the right panel of Figure 2.11.

Taxes and Subsidies
We can get some practice using up or down shifts to analyze a cost change by examining the effect of a $10 oil tax on the supply curve for oil. As far as firms are concerned, a tax on output is the same as an increase in costs. If the government taxes oil producers $10 per barrel, this is exactly the same to producers as an increase in their costs of production of $10 per barrel.

In Figure 2.12, notice that before the tax, firms require $40 per barrel to sell 60 million barrels of oil per day (point *a*). How much will firms require to sell the same quantity of oil when there is a tax of $10 per barrel? Correct, $50. What firms care about is the take-home price. If firms require $40 per barrel to sell 60 million barrels of oil, that's what they require regardless of the tax. When the government takes $10 per barrel, firms must charge $50 to keep their take-home price at $40. Thus, in Figure 2.12, notice that the $10 tax shifts the supply curve up by exactly $10 at *every point* along the curve.

FIGURE 2.12

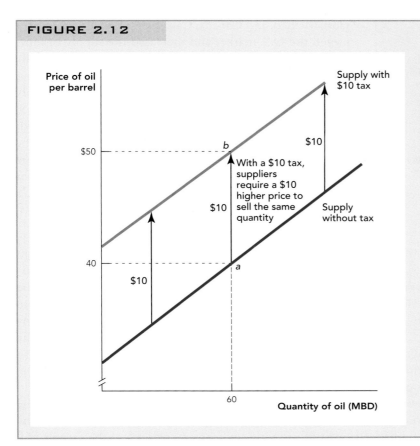

A Tax on Industry Output Shifts the Supply Curve Up by the Amount of the Tax When suppliers pay no tax, they are willing to supply 60 MBD of oil for a price of $40 per barrel. If they must pay a tax of $10 per barrel, they will be willing to supply 60 MBD for $10 more, or $50 a barrel. Thus a tax shifts the supply curve up by the amount of the tax.

It's important to avoid one possible confusion. All we have said so far is that a $10 tax shifts the supply curve for oil up by $10. We haven't said anything about the effect of a tax on the *price* of oil—that's because we have not yet analyzed how market prices are formed. We are saving that topic for Chapter 3.

How does a subsidy, a tax-benefit, or write-off shift the supply curve? We will save that analysis for the end of chapter problems but here's a hint: a subsidy is the same as a negative or "reverse" tax.

Expectations Suppliers who expect that prices will increase in the future have an incentive to sell less today so that they can store goods for future sale. Thus, the expectation of a future price increase shifts today's supply curve to the left as illustrated in Figure 2.13. The shifting of supply in response to price expectations is the essence of *speculation*, the attempt to profit from future price changes.

Entry or Exit of Producers When the United States signed the North American Free Trade Agreement (NAFTA), reducing barriers to trade among the United

FIGURE 2.13

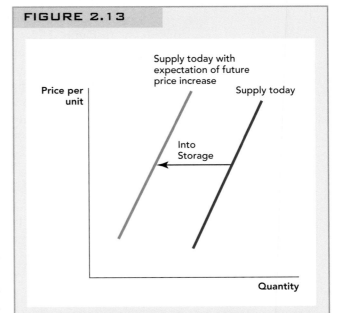

Expectations Can Shift the Supply Curve If sellers expect a higher price in the future, today's supply curve will shift to the left as producers store some of the good for future sale.

FIGURE 2.14

Entry Increases Supply The entry of lower-cost producers increases supply, thus shifting the supply curve to the right and down.

States, Mexico, and Canada, Canadian producers of lumber entered the U.S. market and increased the supply of lumber. We can most easily think about this as a shift to the right of the supply curve.

In Figure 2.14 the domestic supply curve is the supply curve for lumber before NAFTA. The curve labeled domestic supply plus Canadian imports is the supply curve for lumber after NAFTA allowed Canadian firms to sell in the United States with fewer restrictions. The entry of more firms meant that at any price a greater quantity of lumber was available, that is, the supply curve shifted to the right.*

In a later chapter, we discuss the effects of foreign trade at greater length.

Changes in Opportunity Costs The last important supply shifter, changes in opportunity costs, is the trickiest to understand. Recall from Chapter 1 that when the unemployment rates increase more people tend to go to college. If you can't get a job, you aren't giving up many good opportunities by going to college. Thus, when the unemployment rate increases, the (opportunity) cost of college falls and so more people attend college. Notice that to understand how people behave, you must understand their opportunity costs.

Now suppose that a farmer is currently growing soybeans but that he could also use his land to grow wheat. If the price of *wheat* increases, then the farmer's opportunity cost of growing soybeans increases and the farmer will want to shift land from soybean production into the more profitable alternative of wheat production. As land is taken out of soybean production, the supply curve for soybeans shifts up and to the left.

In Figure 2.15, notice that before the increase in the price of wheat, farmers would be willing to supply 2,800 million bushels of soybeans at a price of $5 per bushel (point *a*). But when the price of wheat increases, farmers are only willing to supply 2,000 million bushels of soybeans at a price of $5 per bushel because an alternative use of the land (growing wheat) is now more valuable. Equivalently, before the increase in the price of wheat, farmers were willing to sell 2,800 million bushels of soybeans for $5 per bushel but after their opportunity costs increase farmers require $7 per bushel to sell the same quantity (point *c*).

Similarly, a decrease in opportunity costs shifts the supply curve down and to the right. If the price of wheat falls, for example, the opportunity cost of growing soybeans falls and the supply curve for soybeans will shift down and

---

* It is equally correct to think of new entrants as shifting the supply curve down. Remember, it's ultimately costs that shift supply and what increases supply is entry of *lower-cost* producers. Industry costs fell when Canadian producers entered the market because many Canadian producers had lower costs than some U.S. producers. As lower-cost Canadian producers entered the industry, higher-cost U.S. producers exited the industry and industry costs decreased, thus shifting the supply curve down.

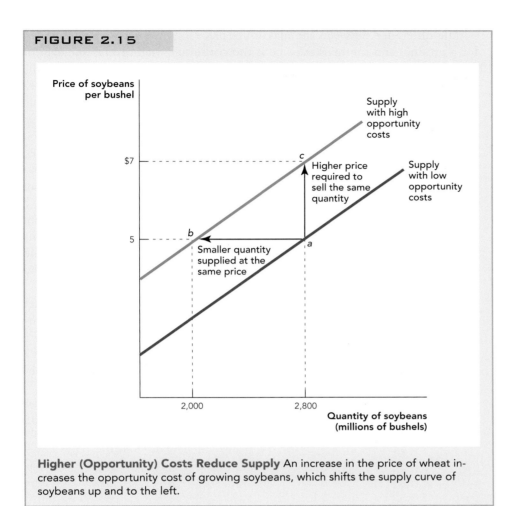

FIGURE 2.15

Price of soybeans per bushel

Supply with high opportunity costs

$7 — c

Higher price required to sell the same quantity

Supply with low opportunity costs

5 — b

Smaller quantity supplied at the same price

a

2,000   2,800

Quantity of soybeans (millions of bushels)

Higher (Opportunity) Costs Reduce Supply An increase in the price of wheat increases the opportunity cost of growing soybeans, which shifts the supply curve of soybeans up and to the left.

to the right. It's just another example of a running theme throughout this chapter, namely that both supply and demand respond to incentives.

□ Takeaway

In this chapter we have presented the fundamentals of the demand curve and the supply curve. The next chapter and much of the rest of this book build on these fundamentals. We thus give you fair warning. If you do not understand this chapter and the next, you will be lost!

    Key points to know are that a demand curve is a function that shows the quantity demanded at different prices. In other words, a demand curve shows how customers respond to higher prices by buying less and to lower prices by buying more. Similarly, a supply curve is a function that shows the quantity supplied at different prices. In other words, a supply curve shows how producers respond to higher prices by producing more and to lower prices by producing less.

CHECK YOURSELF

> Technological innovations in chip making have driven down the costs of producing computers. What happens to the supply curve for computers? Why?

> The U.S. government subsidizes making ethanol as a fuel made from corn. What effect does the subsidy have on the supply curve for ethanol?

The difference between the maximum price a consumer is willing to pay for a product and the market price is the consumer's gain from exchange or consumer surplus. The difference between the market price and the minimum price at which a producer is willing to sell a product is the producer's gain from exchange or producer surplus. You should be able to identify total consumer and producer surplus on a diagram, again as we have outlined in the chapter.

When it comes to what shifts the supply and demand curves, we have listed some factors in this chapter. Yes, you should know these lists but more fundamentally you should know that an increase in demand *means* that buyers want a greater quantity at the same price or, equivalently, they are willing to pay a higher price for the same quantity. Thus, anything that causes buyers to want more at the same price or be willing to pay more for the same quantity increases demand. In a pinch, just think about some of the factors that would cause you to want more of a good at the same price or that would make you willing to pay more for the same quantity.

Similarly, an increase in supply *means* that sellers are willing to sell a greater quantity at the same price or, equivalently, they are willing to sell a given quantity at a lower price. Again, what would make you willing to sell more of a good for the same price or sell the same quantity for a lower price? (Here's a hint—you might be willing to do this if your costs had fallen.) Supply and demand curves are not just abstract constructs, they also shape your life.

In the next chapter, we will use supply curves and demand curves to answer one of the most crucial questions in economics: How is the price of a good determined?

☐ CHAPTER REVIEW

KEY CONCEPTS

Demand curve, p. 13

Quantity demanded, p. 14

Consumer surplus, p. 16

Total consumer surplus, p. 16

Normal good, p. 18

Inferior good, p. 18

Substitutes, p. 18

Complements, p. 18

Supply curve, p. 20

Quantity supplied, p. 20

Producer surplus, p. 23

Total producer surplus, p. 23

FACTS AND TOOLS

1. When the price of a good increases the quantity demanded _____. When the price of a good decreases the quantity demanded _____.

2. When will people search harder for substitutes for oil: When the price of oil is high or when the price of oil is low?

3. Your roommate just bought an iPod for $200. She would have been willing to pay $500 for a machine that could store and replay that much music. How much consumer surplus does your roommate enjoy from the iPod?

4. What are three things that you'll buy less of once you graduate from college and get a good job? What kinds of goods are these called?

5. When the price of Apple computers goes down, what probably happens to the demand for Windows-based computers?

6. **a.** When the price of olive oil goes up, what probably happens to the demand for corn oil?

   b. When the price of petroleum goes up, what probably happens to the demand for natural gas? To the demand for coal? To the demand for solar power?

7. **a.** If everyone thinks that the price of tomatoes will go up next week, what is likely to happen to demand for tomatoes today?

   b. If everyone thinks that the price of gasoline will go up next week, what is likely to happen to the demand for gasoline today? (Note: Is this change in demand caused by consumers or by gas station owners?)

8. Along a supply curve, if the price of oil falls, what will happen to the quantity of oil supplied? Why?

9. If the price of cars falls, are carmakers likely to make more cars or fewer cars, according to the supply curve? (Notice that the "person on the street" often thinks the opposite is true!)

10. When is a pharmaceutical business more likely to hire highly educated, cutting-edge workers and use new, experimental research methods: When the business expects the price of its new drug to be low or when it expects the price to be high?

11. Imagine that a technological innovation reduces the costs of producing high-quality steel. What happens to the supply curve for steel?

12. When oil companies expect the price of oil to be higher next year, what happens to the supply of oil today?

13. Do taxes usually increase the supply of a good or reduce the supply?

THINKING AND PROBLEM SOLVING

1. Consider the following supply curve for oil. Note that MBD stands for "millions of barrels per day," the usual way people talk about the supply of oil:

   a. Based on the above supply curve, fill in the table below:

Price	Quantity Supplied
$12	
	40

   b. If the price for a barrel of oil was $15, how much oil would oil suppliers be willing to supply?

   c. What is the lowest price at which suppliers of oil would be willing to supply 20 MBD?

2. From the following table of prices per 100 pencils and quantities supplied (in hundreds of pencils), draw the supply curve for pencils:

Price	Quantity Supplied
$5	20
$15	40
$25	50
$35	55

3. Suppose LightBright and Bulbs4You were the only two suppliers of 60-watt lightbulbs in Springfield. Draw the supply curve for the 60-watt lightbulb industry in Springfield from the following tables for the two companies. To create this "light bulb industry supply curve," note that you'll add up the *total* number of bulbs that the industry will supply at a price of $1 (15 bulbs), and then do the same for the prices of $5, $7, and $10:

Price	Bulbs Supplied by LightBright	Bulbs Supplied by Bulbs4You
$1	10	5
$5	15	7
$7	25	15
$10	35	20

4. Using the following diagram, identify and calculate total producer surplus if the price of oil is $50 per barrel. Recall that for a triangle, Area = (1/2) × Base × Height. (You never thought you'd use that equation unless you became an engineer, did you?)

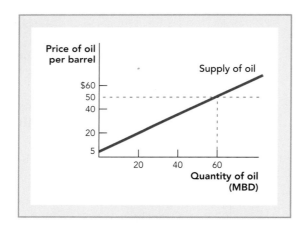

5. In Sucrosia, the supply curve for sugar is as follows:

Price (per 100 pound bag)	Quantity
$30	10,000
$50	15,000
$70	20,000

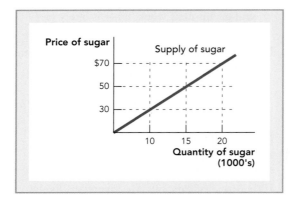

Under pressure from nutrition activists, the government decides to tax sugar producers with a $5 tax per 100 pound bag. Using the figure above, draw the new supply curve. After the tax is enacted, what price will bring forth quantities of 10,000? 15,000? 20,000? Give your answers in the table below.

Price (per 100 pound bag)	Quantity
	10,000
	15,000
	20,000

6. Consider the farmers talked about in the chapter who have land that is suitable for growing both wheat and soybeans. Suppose all farmers are currently farming wheat but the price of soybeans rises dramatically.

   a. Does the opportunity cost of producing wheat rise or fall?

b. Does this shift the supply curve for wheat (as in one of the panels of Figure 2.11), or is it a movement along a fixed supply curve?

What direction is this shift or movement? Illustrate your answer on the figure below:

7. Consider the following demand curve for oil:

a. Using the above demand curve, fill in the following table:

Price	Quantity Demanded
	55
$25	

b. If the price was $10, how much oil would be demanded?

c. What is the maximum price (per barrel) demanders will pay for 20 million barrels of oil?

8. From the following chart, draw the demand curve for pencils (in hundreds):

Price	Quantity Demanded (in hundreds)
$5	60
$15	45
$25	35
$35	20

9. If the price of glass dramatically increases, what are we likely to see a lot less of: Glass windows or glass bottles? Why?

10. Let's think about the demand for plasma TVs.

a. If the price for a 50" plasma TV is $2,010, and Newhart would be willing to pay $3,000, what is Newhart's consumer surplus?

b. Consider the figure below for the total demand for plasma TVs. At $2,010 per TV, 1,200 TVs were demanded, what would be the total consumer surplus? Calculate the total and identify it on the diagram.

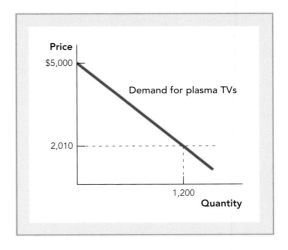

c. Where is Newhart in the figure above?

11. If income increases and the demand for good X shifts as shown below, then is good X a normal or inferior good? Give an example of a good like good X.

12. Assume that butter and margarine are substitutes. What will happen to the demand curve for butter if the price of margarine increases? Why?

13. Cars and gasoline are complements. What will happen to the demand curve for gasoline if the price of cars decreases? Why? (Hint: What happens to the quantity demanded of cars?)

CHALLENGES

1. Michael is an economist. He loves being an economist so much that he would do it for a living even if he only earned $30,000 per year. Instead, he earns $80,000 per year. (Note: This is the average salary of new economists with a Ph.D. degree.) How much producer surplus does Michael enjoy?

2. The economist Bryan Caplan recently found a pair of $10 arch supports that saved him from the pain of major foot surgery. As he stated on his blog (econlog.econlib.org), he would have been willing to pay $100,000 to fix his foot problem, but instead he only paid a few dollars.

   a. How much consumer surplus did Bryan enjoy from this purchase?

   b. If the sales tax was 5 percent on this product, how much revenue did the government raise when Bryan bought his arch supports?

   c. If the government could have taxed Bryan based on his *willingness to pay* rather than on how much he *actually* paid, how much sales tax would Bryan have had to pay?

3. For most young people, working full time and going to school are substitutes: You tend to do one or the other. When it's tough to find a job, does that raise the opportunity cost of going to college or does it lower it? When it's tough to find a job, does the demand for college rise or fall?

4. What should happen to the "demand for speed" (measured by the average speed on highways) once airbags are included on cars?

5. The industrial areas in Northeast Washington, D.C., were relatively dangerous in the 1980s. Over the last two decades, the area has become a safer place to work (although there are still seven times more violent crimes per person in these areas compared to another D.C. neighborhood, Georgetown). When an area becomes a safer place to work, what probably happens to the "supply of labor" in that area?

3

Equilibrium: How Supply and Demand Determine Prices

CHAPTER OUTLINE

Equilibrium and the Adjustment Process

Gains from Trade Are Maximized at the Equilibrium Price and Quantity

Does the Model Work? Evidence from the Laboratory

Shifting Demand and Supply Curves

Terminology: Demand Compared to Quantity Demanded and Supply Compared to Quantity Supplied

Understanding the Price of Oil

Takeaway

I n Chapter 2, we introduced the supply curve and the demand curve. In that chapter, we wrote things like "if the price is $20 per barrel, the quantity supplied will be 50 million barrels per day (MBD)" and "if the price is $50, the quantity demanded will be 120 MBD." But how is price determined?

We are now ready for the big event: Equilibrium. Figure 3.1 puts the supply curve and demand curve for oil together in one diagram. Notice the one point where the curves meet. The price at the meeting point is called the equilibrium price and the quantity at the meeting point is called the equilibrium quantity.

The equilibrium price is $30 and the equilibrium quantity is 65 MBD. What do we mean by equilibrium? We say that $30 and 65 are the equilibrium price and quantity because at any other price and quantity, economic forces are put in play that push prices and quantities toward these values. The equilibrium price and quantity are the only price and quantity that in a free market are stable. The sketch at right gives an intuitive feel for what we mean by equilibrium— the force of gravity pulls the ball down the side of the bowl until it comes to a state of rest. We will now explain the economic forces that push and pull prices toward their equilibrium values.

Equilibrium and the Adjustment Process

Imagine that demand and supply were as in Figure 3.1, but the price was $50, above the equilibrium price of $30—we would then have the situation depicted in the left panel of Figure 3.2.

Thinking about Equilibrium

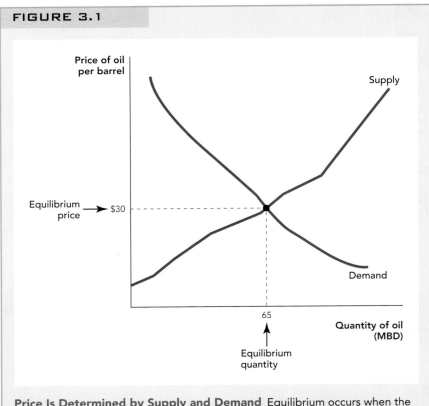

FIGURE 3.1

Price of oil per barrel

Supply

Equilibrium price → $30

Demand

65

Quantity of oil (MBD)

Equilibrium quantity

Price Is Determined by Supply and Demand Equilibrium occurs when the quantity demanded equals the quantity supplied. The quantity demanded equals the quantity supplied only when the price is $30 and the quantity exchanged is 65; hence, $30 is the equilibrium price and 65 the equilibrium quantity.

A **surplus** is a situation in which the quantity supplied is greater than the quantity demanded.

A **shortage** is a situation in which the quantity demanded is greater than the quantity supplied.

The **equilibrium price** is the price at which the quantity demanded is equal to the quantity supplied.

At a price of $50, suppliers want to supply 100, but at that price the quantity demanded by buyers is just 32, which creates an excess supply or **surplus** of 68. What will suppliers do if they cannot sell all of their output at a price of $50? Hold a sale! Each seller will reason that by pricing just a little bit below his or her competitors, he or she will be able to sell much more. *Competition will push prices down whenever there is a surplus.* As competition pushes prices down, the quantity demanded will increase and the quantity supplied will decrease. Only at a price of $30 will equilibrium be restored because only at that price does the quantity demanded (65) equal the quantity supplied (65).

What if price is below the equilibrium price? The right panel of Figure 3.2 shows that at a price of $15 demanders want 95 but suppliers are only willing to sell 24, which creates an excess demand or **shortage** of 71. What will sellers do if they discover that at a price of $15 they can easily sell all of their output and still have buyers asking for more? Raise prices! Buyers also have an incentive to offer higher prices when there is a shortage because when they can't buy as much as they want at the going price, they will try to outbid other buyers by offering sellers a higher price. *Competition will push prices up whenever there is a shortage.* As prices are pushed up, the quantity supplied increases and the quantity demanded decreases until at a price of $30 there is no longer an incentive for prices to rise and equilibrium is restored.

If competition pushes the price down whenever it is above the **equilibrium price** and it pushes the price up whenever it is below the equilibrium price, what happens at the equilibrium price? *The equilibrium price is stable because at the equilibrium*

FIGURE 3.2

A Surplus Drives Prices Down At a price of $50 there is a surplus of oil. When there is a surplus, sellers have an incentive to decrease their price and buyers have an incentive to offer lower prices. The price decreases until at $30 the quantity demanded equals the quantity supplied and there is no longer an incentive for price to fall.

A Shortage Drives Prices Up At a price of $15 there is a shortage of oil. When there is a shortage, sellers have an incentive to increase the price and buyers have an incentive to offer higher prices. The price increases until at a price of $30 the quantity supplied equals the quantity demanded and there is no longer an incentive for the price to rise.

price the quantity demanded is exactly equal to the quantity supplied. Because every buyer can buy as much as he or she wants at the equilibrium price, buyers don't have an incentive to push prices up. Since every seller can sell as much as he or she wants at the equilibrium price, sellers don't have an incentive to push prices down. Of course, buyers would like lower prices, but any buyer who offers sellers a lower price will be scorned. Similarly, sellers would like higher prices, but any seller who tries to raise his or her asking price will quickly lose customers.

Who Competes with Whom?

Sellers want higher prices and buyers want lower prices so the person in the street often thinks that sellers compete *against* buyers.

But economists understand that regardless of what sellers want, what they do when they compete is lower prices. *Sellers compete with other sellers.* Similarly, buyers may want lower prices but what they do when they compete is raise prices. *Buyers compete with other buyers.*

If the price of a good that you want is high, should you blame the seller? Not if the market is competitive. Instead, you should "blame" other buyers for outbidding you.

Gains from Trade Are Maximized at the Equilibrium Price and Quantity

Figure 3.3 on the next page provides another perspective on the market equilibrium. Consider Panel A. At a price of $15 suppliers will voluntarily produce 24 million barrels of oil per day. But notice that this is only enough oil to satisfy

CHECK YOURSELF

> If high gasoline prices lead to a decrease in the demand for large trucks and SUVs, what will automobile companies do to sell the trucks and SUVs already manufactured?

> Consider clothes sold at outlet malls. Have sellers produced too few or too many of the particular items based on demand? What actions are sellers taking to move their goods out the door?

FIGURE 3.3

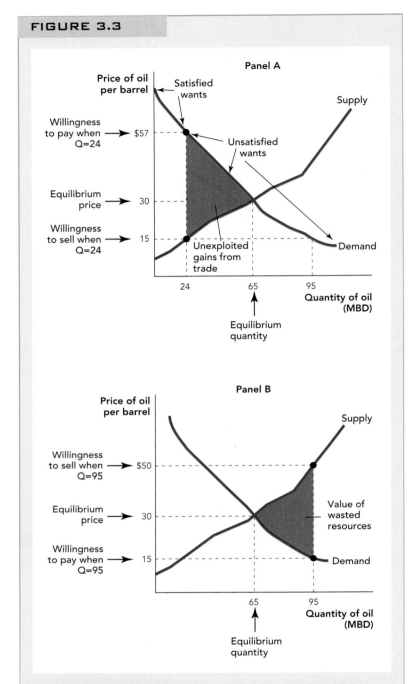

At the Equilibrium Quantity There Are No Unexploited Gains from Trade nor Any Wasteful Trades **Panel A:** Unexploited gains from trade exist when quantity is below the equilibrium quantity. Buyers are willing to pay $57 for the 24th unit and sellers are willing to sell the 24th unit for $15, so not trading the 24th unit leaves $42 in unexploited gain from trade. Only at the equilibrium quantity are there no unexploited gains from trade.
Panel B: Resources are wasted at quantities greater than the equilibrium quantity. Sellers are willing to sell the 95th unit for $50, but buyers are willing to pay only $15 so selling the 95th unit wastes $35 in resources. Only at the equilibrium quantity are there no wasted resources.

some of the buyers' wants. Which ones? The buyers will allocate what oil they have to their highest-valued wants. In Panel A of Figure 3.3, the 24 MBD of oil will be used to satisfy the wants labeled "Satisfied Wants." All other wants will remain unsatisfied. Now suppose that suppliers could be induced to sell just one more barrel of oil. How much would buyers be willing to pay for this barrel of oil? We can read the value of this additional barrel of oil by the height of the demand curve at 24 MBD. Buyers would be willing to pay up to $57 (or $56.99 if you want to be very precise), the value of the first unsatisfied want for an additional barrel of oil when 24 MBD are currently being bought. How much would sellers be willing to accept for one additional barrel of oil? We can read the lowest price at which sellers are willing to sell an additional barrel of oil by the height of the supply curve at 24 MBD. (Since sellers will be just willing to sell an additional barrel of oil when it covers their additional costs we can also read this as the cost of producing an additional barrel of oil when 24 MBD are currently being produced.) Sellers would be willing to sell an additional barrel of oil for as little as $15.

Buyers are willing to pay $57 for an additional barrel of oil, and sellers are willing to sell an additional barrel for as little as $15. Trade at any price between $57 and $15 can make both buyers and sellers better off. There are potential gains from trade so long as buyers are willing to pay more than sellers are willing to accept. Now notice that *there are unexploited gains from trade at any quantity less than the* **equilibrium quantity.** Economists believe that in a free market unexploited gains from trade won't last for long. We expect, therefore, that in a free market the quantity bought and sold will increase until the equilibrium quantity of 65 is reached.

We have shown that gains from trade push the quantity toward the equilibrium quantity. What about a push for trade coming from the other direction? In a free market, why won't the quantity bought and sold *exceed* the equilibrium quantity?

Now consider Panel B of Figure 3.3. Suppose that for some reason suppliers produce a quantity of 95 MBD. At a quantity of 95, it costs suppliers $50 to produce the last barrel of oil (say by squeezing it out of the Athabasca tar sands). How much is that barrel of oil worth to buyers? Again we can read this from the height of the demand curve at 95 MBD. It's only $15 (they get a few extra rubber duckies). So if quantity supplied exceeds the equilibrium quantity, it costs the sellers more to produce a barrel of oil than that barrel of oil is worth to buyers.

The **equilibrium quantity** is the quantity at which the quantity demanded is equal to the quantity supplied.

In a free market, suppliers won't spend $50 to produce something they can sell for at most $15—that's a recipe for bankruptcy.* We expect, therefore, in a free market, the quantity bought and sold will decrease until the equilibrium quantity of 65 MBD is reached.

Suppliers won't try to drive themselves into bankruptcy, but if they did would this be a good thing? Even at the equilibrium quantity, buyers have unsatisfied wants. Wouldn't it be a good idea to satisfy even more wants? No. The reason is that resources are wasted if the quantity exceeds the equilibrium quantity.

Imagine once again that suppliers were producing 95 units, and thus were producing many barrels of oil whose cost exceeded their worth. This would be a loss not just to the suppliers but also to society. Producing oil takes resources—labor, trucks, pipes, and so forth. Those resources, or the value of those resources, could be used to produce something people really are willing to pay for—economics textbooks, for example, or iPods. If we waste resources producing barrels of oil for $50 that are only worth $15, we have less resources to produce goods that cost only $32 but that people value at $75. We have only a limited number of resources and getting the most out of those resources means neither producing too little of a good (as in Panel A of Figure 3.3) or too much of a good (as in Panel B). Markets can help us to achieve this goal.

Figure 3.3 shows why in a free market there tends not to be unexploited gains from trade—at least not for long—nor wasteful trades. Put these two things together and we have a remarkable result. *A free market maximizes the gains from trade.* The gains from trade can be broken down into producer surplus and consumer surplus, so we can also say that *a free market maximizes producer plus consumer surplus.*

Figure 3.4 on the next page illustrates how the gains from trade—producer plus consumer surplus—are maximized at the equilibrium price and quantity. Maximizing the gains from trade, however, requires more than just producing at the equilibrium price and quantity. In addition, goods must be produced at the lowest possible cost and they must be used to satisfy the highest value demands. In Figure 3.4, for example, notice that every seller has lower costs than every non-seller. Also, every buyer has a higher willingness to pay for the good than every non-buyer.

Imagine if this claim were not true; suppose, for example, that Joe is willing to pay $50 for the good and there are two sellers, Alice with costs of $40 and Barbara with costs of $20. It's possible that Joe and Alice could make a deal, splitting the gains from trade of $10. At a price of $44, for example, Joe could earn $6 in consumer surplus ($50–$44) and Alice could earn $4 in producer surplus ($44–$40). But this trade would not maximize the gains from trade because if Joe and Barbara trade, the gains from trade are much higher, $30.

---

* Can you think of when suppliers might do this? What about if they were being subsidized by the government? In that case, the buyers might value the good less than the cost to sellers, but so long as the government makes up the difference the sellers will be happy to sell a large quantity.

FIGURE 3.4

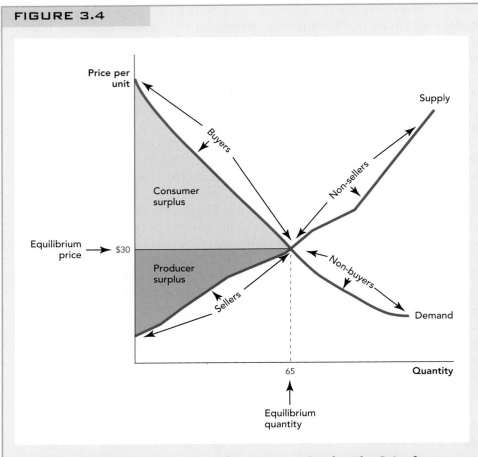

A Free Market Maximizes Producer Plus Consumer Surplus (the Gains from Trade) A free market maximizes the gains from trade because (1) buyers are willing to pay more for the good than non-buyers, (2) sellers are willing to sell the good at a lower price than non-sellers, and (3) there are no mutual profitable deals between non-sellers and non-buyers.

see the
invisible hand

CHECK YOURSELF

> As the price of cars goes up, which marketplace wants will be the first to stop being satisfied? Give an example.

> In the late 1990s, telecommunication firms laid a greater quantity of fiber-optic cable than the market equilibrium quantity (as proven by later events). Describe the nature of the losses from too much investment in fiber-optic cable. What market incentives exist to avoid these losses?

Thus, when we say that a free market maximizes the gains from trade, we mean three closely related things:

1. The supply of goods is bought by the buyers with the highest willingness to pay.
2. The supply of goods is sold by the sellers with the lowest costs.
3. Between buyers and sellers there are no unexploited gains from trade nor any wasteful trades.

Together these three conditions imply that the gains from trade are maximized.

One of the remarkable lessons of economics is that under the right conditions, the pursuit of self-interest leads not to chaos but to a beneficial order. The maximization of the gains from trade in markets populated solely by self-interested individuals is one application of this central idea.

Does the Model Work? Evidence from the Laboratory

It's easy to see the equilibrium price and quantity when we draw textbook supply and demand curves, but in a real market the demanders and sellers do not know the true curves. Moreover, the conditions required to maximize the gains from trade are quite sophisticated. So how do we know whether the model really works?

In 1956, Vernon Smith launched a revolution in economics by testing the supply and demand model in the lab. Smith's early experiments were simple. He took a group of undergraduate students and broke them into two groups, buyers and sellers. Buyers were given a card, which indicated their maximum willingness to pay. Sellers were given a card, which indicated their cost, the minimum price at which they would be willing to sell. The buyers and sellers were then instructed to call out bids and offers ("I will sell for $3.00" or "I will pay $1.50"). Each student could earn a profit by the difference between their willingness to pay or sell and the contract price. For example, if you were a buyer and your card said $3.00 and you were able to make a deal with a seller to buy for $2.00, then you would have made a $1.00 profit.

The students knew only their own willingness to pay or to sell, but Vernon Smith knew the actual shape of the supply and demand curves. Smith knew the curves because he knew exactly what cards he had handed out. Data from one of Smith's first experiments is shown in Figure 3.5. Smith handed out 11 cards to sellers and 11 to buyers. The lowest cost seller had costs of 75 cents, the next lowest cost seller had costs of $1.00. Thus, at any price below 75 cents the quantity supplied on the market supply curve was zero, between 75 cents and $1 the quantity supplied was 1 unit, between $1.00 and $1.25, the next highest cost, 2 units, and so forth. Looking at the figure can you see how many units were demanders willing to buy at a price of $2.65? At a price of $2.65, the quantity demanded is 3 units. (To test yourself, identify, by their willingness to pay, exactly which three buyers are willing to buy at a price of $2.65.)

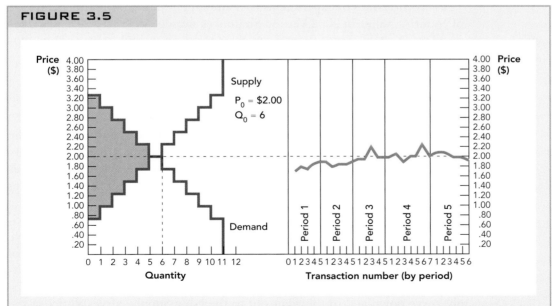

FIGURE 3.5

Economics as an Experimental Science Vernon Smith knew the true demand and supply curves, pictured on the left. On the right are the results from the actual market trades. Prices, quantities, and the gains from trade all converged quickly to those predicted by economic theory.

Source: Smith, Vernon. 1962. An Experimental Study of Competitive Market Behavior. *Journal of Political Economy.* V. 70 (2): 111–137.

The idea of economics as an experimental science came to Vernon Smith in a fit of insomnia in 1956. Nearly 50 years later, Smith was awarded the 2002 Nobel Laureate in Economics.

AP PHOTO/J.SCOTT APPLEWHITE

Smith knew from the graph that the equilibrium price and quantity as predicted by the supply and demand model was $2.00 and 6 units. But what would happen in the real world? Smith ran his experiment for 5 periods, each period about 5 minutes long. The right side of the figure shows the price for each completed trade in each period. The prices quickly converged toward the expected equilibrium price and quantity so that in the last period the average price was $2.03 and the quantity exchanged was 6 units.

Smith's market converged rapidly to the equilibrium price and quantity exactly as predicted by the supply and demand model. But recall that the model also predicts that a free market will maximize the gains from trade. Remember our conditions for efficiency, which in this context are that the supply of goods must be bought by the demanders with the highest willingness to pay, the supply of goods must be sold by the suppliers with the lowest costs, and the quantity traded should be equal to 6 units, neither more nor less.

So what happened in Smith's test of the market model? In the final period, 6 units were bought and sold and the buyers had the six highest valuations and the sellers the six lowest costs—exactly as predicted by the supply and demand model. Producer plus consumer surplus or total surplus was maximized. In fact, in the entire experiment only once was a seller with a cost greater than equilibrium price able to sell and only once was a buyer with a willingness to pay less than the equilibrium price able to buy—so total surplus was very close to being maximized throughout the experiment.

Vernon Smith began his experiments thinking that they would prove the supply and demand model was wrong. Decades later he wrote:

> I am still recovering from the shock of the experimental results. The outcome was unbelievably consistent with competitive price theory. . . . But the results *can't* be believed, I thought. It must be an accident, so I must take another class and do a new experiment with different supply and demand schedules.[1]

Many thousands of experiments later, the supply and demand model remains of enduring value. In 2002, Vernon Smith was awarded the Nobel Prize in Economics for establishing laboratory experiments as an important tool in economic science.

Shifting Demand and Supply Curves

Another way of testing the supply and demand model is to examine the model's predictions about what happens to equilibrium price and quantity when the supply or demand curves shift. Even if the model doesn't give us precise predictions (outside of the lab), we can still ask whether the model helps us to understand the world.

Imagine, for example, that technological innovations reduce the costs of producing a good. As we know from Chapter 2, a fall in costs shifts the supply curve down and to the right as shown in Figure 3.6 on the next page. The result of lower costs is a lower price and an increase in quantity. Begin at the Old Equilibrium Price and Quantity at point *a*. Now a decrease in costs shifts the Old Supply curve down and to the right out to the New Supply curve. Notice at the Old Equilibrium Price there is now a surplus—in other words, now that their costs have fallen, suppliers are willing to sell more at the old price than demanders are willing to buy. The excess supply, however, is temporary. Competition

FIGURE 3.6

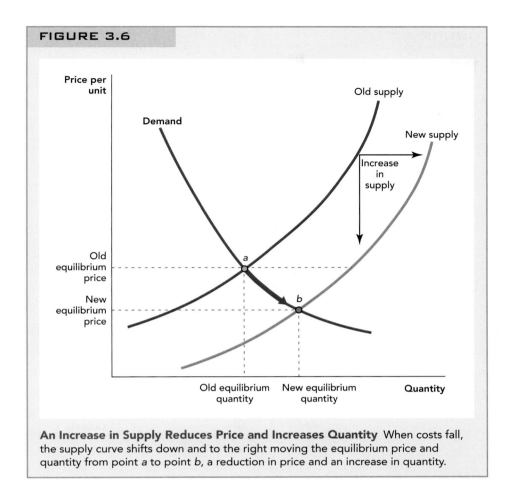

An Increase in Supply Reduces Price and Increases Quantity When costs fall, the supply curve shifts down and to the right moving the equilibrium price and quantity from point *a* to point *b*, a reduction in price and an increase in quantity.

between sellers pushes prices down and as prices fall the quantity demanded increases. Prices fall and quantity demanded increases until the New Equilibrium Price and Quantity are established at point *b*. At the new equilibrium, the quantity demanded equals the quantity supplied.

We can see this process at work throughout the economy. As technological innovations reduce the price of computer chips, for example, prices fall and the quantity of chips—used in everything from computers to cell phones to toys—increases.

What about a decrease in supply? A decrease in supply will raise the market price and reduce the market quantity, exactly the opposite effects to an increase in supply. But don't take our word for it. Draw the diagram. The key to learning demand and supply is not to try to memorize everything that can happen. Instead focus on learning how to use the tools. If you know how to use the tools, you can deduce what happens to price and quantity for any configuration of demand and supply and for any set of shifts simply by drawing a few pictures.

Figure 3.7 on the next page shows the same process for an increase in demand. Begin with the Old Equilibrium Price and Quantity at point *a*. Now suppose that demand increases to New Demand. As a result, the price and quantity are driven up to the New Equilibrium Price and Quantity at point *b*. Notice this time we omitted discussion of the temporary transition. So here's a good test of your knowledge. Can you explain *why* the price and quantity demanded increased with an increase in demand? Hint: What happens at the Old Equilibrium Price after demand has increased to New Demand?

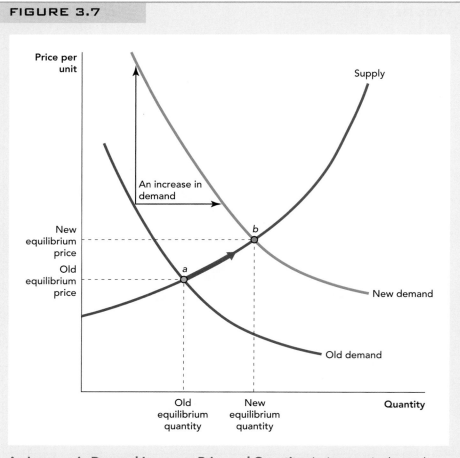

FIGURE 3.7

An increase in demand

Supply

b

New equilibrium price

Old equilibrium price

a

New demand

Old demand

Price per unit

Quantity

Old equilibrium quantity

New equilibrium quantity

An Increase in Demand Increases Price and Quantity An increase in demand shifts the demand curve up and to the right moving the equilibrium from point *a* to point *b*, an increase in price and quantity.

Of course, if we can analyze an increase in demand, then a decrease in demand is just the opposite: a decrease in demand will tend to decrease price and quantity. Once again, draw the diagram!

Do you recall the list of demand and supply shifters that we presented in Chapter 2? We can now put all that knowledge to good use. With demand, supply, and the idea of equilibrium, we have powerful tools for analyzing how changes in income, population, expectations, technologies, input prices, taxes and subsidies, alternative uses of industry inputs, and other factors will change market prices and quantities. In fact, with our tools of demand, supply, and equilibrium, we can analyze and understand *any* change in *any* competitive market.

Terminology: Demand Compared to Quantity Demanded and Supply Compared to Quantity Supplied

Sometimes economists use very similar words for quite different things. (We're sorry but unfortunately it's too late to change terms.) In particular, there is a big difference between demand and quantity demanded. For example, an increase in the quantity demanded is a movement *along* a fixed demand curve. An increase in demand is a *shift* of the entire demand curve (up and to the right).

Don't worry: you are *already* familiar with these differences, we just need to point them out to you and explain the associated differences in terminology. Panel A of Figure 3.8 is a repeat of Figure 3.6, showing that an increase in supply reduces the equilibrium price and increases the equilibrium quantity. But now we emphasize something a little different—the increase in supply pushes the

FIGURE 3.8

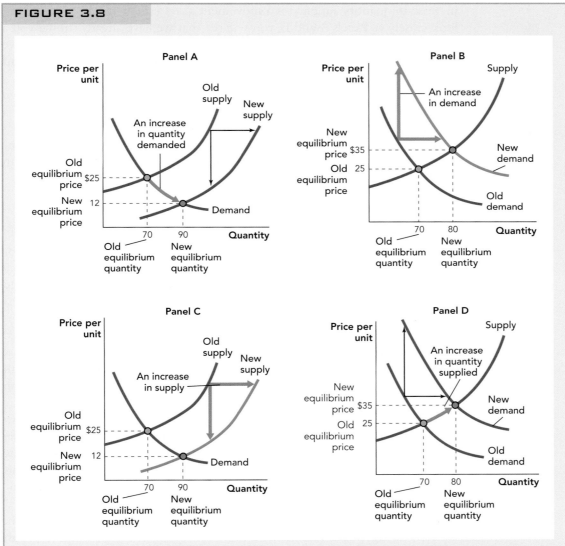

An Increase in Quantity Demanded Compared to an Increase in Demand, and an Increase in Supply Compared to an Increase in Quantity Supplied
Panel A: An increase in quantity demanded is a movement along a fixed demand curve caused by a shift in the supply curve.
Panel B: An increase in demand is a shift in the demand curve up and to the right.
Panel C: An increase in supply is a shift in the supply curve down and to the right.
Panel D: An increase in quantity supplied is a movement along a fixed supply curve caused by a shift in the demand curve.

price down, thereby causing an increase in the *quantity demanded* from 70 units to 90 units. Notice that the increase in the quantity demanded is a movement along the demand curve. In Panel A, the demand has not changed, only the quantity demanded. Notice also that changes in the quantity demanded are always caused by changes in supply. In other words, *shifts* in the supply curve cause movements *along* the demand curve.

Panel B is a repeat of Figure 3.7 and it shows an *increase in demand*. Notice that an increase in demand is a shift in the entire demand curve up and to the right. Indeed, we can also think about an increase in demand as the creation of a new demand curve, appropriately labeled New Demand.

Similarly, an increase in supply is a *shift* of the entire supply curve while an increase in quantity supplied is a movement *along* a fixed supply curve. If you look closely at Panels A and B, you will see that we have already shown you a shift in supply and a change in quantity supplied! But to make things clear, we repeat the analysis for supply in Panels C and D: the graphs are the same but now we emphasize different things.

Panel C shows an increase in supply, a shift in the entire supply curve down and to the right. Panel D shows an increase in quantity supplied, namely a movement from 70 to 80 units along a fixed supply curve.

By comparing Panels A and C we can see that shifts in the supply curve create changes in quantity demanded. And by comparing Panels B and D we can see that shifts in the demand curve create changes in the quantity supplied.

Understanding the Price of Oil

We can use the supply and demand model to understand some of the major events that have determined the price of oil over the past half century. Figure 3.9 on the next page shows the *real price* of oil in 2005 dollars between 1960 and 2005. (The real price corrects prices for inflation—we will cover this process and what it means in Chapter 11).

From the early twentieth century to the 1970s, the demand for oil increased steadily, but major discoveries and improved production techniques meant that the supply of oil increased at an even faster pace leading to modest declines in price. Contrary to popular belief, slightly declining prices over time are common for minerals and other natural resources supplied under competitive conditions.

Although the streets of Baghdad were paved with tar as early as the eighth century, the discovery and development of the modern oil industry in the Middle East was made primarily by U.S., Dutch, and British firms much later. For many decades, these firms controlled oil in the Middle East, giving local governments just a small cut of their proceeds. It's hard to take your oil well and leave the country, however, so the major firms were vulnerable to taxes and nationalization.

The Iranian government nationalized the British oil industry in Iran in 1951.* The Egyptians nationalized the Suez Canal, the main route through which oil flowed to the West, in 1956, leading to the Suez Crisis—a brief war that pitted Egypt against an alliance of the United Kingdom, France, and Israel. Further nationalizations and increased government control of the oil industry occurred throughout the 1960s and early 1970s.

---

* The nationalization was reversed in 1953 when the government of Mohammad Mosaddeq was toppled by a CIA-backed coup that brought the king, Mohammad Reza Pahlavi, back to power. The coup would have repercussions a quarter century later with the coming of the Iranian revolution, when the American-backed government was overthrown by Islamic radicals.

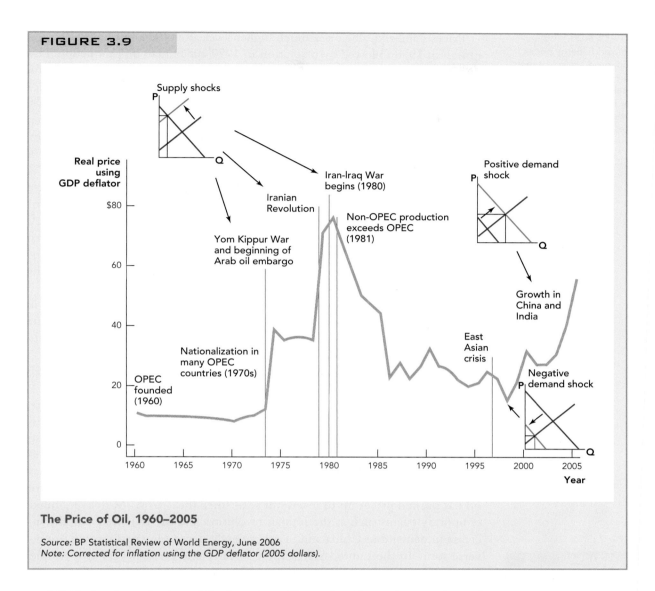

FIGURE 3.9

The Price of Oil, 1960–2005

Source: BP Statistical Review of World Energy, June 2006
Note: Corrected for inflation using the GDP deflator (2005 dollars).

OPEC, the Organization of the Petroleum Exporting Countries, was formed in 1960.* Initially OPEC restricted itself to bargaining with the foreign nationals for a larger share of their oil revenues. By the early 1970s, however, further nationalizations in the OPEC countries made it possible for OPEC countries to act together in order to reduce supply and raise prices.

A triggering event for OPEC was the Yom Kippur War. Egypt and Syria attacked Israel in 1973 in an effort to regain the Sinai Peninsula and the Golan Heights, which Israel had captured in 1967. In an effort to punish Western countries that had supported Israel, a number of Arab exporting nations cut oil production. Supply had been increasing by about 7.5 percent per year in the previous decade, but between 1973 and 1974 production was dead flat. Prices shot up, increasing in real dollars from $14.50 to $46 per barrel in just one year. The large increase in price from a small decline in supply (relative to what it would have been without the cut in production) demonstrated how much the world depended on oil.

* OPEC was founded by Iran, Iraq, Kuwait, Saudi Arabia, and Venezuela, later joined by Qatar (1961), Indonesia (1962), Libya (1962), United Arab Emirates (1967), Algeria (1969), Nigeria (1971), Ecuador (1973–1992), and Gabon (1975–1994). More recently, Ecuador rejoined OPEC in 2007, Angola joined in 2007, and Indonesia left in 2008.

►►SEARCH ENGINE
Statistics on world energy prices, consumption, production, reserves and other areas can be found at the **BP Statistical Review of World Energy**. The **Energy Information Administration** focuses on the United States.

Prices stabilized, albeit at a much higher level, after 1974, but political unrest in Iran in 1978 followed by revolution in 1979 cut Iranian oil production. This time the reduction in supply was accidental rather than deliberate, but the result was the same—sharply higher prices. When Iraq attacked Iran in 1980, production in both countries diminished yet again, pushing prices to their highest level in the twentieth century—$75.31 in 2005 dollars. Prices might have been driven even higher if demand had not been reduced by a recession in the United States.

Higher prices attract entry. In 1972, the United Kingdom produced 2,000 barrels of oil per day. By 1978, with the opening of the North Sea wells, the UK was producing one million barrels per day. In the same period, Norway increased production from 33,000 to 287,000 barrels per day and Mexico doubled its production from 506,000 barrels per day to just over one million barrels per day. By 1982, non-OPEC production exceeded OPEC production for the first time since OPEC was founded. Iranian production also began to recover, increasing by one million barrels per day in 1982. Prices began to fall during the 1980s and 1990s.

Prices can also fluctuate with shifts in demand. A sharp fall in prices came in 1997 when the economy of South Korea (the tenth largest economy in the world) and that of Indonesia, Thailand, and other East Asian countries went into a severe recession. Income fell, reducing the demand for oil and reducing oil prices. As these countries recovered, however, the demand for oil increased along with prices.

The economies of China and India have surged in the early twenty-first century to the point where millions of people are for the first time in the history of their country able to afford an automobile. In 1949, the communists confiscated all the private cars in China. As late as 2000, there were just 6 million cars in all of China, but by 2005 there were 20 million. Total highway miles more than doubled in the same five years.[2] This increased demand for oil has pushed prices up to levels not seen since the 1970s.[*] Moreover, unlike temporary events such as the Iranian revolution and the Iran-Iraq war, the increase in demand in China and in other newly developing nations will not reverse soon. In the United States, there's nearly one car for every two people. China has a population of 1.3 billion people, so there is plenty of room for growth in the number of cars and thus the demand for oil. What is your prediction for future oil prices?

CHECK YOURSELF
> In Figure 3.9, you will notice a jump in oil prices around 1991. What happened in this year to increase price? Was it a supply shock or a demand shock?
> In Figure 3.9, during what period would you include a small figure for positive supply shocks (increases in supply)? Explain the causes behind the positive supply shocks and the effect of these shocks on the price of oil.

□ Takeaway

Now that you have finished reading this chapter you should read it again. Really. Understanding supply and demand is critical to understanding economics, and in this chapter we have covered the most important aspects of the supply and demand model, namely how supply and demand together determine equilibrium price and quantity. You should understand, among other ideas, the following:

1. Market competition brings about an equilibrium in which the quantity supplied is equal to the quantity demanded.

[*] Improved technology is continually lowering the cost of discovering and producing oil (shifting the supply curve down and to the right), so what has happened in recent years is not simply an increase in demand but an increase in demand that has outstripped the increase in supply.

2. Only one price/quantity combination is a market equilibrium and you should be able to identify this equilibrium in a diagram.

3. You should understand and be able to explain the incentives that enforce the market equilibrium. What happens when the price is above the equilibrium price? Why? What happens when the price is below the equilibrium price? Why?

4. Gains from trade are maximized at the equilibrium price and quantity and no other price/quantity combination maximizes the gains from trade.

5. You should know from Chapter 2 the major factors that shift demand and supply curves and from this chapter be able to explain and predict the effect of any such shift on the equilibrium price and quantity.

6. A "change in demand [the demand curve]" is not the same thing as "a change in quantity demanded"; a "change in supply [the supply curve]" is not the same thing as "a change in quantity supplied."

Most important, you should be able to work with supply and demand to answer questions about the world.

□ CHAPTER REVIEW

KEY CONCEPTS

Surplus, p. 34

Shortage, p. 34

Equilibrium price, p. 34

Equilibrium quantity, p. 37

FACTS AND TOOLS

1. If the price in a market is above the equilibrium price, does this create a surplus or a shortage?

2. When the price is above the equilibrium price, does greed (in other words, self-interest) tend to push the price down or does it push it up?

3. Jon is on eBay, bidding for a first edition of the influential Frank Miller graphic novel *Batman: The Dark Knight Returns*. In this market, who is Jon competing with: the seller of the graphic novel or the other bidders?

4. Now, Jon is in Japan, trying to get a job as a full-time translator; he wants to translate English TV shows into Japanese and vice versa. He notices that the wage for translators is very low. Who is the "competition" that is pushing the wage down: Does the competition come from businesses who hire the translators or from the other translators?

5. Jules wants to purchase a Royale with cheese from Vincent. Vincent is willing to offer this tasty burger for $3. The most Jules is willing to pay for the tasty burger is $8 (after all, his girlfriend is a vegetarian, so he doesn't get many opportunities for tasty burgers).

   a. How large are the potential gains from trade if Jules and Vincent agree to make this trade? In other words, what is the sum of producer and consumer surplus if the trade happens?

   b. If the trade takes place at $4, how much producer surplus goes to Vincent? How much consumer surplus goes to Jules?

   c. If the trade takes place at $7, how much producer surplus goes to Vincent? How much consumer surplus goes to Jules?

6. What happened in Vernon Smith's lab? Choose the right answer:

   a. The price and quantity were close to equilibrium but gains from trade were far from the maximum.

   b. The price and quantity were far from equilibrium and gains from trade were far from the maximum.

   c. The price and quantity were far from equilibrium but gains from trade were close to the maximum.

   d. The price and quantity were close to equilibrium and gains from trade were close to the maximum.

7. When supply falls, what happens to quantity demanded in equilibrium? (This should get you

to notice that both suppliers *and* demanders change their behavior when one curve shifts.)

8. **a.** When demand increases what happens to price and quantity in equilibrium?

   b. When supply increases what happens to price and quantity in equilibrium?

   c. When supply decreases what happens to price and quantity in equilibrium?

   d. When demand decreases what happens to price and quantity in equilibrium?

9. **a.** When demand increases what happens to price and quantity in equilibrium?

   b. When supply increases what happens to price and quantity in equilibrium?

   c. When supply decreases what happens to price and quantity in equilibrium?

   d. When demand decreases what happens to price and quantity in equilibrium?

   No, this is not a mistake. Yes, it is that important.

10. What's the best way to think about the rise in oil prices in the 1970s, when wars and oil embargoes wracked the Middle East? Was it a rise in demand, a fall in demand, a rise in supply, or a fall in supply?

11. What's the best way to think about the rise in oil prices in the last 10 years, as China and India have become richer: Was it a rise in demand, a fall in demand, a rise in supply, or a fall in supply?

THINKING AND PROBLEM SOLVING

1. Suppose the market for batteries looks as follows:

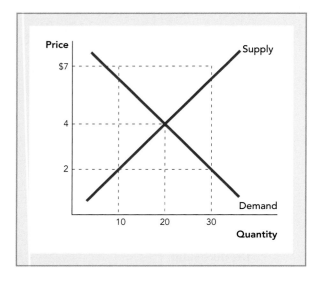

What is the equilibrium price and quantity?

2. Consider the following supply and demand tables for bread. Draw the supply and demand curves for this market. What is the equilibrium price and quantity?

Price of One Loaf	Quantity Supplied	Quantity Demanded
$0.50	10	75
$1	20	55
$2	35	35
$3	50	25
$5	60	10

3. If the price of a one-bedroom apartment in Washington, D.C., is currently $1,000 per month, but the supply and demand curves look as follows, then is there a shortage or surplus of apartments? What would we expect to happen to prices? Why?

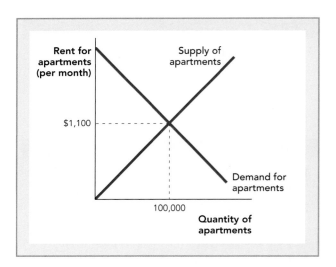

4. Determine the equilibrium quantity and price without drawing a graph.

Price of Good X	Quantity Supplied	Quantity Demanded
$22	100	225
$25	115	200
$30	130	175
$32	150	150
$40	170	110

5. In the figure below how many pounds of sugar are sellers willing to sell at a price of $20? How much is demanded at this price? What is the buyer's willingness to pay when the quantity is 20 lbs? Is this combination of $20 per pound and a quantity of 20 pounds an equilibrium? If not, identify the unexploited gains from trade.

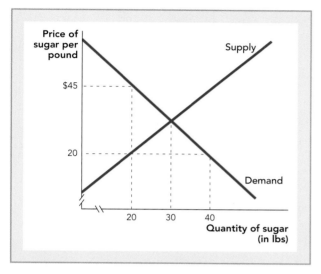

6. The market for marbles is represented in the graph below. What is the total producer surplus? The total consumer surplus? What are the total gains from trade?

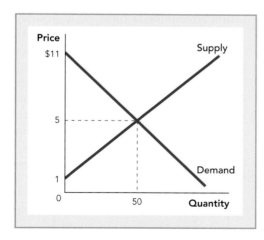

7. Suppose you decided to follow in Vernon Smith's footsteps and conducted your own experiment with your friends. You give out 10 cards, 5 cards to buyers with the figures for willingness to pay of $1, $2, $3, $4, and $5, and 5 cards to sellers with the amounts for costs of $1, $2, $3, $4, and $5. The rules are the same as Vernon Smith implemented.

a. Draw the supply and demand curves for this market. At a price of $3.50 how many units are demanded? And supplied?

b. Assuming the market works as predicted, and the market moves to equilibrium, will the buyer who values the good at $1 be able to purchase? Why or why not?

8. If the price of margarine decreases, what happens to the demand for butter? What happens to the equilibrium quantity and price for butter? What would happen if butter and margarine were not substitutes? Use a supply and demand diagram to support your answer.

9. The market for sugar is diagramed below:

a. What would happen to the equilibrium quantity and price if the wages of sugar cane harvesters increased?

b. What if a new study was published that emphasized negative health effects of consuming sugar?

10. If a snowstorm was forecast for the next day, what would happen to the demand for snow shovels? Is this a change in quantity demanded or a change in demand? This shift in the demand curve would affect the price; would this cause a change in quantity supplied or a change in supply?

11. In the 1990s, the Atkins diet, which emphasized eating more meat and fewer grains, became very popular. What do you suppose that did to the price and quantity of bread? Use supply and demand analysis to support your answer.

12. In recent years, there have been news reports that toys made in China are unsafe. When those news reports show up on CNN and Fox News, what probably happens to the demand for toys made in China? What probably happens to the equilibrium price and quantity of toys made in China? Are Chinese toymakers probably better or worse off when such news comes out?

CHALLENGES

1. For many years it was illegal to color margarine yellow (margarine is naturally white). In some states, margarine manufacturers were even required to color margarine pink! Who do you think supported these laws? Why? Hint: Your analysis in question 8 from the previous section is relevant!

2. Think about two products, "safe cars" (a heavy car such as a BMW 530xi with infrared night vision, four-wheel antilock brakes, and electronic stability control), and "dangerous cars" (a lightweight car such as _____ (name removed for legal reasons, but you can fill in as you wish)).

   a. Are these two products substitutes or complements?

   b. If new research makes it easier to produce safe cars, what happens to the supply of safe cars? What will happen to the equilibrium price of safe cars?

   c. Now that the price of safe cars has changed, how does this impact the demand for dangerous cars?

   d. Now let's tie all of these links into one simple sentence:

   "In a free market, as engineers and scientists discover new ways to makes cars safer, the number of dangerous cars sold will tend to _____."

3. Many clothing stores often have clearance sales at the end of each season. Using the tools you learned in this chapter can you think of an explanation why?

4. a. If oil executives read in the newspaper that massive new oil supplies have been discovered under the Pacific Ocean but will likely only be useful in 10 years, what is likely to happen to the supply of oil *today*? What is the likely equilibrium impact on the price and quantity of oil *today*?

   b. If oil executives read in the newspaper that new solar-power technologies have been discovered but will likely only become useful in 10 years, what is likely to happen to the supply of oil *today*? What is the likely equilibrium impact on the price and quantity of oil *today*?

   c. What's the short version of the above scenarios? Fill in the blank: If we learn *today* about promising *future* energy sources, today's price of energy will _____ and today's quantity of energy will _____.

5. Economists often say that prices are a "rationing mechanism." If the supply of a good falls, how do prices "ration" these now-scarce goods in a competitive market?

6. When the crime rate falls in the area around a factory, what probably happens to wages at that factory?

7. Let's take the idea from the previous question and use it to explain why businesses sometimes try to make their employees happy. If a business can make the job seem fun (by having inexpensive pizza parties) or at least safe (by nagging the city government to put police patrols around the factory), what probably happens to the supply of labor? What happens to the equilibrium wage if a factory or office or laboratory becomes a great place where people "really want to work?" How does this explain why the hourly wage for the typical radio or television announcer is only $13 per hour, lower than almost any other job in the entertainment or broadcasting industry?

   (*Source:* Bureau of Labor Statistics, *National Occupational Employment and Wage Estimates*, available online.)

4

Elasticity and Its Applications

CHAPTER OUTLINE

The Elasticity of Demand

The Elasticity of Supply

Using Elasticities for Quick Predictions (Optional)

Takeaway

Appendix 1: Using Excel to Calculate Elasticities

Appendix 2: Other Types of Elasticities

In fall 2000, Harvard sophomore Jay Williams flew to the Sudan where a terrible civil war had resulted in many thousands of deaths. Women and children captured in raids by warring tribes were being enslaved and held for ransom. Working with Christian Solidarity International, Williams was able to pay for the release of 4,000 people. But did Williams do the right thing? It's a serious question and one that is surprisingly complex, both morally and economically. By paying for the release of slaves, could Williams have encouraged more people to be enslaved? If so, by how much? Slavery is an abomination. Because of the terrible effects of slavery, careful thought about the best way to deal with the problem is essential. Perhaps surprisingly, the economic concept of elasticity can help people think clearly about the most effective policies to adopt to end slavery.

In this chapter, we develop the tools of demand and supply elasticity. To be honest, at first these tools will seem rather dry and technical. Stick with us, however, and you will see how the concept of elasticity is useful for dealing with the economic complexity of important questions such as how best to help people held as slaves for ransom, why the war on drugs can generate violence, why gun buyback programs are unlikely to work, and how to evaluate proposals to increase drilling in the Arctic National Wildlife Refuge (ANWR).

In Chapter 3, we discussed how to shift the supply and demand curves to produce *qualitative* predictions about changes in prices and quantities. Estimating elasticities of demand and supply is the first step in *quantifying* how changes in demand and supply will affect prices and quantities.

The Elasticity of Demand

The **elasticity of demand** measures how responsive the quantity demanded is to a change in price; more responsive equals more elastic.

When the price of a good increases, individuals and businesses will buy less. But how much less? A lot or a little? The **elasticity of demand** measures how responsive the quantity demanded is to a change in price—the more responsive quantity demanded is to a change in the price, the more elastic is the demand curve. Let's start by comparing two different demand curves.

In Figure 4.1, when the price increases from $40 to $50, the quantity demanded decreases from 100 to 20 along demand curve E but only from 100 to 95 along demand curve I—thus, demand curve E is more elastic than demand curve I.

FIGURE 4.1

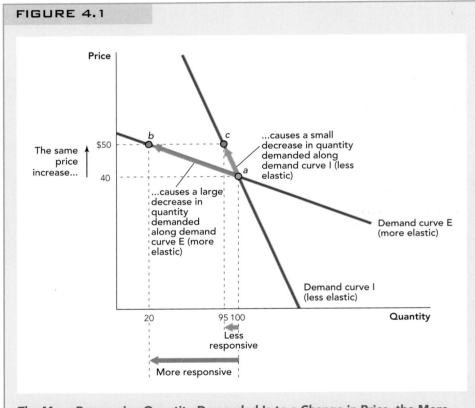

The More Responsive Quantity Demanded Is to a Change in Price, the More Elastic Is the Demand Curve Beginning at point *a*, an increase in price from $40 to $50 causes a big decrease in quantity demanded along demand curve E, from 100 units to 20 units at point *b*. But the same increase in price causes only a small decrease in quantity demanded along demand curve I from 100 to 95 units at point *c*. Since the quantity demanded is more responsive to a change in price along demand curve E, demand curve E is more elastic than demand curve I.

Elasticity is not the same thing as slope, but they are related and for our purposes you won't make any mistakes if you follow the elasticity rule:

> *Elasticity rule:* If two linear demand (or supply) curves run through a common point, then at any given quantity the curve that is flatter is more elastic.

Determinants of the Elasticity of Demand

Of the two curves in Figure 4.1, which do you think would best represent the demand curve for oil?

The demand curve for oil is not very elastic, which means that the quantity demanded falls by only a little even when the price increases by a lot. Thus, demand curve I would best represent the demand curve for oil. The demand for oil is not very elastic because there are *few substitutes* for oil in its major use, transportation.

The fundamental determinant of the elasticity of demand is how easy it is to substitute one good for another. The fewer substitutes for a good, the less elastic the demand. The more substitutes for a good, the more elastic the demand.

When the price of oil goes up people grumble, but few stop using cars, at least not right away. But what happens to the elasticity of the demand for oil over time? The demand for oil tends to become more elastic over time because the more time people have to adjust to a price change, the better they can substitute one good for another. In other words, there are more *substitutes* for oil in the long run than in the short run. Since the OPEC oil price increases in the 1970s (see Figure 3.9 in Chapter 3), the U.S. economy has slowly substituted away from oil by moving toward other sources of energy such as coal, nuclear, and hydroelectric. It took many years, but today the U.S. economy uses about half the amount of oil per dollar of GDP than it did in the 1970s.[1]

In the long run, there are even substitutes for oil in transportation. One reason that mopeds are more popular and SUVs less popular in Europe than in the United States is that taxes make the price of gasoline much higher in Europe than in the United States. Europeans have adjusted by buying more mopeds and smaller cars and driving fewer miles—Americans would do the same if the price of gasoline were expected to increase permanently.

If the price of oil increases by a significant amount for a long period, then even the organization of cities will change as people move from suburbia toward apartments and townhouses located closer to work. It may seem odd to think of moving closer to work as a "substitute for oil," but people adjust to price increases in many ways and economists think of all these adjustments as involving substitutes. If the price of cigarettes goes up and people decide to satisfy their oral cravings by chewing carrots, then carrots are a substitute for cigarettes.

In short, the more time people have to adjust to a change in price the more elastic the demand curve will be.

Let's compare the demand for Orange Crush, a particular brand of orange soda, with the demand for orange soda. There are many good substitutes for Orange Crush, including Orangina, Fanta, and Slice (Wikipedia lists 24 types of orange soda). As a result, the demand for Orange Crush is very elastic because even a small increase in the price of Orange Crush will result in a large decrease in the quantity demanded as people switch to the substitutes. The demand curve for orange soda, however, is less elastic because there are fewer substitutes for orange soda than there are for Orange Crush and the substitutes such as root beer or cola are not as good. We illustrate in Figure 4.2 on the next page. The general point is that the demand for a specific brand of a product is more elastic than the demand for a product category. We come back to this point when we look in more depth at competition and monopoly in Chapters 10 and 11.

FIGURE 4.2

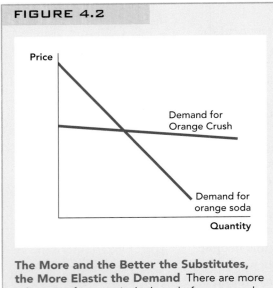

The More and the Better the Substitutes, the More Elastic the Demand There are more substitutes for a particular brand of orange soda, such as Orange Crush, than there are for orange soda. Thus, the demand for Orange Crush is more elastic than the demand for orange soda.

TABLE 4.1 Some Factors Determining the Elasticity of Demand

Less Elastic	More Elastic
Fewer substitutes	More substitutes
Short run (less time)	Long run (more time)
Categories of product	Specific brands
Necessities	Luxuries
Small part of budget	Large part of budget

What counts as a good substitute depends on a buyer's preferences as well as on objective properties of the good. If the price of Coca-Cola increases at the supermarket, many people will buy Pepsi but others will keep on buying Coca-Cola because for them Pepsi is *not* a good substitute. So, some people have a more elastic demand for Coca-Cola while other people have a less elastic demand. A closely related idea is that demand is less elastic for goods that people consider to be "necessities" and is more elastic for goods that are considered "luxuries." Of course, for some people the morning coffee at Starbucks is a necessity and for others it's a luxury. Let's summarize by saying that the demand for necessities—however a person defines that term—tends to be less elastic and the demand for luxuries tends to be more elastic.

The higher a person's income, the less concerned they are likely to be with the price of an item, thus higher income makes demand less elastic. In 2008, the price of wheat tripled and all around the world fewer people bought bread but neither of the authors of this book cut back much on their consumption of bread. The price of bread is too small a portion of our budgets to worry very much about its price so our consumption of bread is not very elastic. On the other hand, when the price of housing increases, we buy smaller houses just like everyone else. Thus, the larger the share of a person's budget devoted to a good, the more elastic their demand for that good is likely to be.

We summarize the determinants of the elasticity of demand in Table 4.1.

Calculating the Elasticity of Demand

The elasticity of demand has a precise definition with important properties. The elasticity of demand is the percentage change in the quantity demanded divided by the percentage change in price.

$$\text{Elasticity of demand} = E_d = \frac{\text{Percentage change in quantity demanded}}{\text{Percentage change in price}}$$

$$= \frac{\%\Delta Q_{Demanded}}{\%\Delta Price}$$

Where delta, Δ, is the mathematical symbol for "change in."

> If the price of oil increases by 10 percent and over a period of several years the quantity demanded falls by 5 percent, then the long-run elasticity of demand for oil is $-5\%/10\% = -0.5$, or 0.5 in absolute terms.

> If the price of Minute Maid orange juice falls by 10 percent and the quantity of Minute Maid orange juice demanded increases by 17.5 percent, then the elasticity of demand for Minute Maid OJ is $17.5\%/-10\% = -1.75$, or 1.75 in absolute terms.[2]

Elasticities of demand are always negative because when the price goes up, the quantity demanded always goes down (and vice versa), which is why economists sometimes drop the negative sign and work with the absolute value instead.

When the absolute value of the elasticity is less than 1, the demand is not very elastic or economists say the demand is **inelastic;** if it is greater than 1 economists say that demand is **elastic,** and if it is exactly equal to one economists say that demand is **unit elastic.** So in our calculations above, oil has inelastic demand and Minute Maid orange juice has elastic demand.

The **elasticity of demand** is a measure of how responsive the quantity demanded is to a change in price. It is computed by

$$E_d = \frac{\%\Delta Q_{Demanded}}{\%\Delta Price}.$$

$|E_D| > 1 = $ **Elastic**
$|E_D| < 1 = $ **Inelastic**
$|E_D| = 1 = $ **Unit Elastic**

Using the Midpoint Method to Calculate the Elasticity of Demand

To calculate an elasticity, you need to know how to calculate the percentage change in quantity and the percentage change in price. That is a bit trickier than it sounds. To see why, let's suppose that you observe the price, quantity pairs shown in the table at right (careful readers will note that these points correspond to points a and b along demand curve E in Figure 4.1).

If you think of moving from point *a* to point *b* (let's call this moving from "before" to "after"), then the quantity demanded falls from 100 to 20 so the change in quantity demanded is −80. What is the percentage change in quantity demanded?

If the beginning quantity, Q_{Before}, is 100 and the ending quantity, Q_{After}, is 20, it seems natural to calculate the percentage change in quantity like this:

	Price	Quantity Demanded
Point a	$40	100
Point b	$50	20

$$\frac{\Delta Q}{Q} = \frac{Q_{After} - Q_{Before}}{Q_{Before}} = \frac{20 - 100}{100} = \frac{-80}{100} = -0.8 = -80\%$$

But now think of moving from point *b* to point *a*. In this case, quantity demanded increases from 20 to 100 and it now seems natural to calculate the percentage change in quantity like this:

$$\frac{\Delta Q}{Q} = \frac{Q_{After} - Q_{Before}}{Q_{Before}} = \frac{100 - 20}{20} = \frac{80}{20} = 4 = 400\%$$

In the first case, we are thinking of a percentage decrease in quantity and in the second of a percentage increase in quantity so it's easy to see why one number is negative and the other positive. But why are the numbers so different when we are calculating exactly the same change?

The different values occur because the base of the calculation changes. If you are driving 100 mph and decrease speed to 20 mph, it's natural to say that your speed went down by 80 percent because you calculate using a base of 100. But if you are driving 20 mph and you increase speed to 100 mph, it's natural to say that you increased your speed by 400 percent since you now use 20 as the base. Economists would like to calculate the same number for elasticity whether the quantity (or speed) decreases from 100 to 20 or increases from 20 to 100.

To avoid problems with the choice of base, economists calculate the percentage change in quantity by dividing the change in quantity by the *average or midpoint quantity*—the base is thus the same whether you think about quantity as increasing or decreasing.

Here is the formula:

$$\text{Elasticity of demand} = E_d = \frac{\%\Delta Q_{Demanded}}{\%\Delta Price}$$

$$= \frac{\dfrac{\text{Change in quantity demanded}}{\text{Average quantity}}}{\dfrac{\text{Change in price}}{\text{Average price}}} = \frac{\dfrac{Q_{After} - Q_{Before}}{(Q_{After} + Q_{Before})/2}}{\dfrac{P_{After} - P_{Before}}{(P_{After} + P_{Before})/2}}$$

In this case, we calculate the percentage change in quantity demanded as $\dfrac{-80}{(100 + 20)/2} \times 100 = -133.3\%$ and we also use the midpoint formula for the percentage change in price, which is $\dfrac{(50 - 40)}{(50 + 40)/2} \times 100 = 22.2\%$. With these two numbers, we can now calculate the elasticity of demand over this portion of the demand curve:

$$E_d = -133.3\%/22.2\% = -6$$

Notice that the absolute value of the elasticity, 6, is greater than 1 so the demand is elastic over this range.

It's more important that you understand the concept of elasticity. To calculate an elasticity, don't worry too much; just remember where the formula is located and plug in the numbers. In the first appendix to this chapter, we show how to create a simple Excel spreadsheet to calculate elasticity so you need not even worry about making calculation mistakes (at least not on your homework!).

Total Revenues and the Elasticity of Demand

A firm's revenues are equal to price per unit times quantity sold.

$$\text{Revenue} = \text{Price} \times \text{Quantity, or } R = P \times Q$$

Elasticity measures how much Q goes down when P goes up, so you might suspect that there is a relationship between elasticity and revenue. Indeed, the relationship is remarkably useful: If the demand curve is inelastic, then revenues go up when the price goes up. If the demand curve is elastic, then revenues go down when the price goes up.

Let's give some intuition for this result. Imagine that the demand curve is inelastic, thus not responsive to price. This means that when P goes up by a lot, Q goes down by a little, like this

$$\overset{\uparrow}{P} \times \underset{\downarrow}{Q}$$

So when the demand curve is inelastic, what will happen to revenues? If P goes up by a lot and Q goes down by a little, then revenues will go up,

FIGURE 4.3

Elasticities and Revenues When the price increases what happens to total revenue? If demand is inelastic, an increase in price increases revenues. In the left panel, an increase in the price from $40 to $50 increases revenues from $4,000 to $4,750 so demand is inelastic. If the demand is elastic, then an increase in price decreases revenues. In the right panel, an increase in price from $40 to $50 decreases revenues from $4,000 to $1,000 so demand is elastic.

$$\overset{\uparrow}{\underset{}{R}} = \overset{\uparrow}{P} \times \overset{}{\underset{\downarrow}{Q}}$$

Thus, when the demand curve is inelastic, revenues go up when the price goes up and, of course, revenues will go down when the price goes down.

We can also show the relationship in a diagram. Figure 4.3 shows an inelastic demand curve on the left and an elastic demand curve on the right.* Revenue is P × Q so revenue is equal to the area of a rectangle with height equal to price and width equal to the quantity; for example, when the price is $40 and the quantity is 100, revenues are $4,000, or the area of the blue rectangle (note that the blue and green rectangles overlap).

In both diagrams, the blue rectangles show revenue at a price of $40 and the green rectangles show revenues at the higher price of $50. Compare the size of the green and blue rectangles when the demand curve is inelastic (on the left) and when the demand curve is elastic (on the right). What do you see? When the demand curve is inelastic, an increase in price increases revenues (the green rectangle

---

* These curves are the same curves as in Figure 4.1 so they run through a common point and thus we can apply our elasticity rule, which tells us that at any given quantity the flatter curve is more elastic than the steeper curve.

is bigger than the blue rectangle), but when the demand curve is elastic, an increase in price decreases revenues (the green rectangle is smaller than the blue rectangle).

Of course, the relationships hold in reverse as well. If the demand curve is inelastic, a price decrease causes a decrease in revenues, and if the demand curve is elastic a price decrease causes an increase in revenues.

Can you guess what happens to revenues when price increases or decreases when the demand curve is unit elastic? Right, nothing! When the demand curve is unit elastic, a change in price is exactly matched by an equal and opposite percentage change in quantity so revenues stay the same. Unit elasticity is the dividing point between elastic and inelastic curves.

You should be able to use all of these relationships on an exam. Table 4.2 summarizes what we have covered so far.

TABLE 4.2 Elasticity and Revenue		
Absolute Value of Elasticity	Name	How Revenue Changes with Price
$\left\lvert E_d \right\rvert < 1$	Inelastic	Revenue and price move together.
$\left\lvert E_d \right\rvert > 1$	Elastic	Revenue and price move in opposite directions.
$\left\lvert E_d \right\rvert = 1$	Unit Elastic	Revenue stays the same when price changes.

If you must, memorize the table. At least one of your textbook authors, however, can never remember the relationship between elasticity and total revenue. So, instead of memorizing the relationship, he always derives it by drawing little diagrams like those in Figure 4.3. If you can easily duplicate these diagrams, you too will always be able to answer questions involving elasticity and total revenue.

Applications of Demand Elasticity

Let's put to work what you have learned so far about demand elasticity. Here are two applications.

How American Farmers Have Worked Themselves Out of a Job   Using the same inputs of land, labor, and capital, American farmers can produce more than twice as much food today as they could in 1950—that's an amazing increase in productivity. The increase in productivity means that Americans can produce more food per person today than in 1950. But how much more food can Americans eat? Although it doesn't always seem this way, Americans want to consume only so much more food even if the price falls by a lot. So what type of demand curve does this suggest? An inelastic demand curve; and remember, when the demand curve is inelastic, a fall in price means a fall in revenues.

The left panel of Figure 4.4 shows how the American farmer has worked himself (and herself) out of a job. Increases in farming productivity have reduced cost, shifting the supply curve down and reducing the price of food. But since the demand curve for food is inelastic, the quantity of food demanded has increased by a smaller percentage than the price has fallen. As a result, farming revenues have declined. Notice that in the left panel of Figure 4.4, the blue rectangle (farm revenues today) is smaller than the green rectangle (revenues in 1950)—just as we showed in Figure 4.3.

FIGURE 4.4

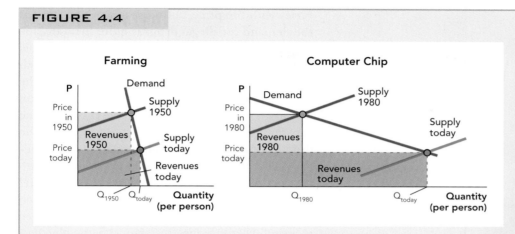

Farming/Computer Chips
Productivity improvements have increased the supply of food and the supply of computer chips, thus reducing the prices of these goods. The demand for food, however, is inelastic while the demand for computer chips is elastic. As a result, the decrease in the price of food has driven down farm revenues while the decrease in the price of computer chips has driven up computer chip revenues.

Increases in productivity, however, do not always mean that revenue falls. In the last several decades, productivity has increased in computer chips even faster than in farming. But as the price of computer chips has fallen, the quantity of computer chips demanded has increased even more. Computer chips are now not just in computers but in phones, televisions, automobiles, and toys. As a result, revenues for the computer chip industry have increased and made computing a larger share of the American economy. What type of demand curve does this suggest? An elastic demand curve. The right panel in Figure 4.4 illustrates how an increase in productivity in computing has shifted the supply curve down and reduced prices, but the quantity of computer chips demanded has increased by an even greater percentage than the price has fallen. As a result, computer chip revenues have increased.

The lesson is that whether a demand curve is elastic or inelastic has a tremendous influence on the how an industry evolves over time. If you want to be in on a growing industry, it helps to know the elasticity of demand.

Why the War on Drugs Is Hard to Win

It's hard to defeat an enemy that grows stronger the more you strike against him or her. (See the movies *Rocky I, II, III, IV, V,* and *VI.*) The war on drugs is like that. We illustrate with a simple model.

The U.S. government spends over $33 billion a year arresting over 1.5 million people and deterring the supply of drugs with police, prisons, and border patrols.[*] This, in turn, increases the cost of smuggling and dealing drugs. (The war on drugs also increases the costs of buying drugs. We could include this factor in our model but to keep the model simple we will focus on increases in the costs of supplying drugs.) When costs go up, suppliers require a higher price to supply any given quantity so the supply curve shifts up—in Figure 4.5 (on the next page) from "Supply with no prohibition" to "Supply with prohibition."[†]

The most important assumption in Figure 4.5 is that the demand curve is inelastic. It's hard to get good data on how the quantity of drugs demanded

SERGIO PITAMITZ/ROBERT HARDING WORLD IMAGERY/CORBIS

High Prices?

How do we know how much prohibition has raised the price of illegal drugs? In the Netherlands, small quantities of marijuana can be bought openly at "coffee shops" and the price is roughly the same as it is in the United States.

It may seem surprising that prohibition doesn't raise prices more, but prohibition raises some costs of selling illegal drugs while lowering others. Marijuana shops in the Netherlands, for example, pay taxes while most drug dealers in the United States do not.

---

[*]See Miron, Jeffrey A. 2004. *Drug War Crimes: The Consequences of Prohibition* (Oakland, CA: Independent Institute) and MacCoun, Robert J. and Peter Reuter. 2001. *Drug War Heresies: Learning from Other Vices, Times, and Places.* (Cambridge: Cambridge University Press) for two good analyses of the war on drugs from an economic perspective.

[†]Note that we have assumed that the supply of drugs is perfectly elastic, which is plausible for an agricultural product whose production can be expanded or contracted very easily without an increase in costs. We discuss the elasticity of supply at greater length in the next section.

FIGURE 4.5

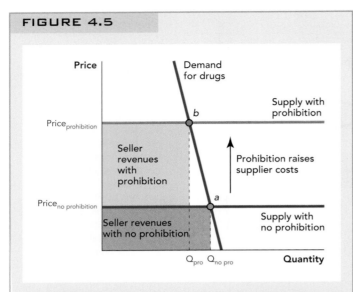

The Drug War Is Hard to Win Because Seller Revenues Increase with Greater Enforcement Without drug prohibition, the market equilibrium is at point a with seller revenues given by the blue area. Prohibition raises the costs of supply pushing up the supply curve and moving the equilibrium to point b. At point b, seller revenues are the larger green area. Prohibition in this graph reduces the quantity of drugs consumed a little, from $Q_{no\ pro}$ to Q_{pro} but it raises seller revenues by a lot.

UNDERSTAND YOUR **world**

CHECK YOURSELF

> Which is more elastic, the demand for computers or the demand for Dell computers?

> The elasticity of demand for eggs has been estimated to be 0.1. If the price of eggs increases by 10 percent, what will happen to the total revenue of egg producers or in other words the total spending on eggs? Will it go up or down?

> If a fashionable clothing store raises its prices by 25 percent, what does that tell you about the store's estimate of the elasticity of demand for its products?

The **elasticity of supply** measures how responsive the quantity supplied is to a change in price.

varies with the price, but most studies suggest that the demand for illegal drugs is quite inelastic, approximately 0.5. Inelastic demand is also plausible from what we know intuitively about how much people are willing to pay for drugs even when the price rises. Economists have much better data on the elasticity of demand for cigarettes, which one can think of as the elasticity of demand for the drug nicotine and it too is about 0.5.[3]

What happens to seller revenues when the demand curve is inelastic and the price rises? (Review Figure 4.3 if you don't know immediately.) When the demand curve is inelastic, an increase in price increases seller revenues. In Figure 4.5, the blue rectangle is seller revenues at the no prohibition price; the much larger green rectangle is seller revenues with prohibition. Prohibition increases the cost of selling drugs, which raises the price, but at a higher price, revenues from drug selling are greater even if the quantity sold is somewhat smaller.

The more effective prohibition is at raising costs, the greater are drug industry revenues. So, more effective prohibition means that drug sellers have more money to buy guns, pay bribes, fund the dealers, and even research and develop new technologies in drug delivery (like crack cocaine). It's hard to beat an enemy that gets stronger the more you strike against him or her.

The war on drugs is difficult to win, but that doesn't necessarily mean that it's not worth fighting. Nobel Prize-winning economist Gary S. Becker, however, does suggest a change in tactics. Suppose drugs were legal but taxed, much as alcohol is today. Becker suggests that the tax could be set so that it raised seller costs exactly as much as did prohibition (in Figure 4.5 simply relabel "Supply with prohibition," as "Supply with tax"). Since the tax raises costs by the same amount, the quantity of drugs sold would be the same under the tax as under prohibition. The only difference would be that instead of increasing seller revenues, a tax would increase government revenues (by the green rectangle *not* including the overlap with the blue rectangle). Many of the unfortunate spillovers of the war on drugs—things like gangs, guns, and corruption—could be greatly reduced under a "legal but taxed" system.*

Let's turn now to the elasticity of supply.

The Elasticity of Supply

When the price of a good like oil increases, suppliers will increase the quantity supplied, but by how much? Will the quantity supplied increase by a lot or by a little? The **elasticity of supply** measures how responsive the quantity supplied is to a change in price. To see the intuition, let's take a look at Figure 4.6 on the next page, which shows two different supply curves.

---

*On the benefits of a tax system for currently illegal drugs, see Becker, Gary S., Kevin M. Murphy, and Michael Grossman. 2006. "The Market for Illegal Goods: The Case of Drugs." *Journal of Political Economy* 114(1):38–60.

FIGURE 4.6

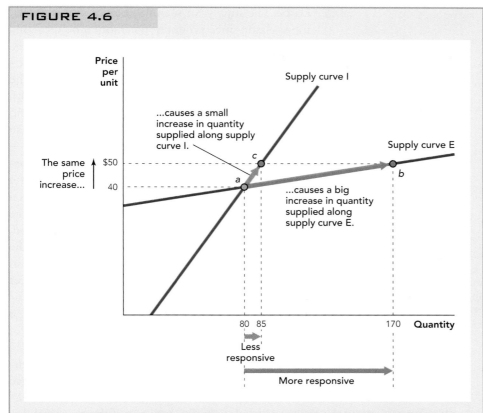

The More Responsive Quantity Supplied Is to a Change in Price, the More Elastic the Supply Curve Beginning at point *a*, an increase in price from $40 to $50 causes a small increase in quantity supplied along supply curve I, from 80 to 85 units (at point *c*). But the same increase in price causes a big increase in quantity supplied along supply curve E, from 80 to 170 units (at point *b*). Since the quantity supplied is more responsive to a change in price, supply curve E is more elastic than supply curve I.

In Figure 4.6, when the price increases from $40 to $50, the quantity supplied increases from 80 to 85 along supply curve I but a much larger amount from 80 to 170 along supply curve E. Since the quantity supplied is more responsive to a change in price, supply curve E is more elastic than supply curve I.

Determinants of the Elasticity of Supply

Which supply curve, supply curve I or supply curve E, do you think would better represent the supply curve for oil? Even large increases in the price of oil will not increase the quantity of oil supplied by very much because it's not easy to quickly increase the production of oil. Producing more oil requires time and a significant increase in the costs of exploration and drilling. Thus, the supply curve for oil is not very elastic (we could also say inelastic) and would be better represented by supply curve I.

The fundamental determinant of the elasticity of supply is how quickly per-unit costs increase with an increase in production. If increased production requires much higher per-unit costs, then supply will be less elastic—or inelastic. If production can increase with constant per-unit costs, then supply will be elastic.

It's usually difficult to increase the supply of raw materials like oil, coal, and gold without increasing costs—remember from Chapter 2 that the higher the price, the deeper the mine—so the supply of raw materials is often not very

FIGURE 4.7

A perfectly inelastic supply curve

Price

Quantity

The supply of Picasso paintings is very inelastic.

A perfectly elastic supply curve

Price

Quantity

The supply of toothpicks is very elastic.

The Elasticity of Supply of Toothpicks and Picasso Paintings The supply of Picasso paintings is very inelastic because Picasso won't paint any more no matter how high the price rises. The supply of toothpicks is very elastic because it's easy for suppliers to make more in response to even a small increase in price.

Guernica—never again

Guernica (detail) by Pablo Picasso

elastic. The supply for manufactured goods is usually more elastic since production can often be increased at the same cost per unit by building more factories. To fully understand the elasticity of supply, let's consider two goods that represent polar cases of the elasticity of supply: Picasso paintings and toothpicks.

Picasso won't be painting any more *Guernica*s no matter how high the price of his paintings rises so the supply of Picasso paintings is not at all elastic—perfectly inelastic would be a good working assumption.* A perfectly inelastic supply curve is a vertical line. We show an example in the left panel of Figure 4.7, which indicates that even a very large increase in price won't increase the quantity supplied.

Toothpick manufacturers, however, can increase the supply of toothpicks without an increase in their costs per toothpick by cutting down just a few more trees and running them through the mill. Thus, a small increase in the price of toothpicks will generate a large increase in quantity supplied; that is, the supply of toothpicks will be very elastic—perfectly elastic would be a good working assumption. A perfectly elastic supply curve is flat, which indicates that even a tiny increase in price increases the quantity supplied by a very large amount. We show a perfectly elastic supply curve in the right panel of Figure 4.7.

It's easy to expand the supply of toothpicks because even if the toothpick industry doubles in size, the increases in the demand for wood will be negligible, so the toothpick industry can expand without pushing up the price of its primary input, wood. But if the housing industry were to double in size, the demand for wood would increase dramatically, and since it takes time to plant and harvest new trees, the price of wood and thus the price of houses would increase in the short run. More generally, supply is more elastic when the industry can be expanded without causing a big increase in the demand for that industry's inputs.

A closely related point is that the local supply of a good is much more elastic than the global supply. The supply of oil to the world is inelastic because world production won't increase without a significant increase in the cost of production per barrel. But imagine that more people move to Austin, Texas, increasing the demand for oil in that city. It's very easy to ship more oil to Austin from other parts of the United States so the supply of oil to Austin is well approximated by a perfectly elastic supply curve.

As with demand, supply tends to be more elastic in the long run than in the short run because in the long run, suppliers have more time to adjust. Suppliers can respond to an increase in the price of bicycles fairly quickly by running currently existing factories at higher capacity. Given more time, however, suppliers can increase output at lower cost by building new factories.

For some goods, it's almost impossible to increase output much in the short run. The best Scotch whisky, for example, is aged in oak barrels for 10, 20, or even 30 years. If the price of such high-quality Scotch whisky increases today, it will be at least 10 years before supply can increase.

---

*Why isn't the supply of Picasso paintings perfectly inelastic for certain? The supply of newly created Picasso paintings is perfectly inelastic, but with a higher price more people will be induced to sell their Picasso paintings so the market supply of Picasso paintings will be very inelastic but not necessarily perfectly inelastic.

TABLE 4.3 Primary Factors Determining the Elasticity of Supply

Less Elastic	More Elastic
Difficult to increase production at constant unit cost (e.g., some raw materials)	Easy to increase production at constant unit cost (e.g., some manufactured goods)
Large share of market for inputs	Small share of market for inputs
Global supply	Local supply
Short run	Long run

We summarize the primary factors that determine the elasticity of supply in Table 4.3.

Calculating the Elasticity of Supply

The elasticity of supply also has a precise definition. The **elasticity of supply** is the percentage change in the quantity supplied divided by the percentage change in price.

Examples:

> If the price of cocoa rises by 10 percent and the quantity supplied increases by 3 percent, then the elasticity of supply for cocoa is $\frac{3\%}{10\%} = 0.3$.

> If the price of coffee falls by 10 percent and the quantity supplied of coffee falls by 1.5 percent, then the elasticity of supply for coffee is $\frac{-1.5\%}{-10\%} = 0.15$.[4]

Using the Midpoint Method to Calculate the Elasticity of Supply As with demand elasticities, it's important to calculate percent changes for supply elasticities using the midpoint method. Here is the midpoint formula for the elasticity of supply.

The **elasticity of supply** is a measure of how responsive the quantity supplied is to a change in price. It is computed by

$$E_s = \frac{\%\Delta Q_{Supplied}}{\%\Delta Price}.$$

$$\text{Elasticity of supply} = E_s = \frac{\%\Delta Q_{Supplied}}{\%\Delta Price}$$

$$= \frac{\dfrac{\text{Change in quantity supplied}}{\text{Average quantity}}}{\dfrac{\text{Change in price}}{\text{Average price}}} = \frac{\dfrac{Q_{After} - Q_{Before}}{(Q_{After} + Q_{Before})/2}}{\dfrac{P_{After} - P_{Before}}{(P_{After} + P_{Before})/2}}$$

Applications of Supply Elasticity

Let's examine two important issues in public policy, gun buybacks and slave redemption. In both cases, understanding the elasticity of supply is critical if people are to evaluate these policies wisely.

Gun Buyback Programs The police in Washington, D.C., bought over 6,000 guns, *no questions asked*, from anyone coming to one of their gun buybacks held between August 1999 and December 2000. The program got a big assist from President Clinton and the Department of Housing and Urban Development, which paid most of the buyback's $528,000 cost. Millions of dollars more were spent buying guns in Chicago, Sacramento, Seattle, and dozens of other cities around the country.[5]

The theory of gun buybacks is that gun buybacks (1) reduce the number of guns in circulation and (2) reductions in the number of guns in circulation reduces crime. It's not obvious that point (2) is true—guns are used for self-defense as well as for crime so fewer guns could mean more crime. But we don't have to decide that controversial question here because simple economic theory suggests that point (1) is false—gun buybacks in a city like Washington, D.C., are unlikely to reduce the number of guns in circulation. Let's see why.

We can analyze the effect of this program with a few questions. What kinds of guns are most likely to be sold at the gun buyback, high quality or low quality guns? And, what is the elasticity of supply of such guns to a city like Washington, D.C.?

What type of gun is most likely to be sold at a gun buyback? The best gun to sell at a buyback is one that you can't sell anywhere else, so buybacks attract low-quality guns. In one Seattle buyback, 17 percent of the guns turned in didn't even fire.[6]

Now here is the key question. What is the elasticity of supply of low-quality guns to a city like Washington, D.C.? Recall from Table 4.3 that local supply curves are typically more elastic than global or national supply curves. It's estimated that there are 150 to 200 million guns in the United States so there are plenty of low-quality guns. So many that the supply of such guns to Washington, D.C., will be very elastic—elastic enough to make perfectly elastic a good working assumption.

Now that we know that the supply of low-quality guns to Washington, D.C., is very elastic, let's draw the diagram and analyze the policy. In Figure 4.8, we draw a perfectly elastic supply curve. With no buyback, the price of a low-quality, used gun is $84 and 1,000 guns are traded in Washington. The gun buy-back program increases the demand for used guns, shifting the demand curve outward, and the increase in demand pushes up the quantity of guns supplied in

Washington, D.C., to 6,000 units. But the supply is so elastic that the price of guns doesn't increase so even though the police buy 5,000 guns, the quantity of guns traded on the streets stays at 1,000. In other words, there is no net change in the number of guns on the streets of DC.

If this seems difficult to believe, imagine that instead of guns the Washington police decided to buy back shoes. Remember, the idea of a gun buyback is to reduce the number of people in Washington, D.C., with guns. Now, do you think that a shoe buyback would reduce the number of people in Washington, D.C., with shoes? Of course not. What will happen? People will sell their old shoes, the ones they don't wear anymore. Some enterprising individuals might even buy old shoes from thrift shops and sell those to the police. (In one Oakland gun buyback, some enterprising gun dealers from Reno, Nevada, drove to Oakland and sold the police more than 50 low-quality guns.[7]) The shoe buyback is unlikely to cause people to go shoeless, and for the same reasons a gun buyback is unlikely to cause people to go gunless.

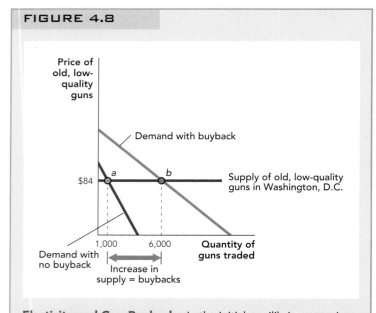

FIGURE 4.8

Elasticity and Gun Buybacks In the initial equilibrium at point a, 1,000 low-quality guns are traded. When police buy guns, the demand for guns increases, but since the supply of guns to a local region is very elastic, the street price of guns does not increase. As a result, the police can buy as many guns as they want, but there is no decrease in guns on the street.

The key point is that if the police can't drive up the price of guns, then they can't reduce the quantity of guns demanded on the streets. And the price of guns is determined not in Washington, D.C., but in the national market for guns where millions of guns are bought and sold so a police buyback of 5,000 guns is too small to influence the price.

It's even possible that gun buybacks will *increase* the number of guns in circulation. Suppose that gun buybacks become a common and permanent feature of the market for guns. Before the gun buyback, a purchaser of a new gun expects that it will eventually wear out or otherwise fall in value until it becomes worthless. But when gun buybacks are common, someone buying a gun knows that if it stops working he can always sell it to the government. A buyback makes new guns more valuable; now they come with an insurance policy protecting against declines in value which increases the demand for new guns.[8] You have probably experienced the same effect—students are more willing to buy an expensive textbook if they know they can easily sell it at the end of the semester—but do keep this book forever!

Given the economic analysis, it's not surprising that studies of gun buybacks have shown them to be completely ineffective at reducing crime.[9]

UNDERSTAND YOUR world

The Economics of Slave Redemption   Let's return to our opening example. Recall that Harvard sophomore Jay Williams flew to the Sudan in fall 2000 to buy the freedom of people who had been enslaved. Working with Christian Solidarity International, Williams was able to buy and free 4,000 people. Donations came from all over the United States, including a fourth grade class in Denver.[10]

The policy of slave redemption has been controversial. Some groups such as Christian Freedom International, equally as humanitarian as Christian Solidarity International, have argued that slave redemption can make a bad situation even worse. Perhaps surprisingly, at the heart of the controversy is the concept of the elasticity of supply. If groups who pay to free people from slavery increase the demand for slaves, what effect will this have on the price of slaves and on the incentives of those who traffic in people?

In Figure 4.9 on the next page, we show the best case for slave redemption, when the supply curve is perfectly inelastic (vertical). When the supply curve is perfectly inelastic, there is a fixed number of slaves no matter what the price. As a result, every person ransomed and freed is one less slave held in captivity. This may be the case that people like Jay Williams were implicitly thinking of when they flew to the Sudan.

Let's take a closer look at Figure 4.9. Before the slave redemption program begins, the price of a slave is $15, a realistic number for slaves in Sudan, and there are 1,000 slaves bought and held in captivity every year (point *a*). With the redemption program, the demand for slaves increases (shifts outward), which pushes the price of slaves up to $50 (point *b*). Now here is the key: At a price of $50, the quantity of slaves demanded by potential slave owners decreases to 200 (point *c*). The remaining 800 slaves are bought and freed by the redeemers. Because there is no increase in the quantity supplied in this case, every slave purchased means one less person held in slavery. Note that slave redemption works by driving up the price of slaves so high that potential owners cannot afford to buy slaves. In other words, to work well, slave redeemers must outbid potential slave owners.

Unfortunately, the supply of slaves is unlikely to be perfectly inelastic. We are back again to one of the primary lessons of this book, incentives. When people enter the market to buy back slaves and increase the price of slaves, they increase the incentive to capture more slaves.

Jay Williams (right) in the Sudan

FIGURE 4.9

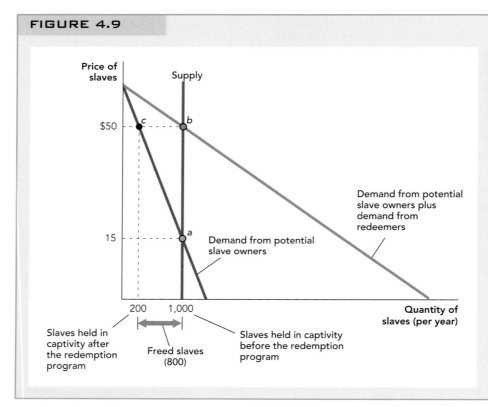

Slave Redemption Works Best When the Supply Curve for Slaves Is Perfectly Inelastic In the initial equilibrium at point *a*, potential slave owners purchase 1,000 slaves at a price of $15. The increase in demand from the redeemers pushes up the price of slaves to $50 at point *b*. At the higher price, the quantity of slaves demanded by potential slave owners is just 200 so the redeemers are able to free 800 slaves. Since there is no increase in the quantity supplied, every slave purchased is a slave freed.

Figure 4.10 analyzes the more realistic case when the supply curve is not perfectly inelastic. In the initial equilibrium, the price of slaves is $15 and potential owners buy 1,000 slaves (point *a*). When the redeemers enter the market, the demand for slaves increases and the price increases from $15 to $30 (point *b*). The price of slaves does not increase as much as when the supply curve was perfectly inelastic because some of the increased demand for slaves is met by a greater quantity supplied. At a price of $30, the quantity of slaves demanded by potential owners falls from 1,000 to 600 (point *c*) but notice also that the total number of people captured by human traffickers increases by 1,200 to 2,200 (point *b*). Of these 2,200, 1,600 are freed by the redeemers, leaving 600 held in captivity.

Let's summarize: Before redemption, 1,000 slaves were demanded by slave owners. After redemption, demand has dropped to 600 slaves from these slave owners. This is the good result of the redemption program. But due to the higher price of slaves, slave traffickers increase the quantity of slaves from 1,000 to 2,200. The redeemers free 1,600 of these 2,200 slaves, but 1,200 of these would not have been enslaved had it not been for the increase in demand. Thus, on net, the slave redeemers free just 400 slaves.

The key point is this: The additional demand for slaves from those who wish to free slaves pushes up the price of slaves, which reduces the quantity demanded— that's good. But the higher price also pushes up the quantity supplied—that's bad.

Thus, slavery redemption programs create a true dilemma. The groups that buy freedom can reduce the number of slaves held in captivity, but only at the price of increasing the number of people who are enslaved for at least some period. An economist can point to this dilemma but economics does not offer a solution (and unfortunately neither does anyone else).

Is there any evidence on the effect of slave redemption programs? Remember that one sign of whether the redemption program is working is how much the

FIGURE 4.10

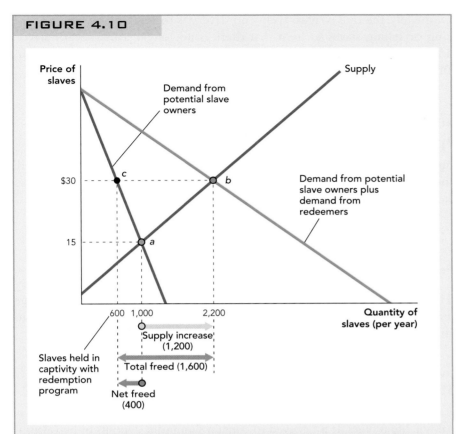

Slave Redemption When the Supply Curve Is Not Perfectly Inelastic When the slave redeemers enter the market, the demand for slaves increases and the price rises from $15 at point *a* to $30 at point *b*. At the higher price, potential slave owners demand just 600 slaves, or 400 fewer than before—that's the good aspect of slave redemption. But at the higher price, slave traffickers increase the quantity of slaves supplied from 1,000 to 2,200. The slave redeemers free 1,600 slaves, but 1,200 of these people would not have been enslaved had it not been for the increase in demand; thus, on net just 400 slaves are freed.

program *increases* the price of slaves. Higher prices mean that the redeemers are outbidding potential slave traffickers. Data on slave prices in the Sudan are unreliable, but the fragmentary data that does exist is not encouraging. Although the redemption program initially appeared to raise prices, prices soon began to fall.[11] Recall that supply tends to be more elastic in the long run—thus, the data on prices is consistent with a supply curve that became more elastic over time. Since redemption programs are less effective when the elasticity of supply is greater, the data on prices suggest that the program became less effective over time.

Finally, let us note some further complications. Slavery in the Sudan is part of a larger civil war—the government in Khartoum permits and even encourages slave traffickers who attack the government's enemies. When redeemer groups buy slaves, they are funding not simply slave traffickers but shock troops in a civil war. Guns bought with money received from selling slaves can be used to kill as well as to enslave. Even if we concluded that slave redemption was on average good for the slaves, it might not be good once we account for all of the *external effects* of enriching slave raiders. (We explain the idea of external effects at greater length in Chapter 9.)

> A computer manufacturer makes an experimental computer chip that critics praise, leading to a huge increase in the demand for the chip. How elastic is supply in the short run? What about the long run?

> Will the same increase in the demand for housing increase prices more in Manhattan or in Des Moines, Iowa?

Ultimately, the only way to truly end slavery is to raise the punishment for buying or selling slaves so high that there is no longer a market for slaves. Doing this in the Sudan will require an end to the civil war and the establishment of the rule of law.*

Using Elasticities for Quick Predictions (Optional)

Economists are often asked to predict how shifts in demand and supply will change market prices. Two simple price-change formulas make it possible to make quick predictions for price changes using elasticities.[12]

> Percent change in price from a shift in demand $= \dfrac{\text{Percent change in demand}}{E_d + E_s}$

> Percent change in price from a shift in supply $= -\dfrac{\text{Percent change in supply}}{E_d + E_s}$

These formulas are approximations that work well when the percent change in demand or supply is small, say 10 percent or less.[13] Let's apply the formula to an interesting problem.

How Much Would the Price of Oil Fall if the Arctic National Wildlife Refuge Were Opened Up for Drilling?

The Arctic National Wildlife Refuge (ANWR) is the largest of Alaska's 16 national wildlife refuges. It is believed to contain significant deposits of petroleum. Former President George W. Bush argued in favor of drilling in ANWR.

> Increasing our domestic energy supply will help lower gasoline prices and utility bills. We can and should produce more crude oil here at home in environmentally responsible ways. The most promising site for oil in America is a 2,000 acre site in the Arctic National Wildlife Refuge, and thanks to technology, we can reach this energy with little impact on the land or wildlife.[14]

Some environmentalists disagree about whether the oil can be produced in environmentally-responsible ways. We will leave that debate to others. What do economists say about the president's assertion that "Increasing our domestic energy supply will help lower gasoline prices and utility bills"? An increase in supply will lower prices, but by how much?

The Department of Energy's Energy Information Service (EIS) predicts that production from ANWR will average about 800,000 barrels per day, or a little bit less than 1 percent of worldwide oil production (82 million barrels per day in 2004 and increasing slowly over time). Let's be generous and suppose that ANWR increases world supply by 1 percent. Since the elasticity of demand for oil is about 0.5 and the best estimate of the elasticity of supply is about 0.3, using our price formula we have:

At what price should we drill for oil in ANWR?

Percent change in price of oil from a 1% increase in supply $= -\dfrac{1\%}{0.5 + 0.3}$
$$= -1.25\%$$

*For more on the difficult ethics and economics of slave redemption, see the essays in Kwame Anthony Appiah and Martin Bunzl. 2007. *Buying Freedom: The Ethics and Economics of Slave Redemption.* Princeton: Princeton University Press. See especially, Chapter 1, Some Simple Analytics of Slave Redemption, by Dean S. Karlan and Alan B. Krueger, for an incisive economic analysis that we have drawn on.

A 1.25 percent fall in price won't seem like very much when *you* are gassing up at the pump but don't forget that *every user of oil in the world* will benefit from the fall in price—so a fall of 1.25% is nothing to sneeze at.

In the past decade, the price of oil has varied from around $20 a barrel to over $140 a barrel. It's difficult to know the value of conservation in Alaska or how much the environment might be damaged by drilling, but we do know that the higher the price of oil, the stronger the case for drilling.

UNDERSTAND YOUR **world**

☐ Takeaway

The elasticity of demand measures how responsive the quantity demanded is to a change in price—the more responsive, the more elastic the demand. Similarly, the elasticity of supply measures how responsive the quantity supplied is to a change in price—the more responsive, the more elastic the supply.

In Chapter 3, we learned how to shift the supply and demand curves to produce *qualitative* predictions about changes in prices and quantities. Estimating elasticities of demand and supply is the first step in *quantifying* how changes in demand and supply will affect prices and quantities. You should know how to calculate elasticities of demand and supply using data on prices and quantities.

The elasticity of demand tells you how revenues respond to changes in price along a demand curve. If the $|E_d| < 1$, then price and revenue move together, and if $|E_d| > 1$ then price and revenue move in opposite directions. We used these relationships to explain why decreases in the price of food have made farming a smaller share of the economy, but decreases in the price of computer chips have made computing a larger share of the economy. We also used the same relationship to explain why the war on drugs can arm the very people it is trying to weaken.

You don't need to do statistical studies of demand and supply to get useful information about elasticities. Once you understand the concept, a little common sense will tell you that the supply curve for low-quality guns in Washington, D.C., is very elastic. And, if you can reason that the supply of low-quality guns to Washington, D.C., is very elastic, a little economics will tell you that gun buyback programs are a waste of taxpayer dollars. Similar reasoning suggests how slave redemption programs might harm more people than they benefit.

Elasticity is a bit dry but it's a useful concept and it will appear again in this book when we come to discuss taxes in Chapter 7 and monopoly in Chapter 11.

☐ CHAPTER REVIEW

KEY CONCEPTS

Elasticity of demand, p. 52

Inelastic, p. 55

Elastic, p. 55

Unit elastic, p. 55

Elasticity of supply, p. 60

FACTS AND TOOLS

1. For each of the following pairs, which of the two goods is more likely to be inelastically demanded and why? Table 4.1 should help:

a. Demand for tangerines vs. demand for fruit.

b. Demand for beef next month vs. demand for beef over the next decade.

c. Demand for Exxon gasoline at the corner of 7th and Grand vs. demand for gasoline in the entire city.

d. Demand for insulin vs. demand for vitamins.

2. For each of the following pairs, which of the two goods is more likely to be elastically supplied? Table 4.3 should help:

a. Supply of apples over the next growing season vs. supply of apples over the next decade.

b. Supply of construction workers in Binghamton, New York, vs. supply of construction workers in New York state.

c. Supply of breakfast cereal vs. supply of food.

d. Supply of gold vs. supply of computers.

3. Indicate whether the demand for the good would become more elastic or less elastic after each of the following changes. (Note that in each of these cases the demand curve may also shift inward or outward but in this question we are interested in whether the demand becomes more or less elastic.) Briefly justify your answer.

a. The demand curve for soap after wide understanding that bacteria and other organisms cause and spread disease.

b. The demand curve for coal after the invention of nuclear power plants.

c. The demand curve for cars as more employers allow employees to telecommute.

d. The demand curve for a new television during an economic boom.

4. For each of the following, indicate if the supply for the good would become more elastic or less elastic as a result of each change and briefly justify your answer (once again, in each case the supply curve will also shift but we are interested in changes in the elasticity).

a. The supply curve for diamonds if a new process for *manufacturing* diamonds is created.

b. The supply curve for food if pesticides and fertilizers were banned.

c. The supply curve for plastic if a very large share of oil output was used to make plastic.

d. The supply curve for nurses after several years of increasing wages in nursing.

5. Let's work out a few examples to get a sense of what elasticity of demand means in practice. Remember that in all of these cases, we're moving along a fixed demand curve—so think

of supply increasing or decreasing while the demand curve is staying in the same place.

a. If the elasticity of demand for college textbooks is −0.1 and the price of textbooks increases by 20 percent, how much will the quantity demanded change, and in what direction?

b. In your answer to part a, was your answer in percentages or in total number of textbooks?

c. If the elasticity of demand for spring break packages to Cancun is −5, and if you notice that this year in Cancun the quantity of packages demanded increased by 10 percent, then what happened to the price of Cancun vacation packages?

d. In your college town, real estate developers are building thousands of new student-friendly apartments close to campus. If you want to pay the lowest rent possible, should you hope that demand for apartments is elastic or inelastic?

e. In your college town, the local government decrees that thousands of apartments close to campus are uninhabitable and must be torn down next semester. If you want to pay the lowest rent possible, should you hope that demand for apartments is elastic or inelastic?

f. If the elasticity of demand for ballpoint pens with blue ink is −20, and the price of ballpoint pens with blue ink rises by 1 percent, what happens to the quantity demanded?

g. What's an obvious substitute for ballpoint pens with blue ink? (This obvious substitute explains why the demand is so elastic.)

6. It's an important tradition in the Santos family that they eat the same meal at their favorite restaurant every Sunday. By contrast, the Chen family spends exactly $50 for their Sunday meal at whatever restaurant sounds best.

a. Which family has a more elastic demand for restaurant food?

b. Which family has a unit elastic demand for restaurant food? (Hint: How would each family respond to an increase in food prices?)

7. The U.S. Department of Agriculture (USDA) has been concerned that Americans aren't eating enough fruits and vegetables, and they've considered coupons and other subsidies to encourage people—especially lower-income

people—to eat these healthier foods. Of course, if people's demand for fruits and vegetables is perfectly inelastic, then there's no point in giving out coupons (Thought question: Why?). If instead the demand is only somewhat elastic, there may be better ways to spend taxpayer dollars.

This is clearly a situation where you'd want to know the elasticity of fruit and vegetable demand: If people respond a lot to small changes in price, then government-funded fruit and vegetable coupons *could* make poorer Americans a lot healthier, which *might* save taxpayers money *if* they don't have to pay for expensive medical treatments for unhealthy eaters. There are a lot of links in this chain of reasoning—all of which are covered in more advanced economics courses—but the first link is whether people actually have elastic demand for fruits and vegetables. The USDA's Economic Research Service employs economists to answer these sorts of questions, and a recent report contained the following estimated elasticities (*Source:* Diansheng Dong and Biing-Hwan Lin. 2009. "Fruit and Vegetable Consumption by Low-Income Americans: Would a Price Reduction Make a Difference?" *Economic Research Report* 70, USDA).

Fruit	Elasticity of Demand
Apple	−0.16
Banana	−0.42
Grapefruit	−1.02
Grapes	−0.91
Orange	−1.14

a. Based on these demand elasticity estimates, which fruit is most inelastically demanded? Which is most elastically demanded?

b. For which of these fruits would a 10 percent drop in price cause an increase in total revenue from the sale of that fruit?

c. If the government could only offer "10 percent off" coupons for three of these fruits, and it wanted to have the biggest possible effect on quantity demanded, which three fruits should get the coupons?

d. Overall, the authors found that for the average fruit, the elasticity of demand was about −0.5. Is the demand for fruit elastic or inelastic?

8. On average, old cars pollute more than newer cars. Therefore, every few years, a politician proposes a "cash for clunkers" program: The government offers to buy up and destroy old, high-polluting cars. If a "cash for clunkers" program buys 1,000 old, high-polluting cars, is this the same as saying that there are 1,000 fewer old, high-polluting cars on the road? Why or why not?

9. As we noted in the chapter, many economists have estimated the short-run and long-run elasticities of oil demand. Let's see if a rise in the price of oil hurts oil revenues in the long run. Cooper, the author cited in this chapter, found that in the United States, the long-run elasticity of oil demand is −0.5.

a. If the price of oil rises by 10 percent, how much will the quantity of oil demanded fall: By 5 percent, by 0.5 percent, by 2 percent, or by 20 percent?

b. Does a 10 percent rise in oil prices increase or decrease total revenues to the oil producers?

c. Some policymakers and environmental scientists would like to see the United States cut back on its use of oil in the long run. We can use this elasticity estimate to get a rough measure of how high the price of oil would have to permanently rise in order to get people to make big cuts in oil consumption. How much would the price of oil have to permanently rise in order to cut oil consumption by 50 percent?

d. France has the largest long-run elasticity of oil demand (−0.6) of any of the large, rich countries, according to Cooper's estimates. Does this mean that France is better at responding to long-run price changes than other rich countries, or does it mean France is worse at responding?

10. Figure 4.3 and Table 4.2 both set out some important but tedious rules. Let's practice them, since they are quite likely to be on an exam. For each of the cases below, state whether the demand curve is relatively steep or flat, and whether a *fall* in price will raise total revenue or lower it. In this case, note that we present the elasticity in terms of its absolute value.

a. Elasticity of demand = 0.2

b. Elasticity of demand = 2.0

c. Elasticity of demand = 10.0

d. Elasticity of demand = 1.1

e. Elasticity of demand = 0.9

11. A lot of American action movies are quests to eliminate a villain. If in real life villains are elastically supplied (like guns for buyback programs), should we care whether the hero captures a particular villain? Why or why not?

THINKING AND PROBLEM SOLVING

1. During the Middle Ages, the African city of Taghaza quarried salt in 200-pound blocks to be sent to the salt market in Timbuktu, in present-day Mali. Travelers report that Taghazans used salt instead of wood to construct buildings.

Compared to other towns without big salt mines, was the demand for *wood* more elastic or less elastic in Taghaza? How do you know?

2. Suppose that drug addicts pay for their addiction by stealing: So the higher the total revenue of the illegal drug industry, the higher the amount of theft. If a government crackdown on drug suppliers leads to a higher price of drugs, what will happen to the amount of stealing if the demand for drugs is elastic? What if the demand for drugs is inelastic?

3. Henry Ford famously mass produced cars at the beginning of the twentieth century, starting Ford Motor Company. He made millions because mass production made cars cheap to make, and he passed some of the savings to the consumer in the form of a low price. Cars became a common sight in the United States thereafter. Keeping total revenue and its relationship with price in mind, do you expect the demand for cars to be elastic or inelastic given the story of Henry Ford?

BETTMANN/CORBIS

4. In Chapter 9, you'll see that we recently purchased permits to pollute the air with sulfur dioxide (SO_2). We didn't use the permits: Instead, we threw them out. In other words, we bought permits for the same reason the government buys guns in gun buyback programs—to prevent what we bought from being used. As we discussed in the chapter, gun buyback programs have failed. So why is our plan to buy permits more likely to get SO_2 out of the air than the government's plan to get guns off the street?

5. How might elasticities help to explain why people on vacation tend to spend more for food and necessities than the local population?

6. In the short run, the price elasticity of the demand and supply of electricity can be very low.

a. How might revenue for the electricity industry change if one power plant were shut down for maintenance, reducing supply?

b. If one power company owned many power plants, would it have a short-term incentive to keep all of its plants running, or could it have a short-term incentive to shut down a power plant now and then?

7. Immigration is a fact of life in the United States. This will lead to a big boost in the labor supply. What field would you rather be in: A field where the demand for your kind of labor is elastic or a field where the demand for your kind of labor is inelastic?

8. In the world of fashion, the power to imitate a trendy look is the power to make money. Stores such as H&M and Forever 21 focus on imitating fashions wherever possible: As soon as they see that a new look is coming along, something people are willing to pay a high price for, they start cranking out that look. Do these imitation-centered stores make the supply of clothing more elastic or less elastic? How can you tell?

9. Let's practice the midpoint formula. Calculate the elasticity of demand for each of the following goods or services.

Good or Service	Beginning Price	Beginning Quantity	Ending Price	Ending Quantity	Elasticity
Daily movie ticket sales in Denver, Colorado	$6	50,000	$10	40,000	
Weekly milk sales at Loma Vista Elementary School	$1	1,000	$1.50	800	
Weekly round-trip ticket sales, New York to San Francisco	$500	10,000	$1,000	9,000	
Annual student enrollments, Upper Tennessee State University	$6,000	40,000	$9,000	39,000	

CHALLENGES

1. In this chapter, we've emphasized that the elasticity of supply is higher in the long run than in the short run. In a lot of cases, this is surely true: If you see that jobs pay more in the next state over, you won't move there the next week but you might move there next year. But sometimes the short-run elasticity will be *higher* than the long-run elasticity.

   Austan Goolsbee found an interesting example of this when he looked at the elasticity of income of highly paid executives with respect to taxes. In 1993, President Clinton passed a law raising income taxes. This tax hike was fully expected: He campaigned on it in 1992.

   a. What do you expect happened to executive income in the first year of the tax increases? What about in subsequent years?

      Here's a hint: Top executives have a lot of power over when they get paid for their work: They can ask for bonuses a bit earlier, or they can cash out their stock options a bit earlier. Literally, this isn't their "labor supply," it's more like their "income supply."

   (*Source:* Goolsbee. Austan. 2000. "What Happens When You Tax the Rich? Evidence from Executive Compensation". *Journal of Political Economy* 108(2), pages 352–378. For a book on the topic written by leading economists, see Joel Slemrod., ed. 2000. *Does Atlas Shrug?* Cambridge, MA: Harvard University Press.

   b. Goolsbee estimated that the short-run elasticity of "income supply" for these executives was 1.4, while the long-run elasticity of "income supply" was 0.1. (Note: Goolsbee used a variety of statistical methods to look for these elasticities, and all came to roughly the same result.) If taxes pushed down their take-home income by 10 percent, how much would this cut the amount of income supplied in the short run? In the long run?

   c. You are a newspaper reporter. Your editor tells you to write a short story with this title: "Goolsbee's research proves that tax hikes make the rich work less." Make your case in one sentence.

   d. You are a newspaper reporter. Your editor tells you to write a short story with this title: "Goolsbee's research proves that tax hikes have little effect on work by the wealthy." Make your case in one sentence.

   e. Which story is more truthful?

2. We saw that a gun buyback program was unlikely to work in Washington, D.C. If the entire United States ran a gun buyback program, would that be better at eliminating guns or worse? Why? What about if the gun buyback was also accompanied by a law making (at least some) guns illegal?

3. Using the data from the ANWR example, what will be the percentage increase in quantity supplied if ANWR raises supply by 1 percent? No, this isn't a trick question, and the formula is already there in the chapter. Why isn't this number just 1 percent?

APPENDIX 1

Using Excel to Calculate Elasticities

Let's use a spreadsheet to compute the elasticity of demand along the two demand curves illustrated in Figure 4.1.

The first step is to input the basic data into the spreadsheet. For the demand curve labeled demand curve I, we have Q Before=100, Q After=95, P Before=$40, and P After=$50 and for the demand curve labeled demand curve E, we have Q Before=100, Q After=20, P Before=$40, and P After=$50. (By the way, it doesn't matter which price-quantity pair you call before and which after.) Your spreadsheet should like look Figure A4.1.

FIGURE A4.1

	A	B
1	Q Before	Q After
2	100	95
3	P Before	P After
4	40	50
5		
6		
7	Q Before	Q After
8	100	20
9	P Before	P After
10	40	50
11		

Now remember our formula for calculating an elasticity:

$$\text{Elasticity of demand} = E_d = \frac{\%\Delta Q_{Demanded}}{\%\Delta Price} = \frac{\dfrac{Q_{After} - Q_{Before}}{(Q_{After} + Q_{Before})/2}}{\dfrac{P_{After} - P_{Before}}{(P_{After} + P_{Before})/2}}$$

Let's input the formula in two parts: the $\%\Delta Q$ on the top and $\%\Delta Price$ on the bottom as in Figure A4.2.

FIGURE A4.2

	C2	▼	f_x =(B2-A2)/((B2+A2)/2)*100		
	A	B	C	D	E
1	Q Before	Q After	%Change in Quantity		
2	100	95	-5.12821		
3	P Before	P After	%Change in Price		
4	40	50	22.22222		
5					
6					
7	Q Before	Q After	%Change in Quantity		
8	100	20	-133.333		
9	P Before	P After	%Change in Price		
10	40	50	22.22222		
11					

Notice the formula in cell C2, $=(B2 - A2)/((B2 + A2)/2) \times 100$ that's the percentage change in quantity along demand curve I. There is a similar formula in C4 for the percentage change in price and then these are repeated for demand curve E.

We can then finish off the spreadsheet by dividing C2/C4 and taking the absolute value, which gives us Figure A4.3.

FIGURE A4.3

	F2	▼	f_x =ABS(C2/C4)			
	A	B	C	D	E	F
1	Q Before	Q After	%Change in Quantity			
2	100	95	-5.12821		Elasticity	0.230769
3	P Before	P After	%Change in Price			
4	40	50	22.22222			
5						
6						
7	Q Before	Q After	%Change in Quantity			
8	100	20	-133.333		Elasticity	6
9	P Before	P After	%Change in Price			
10	40	50	22.22222			
11						

Fortunately, the answer is consistent with what we said earlier in the chapter! Along this region of the curve labeled demand curve I the elasticity is $0.231 < 1$, or inelastic and along this region of demand curve E the elasticity is $6 > 1$, or elastic.

APPENDIX 2

Other Types of Elasticities

Economists often compute elasticities any time one variable is related to another variable. Klick and Tabarrok, for example, find that a 50 percent increase in the number of police on the streets reduces automobile theft and theft from automobiles by 43 percent so the elasticity of auto crime with respect to police is $-43\%/50\% = -.86$. Gruber studies church attendance and he finds an interesting relationship: The more people give to their church, the less likely they are to attend! In other words, people regard money and time as substitutes and those who give more of one are likely to give less of the other. Gruber calculates that a 10 percent increase in giving leads to an 11 percent decline in attendance or an elasticity of attendance with respect to giving of $-11\%/10\% = -1.1$.[15]

Thus, any time there is a relationship between two variables A and B, you can always express the relationship in terms of an elasticity. Two other frequently used elasticities in economics are the cross-price elasticity of demand and the income elasticity of demand.

The Cross-Price Elasticity of Demand

The cross-price elasticity of demand measures how responsive the quantity demanded of good A is to the price of good B.

Cross-price elasticity of demand =

$$\frac{\text{Percentage change in quantity demanded of good A}}{\text{Percentage change in price of good B}} = \frac{\%\Delta Q_{Demanded,\ A}}{\%\Delta P_{Price,\ B}}$$

Given data on the quantity demanded of good A at two different prices of good B, the cross-price elasticity can be calculated using the following formula:

$$\frac{\dfrac{\text{Change in quantity demanded A}}{\text{Average quantity A}}}{\dfrac{\text{Change in price B}}{\text{Average price B}}} = \frac{\dfrac{Q_{After,\ A} - Q_{Before,\ A}}{(Q_{After,\ A} + Q_{Before,\ A})/2}}{\dfrac{P_{After,\ B} - P_{Before,\ B}}{(P_{After,\ B} + P_{Before,\ B})/2}}$$

The cross-price elasticity of demand is closely related to the idea of substitutes and complements. If the cross-price elasticity is positive, an increase in the price of good B increases the quantity of good A demanded so the two goods are substitutes. If the cross-price elasticity is negative, an increase in the price of good B decreases the quantity of good A demanded so the two goods are complements.

> If the Cross-price elasticity > 0, then goods A and B are substitutes.
> If the Cross-price elasticity < 0, then goods A and B are complements.

The Income Elasticity of Demand

The income elasticity of demand measures how responsive the quantity demanded of a good is with respect to changes in income.

$$\text{Income elasticity of demand} = \frac{\text{Percentage change in quantity demanded}}{\text{Percentage change in income}}$$

$$= \frac{\%\Delta Q_{Demanded}}{\%\Delta Income}$$

As usual, given data on the quantity demanded at two different income levels, the income elasticity of demand can be calculated as:

$$\frac{\dfrac{\text{Change in quantity demanded}}{\text{Average quantity}}}{\dfrac{\text{Change in income}}{\text{Average income}}} = \frac{\dfrac{Q_{After} - Q_{Before}}{(Q_{After} + Q_{Before})/2}}{\dfrac{I_{After} - I_{Before}}{(I_{After} + I_{Before})/2}}$$

The income elasticity of demand can be used to distinguish normal from inferior goods. Recall from Chapter 2 when an *increase* in income *increases* the demand for a good, we say the good is a *normal good*. And a good like Ramen noodles, for which an *increase* in income *decreases* the demand, is called an *inferior good*.

> If the Income Elasticity of Demand > 0, then the good is a normal good.

> If the Income Elasticity of Demand < 0, then the good is an inferior good.

Sometimes economists also distinguish normal from "luxury" goods, where a luxury good is defined as one where say a 10 percent increase in income causes more than a 10 percent increase in the quantity of the good demanded. Thus,

> If the Income Elasticity of Demand > 1, then the good is a luxury good.

5

The Price System: Signals, Speculation, and Prediction

CHAPTER OUTLINE

Markets Link the World

Markets Link to Each Other

Solving the Great Economic Problem

A Price Is a Signal Wrapped Up in an Incentive

Speculation

Signal Watching

Prediction Markets

Takeaway

Chaos, conflict, and war may dominate the news, but it's heartening to know that there is also an astounding amount of world *cooperation*. The next time you are in your local supermarket, stop and consider how many people cooperated to bring the fruits of the world to your table: kiwis from New Zealand, dried apricots from Turkey, dates from Egypt, mangoes from Mexico, bananas from Guatemala. How is it that a farmer in New Zealand wakes up at 5 AM to work hard tending his or her fields so that you, on the other side of the world, may enjoy a kiwi with your fruit salad?

This chapter is about a central feature of our world, the connection of markets. It's about how you eat well every day yet have little knowledge of farming, it's about how you cooperate with people whom you will never meet, and it's about how civilization is made possible. In this chapter, you'll see how one market influences another and then how an entire series of markets in a global economy fit together. We're also going to say more about prices. Seemingly simple but amazingly complex, prices are a key force integrating markets. What is a price? A price is a signal wrapped up in an incentive. That may sound a little abstract, but it's one of the most important insights in economics and after this chapter it should have a very concrete meaning in your mind. We will have plenty of examples in this chapter, but keep your eye on the primary theme: The rich connections between markets enable societies to mobilize vast amounts of knowledge toward common ends, yet without a central planner.

Markets Link the World

Let's take a closer look at the story of just one product. It's Valentine's Day. You have just given your boyfriend or girlfriend a beautiful, single-stemmed rose,

Kenyan women harvesting roses

A small part of the world's largest flower market in Aalsmeer, Holland

The world is linked in fascinating ways. In Peru, workers roam the hillsides collecting millions of female cochineal bugs from their cactus pad nests. After dunking in hot water, drying and grinding, the bugs make an excellent red dye. The dye is used to color many products including yogurt (look for carmine in the ingredients), red Smarties, and even lipstick!

one of 180 million that will be sold today.[1] Where did the rose come from and how did it get to your hands?

Chances are good that your rose was grown in Kenya in the Lake Naivasha area to the northwest of Nairobi.[2] Over 50,000 tons of roses are grown in Kenya every year, almost all for export. The Kenyan women who do most of the fieldwork know very little about the strange Western celebration of love called Saint Valentine's Day, but they don't have to. What they do know is that they get paid more when the roses are debudded so that they bloom just in time for delivery on February 14.

No one wants to give (or receive) a wilted rose, so everyone involved in the rose business has an incentive to move quickly. In a matter of hours after picking, the roses travel in cooled trucks from the field to the airport in Nairobi, where they are loaded onto refrigerated aircraft. Within a day, the flowers are in Aalsmeer, Holland.

Aalsmeer is the home of the world's largest flower market. On a typical working day, 20 million flowers are flown into this tiny Dutch town. The flowers are paraded in lots before large clocks, clocks that measure not time but prices. Beginning with a high price, the clocks quickly tick downward until a bidder stamps a button indicating that he or she is willing to buy at that price. By the end of the day, 20 million flowers have been sold, and they are once again packed onto cooled airplanes to be flown to the world's buyers in London, Paris, New York, and Topeka. From Kenya to your girlfriend's or boyfriend's hand in 72 hours.[3]

The worldwide market links romantic American teenagers with Kenyan flower growers, Dutch clocks, British airplanes, Colombian coffee (to keep the pilots awake), Finnish cell phones, and much, much more. To bring just one product to your table requires the cooperative effort of millions.

Moreover, this immense cooperation is voluntary and undirected. Each of millions of people acting in their own self-interest play a role, but no one knows the full story of how a Kenyan rose becomes a gift of love in Topeka because the full story is too complex. Nevertheless, every Valentine's Day you can count on the fact that your local florist will have roses for sale.

The market is the original Web, and it's more dense, interconnected, and alive with intelligence than its computer analog.

Markets Link to Each Other

In Chapters 2 and 3, we showed how the supply and demand for oil determine the price of oil. Now we return to oil but this time as an example of how shifts in supply and demand in one market ripple across the worldwide market, changing distant people and products in ways that no one can foresee.

The Kenyan flower industry was one unforeseen consequence of changes in the market for oil. Prior to the 1970s, roses were grown in American greenhouses. Higher prices for oil raised heating costs so much that it became cheaper to grow roses in warm countries and ship them to cold countries.* If roses had

---

* The shift of flower production from America to Kenya and other equatorial countries like Colombia and Ecuador in the 1980s is part of a trend. Two decades earlier, declines in transportation costs and relative increases in the relative costs of heating, land, and labor moved flower production from New York and Pennsylvania to Florida and California. On the evolution of the cut flower industry, see Mendez, Jose A. 1991. "*The Development of the Colombian Cut Flower Industry.*" The World Bank. WPS 660.

been heavier, the higher costs of transportation might have outweighed the lower costs of heating, but even with higher fuel costs, transportation costs in the modern world have been falling.

It's not obvious that the right way to respond to an increased scarcity of oil is to move flower production from California to Kenya. No one planned such a response in advance. Instead, creative entrepreneurs responded to the increase in the price of oil in ways that no one predicted or planned. Entrepreneurs are constantly on the lookout for ways to lower costs, and their cost-cutting measures link markets that at first seem like they are a world away.

From Oil to Candy Bars and Brick Driveways

How does the price of oil affect the price of candy bars? One way is obvious: higher energy costs increase the cost of producing most products, including candy bars. But the market also links oil and candy bars in more subtle ways. For instance, ethanol is the active ingredient in alcoholic beverages, but it's also a good fuel that can be made from a variety of crops like corn or sugar cane. Brazil is the largest producer and consumer of fuel ethanol in the world, so much so that it has managed to reduce its gasoline consumption by 40 percent by adopting flexible fuel vehicles that can run on ethanol, gasoline, or any combination of the two.[4] Brazil is also the largest producer of sugar in the world.

Can you see the connection between the price of oil and the price of candy bars now? As the price of oil has increased, the Brazilians have shifted sugar cane from sugar production to ethanol production, thereby holding down fuel costs but increasing the price of sugar.[5]

What about brick driveways? A 42-gallon barrel of crude oil is refined into approximately 19.5 gallons of gasoline, 9.7 gallons of fuel oil, 4 gallons of jet fuel, 1.4 gallons of asphalt, and a number of other products.[6] To some extent, these divisions are fixed. (Asphalt is what you get after you separate out the other products.) But oil refiners do have some flexibility, and when the price of gasoline is relatively high, it pays for them to pull every last drop of gasoline out of a barrel of crude, leaving less crude to make the remaining products. A higher price of gasoline, therefore, means a reduced supply of asphalt. A reduced supply of asphalt pushes up the price of asphalt. When the price of oil rose to $70 a barrel in 2006, for example, the price of using asphalt to pave an average-sized driveway rose by $300.[7] Seeing the higher price, homeowners turned to substitutes such as concrete, cobblestones, and brick.

Solving the Great Economic Problem

Markets around the world are linked to each other. A change in supply and demand in one market can influence markets for entirely different products thousands of miles away. But what does all this linking accomplish? The **great economic problem** is to arrange our limited resources to satisfy as many of our infinite wants as possible. Let's imagine that war in the Middle East reduces the supply of oil. We must economize on oil. But how? It would be foolish to reduce oil equally in all uses—oil is more valuable in some uses than in others. We want to shift oil out of low-valued uses, where we can do without or where good substitutes for oil exist, so that we can keep supplying oil for high-valued uses, where oil has few good substitutes.

MARTIN SHIELDS / ALAMY

Surprised? Corn and oil are substitutes.

CHECK YOURSELF

> The U.S. government offers a subsidy for converting corn to ethanol. If farmers receive a higher price for turning corn into ethanol, what will happen to the price of corn used in cornbread? How will cafeterias and restaurants respond?

> Sawdust is used for bedding milk cows. What did the end of the housing boom in 2007 do to the price of milk? Search for "sawdust" at http://www. MarginalRevolution.com if you need a hint.

The great economic problem is to arrange our limited resources to satisfy as many of our infinite wants as possible.

One way to make this shift would be for a central planner to issue orders. The central planner would order so much oil to be used in the steel industry, so much for heating and so much for Sunday driving. But how would the central planner know the value of oil in each of its millions of uses? No one knows for certain all the uses of oil, let alone which uses of oil are high-valued uses and which are low-valued uses. Is the oil used to produce steel more valuable than the oil used to produce vegetables? Even if steel is worth more than vegetables, the answer isn't obvious because electricity might be a good substitute for oil in producing steel but not for producing vegetables. To estimate the value of oil in different uses, therefore, the central planner would have to gather information about all the uses of oil and all of the substitutes for oil in each use (and all of the substitutes for the substitutes!). Using this information, the central planner would then have to somehow compute the optimal allocation of oil and then send out thousands of orders directing oil to its many uses in the economy.

The task of central planning is impossibly complex and we haven't yet discussed incentives. Why would anyone have an incentive to send truthful information to the central planner? Each user of oil would surely announce that their use is the high-valued use for which no substitute is possible. And what incentive would the central planner have to actually direct oil to its high-value uses?

The U.S. government briefly tried to centrally plan the allocation of oil during the 1973–1974 oil crisis. President Nixon even went so far as to forbid gas stations from opening on Sundays in an attempt to reduce Sunday driving! We describe the consequences of this approach to the oil crisis at greater length in the next chapter. The Soviet Union and China went much further than the United States and tried to centrally plan entire economies. Central planning on a large scale, however, failed and has now been abandoned throughout virtually all the world (Cuba and North Korea, both very poor countries, are the exceptions).

The central planning approach failed because of problems of *information* and *incentives*. We need a better approach.

Users of oil have a lot of information about the value of oil in their own uses, much more information than could ever be communicated to a central planner. We need to take advantage of this information without attempting to communicate it to a central bureaucracy. Ideally each user of oil would compare the value of oil in their use with the value of oil in alternative uses, and each user of oil would have an incentive to give up the oil if it has a lower value in their use than in alternative uses. This is exactly what the price system accomplishes.

Let's go back to the person thinking about whether to pave the driveway with asphalt or brick. This person knows the value of a paved driveway, but they don't know what uses the asphalt has elsewhere in the economy. They do know the price of asphalt, and *in a free market, the price of asphalt is equal to the value of the asphalt in its next highest-value use.* Take a look at Figure 5.1, which is just the now-familiar supply and demand diagram. Remember that the value of a good in its various uses is given by the height of the demand curve. Notice that the equilibrium price splits the uses of the good into two—above the equilibrium price are the high-value, satisfied demands, below the price are the low-value, unsatisfied demands. Now what is the value of the highest-value demand that is *not* satisfied? It's just equal to the market price (or if you like, "just below" the market price). In other words, if one more barrel of oil became available the highest-value use of that barrel would be to satisfy the first presently unsatisfied demand. The market price tells us the value of the good in its next highest-valued use.

FIGURE 5.1

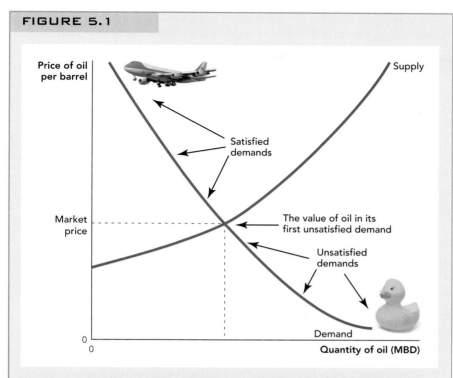

The Market Price and Opportunity Cost The market price splits the uses of oil into two. Above the price are the uses of oil whose value is greater than the price; in a free market, these demands will be satisfied. Below the price are the uses of oil whose value is less than the price; in a free market, these are the unsatisfied demands. Notice the value of oil in the first unsatisfied demand is just slightly below the market price.

(Top photo: EuroStyle Graphics/Alamy)

(Bottom: Lew Robertson/Corbis)

When a consumer compares the price of asphalt to the value of asphalt for paving his driveway, he is comparing *the value of asphalt on his driveway to its opportunity cost*. And remember, because markets are linked, the price of asphalt is linked to the price of oil, and the price of oil is linked to the demand for automobiles in China and the supply of ethanol and the price of sugar.... So when the consumer compares the value of asphalt in paving his driveway to the price of asphalt, he may be comparing the value of asphalt in paving his driveway to the value of 500 gallons of gasoline used by a motorist in Brazil. Or, in other words, when you decide whether or not to drive to school or take the bus, you are deciding whether your use of oil is more valuable than the billions of other uses of oil in the world that are presently unsatisfied!

The market solves the information problem by collapsing all the relevant information in the world about the uses of oil into a single number, the price. As Nobel Laureate Friedrich Hayek wrote[*]:

> The most significant fact about this system is the economy of knowledge with which it operates ... by a kind of symbol [the price], only the

OLEKSIY MAKSYMENKO/ ALAMY

COMPLIMENTS OF JOHN DEERE

Opportunity cost. The true cost of a motorcycle is not its money price but rather a lawnmower. The true cost is the *opportunity cost*— what the resources that went into the motorcycle could have produced had the motorcycle not been built.

It is part of the marvel of a free market that, under the right conditions, the money price of the motorcycle exactly represents the value of the resources that went into producing the motorcycle, namely the value those resources would have had in their next highest-valued use.

[*] Hayek's classic paper, "The Use of Knowledge in Society," is deep but easy to read. You can find it online by searching for "Hayek use of knowledge in society." The original citation is Hayek, A. Friedrich, 1945. The use of knowledge in society. *American Economic Review*. XXXV, 4:519–530.

most essential information is passed on and passed on only to those concerned. . . . The marvel is that in a case like that of a scarcity of one raw material, without an order being issued, without more than perhaps a handful of people knowing the cause, tens of thousands of people whose identity could not be ascertained by months of investigation, are made to use the material or its products more sparingly; *i.e.*, they move in the right direction.

In addition to solving the information problem, the price system also solves the incentive problem. It's in a consumer's interest to pay attention to prices! When the price of an oil product like asphalt increases, consumers have an incentive to turn to substitutes like bricks and, in so doing, they free up oil to be used elsewhere in the economy where it is of higher value.

The worldwide market accomplishes this immense task of allocating resources without any central planning or control. No one knows or understands all the links between oil, sugar, and brick driveways, but the links are there and the market works even without anyone's understanding or knowledge. Amazed by what he saw, Adam Smith said the market works as if "an invisible hand" guided the process.

Nobel Laureate Vernon Smith, whom we met in Chapter 3, put it this way:

> At the heart of economics is a scientific mystery: How is it that the pricing system accomplishes the world's work without anyone being in charge? Like language, no one invented it. None of us could have invented it, and its operation depends in no way on anyone's comprehension or understanding of it. . . . The pricing system—How is order produced from freedom of choice?—is a scientific mystery as deep, fundamental and inspiring as that of the expanding universe or the forces that bind matter.[8]

A Price Is a Signal Wrapped Up in an Incentive

How is order produced from freedom of choice? That is a scientific mystery, and prices are the biggest clue to the solution. Prices do much more than tell people how much they must shell out for a burger and fries. Prices are incentives, prices are signals, prices are predictions. To understand the market, you need to better understand prices.

When the price of oil rises, all users of oil are encouraged to economize—perhaps by simply using less but also by thinking about substitutes: everything from electric cars to moving flower cultivation overseas. An increase in the price of oil is also a signal to suppliers to invest more in exploration, look for alternatives like ethanol, and to increase recycling. Do you know the most recycled product in America? It's asphalt.[9]

Politicians and consumers sometime fail to understand the signaling role of prices. After a hurricane, the prices of ice, generators, and chainsaws often skyrocket. Consumers complain of price gouging, and politicians call for price controls. That's understandable, because it can seem doubly harsh to be hit by a hurricane *and* high prices. But the price system is just doing its job. A skyrocketing price is like a flare being shot into the night sky that shouts—bring ice here! A price control eliminates the signal to bring ice into the devastated area as quickly as possible.

The high price of ice in a hurricane-devastated area signals a profit opportunity for ice suppliers. Buy ice where the price is low and ship it to where the price is high. As the supply of ice in the hurricane-devastated area increases, the

Friedrich A. Hayek (1899–1992) explained the marvel of the price system.

see the
invisible hand

CHECK YOURSELF

> Peanuts are used primarily for food dishes, but they are also used in bird feed, paint, varnish, furniture polish, insecticides, and soap. Rank these uses from higher to lower value taking into account in which use the peanuts are critical and in which uses there are good substitutes. Don't obsess over this, we know you are not a peanut expert, but see if you can come up with a sense of higher and lower value.

> Imagine that there is a large peanut crop failure in China, which produces over one-third of the world's supply. Which of the uses that you ranked in the previous question will be cut back?

A skyrocketing price is a signal to bring resources here!

price will fall. More generally, price signals and the accompanying profits and losses tell entrepreneurs what areas of the economy consumers want expanded and what areas they want contracted. If consumers want more computers, prices and profits in the computer industry will increase and the industry will expand.

Losses may be an even more important signal than profits. Entrepreneurs who fail to compete with lower costs and better products take losses and their businesses contract or even go bankrupt. Bankruptcy is bad for a business but can be good for capitalism. Ever heard of Smith Corona, Polaroid, Pan Am, or Hechingers? At one point, each of these companies led their industry, but today they are either bankrupt or much smaller than at their peak. In a free market, no firm is so powerful that it does not daily face the market test. As a result, *in a successful economy there will be many unsuccessful firms.*

Speculation

Suppose that you expect that a war in the Middle East is likely next year and that if it should occur the supply of oil will decrease, thereby pushing up the price of oil. How could you profit from your expectation? The way to make money is to buy low and sell high, so you should buy oil today when the price is low, hold the oil in storage, and then sell it next year after war breaks out, when the price is higher. Figure 5.2 on the next page shows this process, which is called **speculation**. We have used vertical supply curves, meaning that the amount of oil is fixed, to simplify the diagram.

The top panel shows what happens without speculation. Production today is high and today's price is low (point *a*). Future production, however, will be disrupted by the war, pushing up the future price (point *b*). Notice that without speculation, the war disrupts the oil market and prices jump from point *a* to point *b*.

The bottom panel shows what happens with speculation. Speculators buy oil today and they put it into storage—this reduces the quantity available for consumption today and pushes up today's price (point *c*). Next year, however, when the war occurs, production is low but consumption is higher than it would have been without speculation and prices are lower because the speculators sell oil from their inventories (point *d*). Notice that with speculation, preparations are made for any disruption in oil production and oil prices are smoothed.

Speculators raise prices today but lower prices in the future. As a result, speculators have an image problem because the media often report when speculators raise prices but rarely do they report when speculators lower prices. Overall, however, society is better off from speculation because speculators move oil from when it has low value (today) and move it to when it has high value (the future). When producers put oil in storage, society doesn't get to consume that oil so some wants become unsatisfied—the loss in value from these unsatisfied wants is measured by the blue area in the (bottom) left panel of Figure 5.2 (once again, the value of the good in its various uses is measured by the height of the demand curve). But when the speculators sell that oil in the future, consumption increases—more wants are satisfied—and the value of this increase in consumption is measured by the much larger blue area in the right panel. Thus, when speculators are right they move oil from today, where it has low value, to the future where the value of oil is much higher, in the process making society better off.

CHECK YOURSELF

> Imagine that whenever the supply of oil rose or fell, the government sent text messages to every user of oil asking them to use more or less oil as the case warranted. Suppose that the messaging system worked very well. Is such a messaging system likely to allocate resources as well as prices? Why or why not? What is the difference between the message system and the price system?

> Firms in the old Soviet Union never went bankrupt. How do you think this influenced the rate of innovation and economic growth?

Speculation is the attempt to profit from future price changes.

FIGURE 5.2

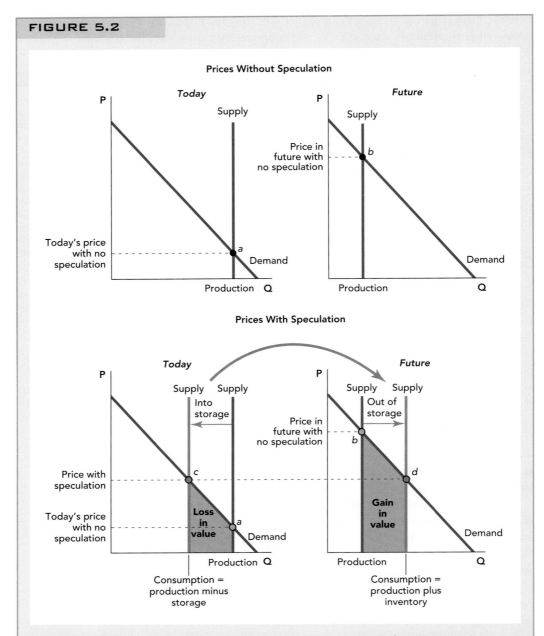

Prices Without Speculation

Speculation Tends to Smooth Prices over Time and Increase Welfare The top panel shows the price of oil, oil consumption, and oil production in an economy without speculation. In the panel on the left, Today, the equilibrium is at point *a*, the price is low and oil consumption and production are high. In the panel on the right, Future, the price of oil is high because the disruption has reduced the production of oil. Since no oil was stored from the previous period, the consumption of oil is also reduced.

The bottom panel shows what happens with speculation. In the left panel, labeled Today, oil speculators buy oil and put it into storage pushing up the price of oil and reducing consumption today—thus, the equilibrium shifts from point *a* to point *c*. In the future when the price of oil is high (at point *b*), speculators sell their oil from storage. The oil flowing out of storage pushes the price down and allows people to consume more oil even though production is low.

The value of oil to consumers (in blue) falls today when oil is put into storage but rises by an even larger amount in the future when oil is in short supply and speculators move their stocks out of storage.

Speculators, of course, don't always guess correctly. But speculators put their money where their mouth is. They have strong incentives to be as accurate as possible because when they are wrong they lose money, a lot of money. Furthermore, bad speculators soon find themselves poor. Anyone who is able to be a speculator for a long time is either very, very lucky or just very good. So, on net, speculators tend to make prices more informative, even though in particular instances many speculators are wrong.

A careful observer of Middle East politics might have very good information about the probability of war in the Middle East but have no easy way to store oil. Fortunately, the market provides a way to speculate in oil without having to build oil tanks in your backyard.

A speculator can buy oil **futures**. Oil futures are contracts to buy or sell a given quantity of oil at a specified price with delivery set at a specified time and place in the future. On the New York Mercantile Exchange (NYMEX), you can buy futures for light, sweet crude oil to be delivered in Cushing, Oklahoma, at 30, 36, 48, 72, or 84 months in the future at a price agreed on today. What makes futures contracts important is that despite specifying delivery and acceptance in Cushing, almost all futures contracts actually settle in cash.

Let's see how this works. Suppose Tyler believes that the price of oil will be higher in the future than what other people are expecting. Tyler buys an oil contract that gives him the right to 1,000 barrels of oil to be delivered (in Cushing) 30 months in the future. Tyler agrees that on delivery he will pay the seller, Alex, $50 per barrel or $50,000. Similarly, Alex has agreed to deliver 1,000 barrels of oil in Cushing in 30 months. Thirty months from now, Tyler's expectation is proven correct—the actual or "spot" price of oil is $82. If Tyler went to Cushing, he could physically accept the oil from Alex, give him $50,000 and then turn around and sell the oil to someone else for $82 per barrel for a profit of $32 per barrel or $32,000. Instead of doing that, however, Tyler and Alex could agree to *cash settlement*. Alex has agreed to give Tyler 1,000 barrels of oil, which are currently worth $82,000, for a price of $50,000. Instead of giving Tyler the oil, suppose that Alex gives Tyler the cash difference, $32,000, and they call it even. The advantage of cash settlement is that Tyler and Alex can both speculate on the price of oil without ever accepting or delivering oil. Moreover, neither Tyler nor Alex ever have to go to Cushing, which is sadly lacking in good ethnic restaurants.*

Futures markets are used not only for speculation but also for reducing risk. An airline that wants to know in advance what its fuel costs are going to be next year can lock in the price by buying oil on the futures market. Instead of buying futures, farmers can sell futures. A soybean farmer plants the crop today but does not harvest it until next year when the soybean price could be quite different than today's spot price. To avoid the price risk, the farmer can sell futures, that is, agree

Futures are standardized contracts to buy or sell specified quantities of a commodity or financial instrument at a specified price with delivery set at a specified time in the future.

---

* Technically this describes a forward contract. The difference between forward and futures contracts is not important for making the point that cash settlement allows anyone to speculate in oil even if they neither want nor have any oil to trade.

The technical difference between futures and forwards is that in a futures contract the buyer and the seller do not contract directly but rather each works through a middleman, the New York Mercantile Exchange (NYMEX). NYMEX guarantees that neither the buyer nor the seller will cheat on the deal. NYMEX does this by *marking the contract to market* on a daily basis, which means that there is a small cash settlement every day until the final day. For example, if the day after Tyler and Alex signed the contract the spot price moved to $51, then Alex would have to pay some extra money to NYMEX. If the day after the contract was signed, the spot price moved to $49, then Tyler would have to pay some extra money to NYMEX. NYMEX holds onto the money, keeping a running tab, until the final day when they release the total to the party with the net gain. In this way, NYMEX's losses are limited even if one party refuses to honor the deal.

> Speculation occurs in stocks as well as commodities. In 2008, Lehman Brothers, a Wall Street investment banking firm, complained that speculators were driving the price of its stock lower and lower. During this time, Lehman continued to give rosy forecasts. Later in 2008, Lehman Brothers went bankrupt. Why was the forecast of the speculators more informative on net than the statements being issued from Lehman?

DOUGLAS PULSIPHER/ ACCLAIM IMAGES

Markets see the future with futures markets.

A **prediction market** is a speculative market designed so that prices can be interpreted as probabilities and used to make predictions.

to sell so many soybeans at harvest time at a price agreed on today. Futures markets are also common in currencies. Suppose that Ford expects to sell 1,000 cars in Germany for 25,000 euros each. At the end of the year, how many dollars will Ford make? Ford doesn't know because the euro/dollar exchange rate can fluctuate. By selling euro futures, Ford can lock in the exchange rate.

Signal Watching

Speculators who think that a war in the Middle East is likely will buy oil futures, pushing up the futures price (the price agreed on today for delivery in the future). If the futures price is much higher than the spot or current price, that is a sign that smart people with their own money on the line think that supply disruptions may soon occur. Futures prices for oil, currencies, and many commodities can be found in a newspaper or online, so anyone who wants to forecast events in the Middle East can benefit from reading price signals.

Futures prices can be extraordinarily informative about future events. The major factor determining the price of orange juice futures, for example, is the weather. If bad weather is expected to cause a frost destroying many oranges, the price of OJ futures will be high. If good weather and a bumper crop is expected, the price will be low. The economist Richard Roll found that the futures price for OJ was so sensitive to the weather that it could be used to improve the predictions of the National Weather Service![10]

It's not hard to see the future if you know where to look. In December 1991, the United Nations and the Worldwatch Institute warned that wheat would be very scarce in the coming year. Economist Paul Heyne looked in the newspaper and found that on that day the price of wheat was $4.05 a bushel. But the futures price for the following December was $3.51. Speculators, unlike the Worldwatch Institute, were not forecasting increased scarcity. In whose forecast would you put more confidence: that of the Worldwatch Institute or that of wheat speculators? Why?*

The futures price of oil can be used to predict war in the Middle East, but that is a side benefit of the futures market and not its purpose. Factors other than war (e.g., the decisions of OPEC, oil discoveries, and the demand for oil) also affect oil futures, so the futures price of oil is a *noisy signal* of war in the Middle East. A phone line with static—that's a noisy signal. Electrical engineers work to increase the signal-to-noise ratio on cell phones. More recently, economic engineers have begun to design markets to increase the signal-to-noise ratio of prices.

Prediction Markets

If markets are good at predicting the future even though they evolved to do something else, imagine how useful they might be if they were designed to predict. Beginning in the late 1980s, economic engineers began to design **prediction markets,** speculative markets designed so that prices can be interpreted as probabilities and used to make predictions.[11]

The best known prediction market is the Iowa Electronic Markets. The Iowa market lets traders use real money to buy and sell "shares" of political candidates.

* By the way, Heyne's forecast was correct—wheat was not especially scarce in 1992. Did you put your confidence in the right place?

During the 2008 election, for example, traders on the Iowa Electronic Markets could buy shares in John McCain and Barack Obama. A share in Barack Obama, for example, would pay $1 if Barack Obama won the election and nothing otherwise. Suppose that the market price of an Obama share is 75 cents. What does this market price suggest about the probability of Barack Obama winning the election?

To answer this question, think about each share as a bit like a lottery ticket. The ticket pays $1 if Obama wins and nothing if he loses. How much would you be willing to pay for this lottery ticket if Obama has a 20 percent chance of winning? How much would you be willing to pay for this lottery ticket if Obama has a 75 percent chance of winning? If Obama has a 20 percent chance of winning, then a lottery ticket that pays $1 if he wins, and nothing otherwise, is worth about 20 cents on average (0.2 × $1). If Obama has a 75 percent chance of winning, then the lottery ticket is worth about 75 cents (0.75 × $1). Thus, working backward, if we see that people are willing to pay 75 cents for an Obama lottery ticket, we can infer that they think that Obama has about a 75 percent probability of winning the election. In this way, we can use market prices to predict elections!

The Iowa markets correctly predicted the Obama win in 2008 and they were very close about Obama's vote share as well. The future can never be predicted perfectly, but in some 20 years of predicting U.S. and foreign elections, primaries, and other political events, the Iowa markets have proven to be more accurate than alternative institutions such as polls.[12] In tight elections, professional bond traders—who often have millions of dollars riding on postelection economic policies—monitor the Iowa markets for clues about future events.

Hewlett-Packard has used a similar market approach to help predict future hardware sales. Members of HP's sales team bought and sold shares that paid off when sales fell within a certain range. A typical security would pay out $1, if and only if future sales were, say, between 10,000 and 15,000 units. Another might pay off if sales were between 15,000 and 20,000 units. The market contained 10 types of securities—a range broad enough to include all the relevant possible sales outcomes.

By examining the prices of all 10 shares, HP could assign a probability to any combination of outcomes. For example, if the price of the 5,000–10,000 unit sales security was 10 cents and the price of the 10,000–15,000 unit sales security was 20 cents, this suggests that the probability of selling 5,000–15,000 units was 30 percent.

HP compared the forecasts made by the prediction market with its own official forecasts and with actual sales figures. In 15 out of 16 trials, the mean market-based prediction was significantly closer to the actual sales figure than the official forecast. In the one remaining trial, the mean market-based prediction and the official forecast were equally close. Encouraged by these results, HP created its own experimental economics laboratory.

Another advantage of prediction markets is that they encourage traders to put their money where their mouths are *not*. While the members of a company's sales team may know better than anyone that next quarter's sales will be lower than expected, they rarely have incentives to relay this information to their bosses.

Prediction markets can help to overcome the "yes-man" phenomenon that makes it difficult for information to move from the field and into the hands of the senior decision makers.

The Hollywood Stock Exchange (http://www.HSX.com) is also proving that the innovative use of markets can be profitable. The Hollywood Exchange lets traders buy and sell shares and options in movies, music, and Oscar contenders. Trading on the Hollywood Exchange is conducted in make-believe "Hollywood Dollars," but the goal of the HSX—which is owned by a subsidiary of the Wall Street firm Cantor Fitzgerald—is profit. Some 800,000 people trading on HSX for fun have proven that HSX prices are reliable predictors of future film profits. Figure 5.3 graphs market predictions of opening revenues on the x-axis against actual opening revenues on the y-axis. If all predictions were perfect, then predicted revenues would be exactly equal to actual revenues and all the observations would lie on the 45-degree red line. No one can predict the future perfectly, of course. Movies above the red line did better than predicted and movies below the red line did worse than predicted. The market predicted that *The Adventures of Pluto Nash,* a 2002 movie starring Eddie Murphy, would take in opening weekend revenues of over $10 million. In fact, *The Adventures* was the biggest financial bomb of all time with costs of $100 million and revenues of $4.41 million, just over half of that generated on the opening weekend before word of mouth sent it straight to the reject pile. Director Spike Lee's *The Original Kings of Comedy,* however, was an unexpected hit with actual opening revenues of nearly $12 million compared to predicted revenues of just $4.7 million. Although market predictions are sometimes a little high and sometimes a little low, they are centered around the 45-degree line, which means that they are correct on average. The market, for example, predicted that *American Pie 2* would have opening revenues of $45.1 million and actual

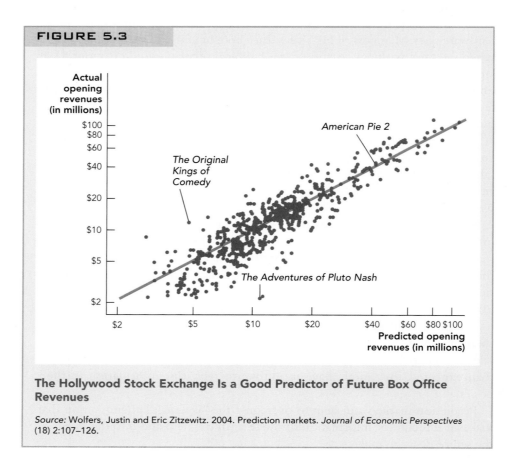

FIGURE 5.3

The Hollywood Stock Exchange Is a Good Predictor of Future Box Office Revenues

Source: Wolfers, Justin and Eric Zitzewitz. 2004. Prediction markets. *Journal of Economic Perspectives* (18) 2:107–126.

revenues were $45.3 million. Perhaps the biggest sign of the accuracy of the HSX market is that HSX sells its data to Hollywood studios eager to improve their predictions about future blockbusters.

The use of prediction markets is expanding rapidly, but what's important for our purposes is that prediction markets help to illustrate how *all* markets work. Market prices are signals that convey valuable information. Buyers and sellers have an incentive to pay attention to and respond to prices and in so doing they direct resources to their highest-value uses. That means everyone can make the most out of limited resources.

□ Takeaway

No market is an island. Markets are linked geographically, through time and across different goods. The price of gasoline at your local gasoline station is linked to the market for oil in China. The price of oil today is linked to the expectations about the market for oil in the future and, through investment, to the market for oil in the past. Markets in one good are linked to markets in other goods. The supply and demand of flowers, asphalt, and candy bars are all linked through the worldwide market.

The worldwide market is neither designed nor, because it is so complex, is it ever completely understood. The market acts like a giant computer to arrange our limited resources to satisfy as many of our limitless wants as possible. Prices are the heart of the market process. Prices signal the value of resources to consumers, suppliers, and entrepreneurs, and they encourage everyone to take appropriate actions to respond to scarcity and changing circumstances.

Free market prices work as signals because through buying and selling, prices come to reflect important pieces of information. The futures price of oil, for example, can signal war in the Middle East and the futures price of orange juice can tell us about the weather in Florida. Market prices can be so informative that new markets (prediction markets) are being created to help businesses, governments, and scientists predict future events.

□ CHAPTER REVIEW

KEY CONCEPTS

The great economic problem, p. 81

Speculation, p. 85

Futures, p. 87

Prediction market, p. 88

FACTS AND TOOLS

1. a. Suppose you'd like to do five different things, each of which requires exactly one orange. Complete the following table, ranking your highest-valued orange-related activity (1) to your lowest-valued activity (5).

Activity	Rank of Preference
Give a friend the orange.	
Throw the orange at a person you don't like.	
Eat the orange.	
Squeeze the orange to drink the juice.	
Use the orange as decorative fruit.	

b. Suppose the price per orange is high enough that you buy only four. What activity do you not do?

c. How low would the price of oranges have to fall for you to purchase five oranges? What does the price at which you would just purchase the fifth orange tell us about the value you receive from the fifth-ranked activity?

2. The supply and demand for copper changes constantly. New sources are discovered, mines collapse, workers go on strike, products that use it wane in and out of popularity, weather affects shipping conditions, and so on.

a. Suppose you learned that growing political instability in Chile (the largest producer of copper) will greatly reduce the productivity of its mines in two years. Ignoring all other factors, which curve (demand or supply) will shift which way in the market for copper two years from now?

b. Will the price rise or fall as a result of this curve shift?

c. Given your answer in part b, would a reasonable person buy copper to store for later? Why or why not? Ignore storage costs.

d. As a result of many people imitating your choice in part c, what happens to the current price of copper?

e. Does the action in parts c and d encourage people to use more copper today or less copper today?

3. In this chapter, we noted that successful economies are more likely to have many failing firms. If a nation's government instead made it impossible for inefficient firms to fail by giving them loans, cash grants, and other bailouts to stay in business, why is that nation likely to be poor? (Hint: Steven Davis and John Haltiwanger. 1999. Gross job flows, *Handbook of Labor Economics* (North-Holland) found that in the United States, 60 percent of the increase in U.S. manufacturing efficiency was caused by people moving from weak firms to strong firms.)

4. For you, personally, what is your opportunity cost of doing this homework?

5. Suppose you are bidding on a used car and someone else bids above the highest amount that you are willing to pay. What can you say for sure about that person's monetary value of the good compared to yours?

6. Sometimes speculators get it wrong. In the months before the Persian Gulf War, speculators drove up the price of oil: the average price in October 1990 was $36 per barrel, more than double its price in 1988. Oil speculators, like many people around the world, expected the Gulf War to last for months, disrupting the oil supply throughout the Gulf region. Thus, speculators either bought oil on the open market (almost always at the high speculative price) or they already owned oil and just kept it in storage. Either way, their plan was the same: to sell it in the future, when prices might even be higher.

As it turned out, the war was swift: After one month of massive aerial bombardment of Iraqi troops and a 100-hour ground war, President George H. W. Bush declared a cessation of hostilities. Despite the fact that Saddam Hussein set fire to many of Kuwait's oil fields, the price of oil plummeted to about $20 per barrel, a price at which it remained for years.

In 1991, speculators bet that a war against Saddam Hussein's regime would raise the price of oil for years. Wrong decade, perhaps.

a. Is buying oil for $36 a barrel and selling it for $20 per barrel a good business plan? How much profit did speculators earn, or how much money did they lose, on each barrel?

b. Why did the speculators follow this plan?

c. When the speculators sold their stored oil in the months after the war, did this massive resale tend to increase the price of oil or decrease it?

d. Do you think that many consumers complained about speculators or even realized that speculators were influencing the price of oil in spring 1991?

7. You manage a department store in Florida, and one winter day you read in the newspaper that orange juice futures have fallen dramatically in price. Should your store stock up on more sweaters than usual, or should your store stock up on more Bermuda shorts?

8. Take a look at Figure 5.3. If investors in the Hollywood Stock Exchange were too optimistic on average, would the dots tend to cluster above the red diagonal line or below it? How can you tell?

9. Let's see if the forces of the market can be as efficient as a benevolent dictator. Since laptop computers are increasingly easy to build and since they allow people to use their computers wherever they like, an all-wise benevolent dictator would probably decree that most people buy laptops rather than desktop computers. This is especially true now that laptops are about as powerful as most desktops. In answering questions a–c, answer in words as well as by shifting the appropriate curves in the figures below.

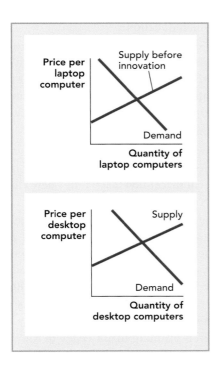

a. Since it's become much easier to build better laptops in recent years, laptop supply has increased. What does this do to the price of laptops?

b. Laptops and desktops are substitutes. Now that the price of laptops has changed, what does this do to the demand for desktop computers?

c. And how does that affect the quantity supplied of desktop computers?

d. Now let's look at the final result: Once it became easier to build good laptops, did "invisible hand" forces push more of society's resources into making laptops and push resources away from making desktops? (Note: Laptop sales first outnumbered desktop sales in 2008.)

THINKING AND PROBLEM SOLVING

1. Andy enters in a futures contract, allowing him to sell 5,000 troy ounces of gold at $1,000 per ounce in 36 months. After that time passes, the market price of gold is $950 per troy ounce. How much does Andy make or lose?

CRAIG AURNESS/CORBIS

2. Two major-party presidential candidates are running against each other in the 2016 election. The Democratic party candidate promises more money for corn-based ethanol research, and the Republican party candidate promises more money for defense contractors. In the weeks before the election, defense stocks take a nosedive.

a. Who is probably going to win the election: the pro-ethanol candidate or the pro-defense spending candidate?

b. We talked about how price signals are sometimes noisy. Think of two or three other markets you might want to look at in order to see if your answer to question a is correct.

3. In circa 1200 BCE, a decreasing supply of tin due to wars and the breakdown of trade led to a drastic increase in the price of bronze in the Middle East and Greece (tin being necessary for its production). It is around this time that blacksmiths developed iron- and steel-making techniques (as substitutes for bronze).

  a. How is the increasing price of bronze a signal?

  b. How is the increasing price an incentive?

  c. How do your answers in questions a and b help explain why iron and steel became more common around the same time as the increase in price?

  d. After the development of iron, did the supply or demand for bronze shift? Which way did it shift? Why?

4. In 1980, University of Maryland economist Julian Simon bet Stanford entomologist Paul Ehrlich that the price of any five metals of Ehrlich's choosing would fall over 10 years. Ehrlich believed that resources would become scarcer over time as population grew, while Simon believed that people would find good substitutes, just as earlier people developed iron as a substitute for scarce bronze. The price of all five metals that Ehrlich chose (nickel, tin, tungsten, chromium, and copper) fell over the next 10 years and Simon won the bet. Ehrlich, an honorable man, sent a check in the appropriate amount to Simon.

  a. What does the falling price tell us about the relative scarcity of these metals?

  b. What *could have* shifted to push these prices down: demand or supply? And would demand have increased or decreased? And supply?

5. In this chapter, we explored how prices tie all goods together. To illustrate this idea, suppose new farming techniques drastically increased the productivity of growing wheat.

  a. Given this change, how would the price of wheat change?

  b. Given your answer in question a, how would the price of cookbooks specializing in recipes using wheat flour change?

  c. Given your answer in question b, how would the price of paper change?

  d. Given your answer in question c, how would the price of pencils change? (Hint: Are paper and pencils substitutes or complements?)

  e. Given your answer in question d, how would the quantity of graphite (used in pencils) consumed change?

6. The "law of one price" states that if it's easy to move a good from one place to another, the price of identical goods will be the same because traders will buy low in one region and sell high in another. How is our story about the effect of speculators similar to the lesson about the "law of one price?"

7. Let's build on this chapter's example of asphalt. Suppose a new invention comes along that makes it easier and much less expensive to recycle clothing: perhaps a new device about the size of a washing machine can bleach, re-weave, and re-dye cotton fabric to closely imitate any cotton item you see in a fashion magazine. Head into the laundry room, drop in a batch of old clothes, scan in a couple of pages from *Vogue*, and come back in an hour.

  a. If you think of the "market for clothing" as "the market for new clothing," does this shift the demand or the supply curve, and in which direction?

  b. If you think of the "market for clothing" as "the market for clothing, whether it's new or used," does this shift the demand or the supply curve, and in which direction?

  c. What will this do to the price of new, unrecycled clothing?

  d. After this invention, will society's scarce productive resources (machines, workers, retail space) flow *toward* the "new clothing" sector or away from it?

(Note: This question might sound fanciful but three-dimensional printers, which can create plastic or plaster prototypes of small items such as toys, cups, etc., have fallen dramatically in price. Every day, you're getting just a little bit closer to having your own personal *Star Trek* replicator.)

8. Robin is planning to ask Peggy to the Homecoming dance. Before he asks her, he wants to know what the chances are that she'll say "yes." Robin is a scientist so he considers two paths to estimate the probability that Peggy will say yes.

I. Ask 10 of his friends, "Do you think she'll really say yes?"

II. Tell another 10 of his friends, "I'm starting a betting market. I'll pay $10 if she says yes, $0 if she says no. I'm only offering this bet once, to the highest bidder. Start bidding against each other for a chance at $10!"

   a. According to the evidence in this chapter, one of these methods will work better. Which one, and why?

   b. If the highest bid from Group II is $1 (along with a few lower bids of $0.75, $0.50, and zero), then roughly what's the chance that Peggy will say yes to Robin?

   c. If the highest bid from Group II quickly shoots up to about $9, then what's the chance that Peggy will say yes to Robin?

9. A classic essay about how markets link to each other is entitled "I, Pencil," written by Leonard E. Read (his real name). It is available for free online at the *Library of Economics and Liberty*. As you might suspect, it is written from the point of view of a pencil. One line is particularly famous: "no single person on the face of this earth knows how to make me." Based on what you've learned in this chapter about how markets link the world, how is this true?

CHALLENGES

1. In *The Fatal Conceit*, economist Friedrich A. Hayek, arguing against central planning, wrote: "The curious task of economics is to demonstrate to men how little they really know about what they imagine they can design." In other words, people generally assume that they can plan out the best procedure for producing a good (such as the Valentine's Day rose mentioned at the beginning of the chapter) but as we learned, that's not true. What are some of the different roles that the price system plays in creating this order? (Hint: Key words are "links," "signals," and "incentives.")

2. One question that economics students often ask is "In a market with a lot of buyers and sellers, who sets the price of the good?" There are two possible correct answers to this question: "Everyone" and "No one." Choose one of the two as your answer, and explain in one or two sentences why you are correct.

3. This chapter emphasized the ability of an orderly system to emerge without someone explicitly designing the entire system. How does the evolution of language illustrate a type of spontaneous order?

4. Are you in favor of "price gouging" during natural disasters? Why or why not?

5. What is the opportunity cost of the economics profession?

6

Price Ceilings

CHAPTER OUTLINE

Price Ceilings

Rent Control (Optional Section)

Arguments for Price Controls

Universal Price Controls

Takeaway

O n a quiet Sunday in August 1971, President Richard Nixon shocked the nation by freezing all prices and wages in the United States. It was now illegal to raise prices—even if both buyers and sellers voluntarily agreed to the change. Nixon's order, one of the most significant peacetime interventions into the U.S. economy ever to oc-cur, applied to almost all goods, and even though it was supposed to be in ef-fect for only 90 days, it would have lasting effects for over a decade.

In Chapter 5, we explained how a price is "a signal wrapped up in an in-centive," that is, we explained how prices signal information and create incentives to economize and seek out substitutes. We also explained how markets are linked geographically, across different products, and through time. In this chapter and the next, we show how price controls—laws making it illegal for prices to move above a maximum price (price ceilings) or below a minimum price (price floors)—interfere with all of these processes. We begin by explaining how a price control affects a single market, and then we turn to how price controls delink some markets and link others in ways that are counterproductive.

Price Ceilings

Nixon's price controls didn't have much effect immediately because prices were frozen near market levels. But the economy is in constant flux and market prices soon shifted. At the time of the freeze prices were rising due to inflation, so the typical situation came to resemble that in Figure 6.1 on the next page with the controlled price below the uncontrolled or market equilibrium price.

FIGURE 6.1

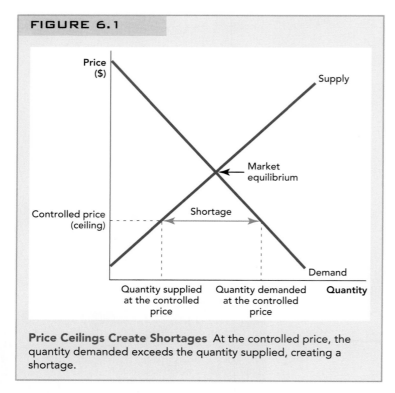

Price Ceilings Create Shortages At the controlled price, the quantity demanded exceeds the quantity supplied, creating a shortage.

A **price ceiling** is a maximum price allowed by law.

A shortage of vinyl in 1973 forced Capitol Records to melt down slow sellers so they could keep pressing Beatles' albums.

When the maximum price that can be legally charged is below the market price we say that there is a **price ceiling**. Economists call it a price ceiling because prices cannot legally go higher than the ceiling. Price ceilings create five important effects:

1. Shortages
2. Reductions in product quality
3. Wasteful lines and other search costs
4. A loss of gains from trade
5. A misallocation of resources

Shortages

When prices are held below the market price, the quantity demanded exceeds the quantity supplied. Economists call this a shortage. Figure 6.1 shows that the shortage is measured by the difference between the quantity demanded at the controlled price and the quantity supplied at the controlled price. Notice also that the lower the controlled price is relative to the market equilibrium price, the larger the shortage.

In some sectors of the economy, shortages appeared soon after prices were controlled in 1971. Increased demand in the construction industry, for example, meant that price controls hit that sector especially hard. Ordinarily, increased demand for steel bars, for example, would increase the price of steel bars, encouraging more production. But with a price ceiling in place, demanders could not signal their need to suppliers nor could they provide suppliers with an incentive to produce more. As a result, shortages of steel bars, lumber, toilets (for new homes), and other construction inputs were common. By 1973, there were shortages of wool, copper, aluminum, vinyl, denim jeans, paper, plastic bottles, and more.

Reductions in Quality

At the controlled price, demanders find that there is a shortage of goods—they cannot buy as much of the good as they would like. Equivalently, at the controlled price, sellers find that there is an excess of demand or, in other words, *sellers have more customers than they have goods*. Ordinarily, this would be an opportunity to profit by raising prices, but when prices are controlled, sellers can't raise prices without violating the law. Is there another way that sellers can increase profits? Yes. It's much easier to evade the law by cutting quality than by raising price, so when prices are held below market levels, quality declines.

Thus, even when shortages were not apparent, quality was reduced. Books were printed on lower-quality paper, 2" × 4" lumber shrank to $1\frac{5}{8}$" × $3\frac{5}{8}$", and new automobiles were painted with fewer coats of paint. To help deal with the shortage of paper some newspapers even switched to a smaller font size.

Another way quality can fall is with reductions in service. Ordinarily sellers have an incentive to please their customers, but when prices are held below market levels, sellers have more customers than they need *or want*. Customers without potential for profit are just a pain so when prices cannot rise we can expect service quality to fall. The full service gasoline station, for example, disappeared with price controls in 1973 and instead of staying open for 24 hours, gasoline stations would close whenever the owner wanted a lunch break.

Wasteful Lines and Other Search Costs

The most serious shortage during the 1970s was for oil. The OPEC embargo in 1973 and the reduction in supply caused by the Iranian revolution in 1979 increased the world price of oil, as we saw in Chapter 3. In the United States, however, price controls on domestically produced oil had not been lifted and thus the United States faced intense shortages of oil and the classic sign of a shortage, lines.

Figure 6.2 focuses on the third consequence of controlling prices below market prices: wasteful lines.

The Great Matzo Ball Debate

In 1972, AFL-CIO boss George Meany complained that the number of matzo balls in his favorite soup had sunk from four to three, in effect raising the price.

C. Jackson Grayson, chairman of the U.S. Price Commission, was worried about the bad publicity, so on *Face the Nation* he triumphantly held aloft a can of Mrs. Adler's soup claiming that his staff had opened many cans and concluded there were still four balls per can.

Whoever was right about the soup, Meany was certainly the better economist: price ceilings reduce quality.

FIGURE 6.2

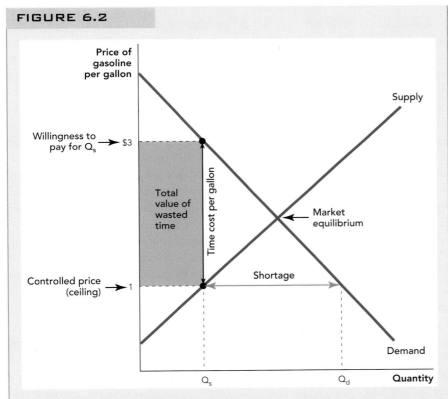

Price Ceilings Create Wasteful Lines At the controlled price, the quantity of gasoline supplied is Q_s and buyers are willing to pay as much as $3 for a gallon of gasoline. But the maximum price that sellers can charge is $1. The difference between what buyers are willing to pay and what sellers can charge encourages buyers to line up to buy gasoline. Buyers will line up until the total price of gasoline, the out-of-pocket price plus the time cost, increases to $3 per gallon. Time spent waiting in line is wasted time. The total value of wasted time is given by the time cost per gallon multiplied by the quantity of gallons bought.

At the controlled price of $1, sellers supply Q_s units of the good. How much are demanders willing to pay (per unit) for these Q_s units? Recall that the demand curve shows the willingness to pay, so follow a line from Q_s up to the demand curve to find that demanders are willing to pay $3 per unit for

Q_s units. The price controls, however, make it illegal for demanders to offer sellers a price of $3, but there are other ways of paying for gas.

Knowing that there is a shortage, some buyers might bribe station owners (or attendants) to fill up their tanks. Suppose that the average tank holds 20 gallons. Buyers would then be willing to pay $60 for a fill-up, the legal price of $20 plus a $40 under-the-table bribe. Thus, if bribes are common the total price of gasoline—the legal price plus the bribe price—will rise to $3 per gallon ($60/20 gallons).

Corruption and bribes can be common, especially when price controls are long lasting, but they were not a major problem during the gasoline shortages of the 1970s. Nevertheless, the total price of gasoline did rise well above the controlled price. Instead of competing by paying bribes, buyers competed by their willingness to wait in line. Remember that at the controlled price the quantity of gasoline demanded is greater than the quantity supplied, so some buyers are going to be disappointed—they are going to get less gasoline than they want and some buyers may get no gasoline at all. Buyers will compete to avoid being left with nothing. Let's assume that all gasoline station owners refuse bribes. Unfortunately, honesty does not eliminate the shortage. A "first-come, first-served" system is honest, but buyers who get to the gasoline station early will get the gas, leaving the latecomers with nothing. Under this situation, how long will the lineups get?

Suppose that buyers value their time at $10 an hour and, as before, the average fuel tank holds 20 gallons. Eager to obtain gas during the shortage, a buyer arrives at the station early, perhaps even before it opens, and must wait in line for an hour before he is served. His total price of gas is $30, $1 per gallon for 20 gallons in out-of-pocket cost plus $10 in time cost. Since the total value of the gas is $60, that's still a good deal. But if it's a good deal for him, it's probably a good deal for other buyers too; so the next time he wants to fill up he is likely to discover that others have preceded him and now he has to wait longer. How much longer? Following the logic to its conclusion we can see that the line will lengthen until the total cost for 20 gallons of gasoline is $60, $20 in cash paid to the station owner plus $40 in time costs. The price per gallon, therefore, rises to $3 ($60/20 gallons)—exactly as occurred with bribes!

Price controls do not eliminate competition. They merely change the form of competition. Is there a difference between paying in bribes and paying in time? Yes. Paying in time is much more wasteful. When a buyer bribes a gasoline station owner $40, at least the gasoline station owner gets the bribe. But when a buyer spends $40 worth of time or four hours waiting in line, the gasoline station owner doesn't get to add four hours to his life. The bribe is transferred from the buyer to the seller, but the time spent waiting in line is simply lost. Figure 6.2 shows that when the quantity supplied is Q_s, the total price of gasoline will tend to rise to $3, a $1 money price plus a time-price of $2 per gallon. The total amount of waste from waiting in line is given by the shaded area, the per gallon time price ($2) multiplied by the number of gallons bought (Q_s).*

When the quantity demanded exceeds the quantity supplied, someone is going to be disappointed.

---

* We need to qualify this slightly. If *every* buyer has a time value of $10 per hour, then the total time wasted will be the area as shaded in the diagram. If some buyers have a time value lower than $10, say $5 per hour, they will wait in line for 4 hours, paying $20 in out-of-pocket costs but only $20 in time costs. If these buyers value the gasoline as high as does the marginal buyer, at $60 for 20 gallons, they will earn what economists call a "rent" of $20; thus, not all of the rectangle would be wasted. Regardless of whether all of the rectangle or just some of the rectangle is wasted, it's important to see that (1) price ceilings generate shortages and line-ups, (2) the lineups mean that the total price of the controlled good is higher than the controlled price (and perhaps even higher than the uncontrolled price), and (3) the time spent waiting in line is wasted.

Lost Gains from Trade

Price controls also reduce the gains from trade. In Figure 6.3, at the quantity supplied, Q_s, how much would demanders pay for one *additional* gallon of gasoline? The willingness to pay for a gallon of gas at Q_s is $3, so demanders would be willing to pay just a little bit less, say $2.95, for an additional gallon. How much would suppliers require to sell an additional gallon? Supplier cost is read off the supply curve, so reading up from the quantity Q_s to the supply curve we find that the willingness to sell at Q_s is $1; suppliers would be willing to supply an additional unit for just a little bit more, say $1.05.

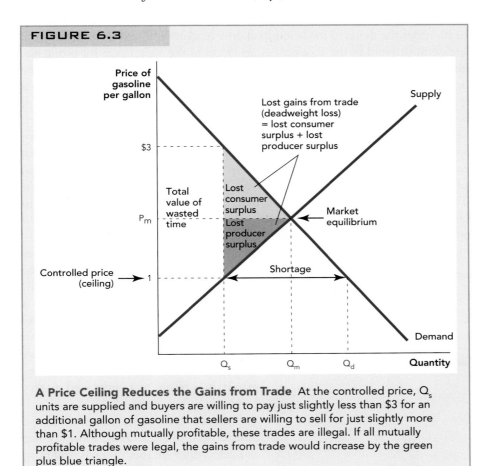

FIGURE 6.3

A Price Ceiling Reduces the Gains from Trade At the controlled price, Q_s units are supplied and buyers are willing to pay just slightly less than $3 for an additional gallon of gasoline that sellers are willing to sell for just slightly more than $1. Although mutually profitable, these trades are illegal. If all mutually profitable trades were legal, the gains from trade would increase by the green plus blue triangle.

Demanders are willing to pay $2.95 for an additional gallon of gas, suppliers are willing to sell an additional gallon for $1.05, and so there is $1.90 of potential gains from trade to split between them. But it's illegal for suppliers to sell gasoline at anything more than $1. Buyers and sellers want to trade, but they are prevented from doing so by the threat of jail. If the price ceiling were lifted and trade were allowed, the quantity traded would expand from Q_s to Q_m and buyers would be better off by the green triangle labeled "Lost consumer surplus," while sellers would be better off by the blue triangle labeled "Lost producer surplus." But with a price ceiling in place, the quantity supplied is Q_s and together the lost consumer and producer surplus are lost gains from trade (economists also call this a **deadweight loss**).

Recall from Chapter 3 that we said that in a free market the quantity of goods sold maximizes the sum of consumer and producer surplus. We can now

A **deadweight loss** is the total of lost consumer and producer surplus when not all mutually profitable gains from trade are exploited. Price ceilings create a deadweight loss.

see that in a market with a price ceiling, the sum of consumer and producer surplus is not maximized because the price control prevents mutually profitable gains from trade from being exploited.

In addition to these losses, price controls cause a misallocation of scarce resources; let's see how that works in more detail.

Misallocation of Resources

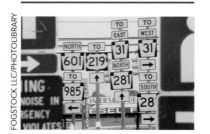

Distorted signals cause resources to be misallocated.

In Chapter 5, we explained how a price is a signal wrapped up in an incentive. Price controls distort signals and eliminate incentives. Imagine that it's sunny on the West Coast of the United States, but on the East Coast there is a cold winter that increases the demand for heating oil. In a market without price controls, the increase in demand in the East pushes up prices in the East. Eager for profit, entrepreneurs buy oil in the West, where the oil is not much needed and the price is low, and they move it to the East, where people are cold and the price of oil is high. In this way, the price increase in the East is moderated and supplies of oil move to where they are needed most.

Now consider what happens when it is illegal to buy or sell oil at a price above a price ceiling. No matter how cold it gets in the East, the demanders of heating oil are prevented from bidding up the price of oil, so there's *no signal* and *no incentive* to ship oil to where it is needed most. Price controls mean that oil is misallocated. Swimming pools in California are heated while homes in New Jersey are cold. In fact, this was exactly what occurred in the United States, especially in the harsh winter of 1972–1973.

Once again recall from Chapter 3 that we said that in a free market the supply of goods is bought by the demanders who have the highest-willingness to pay. We can now see that in a market with a price ceiling demanders with the highest-willingness to pay have no easy way to signal their demands nor do suppliers have an incentive to supply their demands. As a result, in a controlled market goods are misallocated.

Price controls cause resources to be misallocated not just geographically, but also across different uses of oil. Recall from Chapter 2 that the demand curve for oil shows the uses of oil from the highest-valued uses to the lowest-valued uses. In case you forgot, Figure 6.4 shows the key idea: high-valued uses are at the top of the curve and low-valued uses at the bottom. Without market prices, however, we have no guarantee that oil will flow to its highest-valued uses. As we have just seen, in a situation with price controls, it's possible to have plenty of oil to heat swimming pools in California (hello, rubber ducky!) and not enough oil for heating cold homes in New Jersey. Similarly, in 1974 *Business Week* reported, "While drivers wait in

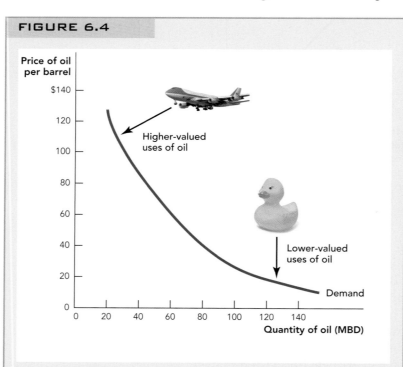

FIGURE 6.4

Price of oil per barrel

Higher-valued uses of oil

Lower-valued uses of oil

Demand

Quantity of oil (MBD)

The Demand for Oil Depends on the Value of Oil in Different Uses
When the price of oil is high, oil will only be used in the higher-valued uses. As the price falls, oil will also be used in lower-valued uses.

(Top photo: EuroStyle Graphics/Alamy)

(Bottom: Lew Robertson/Corbis)

three-hour lines in one state, consumers in other states are breezing in and out of gas stations."[1]

Figure 6.5 illustrates the problem more generally. As we know, at the controlled price, the quantity demanded (Q_d) exceeds the quantity supplied (Q_s) and there is a shortage. Ideally, we would like to allocate the quantity of oil supplied (Q_s), to its highest-valued uses; these are illustrated at the top of the demand curve by the thick line. But the potential consumers of the oil with the highest-valued uses are legally prevented from signaling their high value by offering to pay oil suppliers more than the controlled price. Oil suppliers, therefore, have no incentive to supply oil to just the highest-valued uses. Instead, oil suppliers will give the oil to any user who is willing to pay the controlled price—but most of these users of oil have lower-valued uses. Like the lines at the gas station, it's first-come, first-served. In fact, the only uses of oil that definitely will not be satisfied are the least-valued uses. (Why not? The users with the least-valued uses are not even willing to pay the controlled price.)

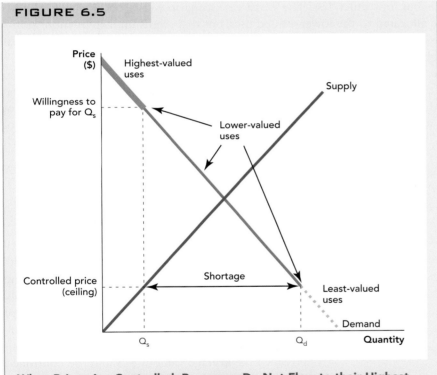

FIGURE 6.5

When Prices Are Controlled, Resources Do Not Flow to their Highest Valued Uses Gains from trades are maximized when goods flow to their highest valued uses. A price control prevents the highest-valued uses from outbidding lower valued uses so some oil flows to lower-valued uses even though it would be more valuable if used elsewhere.

When a crisis in the Middle East reduces the supply of oil, the price system rationally responds by reallocating oil from lower valued uses to the highest-value uses. In contrast, when the supply of oil is reduced and there are price ceilings, oil is allocated according to random and often trivial factors. The shortage of heating oil in 1971, for example, was exacerbated by the fact that President Nixon happened to impose price controls in *August* when the price of heating oil was near its seasonal low.[2] Since the price of heating oil was controlled at a low price while gasoline was controlled at a slightly higher price, it was more profitable to turn crude oil into gasoline than into heating oil. As winter approached, the price of heating oil would normally have risen and refiners would have turned away from gasoline production to the production of heating oil, but price controls removed the incentive to respond rationally.

see the invisible hand

Advanced Material: The Loss from Random Allocation If there were no misallocation, then under a price control consumer surplus would be the area between the demand curve and the price up to the quantity supplied, the green area in Figure 6.6. (Of course, some of this surplus will likely be eaten up by bribes, time spent waiting in line, and so forth as we discussed above.)

Under a price control, however, the good is not necessarily allocated to the highest-valued uses. As a result, consumer surplus will be less than the green area—but how much less? The worst case scenario would occur if all the goods were allocated to the lower-valued uses, but that seems unlikely. A more realistic assumption is that under price controls, goods are allocated randomly so that a high-valued use is as likely as a low-valued use to be satisfied.

In Figure 6.7 we show two uses. The highest-valued use has a value of $30 and the lowest-valued use has a value of $6. Now imagine that one unit of the good is allocated randomly between these two uses. Thus, with a probability of 1/2 it will be allocated to the use with a value of 30 and with a probability of 1/2 it will be allocated to the use with a value of 6. On average how much value will this unit create? The average value will be

$$\text{Average value} = \frac{1}{2} \times \$30 + \frac{1}{2} \times \$6 = \$18$$

Extending this logic, it can be shown that if every use between the highest-valued use and the lowest-valued use is *equally* likely to be satisfied, then the average value is $18. Thus on average a randomly allocated unit of the good will create a value of $18. If there are, say, 10 units allocated, then the total value of those units will be $10 \times \$18 = \$180$. Since the average value is $18 and the controlled price is $6, consumer surplus is the green area in Figure 6.7 labeled total consumer surplus under random allocation. But notice that the green area in Figure 6.7, consumer surplus under random allocation, is much less than the green area in Figure 6.6, consumer surplus under allocation to the highest value uses. The difference is the red area in Figure 6.7, the loss due to random allocation.

FIGURE 6.6

Price

$30 — Highest valued uses

Supply

Consumer surplus

Controlled price 6 — Shortage

Demand

0   Q_s   Q_d   Quantity
          10   45

In a Free Market Goods Flow to Their Highest Value Uses
If all units of the good are allocated to the highest valued uses, then consumer surplus is the area between the demand curve and the price up to the quantity supplied.

Misallocation and Production Chaos Shortages in one market create breakdowns and shortages in other markets, so the chaos of price controls expands even into markets without price controls. In ordinary times, we take it for granted that products will be available when we want them, but in an economy with many price controls, shortages of key inputs can appear at any time. In 1973, for example, million-dollar construction projects were delayed because a few thousand dollars worth of steel bar was unavailable.[3]

Perhaps the height of misallocation occurred when shortages of steel drilling equipment made it difficult to expand oil production; this mistake took place even as the United States was undergoing the worst energy crisis in its history.[4]

As the shortages and misallocations grew worse, schools, factories, and offices were forced to close, and the government stepped in to allocate oil by command. President Nixon ordered gasoline stations to close between 9 P.M. Saturday and 12:01 A.M. Monday.[5] The idea was to prevent "wasteful" Sunday driving, but the ban simply encouraged people to fill their tanks earlier. Daylight savings time and a national 55 mph speed limit were put into place (the latter not to be repealed until 1995). Some industries, such as agriculture, were given priority treatment for fuel allocation, while others were forced to endure cutbacks. Fuel for noncommercial aircraft, for example, was cut by 42.5 percent in November of 1973, sending the local economy of Wichita, Kansas, where aircraft producers Cessna, Beech, and Lear were located, into a tailspin.[6]

Some of these ideas for conserving fuel were probably sensible while others were not, but without market prices, it's hard to tell which is which. The subtlety of the market process in allocating oil and taking advantage of links between markets is difficult, even impossible, to duplicate. C. Jackson Grayson was chairman of President Nixon's Price Commission, but after seeing how controls worked in practice he said:

> Our economic understanding and models are simply not powerful enough to handle such a large and complex economic system better than the marketplace.[7]

FIGURE 6.7

Consumer Surplus Falls under Random Allocation When there is a price control, the buyers with the highest valued uses cannot outbid other buyers, so goods will flow to *any* buyer willing to pay more than the controlled price of $6. If goods are allocated randomly to buyers with values between $30 and $6, the average value will be $18. Consumer surplus under random allocation is the green area. If goods were allocated to the highest valued uses, consumer surplus would be larger, the red plus green areas. Thus, a price control misallocates resources, reducing consumer surplus.

President Nixon said no to commercial holiday lights during the Christmas of 1973.

UNDERSTAND YOUR **world**

The End of Price Ceilings

Price controls for most goods were lifted by April 1974, but controls on oil remained in place. Over the next 7 years, controls on oil would be eased but at the price of substantial increases in complexity and bureaucracy. In September 1973, for example, price controls were lifted on new oil. "New oil" was defined as oil produced on a particular property in excess of the amount that had been produced in 1972. Decontrol of new oil was a good idea because it increased the incentive to develop new deposits. The two-tier system, however, also created wasteful gaming as firms shut down some oil wells only to drill "new" wells right next door.[8] The battle between entrepreneurs and regulators was met with increasingly complex rules. Thus, the two-tier program was extended to three tiers, then five, then eight, then eleven.

Price controls on oil ended as abruptly as they had begun when on the morning of January 20, 1981, Ronald Reagan was inaugurated as president, and before lunch with Congress, he performed his first act as president—eliminating all controls on oil and gasoline. As expected, the price of oil in the United States rose a little but the shortage ended overnight. Within a year, prices began to fall as supply increased and within a few years they were well below the levels of 1979. Fluctuations in the price of oil have continued to occur, of course, but since the ending of controls, there has been no shortage of oil in the United States.

Rent Controls (Optional Section)

A **rent control** is a price ceiling on rental housing such as apartments so everything we have learned about price ceilings also applies to rent controls. Rent controls create shortages, reduce quality, create wasteful lines and increase the costs of search, cause a loss of gains from trade, and misallocate resources.

Shortages

Rent controls usually begin with a "rent freeze," which prohibits landlords from raising rents. Since rent controls are often put into place when rents are rising, the situation quickly comes to look like Figure 6.8 with the controlled rent below the market equilibrium rent.

CHECK YOURSELF

> Nixon's price controls set price ceilings below the market price. What would have happened if the price ceilings had been set above market prices?

> Under price controls why were the shortages of oil in some local markets much more severe than in others?

A **rent control** is a price ceiling on rental housing.

FIGURE 6.8

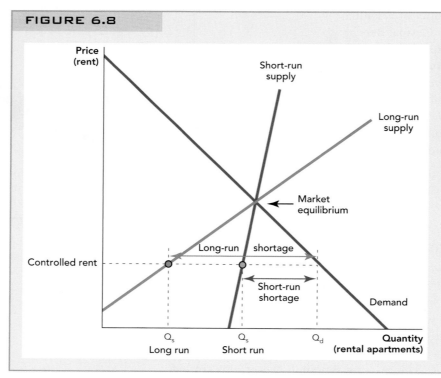

Rent Control Creates Larger Shortages in the Long Run than in the Short Run A rent control below the equilibrium price generates a shortage. The short-run shortage is small since the apartment units are already built. In the long run, fewer new units are built and old apartments are torn down or turned into condominiums so the long-run shortage is much greater.

Apartments are long-lasting goods that cannot be shipped elsewhere, so when rent controls are first imposed, owners of apartment buildings have few alternatives but to absorb the lower price. In other words, the short-run supply curve for apartments is inelastic. Thus, Figure 6.8 shows that even though the rent freeze may result in rents well below the market equilibrium level, there is only a small reduction in the quantity supplied in the short run.

In the long run, however, fewer new apartment units are built and older units are turned into condominiums or torn down to make way for parking garages or other higher-paying ventures. Thus, the long-run supply curve is much more elastic than the short-run supply curve, and the shortage grows over time from the short-run shortage to the long-run shortage.

Although old apartment buildings can't disappear overnight, future apartment buildings can. Developers look for profits over a 30 year or longer time frame, so even a modest rent control can sharply reduce the value of new apartment construction. Developers who fear that rent controls are likely will immediately end their plans to build. In the early 1970s, for example, rent control was debated in Ontario, Canada, and put into place in 1975. In the five years before controls were put into place, developers built an average of 27,999 new apartments per year. In the five years after controls were put into place, developers built only 5,512 apartments per year. Figure 6.9 graphs the number of new apartment starts and the number of new house starts per year from 1969 to 1979. The sharp drop in new apartment construction in the years when rent controls first started to be debated is obvious. But perhaps the drop was due to other factors like the state of the economy. To test

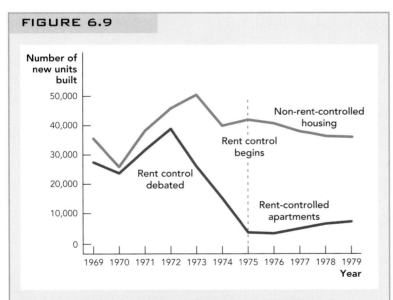

FIGURE 6.9

Rent Control Reduces the Building of New Apartments As rent control began to be debated in Ontario, the construction of new apartments plummeted. After rent control was put into place, fewer apartments were built compared to non-rent-controlled homes.

Source: Smith, Lawrence B. 1988. "An Economic Assessment of Rent Controls: The Ontario Experience." *Journal of Real Estate Finance and Economics* 1: 217–231.
Note: These figures are for private, unsubsidized housing.

for this possibility, we also graph the number of new houses that were built annually during this time. The demand for houses and the demand for apartments respond similarly to the economy, but price controls on houses were never debated or imposed. We can see from Figure 6.9 that prior to 1972 the number of new apartment starts was similar to the number of new house starts. But when rent control became a possibility, apartment construction fell but the construction of houses did not. Thus, it's likely that rent control and not the general state of the economy (which would also have affected house starts) was responsible for the sharp drop in the number of new apartments built.

Reductions in Product Quality

Rent controls also reduce housing quality, especially the quality of low-end apartments. When the price of apartments is forced down, owners attempt to stave off losses by cutting their costs. With rent controls, for example, owners mow the lawns less often, replace lightbulbs more slowly, and don't fix the elevators so quickly. When the controls are strong, cheap but serviceable apartment buildings turn into slums and then slums turn into abandoned and hollowed-out apartment blocks. In Manhattan, for example, 18 percent of the rent-controlled housing is "dilapidated or deteriorating," a much higher percentage than in the uncontrolled sector.[9] Rent controls in European countries have tended to be more restrictive than in the United States, leading the economist Assar Lindbeck to remark, "Rent control is the most effective method we know for destroying a city, except for bombing it."[10] Lindbeck, however, was wrong, at least according to Vietnam's foreign minister who in 1989 said, "The Americans couldn't destroy Hanoi, but we have destroyed our city by very low rents."[11]

Wasteful Lines, Search Costs, and Lost Gains from Trade

Lines for apartments are not as obvious as for gasoline, but finding an apartment in a city with extensive rent controls usually involves a costly search. New Yorkers have developed a number of tricks to help them, as Billy Crystal explained in the movie *When Harry Met Sally*:

> What you do is, you read the obituary column. Yeah, you find out who died, and go to the building and then you tip the doorman. What they can do to make it easier is to combine the obituaries with the real estate section. Say, then you'd have "Mr. Klein died today leaving a wife, two children, and a spacious three bedroom apartment with a wood burning fireplace."

Search can be especially costly for people that landlords think are not "ideal renters." At the controlled price, landlords have more customers than they have apartments, so they can pick and choose among prospective renters. Landlords prefer to rent to people who are seen as being more likely to pay the rent on time and not cause trouble for other tenants, for example, older, richer couples without children or dogs. Landlords might also discriminate on racial or other grounds. Indeed, a landlord who doesn't like your looks can turn you down and immediately rent to the next person in line. Landlords can discriminate even if there are no rent controls, but without rent controls, the vacancy rate will be higher because the quantity of apartments will be larger and turnover will be more common, so landlords who turn down prospective renters will lose money as they wait for their ideal renter. Rent controls reduce the price of discrimination, so remember the law of demand: when the price of discrimination falls, the quantity of discrimination demanded will increase.

Bribing the landlord or apartment manager to get a rent-controlled apartment is also common. Bribes are illegal but they can be disguised. An apartment might rent for $500 a month but come with $5,000 worth of "furniture." Renters refer to these kind of tie-in sales as paying "key money," as in the rent is $500 a month but the key costs extra. Nora Ephron, the screenwriter for *When Harry Met Sally,* lived for many years in a five-bedroom luxury apartment that thanks to rent control cost her just $1,500 a month. She did, however, have to pay $24,000 in key money to get the previous renter to move out!

The analysis of lost gains from trade from rent controls is exactly the same as we showed in Figure 6.3 for price controls on gasoline. At the quantity supplied under rent control, demanders are willing to pay more for an apartment than sellers would require to rent the apartment. If buyers and sellers were free to trade, they could both be better off, but under rent control these mutually profitable trades are illegal and the benefits do not occur.

A rent-controlled apartment—furnished.

Misallocation of Resources

As with gasoline, apartments under rent control are allocated haphazardly—some people with a high willingness to pay can't buy as much housing as they want even as others with a low willingness to pay consume more housing than they would purchase at the market rate. The classic example is the older couple who stay in their large rent-controlled apartment even after their children have moved out. It's a great deal for the older couple, but not so good for the young couple with children who as a result are stuck in a cramped apartment with nowhere to go.

Economists can estimate the amount of misallocation by comparing the types of apartments that renters choose in cities like New York, which has had rent controls since they were imposed as a "temporary" measure in World War II, with the types of apartments that people choose in cities like Chicago, which has a free market in rental housing. In one recent study of this kind, Edward Glaeser and Erzo Luttmer found that as many as 21 percent of the renters in New York City live in an apartment that has more or fewer rooms than they would choose if they lived in a city without rent controls.[12] This misallocation of resources creates significant waste and hardship.

Rent Regulation

In the 1990s, many American cities with rent control changed policy and began to eliminate or ease rent controls. Some economists refer to these new policies not as rent control but as "rent regulation." A typical rent regulation limits price increases without limiting prices. Prices increases, for example, might be limited to say 10 percent per year. Thus, rent regulations can protect tenants from sharp increases in rent while still allowing prices to rise or fall over several years

CHECK YOURSELF

> If landlords under rent control have an incentive to do only the minimum upkeep, what inevitably must accompany rent control? Think of a tenant with a dripping faucet: how does it get fixed?

> New York City has had rent control for decades. Assume you are appointed to the mayor's housing commission and convince your commission members that rent control has been a bad thing for New York. How would you get rid of rent control, considering the vested interests?

Iraq 2003. Gasoline is a bargain at 5 cents a gallon. If you can afford the wait.

UNDERSTAND YOUR
world

in response to market forces. Rent regulation laws usually also allow landlords to pass along cost increases so the incentive to cut back on maintenance is reduced. Economists are almost universally opposed to rent controls but some economists think that moderate rent regulation could have some benefits.[13]

Arguments for Price Controls

Without price controls on oil in 1973, some people might not have been able to afford to heat their homes. Without rent controls, some people may not be able to afford appropriate housing. It's not obvious that the poor are better off with shortages than with high prices. Nevertheless, *if* price controls were the *only* way to help the poor, then this would be an argument in favor of price controls.

Price controls, however, are never the only way to help the poor and they are rarely the best way. If affordable housing is a concern, for example, then a better policy than rent controls is for the government to provide housing vouchers. Housing vouchers, which are used extensively in the United States, give qualifying consumers a voucher worth say $500 a month that can be applied to any unit of housing.[14] Unlike rent controls, which create shortages, vouchers *increase* the supply of housing. Vouchers can also be targeted to consumers who need them, whereas rent controls in New York City have subsidized millionaires.

There are a few other sound arguments for price controls. The best case for price controls is to discipline monopolies. Alas, this explanation does not fit price controls on gasoline, apartments, bread, or almost all of the goods that price controls are routinely placed on. We will look at this special case more extensively in Chapter 11.

One of the primary reasons for price controls may be that the public, unlike economists, do not see the consequences of price controls. People who have not been trained in economics rarely connect lineups with price controls. During the gasoline shortages of the 1970s, probably not one American in 10 understood the connection between the controls and the shortage—most consumers blamed big oil companies and rich Arab sheiks. Americans are not alone in blaming shortages on foreigners. The demand for price controls is a recurring and common event in history. Consider, for example, the situation in Iraq in 2003:

> The line of cars waiting to fill up at the Hurreya gas station on Monday snaked down the right lane of a busy thoroughfare, around a traffic circle, across a double-decker bridge spanning the Tigris River and along a potholed side street leading to one of Iraq's three oil refineries.

> At the end, almost two miles from the station, was Mohammed Adnan, a taxi driver who could not comprehend why he would have to wait seven hours to fuel his mud-spattered Chevrolet Beretta. "This is Iraq," he noted wryly. "Don't we live on a lake of oil?" . . .

> "Maybe it's the black marketeers," Adnan said. "They're taking all our fuel."

> Bayar was more certain. "It's the refineries," he said. "They're not producing enough gasoline."

> The driver of the next car in line scoffed at both explanations. "It's the Americans, for sure," said Hassan Jawad Mehdi. "They are taking our oil back to America."[15]

Each of these explanations might help to explain why Iraq in 2003 was producing less gasoline than before the war. But reductions in supply create high prices, not shortages. To generate a shortage, you need a price control, and in Iraq in 2003 the price of gasoline was controlled at 5 cents per gallon.[16]

Universal Price Controls

We have seen that price controls in the United States caused shortages, lineups, delays, quality reductions, misallocations, bureaucracy, and corruption. And the U.S. experience with extensive price controls was short, just a few months for most goods, and a few years for oil and a handful of other goods. What would happen if price controls on all goods remained in place for a lengthy period of time? An economy with permanent, universal price controls is in essence a "command economy," much as existed in the communist countries prior to the fall of the Berlin Wall. In *The Russians*, Hedrick Smith described what it was like for consumers living in the Soviet Union in 1976[17]:

> The list of scarce items is practically endless. They are not permanently out of stock, but their appearance is unpredictable . . . . Leningrad can be over-stocked with cross-country skis and yet go several months without soap for washing dishes. In the Armenian capital of Yerevan, I found an ample supply of accordions but local people complained that they had gone for weeks without ordinary kitchen spoons or tea samovars. I knew a Moscow family that spent a frantic month hunting for a child's potty while radios were a glut on the market. . . .
>
> The accepted norm is that the Soviet woman daily spends two hours in line, seven days a week . . . . I have known of people who stood in line 90 minutes to buy four pineapples . . . three and a half hours to buy three large heads of cabbage only to find the cabbages were gone as they approached the front of the line, 18 hours to sign up to purchase a rug at some later date, all through a freezing December night to register on a list for buying a car, and then waiting 18 months for actual delivery, and terribly lucky at that.

In the Soviet Union never-ending shortages meant that lining up for hours to get bread, shoes or other goods was normal.

The never-ending shortage of goods in the Soviet Union suggests another reason why price controls are not eliminated even when doing so would make most people better off. Shortages were beneficial to the very same party elite who controlled prices. With all goods in permanent shortage, how did anyone in the Soviet Union obtain goods? By using *blat*. Blat is a Russian word meaning having connections that can be used to get favors. As Hedrick Smith put it:

> In an economy of chronic shortages and carefully parceled-out privileges, blat is an essential lubricant of life. The more rank and power one has, the more blat one normally has . . . each has access to things or services that are hard to get and that other people want or need.

Consider the manager of a small factory that produces radios. Music may be the food that feeds people's souls but the manager would also like some beef. Shortages mean that the manager's salary is almost useless in helping him to obtain beef but what does he have of value? He has access to radios. If the manager can find a worker in a beef factory who loves music, he will have blat, a connection and something to trade. Even if he can't find someone with the exact opposite wants as he has, access to radios gives the manager power because people will want to do favors for him. But notice that the manager of the radio factory only has blat because of a shortage of radios. If radios were easily available at the market price, then the manager's access would no longer be of

CHECK YOURSELF

> In the 1984 movie *Moscow on the Hudson*, a Soviet musician defects to the United States. Living in New York, he cannot believe the availability of goods and finds that he cannot break away from previous Soviet habits. In one memorable scene, he buys packages and packages of toilet paper. Why? Using the concepts from this chapter, explain why hoarding ocurrs under price controls and why it is wasteful.

> Shortages in the Soviet Union were very common, but why were there also surpluses of some goods at some times?

special value. The manager of the radio factory wants low prices because then he can legally buy radios at the official price and use them to obtain goods that he wants. Ironically, the managers and producers of beef, purses, and televisions all want shortages of their own good even though all would benefit if the shortages of all goods were eliminated.

Blat is a Russian word but it's a worldwide phenomena. Even in the United States, where by world standards corruption is low, blat happens. During the 1973–1974 oil crisis, for example, when the Federal Energy Office controlled the allocation of oil, it quickly became obvious that the way to get more oil was to use blat. Firms began to hire former politicians and bureaucrats who used their connections to help the firms get more oil. Today, the blat economy is much larger—about half of all federal politicians who leave office for the private sector become lobbyists.

☐ Takeaway

Price ceilings have five important effects. They create:

1. Shortages
2. Reductions in product quality
3. Wasteful lines and other search costs
4. Lost gains from trade
5. A misallocation of resources

After reading this chapter, you should be able to explain all of these effects to your uncle. Also, to do well on the exam, you should be able to draw a diagram showing a price ceiling and correctly labeling the shortage. On the same diagram, can you locate the wasteful losses from waiting in line and the lost gains from trade? Review Figure 6.3 if you are having trouble with these questions. You should also understand why a price ceiling reduces product quality and how price ceilings misallocate resources, not just in the market with the price ceiling but potentially throughout the economy.

In Chapter 5, we explained that prices send signals both to buyers and to sellers—signals that communicate information about the relative scarcity of goods and services, signals that coordinate and harmonize the economic plans of the millions of prospective buyers and sellers in the economy. In the present chapter we have explained that impeding those signals by imposing price controls can have serious negative consequences. More often than not, price ceilings are supported by those who are ignorant of these consequences. Prices have important things to tell us, but if we turn a deaf ear to them, we do so at our own peril.

☐ CHAPTER REVIEW

KEY CONCEPTS

Price ceiling, p. 98

Deadweight loss, p. 101

Rent control, p. 106

FACTS AND TOOLS

1. How does a free market eliminate a shortage?

2. When a price ceiling is in place keeping the price below the market price, what's larger: quantity demanded or quantity supplied? How does this explain the long lines and wasteful searches we see in price-controlled markets?

3. Suppose that the quantity demanded and quantity supplied in the market for milk is as follows:

Price per gallon	Quantity Demanded	Quantity Supplied
$5	1000	5000
$4	2000	4500
$3	3500	3500
$2	4100	2000
$1	6000	1000

   a. What is the equilibrium price and quantity of milk?

   b. If the government places a price ceiling of $2 on milk, will there be a shortage or surplus of milk? How large will it be? How many gallons of milk will be sold?

4. If a government decides to make health insurance affordable by requiring all health insurance companies to cut their prices by 30 percent, what will probably happen to the number of people covered by health insurance?

5. The Canadian government has wage controls for medical doctors. To keep things simple, let's assume that they set one wage for all doctors: $100,000 per year. It takes about 6 years to become a general practitioner or a pediatrician, but it takes about 8 or 9 years to become a specialist like a gynecologist, surgeon, or ophthalmologist. What kind of doctor would

you want to become under this system? (Note: the actual Canadian system does allow specialists to earn a bit more than general practitioners, but the difference isn't big enough to matter.)

6. Between 2000 and 2008, the price of oil increased from $30 per barrel to $140 per barrel, and the price of gasoline in the United States rose from about $1.50 per gallon to over $4.00 per gallon. Unlike in the 1970s when oil prices spiked, there were no long lines outside gas stations. Why?

7. Price controls distribute resources in many unintended ways. In the following cases, who will probably spend more time waiting in line to get scarce, price-controlled goods? Choose one from each pair:

   a. Working people or retired people?

   b. Lawyers who charge $800 per hour or fast-food employees who earn $8 per hour?

   c. People with desk jobs or people who can disappear for a couple of hours during the day?

8. In the chapter, we discussed how price ceilings can put goods in the wrong *place,* as when too little heating oil wound up in New Jersey during a harsh winter in the 1970s. Price controls can also put goods in the wrong *time* as well. If there are price controls on gasoline, can you think of some time periods during which the shortage will get worse? Here's a hint: Gas prices typically rise during the busy Memorial Day and Labor Day weekends.

9. a. Consider Figure 6.8. In a price-controlled market like this one, when will consumer surplus be larger: in the short run or in the long run?

   b. In this market, supply is more elastic, more flexible, in the long run. In other words, in the longer term, landlords and homebuilders can find something else to do for a living. In light of this and in light of the geometry of producer surplus in this figure, do rent controls hurt landlords and homebuilders more in the short run or in the long run?

10. Business leaders often say that there is a "shortage" of skilled workers, and so they argue that immigrants need to be brought in to do these jobs. For example, a recent AP article was entitled "New York farmers fear a shortage of skilled workers," and went on to point out that a

special U.S. visa program, the H–2A program, "allows employers to hire foreign workers temporarily if they show that they were not able to find U.S. workers for the jobs."

(*Source:* Thompson, Carolyn. 2008. "N.Y. farmers fear a shortage of skilled workers" *Associated Press,* May 13.)

a. How do unregulated markets cure a "labor shortage" when there are no immigrants to boost the labor supply?

b. Why are businesses reluctant to let unregulated markets cure the shortage?

11. a. If the government forced all bread manufacturers to sell their products at a "fair price" that was half the current, free-market price, what would happen to the quantity supplied of bread?

b. To keep it simple, assume that people must wait in line to get bread at the controlled price. Would consumer surplus rise, fall, or can't you tell with the information given?

c. With these price controls on bread, would you expect bread *quality* to rise or fall?

THINKING AND PROBLEM SOLVING

1. In rich countries, governments almost always set the fares for taxi rides. The prices for taxi rides are the same in safe neighborhoods and in dangerous neighborhoods. Where is it easier to find a cab? Why? If these taxi price controls were ended, what would probably happen to the price and quantity of cab rides in dangerous neighborhoods?

2. When the United States had price controls on oil and gasoline, some parts of the United States had a lot of heating oil while other states had long lines. As in the chapter, let's assume that winter oil demand is higher in New Jersey than in California. If there had been *no* price controls, what would have happened to the prices of heating oil in New Jersey and in California and how would "greedy businesspeople" have responded to these price differences?

3. On January 31, 1990, the first McDonald's opened in Moscow, capital of the then-Soviet Union. Economists often described the Soviet Union as a "permanent shortage economy," where the government kept prices permanently low in order to appear "fair."

"An American journalist on the scene reported the customers seemed most amazed at the 'simple sight of polite shop workers . . . in this nation of commercial boorishness.'"

(*Source:* http://www.history.com/this-day-in-history.do?action=Article&id=2563)

a. Why were most Soviet shop workers "boorish" when the McDonald's workers in Moscow were "polite"?

b. What does your answer to the previous question tell you about the power of economic incentives to change human behavior? In other words, how entrenched is "culture"?

McDonald's in Moscow: The First Day

4. Let's count the value of lost gains from trade in a regulated market. The government decides it wants to make basic bicycles more affordable, so it passes a law requiring that all one-speed bicycles sell for $30, well below the market price. Use the data below to calculate the lost gains from trade, just as in Figure 6.3. Supply and demand are straight lines.

a. What is the total value of wasted time in the price-controlled market?

b. What is the value of the *sum* of lost consumer surplus and lost producer surplus?

c. Note that we haven't given you the original market price of simple bicycles—why don't you need to know it? (Hint: The answer is a mix of geometry and economics.)

5. During a crisis such as Hurricane Katrina, governments often make it illegal to raise the price of emergency items like flashlights and bottled water. In practice, this means that these items get sold on a first-come, first-served basis.

a. If a person has a flashlight that she values at $5, but its price on the black market is $40, what gains from trade are lost if the government shuts down the black market?

b. Why might a person want to sell a flashlight for $40 during an emergency?

c. Why might a person be willing to pay $40 for a flashlight during an emergency?

d. When will entrepreneurs be more likely to fill up their pickup trucks with flashlights and drive into a disaster area: When they can sell their flashlights for $5 each or when they can sell them for $40 each?

6. A "black market" is a place where people make illegal trades in goods and services. For instance, during the Soviet era, it was common for American tourists to take a few extra pairs of Levi's jeans when visiting the Soviet Union: They would sell the extra pairs at high prices on the illegal black market.

Consider the following claim: "Price-controlled markets tend to create black markets." Let's illustrate with the figure below. If there is a price ceiling in the market for

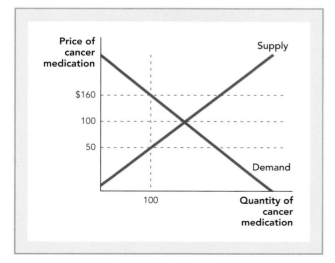

cancer medication of $50 per pill, what is the *widest* price range within which you can *definitely* find both a buyer and a seller who would be willing to illegally exchange a pill for money? (There is only one correct answer.)

7. So, knowing what you know now about price controls, are you in favor of setting a $2 per gallon price ceiling on gasoline? Create a pro-price control and an anti-price control answer.

8. a. As we noted, Assar Lindbeck once said, "Short of aerial bombardment, the best way to destroy a city is through rent control." What do you think Lindbeck might mean by this?

b. How does paying "key money" to a landlord reduce the severity of Lindbeck's "bombardment?"

9. In the town of Freedonia, the government declares that all street parking must be free: There can be no parking meters. In an almost identical town of Meterville, parking costs $5 per hour (or $1.25 per 15 minutes).

a. Where will it be easier to find parking: In Freedonia or Meterville?

b. One town will tend to attract shoppers who hate driving around looking for parking. Which one?

c. Why will the town from part b also attract shoppers with higher incomes?

10. In the late 1990s, the town of Santa Monica, California, made it illegal for banks to charge people ATM fees. As you probably know, it's almost always free to use your own bank's ATMs, but there's usually a fee charged when you use another bank's ATM. (*Source:* "The War on ATM Fees," *Time,* November 29, 1999.) As soon as Santa Monica passed this law, Bank of America stopped allowing customers from other banks to use their ATMs: In bank jargon, B of A banned "out-of-network" ATM usage.

In fact, this ban only lasted for a few days, after which a judge allowed banks to continue to charge fees while awaiting a full court hearing on the issue. Eventually, the court declared the fee ban illegal under federal law. But let's imagine the effect of a full ban on out-of-network fees.

a. In the figure below, indicate the new price per out-of-network ATM transaction after the fee ban. Also clearly indicate the amount of the shortage.

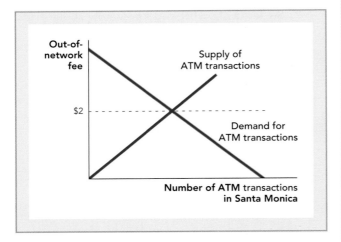

b. Calculate the exact amount of producer and consumer surplus in the out-of-network ATM market in Santa Monica after the ban. How large is producer surplus? How large is consumer surplus?

11. Consider Figure 6.9. Your classmate looks at that chart and says, "Apartment construction slowed down years before rent control was passed, and after rent control was passed, more apartments were built. Rent control didn't cut the number of new apartments, it raised it. This proves that rent control works." What is wrong with this argument?

12. Rent control creates a shortage of housing, which makes it hard to find a place to live. In a price-controlled market, people have to waste a lot of time trying to find these scarce, artificially cheap products. Yet Congressman Charles B. Rangel, the chairman of the powerful House Ways and Means Committee, lived in *four* rent-stabilized apartments in Harlem. Why are powerful individuals often able to "find" price-controlled goods much more often than the nonpowerful? What does this tell us about the political side effects of price controls? (*Source:* "Republicans Question Rangel's Tax Break Support," *The New York Times*, November 25, 2008.)

CHALLENGES

1. If a government decided to impose price controls on gasoline, what could it do to avoid the time wasted waiting in lines? There is surely more than one solution to this problem.

BETTMANN/CORBIS

2. In New York City, some apartments are under strict rent control, while others are not. This is a theme in many novels and movies about New York, including *Bonfire of the Vanities* and *When Harry Met Sally*. One predictable side effect of rent control is the creation of a black market. Let's think about whether it's a good idea to allow this black market to exist.

a. Harry is lucky enough to get a rent-controlled apartment for $300 per month. The market rent on such an apartment is $3,000 per month. Harry himself values the apartment at $2,000 per month, and he'd be quite happy with a regular, $2,000 per month New York apartment. If he stays in the apartment, how much consumer surplus does he enjoy?

b. If he illegally subleases his apartment to Sally on the black market for $2,500 per month and instead rents a $2,000 apartment, is he better off or worse off than if he obeyed the law?

3. Suppose that the market for coats can be described as follows:

Price	Quantity Demanded (millions)	Quantity Supplied (millions)
$120	16	20
$100	18	18
$80	20	16
$60	22	14

a. What are the equilibrium price and quantity of coats?

b. Suppose the government sets a price ceiling of $80. Will there be a shortage, and if so, how large will it be?

c. Given that the government sets a price ceiling of $80, how much will demanders be willing to pay per unit of the good (i.e., what is the true price)? Suppose that people line up to get this good and that they value their time at $10 an hour. For how long will people wait in line to obtain a coat?

4. Let's measure consumer surplus if the government imposes price controls and goods ended up being randomly allocated among those consumers willing to pay the controlled price. If the demand and supply curves are as in the figure below, then

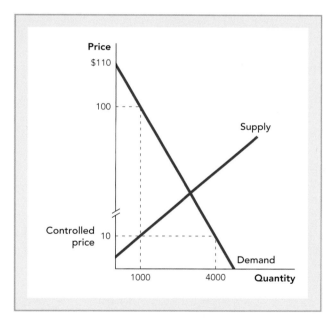

a. What is consumer surplus under the price control?

b. What would consumer surplus be if the quantity supplied were 1,000 but there were no price control?

5. Antibiotics are often given to people with colds (even though they are not useful for that purpose), but they are also used to treat life-threatening infections. If there were a price control on antibiotics, what do you think would happen to the allocation of antibiotics across these two uses?

6. In a command economy, such as the old Soviet Union, there were no prices for almost all goods. Instead, goods were allocated by a "central planner." Suppose that a good like oil becomes more scarce. What problems would a central planner face in reallocating oil to maximize consumer plus producer surplus?

7

Price Floors, Taxes, and Subsidies

CHAPTER OUTLINE

Price Floors

Commodity Taxes

Subsidies

Takeaway

When governments control prices, it is usually with a price ceiling designed to keep prices below market levels, but occasionally the government intervenes to keep prices above market levels. Can you think of an example? Here's a hint. Buyers usually outnumber sellers, so it's probably no accident that governments intervene to keep prices below market levels more often than they intervene to keep prices above market levels. The most common example of a price being controlled above market levels is the exception that proves the rule because it involves a good for which sellers outnumber buyers. Here's another hint. You own this good.

The good is labor and the most common example of a price controlled above the market level is the minimum wage.

In this chapter, we start by examining price floors, such as the minimum wage, and then turn to taxes and subsidies. All of these topics can be analyzed using supply and demand so this chapter and the previous one will give you a good introduction to these tools. The topics are also related: one of the goals of a minimum wage is to raise the wages of low-income workers. But some economists believe that the minimum wage is not very effective at increasing low-wage incomes and in some respects may be counterproductive. An alternative approach is to raise the wages of low-income workers using wage subsidies. Thus, we conclude this chapter with a comparison of minimum wages and wage subsidies.

Price Floors

When the minimum price that can be legally charged is above the market price, we say that there is a **price floor.** Economists call it a price floor

A **price floor** is a minimum price allowed by law.

119

because prices cannot legally go below the floor. Price floors create four important effects:

1. Surpluses

2. Lost gains from trade (deadweight loss)

3. Wasteful increases in quality

4. A misallocation of resources

Surpluses

Figure 7.1 graphs the demand and supply of labor and shows how a price held above the market price creates a surplus, a situation where the quantity of labor supplied exceeds the quantity demanded. We have a special word for a surplus of labor: unemployment.

The idea that a minimum wage creates unemployment should not be surprising. If the minimum wage did not create unemployment, the solution to poverty would be easy—raise minimum wages to $10, $20, or even $100 an hour! But at a high enough wage, none of us would be worth employing.

Can a more moderate minimum wage also create unemployment? Yes. A minimum wage of $5.85 an hour, the federal minimum in 2007, won't affect most workers who, because of their productivity, already earn more than $5.85 an hour. In the United States, for example, about 97 percent of all workers paid by the hour already earn more than the minimum wage. A minimum wage, however, will decrease employment among low-skilled workers. The more employers have to pay for low-skilled workers, the fewer low-skilled workers they will hire.

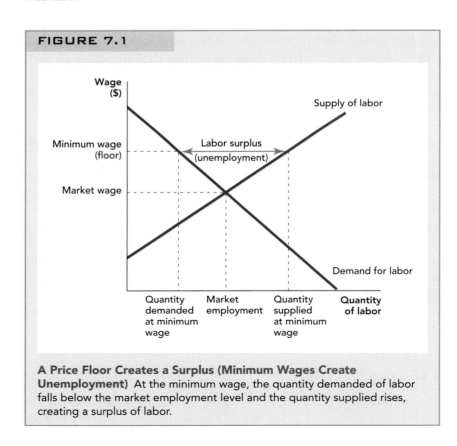

FIGURE 7.1

A Price Floor Creates a Surplus (Minimum Wages Create Unemployment) At the minimum wage, the quantity demanded of labor falls below the market employment level and the quantity supplied rises, creating a surplus of labor.

Young people, for example, often lack substantial skills and are more likely to be made unemployed by the minimum wage. About a quarter of all workers earning the minimum wage are teenagers (ages 16–19) and more than half are less than 25 years of age.[1] Studies of the minimum wage verify that the unemployment effect is concentrated among teenagers.[2]

In addition to creating surpluses, a price floor, just like a price ceiling, reduces the gains from trade.

Lost Gains from Trade

Notice in Figure 7.2 that at the minimum wage employers are willing to hire Q_d workers. Employers would hire more workers if they could offer lower wages and, importantly, workers would be willing to work at lower wages if they were allowed to do so. If employers and workers could bargain freely, the wage would fall and the quantity of labor traded would increase to the level of market employment. Notice that at the market employment level, the gains from trade increase by the green and blue triangles. The green triangle is the increase in consumer surplus (remember that in this example it is the employers who are the consumers of labor) and the blue triangle is the increase in producer (worker) surplus.

Although the minimum wage creates some unemployment and reduces the gains from trade, the influence of the minimum wage in the American economy

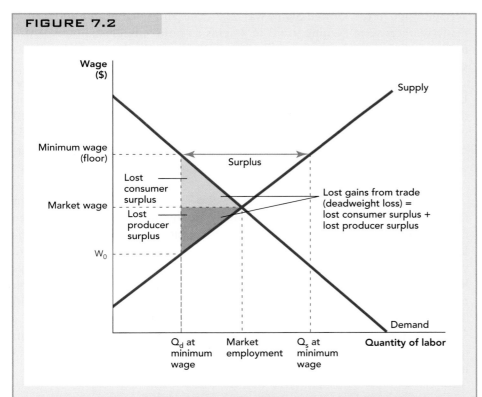

FIGURE 7.2

A Price Floor Reduces the Gains from Trade At the minimum wage, employers are willing to hire more workers at just less than the minimum wage and workers are willing to work additional hours for just more than W_0. Although mutually profitable, these trades are illegal. If all mutually profitable trades were legal, the gains from trade would increase by the green plus blue triangles.

is very small. Even for the young, the minimum wage is not very important because although most workers earning the minimum wage are young, most young workers earn more than the minimum wage. As we noted above, a majority of workers earning the minimum wage are younger than 25 years old but 93.9 percent of workers younger than 25 earn more than the minimum wage.[3]

These facts may surprise you. The minimum wage is hotly debated in the United States. Democrats often argue that the minimum wage must be raised to help working families. Republicans respond that a higher minimum wage will create unemployment and raise prices as firms pass on higher costs to customers. Neither position is realistic. At best, the minimum wage will raise the wages of some teenagers and young workers whose wages would increase anyway as they improve their education and become more skilled. At worst, the minimum wage will raise the price of a hamburger and create unemployment among teenagers, many of whom will simply choose to stay in school longer (not necessarily a bad thing). The minimum wage debate is more about rhetoric than reality.

Even though small increases in the U.S. minimum wage won't change much, large increases would cause serious unemployment. A large increase in the minimum wage is unlikely in the United States, but it has happened elsewhere. In 1938, Puerto Rico was surprised to discover that it was bound by a minimum wage set well above the Puerto Rican average wage for unskilled labor.

Puerto Rico has a peculiar political status; it's an unincorporated U.S. territory classified as a commonwealth. In 1938, Congress passed the Fair Labor Standards Act, which set the first U.S. minimum wage at 25 cents an hour. At the time, the average wage in the United States was 62.7 cents an hour, but in Puerto Rico many workers were earning just 3 to 4 cents an hour. Congress, however, had forgotten to create an exemption for Puerto Rico so what was a modest minimum wage in the United States was a huge increase in wages in Puerto Rico.

Puerto Rican workers, however, did not benefit from the minimum wage. Unable to pay the higher wage, Puerto Rican firms went bankrupt, creating devastating unemployment. In a panic, representatives of Puerto Rico pleaded with the U.S. Congress to create an exemption for Puerto Rico. "The medicine is too strong for the patient," said Puerto Rican Labor Commissioner Prudencio Rivera Martinez. Two years later Congress finally did establish lower rates for Puerto Rico.[4]

Minimum wages in other countries are also sometimes considerably higher than in the United States. France combines a high minimum wage—nearly twice as high relative to the median wage than in the United States—with labor regulations that make it difficult to fire workers. As a result, firms are reluctant to hire young workers both because they are less productive than older workers, and thus less employable at a high minimum wage, and because hiring someone that you can't fire is more risky when the person doesn't have a history of employment. In 2005, 23 percent of French workers under 25 years old were unemployed.

To explain the other important effects of price floors—wasteful increases in quality and a misallocation of resources—we turn from minimum wages to airline regulation.

Wasteful Increases in Quality

Many years ago, flying on an airplane was extremely pleasurable; seats were wide, service was attentive, flights weren't packed, and the food was good.

So airplane travel in the United States must have gotten worse, right? No, it has gotten better. Let's explain.

The Civil Aeronautics Board (CAB) extensively regulated airlines in the United States from 1938 to 1978. No firm could enter or exit the market, change prices, or alter routes without permission from the CAB. The CAB kept prices well above market levels, sometimes even denying requests by firms to lower prices!

We know that prices were kept above market levels because the CAB only had the right to control airlines operating *between* states. In-state airlines were largely unregulated. Using data from large states like Texas and California, it was possible to compare prices on unregulated flights to prices on regulated flights of the same distance. Prices on flights between San Francisco and Los Angeles, for example, were half the price of similar length flights between Boston and Washington, D.C.

In Figure 7.3, firms are earning the CAB-regulated fare on flights that they would be willing to sell at the much lower price labeled "Willingness to sell." Initially, therefore, regulation was a great deal for the airlines, who took home the red area as producer surplus.

A price floor means that prices are held *above* market levels, so firms want more customers. The price floor, however, makes it illegal to compete for more

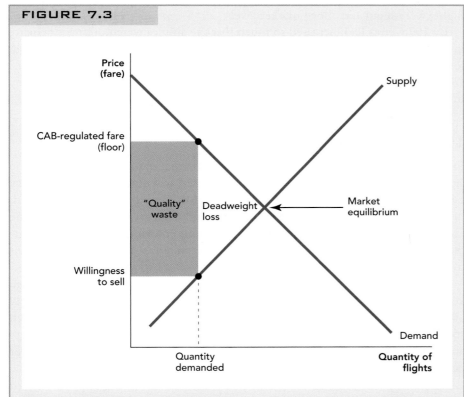

FIGURE 7.3

A Price Floor Creates Quality Waste At the CAB-regulated fare, price is well above a seller's willingness to sell. Sellers cannot compete by offering lower prices so they compete by offering higher quality. Higher quality raises costs and reduces seller profit. Buyers enjoy the higher quality but would prefer less quality at a lower price. Thus, the price floor encourages sellers to waste resources by producing more quality than buyers are willing to pay for.

customers by lowering prices. So how do firms compete when they cannot lower prices? Price floors cause firms to compete by offering customers higher quality.

When airlines were regulated, for example, they competed by offering their customers bone china, fancy meals, wide seats, and frequent flights. Sounds good, right? Yes, but don't forget that the increase in quality came at a price. Would you rather have a fine meal on your flight to Paris or a modest meal and more money to spend at a real Parisian restaurant?

If consumers were willing to pay for fine meals on an airplane, airlines would offer that service. But if you have flown recently, you know that consumers would rather have a lower price. An increase in quality that consumers are not willing to pay for is a wasteful increase in quality. Thus, as firms competed by offering higher quality, the initial producer surplus was wasted away in frills that consumers liked but would not be willing to pay for—hence, the red area in Figure 7.3 is labeled "Quality" waste.

Airline costs increased over time for another reason. The producer surplus initially earned by the airlines was a tempting target for unions who threatened to strike unless they got their share of the proceeds. The airlines didn't put up too much of a fight because, when their costs rose, they could apply to the CAB for an increase in fares, thus passing along the higher costs to consumers. Many of the problems that older airlines have faced in recent times are due to generous pension and health benefits, which were granted when prices of flights were regulated above market levels.

By 1978, costs had increased so much that the airlines were no longer benefiting from regulation and were willing to accede to deregulation.[5] Deregulation lowered prices, increased quantity, and reduced wasteful quality competition.[6] Deregulation also reduced waste and increased efficiency in another way—by improving the allocation of resources.

The Misallocation of Resources

Regulation of airline fares could not have been maintained for 40 years if the CAB had not also regulated entry. Firms wanted to enter the airline industry because the CAB kept prices high, but the CAB knew that if entry occurred, prices would be pushed down. So under the influence of the older airlines, the CAB routinely prevented new competitors from entering. In 1938, for example, there were 16 major airlines; by 1974 there were just 10 despite 79 requests to enter the industry.

Restrictions on entry misallocated resources because low-cost airlines were kept out of the industry. Southwest Airlines, for example, began as a Texas-only airline because it could not get a license from the CAB to operate between states. (Lawsuits from competitors also nearly prevented Southwest from operating in Texas.) Southwest was able to enter the national market only after deregulation in 1978.

The entry of Southwest was not just a case of increasing supply. One of the virtues of the market process is that it is open to new ideas, innovations, and experiments. Southwest, for example, pioneered consistent use of the same aircraft to lower maintenance costs, greater use of smaller airports like Chicago's Midway, and long-term hedging of fuel costs. Southwest's innovations have made it one of the most profitable and largest airlines in the United States. Southwest's innovations have spread in turn to other firms

MUSEUM OF FLIGHT/CORBIS

Despite being more efficient than its rivals, airline regulation prevented Southwest from entering the national market until deregulation in 1978. Today, Southwest Airlines is one of the largest airlines in the world.

UNDERSTAND YOUR world

such as JetBlue Airways, easyJet (Europe), and WestJet (Canada). Regulation of entry didn't just increase prices, it increased costs and reduced innovation. Deregulation improved the allocation of resources by allowing low-cost, innovative firms to expand nationally. Deregulation is the major reason why, today, flying is an ordinary event for most American families, rather than the province of the wealthy.

Commodity Taxes

Commodity taxes are taxes on goods. Well-known commodity taxes include those on fuel, liquor, and cigarettes, although in the United States most commodities are taxed in one way or another. We will emphasize the following truths about commodity taxation.

1. Who ultimately pays the tax does *not* depend on who writes the check to the government.

2. Who ultimately pays the tax *does* depend on the relative elasticities of demand and supply.

3. Commodity taxation raises revenue and creates lost gains from trade (deadweight loss).

Who Ultimately Pays the Tax Does Not Depend on Who Writes the Check

Imagine that the government is considering a tax on apples. The government can collect the tax in either of two different ways (assume that each method is equally costly to implement). The government can tax apple sellers $1 for every basket supplied or they can tax apple buyers $1 for every basket of apples bought. Which tax scheme is better for apple buyers?

Surprisingly, the answer is that the tax has exactly the same effects whether it is "paid" for by sellers or "paid" for by buyers. It is one of the great insights of economics that who ultimately pays a tax is determined not by the laws of Congress but by the laws of supply and demand.

Let's consider the effect of a $1 tax on apple sellers, which we analyze beginning with the left panel of Figure 7.4 on the next page. As we discussed in Chapter 2, as far as sellers are concerned, a tax is the same as an increase in costs. Thus, if with no tax sellers require a minimum of $1 per basket to sell 250 baskets of apples, then with a $1 tax they will require $2 per basket to sell the same quantity—$1 for their regular costs and $1 for their tax cost. Similarly, if with no tax sellers require a minimum of $3 per basket to sell 1,250 baskets, then with a $1 tax they will require $4 per basket. Following through on this logic, we see that a $1 tax shifts the supply curve up at every quantity by exactly $1.

The right panel of Figure 7.4 adds a demand curve to show the effect of the tax on the market for apples. With no tax, the equilibrium is at point *a* with a price of $2 per basket and a quantity of 700. If apple sellers must pay a $1 tax for every basket supplied, the supply curve shifts up by $1 and the new equilibrium is at point *b* with a higher price of $2.65 and a smaller quantity consumed of 500.

Students are sometimes surprised that a $1 tax does not necessarily raise the price by $1. To see why, imagine that the price did rise by $1. In that case, the price would rise to $3 at point *c*. But is point *c* an equilibrium?

CHECK YOURSELF

> The European Union guarantees its farmers that the price of butter will stay above a floor, the floor price is often above the market equilibrium price. What do you think has been the result of this?

> The United States has set a price floor for milk above the equilibrium price. Has this led to shortages or surpluses? How do you think the U.S. government has dealt with this? (Hint: remember the cartons of milk you had in elementary school and high school? What was their price?)

FIGURE 7.4

Panel A

Panel B

A Tax on Apple Sellers
Panel A: A $1 tax on apple sellers shifts the supply curve up by $1.
Panel B: A $1 tax on apple sellers shifts the supply curve up by $1, changing the equilibrium from point *a* to point *b*.

No. Point *c* is not an equilibrium because at point *c*, the quantity supplied is greater than the quantity demanded. In other words, apple sellers in this market find that if they try to pass all of the tax onto apple buyers by raising the price to $3 per basket, there are not enough buyers to purchase 700 baskets, so sellers have excess supply. What incentives does this create? As they compete to obtain buyers, sellers must bid the price down. As the price falls, sellers supply fewer apples until the new equilibrium is reached at point *b*.

With the tax, buyers pay $2.65 per basket and sellers receive $1.65 per basket ($2.65 minus the $1 tax they must send to the government). Notice that the difference between the price that buyers pay and the price that sellers receive is equal to the tax. In fact, so long as the tax doesn't drive the industry out of existence, it will always be the case that:

The tax = Price paid by buyers − Price received by sellers

What happens if instead of taxing sellers, the government taxes buyers? We illustrate beginning with the left panel of Figure 7.5. Imagine that before the tax buyers were willing to pay up to $4 per basket to purchase 100 baskets. If buyers must pay a $1 tax *on top of the price,* what is the most that they will now be willing to pay? Correct, $3. That is, if the buyers value the apples at $4 per basket but they must pay a tax of $1 to the government, then the most the buyers will be willing to pay the apple suppliers is $3 per basket (since the total price including the tax will now be $4). Similarly, if before the tax buyers were willing to pay up to $2 per basket to purchase 700 baskets, then after the $1 tax they will be willing to pay to the sellers at most $1 per basket for the same quantity. Following through on this logic, we see that a tax of $1 on buyers shifts the demand curve down at every quantity by $1.

FIGURE 7.5

A Tax on Apple Buyers
Panel A: A $1 tax on apple buyers shifts the demand curve down by $1.
Panel B: A $1 tax on apple buyers shifts the demand curve down by $1, changing the equilibrium from point *a* to point *d*.

The right panel shows the market for apples. With no tax, the equilibrium is at point *a* with a price of $2 and a quantity of 700. With the $1 tax on apple buyers, the demand curve shifts down by $1 and the new equilibrium is at point *d* with a price of $1.65 and a quantity of 500.

Notice that with the tax apple buyers pay a total price of $2.65 ($1.65 in market price plus $1 tax) and apple sellers receive $1.65. In other words, the price buyers pay, the price sellers receive, and the quantity traded (500 baskets) are identical to what they were when the tax was placed on apple sellers.

We can see what is going on by also showing in panel B of Figure 7.5 a dotted supply curve, the supply curve *if* there were a $1 tax on sellers (exactly as in Figure 7.4). If the $1 tax is placed on sellers, the equilibrium is at point *b*. If the tax is placed on buyers, the equilibrium is at point *d*. The only difference between points *b* and *d* is that when the tax is placed on suppliers, the market price ($2.65) *includes* the tax, but when the tax is placed on buyers, the market price ($1.65) does not include the tax. The tax must be paid, however, so in either case the final price paid by buyers is $2.65 and the final price received by sellers is $1.65.

We have just shown something quite surprising. Who pays a tax does not depend on who must send the check to the government. Don't be fooled; a tax on apple sellers has exactly the same effects as a tax on apple buyers.

Who pays the tax does not depend on who gets hit by the tax first.

Who Ultimately Pays the Tax Depends on the Relative Elasticities of Supply and Demand

We have just seen that whether the $1 apple tax is placed on buyers or sellers, the price to buyers ends up being $2.65 and the price received by sellers ends up being $1.65. But why is it that with the tax, buyers pay 65 cents more ($2.65 − $2) while sellers receive 35 cents less ($2 − $1.65)? What determines how the burden of the tax is shared between buyers and sellers? To answer this question, we introduce the *wedge shortcut.*

The Wedge Shortcut The most important effect of a tax is to drive a wedge between the price paid by buyers and the price received by sellers. Recall that:

$$\text{The tax} = \text{Price paid by buyers} - \text{Price received by sellers}$$

If we focus on the wedge aspect of a tax, we can simplify our tax analysis. In Figure 7.6, instead of shifting curves, we start with a tax of $1 and we "push" this vertical "tax wedge" into the diagram until the top of the wedge just touches the demand curve and the bottom of the wedge just touches the supply curve. The top of the wedge at point *b* gives us the price paid by the buyers ($2.65), the bottom of the wedge at point *d* gives us the price received by sellers ($1.65), and the quantity at which the wedge "sticks" is 500 baskets, exactly as before.

Using the wedge shortcut, we show that whether buyers or sellers pay a tax is determined by the relative elasticities of demand and supply. Recall from Chapter 4 that the elasticity of demand measures how responsive the quantity demanded is to a change in price and the elasticity of supply measures how responsive the quantity supplied is to a change in price. We show that *when demand is more elastic than supply, demanders pay less of the tax than sellers. When supply is more elastic than demand, suppliers pay less of the tax than buyers.*

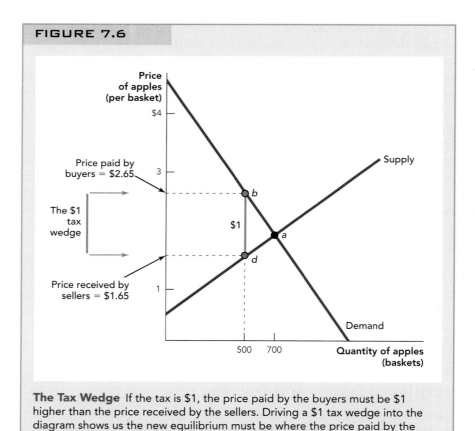

FIGURE 7.6

The Tax Wedge If the tax is $1, the price paid by the buyers must be $1 higher than the price received by the sellers. Driving a $1 tax wedge into the diagram shows us the new equilibrium must be where the price paid by the buyers is $2.65, the price received by the sellers is $1.65, and the quantity traded is 500.

FIGURE 7.7

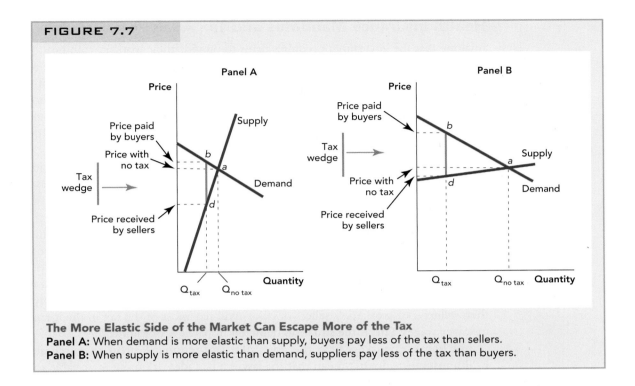

The More Elastic Side of the Market Can Escape More of the Tax
Panel A: When demand is more elastic than supply, buyers pay less of the tax than sellers.
Panel B: When supply is more elastic than demand, suppliers pay less of the tax than buyers.

In the left panel of Figure 7.7, we draw a demand curve that is more elastic than the supply curve. So who will pay most of the tax? Sellers. To see why sellers will pay most of the tax, push the tax wedge into the diagram. Notice that at the quantity that the tax wedge sticks, the price paid by buyers is only a small amount above the price with no tax. The price received by sellers, however, falls well below the price with no tax. Thus, when demand is more elastic than supply, buyers pay less of the tax than sellers.

In the right panel of Figure 7.7, we draw a supply curve that is more elastic than the demand curve. So who will pay most of the tax? Buyers. To see why buyers will pay most of the tax, take the tax wedge and push it into the diagram. At the point that the wedge "sticks," notice that the price paid by buyers has risen far above the price with no tax. The price received by sellers, however, has fallen only just below the price with no tax. Thus, when supply is more elastic than demand, buyers pay more of the tax.

The intuition for these results is simple. An elastic demand curve means that demanders have a lot of substitutes and you can't tax someone who has a good substitute because they will just buy the substitute! Thus, when demand is elastic, sellers will end up paying most of the tax. An elastic supply curve has a similar interpretation. It means that the workers and capital in the industry can easily find work in another industry—so if you try to tax an industry with an elastic supply curve the industry inputs will escape to other industries. Just remember, therefore, that *elasticity* = *escape*. So long as the industry is not taxed out of existence, however, someone must pay the tax so whether buyers or sellers pay most depends on who can escape the best—that is, which curve is *relatively* more elastic.

Bearing in mind our rule that the more elastic side of the market can better escape the tax, let's take a look at some taxes to see whether it is buyers or sellers who will bear the greater burden.

Health Insurance Mandates and Tax Analysis

Imagine that the government requires firms to provide their workers with health insurance. It's good to have health insurance and it's even better if someone else is paying for it. But who really pays? The law requires that firms buy health insurance for every worker hired so we can think of the law as a tax on labor. Who pays the tax? As we now know, who pays more of the tax depends on whether supply or demand is more elastic. So consider, is it easier for firms to escape the tax by not employing or for workers to escape the tax by not working?

Can firms escape the tax? Yes, in a lot of ways. If the tax on labor gets too high, firms can substitute capital (machines) for labor, they can move overseas, or they can close up shop altogether. Can workers escape the tax? It's not so easy. Most workers would continue to work even if their wages were lower because the costs of leaving the labor force are high. Thus, for most workers, the elasticity of labor supply is low (this is especially true for working-age men; men nearing retirement and married women tend to have higher elasticities of labor supply). The demand for labor, therefore, is likely to be more elastic than the supply of labor. Remember that when demand is more elastic than supply then sellers (i.e., workers = sellers of labor) will pay most of the tax in the form of lower wages. This is the situation depicted in panel A of Figure 7.7.

Just because workers bear the costs of a law requiring firms to purchase health insurance, doesn't mean that the law is a bad idea. It's quite reasonable to want everyone in society to have health insurance and requiring employers to purchase health insurance is one way, albeit not necessarily the best way, to move toward this goal. What is important is that citizens not be fooled into thinking that the law is a free lunch at the expense of their employer. Tax analysis is useful because it helps us to see the true benefits and costs of economic policy and thus to choose wisely.

Who Pays the Cigarette Tax?

States tax cigarettes at rates ranging from $2.57 per pack in New Jersey to 7 cents per pack in South Carolina. Who ultimately pays the cigarette tax? Buyers or sellers? As usual, who pays depends on the relative elasticities of demand and supply.

As you might expect, given the addictive nature of nicotine, smokers have an inelastic demand for cigarettes, around −0.5. What about suppliers? Before you answer, remember that we are analyzing *state* cigarette taxes so the relevant question is how easily can a cigarette manufacturer escape a state tax?

A manufacturer can easily escape a state tax by selling elsewhere. In fact, because it's so easy for a cigarette manufacturer to ship its product around the country, the elasticity of supply to any one state is very large, which means that buyers will bear almost all of the tax—as illustrated in panel B of Figure 7.7.

If the price paid by buyers increases by almost the amount of the tax, then the price received by sellers must be almost the same in all states regardless of the tax. To see why this makes sense, imagine what would happen if manufacturers earned less money per pack selling cigarettes in a high-tax state like New Jersey than in a low-tax state like South Carolina. If this happened, manufacturers would ship fewer cigarettes to New Jersey and more to South Carolina, and this would continue until the after-tax price was the same in both states.

We can easily test this theory. A pack of cigarettes sells for about $3.35 in South Carolina and $6.45 in New Jersey so the price to buyers is nearly twice

ENVISION/CORBIS

What a drag it is being taxed
Heavy taxes encourage smokers to smoke fewer cigarettes, but they also encourage smokers to choose cigarettes with higher nicotine levels. High cigarette taxes have also been shown to increase smoking intensity—when taxes are high, smokers inhale more deeply and they smoke down to the butt.

as high in New Jersey as in South Carolina. But the after-tax price received by sellers is about the same, $3.28 in South Carolina ($3.35 − $0.07) versus $3.88 in New Jersey ($6.45 − $2.57). (The small differences can probably be accounted for by other costs of doing business that differ between New Jersey and South Carolina.)

By the way, one argument for high cigarette taxes is that the government should discourage smoking. State taxes, however, are a bad method of discouraging smoking in the United States. A New Jersey tax will discourage smoking by residents of New Jersey but, as we have seen, to escape the NJ tax, cigarette manufacturers will ship more cigarettes to other states, which pushes cigarette prices down in those states, thereby increasing the quantity demanded. A New Jersey tax, therefore, will decrease smoking in New Jersey but this will be partially offset by increased smoking in other states. It's more difficult for cigarette manufacturers to escape federal taxes than state taxes so if the goal is to reduce national consumption, a federal tax is superior to a state tax.

A Commodity Tax Raises Revenue and Creates Lost Gains from Trade (Deadweight Loss)

A tax generates revenues for the government but also reduces the gains from trade. In the left panel of Figure 7.8, we show the apple market with no tax; the equilibrium price is $2 and the equilibrium quantity is 700. Consumer surplus

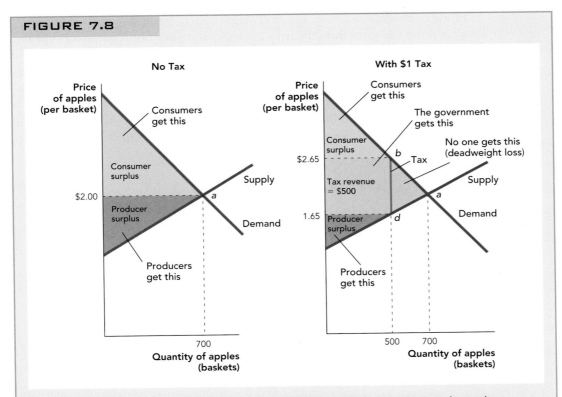

FIGURE 7.8

A Tax Generates Revenue and Creates a Deadweight Loss With no tax, producer plus consumer surplus is maximized in the left panel. With the tax, consumer surplus and producer surplus are smaller and tax revenues are larger. But tax revenues increase by less than producer and consumer surplus fall. As a result, the tax creates a net loss or deadweight loss shown by the grey area in the right panel.

is shown in green and producer surplus is shown in blue. As we emphasized in Chapter 3, in a free market trade occurs whenever the buyer's willingness to pay exceeds the supplier's willingness to sell (i.e., whenever the demand curve lies above the supply curve). A free market maximizes the gains from trade, the sum of consumer and producer surplus.

In the right panel, we show the same market with a $1 tax (this is identical to Figure 7.6 only this time we have labeled some of the areas). The tax is $1 per basket and 500 baskets are traded, so tax revenues are shown by the purple rectangle and are equal to $500 = $1 × 500.

The tax decreases consumer and producer surplus, as you can see by comparing the green and blue areas in the left and right panels. *Some* of the consumer and producer surplus is transferred to the government in the form of tax revenues, but notice that consumer and producer surplus together decrease by more than government revenue increases—the difference is the grey triangle labeled "deadweight loss."

To understand why a tax creates a deadweight loss, let's take a simple case. Imagine that you are willing to pay $50 for a bus ride to New York City when the price of a ticket is $40. Thus, you take the trip and earn $10 in consumer surplus ($50 − $40). Now suppose the government imposes a $20 tax, which increases the price of the ticket to $60. Do you take the trip? No, since the price of the ticket now exceeds your willingness to pay, you do not go to New York City. Thus, you lose $10 in consumer surplus. Does the government gain any tax revenue? No. Your loss of $10 is not compensated for by any increase in government revenue and, thus, is a deadweight loss. In short, the deadweight loss of a tax is the lost gains from the trips (trades) that do not occur because of the tax.

A key factor determining deadweight loss is the elasticities of supply and demand. Figure 7.9, for example, shows that the deadweight loss from taxation is larger the more elastic the demand curve. To understand why, remember that deadweight loss is the lost gains from trade. If the demand curve is relatively elastic, as in the left panel of Figure 7.9, then the tax deters a lot of trades, Q_{tax} is much less than $Q_{no\ tax}$, so the lost gains from trade are large. It's

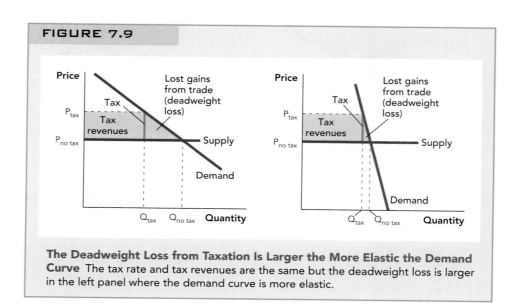

FIGURE 7.9

The Deadweight Loss from Taxation Is Larger the More Elastic the Demand Curve The tax rate and tax revenues are the same but the deadweight loss is larger in the left panel where the demand curve is more elastic.

just like the bus story—if the demand curve is elastic, then the tax means many lost bus trips.

If the demand is relatively inelastic, however, as in the right panel of Figure 7.9, then the tax does not deter many trades. Notice that Q_{tax} is only slightly smaller than $Q_{no\ tax}$. Since nearly the same number of trades occur, there are few lost gains from trade. Again, let's go back to the bus. Imagine that you were willing to pay $100 to go to New York. In that case, if the government taxes you $20, you still take the trip. True, your consumer surplus falls by $20, but the government's revenues increased by $20—since the trip was not deterred, there is no deadweight loss in this case.

The same intuition also explains why the deadweight loss from taxation (holding tax revenue constant) is lower the less elastic the supply curve. If the supply curve is elastic, then the tax deters many trades, but if the supply curve is inelastic, there is little deterrence and, thus, few lost gains from trade.

Even though taxes create a deadweight loss, they also pay for beneficial goods and services. In Chapter 17, we discuss in more detail when the goods that taxation provides are likely to have benefits that exceed the deadweight loss caused by taxation.

Subsidies

A subsidy is a reverse tax: instead of taking money away from consumers (or producers), the government gives money to consumers (or producers). The close connection between subsidies and taxes means that their effects are analogous. We emphasize the following facts about commodity subsidies.

1. Who gets the subsidy does *not* depend on who gets the check from the government.

2. Who benefits from a subsidy *does* depend on the relative elasticities of demand and supply.

3. Subsidies must be paid for by taxpayers and they create inefficient *increases* in trade (deadweight loss).

With a tax, the price paid by the buyers exceeds the price received by sellers. A subsidy reverses this relationship so the price *received* by sellers exceeds the price *paid* by buyers, the difference being the amount of the subsidy. In other words:

The subsidy = Price received by sellers − Price paid by buyers

We can analyze subsidies using the same wedge shortcut as before, except now we push the wedge from the right side of the diagram toward the left side. In Figure 7.10 on the next page, we show that with a $1 subsidy, sellers of apples will receive $2.40 per basket, but buyers will pay only $1.40, the difference of $1 being the subsidy amount.

A subsidy means that the sellers are receiving more than buyers are paying, so who is making up the difference? Taxpayers. The cost to taxpayers is the amount of the subsidy times the number of units subsidized. In Figure 7.10, this is $1 × 900 or $900.

Just like a tax, a subsidy also creates a deadweight loss. A tax creates a deadweight loss because with the tax some beneficial trades fail to occur. A subsidy

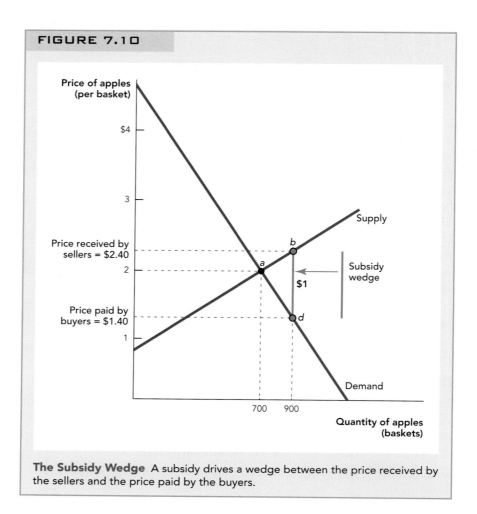

FIGURE 7.10

Price of apples
(per basket)

$4

3

Supply

Price received by
sellers = $2.40

b

a

2

Subsidy
wedge

$1

Price paid by
buyers = $1.40

d

1

Demand

700   900

Quantity of apples
(baskets)

The Subsidy Wedge A subsidy drives a wedge between the price received by
the sellers and the price paid by the buyers.

creates a deadweight loss for the reverse reason: with the subsidy, some nonbeneficial trades do occur. In Figure 7.10, notice that for the baskets between 700 and 900 the supply curve lies above the demand curve (i.e., line segment *ab* lies above line segment *ad*). The height of the supply curve tells us the cost of producing these baskets. The height of the demand curve tells us the value of these baskets to buyers. Producing baskets for which the cost exceeds the value creates waste, a deadweight loss measured by the triangle *abd*. In other words, the resources used to produce those extra baskets have an opportunity cost, and they could produce more value in some other part of the economy.

As with taxes, the wedge analysis shows that it doesn't make a difference whether buyers are subsidized $1 for every unit bought or sellers are subsidized $1 for every unit sold.

Similarly, we showed that who bears the burden of a tax depends on the relative elasticities of supply and demand. Exactly the same forces determine who gets the benefit of a subsidy. The rule is simple: *Whoever bears the burden of a tax receives the benefit of a subsidy.* Figure 7.11 illustrates the intuition for the case where the elasticity of supply is less than the elasticity of demand. In this case, suppliers bear the burden of the tax but receive the benefit of a subsidy.

Let's analyze two examples of subsidies in action.

FIGURE 7.11

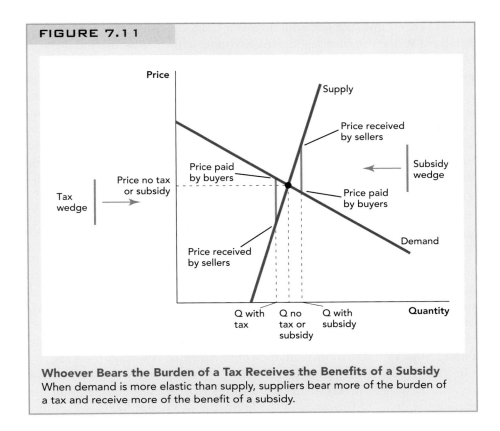

Whoever Bears the Burden of a Tax Receives the Benefits of a Subsidy
When demand is more elastic than supply, suppliers bear more of the burden of a tax and receive more of the benefit of a subsidy.

King Cotton and the Deadweight Loss of Water Subsidies

In California, Arizona, and other western states, there are very large subsidies to water used in agriculture. In California, for example, cotton, alfalfa, and rice farmers in the Central Valley area typically pay $20–$30 an acre-foot for water that costs $200–$500 an acre-foot (an acre-foot is the amount of water needed to cover one acre one foot deep). The difference is made up by a government subsidy.

Farmers use the subsidized water to transform desert into prime agricultural land. But turning a California desert into cropland makes about as much sense as building greenhouses in Alaska! America already has plenty of land on which cotton can be grown cheaply. Spending billions of dollars to dam rivers and transport water hundreds of miles to grow a crop that can be grown more cheaply in Georgia is a waste of resources, a deadweight loss. The water used to grow California cotton, for example, has much higher value producing silicon chips in San Jose or as drinking water in Los Angeles than it does as irrigation water.

Recall from Chapter 3 that one of the conditions for maximizing the gains from trade in a free market is that there are no wasteful trades. We can now see how in some situations a subsidy can create wasteful trades.

The waste created by water subsidies is compounded with a variety of agricultural subsidies. Some farmers in the Central Valley are "double-dippers"—they use subsidized water to grow subsidized cotton. Some are even "triple-dippers"—they use subsidized water to grow subsidized corn to feed cows to produce subsidized milk!

Who benefits from the water subsidy? Is it California cotton suppliers or cotton buyers? Remember that suppliers receive more of the benefit of a subsidy than buyers when the elasticity of demand is greater than the elasticity of supply (as in Figure 7.11). Can you explain why the elasticity of demand for California cotton is much greater than the elasticity of supply? The elasticity of demand for *California* cotton is very high since cotton grown elsewhere is almost a perfect substitute. In other words, the price of cotton is determined on the world market for cotton and California production is too small to have much of an influence on the world price. It's not surprising, therefore, that it's not cotton consumers who lobby for water subsidies but the farmers in California's Central Valley. Central Valley California farmers are politically powerful and they have been subsidized since 1902!

Wage Subsidies

It's difficult to see why California cotton should be subsidized when cotton from Georgia (or India, China, or Pakistan) is just as good, but subsidies are not *always* bad for social welfare. Just as a tax might be beneficial if it reduced smoking, a subsidy might be beneficial if it increased something of special importance (see Chapter 9 for more on when taxes and subsidies might be beneficial). Nobel prize winner Edmund Phelps, for example, is a strong advocate of using wage subsidies to increase the employment of low-wage workers.

In Phelps' plan, firms would be subsidized for every low-wage worker that they hire. A subsidy makes hiring a low-wage worker even cheaper, thus increasing the demand for labor. In the left panel of Figure 7.12, a wage subsidy increases the demand for labor, which pushes up the wage received by workers. Note especially that with the subsidy employment is *increased* from Q_m to Q_s.

In his book, *Rewarding Work,* Phelps argues that wage subsidies are a better way to help low-skilled workers than the minimum wage. The minimum wage

FIGURE 7.12

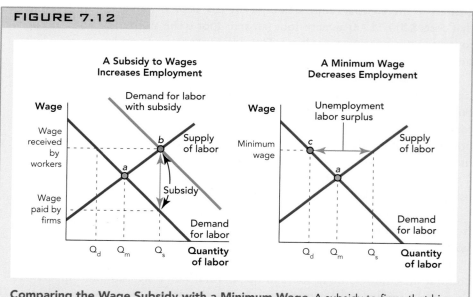

Comparing the Wage Subsidy with a Minimum Wage A subsidy to firms that hire low-wage workers shifts the demand for labor outwards increasing the wage and employment thus moving the equilibrium from point *a* to point *b*. The minimum wage increases the wage but reduces employment, thus moving the equilibrium from point *a* to point *c*.

and wage subsidies both increase the wage, but they have opposite effects on employment: the minimum wage decreases employment while wage subsidies increase employment. In the right panel of Figure 7.12, we show the minimum wage with the minimum set at the same level as wages would be with a subsidy. The minimum wage raises the wage but only for those Q_d workers lucky enough to get jobs—other low-skill workers, perhaps the least skilled, are made unemployed by the higher wage. Thus, employment with the minimum wage *decreases* from Q_m to Q_d.

A wage subsidy increases employment and a minimum wage decreases employment. Workers and employers, therefore, will always prefer a wage subsidy to an equal-wage minimum wage. Taxpayers, however, may prefer a minimum wage. The reason is that a minimum wage has no direct cost to taxpayers, but they must pay for the subsidy. In Figure 7.12, the total cost to taxpayers is the subsidy amount times Q_s.

Wage subsidies, however, could have offsetting benefits to taxpayers, making their total cost less than at first appears. Phelps argues, for example, that if wages and employment among low-skilled workers were higher then welfare payments would be lower. He also suggests that encouraging work among those with the least skills would reduce crime, drug dependency, and the culture of "rational defeatism" that keeps many people in poverty.

The United States does have one program that is similar to a wage subsidy. It's called the Earned Income Tax Credit (EITC). The EITC is a cash-subsidy to the earnings of low-income workers. The main difference between the EITC and a Phelps wage-subsidy is that Phelps would like to subsidize all low-wage workers. The EITC, however, is targeted at families with children—the subsidy is much smaller for workers without children. The EITC has been successful at increasing employment among single mothers, but it doesn't do much for single men or single women without children.

☐ Takeaway

Using the tools of supply and demand you should be able to explain why a price floor creates a surplus, a deadweight loss, and a wasteful increase in quality. You should be able to label these areas on a diagram. You should also be able to explain how price floors (and price ceilings) cause resources to be misallocated.

We used supply and demand to explain the effects of taxes and subsidies. Using the wedge shortcut, you should be able to show that taxes decrease the quantity traded, subsidies increase the quantity traded, and both taxes and subsidies create a deadweight loss. Surprisingly, we showed that the burden of a tax and the benefit of a subsidy do not depend on who sends or receives the government check. Instead, who bears the burden of a tax and who receives the benefit of a subsidy depends on the relative elasticities of supply and demand. In particular, if you remember that *elasticity = escape,* then you will know that the side of the market (buyers or sellers) with the more elastic curve will escape more of the tax. We also showed that elasticities of demand and supply determine the deadweight loss of a tax. The more elastic either the demand or the supply curve is, the more a tax deters trade, and the more trades that are deterred, the greater the deadweight loss (for a given amount of tax revenue).

The tools of supply and demand are very powerful. In this chapter and the previous one, we have shown how we can use these tools to understand price ceilings, price floors, taxes, and subsidies.

CHECK YOURSELF

> To promote energy independence, the U.S. government provides a subsidy to corn growers if they convert the corn to ethanol, a fuel used in some cars. Because of this subsidy, what happens to the quantity supplied of ethanol, and what happens to the price received by corn growers and the price paid by ethanol buyers?

> The U.S. government subsidizes college education in the form of Pell grants and lower-cost government Stafford loans. How do these subsidies affect the price of college education? Which is relatively more elastic: supply or demand? Who benefits the most from these subsidies, suppliers (colleges) or demanders of education (students)?

□ CHAPTER REVIEW

Price floor, p. 119

1. First, a review of the jargon: Is the minimum wage a "price ceiling" or a "price floor?" What about rent control?

2. How do U.S. business owners change their behavior when the minimum wage rises? How does this impact teenagers?

3. The basic idea of deadweight loss is a willing buyer and a willing seller can't find a way to make an exchange. In the case of the minimum wage law, the reason they can't make an exchange is because it's illegal for the buyer (the firm) to hire the seller (the worker) at any wage below the legal minimum. But how can this really be a "loss" from the worker's point of view? It's obvious why business owners would love to hire workers for less than the minimum wage, but if all companies obey the minimum wage law, why are some workers still willing to work for less than that?

4. As we saw in Chapter 3, economists' idea of "equilibrium" borrows a lot from physics. Let's push the physics metaphors a bit further. Here, we focus just on the supply side. For each set of words in brackets, circle the correct choice:

  a. When the government subsidizes an activity, resources such as labor, machines, and bank lending will tend to gravitate [toward/away from] the activity that is subsidized and will tend to gravitate [toward/away from] activity that is not subsidized.

  b. When the government taxes an activity, resources such as labor, machines, and bank lending will tend to gravitate [toward/away from] the activity that is taxed and will tend to gravitate [toward/away from] activity that is not taxed.

5. Junk food has recently been criticized for being unhealthy and too cheap, enticing the poor to adopt unhealthy lifestyles. Suppose that the state of Oklakansas imposes a tax on "junk" food.

  a. What needs to be true for the tax to actually deter people from eating junk food: Should junk food demand be elastic or should it be inelastic?

  b. If the Oklakansas government wants to strongly discourage people from eating junk food, when will it need to set a higher tax rate: When junk food demand is elastic or when it is inelastic?

  c. But hold on a moment: The supply side matters as well. If junk food supply is highly elastic—perhaps because it's not that hard to start selling salads with low-fat dressing instead of mayonnaise- and cheese-laden burgers—does that mean that a junk food tax will have a bigger effect than if supply were inelastic? Or is it the other way around?

  d. Let's combine these stories now: If a government is hoping that a small tax can actually discourage a lot of junk food purchases, it should hope for:

     I. Elastic supply and inelastic demand.
    II. Elastic supply and elastic demand.
   III. Inelastic supply and elastic demand.
   IV. Inelastic supply and inelastic demand.

6. As we saw in the chapter, a lot turns on elasticity. Decades ago, Washington, D.C., a fairly small city, wanted to raise more revenue by increasing the gas tax. Washington, D.C., shares borders with Maryland and Virginia, and it's very easy to cross the borders between these states without even really noticing: The suburbs just blend together.

  a. How elastic is the demand for gasoline *sold at stations within D.C.?* In other words, if the price of gas in D.C. rises, but the price in Maryland and Virginia stays the same, will gasoline sales at D.C. stations fall a little, or will they fall a lot?

  b. Take your answer in part a into account when answering this question. So, when Washington, D.C. increased its gasoline tax, how much revenue did it raise: Did it raise a little bit of revenue, or did it raise a lot of revenue?

  c. How would your answer to b change if D.C., Maryland, and Virginia all agreed to raise their gas tax simultaneously? These states have heavily populated borders with each other, but they don't have any heavily populated borders with other states.

7. In Figure 7.8, what is the total revenue raised by the tax, in dollars? What is the deadweight loss from the tax, in dollars? (Note: You've seen the formula for the latter before. We'll let you look around a little for this one.)

8. **a.** Once again: Why does the text say that *elasticity = escape*? (This is worth remembering: Elasticity is one of the toughest ideas for most economics students.)

   b. Which two groups of workers did we say have a relatively high elasticity of labor supply? Keep this in mind as politicians debate raising or lowering taxes on different types of workers: These two groups are the ones most likely to make big changes in their behavior.

THINKING AND PROBLEM SOLVING

1. In the 1970s, AirCal and Pacific Southwest Airlines flew only within California. As we mentioned, the federal price floors didn't apply to flights within just one state. A major route for these airlines was flying from San Francisco to Los Angeles, a distance of 350 miles. This is about the same distance as from Chicago, Illinois, to Cleveland, Ohio. Do you think AirCal flights had nicer meals than flights from Chicago to Cleveland? Why or why not?

2. Some people with diabetes absolutely need to take insulin on a regular basis to survive. Pharmaceutical companies that make insulin could find a lot of other ways to make some money.

   a. If the U.S. government imposes a tax on insulin producers of $10 per cubic centimeter of insulin, payable every month to the U.S. Treasury, who will bear most of the burden of the tax: Insulin producers, people with diabetes, or can't you tell with the information given?

   b. Suppose instead that because of government corruption, the insulin manufacturers convince the U.S. government to pay the insulin makers $10 per cubic centimeter of insulin, payable every month *from* the U.S. Treasury. Who will get most of the benefit

of this subsidy: Insulin producers, people with diabetes, or can't you tell with the information given?

3. President Jimmy Carter didn't just deregulate airline prices. He also deregulated much of the trucking industry as well. Trucks carry almost all of the consumer goods that you purchase, so almost every time you purchase something, you're paying money to a trucking company.

   a. Based on what happened in the airline industry after prices were deregulated, what do you think happened in the trucking industry after deregulation? You can find some answers here:

   http://www.econlib.org/Library/Enc1/TruckingDeregulation.html

   For another look that is critical of trucking deregulation but comes to basically the same answers, see Michael Belzer, 2000. *Sweatshops on Wheels: Winners and Losers in Trucking Deregulation*, Thousand Oaks, CA: Sage

   b. Who do you think asked Congress and the president to keep price floors for trucking: consumer groups, retail shops like Wal-Mart, or the trucking companies?

4. Suppose you're doing some history research on shoe production in ancient Rome, during the reign of the famous Emperor Diocletian. Your records tell you how many shoes were produced each year in the Roman Empire, but it doesn't tell you the price of shoes. You find a document that says that in the year 301, Emperor Diocletian issued an "Edict on Prices," but you don't know whether he imposed price *ceilings* or price *floors*—your Latin is a little rusty. However, you can clearly tell from the documents that the number of shoes actually exchanged in markets fell dramatically, and that both potential shoe sellers and potential shoe buyers were unhappy with the edict. With the information given, can you tell whether Diocletian imposed a ceiling or a floor? If so, which is it? (Yes, there really was an Edict of Diocletian, and Wikipedia has excellent coverage of ancient Roman history.)

5. In the market depicted below there is either a price ceiling or a price floor—surprisingly, it doesn't matter which one it is: Whether it's an $80 price floor or a $30 price ceiling, the chart looks the same.

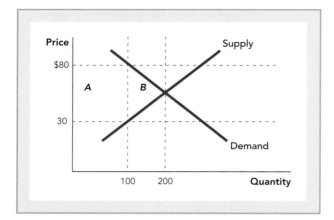

In the chart, there's a rectangle and a triangle. One represents the value lost from the "deals that don't get made" and one represents the value lost from "the deals that do get made." Which is which?

6. We noted that in the 1970s price floors on airline tickets caused wasteful increases in the quality of airline trips. Does the minimum wage cause wasteful increases in the quality of workers? If so, how? In other words, how are minimum-wage workers like airplane trips?

7. Let's see if we can formulate any real laws about the economics of taxation. Which of the following *must* be true, as long as supply and demand curves have their normal shape (i.e., they aren't perfectly vertical or horizontal, and demand curves have a negative slope while supply curves have a positive slope). More than one may be true.

   If there is a tax:

   a. The equilibrium quantity must fall, and the price that buyers pay must rise.

   b. The equilibrium quantity must rise, and the price that sellers pay must rise.

   c. The equilibrium quantity must fall, and the price that sellers receive must fall.

   d. The equilibrium quantity must rise, and the price that buyers receive must fall.

   (Note: The correct answer(s) to this question was actually controversial until Nobel Laureate Paul Samuelson created a simple mathematical proof in his legendary graduate textbook, *Foundations of Economic Analysis*.)

8. Using the following diagram, use the wedge shortcut to answer these questions:

   a. If a tax of $2 were imposed, what price would buyers pay and what price would suppliers receive? How much revenue would be raised

by the tax? How much deadweight loss would be created by the tax?

   b. If a subsidy of $5 were imposed, what price would buyers pay and what price would suppliers receive? How much would the subsidy cost the government? How much deadweight loss would be created by the subsidy?

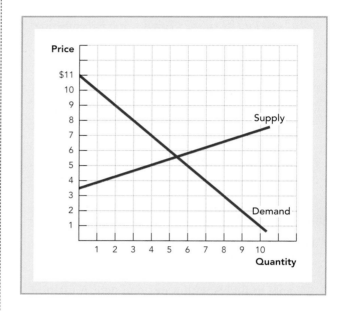

CHALLENGES

1. Let's apply the economics of taxation to romantic relationships.

   a. What does it mean to have an inelastic demand for your boyfriend or girlfriend? How about an elastic demand?

   b. Sometimes relationships have taxes. Suppose that you and your boyfriend or girlfriend live one hour apart. Using the tools developed in the chapter, how can you predict which one of you will do most of the driving? That is, which one of you will bear the majority of the relationship tax?

2. Labor unions are some of the strongest proponents of the minimum wage. Yet in 2008, the median full-time union member earned $886 per week, an average of over $22 per hour (http://www.bls.gov/news.release/union2.nr0 .htm). Therefore, a rise in the minimum wage doesn't directly raise the wage of many union workers. So why do unions support minimum wage laws? Surely, there's more than one reason why this is so, but let's see if economic theory can shed some light on the subject.

a. Skilled and unskilled labor are substitutes: For example, imagine that you can hire four low-skilled workers to move dirt with shovels at $5 an hour, or you can hire one skilled worker at $24 an hour to move the same amount of dirt with a skid loader. Using the tools developed in Chapter 2, what will happen to the demand for skilled labor if the price of unskilled labor increases to $6.50 per hour?

CHRISTIE & COLE/CORBIS

GEHL COMPANY/CORBIS

b. If the minimum wage rises, will that increase or decrease the demand for the average union worker's labor? Why?

c. Now, let's put the pieces together: Why might high-wage labor unions support an increase in the minimum wage?

3. a. In the opening scene of the classic Eddie Murphy comedy *Beverly Hills Cop,* Axel Foley, a Detroit police officer, is stopping a cigarette smuggling ring. Of course, smugglers don't pay the tax when the cigarettes crossed state lines. Which way do you suspect the smugglers were moving the cigarettes, based on economic theory? From the high-tax North to the low-cost South, or vice versa?

b. In our discussion of taxation, we've acted as if it were effortless to pass and enforce tax laws. But of course, law enforcement officials including the Internal Revenue Service put a lot of effort into enforcing tax laws. Let's think for a moment about what kind of taxes are easiest to collect, just based on the basic ideas we've covered. Who will make the most effort to escape a tax: The party who is elastic or the party who is inelastic? (Hint: It doesn't matter whether we're talking about suppliers or demanders.)

(Note: Public administration researchers know the most about this topic: Carolyn Webber and Aaron Wildavsky's surprisingly enjoyable classic, *A History of Taxation and Expenditure in the Western World,* sets out just how difficult it's been for most Western governments to collect taxes.)

4. Let's get some practice with the "wedge trick," and use it to learn about the relationship between subsidies and lobbying. The U.S. government has many subsidies for alternative energy development: some are just called subsidies, some are called tax breaks instead. Either way, they work just like the subsidies we studied in this chapter. We'll look at the market for windmills.

a. In the two figures below, one is a case where the sellers of windmills have an elastic supply and the buyers of windmills (local power companies) have inelastic demand. In the other case, the reverse is true. Which is which?

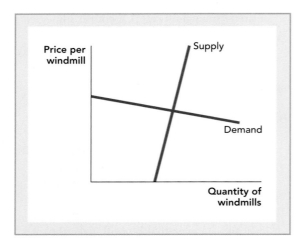

b. In which case will a subsidy cut the price paid by the buyers the most: When demand is elastic or when it is inelastic? (It'll be easiest if you use the "wedge trick.") Is this the first or second graph?

c. In which case will a subsidy increase the price received by the sellers the most: When supply is elastic or when it is inelastic? Again, which graph is this?

d. Now look at how producer surplus and consumer surplus change in these two cases. To see this, remember that producer surplus is the area *above* the supply curve and below the price, and consumer surplus is the area *below* the demand curve and above the price. So in the first graph, who gets the lion's share of any subsidy-driven extra surplus: Suppliers or demanders? Is that the inelastic group or the elastic group? In other words, whose surplus triangle gets bigger faster as the quantity increases? (You might try shading in these triangles just to be sure.)

e. Now it's time for the second graph. Again, who gets the lion's share of any subsidy-driven extra surplus: Suppliers or demanders? Is that the inelastic group or the elastic group?

f. There's going to be a pattern here in parts d and e: The more [elastic or inelastic?] side of the market gets most of the extra surplus from the subsidy.

g. When Congress gives subsidies for the alternative energy market, it is hoping that a small subsidy can get a big increase in output: In other words, they are hoping that the equilibrium quantity will be *elastic*. At the same time, the groups most likely to lobby Congress for a big alternative energy subsidy are going to be the groups that get the most extra surplus from any subsidy. After all, if the subsidy doesn't give them much surplus, they're not likely to ask Congress for it.

So here's the big question: Will the groups that are most likely to *lobby for* a subsidy be the same groups that are most likely to *respond to* the subsidy? (Note: this is a general lesson about the incentives for lobbying: It's not just a story about the alternative energy industry.)

8

International Trade

CHAPTER OUTLINE

Why Trade?

Analyzing Trade with Supply and Demand

The Costs of Protectionism

Arguments against International Trade

Trade and Globalization

Takeaway

Economics textbooks should never have chapters on "International Trade." The word "international" suggests that international trade is a special type of trade requiring new principles and arguments. But when Joe and Frank trade, Joe and Frank are made better off. When Joe and Francisco trade, Joe and Francisco are made better off. The politics are different but the economics doesn't change much if Frank lives in El Paso and Francisco lives in Ciudad Juarez. International trade is trade. Thus, the real subject of this chapter is the economics of trade and the politics of international trade. We begin by asking "why trade?" We then explain how trade can be analyzed using the tools you already know, namely demand and supply. We close by evaluating some of the arguments, both economic and political, against international trade.

Why Trade?

We will focus on three benefits of trade:

> The division of knowledge

> Economies of scale and creating competition

> Comparative advantage

The Division of Knowledge

Without trade, civilization would collapse and billions of people would starve. How long could you survive if you had to grow your own food? Yet most of us can make enough money in a day to buy more food than we could grow in a year. *Specialization* followed by trade vastly increases productivity. Why? Farmers have two immense advantages in producing food compared to economics

143

Contra Episode 61, even Spock's brain could not come close to running a modern economy. For this reason, some economists consider "Spock's Brain" to be the worst *Star Trek* episode *ever*.

professors or students: they know more about farming and they can afford to buy large-scale farming machines. Both of these advantages flow from specialization and trade.

The human brain is limited and there is much to know. Thus, it makes sense to divide knowledge across many brains and then trade. In a primitive agricultural economy in which each person or household farms for themselves, each person has about the same knowledge as the person next door. In this case, the combined knowledge of a society of one million people barely exceeds that of a single person.[1] A society run with the knowledge of one brain is a poor and miserable society.

In a modern economy, many millions of times more knowledge is used than could exist in a single brain. In the United States, for example, we don't just have doctors—we have neurologists, cardiologists, gastroenterologists, gynecologists, and urologists, to name just a few of the many specializations in medicine. Knowledge increases productivity so specialization increases total output. All of this knowledge is productive, however, only because each person can specialize in the production of one good and then trade for all other desired goods. Without trade, specialization is impossible.

The extent of specialization in a modern economy explains why no one knows the full details of how even the simplest product is produced. A Valentine's Day rose may have been grown in Kenya, flown to Amsterdam on refrigerated airplanes, and trucked to Topeka by drivers staying awake with Colombian coffee. Each person in this process knows only a small part of the whole but with trade and market coordination, they each do their part and the rose is delivered without anyone needing to understand the whole process.

The extent of specialization in modern society is remarkable. We have already mentioned the many specializations in medicine. We also have dog walkers, closet organizers, and manicurists. It's common to dismiss the latter jobs as frivolous, but trade connects all markets. It's the dog walkers, closet organizers, and manicurists who give the otolaryngologists—specialists in the nose, ear, and throat—the time they need to perfect their skills.

The division of knowledge increases with the extent of the market. Economic growth in the modern era is primarily due to the creation of new knowledge. Thus, one of the most momentous turning points in the division of knowledge happens when trade is extensive enough to support large numbers of scientists, engineers, and entrepreneurs, all of whom specialize in producing new knowledge.

Consider the many ideas and innovations that make life better, from antibiotics, to high-yield, disease-resistant wheat, to the semiconductor. Insofar as those goods have originated in one place and then been spread around the world, improving the lives of millions or billions, it is because of trade.

Reducing trade barriers, Berlin 1989

Every increase in world trade is an opportunity to increase the division of knowledge and extend the power of the human mind. During the communist era, for example, China was like an island cut off from the world economy: one billion people who neither traded many goods nor many ideas with the rest of the world. The fall of the Berlin Wall and the opening to the world economy of China, Russia, Eastern Europe, and other nations greatly adds to the productive stock of scientists and engineers and is one of the most promising signs for the future of the world. Billions of minds have been added to the division of knowledge and cooperation has been extended further around the world than ever before.

Economies of Scale and Creating Competition

One way that specialization and trade increase total production is by increasing knowledge. Specialization and trade also make it profitable to use specialized machines. A person who must grow his own wheat and bake his own bread cannot afford a combine thresher or ovens that bake bread in assembly line fashion. A combine thresher that speeds the separation of grain from husk by 20 percent, for example, isn't worth the expense when you have just 10 acres to thresh, but at 1,000 acres, the savings can be significant. Similarly, the cost per loaf of bread is lower when 25,000 loaves of bread are produced an hour, as is true in a modern bakery, than when 100 loaves of bread are produced in a day. By specializing and trading, people can take advantage of the cost savings associated with large-scale production. Economists call those cost savings **economies of scale.**

Economies of scale mean that costs per unit fall with increases in production.

Taking advantage of economies of scale is one reason why many European countries have joined the European Union (EU), an agreement to remove many trade barriers between member nations by creating a single market. The EU was inspired by the creation of a single market called the "United States" by the original American states and it has many of the same benefits. It makes no more sense for every country to have its own automobile or aircraft manufacturer than it does for every U.S. state to have its own auto and aircraft manufacturer. Instead, by forming a single market, countries in the EU can specialize and every country can benefit from the cost savings that occur when automobiles and aircraft are produced with specialized, large-scale production techniques.

Economies of scale are closely related to another advantage of international trade, creating competition. If an industry enjoys large economies of scale but trade barriers prevent competition from foreign producers, there will be only a few domestic firms. Without foreign competition, these firms will have the ability to raise prices and reduce output.

In the 1980s, for example, so-called voluntary export restraints reduced imports of Japanese automobiles into the United States. As a result, U.S. consumers had to pay more for Japanese automobiles, about $1,300 extra. But it wasn't only buyers of Japanese automobiles who faced higher prices. Buyers of domestic automobiles also had to pay more, about $660 more per car. Prices of domestic cars increased because GM, Ford, and Chrysler knew that with less pressure from international competition, they could increase prices. The profits of the big three went up during this period and consumers bore the costs.

International trade keeps domestic firms competitive and on their toes. Interestingly, so long as domestic firms know that foreign firms stand ready to compete, domestic firms cannot raise their prices by much. Thus, consumers can benefit from a free trade policy even if no trade actually occurs!

Comparative Advantage

A third reason to trade is to take advantage of differences. Brazil, for example, has a climate ideally suited to growing sugar cane, China has an abundance of low-skilled workers, and the United States has one of the best-educated workforces in the world. Taking advantage of these differences suggests that world production can be maximized when Brazil produces sugar, China assembles iPods, and the United States devotes its efforts to designing the next generation of electronic devices.

Absolute advantage is the ability to produce the same good using fewer inputs than another producer.

Comparative advantage: It's a good thing

Martha Stewart may be the world's best ironer but she doesn't do her own ironing. Every hour Martha spends ironing is an hour less she has to run her billion-dollar business. The cost of ironing is too high for Martha Stewart, even if she is the world's best.

Martha can be most productive if she does what she does *most* best.

A country has a **comparative advantage** in producing goods for which it has the lowest opportunity cost.

Taking advantage of differences is even more powerful than it looks. We say that a country has an **absolute advantage** in production if it can produce the same good using fewer inputs than another country. But to benefit from trade, a country need not have an absolute advantage in production. For example, even if the United States did have the world's best climate for growing sugar, it might still make sense for Brazil to grow sugar and for the United States to design iPods, if the U.S. had a bigger advantage in designing iPods than it did in growing sugar.

Here's another example of what economists call comparative advantage. Martha Stewart doesn't do her own ironing. Why not? Martha Stewart may in fact be the world's best ironer but she is also good at running her business. If Martha spent more time ironing and less time running her business, her blouses might be pressed more precisely but that would be a small gain compared to the loss from having someone else run her business. It's better for Martha if she specializes in running her business and then trades some of her income for other goods, such as ironing services, and of course many other goods and services as well.

The idea of comparative advantage is subtle but important. In order to give a precise definition, let's explore comparative advantage using a simple model. Suppose that there are just two goods, computers and shirts, and one input, labor. Assume that in Mexico, it takes 12 units of labor to make one computer and 2 units of labor to produce one shirt, and in the United States it takes 1 unit of labor to produce either good. Notice that the United States can produce both computers and shirts using less labor than in Mexico. Thus, in this example, the United States has an absolute advantage in both computers and shirts. Table 8.1 summarizes.

Since the United States can produce computers and shirts using less labor than Mexico, it's natural to wonder whether the United States has anything to gain from trade with its less productive neighbor. Mexicans may similarly wonder whether they have everything to lose from trading with their more productive neighbor. Both of these fears are unfounded. Mexico and the United States can each benefit from trade. Let's see how.

First, let's use the information in Table 8.1 to calculate the cost of shirts and computers. But remember from Chapter 2 that the real cost of producing a good is not the money cost but the *opportunity cost,* the best alternative that society must give up to get the good. Thus, we will calculate the opportunity cost of shirts and computers. We begin with shirts in the United States because that case is easy and requires only some easy-to-use ratios. The United States can produce one additional shirt by producing one less computer so the opportunity cost of a shirt in the United States is one computer.

What about Mexico? Mexico can produce an additional shirt by producing one-sixth less of a computer. In other words, by moving 2 units of labor—which could produce one-sixth of a computer—from computer production to shirt production, Mexico can produce one additional shirt.

Now here is the key. The (opportunity) cost of a shirt in the United States is one computer but the (opportunity) cost of a shirt in Mexico is just one-sixth of a computer. Thus, even though Mexico is less productive than the United States, Mexico has a lower cost of producing shirts! Since Mexico has the lowest opportunity cost of producing shirts, we say that Mexico has a **comparative advantage** in producing shirts.

TABLE 8.1 Labor Units Required to Produce Computers and Shirts in Mexico and the United States

Country	1 Computer	1 Shirt
Mexico	12	2
United States	1	1

Now let's look at the opportunity cost of producing computers. Again, the trade-off for the United States is easy to see: It can produce one additional computer by giving up one shirt so the cost of one computer is one shirt. But to produce one additional computer in Mexico requires giving up six shirts! Thus, the United States has the lowest cost of producing computers or, economists say, it has a comparative advantage in producing computers. Table 8.2 summarizes.

We now know that the United States has a high cost of producing shirts and a low cost of producing computers. In Mexico, it's the reverse: Mexico has a low cost of producing shirts and a high cost of producing computers.

The theory of comparative advantage says that to increase its wealth a country should produce the goods it can make at low cost and buy what it can make only at high cost. Thus, the theory says the United States should make computers and buy shirts. Similarly, the theory says that Mexico should make shirts and buy computers. Let's use some numbers to see whether the theory holds up in our example.

Suppose that both Mexico and the United States have 24 units of labor and they each devote 12 units to producing computers and 12 units to producing shirts. Using the figures from Table 8.1, we can see that Mexico will produce one computer and six shirts and the United States will produce 12 computers and 12 shirts. At first, there is no trade so production in each country is equal to consumption. Table 8.3 summarizes.

Notice that total production is 13 computers and 18 shirts. Now, can Mexico and the United States make themselves better off through trade? Yes.

Imagine that Mexico moves 12 units of its labor out of computer production and into shirt production. Thus, Mexico specializes completely by allocating all 24 units of its labor to shirt production, thereby producing 12 shirts. Similarly, suppose that the United States moves 2 units of its labor out of shirt production and into computers—thus producing 14 computers and 10 shirts. The situation is now as in Table 8.4.

Now compare total production in Table 8.3 with total production in Table 8.4. Total production has increased with specialization! By specializing as comparative advantage would dictate, the two countries can increase total production by one computer and four shirts.

So to finish the story, can you now see a way in which both Mexico and the United States can be made better off? Sure! Imagine that the United States trades one computer to Mexico in return for three shirts. Mexico is now able to consume one computer and nine shirts (three more shirts than before trade; compare with Table 8.3), while the United States is able to consume 13 computers (one more than before

TABLE 8.2 Opportunity Costs

Country	Opportunity Cost of 1 Computer	Opportunity Cost of 1 Shirt
Mexico	6 Shirts	1/6 of a Computer
United States	1 Shirt	1 Computer

Mexico is the low cost producer of shirts.

The United States is the low cost producer of computers.

TABLE 8.3 Production = Consumption in Mexico and the United States (No Trade)

Country labor allocation (computers, shirts)	Computers	Shirts
Mexico (12, 12)	1	6
United States (12, 12)	12	12
Total Production	13	18

TABLE 8.4 Production in Mexico and the United States (Specialization)

Country labor allocation (computers, shirts)	Computers	Shirts
Mexico (0, 24)	0	12
United States (14, 10)	14	10
Total Production	14	22

trade) and 13 shirts (one more than before trade). Both Mexico and the United States are better off, as Table 8.5 illustrates.

TABLE 8.5 Consumption in Mexico and the United States (Specialization and Trade)

Country	Computers	Shirts
Mexico	1	9 (+3)
United States	13 (+1)	13 (+1)
Total Consumption	14	22

Thus, when each country produces according to its comparative advantage and then trades, total production and consumption increase. Importantly, both Mexico and the United States gain from trade even though the United States is more productive than Mexico at producing *both* computers and shirts.

The theory of comparative advantage not only explains trade patterns but it also tells us something remarkable: a country (or a person) will *always* be the low-cost seller of some good. The reason is clear: the greater the advantage a country has in producing A, the greater the cost to it of producing B. If you are a great pianist, the cost to you of doing anything else is very high. Thus, the greater your advantages in being a pianist, the greater the incentive you have to trade with other people for other goods. It's the same way for countries. The more productive the United States is at producing computers, the greater its demand will be to trade for shirts. Thus, countries with high productivity can always benefit by trading with lower productivity countries, and countries with lower productivity need never fear that higher productivity countries will outcompete them in all goods.

When people fear that a country can be outcompeted in everything, they are making a common mistake, namely confusing absolute advantage with comparative advantage. A producer has an absolute advantage over another producer if it can produce more output from the same input. But what makes trade profitable is differences in comparative advantage, and a country will always have some comparative advantage.

Thus, everyone can benefit from trade. From the world's greatest genius down to the person of below average ability, no person or country is so productive or so unproductive that they cannot benefit by inclusion in the worldwide division of labor. The theory of comparative advantage tells us something vital about world trade and about world peace. Trade unites humanity.

see the
invisible hand

Comparative Advantage and Wages Comparative advantage is a difficult story to grasp. Most of the world hasn't got it yet so don't be too surprised if it takes you some time as well. You may at first be bothered by the fact that we did not explicitly discuss wages. Won't a country like the United States be uncompetitive in trade with low-wage countries like Mexico?

In fact, wages are in our model, we just need to bring them to the surface. Doing so will provide another perspective on comparative advantage.

In our model, there is only one type of labor that can be used to produce either computers or shirts. In a free market, all workers of the same type will earn the same wage.* So, in this model there is just one wage in Mexico and one wage in the United States. We can calculate the wage in Mexico by summing up the total value of *consumption* in Mexico and dividing by the number of workers.† We can perform a similar calculation for the United States. To do

---

* In a free market, the same good will tend to sell for the same price everywhere. Imagine that the wages in computer manufacturing exceed the wages in shirt manufacturing. Everyone wants a higher wage so workers in the shirt industry will try to move to the computer industry. As the supply of workers in computer manufacturing increases, however, wages in the computer sector will fall. And, as the supply of workers in shirt manufacturing decreases, wages in that sector will increase. Only when workers of the same type are paid the same wage is there no incentive for workers to move.
† We calculate the value of consumption because at the end of the day workers care about what they consume, not what they produce.

this, we need only a price for computers and a price for shirts. Let's suppose that computers sell for $300 and shirts for $100 (this is consistent with trading one computer for three shirts as we did earlier). Let's look first at the situation with no trade (see Table 8.3). The value of Mexican consumption is 1 × $300 plus 6 × $100 for a total of $900. Since there are 24 workers, the average wage is $37.50. The value of U.S. consumption is 12 × $300 + 12 × $100 = $4,800 so the U.S. wage is $200.

Now consider the situation with trade (see Table 8.5). The value of Mexican consumption is now 1 × $300 + 9 × $100 = $1,200 for a wage of $50 while the U.S. wage is now $216.67 (check it!). Wages in both countries have gone up, just as expected.

But notice that the wage in Mexico is lower than the wage in the United States, both before and after trade. The reason is that the productivity of labor is lower in Mexico. Ultimately, it's the productivity of labor that determines the wage rate. Specialization and trade lets workers make the most of what they have—it raises wages as high as possible given productivity—but trade does not directly increase productivity.* Trade makes both Einstein and his less clever accountant better off, but it doesn't make the accountant a skilled scientist like Einstein.

In summary, workers in the United States often fear trade because they think that they cannot compete with low-wage workers in other countries. Meanwhile, workers in low-wage countries fear trade because they think that they cannot compete with high productivity countries like the United States! But differences in wages reflect differences in productivity. High productivity countries have high wages, low productivity countries have low wages. Trade means that workers in both countries can raise their wages to the highest levels allowed for by their productivities.

Adam Smith (1723–1790) author of the *Wealth of Nations* and one of the greatest economists of all time. When Smith could not finish teaching one semester, he told his students he would refund their tuition. When the students refused the refund saying they had learned so much already, Smith wept. We, however, will not refund the purchase price of this book even if you only read half of it. We are not as good economists as was Adam Smith.

Adam Smith on Trade

As promised, we have so far talked about trade without distinguishing it much from "international trade." Adam Smith had an elegant summary connecting the argument for trade to that for international trade:

> It is the maxim of every prudent master of a family never to attempt to make at home what it will cost him more to make than to buy. The tailor does not attempt to make his own shoes, but buys them of the shoemaker. The shoemaker does not attempt to make his own clothes, but employs a tailor. What is prudence in the conduct of every private family can scarce be folly in that of a great kingdom. If a foreign country can supply us with a commodity cheaper than we ourselves can make it, better buy it of them with some part of the produce of our own industry employed in a way in which we have some advantage.[2]

Analyzing Trade with Supply and Demand

Now that we have discussed some of the fundamental reasons for trade, let's look at trade—and trade restrictions—using tools that you are already familiar with: demand and supply.

CHECK YOURSELF

> What does specialization do to productivity? Why?

> How does trade let us benefit from the advantages of specialization?

> Alex Rodriguez is a premier baseball player. Being so athletic, he also would be very good at mowing his lawn, much better than Harry who mows lawns for a living. Why would Alex Rodriguez pay Harry to do his lawn rather than do it himself?

★ Trade can increase productivity by allowing for exploitation of economies of scale, improving the division of knowledge, and diffusing information about advanced production techniques. These advantages of trade are important but the logic of comparative advantage does not require an increase in productivity.

Figure 8.1 shows a domestic demand curve and a domestic supply curve for semiconductors. If there were no international trade the equilibrium would be, as usual, at $P^{\text{no trade}}$, $Q^{\text{no trade}}$. Suppose, however, that this good can also be bought in the world market at the world price. To simplify, we will assume that the U.S. market is small relative to the world market, so U.S. demanders can buy as many semiconductors as they want without pushing up the world price. In terms of our diagram, the world supply curve is flat (perfectly elastic) at the world price.

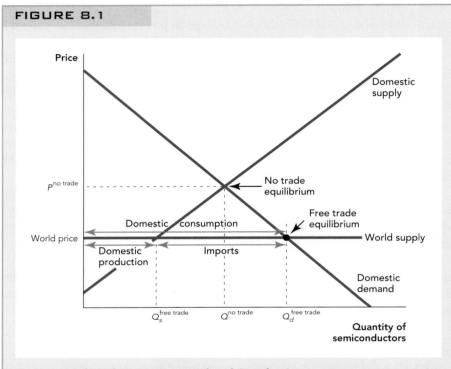

FIGURE 8.1

International Trade Using Demand and Supply If there were no international trade, the equilibrium would be found, as usual, at the intersection of the domestic demand and domestic supply curves at $P^{\text{no trade}}$, and $Q^{\text{no trade}}$. With trade, U.S. consumers can buy as many semiconductors as they want at the world price and at this price U.S. consumers demand $Q_d^{\text{free trade}}$ units. At the world price, the difference between domestic demand, $Q_d^{\text{free trade}}$, and domestic supply, $Q_s^{\text{free trade}}$, is made up by imports.

Given that U.S. consumers can buy as many semiconductors as they want at the world price, how many will they buy? As usual, we read the quantity demanded off the domestic demand curve so at the world price, U.S. consumers will demand $Q_d^{\text{free trade}}$ semiconductors. How many semiconductors will be supplied by *domestic* suppliers? As usual, we read the quantity supplied off the domestic supply curve so domestic suppliers will supply $Q_s^{\text{free trade}}$ units. Notice that $Q_d^{\text{free trade}} > Q_s^{\text{free trade}}$, so where does the difference come from? From imports. In other words, with international trade, domestic consumption is $Q_d^{\text{free trade}}$ units; $Q_s^{\text{free trade}}$ of these units are produced domestically and the remainder, $Q_d^{\text{free trade}} - Q_s^{\text{free trade}}$, are imported.

Analyzing Tariffs with Demand and Supply

Many countries, including the United States, restrict international trade with tariffs, quotas, or other regulations that burden foreign producers but not domestic producers—this is called **protectionism**. A **tariff** is simply a tax on imports.

Protectionism is the economic policy of restraining trade through quotas, tariffs, or other regulations that burden foreign producers but not domestic producers.

A **tariff** is a tax on imports.

A **trade quota** is a restriction on the quantity of foreign goods that can be imported: Imports greater than the quota amount are forbidden or heavily taxed.

Figure 8.2 shows how to analyze a tariff. The figure looks imposing but it's really the same as Figure 8.1 except that now we analyze domestic consumption, production, and imports before and after the tariff. Before the tariff, the situation is exactly as in Figure 8.1, $Q_d^{\text{free trade}}$ units are demanded, $Q_s^{\text{free trade}}$ units are supplied by domestic producers, and imports are $Q_d^{\text{free trade}} - Q_s^{\text{free trade}}$.

A **trade quota** is a restriction on the quantity of goods that can be imported: Imports greater than the quota amount are forbidden or heavily taxed.

FIGURE 8.2

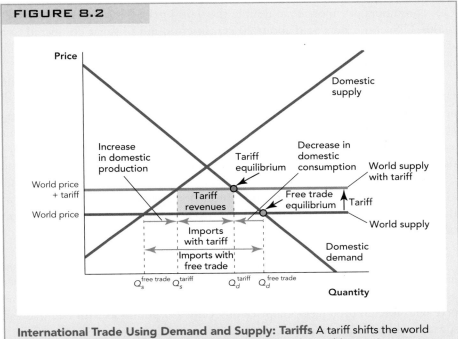

International Trade Using Demand and Supply: Tariffs A tariff shifts the world supply curve up by the amount of the tariff, thus raising the world price. In response to the higher price, consumers reduce their purchases from $Q_d^{\text{free trade}}$ to Q_d^{tariff} and domestic suppliers increase their production from $Q_s^{\text{free trade}}$ to Q_s^{tariff}. Since domestic consumption decreases and domestic production increases the quantity of imports falls from $Q_d^{\text{free trade}} - Q_s^{\text{free trade}}$ to $Q_d^{\text{tariff}} - Q_s^{\text{tariff}}$.
The government collects revenues from the tariff equal to the tariff × the quantity of imports, which is shown as the blue area.

The tariff is a tax on imports so—just as you learned in Chapter 2—the tariff (tax) shifts the world supply curve up by the amount of the tariff. For example, if the world price of semiconductors is $2 per unit and a new tariff of $1 per semiconductor is imposed, then the world supply curve shifts up to $3 per unit.

At the new, higher price of semiconductors, two things happen. First, there is an increase in the domestic production of semiconductors as domestic suppliers respond to the higher price by increasing production. In the diagram, domestic production increases from $Q_s^{\text{free trade}}$ to Q_s^{tariff}. Second, there is a decrease in domestic consumption from $Q_d^{\text{free trade}}$ to Q_d^{tariff} as domestic consumers respond to the higher price by buying fewer semiconductors. Since the quantity produced by domestic suppliers rises and the quantity demanded by domestic consumers falls, the quantity of imports falls. Specifically, imports fall from $Q_d^{\text{free trade}} - Q_s^{\text{free trade}}$ to the smaller amount $Q_d^{\text{tariff}} - Q_s^{\text{tariff}}$.

Figure 8.2 illustrates one more important idea. A tariff is a tax on imports so tariffs raise tax revenue for the government. The revenue raised by a tariff is the tariff amount times the quantity of imports (the quantity taxed). Thus, in Figure 8.2 the tariff revenue is given by the blue area.

The Costs of Protectionism

Now that we know that a tariff on an imported good will increase domestic production and decrease domestic consumption, we can analyze in more detail the costs of protectionism. The U.S. government, for example, greatly restricts the amount of sugar that can be imported into the United States. As a result, U.S. consumers pay more than double the world price for sugar—in the early 2000s, U.S. consumers paid about 20 cents per pound of sugar compared to a world price of around 9 cents per pound. So, let's look in more detail at the costs of sugar protectionism.

To simplify our analysis, we make two assumptions. First, we assume that the tariff is so high that it completely eliminates all sugar imports. Although a small amount of sugar is allowed into the United States at a low tariff rate, anything above this small amount is taxed so heavily that no further imports occur. Our assumption that the tariff eliminates all sugar imports is not a bad approximation to what actually happens. Second, we assume that if we had complete free trade, all sugar would be imported. This is also a reasonable assumption because, as we will explain shortly, sugar can be produced elsewhere at much lower cost than in the United States. Making these two assumptions will focus attention on the key ideas. See Challenge Question 1 in the end of chapter questions for a more detailed analysis.

In Figure 8.3, we show the market for sugar. If there were complete free trade in sugar, U.S. consumers would be able to buy at the world price of 9 cents per pound and they would purchase 24 billion pounds. U.S. producers cannot compete with foreign producers at a price of 9 cents per pound so with free trade all sugar would be imported.

The tariff on sugar imports is so high that with the tariff there are no imports and the U.S. price of sugar—found at the intersection of the domestic demand and domestic supply curve—rises to 20 cents per pound.

Recall that a tariff has two effects: it increases domestic production and reduces domestic consumption. Each of these effects has a cost. First, the increase in domestic production may sound good—and it is good for domestic producers as we shall see below—but domestic producers have higher costs of production than foreign producers. Thus, the tariff means that sugar is no longer supplied by the lowest-cost sellers and resources that could have been used to produce other goods and services are instead wasted producing sugar. Second, due to higher costs the price of sugar rises and fewer people buy sugar, reducing the gains from trade. Let's look at each of these costs in more detail.

Sugar costs more to grow in the United States than in say Brazil, the world's largest producer of sugar, because the climate in the U.S. mainland is not ideal for sugar growing and because land and labor in Florida, where a lot of U.S. sugar is grown, have many alternative uses that are high in value. Sugar farmers in Florida, for example, have to douse their land with expensive fertilizers to increase production—in the process creating environmental damage in the Florida Everglades.[3] The excess resources—the fertilizer, land, and labor—that go into producing U.S. sugar could have been used to produce other goods like oranges and theme parks for which the United States and Florida are better suited.

Recall from Chapter 2 that the supply curve tells us the cost of production so at the equilibrium price the cost of producing an additional pound of sugar

▶▶ **SEARCH ENGINE**

Information on sugar and the U.S. sugar tariff can be found from the *USDA Economic Research Service, Sugar Briefing Room.*

FIGURE 8.3

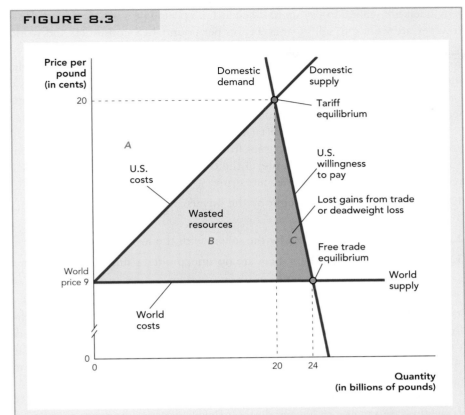

A Restriction on Trade Wastes Resources and Creates Lost Gains from Trade
With free trade domestic production of sugar is 0 billion pounds. When imports are restricted the domestic industry expands to 20 billion pounds but U.S. costs are above World costs so the expansion of the domestic industry creates Wasted resources (area B). At the higher price of sugar, less sugar is bought so the import restriction also creates Lost gains from trade (area C).

How to smuggle sugar

The high price of U.S. sugar has encouraged smuggling and attempts to circumvent the tariff. In the 1980s when the U.S. price was four times the world price, Canadian entrepreneurs created super-high-sugar iced tea. The "tea" was shipped into the United States and then sifted for the sugar, which was resold.

To combat this entrepreneurship, the U.S. government created even more tariffs for sugar-containing products like iced tea, cake mixes, and cocoa.

Source: Economic Report of the President 1986, Chapter 4.

in the United States is exactly 20 cents. In other words, in the United States it takes 20 cents worth of resources like land and labor to produce one additional pound of sugar. That same pound of sugar could be bought in the world market for just 9 cents so the tariff causes 11 cents worth of resources to be wasted in producing that last pound of sugar.

The total value of wasted resources is shown in Figure 8.3 by the yellow area labeled Wasted resources; that area represents the difference between what it costs to produce 20 billion pounds of sugar in the United States and what it would cost to buy the same amount from abroad. We can calculate the total value of wasted resources using our formula for the area of a triangle.

The height of the yellow triangle is 20 − 9 or 11 cents per pound, the base is 20 billion pounds, so the area is 110 billion cents, or $1.1 billion. The sugar tariff wastes $1.1 billion worth of resources.

Notice that if the sugar tariff were eliminated, the price of sugar in the United States would fall to the world price of 9 cents per pound and U.S. production would drop from 20 billion pounds to 0 pounds. It's important to see that the reduction in U.S. production is a *benefit* of eliminating the tariff because it frees up resources that can be used to produce other goods and services.

There is another cost to the tariff. Remember from Chapter 2 that the demand curve tells us the value of goods to the demanders, so at the equilibrium price

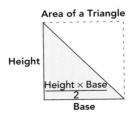

demanders are willing to pay up to 20 cents for a pound of sugar. World suppliers, however, are willing to sell sugar at 9 cents per pound. U.S. consumers and world suppliers could make mutually profitable gains from trade, but they are prevented from doing so by the threat of punishment. The value of the lost gains from trade, which economists also call a deadweight loss, is given by the pink area. Again, we can calculate this area using our formula for the area of a triangle ((20 − 9) cents per pound × 4 billion pounds divided by 2) = 22 billion cents or $0.22 billion.

Thus, the total cost of the sugar tariff to U.S. citizens is $1.1 billion of wasted resources plus $0.22 billion of lost gains from trade for a total loss of $1.32 billion.

Do you remember from Chapter 3 the three conditions that explain why a free market is efficient? Here they are again:

1. The supply of goods is bought by the buyers with the highest willingness to pay.
2. The supply of goods is sold by the sellers with the lowest costs.
3. Between buyers and sellers there are no unexploited gains from trade nor any wasteful trades.

A tariff or quota that restricts consumers from trading with foreign producers means that the market is not free, so we should expect some of the conditions in our list to be violated. In this case, conditions 2 and 3 are violated. A tariff reduces efficiency because the supply of goods is no longer sold by the sellers with the lowest costs and with a tariff there are unexploited gains from trade between buyers and sellers.

Some of these benefits of trade may sound pretty abstract, but for a lot of people they are a matter of life and death. If Brazilian sugar cane farmers could sell more of their products to U.S. consumers, many more of the farmers could afford to eat better or to improve their housing with proper water and sewage. But don't think the United States is the only party at fault here. The Brazilian government places a lot of tariffs on foodstuffs from the United States and for many Brazilians, including the very poor, this makes food more expensive. The end result is that U.S. consumers pay a high price for sugar and poor Brazilians have less to eat and less money to spend when they need to take their kids to the doctor.

Winners and Losers from Trade

We can arrive at this same total loss in another revealing way. The sugar tariff raises the price of sugar to U.S. consumers, which reduces consumer surplus. Recall from Chapter 2 that consumer surplus is the area underneath the demand curve and above the price. Thus, consumer surplus with the tariff is the area above the price of 20 cents and below the demand curve (not all of which is shown in Figure 8.3). As the price falls from 20 cents to 9 cents, consumer surplus increases by area A + B + C, which has a value (check it!) of $2.42 billion. Or, put differently, the tariff costs consumers $2.42 billion in lost consumer surplus.

The tariff increases price which increases producer surplus, the area above the supply curve and below the price. Thus, the tariff increases U.S. producer surplus by area A, which has a value of $1.10 billion.

Notice that U.S. consumers lose more than twice as much from the tariff as U.S. producers gain. The loss to U.S. citizens in total is $2.42 billion of consumer loss minus $1.10 billion of U.S. producer gain, for a total loss of $1.32 billion a year, *exactly as we found before.*

Our two methods of analyzing the cost of the sugar tariff are equivalent, but they emphasize different things. The first method calculates social loss directly and emphasizes where the loss comes from: wasted resources and lost gains from trade. The second method focuses on *who* gains and *who* loses. Domestic producers gain but U.S. consumers lose even more.

Why does the government support the U.S. sugar tariff when U.S. consumers lose much more than U.S. producers gain? One clue is that the costs of the sugar tariff are spread over millions of consumers so the costs per consumer are small. The benefits of the tariff, however, flow to a small number of producers, each of whom benefits by millions of dollars. As a result, the producers support and lobby for the tariff much more actively than consumers oppose the tariff.

The costs of all this lobbying point our attention to yet another cost of protectionism. When a country erects a lot of tariffs against foreign competition, the producers in that country will spend a lot of their time, energy, and money lobbying the government for protection. Those same resources should be spent on production and innovation, not lobbying. Protectionism tends to create a society that pits one interest group against the other and seeds social discord. Free trade, in contrast, creates incentives for people to cooperate toward common and profitable ends.

Arguments against International Trade

It would take several books to analyze all the arguments against international trade. We will take a closer look at some of the most common arguments:

> Trade reduces the number of jobs in the United States.

> It's wrong to trade with countries that use child labor.

> We need to keep certain industries at home for reasons of national security.

> We need to keep certain "key" industries at home because of beneficial spillovers onto other sectors of the economy.

> We can increase U.S. well-being with strategic trade protectionism.

Trade and Jobs

When the United States reduces tariffs and imports more shirts from Mexico, the U.S. shirt industry will contract. As a result, many people associate free trade deals with lost jobs. As economists, however, we want to trace the impact of lower tariffs beyond the most immediate and visible effects. So let's trace what happens when a tariff is lowered, paying particular attention to the effect on jobs.

When the price of shirts falls, U.S. consumers have more money in their pockets that they can use to buy other goods. The increased consumer spending on Scotch tape, bean bag chairs, X-ray tests, and thousands of other goods leads to increased jobs in these industries. These jobs gains may be more difficult to see than the job losses in the U.S. shirt industry but they are no less real. But what about the money that is now going to Mexican shirt producers instead of to U.S. shirt producers? Isn't it better to "Buy American" and keep this money at home?

When Mexican producers sell shirts in the United States they are paid in dollars. But what do Mexicans want dollars for? Ultimately, everyone sells in order to buy. Mexican producers might use their dollars to buy U.S. goods. In this case, the increased U.S. spending on imports of Mexican shirts leads directly to increased Mexican spending on U.S. goods (i.e., U.S. exports).

UNDERSTAND YOUR world

CHECK YOURSELF

> Who benefits from a tariff? Who loses?

> Why does trade protectionism lead to wasted resources?

> If there are winners and losers from trade restrictions, why do we hear more often from the people who gain from trade restrictions than from the people who lose?

But what happens if the Mexican shirt producers want to buy Mexican goods or European goods rather than U.S. goods? In order to buy Mexican or European goods, the Mexican shirt producers will need pesos or euros. Fortunately, they can trade their dollars for pesos or euros on the foreign exchange market. Suppose the Mexicans trade their dollars to someone in Germany who in return gives them euros. Why would a German want to trade euros for dollars? Remember that people sell in order to buy. Thus, Germans want dollars so that they can buy U.S. goods. So once again, the increased spending on Mexican shirt imports leads to an increase in U.S. exports (in this case to Germany) and thus an increase in jobs in U.S. exporting industries.

Our thought experiment reveals an important truth: *We pay for our imports with exports.* Think about it this way: Why would anyone sell us goods if not to get goods in return? Thus, trade does not eliminate jobs—it moves jobs from import-competing industries to export industries.

When a tariff on shirts is reduced, it's easy to see the jobs lost at a local shirt factory. It's more difficult to see the jobs gained in export industries such as computer production, but the increase in jobs is no less real. And remember although trade does not change the number of jobs it does raise wages, as we demonstrated in the section on comparative advantage.

Of course, it's traumatic to lose a job and not all workers can easily transfer from shirt making to computer production. But in a dynamic and growing economy, job loss and job gain are two sides of the same coin. Thomas Edison ended the whale oil industry with his invention of the electric lightbulb in 1879. This was bad for whalers but good for people who like to read at night (and very good for the whales). The phonograph destroyed jobs in the piano industry (darn that Edison, again!), CDs destroyed jobs in the record industry, and today MP3s are destroying jobs in the CD industry. And, yet somehow with all these jobs being destroyed, employment and the standard of living keep trending upward.

Job destruction is ultimately a healthy part of any growing economy, but that doesn't mean we have to ignore the costs of transitioning from one job to another. Unemployment insurance, savings, and a strong education system can help workers respond to shocks. Trade restrictions, however, are not a good way to respond to shocks. Trade restrictions save *visible* jobs, but they destroy jobs that are just as real but harder to see.

Thomas Edison, destroyer of jobs or benefactor of humanity? Yes.

Child Labor

Is child labor a reason to restrict trade? In part, this is a question of ethics on which reasonable people can disagree but our belief, for which we will give reasons, is that the answer is no.

In 1992, labor activists discovered that Wal-Mart was selling clothing that had been made in Bangladesh by subcontractors who had employed some child workers. Senator Tom Harkin angrily introduced a bill in Congress to prohibit firms from importing any products made by children under the age of 15. Harkin's bill didn't pass, but in a panic the garment industry in Bangladesh dismissed 30 to 50 thousand child workers. A success? Before we decide, we need to think about what happened to the children who were thrown out of work. Where did these children go? To the playground? To

The Pin Factory
Lewis Hine photograph of bowling alley boys in New Haven, Conn. Circa 1910.

school? To a better job? No. Thrown out of the garment factories, the children went to work elsewhere, many at jobs like prostitution with worse conditions and lower pay.[4]

In 2009, about 18 percent of all children aged 5–14 around the world work for a significant number of hours. The vast majority of these children work in agriculture, often alongside their parents, and not in export industries. Restrictions on trade, therefore, cannot directly reduce the number of child workers and by making a poor country poorer, trade restrictions may increase the number of child workers. In fact, studies have shown that more openness to trade increases income and reduces child labor.[5]

Child labor is more common in poor countries and it was common in nineteenth century Great Britain and the United States when people were much poorer than today. Child labor declined in the developed world as people got richer.

The forces that reduced child labor in the developed world are also at work in the developing world. The vertical axis of Figure 8.4 shows the percentage of children ages 10–14 who are laboring in 132 countries across the world. Real GDP per capita is shown on the horizontal axis. The size of the circles is proportionate to the total number of child laborers so although the percentage of child laborers is much higher in Burundi (48.5 percent) than in India (12 percent), there are many more child laborers in India. The lesson of Figure 8.4 is that economic growth reduces child labor.

FIGURE 8.4

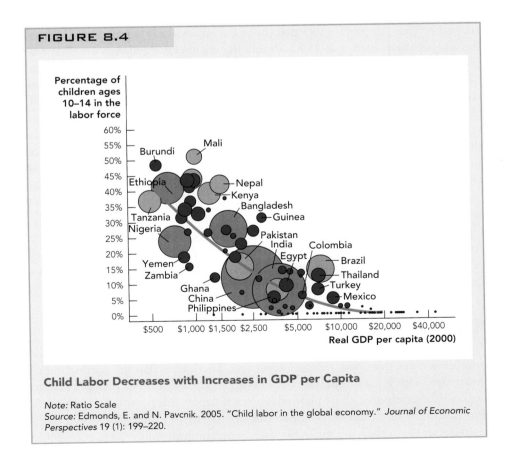

Child Labor Decreases with Increases in GDP per Capita

Note: Ratio Scale
Source: Edmonds, E. and N. Pavcnik. 2005. "Child labor in the global economy." Journal of Economic Perspectives 19 (1): 199–220.

The real cause of child labor is poverty, not trade. Thus, to reduce child labor, we should focus on reducing poverty rather than on reducing trade; putting up trade barriers is likely to be ineffective or even counterproductive.

Governments and nonprofits from the developed world can help developing countries reduce child labor by helping them to improve the quality of schooling and to lower the opportunity cost of education. In Bangladesh, at about the same time that child workers were being thrown out of work by the Harkin bill, the government introduced the Food for Education program. The program provides a free monthly stipend of rice or wheat to poor families who have at least one child attending school that month. The program has been very successful at encouraging school attendance. Even more important, increased education of children today means richer parents tomorrow—parents who will no longer feel crushed by the forces of poverty, or in other words parents who will have enough wealth to feed their children *and* send them to school.[6]

Trade and National Security

If a good is vital for national security but domestic producers have higher costs than foreign producers, it can make sense for the government to tax imports or subsidize the production of the domestic industry. It may make sense, for example, to support a domestic vaccine industry. In 1918, more than a quarter of the U.S. population got sick with the flu and more than 500,000 died, sometimes within hours of being infected. The young were especially hard hit and as a result life expectancy in the United States dropped by 10 years. No place in the world was safe, as between 2.5 percent to 5 percent of the entire world population died from the flu between 1918 and 1920. Producing flu vaccine requires an elaborate process in which robots inject hundreds of millions of eggs with flu viruses. In an ordinary year there are few problems with buying vaccine produced in another country, but if something like the 1918 flu swept the world again it would be wise to have significant vaccine production capacity in the United States.[7]

Don't be surprised, however, if every domestic producer in trouble claims that their product is vital for national security. Everything from beeswax to mohair, not to mention steel and computer chips, has been protected in the name of national security. It's common for protectionists to lobby under the guise of some other motive. Many people are legitimately concerned about working conditions in developing countries but does it surprise you that U.S. labor unions are often the biggest lobbyists for bills to restrict trade on behalf of "oppressed foreign workers"? As Youssef Boutros-Ghali, Egypt's minister for trade put it, "The question is why all of a sudden, when third world labor has proved to be competitive, why do industrial countries start feeling concerned about our workers? .... It is suspicious."[8]

NORM EGGERT

Vital for National Security?
In 1954 the U.S. government declared that mohair, the fleece of the Angora goat, was vital for national security (it can be used to make military uniforms). For nearly forty years mohair producers received millions of dollars in annual payments. Finally, after much ridicule, the program was eliminated in 1993 . . . only to be reestablished in 2002. Hard to believe? Yes, but we aren't kidding around.

Key Industries

Another argument that in principle could be true is the "it's better to produce computer chips than potato chips" argument. The idea is that the production of computer chips is a key industry because it generates spillovers, benefits that go beyond the computer chips themselves (see Chapter 9 for more on spillovers). Protectionism isn't the best policy in this case (in theory, a subsidy would work better), but if a subsidy isn't possible then protectionism might be a second best policy with some net benefits.

The words "in principle," and "might" are well chosen. The "computer chips are better than potato chips" argument can't be faulted on logic alone, but it's not very compelling. To address this particular example, most computer chips today are cheap, mass-manufactured commodities. The United States rightly doesn't specialize in this type of manufacturing and is better off for it, even though this used to be a common argument for protectionism against foreign computer chips.

Second, no one knows which industries are the ones with the really important spillovers. In the late 1980s, many pundits argued that HDTV would be a technology driver for many related industries. Japan and the European Union subsidized their producers to the tune of billions of dollars. The United States lagged behind. In the end, however, Japan and the EU chose an analog technology that is now considered obsolete and HDTV has yet to produce significant benefits for the broader economy, even if it does give you a really nice picture at home.

Strategic Trade Protectionism

In some cases, it's possible for a country to use tariffs and quotas to grab up a larger share of the gains from trade than would be possible with pure free trade policy. The idea is for the government to help domestic firms to act like a cartel when they sell to international buyers. Oddly, the way to do this is to limit or tax exports. A tax or limit on exports reduces exports but can drive up the price enough so that net revenues increase. Of course, this can only work if international buyers have few substitutes for the domestic good. Could this work in practice? Yes, in many ways OPEC is a possible example. OPEC limits exports and because the demand for oil is inelastic this increases oil revenues.

Oil is a special good, however, because it is found in large quantities in just a few places in the world. The United States would have a much harder time using strategic trade protectionism because there are more substitutes for U.S. produced goods. The U.S. economy, or any advanced economy, would also have another problem. Oil is Saudi Arabia's only significant export so when they raise the price of oil, the rest of the world can't threaten to retaliate by putting tariffs on Saudi Arabia's other exports. But if the United States were to try to grab up a larger share of the gains from trade, in say computers, other countries could respond with tariffs on our grain exports. A trade war could easily make both countries worse off. Trying to divide the pie in your favor usually makes the pie smaller.

Trade and Globalization

Having trouble understanding the theory of international trade? GrowingStars. com offers online tutors who are available 24 hours a day, 7 days a week to help you understand difficult topics in economics.* GrowingStars tutors ought to understand international trade: The tutors live in India.[10]

Declines in transportation costs, integration of world markets, and increased speed of communication have made the world a smaller place. But globalization is not new; rather it has been a theme in human history since at least the Roman Empire, which knit together different parts of the world in a common economic and political area. When these trade networks later fell apart, the subsequent era was named "The Dark Ages."

Later, the European Renaissance arose from revitalized trade routes, the rebirth of commercially based cities, and also the spread of science from China,

COURTESY WAL-MART STORES, INC.

Wal-Mart: SuperProductivity
Surprisingly, the biggest factor in the productivity boom of the 1990s was not a Silicon Valley high-tech firm but improvements in the retail and wholesale sector. Wal-Mart alone was responsible for one-eighth of these productivity gains and Wal-Mart innovations in warehouse logistics, wireless bar code scanning, and database integration spread throughout the retail industry. Computer chips may be better than potato chips, but apparently *selling* potato chips is best of all.[9]

CHECK YOURSELF

> Over the past 30 years, most U.S. garment manufacturing has moved overseas, to places such as India and China, where wages are lower. The result of this shift has been a sizeable drop in the number of garment workers in the United States. While bad for these workers, why has this trend been a net benefit for the United States?

> What would happen if the U.S. government decided that computer chip manufacturing was a strategic national industry and provided monetary grants to Silicon Valley companies? Trace the effects of this policy on Silicon Valley companies, foreign competitors, and the cost and benefit to U.S. taxpayers and consumers.

---

* We are using GrowingStars as an example of globalization. We have not evaluated the services of GrowingStars or any online tutors and make no recommendation for or against any such service.

India, and the Middle East. Periods of increased trade, and the spread of ideas, have been among the best for human progress. As economist Donald Boudreaux puts it "globalization is the advance of human cooperation across national boundaries."[11]

□ Takeaway

Specialization and trade create enormous increases in productivity. Without trade, the knowledge used by an entire economy is approximately equal to the knowledge used by one brain. With specialization and trade, the total sum of knowledge used in an economy increases tremendously and far exceeds that of any one brain. Specialization and trade also let us take advantage of economies of scale.

International trade is trade across political borders. The theory of comparative advantage explains how a country, just like a person, can increase its standard of living by specializing in what it can make at low (opportunity) cost and trading for what it can make only at high cost. When we apply the logic of opportunity cost to trade, we discover that everyone has a comparative advantage in something so everyone can benefit from inclusion in the worldwide market.

Restrictions on trade waste resources by transferring production from low-cost foreign producers to high-cost domestic producers. Restrictions on trade also prevent domestic consumers from exploiting gains from trade with foreign producers. Domestic producers can benefit from trade restrictions, but domestic consumers lose more than the producers gain. Trade restrictions sometimes persist because the benefits from restrictions are often concentrated on small groups who lobby for protection, while the costs of restrictions are spread over millions of consumers and can be small for each individual.

High productivity countries have high wages, low productivity countries have low wages. Trade means that workers in both countries can raise their wages to the highest levels allowed for by their productivities. International trade does not raise productivity directly but can help poor countries raise their productivity indirectly by diffusing knowledge and capital.

We have set out various common arguments for restricting trade. Some of these arguments are valid but they are usually of limited applicability.

Globalization is not new but an important theme in history and one connected with human progress.

□ CHAPTER REVIEW

KEY CONCEPTS

Economies of scale, p. 145

Absolute advantage, p. 146

Comparative advantage, p. 146

Protectionism, p. 150

Tariff, p. 150

Trade quota, p. 151

FACTS AND TOOLS

1. Use the idea of the "division of knowledge" to answer the following questions.

   a. Which country has more knowledge: Utopia, where in the words of Karl Marx, each person knows just enough about hunting, fishing, and cattle raising to "hunt in the morning, fish in the afternoon, [and] rear cattle in the evening," or Drudgia, where one-third of the population learns only about hunting, one-third only about fishing, and one-third only about cattle raising?

b. Which planet has more knowledge: Xeroxia, each of whose one million inhabitants knows the same list of one million facts, or Differentia, whose one million inhabitants each know a different set of one million facts? How many facts are known in Xeroxia? How many facts are known in Differentia?

2. In the *Wealth of Nations*, Adam Smith said that one reason specialization makes someone more productive is because "a man commonly saunters a little in turning his hand from one sort of employment to another." How can you use this observation to improve your pattern of studying for your four or five college courses this semester?

3. "Opportunity cost" is one of the tougher ideas in economics. Let's make it easier by starting with some simple examples. In the examples below, find the opportunity cost: Your answer should be a *rate*, as in "1.5 widgets per year" or "6 lectures per month." Ignoring Adam Smith's insight from the previous question, assume that these relationships are simple linear ones, so that if you put in twice the time you get twice the output, and half the time yields half the output.

a. Erin has a choice between two activities: She can repair one transmission per hour or she can repair two fuel injectors per hour. What is the opportunity cost of repairing one transmission?

b. Katie works at a customer service center and every hour she has a choice between two activities: Answering 200 telephone calls per hour or responding to 400 emails per hour. What is the opportunity cost of responding to 400 phone calls?

c. Deirdre has a choice between writing one more book this year or five more articles this year. What is the opportunity cost of writing half of a book this year, in terms of articles?

4. a. American workers are typically paid much more than Chinese workers. *True or false:* This is largely because American workers are typically more productive than Chinese workers.

b. Julia Child, an American chef (and World War II spy) who reintroduced French cooking to Americans in the 1960s, was paid much more than most American chefs. *True or false:* This was largely because Julia Child was much more productive than most American chefs.

5. The Japanese people currently pay about four times the world price for rice. If Japan removed its trade barriers so that Japanese consumers could buy rice at the world price, who would be better off and who would be worse off: Japanese consumers or Japanese rice farmers? If we added all the gains and losses to the Japanese, would there be a net gain or net loss? Who would make a greater effort lobbying, for or against, this reduction in trade barriers: Japanese consumers or Japanese rice farmers?

6. The supply curve for rice in Japan slopes upward, just like any normal supply curve. If Japan eliminated its trade barriers to rice, what would happen to the number of workers employed in the rice-producing industry in Japan: Would it rise or fall? What would these workers probably do over the next year or so? Will they ever work again?

7. In Figure 8.3, consider triangles B and C. One of these could be labeled "Workers and machines who could be better used in another sector of the economy," while the other could be labeled "Consumers who have to pay more than necessary for their product." Which is which?

8. In his book *The Choice,* economist Russ Roberts asks how voters would feel about a machine that could convert wheat into automobiles.

a. Do you think that voters would complain that this machine should be banned, since it would destroy jobs in the auto industry?

b. Would this machine *in fact* destroy jobs in the auto industry? If so, would roughly the same number of jobs eventually be created in other industries?

c. Here is Roberts's punch line: If voters were told that the wonder machine was in fact just a cargo ship that exported wheat and imported autos from a foreign country, how would voters' attitudes toward this machine change?

9. According to the *Wall Street Journal* (August 30, 2007, "In the Balance"), it takes about 30 hours to assemble a vehicle in the United States. Let's use that fact plus a few invented numbers to sum up the global division of labor in auto manufacturing. In international economics, "North" is shorthand for the high-tech developed countries of East Asia, North America, and Western Europe, while "South" is shorthand for the rest of the world. Let's use that shorthand here.

   a. Consider the productivity table below: Which region has an absolute advantage at making high-quality cars? And low quality cars?

	Number of Hours to Make One High-Quality Car	Number of Hours to Make One Low-Quality Car
North	30	20
South	60	30

   b. Using the information in the productivity table above, estimate the opportunity cost of making high- or low-quality cars in the North and in the South. Which region has a comparative advantage (i.e., lowest opportunity cost) for manufacturing high-quality cars? For low-quality cars?

	Opportunity Cost of Making One High-Quality Car	Opportunity Cost of Making One Low-Quality Car
North	_____ low-quality cars	_____ high-quality cars
South	_____ low-quality cars	_____ high-quality cars

   c. There are one million hours of labor available for making cars in the North, and another one million hours of labor available for making cars in the South. In a no-trade world, let's assume that two-thirds of the auto industry labor in each region is used to make high-quality cars and one-third is used

to make low-quality cars. Solve for how many of each kind of car will be produced in North and South, and add up to determine total global output of each type of car. (Why will both kinds of cars be made? Because the low-quality cars will be less expensive.)

	Output of High-Quality Cars	Output of Low-Quality Cars
North		
South		
Global output		

   d. Now, allow specialization. If each region completely specializes in the type of car in which they hold the comparative advantage, what will global output of high-quality cars be? Of low-quality cars? In the table below, report your answers. Is global output in each kind of car higher than before? (We'll solve a problem with the final step of trade in the Thinking and Problem Solving section.)

	Output of High-Quality Cars	Output of Low-Quality Cars
North		
South		
Global output		

THINKING AND PROBLEM SOLVING

1. Fit each of the following examples into one of the three reasons for trade:

   I. Division of knowledge

   II. Economies of scale/creating competition

   III. Comparative advantage

     a. It is the 1950s. The American auto industry makes mediocre cars at high prices. The main reason they can do this is because they face little pressure to improve. Once the Japanese start making mediocre cars at low prices in the 1970s, American firms feel a pressure to improve their products.

b. Two recently abandoned cats, Bingo and Tuppy, need to quickly learn how to catch mice in order to survive. If they also remain well groomed, they stand a better chance of surviving: Good grooming reduces the risk of disease and parasites. Each cat could go it alone, focusing almost exclusively on learning to catch mice. The alternative would be for Bingo to specialize in learning how to groom well and for Tuppy to specialize in learning how to catch mice well.

c. Former President Bill Clinton, a graduate of Yale Law School, hires attorneys who are less skilled than himself to do routine legal work.

2. Let's see how important "economies of scale" can be. Assume that it costs $1 billion to build a new computer chip facility. (The true cost would be more like $3 billion, as an Internet news search for "computer chip factory cost" will demonstrate.) Once the factory is open, it costs only $1 to produce an additional chip.

a. What is the total cost of producing one chip? (Be sure to include the cost of building the factory.)

b. What is the total cost of producing 100,000 chips? What is the average cost per chip? (Average cost equals total cost divided by number of chips.)

c. What is the average cost per chip of producing 1 million chips? The average cost per chip if the company makes one billion chips? (Notice how this is similar to Chapter 11's discussion of the positive relationship between market size and research activity. Such "scale effects" are common in economics.)

d. Just to make a profit, the price of a computer chip must be more than the average cost of making that chip ($P > AC$, as they say in microeconomics). Canada's population is 34 million: If Canada had to

make its own computer chips in a billion-dollar factory, and it needed to make one chip per person, could computer chips sell for less than $10 each? Could they sell for less than $100 each?

3. Nobel Laureate Paul Samuelson said that comparative advantage is one of the few ideas in economics that is both "true and not obvious." Since it's not obvious, we should practice with it a bit. In each of the cases below, who has the absolute advantage at each task, and who has the comparative advantage?

a. In 30 minutes, Kana can either make miso soup or she can clean the kitchen. In 15 minutes, Mitchell can make miso soup; it takes Mitchell an hour to clean the kitchen.

b. In one hour, Ethan can bake 20 cookies or lay the drywall for two rooms. In one hour, Sienna can bake 100 cookies or lay the drywall for three rooms.

c. Kara can build two glass sculptures per day or she can design two full-page newspaper advertisements per day. Sara can build one glass sculpture per day or design four full-page newspaper ads per day.

d. Data can write 12 excellent poems per day or solve 100 difficult physics problems per day. Riker can write one excellent poem per day or solve 0.5 difficult physics problems per day.

4. a. Just to review: Back in Chapter 6 on price ceilings, we illustrated price ceilings with a horizontal line below the equilibrium price. Did price ceilings create surpluses or shortages?

b. The horizontal line in Figure 8.1 doesn't represent a surplus or a shortage. What does it represent?

c. Figure 8.1 considers the case of a country that can buy as many semiconductors as it wants at the same world price. Why do people in this country only buy $Q_d^{\text{Free Trade}}$ units? Why don't they buy more of this inexpensive product?

5. Figure 8.1 looks at a case where the world price is below the domestic no-trade price. Let's look at the case where the world price is *above* the domestic no-trade price. We'll work with the market for airplanes shown in the figure below.

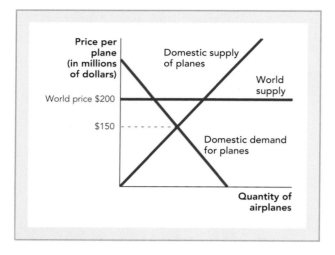

a. In the above figure, use the Quantity axis to label $Q_S^{\text{free trade}}$ and $Q_D^{\text{free trade}}$. This is somewhat similar to Figure 8.1.

b. What would you call the gap between $Q_S^{\text{free trade}}$ and $Q_D^{\text{free trade}}$?

c. Also following Figure 8.1, label "domestic consumption" and "domestic production."

d. Will domestic airplane buyers—airlines and delivery companies like FedEx—have to pay a higher or a lower price under free trade compared to the no-trade alternative? Will domestic airplane buyers purchase a higher or a lower quantity of planes if there's free trade in planes?

e. Based on your answer to part d, would you expect domestic airplane demanders to support free trade in planes or oppose it?

6. The federal education reform law known as No Child Left Behind requires every state to create standardized tests that measure whether students have mastered key subjects. Since the same test is given to all students in the same grade in the state, this encourages all schools within a state to cover the same material. According to the division of knowledge model, what are the costs of this approach?

7. In the text, we discuss sugar farmers in Florida who use unusually large amounts of fertilizer to produce their crops; they do so because their land isn't all that great for sugar production. If we translate this into the language of the supply curve, would these Florida sugar farms be those

on the lower-left part of a supply curve, or those along the upper-right of the supply curve? Why?

8. In this chapter, we've often emphasized how specialization and exchange can create more *output*. But sometimes the output from voluntary exchange is difficult to measure and doesn't show up in GDP statistics. In each of the following cases, explain how the two parties involved might be able to make themselves *both* better off just by making a voluntary exchange.

a. Alan received two copies of *Gears of War* as birthday gifts. Burton received two copies of *Halo* as birthday gifts.

b. Jeb has a free subscription to *Field and Stream* but isn't interested in hunting. George has a free subscription to the *Miami Herald* but isn't all that interested in Florida news.

c. Pat has a lot of love to give, but it is worthless unless received by another. Terry is in the same sad situation.

9. According to Chinese government statistics, China imported 140,000 sedans in 2007. Let's see what would happen to consumer and producer surplus if China were to ban sedan imports. To keep things simple, let's assume that if sedan imports were banned, the equilibrium price of sedans (holding quality constant!) would rise by $5,000.

a. In the figure below, shade the area that represents the total gains when sedan imports are allowed into China.

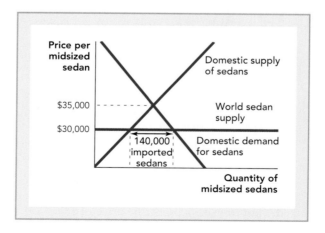

b. Once China bans the import of sedans, what is the dollar value of the lost gains from trade? (Hint: The chapter provides the formula.)

c. If sedan imports are banned, Chinese sedan producers will be better off and Chinese sedan consumers will be worse off. A polygon in the figure above shows the surplus that will shift from consumers to producers. Write the word "transfer" in this polygon. (Hint: It's not the area you calculated in part b.)

10. Here's another specialization and exchange problem. This problem is wholly made-up, so that you won't be able to use your intuition about the names of countries or the products to figure out the answer.

   a. Consider the productivity table below: Which country has an absolute advantage at making rotids? At making taurons?

	Number of Hours to Make One Rotid	Number of Hours to Make One Tauron
Mandovia	50	100
Ducennia	150	200

   b. Using the information in the productivity table above, estimate the opportunity cost of making rotids and taurons in Mandovia and Ducennia. Which country has a comparative advantage at manufacturing rotids? At making taurons?

	Opportunity Cost of Making One Rotid	Opportunity Cost of Making One Tauron
Mandovia	____taurons	____rotids
Ducennia	____taurons	____rotids

   c. There are one billion hours of labor available for making products in Mandovia, and two billion hours of labor available for making products in Ducennia. In a no-trade world, let's assume that half the labor in each country gets used to make each product. (In a semester-long international trade course, you'd build a bigger model that would determine just how the workers get divided up according to the forces of supply and demand.) Fill in the table.

	Output of Rotids	Output of Taurons
Mandovia		
Ducennia		
Total output		

   d. Now, allow specialization. If each country completely specializes in the product in which they hold the comparative advantage, what will total output of rotids be? Of taurons? Is total output of each product higher than before?

	Output of Rotids	Output of Taurons
Mandovia		
Ducennia		
Total output		

   e. Finally, let's open up trade. Trade has to make both sides better off (or at least no worse off), and in this problem as in most negotiations, there's more than one price that can do so (just think about haggling over the price of a car or a house). Let's pick out a case that makes one side better off, and leaves the other side just as well off as in a no-trade world. The price both sides agree to is three rotids for two taurons. Ship 5 million taurons in one direction, and 7.5 million rotids in the other direction (You'll have to figure out on your own which way the trade flows). In the table below calculate the amount that each country gets to consume. Which country is better off under this set of prices? Which one is exactly as well off as before?

	Consumption of Rotids	Consumption of Taurons
Mandovia		
Ducennia		
Total consumption		

f. This time, the trade negotiations turn out differently: It's two rotids for one tauron. Have the correct country ship 10 million rotids, have the other send 5 million taurons, and fill out the table below. One way to make sure you haven't made a mistake is to make sure that "total consumption" is equal to "total output" from part d: We can't create rotids and taurons out of thin air! Are both countries better off than if there were no trade? Which country likes this trade deal better than the deal from part e?

	Consumption of Rotids	Consumption of Taurons
Mandovia		
Ducennia		
Total consumption		

CHALLENGES

1. In the chapter, we focused on a sugar tariff that eliminated all imports. Let's now take a look at the case where the sugar tariff eliminates some but not all imports. We will also examine the closely related case of a quota on sugar imports. The figure below shows a tariff on sugar that raises the U.S. price to 20 cents per pound but at that price some sugar is imported even after the tariff.

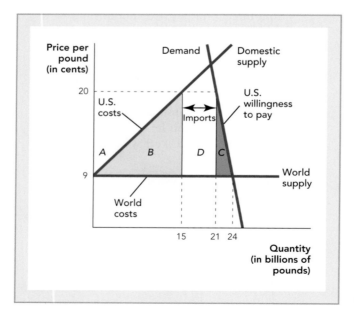

a. Label the free trade equilibrium, the tariff equilibrium, wasted resources, lost gains from trade, and tariff revenues.

b. Now imagine that instead of a tariff, the U.S. government uses a quota that forbids imports of sugar greater than 6 billion pounds. (Equivalently imagine a tariff that is zero on the first 6 billion pounds of imports but then jumps to a prohibitive level after that quantity of imports—this is closer to how the system works in practice.) Under the quota system what does area D represent? Would importers of sugar prefer a tariff or a quota?

c. The sugar quota is allocated to importing countries based on imports from these countries between 1975 and 1981 (with some subsequent adjustments). For example, in 2008 Australia was given the right to export 87 thousand metric tons of sugar to the United States at a very low tariff rate while Belize was given the right to export 11.5 thousand metric tons of sugar to the United States at a very low tariff rate. How do you think these rights are allocated to firms within the sugar-exporting countries?

d. Discuss how the quota and the way it is allocated could create a misallocation of resources that would further reduce efficiency relative to a tariff that resulted in the same quantity of imports.

2. In a 2005 *Washington Post* article ("The Road to Riches Is Called K Street"), Jeffrey Birnbaum noted that there were 35,000 registered lobbyists in Washington, D.C., people whose primary job is asking the federal government for something. A lobbyist who comes with long experience as an aide to a powerful politician will earn at least $200,000 per year. Many lobbyists (not all) are attempting to restrict trade in order to turn consumer surplus into producer surplus.

a. Let's focus just on the lobbyists who are restricting trade. If the United States were to amend the Constitution to permanently ban all tariffs and trade restrictions, these lobbyists would lose their jobs, and they'd have to leave Washington to get "real jobs." Would this job change raise U.S. productivity or lower it?

b. Would most of these lobbyists likely earn more after the amendment was enacted or less?

c. How can you reconcile your answers to parts a and b?

3. Let's think a little more about Thinking and Problem Solving question 9. If quality *weren't* held constant, what would you expect to happen to the additional Chinese sedans produced after the import ban? Would they be as good as the ones that used to be imported? (Hint: Which types of sedans do you think that China imports? Low quality or high quality? Why?)

4. In Facts and Tools question 9, we didn't do the final step: trade. There's more than one price at which both sides would agree to an exchange. What is the *complete* price range (number of low-quality cars per high-quality car) that would make both sides better off?

9

Externalities: When Prices Send the Wrong Signals

CHAPTER OUTLINE

External Costs, External Benefits, and Efficiency

Private Solutions to Externality Problems

Government Solutions to Externality Problems

Takeaway

On a sunny day in June 1924, a young man developed a blister on his toe after playing a game of tennis. A week later, he was dead from a bacterial infection. The young man had been given the best medical care possible: he was the son of the president of the United States, Calvin Coolidge. President Coolidge wept when he learned that all the "power and the glory of the presidency" could not prevent the death of his son from a simple blister.

The president's son, Calvin Jr., was probably killed by a bacterium called *Staphylococcus aureus* or *staph* for short. Penicillin could easily have cured him, but penicillin was not discovered until 1928. When penicillin and other antibiotics became widely available in the 1940s, they were hailed as miracle drugs. Dying from a blister became a thing of the past—until recently.

Staph has evolved. Today it is resistant to penicillin and some "superbug" strains are resistant to almost all antibiotics. In 2007, five healthy high school athletes died from infections much like those that killed Calvin Jr. Multidrug-resistant *Staphylococcus aureus* is now spreading around the globe.

Antibiotic resistance is a product of evolution. Any population of bacteria includes some bacteria with unusual traits, such as the ability to resist an antibiotic's attack. When a person takes an antibiotic, the drug kills the defenseless bacteria, leaving the unusually strong bacteria behind. Without competition for resources, these stronger bacteria multiply rapidly. When the same antibiotic is applied again and again, the stronger bacteria get even stronger until after many generations of bacteria, the antibiotic loses its power to perform miracles.

Evolution is a powerful force so it was inevitable that staph would grow resistant to penicillin eventually, but staph has grown more resistant more quickly than was necessary. The problem is that antibiotics are overused.

A **private cost** is a cost paid by the consumer or the producer.

An **external cost** is a cost paid by people other than the consumer or the producer trading in the market.

The **social cost** is the cost to everyone, the private cost plus the external cost.

Externalities are external costs or external benefits, costs or benefits that fall on bystanders.

Social surplus is consumer surplus plus producer surplus plus everyone else's surplus.

Antibiotic users get all the benefits of antibiotics but they do not bear all of the costs. The patient or the farmer who demands an antibiotic must pay a **private cost** for the antibiotic, the market price. But because bacteria spread widely, each use of an antibiotic creates a small increase in bacterial resistance, which raises the probability that other people could die from a simple infection. For example, when a teenager takes tetracycline for acne there is an increase in antibiotic-resistant bacteria on the skin of *other* members of his or her family. Antimicrobial detergents that are washed down the sink enter into the environment where they increase the proportion of resistant bacteria for us all. Almost half of all antibiotics are used on farm animals, not to treat disease but primarily because they increase and accelerate growth. Bacteria that develop resistance on the farm travel onto and into human beings where they may cause incurable infections.

In a sense, each use of antibiotics pollutes the environment with more resistant and stronger bacteria. Thus, each use of antibiotics creates an **external cost**, a cost that is paid not by the consumers or producers of antibiotics but by bystanders to the transaction. The **social cost** of antibiotic use is the cost to everyone, the private cost plus the external cost.

Since the external cost is not paid by consumers or producers, it is not built into the price of antibiotics. So when patients or farmers choose whether to use more antibiotics, they compare their private benefits with the market price, but they ignore the external costs just as a factory will ignore the cost of the pollution that it emits into the atmosphere (assuming there are no regulations forbidding this). Since antibiotic users ignore some relevant costs of their actions, antibiotics are overused. Alternatively stated, since the price of antibiotics does not include all the costs of using antibiotics, the price sends an imperfect signal—the price is too low and so antibiotics are overused. Thus, the problem of antibiotic resistance is about evolution *and* economics. Evolution drives antibiotic resistance, but the process is happening much faster than we would like because antibiotic users do not take into account the external costs of their choices.

External Costs, External Benefits, and Efficiency

This chapter is about products, like antibiotics, for which some of the costs or benefits of the product fall on bystanders. These costs or benefits are called external costs or external benefits or, for short, **externalities.** When externalities are significant, markets work less well and government action can increase social surplus.

In Chapter 3, we showed that a market equilibrium maximizes consumer plus producer surplus (the gains from trade). But maximizing consumer plus producer surplus isn't so great if bystanders are harmed in the process. Everyone counts, not just the consumers and producers of a particular product. So, when we evaluate how well a market with externalities is working we want to look at **social surplus,** namely consumer surplus plus producer surplus plus everyone else's surplus.

To show why a market with externalities *does not* maximize *social surplus,* it's useful to briefly review why a market equilibrium *does* maximize *consumer plus producer surplus* (see also Chapter 3). The key is to remember that you can read the value of the nth unit of a good from the height of the demand curve and the cost of the nth unit of a good from the height of the supply curve. For example, imagine that buyers and sellers are currently exchanging 99 units of a good. What is the value to buyers and the costs to sellers of one additional unit, the 100th unit? In Figure 9.1, you can read the value to buyers from the height of the demand curve at the 100th unit, namely $22. You can read the cost to sellers from the height of the supply curve at the 100th unit, namely $10. Since the value of the 100th unit exceeds the additional cost of the 100th unit, there is an incentive to trade, namely an opportunity to increase consumer and producer surplus. Following this logic, trade is mutually profitable up until the 210th unit is sold. The value to buyers of the 210th unit is $13 and the cost to sellers of producing that additional unit is $13 so at this point there are no further incentives to trade. If any fewer units were traded, gains from trade would be left on the table. If any more units were traded, the cost of those units would exceed their value. Thus, gains from trade are maximized at the market equilibrium of 210 units.

Let's call the price and quantity that maximize social surplus the **efficient equilibrium**. If there are no significant externalities, the market equilibrium is also the efficient equilibrium (because if there are no significant external costs or benefits, maximizing producer plus consumer surplus is the same as maximizing everyone's surplus). But if there are significant externalities, the market equilibrium is no longer the efficient equilibrium, as we will now show.

FIGURE 9.1

Reviewing Gains from Trade The value of the 100th unit to buyers is $22. The cost of the 100th unit to sellers is $10. At the 100th unit, there is a $12 gain from exchange. Gains from trade are maximized when a total of 210 units are exchanged. Notice that the value of the 210th unit is just equal to the cost of the 210th unit.

The **efficient equilibrium** is the price and quantity that maximizes social surplus.

External Costs

The left panel of Figure 9.2 on the next page shows the market equilibrium for antibiotics. As usual, the market equilibrium maximizes consumer plus producer surplus. But now the use of antibiotics creates an external cost, a cost to people who are neither buying nor selling antibiotics. At the market equilibrium, the price of a round of antibiotics—such as your doctor would prescribe to cure an infection—is $5 and we will assume that the external cost of antibiotic use is $7, a number that is consistent with a recent study of the matter.[1] The private cost plus the external cost is the social cost of antibiotic use.

In the right panel of Figure 9.2, we add the external cost to the supply curve to show the social cost curve. The social cost curve takes into account *all* of the costs of antibiotic use so it's the social cost curve that we use to figure out the **efficient quantity**, the quantity that maximizes social surplus. The efficient quantity, $Q_{Efficient}$, is found where the demand curve intersects the social cost curve.

To see exactly why the market equilibrium is *not* efficient, let's consider the value to buyers and the social costs of the Q_{Market} unit of the good. The height of the demand curve at the Q_{Market} unit (the black arrow labeled Private value) tells us that this unit has a private value of $5. The height of the social cost curve at Q_{Market} (the green arrow labeled Social cost) tells us that this unit has a social cost of $12. Thus, producing this unit creates a social loss or deadweight loss of $7. Following this logic, you can see that reducing output increases social surplus so long as the social cost of an additional prescription of antibiotics

The **efficient quantity** is the quantity that maximizes social surplus.

FIGURE 9.2

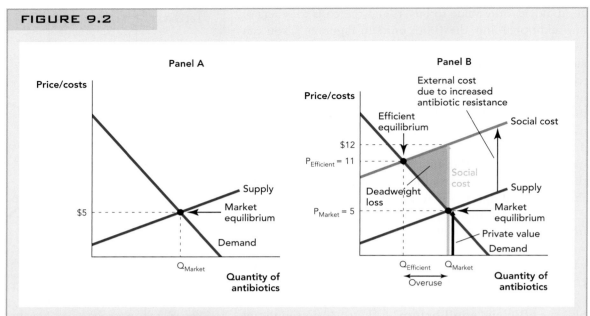

When External Costs Are Significant, Output Is Too High
Panel A: The market equilibrium is found, as usual, where the supply and demand curves intersect. The market equilibrium maximizes consumer plus producer surplus.
Panel B: We add external costs to the supply curve to find the social cost curve. Notice that the social cost of the Q_{Market} unit exceeds the private value of this unit. The efficient equilibrium is found where the social cost and demand curves intersect. $Q_{Efficient}$ is less than Q_{Market} so the market overproduces goods with significant external costs.

exceeds the buyer value, that is, so long as the social cost curve lies above the demand curve. Thus, to maximize social surplus, output should be reduced to $Q_{Efficient}$, the point at which the social cost curve intersects the demand curve and where the social costs of an additional unit just equal the value.

A final way of illustrating the overuse of antibiotics is to notice that *if* the users did bear all the costs of antibiotic use, that is, *if* the private cost included the $7 external cost, then the supply curve would shift upward and would be the same as the social cost curve. The market equilibrium would then be the same as the efficient equilibrium, that is, buyers would purchase $Q_{Efficient}$ units. But for determining efficient quantities, *who* bears the costs is irrelevant—*costs are costs regardless of who bears them.* Thus, $Q_{Efficient}$ is the efficient quantity when antibiotic users pay all of the costs *and* when they pay only some of the costs—the only difference is that when other people bear some of the costs, antibiotic users purchase more antibiotics, so $Q_{Market} > Q_{Efficient}$.

The last way of explaining why antibiotics are overused suggests one potential solution to the problem of external costs. If antibiotic users had to pay a tax just equal to the external costs, $7, they would demand only the amount $Q_{Efficient}$. Remember from Chapter 7 that a tax on suppliers will shift the supply curve up by the amount of the tax. Thus, in Figure 9.2, notice that a tax set equal to the level of the external cost would shift the supply curve up so that it exactly over-lays the social cost curve. The market quantity would then fall from Q_{Market} to $Q_{Efficient}$. Thus, a tax set equal to the external cost would once again mean that the market equilibrium was the efficient equilibrium!

A tax on an ordinary good increases deadweight loss, as we discussed in Chapter 7, but a tax on a good with an external cost reduces deadweight loss and raises revenue. For these reasons, there is a strong argument for taxing goods with external costs. Such taxes are often called **Pigouvian taxes,** after the economist Arthur C. Pigou (1877–1959) who first focused attention on externalities and how they might be corrected with taxes. We will return to look at solutions to external cost problems in more detail after we have examined a parallel issue, namely that of external benefits.

A **Pigouvian tax** is a tax on a good with external costs.

External Benefits

An **external benefit** is a benefit to people other than the consumers or the producers trading in the market. Consider, for example, another medical good, vaccines. Vaccines benefit the person who is vaccinated but they also create an external benefit for other people because people who have been vaccinated are less likely to harbor and spread disease-causing viruses.*

An **external benefit** is a benefit received by people other than the consumers or producers trading in the market.

In a typical year, for example, some 36,000 Americans die from the flu, a contagious respiratory disease caused by influenza viruses. Fortunately, millions of Americans get a yearly vaccination—a "flu shot"—that is usually effective at preventing the flu. Flu viruses spread from person to person when someone who *already has the flu* coughs or sneezes. As a result, when one person gets a flu shot, the expected number of people who get the flu falls by more than one. So getting a flu shot is a real public service. Get a flu shot. The life you save may not be your own.

So what's the problem? The problem is not the millions of Americans who get a flu shot—it's the even larger number of Americans who don't get one. When an individual compares the private costs and benefits of getting a flu shot, it may be quite sensible not to get one. It takes time to get a shot, it costs money, and there is often a slight fever and ache. The problem is that the person getting the shot bears all these costs but doesn't receive all the benefits. As a result, fewer people get flu shots than is efficient.

In Figure 9.3 on the next page, for example, we show the demand and supply of vaccines. Demanders compare their private value of vaccines with their private costs and purchase Q_{Market} units at the price P_{Market}. Vaccination, however, reduces the probability that a disease spreads so there are external benefits from vaccination. The social value curve counts *all* the benefits of vaccine use, the private value plus the external benefits, so the efficient quantity is found where the social value curve intersects the supply curve.

To see exactly why the market equilibrium is not efficient, consider in Figure 9.3 the private and social value of the Q_{Market} unit of vaccination. This unit has a private cost of $20 (the black arrow labeled Private cost) but it has a social value of $40 (the green arrow labeled Social value). Thus, consuming more units would increase social surplus. Following this logic, you can see that increasing output increases social surplus so long as the social value of an additional flu shot exceeds the private cost, that is, so long as the social value curve is above the supply curve. Thus, to maximize social surplus output should increase to $Q_{Efficient}$, the unit for which social value just equals the costs of production.

A final way of illustrating the underuse of vaccines is to notice that *if* people who got a flu shot did receive all the benefits of vaccination, then their demand

---

* An antibiotic could also have an external benefit in the case of infections that can be easily transmitted. Not all infections are easily transmitted, however, and the external costs due to antibiotic resistance appear to be much larger than any external benefits.

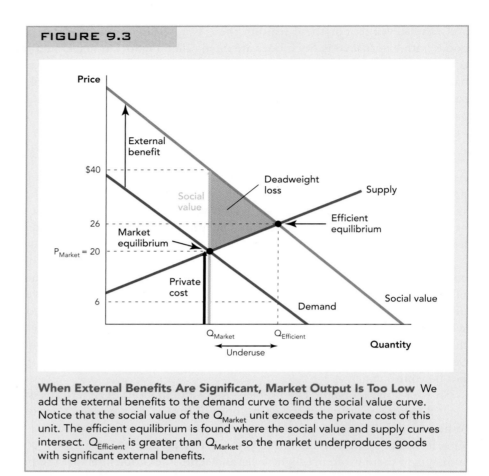

FIGURE 9.3

When External Benefits Are Significant, Market Output Is Too Low We add the external benefits to the demand curve to find the social value curve. Notice that the social value of the Q_{Market} unit exceeds the private cost of this unit. The efficient equilibrium is found where the social value and supply curves intersect. $Q_{Efficient}$ is greater than Q_{Market} so the market underproduces goods with significant external benefits.

curve would shift upward by $20 and would be the same as the social value curve. The market equilibrium would then be the same as the efficient equilibrium, that is, buyers would purchase $Q_{Efficient}$ units. But for determining efficiency *who* receives the benefits is irrelevant—benefits are benefits regardless of who receives them. Thus, $Q_{Efficient}$ is the efficient quantity when vaccine users receive all of the benefits of vaccination *and* when they receive only some of the benefits—the only difference is that when other people receive some of the benefits fewer people purchase flu shots, so $Q_{Market} < Q_{Efficient}$.

The last way of thinking about the problem of external benefits also suggests one potential solution. If every time someone was vaccinated they were given a subsidy of $20, the monetary equivalent of the external benefit, they would demand the amount $Q_{Efficient}$. Recall from Chapter 7 that a subsidy to buyers will shift up the demand curve by the amount of the subsidy. Thus, in Figure 9.3, notice that a subsidy set equal to the level of the external benefit would shift the demand curve up and increase the market quantity from Q_{Market} to $Q_{Efficient}$. In other words, if set correctly, a subsidy will make the market equilibrium equal to the efficient equilibrium. In addition, unlike in Chapter 7 where we looked at subsidies on ordinary goods, a subsidy on a good with an external benefit will reduce deadweight loss, thereby increasing social surplus.

A **Pigouvian subsidy** is a subsidy on a good with external benefits.

A subsidy on a good with an external benefit is often called a **Pigouvian subsidy,** again after Pigou, who first discussed these issues. Another way of thinking about Pigouvian taxes and subsidies is to recall from Chapter 5 that market prices are signals. But when there are external costs or benefits, the market price sends the wrong signal. If there are external costs the market price is too low, thus resulting in overproduction. A Pigouvian tax increases the price so that the after-tax price sends the correct signal. Similarly, if there are external benefits the market price is too high, thus resulting in underproduction. A Pigouvian subsidy reduces the price so that the after-subsidy price sends the correct signal.

Let's look in more detail at how to solve problems caused by external costs or benefits. We will discuss private solutions to problems created by externalities and three types of solutions involving government: taxes and subsidies (which we have mentioned already), command and control, and tradable permits.

Private Solutions to Externality Problems

In a classic paper on externalities, the Nobel Prize-winning economist James Meade wrote that the market for honey was inefficient. As they make honey, bees pollinate fruits and vegetables, which is an important benefit to farmers. Since pollination is an external benefit of honey production, Meade argued there was too little honey being made.

Meade was right about the bees, but wrong about the market for honey. Bee pollination is a thriving business for which beekeepers are paid. In fact, in the United States, beekeepers manage around half a billion bees that they truck around the country to rent out to farmers. Since farmers pay beekeepers to pollinate their crops, the "external benefit" becomes internalized—the beekeepers earn money from the pollination of fruits and vegetables and so expand production toward the efficient quantity, the quantity that takes into account the benefits of bees for honey production and for fruit and vegetable production.[2]

The market in pollination is quite sophisticated. When bees pollinate almonds, for example, the honey that they produce doesn't taste good so beekeepers charge almond growers $75 per colony of bees, but they only charge apple growers $25 per colony because the honey produced tastes better and can be sold. In this way, the price of pollination adjusts to take into account not only the external benefit of honey production on fruit production but also the external benefit of fruit production on honey production.

The lesson of the bees is that our earlier story was a bit too pessimistic. The market equilibrium can be efficient even when there are externalities, *if* there is systematic trading in those externalities. To see which externalities the market can handle, let's take a closer look at why the market for pollination works reasonably well.

The market for pollination works because transaction costs are low and property rights are clearly defined. **Transaction costs** are all the costs necessary to reach an agreement. The costs of identifying and bringing buyers and sellers together, bargaining, and drawing up a contract are all transaction costs. Transaction costs are low for beekeepers and farmers because farms are large and bees don't fly that far. So when a beekeeper places bees in the center of a large farm the beekeeper and the farmer know that the bees will pollinate the crops owned by the farmer who is paying and not pollinate some other farmer's crops. As a result, the externality from bees is limited to one farmer at a time and can be internalized with one transaction.

CHECK YOURSELF

> In our discussion of Pigouvian taxes, we assumed that the government set the correct tax to achieve the efficient equilibrium. What if government overshoots and adds a tax that is too high? Will the equilibrium quantity be higher or lower than the efficient equilibrium?

> In our discussion of Pigouvian subsidies, we assumed that government set the correct subsidy amount to achieve the efficient equilibrium. What if the government undershoots and provides a subsidy that is too low? Will the equilibrium quantity be higher or lower than the efficient equilibrium?

STEFFEN SCHMIDT/ EPA/CORBIS

Bees create external beenefits.

Transaction costs are all the costs necessary to reach an agreement.

Property rights over farms and bees are also clearly defined. Everyone knows that the beekeeper has the right to the benefits created by bee pollination, so if the farmer wants bees to pollinate his crops he must pay the beekeeper. This works for beekeepers and farmers, but as you will see property rights in other externalities are not as clearly defined and this makes transactions more difficult; you might say that unclear property rights are a type of transaction cost, since they make it harder to trade.

It's not so hard for beekeepers to trade with farmers, but how many transactions would it take to internalize the external benefit created when someone has a flu shot? When one person is vaccinated, thousands of other people benefit by a small amount, especially if the vaccinated person spends a lot of time in airports. When Alex has the flu and coughs while boarding a plane, he could spread the flu virus to dozens of other people, each of whom could in turn pass it on to many others. If Alex receives a flu shot, all these people are better off. In theory, if each of these people paid Alex a small amount for getting a flu shot, Alex would be more likely to get a flu shot. But the transaction costs of arranging a deal like this are enormous—simply to identify the beneficiaries is difficult and getting thousands of them to send a check to Alex is next to impossible (trust us, we have tried!).

What about property rights? We assumed above that other people might be willing to pay Alex to get a flu shot because the flu shot creates an external benefit. But when Alex spreads the flu, he imposes an external cost on other people. Maybe Alex should have to pay other people when he doesn't get a flu shot! Even when other transaction costs are low, if property rights are not well defined—namely the question of who should have to pay whom—it will be difficult to solve externality problems with bargaining.

Ronald Coase, another Nobel Prize winner, summarized the situations where markets alone can solve the externality problems in what has come to be called the **Coase theorem**. The Coase theorem says that if transaction costs are low and property rights are clearly defined, then private bargains will ensure that the market equilibrium is efficient even when there are externalities. In other words, in these cases trading makes sure that just the right amount of the externality is produced. If there were either too little or too much of the externality, trading would push the quantity to the optimum level.

Recall that in a free market, the quantity of goods sold maximizes the sum of consumer and producer surplus. If the conditions of the Coase theorem are met, we can replace this with the even stronger conclusion that in a free market, the quantity of goods sold will maximize social surplus, the sum of consumer, producer, and everyone else's surplus.

But the conditions of the Coase theorem are often *unlikely* to be met. Transaction costs for many externalities are high and property rights are often not clearly defined. Thus, markets alone will *not* solve all externality problems.

The importance of the Coase theorem lies not in suggesting that markets alone might solve externality problems, but in suggesting a solution—the creation of new markets. If property rights can be clearly defined and transaction costs reduced, then a market for externalities might develop. If such a market does develop, we know from the Coase theorem that it will have all the efficiency properties of ordinary markets. Not only will this market maximize social surplus (consumer + producer + everyone else's surplus) but it will also ensure that the supply of goods will be bought by the demanders with the highest willingness to pay and sold by the suppliers with the lowest costs.

The **Coase theorem** posits that if transaction costs are low and property rights are clearly defined, private bargains will ensure that the market equilibrium is efficient even when there are externalities.

Government can play a role in defining property rights and reducing transaction costs. In fact, in recent years governments have helped to create working markets in many externalities, verifying the insights of the Coase theorem. Further below we discuss one of these new markets, a market in the right to emit pollution.

CHECK YOURSELF

> You want to hold a Saturday night party at your house but are worried that your elderly neighbors will complain to the police about the noise. Suggest a solution to this problem using what you know about the Coase theorem.

> Consider a factory near you that pollutes. What are the transaction costs involved in you and your neighbors negotiating with the factory to reduce the pollution? Is a private solution possible?

Government Solutions to Externality Problems

We have already discussed one kind of government solution to externality problems, namely taxes and subsidies. Two other solutions are also common: command and control and tradable allowances for the activity in question. We will look at both of these solutions in the context of another externality, acid rain, and we will also offer some comparisons with taxes and subsidies.

Acid rain damages forests and lakes, it corrodes metal and stone, and in the form of particulates, it creates haze and increased lung diseases such as asthma and bronchitis. Acid rain is caused when sulfur dioxide (SO_2) and nitrogen oxides (NO_x) are released into the atmosphere. A majority of SO_2 and a significant fraction of NO_x is created in the process of generating electricity from coal. Let's look at how the government has reduced the external cost of acid rain.

Command and Control

When external costs are significant, we know that $Q_{Market} > Q_{Efficient}$, so the most obvious (but not necessarily the best) method to reduce the external cost of electricity generation is for the government to order firms to use (or make) less electricity. This is called a command and control method. Command and control methods are not always efficient. The government, for example, recently required manufacturers to make clothes washers that use less electricity. *Consumer Reports* reviewed the clothes washers produced under this new standard and the reviewers were not happy with the results.[3]

> Not so long ago you could count on most washers to get your clothes very clean. Not anymore. Our latest tests found huge performance differences among machines. Some left our stain-soaked swatches nearly as dirty as they were before washing. For best results, you'll have to spend $900 or more.

> What happened? As of January [2007], the U.S. Department of Energy has required washers to use 21 percent less energy, a goal we wholeheartedly support. But our tests have found that traditional top-loaders, those with the familiar center-post agitators, are having a tough time wringing out those savings without sacrificing cleaning ability, the main reason you buy a washer.

The problem with command and control is that there are typically many methods to achieve a goal and the government may not have enough information to choose the least costly method. Let's suppose, for example, that the Department of Energy's regulation on clothes washers reduces electricity consumption by 1 percent (this number is too large but it will do for our purposes). Now let's compare command and control with a tax on electricity consumption that causes people to reduce their electricity consumption by *exactly the same amount*, 1 percent.[4] Faced with an increase in price, how would people choose to reduce their electricity consumption?

If the price of electricity increased, some people would choose to cut back on electricity by turning their lights off more often or by switching to lower-consumption fluorescent lightbulbs. Other people would respond by turning down the heat or the air conditioning or by buying a cover for their pool, or by installing insulation in their attic. The ways in which people would reduce electricity consumption are as different as the people themselves. But notice that probably very few people would respond to an increase in the price of electricity by spending a *lot* more on a clothes washer that saves electricity or by buying a clothes washer that saves electricity but doesn't clean very well. Thus, the government's method of reducing electricity consumption is not the lowest cost method.

A tax on electricity can reduce the consumption of electricity by exactly the same amount as a regulation on clothes washers but a tax will cost less. The tax costs less because a tax gives people the flexibility to reduce consumption in the way that is least costly to them. Recall from Chapter 5 that prices are signals. A tax on electricity sends a signal to every user of electricity that says "Economize!" But the tax leaves it to each person to use his or her local knowledge and unique preferences to choose the least costly method of economizing.

It's better to reduce electricity consumption with a tax than with a regulation on clothes washers, but we can do even better. After all, we don't really want to reduce *electricity*—we want to reduce *pollutants* like SO_2 and NO_x. It's true that pollutants are a by-product of electricity generation but there are many ways of reducing SO_2 and NO_x other than by producing less electricity. Thus, taxing the pollutants directly is a better way of creating incentives to reduce pollution than is taxing electricity. Taxing the pollutants directly gives firms the maximum flexibility to adopt the least costly methods of reducing pollution. Remember it's the pollutants that are creating the external cost so taxing the pollutants sends the right signal.

Command and control is not always a bad idea. The advantage of using incentives like taxes to control an externality is flexibility. The government corrects the price with a tax or subsidy so the price sends the right signal and people adapt using their own information and preferences (with all the benefits of the price system that we described in Chapters 3 and 5). But flexibility is not always desirable. Consider, for example, one of the great triumphs of humanity—the eradication of smallpox. Smallpox killed 300–500 million people in the twentieth century alone. As late as 1967, 2 million people died and millions more were scarred and blinded from smallpox, but in that year the World Health Organization (WHO) launched a program of mass vaccination, intensive surveillance, and immediate quarantine. The WHO program relied on command and control because so long as *any* reservoir of smallpox remained anywhere on the planet, the virus could reemerge and spread worldwide. To be successful, the WHO could not rely on taxes because it needed everyone to follow its policies—flexibility was not desirable. Fortunately, the WHO program was successful and by 1978 smallpox was extinct—the first and so far the only infectious disease to be stopped dead in its tracks.*

The bottom line is that command and control can be useful if the best approach to a problem is well known and if success requires very strong

---

* Command and control continues to be used today in handling other infectious diseases. Before registering for classes, for example, school-age children and college and university students must show that they have had their MMR vaccine (measles, mumps, rubella).

compliance. If it's important to control the externality at the least possible cost and if the government doesn't have full information, then more flexible approaches such as taxes and subsidies are preferable.

Tradable Allowances

Another type of command and control program is to require that firms reduce pollutants by a specific quantity. In the 1970s, for example, the government limited SO_2 from all generators of electricity to a maximum rate. The problem with this approach is that because of differences in location, fuel, and technology, it's much cheaper to reduce emissions of SO_2 from some firms than from others. By treating all firms the same, the government reduced flexibility and increased the cost of eliminating a given amount of pollution.

A simple example illustrates the problem with quantity restrictions and a potential solution. Suppose that there are two firms. We begin with a command and control regulation that limits each firm to 100 tons of SO_2 emissions in a year. Now imagine that reducing pollution at High Cost Industries is expensive, so High could save $1,100 if it were allowed to produce 101 tons of SO_2 instead of being limited to 100 tons. Low Cost Industries can control its pollution quite cheaply, so if Low reduces its pollution level even further to 99 tons, its costs increase by only $200.

Now imagine that the CEOs of High and Low approach the head of the Environmental Protection Agency with a proposal. The CEOs suggest that High be allowed to increase its pollution level by 1 ton to 101 tons. High will also pay $500 to Low. In return, Low will cut its pollution level by 1 ton to 99 tons. It's clear why High and Low want the deal—it's profitable. High cuts its pollution control costs by $1,100 for which it pays $500 for a net increase in profit of $600. Low increases its pollution control costs by $200, but it receives a $500 payment for a net increase in profit of $300. But should the EPA accept this deal?

Yes, if the EPA cares about social surplus it should accept the deal. Notice that pollution stays exactly the same, 200 units, so the deal does not harm the environment. The deal, however, does increase profits by $900 ($600 to High and $300 to Low). Should the EPA care about firm profits? Maybe not directly, but notice *why* profits increase in this example. Profits increase because the costs of reducing pollution fall. By trading, the firms reduce the cost of eliminating the last unit of pollution from $1,100 to just $200—a $900 fall in costs and that represents an increase in resources available to society.

So, we can now ask our question in a different way. Should the EPA care about decreasing the costs of reducing pollution? Of course the answer is yes. If we can reduce the same amount of pollution at lower cost that means more resources are available for other goods. And, the lower the costs of eliminating pollution, the more pollution it makes sense to eliminate.

What we have shown is that trading pollution allowances is like a new technology that reduces pollution at lower cost. The EPA should always be in favor of new technologies to reduce pollution and so they should also be in favor of trades in the right to pollute.

Tradable Allowances in Practice   A formal version of the tradable allowances system that we have just described was created by the Clean Air Act of 1990. Under this reform, the EPA distributes pollution allowances to generators of electricity, and each allowance gives the owner the right to emit one ton of SO_2.

FIGURE 9.4

Percentage of
1990 level

Electricity generation (MWH)

Sulfur dioxide

Since the 1990 Clean Air Act, Electricity Generation Has Increased and Sulfur Dioxide Emissions Have Decreased

Source: U.S. Energy Information Administration

Firms may trade allowances as they see fit and they have organized sophisticated markets in tradable allowances. Firms can even bank allowances for future use. The EPA monitors each firm's emissions of SO_2, and they also track how many allowances each firm owns so no firm can emit more pollution than it has allowances. Congress sets the total number of allowances.

The EPA's tradable allowances program has been very successful, as SO_2 emissions have been reduced by over 5 million tons or 35 percent since 1990. Air quality has improved and illness has been reduced.[5] The number of allowances is scheduled to fall so that by 2010, SO_2 emissions from power plants will be roughly half what they were in 1980. Remarkably, as shown in Figure 9.4, electricity generation has increased even as SO_2 emissions have decreased.

The EPA's system of tradable allowances is a successful application of the Coase theorem. Recall that the Coase theorem says that markets can internalize externalities when transaction costs are low and property rights are clearly defined. The Clean Air Act of 1990 clearly defined rights to emit SO_2, and the EPA has reduced transaction costs by distributing the allowances, monitoring emissions, and by creating a database that tracks ownership. Trading in markets has then allocated the allowances among firms in the way that minimizes the costs of reducing pollution.

One of the most interesting aspects of the market in rights to emit sulfur dioxide is that anyone can participate in this market, not just generators of electricity. We recently bought the right to emit 30 pounds of SO_2. We don't intend to emit any pollutants; rather we bought the rights and ripped them up in order to create more clean air. Environmentalists and industry often oppose one another, but when markets in externalities are created, environmentalists can buy pollutants and industry is happy to sell—as always, trade makes both parties better off.

An important result of the SO_2 trading program is that firms that generate electricity from relatively clean sources such as solar power can make money by selling their pollution allowances. In contrast, firms that generate electricity from relatively dirty sources must buy allowances. In essence, clean energy is subsidized and dirty energy is taxed—thus, a program of tradable allowances correctly reflects the fact that clean energy has lower social costs than dirty energy.

The success of the acid rain program in reducing SO_2 emissions at low cost and concern over global climate change motivated President Obama to propose a tradable allowances plan for carbon dioxide, a greenhouse gas that contributes to global warming. Tradable allowances in carbon dioxide would change the economics of all energy, not just electricity, and would create incentives for firms to move toward nuclear, solar, and biomass fuels which contribute less to global warming. Since global warming is a worldwide problem, tradable allowances ideally would be distributed and bought and sold on a worldwide basis. As of yet, however, not enough cooperation exists in the world community to establish such a system. Why not? Transaction costs again—in moving to a tradable allowance system, some countries and industries will be harmed and others will benefit. If moving to such a system would prevent global climate change, the overall outcome is good, but even if the overall outcome is good no one wants to bear a large share of the costs.

Comparing Tradable Allowances and Pigouvian Taxes—Advanced Material

There is a close relationship between using Pigouvian taxes and tradable allowances to solve externality problems. A tax set equal to the level of the external cost is equivalent to tradable allowances where the number of allowances is set equal to the efficient quantity. To achieve the efficient equilibrium in Figure 9.5, for example, the government can either use taxes to raise the price to the efficient price or it can use allowances to reduce the quantity to the efficient quantity. The equilibrium is identical no matter which method is used.

Differences between Pigouvian taxes and tradable allowances do occur when there is uncertainty. Imagine, for example, that we know that any quantity above a certain threshold level of SO_2 will acidify thousands of lakes and thus cause an environmental disaster. Any level below the threshold, however, will be acceptable or at least tolerable. In this case, tradable allowances are best because we can set the allowance below the threshold level and be certain that we will avoid disaster. If we set a tax, however, and we don't know the exact position of the supply curve, then we could easily set the tax too low, leading to SO_2 emissions above the threshold level. A fixed quantity, even if tradable, is like a command and control regulation and just as in our discussion of eliminating smallpox the best argument for command and control is when flexibility is not a virtue.

On the other hand, sometimes we know a lot about the cost that a unit of SO_2 creates but we aren't sure about the efficient quantity of pollution because demand and supply are changing. If the supply curve in Figure 9.5 were to shift down, for example if the cost of producing electricity falls, the efficient quantity will increase. With a Pigouvian tax, the adjustment to the new equilibrium occurs automatically but with allowances we could be stuck with a quantity of allowances that is much lower than the new efficient quantity. In this case, a Pigouvian tax is best because it can more easily adjust to changes in demand and supply.

The second difference between taxes and pollution allowances is not economic but political. With a tax, firms must pay the government for each ton of pollutant that they emit. With pollution allowances, firms must either use the pollution allowances that they are given or, if they want to emit more, they must buy allowances from other firms. Either way, firms that are given allowances in the initial allocation get a big benefit compared to having to pay taxes. Thus, some people say that pollution allowances equal corrective taxes plus corporate welfare.

That's not necessarily the best way of looking at the issue, however. First, allowances need not be given away; they

FIGURE 9.5

Comparing Tradable Allowances and Pigouvian Taxes If we knew the exact positions of the supply and demand curves, then we could always use tradable allowances to hit the Efficient quantity or a tax to hit the Efficient price and the equilibrium would be identical.

could be auctioned to the highest bidder, as under some proposed tradable allowance programs for carbon dioxide—this would also raise significant tax revenue. To make progress against global warming, moreover, may require building a political coalition. A carbon tax pushes one very powerful and interested group, the large energy firms, into the opposition. If tradable allowances are instead given to firms initially, there is a better chance of bringing the large energy firms into the coalition. Perhaps it's not fair that politically powerful groups must be bought off but as Otto von Bismarck, Germany's first chancellor, once said, "Laws are like sausages, it is better not to see them being made." We can only add that producing both laws and sausages requires some pork.

□ Takeaway

In a free market, the quantity of goods sold maximizes consumer plus producer surplus. When the consumers and producers bear all the significant costs and benefits of trading, the market quantity is also the efficient quantity. But when there are external costs or benefits, the market quantity is not the efficient quantity. If it doesn't bear all the costs of pollution, an electricity generator will emit too much pollution. If a person doesn't receive all the benefits of a flu shot, he or she will choose too few flu shots.

There are three types of government solutions to externality problems: taxes and subsidies, command and control, and tradable allowances. Market prices do not correctly signal true costs and benefits when there are significant external costs or benefits. Taxes and subsidies can adjust prices so that they do send the correct signals. When external costs are significant, the market price is too low, so an optimal tax raises the price. When external benefits are significant, the market price is too high, so an optimal subsidy lowers the price.

Command and control solutions can work but are often high cost because they are inflexible and do not take advantage of differences in the costs and benefits of eliminating and producing the externality.

The Coase theorem explains that the ultimate source of the externality problem is too few markets. If property rights can be clearly defined and transaction costs reduced, then markets in the externality will solve the problem and will do so at the lowest cost. In recent years, successful markets have been created in the right to emit sulfur dioxide and new markets are being proposed to reduce the gases that contribute to global warming.

UNDERSTAND YOUR
world

CHECK YOURSELF

> Government sets a total quantity of tradable pollution allowances and auctions them off. After the auction, the price for an individual allowance is high. Over time, the price falls dramatically. What does this tell you?

> The local government has decided to set and apportion tradable allowances for pollution in your neighborhood. Name three groups that would press for a large total quantity of allowances. Name three groups that would press for a smaller total quantity of allowances. Considering these groups, how likely is it that government would set a total quantity of allowances that would achieve an efficient equilibrium?

□ CHAPTER REVIEW

KEY CONCEPTS

Private cost, p. 170

External cost, p. 170

Social cost, p. 170

Externalities, p. 170

Social surplus, p. 170

Efficient equilibrium, p. 171

Efficient quantity, p. 171

Pigouvian tax, p. 173

External benefit, p. 173

Pigouvian subsidy, p. 174

Transaction costs, p. 175

Coase theorem, p. 176

FACTS AND TOOLS

1. Let's sort the following eight items into private costs, external costs, private benefits, or external benefits. There's only one correct answer for each of questions a–h.

   a. The price you pay for an iTunes download.

   b. The benefit your neighbor receives from hearing you play your pleasant music.

   c. The annoyance of your neighbor because she doesn't like your achingly conventional music.

   d. The pleasure you receive from listening to your iTunes download.

   e. The price you pay for a security system for your home.

   f. The safety you enjoy as a result of having the security system.

   g. The crime that is more likely to occur to your neighbor once a criminal sees a "Protected by alarm" sticker on your window.

   h. The extra safety your neighbor might experience because criminals tend to stay away from neighborhoods that have a lot of burglar alarms.

2. If the students at your school started saying "thank you" to friends who got flu shots, would this tend to reduce the undersupply of people who get flu shots? Why or why not?

3. **a.** Consider a factory, located in the middle of nowhere, producing a nasty smell. As long as no one is around to experience the unpleasant odor, are any externalities produced?

   b. Suppose that a family moves in next door to the smelly factory. Do we now have an externalities problem? If so, who is causing it: the factory by producing the smell, the family by moving in next door, or both?

   c. Suppose that the family clearly possesses the right to a pleasant-smelling environment. Does this mean that the factory will be required to stop producing the bad smell? What could happen instead? There are many right answers. (Hint: Think about the Coase theorem. Actually, it's *always* a good idea to think about the Coase theorem, whether the topic is smelly factories, labor-management disputes, international peace negotiations, or divorce settlements.)

4. Considering what we've learned about externalities, should human-caused global warming be *completely* stopped? Explain, using the language of social benefits and social costs.

5. In the following cases, the markets are in equilibrium, but there are externalities. In each case, determine whether there is a positive or negative externality, and estimate the external benefit or cost. Finally, decide between a tax or a subsidy as a simple way to compensate for the externality. Fill out the table below with your answers.

   a. In the market for automobiles, the private benefit of one more small SUV is $20,000 and the social cost of one more small SUV is $30,000.

   b. In the market for fashionable clothes, the marginal social benefit of one more dress per person is $100, and the marginal private benefit is $500. Bonus: Can you tell an externality story that makes sense of these numbers?

   c. In the market for really good ideas, ideas that will dramatically change the world for the better, the private benefit of one more really good idea (from speaker's fees, book sales, patents, etc.) is $1,000,000. The marginal social benefit is $100,000,000.

Case	External Cost or Benefit?	Size of External Benefit (or Cost if Negative)	Tax It or Subsidize It?
a. SUVs			
b. Fashionable clothes			
c. Ideas			

6. In which cases are the Coase theorem's assumptions likely to be true? In other words, when will the parties be likely to strike an efficient bargain? How do you know?

   a. My neighbor wants me to cut down an ugly shrub in my front yard. The ugly shrub, of course, imposes a negative externality on him and on his property value.

   b. My neighbors all would love for me to get that broken-down Willys Jeep off my front lawn. It's been years now, after all. And would it be too much for me to paint the house and fill up that 6-foot deep ditch in the front yard? The whole neighborhood is just annoyed.

    c. A coal-fired electricity plant dumps its leftover hot water into the nearby lake, killing the naturally occurring fish. Thousands of homes line the banks of the lake.

    d. A coal-fired electricity plant dumps its leftover hot water into the nearby river, killing the naturally occurring fish downstream. There is one large fishery one mile downstream affected by this. After that, the water cools enough so it's not a problem.

7. With electricity, we saw that it was important to tax the pollutant rather than the final product itself. In the following cases, will the proposed taxes actually hit at the source of the negative externality, or will it only land an inefficient glancing blow? What kind of tax might be better?

    a. Gas-guzzling cars create more pollution, so the government should tax big SUVs at a higher rate.

    b. All-night liquor stores seem to generate unruly behavior in nearby neighborhoods, so owners of all-night liquor stores should pay higher property taxes.

    c. Bell-bottom jeans insist on coming back every few years, and their ugliness creates negative externalities for all who see them. Therefore, bell-bottom jeans should be taxed heavily.

    d. American parents are worried about their children seeing too much profanity on television. Congress decides to tax TV shows based on the number of profane words used on the shows.

8. When the government expands the number of pollution allowances, does that increase the cost of polluting or cut it? What about when the number of pollution allowances is cut back?

9. Maxicon is opening a new coal-fired power plant, but the government wants to keep pollution down.

    a. Based on what we've seen in this chapter, which is a more efficient way to reduce pollution: commanding Maxicon to use one particular air-scrubbing technology that will reduce pollution by 25 percent or commanding Maxicon to reduce pollution by 25 percent?

    b. If a corrupt government just grants Maxicon all of the (tradable) pollution permits in the entire nation (even though there are many energy companies), does this guarantee that Maxicon will engage in an enormous amount of pollution? Why or why not?

THINKING AND PROBLEM SOLVING

1. When someone is sick, the patient's decision to take an antibiotic imposes costs on others—it helps bacteria evolve resistance faster. But it also gives free benefits to others: it may slow down the spread of infectious disease the same way that vaccinations do. Thus, antibiotics can create external *costs* as well as external *benefits*. In theory, these could cancel each other out, so that just the right amount of antibiotics are being used. But economists think that on balance, there is overuse of antibiotics, not underuse. Why? Here's one hint—think on the margin!

2. A flu shot typically costs about $25–$50 but some firms offer their employees free flu shots. Why might a firm prefer to offer its employees free flu shots if the alternative is an equally costly wage increase?

3. "The environment is priceless." What evidence do you have that this statement is incorrect?

4. Cultural influences often create externalities, for good and ill. A happy movie might make people smile more, which improves the lives of people who don't see the movie. A fashion trend for tight-fitting clothing might hurt the body image of people who think they won't look good in the trendy clothing.

    Let's consider the market for one cultural good that unrealistically raises expectations about the opposite sex: the romance novel. In romance novels, men are dangerous yet safe, wealthy yet never at work, they ride high-speed motorcycles yet never get in terrible accidents, they look fantastic even though they never waste endless hours at the gym, and so on. (Of course, advertising that focuses on sexy female models may also unrealistically raise expectations about the opposite sex so feel free to change our example as you see best.)

    a. Consider the market below. Romance novels impose an external cost on men, who have to try to live up to these unrealistic expectations.

Illustrate the effect of this external cost on the figure below.

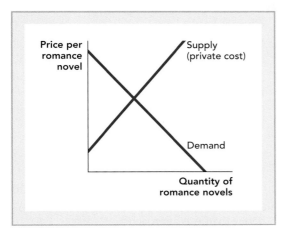

b. Illustrate on the above figure the deadweight loss from the externality, before a tax or other solution is imposed.

c. If the government decides to compensate for the externality by putting a tax on romance novels, should the tax be high enough to stop everyone from reading the novels? Why or why not?

d. Show graphically how big the tax should be per novel.

e. As long as the government spends the money efficiently, does it matter what the government spends the money from the "romance novel tax" on? In other words, could the government just use the money to pay for necessary roads and bridges, or does it need to spend the money to fix the harmful social effects of romance novels?

5. Green Pastures Apartments wants to build a playground to increase demand for its larger-sized apartments but is worried that it will be overcrowded with tenants from the Still Waters Mobile Estates and Twin Pines Townhomes developments nearby.

 a. What type of externality is the playground: Positive or negative?

 b. What type of compromise might Green Pastures be able to make with Still Waters and Twin Pines so that all three developments will benefit from the playground? More than one answer is possible, but give just one based on reasoning from this chapter.

6. In Chapter 7, we said that taxes create deadweight losses. When we tax goods with negative externalities should we worry about deadweight losses? Why or why not?

7. Economists have found that increasing the proportion of girls in primary and secondary school leads to significant improvement in students' cognitive outcomes (Victor Lavy and Analia Schlosser. 2007. *"Mechanisms and impacts of gender peer effects at school,"* NBER Working Paper 13292). One key channel seems to be that on average boys create more trouble in class, which makes it harder for everyone to learn. In newspaper English, we'd say that "boys are a tax on every child's education."

 a. Using the tools of this chapter, do girls in a classroom provide positive or negative externalities? What about boys?

 b. Just based on this study, if you are a parent of a boy, would you rather your son be in a class with mostly boys or mostly girls? What if you are the parent of a girl?

 c. Who should be taxed in this situation? Can you see any problems implementing this tax?

8. In the example of honeybees, we said that the farmers pay the beekeepers for pollination services. But why don't the beekeepers pay the fruit farmers? After all, the beekeepers need the fruit farmers to make honey, so why does the payment go one way and not the other? (Hint: The almond example has some clues.)

9. A government is deciding between command and control solutions versus tax and subsidy solutions to solve an externality problem. In each case, explain why you think one is better, using arguments from the chapter.

 a. Suppose that whales are threatened with extinction because a large number of people like to eat whale meat. Governments are torn between banning all whaling except for certain religious ceremonies, and heavily taxing all whale meat. Assume there are only a few countries in the world who consume whale meat, and that they have fairly efficient governments.

 b. Fires create external costs because they spread from one building to another. Should governments encourage subsidies to sprinkler systems or should they just mandate that everyone have sprinklers?

c. Pets who procreate can create external costs due to problems with stray animals. Strays are extremely common on the streets of poor countries. Sterilization can solve the problem but is a tax/subsidy or command and control a better method to encourage sterilization? Does the best solution depend on the sex of the animal?

CHALLENGES

1. Before Coase presented his theorem, economists who wanted economic efficiency argued that people should be responsible for the damage they do—they should pay for the social costs of their actions. This advice fits nicely with notions of personal responsibility. Explain how the Coase theorem refutes this older argument.

2. A government is torn between selling annual pollution allowances and setting an annual pollution tax. Unlike in the messy real world, this government is quite certain that it can achieve the same price and quantity either way. It wants to choose the method that will pull in more government tax revenue. Is selling allowances better for revenues or is setting a pollution tax better, or will both raise exactly the same amount of revenue? (Hint: Recall that tax revenue is a rectangle. Compare the size of the tax rectangle in Figure 9.5 with the most someone will pay for the right to pollute at the efficient level.)

3. Palm Springs, California, was once the playground of the rich and famous—for example, the town has a Frank Sinatra Drive, a Bob Hope Drive, and a Bing Crosby Drive. The city once had a law against building any structure that could cast a shadow on anyone else's property between 9 A.M. and 3 P.M. (Source: Armen Alchian and William Allen. 1964. *University Economics*, Belmont, CA: Wadsworth). What are some alternatives to this command and control solution? Are they any better than this approach?

4. At indoor shopping malls, who makes sure that no business plays music too loud, no store is closed too often, and that the common areas aren't polluted with garbage? What incentive does this party have to prevent these externalities? Does your answer help explain why parents are quite happy to let their preteen and teen children stroll the malls, as in the Kevin Smith movie *Mallrats*?

10

Profits, Prices, and Costs under Competition

CHAPTER OUTLINE

What Price to Set?

What Quantity to Produce?

Invisible Hand Property #1:
The Minimization of the Total Costs of Production

Profits and the Average Cost Curve

When to Enter and Exit an Industry

Entry and Exit with Uncertainty and Sunk Costs

Invisible Hand Property #2: The Balance of Industries

Deriving Industry Supply Curves

Takeaway

Appendix: Using Excel to Graph Cost Curves

In Chapter 5, we explained that price signals and the accompanying profits and losses tell entrepreneurs where to direct their labor and capital. If health concerns decrease the demand for cigarettes and increase the demand for 24-hour gyms, entrepreneurs will invest less in tobacco farms and more in StairMasters. If the price of oil increases, entrepreneurs will invest more in researching and developing solar panels and less in building gas-guzzling SUVs. We now investigate business decisions more closely, paying particular attention to profits, prices, and costs under competitive conditions.

In this chapter, we focus on three key decisions that a firm must make:

> What price to set?

> What quantity to produce?

> When to enter and exit an industry?

To answer these questions, we assume that a firm's only goal is to maximize profits. What firms aim for and what they achieve, however, can be quite different. Thus, we will also look at what happens in an industry when *all* firms pursue profits. When all firms pursue above-normal profits, for example, none of them achieve more than normal profits!

Most important, the pursuit of profit in competitive markets leads to two remarkable and highly beneficial consequences. First, in a competitive market, production is divided *across firms* in just such a way that the total costs of production are minimized. Second, in a competitive economy, resources move across industries in just such a way that the total value of production is maximized.

We call these two properties of markets, "invisible hand properties," because no firm intends to produce these beneficial properties but it looks as if firms have been led to do so by "an invisible hand," to use Adam Smith's metaphor (see Chapter 1). Together, these ideas explain how competitive markets help to solve the great economic problem of arranging limited resources to satisfy as many of people's infinite wants as possible.

The first question of the three we set out above, what price should a firm set, is the easiest to answer because under some conditions the firm doesn't set prices, it simply accepts the price that is given by the market. So let's start with the pricing decision.

What Price to Set?

A Nodding Donkey

Drive through the Texas countryside and standing alone in a field of wheat you will often see a nodding donkey. In Texas, a nodding donkey isn't an animal but an oil pump. Most oil comes from giant oil fields, but in the United States there are over 400,000 "stripper oil wells," oil wells that produce 10 barrels or less per day. That's not much per well but it adds up to nearly a million barrels of oil a day or about 19 percent of all U.S. production.[1]

Imagine that you are the owner of a stripper oil well. What price should you set for your oil? If the price of oil is $50 per barrel, will you be able to sell your oil for $100 a barrel? Of course not. Oil is pretty much the same wherever it is found in the world (this is not quite true but it's close enough for our purposes) so even your mother probably won't pay much extra just because it's *your* oil. Thus, you can't charge appreciably more than $50 a barrel. What about charging a lower price? You could charge less but why would you? The world market for oil is so large that you can easily sell all that you can produce at the market price. Thus, your pricing decision is easy; you can't sell *any* oil at a price above the market price and you can sell *all* your oil at the market price. Thus, to maximize profit you sell at the market price.

To better understand this result, let's recall an insight about the elasticity of demand from Chapter 4: the more and the better the substitutes, the more elastic the demand. With over 400,000 oil wells in the United States alone, the substitutes for your oil are so plentiful that a useful approximation is to think of the demand for your oil as perfectly elastic (flat) at the world price. In Figure 10.1, we compare the world market for oil on the left with the demand for *your* oil on the right.

The price of oil is determined in the world market where approximately 82 million barrels are bought and sold every day. Your stripper well, however, can at best produce a tiny fraction of world demand, perhaps 10 barrels of oil per day. As a result, the world price of oil won't change by a noticeable amount whether you produce 2, 7, or 10 barrels of oil a day.[*] This is why in the right panel of Figure 10.1 we draw the demand curve for your oil as flat at the market price— whether you choose to sell 2, 7, or 10 barrels, the price is the same, $50 per barrel.

Your job as an entrepreneur is greatly simplified if you don't have to decide on the price and so is our job as economists trying to understand firm behavior.

---

[*] How much is not a noticeable amount? Recall from Chapter 4 that the elasticity of demand is $E_D = \dfrac{\%\Delta Q}{\%\Delta P}$ or rearranging $\%\Delta P = \dfrac{\%\Delta Q}{E_D}$. Suppose that the elasticity of demand for oil is 0.5. This means that a 10 percent increase in the quantity of oil will reduce price by $20\% = \dfrac{10\%}{0.5}$. An increase in the supply of oil of 10 barrels a day is a percentage increase of $\dfrac{10}{82,000,000} \times 100 = 0.000012195122\%$ so price falls by $\dfrac{0.000012195122}{0.5} = 0.0000243902439\%$. At a price of $50 per barrel, an increase of 10 barrels of oil would reduce price to 49.9999987, that is, not noticeable.

FIGURE 10.1

Market Demand and Firm Demand The price of oil is determined in the world market for oil. You cannot sell oil at a price above the market price. At the market price, you can sell as many barrels as you want.

Thus, in this chapter we simplify by assuming that the demand for a firm's product is perfectly elastic at the market price.

A stripper well doesn't have much influence on the price of oil because there's nothing special about oil from a particular producer, and there are many buyers and sellers of oil, each small relative to the total market. Generalizing, a perfectly elastic demand curve for firm output is a reasonable approximation when the product being sold is similar across different firms and there are many buyers and sellers, each small relative to the total market. The markets for gold, wheat, paper, steel, lumber, cotton, sugar, vinyl, milk, trucking, glass, Internet domain name registration, and many other goods and services satisfy these conditions.

In addition, don't forget another lesson from Chapter 4: demand curves are more elastic in the long run. This is especially true when you consider the demand curve that faces a particular firm because in the long run other sellers can enter the market. Imagine that you are the owner of the only grocery store in a small town. Can you raise prices to exorbitant levels reasoning that everyone needs food and you are the only seller? Not likely. If you raise prices too high, other sellers will set up shop and your business will be wiped out. Thus, even when there aren't many sellers, there may be many *potential sellers* so a perfectly elastic demand curve can be a reasonable assumption, at least in the long run.

Summarizing, economists say that an industry is competitive (or sometimes "perfectly competitive") when firms don't have much influence over the price of their product. This is a reasonable assumption under at least the following conditions:

> The product being sold is similar across sellers

> There are many buyers and sellers, each small relative to the total market

Or

> There are many potential sellers

When *do* firms have a lot of influence on the price of their product? We say more about this in the next chapter on monopoly. Briefly, for purposes of comparison, a firm selling a unique product for which there are neither many other sellers nor potential sellers has considerable freedom to choose its price. An example would be a firm with a patent on a uniquely useful pharmaceutical. Similarly, a firm that controls a large share of the market for a homogeneous product could also have significant control over the price. The Saudis, for example, have significant control over the price of oil because their output is a significant share of the total market output. In Chapters 11, 12, and 13, we analyze how firms choose price and output under these conditions.

A competitive firm will sell its output at the market price but what quantity will it choose to produce?

What Quantity to Produce?

What quantity of oil should a stripper well produce if it wants to maximize profit? Profit is total revenue minus total cost, so the firm wants to maximize the difference between total revenue and total cost.

$$\text{Profit} = \pi = \text{Total Revenue} - \text{Total Cost}$$

Total revenue is price times quantity sold: $TR = P \times Q$

Total cost is the cost of producing a given quantity of output.

In Figure 10.2, we present data on the total revenue and total cost of a typical stripper oil well. **Total revenue** is simply price times quantity $(P \times Q)$. If the price of oil is $50 per barrel, then total revenue is $50 per day if 1 barrel is produced per day, $100 if 2 barrels are produced, $150 if 3 barrels are produced, and so forth.

We have also given some figures on total cost. **Total cost** is simply the cost of producing a given quantity of output. Let's break total cost into two components. To produce oil, the well must be drilled then the oil must be pumped out of the ground and delivered to customers. Let's assume that the firm borrows the money it needs to drill the well and, as a result, it must pay interest of $30 per day on its loan. Notice that the firm must pay $30 per day even if it pumps no oil, hence the entry in the table for Total Cost for 0 barrels of oil is $30. In fact, the firm must pay $30 per day for its loan however many barrels of oil it produces. Thus, we say that the firm has $30 per day of **fixed costs,** costs that do not vary with quantity.

Fixed costs are costs that do not vary with output.

The firm must pay additional costs when it runs the oil pump. To pump the oil, the firm must pay for electricity, maintenance, costs for the barrels to store the oil, trucking costs to deliver the oil, and so forth. These costs are called **variable costs,** since they vary with quantity. Total costs are therefore equal to fixed costs plus variable costs. We will say more about costs later in the chapter but for now the key point is simply that total costs increase with output: it costs more to make more.

Variable costs are costs that do vary with output.

Profit is the difference between total revenue and total cost and it is shown in the fourth column. Thus, to find the maximum profit, one method is to look for the quantity that maximizes $TR - TC$. Using the table in Figure 10.2, we can see that the profit-maximizing quantity is 8 barrels of oil per day.

Marginal revenue, MR, is the change in total revenue from selling an additional unit.
$$MR = \frac{\Delta TR}{\Delta Q}$$
For a firm in a competitive industry $MR = \text{Price}$.

It turns out to be useful, especially in order to create graphs, to use a second method to find the quantity that maximizes profit. Instead of looking at total revenue and total cost we compare the increase in revenue from selling an additional barrel of oil, called **marginal revenue,** with the increase in cost from selling an additional barrel, called **marginal cost.** To maximize profit we will show that the firm wants to keep producing oil so long as marginal revenue is

Marginal cost, MC, is the change in total cost from producing an additional unit.
$$MC = \frac{\Delta TC}{\Delta Q}$$

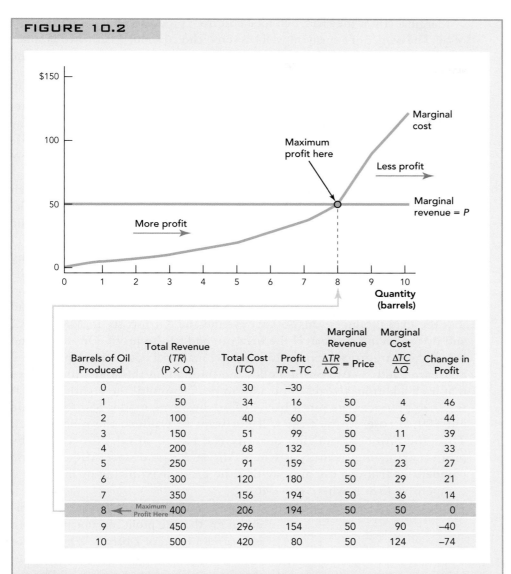

FIGURE 10.2

Barrels of Oil Produced	Total Revenue (TR) (P × Q)	Total Cost (TC)	Profit TR – TC	Marginal Revenue $\frac{\Delta TR}{\Delta Q}$ = Price	Marginal Cost $\frac{\Delta TC}{\Delta Q}$	Change in Profit
0	0	30	–30			
1	50	34	16	50	4	46
2	100	40	60	50	6	44
3	150	51	99	50	11	39
4	200	68	132	50	17	33
5	250	91	159	50	23	27
6	300	120	180	50	29	21
7	350	156	194	50	36	14
8	400	206	194	50	50	0
9	450	296	154	50	90	–40
10	500	420	80	50	124	–74

Profit Is Maximized by Producing Until MR = MC To maximize profit a firm compares the revenue from selling an additional unit, marginal revenue (for a firm in a competitive industry this is equal to the price) to the costs of selling an additional unit, marginal cost. Profit increases from an additional sale whenever MR > MC so profit is maximized by producing up until the point where MR = MC.

greater than marginal cost, which means that the last drop of oil that the firm produces should be the one where marginal revenue equals marginal cost. Let's walk through this argument.

Marginal revenue is the change in total revenue from selling an additional barrel of oil. Suppose that the price of a barrel of oil is $50. Then what is marginal revenue? If the owner sells an additional barrel of oil, his revenues increase by $50 so marginal revenue is just equal to $50, the price. That was easy because we assumed that price of oil doesn't change as the firm sells more barrels, in other words, we used our assumption that a stripper oil well is in a competitive industry and thus faces a perfectly elastic demand curve at the market price. Thus, we have a simple rule: for a firm in a competitive industry, $MR = P$.

Marginal cost is the change in total cost from producing an additional barrel of oil. The owner of a small oil well has some choice about whether to produce a little bit more or a little bit less. The owner, for example, can increase the pump rate and produce more oil per day but only by spending more on electricity, on maintenance, and on more frequent pickup and shipping of the oil. The extra costs that come with a little additional production are called marginal costs. Notice, for example, that if the well produces 2 barrels of oil per day total cost is $40 and if the well produces 3 barrels per day total cost is $51. Thus, producing the third barrel of oil increases costs by $11, that is the marginal cost of the third barrel of oil is $11.

At some point marginal cost must increase because you can only get so much blood out of a stone and only so much oil out of rock. The well, for example, cannot be pumped more than 24 hours a day. As the well reaches capacity the marginal cost of an additional barrel approaches infinity!

We can now use the data in Figure 10.2 to find the profit-maximizing quantity using our second method. The firm should keep producing additional barrels so long as the revenue from producing an additional barrel exceeds the cost of producing an additional barrel. The first barrel of oil that the firm produces adds $50 to revenue and $4 to costs, so $MR > MC$, and by producing that barrel the firm can add $46 to profit. On the second barrel the marginal revenue is $50 and the marginal cost is $6 so producing that barrel adds $44 to profit. Following through on this logic, you can see that each additional barrel of oil adds to profit up until the eighth barrel. If the firm produces the ninth barrel of oil, however, it adds $50 to revenue but $90 to costs so the firm will not want to produce the ninth barrel. Thus, the profit-maximizing quantity is 8 barrels of oil. Notice that the profit maximizing quantity is where $MR = MC$ and since $MR = P$ for a competitive firm we can also say that the profit maximizing quantity for a competitive firm is where $P = MC$.

Students are often confused by why economists say that the profit maximizing output is 8 barrels instead of 7 barrels. Why produce the eighth barrel where $P = MC$ and thus there is no addition to profit? Consider the graph above the table. Notice that wherever $P > MC$, producing additional barrels means more profit, and wherever $MC > P$, producing more barrels means less profit. Now think about producing oil not in barrels but in drops. Then, the graph says that at 7.9999 barrels you still want to add a drop or two, but at 8.0001 barrels you want to take away a drop or two. The reason we say profit is maximized where $P = MC$ is that $P = MC$ is the "just right" point between too little and too much.

As the price changes so does the profit maximizing quantity, as shown in Figure 10.3. When the price is $50 the profit maximizing quantity is 8. If the price of oil rises to $100 per barrel, then the firm will expand production. But by how much? The firm will expand

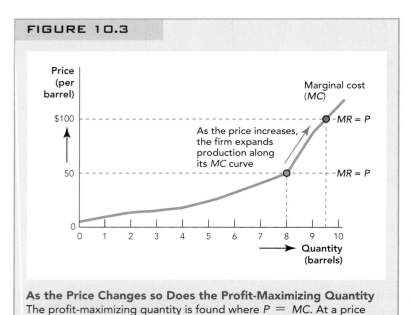

FIGURE 10.3

As the price increases, the firm expands production along its *MC* curve

As the Price Changes so Does the Profit-Maximizing Quantity
The profit-maximizing quantity is found where $P = MC$. At a price of $50, the profit-maximizing quantity is 8. As the price rises to $100, the firm expands. At $100, the profit-maximizing quantity is approximately 9.4 barrels per day.

until it is once again maximizing profit when $P = MC$. In Figure 10.3, we show how the firm expands production along its MC curve as the price of oil increases from $50 to $100 per barrel.

We have now answered our second question: To maximize profit, the firm should produce the quantity such that $MR = MC$, which for a firm in a competitive industry means produce up until $P = MC$.

Our third question is whether to enter or exit the industry. Before turning to it, we pause to emphasize an important and remarkable consequence of the fact that a profit-maximizing firm increases output until $P = MC$.

Invisible Hand Property #1: The Minimization of the Total Costs of Production

We know that a firm in a competitive industry increases output until $P = MC$. What's even more important is that every firm in the same industry faces the *same* price. Thus, in a competitive market with N firms the following will be true:

$$P = MC_1 = MC_2 = ... = MC_N$$

where MC_1 is the marginal cost of firm 1, MC_2 is the marginal cost of firm 2, and so forth. To understand the importance of this condition, let's briefly consider a seemingly different problem. Suppose that you own two farms on which you can grow corn. Farm 1 is in a hilly region that is costly to seed and plow. Farm 2 is on land ideal for growing corn. The marginal cost of growing corn on each of these farms is illustrated in Figure 10.4.

> Let's check our $MR = MC$ rule for maximizing profit. Look at the last column in Figure 10.2, which shows the change in profit. When the firm produces 4 barrels rather than 3, how much additional profit is made? How about when it goes from 7 barrels to 8 barrels? From 8 barrels to 9 barrels? Now look at the MR and MC columns and find the profit maximizing quantity. How does it compare to what you observe in the last column of the table?

CHECK YOURSELF

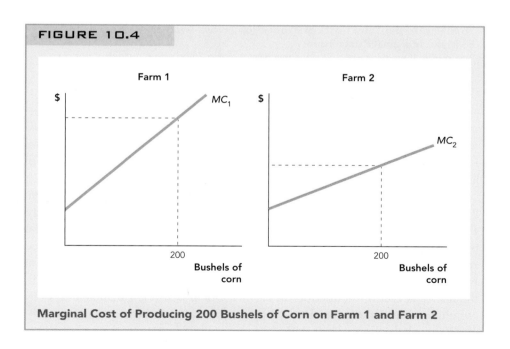

FIGURE 10.4

Farm 1

Farm 2

MC_1

MC_2

200

200

Bushels of corn

Bushels of corn

Marginal Cost of Producing 200 Bushels of Corn on Farm 1 and Farm 2

Let's say that you would like to grow 200 bushels. It might seem that the lowest cost way to produce 200 bushels is to produce all 200 bushels on Farm 2. After all, the marginal costs of production on Farm 2 are lower than on Farm 1 for any level of output.

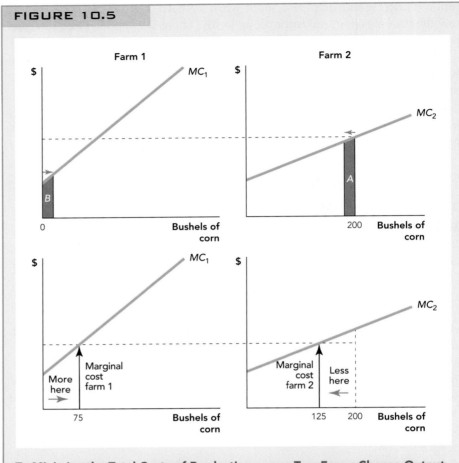

FIGURE 10.5

To Minimize the Total Costs of Production across Two Farms Choose Output to Make Marginal Costs Equal
Top panel: If we produce a few bushels less on Farm 2 and a few bushels more on Farm 1, costs fall by area A and rise by the smaller area B so total costs fall.
Bottom panel: Therefore, to minimize total production costs set output on the two farms so that marginal costs are equal.

Assume that you did produce all 200 bushels on Farm 2 and no bushels on Farm 1 as illustrated in the top panel of Figure 10.5. Can you see a way of lowering your total costs of production?

Let's think in marginal terms. Instead of producing all 200 bushels on Farm 2, what would happen to your total costs of production if you produced, say, 197 bushels on Farm 2 and 3 bushels on Farm 1? Notice that when you produce less on Farm 2 your costs of production decrease by the blue shaded area labeled A—this is the marginal cost of producing those last few bushels on Farm 2. By producing those bushels on Farm 1, your costs increase by area B, the marginal cost of production on Farm 1. But area B is less than area A, so by switching some production from Farm 2 to Farm 1 your total costs of producing 200 bushels of corn goes down.

How far can you extend this logic? Clearly you should continue producing fewer bushels on Farm 2 and more on Farm 1 if the marginal cost of production on Farm 2 exceed that on Farm 1, that is, produce less on Farm 2 and more on Farm 1 if $MC_2 > MC_1$. By the same logic, you should switch production from Farm 1 to Farm 2 if $MC_1 > MC_2$. Put these two statements together and it follows that the way to minimize the total costs of production is to produce just so much on each farm so that the marginal costs of production are equalized, $MC_1 = MC_2$. In the bottom panel of Figure 10.5, we show that the cost minimizing way to produce 200 bushels is to produce 75 bushels of corn on Farm 1 and 125 bushels of corn on Farm 2.

Now for the really important part. If you own both farms, you can act as a "central planner" and allocate production across the two farms so that the marginal costs of production are equal and thus the total costs of production are minimized. But now suppose that Farm 1 is in North Carolina and Farm 2 is in Iowa, and let's say Farm 1 is owned by Sandy and Farm 2 by Pat. Let's further suppose that Sandy and Pat will live their entire lives without ever meeting. Is there any way to organize production so that the output is split in exactly the way that you would split it if you owned both farms? Amazingly, there is.

Sandy and Pat sell their corn in the same market so each of them sees the same price of corn. How will Sandy maximize profits? How will Pat maximize profits? To maximize profits, Sandy will set $P = MC_1$ and Pat will set $P = MC_2$, which means that $MC_1 = MC_2$! But we know from above if $P = MC_1 = MC_2$, then the total costs of production are minimized. Amazingly, in pursuit of their own profit, Sandy and Pat will allocate output across their two farms in exactly the way that a central planner would to minimize the total costs of production!

It's remarkable that a free market could mimic an ideal central planner. What's even more remarkable is that a free market can allocate production across the two farms to minimize total costs even when an ideal central planner could not! Imagine, for example, that only Sandy knows MC_1 and that only Pat knows MC_2. For a free market, this is no problem, Sandy and Pat each acting in their own self-interest choose the output levels that minimize total costs. But a central planner cannot allocate production correctly if it lacks knowledge of MC_1 or MC_2.

The insight that a free market minimizes the total costs of production is one of the most surprising and deepest in all of economics. In a famous quotation in *The Wealth of Nations*, Adam Smith described a similar situation saying that each individual "in this, as in many other cases, [is] led by an invisible hand to promote an end which was no part of his intention." Sandy and Pat don't intend to minimize the total costs of producing 200 bushels of corn, they intend only to make a profit, but this beneficial outcome is the result of their action. Indeed, until Adam Smith and other economists began to study markets, not only did no one intend to minimize industry costs, no one even *knew* that individuals acting to maximize their own profits would minimize industry costs.

Invisible hand property #1 provides another perspective on free trade. In Chapter 8, we explained that free trade increased wealth by letting the United States buy goods from the lowest cost producers. We can now see this principle in another way. Remember that costs are minimized when $MC_1 = MC_2$ so costs are *not* minimized when $MC_1 \neq MC_2$. Now imagine that Farm 1 and Farm 2 are in different countries with no free trade between them. Sandy and Pat, therefore, face *different* prices for corn. Since Sandy and Pat face different prices, $MC_1 \neq MC_2$ and thus the total costs of producing corn cannot be at a minimum.

The Invisible Hand

Invisible hand property #1 says that even though no actor in a market economy intends to do so, in a free market $P = MC_1 = MC_2 = \ldots = MC_N$ and as a result the total costs of production are minimized.

CHECK YOURSELF

> If the MC of production on Sandy's farm is higher than on Pat's farm, how should production be rearranged to minimize the total costs of production?

Profits and the Average Cost Curve

We have shown that the firm maximizes profits by producing the quantity such that $P = MC$, but a firm can maximize profits and still have low or even negative profits. Just because the firm is doing the best it can doesn't mean that it is doing very well. We would like, therefore, to be able to show profits in a diagram. To do this, we need to introduce the average cost curve.

The **average cost** of production is simply the cost per barrel, that is, the average cost of producing Q barrels of oil is the total cost of producing Q barrels divided by Q, $AC = \dfrac{TC}{Q}$. For example, in Figure 10.6, we can read from the table that the total cost of producing 6 barrels of oil per day is $120, thus the cost per barrel is $120/6 = $20. Figure 10.6 computes average cost (in the last column) and graphs the average cost curve alongside the price and marginal cost curves.

The **average cost** of production is the total cost of producing Q units of output divided by Q, $AC = \dfrac{TC}{Q}$.

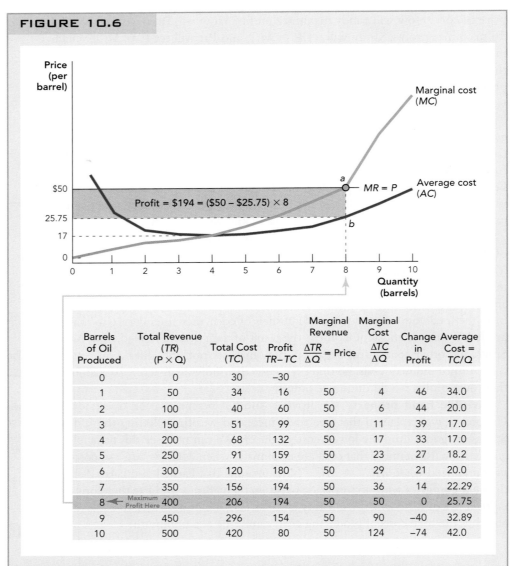

FIGURE 10.6

Barrels of Oil Produced	Total Revenue (TR) (P × Q)	Total Cost (TC)	Profit TR−TC	Marginal Revenue $\frac{\Delta TR}{\Delta Q}$ = Price	Marginal Cost $\frac{\Delta TC}{\Delta Q}$	Change in Profit	Average Cost = TC/Q
0	0	30	−30				
1	50	34	16	50	4	46	34.0
2	100	40	60	50	6	44	20.0
3	150	51	99	50	11	39	17.0
4	200	68	132	50	17	33	17.0
5	250	91	159	50	23	27	18.2
6	300	120	180	50	29	21	20.0
7	350	156	194	50	36	14	22.29
8 ← Maximum Profit Here	400	206	194	50	50	0	25.75
9	450	296	154	50	90	−40	32.89
10	500	420	80	50	124	−74	42.0

Profit = (P − AC) × Q Profit is $(P − AC) \times Q$, profit per barrel times the number of barrels produced. When the price is $50 and 8 barrels of oil are produced, profit is shown on the graph as the shaded area. Notice that the price is the height of point a, AC is the height of point b so that the area $(a − b) \times Q$ is equal to profit or $194 = ($50 − $25.75) \times 8$.

With a little bit of work, we can now show profit on our graph. Recall that:

$$\text{Profit} = \text{Total Revenue} - \text{Total Cost} = TR - TC$$

so we can also write:

$$\text{Profit} = \left(\frac{TR}{Q} - \frac{TC}{Q}\right) \times Q$$

or

$$\text{Profit} = (P - AC) \times Q$$

(To get to the last statement notice that we used the two definitions, $TR = P \times Q$ and $AC = \dfrac{TC}{Q}$.)

The last statement says that profit is equal to the average profit per barrel, $(P - AC)$, times the number of barrels sold, Q.

We already know that 8 barrels is the profit-maximizing quantity when the price is $50, but now we can show profit on our graph in Figure 10.6. To illustrate profit, begin at a quantity of 8 barrels and move up to find the price of $50 at point a. Now reading down from point a, find the average cost from the AC curve at point b, which is $25.75. (You can also check this by examining the table below the diagram for the AC of producing 8 barrels.) The average profit per barrel, $P - AC$, is ($50.00 - $25.75) or $24.25 per barrel. Finally, since production is 8 barrels, the total profit is $(P - AC) \times Q$ or $24.25 \times 8 = $194 per day, the shaded area in the diagram.

As we said earlier, just because a firm is maximizing profits doesn't mean that it is making profits. If the price of oil were to drop to $4 per barrel, what happens? Price equals $4 and the firm maximizes profit by producing at $P = MC$. Looking at the MC column in the table, $MC = $4 at one barrel of oil. So at a price of $4, the firm produces one barrel of oil. But at this price, the firm is taking a loss because $P < AC$. Figure 10.7 on the next page illustrates.

What is the lowest price per barrel that will give the firm a profit (not make a loss)? The firm will stop making a loss only when price is no longer less than average cost. Looking at the last column in Figure 10.6, we can see that the firm will be making a loss if the price of oil is anywhere below $17. Recall that profit is $(P - AC) \times Q$, thus—assuming that the firm is profit maximizing so $P = MC$ at all times—when $P > AC$ the firm is making a profit and when $P < AC$ the firm is making a loss. The minimum point of the AC curve is at $17 so at any price below $17 the firm must be making a loss.

One more technical point is worth noting. Take a look again at Figure 10.7 and notice that the marginal cost curve meets the average cost curve at the minimum of the average cost curve. This is not an accident but a mathematical certainty. We won't delve into this in detail but suppose that your average grade in a class is 75 percent and that on the next test, the marginal test, you earn a grade below your average, 60 percent. What happens to your average grade? It falls. So whenever your marginal grade is below your average grade, your average falls. Now suppose that your average grade is 75 percent and on the next test, the marginal test, you earn a grade above your average, 80 percent. What happens to your average? It rises. So whenever your marginal grade is above your average grade your average rises. What is true for your average and marginal grade is equally true for average and marginal cost. So think about what must happen around the point where the MC and AC curves meet. When

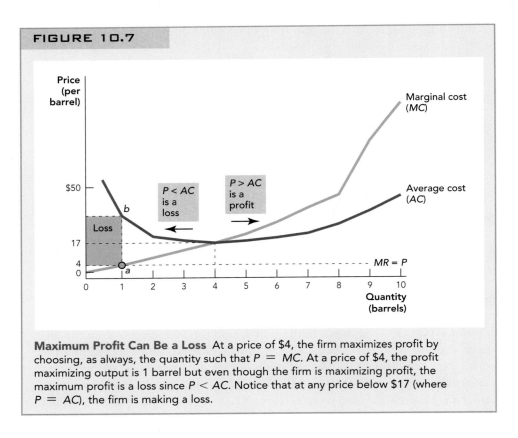

FIGURE 10.7

Maximum Profit Can Be a Loss At a price of $4, the firm maximizes profit by choosing, as always, the quantity such that $P = MC$. At a price of $4, the profit maximizing output is 1 barrel but even though the firm is maximizing profit, the maximum profit is a loss since $P < AC$. Notice that at any price below $17 (where $P = AC$), the firm is making a loss.

marginal cost is just below average cost, the average cost curve is falling and when marginal cost is just above average cost, the average cost curve is rising, so AC and MC must meet at the minimum of the AC curve.

We are now ready to turn to our third question, when should the firm enter or exit the industry.

When to Enter and Exit an Industry

We now know that firms will be profitable when $P > AC$ and unprofitable when $P < AC$. Firms seek profits so the basic idea is very simple. In the long run, firms will enter profitable industries ($P > AC$), and exit unprofitable industries ($P < AC$). Notice that at the intermediate point, when $P = AC$, profits are zero and there is neither entry nor exit.

In Figure 10.7, we can see that at a price of $4 the firm is taking losses. Thus, in the long run, this firm will exit the industry. In fact, at any price below $17, the maximum profit is still a loss. Thus, at any price below $17, the firm will exit the industry in the long run. At any price above $17, firms will be making profits and will enter the industry.

Only when $P = AC$, in this case when $P = \$17$, will firms be making zero profits and there will be no incentive to either enter or exit the industry. Students often wonder why firms would remain in an industry when profits are zero. The problem is the language of economics. By **zero profits** economists simply mean what everyone else means by *normal* profits. Remember that average cost includes wages and payments to capital so even when the firm earns "zero profits," labor and capital are being paid what they could earn in another

---

CHECK YOURSELF

> Use average costs to define profit for the competitive firm.

> Using average cost, describe all the prices at which the firm would make a profit and all the prices at which the firm would make a loss.

Zero profits or normal profits occur when $P = AC$. At this price the firm is covering all of its costs including enough to pay labor and capital their ordinary opportunity costs.

industry, their opportunity cost. Thus, when we say that a firm is earning zero profits we mean that the price of output is just enough to cover normal payments to the labor and capital in that industry.

The simple insight that firms will exit unprofitable industries and enter profitable industries has important implications. The movement of resources from low-profit to high-profit industries increases the value of production and in the long run this movement balances industries in a way that maximizes the total value of production. The balance of industries and the maximization of the total value of production is a second invisible hand property of markets that we discuss at further length below. Before turning to our second invisible hand property, however, we investigate the entry and exit decision in greater detail from the perspective of a businessperson.

Entry and Exit with Uncertainty and Sunk Costs

The entry and exit rules that we have given are useful for understanding the principles of economics but there are significant complications that we have ignored that firms in the real world must take into account. We said above that if $P < AC$ the firm will want to exit in the long run but what about the short-run? If P dips below AC will the firm shut down immediately? Not necessarily. Let's explain why.

If the price dips below average cost, a firm will not necessarily shut down immediately for two reasons. First, shutdown does not immediately eliminate all costs. Consider, for example, a hotel in Cape Cod. During the summer months there are plenty of tourists and the hotel is profitable. But during the winter months there are fewer tourists and revenues don't cover all of the hotel's costs. Should the hotel shut down in the winter? Not

TABLE 10.1 A firm should stay open in the short run if it can cover its variable costs

Decision	Fixed Costs	Variable Costs	Winter Revenues	Profits
Shut down	100	0	0	−100
Stay open	100	50	75	−75

necessarily. If the hotel shuts down in the winter it can reduce its variable costs—the hotel won't have to pay its bellmen and cleaning staff, for example. But the hotel still must pay its fixed costs, the costs that do not vary with output, such as rent on the land and the interest on the loan that the firm took out to construct the hotel. If revenues in the winter are large enough to cover the hotel's variable costs—the bellmen and the cleaning staff—and *some* of its fixed costs, the hotel will make a smaller loss staying open than closing so even though its unprofitable in the winter it's in the hotel's interest not to shut down. Table 10.1 provides a simple illustration. Notice that if the hotel shuts down in the winter its variable costs are zero but so are its revenues—if the hotel stays open its variable costs increase to 50 but revenues increase to 75 so by staying open the hotel covers its variable costs and some of its fixed costs and this reduces its winter losses.

The second reason why a firm may not shut down immediately when $P < AC$ is that shutdown can itself be costly. Imagine, for example, that you have to pay fired workers a severance payment and suppose that when you hire new workers you have to spend resources training them. If you hold on to your workers during bad times you can avoid these hiring and firing costs. So, *if* you expect your firm to be profitable in the future it can sometimes make sense to keep workers on even when it is not profitable to do so today.

A **sunk cost** is a cost that once incurred can never be recovered.

For exactly the same reasons it doesn't always make sense to enter an industry immediately when $P > AC$. Let's return to an oil firm to illustrate. We said above that if the price of oil rises to just above $17 the firm will enter the industry (since at this point $P > AC$) but entering the industry means drilling an oil well. The costs of drilling an oil well are **sunk costs** (literally!) which means that once paid these costs can never be recovered. If the price of oil rises to say $18 but then quickly falls back below $17 the oil firm is unlikely to make enough money to cover its sunk costs. Thus, for entry to be profitable the price must rise above $17 and the firm must *expect* the price to stay above $17 for long enough for it to recover its sunk costs.

Let's generalize the above ideas. If a firm could instantly and costlessly enter and exit an industry then our simple rule, enter when $P > AC$ and exit when $P < AC$, would be exactly correct. But when it's costly to enter and exit and there is uncertainty about future prices, firms must estimate the effect of their decisions on their *lifetime expected profit*. That's not an easy calculation. It can cost Exxon a hundred million dollars to drill an oil well off the Gulf of Mexico. Whether such an oil well will be profitable depends on the price of oil over perhaps the next 20 years. Since the price of oil is volatile, the price may have to rise to a very high level before Exxon sinks its money.

In short, whenever there is uncertainty and sunk costs to entering or exiting an industry, the best entry or exit decision requires a forecast of future prices and the correct decision is not always obvious.

CHECK YOURSELF

> Suppose that it costs $100 million to drill an oil well in the Mexican gulf. The well will be profitable if oil is priced at $60 a barrel or higher. The price of oil hits $65 a barrel. Is it time to start drilling? Suggest why or why not.

Invisible Hand Property #2: The Balance of Industries

Profits encourage entry but what happens to price and profits when firms enter an industry? As firms enter, supply increases and the price declines, which reduces profits. Losses encourage exit but what happens to price and profits when firms exit an industry? As firms exit, supply decreases and the price increases, which increases profit (reduces losses).

These dynamics illustrate a general feature of competitive markets that we call the **elimination principle**: *above normal profits are eliminated by entry and below normal profits are eliminated by exit.*

Earlier we showed that in a free market $P = MC_1 = MC_2 = \ldots = MC_N$ and as a result the total costs of production are minimized. But we could minimize the total costs of producing corn and yet still have too much or too little corn. It's good to know that if 20 or 200 million bushels of corn are produced that we get those bushels at least cost, but how many bushels is the right amount? It's the third key idea discussed in this chapter—entry and exit decisions—that ensure that the right amount of corn is produced.

Consider two industries, the car industry and the computer industry. Both industries use labor and capital to produce goods. Labor and capital, however, are limited. Recall from Chapter 5 that the great economic problem is to arrange limited resources to satisfy as many of people's infinite wants as possible. So how is limited labor and capital allocated across the computer and car industry in order to satisfy as many of people's wants as possible?

The **elimination principle** states that above normal profits are eliminated by entry and below normal profits are eliminated by exit.

PHOTO BY CAMERON QUINN

Profits pop up all the time, but in a dynamic economy entry of new firms quickly whacks them down again.

Profit in the computer industry is total revenue minus total cost. Total revenue measures the value of the output of the computer industry, the computers. Total cost measures the value of the inputs to the computer industry, the labor and capital. High profits, therefore, mean that outputs of high value are being created from inputs of low value. Profit is a signal that limited labor and capital are being used productively in satisfying wants.

Now suppose that profits are higher in the computer industry than the car industry—then the same inputs of labor and capital are creating more valuable output in the computer industry than in the car industry. What we would like, therefore, is for labor and capital to move to the computer industry from the car industry. Or, in other words, to use limited resources most effectively, we would like resources to flow to their highest valued uses.

Fortunately, entrepreneurs have a strong incentive to move resources to their highest valued uses. An entrepreneur must pay labor and capital their opportunity cost, what they could earn in a normal-profit industry. So an entrepreneur who hires labor and capital from the low-value car industry in order to produce high-value computers is buying low (the inputs) and selling high (the output) and in the process pocketing the difference, the profit! Thus, entrepreneurs can profit by moving resources from low-value to high-value industries. In the process, the total value of production is increased.

Change is constant so profitable industries are always popping up and unprofitable industries as well. So we never solve the great economic problem completely but the elimination principle means that in a dynamic economy resources are always moving toward an increase in the value of production. In a dynamic economy, entrepreneurs listen to price signals and they move capital and labor from unprofitable industries to profitable industries. Invisible hand property #1 showed how self-interest worked to minimize the total costs of production. **Invisible hand property #2** shows how the self-interest of entrepreneurs in pursuing profits works to balance production across industries in just such a way that the total value of production is maximized.

Creative Destruction

The elimination principle says that above normal profits are temporary. Great ideas are soon adopted by others; they diffuse throughout the economy and became commonplace. Since no one profits from the commonplace, *to earn above normal profits an entrepreneur must innovate.*

The economist Joseph Schumpeter was eloquent on this point. In the textbooks, he said, competition is about pushing price down to average cost.

> [But] in capitalist reality as distinguished from its textbook picture, it is not that kind of competition which counts but the competition from the new commodity, the new technology, the new source of supply, the new type of organization . . . competition which commands a decisive cost or quality advantage and which strikes not at the margins of the profits and the outputs of the existing firms but at their foundations and their very lives. . . . This process of creative destruction is the essential fact about capitalism.[2]

Invisible hand property #2 says that entry and exit decisions not only work to eliminate profits and losses, they work to ensure that labor and capital move across industries to optimally balance production so that the greatest use is made of our limited resources.

BETTMANN/CORBIS

Joseph Schumpeter (1883–1950)

In his youth Schumpeter said he wanted to be "the greatest lover in Vienna, the best horseman in Europe, and the greatest economist in the world." He later claimed to have achieved two of the three, adding that he and horses just didn't get along.

An **Increasing cost industry** is an industry in which industry costs increase with greater output; shown with an upward sloped supply curve.

A **Constant cost industry** is an industry in which industry costs do not change with greater output; shown with a flat supply curve.

A **Decreasing cost industry** is an industry in which industry costs decrease with an increase in output; shown with a downward sloped supply curve.

Thus, the elimination principle serves as both a warning and an opportunity to entrepreneurs. Stand still and fall behind. Leap ahead and profits may follow.

Deriving Industry Supply Curves

Now that we have examined the *MC* curves for competitive firms and their entry and exit decisions, we can put these all together in order to derive the industry supply curve, which you have been working with since Chapter 2. Supply curves can slope upward, be flat, or in rare circumstance can even slope downward. We show that the slope of the supply curve can be explained by how costs change as industry output increases or decreases.

In an **increasing cost industry**, costs increase with greater industry output and this generates an upward sloping supply curve. In a **constant cost industry**, costs do not change with changes in industry output and this generates a flat supply curve. In a **decreasing cost industry**, costs decrease with greater industry output and this generates a downward sloping supply curve. Decreasing cost industries are rare. Figure 10.8 summarizes the different possibilities for supply curves.

Let's start with constant cost industries, which are conceptually the simplest.

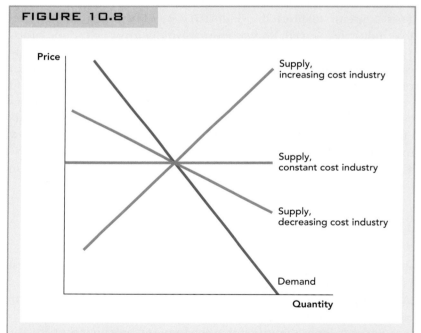

FIGURE 10.8

Increasing, Constant, and Decreasing Cost Industries An upward sloped curve implies that costs increase with greater industry output, an increasing cost industry. A flat supply curve indicates that costs do not change with industry output, a constant cost industry. A downward sloping curve implies that costs fall with greater industry output, a decreasing cost industry.

Constant Cost Industries

Consider the industry of domain name registrars. Web pages on the Internet have a conventional name, called a domain name, such as eBay.com, MarginalRevolution.com, or the web page for this book, which has the domain name SeeTheInvisibleHand.com. But the conventional names are just masks for more difficult to remember numbers called IP (Internet Protocol) addresses. When you type www.SeeTheInvisibleHand.com into a browser the browser sends a message to the Domain Name System (DNS), which looks up and returns the corresponding IP address, in this case 208.64.177.102. The IP address tells your browser where to find the information that is www.SeeTheInvisibleHand.com. So in order to work, every domain name must be registered with the DNS and assigned an IP address. Domain name registrars are firms that manage and register domain names.

The domain name registration industry has two important characteristics. First, domain name registration satisfies all of the conditions for a competitive industry.

> The product being sold is similar across sellers

> There are many buyers and sellers, each small relative to the total market

> There are many potential sellers

As far as the user is concerned, there is little difference between registering with GoDaddy.com or GetRealNames.com so the product is similar across sellers. There are many buyers and many sellers. There are hundreds of registrars in the United States alone. Indeed, GoDaddy.com is based in the United States and GetRealNames.com is based in India, thus, there is *world* free trade in domain name registration. Furthermore, not only are there many competitors in the industry but just about anyone in the world can become an accredited registrar with an investment of a few thousand dollars, so there are many potential competitors.

The second important characteristic of the domain name industry is that the major input for domain name registration is a bank of computers, but all the computers of all the domain name registrars in all the world don't add up to much compared to the world supply of computers. The domain name industry, therefore, can expand without pushing up the prices of its major inputs and thus without raising its own costs. An industry that can expand or contract without changing the prices of its inputs is called a constant cost industry.

These two characteristics, free entry and that the industry demands only a small share of its major inputs, produce the following properties: (1) The price for domain name registration is quickly driven down to the average cost of managing and assigning a domain name so profits are quickly driven to normal levels (the elimination principle) and (2) because average costs don't change much when the industry expands or contracts the price of domain name registration doesn't change much when the industry expands or contracts so the long-run supply curve is very elastic (flat).

Let's examine these characteristics in turn. One of the largest registrars is GoDaddy.com, which charges $6.99 to register a domain name for one year. What would happen if it raised its price to $14.95 a year? GoDaddy would quickly lose a significant fraction of its business. New customers would choose other firms and since domains must be renewed every few years, old customers would soon also switch. As a result of this competition, GoDaddy and every other firm in the industry price their services at near average cost and earn a zero or normal profit.

Now consider what happens when the demand for domain names increases. In 2005, there were over 60 million domain names. Just one year later there were over 100 million domain names. If the demand for oil nearly doubled, the price of oil would rise dramatically, but despite nearly doubling in size, the price of registering a domain name has not increased. When an increase in demand hits a constant cost industry, the price rises in the short run as each firm moves up its MC curve. But the expansion of old firms and the entry of new firms quickly pushes the price back down to average cost.

Figure 10.9 illustrates how a constant cost industry responds to an increase in demand. The figure looks imposing but if we take it in steps the logic of the story will be clear. In the top panel, we have the initial equilibrium. On the left side of the panel, we illustrate the industry. The market price is P_{lr}, $6.99 in the case of domain name registration, the market quantity is Q_1, and the quantity

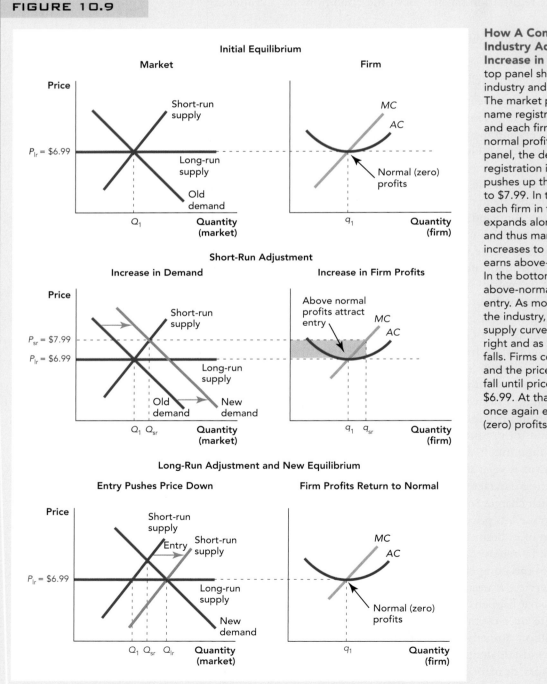

FIGURE 10.9

How A Constant Cost Industry Adjusts to an Increase in Demand The top panel shows the initial industry and firm equilibrium. The market price for domain name registration is $6.99 and each firm is making a normal profit. In the middle panel, the demand for registration increases, which pushes up the market price to $7.99. In the short run, each firm in the industry expands along its MC curve and thus market quantity increases to Q_{sr}. Each firm earns above-normal profits. In the bottom panel, the above-normal profits attract entry. As more firms enter the industry, the short-run supply curve shifts to the right and as it does price falls. Firms continue to enter and the price continues to fall until price returns to $6.99. At that price, firms are once again earning normal (zero) profits since $P = AC$.

demanded is exactly equal to the quantity supplied so the industry is in equilibrium. On the right side of the panel, we have a typical firm in the industry. The firm is profit maximizing because $P = MC$ and it is making a zero or normal profit because $P = AC$. Note that the industry output is Q_1, but the firm output is q_1, which indicates that each firm in the industry produces only a small share of total industry output.

In the middle panel on the left, we illustrate an increase in demand from the old demand curve to the new demand curve. In the short run, the increase in demand increases price to P_{sr}, $7.99, where new demand and short-run supply meet. The industry quantity increases to Q_{sr}. Where does the increase in quantity come from? It comes from many firms in the industry, each of which produces a little bit more by increasing production along its MC curve. In the middle panel on the right, we show that the typical firm in the industry expands to q_{sr} and since the price is above average cost the firm earns profits as illustrated by the shaded area $(P - AC) \times q_{sr}$.

Before turning to the bottom panel let's clarify a few points. What do we mean by the **short run?** The short run is simply the time period before entry occurs. In the middle panel, we are illustrating the *first* response to an increase in demand, which is that the price rises and every firm in the industry responds by increasing production along its marginal cost curve. (Indeed, the short-run supply curve is simply the sum of the MC curves for each firm in the industry.)

The short run is the time period before entry occurs.

The increase in price generates above-normal profits for each firm in the industry. In the **long run,** the above-normal profits attract new investment and entry. Entry is the *second* response to the increase in demand. In some industries, like the domain name registration industry, entry might take a matter of a few months or even as little as a few weeks while in other industries it could take several years before significant entry occurs.

The long run is the time it takes for substantial new investment and entry to occur.

When entry does occur, the short run supply curve shifts to the right and as it does so the price falls and profits are reduced as shown in the bottom left panel of Figure 10.9. Entry doesn't stop until profits return to normal levels so entry continues until price is pushed down to AC (the elimination principle). Since the prices of the industry inputs don't change when the industry expands, the AC curve of each firm in the industry doesn't change so in the new industry, equilibrium price is again equal to P_{lr}, $6.99. Notice that although the typical firm produces q_1 as shown in the bottom right panel of Figure 10.9, just as it did before the increase in demand, the industry quantity has increased to Q_{lr} because there are now more firms in the industry.

Thus, the key to a constant cost industry is that it is small relative to its input markets so when the industry expands it does not push up the price of its inputs and thus industry costs do not increase.

Increasing Cost Industries

In an increasing cost industry, costs rise as industry output increases. The oil industry is an increasing cost industry because greater quantities of oil can only be produced by using more expensive methods such as drilling deeper, drilling in more inhospitable spots, or extracting the oil from tar sands.

To illustrate, let's focus on just two firms. Firm 1 is the firm that we examined earlier. Its oil is located near the surface so its average costs are low and it enters the industry when the price of oil rises to just $17. Firm 2's oil, however, is located deeper than Firm 1's and so Firm 2's fixed costs of drilling are higher and its average cost curve is higher than that of Firm 1. As a result, Firm 2 will not enter the industry until the price of oil reaches $29. We can now build the industry supply curve.

At any price below $17 what is the quantity supplied? Zero. At a price less than $17 profits are negative so no firm enters the industry and the industry supply curve, indicated in the rightmost panel of Figure 10.10 by the bold line, shows a quantity supplied of zero. When the price of oil hits $17, Firm 1 enters the industry at its profit maximizing quantity of 4 barrels of oil and thus industry supply at a price of $17 jumps to 4 barrels. As the price rises, Firm 1 expands along its *MC* curve and so does industry supply. When the price hits $29, Firm 2 enters the industry with its profit maximizing quantity of 5 barrels of oil. To find the quantity supplied by the industry we sum the quantity supplied by each firm in the industry. At a price of $29, Firm 1 supplies 6 barrels of oil and Firm 2 supplies 5 barrels of oil so industry supply is 11 barrels of oil. As the price rises further, both firms now expand along their respective *MC* curves. Once again, industry supply at any price is found by adding up the quantity supplied by each firm at that price. Thus, at a price of $50, Firm 1 produces 8 barrels of oil and Firm 2 produces 7 barrels of oil so industry supply at a price of $50 is 15 barrels of oil.

FIGURE 10.10

To Find the Quantity Supplied by the Industry, Add the Quantities Supplied by each Firm in the Industry At any price below $17, profits for both Firm 1 and Firm 2 are negative so industry output is 0. At a price of $17, Firm 1 enters the industry with a profit-maximizing quantity of 4 barrels so industry output jumps to 4 barrels. As price rises further, Firm 1 expands along its *MC* curve. At a price of $29, Firm 2 enters the industry with a profit-maximizing quantity of 5 barrels so total industry output is 11 barrels (6 from Firm 1 and 5 from Firm 2). As price rises further, both firms expand along their marginal cost curve. At any price, industry output is the sum of each firm's output. At a price of $50, what quantity does Firm 1 produce? What quantity does Firm 2 produce? What is industry output?

Our explanation of the supply curve is simply a more detailed version from Chapter 2. At a low price, the only oil that is profitable to exploit is the oil that can be recovered at low cost from places like Saudi Arabia. As the price of oil rises, it becomes profitable to supply oil from the North Sea, the Athabasca tar sands, and other higher cost sources. The analysis in Chapter 2 focused on how a higher price encourages entry from higher cost producers. This chapter adds to the entry story the idea that as the price increases, each firm expands along its marginal cost curve.

More generally, any industry that buys a large fraction of the output of an increasing cost industry will also be an increasing cost industry. The gasoline industry, for example, is an increasing cost industry because greater demand for gas will push up the price of oil, which in turn raises the price of gas. The electricity industry is an increasing cost industry because greater demand for electricity requires more coal and coal is an increasing cost industry for the same reasons as oil.

The elimination principle works slightly differently in an increasing cost industry than in a constant cost industry. In a constant cost industry, the elimination principle means that above-normal profits are eliminated for *all* firms, since all firms have the same average cost curve. In the case of the two oil firms, however, Firm 1 has a lower average cost curve than Firm 2 because it has access to an input that cannot be duplicated, namely the land and the oil pool underneath the land. Firm 1's land lets it produce oil at a low average cost so its profits are not eliminated by entry. As the price rises, however, firms will enter until the marginal firm earns a zero profit (normal profit). Thus, just as before, invisible hand property #2 continues to hold: as labor and capital move from unprofitable to profitable industries, the greatest use is made of our limited resources.

A Special Case: The Decreasing Cost Industry

In a constant cost industry, firm costs are constant as the industry expands and thus the long-run supply curve is flat. In an increasing cost industry, firm costs increase as the industry expands and thus the supply curve slopes upward. Could firm costs decrease as the industry expands, creating a decreasing cost industry with a downward sloped supply curve? Yes. To see how, we must ask the question: Why is Dalton, Georgia, the "carpet capital of the world?"

An amazing 72 percent of the $12 billion worth of carpets produced in the United States every year is produced in Dalton and the surrounding area. Dalton is home to 150 carpet plants and hundreds of machine shops, cotton mills, dye plants, and other related industries. Why Dalton? Dalton is not like Saudi Arabia: it has no outstanding natural advantages for producing carpets, so why is Dalton the carpet capital of the world? The answer is nothing more than an accident of history that launched a virtuous circle.

The Dalton carpet industry began in 1895 with one teenage girl who crafted an especially beautiful bedspread for her brother's wedding. Wedding guests saw the bedspread and asked her to make more. To meet the demand she hired workers and trained them in her innovative techniques. As demand grew even further, these workers and others went into business for themselves creating a bedspread industry. The skills needed to make bedspreads were also useful for making carpets so carpet firms began to locate in Dalton. With so many carpet firms located in Dalton, it became profitable to open trade schools to teach carpet-making skills. In turn, the trade schools made it even more cost efficient for carpet firms to move to Dalton. Similarly, machine shops, cotton mills, and dye plants moved to Dalton to be close to their customers, and the ready access to machine shops, cotton mills, and dye plants made it even less costly for carpet firms to make carpets in Dalton. The resulting virtuous circle made Dalton the cheapest place to make carpets in the United States—not because Dalton had natural advantages but because it was cheaper to make carpets in a place where there already were a lot of carpet makers.

Decreasing cost industries are important but very special because costs cannot decrease forever. Dalton became the cheapest place to produce carpets in the United States many years ago and that is unlikely to change any time soon. But if the demand for carpets were to increase today, the costs of making carpets in Dalton would not fall further. The costs of making carpets in Dalton fall when the local industry expands from 1 to 100 firms but they don't fall by nearly as much when the industry expands from 100 to 200 firms.

Economists use the idea of a decreasing cost industry to explain the history of industry clusters: not just carpets in Dalton, Georgia, but computer technology in Silicon Valley, movie production in Hollywood, and flower distribution in Aalsmeer, Holland. Once the cluster is established, however, constant or increasing costs are the norm. If the demand for carpet were to increase today, for example, the price of carpets would rise, not fall.

In summary, industry supply curves typically slope upwards but they can be flat over some range if the industry is small relative to its input industries. Industry supply curves can even slope downward but this is rare and temporary although the idea of a decreasing cost industry is important for explaining the existence of industry clusters.

CHECK YOURSELF

> Is the automobile manufacturing industry a constant cost, increasing cost, or decreasing cost industry? Why?

> Where are most U.S. films made? Why do you think the film industry is concentrated in such a small region?

□ Takeaway

We have now answered the three questions that opened the chapter. What price to set? Answer: A firm in a competitive industry sets price at the market price. What quantity to produce? Answer: To maximize profit, a competitive firm should produce the quantity that makes $P = MC$. When to exit and enter an industry? Answer: In the long run, the firm should enter if $P > AC$ and exit if $P < AC$.

A competitive industry is one where the product being sold is similar across sellers, there are many buyers and sellers, each small relative to the total market, or there are many potential sellers.

We have also shown how profit maximization and entry and exit decisions are the foundation of supply curves. In an increasing cost industry, costs rise as more firms enter so supply curves are upward sloped. In a constant cost industry, costs remain the same as firms enter so the long-run supply curve is flat. And in the rare case of a decreasing cost industry, costs fall as firms enter so supply curves are downward sloping.

The elimination principle tells us that above normal profits are eliminated by entry and below normal profits are eliminated by exit. Perhaps even more important, the elimination principle tells you that to earn above normal profits a firm must innovate.

We have also covered two "invisible hand properties." Invisible hand property #1 says that even though no actor in a market economy intends to do so, in a free market $P = MC_1 = MC_2 = ... = MC_N$ and as a result the total costs of production are minimized. Invisible hand property #2 says that entry and exit decisions not only work to eliminate profits and losses, they work to ensure that labor and capital move across industries to optimally balance production so that the greatest use is made of our limited resources.

□ CHAPTER REVIEW

KEY CONCEPTS

Total revenue, p. 190

Total cost, p. 190

Fixed costs, p. 190

Variable costs, p. 190

Marginal revenue, *MR*, p. 190

Marginal cost, *MC*, p. 190

Invisible hand property #1, p. 195

Average cost, p. 196

Zero profits, p. 198

Sunk cost, p. 200

Elimination principle, p. 200

Invisible hand property #2, p. 201

Increasing cost industry, p. 202

Constant cost industry, p. 202

Decreasing cost industry, p. 202

Short run, p. 205

Long run, p. 205

FACTS AND TOOLS

1. You've been hired as a management consultant to four different companies in competitive industries. They're each trying to figure out if they should produce a little more output or a little bit less in order to maximize their profits. The firms all have typical marginal cost curves: They rise as the firm produces more.

   Your staff did all the hard work for you of figuring out the price of each firm's output and the marginal cost of producing one more unit of output *at their current level of output*. However, they forgot to collect data on how much each firm is actually producing at the moment. Fortunately, that doesn't matter. In your final report, you need to decide which firms should produce more output, which should produce less, and which are producing just the right amount:

   a. WaffleCo, maker of generic-brand frozen waffles. Price = $4 per box, marginal cost = $2 per box.

   b. Rio Blanco, producer of copper. Price = $32 per ounce, marginal cost = $45 per ounce.

   c. GoDaddy.com, domain name registry. Price = $5 per website, marginal cost = $2 per website.

   d. Luke's Lawn Service. Price: $80 per month, marginal cost = $120 per month.

2. In the competitive electrical motor industry, the workers at Galt Inc. threaten to go on strike. In order to avoid the strike, Galt Inc. agrees to pay its workers more. At all other factories, the wage remains the same.

   a. What does this do to the marginal cost curve at Galt Inc.? Does it rise, does it fall, or is there no change? Illustrate your answer in the figure below.

   b. What will happen to the number of motors produced by Galt Inc.? Indicate the "before" and "after" levels of output on the x-axis in the figure above.

   c. In this competitive market, what will the Galt Inc. labor agreement do to the price of motors?

   d. Surely, more workers will *want* to work at Galt Inc. now that it pays higher wages. Will more workers *actually* work at Galt Inc. after the labor agreement is struck? Why or why not?

3. In Figure 10.9, you saw what happens in the long run when demand rises in a constant-cost industry. Let's see what happens when demand falls in such an industry: For instance, think about the market for gasoline or pizza in a small city after the city's biggest textile mill shuts down. In the figure below, indicate the price and quantity of output at three points in time:

   I. In the long run, before demand falls.

   II. In the short run, after demand falls.

III. In the long run, after demand falls.

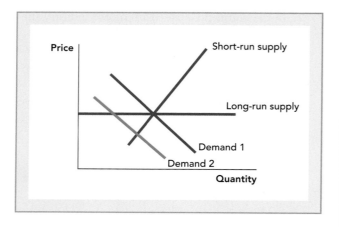

Also, answer the following questions about the market's response to this fall in demand.

a. When will the marginal cost of production be lowest: At stage I, II, or III?

b. When firms cut prices, they often do so in dramatic ways. During which stage will the local pizza shops offer "Buy one get one free" offers? During which stage will the local gas station be more likely to offer "Free car wash with fill-up?"

c. When is P > AC? P < AC? P = AC?

d. Restating the previous question: When are profits positive? Negative? Zero?

e. Roughly speaking, will the long-run response mostly involve firms leaving the industry, or will it mostly involve individual firms shrinking? The "firm" column of Figure 10.9 should help you with the answer.

4. We mentioned that carpet manufacturing looks like a decreasing cost industry. In American homes, carpets are much less popular than they were in the 1960s and 1970s, when "wall-to-wall carpeting" was fashionable in homes. Suppose that carpeting became even less popular than it is today: What would this fall in demand probably do to the price of carpet in the long run?

5. Replacement parts for classic cars are expensive, even though these parts aren't any more complicated than parts for new cars.

a. What kind of industry is the market for old car parts: An increasing cost industry, a constant cost industry, or a decreasing cost industry? How can you tell?

b. If people began recycling old cars more in the United States—repairing them rather than

sending them off to junkyards—would the cost of spare parts probably rise or probably fall in the long run? Why do you think so?

6. We've claimed that the efficient way to spread out work across firms in the same industry is to set the marginal cost of production to be the same across firms. Let's see if this works in an example.

Consider a competitive market for rolled steel (measured by the ton) with just two firms: SmallCo and BigCo. If we wanted to be more realistic, we could say there were 100 firms like SmallCo and 100 firms like BigCo, but that would just make the math harder without generating any insight. The two firms have marginal cost schedules like this:

Q	Marginal Cost SmallCo	BigCo
1	$10	$10
2	$20	$10
3	$30	$10
4	$40	$10
5	$50	$20
6	$60	$30
7	$70	$40
8	$80	$50

a. We'll ignore fixed costs of starting up the firms just to make things a little simpler. What is the total cost at each firm of producing each level of output? Fill in the table.

Q	Total Cost SmallCo	BigCo
1	$10	$10
2	$30	$20
3	$60	
4		
5		
6		
7		
8		

b. What's the cheapest way to make 11 tons of steel? 5 tons?

c. What would the price have to be in this competitive market for these two firms to produce a total of 11 tons of steel? 5 tons?

d. Suppose that a government agency looked at BigCo and SmallCo's cost curves. Which firm looks like the low-cost producer to a government agency? Would it be a good idea, an efficient policy, for the government to shut down the high-cost producer? In other words, could a government intervention do better than the invisible hand in this case?

e. Let's make part d a little more concrete: What would the total cost be if BigCo were the only firm in the market, and it had to produce 7 tons of rolled steel? What would marginal and total cost be if SmallCo and BigCo let the invisible hand divvy up the work between them?

7. Let's review the basic mechanism of the elimination principle.

a. When demand rises in Industry X, what happens to profits? Do they rise, fall, or remain unchanged?

b. When that happens, do firms, workers, and capital tend to enter Industry X, or do they tend to leave?

c. Does this tend to increase short-run supply in Industry X or reduce it?

d. In the long run, after this rise in demand, what will profits typically be in Industry X?

8. Arguing about economics late one night in your dorm room, your friend says, "In a free market economy, if people are willing to pay a lot for something, then businesses will charge a lot for it." One way to translate your friend's words into a model is to think of a product with highly inelastic demand: Items like life-saving drugs or basic food items. Let's consider a market where costs are roughly constant: Perhaps they rise a little or fall a little as the market grows, but not by much.

a. In the long run, is your friend right?

b. In the long run, what has the biggest effect on the price of a good that people really want: The location of the average cost curve or the location of the demand curve?

9 a. In the highly competitive TV manufacturing industry, a new innovation makes it possible to cut the average cost of a 50-inch plasma TV from $1,000 to $400. Most TV manufacturers quickly adopt this new innovation, earning massive short-run profits. In the long run, what will the price of a 50-inch plasma TV be?

b. In the highly competitive memory key industry, a new innovation makes it possible to cut the average cost of a 20-megabyte memory key, small enough to fit in your pocket, from $5 to $4. In the long run, what will the price of a 20-megabyte memory key be?

c. Assume that the markets in parts a and b are both constant cost industries. If demand rises massively for these two goods, why won't the price of these goods rise in the long run?

d. In constant cost industries, does demand have any effect on price in the long run?

e. When average cost falls in *any* competitive industry, regardless of cost structure, who gets 100 percent of the benefits of cost cutting in the long run: Consumers or producers?

THINKING AND PROBLEM SOLVING

1. Suppose Sam sells apples in a competitive market, apples picked from his apple tree. Assume all apples are equal in quality, but grow at different heights on the tree. Sam, being fearful of heights, demands greater compensation the higher he goes: So for him, the cost of grabbing an apple rises higher and higher, the higher he must climb, as shown in the Total Cost column below. The market price of an apple is $0.50.

a. What is Sam's marginal revenue for selling apples?

b. Which apples does Sam pick first? Those on the low branches or high branches? Why?

c. Does this suggest that the marginal cost of apples is increasing, decreasing, or staying the same as the quantity of apples picked increases? Why?

d. Complete the table below.

Apples	Total Cost	Marginal Cost	Marginal Revenue	Change in Profit
1	$0.10	$0.10	$0.50	$0.40
2	$0.22			
3	$0.50			
4	$1.00			
5	$1.73			
6	$2.78			

e. How many apples does Sam pick?

2. How long is the "long run?" It will vary from industry to industry. How long would you estimate the long run is in the following industries?

   a. The market for pretzels and soda sold from street carts in the Wall Street financial district in New York.

   b. The market for meals at newly trendy Korean porridge restaurants.

   c. The market for electrical engineers.

   d. After 1999, the market for movies that are suspiciously similar to *The Matrix*.

3. In the process of creative destruction, what gets destroyed? Is it

   Firms

   Workers

   Machines

   Buildings

   Business plans

   Valuable relationships

   Or some combination of these? The chapter itself contains quite a few ideas about how to answer this question, but you'll have to think hard about the "opportunity cost" for each item on this list.

4. In this chapter, we discussed the story of Dalton, Georgia, and its role as the "carpet capital of the world." A similar story can be used to explain why some 60 percent of the motels in the United States are owned by people of Indian origin or why, as of 1995, 80 percent of doughnut shops in California were owned by Cambodian immigrants. Let's look at the latter case. In the 1970s, Cambodian immigrant Ted Ngoy began working at a doughnut shop. He then opened his own store (and later stores).*

Ngoy was drawn to the doughnut industry because it required little English, startup capital, or special skills. Speaking the same language as your workers, however, helps a lot.

   a. As other Cambodian refugees came to Los Angeles fleeing the tyrannical rule of the Khmer Rouge, which group—the refugees or existing residents—was Ngoy more likely to hire from? Why?

   b. Did this make it more or less likely that other Cambodian refugees would open doughnut shops? Why?

   c. As more refugees came in, did this encourage a virtuous cycle of Cambodian-owned doughnut shops? Why?

   d. At this point in the story, what sort of cost industry (constant, increasing, or decreasing) would you consider doughnut shops owned by Cambodians to be? Why?

   e. Why did this cycle not continue forever? What kind of cost structure are Californian doughnut shops probably in now?

5. Every year, American television introduces many new shows, only about a third of which survive past their first season.[3] The few shows that last, however, prove to be very profitable.

   a. How does creative destruction explain why studios bother to make new shows if most of them will fail?

   b. In 2000, CBS premiered *Survivor*, an immensely popular reality show about everyday people living on an island. How did CBS and other networks respond to this surprise hit?

   c. What happened over the next several years to profits from *Survivor*? You don't need to check CBS's financial statements to get the answer, use the elimination principle!

* Not only are 60 percent of the small motels and hotels in the United States owned by East Indians, nearly a third of these owners have the surname, Patel; see http://news.bbc.co.uk/2/hi/south_asia/3177054.stm. The story of Cambodian doughnut shops in Los Angeles is from Postrel, Virginia. 1999. *The Future and Its Enemies,* by New York: Touchstone, pp. 49–50.

6. Ralph opened a small shop selling bags of trail mix. The price of the mix is $5, and the market for trail mix is very competitive. Ralph's cost curves are shown in the figure below.

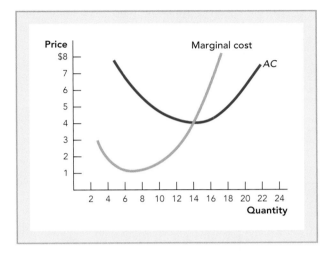

a. At what quantity will Ralph produce? Why?

b. When the price is $5, shade the area of profit or loss in the graph provided and calculate Ralph's profit or loss (round up).

c. If all other sellers of trail mix have the same marginal and average costs as Ralph, should he expect more or fewer competitors in the future? In the long run, will the price of trail mix rise or fall? How do you know? What will the price of trail mix be in the long run?

7. Let's suppose that the demand for allergists increases in California. How does the invisible hand respond to this demand? There is more than one correct answer to this question: Try to come up with two or three.

8. In the competitive children's pajama industry, a new government safety regulation raises the average cost of children's pajamas by $2 per pair.

a. If this is a constant cost industry, then in the long run, what *exactly* happens to the price of children's pajamas?

b. If this is an increasing cost industry, will the long-run price of pajamas rise by more than $2 or less? (Hint: The long-run supply curve will be shaped just like an ordinary supply curve from the first few chapters. If you treat this like a $2 tax per pair, you'll get the right answer.)

c. If this is an increasing cost industry, how much will this new safety regulation change the average pajama maker's profits in the long run?

d. Given your answer to part c, why do businesses in competitive industries often oppose costly new regulations?

9. In the ancient western world, incense was one of the first commodities transported long distances. It grew only in the south of the Arabian Peninsula (modern day Yemen, known then as Arabia Felix), which was transported by camel to Alexandria and the Mediterranean civilizations, notably the Roman Republic. As the republic expanded into a richer and larger empire, the demand for incense grew and planters in Arabia added a second and then a third annual crop (though this incense was not as high of a quality). Cultivation also crossed to the Horn of Africa (modern day Oman) even though such fields were farther away from Rome.[4]

a. How does the lower quality of the additional annual crops illustrate incense as an increasing cost industry? (Hint: Think in terms of an amount of good crop produced per unit of currency.)

b. How does the added distance of incense grown in the Horn of Africa illustrate incense as an increasing cost industry?

c. It's more costly to grow incense in Eastern Africa than in Arabia Felix. Which region would you expect to see more incense grown in?

d. As described in this chapter, the invisible hand allocates productivity between competing producers. Since each grower of incense competed fiercely with each other grower, what eventually happened to their respective marginal costs?

10. You run a small firm. Two management consultants are offering you advice. The first says that your firm is losing money on every unit that you produce. In order to reduce your losses, the consultant recommends that you cut back production. The second consultant says that if your firm sells another unit, the price will more than cover your increase in costs. In order to reduce losses, the second consultant recommends that you should increase production.

a. As an economist, can you explain why both facts that the consultants rely on could be true?

b. Which consultant is offering the correct advice?

11. Paulette, Camille, and Hortense each own wineries in France. They produce inexpensive, mass-market wines. Over the last few years, such wines sold for 7 euros per bottle; but with a global recession, the price has fallen to 5 euros per bottle. Given the information below, let's find out which of these three winemakers (if any) should shut down temporarily until times get better. Remember: whether or not they shut down, they still have to keep paying fixed costs for at least some time (that's what makes them "fixed").

To keep things simple, let's assume that each winemaker has calculated the optimal quantity to produce if they decide to stay in business; your job is simply to figure out if she should produce that amount or just shut down.

Annual income statement when Price = 5 euros				
Winemaker	Fixed costs	Variable Costs	Recession Revenues	Profits
Paulette	50,000	80,000	120,000	
Camille	100,000	40,000	70,000	
Hortense	200,000	250,000	200,000	

a. First, calculate each winemaker's profit.

b. Which of these women, if any, earned a profit?

c. Who should stay in business in the short run? Who should shut down?

d. Fill in the blank: Even if profit is negative, if revenues are _____ variable costs, then it's best to stay open in the short run.

e. For which of these wineries, if any, is $P > AC$? You don't need to calculate any new numbers to answer this.

12. Sandy owns a firm with annual revenues of $1,000,000. Wages, rent, and other costs are $900,000.

a. Calculate Sandy's accounting profit.

b. Suppose that instead of being an entrepreneur Sandy could get a job with one of the following annual salaries i) $50,000, ii) $100,000 or iii) $250,000. Assume that a job would be as satisfying to Sandy as being an entrepreneur. Calculate Sandy's economic profit under each of these scenarios.

CHALLENGES

1. The demand for most metals tends to increase over time. Moreover, as we discussed in this Chapter and also in Chapter 4 these types of natural resource industries tend to be increasing cost industries. And yet the price of metals compared to other goods has tended to fall slowly over time (albeit with many spikes in between). The following figure, for example, shows an index of prices for aluminum, copper, lead, silver, tin, and zinc from 1900 to 2003 (adjusted for inflation). The trend is downward. Why do you think this is the case?

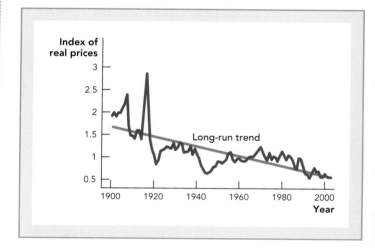

2. Frequent moviegoers often note that movies are rarely based on original ideas. Most of them are based on a television series, a video game, or, most commonly, a book. Why? To help you answer this question, start with the following.

a. Does a movie or a book have a higher fixed cost of production?

b. In 2005, American studios released 563 movies[5] and American publishers produced 176,000 new titles.[6] How does your answer in part a explain such a wide difference? Which is riskier: publishing a book or producing a movie?

c. How does the difference in fixed costs and risk of failure explain why so many movies are based on successful books? As a result, where do you expect to see more innovative plots, dialogues, and characters: In novels or movies?

3. **a.** In the nineteenth century, economist Alfred Marshall wrote about decreasing cost industries, writing in his *Principles of Economics* (available free online) that "When an industry has thus chosen a locality for itself . . . .[t]he mysteries of the trade become no mysteries; but are as it were in the air." In Chapter 9, we had a concept for benefits that are not internal to a firm but are "as it were in the air." What specific concept from Chapter 9 is at work in a business cluster?

   b. In the twenty-first century, economist Michael Porter of the Harvard Business School writes about decreasing cost industries as well: He calls them "business clusters." Porter's work has been very influential among city and town governments who argue that carefully targeted tax breaks and subsidies can attract investment and create a business cluster in their town that will subsequently reap the benefits of decreasing costs. Is this argument correct? Be careful, it's tricky!

4. In Kolkata, India, it is very common to see beggars on the streets. Imagine that the visitors and residents of Kolkata become more generous in their donations; what will be the effect on the standard of living of beggars in Kolkata? Answer this question using supply and demand, making assumptions as necessary.

CHAPTER APPENDIX

Using Excel to Graph Cost Curves

We can use a spreadsheet such as Excel to take some of the drudgery out of graphing and calculating things like marginal revenue and marginal cost. In Figure A10.1 we show some of the data from the Chapter on revenues and costs for the oil well. Notice that in cell B5 we show the Excel formula "=$A$2*A5" which takes the price from cell A2 and multiplies it by the quantity in cell A5 to produce total revenue. We then copy and paste this formula into the remainder of the column. We use the $ sign in $A$2 to tell Excel not to adjust the cell reference when we copy and paste (A5 doesn't have dollar signs so it is automatically adjusted to A6, A7, etc. when we copy and paste).

FIGURE A10.1

	B5	▼		f_x =$A$2*A5	
	A	B	C	D	
1	Price				
2	50				
3					
4	Barrels of Oil Produced	Total Revenue (P * Q)	Total Cost		
5	0	0	30		
6	1	50	34		
7	2	100	40		
8	3	150	51		
9	4	200	68		
10	5	250	91		
11	6	300	120		
12	7	350	156		
13	8	400	206		
14	9	450	296		
15	10	500	420		
16					

With total revenue and total cost inputted it's easy to create the other data that we need. Profit is just total revenue minus total cost which in Figure A10.2 we show in column D. Marginal revenue and marginal cost are defined as $MR = \frac{\Delta TR}{\Delta Q}$ and $MC = \frac{\Delta TC}{\Delta Q}$. We show in cell F4 how to implement these formulas in Excel. The formula "=(C4-C3)/(A4-A3)" takes the cost of producing 2 barrels of oil from cell C4 and subtracts the cost of producing 1 barrel of oil from C3; we then divide by the increase in the number of barrels as we move from producing 1 to 2 barrels. In this case, MC = (40-34)/(2-1) = 6. The formula for MR is entered into Excel in similar manner.

FIGURE A10.2

	F4	▼	f_x =(C4-C3)/(A4-A3)				
	A	B	C	D	E	F	G
1	Barrels of Oil Produced	Total Revenue (P * Q)	Total Cost	Profit	Marginal Revenue (Price)	Marginal Cost	
2	0	0	30	-30			
3	1	50	34	16	50	4	
4	2	100	40	60	50	6	
5	3	150	51	99	50	11	
6	4	200	68	132	50	17	
7	5	250	91	159	50	23	
8	6	300	120	180	50	29	
9	7	350	156	194	50	36	
10	8	400	206	194	50	50	
11	9	450	296	154	50	90	
12	10	500	420	80	50	124	
13							
14							

Average cost is $AC = \dfrac{TC}{Q}$ and we show this calculation in Figure A10.3.

FIGURE A10.3

	G13	▼	f_x =C13/A13				
	A	B	C	D	E	F	G
1	Price						
2	50						
3							
4	Barrels of Oil Produced	Total Revenue (P * Q)	Total Cost	Profit	Marginal Revenue (Price)	Marginal Cost	Average Cost
5	0	0	30	-30			
6	1	50	34	16	50	4	34
7	2	100	40	60	50	6	20
8	3	150	51	99	50	11	17
9	4	200	68	132	50	17	17
10	5	250	91	159	50	23	18.2
11	6	300	120	180	50	29	20
12	7	350	156	194	50	36	22.28571
13	8	400	206	194	50	50	25.75
14	9	450	296	154	50	90	32.88889
15	10	500	420	80	50	124	42
16							

It's now easy to graph MR, MC, and AC. By highlighting the Marginal Revenue, Marginal Cost, and Average Cost columns, including the labels, and clicking Insert and then Line Chart, we can produce a graph similar to that shown in Figure A10.4 (to get the exact graph you must also tell Excel to use the barrel numbers in Column 1 on the X axis—you can do this by clicking on the graph, clicking Select Data, and then Edit, Horizontal (Category) Axis Labels; this is for Excel 2007, Excel 2003 works similarly).

Remember that the profit maximizing quantity is found where MR = MC. You can check this by looking at the table. You can see what happens to the profit maximizing quantity when price changes simply by changing the price in cell A2; the graph will change automatically.

FIGURE A10.4

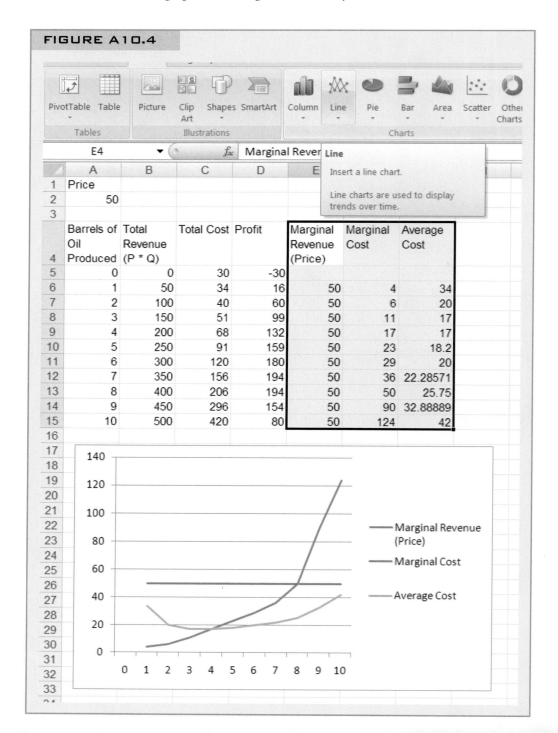

11

Monopoly

CHAPTER OUTLINE

Market Power

How a Firm Uses Market Power to Maximize Profit

The Costs of Monopoly: Deadweight Loss

The Costs of Monopoly: Corruption and Inefficiency

The Benefits of Monopoly: Incentives for Research and Development

Economies of Scale and the Regulation of Monopoly

Other Sources of Market Power

Takeaway

On June 5, 1981, the Centers for Disease Control and Prevention reported that a strange outbreak of pneumonia was killing young, healthy, homosexual men in Los Angeles. Alarm spread as similar reports streamed in from San Francisco, New York, and Boston. What had at first looked like a disease peculiar to homosexual men turned out to be a worldwide killer caused by HIV (human immunodeficiency virus). Since 1981, AIDS (Acquired Immune Deficiency Syndrome) has killed more than 25 million people.

There is no known cure for AIDS, but progress has been made in treating the disease. In the United States, deaths from AIDS dropped by approximately 50 percent between 1995 and 1997. The major cause of the falling death rate was the development of new drugs called combination antiretrovirals, such as Combivir.[1] The drugs only work, however, if one can afford to take them, and they are expensive. A single pill of Combivir costs $12.50—at two per day, every day, that's nearly $10,000 dollars per year.[2] If you have the money, $10,000 a year is a small price to pay for life, but there are 38 million people worldwide living with HIV and most of them don't have $10,000.[3]

If HIV drugs were expensive because production costs were high, economists would have little to say about drug pricing. But it costs less than 50 cents to produce a pill of Combivir—thus, the price of one pill is about 25 times higher than the cost.[4] In earlier chapters, we emphasized how competitive markets drive the price of a good down to marginal cost. Why hasn't that process worked here? There are three reasons why HIV drugs are priced well above cost.

1. Market power

2. The "you can't take it with you" effect

3. The "other people's money" effect

The cause of AIDS, the human immunodeficiency virus (HIV).

MEDICALRF.COM/VISUALS UNLIMITED, INC.

The primary reason that AIDS drugs are priced well above costs is monopoly or market power, the subject of this chapter. The "you can't take it with you" and "other people's money" effects, which we will also discuss in this chapter, make market power especially strong in the pricing of pharmaceuticals.

Market Power

GlaxoSmithKline, the world's largest producer of AIDS drugs, owns the patent on Combivir. A patent is a government grant that gives the owner the exclusive rights to make, use, or sell the patented product. GlaxoSmithKline (GSK), for example, is the only legal seller of Combivir. Even though the formula to manufacture it is well known and easily duplicated, competitors who try to make Combivir or its equivalent will be jailed, at least in the United States and other countries where the patent is enforced.

GSK's patent on Combivir gives GSK **market power,** the power to raise price above marginal cost without fear that other competitors will enter the market. A **monopoly** is simply a firm with market power.

India does not recognize the Combivir patent, so in that country competition prevails and an equivalent drug sells for just 50 cents per pill.[5] Thus, economics correctly predicts that competition will drive price down to the marginal cost of production; it's just that GSK's patent prevents competition from operating.

Patents are not the only source of market power. Government regulations other than patents, as well as economies of scale, exclusive access to an important input, and technological innovation can all create firms with market power. We discuss the sources of market power and appropriate responses at greater length later on in the chapter. For now, we want to ask how a firm will use its market power to maximize profit.

> **Market power** is the power to raise price above marginal cost without fear that other firms will enter the market.
>
> A **monopoly** is a firm with market power.

How a Firm Uses Market Power to Maximize Profit

We know that a firm with market power will price above cost—but how much above cost? Even a firm with no competitors faces a demand curve, so as it raises its price it will sell fewer units. Higher prices, therefore, are not always better for a seller—raise the price too much and profits will fall. Lower the price and profits can increase. What is the profit-maximizing price?

To maximize profit, a firm should produce until the revenue from an additional sale is equal to the cost of an additional sale. This is the same condition that we discovered in Chapter 10: produce until **marginal revenue** equals **marginal cost** ($MR = MC$). In Chapter 10, however, calculating marginal revenue was easy because even if a small oil well increases production significantly, the effect on the world price of oil is so small it can be ignored. For a small firm, therefore, the revenue from the sale of an additional unit is the market price ($MR = $ Price). But when a firm's output of a product is large relative to the entire market's output of that product (or very close substitutes), a significant increase in the firm's output will cause the market price of that product to fall. When the Saudis boost oil production, for example, the price of oil falls. Thus, for a firm that produces a large share of the market's total output of a product, the revenue from the sale of an additional unit is less than the current market price ($MR < $ Price).

> **Marginal revenue, MR,** is the change in total revenue from selling an additional unit.
>
> **Marginal cost, MC,** is the change in total cost from producing an additional unit. To maximize profit, a firm increases output until $MR = MC$.

To understand how a firm with market power will price its product, we need to calculate marginal revenue for a firm that is large enough to influence the price of its product.

We show how to calculate marginal revenue in the table in the left panel of Figure 11.1. Suppose that at a price of $16 the quantity demanded is 2 units, so that total revenue is $32 (2 × $16). If the monopolist reduces the price to $14, it can sell 3 units for a total revenue of $42 (3 × $14). Marginal revenue, the change in revenue from selling an additional unit, is therefore $10 ($42 − $32). Thus we can always calculate *MR* by looking at the change in total revenue when production changes by one unit.

FIGURE 11.1

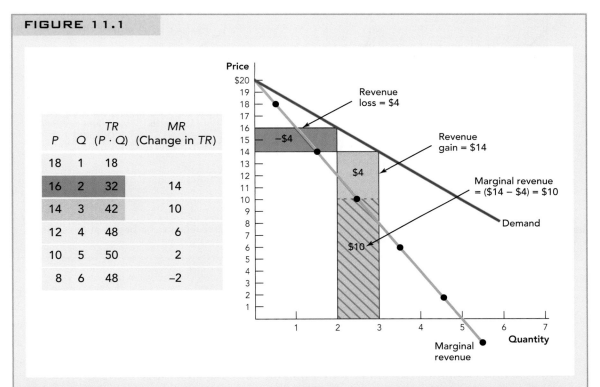

P	Q	TR (P · Q)	MR (Change in TR)
18	1	18	
16	2	32	14
14	3	42	10
12	4	48	6
10	5	50	2
8	6	48	−2

Marginal Revenue The table on the left shows that marginal revenue is the change in total revenue when quantity sold increases by 1 unit. When the quantity sold increases from 2 units to 3 units, for example, total revenue increases from $32 to $42 so marginal revenue, the change in total revenue, is $10.

The figure on the right shows how we can break down the change in total revenue into two parts. When the firm lowers the price from $16 to $14, it sells one more unit and so there is a gain in revenue of $14 but since the firm had to lower the price it loses $2 on each of its two previous sales so there is a revenue loss of $4. Thus, marginal revenue is the revenue gain on new sales plus the revenue loss on previous sales.

The right panel of Figure 11.1 shows another way of thinking about marginal revenue. When the monopolist lowers its price from $16 to $14, it makes one additional sale, which increases revenues by $14—the green area. But to make that additional sale, the monopolist had to lower its price by $2, so it loses $2 on *each* of the two units that it was selling at the higher price for a revenue loss of $4—the red area. Marginal revenue is the revenue gain (green, $14) plus the revenue loss (red, −$4) or $10 (green striped area). Notice that *MR* ($10) is less than price ($14)—once again, this is because to sell more units the monopolist must lower the price so there is a loss of revenue on previous sales.

Now that you understand the idea of marginal revenue, here's a shortcut for finding marginal revenue. If the demand curve is a straight line, then the marginal revenue curve is a straight line that begins at the same point on the vertical axis as the demand curve but with twice the slope.* Figure 11.2 shows three demand curves and their associated marginal revenue curves. Notice that if the demand curve cuts the horizontal axis at, say, Z, then the marginal revenue curve will always cut the horizontal axis at half that amount, Z/2.

FIGURE 11.2

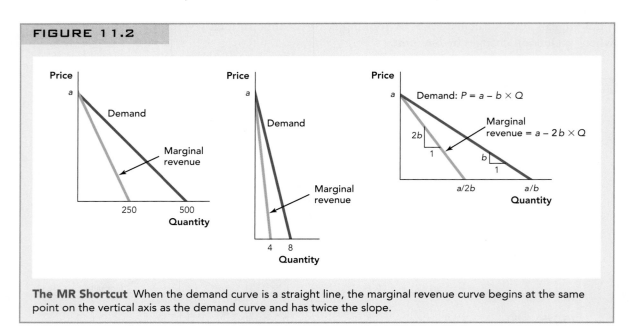

The MR Shortcut When the demand curve is a straight line, the marginal revenue curve begins at the same point on the vertical axis as the demand curve and has twice the slope.

Figure 11.3 sketches the demand, marginal revenue, marginal cost, and average cost curve for a firm with market power, like GlaxoSmithKline. GSK maximizes profit by producing the quantity where $MR = MC$. In Figure 11.3, this is at point a, a quantity of 80 million units. What is the maximum price at which the monopolist can sell 80 million units? To find the maximum that consumers will pay for 80 million units, remember that we read up from the quantity supplied of 80 million units to the *demand curve* at point b. Consumers are willing to pay as much as $12.50 per pill when the quantity supplied is 80 million pills, so the profit-maximizing price is $12.50.

We can also use Figure 11.3 to illustrate the monopolist's profit. Remember from Chapter 10 that profit can be calculated as $(P - AC) \times Q$. At a quantity of 80 million units, the price is $12.50 (point b), the average cost (AC) is $2.50 (point c), and thus profit is ($12.50 - $2.50) $\times$ 80 million units or $800 million as illustrated by the green rectangle. (By the way, the fixed costs of producing a new pharmaceutical are very large so the minimum point of the AC curve occurs far to the right of the diagram.) Recall that a competitive firm earns zero or normal profits but a monopolist uses her market power to earn positive or *above normal* profits.

---

* It's possible to prove why the MR shortcut is true using calculus. Let the demand curve be written in the form $P = a - bQ$ so the slope is b. Total revenue is $P \star Q = TR = aQ - bQ^2$. Marginal revenue is the derivative of total revenue with respect to quantity or $MR = \dfrac{dTR}{dQ} = a - 2bQ$. Notice that the slope of the MR curve is $2b$, twice the slope of the demand curve.

FIGURE 11.3

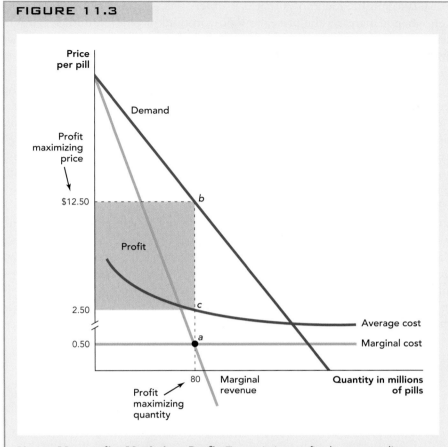

How a Monopolist Maximizes Profit To maximize profit, the monopolist produces until *MR* = *MC* (point *a*). Reading down from point *a*, we find the profit-maximizing quantity, 80 million pills. Reading upward from point *a*, we find the profit-maximizing price on the demand curve, $12.50. Profit is (*P* − *AC*) × *Q* and is given by the green rectangle.

The Elasticity of Demand and the Monopoly Markup

Market power for pharmaceuticals can be especially powerful because of the two other effects we mentioned earlier: the "you can't take it with you" effect and the "other people's money" effect. If you are dying of disease, what better use of your money do you have than spending it on medicine that might prolong your life? If you can't take it with you, then you may as well spend your money trying to stick around a bit longer. Consumers with serious diseases, therefore, are *relatively insensitive to the price of life-saving pharmaceuticals.*

Moreover, if you are willing to spend *your* money on pharmaceuticals, how do you feel about spending *other people's money*? Most patients in the United States have access to public or private health insurance, so pharmaceuticals and other medical treatments are often paid by someone other than the patient. Thus, both the "you can't take it with you" and the "other people's money" effects make consumers with serious diseases relatively insensitive to the price of life-saving pharmaceuticals—that is, they will continue to buy in large quantities even when the price increases.

If GlaxoSmithKline knows that consumers will continue to buy Combivir even when it increases the price, how do you think it will respond? Yes, it will increase the price! When consumers are relatively insensitive to the price, what sort of demand curve do we say consumers have? An inelastic demand curve. The "you can't take it with you" effect and the "other people's money" effect make the demand curve more *inelastic*. Thus, we say that the more inelastic the demand curve, the more a monopolist will raise its price above marginal cost.

Is it ethically wrong for GSK to raise its price above marginal cost? Perhaps, but keep in mind that in the United States it costs nearly a billion dollars to research and develop the average new drug. Once we better understand how monopolies price, we will return to the question of what, if anything, should be done about market power.

Figure 11.4 illustrates that the more inelastic the demand curve, the more a monopolist will raise its price above marginal cost. On the left side of the figure, the monopolist faces a relatively elastic demand curve, and on the right side a relatively inelastic demand curve. As usual, the monopolist maximizes profit by choosing the quantity at which $MR = MC$ and the highest price that consumers will pay for that quantity. Notice that even though the marginal cost curve is identical in the two panels, the markup of price over marginal cost is much higher when the demand curve is relatively inelastic.

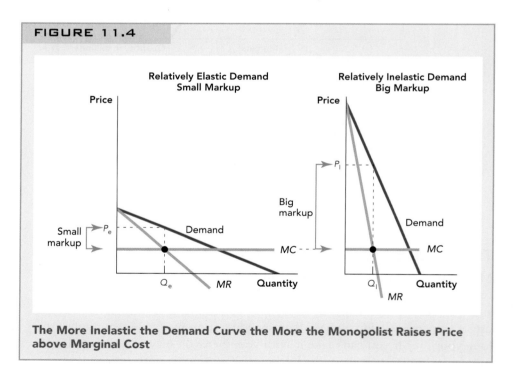

FIGURE 11.4

The More Inelastic the Demand Curve the More the Monopolist Raises Price above Marginal Cost

Remember from Chapter 4 that the fewer substitutes that exist for a good, the more inelastic the demand curve. With that in mind, consider the following puzzle. In December 2006, American Airlines was selling a flight from Washington, D.C., to Dallas for $733.30. On the same day, it was selling a flight from Washington to San Francisco for $556.60. That's a little puzzling. You would expect the shorter flight to have lower costs, and Washington is much closer to Dallas than to San Francisco. The puzzle, however, is even deeper. The flight from Washington to San Francisco stopped in Dallas. In fact, the Washington-to-Dallas leg of the journey was on exactly the same flight![6]

Thus, a traveler going from Washington to Dallas was being charged nearly $200 *more* than a traveler going from Washington to Dallas and then on to San Francisco even though both were flying to Dallas on the same plane. Why?

Here's a hint. Each of the major airlines flies most of its cross-country traffic into a hub, an airport that serves as a busy "node" in an airline's network of flights, and most hubs are located near the center of the country. Delta's hub, for example, is in Atlanta. So if you fly cross-country on Delta, you will probably travel through Atlanta. United's hub is in Chicago and American Airlines has its hub in Dallas. Have you solved the puzzle yet?

Eighty-four percent of the flights into the Dallas–Fort Worth airport are on American Airlines, so if you want to fly from Washington to Dallas at a convenient time, you have few choices of airline. But if you want to fly from Washington to San Francisco, you have many choices. In addition to flying on American Airlines, you can fly Delta, United, or Jet Blue. Since travelers flying from Washington to Dallas have few substitutes their demand curve is inelastic, like the demand curve in the right panel of Figure 11.4. Since travelers flying from Washington to San Francisco have many substitutes, their demand curve is more elastic, like the one in the left panel of Figure 11.4. As a result, travelers flying from Washington to Dallas (inelastic demand) are charged more than those flying from Washington to San Francisco (elastic demand).

You are probably asking yourself why someone wanting to go from Washington to Dallas doesn't book the cheaper flight to San Francisco and then exit in Dallas? In fact, clever people try to game the system all the time—but don't try to do this with a round-trip ticket or the airline will cancel your return flight. As a matter of contract, most airlines prohibit this and similar practices—their profit is at stake!

The Costs of Monopoly: Deadweight Loss

What's wrong with monopoly? The question may seem absurd—isn't it the high prices? Not so fast. The high price is bad for consumers, but it's good for the monopolist. And what's so special about consumers? Monopolists are people too. So if we want to discover whether monopoly is good or bad, we need to count the gains to the monopolist equally with the losses to consumers. It turns out, however, that the monopolist gains less from monopoly pricing than the consumer loses. So monopolies are bad—they are bad because, compared to competition, monopolies reduce *total surplus*, the total gains from trade (consumer surplus plus producer surplus).

In Figure 11.5 on the next page, we compare total surplus under competition with total surplus under monopoly. In the left panel, the competitive equilibrium price and quantity are P_c and Q_c. We also label Q_c the optimal quantity because it is the quantity that maximizes total surplus (recall from Chapter 3 that a competitive market maximizes total surplus). For simplicity, we assume a constant cost industry so the supply curve is flat ($MC = AC$) and producer surplus is zero. Total surplus is thus the same as consumer surplus and is shown by the blue triangle.

The right panel shows how a monopolist with the same costs would behave. Setting $MR = MC$, the monopolist produces Q_m, which is much less than Q_c, and prices at P_m. Consumer surplus is now the much smaller blue triangle. Now here is the key point: *Some* of the consumer surplus has been transferred to the monopolist as profit, the green area. But some of the consumer surplus

CHECK YOURSELF

> As a firm with market power moves down the demand curve to sell more units, what happens to the price it can charge on *all* units?

> What type of demand curve does a firm with market power prefer to face for its products: elastic or inelastic? Why?

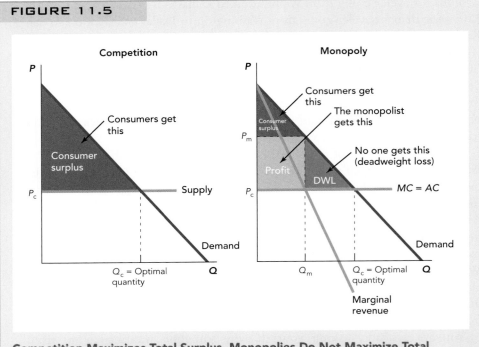

FIGURE 11.5

Competition Maximizes Total Surplus, Monopolies Do Not Maximize Total Surplus The left and right panels compare a competitive market with a monopolized market with the same demand and cost curves. Under monopoly, the price increases from P_c to P_m, consumer surplus falls, and profit increases. Importantly, consumer surplus falls by more than profit increases—the difference is the deadweight loss from monopoly.

is not transferred, it goes to neither the consumers nor to the monopolist; it goes to no one and is lost. We call the lost consumer surplus *deadweight loss*.

To better understand deadweight loss, remember that the height of the demand curve tells you how much consumers are willing to pay for the good, and the height of the marginal cost curve tells you the cost of producing the good. Now notice that in between the amount that the monopolist produces, Q_m, and the amount that would be produced under competition, Q_c, the demand curve is above the marginal cost curve. In other words, consumers value the units between Q_m and Q_c more than their cost; so if these units were produced, total surplus would increase. But the monopolist does not produce these units. Why not? Because to sell these units, the monopolist would have to lower its price; and if it did so, the increase in revenue would not cover the increase in costs, that is, MR would be less than MC, so the monopolist's profit would decrease.

Let's look at deadweight loss in practice. GlaxoSmithKline prices Combivir at $12.50 a pill, the profit-maximizing price. There are plenty of consumers who can't pay $12.50 a pill but would gladly pay more than the marginal cost of 50 cents a pill. Deadweight loss is the value of the Combivir sales that do not occur because the monopoly price is above the competitive price.

CHECK YOURSELF

> Does the monopolist price its product above or below the price of a competitive firm?

> Does the monopolist produce more or less than competitive firms? Why?

The Costs of Monopoly: Corruption and Inefficiency

Sadly, around the world today many monopolies are government created and born of corruption. Indonesian President Suharto (in office from 1967 to 1998), for example, gave the lucrative clove monopoly to his playboy son, Tommy Suharto.

Cloves may sound inconsequential, but they are a key ingredient in Indonesian cigarettes, and the monopoly funneled hundreds of millions of dollars to Tommy. A lot of rich playboys buy Lamborghinis—Tommy bought the entire company.

Monopolies are especially harmful when the goods that are monopolized are used to produce other goods. In Algeria, for example, a dozen or so army generals each control a key good. Indeed, the public ironically refers to each general by the major commodity that they monopolize—General Steel, General Wheat, General Tire, and so forth.

Steel is an input into automobiles, so when General Steel tries to take advantage of his market power by raising the price of steel, this increases costs for General Auto. General Auto responds by raising the price of automobiles even more than he would if steel were competitively produced. Similarly, General Steel raises the price of steel even more than he would if automobiles were competitively produced. Throw in a General Tire, a General Computer and, let's say, a General Electric and we have a recipe for economic disaster. Each general tries to grab a larger share of the pie, but the combined result is that the pie gets much, much smaller.

Compare a competitive market economy with a monopolized economy: Competitive producers of steel work to reduce prices so they can sell more. Reduced prices of steel result in reduced prices of automobiles. Cost savings in one sector are spread throughout the economy resulting in economic growth. In a monopolized economy, in contrast, the entire process is thrown into reverse. Each firm wants to raise its prices, and the resulting cost increases are spread throughout the economy, resulting in poverty and stagnation.

One of the great lessons of economics is to show that good institutions channel self-interest toward social prosperity whereas poor institutions channel self-interest toward social destruction. Business leaders in the United States are no less self-interested than generals in Algeria. So why are the former a mostly positive force while the latter are a mostly negative force? It's because competitive markets channel the self-interest of business leaders toward social prosperity whereas the political structure of Algeria channels self-interest toward social destruction.

The Benefits of Monopoly: Incentives for Research and Development

GlaxoSmithKline prices its AIDS drugs above marginal cost. If GSK didn't have a monopoly, competition would push prices down, more people could afford to buy Combivir, and total surplus would increase (i.e., deadweight loss would decline). So isn't the solution to the monopoly problem obvious? Open up the industry to competition by refusing to enforce the firm's patent or force GlaxoSmithKline to lower its price.

In fact, many countries pursue one or the other of these policies. India, for example, has traditionally not offered strong patent protection, and Canada controls pharmaceutical prices. India's and Canada's policies have successfully kept pharmaceutical prices low in those countries. Many people argue that the United States should also control pharmaceutical prices. Unfortunately, the story is not so simple. We need to revisit our question, what's wrong with monopoly?

In the United States, researching, developing, and successfully testing the average new drug costs nearly one billion dollars.[7] Firms must be compensated for

Monopoly profit

Thomas Edison spent years experimenting with thousands of materials before he discovered that carbonized bamboo filament would make a long-lasting lightbulb. If anyone could have capitalized on his idea, Edison would not have been able to profit from his laborious research and development and perhaps he would not have done the necessary research in the first place.

Profit fuels the fire of invention.

these expenses if people expect them to invest in the discovery process. But if competition pushes the price of a pill down to the marginal cost, nothing will be left over for the cost of invention. And he who has no hope of reaping will not sow.

Patents are one way of rewarding research and development. Look again at Figure 11.3, which shows the green rectangle of monopoly profit. It's precisely the expectation (and hope) of enjoying that monopoly profit that encourages firms to research and develop new drugs.

If pharmaceutical patents are not enforced, the number of new drugs will decrease. India is poor and Canada is small, so neither contributes much to the global profit of pharmaceutical firms. But if the United States were to limit pharmaceutical patents significantly or to control pharmaceutical prices, the number of new drugs would decrease significantly.[8] But new drugs save lives. As noted in the introduction, antiretrovirals like Combivir were the major cause of the 50 percent decrease in AIDS deaths in the United States in the mid-1990s. We should be careful that in pushing prices closer to marginal cost we do not lose the new drug entirely.

In evaluating pharmaceutical patents, you should keep in mind that patents don't last forever. A patent lasts for at most 20 years and by the time a new drug is FDA approved the effective life is typically only 12–14 years. Once the drug goes off patent, generic equivalents appear quickly and the deadweight loss is eliminated.

Pharmaceuticals are not the only goods with high development costs and low marginal costs. Information goods of all kinds often have the same cost structure. Video games like Halo, Madden NFL, and The Sims have typical development costs of $7 million to $10 million and Grand Theft Auto IV cost more than $100 million to develop. Once the code has been written, however, the marginal cost of printing a manual and writing a DVD or CD might be $2. Prices, typically $40–$60, are therefore well above marginal costs. Since prices exceed marginal costs there is a deadweight loss, which in theory could be reduced by a price control. Reducing prices, however, would reduce the incentive to research and develop new games. What would you rather have, Pong at $2, or, for $50 a game, a constant stream of new and better games?

Video games may seem trivial, but the trade-off between lower prices today at the expense of fewer new ideas in the future is a central one in modern economies. In fact, modern theories of economic growth emphasize that monopoly—*when it is used to protect innovation*—may be necessary for economic growth.

Nobel Prize-winning economic historian Douglass North argues that economic growth was slow and sporadic until laws, including patent laws, were created to protect innovation:

> [T]hroughout man's past he has continually developed new techniques, but the pace has been slow and intermittent. The primary reason has been that the incentives for developing new techniques have occurred only sporadically. Typically, innovations could be copied at no cost by others and without any reward to the inventor or innovator. The failure to develop systematic property rights in innovation up until fairly modern times was a major source of the slow pace of technological change.[9]

Patent Buyouts—A Potential Solution?

Is there a way to eliminate the deadweight loss without reducing the incentive to innovate? Economist Michael Kremer has offered one speculative idea.[10]

HANDOUT/EPA/CORBIS

Eyes on the prize

Prizes are another way of rewarding research and development without creating monopolies. SpaceShipOne, pictured here, won the $10 million Ansari X Prize for being the first privately developed manned rocket capable of reaching space and returning in a short time. Netflix, the DVD distribution firm, offered and paid a $1 million prize for improvements to its movie recommendation system. The Department of Defense has sponsored prizes for driverless vehicles and Congress recently established the H-Prize for advances in hydrogen technology.

Take a look again at Figure 11.3. The green profit rectangle is the value of the patent to the patent owner, $800 million. Suppose that the government were to offer to buy the rights to the patent at, say, $850 million? The monopolist would be eager to sell at this price. What would the government do with the patent? Rip it up! If the government ripped up the patent, competitors would enter the field, drive the price down to the average cost of production and eliminate the deadweight loss. In other words, Combivir would fall from $12.50 a pill to 50 cents a pill, and more of the world's poor could afford to be treated for AIDS.

The great virtue of Kremer's proposal is that it reduces the price of new drugs without reducing the incentive to develop more new drugs. Indeed, by offering more than the potential profit, the government could even increase the incentive to innovate! As usual, however, there is no such thing as a free lunch. To buy the patent, the government must raise taxes, and we know from Chapter 7 that taxes, just like monopolies, create deadweight losses. Also determining the right price to buy the patent is not easy and some people worry that corruption could be a problem.

Kremer's idea has never been tried on a widespread basis but despite these problems economists are becoming increasingly interested in patent buyouts and the closely related idea of prizes as a way to encourage innovation without creating too much deadweight loss.

Economies of Scale and the Regulation of Monopoly

Governments are not the only source of market power. Monopolies can arise naturally when economies of scale create circumstances where one large firm (or a handful of large firms) can produce at lower cost than many small firms. When a single firm can supply the entire market at lower cost than two or more firms, we say that the industry is a **natural monopoly.**

A subway is a natural monopoly because it would cost twice as much to build two parallel subway tunnels than to build one but even though costs would be twice as high, output (the number of subway trips) would be the same. Utilities such as water, natural gas, and cable television are typically natural monopolies because in each case it's much cheaper to run one pipe or cable than to run multiple pipes or cables to the same set of homes.

In Figure 11.5, we compared competitive firms with an *equal cost* monopoly and showed that total surplus was higher under competition. The comparison between competitive firms and natural monopoly is more difficult. Even though natural monopolies produce less than the optimal quantity, competitive firms would also produce less than the optimal quantity because they could not take advantage of economies of scale.

If the economies of scale are large enough, it's even possible for price to be lower under natural monopoly than it would be under competition. Figure 11.6 on the next page shows just such a situation. Notice that the average cost curve for the monopoly is so far below the average cost curves of the competitive firms that the monopoly price is below the competitive price. It's possible, for example, for every home to produce its own electric power with a small generator or solar panel but the costs of producing electricity in this way would be higher than buying electricity produced from a dam even if the dam was a natural monopoly.

CHECK YOURSELF

> Name some firms with market power that plausibly encourage innovation. Name some firms with market power that do not seem to encourage innovation.

> If we rewarded innovation with prizes instead of patents, how large do you think the prize should be for a new cancer drug?

A **natural monopoly** is said to exist when a single firm can supply the entire market at a lower cost than two or more firms.

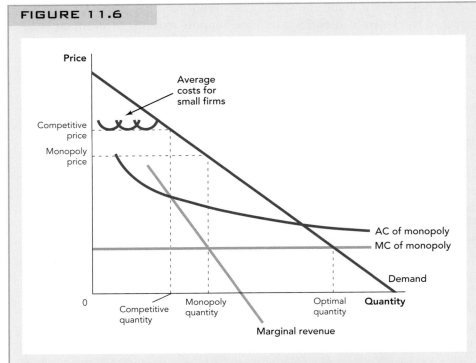

FIGURE 11.6

A Monopoly with Large Economies of Scale Can Have a Lower Price than Competitive Firms Economies of scale mean that a monopoly producer can have lower costs of production than competitive firms. It's cheaper to produce electricity for 100,000 homes with one large dam, for example, than with a solar panel for each home. If economies of scale are large enough, the monopoly price can be lower than the competitive price and the monopoly output can be higher than the competitive output.

Is there any way to have our cake and eat it too? That is, is there a way to have prices equal to marginal cost and to take advantage of economies of scale?

In theory the answer is yes, but it's not easy. In Chapter 6, we showed that a price control set below the market price would create a shortage. But surprisingly when the market price is set by a monopolist, a price control can increase output. Let's see how.

Suppose that the government imposes a price control on the monopolist at level P_R as in Figure 11.7. Imagine that the monopolist sells 2 units and suppose it wants to sell a third. What is the marginal revenue on the third unit? It's just P_R. In fact, when the price is set at P_R, the monopolist can sell up to Q_R units without having to lower the price. Since the monopolist doesn't have to lower the price to sell more units, the marginal revenue for each unit up to Q_R is P_R. Notice that we have drawn the new marginal revenue curve in Figure 11.7 equal to P_R in between 0 and Q_R (after that point, to sell an additional unit, the monopolist has to lower the price on all previous units so the *MR* curve jumps down to the level of the old *MR* curve and becomes negative). Now the problem is simple because, as always, the monopolist wants to produce until *MR* = *MC*, so Q_R is the profit-maximizing quantity.

Notice that the monopolist produces *more* as the government regulated price of its output *falls*.

So what price should the government set? Since the optimal quantity is found where *P* = *MC*, the natural answer is that the government should set P_R = *MC*. Unfortunately, that won't work when economies of scale are large

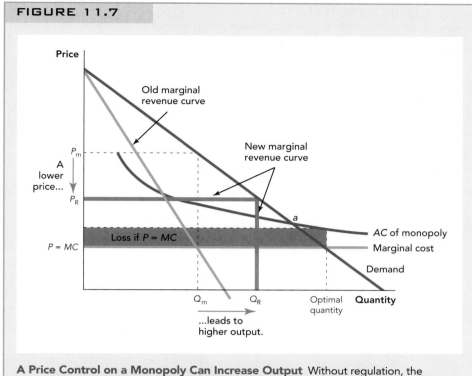

FIGURE 11.7

A Price Control on a Monopoly Can Increase Output Without regulation, the monopoly maximizes profit by choosing P_m, Q_m. If the government imposes a price control at P_R the monopolist chooses Q_R, a larger quantity. The optimal price is at $P = MC$, but at this price the monopolist is making a loss and will exit the industry. The lowest price that will keep the monopolist in the industry is $P = AC$ at point a. At that price the monopolist makes a zero (normal) profit.

because if the price is set equal to marginal cost, the monopolist will be making a loss. Remember that Profit $= (P - AC) \times Q$ so setting P_R equal to marginal cost creates a loss illustrated by the red area in Figure 11.7.

The government could subsidize the monopolist to make up for the loss when $P_R = MC$ but, once again, taxation has its own deadweight losses. If the government set $P_R = AC$ at point a where the AC curve intersects the demand curve, the monopolist would just break even; output would then be larger than the monopoly quantity but less than the optimal quantity. This seems like a pretty good solution but there are other problems with regulating a monopolist. When the monopolist's profits are regulated, it doesn't have much incentive to increase quality with innovative new products or to lower costs. The strange history of cable TV regulation and California's ill-fated efforts at electricity deregulation illustrate some of the real problems with regulating and deregulating monopolies.

I Want My MTV

Regulation of retail subscription rates for cable TV seemed to keep prices low in the early years of television, when there were basically only three channels, ABC, CBS, and NBC. In the 1970s, however, new technology made it possible for cable operators to offer 10, 20, or even 30 channels. But if subscription rates were fixed at the low levels, thereby limiting profit rates, the cable operators would have little incentive to add channels. Recognizing this, Congress lifted caps on pay TV rates in 1979 and on all cable television in 1984.

Quality comes at a price.

UNDERSTAND YOUR **world**

Deregulation of cable TV rates led to higher prices, just as the theory of natural monopoly predicts, but something else happened—the number of television stations and the quality of programming increased dramatically. And, contrary to natural monopoly theory, consumers seemed to appreciate the new channels more than they disliked the higher prices. This is evident because even as prices rose, more people signed up for cable television.[11]

Congress re-regulated "basic cable" rates in 1992 but left "premium channels" unregulated. *Wayne's World* was the result. Let's explain: Cable operators were typically required to carry a certain number of channels in the basic package, but they had some choice over which channels were included in the package. So when basic cable was re-regulated, the cable operators moved some of the best channels to their unregulated premium package. To fill the gaps in the basic package, they added whatever programs were cheap, including television shows created by amateurs on a shoestring budget. *Wayne's World,* a Saturday Night Live comedy sketch, mocked the proliferation of these amateur cable shows.

Rates were mostly deregulated again in 1996. Not entirely coincidentally, this was the first year that HBO won an Emmy. Today, "basic tier cable" is regulated by local governments, but anything beyond the most basic service is predominantly free of regulation and cable companies can charge a market rate. As before, prices have risen since deregulation, but so have the number of television channels and the quality of programming.

If you like *The Sopranos, Entourage,* and *Veronica Mars,* then cable deregulation has worked well. Deregulation of electricity, however, has proven shocking.

Electric Shock

Government ownership is another potential solution to the natural monopoly problem. In the United States, there are some 3,000 electric utilities, and two-thirds of them are government owned (the remainder are heavily regulated). Government ownership of utilities began early in the twentieth century with municipalities owning local distribution companies. In the 1930s, the federal government became a major generator of electricity with the construction of the then largest manmade structures ever built, the Hoover Dam in 1936 and the even larger Grand Coulee Dam in 1941.

Government ownership and regulation worked reasonably well for several decades in providing the United States with cheap power. Without the discipline of competition or a profit motive, however, there is a tendency for a government-run or regulated monopoly to become inefficient. Why reduce costs when costs can be passed on to customers? In the 1960s and 1970s, multibillion dollar cost overruns for the construction of nuclear power plants drew attention to industry inefficiencies as the price of power increased.

Historically, a single firm handled the generation, long-distance transmission, and local distribution of electricity. In the 1970s, however, new technologies reduced the average cost of generating electricity at small scales (in Figure 11.6 you can think of the curves labeled Average costs for small firms as moving down). Although the transmission and distribution of electricity remained natural monopolies, the new technologies meant that the generation of electricity was no longer a natural monopoly. Economists began to argue that unbundling generation from transmission and distribution could open up electricity generation to competitive forces, thereby reducing costs.

The Hoover Dam

The natural monopoly that lights Las Vegas.

California's Perfect Storm

Hoping to benefit from lower costs and greater innovation, California deregulated wholesale electricity prices in 1998. In the first two years after deregulation all appeared well. In fact, as the new century was born, California was booming. In Silicon Valley, college students in computer science were being turned into overnight millionaires and billionaires. In 2000, personal income in California rose by a whopping 9.5 percent. Higher incomes and an unusually hot summer increased the demand for electricity. But California's generating capacity, which was old and in need of repair, began to strain. To meet the demand, California had to import power from other states, but other states had little to spare. Hot weather was pushing up demand throughout the West and the supply of hydroelectric power had fallen by approximately 20 percent because of low snowfall the previous winter.

All of these forces and more smashed together in the summer of 2000 to double, triple, quadruple, and finally quintuple the wholesale price of electricity from an average in April of $26 per megawatt hour (MWh) to an August high of $141 per MWh. Prices declined modestly in the fall but jumped again in the winter, reaching for one short period a price of $3,900 per MWh and peaking in December at an average monthly price of $317 per MWh—about 10 times higher than the previous December's rate.[12] Worse yet, when not enough power was available to meet the demand, blackouts threw more than one million Californians off the grid and into the dark. The new century wasn't looking so bright after all.

Mother Nature was not the only one to blame for California's troubles. The combination of increased demand, reduced supply, and a poorly designed deregulation plan had created the perfect opportunity for generators of electricity to exploit market power.

When the demand for electricity is well below capacity, each generator has very little market power. If a few generators had shut down in 1999, for example, the effect on the price would have been minimal because the power from those generators could easily have been replaced with imports or power from other generators. Thus, in 1999, each generator faced an elastic demand for its product. In 2000, however, every generator was critical because nearly every generator needed to be up and running just to keep up with demand. Electricity is an unusual commodity because it is expensive to store and if demand and supply are ever out of equilibrium, the result can be catastrophic blackouts. Thus, when demand is near capacity, a small decline in supply leads to much higher prices as utilities desperately try to buy enough power to keep the electric grid up and running. Thus, in 2000, the demand curve facing each generator was becoming very inelastic. And what happens to the incentive to increase price when demand becomes inelastic? Do you remember the lesson of Figure 11.4, also pictured at right in Figure 11.8?

In the summer and winter of 2000, demand was near capacity and *every* generator was facing an inelastic demand curve. A firm that owned only one generating plant couldn't do much to exploit its market power: if it shut down its plant, the price of electricity would rise but the firm wouldn't have any power to sell! Many firms, however, owned more than one generator, and in

UNDERSTAND YOUR **world**

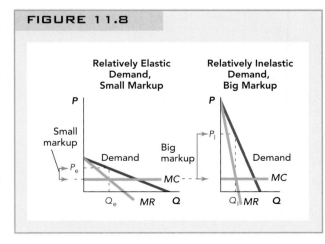

FIGURE 11.8

2000 this created a terrible incentive. A firm with four generators could shut down one, say, for "maintenance and repair," and the price of electricity would rise by so much that the firm could make more money selling the power produced by its three operating generators than it could if it ran all four! Suspiciously, far more generators were taken off-line for "maintenance and repair" in 2000 and early 2001 than in 1999.[13]

California was not the only state to restructure its electricity market in the late 1990s. Other states such as Texas and Pennsylvania had opened up generation to competition and have seen modestly lower electricity prices. Restructuring has also occurred in Britain, New Zealand, Canada, and elsewhere, but California's experience has demonstrated that unbundling generation from transmission and distribution, which remain natural monopolies, is tricky.

Other Sources of Market Power

Table 11.1 summarizes some of the sources of market power. In addition to patents, government regulation and economies of scale, monopolies may be created whenever there is a significant **barrier to entry**, something that raises the cost to new firms of entering the industry. One firm, for example, might own an input that is difficult to duplicate. Saudi Arabia, for example, has some market power in the market for oil because the demand for oil is inelastic and Saudi Arabia controls a significant fraction of the world's oil supply. What makes oil special is that oil is found in large quantities in only a few places in the world so a single firm in the right place can monopolize a significant share of the total supply. The market power of Saudi Arabia is enhanced when instead of competing with other suppliers it joins with them to form a cartel, a group of firms that acts in concert to maximize total profits. We analyze cartels at greater length in Chapter 13.

Brands and trademarks can also give a firm market power because the prestige of owning the real thing cannot be easily duplicated. Timex watches tell the time as well as a Rolex but only the Rolex signals wealth and status.

Monopolies may also arise when a firm innovates and produces a product that no other firm can immediately duplicate. In 2006, Apple had a 70 percent share in the market for MP3 players even though Apple's iPod had many competitors—the iPod was simply better than its rivals.[14] As with patent monopolies, monopolies produced by innovation involve a trade-off: iPods are priced higher than they

CHECK YOURSELF

> Look at Figure 11.7. If regulators controlled the price at $P = AC$ at point a how much would the monopolist produce? Is this better for consumers, the monopolist or society than the unregulated monopoly quantity?

> Telephone service used to be a natural monopoly. Why? Is it a natural monopoly today? Discuss how technology can change what is and isn't a natural monopoly.

Barriers to entry are factors that increase the cost to new firms of entering an industry.

TABLE 11.1 Some sources of market power.

Sources of Market Power	Example
Patents	GSK's patent on Combivir
Laws preventing entry of competitors	Indonesian clove monopoly, Algerian wheat monopoly, U.S. Postal Service
Economies of scale	Subways, cable TV, electricity transmission, major highways
Hard to duplicate inputs	Oil, diamonds, Rolex watches
Innovation	Apple's iPod, Wolfram's Mathematica software, eBay

would be if Apple had better competitors but Apple would have less incentive to innovate if it didn't expect to earn monopoly profits.

☐ Takeaway

After reading this chapter, you should be able to find marginal revenue given either a demand curve or a table of prices and quantities (as in Figure 11.1). Given a demand and marginal cost curve, you should be able to find and label the monopoly price, the monopoly quantity, and deadweight loss. With the addition of an average cost curve, you should be able to find and label monopoly profit. You should also be able to demonstrate why the markup of price over marginal cost is larger the more inelastic the demand—this relationship will also be useful in the next chapter.

What makes monopoly theory interesting and a subject of debate among economists is that it's not always obvious whether monopolies are good or bad. Instead, we are faced with a series of trade-offs. Patent monopolies, such as the one on Combivir, create a trade-off between deadweight loss and innovation. The monopolist prices its product above marginal cost, but without the prospect of monopoly profits, there might be no product at all.

Natural monopolies also involve trade-offs, this time between deadweight loss and economies of scale. Deadweight loss means that monopoly is not optimal but when economies of scale are large, competitive outcomes aren't optimal either. Regulating monopoly seems to offer an escape from this trade-off but as we saw in our analysis of cable TV and electricity regulation, the practice of regulation is much more complicated than the theory. Cable TV regulation kept prices low but it kept quality low as well. Overall, deregulation of cable television rates worked surprisingly well, at least according to the consumers who flocked to cable even as rates rose. In contrast, electricity deregulation left California at the mercy of firms wielding market power.

Economists don't always agree on the best way to navigate the trade-offs between deadweight loss, innovation, and economies of scale. Many monopolies, however, perhaps most on a world scale, are "unnatural"—they neither support innovation nor take advantage of economies of scale—instead they are created to transfer wealth to politically powerful elites. For these monopolies, economics does offer guidance—open the field to competition! Alas, economics offers less clear guidance about how to convince the elites to follow the advice of economists.

CHECK YOURSELF

> Consider ticket prices at major league baseball and professional football parks. How does the term "barrier to entry" help explain their pricing?

> How permanent are barriers to entry in the following cases: music, NBA basketball franchises, U.S. Postal Service delivery of first-class mail, U.S. Postal Service delivery of parcels?

☐ CHAPTER REVIEW

KEY CONCEPTS

Market power, p. 220

Monopoly, p. 220

Marginal revenue, MR, p. 220

Marginal cost, MC, p. 220

Natural monopoly, p. 229

Barriers to entry, p. 234

FACTS AND TOOLS

1. In the following diagram, label the marginal revenue curve, the profit-maximizing price, the profit-maximizing quantity, the profit, and the deadweight loss.

2. **a.** Consider a market like the one illustrated in Figure 11.5, where all firms have the same average cost curve. If a competitive firm in this market tried to set a price above the minimum point on its average cost curve, how many units would it sell?

   b. If a monopoly did the same thing, raising its price above average cost, what would happen to the number of units it sells: Does it rise, fall, or remain unchanged?

   c. What accounts for the difference between your answers to parts a and b?

3. **a.** In the textbook *The Applied Theory of Price,* D. N. McCloskey refers to the equation MR = MC as the rule of rational life. Who follows this rule: monopolies, competitive firms, or both?

   b. Rapido, the shoe company, is so popular that it has monopoly power. It's selling 20 million shoes per year, and it's highly profitable. The marginal cost of making extra shoes is quite low, and it doesn't change much if they produce more shoes. Rapido's marketing experts tell the CEO of Rapido that if it *decreased* prices by 20 percent, it would sell so many more shoes that profits would rise. If the expert is correct, at its current output, is

MC > MR, is MC = MR, or is MR > MC?

   c. If Rapido's CEO follows the experts' advice, what will this do to marginal revenue: Will it rise, fall, or be unchanged? Will Rapido's total revenue rise, fall, or be unchanged?

   d. Apollo, another highly profitable shoe company, also has market power. It's selling 15 million shoes per year, and it faces marginal costs quite similar to Rapido. Apollo's marketing experts conclude that if they *increased* prices by 20 percent, profits would rise. For Apollo, is MC > MR, is MC = MR, or is MR > MC?

4. **a.** When selling e-books, music on iTunes, and downloadable software, the marginal cost of producing and selling one more unit of output is essentially zero: MC = 0. Let's think about a monopoly in this kind of market. If the monopolist is doing its best to maximize profits, what will marginal revenue equal at a firm like this?

   b. All firms are trying to maximize their profits (TR − TC). The rule from part 4a tells us that in the special case where marginal cost is zero, "profit maximization" is equivalent to which of the following statements?

   "Maximize total revenue"

   "Minimize total cost"

   "Minimize average cost"

   "Maximize average revenue"

5. **a.** What's the rule: monopolists charge a higher markup when demand is highly elastic or when it's highly inelastic?

   b. What's the rule: monopolists charge a higher markup when customers have many good substitutes or when they have few good substitutes?

   c. For the following pairs of goods, which producer is more likely to charge a bigger markup? Why?

   I. Someone selling new trendy shoes, or someone selling ordinary tennis shoes?

   II. A movie theater selling popcorn or a New York City street vendor selling popcorn?

   III. A pharmaceutical company selling a new powerful antibiotic or a firm selling a new powerful cure for dandruff?

6. **a.** An answer you can find on the Internet: How high did *SpaceShipOne* fly when it won the Ansari X Prize?

   b. How much did it cost to develop *SpaceShipOne*? Was the $10 million prize enough to cover the costs? Why do you think Microsoft cofounder Paul Allen invested so much money to win the prize? Do Allen's motivations show up in our monopoly model?

7. Which of the following is true when a monopoly is producing the profit-maximizing quantity of output? More than one may be true.

   Marginal revenue = Average cost

   Total cost = Total revenue

   Price = Marginal cost

   Marginal revenue = Marginal cost

8. **a.** Consider a typical monopoly firm like that in Figure 11.3. If a monopolist finds a way to cut marginal costs, what will happen: Will it pass along some of the savings to the consumer in the form of lower prices, will it paradoxically raise prices to take advantage of these fatter profit margins, or will it keep the price steady?

   b. Is this what happens when marginal costs fall in a competitive industry, or do competitive markets and monopolies respond differently to a fall in costs?

9. **a.** Where will profits be higher: when demand for a patented drug is highly inelastic or when demand for a patented drug is highly elastic? (Figure 11.4 might be helpful.)

   b. Which of those two drugs are more likely to be "important?" Why?

   c. Now, consider the lure of profits: If a pharmaceutical company is trying to decide what kind of drugs to research, will it be lured toward inventing drugs with few good substitutes or drugs with many good substitutes?

   d. Is your answer to part c similar to what an all-wise, benevolent government agency would do, or is it roughly the opposite of what an all-wise, benevolent government agency would do?

10. True or False:

    a. When a monopoly is maximizing its profits, price is greater than marginal cost.

    b. For a monopoly producing a certain amount of output, price is less than marginal revenue.

    c. When a monopoly is maximizing its profits, marginal revenue equals marginal cost.

    d. Ironically, if a government regulator sets a fixed price for a monopoly *lower* than the unregulated price, it is typically *raising* the marginal revenue of selling more output.

    e. In the United States, government regulation of cable TV cut the price of premium channels down to average cost.

    f. When consumers have many options, monopoly markup is lower.

    g. A patent is a government-created monopoly.

THINKING AND PROBLEM SOLVING

1. In addition to the clove monopoly discussed in the chapter, Tommy Suharto, the son of Indonesian President Suharto (in office from 1967 to 1998), owned a media conglomerate, Bimantara Citra. In their entertaining book, *Economic Gangsters* (Princeton University Press, 2008), economists Raymond Fisman and Edward Miguel compared the stock price of Bimantara Citra with that of other firms on Indonesia's stock exchange around July 4, 1996, when the government announced that President Suharto was traveling to Germany for a health checkup. What do you think happened to the price of Bimantara Citra shares relative to other shares on the Indonesian stock exchange? Why? What does this tell us about corruption and monopoly power in Indonesia?

2. **a.** Sometimes, our discussion of marginal cost and marginal revenue unintentionally hides the real issue: The entrepreneur's quest to maximize total profits. Here is information on a firm:

   Demand: P = 50 − Q. Fixed cost = 100, marginal cost = 10.

   Using this information, calculate total profit for each of the values in the table below, and then plot total profit in the figure below. Clearly label the amount of maximum profit and the quantity that produces this level of profit.

Quantity	Total Revenue	Total Cost	Total Profit
18			
19			
20			
21			
22			
23			

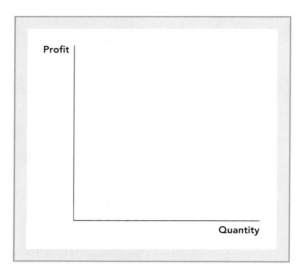

b. If the fixed cost increased from 100 to 200, would that change the shape of this curve at all? Also, would it shift the location of the curve to the left or right? Up or down? How does this explain why you can ignore fixed costs most of the time when thinking about a monopoly's decision-making process?

3. When a sports team hires an expensive new player or builds a new stadium, you often hear claims that ticket prices have to rise to cover the new, higher cost. Let's see what monopoly theory says about that. It's safe to treat these new expenses as fixed costs: Something that doesn't change if the number of customers rises or falls. You have to pay A-Rod the same salary whether people show up or not, you have to make the interest payments on the new Yankee Stadium whether the seats are filled or not. Treat the local sports team as a monopoly in this question, and to keep it simple, let's assume there is only one ticket price.

a. As long as the sports team is profitable, will a mere rise in fixed costs raise the equilibrium ticket price, lower the equilibrium ticket price, or have no effect whatsoever on the equilibrium ticket price? Why?

b. In fact, it seems common in real life for ticket prices to rise after a team raises its fixed costs by building a fancy new stadium or hiring a superstar player: In recent years, it's happened in St. Louis and San Diego's baseball stadiums. What's probably shifting to make this happen? Name *both* curves, and state the direction of the shift.

c. So, do sports teams spend a lot of money on superstars so that they can pass along the costs to the fans? Why *do* they spend a lot on superstars, according to monopoly theory? (Note: Books like *Moneyball* and *The Baseball Economist* apply economic models to the national pastime, and it's common for sports managers to have solid training in economic methods.)

4. Earlier we mentioned the special case of a monopoly where $MC = 0$. Let's find the firm's best choice when more goods can be produced at no extra cost. Since so much e-commerce is close to this model—where the fixed cost of inventing the product and satisfying government regulators is the only cost that matters—the $MC = 0$ case will be more important in the future than it was in the past. In each case, be sure to see whether profits are positive! If the "optimal" level of profit is negative, then the monopoly should never start up in the first place; that's the only way they can avoid paying the fixed cost.

a. $P = 100 - Q$. Fixed cost $= 1,000$.

b. $P = 2,000 - Q$. Fixed cost $= 900,000$. (Driving the point home from part a.)

c. $P = 120 - 12Q$. Fixed cost $= 1,000$.

5. a. Just based on self-interest, who is more likely to support strong patents on pharmaceuticals: Young people or old people? Why?

b. Who is more likely to support strong patent and copyright protection on video games: People who really like old-fashioned videogames or people who want to play the best, most advanced video games?

c. How are parts a and b really the same question?

6. "Common sense" might say that a monopolist would produce more output than a competitive industry facing the same marginal costs. After all, if you're making a profit, you want to sell as much as you can, don't you? What's wrong with this line of reasoning? Why do monopolistic industries sell *less* than competitive industries?

7. In the early part of the twentieth century, it was cheaper to travel by rail from New York to San Francisco than it was to travel from New York to Denver even though the train to San Francisco would stop in Denver on the way.

   a. Denver is a city in the mountains. Suggest alternate ways to get there from New York without taking the train.

   b. San Francisco is a city on the Pacific Ocean. Suggest alternate ways to get there from New York without taking the train.

   c. Why was San Francisco cheaper?

   d. How is this story similar to the one told in this chapter about prices for flights from Washington, D.C., to either Dallas or San Francisco?

8. This chapter told the story of how the 2000 California energy shortage was aggravated by price deregulation.

   a. Suppose you are an entrepreneur who is interested in building a power plant to take advantage of the high prices for energy. Seeing rising energy costs, would price deregulation make it more or less likely you would build a new power plant? Why?

   b. It's very difficult to build and operate a new power plant largely because new plants have to comply with a long list of environmental and safety regulations. Compared to a world with fewer such regulations, how do these rules change the average total cost of building and operating a power plant? Why?

   c. Do these regulations make it more or less likely that you will build a new power plant? Why?

   d. Do these regulations increase or decrease the market power of power plants that already exist?

9. The lure of spices during the medieval period wasn't driven merely by the desire to improve the taste of food (Europe produced saffron, thyme, bay leaves, oregano, and other spices for that). The lure of nutmeg, mace, and cloves came from their mystique. Spices became a symbol of prestige (just as Gucci and Ferrari are today). Most Europeans didn't even know that they grew in the tiny chain of islands called the Spice Islands today.

   a. Suppose you grow much of the spices in the Spice Islands. Knowing that few people could compete with you, how would you adjust your production to maximize your profits?

   b. Suppose you heard rumors that the Europeans to whom you often sell are also becoming fascinated by the mechanical clock, a new invention that was spreading across Europe as a new novelty and as yet another symbol of prestige. How would this change your optimal production? Why?

   c. Once Europeans made contact with the Americas, a new, high-status novelty arose: chocolate. Was this good news or bad news for you, the monopolist in the Spice Islands?

   (The Field Museum in Chicago has more information on the rise of chocolate: http://www.fieldmuseum.org/Chocolate/history_european.html)

10. China developed gunpowder, paper, the compass, water-driven spinning machines, and many other inventions long before their European counterparts. Yet they did not adopt cannons, industrialization, and many other applications until *after* the West did.

    a. Suppose you are an inventor in ancient China and suddenly realize that the fireworks used for celebration could be enlarged into a functioning weapon. It would take time and money to develop, but you could easily sell the cutting-edge result to the government. If there is a strong patent system, would you put a big investment into developing this technology? Why or why not?

    b. Suppose there were no patent system, but you could still sell your inventions to the government. Compared to a world with a good patent law, would you be more inclined, less inclined, or about equally inclined to invest in technological development? Why?

CHALLENGES

1. **a.** For the following three cases, calculate

    I. The marginal revenue curve

    II. The level of output where MR = MC (i.e., set equation I equal to marginal cost, and solve for Q)

    III. The profit-maximizing price (i.e., plug your answer from equation II into the demand curve)

    IV. Total revenue and total cost at this level of output (something you learned in the last chapter)

    V. What entrepreneurs really care about: Total profit

    Case A: Demand: P = 50 − Q.
    Fixed cost = 100, marginal cost = 10.

    Case B: Demand: P = 100 − 2Q.
    Fixed cost = 100, marginal cost = 10.

    Case C: Demand: P = 100 − 2Q.
    Fixed cost = 100, marginal cost = 20.

    b. What's the markup in each case? Measure it two ways: First in dollars, as price minus marginal cost, and then as a percentage markup [100 × (P − MC)/MC, reported as a percent].

    c. If you solved part b correctly, you found that when costs rose from Case B to Case C, the monopolist's optimal price increased. Why didn't the monopolist charge that same higher price when costs were lower? After all, they're a monopolist, so they can charge what price they want. Explain in language that your grandmother could understand.

2. In Challenges question 1, what was the deadweight loss of monopoly in each of the three cases? (Hint: Where does the marginal cost curve cross the demand curve? The same place it does under competition.) Is this number measured in dollars, in units of the good, or in some other way?

3. **a.** In 2006, Medicare Part D was created to subsidize spending on prescription drugs. What effect would you expect this expansion to have on pharmaceutical prices? What principle in the chapter would explain this result?

    b. Given your answer in part a, what effect would you predict on pharmaceutical research and development?

    c. Whatever answer you gave in part a, can you think of an argument for the opposite prediction? Here's a hint that may help you to formulate an answer: In writing the Part D law Congress said that subsidized drug plans must cover all pharmaceuticals in some "protected" classes, such as AIDS drugs, but in other areas subsidized plans could pick and choose which drugs to offer. Understanding this difference may lead to different predictions.

4. In 1983, Congress passed the Orphan Drug Act, which gave firms that developed pharmaceuticals to treat rare diseases (diseases with U.S. patient populations of 200,000 people or fewer) the exclusive rights to sell their pharmaceutical for 7 years, basically an extended patent life. In other words, the act gave greater market power to pharmaceutical firms who developed drugs for rare diseases. Perhaps surprisingly, a patient organization, the *National Organization for Rare Disorders* (NORD), lobbied for the act. Why would a patient group lobby for an act that would increase the price of pharmaceuticals to their members? Why do you think the act was specifically for rare diseases?

5. In order for Kremer's patent buyout proposal (mentioned in the chapter) to work, the government needs to pay a price that's high enough to encourage pharmaceutical companies to develop new drugs. How can the government find out the right price? Through an auction, of course. In Kremer's plan, it works roughly like this: The government announces that it will hold an auction the next time that a company invents a powerful anti-AIDS drug. Once the drug has been invented and thoroughly tested, the government holds the auction. Many firms compete in the auction—just like on eBay—and the highest bid wins.

    Now comes the twist: After the auction ends, a government employee rolls a six-sided die. If it comes up "1," then the highest bidder gets the patent, it pays off the inventor, and it's free to charge the monopoly price. If the die comes up "2" through "6," then the government pays the inventor whatever the highest bid was, and then it tears up the patent. The auction had to be held to figure out how much to pay, but most of the time it's the government that does the paying. Similarly, most of the time, citizens get to pay marginal cost for the drug, but one-sixth of all new drugs will still charge the monopoly price.

a. In your opinion, would taxpayers be willing to pay for this?

b. Using Figure 11.5 to guide your answer, what polygon(s) would these firms' bid be equal to?

c. If the government wins the die roll, what *net* benefits do consumers get, using Figure 11.5's polygons as your answer? (Be sure to subtract the cost of the auction!)

6. a. Let's imagine that the firm with cost curves illustrated in the left panel of the figure below is a large cable TV provider. Assuming that the firm is free to profit maximize, label the profit-maximizing price, quantity, and the firm's profit.

b. Now assume that the firm is regulated and that the regulator sets the price so that the firm earns a normal (zero) profit. What price does the regulator set and what quantity does the firm sell? (Label this price and quantity on the diagram.)

c. Which price and quantity pair do consumers prefer, that in part a or b? Do consumers benefit from price regulation?

d. Imagine that the cable TV provider can invest in fiber optic cable (high definition), better programming, movie downloading or some other service that increases the demand for the product as shown in the right panel. If the firm were regulated as in part b, do you think it would be more or less likely to make these investments?

e. Given your answer in part d, revisit the question of price regulation and make an argument that price regulation could harm consumers once you take into account dynamic factors. Would this argument apply to all consumers or just some? If so, which ones?

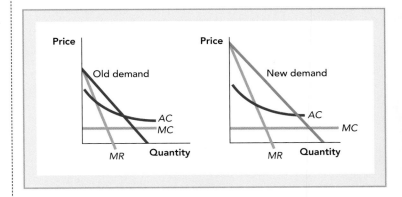

12

Price Discrimination

CHAPTER OUTLINE

Price Discrimination

Price Discrimination Is Common

Is Price Discrimination Bad?

Tying and Bundling

Takeaway

After months of investigation, Interpol police swooped down on an international drug syndicate operating out of Antwerp, Belgium. The syndicate had been smuggling drugs from Kenya, Uganda, and Tanzania into the port of Antwerp for distribution throughout Europe. Smuggling had netted the syndicate millions of dollars in profit. The drug being smuggled? Heroin? Cocaine? No, something more valuable, Combivir. Why was Combivir, the anti–AIDS drug we introduced in Chapter 11, being illegally smuggled from Africa to Europe when Combivir was manufactured in Europe and could be bought there legally?[1]

The answer is that Combivir was priced at $12.50 per pill in Europe and, much closer to cost, about 50 cents per pill in Africa. Smugglers who bought Combivir in Africa and sold it in Europe could make approximately $12 per pill, and they were smuggling millions of pills. But this raises another question. Why was GlaxoSmithKline (GSK), selling Combivir at a much lower price in Africa than in Europe? Remember from Chapter 11 that GSK owns the patent on Combivir and thus has some market power over pricing. In part, GSK reduced the price of Combivir in Africa for humanitarian reasons, but lowering prices in poor countries can also increase profit. In this chapter, we explain how a firm with market power can use **price discrimination**—selling the same product at different prices to different customers—to increase profit.

> **Price discrimination** is selling the same product at different prices to different customers.

Price Discrimination

Figure 12.1 shows how price discrimination can increase profit. In the left panel we show the market for Combivir in Europe and in the right panel the market in Africa. The demand curve in Africa is much lower and more elastic (price sensitive) than in Europe because on average Africans are poorer than Europeans.

243

FIGURE 12.1

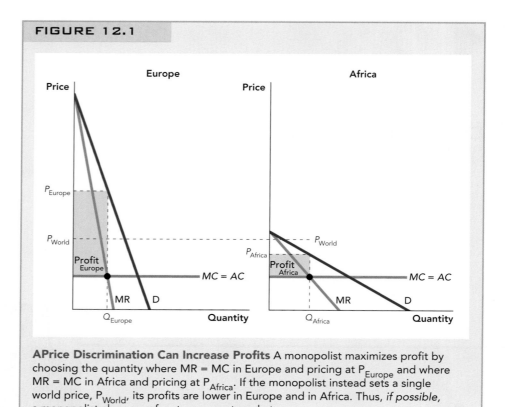

A Price Discrimination Can Increase Profits A monopolist maximizes profit by choosing the quantity where MR = MC in Europe and pricing at P_{Europe} and where MR = MC in Africa and pricing at P_{Africa}. If the monopolist instead sets a single world price, P_{World}, its profits are lower in Europe and in Africa. Thus, *if possible, a monopolist always prefers to segment markets.*

Now let's suppose for the moment that Europe is the only market. What price should GSK set? We know from Chapter 11 that the profit-maximizing quantity is found where marginal revenue equals marginal cost. From MR = MC in the left panel we find that the profit-maximizing quantity is Q_{Europe}. The profit-maximizing price is the highest price that consumers will pay to purchase Q_{Europe} units, which we label P_{Europe}. Profit is given by the green area labeled $Profit_{Europe}$.

Similarly, if Africa were the only market, GSK would choose the profit-maximizing quantity Q_{Africa} and the profit-maximizing price, P_{Africa}, which would generate profit in the amount $Profit_{Africa}$.

But what price should GSK set if it wants to have a single, "world price" for both Europe and Africa? If GSK wants a single world price it should lower the price in Europe and raise the price in Africa, setting a price somewhere between P_{Europe} and P_{Africa}, say at P_{World}. (In a more advanced class, we would solve for the exact profit-maximizing world price, but that level of detail is not necessary here.)

But remember that P_{Europe} is the profit-maximizing price in Europe and P_{Africa} is the profit-maximizing price in Africa, so by lowering the price in Europe, GSK must be reducing profit in Europe. Similarly, by raising the price in Africa, GSK must be reducing profit in Africa. Thus, profit at the single price P_{World} must be less than when GSK sets two different prices earning the combined profit, $Profit_{Europe} + Profit_{Africa}$.

We have now arrived at the first principle of price discrimination: *(1a) If the demand curves are different, it is more profitable to set different prices in different markets than a single price that covers all markets.*

We also know from Chapter 11 and from Figure 12.1 how a monopolist should set prices. Recall that the more inelastic the demand curve, the higher the profit-maximizing price. In this case, the demand for Combivir is more inelastic (less sensitive to price) in the European market than in the African market, so the price is higher in Europe. This really isn't an independent principle; it's an implication of profit maximization, as we showed in Chapter 11. But it's a useful reminder, so we will add to our first principle: (*1b*) *To profit maximize, the monopolist should set a higher price in markets with more inelastic demand.*

The first principle of price discrimination tells us that GSK wants to set a higher price for Combivir in Europe than in Africa. But we also know from the introduction that setting two different prices for Combivir encourages drug smuggling. Smugglers buy Combivir at P_{Africa} and sell at P_{Europe}, which leaves fewer sales for GSK. A smuggler's profit comes out of GSK's pocket.

If smuggling is extensive, GSK will end up selling most of its output at P_{Africa}, which is less profitable than if GSK set a single world price. Thus, if GSK can't stop the drug smugglers, it will abandon its attempt at price discrimination and will instead set a single price—perhaps a single world price such as P_{World} or, if the African market is small, GSK may abandon Africa altogether and set a single price of P_{Europe}.

Smuggling is a special example of a more general (and legal) process that economists call **arbitrage**—buying low in one market and selling high in another market. Thus, we arrive at the second principle of price discrimination: (*2*) *Arbitrage makes it difficult for a firm to set different prices in different markets, thereby reducing the profit from price discrimination.*

We summarize the principles of price discrimination.

Arbitrage is taking advantage of price differences for the same good in different markets by buying low in one market and selling high in another market.

The Principles of Price Discrimination

1a. If the demand curves are different, it is more profitable to set different prices in different markets than a single price that covers all markets.

1b. To maximize profit the firm should set a higher price in markets with more inelastic demand.

2. Arbitrage makes it difficult for a firm to set different prices in different markets, thereby reducing the profit from price discrimination.

The first principle tells us that a firm *wants* to set different prices in different markets. The second principle tells us that a firm may not be *able* to set different prices in different markets. To succeed at price discrimination, the monopolist must prevent arbitrage.

Preventing Arbitrage

If it wants to profit from price discrimination, GSK must prevent Combivir that it sends to Africa from being resold in Europe. GSK has a number of tools to discourage smuggling. GSK, for example, sends red Combivir pills to Africa and sells white Combivir in Europe. If GSK detectives find red Combivir in Europe, they know that a GSK distributor has broken its agreement. Using special bar codes on each package, GSK can then track the smuggled pills back to the distributor who was supposed to distribute them in Africa. Interpol is called in to make arrests.

Markets can differ in more ways than geographically. Rohm and Haas is a producer of plastics. One of its plastics, methyl methacrylate (MM), was used in industry and also in dentistry as a material for dentures. MM had lots of substitutes as an industrial plastic but few as a denture material, so Rohm and Haas sold MM for industrial uses at $0.85 per pound and sold a slightly different version designed for dentures at $22 per pound. At these prices, it wasn't long

Region codes prevent DVDs bought in India from being played on U.S. players. The codes help studios to price discriminate by discouraging arbitrage from low-price regions to high-price regions. Many consumers modify their players so that they can play DVDs from any region. Is this pirating?

before enterprising individuals started buying industrial MM and converting it to denture MM. Just like GSK, Rohm and Haas needed a way to prevent arbitrage between the two markets.

One bold thinker came up with what Rohm and Haas internal documents called "a very fine method of controlling the bootleg situation." The innovator suggested that Rohm and Haas should mix industrial MM with arsenic. This wouldn't reduce the value of MM in industry, but it would surely deter people from making it into dentures! Rohm and Haas's legal department rejected this plan, but the company came up with an idea nearly as good: they planted a *rumor* that industrial MM was mixed with arsenic![2]

Although Rohm and Haas never implemented the poisoning idea, the U.S. government has. The government taxes alcohol but subsidizes ethanol fuel. To prevent arbitrage, that is, to prevent entrepreneurs from buying ethanol fuel and converting it to drinkable alcohol, the government requires that ethanol fuel be poisoned!

It's easier to prevent arbitrage of some products than of others. A masseuse, for example, may easily set different prices for different customers because it's hard for a customer who buys a massage at the low price to resell it to another customer at the higher price. Services, in general, are difficult to arbitrage.

CHECK YOURSELF

> Why does a monopolist want to segment a market?

> Would a price-discriminating firm set higher or lower prices for a market segment with more inelastic demand?

> What is arbitrage? How does arbitrage affect the ability of a monopolist to price discriminate?

Price Discrimination Is Common

Once you know the signs, price discrimination is easy to see. Movie theaters, for example, often charge less for seniors than for younger adults. Is this because theater owners have a special respect for the elderly? Probably not. More likely it's that theater owners realize that young people have a more inelastic demand for movies than seniors. Thus, theater owners charge a high price to young people and a low price to seniors. It would probably be even more profitable if theater owners could charge people who are on a date more than married people (no one likes to look cheap on a date). But it's easy for theater owners to judge age and not so easy for them to figure out who is on a date and who is married.

Students don't always pay higher prices, however. Stata is a well-known statistical software package. It costs a business $1,295 to buy Stata, but registered students pay only $145. Thus, it's not about age—the young sometimes pay more and sometimes pay less—it's about how age correlates with what businesses really care about, which is how much the customer is willing to pay.

Here's another example. Airlines know that businesspeople are typically less sensitive to the price of an airline ticket than are vacationers (i.e., businesspeople have more inelastic demand curves). An airline would like, therefore, to set a high price for businesspeople and a low price for vacationers, as illustrated in Figure 12.2.

But airlines can't very well say to their customers, "Are you flying on business? Okay, the price is $600. Going on a vacation? The price is $200." So how can airlines segment the market?

Airlines set different prices according to characteristics that are correlated with willingness to pay. Vacationers, for example, can easily plan their trips weeks or months in advance. Businesspeople, however, may discover that they need to fly tomorrow. Thus, if a customer wants to fly to Tampa, Florida, in two weeks time they are probably a vacationer and the airline will charge them a low price, but if they want to fly tomorrow the price will be higher. On the day these words were written U.S. Airways was charging $113 to fly from Washington, DC, to Tampa with two weeks notice but

FIGURE 12.2

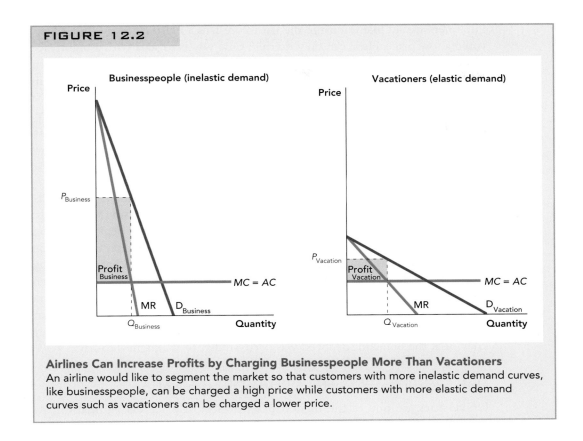

Airlines Can Increase Profits by Charging Businesspeople More Than Vacationers
An airline would like to segment the market so that customers with more inelastic demand curves, like businesspeople, can be charged a high price while customers with more elastic demand curves such as vacationers can be charged a lower price.

more than three times as much, $395, to fly tomorrow. Except for the dates the flights were identical. Figure 12.3 illustrates how one airline charged many different prices for the same flight.

Similarly, publishers know that hard-core fans are willing to pay a high price for the latest Harry Potter book, while others will only buy if the price is low.

FIGURE 12.3

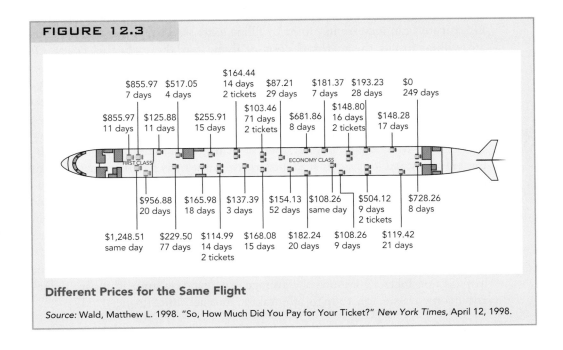

Different Prices for the Same Flight

Source: Wald, Matthew L. 1998. "So, How Much Did You Pay for Your Ticket?" *New York Times*, April 12, 1998.

Publishers would like to charge the hard-core fans a high price and the less de-voted a low price. How can they do this? One way is to start with a high price and then lower it once the hard-core fans have bought their fill. Thus, when *Harry Potter and the Half-Blood Prince* hit the shelves, it retailed at $34.99 in hardback, but when the paperback was released about a year later it sold for just $9.99. Does it cost more to produce a hardback? Yes, but not much more, maybe a dollar or two. The hard-core fans pay a higher price not because costs are higher, but because the publisher knows that they are willing to pay a higher price.

A more subtle form of price discrimination occurs when firms offer differ-ent versions of a product for the purpose of segmenting customers into differ-ent markets. IBM, for example, offered one of its laser printers in two models: the regular version and the Series E (E for economy). The regular version printed at 10 pages per minute, the Series E printed at 5 pages per minute. The regular version was much more expensive than the Series E. What's surprising is that the Series E cost more to produce. In fact, the only difference between the regular and the Series E was that the Series E printer contained an extra chip that slowed the printer down! IBM wasn't charging more for the regular printer because it cost more to produce, they were charging more because they knew that the demand for speed was correlated with willingness to pay.

Universities and Perfect Price Discrimination

Universities are one of the biggest practitioners of price discrimination, al-though they hide this practice under the blanket of "student aid." Student aid is a way of charging different students different prices for the same good. Con-sider Williams College, a small, prestigious liberal arts college. In 2001, some students at Williams paid the sticker price of $32,470 while others paid just $1,683 for exactly the same education. Why the big difference in price?

Part of the story is that Williams College was doing good by offering finan-cial aid to students from poorer families. But Williams College was also doing well. To see why, notice that Williams College is a lot like an airline. If U.S. Air-ways is going to fly an airplane from New York to Los Angeles anyway, then U.S. Airways can increase its profits by filling extra seats so long as its customers are willing to pay the marginal costs of flying (say the extra fuel costs). Of course, if a customer is willing to pay $800 to fly to L.A., then U.S. Airways wants to charge that customer $800 and not less. But if the marginal cost of fly-ing is $100, then U.S. Airways can increase its profits by filling an empty seat so long as the customer is willing to pay at least $101.

UNDERSTAND YOUR **world**

Williams College is a lot like an airline because if Ancient Greek History 101 is going to be taught anyway, then Williams can increase its profits by fill-ing extra seats so long as its students are willing to pay the marginal costs of teaching. Of course, if a student is willing to pay $32,470 for a year of educa-tion at Williams, then Williams wants to charge that student $32,470 and not less. But if the marginal costs of teaching are $1,682 a year, then Williams can increase its profits by filling an empty seat so long as the student is willing to pay at least $1,683.

About half the students at Williams paid the full sticker price of $32,470, but half did not. Table 12.1 shows the average price paid by students in five differ-ent income classes, low to high, after taking into account "financial aid."

TABLE 12.1 Price Discrimination at Williams College, 2001–2002

Income Quintile	Family Income Range	Net Price after Financial Aid
Low	$0–$23,593	$1,683
Lower Middle	$23,594–$40,931	$5,186
Middle	$40,932–$61,397	$7,199
Upper Middle	$61,398–$91,043	$13,764
High	$91,044-	$22,013

Note: Students who did not apply for financial aid paid $32,470.
Source: Hill, Catharine B., and Gordon C. Winston. 2001. *Access: Net Prices, Affordability, and Equity at a Highly Selective College.* Williams College, DP-62.

The difference in price is extreme. Even the airlines, masters of price discrimination, can rarely charge some customers 20 times what they charge other customers. Williams has a big advantage over the airlines, however. Williams has an extraordinary amount of information about its customers.

In order to receive financial aid, Williams demands that students and their parents submit their tax returns to Williams. Williams, therefore, has very detailed information about the income of its customers, and it uses that information to set many different prices. Table 12.1 shows *average* prices within each income class, but, in fact, Williams divided prices even more finely, setting a different price, for example, to a student with family income of $30,000 than one with family income of $35,000. In theory, Williams could offer a different price to each one of it students, charging each student his or her maximum willingness to pay. This is what economists call **perfect price discrimination**.

Figure 12.4 on the next page shows how perfect price discrimination works in a market like education, where each customer buys one unit of the good. Alex values education the highest, Tyler the second highest, Robin the third highest, all the way down to Bryan who thinks that education has very little value. A firm that has a lot of information about Alex, Tyler, Robin, and Bryan can set four different prices, charging each of them their maximum willingness to pay (or, if you like, a penny less than their maximum willingness to pay). Thus, Alex is charged the most and Bryan the least.

Since a perfectly price discriminating (PPD) monopolist charges each consumer his or her maximum willingness to pay, consumers end up with zero consumer surplus. All of the gains from trade go to the monopolist. This is bad for consumers but does have a beneficial side effect: Since the PPD monopolist gets all the gains from trade, the PPD monopolist has an incentive to maximize the gains from trade, and maximizing the gains from trade means no deadweight loss.

In Chapter 11, we showed that a single-price monopoly creates a deadweight loss, but this is not true for a perfectly price discriminating monopoly. In Figure 12.4 notice that whenever a consumer's willingness to pay is higher than marginal cost, then that consumer is sold a unit of the good—but this means that the PPD monopoly produces the efficient quantity! In fact, the perfectly price discriminating monopolist produces until P = MC (i.e., $Q^\star$ units), exactly as does a competitive firm!

Under **perfect price discrimination (PPD)**, each customer is charged his or her maximum willingness to pay.

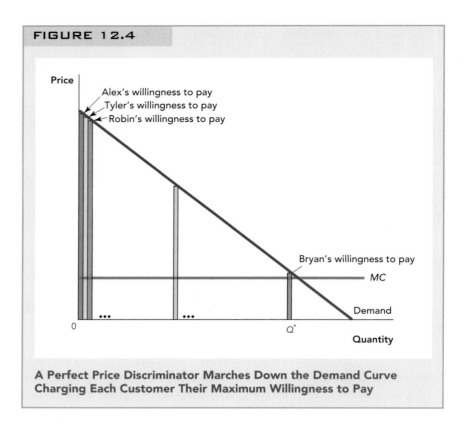

FIGURE 12.4

A Perfect Price Discriminator Marches Down the Demand Curve Charging Each Customer Their Maximum Willingness to Pay

Another way of seeing why the perfectly price discriminating monopolist produces the efficient quantity is to remember that *all* firms want to produce until MR = MC. For a competitive firm MR = P, so the competitive firm produces until P = MC. For a single single-price monopolist MR < P, so the single-price monopolist produces less than the competitive firm. But what is MR for a PPD monopolist? It's P and thus the PPD monopolist also sets P = MC. Can you explain why as a PPD monopolist moves down the demand curve selling to additional customers its MR is always equal to price?

Detailed information about their customers helps Williams College set each student's price close to that student's maximum willingness to pay, thus maximizing Williams' revenue. Ever wonder why many retailers ask for your zip code when they ring up your purchase? More information means more profit. Ever wonder why used car salespeople are so friendly? Sure, friendliness helps to sell cars, but what you think of as friendly talk is really a clever strategy to learn as much about you as possible so the salesperson can price accordingly. When buying a new car, one of the authors of this book always tells the salesperson he is a student. Alas, the ruse is becoming less believable as the years wear on.

CHECK YOURSELF

> Is the early bird special (eating dinner at a restaurant before 6:00 PM or 6:30 PM) a form of price discrimination? If so, what are the market segments? Can you think of another explanation for this type of pricing?

> Why is it much more expensive to see a movie in a theater than to wait a few months and see it at home on DVD? Can you give an explanation based on price discrimination?

Is Price Discrimination Bad?

Price discrimination certainly sounds bad, but we just showed that a perfectly price discriminating monopolist produces more output than a single-price monopolist, and this is good so price discrimination can't always be bad. What about if price discrimination is imperfect? Does a monopolist that sets two (or a handful of) prices raise or lower total surplus? The answer is subtle, but there is a similar intuition to the case of the perfectly price discriminating monopolist. Price discrimination is bad if the total output with price discrimination falls or stays the same, but if output increases under price discrimination then total surplus will usually increase.

To see this, let's return to the case of Combivir in Europe and Africa. Suppose that GSK was forbidden from price discriminating so it had to set one world price. What world price would GSK set, and would this increase or decrease total surplus?

One possibility is that if forced to set a single price, GSK would lower the price enough so that some Africans could buy Combivir—for example, a price like P_{World} in Figure 12.1. A single price of P_{World} is better for Europeans since $P_{World} < P_{Europe}$, but it is worse for Africans since $P_{World} > P_{Africa}$. Thus, depending on exactly how much better off Europeans are and how much worse off Africans are at P_{World}, price discrimination could be better or worse than single pricing.

How likely is it, however, that GSK would lower the price to P_{World}? Two-thirds of the 630 million people living in Africa live on less than a dollar a day. Thus, even when GSK sells Combivir at close to its cost of 50 cents a pill, most Africans with AIDS cannot afford Combivir. GSK, therefore, cannot make up for a low price by selling large volumes of Combivir to Africans. Thus, if GSK cannot set two different prices, it will probably abandon the African market altogether and sell to the world at P_{Europe}. At P_{Europe} only Europeans can afford to buy Combivir.

At the single price of P_{Europe} are Europeans better off than with price discrimination? No, the price to Europeans hasn't changed and thus the quantity of Combivir consumed by Europeans is the same under both pricing systems. What about Africans? At the single price of P_{Europe} Africans pay more for Combivir than with price discrimination and they consume less. Thus, in the most plausible case, forcing GSK to set a single price doesn't help Europeans but does hurt Africans. Alternatively stated, price discrimination in this case increases total surplus because price discrimination increases output—with price discrimination, Europeans consume as much Combivir as with a single price, but Africans increase their consumption from what it would be with a high single-price.

Why Misery Loves Company and How Price Discrimination Helps to Cover Fixed Costs

In industries with high fixed costs, price discrimination has another benefit. To explain why, we ask a strange question. Imagine that there are two diseases that if left untreated are equally deadly. One of the diseases is rare, the other is common. If you had to choose would you rather be afflicted with the rare disease or the common disease? Take a moment to think about this question because there is a definite answer.

It's much better to have the common disease because there are more drugs to treat common diseases than to treat rare diseases, and more drugs means greater life expectancy. Patients diagnosed with a rare disease are 45 percent more likely to die before the age of 55 than patients diagnosed with a more common disease.*

★ "Rare" is defined as a disease in the bottom quarter of incidence in the United States in 1998; "common" is defined as a disease in the top quarter of incidence. See Lichtenberg, Frank R. and Waldfogel, Joel, *Does Misery Love Company? Evidence from Pharmaceutical Markets Before and After the Orphan Drug Act* (June 2003). NBER Working Paper No. W9750. Available at SSRN: http://ssrn.com/abstract=414248

The reason there are more drugs to treat common diseases is because the market is larger. Simply put, it costs about the same to develop a drug for a rare or a common disease but the revenues are much greater for a drug that treats a common disease. Thus, the larger the market the more profitable it is to develop a drug for that market.

The fact that profits increase with market size explains why price discrimination can benefit *Europeans* as well as Africans. We have already shown that Africans benefit from price discrimination because of lower prices. Europeans benefit because price discrimination increases the profit from producing pharmaceuticals, and more profit means more research and development, more new drugs, and greater life expectancy.

Pharmaceuticals are not the only industry with high fixed costs—airlines, chemicals, universities, software, and movies all have a similar cost structure. Low prices for vacationers, for example, can benefit business travelers because the extra profit that airlines earn from selling to vacationers encourages airlines to offer more flights to more places at more times. The synthetic fabric Kevlar is five times stronger by weight than steel and is used to make bulletproof vests as well as auto tires. As a bulletproof vest, Kevlar has few substitutes, but as tire belting it has many. As a result, DuPont charges more for Kevlar used in vests than for Kevlar used in belting. If DuPont had to charge the same price in all markets, Kevlar might not be used for belting at all, and Du Pont would have lower profits and less incentive to innovate.

Tying and Bundling

Everyone knows the airlines charge different prices to different customers for the same flight. Senior citizen and student discounts are obvious. Universities advertise their scholarship policies—even if they don't always advertise that this is a way of increasing profit! But other types of price discrimination are more subtle and difficult to see. Let's take a look at tying and bundling, two types of price discrimination that are hidden to the untrained observer.

Tying

Why are printers so cheap and ink so expensive? As we write this chapter one remarkable Hewlett-Packard (HP) photo printer/scanner/copier sells for just $69. A full set of color ink cartridges, however, will set you back $44. At that price, it almost pays to buy a new printer (which comes with a cartridge) every time you run out of ink! Clearly, HP is pricing their printers low and making their profit from selling ink. HP is not alone in pursuing this strategy. Xbox game consoles are priced below cost, and Xbox games are priced above cost. Cell phones are priced below cost and phone calls are priced above cost. Why?

HP's strategy is a type of price discrimination called **tying**. Think of HP as selling not printers and ink, but the package good, "ability to print color photos." HP wants to charge a high price to consumers with a high willingness to pay and a low price to consumers with a low willingness to pay. Consumers with a high willingness to pay for the "ability to print color photos" probably want to print a lot of color photos. Consumers with a low willingness to pay probably want to print only the occasional color photo. By charging a high price for ink, HP is charging high willingness to pay consumers a high price. Yet, because the

Tying is a form of price discrimination in which one good, called the base good, is tied to a second good called the variable good.

price of printers is low, consumers who have only a low willingness to pay are charged a low price.

HP's pricing scheme is especially brilliant because the price is so flexible. Instead of two prices there are many: one for a consumer who prints 10 photos a month, another for a consumer who prints 15 photos a month, and yet another for a consumer who prints 100 photos a month.

In addition to price discrimination, HP is probably also taking advantage of a bit of consumer irrationality. When comparing printers, consumers *should* look at the total price, printer plus ink, over the entire lifetime of the printer. But it takes some work to estimate the total price, and consumers who are shortsighted may focus on amazingly cheap printers rather than astonishingly expensive ink.

In order for HP's scheme to work, it's critical that no one else but HP be allowed to sell ink for HP printers—HP must *tie* its printers to HP ink cartridges. If competitors could easily enter the market for ink, the price of ink would fall to marginal cost and HP's pricing scheme would fall apart. HP manages to keep competitors out of the market for ink in a clever way—the HP ink cartridge contains not just ink, but also a crucial and patented component of the printer head. Since other firms are forbidden by law from manufacturing the printer head, and since the head and the ink must be packaged together, HP manages to keep competitors out of the market for ink. Well, almost. There is an active market in *refilling* HP printer heads, which is much cheaper than buying them new.

HP's strategy illustrates both the benefits and costs of price discrimination. Price discrimination, as usual, may increase output by lowering the price to users who only want to print the occasional photo. Price discrimination also spreads the fixed costs of research and development—which are extensive for color photo printers—over more users, thus encouraging more innovation. But putting printer heads in the ink cartridge rather than in the printer probably raises the total cost of printing. Although there are some advantages to disposable printer heads, HP is spending the extra money not to benefit consumers but to keep competitors out of the ink business. Since the extra costs of production don't benefit consumers, they are a cost of price discrimination.

Bundling

Goods are **bundled** when they must be bought in a package. Nike doesn't sell right and left shoes individually, Nike only sells shoes in a right and left bundle.* Toyota doesn't sell engines, steering columns, and wheels, it sells a bundle called a car. As the examples suggest, most bundling is easily explained as a way to reduce costs. But why does Microsoft sell Word, Excel, Outlook, Access, and PowerPoint in a bundle called Microsoft Office?

Unlike buying a car piece by piece, it would not be difficult for consumers to buy the Office products individually and assemble them as they wanted. Almost every car buyer wants an engine and four wheels, but not every Office buyer wants Microsoft Access. So why does Microsoft bundle? Note that Microsoft does sell most Office products individually, but the sum of the individual prices far exceeds the price of the bundle so most consumers buy Office.

Bundling is requiring that products be bought together in a bundle or package.

---

* The difference between tying and bundling is that bundled goods are sold one to one. Every right shoe comes with a left shoe. Tied goods are sold one to many. Every HP printer is tied to a variable number of ink cartridges depending on consumer demand.

TABLE 12.2 Maximum Willingness to Pay for Word and Excel

	Amanda	Yvonne
Word	$100	$40
Excel	$20	$90

Bundling is a type of price discrimination. Suppose that we have two consumers, Amanda and Yvonne, whose maximum willingness to pay for Word and Excel is as given in Table 12.2.

Microsoft can sell each product individually or it can sell Word and Excel together as a bundle. Let's calculate profit for each possibility. To make our lives simple we will assume that the marginal costs of production are zero (which is approximately true—it costs very little to write another Word CD).

If Microsoft sets prices individually, there are two sensible choices for the price of Word: $40 or $100. If Microsoft sets a price for Word of $40, both Amanda and Yvonne will buy and profit will be $80. If Microsoft sets a price of $100, Amanda alone will buy but profit will be higher, $100. Similarly, Microsoft can sensibly sell Excel for $20 or $90. Profit is higher at a price of $90 because 2 × $20 = $40 < $90. If Microsoft sets prices individually, therefore, it will charge $100 for Word and $90 for Excel for a total profit of $190 = $100 + $90.

TABLE 12.3 Maximum Willingness to Pay for Office

	Amanda	Yvonne
Word	$100	$40
Excel	$20	$90
Office = Word + Excel	$120	$130

Now consider bundling Word and Excel and selling them as Office. What price to set? To calculate this, we need to know the maximum amount that Amanda and Yvonne will pay for Word plus Excel. We calculate this in Table 12.3.

Amanda is willing to pay up to $120 for the Office bundle and Yvonne is willing to pay up to $130. What is the profit-maximizing price for the Office bundle? Microsoft will set the bundle price at $120 and sell two Office bundles for a total profit of $240. What has happened to Microsoft's profit compared to when it set prices individually? When Microsoft priced Word and Excel individually, its profit was just $190. When Microsoft sells Word and Excel in a bundle called Office, its profits increase by $50 or 26 percent more. Why?

Notice that in this example bundling is equivalent to a sophisticated scheme of (almost) perfect price discrimination. At a bundle price of $120, we can think of Amanda as being charged $100 for Word and $20 for Excel, and Yvonne as being charged $40 for Word and $80 for Excel. But in order to implement this price discrimination scheme directly, Microsoft would have to know a lot about Amanda's and Yvonne's willingness to pay for Word and Excel and Microsoft would have to prevent Yvonne from buying Word at $40 and reselling it to Amanda (and similarly keep Amanda from reselling Excel to Yvonne). When Microsoft bundles, however, it's easier to price discriminate because although Amanda and Yvonne place very different values on Word and Excel, they have similar values for Office. Microsoft, therefore, knows more about the demand for Office than about the demand for Word or Excel and the more Microsoft knows about demand, the easier it is for Microsoft to price discriminate.

As with other forms of price discrimination, bundling can increase efficiency especially when fixed costs are high and marginal costs are low. In our example, when Microsoft set prices individually, only Amanda bought Word and only Yvonne bought Excel. This is inefficient because Amanda values Excel at $40 and the costs of providing Excel is zero (and similarly for Yvonne and Word). When Microsoft bundles, Amanda and Yvonne buy both Word and Excel, which increases total surplus.

Total surplus without bundling is $190. What is total surplus with bundling? It's $250. Check that you understand where this number came from.

Furthermore, the costs of producing software are primarily the fixed costs of research and development. Bundling means that these fixed costs are spread across more consumers, which raises the incentive to innovate.

Bundling and Cable TV

Bundling is quite common. LexisNexis sells online access to a bundle of thousands of newspapers, journals, and references. Disneyland bundles many attractions and sells them for a single entrance fee. The buffet at China Garden is a bundle of food. Bundling, however, can be controversial. Cable TV operators sell television channels in a bundle. Recently, this practice has come under attack with many politicians arguing for "à la carte" pricing, that is, pricing by the channel. Critics of bundling complain that consumers should not be forced to pay for channels that they don't watch. The claim seems sensible at first, but does it add up? Would the critics also say that the buffet at China Garden forces consumers of kung pao chicken to pay for unwanted egg foo young?

Bundle pricing makes sense for cable operators because customers have a high willingness to pay for some channels and a low willingness to pay for other channels, but the high and low value channels differ by customer. The demand for the bundle, however, is more similar across customers. Since it costs the cable company very little to offer every channel to every customer, bundling can increase profit and efficiency. The idea is exactly the same as we showed with the Office example. In Table 12.3, change Word to the Food Network and Excel to the CW (and see also end-of-chapter Challenge question 1).

As usual, bundling is most likely to be beneficial in a high fixed cost, low marginal cost industry. Cable TV is a high fixed cost, low marginal cost industry. Over the last decade, for example, one cable operator, Comcast, spent $40 billion laying new cable. Once the cable is laid, the marginal cost of carrying another channel is low, especially with high bandwidth fiber-optic cable. In cases like this, bundling doesn't cost the firm very much (and may even be cheaper than individual pricing) and by increasing profit it increases the incentive to spend resources on the fixed costs of development.

□ Takeaway

Price discrimination—selling the same good to different customers at different prices—is a common feature of many markets. The most obvious form of price discrimination is when a firm sets different prices in different markets, as for example when GSK sells Combivir for a high price in Europe and a low price in Africa. Firms also price goods based on characteristics that are correlated with willingness to pay so student and senior discounts are a form of price discrimination, as are the different prices that airlines set for the same flight depending on how far in advance the flight is booked.

Price discrimination isn't always easy. To price discriminate, the firm must prevent consumers who are charged a low price from reselling to consumers

UNDERSTAND YOUR **world**

MODERN PRINCIPLES: MICROECONOMICS
Tyler Cowen • Alex Tabarrok

Textbooks are bundles of chapters.

CHECK YOURSELF

> If cell phone companies were not allowed to tie cell phones with service plans, what would you predict would happen to the price of cell phones and what would you predict would happen to the price of cell phone calls?

> When is bundling likely to increase total surplus?

who would be charged a high price, i.e. prevent arbitrage. Price discrimination also requires that the firm know a lot about its customers. The more the firm knows, the better it can price discriminate. If the firm knew exactly how much each of its customers valued its product and it could prevent arbitrage, it could charge each customer that customer's maximum willingness to pay—this is called perfect price discrimination. Universities come closest to practicing perfect price discrimination because to provide scholarships, the university can demand a lot of information about the income of its students and their families and it's hard to resell an education.

Tying and bundling are less obvious forms of price discrimination. By setting a low price for printers and a high price for ink, HP is setting different prices for the "ability to print color photos"—a low price for those who print only occasionally and a high price for those who print often. Cell phones are priced below cost and cell phone calls are priced above cost for the same reason.

Bundling goods in a package can also be a form of price discrimination. When consumers place very different values on package components but similar values on the package, bundling can increase profits.

Firms want to price discriminate because price discrimination increases profits. Price discrimination may also increase total surplus. Price discrimination is most likely to increase total surplus when it increases output and when there are large fixed costs of development. Price discrimination for pharmaceuticals, for example, lowers the price for consumers in poor countries (thus, increasing output) and, by increasing profits, price discrimination increases the incentive to research and develop new drugs.

□ CHAPTER REVIEW

KEY CONCEPTS

Price discrimination, p. 243

Arbitrage, p. 245

Perfect price discrimination, p. 249

Tying, p. 252

Bundling, p. 253

FACTS AND TOOLS

1. True or False: A business that price discriminates will generally charge some customers more than marginal cost, and it will generally charge other customers less than marginal cost.

2. Two customers, Fred and Lamont, walk into a Grady's Used Pickups. Who probably has a more inelastic demand for one of Grady's pickups: people like Lamont, who are good at shopping around, or people like Fred, who know what they like and just buy it?

3. Who probably has more elastic demand for a Hertz rental car: someone who reserves a car online weeks before a trip, or someone who walks up to a Hertz counter after he walks off an airplane after a 4-hour flight? Who probably gets charged more?

4. When arbitrage is easy in a market of would-be price discriminators, who is more likely to get priced out of the market: those with elastic demand or those with inelastic demand?

5. If Congress passed a privacy law making it illegal for colleges to ask for parents' tax returns, would that tend to help students from high-income families or students from low-income families?

6. Why would a firm hand out coupons for its products rather than just lowering the price? Here's a hint: At your school, what kind of students use coupons to buy their pizza? What kind of students *never* use coupons to buy their pizza?

7. Where will you see more price discrimination: In monopoly-type markets with just a few firms or in competitive markets with many firms? Why?

8. When will a monopoly create more output: when it is allowed and can perfectly price discriminate or when the government bans price discrimination?

9. Some razors, like Gillette's Fusion and Venus razors, have disposable heads. The razor comes with an initial pack with a razor handle plus three or four heads; after that, you need to buy refills separately.

   a. Where do you think Gillette gets more revenue: by selling the initial pack or by selling the refills?

   b. The next time you buy a new razor, are you going to spend more time looking at the price of the razor or at the price of the refills?

THINKING AND PROBLEM SOLVING

1. Subway, the fast-food chain, recently began selling foot-long sandwiches for $5 each in a promotion. However, Subway still sells six-inch sandwiches for considerably more than $2.50 each, i.e. at a higher price per inch of sub.

   a. Can you think of a way that in theory you could make money from Subway's pricing practices? Would this method work in practice? What does this tell you about the limits of arbitrage?

   b. In many of our price discrimination examples, we think that businesses try to break customers into two groups: "more price sensitive," and "less price sensitive." What kinds of Subway customers fit into the first group? Into the second?

   Busy lawyers with 20-minute lunches

   College students

   Health-conscious soccer moms

   Long-haul truck drivers

2. A dry cleaner has a sign in its window: "Free internet coupons." The dry cleaner lists its website, and indeed there are good discounts available with the coupons. Most customers don't use the coupons.

   a. What probably would be the main difference between customers who use the coupons and those who don't?

   b. Some people might think "The dry cleaner offers the coupons to get people in the door to try the place out, but then the customers will pay the normal high price afterward." But the coupons are always there, so even repeat customers can keep using the coupons. Is this a mistake on the business owner's part? Hint: Think about marginal cost.

3. a. When will a firm find it easier to price discriminate: before the existence of eBay or afterward?

   b. Which of the two "principles of price discrimination" does this invoke?

4. As we saw in this chapter, drug companies often charge much more for the same drug in the United States than in other countries. Congress often considers passing laws to make it *easier* to import drugs from these low-price countries (it also considers passing laws to make it illegal to import these drugs, but that's another story).

   If one of these laws passes, and it becomes effortless to buy AIDS drugs from Africa or antibiotics from Latin America—drugs that are made by the same companies and have essentially the same quality controls as the drugs here in the United States—how will drug companies change the prices they charge in Latin America and Africa? Why?

5. Some people think that *businesses* create monopolies by destroying their competition, and there is certainly some truth to that. But as we learned from Obi-Wan Kenobi, "[Y]ou will find that many of the truths we cling to depend greatly on our own point of view." For instance, some people (Convenience Shoppers) love shopping at one particular store and will only switch stores when a product is outrageously expensive, while other people (Bargain Shoppers) will gladly spend hours looking through newspaper advertisements searching for the best deal.

   a. When both kinds of people, the Convenience Shoppers and the Bargain Shoppers, are shopping at the same Wal-Mart, who is more likely to stick to their prearranged shopping list, and who is more likely to splurge on a little something?

   b. Which group does Wal-Mart have monopoly power over? Which group does Wal-Mart have no monopoly power over?

c. Does this mean that the same shop can simultaneously be a "monopolist" to some customers and a "competitive firm" to other customers? Why or why not?

d. Does this mean that Darth Vader really *did* kill Anakin Skywalker?

6. Where are you more likely to see businesses "bundling" a lot of goods into one package: in industries with high fixed costs and low marginal costs (like computer games or moviemaking), or in industries with low fixed costs and high marginal costs (like doctor visits, where the doctor's time is expensive)?

7. Smokey Robinson and Berry Gordy included an insight about price discrimination in the following song, the full lyrics of which you should Google:

Try to get yourself a bargain son/Don't be sold on the very first one/. . . My mama told me . . . "you better shop around."

a. What "market" are Smokey Robinson and the Miracles singing about? (The lyrics are clear about this.)

b. In this market, if a customer "shops around," what does Mama say the customer will get in return? Note: Robinson and Gordy are quite clear about this.

8. Isn't it surprising that movies, with tickets that rarely cost as much as $10, often use vastly more economic resources than stage plays where tickets can easily cost $100?

Compare, for example, a live stage performance of Shakespeare's *Hamlet* with a movie of *Hamlet*.

a. In which field is the marginal cost of one more showing lower: on stage or on screen?

b. "Bundling" in a movie or stage performance might show up in the form of adding special effects, expensive actors, or fancy costumes: Some customers might not be too interested in an Elizabethan revenge drama, but they show up to see Liam Neeson waving an authentic medieval dagger. Is it better to think of these extra expenses as "fixed costs" or "marginal costs"?

c. In which setting will it be easier for a business to cover its total costs: in a "bundled" stage production or in a "bundled" movie production?

9. When is a pharmaceutical company more likely to spend $100 million to research a new drug: When it knows it will be able to charge different prices in different countries or when it knows that it will be required to charge the same price in different countries? Why?

10. True or false: A price-discriminating business will sometimes be willing to spend money to make a product worse.

11. Let's calculate the profit from price discrimination. The average daily demand for dinners at Paradise Grille, an upscale casual restaurant, is as follows:

Demand for dinners by senior citizens: $P = 50 - 0.5Q$. $MR = 50 - Q$

Demand for dinners by others: $P = 100 - Q$. $MR = 100 - 2Q$

Marginal cost = 10 in both cases.

a. What is the profit-maximizing price for each group?

b. Translate this into real-world jargon: If you owned this restaurant, what "senior citizen discount" would you offer, in percent?

c. Ignoring fixed costs, how much profit would Paradise Grille make if it did this?

d. If it became illegal to discriminate on the basis of age, you would face only one demand curve. Adding up these two demand curves turns out to yield:

$$P = 67 - \left(\tfrac{1}{3}\right)Q, MR = 67 - \left(\tfrac{2}{3}\right)Q$$

What is the optimal price and quantity in this unified market? Are the total meals sold in this discrimination-free market higher or lower than in part a?

e. What is the profit in this discrimination-free market?

12. At the Kennedy Center for the Performing Arts in Washington, DC, if you make a $120 donation per year, you are allowed to go to a small room before the concert and drink free coffee and eat free cookies. If you make a donation of $1,200 per year, you are allowed to go to a *different* small room before the concert and drink the *same* free coffee and eat the *same* free cookies. There are always a lot of people in both rooms before the concert: Why doesn't everybody just pay the $120 instead of the higher price?

CHALLENGES

1. In the table below, we consider how Alex, Tyler, and Monique would fare under à la carte pricing and under bundling for cable TV when there are two channels: the CW and the Food Network.

    Alex and Tyler like to watch *Veronica Mars* so they each place a higher value on the CW than on the Food Network. Monique is practicing to be an Iron Chef in her second life and so she places a higher value on the Food Network than on the CW.

Maximum Willingness to Pay			
	Alex	Tyler	Monique
The CW	10	15	3
The Food Network	7	4	9
The Bundle	15	19	12

   a. If the channels are priced individually, the most profitable prices for the cable operator turn out to be 10 for the CW and 7 for the Food Network. At these prices, who buys what channel and how much profit is there?

   b. Let's just check to see if these prices really are profit-maximizing. What would profit be if the cable company raised CW to a price of 11 and Food Network to a price of 8?

   c. At these prices, how much total consumer surplus would there be for the three of them? (Recall that consumer surplus is just each customer's willingness to pay minus the amount each person actually paid.)

   d. Now consider what happens under bundling: Customers get a take-it-or-leave-it offer of both channels or nothing at all. The profit-maximizing bundle price turns out to be 12, and at that price, Alex, Tyler, and Monique all subscribe. How much consumer surplus is there at this price? How much profit? And, most important, what would profit equal if the cable company raised the price to 13 instead?

2. Consider the following seating arrangement for a concert hall:

   The front row only seats two people. Rows B–H, about 50 feet back from the front row, seat 20 people per row.

   a. Would these front-row seats sell for more or for less than the front-row seats at a typical concert hall? Why?

   b. Why don't we see concert halls set up like this?

3. a. In competitive markets in the long run, if there are two kinds of steaks, "regular" and "high-quality Angus beef," and the regular beef sells at a lower price, is this an example of price discrimination?

   b. How is this different from the HP printer story in this chapter?

4. Amanda and Yvonne are thinking of going out to the movies. Amanda likes action flicks more, but Yvonne likes a little bit of romance. Warner Bros. is trying to decide what kind of movies to make this year. Should it make one movie for release this summer, an action flick with a romantic subplot, or should it make two movies for release this summer: an action flick and a romantic drama?

    Here's their willingness to pay for the separate kinds of movies. As you can see, both Amanda and Yvonne are annoyed by the idea of a hybrid movie: Each would rather see their favorite kind of movie.

Maximum Willingness to Pay for a Movie Ticket		
	Amanda	Yvonne
Pure Action	$10	$2
Pure Romance	$2	$10
Action + Romance	$9	$9

Now, let's look at this from Warner Bros. point of view. You're the mid-level executive who has to decide which project to green light. Your marketing people have figured out that there are 5 million people like Amanda and 5 million people like Yvonne in the United States, and they'll only see one film per summer. To make things simple, assume that the marginal cost of showing the movie one more time is zero, and that ticket prices are fixed at $8.

a. If the cost of producing any of the three films is $30 million, what should it do: make the two films or just the one hybrid film? Of course, the right way to find the answer is to figure out which choice would generate the most profit for Warner Bros.

b. Of course, the hybrid might cost a bit more to make. What if the hybrid costs $40 million to make, the pure action flick $30 million, and the romance a mere $15 million? What's the best choice now: one hybrid or two pure films?

c. Let's see how much prices would have to change for the answer to this question to change. Holding all else equal, how low would the cost of the pure romance film have to fall before the two-movie deal would get the green light?

d. (Hard) There's an underlying principle here: The "unbundled" two-movie deal won't get the green light unless its total cost is less than what? The answer is not a number—it's an idea. Is this likely to happen in the real world? Why or why not?

5. Think about the kind of 40 year-old who pulls out a faded, obviously expired student ID to get a discount ticket at a movie theater: What can you predict about his or her willingness to pay for a full-price movie? Is the movie theater making a mistake when it lets him or her pay the student price?

6. We mentioned that airlines charge much more for flights booked at the last minute than for flights booked well in advance, even for exactly the same flight. This is because people who tend to book at the last minute tend to have inelastic demand. Think of other characteristics that airlines use to vary their pricing: Do you think these characteristics are correlated with business travel or any other sort of inelastic demand? (If you don't fly too often, just ask someone who does: "What's the key to getting the lowest possible airfare?")

CHAPTER APPENDIX

Solving Price Discrimination Problems with Excel (Advanced Section)

Excel's Solver tool can be used to solve difficult price discrimination problems. Imagine that there are two groups of customers with the following demand curves.

$$Q_1^D = 330 - 2 \times P_1$$
$$Q_2^D = 510 - 4 \times P_2$$

where Q_1^D is the quantity demanded by Group One when it faces price P_1 and Q_2^D is the quantity demanded by Group Two when it faces price P_2. We could think of these markets as Europe and Africa or business travelers and vacationers, similar to the way we did in the text. The monopolist has the following costs:

$$Costs = 1000 + Q^2$$

where Q is the quantity produced by the monopolist.

The monopolist's goal is simple: it wants to choose prices P_1 and P_2 in order to maximize its profits. We will assume that the two markets are distinct so arbitrage is not possible. Although the goal is simple, the solution is difficult. In fact, this problem is considerably more difficult than any of the problems we dealt with in the text. In the text we assumed that marginal cost was constant (a flat MC curve). Assuming constant marginal costs simplified the problem because it meant that when the monopolist produced more in Market One, the costs of producing another unit in Market Two didn't change. In our problem here, marginal cost is increasing—which means that when the monopolist produces more in Market One its cost of producing an additional unit in Market Two also increases. In an intermediate or graduate economics class you would use calculus to solve a problem like this.

In the real world, business managers and entrepreneurs must solve problems like this every day and they don't all know calculus so we will show you how to solve the problem using Excel. First, let's write down what we know. In Figure A12.1, we highlight the equation for Q_1^D which we enter as "=330-2*B2". We put the price for group one in cell B2. We want to find the profit maximizing price for group one but we don't know what it is so for now we just put a zero in cell B2. The equation and price for group two are entered similarly.

FIGURE A12.1

B3		f_x	=330-2*B2	
	A	B	C	
1		Group One	Group Two	
2	Price	$0.00	$0.00	
3	Quantity Demanded	330.00	510.00	
4				

Now we enter the formula for the monopolist's cost. The total quantity produced by the monopolist is simply the quantity produced for Group One plus the quantity produced for Group Two. Thus, we can rewrite the monopolist's costs as:

$$Costs = 1000 + (Q_1^D + Q_2^D)^2$$

In Figure A12.2, we have entered the monopolist's costs in cell B5 as "=1000+(B3+C3)^2".

FIGURE A12.2

B5	f_x =1000+(B3+C3)^2	
	A	B	C
1		Group One	Group Two
2	Price	$0.00	$0.00
3	Quantity Demanded	330.00	510.00
4			
5	Monopoly Cost	$706,600.00	
6			

It is important to see that what matters here is the formula for costs; the number in the picture, $706,600.00, is simply the monopolist's costs if the monopolist set P_1 and P_2 at zero and produced everything its customers demanded at those prices!

Finally, we enter the formula for profits, as shown in Figure A12.3.

FIGURE A12.3

B6	f_x =B2*B3+C2*C3-B5	
	A	B	C
1		Group One	Group Two
2	Price	$0.00	$0.00
3	Quantity Demanded	330.00	510.00
4			
5	Monopoly Cost	$706,600.00	
6	Monopoly Profit	-$706,600.00	
7			

Profits are revenues minus costs so we enter into Excel ="B2*B3+C2*C3-B5" which is price times the quantity demanded for Group One plus price times quantity demanded for Group Two minus total costs. Excel now has enough information to solve this problem. In Excel 2007 the Solver function is found under the Data tab (but you may first have to add-in the Solver application—see Excel help for instructions on how to do this). Clicking on the Solver button produces Figure A12.4.

FIGURE A12.4

	C6	▼	f_x =B2*B3+C2*C3-B5							
	A	B	C	D	E	F	G	H	I
1		Group One	Group Two						
2	Price	$0.00	$0.00						
3	Quantity Demanded	330.00	510.00						
4									
5	Monopoly Cost	$706,600.00							
6	Monopoly Profit	-$706,600.00							

Solver Parameters ✕

Set Target Cell: B6   Solve

Equal To: ◉ Max   ○ Min   ○ Value of: 0   Close

By Changing Cells:

B2:C2   Guess

Subject to the Constraints: Options

   Add

   Change

   Reset All

   Delete

   Help

Our target is profits so in the Solver box next to "Set Target Cell" we enter B6. We want a maximum of profits so make sure the "Equal to" button is filled in on Max. Finally, we are going to maximize profits by changing prices, so in the box for "By Changing Cells" we enter "B2:C2". Now we click Solve and Excel finds the answer shown in Figure A12.5.

FIGURE A12.5

	B6	▼	f_x =B2*B3+C2*C3-B5	
	A	B	C	D
1		Group One	Group Two	
2	Price	$142.50	$123.75	
3	Quantity Demanded	45.00	15.00	
4				
5	Monopoly Cost	$4,600.00		
6	Monopoly Profit	$3,668.75		
7				

Excel tells us that the profit maximizing prices are $142.50 for Group One and $123.75 for Group Two. At these prices, Group One customers buy 45 units, Group Two customers buy 15 units, and monopoly profits are $3,668.75.

Once you understand the basic ideas, it's easy to make these models even more realistic by adding bells and whistles such as more groups. Notice that we have solved this problem with a combination of economic principles and practical skills (in this case a bit of Excel know how). An important lesson to know is that this combination of principles and practical skills is very powerful and eagerly sought out by employers in a variety of fields.

13

Cartels, Games, and Network Goods

CHAPTER OUTLINE

Cartels

Network Goods

Takeaway

As oil prices neared a historic high in July 1979, President Jimmy Carter spoke to the nation. Quoting a concerned American, Carter said, "Our neck is stretched over the fence and OPEC has a knife." What is OPEC and what power did OPEC have to control the price of oil?

OPEC, which is short for the Organization of the Petroleum Exporting Countries, is a **cartel**, a group of suppliers who try to act together in order to reduce supply, raise prices, and increase profits. In other words, a cartel is a group of suppliers who try to act *as if* they were a monopolist.

We analyzed monopoly in Chapter 11 so we have a good understanding of what cartels are *trying* to achieve, but the question we address in this chapter is when will cartels be *able* to achieve their goal. As we will see, it's not easy for a group of firms to act as if they were a monopolist.

In this chapter, we also introduce a new tool, game theory. Game theory is the study of **strategic decision-making**. An example illustrates what we mean. In Las Vegas, craps players make decisions, but poker players make strategic decisions. Craps is a dice game and deciding when and how much to bet can be complicated, but the outcome depends only on the dice and the bet and not on how other people bet. In contrast, poker is a game of strategy because a good poker player must forecast the decisions of other players, knowing that they in turn are trying to forecast his or her decisions. Game theory is used to model decisions in situations where the players interact.

Although we introduced game theory with an example from poker, a game in the usual sense of the word, game theory is used to study decision making in any situation that is interactive in a significant way. Game theory has also been used to study war, romance, business decisions of all kinds, evolution, voting, and many other situations involving interaction.

A **cartel** is a group of suppliers that tries to act *as if* they were a monopoly.

Strategic decision-making is decision making in situations that are interactive.

265

In this chapter, we use game theory to look at the economics of cartels and network goods. A network good is a good whose value to one consumer increases the more that other consumers use the good. A cell phone is a network good because cell phones are more useful the more people have them. We show that network goods have peculiar and interesting properties. When networks are important, the best product in an absolute sense may not always become the best-selling product. Furthermore, the meaning of competition and monopoly changes in network industries.

Let's begin with cartels.

Cartels

Figure 13.1 shows the price for a barrel of oil from 1960 to 2005.

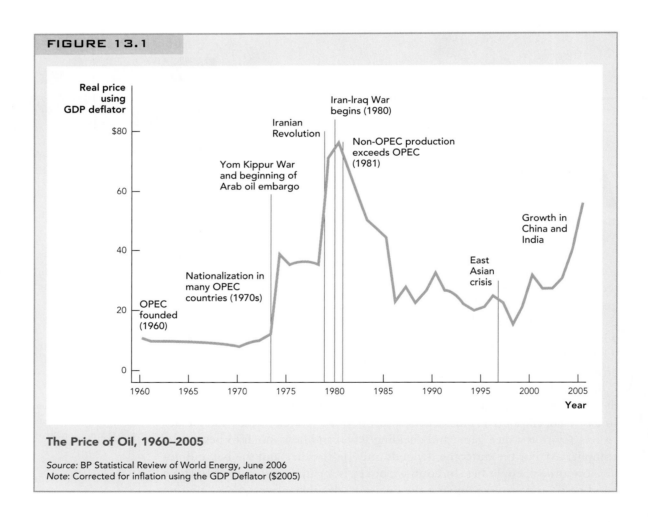

FIGURE 13.1

The Price of Oil, 1960–2005

Source: BP Statistical Review of World Energy, June 2006
Note: Corrected for inflation using the GDP Deflator ($2005)

The patterns are striking. The price of oil is very low and stable for several decades. From 1973 to 1974, the price of oil spikes upward dramatically. From 1979 to 1980, the price of oil spikes upward again. In 1985, the price of oil plummets. From the end of the 1990s to 2007 the price of oil mostly rose.

Why did the price of oil more than triple in 1973–1974, jumping from $8 a barrel to $27 a barrel? The answer is simple: Led by Saudi Arabia, a cartel of oil exporting countries cut back on their production of oil.*

The left panel of Figure 13.2 shows a competitive market in a constant-cost industry so the supply curve is flat (the constant-cost assumption makes the analysis simpler but is not necessary); remember that in a competitive market each supplier earns zero economic profit. The right panel shows the *same market* but now run *as if* it were controlled by a monopolist; profits, shown in green, are maximized. A cartel is not a monopolist, but if all the firms in a market could be convinced to cut supply so that total supply fell from Q_c to Q_m, then each firm could share in the "monopoly" profits. Thus, a cartel is an organization of suppliers that tries to move the market from the left panel of Figure 13.2 to the right panel, that is, from "Competition" toward "As if Controlled by a Monopolist."

FIGURE 13.2

A Cartel Tries to Move a Market from "Competition" Toward "As if Controlled by a Monopolist" The left panel shows price and quantity in a competitive industry. The right panel shows how price is increased, quantity is decreased, and profit is increased if that same industry is monopolized or "centralized," controlled by a cartel that acts as if it were a monopolist.

Very few cartels can move an industry from competition to pure monopoly, but Figure 13.2 shows the basic tendency of cartels to reduce output and raise price.

It might seem from this short look at OPEC that cartels are all powerful. But in reality few cartels—unless they have strong government support—have much control over market price for very long. A cartel is a deal in which businesspeople promise: "I will raise my price and cut back my production if you promise to do the same." But will the promise be kept?

---

* OPEC had been around since 1960, but until the early 1970s it didn't have much success in raising the price of oil. OPEC became more powerful through the 1960s and 1970s as the participating countries nationalized oil fields and as more countries joined OPEC. In 1973, OPEC expanded from Iran, Iraq, Kuwait, and Saudi Arabia to add Qatar, Indonesia, Libya, the United Arab Emirates, Algeria, Nigeria, Ecuador, and Gabon. Ecuador left in 1992 but returned in 2007. Gabon left OPEC in 1995, Angola joined in 2007, Indonesia left in 2009.

Cartels tend to collapse and lose their power for three reasons.

1. Cheating by the cartel members

2. New entrants and demand response

3. Government prosecution

OPEC, although a relatively successful cartel by historical standards, could not keep the price of oil high for very long. By 1985, the price of oil plummeted from its previous heights of $75 per barrel, sometimes falling as low as $10 per barrel; occasionally a Persian Gulf country would sell its oil for as little as $6 a barrel. OPEC nations were unhappy, but there was little they could do to keep oil prices high.

How did this happen? To understand, let's turn to the first reason for why cartels collapse, namely cheating by the cartel members.

Cheating on the OPEC Cartel

OPEC nations have a great deal at stake in the oil market. For instance, when oil prices were relatively high, in 1981, Saudi Arabia pulled in $119 billion in oil revenue. By 1985, when the price of oil was much lower, the Saudis earned only $26 billion. With lower oil revenues, the Saudis had to cut back on public projects, government spending, and allowances for the royal family. The Saudi royals feared that if the oil revenue dried up, the monarchy would lose its legitimacy in the eyes of the public and be overthrown, perhaps even with a few executions.

So it's no surprise that oil-exporting nations might seek to work together to reduce production and raise prices. If the cartel succeeds, cartel members earn high profits on each barrel of oil that comes out of the ground.

But this same desire for profit makes the cartel fall apart. Members will cheat on the cartel agreement. That is, they will promise to reduce production, but when everyone else reduces production and the price of oil rises, some cartel members will cheat by producing more than they promised. If everyone else is keeping their promise, the cheaters will increase their profits. At first, only a few firms might cheat, but the more cheaters, the less profitable it is to reduce production and cheating will soon increase.

Let's look at the logic of cheating with an example. Imagine that oil is produced by 10 countries (which we can think of as firms), each of which produces 10 million barrels of oil a day (MBD) for a total of 100 MBD. At that quantity, let's say the world price of oil is $36 so each country earns 360 million dollars a day (10 million barrels a day × $36 per barrel). We show this information in Table 13.1.

TABLE 13.1 No Cartel

Countries	Output per Country	Output	Revenue per Country (per day)
10	10 MBD	100 MBD	$360 million
	World Output	100 MBD	
	World Price	$36	

Now suppose that the countries form a cartel and they each cut back production to 8 million barrels a day for a world total of 80 MBD. At the lower quantity, the price of oil surges to say $50 a barrel. Instead of $360 million, each country now earns 400 million dollars a day (8 MBD times $50 per barrel). If every country keeps its promise to cut back on production, the cartel will be very profitable as we show in Table 13.2.

TABLE 13.2 Cartel

Countries	Output per Country	Output	Revenue per Country (per day)
10	8 MBD	80 MBD	$400 million
	World Output	80 MBD	
	World Price	$50	

Imagine, however, that *one* of the cartel members cheats by secretly pushing its production back to 10 MBD rather than 8. If one cartel member cheats, world production will increase to 82 MBD and the price of oil will fall to say $47.50.★ Even though the price of oil has fallen a little, the cheater has increased production a lot, so total revenue for the cheater increases to 475 million dollars a day (10 MBD × $47.50 per barrel). The cheater profits! The non-cheaters are not so lucky: their revenues fall from $400 million a day to $380 million a day (8 MBD × $47.50). We illustrate in Table 13.3.

TABLE 13.3 Cartel with One Cheater

Countries	Output per Country	Output	Revenue per Country (per day)
9	8 MBD	72 MBD	$380 million
1	10 MBD	10 MBD	$475 million
	World Output	82 MBD	
	World Price	$47.50	

Every country in the oil cartel can earn more by cheating than by keeping their promises to cut back production. But what happens if many firms cheat? The cartel collapses.

Cheating is profitable when other countries keep their promise to cut back production. But that is not the only problem the cartel faces. Cheating is also profitable when other countries *don't keep* their promise to cut back production.

★You might wonder where the numbers in the example come from. Recall from Chapter 4 that the elasticity of oil demand has been estimated to be approximately −0.5. Thus, if the price of oil is $36 when the quantity is 100 MBD, a 20 percent decrease in quantity (to 80 MBD) will raise the price by 40 percent to $50.40. Similarly, an increase in quantity of 2.5 percent to 82 MBD will reduce the price by 5 percent to $47.50.

I promise never to cheat on you.

Venezuelan President Hugo Chavez (left) hugs Saudi Crown Prince Abdullah bin Abdul Aziz Al Saud during an OPEC summit in 2000.

The logic is simple: a single cartel member does not have extensive monopoly power, so cutting back production doesn't raise the world price enough to make up for its loss of sales.

To see this in more detail, imagine that nine countries cheat and produce 10 MBD while one country keeps its promise and maintains production at 8 MBD. We show this in Table 13.4. With a world quantity of 98 MBD, the price of oil might be $37.50. Each cheater, therefore, earns revenue of $375 million a day (10 MBD × $37.50 per barrel) while the firm that kept its promise to cut back production earns $300 million a day (8 MBD × $37.50 per barrel). Notice that if the last non-cheater increases production to 10 MBD, it brings us back to the situation in Table 13.1 where the price of oil is $36 and the non-cheater's revenues are $360 million a day; in other words, $60 million more per day than when the firm kept its promise to produce 8 MBD.

TABLE 13.4 Cartel with Nine Cheaters and One Non-cheater

Countries	Output per Country	Output	Revenue per Country (per day)
1	8 MBD	8 MBD	$300 million
9	10 MBD	90 MBD	$375 million
	World Output	98 MBD	
	World Price	$37.50	

Thus, cheating pays when others firms keep their promise and cheating pays when others firms cheat!

We can get another perspective on the incentive to cheat by comparing a monopolist with a cartel member. When a monopolist increases quantity beyond the profit-maximizing quantity, the monopolist hurts itself. But when a cartel cheater increases quantity beyond the profit-maximizing quantity, the cheater benefits itself and hurts *other cartel members*. If a cheater hurts the other cartel members, not so many tears will be shed by the cheater. This is especially true for the OPEC cartel. Iran and Iraq, for example, fought a major war from 1980 to 1988, with over 800,000 people killed. The war saw the use of poison gas, chemical weapons, and the use of child soldiers as advance scouts to trigger land mines. While this war was going on, Iran and Iraq were both in OPEC. Each nation, in effect, was promising it would not undercut the other when it came to selling more oil at a lower price. Do you really think they felt obliged to keep their word?

And so have most cartels ended. The more successful the cartel is in raising member profits, the greater the incentive to cheat. And once a cartel falls apart, it is hard to put it back together again. Everyone correctly expects cheating to be the norm.

No One Wins the Cheating Game   It's useful to show the incentive to cheat in another way, using what is called a payoff table. With ten firms, the payoff table would be quite complicated and hard to draw in two dimensions but the same logic of cheating applies if there are just two firms. So imagine that the oil market is dominated by two large firms, Saudi Arabia and Russia.

Saudi Arabia has two choices or strategies, Cooperate (by cutting back production) or Cheat. These strategies are shown in Figure 13.3 by the rows of the payoff table. Russia also has the same two strategies, shown as the columns of the payoff table.

FIGURE 13.3

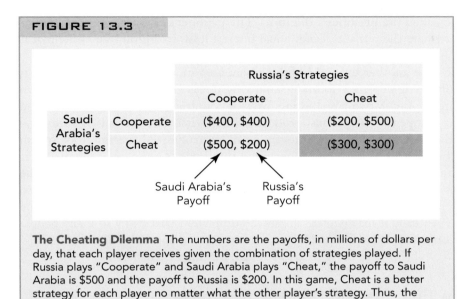

		Russia's Strategies	
		Cooperate	Cheat
Saudi Arabia's Strategies	Cooperate	($400, $400)	($200, $500)
	Cheat	($500, $200)	($300, $300)

Saudi Arabia's Payoff   Russia's Payoff

The Cheating Dilemma The numbers are the payoffs, in millions of dollars per day, that each player receives given the combination of strategies played. If Russia plays "Cooperate" and Saudi Arabia plays "Cheat," the payoff to Saudi Arabia is $500 and the payoff to Russia is $200. In this game, Cheat is a better strategy for each player no matter what the other player's strategy. Thus, the equilibrium of this game (shaded) is (Cheat, Cheat).

The two numbers in each box of the table are the payoffs to the players; the first number is the payoff to Saudi Arabia, the second to Russia. For instance, if both Saudi Arabia and Russia choose to cooperate by cutting back production, the payoff is $400 (million per day) to Saudi Arabia and $400 (million per day) to Russia. If Saudi Arabia cheats and Russia cooperates, then the payoff to Saudi Arabia is $500 and the payoff to Russia is $200.

Now let's see what the "players" will do in this "game." Consider the incentives faced by Saudi Arabia. If Russia cooperates, then Saudi Arabia can choose Cooperate and receive a payoff of $400 or choose Cheat and receive a payoff of $500. Since $500 is more than $400, Saudi Arabia's best strategy *if Russia cooperates* is to cheat.

What is Saudi Arabia's best strategy if Russia cheats? If Russia cheats, Saudi Arabia can cooperate and earn a payoff of $200 or Saudi Arabia can cheat and earn a payoff of $300. Cheat is again the more profitable strategy. A strategy that has a higher payoff than any other strategy, no matter what the other player does, is called a **dominant strategy**. In this setup, cheating is a dominant strategy for Saudi Arabia.

Cheating is also a dominant strategy for Russia. If Saudi Arabia cooperates, Russia earns $500 by choosing Cheat and $400 by choosing Cooperate. If Saudi Arabia cheats, Russia earns $300 by choosing Cheat and $200 by choosing Cooperate. Thus, both Saudi Arabia and Russia will cheat and we shade (Cheat, Cheat) to show that this is the equilibrium outcome of the game.

The logic is compelling but also surprising. When Saudi Arabia and Russia each follow their individually sensible strategy of Cheat, each receives a payoff of $300. If Saudi Arabia and Russia instead both chose to cooperate, a strategy that is not individually sensible, they will receive a higher payoff of $400. Thus,

A **dominant strategy** is a strategy that has a higher payoff than any other strategy no matter what the other player does.

The **prisoner's dilemma** describes situations where the pursuit of individual interest leads to a group outcome that is in the interest of no one.

when Saudi Arabia acts in its interest and Russia acts in its interest, the result is an outcome that is in the interest of neither. That is a dilemma well verified by both theory and evidence.

The analysis we have just given of cartel cheating is part of a branch of economics called game theory and Figure 13.3 is one version of a very famous game called the **prisoner's dilemma**. The prisoner's dilemma describes situations where the pursuit of individual interest leads to a group outcome that is in the interest of no one.

To give another example of this phenomenon, the world's stock of fish is rapidly being depleted. To understand why, replace Saudi Arabia and Russia in Figure 13.3 with two large fishing firms or countries, say the United States and Japan. Cooperate now means "produce less fish" (instead of less oil). If both players choose Cooperate, fishing revenue can be maximized and the stock of fish will be maintained for future generations. But if one player cooperates, the other has an incentive to cheat by overfishing. And, of course, if one player cheats, the other has an incentive to cheat as well. Each player has the same incentive and so both players cheat. That reduces the stock of fish below the best possible outcome and eventually it may deplete the stock completely. That's why so many people are concerned that the world is running out of many species of fish.

We will also have more to say about overfishing in Chapter 17.

New Entrants and Demand Response Break Down Cartels

Cheating is not the only reason why cartels fall apart. Usually the high prices of a cartel will attract new entrants; of course, those entrants do not feel bound by previous agreements. For instance, the high price of OPEC oil encouraged a search for new supplies. Pemex, the Mexican oil company, had been a small player in the industry for many decades. But when oil prices went up, Mexico engaged in more searching, more drilling, and more oil production. In 2006, Mexico was the fifth leading oil producer in the world. Great Britain, the Netherlands, and many African nations also expanded their presence in oil markets. Africa will soon supply more oil than does Saudi Arabia, and Brazil may soon become a major producer as well.[1]

It is not just about oil. High oil prices led to more conservation, more interest in natural gas, more interest in solar energy, and many other adjustments. Taken together, these demand responses make it less profitable for OPEC member nations to increase the price of oil. Cartels will tend to be more successful when there are fewer substitutes for the cartelized good, which of course implies less elastic demand. As we know from Chapter 4, more substitutes are typically available in the long run than in the short run, so demand curves tend to become more elastic over time, thus limiting a cartel's power.

The fact that cartels are challenged by new entrants explains why it is typically easier to maintain a cartel in a natural resource than in a manufactured good. It's hard to stop entry into the production of a good that can be made anywhere in the world. In contrast, some natural resources are found in large quantities in only a few places so if you control those places you control the supply.

Oil and diamonds, two goods where cartels have been partially successful, are good examples of natural resources found in only a few places in the world (but see the sidebar on diamonds!). Similarly, Indonesia and Grenada, taken together, control 98 percent of the world's supply of nutmeg, a hard-to-replace spice used in many baking recipes. The nutmeg cartel has had some success. Copper, however, is a natural resource that is distributed more widely. The copper cartel (Intergovernmental Council of Copper Exporting Countries) controls no more than one-third of the world's copper reserves and as a result has not been able to raise prices in any significant manner. There are also good substitutes for copper in most uses, including plastic, aluminum, and recycled copper. The copper case is more typical than diamonds or oil.[2]

Sustainable Cartels in a Market Setting

It's not just natural resources that may be in limited supply. In some cases, the cartel may control access to some key input that cannot be easily duplicated. In these cases, individual firms may not wish to break with the cartel for fear that they will be cut off from the key input.

Major league sports, for example, are cartelized. For instance, major league basketball—the NBA—consists of 30 teams playing against each other. Those teams compete on the court but they collude off the court. They use the NBA league structure to keep down player salaries, using a "salary cap." The salary cap rules are complex, but in essence the league tells teams they cannot spend any more than a certain amount ($58.68 million in 2008–2009) without facing significant financial penalties ("the luxury tax"). Each team, in joining the league, agrees to limit how much it spends on players. This is a buyer's cartel, and the result is that professional basketball salaries are lower than they otherwise would be. Team owners make more money, but players make less money.

Any team that broke the cartel and paid players more would, in time, be kicked out of the league. Access to the league is the good that the cartel controls to keep its members from cheating. The Phoenix Suns are a wonderful team, but how much fun would it be to watch them beat up on some college players? Not much. Fans want to see the Suns play in the NBA and that is why the Suns have to heed the rules of the league (cartel).

Normal businesses, of course, do not need to cooperate as do sports teams, and so their cartels are not sustainable in this fashion. Maybe an angry camera shop cartel would kick a price-cutting deviant out of the local Chamber of Commerce, but that is hardly a major problem, unlike losing membership in the NBA.

Yes, there probably is cheating on the NBA salary cap. Teams cannot pay players more, but they can give them private airplanes, nice facilities, and many other goodies. Maybe some owners give their players cash under the table or hide extra benefits in complex contracts (give a five-year contract to a player with three years left in his legs). But for the most part, sports cartels keep down salaries and that is why players complain about them. It's no accident that players are initially "drafted" rather than hired.

Of course, the NBA cartel still has to attract the attention of the consumer. NBA games compete against collegiate sports, other professional sports, and of course many other activities, such as computer games, listening to music, or going out for a pickup game. In fact, consumers may benefit from the NBA cartel because the salary cap prevents rich teams from buying up all the great players and reducing the competition that consumers demand. It's this last reason that helps to explain another unusual aspect of the NBA cartel; unlike most other cartels, the NBA cartel is legal.

Is the diamond cartel forever?

Diamonds are found in only a few places in the world. As a result, for decades the DeBeers cartel has been able to keep prices high. The diamonds pictured above, however, were not mined—they were *grown*. Man-made diamonds are as beautiful as natural diamonds—even an expert jeweler cannot tell them apart. Man-made diamonds could break the DeBeers cartel.

Government Prosecution and Regulation

The **antitrust laws** give the government the power to regulate or prohibit business practices that may be anti-competitive.

Most cartels have been illegal in the United States since the Sherman Antitrust Act of 1890. ("Trust" is simply an old word for monopoly. The **antitrust laws** are laws that give the government the power to prohibit or regulate business practices that may be anti-competitive.) In the early 1990s, for example, four firms controlled 95 percent of the world market for lysine, an amino acid used to promote growth in pigs, chickens, and cattle. The firms—Archer Daniels Midland (USA), Ajinomoto (Japan), Kyowa Hakko Kogyo (Japan), and Sewon America Inc. (South Korea)—held secret meetings around the world at which they agreed to act in unison to reduce quantity and raise prices.

WHITACRE: And seven from the FTC.
MIMOTO: Yeah. FTC.
(Laughs).

Members of the lysine cartel secretly meeting in Atlanta to fix prices laugh that the FBI and FTC will also be sending members to their meeting. Little did they know, the FBI had already arrived.

What the conspirators didn't know was that one of them was a mole. A high-ranking executive at ADM informed the FBI of the cartel. Working with FBI equipment, the mole videotaped meetings at which the conspirators discussed how to split the market and keep prices high. You can watch some of the conspiracy videos online by going to our textbook's website www.SeeTheInvisibleHand.com.

With the evidence in hand, the FBI and the Department of Justice put the conspirators on trial. Three executives of Archer Daniels Midland, including the vice president, Michael D. Andreas, were fined and imprisoned. One of the Japanese executives was also sentenced to prison, but he fled the country and is currently a fugitive from U.S. law.

Government-Supported Cartels Governments don't always prosecute cartels and in fact sometimes they support cartels. In fact, most successful cartels operate with clear legal and governmental backing. Governments are the ultimate cartel enforcers because they can throw cheaters in jail. OPEC, for example, is a cartel of oil exporting *governments*. In the United States, government-controlled milk cartels raise the price of milk. This cartel is extremely stable. Any seller who breaks it is fined or sent to jail.[3] In the past, the U.S. government has supported cartels in coal mining, agriculture, medicine, and other areas; some but not all of these restrictions have been lifted.

Got milk?

It will cost you more due to the government-controlled milk cartel.

Government-enforced monopolies and cartels, however, are one of the most serious problems facing poor nations today. They plague Mexico, Russia, Indonesia, most of the poor nations in Africa, and many other locales. In Nigeria, it is common for police officers to set up roadblocks to extract bribes or for teachers to demand payoffs for good grades. Entrepreneurs who start new businesses sometimes find that the law (or threats of violence that the law does not prevent) force them out of competition with the small number of so-called untouchable big men who have cartelized the major sectors of the economy.[4] Recent governments in Nigeria have tried to fight corruption but these problems are severe.

A government-supported cartel usually means higher prices, lower quality of service, and less innovation. People with new ideas find it harder or impossible to enter the market. Furthermore, people spend their energies trying to get monopoly or cartel privileges from governments, rather than innovating or finding new ways to service consumers. Governments become more corrupt. For these reasons, most economists oppose most government-enforced cartels. Those cartels are put in place to serve special interests—usually the

UNDERSTAND YOUR world

politically connected cartel members—rather than consumers or the general citizenry.

Summing Up: Successful Cartels

Recall that cartels collapse because of cheating by the cartel members, new entrants, demand response, and possible legal penalties. Thus, successful cartels occur when these factors are weak rather than strong. Cheating by cartel members is less profitable and easier to detect, for example, the fewer the firms that are in an industry. New entrants can be prevented when the good being cartelized is limited in supply or when the good can only be found in a few places in the world. It's easier and more profitable to cartelize goods with few substitutes; that is one reason DeBeers spends so much money advertising that only a "Diamond Is Forever." Cartels will also be more successful if they are backed by government and the power of the law.

Network Goods

Sometimes market power comes not from a cartel but rather from building or otherwise coordinating a network.

As of 2009, there were over 200 million active users on Facebook. Why post your profile on Facebook? It's simple: Facebook is where everyone else posts a profile or goes to view profiles. If you are a teenager, unless you want to be a hermit, it is better to belong to the same network as your friends. Similarly, Match.com, the largest Internet dating service, claims to have over 20 million users.[5] If you are looking to date or marry, Match.com has the largest selection of potential partners and so you are most likely to use it.

We wrote this book in Microsoft Word and not in some other software package. Why? It's not that we firmly believe that Word is superior to other programs. In fact, we've hardly tried most of the other programs. Instead, we knew that both of us had a copy of Word and we were both familiar with writing in Word. Even more important, we knew that our editor and publisher could work with Word files. Notice that we chose to use Word even though there are other software packages such as OpenOffice that are *free*.

In each of these examples, the value of the good depends on how many other people use the good. Facebook, Match.com, and Microsoft Word are all more valuable to one consumer when other consumers also use these goods. Thus, a **network good** is a good whose value to one consumer increases the more that other consumers use the good.

These examples hint at some of the interesting features of network goods that we will be exploring in the remainder of this chapter. When networks are important, we typically see the following:

Features of Markets for Network Goods

1. Network goods are usually sold by monopolies or oligopolies.
2. When networks are important, the "best" product may not always win.
3. Standard wars are common in establishing network goods.
4. Competition in the market for network goods is "for the market" instead of "in the market."

Let's look at each of these features in turn.

CHECK YOURSELF

> When Great Britain discovered large oil deposits in the North Sea, why didn't it immediately join OPEC?
> What is the surprising conclusion of the prisoner's dilemma?

A **network good** is a good whose value to one consumer increases the more that other consumers use the good.

Network Goods Are Usually Sold by Monopolies or Oligopolies

Microsoft is one of the most profitable corporations on earth. Most of their profit comes from selling their operating system and their software at prices above marginal cost. Microsoft can sell their products at prices above marginal cost not because their products are necessarily the best in some absolute sense but because most people want to use the same software as most other people. Microsoft products are, in most cases, the most likely to be compatible with other products and other readers, writers, and publishers.

The power of coordination in "Office-like" software is so strong that Microsoft can sell Office for hundreds of dollars even though there are *free* alternatives such as OpenOffice, Think Free Office, and Google Docs, all of which are roughly similar in quality to Office. But don't make the mistake of thinking that if one of these products became the dominant standard, we would all enjoy free software. The only reason these products are given away for free is that the owners hope to become the dominant standard so that they can charge a high price!

Sometimes the pressures for coordination are strong, but other factors mean that more than one firm can compete in the market. eBay is the market leader in online auctions and it uses its market power to charge higher prices than would occur in a standard competitive market. But there are a handful of other firms in the industry that offer slightly different features. Craigslist, for example, is able to compete with eBay because it offers buyers and sellers a way to buy and sell locally, which is especially useful for products that are expensive to ship. By the way, economists call a market dominated by a small number of firms an **oligopoly**.

An **oligopoly** is a market dominated by a small number of firms.

The market for Internet dating is an oligopoly simply because most people want to join large networks with many other people. But it's not a monopoly because Yahoo! Personals and eHarmony compete with the market leader Match.com by offering different matching algorithms. In addition, there are competing niche services, such as JDate.com (for those looking for a Jewish partner), but notice that JDate dominates its competitors within that niche.

The "Best" Product May Not Always Win

In markets with network goods, it's possible for the market to "lock in" to the "wrong" product or network. We can illustrate using a coordination game as shown in Figure 13.4, similar in structure to the prisoner's dilemma we showed earlier. Alex and Tyler are choosing whether to use software from Apple or Microsoft to write their textbook. Alex's choices or strategies are the rows, Tyler's are the columns. What Alex and Tyler most want to avoid is making different choices. If Alex chooses Microsoft and Tyler chooses Apple, it will be difficult for them to work together so their payoffs will be low, just (3,3). And the same thing is true if Alex chooses Apple and Tyler chooses Microsoft. Alex and Tyler receive the highest payoffs if both are using the same software. So, if Alex chooses Apple, it will make sense for Tyler to choose Apple, and vice versa. In other words, if Alex and Tyler both choose Apple, then neither will have an incentive to change their strategy.

A **Nash equilibrium** is a situation in which no player has an incentive to change their strategy unilaterally.

More formally, economists say a situation is an equilibrium if no player in the game has an incentive to change his or her strategy unilaterally. This is also called a **Nash equilibrium** after John Nash, the mathematician. His

FIGURE 13.4

		Tyler	
		Apple	Microsoft
Alex	Apple	(11, 11)	(3, 3)
	Microsoft	(3, 3)	(10, 10)

Alex's Payoff   Tyler's Payoff

The Coordination Game The payoffs show the rewards to Alex and Tyler given the combination of strategies that are played. If both Tyler and Alex play Apple, neither has an incentive to change strategy. If both Tyler and Alex play Microsoft, neither has an incentive to change strategy. Thus, (Apple, Apple) and (Microsoft, Microsoft) are both Nash equilibria.

contributions to game theory resulted in a Nobel Prize and his strange life was featured in the movie *A Beautiful Mind*. The outcome (Apple, Apple) is an equilibrium because neither Alex nor Tyler has an incentive to change his strategy unilaterally, that is, neither Alex nor Tyler has an incentive to change, holding constant the choice of the other player.

But notice that (Apple, Apple) is not the only equilibrium. If Alex chooses Microsoft, then Tyler will also want to choose Microsoft, and vice versa. Thus, (Microsoft, Microsoft) is also an equilibrium strategy. The payoffs to the (Microsoft, Microsoft) equilibrium are slightly lower than the payoffs to the (Apple, Apple) equilibrium. Nevertheless, (Microsoft, Microsoft) is still an equilibrium because if Alex and Tyler do choose Microsoft, neither will have an incentive to switch. So which equilibrium, (Apple, Apple) or (Microsoft, Microsoft), will Alex and Tyler end up at?

If Alex and Tyler really are the only players in this game, they could probably talk to one another and coordinate on the best equilibrium, which is (Apple, Apple). But in reality the coordination game is between Alex, Tyler, and many other people. Coordinating on the best equilibrium is not so easy when many people are involved and when they do not all agree about whether Apple really is better than Microsoft. So what will determine the final equilibrium? The classic answer is "accidents of history."

It's an accident of history that computer keyboards are laid out according to the QWERTY design (so-named for the keys on the top left side). But is QWERTY the best possible layout for keyboards? According to some studies, a different layout of the keys called the Dvorak design allows for faster and easier typing. So why is the QWERTY design dominant? QWERTY came first and once people learned to type on a QWERTY keyboard, typewriter manufacturers had an incentive to sell QWERTY typewriters. And, of course, once most manufacturers were selling QWERTY typewriters, it made sense to learn how to type on the QWERTY keyboard. Thus, the QWERTY design became "locked in." If you're wondering, QWERTY is the only way that we know how to type.

The QWERTY story needs to be taken with a grain of salt, however. The first study showing that the Dvorak layout was better than QWERTY was a 1944

The Dvorak keyboard.

Would you type faster?

study by the U.S. Navy. But who authored the 1944 study? None other than Lieutenant-Commander August Dvorak. Any guesses as to who created the Dvorak keyboard? Later studies have failed to show big advantages to either keyboard. Thus, it makes sense that few people bother to learn Dvorak even though it's now easy to reprogram a computer keyboard according to any design.*

When networks are important, product design isn't just about the stand-alone product, it is also about making sure the product fits into the rest of the industry and about making things easy for as many users as possible. Microsoft's competitors like Apple have at times arguably had the superior products in stand-alone terms, but Apple has not been better at ensuring widespread compatibility and an easy-to-use industry standard. Designing products that everyone can use will often mean a certain amount of simplification and a certain number of shortcuts. It is precisely the experts who will be most unhappy with a mass-compatible product. That is one reason why some people say "Microsoft is evil," but in part this charge is wishful thinking that everyone could be an advanced computer user.

Standard Wars Are Common

More common than a coordination game in which a bad equilibrium becomes locked in is a standard war where there are two good equilibria but the players differ over which equilibrium is best.

In recent years, two groups of manufacturers have battled over the standard for high-definition DVD discs. One group, led by Toshiba, supported the HD-DVD standard; the other group, led by Sony, supported Blu-ray. HD-DVD was a less complex and cheaper technology but Blu-ray could store more information. Toshiba and Sony each wanted to win the standard war, but they also knew that consumers wouldn't buy either standard in large numbers until they were certain which standard would win the war. Thus, in Figure 13.5 we show that Toshiba is better off in the (HD-DVD, HD-DVD) equilibrium and Sony is better off in the (Blu-ray, Blu-ray) equilibrium but neither company does well when there are two competing standards.

FIGURE 13.5

		Sony	
		HD-DVD	Blu-ray
Toshiba	HD-DVD	(10, 8)	(0, 0)
	Blu-ray	(0, 0)	(8, 10)

The Standard War There are two Nash equilibria in the standard war (shaded). Sony and Toshiba both prefer that they agree on a standard than having no standard at all but Sony prefers the Blu-ray standard and Toshiba prefers the HD-DVD standard.

*The QWERTY story was made prominent by David, Paul A. 1985. "Clio and the Economics of QWERTY." *American Economic Review* 75:332–337 and is criticized in Liebowitz, Stan J. and Stephen E. Margolis. 1990. "The Fable of the Keys." *Journal of Law & Economics* 33(1):1–25.

In the Blu-ray standard war, Toshiba and Sony battled to get content producers such as Disney, 20th Century Fox, and Universal and distributors like Wal-Mart and Netflix to sign on to one standard or the other. HD-DVD initially had the lead but Sony included Blu-ray players in the PlayStation 3, thus building an audience for their standard. More and more firms began to sign on to Blu-ray. After Warner Brothers announced in January 2008 that it would produce movies for Blu-ray exclusively, Toshiba threw in the towel and ended production of HD-DVD machines.

Competition "For the Market" instead of "In the Market"

The Blu-ray wars illustrate another important feature of network goods, namely that competition occurs "for the market" rather than "in the market." For instance, once there is a winning standard, the losing standard can disappear quite quickly. It's also the case that a winning standard is not guaranteed to last forever or even for very long. Let's look at this in more detail.

Network goods are usually sold by monopolies or oligopolies, but what makes these markets different from standard monopolies and oligopolies is the ease and speed by which the monopoly can change hands. In 1988, the spreadsheet program Lotus 1–2–3 held a 70 percent share of the market, but it faced competition from Quattro Pro and Excel. At first Quattro Pro, with sales twice that of Excel, appeared to be gaining, but comparative reviews of all three programs gave the edge to Excel. By 1998, Excel had 70 percent of the market and Lotus 1–2–3 was heading toward irrelevance.

Microsoft Word is the dominant word processor today but the authors of this book remember when WordStar and then WordPerfect were the market leaders. And have you ever heard of Friendster? In 2003, Friendster, a social networking site, had 20 million members, but it failed to increase quality, and today Facebook and MySpace are much larger.

One, or a handful of firms, has dominated the market for network goods like spreadsheets, word processors, and social networking sites at each point in the history of their evolution but the dominant firm has changed over time. We have had serial monopolies rather than a single, stable monopoly. Microsoft's share of the word processing and spreadsheet market appears to be strong today, but Google is betting that its web-based word processor and spreadsheet can dethrone Microsoft in the future. Maybe this will happen, maybe not, but it's a mistake to think that a large market share, taken alone, implies that competition is absent. Competition for the market can dethrone market leaders very quickly.

In 2000, the Department of Justice brought a lawsuit against Microsoft, on the grounds that the company tried to monopolize operating systems and use its operating system to promote its other products. Windows, for example, was packaged with Internet Explorer, and this helped Internet Explorer replace Netscape as the leading market browser. In 1996, Netscape held 80 percent of the browser market according to some estimates, but by 2002 Internet Explorer had taken almost all of Netscape's market share.[6]

To be sure, it seems that Microsoft was guilty of "intent to monopolize," as defined by the antitrust laws. It is less clear that Microsoft's behavior made consumers worse off. Netscape's open-source spinoff, Firefox, is widely available today as is Google's browser, Chrome, Apple's browser, Safari, and many others.

Thus, there is considerable competition in this market. Switching to another browser is easy, but many of us don't bother because the quality of all browsers is high. More generally, during the 1990s, Microsoft prices fell and the software added many new features. For instance, Windows 95 and Windows XP were much more consumer friendly than their predecessors.

The dilemma facing the antitrust authorities is that we know that the market for network goods will be dominated by a handful of firms. Thus, the question is not monopoly versus competition (in the sense of competition from many firms in the market) but rather it is one monopoly versus another. It's not obvious that consumers are better off when Netscape has a market share of 80 percent than when Internet Explorer has a market share of 80 percent. What is important is that competition *for the market* is not impeded. Regulators claim that Microsoft did impede competition for the market by giving away Internet Explorer for free in a bundle with Windows. Maybe, but that is a tough claim to either prove or to refute.

Microsoft settled with the government in 2001. The agreement was that the company would give its competitors the knowledge and technologies to produce software that would interact seamlessly with Windows. In the European Union, however, many of the antitrust charges against Microsoft remain open.

Music Is a Network Good

Finally, network products aren't just found in high tech. Most people want to listen to music that is popular, so music is a network good. If you listen to music that is popular, you can swap songs with your friends, go to concerts together, and talk about the same people. Thus, music that is popular is a more valuable good; namely, it offers more benefits to the listener than does music that is obscure.

In fact, an ingenious experiment by Duncan J. Watts, a sociologist at Columbia University, demonstrated that tastes in music have a strong social component.[7] Watts asked thousands of people to listen to and rate some bands that they had never heard of. If they liked a song, participants could download it for free. The trick was that some of the participants saw only the names of the songs and bands, but others also saw how many times the songs had previously been downloaded by other participants. If tastes in music are independent of what other people are listening to, knowing how many people had previously downloaded a song should be irrelevant. You should just download the songs you like, right?

But Watts discovered that the more downloads a song had, the more people wanted to download the song! So if a few early participants happened to like and download a song that song got even more downloads. As a result, when participants saw previous downloads, accidents of history turned some songs and bands into big hits while others languished. Even more surprisingly, when Watts ran his experiment again and again, the songs that turned into hits were different every time!

So what does this mean? Well, look at two of the principles we outlined above for network industries, namely that the best product may not always win and that standard wars are important. You'll find both of those phenomena in music markets. Some bands catch a lucky break and become popular pretty quickly. That popularity feeds on itself so a small head start is turned into a big market advantage even if the band is not necessarily the "best." Was Britney Spears ever that good of an entertainer? Standard wars occur when different groups, singers, or genres compete to be seen as the market leader and thus attract the patronage of all those looking to support what is popular. Stars can rise or fall quickly depending on public perceptions of popularity. As with other network goods, at any one point in time a handful of entertainers dominate the airwaves and make the most revenues. But a large market share today is no guarantee of popularity in the future so older stars fear being dethroned by hot, young, new stars.

CHECK YOURSELF

> Does a firm with an established network good, such as Microsoft Office, face competition? Why or why not?

> Consider the Blu-ray versus HD-DVD competition. Why is it useful for you to wait before purchasing when standards are not set? What do you predict will happen to sales once standards *are* set?

□ Takeaway

The OPEC cartel did not exhibit a long-term ability to control the price of oil. Most market cartels are not stable either. Either businesses cheat on the cartel agreement or new competitors enter the market. Governments break up some cartels, but they also enforce many other cartels. When you observe a harmful cartel, you should ask whether some governmental rule or regulation might be at fault. The prisoner's dilemma explains why cheating is common in cartels and more generally how individual interest can make cooperation difficult even when cooperation is better for everyone in the group than noncooperation.

Sometimes a firm may achieve market power by selling or creating a network good, a good whose value to a consumer increases the more other consumers use the good. Once such networks take off, they become large very rapidly and tend to be sold by one or only a handful of firms. Since networks often grow rapidly, many entrepreneurs will try to set the standard for the network, thus leading to standard wars. Although network goods are often sold by monopolies, the identities of the monopolists change over time as new firms innovate and leapfrog the previous market leaders.

□ CHAPTER REVIEW

KEY CONCEPTS

Cartel, p. 265

Strategic decision-making, p. 265

Dominant strategy, p. 271

Prisoner's dilemma, p. 272

Antitrust laws, p. 274

Network good, p. 275

Oligopoly, p. 276

Nash equilibrium, p. 276

FACTS AND TOOLS

1. Let's start off by working out a few examples to illustrate the lure of the cartel. To keep it simple on the supply side, we'll assume that fixed costs

are zero so marginal cost equals average cost. We'll compare the competitive outcome ($P = MC$) to what you'd get if the firms all agreed to act "as if" they were a monopoly. In all cases, we'll use terms from the following diagram:

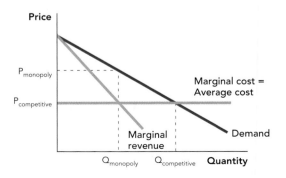

a. First, let's see where the profits are. Comparing this figure to Figure 13.2, shade the rectangle that corresponds to monopoly profit.

b. What is the formula for this rectangle in terms of price, cost, and quantity?

c. Let's look at the market for one kind of apple: Gala. Assume that there are 300 producers of Gala apples and that MC = AC = $0.40 per pound. In a competitive market, price will be driven down to marginal cost. Let's assume that when P = MC, each apple grower produces 2 million pounds of apples for a total market production of 600 million pounds. Now imagine that the apple growers form a cartel and each agrees to cut production to 1 million pounds, which drives the price up to $0.70 per pound. Calculate profit per pound and total industry profit if the apple growers behave "as if" they were a monopoly and are able to produce according to the following table.

$P_{monopoly}$	$Q_{monopoly}$
$0.70/lb.	300 million lbs.
Profit per pound$_{monopoly}$	Total industry profit$_{monopoly}$
_____	_____

d. If a single apple grower broke from the cartel and produced an extra million pounds of apples, how much additional profit (approximately) would this apple grower make?

2. Take a look at the reasons why cartels collapse presented in this chapter. For each pair below, choose the case where the cartel is more likely to stick together.

a. An industry where it's easy for new firms to enter vs. an industry where the same firms stick around for decades.

b. When the government makes it legal for all the firms to agree on prices vs. when the government makes it illegal for all firms in an industry to agree on prices. (Note: The Sherman Antitrust Act made the latter generally illegal in 1890, but President Franklin Roosevelt's National Industrial Recovery Act temporarily legalized price-setting cartels during the Great Depression.)

c. Cartels where all the industry leaders went to the same schools and live in the same neighborhood vs. cartels where the industry leaders don't really know or trust each other. (Hint: As Adam Smith said in the *Wealth of Nations*, "People of the same trade seldom meet together, even for merriment and diversion, but the conversation ends in a conspiracy against the public, or in some contrivance to raise prices.")

d. An industry where it's easy for a firm to sell a little extra product without anyone knowing (e.g., music downloads) vs. an industry where all sales are public and visible (e.g., concert tickets).

e. An industry where a high price spurs new production vs. an industry with highly inelastic supply.

3. The prisoner's dilemma game is one of the most important models in all of social science: Most games of trust can be thought of as some kind of prisoner's dilemma. Here's the classic game: Two men rob a bank and are quickly arrested. The police do not have an airtight case; they have just enough evidence to put each man in prison for one year, a slap on the wrist for a serious crime.

If the police had more evidence, they could put the men away for longer. To get more evidence, they put the men in separate interrogation rooms and offer each man the same deal: If you testify against your accomplice, we will drop all the charges against you (and convict the other guy of the full penalty of 10 years of prison time). Of course, if both prisoners take the deal the police will have enough evidence to put both prisoners away and they will each get 6 years each. And, as noted above, if neither testifies both will get just one year of prison time. What's the best thing for each man to do?

In each cell in the table below, the first number is the number of years Butch will spend in prison, and the second is the number that Sundance will spend in prison given the strategies chosen by Butch and Sundance. If years in prison are minuses, then we can write it like this:

		Sundance	
		Keep quiet	Testify
Butch	Keep quiet	(−1, −1)	(−10, 0)
	Testify	(0, −10)	(−6, −6)

a. If Sundance keeps quiet, what's the best choice (highest payoff) for Butch, keep quiet or testify?

b. If Sundance chooses testify, what's the best choice for Butch, keep quiet or testify?

c. What's the best choice for Butch? What's the best choice for Sundance?

d. Using the definition in the chapter, does Butch have a "dominant strategy?" If so, what is it?

e. What is your prediction about what will happen?

f. How does this help explain why the police never put two suspects in the same interrogation room? (Note the similarity between this question and the earlier Adam Smith quote.)

4. Your professor probably grades on a curve, implicitly if not explicitly. This means that you and your classmates could each agree to study half as much, and you would all earn the same grade you would have earned without the agreement. What do you think would happen if you tried to enact this agreement? Why? Which model in this chapter is most similar to this conspiracy?

5. In many college towns, rumors abound that the gas stations in town collude to keep prices high. If this were true, where would you expect this conspiracy against the public to work best? Why?

a. In towns with dozens of gas stations or in towns with less than 10?

b. In towns where the city council has many environmental and zoning regulations making it hard to open a new gas station or in towns where there is lots of open land for development?

c. In towns where all the gas stations are about equally busy or in towns where half the gas stations are always busy and half tend to be empty?

6. In the following three games, is each a coordination game or a prisoner's dilemma? The best way to check is to see if there is exactly one Nash equilibrium; another way is to see if there is a dominant strategy for each player. To keep it a little challenging, we won't give the actions obvious labels that might give away the answer. Higher numbers are always better:

a.

		Player B	
		Left	Right
Player A	Up	(3, 3)	(5, 5)
	Down	(5, 5)	(1, 1)

b.

		Player B	
		Left	Right
Player A	Up	(100, 100)	(600, 50)
	Down	(50, 600)	(500, 500)

c.

		Player B	
		Left	Right
Player A	Up	(8, 6)	(7, 5)
	Down	(3, 0)	(9, 9)

7. The mantra of Amazon.com CEO Jeff Bezos is "Get big fast." As we saw in Chapter 11 on monopoly one reason to "get big fast" is because in some industries the firm's average cost will plummet as the firm expands—so size helps on the supply side. In this chapter, network effects illustrated how size helps on the demand side. With this in mind, explain the following real world drives to get big fast: Do you think it's mostly about increasing returns or mostly about network effects? Explain why:

a. Second Life, an online virtual world, lets people use many of its features for free. To use the best features, you have to pay for it.

b. Likewise, Match.com, the online dating site, lets people post profiles, look at other people's profiles, and even get mail from other members for free. To send an email to a member, you have to pay.

c. Adobe Acrobat Reader is free, but the software to create sophisticated Adobe documents is not.

d. King Gillette (real name) gave away his first disposable razor blades in 1885. They came free with the purchase of a box of Cuban cigars.

e. Amazon.com itself.

THINKING AND PROBLEM SOLVING

1. Usually, we think of cheating as a bad thing. But in this chapter, cheating turns out to be a very good thing in some important cases.

   a. Who gets the benefit when a cartel collapses through cheating: consumers or producers?

   b. Does this benefit usually show up in a lower price, a higher quantity, or both?

   c. Does cheating increase consumer surplus, producer surplus, or both?

   d. So, is cheating good for the cheaters or good for other people?

2. Firms in a cartel each have an incentive individually to lower the prices they charge.

   a. Suppose there were a government regulation that set minimum prices. Would this regulation tend to strengthen cartels, weaken them, or have no effect?

   b. Another way that one firm can cheat on a cartel is to offer a higher-quality product to consumers. Suppose there were a government regulation that standardized the quality of a good. Would this regulation tend to strengthen cartels, weaken them, or have no effect?

3. Deciding which side of the road to drive on is a kind of coordination game. In some countries, people drive on the right side of the road, and in other countries (notably the United Kingdom and some of its former colonies), they drive on the left. These customs developed hundreds of years ago. If there were a single world standard, car companies could save some money by not having to produce both left and right types and cars would be a little bit cheaper. Why do you think it is that these customs persist? In other words, what keeps the world "locked in" to two separate kinds of cars?

4. In the late-fifteenth century, Europe consumed about 2 million pounds of pepper per year. At this time, Venice (ruled by a small, tightly knit group of merchants) was the major player in the pepper trade. But after Portuguese explorer Vasco da Gama blazed a path around Africa into the Indian Ocean in 1498, Venice found itself competing with Portugal's trade route. By the mid-sixteenth century, Europeans consumed 6 to 7 million pounds per year, much of it through Lisbon. After da Gama's success, the price of pepper fell.

   a. During the fifteenth century, was it likely that a cartel was restricting pepper imports? Why or why not?

   b. If the price of pepper before 1498 had been lower, would da Gama have been more willing or less willing to sail around South Africa's Cape of Good Hope? Why?

   c. Of the three reasons listed in this chapter for why cartels weaken, which one best explains the decline of Venice's influence on the world pepper trade?

   d. The ruling merchants of Venice had no political power in other parts of Europe. Why is that important in understanding how European pepper consumption more than tripled in just over half a century?

5. Suppose you and your friend, Amy, work together to develop a unique magic trick that either of you could perform alone. It turns out to be a tremendously popular trick and both of you make it big as professional magicians. Suppose you decide to conspire together and limit the number of performances featuring the trick. If both of you do only one show a week, each of you earns a profit of $10,000 for that show. If both of you do five shows a week, each of you earns a total profit of $6,000. If one does a single show while the other does five shows, the former gets a profit of $1,000 and the latter gets a profit of $15,000.

   a. Use the information above to complete the table below. (Hint: It'll look a lot like Figure 13.3.)

		Amy	
		1 show	5 shows
You	1 show	,	,
	5 shows	,	,

   b. Suppose Amy does one show. What is your preferred strategy?

   c. Suppose Amy does five shows. What is your preferred strategy?

   d. What is your dominant strategy?

   e. Suppose you do one show. What is Amy's preferred strategy?

   f. Suppose you do five shows. What is Amy's preferred strategy?

   g. What is Amy's dominant strategy?

h. What is the Nash equilibrium?

i. Magicians are famously hesitant to reveal the secrets behind their magic, even to other magicians. Based on what you've learned in this question, why do they act like this? Is letting other magicians in on your secrets an optimal strategy?

6. In 1890, Senator Sherman (of the Sherman Antitrust Act, which we mentioned earlier) pushed through the legislation that bears his name that gave the government significant power to "bust-up" cartels, presumably in order to increase output. Over a century later, economist Thomas J. DiLorenzo examined the industries commonly accused of being cartels and found those industries increased output by an average of 175 percent from 1880 to 1890—seven times the growth rate of the economy at the time.

Suppose the industries were conspiring. Indeed, let's suppose that these cartels grew ever-stronger in the decade before the Sherman Act became law. If that were true, would we expect output in these industries to grow by so much? In other words, is DiLorenzo's evidence consistent with the standard story of the Sherman Antitrust Act?

7. In 2005, economist Thomas Schelling won the Nobel Prize in economics, in part for his development of the concept of the "focal point" in game theory. Focal points are a way to solve a coordination game. If two people both benefit by choosing the same option but cannot communicate, they will choose the most obvious option, called the focal point. Of course, what's obvious will vary from culture to culture. Whether to wear business attire or just shorts and a t-shirt, whether to use Apple or Microsoft products, whether to arrive at meetings on time or late. In all these cases, having a group agree on one focal point is more important than which particular focal point you all agree on. Therefore, people will look for cultural clues so that they can find the focal point. (Note: Schelling wrote two highly readable books that won him the Nobel, *Micromotives and Macrobehavior* and The *Strategy of Conflict*.)

a. Suppose you are playing a game where you and another player have to choose one of three boxes. You can't communicate with the other player until the game is over. One box

is blue and the other two are red. If the two of you choose the same box you win $50; otherwise, you get nothing. Which box do you choose: The blue box or one of the red boxes? Why?

b. Suppose that you and another player have to write down on a slip of paper *any* price in dollars and cents between $90.01 and $109.83. If you both write down the same price, you'll each win that amount of money. If your numbers don't match, you get nothing. Again, you can't communicate with the other player until the game is over. What number will both of you probably choose?

c. Many "slippery slope" arguments are really stories about focal points. In the United States during debates over banning guns or restricting speech, people will argue that *any* limitation follows down a "slippery slope." What do they mean by that? (Hint: Attorneys often worry about "grey areas" and they prefer "bright line tests.")

d. Schelling used the idea of the focal point to explain implicit agreements on the limits to war. Poison gas, for example, was not used in World War II and the agreement was largely implicit. Since focal points have to be obvious, explain why there was no implicit agreement that "some" poison gas would be allowed, but "a lot" of poison gas would not be allowed.

8. Consider the shipping container (the large box that stacks on cargo ships and attaches to trucks). If all containers are the same size and design, then the container can pass seamlessly between ships, trains, trucks, and cranes along the way. Today, the standard dimensions are 8 feet wide, 8.5 feet tall, and 40 feet long. (The recent book *The Box* tells the surprisingly gripping tale of how this size came to be the standard, and how it has cut the cost of shipping worldwide.) Let's see how this standard dimension illustrates the meaning of "Nash equilibrium."

a. Suppose an inventor created a new shipping container that was slightly cheaper to make, as well as stronger, but it *had* to be 41 feet long. Keeping the idea of standardization in mind, would this inventor be successful? Why or why not?

b. Suppose a container manufacturer reduced the strength of the end walls of his containers (saving him $100 per container made). While this makes no difference to containers on a boat, containers on a train are at risk as the container bumps against the flatcar when the train hits the brakes. Who would tend to oppose these weaker, cheaper containers: the company whose products are stored in the container, the train companies who transport the goods, or both?

c. Why does Federal Express, the overnight delivery company, require everyone to use FedEx packaging for most shipments?

9. It's more efficient to go shopping when everyone else is shopping: This is one explanation for the rise of Christmas as a shopping season. Even many people who don't celebrate Christmas do a lot of shopping and gift giving during this season. At the other extreme, a "dead mall" is one of the dreariest sights of modern consumer capitalism. Let's see how a pleasant shopping experience is a network good.

Facebook for those without computers.

a. Part of the pleasure of walking through a mall is the pleasure of seeing and being seen. When will you see more people at the mall: in the months before Christmas or at other times? So if you like seeing people, when will *you* tend to go to the mall? (This is an example of the "multiplier effects" so common in economics.)

b. When you were in high school (or perhaps middle school), you may have spent time hanging out at a mall. How was the mall like Facebook, MySpace, or other social networking websites?

c. Malls will spend more money on decorations and entertainment when they can spread this cost over a large number of consumers. Again, when will you expect to see more of these extra expenses: in the months before Christmas or at other times?

d. If Christmas is so great for malls, why don't they have Christmas every month, spending money on decorations and singers all the time? Of course, they *try* to do this with Easter and back-to-school and Valentine's Day, and so forth, but why do these fail so miserably compared to the big success of Christmas? Answer in the language of network goods. (Hint: Once there's a big chunk of the population committed to using Facebook, what's the benefit to setting up another pseudo-Facebook?)

CHALLENGES

1. Prisoner's dilemmas are common in real life, but not all real-life games are as dismal as the prisoner's dilemma. One game, known as "stag hunt," describes situations where cooperation is possible but fragile. The philosopher Jean-Jacques Rousseau described the game. He said that a lot of social situations are like going hunting with a friend: If you both agree to hunt for a large male deer (a stag), then you each have to hold your positions near each end of a valley so that the animal can't escape. If you both hold to your positions, then you will almost surely get your kill. If one hunter wanders off to hunt the easier-to-find rabbit, however, then the stag will almost surely get away. Rabbit hunting works fine as a solo sport, but to catch a deer you need a team effort. This is the usual way of writing the game:

		Hume	
		Hunt Stag	Hunt Rabbit
Rousseau	Hunt Stag	(5, 5)	(0, 3)
	Hunt Rabbit	(3, 0)	(3, 3)

a. If Rousseau is quite sure that Hume will hunt stag, will he also hunt stag?

b. If Rousseau is quite sure that Hume will hunt rabbit, will Rousseau still hunt stag?

c. There are two Nash equilibria here: What are they? (Check by looking in each box and asking, "Would one player unilaterally change his choice between rabbit and stag? If so, this isn't an equilibrium.")

d. Of these two equilibria, economists call one the "payoff-dominant equilibrium" and the other the "risk-dominant equilibrium." You can figure out which is which by the process of elimination. What do you think is the biggest risk that might push someone to choose the "risk-dominant equilibrium?"

e. Is this a coordination game or is there a dominant strategy?

f. In the coordination games we looked at in the chapter and in previous questions, if you failed to coordinate, things turned out badly. Is that the case here?

g. Anytime someone says "I'll do it as long as I'm not the only one," they're probably describing a stag hunt. Wearing a cocktail dress to a dinner party, making a solid team effort, keeping your lawn mowed—all might be examples of stag hunts. In a stag hunt, if you think the other players are nice, then you'll want to be nice yourself. But if you suspect they're not nice, you'll probably just be a "rugged individualist" and go hunt the rabbit on your own. With this in mind, think of two more examples of stag hunt situations on your own.

(For an excellent, somewhat technical treatment of how people might agree to hunt stag across many areas of life, see Skyrms, Brian. 2004. *The Stag Hunt and the Evolution of Social Structure.* Cambridge: Cambridge University Press. Skyrms is a philosopher who uses the tools of game theory to investigate important social questions.)

2. We mentioned research by Liebowitz and Margolis that poked some holes in the QWERTY story. In particular, they emphasized that in the age when typing first became common, many corporations had large "typing pools," dozens of women (rarely men) who just typed up other people's handwritten notes. If DVORAK had really been faster than QWERTY, then these corporations could have saved millions of dollars in hourly wages by just retraining their workers with a few days on a DVORAK keyboard. In other words, individuals might

choose the wrong standard, but big firms have a tendency to grab the easy money, especially when it's measured in the millions of dollars. That gives these big players a strong incentive to pick the best standard.

a. With this in mind, which major market players might have pushed for the Blu-Ray DVD standard? In other words, which organizations might have a lot of experts around to check every detail of the competing high-definition DVD formats? Which organizations would also care about choosing the format consumers would actually prefer two or three years down the road?

b. In future standard wars, do you expect most of the early sales efforts to be directed at regular consumers or instead at "power users," owners of big retail chains, and other gatekeepers?

3. Why doesn't everyone just switch to one language?

4. Nobel Laureate Paul Krugman once asked "Who would enter a demolition derby without the incentive of a prize?" (Source: Krugman. 1998. "Soft Microeconomics: The Squishy Case Against You-Know-Who," *Slate.*)

a. The "demolition derby" he was talking about was the battle over Internet browsers: Many enter the battle, but only one (or two) survive. But let's take his story literally: If there were two cars in a demolition derby, and each car costs $20,000 to build, and one car will be totally destroyed, how big will the prize probably have to be to get two people to enter if there's a 50–50 chance of losing all your investment?

Netscape?

b. What if we want a really good demolition derby: One where 10 of these cars compete but only one survives. About how big will the prize have to be now?

c. Let's draw the lesson for network goods: Since competition in network good markets is competition "for the market," then it's like winning a prize in a demolition derby. If there's a fixed price of starting up a new social networking website (you need so many computers, so many nerds, so many advertisers), then when would you see a lot of firms competing for the prize: when the prize is large or when the prize is small? Thus, if we want a lot of competition *for the market* do we necessarily want to restrict the profits of the winner?

14

Labor Markets

CHAPTER OUTLINE

The Demand for Labor and the Marginal Product of Labor

Supply of Labor

Labor Market Issues

How Bad Is Labor Market Discrimination, or Can Lakisha Catch a Break?

Takeaway

A janitor in the United States earns about $10 an hour; a typical janitor in India earns less than $1 an hour. Why is there such a difference? Why does one person earn so much more than the other? After all, janitors in both countries do many of the same things: They clean windows and floors, scrub toilets, remove trash, and so forth.

If you think the differences in wages have to do with supply and demand, you are on the right track.

Wages are determined in the market for labor just like other prices are determined.

In this chapter, we look more deeply at the factors underlying the demand for labor and the supply of labor. A deeper understanding explains how wages are determined at a fundamental level, why most Americans earn so much by global standards, why education raises wages, whether and how much labor unions help workers, and how discrimination still shapes labor markets today.

The Demand for Labor and the Marginal Product of Labor

A firm is willing to hire a worker when the worker increases the firm's revenues more than the firm's costs. Economists call the increase in revenue created by hiring an additional worker the **marginal product of labor (MPL).** The increase in costs created by hiring an additional worker is, for a competitive firm, simply the worker's wage (including the cost of other compensation like health benefits). Thus, we can say that a firm is willing to hire a worker when the marginal product of labor is greater than the wage.

The **marginal product of labor (MPL)** is the increase in a firm's revenues created by hiring an additional laborer.

When the Boston Celtics traded for Kevin Garnett, they went from a mediocre record of 24 wins and 58 losses to having the best record in the NBA. Not only did the Celtics win more games when they hired Garnett, their attendance increased and they sold more merchandise. In the long run, the value of their TV contract was much higher too. When the Celtics hired Garnett their revenues increased by a lot—Kevin Garnett had a high marginal product—that's why the Celtics were willing to pay Garnett nearly $24 million a year.

McDonald's considers marginal product when the company hires people to keep its restaurants clean and in good running order. No one wants to eat in a restaurant that looks unclean so a cleaner restaurant increases profit. But how clean is clean enough? At some point, cleanliness costs more than it's worth. Thus, to maximize profit, *McDonald's will hire janitors so long as the increase in revenue from hiring an additional janitor exceeds the janitor's wage.*

To make that more concrete, let's consider the marginal product of labor as we vary the number of janitors, as in Table 14.1.

TABLE 14.1 The Marginal Product of Labor

Number of Cleaners	Task	Marginal Product of Labor (MPL per hour)
One	Clean restrooms, once a day.	$35
Two	Empty trash.	$30
Three	Clean restrooms, twice a day.	$24
Four	Wash floors.	$20
Five	Pick up outside trash.	$16
Six	Clean restrooms, three times a day.	$12
Seven	Clean windows.	$11
Eight	Remove gum from the bottom of tables.	$8

You'll notice a few things about these numbers. First, the marginal product of labor generally declines as more labor is hired. If there is one janitor, he or she will focus on the most important tasks so the marginal product of labor is high. As McDonald's adds janitors, each subsequent janitor is assigned to a less important task so the marginal product of labor falls.

We can see from Table 14.1 that if McDonald's hires three janitors, then the marginal product of labor (per hour) is $24. If McDonald's hires four janitors, the marginal product of labor is $20 and so forth. But how many janitors will McDonald's hire? That depends on the wage.

If a janitor's wage is above $35 an hour, then McDonald's will hire zero janitors. If the wage falls to say $32 an hour, McDonald's will compare the additional revenues from hiring a janitor (the MPL), $35 an hour, with the cost of hiring the janitor, $32 an hour. Since the MPL is greater than the wage, W, McDonald's will make the hire. If the wage falls to $28, McDonald's will hire a second janitor. If the wage falls to $22, McDonald's will hire a third janitor and so forth.

Notice that when the wage falls, McDonald's hires more janitors and assigns them to less important tasks so as the wage falls so does the MPL. The wage and the marginal product of labor will always be very close together since McDonald's will keep hiring workers so long as the MPL is greater than W.

If we know the marginal product of labor, we can derive the demand curve for labor. In Figure 14.1, for example, we show McDonald's demand curve for janitors. From the figure and from Table 14.1 you can see that if the wage is $10 then McDonald's will hire seven janitors.

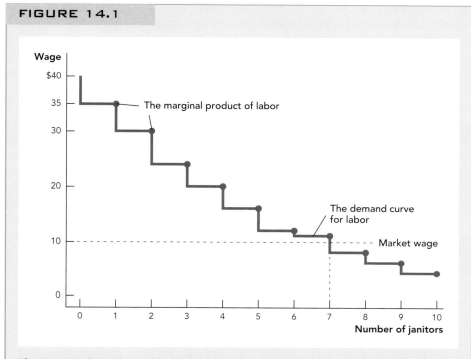

FIGURE 14.1

The Marginal Product of Labor Determines a Firm's Demand Curve for Labor
The marginal product of the first janitor is $35. If the wage is above $35, McDonald's will hire no janitors. If the wage falls to just below $35, McDonald's will find it profitable to hire one janitor. The marginal product of the second janitor is $30. If the wage falls below $30, McDonald's will hire its second janitor. If the wage falls below $24, McDonald's will find it profitable to add a third janitor and so forth.

Of course, we still have not explained what determines the wage. To do that we need to remember that many firms demand janitors, so the wage of janitors will be determined by the *market* demand and supply of janitors. But don't worry, the market demand for janitors is very similar to McDonald's demand for janitors. At a high wage, only some firms (and some consumers, such as the very wealthy) will demand janitors. As the wage falls, more and more firms will demand janitors and each firm will demand more janitors, as we saw with McDonald's. Thus, the market demand for cleaners is downward sloping as usual.

Supply of Labor

The market supply curve for labor will be upward sloping, again as usual. In other words, high wages encourage a greater supply of labor. That's intuitive but we do have to take into account one complication. An *individual's* labor supply curve need not slope upward throughout its range. When Bruce Springsteen was

CHECK YOURSELF

> Why does the marginal product of labor fall as more workers are hired?

paid $100 a night, he toured constantly just to pay the rent. Now that he is paid hundreds of thousands of dollars a night, Springsteen tours less often. If his wage is already high, even Joe the cleaner might decide that he would prefer to spend more time with his family to working more hours at an even higher wage rate.

Figure 14.2 illustrates. In Panel A, if the wage is between $7 and $16 an hour, Joe works 40 hours a week so over this range Joe's supply curve for labor is vertical. If the wage rises to $20 an hour, Joe is willing to work overtime and he puts in 50 hours a week (a positively-sloped labor supply curve). At $20 an hour, Joe is making a comfortable income—enough so that if his wage rises even further Joe would prefer to work fewer hours and instead enjoy the money he is making by taking more leisure time. Thus, it is quite plausible that as the wage rises to $28 an hour, Joe asks his bosses for less overtime (a negatively-sloped or backward-bending labor supply curve).

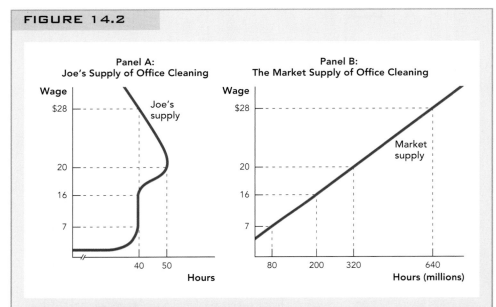

FIGURE 14.2

The Individual and Market Supply of Labor
Panel A: For a wage between $7 and $16 an hour, Joe works 40 hours a week. For $20 an hour, however, Joe is willing to work 50 hours a week but as the wage increases, Joe takes more of his income in the form of leisure and works less—thus, over a higher range, Joe's labor supply curve may be backward bending.
Panel B: The labor supply curve for the market is positively-sloped throughout because even if Joe works less as the wage rises (over some range), many other workers enter the office cleaning industry as the wage rises.

Although Joe's supply curve for labor could have a zero, positive, or even negative slope the market supply curve for labor is very likely to be positively sloped. Why? Let's go back to when Joe was earning $7 an hour and putting in 40 hours a week. When the wage rises to $16 an hour, Joe doesn't work more hours; but, at a higher wage, Mary, who was working in the restaurant business, is likely to switch into office cleaning. Thus, in Panel B we show the market supply of janitors. When the wage increases, the market supply increases for two reasons: First, some workers—although not all—are likely to work more as the wage increases. Second, and more important, when the wages of janitors increases that attracts workers from other industries. Together these two factors mean that even if some individuals supply less labor at a higher wage, a higher wage increases the quantity of labor supplied overall.

Thus, an upward sloping *market* supply curve is the normal situation.

We can now put together the supply and demand for janitors in the usual fashion to represent the market for janitors.

In the United States, there are about 4.2 million janitors each working about 40 hours a week (168 million hours a week in total) who earn an average wage of $10 an hour. Thus, the market for janitors can be represented in Figure 14.3. As usual, the price (wage) is found at the intersection of the demand for janitors and the supply of janitors.

By the way, recall that we said earlier that the wage and the marginal product of labor will always be very close together. That is because a firm will keep hiring workers so long as the MPL is greater than W. When we think about many firms and many workers it often simplifies things to say that the MPL = W. Thus, we know that in the United States, the marginal product of a janitor is about $10 an hour.

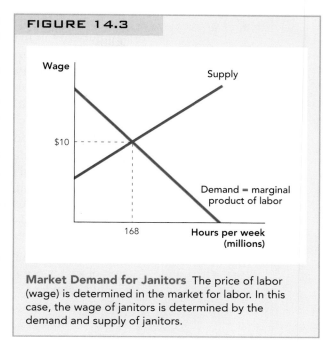

FIGURE 14.3

Market Demand for Janitors The price of labor (wage) is determined in the market for labor. In this case, the wage of janitors is determined by the demand and supply of janitors.

CHECK YOURSELF

> Why might an individual's supply of labor curve be backward bending? Explain.

Labor Market Issues

Now that we know the basic principles underlying the demand and supply of labor, let's turn to some specific questions and issues that our principles can help us to understand.

Why Do Janitors in the United States Earn More Than Janitors in India even When They Do the Same Job?

The short answer for why janitors in the United States earn more for the same type of work as janitors in India is that the janitors in the United States are working for very productive firms, such as McDonald's. The productivity of American firms and offices in general raises the marginal product of labor and thus the wages of American janitors. Indian janitors might work as hard or harder than American janitors but they are less productive and have lower wages because they work in a less productive economy.

Let's look at the differences between the typical American and Indian office building a little more closely. The American office building has more and better equipment, more fax machines, more computers, and more copiers. Overall, there is more capital invested in the American workplace, and American office workers on average are better educated than office workers in India. That makes the American office building more productive. The American office building also has a better marketing department, longer global reach for its sales force, and greater investment in building up the brand name of the product. Most important, the American office is producing a more valuable product.

Since it's more valuable to keep a productive workplace clean than to keep a less productive workplace clean, the wages of American janitors are higher than those in India.

To put it in a single sentence, the American janitor gets the benefit of productivity in many other sectors of the American economy. A typical janitor in India might earn less than $1,000 per year. That same worker, if he wins the green card lottery and comes to the United States, might instead earn over $20,000 in a similar job or even up to $30,000, depending on location and hours. It's not that he has suddenly learned new cleaning techniques but rather that he is working in a more productive economy.

There is no doubt that you are a very productive person—perhaps you know how to use a computer, you have some artistic talents and can write well. Now look around the world—how much would these skills earn you in another country? Your skills are yours alone but your wage is determined not by your skills alone but by the productivity of the entire economy.

Of course, wages are about supply as well as demand. India has more workers than the United States, but what's more important than India's total population is that India has a great many low-skilled workers who eagerly compete for the job of janitor. A much greater proportion of Indians than Americans, for example, would consider a cleaning job in a modern office building to be a very attractive job. Since many Indians compete for the job of janitor, the wages of janitors are pushed down.

Figure 14.4 shows the two reasons why the wages of janitors are lower in India than in the United States. First, the demand for janitors is higher in the

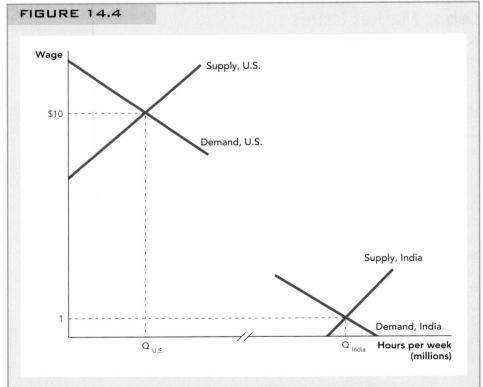

FIGURE 14.4

Wages for Janitors in India and the United States Wages for janitors are higher in the United States than in India because (a) U.S. firms overall are more productive than Indian firms, which raises the demand for janitors and (b) the supply of low-skilled labor is much larger in India than in the United States.

United States because U.S. firms are more productive than firms in India overall. Second, the supply of low-skilled labor in India is higher than in the United States.

Human Capital

Americans are fortunate to work in a productive economy. But high wages are not just the result of fortunes of birth. Wages within America differ greatly from worker to worker so let's look at some of the reasons why.

Some workers have higher wages than others because they have more human capital. Physical capital is tools like computers, bulldozers, and fax machines. **Human capital** is tools of the mind, the stuff in people's heads that makes them productive. Human capital is not something we are born with—it is produced by investing time and other resources in education, training, and experience.

Of course, investing in human capital usually costs money; it costs not just what a doctor spends on medical school tuition but what he or she could have earned during those eight years in medical school, namely, opportunity cost. But, in general, investments in human capital bring a good return in the United States. In recent years, college graduates have made almost twice as much as high school graduates.

The left panel of Figure 14.5 shows annual wages by education level in 2005. Clearly more education, on average, brings a higher wage.

The right panel shows that the return to a college education has been rising over time. College pays off much more now than ever before. The top line is

Human capital is tools of the mind, the stuff in people's heads that makes them productive.

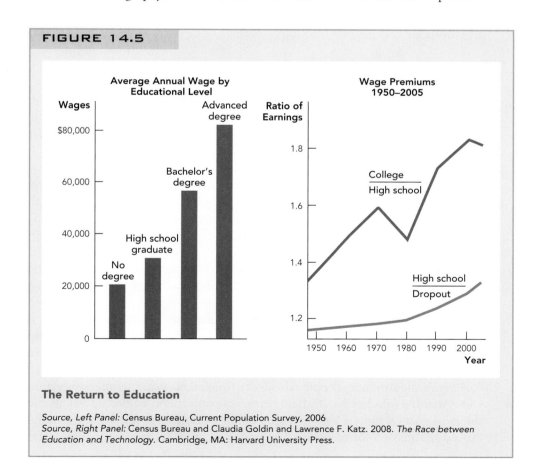

FIGURE 14.5

The Return to Education

Source, Left Panel: Census Bureau, Current Population Survey, 2006
Source, Right Panel: Census Bureau and Claudia Goldin and Lawrence F. Katz. 2008. *The Race between Education and Technology.* Cambridge, MA: Harvard University Press.

the ratio of the wages of college graduates to that of high school graduates, or the "college wage premium." The bottom line reflects how much it is worth to have a high school diploma, relative to dropping out. The returns to education are rising across the board, but nowadays college is especially important.

Why is the return to human capital rising so strongly? Some economists believe that the ability to work with computers has made an education more valuable than in times past, but overall we do not know for sure. Another hypothesis is that bottlenecks in the U.S. system of grade school education are lowering student quality and thus limiting the flow of new people into the ranks of the college educated, thus raising the return to a college education. In any case, it's more important to finish college than it used to be, at least in terms of the wages you can expect to earn.

We should also mention that the return to education is not just about human capital. Have you ever wondered why an art history major earns a higher income than a high school graduate even though neither works in the field of art history? An employer may want to hire someone with a college degree not because of anything they learn at college but because the very fact that they have earned a degree signals to the employer something good about the job candidate, namely that they have enough intelligence, competence, and conscientiousness to earn a college degree. For the same reasons, if you have ever run an Ironman triathlon you might want to subtly indicate that on your resume (say under interests) even if the job you are applying for requires no athletic ability. Competing in an Ironman triathlon doesn't increase your productivity at say managing an advertising department, but it does indicate that you are the type of person who doesn't give up easily and that is a characteristic that employers are seeking.

Compensating Differentials

The supply of labor depends on the real wage but the real wage of a job includes not just the monetary pay but also how fun the job is. Some people work for nice bosses; others work for tyrants. Some jobs are dangerous; others are very safe. Some jobs are fun; others are a bore.

Right now being a fisherman is the most dangerous job in the United States, more dangerous than being a police officer or a firefighter. There are a lot of accidents out on the water. Most of all, a lot of people just slip and fall overboard. Being a truck driver is dangerous too, mostly because of road accidents. That's why those professions earn relatively high wages, especially given that they do not demand a college degree.[1]

It's simple supply and demand. The danger of a dangerous job reduces the supply of labor, pushing the supply curve for labor to the left and up, as shown in Figure 14.6.

The resulting wage is higher than it otherwise would be, and that is what economists call a compensating differential. It is called a **compensating differential** because a difference in wages compensates for the difference in working conditions.

A **compensating differential** is a difference in wages that offsets differences in working conditions.

There's a lesson here. People talk all the time about wanting interesting, fun, and rewarding jobs but *beware*: Being an accountant might be boring but all else the same that's a sign of higher wages. Being a musician is fun but most musicians don't make a lot of money. The higher wage of accountants compensates for the lack of fun or, equivalently, the greater fun of being an artist compensates for the lack of money.

To see this in more detail, consider the following principle: *similar jobs must have similar compensation packages*. Imagine that being an accountant and a musician require similar amounts of skill, education, training, and so forth. Now what would happen if musicians were paid higher wages than accountants? Higher wages *and* more fun can't be beat so the supply of musicians will increase and the supply of accountants will decrease. But the increased supply of musicians will drive the wages of musicians down and the decreased supply of accountants will drive the wages of accountants up. In fact, musician wages will fall and accountant wages will rise until a typical young person deciding on a career will be more or less indifferent: higher wages and less fun equals lower wages and more fun. Figure 14.7 illustrates the main idea.

Every job has a different combination of wages, benefits, fun, risk, and other conditions. Some workers will choose jobs with less risk but lower wages while others will prefer jobs with more risk but higher wages. In fact, workers who choose the less risky jobs are "buying" safety with a reduction in their wages. Now consider, who is more likely to buy safety, a rich worker or a poor worker?

FIGURE 14.6

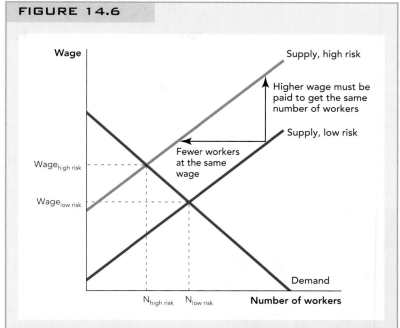

Riskier Jobs Pay More, All Else Being Equal Increased risk reduces the supply of labor—that is, the supply curve for labor shifts up and to the left—increasing the wage.

FIGURE 14.7

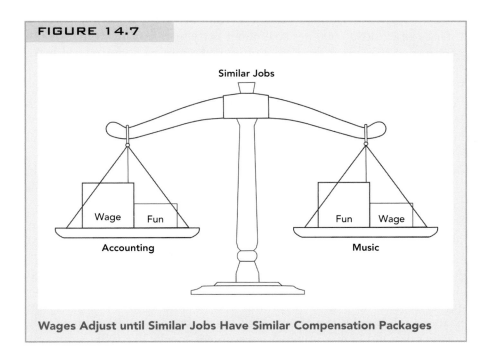

Wages Adjust until Similar Jobs Have Similar Compensation Packages

The rich buy more safety for the same reason they buy more BMWs—buying safety is one of the things that money is good for! We've already noted that being a fisherman is a dangerous job. It should come as no surprise that many of these fishermen are recent immigrants to the United States. But it's not the immigrants from wealthy Sweden who take the fishing jobs. Instead it's poor immigrants from Honduras who concentrate in the fishing trade. These poorer immigrants need the money the most and are less willing to buy safety by taking jobs with lower wages.

The same reasoning explains why jobs in the United States are much safer than similar jobs in poorer countries. Workers in the United States use their wealth to buy more smoke detectors, fire extinguishers, and airbags on their cars and they also "buy" more job safety. Thus, one of the most important reasons why job safety increases over time is economic growth.

In other words, workers become less willing to accept risk as economic growth makes them wealthier. You might take a dangerous job if you need the money to feed your family but not if you need the money to feed your family at *The French Laundry*, one of the best and most expensive restaurants in the United States.

Coal mining is a tough job anywhere, but in China the death rate per ton of coal is more than 100 times higher than in the United States.

Government regulation has improved the quality of American jobs as well (see further below), but increasing wealth and the profit incentive are the main drivers behind this process. Are you surprised that the pursuit of profit leads to *greater* job safety? Remember that firms must pay workers to take on higher risks, the compensating differentials we talked about earlier. But the process works the other way just as well—when firms make jobs safer they can pay lower wages, thus increasing their profits.

Take a job like coal mining. An American coal miner will earn between $50,000 to $80,000 annually, let's say for purposes of argument $70,000.[2] If that sounds like a pretty good wage to you, it is because coal mining is not especially fun. But how much would wages have to be if coal mining in the United States were as dangerous as in China, where the mortality rate per ton of coal is 100 times higher? Coal miners might demand $100,000 to take on the extra risk. That's an extra $30,000 per coal miner per year that firms would have to pay because of riskier working conditions. If the mining company can make the mines safer for less than that, obviously their incentive is to invest in safety.

Economists have estimated how much more firms must pay American workers to take on risk and the numbers are very large, by one estimate $245 billion in recent years. In comparison, OSHA, the Occupational Safety and Health Administration, which oversees workplace safety, levies fines every year of about $150 million. These numbers imply that fear of government fines is not that big a cost, compared to having to pay higher wages for riskier jobs. In other words, market competition—employers luring laborers by paying wages—is the major factor in making jobs safer.

So, as workers become wealthier and less willing to take on risk, firms have greater incentives to increase job safety—which explains why jobs are safer today than they were in the past and why jobs are safer in wealthier countries than in poorer countries. The pursuit of profit doesn't always lead to greater safety, which is why government regulation also has a role to play. Compensating differentials give firms an incentive to increase safety only if workers *know* that a job is risky. If workers don't know about or underestimate risk, they won't demand higher wages. A government agency like OSHA can help to ensure that firms do not hide job risks. Even more important, in the

United States, firms are required to buy workers compensation insurance—which pays workers for on-the-job injuries. Crucially, the premiums that firms must pay to buy this insurance are *experienced-based,* which means that the more injuries a firm has, the more it must pay for insurance. Thus, workers compensation programs give firms an incentive to reduce risk so they can save money on insurance. Since the insurance premiums a firm must pay are based on actual injuries, this incentive works even when workers do not know or underestimate risk.

Do Unions Raise Wages?

It is commonly suggested that unions are a fundamental reason why wages are so high in some countries and so low in other countries. Yet the evidence does not bear out this view. The more unionized countries do not obviously have higher levels of wages. For instance, the United States and Switzerland have much lower levels of unionization (13 percent and 25 percent, respectively, as of 2009) than does most of Western Europe, where unionization rates can run between 30 percent and 80 percent. Yet the United States and Switzerland have equally high or higher wage levels.

It is true that wages in unionized jobs tend to be higher than in nonunionized jobs for similar workers. Studies that compare the wage of unionized electricians to the wages of nonunionized electricians, for example, typically find that unionized electricians have wages about 10 to 15 percent higher than nonunionized electricians. But this doesn't mean that unions could raise wages in all jobs because the primary method that unions use to raise wages is to reduce industry employment.[3]

If you are wondering how unions raise wages and reduce employment, it is easy to see on a supply and demand graph. By restricting their membership and threatening to strike unless employers hire union labor, unions reduce the supply of labor to an industry. The reduction in labor supply shifts the supply curve for labor to the left and up as shown in Figure 14.8. Notice that the reduction in the supply of labor increases wages but reduces employment from $N_{without\ union}$ to $N_{with\ union}$.

Unions can be beneficial in ensuring that employees are treated fairly and by improving labor/management relations, but the main reason that unions raise wages is through restricting the supply of labor. In this respect, a union is quite similar to a cartel, like those we discussed in Chapter 13. The OPEC oil cartel raises the price of oil by restricting the supply of oil and unions raise the wages of labor by restricting the supply of labor.

Unions also can lower wages, although this effect is harder to see. First, consider what happens to the workers who are not hired in the unionized industry—these workers must seek employment in other

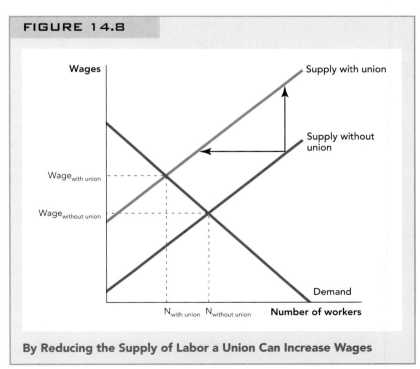

FIGURE 14.8

By Reducing the Supply of Labor a Union Can Increase Wages

industries, which increases the supply of labor to those other industries and drives wages down. Second, unions sometimes bring strikes and work stoppages, which can slow down an entire economy. For instance, the British economy was highly unionized from 1970 to 1982; this coincided with Britain's period of long economic decline relative to other nations.[4] In 1970, dockworkers were on strike for so long that it shut down almost all of Britain's main ports. Coal miners went on strike in 1972, which led to a shortage of electricity. A three-day workweek was implemented for a short time to save power. In 1974, the miners went on strike again and a shortened workweek was implemented again. Ten years later, they had another strike that lasted for almost one year. Prime Minister Margaret Thatcher limited the government-supplied privileges of the British unions during the 1980s. Since that time, Britain has grown rapidly and is now a wealthier country than the more unionized France or Germany.

You've probably also experienced or heard about work stoppages in professional sports (baseball players struck in 1972, 1980, 1981, 1985, and 1994–1995; the NBA lockout of 1998–1999; the NFL strike of 1987), or you may remember the Hollywood writer's strike of 2007–2008. When they don't broadcast your favorite TV shows, the quality of your cable TV package goes down, or in other words its real price goes up. That means that the real wages of everyone buying cable TV are worth that much less. That's just one small example, but enough work stoppages of this kind and the entire economy is much poorer. So labor unions can hurt workers just as they can help them; it's just that the help is immediately evident while the harm is longer term and harder to see.

When people think of unions they often think of the longshoreman's union or a union of electricians, but it's important to remember that doctors, lawyers, dentists, accountants, and other professionals have their own type of union, called a professional association. The American Medical Association (AMA), for example, works to restrict the supply of physicians for the same reason that an electrician's union works to reduce the supply of electricians. It's very difficult to get into a medical school, for example. The AMA says that restricting the supply of physicians is necessary to maintain high standards. Maybe that is true, but restricting the supply of physicians also maintains high wages. The AMA lobbies for laws that make competing against physicians more difficult; for instance they restrict the procedures that can be legally performed by nurse practitioners, midwives, chiropractors, and pharmacists and they make it more difficult for foreign-educated physicians to practice in the United States. As noted, the AMA says that restrictions are necessary to maintain quality and there is some truth to this claim but as always you should be somewhat skeptical when members of a group claim that their high wages are good for you!

The bottom line is this: Unions can raise the wages of particular classes of workers, but unions are not the fundamental reason why wages are high in the wealthy countries.

How Bad Is Labor Market Discrimination, or Can Lakisha Catch a Break?

We all think we know what discrimination is. Discrimination is *bad*. Discrimination is what racists and bigots do. And, yes, that is partly right: Discrimination

CHECK YOURSELF

> Suppose a new and cheap technology increases mine safety. What do you predict will happen to the wages of mine workers?

> Firms often help their employees improve their human capital by offering courses on things such as inventory management or underwriting the tuition for advanced degrees such as an MBA. Firms often attach strings for the MBA education, such as requiring that a supported-MBA stay at the firm for an additional five years. Firms usually do not attach any strings for an inventory management course. Why the difference?

often is morally objectionable. It's also true that there are different types of discrimination and not all discrimination is motivated by prejudice. Let's take a closer look at two major types of discrimination, statistical discrimination and preference-based discrimination.

Statistical Discrimination

Let's say you are walking down a dark alley, late at night, in the warehouse district of your city. Suddenly you hear footsteps behind you. You turn around and you see an old lady walking her dachshund. Do you breathe a sigh of relief? Probably. Would you breathe the same sigh of relief if you saw an angry young man in a dark leather jacket, muttering to himself? What if he was holding a knife? What if he was walking with his two-year-old daughter in a baby stroller?

One way of reading this story is to claim that you are discriminating against young men, relative to old ladies, or relative to young men with baby girls at their side. Another way of describing this story is that you are using information rationally. An angry young man in a leather jacket is far more likely to mug you than is an old lady walking her dachshund. Maybe both descriptions capture some aspect of the reality, but suddenly discrimination isn't so simple a concept anymore.

Statistical discrimination is using information about group averages to make conclusions about individuals. Not every young man in a leather jacket walking the warehouse district late at night is a mugger and not every young man with a baby girl at his side is safe, but that's the way to bet. While statistical discrimination is a useful shorthand for making some decisions, it also causes people to make many errors. They refuse to deal with some people that they really ought to be dealing with. They may refuse to hire some people who deserve the job. We gave one example of this earlier—employers may not look carefully at workers without college degrees even though some of these workers are just as intelligent and industrious as those with college degrees. It is called statistical discrimination because, in essence, the employer is treating the worker as an abstract statistic. Even though statistical discrimination is not motivated by malice, its long-run consequences can be harmful to the penalized groups.

Over time, markets tend to develop more subtle and more finely grained ways of judging people and judging job candidates. An employer can give prospective employees multiple interviews, psychological tests, Google previous histories or writings, look up people on Facebook, ask for more references, and so on, all to get an accurate picture of the person. Eventually these practices break down the crudest methods of statistical discrimination but, of course, some statistical discrimination always remains.

Statistical discrimination tends to be most persistent when people meet in purely casual settings with no repeat interactions, such as in a dark alley late at night. It is profit-seeking employers, who make money from finding and keeping the best workers, who have the greatest incentive to overcome unfairness.

Preference-based Discrimination

A second kind of discrimination—preference-based discrimination—is based on a plain, flat-out dislike of some group of people, such as a race, religion, or

Statistical discrimination is using information about group averages to make conclusions about individuals.

How many times a day do you discriminate?

gender. We're going to lay out three different kinds of preference-based discrimination: discrimination by employers, discrimination by customers, and discrimination by employees. The first of these is easiest for a market economy to overcome while the last is the most difficult to solve.

Discrimination by Employers When most people think of discrimination, they think of an employer with bigoted tastes. Some employers just don't want to hire people of a particular race, ethnicity, religion, or gender. If this discrimination is widespread, the wages of people who are discriminated against will fall since the demand for their labor falls. But fortunately, this kind of discrimination, if taken alone, tends to break down for two reasons: employer discrimination is expensive to the employer and it leaves the bigot open to being outcompeted.

Imagine, for example, that black workers are widely discriminated against and thus that their wages are lower than white workers. Say that a firm can hire white workers for $10 an hour or equally productive black workers for $8 an hour. Imagine that the firm needs 100 workers. If it hires black workers instead of white workers, the firm can increase its profits by $2 per hour per worker. Thus, by hiring black workers, the firm can increase its profits by $1,600 per day ($2 saving per hour for 100 workers for 8 hours a day), $8,000 per week (5 days a week), or $400,000 in a year (50 working weeks). That's a lot of money to give up just so the employer can indulge his or her prejudice.

Even if some employers discriminate, that gives other employers a chance to hire black workers and increase their profits. As profit-hungry employers compete for underpaid, discriminated against workers, the wages of those workers will rise until wages are close to marginal product for all workers, as we described above.

In 1947, Brooklyn Dodgers General Manager Branch Rickey hired Jackie Robinson to be the first black player in modern major league baseball. Robinson already had extensive experience in what were then called the Negro Leagues, and he proved to be an immediate star. Robinson won the Rookie of the Year award and then in his third season he won the MVP award. The first black player in the American League, Larry Doby, proved to be a star for the Cleveland Indians. The baseball teams that moved first to hire black players had a competitive advantage and eventually all the teams had to follow, whether or not they were run by bigots.

Of course, that story is about baseball, but it applies to the broader world of business as well. If employer-driven discrimination is unjustly depressing the wages of a group of people, you can make money by hiring them.

If the pursuit of profit raises wages so that all workers earn their marginal product, why do women earn less than men? It's often said, for example, that women earn about 80 cents per dollar earned by men. The trouble with this widely reported statistic, however, is that it compares the wages of all women with those of all men—the statistic does not mean that a woman with the same qualifications earns less than a man for doing the same job.

One factor lowering wages for women as a group is that women tend to have less job experience than men of the same age because they sometimes leave the job force, typically to take care of children. In fact, if we compare the wages of single men and single women, single women earn just as much as single men. Married women without children also earn about as much as married men without children.

An All-Star Game to Remember (left to right): Roy Campanella, Larry Doby, Don Newcombe, and Jackie Robinson.

Men may also have specialized in higher-paying fields and they take more dangerous jobs. Remember those coal miners we discussed earlier with an average wage of $70,000? Most of them are men, perhaps because women prefer jobs with lower wages but less risk.

Over time, women have moved toward higher-paying sectors (more lawyers and economists, for instance) and there has been a long decline in the birth rate. Since women are having fewer children and they are having their children at later ages, that is helping women earn higher wages.

Nevertheless, some discrimination against women may yet remain but it is probably more subtle than employer discrimination. We need to look at the roles of customers and employees to better understand other forms of discrimination.

Discrimination by Customers   When the customers drive discrimination, owners are not always so keen to hire undervalued, victimized workers. If employing underpaid black workers upsets the customers, it's not a surefire way for an employer to earn more money.

Let's revisit the story of Jackie Robinson and Branch Rickey, discussed above. You might wonder why Branch Rickey hired Robinson in 1947 but not 1946. It's not that one day Branch Rickey stopped being prejudiced against African Americans; he may not have been prejudiced in the first place. Rather in 1947, Rickey sensed that his ticket-buying customers were ready for the idea of watching a black man play baseball in a Brooklyn Dodgers uniform. The lesson is that sometimes discrimination comes from the customers of a business, not always from the owners or managers.

Or, let's consider a lunch counter or hamburger joint in the Deep South in 1957, before the civil rights movement had much influence. Part of the problem was that state laws did not allow mixed-race establishments. But part of the problem came from customers as well. At that time, many white customers didn't like the idea of eating a hamburger while sitting next to a black man. These white customers demanded separate facilities, so usually there were separate lunch counters and separate restaurants for white and black people in many parts of the United States. The entrepreneur running the lunch counter may or may not have been racist, but in any case the preferences of his customers encouraged him to discriminate and to keep out black patrons.

Don't make the mistake of thinking customer-based discrimination has vanished from modern America. It's usually done in a more subtle manner, but many country clubs, restaurants, and other businesses try to encourage "the right kind of customers." They're not always concerned about race per se, but often they seek customers who dress a certain way, have the right kind of jobs, come from the right part of town, and so on. The result is sometimes a de facto segregation, even though the restaurant or country club owner is simply responding to the preferences of his consumers for a particular cultural style or "feel."

By the way, the decline of employer-based discrimination, through market forces, also tends to weaken customer-based discrimination. Marketplace transactions bring different groups into regular contact with each other. Many white people who started listening to black music on the jukebox in the 1950s, or who saw Jackie Robinson play baseball, started asking themselves what was so wrong with integrated lunch counters. Discrimination is also weakened by economic growth more generally. For instance, declining costs of production make it possible for businesses to take more chances. If a small town has only two lunch counters, maybe neither will take a chance with integration. If the town grows and also the costs of starting a new business fall, suddenly there are seven lunch counters. Maybe one will experiment with integration. In the long run, no successful market economy has succeeded in maintaining formal segregation on a widespread basis.

Discrimination by Employees   Customers and employers aren't the only possible sources of discrimination. Sometimes workers don't want to mix with people from different groups. In India, many workers don't want to work alongside Dalits, workers from a low caste who are considered impure. In the United States, some firefighters—rightly or wrongly—don't want women to have equal status in the firehouse. Similarly, some men in the armed forces don't think that women should serve in combat and some men are looked on with suspicion if they want to work at a daycare center.

The profit incentive doesn't necessarily break down discrimination of this kind. An employer in India who hires Dalits, for example, may find that he has to pay other workers a higher wage to compensate them for the negative of working with Dalits. As a result, it's cheaper to discriminate than to hire everyone equally. Similarly, if you hire a woman into an all-male firehouse that doesn't want women, morale may fall and some men may leave for other jobs. As a result, employers are less likely to hire a person, even a productive person, from the victimized group.

Of course, an employer might hire only Dalits or if women are not welcome in firehouses an employer may set up an entirely new firehouse, one equipped with women and non-prejudicial men, but starting from scratch in this fashion isn't always so easy to do.

Discrimination of this kind can be self-reinforcing and difficult to identify. If it's unpleasant for women to work in firehouses, then many women who want to be firefighters won't want to work in firehouses. Few women are hired but employers might say that's because few women are applying. Maybe it won't look like discrimination at all but discrimination will still be a force at work.

Discrimination by Government   So far we've been talking about discrimination in markets but it's important to remember that governments discriminate too. Government is sometimes part of the problem rather than part of the solution. We've already mentioned that pro-segregation policies in the American South, before the civil rights movement, often came from governments. Governments required separate hospitals for black and white patients, separate public and private schools, separate churches, separate cemeteries, separate public restrooms, and separate restaurants, hotels, and train service. Before pro-segregation laws were passed after the Civil War, many parts of the South were moving (albeit sometimes hesitantly) toward more integration.

The best-known example of widespread government segregation was the apartheid system of South Africa, which was enforced from 1948 until the early 1990s. ("Apartheid" is a word in the Afrikaaner language; it translates literally as "apartness.") Under this arrangement, black people had to live in special areas and could not compete with white workers for many jobs. But this highly unjust situation was enforced by government laws, and enacted by white minority governments (black citizens also couldn't vote). Once those laws were removed, black people moved into many jobs and received higher wages. Many forms of implicit segregation continue in South Africa, but many of the most egregious examples of discrimination have fallen away. Many employers are happy to hire the most productive workers they can find, regardless of the skin color or ethnic background of those workers.

Why Discrimination Isn't Always Easy to Identify

Two economists had a neat idea. They sent around two sets of identical resumes. On one set of resumes, the names were quite traditional and did not identify the background of the person applying. An applicant named "John Smith," for instance, could be either white or black. The second set of resumes had more unusual names on them. They had names like "Lakisha Washington" or "Jamal Jones." As you may know, those are names closely associated with African Americans. Names can tell you a lot about who a person is. In recent years, more than 40 percent of the black girls born in California were given names that, in those same years, not one of the roughly 100,000 white newly born California girls was given.*

The result was striking: The resumes with the black names received many fewer interview requests. The job applicants with the "whiter" names received 50 percent more calls.

But that is not the end of the story. Steven Levitt (of *Freakonomics* fame) and Roland Fryer, a Harvard professor and an African American, set out to test how much African American names really mattered in the long run for earnings. It seems that having a "black name" does not appear to hurt a person's chances in life, once the neighborhood that person comes from is controlled for. In other words, the number of interviews a person gets at first may not matter so much in the long run. Levitt and Fryer consider two possibilities. It may be that the so-called black names get fewer interviews, but they end up with jobs of equal quality. Alternatively, people with African American sounding names may have fewer chances in white communities but greater chances in black communities; the two tendencies might balance each other out.

One point to note is that in the resume experiment by far the most common outcome of submitting a resume, for both the white and black candidates and regardless of name, was not getting any interview requests at all. The lesson is that just about everyone can expect a lot of rejection before they find the job that is right for them.

Other economists have tested labor market discrimination in the world of sports. Basketball teams, it seems, do not discriminate against black players. Depending on how racial categories are defined, about 75 percent to 80 percent of the NBA is black, which includes African Americans, Africans, and Brazilians of African descent. If anything, there has been statistical discrimination against (usually white) European players, who are sometimes considered, rightly or wrongly, as "soft on defense." In baseball, large numbers of players from the Dominican Republic have ended up as shortstops, including superstars Miguel Tejada and Alex Rodriguez (before moving to third base) and more recent notables Jose Reyes and Hanley Ramirez.

*That is from Bertrand, Marianne and Sendhil Mullainathan. 2004. "Are Emily and Greg More Employable than Lakisha and Jamal? A Field Experiment on Labor Market Discrimination." *The American Economic Review*, 94(4):991–1013. For the earnings study, see Fryer, Jr., Roland G. and Steven D. Levitt. 2002. "The Causes and Consequences of Distinctively Black Names." *Quarterly Journal of Economics*, 119(3):767–805.

Did the man on the left get the better deal?

> From a profit-making perspective, why is employer discrimination just plain dumb?

> Of the three types of discrimination—employer, customer, employee—which has been affected most by market economies? Which has been affected least? Why?

CHECK YOURSELF

Did you know that good-looking people earn more, even if they have the same job credentials? That's right, good-looking people earn about 5 percent more. Tall people earn more too, again if they are compared to shorter people with the same paper credentials. Under one account, an extra inch in height translates into a 1.8 percent increase in wages.[*]

But these studies also show just how hard it is to identify true discrimination. For instance, maybe tall people are paid more because they are more self-confident and not because anyone discriminates against shorter people. One study found that what best predicts wages, in this context, is *the height a man had at the time of high school* and not the height he ends up with as an adult. So if you were a tall person in high school, maybe that built up your self-confidence and makes you a better leader today, even if you stopped growing while your friends kept on getting taller.[†]

One question is why employers might prefer to hire tall people and to pay them more. One possibility is simply that the employer has an unreasonable preference against shorter people. Another possibility is that the employer is subconsciously tricked into thinking the taller leader is better, without ever realizing it. Yet another option is that the taller leader really is better (for the firm), because subordinates are more likely to pay that person respect. Again, we don't know the right answer, and this illustrates just how difficult it is to estimate the scope of labor market discrimination.

In many cases, market forces have succeeded in making some discrimination go away, or at least markets have minimized some of the bad effects of discrimination. But few people doubt that discrimination remains a feature of our world today.

□ Takeaway

It is no accident that workers in some countries earn much more than workers in other countries. Workers in wealthy, high-wage countries work with more physical capital, they have more education and training (human capital), and they work in a more efficient and flexible setting. Those are the fundamental reasons why wages are high.

The theory of compensating differentials explains why fun jobs pay less and dangerous jobs pay more. As wealth increases, workers become more willing to give up money for safety and so job safety increases over time and is higher in wealthier countries than in poorer countries.

Unions can raise some workers' wages, often at the expense of other workers, but unions are not a fundamental reason why wages are high in wealthy countries.

At least two kinds of discrimination occur in labor markets, statistical discrimination and preference-based discrimination. Markets tend to break down discrimination over time, because profit-seeking employers are looking to hire the most productive workers. Nonetheless, this force is imperfect and often discrimination persists.

---

[*] For a survey of this literature, see Engemann, Kristie M. and Michael T. Owyang. April, 2005. "So Much for That Merit Raise: The Link between Wages and Appearance." *The Regional Economist.* http://www.stlouisfed.org/publications/re/2005/b/pdf/appearance.pdf
[†] Persico, Nicola; Andrew Postlewaite, and Dan Silverman. 2004. "The Effect of Adolescent Experience on Labor Market Outcomes: The Case of Height." *Journal of Political Economy,* 112(5):1019–1053.

☐ CHAPTER REVIEW

Marginal product of labor (MPL), p. 289

Human capital, p. 295

Compensating differential, p. 296

Statistical discrimination, p. 301

FACTS AND TOOLS

1. In Chapter 2, we listed six important demand shifters. Since the demand for labor is like the demand for any other good, those same factors apply here. Let's look at factors that might shift the demand for janitors at the McDonald's we discussed. For each case below, state whether labor demand will rise or fall, and also state which of the six factors seems to be causing the shift in demand.

   a. A new junior high school opens up across the street from the McDonald's.

   b. Customers become much more concerned about clean restaurants: They'll walk out if there's dirt on the floor.

   c. As robots like the Roomba vacuum cleaner become cheaper, the McDonald's buys some robots to do half of the janitors' work.

2. Now let's do the same with shifts in Joe's labor supply from Figure 14.2. We listed five important supply shifters in Chapter 2. For each example below, state whether you think Joe's labor supply will tend to increase or decrease as a result of the change, and state which of the five factors seem to cause the supply shift.

   a. The government raises Joe's income tax rate, so now he pays 20 percent of his wages to the government instead of the old 10 percent.

   b. The price of comfortable work shoes falls dramatically. Now, his feet won't ache nearly as much after a full day of work.

   c. While in Las Vegas for the weekend, Joe wins a $1 million jackpot.

3. Let's apply the idea of compensating differentials to janitorial jobs. Suppose there are two quite similar restaurants in the same town, OrangeBee's and the City Inn. Both have the same demand for janitorial labor. But all the janitors in town know that it's much more fun to work at City Inn.

   a. Which restaurant will pay a higher wage for janitors? Why?

   b. Which restaurant will hire more janitors? Why?

4. According to the theory of compensating differentials, which low-skilled jobs in the United States will tend to pay the most:

   a. The safe jobs or the dangerous jobs?

   b. The fun jobs or the boring jobs?

   c. The dead-end jobs or the first-rung-on-the-ladder jobs?

5. As we mentioned, OSHA fines companies for less safe workplaces. At the same time, the labor market also "fines" companies that give their workers dangerous jobs. The fines of the marketplace are larger than the U.S. government's fines by about what factor: A factor of 10, of 100, of 1,000, or of 10,000?

6. The director of human resources at ToyCo is hiring new engineers. She's got a stack of 250 applications, and she's going to do a little research. She sits down and does a little cyber-snooping on all 250, and she finds the following:

   I. Of the 150 who have Facebook pages, 50 are holding a bottle of beer in their profile photo, and 100 aren't.

   II. Of the 100 who have their own websites, 20 have more than two typos.

   III. Of the 150 who have Facebook pages, 25 have at least two friends who have apparently spent time in prison, according to a quick check of public records.

   a. Each of these are cases of sending bad signals. In each case, describe what you think these might be signals of.

   b. In each case, is the bad signal 100 percent correct? For example, is every applicant with three or four typos on their Facebook page worse than every applicant with an error-free page?

   c. In each case, is the bad signal probably better or probably worse than having no signal at all? In other words, should the bad signal get at least a little bit of weight in the balance if the HR director's only goal is to hire the best workers?

7. It is commonly said that women earn 80 cents for every dollar that a man earns, even when doing the same job. Let's assume this is literally

true in order to see how an entrepreneur would respond to this fact.

   a. Netrovia, a battery manufacturer, has an all-male workforce. It pays $10 million per year in salary to these men, and has annual profits of $1 million. You've just been hired as an outside consultant to help Netrovia raise its profits. Your advice is to fire all the men and replace them with women. If Netrovia followed your advice, what would Netrovia's salary costs fall to? How much would this decision raise Netrovia's profits?

   b. After your success at Netrovia, you start getting a lot more consulting jobs. You give the same advice to all the companies looking to boost profits: Fire your men and hire an all-female workforce for 20 percent less. What will this do to the demand for female labor? And what will this tend to do to women's wages?

8. Michael Lynn, a social psychologist in Cornell's School of Hotel Administration, has spent years studying tipping (his homepage has well-tested advice on how to increase your tips). He finds that men tip more when they have a female server, while women tend to tip more when they have a male server. This sounds a lot like discrimination by customers.

   a. If this is a fact, who will tend to apply for jobs waiting tables at truck stops: mostly men or mostly women?

   b. If this is a fact, who will tend to apply for jobs waiting tables at steakhouses: mostly men or mostly women?

   c. If this is a fact, who will tend to apply for jobs waiting tables at vegetarian restaurants: most men or mostly women?

   d. In these three cases, does your experience match up with what this simple theory predicts? If there's a contradiction, what do you think the simple model is missing?

9. True or false:

   a. The marginal product of labor is the amount of extra profit that a firm will earn if it hires one more worker.

   b. The benefit of having a college education has increased since the 1960s.

   c. The wage gap between high school graduates and high school dropouts has fallen since the 1960s.

   d. By definition, a labor supply curve cannot have a negative slope.

   e. Compensating differentials is a government program that pays injured workers.

   f. The main reason that an immigrant earns more when he moves from Algeria to France is because the French have strong labor unions.

   g. If customers are racist and sexist, then self-interest will tend to push entrepreneurs to engage in racist and sexist hiring.

   h. If some employers are bigots but others are not, the bigoted employers will be able to hire good workers for less money and will tend to drive the fair-minded employers out of business.

THINKING AND PROBLEM SOLVING

1. Construction jobs in New Chongqing pay $20 per hour. The job isn't that safe: a lot of sharp objects, a lot of ways to fall off a building. The city council of New Chongqing decides to set some job safety regulations for the construction industry. Let's assume that the government enforces these new regulations effectively and fairly, so that half as many workers get hurt on the job. Let's also assume that the city council makes the taxpayers pay the cost of making these jobs safer, so there's no noticeable shift in the labor demand curve.

   a. After these new job safety regulations come into effect, will workers be more willing to take these jobs than before or less willing than before?

   b. Is that like a rise in the supply of labor or like a fall in the supply of labor?

   c. Let's put it all together: What will these job safety regulations do to the wage for construction jobs in New Chongqing?

   d. What principle from this chapter does this illustrate?

   e. In the United States, OSHA doesn't make the taxpayers pay the cost of making the jobs safer. Instead, OSHA requires employers to spend the money themselves to make the jobs safer. Thus, OSHA requirements work like a tax on labor demand. What would this probably do to the demand curve for construction labor: Would it increase or decrease construction labor demand?

2. One way to think about wages for different jobs is to see it as another application of the law of one price. We came across this law when we discussed speculation in Chapter 5, and it came up again when we discussed international trade in Chapter 8. The basic idea is that the supply of workers will keep adjusting until jobs that need the same kinds of workers earn the same wage. If *similar* workers earned *different* wages, then the workers in the low-paid jobs would reduce their labor supply, and the workers in the high-paid jobs would face more competition from those low-paid workers.

Let's look at 100 computer programmers who are trying to decide whether to work for one of two companies: Robotron or Korrexia. To keep things simple, assume that both companies are equally fun to work for, so you don't need to worry about compensating differentials here. The marginal product of labor (per additional hour of work) is in the table below:

Number of Programmers per Firm	Robotron's MPL	Korrexia's MPL
10	$200	$110
20	$150	$80
30	$120	$60
40	$110	$50
50	$80	$40
60	$60	$20
70	$50	$10
80	$40	$0
90	$20	$0
100	$10	$0

a. These two firms are the whole market for programmer labor. In the table below, estimate the programmer demand curve by adding up the quantity of programmers demanded at each wage. For example, at a wage of $80 per hour, Robotron would hire 50 workers (since the first 50 workers have a MPL ≥ 80) and Korrexia 20, so the total demand is 70 workers.

Wage	Number of Programmers Demanded
$200	10
$150	
$120	
$110	
$80	50 + 20 = 70
$60	
$50	
$40	
$20	
$10	

b. The programmers in this town are going to work at one of these two places for sure: Their labor supply is vertical, or in other words perfectly inelastic, with supply = 100. So, what will the equilibrium wage be? Just as in Figure 14.1, the numbers may not work out exactly—so use your judgment to come up with a good answer.

c. Now, head back to the first table: About how many programmers will work at Robotron and how many at Korrexia? Again, use your judgment to come up with a good answer.

d. Suppose 50 more programmers come to town. What will the wage be now? And how many will work at each firm?

3. We've seen what happens when job safety regulations are imposed. Now let's see what happens when they're taken away.

a. If a radical free market, antiregulation government comes to power in the land of Pelerania, and they begin dismantling job safety regulations, what will this tend to do to the supply of labor for dangerous jobs in Pelerania: will it increase or decrease?

b. Will that push wages in dangerous jobs up or down?

c. What will this do to the supply of labor in safer jobs? And to the number of people working in safer jobs?

d. Overall, will employers have to pay for their decision to offer dangerous jobs, or will they have a free lunch handed to them by the new government?

4. As we saw, unions can raise wages in a sector of the economy by restricting the number of workers in that sector. Let's see what tends to happen to the workers who don't get jobs in those favored unionized sectors. We'll recycle the computer programmer data to illustrate:

Number of Programmers per Firm	Robotron's MPL	Korrexia's MPL
10	$200	$110
20	$150	$80
30	$120	$60
40	$110	$50
50	$80	$40
60	$60	$20
70	$50	$10
80	$40	$0
90	$20	$0
100	$10	$0

a. As before, there are 100 workers. In 2084, after decades of complaining about low wages, the programmers at Robotron have a secret-ballot vote and form a union. Their new union bargains for a wage of $80 per hour, and the newly unionized programmers are very excited. How many workers will Robotron hire at the new, higher wage?

b. How many Robotron workers just got laid off? Compare your answer to part a against the answer to question 2c to find out.

c. A natural choice for the other programmers is to look for work at Korrexia: As before, the remaining workers have perfectly inelastic labor supply, so all 100 workers are going to work at one of the two firms. What's the wage for the nonunion Korrexia workers? How many programmers work for Korrexia?

d. You might think that one solution is to unionize both firms and lift wages for all the programmers. If the unions negotiate a high-wage contract and unionized wages

rise to $110 at both firms, how many of the 100 workers will have jobs?

5. Suppose that we tax CEO salaries very highly, as some are proposing in the United States. What is your prediction about CEO perks such as jets and in-house chefs?

6. a. The average person doesn't like working the night shift. According to the theory of compensating differentials, are night shift wages probably higher or lower than day shift wages?

b. Most companies do their high-skilled work during the day shift: The big meetings, the major deliveries, the crucial repair work gets done during the day. As a result, firms prefer to hire workers with more human capital during day shift work, and they prefer to hire less-skilled workers at night. According to the theory of human capital, are night shift wages probably higher or lower than day shift wages?

c. Just based on these two theories, will night shift work pay more than day shift work on average, will it pay less on average, or can't you tell with the information given?

d. Economist Peter Kostiuk, in a 1990 article in the *Journal of Political Economy*, wanted to see whether the theory of compensating differentials was true for U.S. workers. He had information on the wages, education backgrounds, and work experience of U.S. workers, and he knew whether they worked the day shift or the night shift. On average, those who worked the night shift actually earned about 4 percent *less* than workers on the day shift. Is this probably because of compensating differentials or is it probably because of human capital differences?

e. Kostiuk then used statistical techniques to simulate how much a typical low-skilled worker would earn if he were switched from the day shift to the night shift. The answer? The low-skilled worker would earn 44 percent *more* money on average. Is this 44 percent wage increase caused by lower supply of night shift labor or is it caused by a higher demand for night shift labor?

7. True or false: Morticians are paid lower wages than other workers because very few people want to work with dead bodies.

8. One way that Jim Crow segregation laws operated was by providing worse government schools for black students. This widened the human capital gap between black workers and white workers (this human capital gap has narrowed dramatically since the successes of the 1960s civil rights movement). Would this form of government segregation tend to increase statistical discrimination on the basis of race or lower it? How can you tell?

9. In the United States, it's legal to work for free: We call this an "unpaid internship."

   a. Why will college students take these zero-wage jobs when they could get a minimum wage job instead?

   b. Which idea in this chapter does this sound like?

   c. Just for thought: Why do you think federal law allows people to work for free, but not for $1 per hour? Is it just an oversight on the part of government, or do you think there's some grand design at work?

CHALLENGES

1. In the decades after the Civil War, most streetcar companies in the South discriminated against a class of citizens: smokers. Customers who wanted to smoke had to ride in the back of the car. Around 1900, many governments in the South passed laws mandating segregation by race instead. As Jennifer Roback documented in the *Journal of Economic History* in 1986, many streetcar operators protested against this new form of segregation. Assuming that these entrepreneurs were driven by self-interest alone rather than a desire for equality, why would they do that?

2. We mentioned that "a [college] degree signals. . . something good about the job candidate, namely that they have enough intelligence, competence, and conscientiousness to earn a college degree." This view, put forward by Nobel Laureate Michael Spence, is unsurprisingly known as the signaling theory of education. Taken to the extreme, signaling theorists say that you suffer through college not because you get valuable job skills, but only because it's a good way to prove that you were *already* smart and capable before you started college.

   a. Suppose you want to prove this theory wrong: You want to show that college courses really do make you a better worker, just like the human capital theorists say. How would you go about proving that? Remember, just showing that college graduates earn more isn't evidence!

   b. If that's too hard, at least explain why the following plausible-sounding tests of human capital vs. signaling aren't very good tests at all:

      I. Looking at wages of people with degrees compared to people without degrees

      II. Comparing wages for people whose parents can afford college to wages for people whose parents can't afford college.

3. In a market economy, firms with more workers can make and sell more output—that goes without saying. The marginal product of labor tells you how much extra revenue each extra worker generates. Economists tend to use one particular equation to sum up the link between workers, revenue, and the marginal product of labor: We call it the production function. Let's practice with it just a little here.

   a. At Dunder Mifflin, the hourly revenue production function works like this:

   $$\text{Revenue} = 100 \times \sqrt{(\text{\# of semi-skilled workers})}$$

   This is a way of saying that in order to sell product, you actually need workers to do work. Use this formula to fill out the total revenue column below.

Number of Workers	Total Revenue	Marginal Product of Labor
0	$0	N/A
1	$100	$100
2	$141	$41
3		
4		
5		

   b. As we mentioned in the chapter, the marginal product of labor is the extra revenue that's generated by each extra worker. It's the change in revenue from adding one more worker. Fill out that column as well.

c. If the market wage for semi-skilled workers is $25 per hour, how many workers should Dunder Mifflin hire?

4. In Chapter 7, we analyzed a minimum wage in the usual way, as a price floor, and we showed that a minimum wage creates unemployment. Now suppose that firms must pay the minimum wage but they can adjust the working conditions such as by increasing the pace of work, reducing lunch breaks, cutting back on employee discounts, and so forth. Will the minimum wage create (as much) unemployment if firms adjust in this way? Hint: Think of the balance in Figure 14.7.

15

Getting Incentives Right: Lessons for Business, Sports, Politics, and Life

CHAPTER OUTLINE

Lesson One: You Get What You Pay For

Lesson Two: Tie Pay to Performance to Reduce Risk

Lesson Three: Money Isn't Everything

Takeaway

NBA basketball player Tim Hardaway was promised a big bonus if he made a lot of assists. The incentive plan worked. Hardaway passed the ball a lot, especially toward the end of the season when it looked like he might not make his bonus. But did the team owners encourage the right thing? Hardaway later admitted that to get his bonus he had sometimes passed even when he should have shot the ball.

Incentives matter—this is one of the key lessons of this book—but getting the incentives right is not always easy. Managers of businesses and sports teams, voters, politicians, parents, all must think about and choose incentives. This chapter is all about getting the incentives right and what happens when we get the incentives wrong.

Lesson One: You Get What You Pay For

Every May, Chicago public school students take a standardized test. Students are used to being tested, graded, and rewarded accordingly, but beginning in May 1996 teachers and principals had a lot more than usual on the line: Schools with low scores would be closed, teachers reassigned, and principals fired. The idea, of course, was to give educators stronger incentives to work harder and better. If grading was good for the students, why not for the teachers?

Stronger incentives do give teachers and principals an incentive to put in extra hours and search for better teaching methods. But how else can teachers raise the grades of their students? Here's a hint: some students also use this method. That's right—they cheat. Indeed, teachers can cheat a lot better than students because they know which answers are correct! Two economists who

313

understand incentives, Brian Jacob and Steven Levitt (the latter of *Freakonomics* fame), started to look carefully at test data and asked: would teachers really cheat to raise student grades?[1] Sure enough, Jacob and Levitt found odd patterns in the data—students who got easy answers wrong and hard answers right, groups of students who had exactly the same right and wrong answers, and students who received high grades during a test year but low grades the year after. Most telling for an economist was that the indicators of cheating were much stronger after the penalty for low-performing schools went into effect than before!

Perhaps you think that teachers cheating to raise student grades is a good idea! But it wasn't what the proponents of strong incentives for teachers had in mind. Not all teachers cheated, but cheating was surprisingly common. Jacob and Levitt estimated that cheating occurred in at least 4 percent to 5 percent of classrooms. Other researchers have found that after the introduction of strong incentives a lot more students are declared learning disabled.[2] Why? Test scores of students called "learning disabled" are usually not counted when it comes to rewarding teachers and principals.

Can Incentives Cheat Death?

In the last week of 1999, New York hospitals reported fewer deaths than usual. The following week there were more deaths than usual. Why? Could it be that people willed themselves to live to see the dawn of the twenty-first century?

If death can be postponed for major events, then why not to save on taxes? Two economists, Wojciech Kopczuk and Joel Slemrod found that a $10,000 reduction in the estate tax can postpone death by about a week! To be fair, however, it could also be that the heirs to the inheritance alter death certificates so as to lower their taxes.

Does all this mean that strong incentives for teachers is a bad idea? Not necessarily. Students who learn more, earn more. If strong incentives for teachers do increase true scores, even by a small amount, maybe it's a good idea even if some of the better scores are due to cheating.[3]

A similar example of incentives for cheating comes from corporate finance. In the 1980s, chief executive officers (CEOs) were given much stronger incentives to increase their firm's stock price. Instead of being paid a straight salary, they were awarded stock options. These are complicated financial instruments, but what you need to know is that they pay off only if the stock rises above a certain price. As with strong incentives for teaching, strong incentives encouraged CEOs to work harder and smarter. It also encouraged them to cheat by manipulating earnings reports to make their firms appear more profitable than they really were. Enron and the other scandals of the 1990s and first decade of the 2000s were in part the result. Were strong incentives worth it? If the shareholders thought that on average the costs of cheating exceeded the benefits of encouraging harder work, they would offer their CEOs fewer options and other strong incentives. But so far most of these incentives have stayed in place, albeit with more monitoring of potentially bad behavior.*

---

* The shareholders are not the only ones who are harmed when a corporation like Enron collapses so their choice of CEO incentive scheme may not reflect what is best for society as a whole. In Chapter 9, we discussed problems like this, called externality problems, in more detail.

When designing an incentive scheme remember this: You get what you pay for. That sounds good but there is a problem. What if what you pay for is not exactly what you want? If you pay for higher test scores, you will get higher test scores. But test scores are an imperfect measure of what you really want—more productive teachers and more knowledgeable students. What you pay for is higher stock prices, but what you really want is a more profitable firm. Usually stock prices reflect a firm's fundamental value, but even the market can be fooled sometimes!

The closer "what you pay for" is to "what you want," then the more you can rely on strong incentives. Careful design of an incentive scheme can narrow the gap between what you want and what you can pay for. After Jacob and Levitt published their results, the administrators of Chicago Public Schools, to their credit, fired some teachers and instituted new procedures to make cheating more difficult. After the Enron scandal, investors demanded more independent financial audits. The stronger the incentives, the more it pays to invest in careful measurement and auditing, and vice versa.

If you can't bridge the gap between "what you pay for" and "what you want," then weak incentive schemes can be better than strong incentive schemes.

Prisons for Profit?

Should the management of prisons be contracted out to the private sector? The owners of a private firm have a strong incentive to cut costs and improve productivity because they get to keep the resulting profits. If a public prison cuts costs, there is more money in the public treasury but no one gets to buy a yacht so the incentive to cut costs is much weaker.

In 1985, Kentucky became the first state to contract out a prison to a for-profit firm. Private prisons today hold about 120,000 prisoners in the United States, about 5 percent of all prisoners. Should efficient private prisons replace inefficient public prisons? Three economists—Oliver Hart, Andrei Shleifer, and Robert Vishny (HSV)—say no. HSV don't question that the profit motive gives private prisons stronger incentives than public prisons to cut costs—HSV say that's the problem! Suppose that we care about costs but we also care about prisoner rehabilitation, civil rights, and low levels of inmate and guard violence. What we pay for is cheap prisons, but what we want is cheap but high quality prisons. If we can't measure and pay for quality, then strong incentives could encourage cost cutting at the expense of quality.

The principle is a general one, a strong incentive scheme that incentivizes the wrong thing can be worse than a weak incentive scheme. One car dealer in California advertises that its sales staff is not paid on commission.[4] Why would a store advertise that its sales staff do not have strong incentives to help you? The answer is clear to anyone who has tried to buy a car. High-pressure dealers who pounce on you the moment you enter the showroom and bombard you with high-pressure sales tactics ("I can get you 15 percent off the sticker, but you have to act NOW!") may sell cars to first-time buyers, but the strategy is too unpleasant to win many repeat customers. Car dealers who rely on repeat business usually prefer a low-pressure, informative sales staff.

In theory, a car dealer could have strong incentives *and* repeat business by paying its sales staff based on their "nice" sales tactics, but in practice it's too expensive to monitor how salespeople interact with clients. Cheating by the sales staff would be difficult to detect and thus would be common. Paying the sales staff a salary instead of a commission calms them down a bit. Of course, there is a price to be paid for weak incentives. Imagine that Joe's Honda pays its sales staff on commission while Pete's Subaru pays its staff a straight salary. Which dealership do you expect to be open late at night and on Sundays?

What about prisons? Are HSV correct that weak-incentive public prisons are better than strong incentive private prisons? Not necessarily. HSV assume that cutting quality is the way to cut cost. But sometimes higher quality is also a path to lower costs. Low levels of inmate and guard violence, for example, are likely to reduce costs. And respect for prisoner's civil rights? That can save on legal bills. When quality and cost cutting go together, a private firm has a strong incentive to increase quality.

HSV may also underestimate how well quality can be measured. Measuring output pays off more when incentives are high. Unsurprisingly, therefore, private prison companies and government purchasers have made extensive efforts to measure the quality of private prisons.

Finally, don't forget that weak incentives reduce the incentive to cut costs but they don't increase the incentive to produce high quality! Public prisons might use their slack budget constraints to offer high-quality rehabilitation programs, or they might instead offer prison guards above-market wages. Which do you think is more likely?

Nevertheless, whether HSV are right or wrong about private prisons, their argument is clever. The usual argument against government bureaucracy is that without the profit incentive, public bureaucracies won't have an incentive to cut costs. HSV suggest this is exactly why public bureaucracies may sometimes be better than private firms.[5]

Piece Rates vs. Hourly Wages

A majority of workers are paid by the hour but a significant number are paid by the piece. An hourly wage pays workers for their inputs (of time); a **piece rate** pays workers directly for their output. Agricultural workers, for example, are often paid by the number of pieces of fruit or vegetable that they pick. Garment workers are often paid per item completed. Salespeople are often paid in part by the number of sales that they make. When should workers be paid by the hour and when should they be paid by the piece?

> A **piece rate** is any payment system that pays workers directly for their output.

Piece rates increase the incentive to work hard and can work well when output is easy to measure so "what you pay for" is close to "what you want." Piece rates are common in agricultural work because it's easy to measure the number of apples picked and this is close to what the employer wants. Even in agricultural work, however, the employer wants not just apples but ripe and unbruised apples so piece rates usually require some form of quality control. Piece rates do not work well when quality is important but quality control is expensive.

In the early days of computing, IBM paid its programmers per line of code. Can you see the problem? When IBM paid by the line, IBM programmers produced lots of code but in their rush to earn more money the programmers often wrote low quality code. IBM's incentive scheme rewarded what was measurable—lines of code—at the expense of what IBM really wanted but what was difficult to measure, high quality code. IBM quickly stopped paying its workers by the line and switched to hourly wages. Hourly wages reduced the incentive to work hard but hourly wages also reduced the incentive to rush the work before it was ready.

The advantage of piece rates is that, if used properly, they can greatly increase productivity. The auto-glass installer Safelite Glass Corporation switched from an hourly wage system to a piece rate in 1994. Safelite was able to handle the quality control issue by linking every job with a worker so that if a quality problem arose, the worker who was responsible for that windshield installation had to fix it on his or her own time. Productivity quickly improved by an astonishing 44 percent.[6] About half of the increase in productivity was due to the same workers working harder, including lower absenteeism and fewer sick days, but the other half of the productivity increase was due to another important effect of piece rates. A piece-rate system attracts more productive workers.

Consider two firms, one of which pays workers according to a piece rate, the other pays workers an hourly wage. Now consider two workers, one of which can install five windshields a day, the other just three. Which worker will be attracted to which firm? The piece rate firm will attract the more productive worker because piece rates give productive workers a chance to earn more money. The hourly wage plan will attract workers who are relatively less productive or even "lazy."

The differences between workers in productivity can be surprisingly large. One California wine grower switched from paying grape pickers by the hour to paying by the pound. Previously, the firm had paid its workers $6.20 per hour. Under piece rates the average pay was effectively $6.84 per hour, about the same as before, but some workers were making as much as $24.85 an hour.

When some workers are more productive than other workers, piece rates will tend to increase inequality in earnings. Under the hourly wage, every grape picker earned $6.20 an hour. Under the piece rate some earned $6.84 while others earned $24.85. Information technology is making it easier to measure the output of all kinds of workers, not just grape pickers. As a result, performance pay (piece rates, commissions, bonuses, and other rewards tied directly to output) is becoming more common in the U.S. economy and this is one important reason why the inequality of earnings has also increased.[7]

The increase in effective pay under piece rates explains why both firms and employees can benefit from piece rates. Under hourly wages, workers don't have an incentive to work harder even when they can do so at low cost. Piece rates benefit productive workers by giving them an opportunity to use their skills to make more money. Piece rates also benefit firms by increasing productivity more than wages.

Even though firms and workers can both benefit from piece rates, piece rates are sometimes not implemented because of issues of distrust. Workers fear that if they respond to a new piece rate plan by increasing productivity (and thus wages) that the firm will respond by reducing the piece rate in the next period (for example, paying less per pound of grapes picked). In the old Soviet Union, factory managers who increased productivity in response to new incentives were often denounced because their increased performance proved that they had previously been lazy! Of course, this greatly reduced the incentive to increase productivity. Similarly, workers won't work harder if they expect that higher productivity will be punished with lower piece rates. Firms that want to introduce piece rates must build trust with their workers.

Lesson Two: Tie Pay to Performance to Reduce Risk

Consider an auto dealer who wants to motivate her sales staff. Let's assume that all the auto dealer cares about is sales, so she is not worried that strong incentives will make her sales staff too pushy. Are strong incentives now the best? Maybe not.

Auto sales depend on more than hard work. Sales also depend on factors the staff has no control over, such as the price and quality of the car, the price of gas, and the state of the economy. If the sales staff has strong incentives, they are going to do great when the economy is booming but poorly when the economy is in a recession.

When sales vary for reasons having little to do with hard work, strong incentives may be more expensive than they are worth. Most people don't like risk. Which would you prefer, $100 for sure or a gamble that pays $200 with probability 0.5 and $0 with probability 0.5? Gambling in Las Vegas can be fun but most people will prefer $100 for certain over a gamble with the same expected payoff. Similarly, suppose that there are two jobs: Job one pays $100,000 a year for sure, job two pays $200,000 in a good year but just $0 in a bad year. Suppose also that good and bad years are equally likely so, on average, job two also pays $100,000 a year. Which job would you prefer? If the wages are the same on average most people will prefer job one, the less risky job. How high would the average wage have to be for you to prefer job two? $110,000, $150,000, $175,000? The precise number is less important than the principle: the riskier payments are to workers, the more a firm must pay on average. Thus, if a firm's sales staff has to bear the risk of a bad economy or a low quality car, they will demand a big bonus for every sale. But if staff members demand a big bonus, what is left over for the owner? If the sales staff is sufficiently afraid to face these risks, the owner and the staff might not be able to agree on a mutually profitable strong incentive plan.*

Weak incentives insulate the sales staff from risk. If the owner is better able than the sales staff to bear the risk of a recession (perhaps because she is wealthier), weak incentives may be mutually profitable. In essence, the owner can sell the staff "recession insurance" by paying them with a fixed or nearly fixed salary. The sales staff "buy" the insurance by accepting smaller bonuses but of course their pay stream is more stable.

Bearing the risk of a recession might be worth it if hard work from the sales force is also the critical factor in sales. But if the state of the economy is a significant determinant of sales, then strong incentives have created risk with very little motivational advantage. Imagine if rewards were based solely on luck—what incentive would there be to exert effort? Similarly, if rewards are mostly based on luck, the incentive to exert effort will be low and many potential employees won't want to face those risks at a price the owner is willing to pay.

* Or worse, the sales staff may be eager to sell cars when the economy is good but the staff may quit the day the economy turns sour.

Tournament Theory

When sales depend heavily on outside factors such as the state of the economy, tying bonuses to sales will reward or penalize agents for outcomes that are often beyond their control—thus, shifting risk to the agent but giving the agent little incentive to exert effort. One way a manager can reduce an agent's risk is to tie rewards more closely to actions that a sales agent does control. A surprising way to do this is to pay bonuses based not on a sales agent's absolute number of sales but on their sales relative to other agents—for example, giving a bonus to the sales agents with the highest, second highest, and third highest sales. For obvious reasons, economists call a compensation scheme in which pay is based on relative performance, a **tournament**.

A **tournament** is a compensation scheme in which payment is based on relative performance.

If they are used cleverly, tournaments can tie rewards more closely to actions that an agent controls, thereby improving productivity and pay. To see how a tournament works in the business world, let's start with sports, an area where we are all used to thinking about tournaments.

Imagine a golf game in which players are paid based on the total number of strokes to finish the course (by the nature of golf, fewer strokes mean better play and thus higher payments). If the weather is bad, scores will be high and agents won't earn very much even if they work hard. If the weather is good (clear day, no wind), scores will be low and agents will earn a lot even if they don't work very hard. Either way, when players are paid based on their absolute scores, random forces—such as the weather—will influence how much the players earn.

Now imagine that players are playing in a tournament with a fixed number of prizes, which of course is usually the case. The fixed number of prizes means that the players are competing *against each other* rather than against some external standard of achievement. Since every player plays with the same weather, the weather no longer influences rewards. Thus, a tournament limits the amount of risk from the external environment. A lot of sporting events, not just golf, are organized in the form of tournaments. Tournaments are also common in the business world.

For instance, paying sales agents based on relative sales will reduce environment risk, risk from external factors that are common to all the agents. When sales agents are paid based on relative sales, factors that the agents do not control such as the state of the economy, the quality of the product, and the price of competing products will no longer influence agent rewards. *Here is the key*: When factors that an agent doesn't control no longer influence rewards, then factors that an agent does control—factors like effort—become more important determinants of rewards. Thus, pay for relative performance such as that used in a tournament can reduce risk and tie rewards more closely to actions that an agent controls. This will mean harder work, less risk, more output, and higher pay.

Bonus!

ALAN SMITH/CSM /LANDOV

Improving Executive Compensation with Pay for Relative Performance

A good compensation scheme ties rewards to actions that an agent controls. How would you use the idea of *pay for relative performance* to tie executive pay more closely to actions that executives control?

Today, a large fraction of an executive's pay is tied to the stock price of their firm. When the value of their firm rises, executives are often able to cash in stock options at profitable prices. But many factors other than executive effort or ability influence the price of a stock. When the economy does well, for example, the price of most stocks goes up. Similarly, when the price of oil goes up the stock price of firms in the oil industry tends to go up—and surprisingly so does the pay of executives in the oil industry despite the fact that these executives have no control over the price of oil.[8] Of course, when the price of oil falls these executives are paid less despite the fact that they may be working as hard, or harder, than ever. The bottom line is that quite a bit of executive pay appears to be based on luck. But payment based on luck is not a good compensation scheme on either the upside or downside.

Is there a better way to pay executives? Instead of paying based on how well their stock performs, how about paying executives based on how well their stock performs *relative to other firms in the same industry?* If executives were paid based on relative performance, they wouldn't reap big windfall profits when the industry boomed (due to no virtue of their own) but neither would they necessarily be paid less when the industry declined (due to no fault of their own).

Pay for relative performance seems to make a lot of sense but it has not been widely adopted. As a result, some observers suspect that the complicated stock option schemes currently used to reward executives are less about creating incentives than about creative accounting that takes advantage of shareholders who do not closely monitor how much the executives are being paid. Interestingly, firms that have at least one very large shareholder—and thus at least one shareholder with an incentive to monitor the firm closely—do appear to base more executive pay on relative performance.[9]

Environment Risk and Ability Risk

A tournament insulates rewards from risks due to outside factors that are common to all the players but it adds another type of risk called ability risk. Imagine that you had to compete in a golf game against Tiger Woods. Would you put in more effort if you were paid based on the number of strokes or if you were paid based on who wins the game? The probability that you could beat Tiger Woods at golf is so low that if all you cared about was money, it would make sense to give up right away—why exert effort in a hopeless cause? Of course, for the same reason, Tiger Woods won't need to try very hard either!

Remember, an ideal incentive scheme ties rewards to factors that an agent controls, such as effort. But winning at golf takes more than effort, it also takes ability. As far as an agent is concerned someone else's ability is just like the weather or the state of the economy, it's not under his control. A golf tournament between players with highly unequal abilities doesn't tie rewards to effort, it ties rewards to ability and that often causes people to shirk and slack. Thus, tournaments work best when the risk from the outside environment is more important than ability risk.

Tournaments can be structured to reduce ability risk. At a professional golf tournament, for example, players play in rounds with the weakest players being eliminated in early rounds so when the final and most important round is played the players have similar abilities. Similarly, tournaments are often split into age classes or experience classes (beginner, intermediate, expert) so that abilities are similar and each player has a strong incentive to work hard. In amateur but serious golf games, when players of different ability compete together, the high ability players will often be handicapped, which makes competition more intense for all the players. A manager who wants a lot of effort will also structure tournaments so that rewards are closely tied to effort. A manager, for example, might create junior and senior sales positions with tournaments played within each class of employee.

Tournaments in business might seem a bit unusual but they are quite common. About a third of U.S. corporations evaluate employees based on relative performance.[10] Under the hard-nosed CEO Jack Welch, managers at General Electric were required to divide employees into three groups—the top 20 percent, the middle 70 percent, and the bottom 10 percent—with the bottom 10 percent often being shown the door. Even when employees are not explicitly rewarded based on relative performance, tournaments are often implicit. Lawyers, for example, compete to earn the prize of becoming a partner. Or becoming the president of a corporation is a lot like winning a tournament. Imagine that a corporation has eight vice presidents and one president—the vice presidents compete to become the next president. The fact that moving up the corporate ladder is like competing in a tournament may also shed some light on the large salaries and perks of many corporate presidents. Personal chefs, corporate jets, and lavish parties might be a sign of the abuse of power but the perks of presidency may also motivate the eight vice presidents. In part, corporate presidents are paid a lot to motivate those beneath them.

Tournaments are wonderful at encouraging competition but sometimes competition can be too fierce. In a tournament, when one player falters the others gain, so tournaments can discourage cooperation. One corporate vice president might be unwilling to mentor another if she sees a competitor waiting to take away her job. Thus, as usual, compensation schemes must be carefully designed to balance a variety of goals.

Tournaments and Grades

Let's apply some of the insights from tournament theory to a competition that you are very familiar with, the competition for grades. Some professors grade on a curve while others use an absolute scale. When a professor "grades on a curve," there are a fixed number of "prizes," As, Bs, Cs, for each class. The competition for grades becomes a tournament.

The costs and benefits of being graded on a curve are just like the more general analysis of tournaments. Grading on a curve reduces environment risk but increases ability risk. Can you think of some examples of environment risk? Suppose that your professor is hard to understand—perhaps the professor has an accent or teaches the material too quickly or is simply not a good teacher (unlike us!). Fortunately, if the professor grades on a curve, his or her bad performance doesn't mean you have to fail. Bad teaching will reduce how much you learn but bad teaching harms everyone's performance. If the professor grades on a curve, bad teaching need not reduce your grade or reduce your incentive to study.

A bad teacher who grades on an absolute scale, however, is double trouble. First, bad teaching means that you won't learn much. Second, if the grading is on an absolute scale, not learning much means that even if you work hard you will get a low grade. There isn't much incentive to work hard in that case.

Grading on a curve, however, does have disadvantages—grading on a curve means that you will be competing directly with the other students in the class. If you happen to be in a class with a handful of super-brilliant students, it's like golfing against Tiger Woods (unless *you* are the academic Tiger Woods). Even if

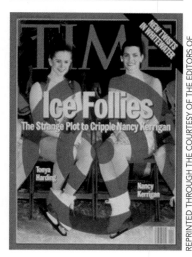

Tournaments can encourage too much competition.

you learn a lot and work hard, you won't get a high grade and that reduces your incentive to study.

Grading on a curve, therefore, creates better incentives to study when the big risk is that the professor will be bad (an environment risk), but it reduces the incentive to study when students are of very different abilities (ability risk). Grading on an absolute scale creates better incentives to study when students are of very different abilities (ability risk) but reduces the incentive to study when the big risk is that professors will be bad (environment risk).

What are some other effects of grading on a curve? Remember, tournaments tend to reduce cooperation. If your professor grades on a curve, other students might be less willing to help you with your homework (or you might be less willing to help them!). Study groups will probably be less common. Some students might even try to sabotage other students. Tournaments can also encourage the wrong kinds of cooperation. If a professor grades on a curve, in theory all the students could get together and agree not to study very much. This probably wouldn't be a problem in a large class, but if two sales agents regularly compete for the "salesman of the month" award they could collude to reduce effort and rotate the prize between them.

Here's another problem for you to think about. Suppose that the environment risk is not bad professors but rather hard material. Imagine, for example, that some classes are more difficult than other classes (quantum physics 101 vs. handball 101). If you really wanted to learn a little about quantum physics, but you were afraid of reducing your GPA, what type of grading system would you prefer? And to ask the classic economist's question: under what conditions? See Thinking and Problem Solving question 6 for further discussion of this question.

Lesson Three: Money Isn't Everything

Incentives are powerful but not all powerful incentives are for money. If you want to keep business or school club meetings short, make everyone stand until the meeting is over. All of a sudden the cost of talking is higher so people have an incentive to talk less.

In addition to money, other powerful rewards include the feeling of identification and belonging that comes from being part of a team, the joy that comes from a job well done, and the status that comes from success on one's own terms. Intrinsic motivation is when you want to do something simply for feelings of enjoyment and pride. Ideally, firms would like their employees to be motivated by intrinsic rewards like pride in a job well done as well as extrinsic rewards like money.

A good manager will get workers to enjoy doing what the manager wants. One way of doing this is to encourage workers to identify with the corporation and its goals in the same way that sports fans identify with their team. Many workers, for example, are given shares of stock in the company they work in. Currently about 20 million American employees own a part of their employers.[11] Since most workers don't have much control over the value of the entire company, this doesn't make sense as a monetary incentive. But workers are more likely to identify with their company if they are also part owners of their company. Workers who identify with their company see corporate success as their success. Bostonians celebrated when the Red Sox won the World Series

CHECK YOURSELF

> At one prominent university, a professor's first name and middle initial are "Harvey C." Undergraduates refer to him as "Harvey C-minus" because he is a notoriously hard grader. What are this professor's incentives to be known as a hard grader? What type of students does he attract? Who does he encourage to stay away? Why might this professor not want to grade on a curve?

> How can a tournament create too much competition? Isn't competition a good thing?

even though the fans didn't receive any monetary rewards. In a company with strong worker identification, high profits are a cause for celebration even if the workers don't receive raises. Workers who identify with their company are more likely to see themselves in the same boat as other workers and to think and act more like a team or sometimes even like a family. This is also why many companies run staff retreats or invest in a softball team.

Successful businesses take great care to create the right **corporate culture.** Corporate culture is the shared collection of values and norms that govern how people interact in an organization or firm. Sometimes it is said that corporate culture is "how things get done around here."

> **Corporate culture** is the shared collection of values and norms that govern how people interact in an organization or firm.

The American military is one of the most successful creators of a powerful "corporate culture." In the military, a team member may sacrifice his or her life for the sake of the team. Business corporations can rarely rely on this intensity of identification but a strong corporate culture can help workers improve. Recall that one of the big problems with monetary incentives is that the firm can't always measure what it wants and a firm that can't measure quality, for example, may be worried about creating strong incentives for quantity. But a firm with workers who value high quality for its own sake can have the best of both worlds—high quantity and high quality. Corporate culture helps firms incentivize what is difficult to measure.

Corporate culture is in part responsible for the ascendancy of Wal-Mart, starting in the 1970s. In the 1970s, CEO Sam Walton spent several days a week visiting each store. He typically would gather the employees together in a rousing corporate cheer. He then walked around the store and encouraged people to tell him what the problems were or what the company was doing wrong. Most managers were encouraged to visit stores and find out what was on the minds of workers. The flow of useful information up to the bosses became a company norm, and workers grew more and more willing to share what they knew. When something in the company went wrong, usually the mistake was discovered quickly and there was someone ready to set it right.

In other cases, corporate culture malfunctions. As Wal-Mart was growing, Kmart, one of its main competitors, was on the road to bankruptcy. At Kmart, employees tended to hide problems from managers rather than volunteer solutions. Usually control was centralized and the attitude was that the home office knows best. Each time the company had a problem it looked for a "quick fix" rather than going to the root of the difficulty. The tradition of failure bred on itself and members of the company simply did not work together very well. Kmart has come out of bankruptcy but it remains unclear whether the company enjoys much of a future. Most customers vote with their feet and go to Wal-Mart.[12]

The importance of morale and good relations extends beyond the business corporation. You can see these same principles at work in your everyday life.

Intrinsic and extrinsic motivation can work together but not always. When intrinsic motivation is strong, people are sometimes insulted by offers of money. If you ask a friend to give you a ride to the airport, the friend would probably say yes (well, *some* friends . . . maybe not all of your friends). Offer your friend $20 for a ride and all of a sudden the friend feels like a taxi driver, not a friend. The friend who might have done it for free will turn down the job for $20. In one advice column, a woman complained that her husband promised to "pay her by the pound" to lose weight (the advice column did not say whether the husband was an economist). This marriage probably was not a happy one, and we should not expect this proposed transaction to succeed.

Similarly, it is not always possible to pay a son or a daughter to do the dirty dishes. Nagging doesn't always work well either but paying money can be worse. When the parents pay money, the daughter feels less familial obligation. Once she says to herself "Doing the dishes is a job for money," the daughter is no more obligated to do her parent's dishes than she is to get a job at a restaurant to do other people's dishes.

In these cases, payment causes external motivation to replace internal motivation. Yet for some tasks, internal motivation is what gets the job done, and in these cases payment can be counterproductive.

Note that payment from a restaurant will get the same daughter to show up for work on time. Having her own job—which is a signal of adulthood and independence—is "cool" and makes the daughter feel like a grown-up. Money from parents, which feels like an allowance for tots, or feels like a means of parental control, will not boost the daughter's internal motivation to do the dishes.

The lesson is this: Monetary rewards are most effective when they are supported by intrinsic motivation and measures of social status. Good entrepreneurs understand these connections, and they design their workplaces so that money, intrinsic motivation, and status incentives work together. Money can't buy you love, however, and sometimes love is the incentive that makes family and personal relationships work well. Money can't buy you duty or honor either so even within firms and other organizations such as the military, monetary incentives must be used with care. Understanding when extrinsic and intrinsic rewards complement one another and when they are at odds is today more of an art than a science. Questions like these are on the cutting edge of social psychology and behavioral economics.

CHECK YOURSELF

> Is Christmas wasteful? Instead of presents, wouldn't it be more efficient to give cash which can be used to buy what the recipient really wants? Why don't we see cash gifts more often?

> Some parents and increasingly some schools are using cash to pay students for good grades. Good idea or not?

□ Takeaway

Incentives are a double-edged sword. When aligned with the social interest, incentives can be powerful forces for good but misaligned incentives can be equally powerful forces for bad. One of the goals of economics is to understand what institutions generate good incentives.

On a less grand level, getting the incentives right is an important goal of managers who want to motivate employees, stockholders who want to motivate managers, parents who want to motivate children, and consumers who want to motivate real estate agents, physicians, or lawyers among many others.

In this chapter, we discussed three lessons to help get the incentives right. Lesson one is: you get what you pay for but what you pay for is not always what you want. Sometimes the gap between what you pay for and what you want arises because the incentive plan is badly designed. More often the gap arises because measuring exactly what you want is difficult so you must pay for something that is more easily measurable but is not exactly what you want. When the gap between what you pay for and what you want is large, strong incentives can be worse than weak incentives. As it becomes easier to measure things like quality, however, strong incentive plans are becoming more common.

Lesson two is tie pay to performance to reduce risk. Strong incentives put more risk on agents from factors beyond their control and to bear this risk the agents will demand greater compensation. Sales agents on commission, for example, bear the risk that the economy goes into a downturn or that the product they sell is of low quality. As a result of this increased financial risk, sales agents on commission must be paid higher average wages than sales agents on salary. A firm must ask whether the strong incentives created by commissions increase sales enough to justify the higher average wages.

A good incentive plan will reduce unnecessary risk by tying rewards to actions that an agent controls and that are effective in increasing output. Different incentive plans like commissions, bonuses, and tournaments impose different types of risks on agents. Which incentive plan is best will depend on which risks are most important.

Lesson three is that money isn't everything. In addition to earning money, workers want to enjoy their work, identify with a team, and be respected. Successful corporations provide these rewards as well as monetary rewards. Monetary rewards can be paid only for what is measurable but a successful corporate culture can help firms incentivize what is difficult to measure. Monetary rewards are most effective when they are supported by intrinsic motivation and measures of social status.

❑ CHAPTER REVIEW

KEY CONCEPTS

Piece rate, p. 316

Tournament, p. 319

Corporate culture, p. 323

FACTS AND TOOLS

1. This chapter had three big lessons. Each of the following situations illustrates one and (we think) only one of those lessons. Which one?

   a. Militaries throughout the world give medals, citations, and other public honors to members of the military who excel in their duties.

   b. People tip for good service after their meal is concluded.

   c. Real estate agents work on commission, but office managers at a real estate office are paid a straight salary.

   d. In Pennsylvania in 2009, two judges received $2.6 million in bribes from a juvenile prison. The more people they sent to jail, the more they received from the prison owners. What tipped off prosecutors was that the judges were sentencing teens to such harsh sentences for relatively minor crimes. One teenager was sent to prison for putting up a Facebook page that said mean things about her school principal; another accidentally bought a stolen bicycle. (Both judges pled guilty.)

2. An American church sends 10 missionaries to Panama for three years to try to find new converts. Every six months, the missionary with the most new converts gets to be the supervising missionary for the next six months. This basically means that he or she gets to drive a car, while the other 9 have to walk or ride bicycles. Clearly, this is a tournament. Now consider the following two cases. For which case will the church's incentive plan work best? (Hint: Think about ability risk vs. environment risk.)

   Case I: Missionaries specialize in different regions: Some stay in rich neighborhoods for the whole six months, others stay in the poor neighborhoods for the whole six months.

   Case II: Missionaries move from region to region every few weeks, so that all missionaries spend a little time in every kind of Panamanian neighborhood.

3. Punishments can be an incentive, not just rewards. Consider an assembly line. Why wouldn't you necessarily want to reward the fastest worker on the assembly line? What other incentive system might work?

4. Many professional athletes get a bonus if they win a championship. Is this kind of incentive better or worse than Tim Hardaway's assist bonus? Why?

5. Let's return to Big Idea Four (thinking on the margin) back in Chapter 1. Why are calls to give harsher penalties to drug dealers and kidnappers often met with warnings by economists?

6. Why are salespeople so much more likely than other kinds of workers to be paid on a "piece rate" (i.e., on commission)? What is it about the kind of work they do that makes the high-commission + low-base-salary combination the equilibrium outcome?

7. Unlike in the previous question, sometimes, piece rates don't work so well. Why might the following incentive mechanisms turn out to be more trouble than they're worth?

   a. An industrial materials company pays welders by the number of welds per hour. Of course, the company only pays for necessary welds.

   b. A magazine publisher pays its authors to write "serial novels" one chapter at a time. The authors are paid by the word (common in the nineteenth century: This is how Dickens and Dostoyevsky made their livings).

8. The typical corporate executive's incentive package offers higher pay when the company's stock does well. One proposal for such executive merit pay is to instead pay executives based on whether their firm's stock price does better or worse than the stock price of the average firm in their own industry. Does this proposal solve an environment risk problem or an ability risk problem? How can you tell?

THINKING AND PROBLEM SOLVING

1. In 1975, economist Sam Peltzman published a study of the effects of recent safety regulations for automobiles. His results were surprising: increased safety standards for automobiles had no measurable effect on passenger fatalities. Pedestrian fatalities in automobile accidents, however, increased. (This is now known as the Peltzman effect and has been tested repeatedly over the decades.)

   a. Why might more *pedestrians* be killed when a car has *more* safety features?

   b. Economists have looked for ways out of Peltzman's dilemma. Here's one possible solution: Gordon Tullock, our colleague at George Mason, has argued that cars could have long spikes jutting out of the steering column pointed directly at the driver's heart. Keeping Peltzman's paper and the role of incentives in mind, would you expect this safety mechanism to result in an increase, decrease, or no change in automobile accident fatalities? Why?

   c. Would a pedestrian who never drives or rides in cars tend to favor Tullock's solution? Why or why not?

2. One reason it's hard for a manager to set up good incentives is because it's easy for employees to lie about how they'll respond to incentives. For example: Simple Books pays Mary Sue to proofread chapters of new books. After an author writes a draft of a book, Simple sends chapters out to proofreaders like Mary Sue to make sure that spelling, punctuation, and basic facts are correct.

   As you can imagine, some books are easy to proofread (perhaps Westerns and romances), while others are hard to proofread (perhaps engineering textbooks). But what's hard or easy is often in the eye of the beholder: Simple can't tell which books are particularly easy for Mary Sue to proof, so they have to take her word for it. Let's see how this fact influences the publishing industry.

   In the figure below, Q★ is the number of chapters in the new book, *Burned: The Secret History of Toast.* It's a strange mix of chemistry and history, so Simple isn't sure how Mary Sue will feel about proofing it. The marginal cost curve shows Mary Sue's true willingness to work: The more chapters she has to read, the more you have to pay her. If Simple offers to pay her $50 per chapter, as shown, she'll actually finish the job.

a. If Mary Sue wants to bluff, claiming that the book is actually painful to read, what is that equivalent to?

Supply curve shifting left

Supply curve shifting right

Demand curve shifting down

Demand curve shifting up

Once you decide, make the appropriate shift in the figure above.

b. The publisher just *has* to have Mary Sue proof all Q^* chapters of *Burned*: All the other proofreaders are busy. They'll pay what they need to for her to finish the book. This is the same as another curve shift in a certain direction: Draw in this shift in the figure above.

c. What did Mary Sue's complaining do to her price per chapter? What did it do to her work load?

d. (Bonus) You've seen how Mary Sue's bluffing influenced the outcome. What are some things that Simple might do to keep this from happening?

3. Who do you think is in favor of forbidding baseball player contracts from including bonuses based on playing skill? Owners or players? Why?

4. In the short, readable classic *Congress: The Electoral Connection*, David Mayhew uses the basic ideas of incentives and information as a pair of lenses through which to view members of Congress. What he saw was quite simple: The urge for reelection drives everything. Thus, members are driven by self-interest to give the voters in their home district as much as possible. Of course, voters face the same problem in judging members of Congress that any manager faces when evaluating an employee: Some

outputs are harder to measure than others, so voters focus on measurable outputs. With that in mind, what will voters be most likely to care about? Choose one from each pair and briefly explain why you made that choice.

a. How many dollars come to the district for new hospitals and highways vs. how many dollars are spent on top-secret military research.

b. How well the member behaved in private meetings with Chinese leaders vs. how the member sounded on *Meet the Press*.

c. How well the member did in reforming the Justice Department vs. how well the member did at the Turkey Toss back in the district last Thanksgiving.

(As you've seen, voters' focus on the visible can easily drive the member's entire career. Mayhew's book was an important early work in "public choice," the use of basic microeconomic ideas like self-interest and strategy to study political behavior. For more on the topic, Kenneth Shepsle and Mark Bonchek's short textbook *Analyzing Politics* is highly recommended. See also Chapter 19 of this textbook.)

5. In the movie business, character actors are typically paid a fixed fee while movie "stars" are typically paid a share of the box office revenues. Why the difference? Try to give *two* explanations based on the ideas in this chapter.

6. Let's return to the question we posed in the chapter: Suppose that the big environment risk is not bad professors but rather hard material. Imagine, for example, that some classes are more difficult than other classes (quantum physics 101 vs. handball 101). If you really wanted to learn a little about quantum physics but you were afraid of reducing your GPA, you'd face a tough choice. A curve is better for you than an absolute scale but even if your professor grades on a curve, you're probably still sitting in a class with other well-trained physics majors. Let's see if we can find a work-around.

a. At your school, are there certain times of the day when the less serious, more fun-loving tend to take their classes? If so, when is it? If you sign up for a section scheduled then, you might look better on the curve.

b. Some schools offer simplified (we won't say "dumbed down") versions of some hard courses. Does your school offer anything like this? If so, does it allow majors to take the same sections as the non-majors? How is this sorting related to tournament theory?

   c. If you were a professor, which teaching schedule would you rather have: Two sections where the majors and non-majors are mixed together, or one section with the majors, and one with the non-majors?

7. When an accused defendant is brought before a judge to schedule a trial, the judge may release the defendant on his or her "own recognizance" or the judge may demand that the defendant post bail, an amount of cash that the defendant must give to the court and that will be forfeited if the defendant fails to appear. Many defendants don't have the cash so they borrow the money from a bail bondsperson. So if the defendant fails to appear, the bail bondsperson is out the money, unless the defendant is recaptured within 90–180 days. To recover their money, a bail bondsperson will hire bail enforcement agents, also known as bounty hunters, to track down the missing defendant. If the bounty hunters don't find the defendant, they don't get paid.

This Dog knows how to hunt.

   a. If defendants released on their own recognizance fail to appear, they are pursued by the police, but if they are released on bail borrowed from a bondsperson and they fail to appear they will be pursued by bounty hunters. Which type of defendant do you think is more likely to fail to appear and which type is more likely to be recaptured if they do fail to appear? Why?

   b. Perhaps surprisingly, bounty hunters tend to be quite courteous and respectful even to defendants who have tried to skip town. Can you think of one reason why?

8. a. Why do so many charitable activities like marathons, walks, and 5K runs give the participants "free" t-shirts, wristbands, hats, bumper stickers, and so forth?

   b. Charitable organizations could probably make a lot of money for their cause by selling these items on their websites, but you usually have to actually attend the "2012 Cancer Run" in order to get the "2012 Cancer Run" t-shirt. Why?

CHALLENGES

1. Let's tie together this chapter's story on incentives with Chapter 13's story about cartels. Suppose your economics professor grades on a curve: The average score on each test becomes a B–. If all of the students in your class form a conspiracy to cut back on studying, point out how this cartel might break down just like OPEC's cartel breaks down during some decades.

2. What type of systems in the United States help overcome the incentives of physicians to order medically unnecessary tests?

3. In his path-breaking book *Managerial Dilemmas,* political scientist Gary Miller says that a good corporate culture is one that gets workers to work together even when they face prisoner's dilemmas (we discussed the prisoner's dilemma in detail in Chapter 13). In a healthy corporate culture, you feel guilty if you're being lazy while your buddy is working. Let's sum up "guilt" as simply as possible: It's some number "X" that represents how you feel. These figures are adapted from Figure 13.3.

		Stan	
		Work	Shirk
Kyle	Work	(4, 4)	(2, X)
	Shirk	(X, 2)	(3, 3)

a. What does X have to be in order to keep this from being a prisoner's dilemma? Answer with a range (e.g., greater than 12.5, less than −2).

b. Now, there are two Nash equilibria in this problem. What are they? Using the language of Chapter 13, what kind of game has this just become?

c. There's an idea buried in the questions from Chapter 13 that will "point" Stan and Kyle toward the best possible outcome. What is it? (Keep in mind that a good corporate culture can help with this part, too.)

4. a. Many HMOs pay their doctors based, in part, on how many patients the doctor sees in a day. What problems does this incentive system create?

b. If HMOs pay their doctors a fixed salary, what problems does this incentive system create?

c. Ideally, we would like to pay doctors based on how long their patients live! What problems exist in implementing this type of system?

16

Stock Markets and Personal Finance

CHAPTER OUTLINE

Passive vs. Active Investing

How to Really Pick Stocks, Seriously

Other Benefits and Costs of Stock Markets

Takeaway

In 1992, television reporter John Stossel decided to challenge the experts of Wall Street. As a student, Stossel had taken classes from economist Burton Malkiel whose book, *A Random Walk Down Wall Street,* claimed that the money and fame that went to stock-picking gurus was a sham and a waste. According to Malkiel: "a blindfolded monkey throwing darts at a newspaper's financial pages could select a portfolio that would do just as well as one carefully selected by experts."[1]

Instead of using a monkey, Stossel himself threw darts at a giant wall-sized version of the stock pages of the *Wall Street Journal*. Stossel followed his portfolio for nearly a year and compared the return to the portfolios picked by major Wall Street experts. Stossel's portfolio beat 90 percent of the experts! Not surprisingly, none of the experts would speak to him on camera about their humiliating loss. The lesson, according to Stossel, is that if you are paying an expert a lot of money to pick your stocks, it is probably you who are the monkey.

In this chapter, we explain why Stossel's amusing experiment is backed up by economic theory and by many careful empirical studies. We will also be giving you some investment advice in this chapter. No, we can't promise you the secret to getting rich. Most of the get rich quick schemes sold in books, investment seminars, and newsletters are scams. Economics, however, does provide some important lessons for investing wisely. We won't tell you how to get rich quick, but we can perhaps help you to get richer slowly.

Throughout this chapter, we emphasize a core principle of economics: there's no such thing as a free lunch. That's just another way of saying that you shouldn't expect something for nothing, or trade-offs are everywhere. Let's see how the principle applies to personal finance.

Passive vs. Active Investing

Many people invest in the stock market through a mutual fund. A mutual fund pools money from many customers and invests the money in many firms, in

Better than the experts?

UNDERSTAND YOUR **world**

return, of course, for a management fee. Some of these mutual funds, called "active funds," are run by managers who try to pick stocks—these mutual funds often charge higher than average fees. Other mutual funds are called "passive funds" because they simply attempt to mimic a broad stock market index such as Standard and Poor's 500 (S&P 500), a basket of 500 large firms broadly representative of the U.S. economy.

Figure 16.1 shows that in a typical year passive investing in the S&P 500 Index beats about 60 percent of all mutual funds. In any given year, some mutual funds beat the index, but what is telling is that the funds that beat the index are different nearly every year! In other words, the funds that beat the index in one year probably just got lucky that year. One study that looked over 10 years found that passive investing beat 97.6 percent of all mutual funds![1] Overall, it is clear that very few mutual fund managers can consistently beat the market averages.

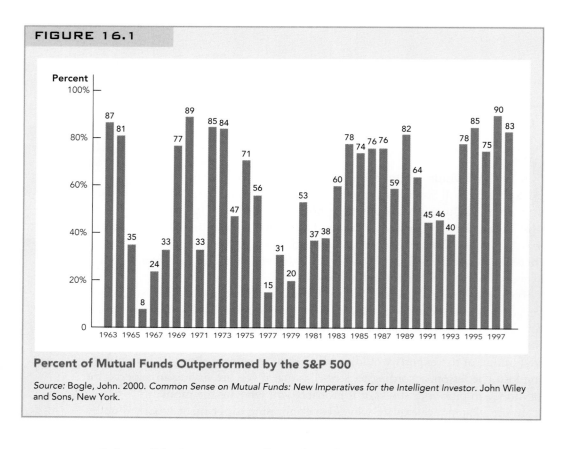

FIGURE 16.1

Percent of Mutual Funds Outperformed by the S&P 500

Source: Bogle, John. 2000. Common Sense on Mutual Funds: New Imperatives for the Intelligent Investor. John Wiley and Sons, New York.

It is possible that a very small number of experts can systematically beat the stock market. Sometimes Warren Buffett, who promotes long-term investing for value, is cited as an example of a person who sees farther than the rest of the market. He started out as a paperboy and worked his way up to $52 billion by purchasing undervalued stocks.

Some economists even think that Buffett, and a few others like him, just got lucky. If enough people are out there trying to pick stocks, you're going to have a few who get lucky many times in a row. Take a look at Figure 16.2. At the top of the figure, we start out with one thousand experts, each of whom flips a coin to predict whether the market will go up in the following year or down. After one year, 500 of the experts will turn out to be right. After two years, 250 experts

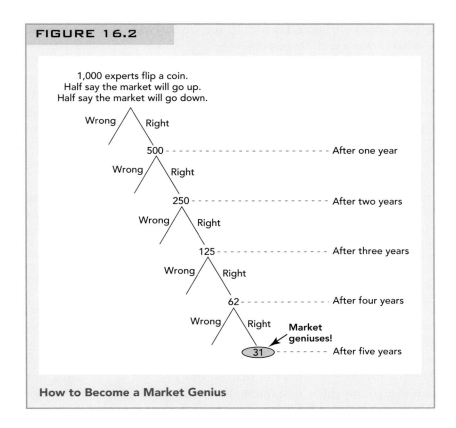

FIGURE 16.2

1,000 experts flip a coin.
Half say the market will go up.
Half say the market will go down.

Wrong / Right
500 ------------------------------ After one year

Wrong / Right
250 ------------------------------ After two years

Wrong / Right
125 ------------------------------ After three years

Wrong / Right
62 ------------------------------ After four years

Wrong / Right
Market geniuses!
31 ------------------------------ After five years

How to Become a Market Genius

will have been right two years in a row. At the end of 5 years, just 31 out of 1,000 experts will have been right five years in a row. The experts who get it correct every time will be lauded as geniuses on CNBC and their advice will be eagerly sought. But the reality is that they just got lucky.

Is Buffett skilled or lucky? We're not so sure, but we do know this: Right now there is a small industry of people following the moves of Warren Buffett, trying to guess what he will say and do next. It is harder and harder for Buffett to get a big jump on the rest of the stock market. Even if Buffett could beat the market at first, it is not so clear he can beat the market any longer.

CHIP SOMODEVILLA/
GETTY IMAGES

Warren Buffett: Genius investor or lucky as a monkey?

Why Is It Hard to Beat the Market?

These results aren't just an accident. Nor is it a statement about the stupidity of mutual fund managers. We know a few of these managers and most of them are pretty smart. Rather, the difficulty of beating the stock market is a tribute to the power of markets and the ability of market prices to reflect information.

Think about it this way: for every buyer of a stock there is a seller. The buyer thinks the price is going up, the seller thinks the price is going down. There is a disagreement. On average, who do you think is more likely to be correct, the buyer or the seller? Of course, the answer is neither. But if on average buyers and sellers have about the same amount of information, stock picking can't work very well.

Consider the following bit of pseudo-investment advice. The number of senior citizens will double by 2020. So the way to make money is to invest in companies that produce goods and services that senior citizens want, things like assisted living facilities, medical care for the elderly, and retirement homes.

The baby boom can be a boom for you, If You Invest Now! Sounds plausible right? So, what's wrong with this argument?

All the premises in the argument are true: the baby boomers are retiring and the demand for goods and services that senior citizens want will increase in the future. But investing in firms that produce goods and services for senior citizens is not a sure road to riches. Why not? If it were, why would anyone sell their stock in these firms? Remember, for every buyer there is a seller. If you think the stock is a good buy, why is the seller selling? It's not a secret that the baby boomers are retiring so the stock price of firms that are likely to do well in the future *already* reflects this information.

Since for every buyer there is a seller, you can't get rich by buying and selling on *public information*. This idea is the foundation of what is called the **efficient markets hypothesis.** The best-known form of this hypothesis states:

> The prices of traded assets, such as stocks and bonds, reflects all publicly available information. Unless an investor is trading on inside information, he or she will not systematically outperform the market as a whole over time.

Let's be clear on what this means. It doesn't mean that market prices are always right, that markets are all powerful, or that traders are calm, cool, and rational people. It just means it is hard for ordinary investors (that probably means you too!) to systematically outperform the market, again unless a trader has inside information—information that no one else has. It's restating our above point that you might as well throw darts at the stock pages as try to figure out which companies will beat the market. The efficient markets hypothesis is just another way of saying there is no such thing as a free lunch.

So what happens if you do have some information that no one else has, then can you make money in the stock market? Yes, but you have to act very quickly. Within *minutes* of the news that the Russian nuclear power plant at Chernobyl had melted down, shares in U.S. nuclear power plant companies tumbled, the price of oil jumped as did the price of potatoes. Why potatoes? Clever traders on Wall Street figured out that the disaster at Chernobyl meant that the Ukrainian potato crop would be contaminated so they bought American potato futures to profit from the coming rise in prices. The traders who acted quickly made a lot of money, but as they bought and sold, prices changed and signaled to other people that something was up. Quite quickly the inside information became public information and the opportunities for profit evaporated.

The only way you can take advantage of information that other people don't have is to start buying or selling large numbers of shares. But once you start the buying or selling, the rest of the market knows something is up. That is why secrets do not last very long in the stock market and that is another reason why it is so hard to beat the market as a whole.

Some people believe that they have found exceptions to the efficient markets hypothesis. For instance, it is commonly believed that you can make more money by buying stocks when prices are low, or by buying right after prices have fallen. That sounds good, doesn't it? Buying at lower prices. It feels like what you do when you go to Wal-Mart. But a stock isn't like buying a lawn chair or a banana. The value of a stock is simply what its price will be in future periods of time. The banana, in contrast, you can simply eat for pleasure, no matter what the future price of bananas. Often lower prices mean that prices are going to stay low or fall even more and that means lower returns on owning stocks. Some studies find that you can do slightly better with your investments

---

The **efficient markets hypothesis** says that the prices of traded assets reflect all publicly available information.

by buying right after prices have fallen. But do you know what? If you adjust those higher returns to account for the broker commissions that you have to pay for the extra trading, the higher returns pretty much go away.

A field of study known as "technical analysis" looks for much deeper patterns in stock and asset prices. Maybe you've heard on the financial news that stocks have "broken through a key support point," or "moved into a new trading range." If you dig deeper, you will find a claim that stock prices exhibit predictable mathematical patterns. For instance, if a stock hovers in the range of $100 a share but does not exceed that level, and one day goes over $100, it might be claimed that the stock is now expected to skyrocket to a much higher level. Hardly. One nice thing about studying the stock market is that there is a lot of very good data. One team of economists studied 7,846 different strategies of technical analysis. Their conclusion was that none of them systematically beat the market over time.[2]

For most investors, the efficient markets hypothesis looks like a pretty good description of reality.

CHECK YOURSELF

> Is it better to invest in a mutual fund that has performed well for five years in a row or one that has performed poorly for five years in a row? Use the efficient markets hypothesis to justify your answer.

How to Really Pick Stocks, Seriously

Okay, you probably can't beat the market without a lot of luck on your side. But we do still have four pieces of important advice. *Very* important advice. If you apply this advice over the course of your life, you will probably save thousands of dollars and if you become rich, you may save millions of dollars. (Suddenly this textbook seems like a real bargain!) No, we don't have a get rich quick formula for you, but there are a few simple mistakes you can avoid to your benefit and at no real cost, other than a bit of time and attention. Let's go through each piece of advice in turn.

Diversify

The first secret to picking stocks is to pick lots of them! Since picking stocks doesn't work well, the "secret" to wise investing is to invest in a large basket of stocks—to diversify. Diversification lowers the risk of your portfolio, how much your portfolio fluctuates in value over time.

By picking a lot of stocks, you limit your overall exposure to things going wrong in any particular company. When the energy company Enron went bankrupt in 2001, many Enron employees had put most of their life's wealth in . . . can you guess . . . Enron stock. That's a huge mistake, whether you work at the company or not. If you put all your eggs in one basket, it is a disaster if the handle on that basket breaks. Instead, you should buy many different stocks, in many different sectors of the economy, and, yes, in many countries too. You'll end up with some Enrons, but you'll also have some big winners, such as Google and Microsoft. And if Google and Microsoft have become Enrons and gone under since this book was published, well, that is just further reason why you should diversify!

Modern financial markets have made diversification easy. Mutual funds let you invest in hundreds of stocks with just one purchase. And since stock picking doesn't work well, diversification has no downside—it reduces risk without reducing your expected return.

We are focusing on diversification across stocks but there are all kinds of risks in the world and you should diversify across as many as possible. U.S. stocks, for

To buy and hold is to buy stocks and then hold them for the long run, regardless of what prices do in the short run.

example, tend to fluctuate in value along with the growth rate of the U.S. economy. You can reduce this source of risk by including a large number of international firms in your portfolio. Bonds, art, housing, and human capital (your knowledge and skills) all have associated returns and risks and for a given amount of return, you minimize your risk by diversifying across many assets.

If you accept the efficient markets hypothesis, and you accept the value of diversification, your best trading strategy can be summed up very simply. It is called **buy and hold**. That's right, buy a large bundle of stocks and just hold them. You don't have to do anything more. You will be diversified, you will not be trying to beat the market, and you can live a peaceful, quiet life.

Some of the simplest ways to buy and hold mean that you replicate the well-known stock indexes. Just for your knowledge, here are a few of those indexes:

The Dow Jones Industrial Average (or the Dow for short) is the most famous stock price index. The Dow is composed of 30 leading American stocks, each of these counted equally, whether the company is large or small. The Dow is not a very diversified index.

The Standard and Poor's 500 (S&P 500) is a much broader index of stock prices than the Dow; as the name indicates it consists of the prices of five hundred different stocks. Unlike in the Dow, the larger companies receive greater weight in the index than the smaller companies. The S&P 500 is a better indicator of the market as a whole than is the Dow.

The NASDAQ Composite Index averages the prices of all the companies traded on NASDAQ, or National Association of Securities Dealers Automated Quotations. This usually amounts to a few thousand securities, as of 2009 2,916, but of course the number changes all the time. The NASDAQ index gives especially high weight to small stocks and high-tech stocks, at least relative to the Dow or the S&P 500.

Notice that diversification changes our understanding of what makes a stock risky, or not risky. You might at first think that a risky stock is one whose price moves up and down a lot. Not exactly. If investors are diversified, and indeed most of them are, their risk depends on how much their portfolio moves up and down, not how much a single stock moves up and down. A single stock might move up and down all the time but still an overall diversified portfolio won't change in value much if some of your stocks are moving up while others are moving down.

According to finance economists, the riskiest stocks are those that move up and down in harmony with the market. For instance, many real estate stocks are risky because they are highly cyclical. They move up a lot when times are good (and the rest of the market is high) and they move down a lot when times are bad. When a recession comes, a lot of people just can't afford to buy a new house. In contrast, for an example of a relatively safe stock, consider Wal-Mart, the discount outlet. When bad times come, yes, Wal-Mart loses some business. But Wal-Mart also gains some business because people who used to shop at Nordstrom now have less money and some of them will now shop at Wal-Mart. In this regard, Wal-Mart is partly protected from business downturns.[3] Many health care stocks are safe in a similar way. Even if times are bad, you're probably not going to postpone that triple bypass operation; if you do, you won't be around to see when times are good again. In other words, if you care about the risk of a stock, don't just look at how the price of that stock moves. Look at how the price varies with the rest of the market. In the language of finance economists or statisticians, the riskiest stocks are those with the highest *covariance* with the market as a whole.

The lesson here is that if you are worried about risk, think about your portfolio as a whole, rather than obsessing over any single stock. Or let's be more specific: if you are going to become an aerospace engineer, don't buy a lot of stock in aerospace companies. The value of your human capital—which is worth a lot—is already tied up in that industry. Don't make your overall portfolio riskier by putting more eggs in that basket. If anything, buy stocks that do well when aerospace does poorly. More generally, finance theorists say that the least risky assets *for you* are assets that are *negatively correlated* with *your portfolio*. What this means is that you should try to buy assets that rise in value when the rest of your portfolio is falling in value. Are you afraid that high energy prices will cripple the prospects for your career? Buy stock in a company that builds roads in Saudi Arabia. If oil prices stay high, the gains of that road-building company will partially offset your other losses. The lesson applies to more than stocks. If you become a dentist, you run the risk that a new technology will eliminate cavities. So try to limit your risk by diversifying your portfolio: marry an optician or an engineer, not another dentist!

Avoid High Fees

We have some other advice for picking stocks. Avoid investments and mutual funds that have high fees or "loads," as they are sometimes called. It simply isn't worth it.

Let's say for instance that you wish to invest in the S&P 500. Some funds charge management and administrative fees of 0.09 percent of your investment but other funds can charge up to 2.5 percent per year for what is really the same thing! Table 16.1 shows some of the different options for investing in the

TABLE 16.1 Don't Pay Higher Fees for the Same Service

S&P Index Fund	Expense Ratio
Vanguard 500 Index Mutual Fund Admiral Shares (VFIAX)	0.09%
Fidelity Spartan 500 Index Mutual Fund (FSMKX)	0.10%
State Street Global Advisors S&P 500 Index Fund (SVSPX)	0.16%
United Association S&P 500 Index Fund II (UAIIX)	0.16%
USAA S&P 500 Index Mutual Fund Member Shares (USSPX)	0.18%
Schwab S&P 500 Index Fund—Select Shares (SWPPX)	0.19%
Vantagepoint 500 Stock Index Mutual Fund Class II Shares (VPSKX)	0.25%
T. Rowe Price Equity Index 500 Mutual Fund (PREIX)	0.35%
California Investment S&P 500 Index Mutual Fund (SPFIX)	0.36%
MassMutual Select Indexed Equity A (MIEAX)	0.67%
MassMutual Select Indexed Equity N (MMINX)	0.97%
ProFunds Bull Svc, Inv (BLPSX)	2.50%

S&P 500 and their expense ratios, the yearly percentage of your investment that you must pay in fees to the fund's managers.

The funds with the higher fees don't give you much of value in return. The lesson is simple: don't pay the higher fees!

Often when your broker calls you up to make a stock purchase, that purchase involves a relatively high fee (have you ever wondered why the broker is making the call?). Before buying or selling a stock in these circumstances, you should ask what the fee is to make the transaction. Understand the incentives of the person you are dealing with and that means understand that the broker usually earns more, the greater the number of transactions he or she can get you to make. Might that explain why he or she is telling you to buy or sell? Or maybe this really is a "once in a lifetime opportunity."

Even small fees can add up to large differences in returns over time. Let's say you are investing $10,000 over 30 years. If you invest with a firm that charges 0.10 percent a year in fees and the stock market gives a real return of 7 percent a year, then in 30 years you will have earned $74,016. If you invest in a firm that charges 1 percent a year, then in 30 years you will have about $57,434. The higher fees cost you $16,582 and, as we showed above, you probably got nothing for your extra fees. Small differences in growth or loss rates, when compounded over time, make for a big difference. The same is true for your portfolio.

That brings us to a corollary principle, to which we now turn.

Compound Returns Build Wealth

If one investment earns a higher rate of return each year than another investment, in the long run that makes a big difference. Imagine you buy a well-diversified portfolio of stocks and every year you reinvest all of your dividends. A simple approximation, called the rule of 70, explains how long it will take for your investment to double in value given a specified rate of return.

Rule of 70: If the rate of return (annual increase in value including dividends) of an investment is x percent, then the doubling time is $70/x$ years.

Table 16.2 illustrates the rule of 70 by showing how long it takes for an investment to double in value given different returns. With a return of 1 percent, an investment will double approximately every 70 years ($70/1 = 70$). If returns increase to 2 percent, the value of your investment will double every 35 years ($70/2 = 35$). Consider the impact of a 4 percent return. If this rate of return is sustained, then the value of an investment doubles every 17.5 years ($70/4 = 17.5$). In 70 years, the value doubles 4 times reaching a level 16 times its starting value!

The rule of 70 is just a mathematical approximation but it bears out the key concept that when compounded, small differences in investment returns can have a large effect. To make this more concrete, if you have a long time horizon you probably should invest in (diversified) stocks rather than bonds.

In the long run, stocks offer higher returns than bonds. Since 1802, for example, stocks have had an average real rate of return of about 7 percent per year while bonds have paid closer to 2 percent per year.[4]

TABLE 16.2 Years to Double Using the Rule of 70	
Annual Return	Years to Double
0%	Never
1%	70
2%	35
3%	23.3
4%	17.5

Using our now familiar rule of 70, we know that money that grows at 7 percent a year will double in 10 years, but money that grows at 2 percent a year won't double for 35 years. Alternatively, growing at 7 percent a year, $10,000 will return $76,122 in 30 years but if it grows at 2 percent a year, the return will be only $18,113.

Stocks, however, have the potential for greater losses than do bonds because bond holders and other creditors are always paid before shareholders. You are unlikely to lose much money if you buy high grade corporate or government bonds, but the stock market is highly volatile and it does periodically crash. Nonetheless, in American history stocks almost always outperform bonds over any 20-year time period you care to examine, including the period of the Great Depression and World War II. Stocks are usually the better long-term investment.

Of course, that doesn't mean that everyone should invest so heavily in stocks. In any particular year, or even over the course of a month, week, or day, stocks can go down in value quite a bit. If you are 80 years old and managing your retirement income, you probably shouldn't invest much in stocks. If you have to send your twins to college in two years' time, you might want some safer investments as well. Nor does the past necessarily predict the future—just because stocks outperformed bonds in the past doesn't mean that will continue to happen. Remember to diversify!

The No Free Lunch Principle or No Return Without Risk

The differences between stocks and bonds, as investment vehicles, reflect a more general principle. There is a systematic **trade-off between return and risk**. Figure 16.3, for example, shows the trade-off between return and risk on four asset classes. U.S. T-bills are safe but have low returns. You can get a higher return by buying stock in a group of large firms such as in the S&P 500, but the value of those firms fluctuates a lot more than the value of T-bills so to get the higher return you need to bear higher risk.*

The **risk-return trade-off** means higher returns come at the price of higher risk.

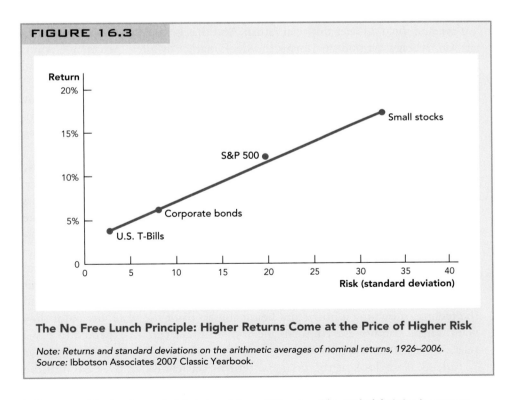

FIGURE 16.3

The No Free Lunch Principle: Higher Returns Come at the Price of Higher Risk

Note: Returns and standard deviations on the arithmetic averages of nominal returns, 1926–2006. Source: Ibbotson Associates 2007 Classic Yearbook.

* We measure risk using the standard deviation of the portfolio return. The standard deviation is a measure of how much the return tends to fluctuate from its average level: thus, the larger the standard deviation, the greater the risk. A rule of thumb is that there is a 68 percent probability of being within ±1 standard deviation of the mean return. For the S&P 500, for example, the mean return is about 12 percent and the standard deviation is about 20 percent so in any given year there is a 68 percent probability that the return will be between −8 percent and 32 percent. Of course, something else could happen with probability 32 percent! But beware! The rule of thumb is only an approximation. Risk in the real world can rarely be modeled with perfect mathematical accuracy.

If you want even more risk than an investment in the stock market, numerous schemes give you a chance of making a killing. The simplest of such strategies is to take all your money, fly to Las Vegas, and bet on "black" for a spin of the roulette wheel. Yes, there is a 47.37 percent chance that you double your wealth. That's a high return, sort of. Sadly, there is also a 52.63 percent chance that you will lose everything you have, including your credit rating and the trust of your spouse and children. That's what we call high risk.

Remember this story when you hear about a high-flying "hedge fund" or other fancy investment device. It's easy to generate high returns for a few years by getting lucky and doubling down (betting all your winnings again). Take a look again at Figure 16.2. But higher returns come at the expense of higher risk.

This no free lunch principle can help you evaluate some other investments as well. Let's say you come into a tidy sum of money and you start wondering whether or not you should invest in art. Overall, should you expect art to be a better or inferior financial investment, compared to the market as a whole?

A lot of people—probably most people—buy art because they want to look at it. They enjoy hanging it on their walls. In the language of economics, art yields "a nonmonetary return," which is just our way of saying it is fun to look at. Now suppose that investments in art earned just as high a return as investments in stocks. In that case, art would be fun to have on the wall and would be an excellent investment. But wait, that sounds like a free lunch doesn't it? So what does the no free lunch principle predict?

We know that the expected returns on different assets, adjusted for risk, should be equal. So if some asset yields a higher "fun" return those assets should, on average, yield a lower financial return. And that is exactly what we find with art. On average, art underperforms the stock market by a few percentage points a year. You can think of the lower returns as the price of having some beautiful art on your wall. Again, it's the no free lunch principle in action.

This kind of analysis applies not just to art but also to real estate. Let's say you want to buy a home. Can you expect superior or inferior financial returns over time? This question is a little trickier than the art question because two different and opposing forces operate. Let's look at each in turn.

First, a home tends to be a risky asset for most purchasers. Let's say you buy a $300,000 home by putting down $200,000 and borrowing the remainder. That home is probably a pretty big chunk of your overall wealth and it puts you in a relatively nondiversified position. That's risk, people don't usually like risk, and as we saw above riskier assets earn, all other things equal, higher expected returns (the risk-return trade-off).

Second, and probably more important, if you buy a house you get to live in it. The house, like the painting, provides you with personal services and in this case those services are pretty valuable. Many people enjoy their backyard and the feeling of owning a home and being able to paint the walls any color they want. These nonmonetary returns mean that houses can be expected to pay a relatively low financial return.

Indeed, if we look at the financial returns on real estate over a long time horizon, it turns out they are pretty low. In fact, for pretty long periods of time the average financial rate of return on real estate is not much different than zero. One lesson is that houses must be lots of fun!

If you want to see that the downside of real estate investments is not just a recent phenomenon, take a look at Figure 16.4.

FIGURE 16.4

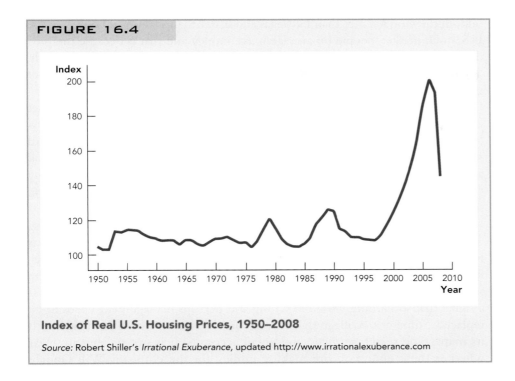

Index of Real U.S. Housing Prices, 1950–2008

Source: Robert Shiller's *Irrational Exuberance*, updated http://www.irrationalexuberance.com

In the 50 years from 1947 to 1997, real housing prices hardly changed at all with some blips upward in the late 1970s and late 1980s. Beginning in 1997, a housing boom pushed prices well above any before seen in U.S. history. As you probably know, however, since 2006 prices have tumbled and may be even lower by the time you read this book.

The lesson is that most of the time a house is a good place to live but not a good place to invest. When prices started to rise in 1997 and kept rising year after year, many people thought that real estate was the investment of the century—"they ain't making any more," people said. But the no free lunch principle tells us that precisely because houses are a good place to live, we should not also expect them to be a good investment. All other things equal, fun activities yield lower financial returns than non-fun activities.

When prices rose, some people got lucky and made a killing, but other people tried to do the same and ended up bankrupt. So don't expect to make a killing in the real estate market and remember to diversify! One more point. Are you one of these people who doesn't like to mow the lawn? Do you dread the notion of choosing homeowner's insurance or worrying about when your roof will fall in? The lesson is simple: don't buy a house, you won't have fun and the financial returns won't make it worth your while.

Other Benefits and Costs of Stock Markets

Throughout this chapter we've recommended against gambling with all or most of your money. We've recommended buy and hold, based on a diversified portfolio. But hey, maybe some of you are into gambling. You know what? If you want to take risk for the sake of risk alone, the U.S. stock market offers the best

UNDERSTAND YOUR

CHECK YOURSELF

> How does investing in stocks of other countries help to diversify your investments?

> Many people dream of owning a football or baseball team. Would you expect the return on these assets to be relatively high or low?

odds in the world, better than Las Vegas and better than your local bookie. In the U.S. stock market, people on average make money and that is because the productive capacity of the U.S. economy is expanding through economic growth. There is more profit to go around and that means you have a good chance of making some really lucrative investments.

Stocks markets have uses beyond investment. First, new stock and bond issues are an important means of raising capital for new investment (investment now in the economic sense of increasing the capital stock). Stock markets also reward successful entrepreneurs and thus encourage people to start companies and look around for new ideas. The founders of Google are now very rich and selling company shares to the stock market helped make them so. A well-functioning stock market helps companies such as Google get going or expand.

Second, the stock market gives us a better idea of how well firms are run. The stock price is a signal about the value of the firm. When the stock price is increasing, especially when it is increasing relative to other stocks, this is a signal that the firm is making the right investments for future profits. When the stock is declining, especially when it is declining relative to other stocks, this is a signal that something has gone wrong and perhaps management needs to be replaced. Some critics allege that Google has dominated search but failed with its maps, blog search services, and email accounts. It is not necessarily clear whether these endeavors are making money for the company. Will Google make YouTube into a profitable venture? Are the charges true that "Google has lost it"? It's hard to say in the abstract. But we can look at Google's share price and see if it is going up or down. Market prices give the public a daily report on whether the managers of a company are succeeding or failing.

Third, stock markets are a way of transferring company control from less competent people to more competent people. If a group of people think they know the right way to run a company, they can buy it and put their money where their mouth is, so to speak. Maybe a company should be merged, broken up, or simply look for a new direction. The stock market is the ultimate venue where people bid for the right to make these decisions.

Bubble, Bubble, Toil, and Trouble

It's worth pointing out that stock markets (and other asset markets) have a downside, namely that they can encourage speculative bubbles. A speculative bubble arises when stock prices rise far higher, and more rapidly, than can be accounted for by the fundamental prospects of the companies at hand. Bubbles are based in human psychology and often they are hard to understand, but it seems that at times investors simply get carried away by the prospects for gain and they are not sufficiently sensitive toward the prospects for loss. For instance, many of the new Internet or dot.com stocks had very high prices, circa 2000, even though many of these companies had never earned a dime of profit or for that matter any revenue. Many of the tech stocks were listed on the NASDAQ stock exchange. As you can see in Figure 16.5, in the space of five years the NASDAQ Composite Index more than tripled from a monthly average of about 1,200 to over 4,000 before falling back down again. Many people made a lot of money on the ride up and many people—maybe the same people, maybe others—lost a lot of money on the ride down.

If you can spot speculative bubbles on a consistent basis, yes, you can become very wealthy. But, of course, a speculative bubble is usually easier to detect with hindsight than at the time. Microsoft and Google might have looked

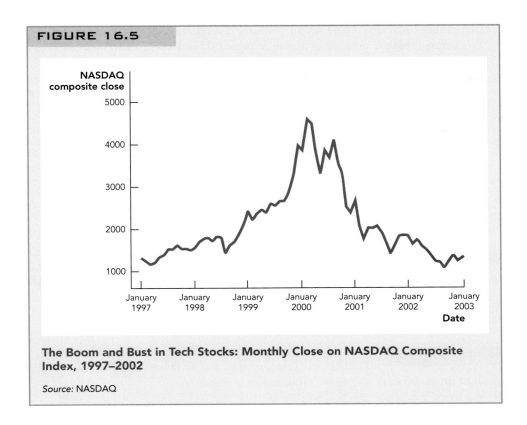

FIGURE 16.5

The Boom and Bust in Tech Stocks: Monthly Close on NASDAQ Composite Index, 1997–2002

Source: NASDAQ

like speculative bubbles too; the only problem is that they never burst. Betting too soon that high prices will end is also one way to go bankrupt.

Speculative bubbles, and their bursting, can hurt an economy. During the rise of the bubble, capital is invested in areas where it is not actually very valuable. This was the case with many .com firms circa 2000 and also the case with real estate in the years leading up to the crash of the real estate bubble in 2007–2008. That bubble, by the way, had less to do with stocks but a lot to do with financial assets that were backed by portfolios of mortgages. The analysis of these "asset-backed securities" is similar to that for stocks.

A second wave of problems comes when the bubble crashes. Lower stock prices (or lower home prices) mean that people feel poorer and so they will spend less. The collapse of the bubble also means that workers must move from one sector to another, such as from high tech to retailing, or from real estate to export industries. Shifting labor from one sector of an economy to another creates labor adjustment costs.

Yes, bubbles can be a problem, but few people doubt that we are better off with active trading in stock and asset markets. One partial solution is to have greater transparency in assessing the value of companies and assets. But at least for now there is no surefire solution for getting rid of asset bubbles.

CHECK YOURSELF

> The Federal Reserve has been criticized for not stepping in and bursting the housing bubble, which would have prevented the housing collapse. Do you think this criticism is valid, based on what you read in this section?

☐ Takeaway

We have stressed some simple and practical points. It is hard for an investor to consistently beat the market over long periods. You are well advised to diversify your investments. Avoid fees and try to generate a high compound return over time. Understand that the promise of higher returns is often accompanied by higher risk.

Viewed as a whole, stock markets and other trading markets give investors a chance to earn money, diversify their holdings, express opinions on the course of the market, and hedge risks. Stock markets also play a role in financing innovative new firms. Stock markets appear to be subject to speculative bubbles, but active stock markets are an important part of a healthy growing economy.

□ CHAPTER REVIEW

KEY CONCEPTS

Efficient markets hypothesis, p. 334

Buy and hold, p. 336

Risk-return trade-off, p. 339

FACTS AND TOOLS

1. Before we plunge into the world of finance, let's review the rule of 70. Suppose your rich aunt hands you a $3,000 check at the end of the school year. She tells you it's for your education. But what should you *really* do with that extra money? Let's see how much it would be worth if you saved it for a while.

   a. If you put it in a bank account earning 2 percent real annual return on average, how many years would it take before it was worth $6,000? Until it was worth $12,000?

   b. If you put it in a Standard and Poor's 500 (S&P 500) mutual fund earning an average 7 percent real return every year, how many years would it take before it was worth $6,000? Until it was worth $12,000? (Note: $3,000 is the minimum investment for many low-fee mutual funds.)

   c. Suppose you invest a little less than half your money in the bank and a little more than half in a mutual fund, just to play it somewhat safe, so that you can expect a 5 percent real return on average. How many years now until you reach $6,000 and $12,000? (Yes, ignore the fact that you won't have enough money to make the $3,000 minimum investment in the mutual fund.)

2. Let's do something boring just to drive home a point: Count up the number of years in Figure 16.1 where more than half of the mutual funds managed to beat the S&P 500 index. (Recall that the Standard and Poor's 500 is just a list of 500 large U.S. corporations—it's a list that overlaps a lot with the Fortune 500). What percentage of the time did the experts actually beat the S&P 500?

3. Consider the supply and demand for oranges. Orange crops can be destroyed by below-freezing temperatures.

   a. If a weather report states that oranges are likely to freeze in a storm later this week, what probably happens to the demand for oranges *today*, before the storm comes?

   b. According to a simple supply-and-demand model, what happens to the price of oranges today given your answer to part a.

   c. How does this illustrate the idea that stock prices *today* "bake in" information about *future* events? In other words, how is a share of Microsoft like an orange? (Note: Wall Street people often use the expression "That news is already baked into the price" when they talk about the efficient markets hypothesis.)

4. In the United States, high-level corporate officials have to publicly state when they buy or sell a large number of shares in their own company. They have to make these statements a few days after their purchase or sale. What do you think probably happens (choose a, b, c or d below) when newspapers report these true "insider trades?" (Note: The right answer according to theory is actually true in practice.)

   a. When insiders sell, prices rise, since investors increase their demand for the company's shares.

   b. When insiders sell, prices fall, since investors increase their demand for the company's shares.

c. When insiders sell, prices fall, since investors decrease their demand for the company's shares.

d. When insiders sell, prices rise, since investors decrease their demand for the company's shares.

5. Let's see how fees can hurt your investment strategy. Let's assume that your mutual fund grows at an average rate of 7 percent per year—before subtracting off the fees. Using the rule of 70:

a. How many years will it take for your money to double if fees are 0.5 percent per year?

b. How many years will it take for your money to double if fees are 1.5 percent per year (not uncommon in the mutual fund industry)?

c. How many years to double if fees are 2.5 percent per year?

6. a. If you talk to a broker selling the high-fee mutual fund, what will he or she probably tell you when you ask them, "Am I getting my money's worth when I pay your high fees?"

b. According to Figure 16.1, is your broker's answer likely to be right most of the time?

THINKING AND PROBLEM SOLVING

1. Your brother calls you on the phone telling you that Google's share price has fallen by about 25 percent over the past few days. Now you can own one small slice of Google for only $430 a share (the price on the day this question was written). Your brother says he is pretty sure the stock is going to head back up to $600 very soon and you should buy.

Should you believe your brother? Hint: Remember someone is selling shares whenever someone else is buying.

2. In most of your financial decisions early in life, you'll be a buyer, but let's think about the incentives of people who sell stocks, bonds, bank accounts, and other financial products.

a. Walking in the shopping mall one day, you see a new store: The Dollar Store. Of course, you've seen plenty of dollar stores before, but none like this one: The sign in the window says "Dollars for sale: Fifty cents each." Why will this store be out of business soon?

b. If business owners are self-interested and fairly rational people, will they ever open up this "Dollar Store" in the first place? Why or why not?

c. This "Dollar Store" is similar to stories people tell about "cheap stocks" that you might hear about on the news. Fill in the blank with any prices that make sense: "If the shares of this company were really worth _____, no one would really sell it for _____."

3. How is "stock market diversification" like putting money in a bank account?

4. Warren Buffett often says that he doesn't want a lot of diversification in his portfolio. He says that diversification means buying stocks that go up along with stocks that go down; but he only wants to buy the stocks that go up! From the point of view of the typical investor, what is wrong with this reasoning?

5. You own shares in a pharmaceutical company, PillCo. Reading the Yahoo! Finance website, you see that PillCo was sued this morning by users of PillCo's new heart drug, Amphlistatin. PillCo's stock has already been trading for a few hours today.

a. When the bad news about the lawsuits came out, what probably happened to the price of PillCo shares within just a few minutes?

b. According to the efficient markets hypothesis, should you sell your shares in PillCo now, a few hours after the bad news came out?

c. In many statistical studies of the stock market, the best strategy turns out to be "buy and hold." This means just what it sounds like: You buy a bunch of shares in different companies and hold them through good times and bad. People often have a tough time with the "bad" part of "holding through good times and bad." What does your answer to part b tell you about this idea?

CHALLENGES

1. What is so bad about bubbles? If the price of Internet stocks or housing rises and then falls, is that such a big problem? After all, some people say, most of the gains going up are "paper gains" and most of the losses going down are "paper losses." Comment on this view.

17

Public Goods and the Tragedy of the Commons

CHAPTER OUTLINE

Four Types of Goods

Private Goods and Public Goods

Nonrival Private Goods

Common Resources and the Tragedy of the Commons

Takeaway

Appendix: The Tragedy of the Commons: How Fast?

Armageddon almost happened on September 29, 2004. We aren't talking about the final battle described in the Bible, but what happened in *Armageddon* the movie. In *Armageddon,* an asteroid is discovered to be on a collision course with earth and NASA recruits a group of roughneck oil drillers to rocket into space, deflect the asteroid, and save civilization. *Armageddon* the movie is a bit absurd, but it got a few things right. Even an asteroid the size of an apartment building would hit the earth with the force of a 4-megaton nuclear bomb. On September 29, 2004, an asteroid called Toutatis, 2.9 *miles* long by 1.5 *miles* wide, narrowly missed the earth. If Toutatis had hit, it would have meant the end of civilization.

The probability of death by asteroid is remarkably high, by some calculations about the same as death by passenger aircraft crash. How can this be? Although the probability of an asteroid hitting the earth is very small, a lot of people would be killed if one did hit so the probability of death by asteroid is much larger than most people imagine. It doesn't happen very often but watch out when it does.*

Let's assume that we have convinced you that the danger from an asteroid collision is real and thus that asteroid deflection would be a valuable good to have. Markets provide us with all kinds of valuable goods like food, clothing, cell phones, and video games but you can't buy asteroid deflection in the market. Even if everyone were to become convinced of the benefits of asteroid deflection, you probably will *never* be able to buy asteroid deflection in the market. To see

Toutatis: Harbinger of Armageddon?

STEVE OSTRO, JPL

---

* Everyone dies from something. In the United States the probability of death by car crash is about 1 in 100 and the probability of death by commercial airplane crash is about 1 in 20,000. Chapman and Morrison (1994) estimate that the probability of death by asteroid collision is also about 1 in 20,000. See Chapman, Clark and David Morrison. 1994. "Impacts on the Earth by Asteroids and Comets: Assessing the Hazard." *Nature* 367, 33–40.

347

why, we need to take a closer look at some of the common properties of ordinary goods and some of the special properties of asteroid deflection.

When you spend $100 on a new pair of jeans, you get the exclusive use of a new pair of jeans. If you don't spend $100 on a new pair of jeans, you are excluded from using the jeans. In other words, the $100 makes a big difference in whether or not you get the jeans. That's obvious.

Now consider paying $100 toward asteroid deflection. What do you get for your $100? There are really only two situations to consider: Either enough other people pay for asteroid deflection so that the asteroid will be deflected even without your $100 or so few other people pay that the asteroid will not be deflected even with your $100.* Either way, your $100 makes no appreciable difference to the amount of asteroid deflection that you will receive. In other words, you get the same amount of asteroid deflection whether you pay or don't pay.

Since your $100 doesn't get you more asteroid deflection but it does get you a new pair of jeans, most people will buy the jeans rather than the asteroid deflection. As a result, we see a lot of firms selling jeans and none selling asteroid deflection. That's a problem because asteroid deflection is an important threat to everyone on the planet.

Jeans are an example of a private good. Asteroid deflection is an example of what economists call a public good, a good that markets are unlikely to produce in efficient quantities. Let's look more closely at these terms and the differences between jeans and asteroid deflection.

Four Types of Goods

Jeans are different from asteroid deflection for two reasons. First, as we said, people are willing to pay for jeans because paying makes the difference between getting the jeans or not—non-payers can be cheaply excluded or prevented from consuming jeans. But people aren't willing to pay for asteroid deflection because paying makes no appreciable difference to how much asteroid deflection you consume—non-payers cannot be excluded from consuming the benefits of asteroid deflection. When a person can cheaply be prevented from using a good economists say the good is excludable. When a person cannot be cheaply prevented from using a good, economists say the good is **nonexcludable.** Jeans are excludable; asteroid deflection is nonexcludable.

A good is **nonexcludable** if people who don't pay cannot be easily prevented from using the good.

The second reason why asteroid deflection is different from jeans is that when one person is wearing a pair of jeans, it's not easy for a second person to wear the same jeans. But two people can enjoy the benefits of the same asteroid deflection. In fact, billions of people can enjoy the benefits of the same asteroid deflection. But don't try fitting a billion people into the same pair of jeans!

When one person's use of a good reduces the ability of another person to use the same good, economists say the good is rival. When one person's use of a good does not reduce the ability of another person to use the same good, economists say the good is **nonrival.** Jeans are rival; asteroid deflection is nonrival.

A good is **nonrival** if one person's use of the good does not reduce the ability of another person to use the same good.

These two factors, whether a good is excludable or nonexcludable and whether it is rival or nonrival can be used to divide goods into four types, as in

---

* The probability that your $100 makes the difference between a successful asteroid deflection and an unsuccessful asteroid deflection is so small that we can ignore it.

TABLE 17.1 Four Types of Goods

	Excludable	Nonexcludable
Rival	**Private Goods**	**Common Resources**
	Jeans	Tuna in the ocean
	Hamburgers	The environment
	Contact lenses	Public roads
Nonrival	**Nonrival Private Goods**	**Public Goods**
	Cable TV	Asteroid deflection
	Wi-Fi	National defense
	Digital music	Mosquito control

Table 17.1. We have already given an example of a private good, a good that is excludable and rival. Jeans are a private good, hamburgers and contact lenses are other familiar examples. We have also given one example of a public good, a good that is nonexcludable and nonrival. Asteroid deflection is nonexcludable and nonrival. National defense is another example. Let's take a closer look at the differences between private and public goods and then we will examine the other two categories of goods, nonrival private goods and common resources.

Private Goods and Public Goods

Private goods are excludable and rival. Since private goods are excludable, they can be provided by markets—someone who doesn't pay, doesn't get; so there is an incentive to pay for and thus to produce these goods. Furthermore, since the goods are rival, excludability doesn't result in inefficiency—in a competitive market the only people who will be excluded from consuming a private good are the people who are not willing to pay what it costs to produce the good, and that's efficient.

Public goods are nonexcludable and nonrival. Since public goods are nonexcludable, it's difficult to get people to pay for them voluntarily. Markets, therefore, will tend to underprovide public goods.

Public goods are also nonrival, which means that one person's use doesn't reduce the ability of another person to use the good. As a result, 7 billion people can be protected from an asteroid strike for the same cost as protecting 1 million people. Since public goods are nonrival, the losses from the failure to provide these goods can be especially large.

Let's look at another public good, mosquito control. Mosquitoes are annoying insects. With the spread of West Nile virus in the United States, they are also dangerous. Mosquitoes can be killed by spraying, but spraying just one house won't do much good to the owners because mosquitoes from other areas will quickly repopulate any small region, so you have to spray a city or neighborhood. But who will pay to spray a city or neighborhood? If some people do pay, then many others are likely to **free ride,** sit back and enjoy the benefits without contributing to their share of the costs. Fewer mosquitoes mean fewer mosquitoes for everyone, not just those who pay for mosquito control. If a lot

Private goods are excludable and rival.

Public goods are nonexcludable and nonrival.

A **free rider** enjoys the benefits of a public good without paying a share of the costs.

of people free ride, then mosquito control will be underprovided by the market even though it is a valuable good.

The benefits of public goods provide an argument for taxation and government provision. By taxing everyone and producing the public good, government can make people better off. Many cities and counties, for example, pay for mosquito control from government tax revenues. National defense is another example of a public good that would be difficult to provide voluntarily but is provided by government.

It may seem paradoxical that people can be made better off by requiring them to do something that they would not choose to do voluntarily but the paradox can be resolved. Imagine that there are a million people all of whom want national defense but none of whom chooses to voluntarily contribute to national defense because of the incentive to free ride. Now imagine that this group is offered a plan "The government will tax each of you and use the proceeds to pay for national defense but only if you all agree to the plan." It's quite possible that even though none contribute voluntarily all will agree to be taxed, *so long as everyone else is also taxed.*

Of course just because everyone *can* be made better off by taxation does not mean that everyone *will* be made better off. Some people want more national defense, some people want less, pacifists want none. So, taxation means that some people will be turned into **forced riders,** people who must contribute to the public good even though their benefits from the public good are low or even negative.

What quantity of the public good should the government produce? In principle, the government should produce the amount that maximizes consumer plus producer surplus or the total benefits of the public good minus the total costs. But, in practice, figuring this out is very difficult. The total benefit of a public good, for example, is the sum of the benefits to each individual. But some individuals value the public good more than others and there is no easy way to finding out exactly how much each person values the good.

We showed in Chapter 3 that (under certain conditions) a market automatically produces the quantity of a good that maximizes consumer plus producer surplus. We now know that one of the required conditions is that the good be a private good, a good that is rival and excludable. Unfortunately, no one has yet discovered a workable process that, as if guided by an "invisible hand," produces optimal amounts of nonrival and nonexcludable goods, i.e., public goods.

Voting and other democratic procedures can help to produce information about the demand for public goods, but these processes are unlikely to work as well at providing the optimal amounts of public goods as do markets at providing the optimal amounts of private goods (see Chapter 19 for more). Thus, we have more confidence that the optimal amount of toothpaste is purchased every year ($2.3 billion worth in recent years) than the optimal amount of defense spending ($549 billion) or the optimal amount of asteroid deflection (close to $0). In some cases, we could get too much of the public good with many people being forced riders and in other cases we could get too little of the public good. Nevertheless, since the market fails to provide public goods, we are probably fortunate that government can provide public goods even if the method is imperfect.

One final point about public goods: a public good is *not* defined as a good produced in the public sector. If the government started to produce jeans, for

A **forced rider** is someone who pays a share of the costs of a public good but who does not enjoy the benefits.

TIME LIFE PICTURES/MANSEL/TIME LIFE PICTURES/GETTY IMAGES

The English philosopher Thomas Hobbes (1588–1679) explained under what conditions individuals might voluntarily give up their rights.

"I authorise and give up my right of governing myself to this man, or to this assembly of men, on this condition; that thou give up, thy right to him, and authorise all his actions in like manner."

Leviathan, Chapter 17.

example, that does not make jeans a public good. The government does produce mail delivery even though mail delivery is not a public good. Similarly, asteroid deflection is a public good even though, as of yet, the government does not produce very much asteroid deflection.

Nonrival Private Goods

Nonrival private goods are goods that are excludable but nonrival. A television show like *The Sopranos*, for example, is excludable—you must buy HBO to watch the show, at least in its first run—but it's also nonrival because when one person watches this does not reduce the ability of another person to watch. Clearly, markets can provide goods that are excludable but nonrival, but they do so at the price of some inefficiency. HBO prohibits some people from watching *The Sopranos*, for example, even though they would be willing pay the cost (close to zero for an additional viewer) but not the price (say $25.99 a month).

Nonrival private goods are goods that are excludable but nonrival.

In practice, the inefficiency from the underprovisioning of most nonrival private goods like television, music, and software is not that big a deal. The fixed costs of producing these goods must be paid somehow and we do not want to lose the diversity, creativity, and responsiveness provided by markets.

Entrepreneurs are constantly looking for ways to turn nonexcludable, nonrival goods such as television into nonrival, private (excludable) goods such as cable television, so that they can be provided at a profit. Furthermore, entrepreneurs can sometimes find clever ways of profiting from nonrival goods *even without relying on exclusion.*

The Peculiar Case of Advertising

Radio and television are peculiar goods because although they are public goods, nonrival *and* nonexcludable, they are provided in large quantities by markets. How is this possible? When radio first appeared, no one could figure out how to make a profit from it and most people thought that government provision would be necessary if people were to benefit from this amazing discovery. After much experimentation, however, entrepreneurs did discover how to give radio away for free (the efficient solution) and yet still make a profit—they discovered advertising. Advertisers pay for the costs of programming that is then given away for free.

Advertising, of course, is not a perfect solution to the problem of nonexcludability and nonrivalry, but for radio and broadcast television it has worked pretty well. Advertising works so well that some nonrival goods are provided without exclusion even when exclusion would be cheap. Google, for example, spends billions of dollars indexing the web and developing search algorithms and then they offer their product to anyone in the world for free. Google could exclude people who don't pay for its service, but it has discovered that selling advertising and providing its services for free is more profitable.

Finally, Wi-Fi is an interesting example of a nonrival but potentially excludable public good because it is currently provided in just about every possible manner. Wi-Fi is sold by private firms like Sprint who exclude non-payers by requiring security codes. Other firms offer Wi-Fi for free but only if you watch advertising. Cafes such as Panera Bread offer free Wi-Fi to help attract customers. Wi-Fi is also given away by people who choose not to close their

> Could advertising be used to pay for the upkeep of public parks? Where would the advertising be seen?

> Many airports have pay-for Wi-Fi. Why don't they offer free Wi-Fi?

Common resources are goods that are nonexcludable but rival.

The **tragedy of the commons** is the tendency of any resource that is unowned and hence nonexcludable to be overused and undermaintained.

access points. In Philadelphia, the government taxes citizens to pay for the network and then offers free access. Each of these methods has its advantages and disadvantages.

Common Resources and the Tragedy of the Commons

Common resources are goods that are nonexcludable but rival. An example is tuna in the ocean. Until they are caught the tuna are unowned hence nonexcludable and it's difficult to prevent anyone from fishing for tuna. But tuna are not public goods since when one person catches and consumes a tuna that leaves less tuna for other people. The result of nonexcludability and rivalry is often the **tragedy of the commons**, overexploitation and undermaintenance of the common resource. As a result of the tragedy of the commons, tuna are being driven toward extinction.

Since 1960, the tuna catch has decreased by 75 percent (see Figure 17.1). The southern bluefin is highly prized as sushi and demand has increased as sushi has become more trendy. The increase in demand and the decrease in the catch have driven up prices so a single choice tuna can now fetch $50,000 or more at the Tokyo fish market. As a result of the high price, corporations hunt tuna across the oceans in fast ships using satellites, sophisticated radar, and on-board helicopters. The sad truth is that so many fish are caught that many types of sushi may soon be a thing of the past.

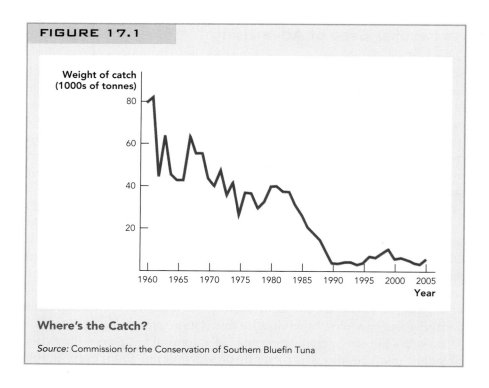

FIGURE 17.1

Where's the Catch?

Source: Commission for the Conservation of Southern Bluefin Tuna

Tuna isn't the only fish headed toward extinction. A 2006 paper in *Science* estimated that if the long-term trend continues, *all* of the world's major seafood stocks will collapse by 2048. Already nearly 30 percent of seafood species have collapsed (defined as a decline in the catch of 90 percent). As seafood species decline so do all the species that depend on them in the food chain. Overfishing is draining the oceans of fish.

Overfishing, however, is not primarily caused by increased demand. People like to eat chickens even more than they like to eat tuna but chickens are not going extinct. Why not? The difference is that chickens are owned and tuna, "chickens of the sea," are unowned.

To see why ownership means that chickens are plentiful and tuna are scarce, let's take a closer look at the incentives of fishermen and chicken ranchers.

Everyone, including the fishermen whose livelihoods depend on tuna, knows that tuna are being fished to extinction. So, you might think that the logical thing for a tuna fisherman to do is to fish less. But that's not correct. If Haru, a Japanese tuna fisherman, fishes less will there be more tuna for him to catch in the future? No, if Haru fishes less, that just leaves more tuna for other fishermen to catch—fishing less doesn't help Haru because he doesn't own the tuna until it's in the hold of his ship. Since Haru doesn't own the tuna in the ocean, he has no way of securing the fruits of his restraint.

The Difference Is Ownership

Chickens
(owned, not endangered)

"Chickens of the Sea"
(unowned, endangered)

Compare the incentives facing Haru with those facing Frank Perdue, the legendary chicken entrepreneur. Will Frank Perdue ever let his chickens go extinct? Of course not, Perdue makes money from his chickens, so to maximize profits Perdue will keep his stock of chickens healthy and growing. If Perdue "overfishes" his chickens, he pays the price. If Perdue exercises restraint and grows his flock, he gets the benefit. In short, Frank Perdue will never kill the ~~goose~~ chicken that lays his golden eggs.

The problem of overfishing is one example of the *tragedy of the commons*, the tendency for any resource that is unowned to be overused and undermaintained. The theory goes back at least to Aristotle who in criticizing Plato's idea of raising children in common said "that which is common to the greatest number has the least care bestowed upon it."[1]

Do you live with other students? Take a look at your kitchen—that's the tragedy of the commons. Other examples of the tragedy of the commons include the slaughter of the open-range buffalo during the nineteenth century, deforestation in the African Sahel region, and the hunting of elephants to near extinction.

The tragedy of the commons

The tragedy of the commons applies especially strongly to resources like fish, forests, and agricultural land because these resources must be carefully maintained to remain useful. But when resources are unowned, the users do not have strong incentives to invest in maintenance because maintenance mostly creates an external benefit not a private benefit. In other words, the fisherman who throws the small fish back mostly increases other people's future catch, not his own. The tragedy of the commons is thus a type of externality problem like those we examined in Chapter 9.

We typically call something a *tragedy* of the commons when the lack of maintenance is so severe that exploitation is pushed beyond the point where the resource reproduces itself. To maintain a healthy stock of fish, for example, the yearly catch of fish must be no more than the yearly increase in fish population. If a population of 100 fish grows by 10 percent every year, then fishermen can catch 10 fish *forever*. But if the fishermen catch just one more fish, 11 fish per year, the stock of fish will be extinct in just 26 years. (See the appendix for a proof.) So, the fishermen who overfish are not just driving the fish into extinction, they are driving *their own way of life* into extinction—that's a tragedy.

Happy Solutions to the Tragedy of the Commons

The tragedy of the commons can sometimes by averted in small groups. Small tribes and villages have avoided the tragedy of overfishing a lake or overgrazing a pasture through the enforcement of norms. A tribe member who takes too many fish from the common lake will be shunned, like someone who litters in a public park. A tribe member who exercises restraint and throws the small fish back will be respected. Tragedy of the commons problems, however, are harder to solve when a lot of unrelated people have access to the common good.

Command and control and more recently tradable allowances have been used to solve tragedy of the commons problems, just as they have been used to solve other externality problems as we discussed in Chapter 9. When fishing stocks have neared depletion, for example, governments have tried command and control solutions like limiting the number of fishing boats. To protect their salmon fishery, British Columbia limited the number of boats in 1968. Unfortunately, the scheme did not work well because the fishermen installed more powerful engines and better electronics for finding fish—this is often called "capital stuffing" because the fishermen stuffed their boats with expensive capital so those boats could be more effective. As a result of capital stuffing, the value of the typical fishing boat tripled in just 10 years; not surprisingly the salmon fishery continued to decline. Similar problems have occurred when governments have restricted the number of days that fishing is allowed.

New Zealand pioneered an alternative approach in 1986 with individual transferable quotas (ITQs). ITQs are just like the pollution allowances that we looked at in Chapter 9; the owner of an ITQ has the right to catch a certain tonnage of fish. The sum of the individual ITQs adds up to the total allowable catch, which is set by the government.[2] ITQs can be bought and sold and the government does not restrict the types of boats or equipment that the fishermen use so resources are not wasted by capital stuffing.

The ITQ system has been very successful. Figure 17.2 shows that after the ITQ system was put into place the fish catch in New Zealand increased—in other words, preventing the fishermen from overfishing *increased* the amount of fish that they caught! This may seem paradoxical but it's just a reminder of why the tragedy of the commons is a tragedy—when each fisherman chooses to fish rather than restrain themselves the net result is less fish for everyone.*

New Zealand was able to create an ITQ system and rescue its fishery because most of the New Zealand fish live and spawn within 200 miles of New Zealand's shore—the economic zone that international law assigns exclusively to New Zealand. Thus, the New Zealand government was able to create property rights and exclude anyone who didn't have the right to fish (i.e., an ITQ) from catching fish within its waters. Property rights in other common resources such as African elephants have also been created and have resulted in substantial improvements.

Unfortunately it's not easy to create property rights in all common resources. Southern bluefin tuna, for example, migrate throughout the Pacific, and some have been tagged and tracked across thousands of miles of ocean. So any solution to the tragedy of the tuna commons will require a multi-country agreement. That's not impossible. In the 1970s, scientists discovered that certain

---

* Thus, the tragedy of the commons can also be understood as a prisoner's dilemma, which we introduced in Chapter 13.

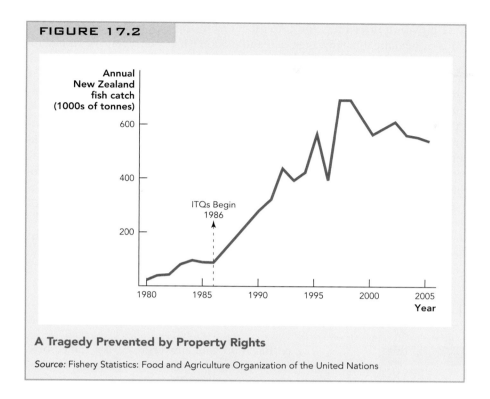

FIGURE 17.2

A Tragedy Prevented by Property Rights

Source: Fishery Statistics: Food and Agriculture Organization of the United Nations

chemicals commonly used in aerosols could disrupt the ozone layer, which protects the earth from UV-B radiation. Protecting the ozone layer is a public good since it is nonexcludable and nonrival. Fortunately, an international treaty called the Montreal Protocol has been signed by 195 of the 196 United Nations member states and it restricts the use of chemicals that damage the ozone layer. The treaty is widely regarded as the most successful environmental treaty as emissions of ozone-depleting chemicals have declined and the ozone layer has begun to recover.[3]

Similarly, if there were world agreement, technology could be used to tag tuna and create property rights but as we know from our discussion of the Coase theorem in Chapter 9, the more parties required to make an agreement, the greater the transactions costs and the less likely a solution. Moreover, rather than working to create property rights or restrict fishing to sustainable levels, most major governments today subsidize fishing extensively, which is making the tragedy of the commons worse. Thus, the tragedy of the tuna commons may not have a happy solution any time soon, either for sushi lovers or for tuna.

☐ Takeaway

Public goods are valuable but markets will often undersupply these goods. As we have seen "nonexcludability" and "nonrivalry" are important qualities of public goods, but nonexcludability is usually the more important problem. Nonrival but excludable goods such as Cable TV or digital music can often be provided privately. Although there may be some inefficiency when nonpayers are excluded,

CHECK YOURSELF

> Why do small communities find it easier to deal with common resource problems than a state or a country?

> Why is the establishment of property rights a key way to solve the problem of some common resources?

private provision does allow for entrepreneurship and market discovery. When a good is nonexcludable, however, demanders don't have an incentive to pay for the good and as a result suppliers don't have an incentive to supply the good. That's why, for instance, the world doesn't have enough protection against an asteroid strike. The benefit of providing public goods is an argument for government taxation and supply.

A resource that is nonexcludable but rival will tend to be overused and under-maintained. The tragedy of the commons explains many of the major environmental problems facing the world today. Sometimes there are creative solutions to the tragedy of the commons, such as instituting new property rights. Unfortunately, creating property rights is not automatic and may require extensive understanding of economic principles and agreement among many of the world's governments.

In short, many of the world's problems arise when property rights to goods are either not possible, not protected or not easily implemented.

□ CHAPTER REVIEW

KEY CONCEPTS

Nonexcludable, p. 348

Nonrival, p. 348

Private good, p. 349

Public good, p. 349

Free rider, p. 349

Forced rider, p. 350

Nonrival private good, p. 351

Common resources, p. 352

Tragedy of the commons, p. 352

FACTS AND TOOLS

1. Take a look at the following list of goods and services:

   Apples

   Open-heart surgery

   Cable television

   Farm-raised salmon

   Yosemite National Park

   Central Park, New York

   The Chinese language

   The idea of calculus

   a. Is each item on the list excludable or nonexcludable? Sometimes the border is a little fuzzy, but justify your answer if you think there's any ambiguity.

   b. Rival or nonrival?

   c. Based on your answers to parts a and b, sort each good or service into one of the four categories from Table 17.1.

   d. How do you exclude people from a park?

2. Which of the following are free riders, which are forced riders, and which are just people paying for public goods?

   a. In Britain, Alistair pays a tax to support the British Broadcasting Corporation. He doesn't own a radio or TV.

   b. Monica pays her local property taxes and state income taxes. Police patrol her neighborhood regularly.

   c. Richard, a young boy in 1940s Los Angeles, jumps on board the streetcar without paying.

   d. In the United States, Sara pays taxes to fund children's immunizations. She lives out in the forest, has no family, and rarely sees other people.

   e. In Japan, Dave, a tourist from the United States, enjoys the public parks.

3. **a.** Is education—a college course, for instance—excludable?

   b. Is education a rival good? That is, if your class has more students, do you get a worse education on average? Do students (and parents) typically prefer smaller class sizes? Do professors typically prefer smaller classes? Does it usually cost more for a school to educate more students?

c. According to the standard economists' definition of a public good—the definition we use in this chapter—is education a public good?

d. Which of the four categories from Table 17.1 does education seem to fit best into?

4. Emeril says, "In my economics class, I learned that the only way to fund public goods was to have the government tax citizens to pay for those goods. Is that what you learned?"

Rachel responds, "Actually, in my class, we used *Modern Principles,* and we learned that there are other ways to fund public goods, like _____." Complete Rachel's statement.

5. a. American bison used to freely roam the Great Plains. In the 1820s, there were some 30 million bison in the United States but a survey in 1889 counted just 1,091. Why were the bison driven to near extinction? How were the bison like tuna?

b. At some restaurants and grocery stores, you can buy bison burgers, made from farm-raised bison. Is this good news or bad news if we want more bison around?

6. a. The nation of Alphaville has been hunting its deer population to extinction. The government decrees strict limits on the number of hunters, and on the number of rounds of ammunition that each hunter can take into the hunt. Hunters, like fishermen, are a creative lot: What will "capital stuffing" look like in this case?

b. What would an individual transferable quotas (ITQ) system look like in this case?

c. Do real governments use quotas like this to control deer populations? If you don't know the answer, just ask your classmates: There's probably a hunter or two in your course.

7. This chapter noted that chickens and the "chicken of the sea" (tuna) are fundamentally different in terms of population though they are both food. Indeed, chickens are eaten far more than tuna, and chickens are abundant compared to their ocean-living cousins.

a. What difference between these two species does this chapter identify as the explanation for this seemingly strange puzzle?

b. As population and prosperity has increased, the demand for chicken has increased. What happens to the price of chickens as a result? Why?

c. Because of the rules humans have concerning chickens, what happens to the number of people raising chickens as a result of the price change? Why? What happens to the number of chickens? Why?

d. What happens to the price of tuna as population and prosperity increase? Why?

e. Because of the rules humans have concerning tuna, what happens to the number of people harvesting tuna as a result of the price change? Why?

8. a. Why did the fish catch *increase* in New Zealand after the amount that each fisherman could catch was *limited* by a quota?

b. Given your answer to part a, would an individual fisherman in New Zealand want to catch more fish than he's allowed, if he knew no one would ever catch him?

c. So given your answer to part b, does the New Zealand system depend on government enforcement to work, or will individual fishermen agree out of self-interest to abide by the ITQ?

THINKING AND PROBLEM SOLVING

1. In 2008, Jean Nouvel won the Pritzker Architecture Prize (the highest prize in architecture). One of his most notable works is the Torre Agbar (pictured), a break-through skyscraper that lights up each night thanks to over 4,000 LED devices—a pricey but purely cosmetic feature.

ATLANTIDE PHOTO TRAVEL/CORBIS

a. Many people enjoy looking at the Torre Agbar. Just considering that enjoyment, how would you classify the Torre Agbar: rival or nonrival? Why?

b. The Torre Agbar is the third tallest building in Barcelona. For the purposes of enjoying its illuminated façade, would you classify the building as an excludable or nonexcludable good? Why?

c. Based on your answers, is the LED façade a public good?

d. Companies often hire architects like Nouvel to create beautiful buildings that are expensive to design, build, and maintain yet they cannot charge people to look at them. This chapter offered one possible explanation for this puzzle. What's the explanation and how does it help justify the construction of a widely enjoyed building? (Hint: The building is the headquarters for Grupo Agbar, a company dedicated to the distribution and treatment of water in countries all over the world. For most of you, this is the first time you've heard of this company.)

2. a. "A public good is just a good that provides large positive externalities." Discuss.

b. "A tragedy of the commons occurs when using a good causes massive negative externalities." Discuss. In parts a and b, compare the definitions from Chapter 9 to those from this chapter.

3. a. Has the rise of the Internet and file sharing turned media such as movies and music into public goods? Why?

b. Taking your answer in part a into account, would government taxation and funding of music improve social welfare? In your answer, at least *mention* some of the practical difficulties of doing this.

4. We mentioned that the tragedy of the commons is a form of prisoner's dilemma, something we saw back in Chapter 13. As so often in economics, the same model can apply to many different settings. Let's recycle *Facts and Tools* question 6b from that chapter just to emphasize the point:

		Player B	
		Left	Right
Player A	Up	(100, 100)	(600, 50)
	Down	(50, 600)	(500, 500)

a. We have given you very generic strategies "Up, Down, Left, Right." Relabel the matrix so the game applies to fishermen and the tragedy of the commons.

b. Which set of strategies would give the fishermen the highest joint payoff?

c. Which set of actions would be equivalent to the following choice: "One fisherman decided not to conserve and to catch more than his fair share." (There are two right answers here.)

d. Which set of actions is the one and only Nash equilibrium? How would you describe it in terms of these two fishermen?

5. As we've already mentioned, the line between "public good" and "private good" is genuinely blurry. Electronic tolls on roadways are making excludability a little bit easier every year. In your view, should we continue to think of roads as public goods? (To be more accurate, we really should say, "Should we continue to think of *travel* on uncongested roads as public goods?")

6. The massive stone faces that pepper Easter Island puzzled people for centuries. What happened to the civilization that erected these faces? A clue is that the island currently has no trees. Trees would have been necessary to roll the stones and to make boats to bring the stones to the island. Archeological digs have discovered the island *did* have trees very long ago but it's thought that the natives used up all the trees until they had no choice but to leave. Can you think of an explanation for why people would behave in this way? The following questions may suggest an answer.

JAMES L. AMOS/CORBIS

a. Who bore the cost of planting new trees? Who benefited from planting new trees?

b. As the population of the island grew, what happened to the number of trees? Why?

c. Biologist Jared Diamond, writing on the subject of trees in Easter Island, asked, "What were they thinking when they cut down the last palm tree?"[4] What do you think the person who cut down that last palm tree was thinking, if he acted like a person facing a tragedy of the commons?

7. Economists typically remind people to weigh the costs of an action against the benefits of that action. Let's invent some examples where it's just too expensive or too risky to solve the very real problems discussed in this chapter.

a. It's possible that it would just cost too much to defend the earth from asteroids, where the best option, all things considered, is just to hope for the best. Invent an extreme example where this is the case—your example might take place in a world with different technology, different type of government, and so forth.

b. What about saving the tuna? Invent an example where the best option is to just let the fishermen do what they want, even if tuna go extinct.

CHALLENGES

1. a. Two girls are sharing a cold chocolate milk as in the picture below. How long do you think it will take them to drink all the milk? How long would it take if each girl had their own glass and half the milk? Can you see a problem when the girls drink from a common glass?

SEAN JUSTIC/CORBIS

b. What is going on in this picture of the East Texas oil field in 1919? Can you see the problem?

LOOKING WEST FROM GOLDEN CYCLE - TOWARD THE FAMOUS NORTH WEST POOL THAT SURPASSES IN DIVIDENDS AND ACTIVITY - ANY OIL POOL YET DISCOVERED

AMERICAN PETROLEUM INSTITUTE PHOTOGRAPH AND FILM COLLECTION, ARCHIVES CENTER, NATIONAL MUSEUM OF AMERICAN HISTORY, SMITHSONIAN INSTITUTION

c. Why did we put these two questions together? (Hint: A speech from the movie *There Will Be Blood* gets at the same question—it's based on a 1924 speech by U.S. Senator Albert Fall of New Mexico.)

2. Some media companies (especially in music and movie industries) run ads claiming that downloading or copying media is the same thing as stealing a CD or DVD from a store. Let's see if this is the case.

a. Is a DVD a nonrival good? Why or why not?

b. Suppose someone stole a DVD from a retail outlet. Regardless of how that person values the DVD, does the movie company lose any revenue as a result of the theft? Why or why not?

c. Suppose someone illegally downloaded a movie instead of purchasing it. Also suppose that person placed a high value on the movie (they valued it more than the price required to purchase it legally). Does the movie company lose any revenue as a result of the theft? Why or why not?

d. Suppose someone illegally downloaded a movie instead of purchasing it. Also suppose that person placed a low value on the movie (they valued it less than the price required to purchase it legally). Does the movie company lose any revenue as a result of the theft? Why or why not?

e. How is illegally downloading media like retail theft and how is it not?

3. The economic theory of public goods makes a very clear prediction: If the benefits of some action go to strangers, not to yourself, then you won't do that action. Economists have run dozens of experiments testing out this prediction. Elinor Ostrom sums up the results in a 2000 article in the *Journal of Economic Perspectives*.

A typical "public goods game" is quite simple: Everyone in the experiment is given, say, $5 each, theirs to take home if they like. They're told that if they donate money to the common pool, all the money in the pool will then be doubled. The money in the pool will then be divided equally among all players, whether they contributed to the pool or not. That's the whole game. Let's see what a purely self-interested person would do in this setting. (Hint: A public goods game is just like a prisoner's dilemma, only with more people.)

a. If there are 10 people playing the game, and they all chip in their $5 to the pool, how much will be in the pool *after* it doubles?

b. So how much money does each person get to take home if everyone puts their money in the pool?

c. Now, suppose that you are one of the players, and you've seen that all 9 other players have put in all their money. If you keep your $5, and the pool money gets divided up equally among all 10 of you, how much will you have in total?

d. So are you better or worse off if you keep your money?

e. What if none of the nine had put money into the pot: If you were the only one to put your money in, how much would you have afterward? Is this better or worse than if you'd just kept the money yourself?

f. So if you were a purely self-interested individual, what's the best thing to do regardless of what the other players are doing: Put all the money in, put some of it in, or put none of it in? (Answer in percent.) Do the benefits of donating go to you or to other people?

g. If people just cared about "the group," they'd surely donate 100 percent. In part f, you just said what a purely self-interested person would do. In the dozens of studies that Ostrom summarizes, people give an average of 30 percent to the common pool. So, are the people in these studies closer to the pure self-interest model from part f, or are they closer to the pure altruist model of human behavior?

4. Canada's Labrador Peninsula (which includes modern day Newfoundland and most of modern day Quebec) was once home to an indigenous group, the Montagnes, who, in contrast to their counterparts in the American Southwest, established property rights over land. This institutional change was a direct result of the increase in the fur trade after European traders arrived.[5]

a. Before European traders came, the amount of land in the Labrador Peninsula far exceeded the indigenous people's needs. Hunting animals specifically for fur was not yet widely practiced. What can you conclude about the relative scarcity of land or animals? Why?

b. Before the European arrival, land was commonly held. Given your answer in part a, did the tragedy of the commons play out for the indigenous Montagnes? (Remember, air is also commonly held.)

c. Once the European traders came, the demand for fur increased. Do you expect the tragedy of the commons to play out under these circumstances? Why or why not?

d. The Montagnes established property rights over the fur trade, allocating families' hunting territory. This led to rules ranging from when an animal is accidentally killed in a neighbor's territory to laws governing inheritance. Why did the Montagnes create property rights only after the Europeans traders came?

5. It's one of the ironies of American history that when the pilgrims first arrived at Plymouth Rock they promptly set about creating a communal society in which all shared equally in the produce of their land. As a result, the pilgrims were soon starving to death.

Fortunately, "after much debate of things," Governor William Bradford ended the corn commons, decreeing that each family should keep the corn that it produced. In one of the most insightful statements of political economy ever written, Bradford described the results of the new and old systems.

> [Ending the corn commons] had very good success, for it made all hands very industrious, so as much more corn was

planted than otherwise would have been by any means the Governor or any other could use, and saved him a great deal of trouble, and gave far better content. The women now went willingly into the field, and took their little ones with them to set corn; which before would allege weakness and inability; whom to have compelled would have been thought great tyranny and oppression.

The experience that was had in this common course and condition, tried sundry years and that amongst godly and sober men, may well evince the vanity of that conceit of Plato's and other ancients applauded by some of later times; that the taking away of property and bringing in community into a commonwealth would make them happy and flourishing; as if they were wiser than God. For this community (so far as it was) was found to breed much confusion and discontent and retard much employment that would have been to their benefit and comfort. For the young men, that were most able and fit for labour and service, did repine that they should spend their time and strength to work for other men's wives and children without any recompense. The strong, or man of parts, had no more in division of victuals and clothes than he that was weak and not able to do a quarter the other could; this was thought injustice. The aged and graver men to be ranked and equalized in labours and victuals, clothes, etc., with the meaner and younger sort, thought it some indignity and disrespect unto them. And for men's wives to be commanded to do service for other men, as dressing their meat, washing their clothes, etc., they deemed it a kind of slavery, neither could many husbands well brook it. Upon the point all being to have alike, and all to do alike, they thought themselves in the like condition, and one as

good as another; and so, if it did not cut off those relations that God hath set amongst men, yet it did at least much diminish and take off the mutual respects that should be preserved amongst them. And would have been worse if they had been men of another condition. Let none object this is men's corruption, and nothing to the course itself. I answer, seeing all men have this corruption in them, God in His wisdom saw another course fitter for them.

Bradford, William. *Of Plymouth Plantation, 1620–1647*. Edited by Samuel Eliot Morison. New York: Modern Library, 1967.

a. Imagine yourself a pilgrim under the communal (commons) system. If you worked hard all day in the fields, would that increase your share of the food by a lot or a little? Describe the incentive to work under the communal system.

b. Under this system, what type of good was the pilgrim's harvest?

c. According to Bradford the communal system "retard[ed] much employment that would have been to their benefit and comfort." Why would the communal system reduce something that would have been to the pilgrim's benefit? How would you describe this using the tools of economics?

d. According to Bradford what happened to the amount of food produced and the amount of labor after the communal system was abolished and workers got to keep a larger share of what they produced?

e. Read Bradford's statement carefully. What other effects did the communal system create? (Note that economists typically ignore these kinds of effects.)

CHAPTER APPENDIX

The Tragedy of the Commons: How Fast?

We can use a simple spreadsheet to see how quickly common resources can become tragically overexploited and ruined. Suppose that we start with a stock of 100. This could be 100 million fish or 100 thousand elephants, or 100 units of agricultural quality or other common resource. Let's suppose that this resource grows or reproduces itself by 10 percent every year. We can then set up our spreadsheet as shown in Figure A17.1. The key cell is Cell B3, which contains the formula =B2*(1+$C$2)-$D$2. This formula takes the stock of fish in the previous year from cell B2, multiplies it by one plus the growth rate in Cell C2 (using the dollar signs to make sure that this cell reference stays the same when we copy it elsewhere), and then subtracts the annual catch or usage in Cell D2 (which we initially set at 10) to get the stock in this year.

FIGURE A17.1

	B3			f_x	=B2*(1+$C$2)-$D$2	
	A	B	C		D	E
1	Year	Stock	Natural Growth Rate		Annual Catch	
2	1	100		0.10	10	
3	2	100				
4	3	100				
5	4	100				
6	5	100				
7	6	100				
8	⋮	⋮				
9						
10						

We now copy and paste Cell B3 into Cells B4 onward. It's pretty obvious that if a stock of 100 fish grows by 10 percent every year, then a catch of 10 is sustainable forever and this is what our spreadsheet indicates.

What is more surprising is how quickly an increase in the catch can drive a stock to extinction. If we change the annual catch in Cell D2 to 11, for example, we get the result in Figure A17.2.

FIGURE A17.2

	A	B	C	D
1	Year	Stock	Natural Growth Rate	Annual Catch
2	1	100	0.10	11
3	2	99		
4	3	97.9		
5	4	96.69		
6	5	95.359		
7	6	93.8949		
8	7	92.28439		
9	8	90.51283		
10	9	88.56411		
11	10	86.42052		
12	11	84.06258		
13	12	81.46883		
14	13	78.61572		
15	14	75.47729		
16	15	72.02502		
17	16	68.22752		
18	17	64.05027		
19	18	59.4553		
20	19	54.40083		
21	20	48.84091		
22	21	42.725		
23	22	35.9975		
24	23	28.59725		
25	24	20.45698		
26	25	11.50267		
27	26	1.652941		
28	27	-9.18177		
29				

Notice that the decline starts slowly but by year 27 the stock of fish has gone negative, that is, the fish are extinct. You can experiment with different assumptions about growth rates and catches to see how long stocks can be sustained under different scenarios.

18

Economics, Ethics, and Public Policy

CHAPTER OUTLINE

The Case for Exporting Pollution and Importing Kidneys

Exploitation

Meddlesome Preferences

Fair and Equal Treatment

Cultural Goods and Paternalism

Poverty, Inequality, and the Distribution of Income

Who Counts? Immigration

Economic Ethics

Takeaway

Is it okay to export pollution from rich to poor countries? Larry Summers not only said it was okay when he was chief economist at the World Bank but he said that exporting pollution should be encouraged. Summers, if you don't already recognize the name, is one of the best economists of his generation, a former president of Harvard and secretary of the Treasury, and now a lead advisor to President Obama. In a memo to some of his colleagues, Summers wrote:

> Just between you and me, shouldn't the World Bank be encouraging *more* migration of the dirty industries to the LDCs [Less Developed Countries]? . . .
>
> The measurements of the costs of health impairing pollution depends on the foregone earnings from increased morbidity and mortality. From this point of view a given amount of health impairing pollution should be done in the country with the lowest cost, which will be the country with the lowest wages. I think the economic logic behind dumping a load of toxic waste in the lowest wage country is impeccable and we should face up to that.*

Unfortunately for Summers, his memo didn't remain "just between you and me." When it was leaked to the press there was a firestorm of controversy, not just against Summers but against economics and the type of "impeccable" economic reasoning that Summers found convincing.

If you found Larry Summers's memo disturbing, what about some of the ideas of Nobel Prize-winning economist Gary Becker? Becker says that we

---

*The Summers memo can be widely found online.

Kidney for sale! Kidney for sale!

Positive economics is describing, explaining, or predicting economic events.

Normative economics is recommendations or arguments about what economic policy should be.

should legalize the trade in human kidneys. In fact, in a survey, Robert Whaples found that 70 percent of the economists he surveyed (128 members of the American Economic Association) agreed or strongly agreed with this idea.[1] Right now over 75,000 Americans are waiting for kidney transplants. Many of them will die; others will undergo painful and exhausting dialysis for three days a week, four hours a day. The hospital waiting lists run for five years or more to get a kidney from a willing donor. In case you didn't know, the law won't allow kidneys to be bought and sold, so at a price of zero we have a severe kidney shortage (see Chapter 6 for a discussion of how price controls work).

Becker says that to alleviate the shortage, we should allow people to sell their kidneys (you only need one of the two you have). Many citizens of poorer countries would be willing to sell their kidneys for a few thousand dollars or less; in fact some of these people are selling their kidneys on the black market right now.

Thus, we have two outstanding economists, one of whom says we should export pollution *to* poor countries while the other says we should import kidneys *from* poor countries. No doubt, these two economists would probably also agree with each other!

Economists sometimes draw a distinction between positive economics and normative economics. **Positive economics** is about describing, explaining, or predicting economic events. For instance, if a quota restricts imports of sugar, the price of sugar will increase and people will buy less sugar. That's true whether or not we think that sugar is good for people. **Normative economics** is about making recommendations about what economic policy should be. Is a sugar quota a good policy? That depends on what we think is good and who we think counts most when we measure benefits and costs.

Not all of this chapter is economics—much of it touches on ethics and morals—but it is still important material for understanding economics as a broader approach to the world. First, economics has limitations and you need to know what they are. It helps to know which ethical values are left out of economic theory. Second, sometimes you will hear bad or misleading arguments against economics, and you need to know those too and where they fall short.

We warn you, however, that in this chapter our primary goal is to raise questions rather than provide answers. And, we try not to present our own normative claims. Instead, we consider the normative claims made by other people, especially critics of economics, and how they intersect with the positive economics that you have learned already.

The Case for Exporting Pollution and Importing Kidneys

The case for exporting pollution and importing kidneys is actually a familiar one: Trade makes people better off. One person wants the kidney more than the money; the other wants the money more than the kidney. Both people can be made better off by trade.

Similarly, it's not surprising that the rich are willing to pay the poor to take some of their pollution. On the margin, the rich value health more than money and the poor value money more than health, so both can be made better off by trade.

What's wrong with these trades? Plenty, according to many people who argue that economic reasoning ignores important values. Economists, it has been said, know the price of everything and the value of nothing.

Some of the objections to standard economic reasoning that we will examine are:

1. The problem of exploitation
2. Meddlesome preferences
3. Fair and equal treatment
4. Cultural goods and paternalism
5. Poverty, inequality, and the distribution of income
6. Who counts? Should some count for more?

Let's consider each in turn. You can think of these as the major reasons why not everyone thinks that voluntary exchanges are, in every case, a good idea.

Exploitation

Is the seller of a kidney being exploited? To focus on the difficult issues, let's assume that the seller is in good mind and fully informed about all the risks of donating a kidney. Even in this situation, many people argue that someone selling a kidney is being exploited. Dr. Francis Delmonico, a transplant surgeon and prominent opponent of kidney sales, argues that "Payments eventually result in the exploitation of the individual. It's the poor person who sells."[2]

Delmonico is correct that a poor person is more likely to sell a kidney than a rich person. But does this mean that the poor person who sells a kidney is being exploited? Let's consider three cases.

> Case 1: Alex buys a kidney from Ajay.
> Case 2: Alex pays Ajay to clean his house.
> Case 3: George Mason University pays Alex to grade exams.

In all three cases, the seller would not sell if he were wealthier. So are the sellers (Ajay in the first two cases and Alex in the third) being exploited? We may feel that there is something different about selling a kidney but it's difficult to see the dividing line that separates exploitation from exchange. Many people in rich and poor countries alike take jobs that involve significant risks. The yearly mortality rate for commercial fishermen in Alaska, for example, is seven times higher than the mortality rate for donating a kidney—so why is donating a kidney different than fishing in Alaska?[3]

One response is that for a poor person the money is exploitative because the circumstances of a poor person give them little choice but to sell things they would rather keep. But consider which of the three following cases is most exploitive.

> Case 1: Someone asks you to donate a kidney but offers you nothing in return.
> Case 2: Someone offers you $5,000 to donate a kidney.
> Case 3: Someone offers you $500,000 to donate a kidney.

Few people would say that Case 1 involves exploitation. But what about Case 2 and Case 3? If Case 2 is exploitative, then Case 3 must be even more exploitative—after all, the temptation to sell is many times greater. In fact, many more people, including a great many people in rich countries, would accept an offer of $500,000 to sell one of their kidneys. But it seems odd to say that Case 3 is the *most* exploitative case. The usual story is that buyers exploit sellers by offering them too little, not too much! But if bigger offers are less exploitive, then Case 2 can't be exploitative either because Case 2 is Case 1 plus some money and how can offering someone more be a way to exploit them?

If someone offered you $500,000 to sell your kidney, would you feel exploited? Probably not. After all, you could always say no. But if Case 3 doesn't exploit *you*, it's hard to see how Case 2 exploits Ajay. Maybe Ajay needs the money more than you but imagine, for example, that 10 percent of the people in India would accept $5,000 for a kidney and 12 percent of people in the United States would accept $500,000 for a kidney. Does this make the larger offer more exploitive?

Keep in mind that everyone agrees that abject poverty is itself a problem. Overall, it would be better if people had access to clean water, good health care, and more wealth. The issue is whether it's wrong to offer to buy things from the poor just because they are poor. We will be returning to the issue of poverty and the distribution of income further below.

One more point: We assumed for the sake of argument that the seller of the kidney was in good mind and understood all of the risks. One possible response is to say that no one ever understands the risks well enough to make trades like this. If that is the case, however, then we ought to ban gifts of kidneys as well as sales. In fact, thousands of people voluntarily give one of their kidneys away every year and we generally regard such people as heroes. But we don't allow anyone to buy or sell a kidney, despite the fact that doing so could save many thousands of lives.

Meddlesome Preferences

Even if exploitation isn't an issue, many people have a gut feeling that trading kidneys for money is just wrong. How much should this gut feeling count when thinking about justice?

Consider this: Is it okay to eat a horse? Not in California. Millions of Californians voted for a law that says "No restaurant, cafe, or other public eating place may offer horsemeat for human consumption." The market in horsemeat is open, however, in Europe and Japan where you'll find horse on the menu at many restaurants. In Japan, it's even common to find raw horsemeat for sale, as a kind of sushi. The National Horse Protection League doesn't want anyone eating horses—especially foreigners—so it took out full page ads in the *New York Times* to lobby for a ban on the export of horses to save them from a "brutal fate designed to feed foreign coffers."

In America the horse is, so to speak, a sacred cow (unlike in India where the cow is a sacred cow). So should horsemeat be banned? And if horsemeat is banned because people don't like the idea of someone eating horses, should kidney sales be banned because some people don't like the idea of someone trading kidneys? And what about homosexuality, interracial dating, or various religious practices that do not meet with anything close to universal approval? Often these practices offend someone, so how much should these meddlesome preferences count?

Preferences over what other people do, even when those other people don't interfere in any direct way with what you do, are sometimes called meddlesome preferences. It's often difficult to resolve meddlesome preferences with other values that are considered important such as liberty, rights, or religious freedom. We, Alex and Tyler, don't usually put much normative weight on meddlesome preferences (we think that "live and let live" should be more popular), but that's one of our value judgments, not anything intrinsic to being economists.

Fair and Equal Treatment

The notion of fair and equal treatment also can run up against the value of trade and efficiency. Consider some of the programs to make mass transit accessible to disabled passengers. In New York City, it has long been the case that buses are capable of accepting passengers in wheelchairs. In essence, the bus "kneels down" until the wheelchair can board and then the bus elevates again.

Equipping buses in this fashion was very costly. A study commissioned by Ed Koch, the mayor of New York City at the time of bus conversion, estimated that it would have been cheaper for each wheelchair user or severely handicapped person to take a taxi than refit all buses. Not only would it have cost less, but it would have been more convenient as well. But would that have been the right thing to do? On one side of the equation stands the virtue of efficiency. Taxpayers would have saved money and disabled people, if they were taking taxis, would have had easier and more luxurious transport options. But defenders of the bus investments claimed that the principle of "equal treatment" was more important than buying each disabled person free taxi trips for life. Even if the taxpayers and disabled people both agreed that taxis would have been preferable, the critics were saying that more is involved in mass transit than getting a person from place A to place B. Mass transit was in part about the sacred value of equal treatment and not making people feel different or disadvantaged.

Economics cannot answer questions about the sacred and the profane, but these issues underlie many arguments about public policy. When thinking about trade offs we need to be aware of the resulting tensions and subtleties, many of which are ethical in nature.

Cultural Goods and Paternalism

A closely related issue is whether governments should support some goods even when the public isn't willing to pay for them. The French government, for example, spends 1.5 percent of French GDP a year subsidizing culture and related "higher values."[4] The implicit judgment is that culture is "more valuable" than what people will otherwise spend their money on, and that government is a better judge of "what is best" than are private individuals, at least for these particular sums of money.

The French also place a minimum quota on how many French-language movies must be shown on TV, specifically 40 percent of the total. For a while, there was even a French ministry of rock and roll, to support the production of French-language popular music. Again, the goal has been to give people something different from what they otherwise would have chosen. The government tried to give the French people French rock and roll instead of the American and British rock and roll that the French people were buying. Supporters of the policy say that subsidizing French culture is valuable in its own right, and that the aesthetic judgments of the marketplace should not be the final ones.

The pragmatic criticism of French policy is to argue that these subsidy schemes tend to be counterproductive and wasteful. Maybe French movies would be more successful if they had to appeal to French consumers rather than to the French bureaucrats who hand out the subsidies. The more philosophical criticism is that people should be allowed to spend their money as they choose. In the latter view, freely-chosen values have a moral worth of their own that is to be respected.

The French government sees a dark side to American culture.

Of course, it is not just the French who give special support to some cultures and not others. The American government exempts the Amish, a small religious community living predominantly in Ohio, Pennsylvania and Indiana, from many forms of taxation and compulsory education. America's approximately three hundred Indian reservations have a special legal status, in part because the U.S. government takes special care to preserve those cultures. The U.S. federal government also spends money supporting the arts (though the American government spends less than does the French government), in part, because some people want to encourage a higher quality of art than they think will arise through the marketplace and voluntary charity. In fiscal 2008, the U.S. budget for the National Endowment for the Arts was just over $144 million.

Poverty, Inequality, and the Distribution of Income

Perhaps the problem with kidney sales and exporting pollution to poor countries is not trade per se but the poverty and inequality that makes the trade happen. We might accept that when the poor person sells a kidney to the rich person both are made better off but still rue the fact that the poor person is poor.

But what is a just distribution of income? How much is owed to the poor? How much is owed to the rich? Questions like these are at the heart of many debates about foreign aid, trade, taxation, health care, and immigration, to name just a few controversial areas.

Many economists have turned to moral philosophy to seek support for their normative policy judgments, and three views have proven especially influential: John Rawls's maximin principle, utilitarianism, and Robert Nozick's entitlement theory of justice. These three views have very different implications for how we, as citizens, should judge the distribution of income and the status of voluntary marketplace transactions.

Rawls's Maximin Principle

Rawls's maximin principle says that justice requires maximizing the benefits going to society's most disadvantaged group.

John Rawls's *A Theory of Justice*, published in 1971, argued that questions of income and wealth distribution are keys for evaluating social policy. Rawls, a Harvard philosopher, laid out the **maximin principle**, namely that a government should (without violating people's basic rights) maximize the benefits going to society's most disadvantaged group. The notion of "maximizing the minimum" led to the phrase "maximin." For Rawls, doing well by the worst-off group is more important than improving the lot of better-off groups. Rawls deliberately rejects the economist's idea of trade offs, instead concluding that the worst-off group should be the clear first priority.

Rawls's argument for making the worst off the first priority is that if no one knew what position they held in society, that is, if people were behind a "veil of ignorance" then they would want a rule that maximized the position of the worst off, just in case they turned out to be the worst off! In economic terms, Rawls thought that people were extremely risk averse.

To see how maximin works in practice, consider a simple example with three people, Red, Blue, and Green.

Now let's compare Society A where Red, Blue, and Green have equal incomes of 100 to Society B where the respective incomes are 150, 100, and 50. Rawls's maximin principle implies that Society A is better or more just than

Society B because the worst-off person in Society B, Green, has more income in Society A. Notice that the only difference between Society A and B is that income is more equally distributed in A than in B; average income is identical so it doesn't seem unreasonable to prefer Society A to Society B.

Society	Red	Blue	Green	Average Income
A	100	100	100	100
B	150	100	50	100
C	600	600	99	433
D	1096	102	101	433

But now let's compare Society A with Society C. In Society C, Red and Blue are much better off than in Society A and Green is slightly worse off. Notice that average income in Society C is more than four times as high as in Society A. Which society would you rank as the better society? Which society does maximin rank more highly? The maximin principle says that Society A is better than Society C because the worst-off person in Society C, Green, is better off in Society A. The maximin principle says that the extra income of Red and Blue counts for nothing, only the income of the least well off person counts.

It's sometimes said that the maximin principle favors societies with more equal division of incomes but that is not necessarily true. Let's compare Society A with Society D. Even though income is perfectly egalitarian in Society A, the maximin principle says that Society D is better because, once again, the income of the least well off person is higher. The maximin principle even prefers Society D to Society C, even though Society C has a more equal division of the same average income.

The maximin principle is influential among philosophers but less so among economists who, as you know, tend to think in terms of trade offs between values. A little bit less income for the worst off might be acceptable if it comes with a big enough gain to others. Lower average income might be acceptable if income is a little bit more equally divided and so forth.

Utilitarianism

Under **utilitarianism**, we try to implement the outcome that brings the greatest sum of utility or "happiness" to society. The best known utilitarian philosopher today is Peter Singer, whom you also may know as an advocate of animal rights.

When it comes to redistribution, a utilitarian approach tries to determine which people have the greatest need for some additional income. For instance, an extra dollar for a poor person may go toward a doctor's visit but an extra dollar for a rich person may just go toward buying an extra silk tie. The poor person probably gets greater happiness from the extra dollar. The utilitarian is likely to suggest that some amount of money be redistributed from rich people toward poor people. Unlike Rawls, however, utilitarians are not always trying to make the poorest people as well off as possible. Utilitarians advocate redistributing income only up to the point where the marginal change in utility created from the redistribution is positive. They try to maximize the total sum of utility, not the utility of the worst-off person. So, in principle utilitarianism (unlike maximin) allows the poor to undergo some extra suffering, provided that suffering is outweighed by enough gains elsewhere in the economy.

What might limit the amount of wealth a utilitarian would redistribute from rich to poor? Incentives! Taking money away from richer people decreases their incentive to earn, so more redistribution could reduce overall wealth by enough to reduce total utility. A utilitarian recipe therefore might involve only a modest amount of redistribution, especially if people are very responsive to incentives. Utilitarianism will also take into account the incentive effects of

Utilitarianism is the idea that the best society maximizes the sum of utility.

Some rich people have a very high marginal utility of wealth. Should we give them more?

redistribution on the poor. Giving dollars to poor people is not always the best way to improve their welfare. As Milton Friedman once said, if you pay people to be poor, you're going to have a lot of poor people.

Notice the usual assumption in economics is that a dollar gain is a dollar gain no matter who gets the dollar, so utilitarianism needs to make assumptions that extend beyond those of economic theory. Economic theory does not assume that a dollar is worth more to a rich man than to a poor man and standard economic tools don't give us any easy way to measure happiness or utility. In fact, many economists believe that comparing the happiness of two people is not very scientific. We might think that the poor person gets more happiness than the rich person from an extra dollar of wealth, but perhaps the poor person is a monk who neither needs nor wants money while the rich person really does desire another silk tie. Maybe the rich person is rich precisely because he loves money and worked very hard to get it. We aren't saying that this is the case; we are only pointing out that there is no natural unit of measurement of utility and human beings have very different preferences.

Most economists do believe in a safety net and a welfare state to take care of the poor people in a wealthy society. But this belief doesn't have to be rooted in any very strict comparison of utilities between rich people and poor people. Economists frequently portray the social safety net as a way of obtaining insurance against bankruptcy, major health care problems, and other bad outcomes. If you think that insurance has value, and that private markets might not provide this insurance on their own (this claim has been debated), that provides some case for a social safety net. Utilitarians go further, however, and try to offer very specific recipes for just how much money should be transferred from the rich to the poor.

Robert Nozick's Entitlement Theory

Whether we accept Rawls's maximin principle, or prefer utilitarianism or choose almost any other theory of justice, one thing is clear. There is no guarantee that the distribution of income generated by market forces will be anything like what these theories describe as the just distribution. Most theories of justice, therefore, will call for some amount of taxation and redistribution, using the force of government. One of the few exceptions is Robert **Nozick's entitlement theory of justice**, which is also known as a libertarian theory of justice.

Nozick's entitlement theory of justice says that the distribution of income in a society is just if property is justly acquired and voluntarily exchanged.

Robert Nozick, another Harvard philosopher, laid out a moral system very different from that of Rawls. Nozick was far more sympathetic to the market economy than was Rawls, and he outlined a defense of the market in a 1974 book called *Anarchy, State, and Utopia*. Nozick argued that the pattern of the distribution of income was irrelevant. What mattered was whether income differences were *justly acquired* and thus Nozick focused on the process by which income is distributed.

Nozick argued that if John wishes to trade with Mary, that decision should be up to John and Mary alone, provided they do not infringe on the rights of others. In the words of Nozick, all capitalist acts between consenting adults should be allowed. Nozick admitted and indeed emphasized that such trades, performed on a cumulative basis, would result in different and indeed unequal outcomes and opportunities for people, but he saw nothing wrong with those inequalities. Nozick went further and positively endorsed those inequalities that resulted from freely chosen market transactions, devoid of coercive force or fraud.

Nozick offered a classic rebuttal to Rawlsian and other theories of justice. Nozick said let's imagine that one day we create a world in which the distribution of wealth is exactly as described by some theory of justice. Let's say the distribution of wealth is exactly like that described by *your* theory of justice. Now, Nozick said, imagine someone like J. K. Rowling, the author of the Harry Potter book series (Nozick actually used the example of Wilt Chamberlain, the basketball star of the 1960s and 1970s).

Rowling, let us say, writes another Harry Potter book and she offers to sell a copy to anyone who is willing to buy. Of course, many people are very willing to buy Rowling's book and so person by person money is transferred from book buyers to Rowling. Rowling becomes very rich so at the end of the day (she is the first author ever to become a billionaire by writing), the distribution of wealth will be very different than at the beginning of the day, when by assumption all was just. Yet how can the new distribution of wealth, the one with a very rich J. K. Rowling, be unjust? No one's rights were violated in the process and indeed everyone, including both the fans and Rowling, was made better off every time Rowling sold a book. All that has happened has been voluntary, peaceful trade. Just and rightful trade, Nozick's theory would imply. So why should any outsider disapprove of the resulting pattern of wealth?

Note that this example is not fanciful: when she wrote her first book, J. K. Rowling was an unemployed single mother living on welfare. Today her income is thousands of times higher than that of her average fan.

Nozick's example is a direct criticism of the view that equality of outcome is important. Nozick argues that what we should care about is the justness of the process that leads to differences in wealth—theft is bad and should be condemned and rectified but voluntary, peaceful trade should not be condemned even when it leads to large differences in wealth.

In the libertarian account, what is just is to respect an individual's rights. One way to think of libertarian rights is that they are "side constraints" on possible government actions. The libertarian view corresponds to some common intuitions. For instance, as we discussed above, many people in the world need kidneys, otherwise they will die or require dialysis. Thus, many people need a kidney and you have two good ones. But you need only one kidney to live and be healthy. Is it okay to take a kidney from you, against your will? Is it okay to draft your kidney for the greater good? Is it okay to redistribute kidneys?

If you believe the answer to that question is no, you have taken one big step toward the libertarian theory of justice. If you want to think about the next step, a libertarian would ask, if it's not okay to draft your kidney why is it okay to draft your whole body? And if redistributing kidneys is wrong, isn't redistributing income wrong for similar reasons?

Philosophers continue to debate the relevance of the perspectives of Rawls, utilitarianism, and Nozick, among other ideas. One contribution of the economist is simply to insist that people should be more focused on producing rather than redistributing wealth. Moral philosophers sometimes write as if all the goods were just sitting there on the table ready to be divvied up, but economists know this isn't true. Economists usually stress the importance of producing the wealth in the first place.

KAREN KASMAUSKI/CORBIS

Does his well-being count?

Who Counts? Immigration

When economists evaluate a public policy like trade or immigration they tend to count the benefits and costs to all individuals equally regardless of where they live. But this isn't always how politics works. Usually national governments weigh the preferences of their citizens more heavily, usually much more heavily, than they do the preferences of foreigners.

Immigration is the most salient current issue where the preferences of citizens are counted for much more than the preferences of foreigners. Some people argue that immigration hurts U.S. citizens because low-skilled immigrants reduce the wages of low-skilled Americans. Other people argue that immigrants add to the U.S. economy through their entrepreneurship and their willingness to work at very tough jobs.

On net, careful studies indicate that immigration has some positive and some negative effects, but the U.S. economy is so large that overall immigration is not such a big issue—economists who support and oppose immigration agree on this conclusion. People debate the pluses and minuses of additional immigration, and often this is an emotional issue but again no matter what your view the net cost or benefit is likely small relative to the entire U.S. economy.[5]

So let's assume that immigration is either a small benefit or a small cost to U.S. citizens. Everyone agrees, however, that immigration is a huge benefit to the immigrants. The typical Mexican immigrant today comes from a small village in Chiapas, Guerrero, Oaxaca, or some other very poor part of Mexico. People in those villages usually earn no more than a dollar or two a day. If they come to the United States, they can earn $10 an hour or more. Of course, they send a lot of this money home to their families. Remittances, most of which come from the United States, are Mexico's number one leading "import" industry. Remittances often make the difference between hunger and plenty, or between a collapsing village and a revitalized one. Immigration matters a great deal to the about 400,000 Mexicans who cross the border every year and to those who would come if it were easier to do so.

So, if the United States is making decisions about its immigration policy, how much should it weigh the benefits accruing to Mexicans from immigration? We're talking not just about the Mexicans who arrive in this country (some of whom may become citizens), but also the Mexicans back home receiving the remittances. Economics tends to be cosmopolitan in its implications as it treats all people equally, no matter where those people live. If the gains to foreigners are counted as much as the gains to nationals, then Mexican immigration into the United States will look especially beneficial. But, again, not everyone buys the presumption that foreigners should count for as much as the welfare of U.S. citizens. A presidential candidate who held that assumption as a campaign platform would be unlikely to win election.

Foreign aid is another policy issue where we must ask whether our government should be looking after American citizens or people in other countries. In reality, the amount of money the American government spends on foreign aid is very low. The exact sum is difficult to determine, because in the government budget "foreign aid" and "military assistance" are not completely distinct categories. But, by standard accounts, formal measures of foreign aid amount to less than $30 billion per year, or less than 1 percent of the federal budget.[6] Of course, simply sending money to other countries does not always make them better off; often foreign aid is captured by corrupt elites or used for bad ends. Still you could say the same about some of the money the U.S. government spends at home! The point is this: It remains within the voters' power to have the federal government spend less money on American citizens and more money on needy people overseas. Why not just drop some dollar bills from a helicopter, flying over a poor country?

Whether or not we should do this will depend, in part, on your views as to "who counts?" and "how much?"

Economic Ethics

When economists recommend ideas like exporting pollution or paying for kidneys, they are often said to be ignoring ethics. Economists sometimes agree, perhaps with a bit of pride! But a closer look shows that this is not true. Even though the predictions of economics are independent of any ethical theory, there are ethical ideas behind normative economic reasoning. An economist who rejects the idea of exploitation in kidney purchases, for example, is treating the seller of kidneys with respect—as a person who is capable of choosing for himself or herself even in difficult circumstances.

Similarly, economists don't second-guess people's preferences very much. If people like wrestling more than opera, then so be it; the economist, acting as economist, does not regard some preferences as better than others. In normative terms, economists once again tend to respect people's choices.

Respect for people's preferences and choices leads naturally toward respect for trade—a key action that people take to make themselves better off. As we saw in Chapter 9 on externalities, economists recognize that trade can sometimes make the people who do not trade worse off. Nonetheless, the basic idea that people can make decisions and know their own preferences leads economists to be very sympathetic to the idea of noncoercive trade.

Economists also tend to treat all market demands equally, no matter which person they come from. Whether you are white or black, male or female, quiet or talkative, American or Belgian, your consumer and producer surplus count for the same in an economic assessment of a policy choice.

None of this is to say that economists are always right in their ethical assumptions. As we warned you in the beginning, this chapter has more questions than answers. But the ethical views of economists—respect for individual choice and preference, support for voluntary trade, and equality of treatment—are all ethical views with considerable grounding and support in a wide variety of ethical and religious traditions. Perhaps you have heard that Thomas Carlyle, the Victorian-era writer, called economics the "dismal science." What you may not know is that Carlyle was a defender of slavery and he was attacking the ethical views of economics. Economists like John Stuart Mill thought that all people were able to make rational choices, that trade not coercion was the best route to wealth, and that everyone should be counted equally, regardless of race. As a result, Mill and the laissez-faire economists of the nineteenth century opposed slavery, believing that everyone was entitled to liberty. It was these ethical views that Carlyle found dismal.* We beg to differ.

---

* The Secret History of the Dismal Science is discussed in an excellent article of that title by David M. Levy and Sandra J. Peart available online at http://www.econlib.org/library/Columns/LevyPeartdismal.html#.

□ Takeaway

Economics stresses the core idea of gains from trade. Yet in many circumstances not everyone approves of gains from trade, mostly for ethical reasons. Not everyone thinks that kidneys should be bought and sold and not everyone thinks that pollution should be exported to poor countries. Intuitions about fairness, equitable treatment, distribution, and other matters often clash with the economic notion of increasing gains from trade.

We respect the distinction between positive economics—predicting what will happen—and normative judgments—what should be done. So we haven't tried to answer these ethical dilemmas or give you our sense of the best possible ethical theory. But we do know that you need to understand something about these debates, at least if you wish to make sense of the debates over economics in the real world. Not everyone respects the economic idea of gains from trade and we've tried to give you some idea why.

□ CHAPTER REVIEW

KEY CONCEPTS

Positive economics, p. 366

Normative economics, p. 366

Rawls's Maximin Principle, p. 370

Utilitarianism, p. 371

Nozick's entitlement theory of justice, p. 372

FACTS AND TOOLS

1. **a.** In this chapter, we never actually defined "exploitation." What's a dictionary definition of the word?

   b. Decide whether the six cases of alleged exploitation we discussed earlier in the chapter fit your dictionary's definition. Yes, this will involve quite a bit of personal judgment, as will most of this chapter's questions.

   c. In your opinion, does the dictionary definition go too far or not far enough when it comes to labeling some voluntary exchanges as exploitation?

2. Of the three ethical theories we discuss (Rawlsian, utilitarian, and Nozickian), which two are most different from the third? In what way are the two different from the third?

3. One of Nozick's arguments against utilitarianism was the "utility monster": A person who *always* gets enormous happiness from every extra dollar, more happiness than anyone else in society. If such a person existed, the utilitarian solution would be to give all the wealth in society to Nozick's utility monster; any other income distribution would needlessly waste resources. This possibility was appalling to Nozick. Nozick's argument is intentionally extreme, but we can use it as a metaphor to think about the ethics of real-world income redistribution.

   a. Do you know any utility monsters in your own life: people who get absurdly large amounts of happiness from buying things, owning things, going places? Perhaps a family member or someone from high school?

   b. Do you know any utility misers? That would be people who don't get much pleasure from anything they do or anything they own, even though they probably have enough money to buy what they want.

   c. In your view, would it be ethical for the government to distribute income from real-world utility misers to real-world utility monsters? Why or why not?

4. **a.** Just thinking about yourself, if you did not know in advance whether you were a Red, Blue, or Green person, would you rather live in society A, B, C, or D that is discussed in the Rawls section of the chapter? Why?

   b. Which society would you like least? Why?

5. Rawlsians support government income redistribution to the worst-off members of "society." If "society" means the whole world, how much redistribution might be involved? In other words, what fraction of people in the rich countries might have to give most of their income to people in the poorest countries? Keep in mind that the poorest Americans have clean water, guaranteed food stamps, and free health care, while billions of people around the world lack such guarantees.

6. Would a "global utilitarian" (someone who values the utility of everyone in the world equally, without giving more weight to people in their own country) who lives in America want more immigrants from poor countries or more immigrants from rich countries? Why?

THINKING AND PROBLEM SOLVING

1. To a Rawlsian, would the world be better off without the Harry Potter novels and one additional billionaire?

2. Some people say that the right to equal treatment has no price. But it seems that most people don't really believe that: Those are just polite words that we tell each other. Consider the following cases:

   a. What if it costs $10 million per kneeling bus?

   b. What if it costs $10,000 to hire translators to translate ballots into a rare language spoken by less than 10 voters?

   c. What if it costs the lives of dozens of police officers to ensure the right of a persecuted minority to vote?

   d. At these prices, is the right to equal treatment too expensive for society to buy it? In each case, describe what you think the exact price cutoff should be (in dollars or lives), and briefly explain how you came to that decision. Why not twice the price? Why not half?

3. The line between "having a meddlesome preference" and "recognizing an externality" is not always clear. Both are ways of saying, "What you're doing bothers me." As we used it in this chapter, a "meddlesome preference" is something that reasonable people should just not worry about so much. By contrast, "recognizing an externality" is a way of putting up the subject for public discussion and perhaps even for a vote. In the town you grew up in,

which of the following issues were considered things that should be left to individuals and which were things that should be put up for a vote? Is there a good way of distinguishing between the two?

   a. The amount of pollution emitted by a local factory

   b. How much noise would be allowed after 11 PM

   c. Whether siblings should be allowed to marry, even if it is consensual

   d. Where liquor stores could be located

   e. How people should dress in public

   f. How many children someone should have

4. Let's see how a utilitarian dictator would arrange things for Adam, Eve, and Lilith. One heroic assumption that utilitarians make is that you can actually compare happiness and misery across different people: In reality, brain scans are making this easier to do but it's still a lot of guesswork. Let's suppose that this utilitarian dictator has 8 apples to distribute: The table below shows the utility that each person receives from their first apple (a lot) but extra apples give less extra happiness (apples give diminishing marginal utility, in economic jargon).

Utility per Apple	Adam	Eve	Lilith
1st	1,000	600	1,200
2nd	140	500	200
3rd	20	400	100
4th	1	300	50

   a. So, if the dictator wants to maximize the sum of Adam, Eve, and Lilith's utility, how many apples does each person get?

   b. If instead Lilith received 2,000 units of utility from the first apple, how would this change the optimal utilitarian distribution?

5. a. The "trolley problem" is a famous ethical puzzle created by Philippa Foot: You are the conductor of a trolley (or subway or streetcar or train) that is heading out of control down a track. Five innocent people are tied to the track ahead of you: If you run over them, they will surely die. If you push a lever on your trolley, it will shift onto

another track, where one unfortunate person is tied up. Either you *let* five people die or you *choose* to kill one person: those are your only choices. Which will you choose and why? Which ethical view from this chapter best fits your reasoning? (If you Google "trolley problem" you will find many other interesting ethical dilemmas to debate with your friends.)

b. Another ethical dilemma sounds quite different: You are a medical doctor trying to find five organ donors to save the lives of five innocent people. A new patient comes in for a checkup, and you find that this patient has five organs exactly compatible with the five innocent people. Do you kill the one innocent patient to save the lives of five innocents? Suppose you will never get caught: perhaps you live in a country where people don't care about such things. Is this the same dilemma? Is it the same dilemma from a utilitarian perspective?

6. What do you think best describes the reason that trade in recreational drugs is illegal: fear of exploitation, meddlesome preferences, notions of fairness, paternalism, concerns about equality, or some other factor?

7. Based on the tools from this chapter, how could a person reasonably justify a ban on gambling?

8. Compare a Rawlsian view against a utilitarian view on the question of whether it should be legal to copy movies and music freely.

CHALLENGES

1. Should responsible adults be allowed to sell a kidney? Why or why not? If so, what restrictions would you place on such sales, if any?

2. a. In your view, when should governments enforce a "live and let live" rule: on issues that matter most to people (e.g., matters of life and death, matters of how much income to give to the government, matters of religion, matters of sexuality) or on the issues that matter least to people (e.g., what flavors of spices are permitted at the dinner table, what kind of clothing is acceptable in public)?

b. Europeans fought a lot of wars in the 1500s over the right to meddlesome preferences. Thinking back on your history courses, what preferences did Europeans want to meddle with?

c. What was the usual argument given in the 1500s for why it was right to meddle with other people's preferences?

3. Philosopher Alastair Norcross poses the following question. Suppose that a billion people are suffering from a moderately severe headache that will last a few hours. The only way to alleviate their headache is for one person to die a horrible death. Can the death of this one person ever be justified in a cost-benefit sense?

4. If the rich countries were able to send individual cash payments to people in poor countries, bypassing possibly corrupt governments, would you let rich countries pay people in poor countries to take their high-polluting factories? If so, how high would the annual payment have to be per family? If not, why not?

5. You would probably sacrifice yourself to save all of humanity, but you probably wouldn't sacrifice yourself to save the life of one random stranger. What number is your cutoff: How many lives would you have to save for you to voluntarily face sure death?

6. Some people feel inequality is justified if the people with unequal outcomes accepted risks voluntarily; it was simply the case that some won and some lost. Imagine two people, each spending $10,000 on lottery tickets, but only one of them wins. We end up with one poor person and one multimillionaire.

Is this inequality better or worse than if one person is born into a rich family and the other is born into a poor family? What exactly is the difference and why?

7. Sometimes poor countries have a lot of people; India has over one billion people. Indians are relatively poor and we know that as families become wealthy, they tend to limit their number of children. So, a much wealthier India, over time, would probably have much less than one billion inhabitants. Would this make for a better India or a worse India? Although each Indian would have much more, there would be fewer Indians. As a result, is there any argument for keeping India poor, so as to have a higher number of people? If not, why not? In general, what can economics tell us about the ideal number of people in a society? Anything at all?

8. Let's say that Tom, who is 25 years old, wants to smoke a cigarette. Consider the following two situations.

   a. Tom is smoking. Suddenly the government comes along and tells Tom that he cannot do this. The government claims that Tom is inflicting a "negative externality" on other human beings. Is this a good policy or bad policy?

   b. Tom is smoking a cigarette at home with no one else around. Suddenly the government comes along and tells Tom that he cannot do this. The government claims that Tom is inflicting a "negative externality" on another human being. Tom asks who this might be? The government says that the 65-year-old Tom, will be harmed by the smoking-today-Tom. The government claims that today-Tom isn't doing enough to look out for the well-being of future-Tom. Does this argument make any sense? Is it ethically correct? If so, can and should we trust our government to make these decisions for our future selves?

19

Political Economy

CHAPTER OUTLINE

Voters and the Incentive to Be Ignorant

Special Interests and the Incentive to Be Informed

Voter Myopia and Political Business Cycles

Two Cheers for Democracy

Takeaway

If you have read this far, you may now be asking "What's wrong with the world?" Economists tend to favor free and competitive markets and to be skeptical about policies like price controls, tariffs, command and control regulation, and high inflation rates. Yet around the world, markets are often suppressed, monopolies are supported, and harmful policies, such as those listed above, are quite common. Why do the arguments of economists fall on deaf ears?

One possible answer is that politicians are right to reject mainstream economics. As we explored in Chapter 18, some people do argue that mainstream economics ignores important ethical values. Or perhaps mainstream economics is simply wrong about economics. Of course, that is not our view, so you will have to seek other books to judge that question for yourself. A third answer to what's wrong with the world and the one we will explore in this chapter is . . . can you guess? Bad incentives.

To say it once again (but never enough times!), incentives matter. A good incentive system aligns self-interest with the social interest. In Chapters 5 and 9, we explored the conditions under which markets do and do not align self-interest with the social interest. It's now time to turn to government. The critical question is this: When does the self-interest of politicians and voters align with the social interest and when do these interests collide?

We will begin this chapter looking at some of the major institutions and incentives that govern the behavior of voters and politicians in a democracy. As we will see, democracies have many problems including voter ignorance, control of politics by special interests, and political business cycles. Yet, to quote Winston Churchill, "No one pretends that democracy is perfect or all-wise. Indeed, it has been said that democracy is the worst form of government except all those other forms that have been tried from time to time."[1] Thus, in the latter half of the chapter we look at non-democracies and some of the reasons why non-democracies have typically failed to produce either wealth or political or economic liberty for their citizens.

Let's begin with voters and the question: "Do voters have an incentive to be well informed about politics?"

Voters and the Incentive to be Ignorant

Knowledge is a good thing, but sometimes the price of knowledge is too high. Imagine that your professor changed the grading scheme. Instead of awarding grades based on individual performance, your professor averages test scores and assigns the same grade to everyone. Will you study more or less under this new grading scheme? We think that most people would study less because studying now has a lower payoff. Let's say that before the change an extra few hours of studying would raise your grade by 10 points. What is the payoff to studying under the new system? Imagine that there are 100 people in your class. Then the same hours of studying will now raise your grade by just 10/100 or 0.1 points.* Studying doesn't pay under the second system because your grade is mostly determined by what other people do, not by what you do.

Now let's apply the same idea to politics. When you choose a politician, does studying have a high payoff? No. Studying position papers, examining voting histories, and listening to political speeches is sometimes entertaining, but it doesn't offer much concrete return. Even when studying changes your vote, your vote is very unlikely to change the outcome of the election. Studying politics doesn't pay because the outcome of any election is mostly determined by what other people do, not by what you do.

Economists say that voters are **rationally ignorant** about politics because the incentives to be informed are low.

It's not hard to find evidence that Americans are uninformed about politics. Consider the following questions. Who is the speaker of the U.S. House of Representatives? Who sings *Oops . . . I Did It Again*? Be honest. Which question was it easier for you to answer? And which question is more important? (At the time of writing, Nancy Pelosi was speaker of the House. *Oops . . .* was a Britney Spears's hit.)

Not knowing who the speaker of the House is might not be critical, but Americans are equally uninformed or worse—misinformed—about important political questions. For example, in one survey Americans were asked to name the two largest sources of government spending out of the following six choices.

> Welfare
> Interest on the federal debt
> Defense
> Foreign aid
> Social Security
> Health Care

Rational ignorance occurs when the benefits of being informed are less than the costs of becoming informed.

* It's possible that some people could study more under the new system. Under the old system, studying only raises an individual's grade but under the new system it raises everyone's grades! Thus, if there are some super altruistic students they might study more under the new system. We have not met many such students. Have you?

Amazingly, 41 percent named foreign aid as one of the two biggest programs. But foreign aid is by far the smallest program of the six listed. Do you know the correct answers? The two biggest programs are defense and Social Security. Americans were not even close to the correct answers; for instance, the second most popular choice was welfare, which is at least a large program although still much smaller than defense and Social Security.[2]

Similarly, by their own admission, most Americans know "not much" or "nothing" about important pieces of legislation such as the USA Patriot Act. Most Americans cannot estimate the inflation rate or the unemployment rate to within five percentage points. Hundreds of surveys over many decades have shown that most Americans know little about political matters. Of course, we'd all like to change that—we are glad you are reading this book!—but in the meantime it is simply a fact. And it appears to be a fact which is not easily changed.

Why Rational Ignorance Matters

Ignorance about political matters is important for at least three reasons. First, if voters don't know what the USA Patriot Act says or what the unemployment rate is, then it's difficult to make informed choices. Moreover, voters who think that the unemployment rate is much higher than it actually is are likely to make quite different choices than if they knew the true rate. The difficulty is compounded if voters don't know the positions that politicians take on the issues and it is worse yet if voters don't know much about possible solutions to problems such as unemployment. Voters are supposed to be the drivers in a democracy, but if the drivers don't know where they are or how to get to where they want to go they are unlikely to ever arrive at their desired destination.

Second, voters who are rationally ignorant will often make decisions on the basis of low quality, unreliable, or potentially biased information. Not everyone has read a good principles of economics textbook and those who haven't are likely to vote in ways which are quite different than someone who is better informed.* It's not really surprising, for example, that better looking politicians get more votes even if good looks have nothing to do with policy. Once again, we should not expect too much in the way of wise government policy when voters are rationally ignorant.

The third reason that rational ignorance matters is that not everyone is rationally ignorant. Let's look at this in more detail.

> **CHECK YOURSELF**
>
> \> Would you expect more rational ignorance about national issues among national voters or about local issues among local voters? Make an argument for both possibilities.

Special Interests and the Incentive to Be Informed

Let's return to the sugar quota that we discussed in Chapter 8. As you may recall, the government restricts how much sugar can be imported into the United States. As a result, the U.S. price of sugar is about double the world price. American consumers of candy, soda, and other sweet goods pay more for these goods than they would if the quota was lifted. Why does the government harm sugar consumers, many of whom are voters?

---

* For a superb treatment of this issue, see Caplan, Bryan. 2007. *The Myth of the Rational Voter: Why Democracies Choose Bad Policies*. Princeton, NJ: Princeton University Press.

Although sugar consumers are harmed by the quota, few of them even know of the quota's existence. That's rational because even though the quota costs consumers more than a billion dollars, the costs are diffused over millions of consumers costing each person about $5 or $6 per year. Even if sugar consumers did know about the quota, they probably wouldn't spend much time or effort to oppose it. Will you? After all, just writing a letter to your local newspaper opposing the quota might cost $5 or $6 in time and trouble and what's the probability that your letter will change the policy?

Sugar consumers, therefore, won't do much to oppose the quota but what about U.S. sugar producers? U.S. sugar producers benefit enormously from the quota. As we saw in Chapter 8, if the quota were lifted most sugar producers in Florida would be outcompeted by producers in Brazil where better weather makes sugar cheaper to produce. But with the quota, U.S. producers are shielded from competition and sugar farming in Florida becomes very profitable. Moreover, although there are millions of sugar consumers, sugar production is concentrated among a handful of producers. Each producer benefits from the quota by millions of dollars.

Sugar producers, unlike sugar consumers, have a lot of money at stake so they are *rationally informed*. The sugar producers know when the sugar quota comes up for a vote, they know who is on the House and Senate agricultural committees that largely decide on the quota, they know which politicians are running for reelection and in need of campaign funds, and they act accordingly. Table 19.1, for example, lists the members of the Senate Agricultural Committee in 2008 and the amount of money from 2006 to 2008 that they received from the American Crystal Sugar Political Action Committee (PAC), an industry lobby group in favor of the sugar quota.

As you can see, 13 of the 21 senators on the Agricultural Committee (perhaps not coincidentally just over a majority!), received money from the American Crystal Sugar PAC. Many senators on the committee *also* received money from the American Sugar Cane League, the Florida Sugar Cane League, the American Sugarbeet Growers Association, and the U.S. Beet Sugar Association! Nor is that the end of the story. The owners and executives of the major players in the sugar industry also donate campaign funds as individuals. The "sugar barons" Jose and Alfonso Fanjul, for example, head Florida Crystals Corporation, which is one of the country's largest sugar cane growers. The Fanjuls donate money to the Florida Sugar Cane League and they give money to politicians in their own names. Interestingly, Jose directs most of his support to Republicans while his brother Alfonso supports Democrats. Do you think there is a difference of political opinion between the two brothers?

TABLE 19.1 Special Interests Are Rationally Informed

Senators on the Agriculture Committee, 2008	Donations from the American Crystal Sugar PAC (2006–2008)
Tom Harkin, D-IA	$15,000
Sherrod Brown, D-OH	$15,000
Saxby Chambliss R-GA	$10,000
Mitch McConnell, R-KY	$10,000
Robert Casey, Jr., D-PA	$10,000
E. Benjamin Nelson, D-NE	$8,000
Amy Klobuchar, D-MN	$7,000
Patrick J. Leahy, D-VT	$6,000
Max Baucus, D-MT	$6,000
Pat Roberts, R-KS	$3,000
Kent Conrad, D-ND	$2,000
Ken Salazar, D-CO	$2,000
Debbie Stabenow, D-MI	$1,000
Richard G. Lugar, R-IN	
Thad Cochran, R-MS	
Blanche Lincoln, D-AR	
Lindsey Graham, R-SC	
Norm Coleman, R-MN	
Mike Crapo, R-ID	
John Thune, R-SD	
Charles Grassley, R-IA	

Source: Federal Election Commission data compiled by OpenSecrets.org

Or can you think of another explanation for their pattern of donations? Other Fanjul brothers, wives, daughters, sons, and even sisters-in-law are also active political contributors.

▶▶ SEARCH ENGINE

Extensive information on campaign contributions can be found at www.OpenSecrets.org

One Formula for Political Success: Diffuse Costs, Concentrate Benefits

The politics behind the sugar quota illustrate one formula for political success: diffuse costs and concentrate benefits. The costs of the sugar quota are diffused over millions of consumers so no consumer has much of an incentive to oppose the quota. But the benefits of the quota are concentrated on a handful of producers; they have strong incentives to support the quota. So, the sugar quota is a winning policy for politicians. The people who are harmed are rationally ignorant and have little incentive to oppose the policy, while the people who benefit are rationally informed and have strong incentives to support the policy. Thus, we can see one reason why the self-interest of politicians does not always align with the social interest.

The formula for political success works for many types of public policies, not just trade quotas and tariffs. Agricultural subsidies and price supports, for example, fit the diffused costs and concentrated benefits story. It's interesting that the political power of farmers has *increased* as the share of farmers in the population has *decreased*. The reason? When farmers decline in population, the benefits of, for example, a price support become more concentrated (on farmers) and the costs become more diffused (on non-farmers).

The benefits of many government projects such as roads, bridges, dams, and parks, for example, are concentrated on local residents and producers while the costs of these projects can be diffused over all federal taxpayers. As a result, politicians have an incentive to lobby for these projects even when the benefits are smaller than the costs.

Consider the infamous "Bridge to Nowhere," a proposed bridge in Alaska that would connect the town of Ketchikan (population 8,900) with its airport on Gravina Island (population 50) at a cost to federal taxpayers of $320 million. At present, a ferry service runs to the island but some people in the town complain that it costs too much ($6 per car). If the town's residents had to pay the $320 million cost of the bridge themselves—that's $35,754 each!—do you think they would want the bridge? Of course not, but the residents will be happy to have the bridge if most of the costs are paid by other taxpayers.

As far as the residents of Ketchikan are concerned, the costs of the bridge are *external costs*. Recall from Chapter 9 that when the costs of a good are paid for by other people—rather than the consumers or producers of the good—we get an inefficiently large quantity of the good. In Chapter 9, we gave the example of a firm that pollutes—since the firm doesn't pay all the costs of its production, it produces too much. The same thing is true here except the external cost is created by government. When government makes it possible to push the costs of a good onto other people—to *externalize the cost*—we get too much of the good. In this case, we get too many bridges to nowhere.

The bridge to nowhere is not unique. Representative John Carter (R-Texas), who sits on the House Military Construction Appropriations Subcommittee, included nearly $7 million in funding for a physical fitness center at Fort Hood, which lies within his district. It may be a good idea to provide a physical fitness center for the troops at Fort Hood—but they already have six! One of the fitness centers includes two co-ed saunas, three racquetball courts, an eight-lane, 25-meter swimming pool, and much more.

Given that Fort Hood already has six fitness centers, the benefits of another center are likely to be less than the cost. But since the benefits are concentrated and the costs are diffused over many taxpayers, the project is funded anyway. Special interest provisions like this are very common. Can you guess who supported the $2 million grant for the Charles B. Rangel Center for Public Service? And which senator included $7.5 million in funding for the Harkin Grant Program for the Iowa Department of Education?

The formula for political success works for tax credits and deductions as well as for spending. The federal tax code, including various regulations and rulings, is over 60,000 pages long and it grows every year as politicians add special interest provisions. Tax breaks for various manufacturing industries, for example, have long been common but in 2004 the term "manufacturing" was significantly expanded so that oil and gas drilling as well as mining and timber were included as manufacturing industries. The new tax breaks were worth some $76 billion to the firms involved. One last-minute provision even defined "coffee roasting" as a form of manufacturing. That provision was worth a lot of *bucks* to one famous corporation.

Every year Congress inserts many thousands of special spending projects, exemptions, regulations, and tax breaks into major bills. A multibillion dollar lobbying industry works the system on behalf of their clients and it is not unusual for those lobbies, in essence, to propose and even write up the details of the forthcoming legislation. In 1975, there were more than 3,000 registered lobbyists, by 2000 the number had expanded to over 16,000, and today there are over 35,000 registered lobbyists—all to lobby just 535 politicians (435 representatives and 100 senators) and their staff. Many lobbyists are former politicians who find that lobbying their friends can be very profitable.

When benefits are concentrated and costs are diffuse, resources can be wasted on projects with low benefits and high costs. Consider a special interest group that represents 1 percent of society and a simple policy that benefits the special interest by $100 and costs society $100. Thus, the policy benefits the special interest by $100 and it costs the *special interest* just $1 (if you are wondering where that came from, $1 is 1 percent of the total cost to society). The special interest group will certainly lobby for a policy like this.

But now imagine that the policy benefits the special interest by $100 but costs society twice as much, $200. The policy is very bad for society but it's still good for the special interest which gets a benefit of $100 at a cost (to the lobby) of only $2 ($2 is 1 percent of the total social costs of $200). Indeed, a special interest representing 1 percent of the population will benefit from any policy that transfers $100 in its favor even if the costs to society are nearly 100 times as much!

If each policy, taken on its own, wastes just a few million or billion dollars worth of resources, the country will be much poorer. A country with many inefficient policies will have less wealth and slower economic growth. No society can get rich by passing policies with benefits that are less than costs.

In extreme situations, an economy can falter or even collapse when fighting over the division of the pie becomes more profitable than making the pie grow larger. The fall of the Roman Empire, for instance, was caused in part by bad political institutions. As the Roman Empire grew, courting politicians in Rome became a more secure path to riches than starting a new business. Toward the end of the empire the emperors taxed peasant farmers heavily. Rather than

Many small distortions can tie a giant down.

spending the money on roads or valuable infrastructure, the activities that had made Rome powerful and rich, tax revenues were used to pay off privileged insiders and to placate the public in the city of Rome with "bread and circuses." When the empire finally collapsed in 476 AD, the tax collector was a hated figure and the government enjoyed little respect.[3]

Voter Myopia and Political Business Cycles

We turn now from the microeconomics of political economy to an application in macroeconomics. Rational ignorance and another factor, voter myopia, can encourage politicians to boost the economy before an election in order to increase their chances of reelection.

Presidential elections appear to be fought on many fronts. Candidates battle over education, war, health care, the environment, and the economy. Pundits scrutinize the daily chronicle of events to divine how the candidates advance and retreat in public opinion. Personalities and "leadership" loom large and are reckoned to swing voters one way or other. When the battle is done, historians mark one personality and set of issues as having won the day and reflected the "will of the voters."

But economists and political scientists have been surprised to discover that a simpler logic underlies this apparent chaos of seemingly unique and momentous events. Over the past 100 years the American voter has voted for the party of the incumbent when the economy is doing well and voted against the incumbent when the economy is doing poorly. Voters are so responsive to economic conditions that the winner of a presidential election can be predicted with considerable accuracy, even if one knows nothing about the personalities, issues, or events that seem, on the surface, to matter so much.

The green line in Figure 19.1 shows, for each presidential election since 1948, the share of the two-party vote won by the party of the incumbent (that

CHECK YOURSELF

> President Reagan set up a commission to examine government and cut waste. It had some limited success. If special interest spending is such a problem, why don't we set up another federal commission to examine government waste? Who would push for such a commission? Who would resist it? What will be its prospects for success?

> A local library expanded into a new building and wanted to establish a local history collection and room. The state senator found some state money and had that contributed to the library. Who benefits from this? Who ultimately pays for it?

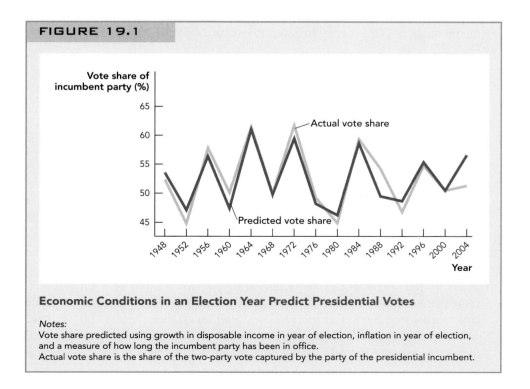

FIGURE 19.1

Economic Conditions in an Election Year Predict Presidential Votes

Notes:
Vote share predicted using growth in disposable income in year of election, inflation in year of election, and a measure of how long the incumbent party has been in office.
Actual vote share is the share of the two-party vote captured by the party of the presidential incumbent.

is, a share greater than 50 percent usually means the presidency stayed with the incumbent party and a share less than 50 percent usually means the presidency switched party). The blue line is the share of the two-party vote predicted by just three variables: growth in personal disposable income (per capita) in the year of the election, the inflation rate in the year of the election, and a simple measure of how long the incumbent party has been in power. Notice that these three variables alone give us great power to predict election results. (But the model did not predict the 2004 election well. Why do you think this might have been the case?)

More specifically, the incumbent party wins elections when personal disposable income is growing, when the inflation rate in the election year is low, and when the incumbent party has not been in power for too many terms in a row. Personal disposable income is the amount of income a person has after taxes. It includes income from wages, dividends, and interest but also income from welfare payments, unemployment insurance, and Social Security payments. The inflation rate is the general increase in prices. The last variable, a measure of how long the incumbent party has been in power, reduces a party's vote share. Voters seem to get tired or disillusioned with a party the longer it has been in power so there is a natural tendency for the presidency to switch parties even if all else remains the same.

Figure 19.1 tells us that voters are responsive to economic conditions, but more deeply it tells us that voters are surprisingly responsive to economic *conditions in the year of an election*. Voters are myopic—they don't look at economic conditions over a president's entire term. Instead, they focus on what is close at hand, namely economic conditions in the year of an election. Politicians who want to be reelected, therefore, are wise to do whatever they can to increase personal disposable income and reduce inflation in the year of an election even if this means decreases in income and increases in inflation at other times. Is there evidence that politicians behave in this way? Yes.

One of the most brazen examples comes from President Richard Nixon. Just two weeks before the 1972 election, he sent a letter to more than 24 million recipients of Social Security benefits. President Nixon's letter read:

Higher Social Security Payments

Your social security payment has been increased by 20 percent, starting with this month's check, by a new statute enacted by Congress and signed into law by President Richard Nixon on July 1, 1972.

The President also signed into law a provision that will allow your social security benefits to increase automatically if the cost of living goes up. Automatic benefit increases will be added to your check in future years according to the conditions set out in the law.

Of course, higher Social Security payments must be funded with higher taxes, but Nixon timed things so that the increase in payments started in October but the increase in taxes didn't begin until January, that is, not until after the election! Nixon was thus able to shift benefits and costs so that the benefits hit before the election and the costs hit after the election.

To be fair, President Nixon's policies were not unique or even unusual. Government benefits of all kinds typically increase before an election while taxes hardly ever do—taxes increase only after an election!

Using 60 years of U.S. data, Figure 19.2 shows the growth rate in personal disposable income in each quarter of a president's 16-quarter term. Growth is much higher in the year before an election than at any other time in a president's term. In fact, in an election year personal disposable income grows on average by 3.01 percent compared to 1.79 percent in a non-election year. The difference is probably not due to chance.

Inflation also follows a cyclical pattern, but since voters dislike inflation, it tends to decrease in the year of an election and increase after the election. These patterns have been observed in many other countries, not just the United States. We also see political patterns at lower levels of politics. Mayors and governors, for example, try to increase the number of police on the streets in an election year, so that crime will fall and people will feel safer.

There are a limited number of things that a president can do to influence the economy so presidents do not always succeed in increasing income during an election year. Presidents can influence transfers and taxes much more readily than they can influence pure economic growth. This is one reason why cyclical patterns are more difficult to see in GDP statistics than they are in personal disposable income.

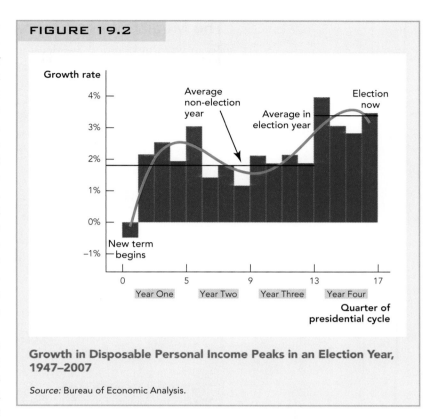

FIGURE 19.2

Growth in Disposable Personal Income Peaks in an Election Year, 1947–2007

Source: Bureau of Economic Analysis.

Two Cheers for Democracy

You might be wondering by now: Why isn't everything from the federal government handed out to special interest groups and why aren't politicians always reelected? Do the voters ever get their way? In fact, voters in a democracy can be very powerful. If you want to think about when voters matter most and when lobbies and special interests matter most, turn to the idea of incentives.

When a policy is specialized in its impact, difficult to understand, and affects a small part of the economy, it is likely that lobbies and special interests get their way. Let's say the question is whether the depreciation deduction in the investment tax credit should be accelerated or decelerated. Even though this issue is important to many powerful corporations, you can expect that most voters have never heard of the issue and that it will be settled behind closed doors by a relatively small number of people.

But when a policy is highly visible, appears often in the newspapers and on television, and has a major effect on the lives of millions of Americans, the voters are likely to have an opinion. The point isn't that voter opinions are always well-informed or rational, but they do care about some of the biggest issues such as Social Security, Medicare, and taxes and when the voters care, politicians have an incentive to serve the voters. But how exactly does voter opinion translate into policy? After all, opinions are divided so which voters will get their way in a democracy?

CHECK YOURSELF

> If voters are myopic, will politicians prefer a policy with small gains now and big costs later or a policy with small costs now but big gains later?

The Median Voter Theorem

To answer this question, we develop a model of voting called the median voter model. Imagine that there are five voters each of whom has an opinion about the ideal amount of spending on Social Security. Max wants the least spending, followed by Sofia, Inez, Peter, and finally Alex who wants the most spending. In Figure 19.3, we plot each voter's ideal policy along a line from least to most spending. We also assume that each voter will vote for the candidate whose policy position is closest to their ideal point.

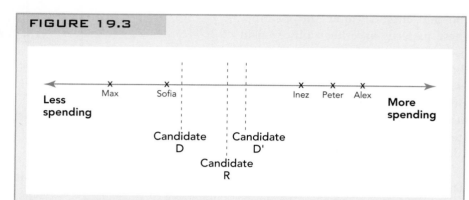

FIGURE 19.3

The Median Voter Theorem Each voter has an ideal policy, marked by an x, on the less to more spending line. Voters will vote for the candidate whose policy is closest to their ideal. The median voter is the voter such that half of the other voters want more spending and half of the other voters want less spending—Inez is the median voter. Under majority rule, the ideal policy of the median voter will beat any other policy. Consider any two candidate policies, such as those of Candidate D and Candidate R. Candidate D will receive two votes (Max and Sofia) and Candidate R will receive three votes (Inez, Peter, and Alex). But Candidate R's position can be beaten by a policy even closer to the ideal policy of the median voter, such as that of Candidate D'. Over time, competition pushes both candidates toward the ideal policy of the median voter, which is the only policy that can not be beaten.

The **median voter theorem** says that when voters vote for the policy that is closest to their ideal point on a line then the ideal point of the median voter will beat any other policy in a majority rule election.

The median voter is defined as the voter such that half of the other voters want more spending and half want less spending. In this case, the median voter is Inez since compared to Inez half of the voters (Paul and Alex) want more spending and half the voters (Max and Sofia) want less spending.

The **median voter theorem** says that under these conditions the median voter rules! Or to put it more formally, the median voter theorem says that when voters vote for the policy that is closest to their ideal point on a line, then the ideal point of the median voter will beat any other policy in a majority rule election.

Let's see why this is true and, as a result, how democracy will tend to push politicians toward the ideal point of the median voter. First, consider any two policies such as those adopted by Candidate D and Candidate R. Which policy will win in a majority rule election? Max and Sofia will vote for Candidate D since D's policy is closer to their ideal point than R's policy. But Inez, Peter, and Alex will vote for Candidate R. By majority rule, Candidate R will win the election. Notice that of the two policies on offer, the policy closest to that of the median voter's ideal policy won the election.

Most politicians don't like to lose. So in the next election Candidate D may shift her position, becoming Candidate D′. By exactly the same reasoning as before, Candidate D′ will now win the election. If we repeat this process, the only policy that is not a *sure loser* is the ideal point of the median voter (Inez). As Candidates D and R converge on the ideal point of the median voter, there will be little difference between them and each will have a 50 percent chance of winning the election.[*]

The median voter theorem can be interpreted quite generally. Instead of thinking about less spending and more spending on Social Security, for example, we can interpret the line as the standard political spectrum of left to right. In this case, the median voter theorem can be interpreted as a theory of democracy in a country such as the United States where there are just two major parties.

The median voter theorem tells us that in a democracy what counts are noses—the number of voters—and not their positions per se. Imagine, for example, that Max decided that he wanted even less spending or that Alex decided that he wanted even more spending. Would the political outcome change? No. According to the median voter theorem, the median voter rules and if the median voter doesn't change, then neither does policy. Thus, under the conditions given by the median voter theorem, democracy does not seek out consensus or compromise or a policy that maximizes voter preferences on average—it seeks out a policy that cannot be beaten in a majority rule election.

The median voter theorem does not always apply. The most important assumption we made was that voters will vote for the policy that is closest to their ideal point. That's not necessarily true. If no candidate offers a policy close to Max's ideal point, he may refuse to vote for anyone, not even the candidate whose policy is (slightly) closer to his own ideal. In this case, a candidate who moves too far away from the voters on his wing may lose votes even if his position moves closer to that of the median voter. As a result, this type of voter behavior means that candidates do not necessarily converge on the ideal point of the median voter.

We have also assumed that there is just one major dimension over which voting takes place. That's not necessarily true either. Suppose that voters care about two issues, such as taxes and war, and assume that we cannot force both issues into a left-right spectrum (so knowing a person's views about taxes doesn't necessarily predict much about his or her views about war). With two voting dimensions, it's very likely that there is *no* policy that beats every other policy in a majority rule contest, so politics may never converge on a stable policy.

To understand why a winning policy sometimes doesn't exist, consider an analogy from sports. Imagine holding a series of (hypothetical) boxing matches to figure out who is the greatest heavyweight boxer of all time. Suppose that Muhammad Ali beats Lennox Lewis and Lewis beats Mike Tyson but Tyson beats Muhammad Ali. So who is the greatest of all time? The question may have no answer if there is more than one dimension to boxing skill so Ali has the skills needed to beat Lewis and Lewis has the skills needed to beat Tyson but Tyson has the skills to beat Ali. In a similar way, when there is more than one dimension to politics, there may be no policy that beats every other policy.

---

[*] In terms of the game theory we discussed in Chapter 13, the ideal policy of the median voter is the only policy that is not dominated by another policy and thus the only Nash equilibrium of a two candidate game is for both candidates to choose this policy.

In terms of politics, the result may be that every vote or election brings a new winner, or alternatively, constitutions and procedural restrictions may slow down the rate of political change. The U.S. Constitution, for example, requires that new legislation must pass two houses of Congress and evade the president's veto, which is more difficult than passing a simple majority rule vote.

As a predictive theory of politics, the median voter theorem is applicable in some but not all circumstances. The theorem, however, does remind us that politicians have substantial incentives to listen to voters on issues that the voters care about. This is a powerful feature of democracy, although of course the quality of the democracy you get will depend on the wisdom of the voters behind it.

Democracy and Non-Democracy

Our picture of democracy so far has been a little disillusioning, at least compared to what you might have learned in high school civics. Yet when we look around the world, democracies tend to be the wealthiest countries and despite the power of special interests, they also tend to be the countries with the best record for supporting markets, property rights, the rule of law, fair government, and other institutions that support economic growth.

Figure 19.4 graphs an index meant to capture good economic policy, called the economic freedom index (with higher numbers indicating greater economic freedom) on the horizontal axis against a measure of the standard of living on the vertical axis (gross national income per capita in 2007). The figure shows two things. First, there is a strong correlation between economic freedom and a higher standard of living. Second, the countries that are most democratic (labeled "Full democracies" and shown in red) are among the wealthiest counties in the world and the countries with the most economic freedom. The only

FIGURE 19.4

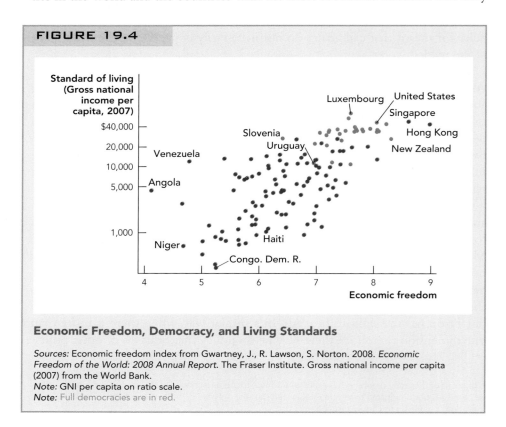

Economic Freedom, Democracy, and Living Standards

Sources: Economic freedom index from Gwartney, J., R. Lawson, S. Norton. 2008. *Economic Freedom of the World: 2008 Annual Report.* The Fraser Institute. Gross national income per capita (2007) from the World Bank.
Note: GNI per capita on ratio scale.
Note: Full democracies are in red.

interesting exceptions to this rule are Singapore and Hong Kong, both of which score very highly on economic freedom and the standard of living but that are not quite full democracies.

Notice, however, that in part there is an association between democracy and the standard of living because greater wealth creates a greater demand for democracy. When citizens have satisfied their basic needs for food, shelter, and security, they demand more cerebral goods, such as the right to participate in the political process. This is exactly what happened in South Korea and Taiwan, two countries that became more democratic as they grew wealthier. Many people think that China may become a more democratic country as it grows wealthier; we will see. But it's not just that wealth brings democracy. Democracy also seems to bring wealth and favorable institutions. Democracies must be doing something right. We therefore need to examine some of the benefits of democratic decision making.

We've already discussed rational ignorance under democracy, but keep in mind that public ignorance is often worse in non-democracies.[4] In many quasi-democracies and in non-democracies, the public is not well informed because the media are controlled or censored by the government.

In Africa, for example, most countries have banned private television stations. In fact, 71 percent of African countries have a state monopoly on television broadcasting. Most African governments also control the largest newspapers in the country. Government ownership and control of the media is also common in most Middle Eastern countries and, of course, the former communist countries controlled the media extensively.

Control of the media has exactly the effects that we would expect from our study of rational ignorance in democracies—it enables special interests to control the government for their own ends. Greater government ownership of the press, for example, is associated with lower levels of political rights and civil liberties, worse regulation (more policies like price controls that economists think are ineffective and wasteful), higher levels of corruption, and a greater risk of property confiscation. The authors of an important study of media ownership conclude that "government ownership of the press restricts information flows to the public, which reduces the quality of the government."[5]

Citizens in democracies may be "rationally ignorant," but on the whole they are much better informed about their governments than citizens in quasi-democracies and non-democracies. Moreover, in a democracy citizens can use their knowledge to influence public policy at low cost by voting. In a democracy, knowledge is power. In non-democracies, knowledge alone is not enough because intimidation and government violence create steep barriers to political participation. Many people just give up or become cynical. Other citizens in non-democracies fall prey to propaganda and come to accept the regime's portrait of itself as a great friend of the people.

The importance of knowledge and the power to vote for bringing about better outcomes is illustrated by the shocking history of mass starvation.

Democracy and Famine

At first glance, the cause of famine seems obvious—a lack of food. Yet the obvious explanation is wrong or at least drastically incomplete. Mass starvations have occurred during times of plenty, and even when lack of food is a contributing factor it is rarely the determining factor of whether mass starvation occurs.

Many of the famines in recent world history have been intentional. When Stalin came to power in 1924, for example, he saw the Ukrainians, particularly the relatively wealthy independent farmers known as kulaks, to be a threat. Stalin collectivized the farms and expropriated the land of the kulaks, turning them out of their homes and sending hundreds of thousands to gulag prisons in Siberia.

Agricultural productivity in the Ukraine plummeted under forced collectivization and people began to starve. Nevertheless, Stalin continued to ship food out of the Ukraine. Peasants who tried to escape starving regions were arrested or turned back at the border by Stalin's secret police. Desperate Ukrainians ate dogs, cats, and even tree bark. Millions died.[6]

The starvation of the Ukraine was intentional and it's clear that it would not have happened in a democracy. Stalin did not need the votes of the Ukrainians and thus they had little power to influence policy. Democratically elected politicians will not ignore the votes of millions of people.

Even unintentional mass starvations can be avoided in democracies. The 1974 famine in Bangladesh was not on the scale of the Ukraine, but still 26,000–100,000 people died of mass starvation. It was probably the first televised starvation and it illustrates some important themes in the relationship between economics and politics.

Floods destroyed much of the rice crop of 1974 at the same time as world rice prices were increasing for other reasons. The flood meant that there was no work for landless rural laborers who in ordinary years would have been employed harvesting the rice.

The lower income from work and the higher rice prices, taken together, led to starvations. Yet in 1974, Bangladesh in the aggregate did not lack for food. In fact, food per capita in 1974 was at an all-time high, as shown in Figure 19.5.

Mass starvation occurred not because of a lack of food per se, but because a poor group of laborers lacked both economic and political power. Lack of economic power meant they could not purchase food. Lack of political power meant that the elites then running Bangladesh were not compelled to avert the famine. Bangladesh continued to pursue bad economic policies; for instance, government regulations made it very difficult to purchase foreign exchange so it wasn't easy for capitalists to import rice from nearby Thailand or India. In fact, rice was even being smuggled out of Bangladesh and into India to avoid price controls and other regulations.

Amartya Sen, the Nobel Prize–winning economist and philosopher, has argued that whether the country has been rich or poor "no famine has taken place in the history of the world in a functioning democracy." The precise claim can be disputed depending on how one defines "functioning democracy" but the lesson Sen draws is correct:

> Perhaps the most important reform that can contribute to the elimination of famines, in Africa as well as in Asia, is the enhancement of democratic practice, unfettered newspapers and—more generally—adversarial politics.[7]

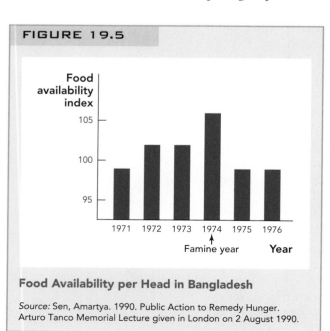

FIGURE 19.5

Food Availability per Head in Bangladesh

Source: Sen, Amartya. 1990. Public Action to Remedy Hunger. Arturo Tanco Memorial Lecture given in London on 2 August 1990.

Economists Timothy Besley and Robin Burgess have tested Sen's theory of democracy, newspapers, and famine relief in India.[8] India is a federal democracy with 16 major states. The states vary considerably in their susceptibility to food crises, newspaper circulation, education, political competition, and other factors.

Besley and Burgess ask whether state governments are more responsive to food crises when there is more political competition and more newspapers. Note that both of these factors are important. Newspapers won't work without political competition and political competition won't work without newspapers. Knowledge and power together make the difference.

Besley and Burgess find that greater political competition is associated with higher levels of public food distribution. Public food distribution is especially responsive in election and pre-election years. In addition, as Sen's theory predicts, government is more responsive to a crisis in food availability when newspaper circulation is higher. That is, when food production falls or flood damage occurs, governments increase food distribution and calamity relief more in states where newspaper circulation is higher. Newspapers and free media inform the public and spur politicians to action.

UNDERSTAND YOUR world

+

=

Democracy, Newspapers and Famine Relief

Democracy and Growth

Democracies have a good record for not killing their own citizens or letting them starve to death. Not killing your own citizens or letting them starve may seem like rather a low standard, but many governments have failed to meet this standard so we count this accomplishment as a serious one favoring democracies. Democracies also have a relatively good record for supporting markets, property rights, the rule of law, fair government, and other institutions that promote economic growth, as we showed in Figure 19.4.

One reason for the good record of democracies on economic growth may be that the *only* way the public as a whole can become rich is by supporting efficient policies that generate economic growth. In contrast, small (non-democratic) elites can become rich by dividing the pie in their favor even if it means making the pie smaller.

Let's first recall why small groups can become rich by dividing the pie in their favor even when this means the pie gets smaller. Recall the special interest group that we discussed earlier that made up 1 percent of the population. Consider a policy that transfers $100 to the special interest at a cost of $4,000 to society. Will the group lobby for the policy? Yes, because the group gets $100 in benefits but it bears only $40 of the costs (1 percent of $4,000).

By definition, oligarchies or quasi-democracies are ruled by small groups. Thus, the rulers in these countries don't have much incentive to pay attention to the larger costs of their policies as borne by the broader public. The incentives of ruling elites may even be to promote and maintain policies that keep their nations poor. An entrenched, non-democratic elite, for example, might not want to support mass education. Not only would a more educated populace compete with the elite, but an informed people might decide that they don't need the elite any more and of course the elite know this. As a result, the elites will often want to keep the masses weak and uninformed, neither of which is good for economic growth or for that matter preventing starvation.

But now let's think about a special interest that represents 20 percent of society. Will this special interest be in favor of a policy that transfers $100 to it at a cost of $4,000 to society? No. The special interest gets $100 in benefits from the transfer but its share of the costs is now $800 (20 percent of $4,000) so the policy is a net loser even for the special interest. Thus, the larger the group, the greater the group's incentives to take into account the social costs of inefficient policies.

Large groups are more concerned about the cost to society of their policies simply because they make up a large fraction of society. Thus, large groups tend to favor more efficient policies. In addition, the more numerous the group in charge, the less lucrative transfers are as a way to get rich. A small group has a big incentive to take $1 from 300 million people and transfer it to themselves. But a group of 100 million that takes $1 from each of the remaining 200 million gets only $2 per person. Even if you took one hundred times as much, $100, from each of the 200 million people and gave it to the 100 million, that's only $200 each. Pretty small pickings. It's usually better for a large group to focus on policies that increase the total size of the pie.

In other words, the greater the share of the population that is brought into power, the more likely that policies will offer something for virtually everybody, and not just riches for a small elite.

The tendency for larger groups to favor economic growth is no guarantee of perfect or ideal policies, of course. As we have seen, rational ignorance can cause trouble. But on the big questions, a democratic leader simply will not want to let things become too bad. That's a big reason why democracies tend to be pretty good—although not perfect—for economic growth.

□ Takeaway

Incentives matter so a good institution aligns self-interest with the social interest. Does democracy align self-interest with the social interest? Sometimes. On the negative side, voters in a democracy have too little incentive to be informed about political matters. Voters are rationally ignorant because the benefits of being informed are small—if you are informed, you are more likely to choose wisely at the polls but your vote doesn't appreciably increase the probability that society will choose wisely, so why bother to be informed? Being informed creates a positive externality because your informed vote benefits everyone, but we know from Chapter 9 that goods with positive externalities are underprovided.

Rational ignorance means that special interests can dominate parts of the political process. By concentrating benefits and diffusing costs, politicians can often build political support for themselves even when their policies generate more costs than benefits.

Incumbent politicians can use their control of the government to increase the probability that they will be reelected. Politicians typically increase spending before an election and only increase taxes after the election. Voters pay attention to current economic conditions even when the prosperity is temporarily and artificially enhanced at the expense of future economic conditions.

Our study of political economy can usefully be considered a study of government failure that complements the theory of market failure we presented in Chapter 9 on externalities and Chapter 11 on monopoly. When markets fail to align self-interest with the social interest, we get market failure. When the institutions of government fail to align self-interest with the social interest we get government failure. No institutions are perfect and tradeoffs are everywhere—this is a key lesson when thinking about markets and government.

A close look at democracy can be disillusioning, but the record of democracies on some of the big issues is quite good. It's hard for politicians in a democracy to ignore the major interests of voters. And if things do go wrong, voters in a democracy can always "throw the bums out" and start again with new ideas. Partially as a result, democracies have a good record on averting mass famines, maintaining civil liberties like free speech, and supporting economic growth. Most of all, democracies tend not to kill their own citizens, who after all are potential voters.

UNDERSTAND YOUR **world**

CHECK YOURSELF

> The free flow of ideas helps markets to function. How does the free flow of ideas help democracies to function?

☐ CHAPTER REVIEW

KEY CONCEPTS

Rational ignorance, p. 382

Median voter theorem, p. 390

FACTS AND TOOLS

1. Which of the following is the smallest fraction of the U.S. federal budget? Which are the two largest categories of federal spending?

   Welfare

   Interest on the federal debt

   Defense

   Foreign aid

   Social Security

   Health Care

2. **a.** How many famines have occurred in functioning democracies?

   b. What percentage of famines occurred in countries without functioning democracies?

3. Around 130 million voters participated in the 2008 U.S. presidential election. Imagine that you are deciding whether to vote in the next presidential election. What do you think is the probability that your vote will determine the outcome of the election? Is it greater than 1 percent, between 1 percent and 0.1 percent, between 0.1 percent and 0.01 percent, or less than 0.01 percent (i.e., less than 1 in 10,000)?

4. If a particular government policy—like a decision to go to war or to raise taxes—only works when citizens are informed, is that an argument for that policy or against that policy?

5. True or false:

   a. During Bangladesh's worst famine, average food per person was much lower than usual.

   b. Democracies are less likely to kill their own citizens than other kinds of governments.

   c. Surprisingly, newspapers aren't that important for informing voters about hungry citizens.

   d. Compared to dictatorship or oligarchy, democracies have a stronger incentive to make the economic pie bigger.

   e. Compared to most other countries, full democracies tend to put a lot of restrictions on markets and property rights.

   f. When it comes to disposable income, American presidents seem to prefer "making a good first impression" rather than "going out with a bang."

   g. When the government owns most of the TV and radio stations, they're motivated to serve the public interest, so voters tend to get better, less-biased information.

6. The "median voter theorem" is sometimes called the "pivotal voter theorem." This is actually a pretty good way to think of the theorem. Why?

7. Let's walk through the median voter theorem in a little more detail. Consider a town with three voters, Enrique, Nandini, and Torsten. The big issue in the upcoming election is how high the sales tax rate should be. As you'll learn in macroeconomics (and in real life), on average a government that wants to do more spending has to bring in more taxes, so "higher permanent taxes" is the same as "higher government spending." Enrique wants low taxes and small government, Nandini is in the middle, and Torsten wants the biggest town government of the three. Each one is a stubborn person, and his or her favorite position—what economic theorists call the "ideal point"—never changes in this problem. Their preferences can be summed up like this, with the x denoting each person's favorite tax rate:

   a. Suppose there are two politicians running for office, N and O. Who will vote for N? Who will vote for O? Which candidate will win the election?

   b. O drops out of the campaign after the local paper reports that he hasn't paid his sales taxes in years. P enters the race, pushing for higher taxes, so it's N vs. P. Voters prefer the candidate who is closest to them, as in the text. Who will vote for N? Who will vote for P? Who will win? Who will lose?

c. In part b, you decided who was heading for a loss. You get a job as the campaign manager for this candidate just a month before election day. You advise her to retool her campaign and come up with a new position on the sales tax. Of course, in politics as in life, there's more than one way to win, so give your boss a choice: Provide her with two different positions on the sales tax, both of which would beat the would-be winner from part b. She'll make the final pick herself.

d. Are the two options you recommended in part c closer to the median voter's preferred option than the loser's old position, or are they further away? So in this case, is the median voter theorem roughly true or roughly false?

8. Perhaps it was in elementary school that you first realized that if everyone in the world gave you a penny, you'd become fantastically rich. This insight is at the core of modern politics. Sort the following government policies into "concentrated benefits" and "diffuse benefits."

a. Social Security

b. Tax cuts for families

c. Social Security Disability Insurance for the severely disabled

d. National Park Service spending for remote trails

e. National Park Service spending on the National Mall in Washington, D.C.

f. Tax cuts for people making over $250,000 per year

g. Sugar quotas

GALEN ROWELL/CORBIS

The trail to Half Dome: diffuse benefits?

THINKING AND PROBLEM SOLVING

1. In Thinking question 4 in Chapter 15, we mentioned David Mayhew's classic book *Congress: The Electoral Connection*. Mayhew argued that members of Congress face strong incentives to put most of their efforts into highly visible activities like foreign travel and ribbon-cutting ceremonies, instead of actually running the government. How does the rational ignorance of *voters* explain why *politicians* put so much effort into these highly visible activities?

2. An initiative on Arizona's 2006 ballot would have handed out a $1 million lottery prize every election: The only way to enter the lottery would be to vote in a primary or general election. How do you think a lottery like this would influence voter ignorance?

3. We mentioned that voters are myopic, mostly paying attention to how the economy is doing in the few months before a presidential election. If they want to be rational, what should they do instead? In particular, should they pay attention to all four years of the economy, just the first year, just the last two years, or some other combination?

4. In his book, *The Myth of the Rational Voter*, our GMU colleague Bryan Caplan argues that not only can voters be rationally ignorant, they can even be rationally irrational. People in general seem to *enjoy* believing in some types of false ideas. If this is true, then they won't challenge their own beliefs unless the cost of holding these beliefs is high. Instead, they'll enjoy their delusion.

Let's consider two examples:

a. John has watched a lot of Bruce Lee movies and likes to think that he is a champion of the martial arts who can whip any other man in a fight. One night, John is in a bar and he gets into a dispute with another man. Will John act on his beliefs and act aggressively or do you think he is more likely to rationally calculate the probability of injury and seek to avoid confrontation?

b. John has watched a lot of war movies and likes to think that his country is a champion of the military arts that can whip any other country in a fight. John's country gets into a dispute with another country. John and everyone else in his country go the polls to vote on war. Will John act on his beliefs and vote for aggression or do you think he is more likely to rationally calculate the probability of defeat and seek to avoid confrontation?

5. In the television show *Scrubs*, the main character J. D. is a competent and knowledgeable doctor. He also has very little information outside of the field of medicine, admitting he doesn't know the difference between a senator and a representative and believes New Zealand is near "Old Zealand."

   a. Suppose J. D. spends some time learning some of these common facts. What benefits would he receive as a result? (Assume there are no benefits for the sake of knowledge itself.)

   b. Suppose instead J. D. spends that time learning how to diagnose a rare disease that has a slight possibility of showing up in one of his patients. What benefits would he receive as a result? (Again, assume there are no benefits for the sake of knowledge itself.)

   c. Make an *economic* argument that even given your answer to question b, voters have too little incentive to be informed about political matters.

6. Driving along America's interstates, you'll notice that few rest areas have commercial businesses. Vending machines are the only reliable source of food or drink, much to the annoyance of the weary traveler looking for a hot meal. Thank the National Association of Truck Stop Operators (NATSO), who consistently lobby the U.S. government to deny commercialization. They argue:

   > Interchange businesses cannot compete with commercialized rest areas, which are conveniently located on the highway right-of-way...rest area commercialization results in an unfair competitive environment for privately-operated interchange businesses and will ultimately destroy a successful economic business model that has proven beneficial for both consumers and businesses.[9]

The sorrow of a land without burgers.

STEVE CRAFT/CORBIS

   a. How does NATSO make travel more expensive for consumers?

   b. Do you think most Americans have heard of NATSO and the legislation to commercialize rest stops? How does your answer illustrate rational ignorance? Do you think that the owners of interchange businesses (i.e., restaurants, gas stations, and other businesses located near but not on highways) have heard of NATSO?

   c. Why does NATSO often succeed in its lobbying efforts despite your answer to part a? Hint: What is the concentrated benefit in this story? What is the diffused cost?

7. The following figure shows the political leanings of 101 voters. Voters will vote for the candidate who is closest to them on the spectrum, as in the typical median voter story. Again as usual, politicians compete against each other, entering the "political market" just as freely as firms enter the economic market back in Chapter 10.

   a. Which group of voters will get their exact wish: the group on the left, the center-left, the center-right, or the right?

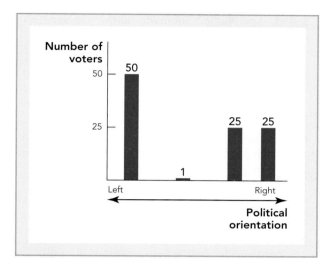

b. Now, four years later, it's time for a new election. Suppose that in the meantime, the two right-leaning groups of voters have merged: The 25 center-right voters move to the far right, forming a far-right coalition. In the new election, whose position will win now?

c. As you've just seen, there's a "pivotal voter" in this model. Who is it?

8. Let's rewrite a sentence from the chapter concerning the Roman Empire: "As the American Empire grew, courting politicians in Washington became a more secure path to riches than starting a new business." Does this seem true today? If it started happening, how would you be able to tell? In your answer, put some emphasis on market signals that could point in favor or against the "decadent empire" theory. (Hint: By some measures, Moscow has the highest real estate prices in the world, and it's probably not due to low housing supply.)

CHALLENGES

1. Is rational ignorance the whole explanation for why voters allow programs like the sugar quota to persist? Perhaps not. In the early 1900s, the government of New York City was controlled by a Democratic Party organization known as Tammany Hall. In a delightful essay entitled "Honest Graft and Dishonest Graft" by George Plunkitt, one of the most successful politicians from the Tammany machine, he argued that voters actually approve of these kinds of government-granted favors. (The essay and the entire book *Plunkitt of Tammany Hall: A Series of Very Plain Talks on Very Practical Politics,* is available for free online.)

For example, Plunkitt said that ordinary voters like it when government workers get paid more than the market wage: "The Wall Street banker thinks it is shameful to raise a [government] clerk's salary from $1500 to $1800, but every man who draws a salary himself says, 'That's all right. I wish it was me.' And he feels very much like votin' the Tammany ticket on election day, just out of sympathy."

a. Plunkitt said this in the early 1900s. Do you think this is more true today than it was back then, or less true? Why?

b. If more Americans knew about the sugar quota, do you think they would be outraged? Or would they approve, saying "That's all right, I wish it was me?" Why?

c. Overall, do you think that real world voters prefer a party that gives special favors to narrow groups, even if those voters aren't in the favored group? Why?

2. a. When a drought hits a country, and a famine is possible, what probably falls more: the demand for food or the demand for haircuts? Why?

b. Who probably suffers more from a deep drought: people who own farms or people who own barbershops? (Note: The answer is on page 164 of Sen's summary of his life's work, *Development as Freedom.*)

c. Sen emphasizes that "lack of buying power" is more important during a famine than "lack of food." How does Sen's barber story illustrate this?

3. Political scientist Jeffrey Friedman and law professor Ilya Somin say that since voters are largely ignorant, that is an argument for keeping government simple. Government, they say, should stick to a few basic tasks. That way, rationally ignorant voters can keep track of their government by simply catching a few bits of the news between reruns of *Two and a Half Men.*

a. What might such a government look like? In particular, what policies and programs are too complicated for today's voters to easily monitor? Just consider the U.S. federal government in your answer.

b. Which current government programs and policies are pretty easy for modern voters to monitor? What programs do you think that you and your family have a good handle on?

c. Are there easy replacements you can think of for the too-complex programs in part a? For instance, cutting one check per farmer and posting the amount on a website might be easier to monitor than the hundreds of farm subsidies and low-interest farm loans that exist today.

4. We mentioned that the median voter theorem doesn't always work, and sometimes a winning policy doesn't exist. This fact has driven economists and political scientists to write thousands of papers and books both proving that fact, and trying to find good workarounds. The most famous theoretical example of how voting doesn't work is the Condorcet paradox. The Marquis de Condorcet, a French nobleman in the 1700s, wondered what would happen if three voters had the preferences like those below. Three friends are holding a vote to see which French economist they should read in their study group. Here are their preferences:

	Jean	Marie	Claude
1st choice	Walras	Bastiat	Say
2nd choice	Bastiat	Say	Walras
3rd choice	Say	Walras	Bastiat

a. They vote by majority rule. If the vote is Walras vs. Say, who will win? Say vs. Bastiat? Bastiat v. Walras?

b. They decide to vote in a single-elimination tournament: Two votes and the winner of the first round proceeds on to the final round. This is the way many sporting events and legislatures work. Now, suppose that Jean is in charge of deciding which order to hold the votes. He wants to make sure that his favorite, Walras, wins the final vote. How should he stack the order of voting to make sure Walras wins?

c. Now, suppose that Claude is in charge instead: how would Claude stack the votes?

d. And Marie? Comment on the importance of being the agenda setter.

(In case you think these examples are unusual, they're not. Any kind of voting that involves dividing a fixed number of dollars can easily wind up the same way—check for yourself! Condorcet himself experienced another form of democratic failure: He died in prison, a victim of the French Revolution that he supported.)

5. In the previous question you showed that sometimes there may be no policy that beats every other policy in a majority rule election and, as a result, the agenda can determine the outcome. In the previous question, all of the policy choices on the agenda were as good as any other, but this is not always the case. Imagine that three voters, L, M, and R are choosing between seven candidates. The preferences of the voters are given in the following table. Voter M, for example, likes Grumpy the best and Doc the least.

Preferences for President of Voters L, M, R			
	Voter L	Voter M	Voter R
1st Choice	Happy	Grumpy	Dopey
2nd Choice	Sneezy	Dopey	Happy
3rd Choice	Grumpy	Happy	Sleepy
4th Choice	Dopey	Bashful	Sneezy
5th Choice	Doc	Sleepy	Grumpy
6th Choice	Bashful	Sneezy	Doc
7th Choice	Sleepy	Doc	Bashful

a. Imagine that we vote according to a given agenda starting with Happy vs. Dopey. Who wins? We will help you with this one. Voter L ranks Happy above Dopey, so voter L will vote for Happy. Voter M prefers Dopey to Happy, so voter M will vote for Dopey. Voter R ranks Dopey above Happy so voter R will vote for Dopey. So _____ wins.

b. Now take the winner from part a and match him against Grumpy. Who wins?

c. Now take the winner from part b and match him against Sneezy. Who wins?

d. Now take the winner from part c and match him against Sleepy. Who wins?

e. Now take the winner from part d and match him against Bashful. Who wins?

f. Finally take the winner from part e and match him against Doc. Who wins?

g. We have now run through the entire agenda so the winner from part f is the final winner. Here is the point. Look carefully at the preferences of the three voters. Compare the preferences of each voter for Happy (or Grumpy or Dopey) to the final winner. Fill in the blank: Majority rule has led to an outcome that _____ regards as worse than some other possible outcome. The answer to this question should shock you.

This question is drawn from the classic and highly recommended introduction to game theory, *Thinking Strategically* by Avinash K. Dixit and Barry J. Nalebuff (W.W. Norton, 1993).

20

GDP and the Measurement of Progress

CHAPTER OUTLINE

What Is GDP?

Growth Rates

Nominal vs. Real GDP

Cyclical and Short-Run Changes in GDP

The Many Ways of Splitting GDP

Problems with GDP as a Measure of Output and Welfare

Takeaway

A visitor to India is immediately struck by the contrast between extreme poverty and rapid economic growth. Squalor in India is obvious, 80 percent of India's population lives on less than $2 a day (as of 2005). Throughout India, you will see people living in the streets, children who have never been to school, fires burning on the sidewalk, and cripples begging for spare change.

But India's growing wealth is also obvious: cell phones are everywhere, new stores are opening, access to clean water is increasing, literacy is rising, and people are better fed. In the cities, there are more restaurants, more clothing shops, more factories, and more cars. India today has at least 100 million people at an American or European standard of living—a remarkable increase from just a few decades ago.

As a rough way of summarizing these changes in economic output and the standard of living, economists look to a country's Gross Domestic Product (GDP) and its gross domestic product per capita, two statistics designed to measure the value of economic production.

Figure 20.1 on the next page shows India's real GDP per capita—or GDP per person—for the 10-year period, 1993–2003. Over this period, India's real GDP per capita grew at an average rate of 4.5 percent a year. If this rate continues, India's GDP per capita will double in just less than 16 years. As we discuss below, real GDP per capita is a rough measure of a country's standard of living. Thus, in the 10 years preceding 2003, the standard of living in India increased by more than 50 percent. That is a notable improvement over India's previous growth performance and it represents the growing wealth of many people in India.

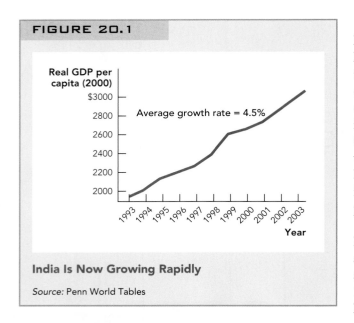

FIGURE 20.1

India Is Now Growing Rapidly

Source: Penn World Tables

TABLE 20.1 The 15 Largest Countries Ranked by GDP (2003)

Rank	Country	GDP (Billions of U.S. Dollars)	GDP per Capita (in U.S. Dollars)
1	United States	$10,205	$34,875
2	China	6,396	4,970
3	India	3,139	2,990
4	Japan	3,070	24,036
5	Germany	2,080	25,188
6	Russia	1,703	11,788
7	United Kingdom	1,544	26,045
8	France	1,540	25,663
9	Italy	1,329	22,924
10	Brazil	1,312	7,204
11	Indonesia	968	4,122
12	Canada	881	27,844
13	Spain	870	20,644
14	South Korea	835	17,597
15	Mexico	828	7,938

Source: Penn World Tables

Table 20.1 lists GDP and GDP per capita for the 15 largest economies circa 2003 (converted into U.S. dollars). In the United States, where GDP was $10.205 trillion and the population was 292.6 million, GDP per capita was $34,875. Although China is the world's second largest economy with a 2003 GDP of $6.4 trillion, it has a population of 1.3 billion people, so per capita GDP is only $4,970, a little bit more than in El Salvador ($4,751) or Guatemala ($3,805). Similarly, India has the world's third largest economy but, after China, it has the world's second largest population, so GDP per capita in India is only $2,990.

Some poorer countries have grown considerably and have achieved a middle-income status between "rich" and "very poor." Examples would be Mexico, Brazil, and Chile; their per capita GDPs are around 9, 8, and 15 thousand dollars respectively. India and China are hoping to make similar gains.

Okay, we can see that GDP per capita gives us a rough guide to a country's standard of living, but what is GDP actually measuring? In this chapter, we will explain:

> What the GDP statistic means and how it is measured

> The difference between the level of GDP and the growth rate of GDP

> The difference between nominal GDP and real GDP

> How growth in per capita real GDP is a standard measure of economic progress

> The use of GDP in business cycle measurement

> Problems with GDP as a measure of output and welfare

What Is GDP?

Gross domestic product (GDP) is the market value of all final goods and services produced within a country in a year. **GDP per capita** is GDP divided by a country's population.

To repeat, GDP is the market value of all final goods and services produced within a country in a year. Let's take each part of this statement in turn.

GDP Is the Market Value . . .

GDP measures an economy's total output, which includes millions of different goods and services. But some goods are obviously more valuable than others: a Ford Mustang is worth more than an iPod. To measure total output, therefore, it doesn't make sense to simply add up quantities. Instead, GDP uses market values to determine how much each good or service is worth and then sums the total.

Gross domestic product (GDP) is the market value of all final goods and services produced within a country in a year.

GDP per capita is GDP divided by population.

For example, in 2005 the U.S. economy produced approximately 12 million cars and light vehicles and 20 million personal computers.[1] If the average price of a car was $28,000 and the average price of a computer was $1,000, the market value of the production of cars was $336 billion ($28,000 × 12 million) and the market value of computer production was $20 billion ($1,000 × 20 million). Using prices in the calculations gives greater weight to goods and services that are more highly valued in the marketplace. Applying this procedure to all final goods and services yields a figure for GDP. In Table 20.2, we show the addition to GDP created by the production of cars and computers.

. . . of All Final . . .

What is a *final* good or service? Some goods and services are sold to firms and then bundled or processed with other goods or services for sale at a later stage. These are called intermediate goods and services. We distinguish these from final goods and services, which are sold to final users and then consumed or held in personal inventories.

TABLE 20.2 GDP Is Calculated by Multiplying the Price of Final Goods and Services by Their Quantities and Adding the Market Values

Final Good	Price	×	Quantity	=	Market Value
Cars	$28,000	×	12 million	=	$336 billion
Computers	$1,000	×	20 million	=	$20 billion
					$356 billion ← **Added to GDP**

A computer chip is one example of an intermediate good. If an Intel chip were counted in GDP when it was sold to Dell, and then counted again when a consumer buys the Dell computer, the value of the computer chip would be counted twice. To avoid double counting, only the computer—the final good—is included in the calculation of GDP.

We do, however, count the production of machinery and equipment used to produce other goods as part of GDP. A tractor, for example, may help to produce soybeans, but the tractor is not part of the final product of soybeans. Thus, both tractor production and soybean production add to GDP, even though the computer chip does not.

. . . Goods and Services . . .

The output of an economy includes both goods and services. Services provide a benefit to individuals without the production of tangible output. For example, paying a consultant to fix a software problem on a computer is a service and its market value is included in GDP. Other services include haircuts, transportation, entertainment, and spending on medical care.

COMEDY CENTRAL/COURTESY: EVERETT COLLECTION

Entertainment is part of GDP

FIGURE 20.2

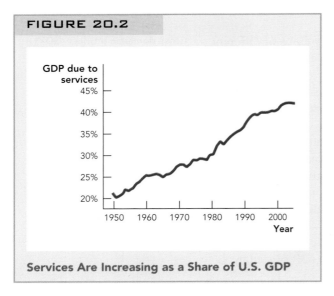

GDP due to services

45%

40%

35%

30%

25%

20%

1950 1960 1970 1980 1990 2000

Year

Services Are Increasing as a Share of U.S. GDP

Since 1950, the portion of U.S. GDP created by the production of services has doubled from 21 to 42 percent (see Figure 20.2). Much of this increase is attributable to spending on medical services and recreational activities, which have both increased to more than 10 times their levels in 1950.[2]

Since U.S. GDP is about $14 trillion (2007), we can tell from the graph that the value of final services is about $5.88 trillion (0.42 × $14) and the value of final goods about $8.12 trillion (0.58 × $14).

. . . Produced . . .

GDP is meant to measure *production* so sales of used goods are not included in GDP. The sale of a used car, for example, is not included in GDP.

Similarly, sales of old houses and sales of financial securities like stocks and bonds are not included in the calculation of GDP. The sale of an old house does not add to GDP because the house was not produced in the year in which it sold. Sales of newly built houses, however, are counted in GDP. Stocks and bonds are claims to financial assets—they are not themselves produced goods or services—so sales of financial assets are not counted in GDP.

Even though the sale of old houses, used goods, and financial assets do not add to GDP the services of real estate agents, used-car salespeople, and brokers do add to GDP because the services provided by these agents are produced in the year in which they are sold.

. . . within a Country . . .

U.S. GDP is the market value of the goods and services produced by labor and property *located* in the United States, regardless of the nationality of the workers or the property owners. A citizen of Mexico who works temporarily in the United States adds to U.S. GDP. By the same reasoning, an American who works temporarily in Mexico contributes to Mexican GDP, not to U.S. GDP.

Gross national product (GNP) is
very similar to GDP but GNP measures what is produced by the labor and property supplied by U.S. permanent residents wherever in the world that labor or property is located, rather than what is produced within the U.S. border. For a large nation like the United States, GDP and GNP are very similar but GDP has evolved into the more commonly used concept.

Gross national product (GNP) is the market value of all final goods and services produced by a country's permanent residents, wherever located, in a year.

. . . in a Year

GDP tells us how much the nation produced in a year, not how much the nation has accumulated in its entire history. You can think of GDP as being analogous to annual wages. Wages are not the same thing as wealth. Some retired people are wealthy even though their wages are low and some people with high wages have very little wealth (perhaps because they are at the beginning of their career or perhaps because they spend everything they earn and never save).

National wealth refers to the value of a nation's entire stock of assets. A tractor built in 1990 and still operating today is part of U.S. wealth but not part of today's GDP. One very crude estimate places U.S. national wealth at $53.3 trillion,[3] which is several times larger than its GDP of about $14 trillion.

Although we typically think of GDP on a yearly basis, it is also calculated every quarter of the year. The calculations are done by the Bureau of Economic Analysis (BEA) which is part of the Department of Commerce and based in Washington, D.C. If you want to see whether you understand what the bureau is up to, try testing yourself with the questions at right.

CHECK YOURSELF

> The Interstate Bakeries Corporation buys wheat flour to make into Wonder Bread. Does the purchase of wheat flour add to GDP?

> On eBay, you sell your collection of Pokémon cards. Does your sale add to GDP?

> An immigrant from Colombia works as a cook in a New York restaurant. Is the money he earns considered part of the GDP of the United States or Colombia?

Growth Rates

GDP tells us how much a country produced in a given year. The growth rate of GDP tells us how rapidly the country's production is rising or falling over time. To compute the growth rate of GDP from 2004 to 2005, for example, you need only two numbers: GDP at the end of both 2004 and 2005. Compute the percentage change as:

$$\frac{GDP_{2005} - GDP_{2004}}{GDP_{2004}} \times 100 = \text{GDP growth rate for 2005}$$

Using actual figures (in billions), we determine:

$$\frac{\$12{,}455 - \$11{,}712}{\$11{,}712} \times 100 = 6.34\%$$

Thus, the U.S. growth rate for 2005 was 6.34 percent.

CHECK YOURSELF

> If GDP in 1990 was $5,803 billion and GDP in 1991 was $5,995 billion, what was the growth rate of (nominal) GDP?

Nominal vs. Real GDP

The rate of growth expressed above did not adjust for price changes and is called the nominal growth rate. The alternative concept is the growth rate of real GDP and here is the background for understanding that distinction.

Nominal GDP is calculated using prices at the time of sale. Thus, GDP in 2005 is calculated using 2005 prices and GDP in 1995 is calculated using 1995 prices. If we want to compare GDP over substantial periods, using nominal GDP creates a problem. GDP in 2005, for example, was $12.4 trillion and GDP in 1995 was $7.4 trillion. Should we celebrate this roughly 70 percent increase in GDP $\left(\frac{12.4 - 7.4}{7.4} \times 100 = 67.6\%\right)$? Not so fast! Before we celebrate, we would like to know whether the increase was due mostly to greater production—more cars and computers—or to increases in prices between 1995 and 2005.

Economists usually are more interested in increases in production than increases in prices because only increases in production are true increases in the standard of living. But how can we measure increases in production while controlling for increases in prices? Here is what we know so far:

Nominal variables, such as nominal GDP, have not been adjusted for changes in prices.

2005 Nominal GDP = 2005 Prices × 2005 Quantities = $12.4 trillion
1995 Nominal GDP = 1995 Prices × 1995 Quantities = $7.4 trillion

Can you see how to compare the increase in production from 1995 to 2005? Suppose we calculate GDP in 1995 using 2005 prices instead of 1995 prices:

2005 GDP in 2005 Dollars = 2005 Prices × 2005 Quantities = $12.4 trillion

1995 GDP in 2005 Dollars = 2005 Prices × 1995 Quantities = $9.0 trillion

What this tells us is that if prices in 1995 were the same as in 2005, then GDP in 1995 would have been measured as $9.0 trillion. Economists also say that 1995 GDP in 2005 dollars is **real GDP** in 2005 dollars. Since 2005 GDP is already in 2005 dollars, it's also real GDP in 2005 dollars.

Now that we have real GDP in 1995 and real GDP in 2005, we can find the increase in real GDP. Between 1995 and 2005, the increase in real GDP was 37.8 percent $\left(\frac{12.4 - 9.0}{9.0} \times 100 = 37.8\%\right)$. Thus in 2005 the economy produced 37.8 percent more stuff, more goods and services, than in 1995. That's a good performance but it's less than the value we calculated earlier—67.6 percent—because prices also increased during this period.

When the media report that fourth quarter 2006 GDP growth was 2.2 percent, we are typically being told about the growth rate of nominal GDP. But if we want to compare GDP over time, we should always compare real GDP, that is, GDP calculated using the *same prices in all years*. Interestingly, it doesn't matter much what prices we use to calculate real GDP, so long as we use the same prices in all years.

Real GDP calculations become trickier, the longer the period we compare. In 1925, for example, what was the price of a computer? Economists and statisticians involved in computing real GDP must worry about the value of new goods and changes in the quality of old goods. The more years that pass, the harder it is to determine how to adjust for those quality changes.

Real variables, such as real GDP, have been adjusted for changes in prices by using the same set of prices in all time periods.

The real versus nominal distinction is an important one in economics and it will recur throughout this book. A **real variable** is one that corrects for inflation, namely a general increase in prices over time. In later chapters, we will discuss the real price of housing, real wages, and the real interest rate and we will show in more detail how to convert nominal data into real data.

Real GDP Growth

If pressed to choose a single indicator of *current* economic performance, most economists would probably choose real GDP growth. Figure 20.3 shows the annual percentage changes in real GDP for the United States from 1948 to 2007. U.S. real GDP growth was high during the 1960s, but rising inflation and the 1973 and 1979 oil price shocks lowered growth in the 1970s and early 1980s. Growth has been more solid since the mid-1980s, but is still somewhat lower than in the 1960s. Note that the long-term (since 1948) average growth of real U.S. GDP has been about 3.5 percent per year. You can use these figures as benchmarks to gauge current growth rates.

Real GDP Growth per Capita

Growth in real GDP per capita is usually the best reflection of changing living standards. Growth in GDP typically gives the same broad idea of how economic conditions are changing as growth in GDP per capita, but there can be

FIGURE 20.3

The Growth Rate of Real GDP (United States, 1948–2007)

Source: Bureau of Economic Analysis

big differences for countries with rapidly growing populations. For instance, between 1993 and 2003, Guatemala experienced real GDP growth of about 3.6 percent a year. That might sound good but over that same period population grew at 2.8 percent a year, so real GDP per capita in Guatemala grew at just 0.8 percent a year. In comparison, real GDP per capita in the United States typically grows by about 2.1 percent a year. Thus, not only is the United States richer than Guatemala, people in the United States are getting richer faster.

Figure 20.4 shows long-term growth rates of real GDP per capita across the globe over the 50-year period ending in 2003. The green-colored nations

FIGURE 20.4

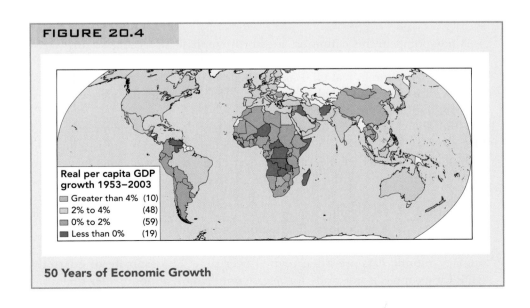

50 Years of Economic Growth

experienced growth rates of greater than 2 percent over the entire period. Taiwan, for example, averaged 6 percent growth of real GDP per capita per year. On the other end of the spectrum, the nations in dark red were growth disasters: they saw no growth or they even saw declines in GDP per capita over this period.

Nigeria is a tragic example of a growth disaster. In 1960, when Nigeria gained its independence from Great Britain, vast deposits of oil were discovered and the future looked bright. But a vicious civil war, dictatorship, and massive corruption meant that the oil wealth disappeared in arms purchases and secret Swiss bank accounts. Incredibly for an economy in the modern era, real GDP per capita in Nigeria was a little bit lower in 2000 than it had been in 1960.

Although it seems shocking that a country could be no richer in 2000 than in 1960, it's important to remember that throughout most of human history a failure to grow is *normal*. In the next chapter, we will begin to explain not just why some nations are poor but the truly mysterious question: Why are any nations rich?

CHECK YOURSELF

> Name a country with a high GDP but a low GDP per capita.
> Name a country with a low GDP but a high GDP per capita.
> Why do we often convert nominal variables into real variables?

A **recession** is a significant, widespread decline in real income and employment.

Business fluctuations or **business cycles** are the short-run movements in real GDP around its long-term trend.

Cyclical and Short-Run Changes in GDP

So far we have focused on GDP as a way to compare economic output across countries and over long periods. GDP is also used to measure short-run volatility in an economy, namely the ups and downs in economic growth that occur within the space of a few years. As we saw in Figure 20.3, U.S. growth rates varied considerably from 1948 to 2007. In some years, such as 1982, the growth rate was negative. **Recessions**—significant, widespread declines in real income and employment—are of special concern to policy makers and the public.

The National Bureau of Economic Research (NBER), a research organization based in Cambridge, Massachusetts, is considered the most authoritative source on identifying U.S. recessions. The official NBER definition of a recession is as follows:

> A recession is a significant decline in economic activity spread across the economy, lasting more than a few months, normally visible in real GDP, real income, employment, industrial production, and wholesale-retail sales.

A few points in this definition are worth emphasizing. A recession is widespread not only geographically but also across different sectors of the economy. Although a decline in real GDP is the single best indicator of a recession, declines will usually also be observed in income, employment, sales, and other measures of the health of an economy.

How often do recessions occur? Figure 20.5 plots real GDP growth and official U.S. recessions since 1948—this time using quarterly data (expressed as annualized rates) so we can better see the variability over time. There have been 11 recessions since 1948, indicated by the shaded bars. Notice that in addition to recessions, the figure illustrates expansions or booms when real GDP grows at a faster rate than normal. We call the fluctuations of real GDP around its long-term trend or "normal" growth rate **business fluctuations** or **business cycles**.

Defining when a recession begins and ends is not always obvious in part because economic data are often revised over time. The estimate of quarterly GDP, for example, is not ready for release until almost a month after the quarter is over. After that, additional rounds of updated estimates are published in

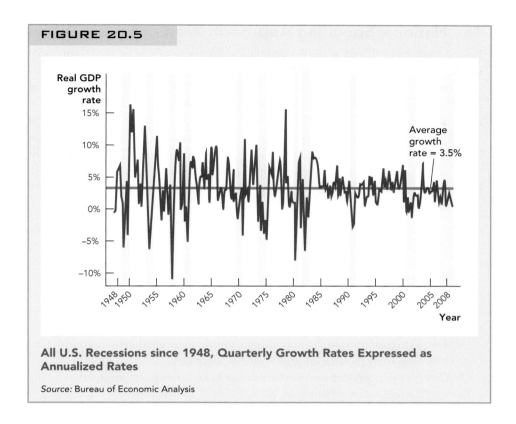

FIGURE 20.5

All U.S. Recessions since 1948, Quarterly Growth Rates Expressed as Annualized Rates

Source: Bureau of Economic Analysis

the following two months. The government often makes significant changes in GDP estimates between the original estimate and the final estimate. For example, the estimates of GDP for the fourth quarter of 2005 increased by $15 billion over the course of the three releases (from growth of $31.2 billion to growth of $46 billion). Updates can even occur years after the first estimates are released. This delay dampens the effectiveness of GDP as a timely indicator and means that understanding recessions and analysis of when they occurred can change over time.

There is debate, for example, about when the 2001 recession started. The official NBER starting date is March 2001, but data revisions have led many people to conclude that the recession actually started in late 2000. Why all the fuss about the timing? If you recall, the presidency changed at the beginning of 2001. Democrats would like to claim that the recession was caused by Republican economic policies, while Republicans want to show that the recession began during President Clinton's final term, before President Bush assumed office.

The Many Ways of Splitting GDP

Another way of understanding GDP is to study its components and how they fit together. Economists split the production of goods and services in many different ways depending on the questions they are asking. We present two common ways of splitting GDP:

1. National spending approach to GDP: $Y = C + I + G + NX$

2. Factor income approach to GDP: $Y = \text{Wages} + \text{Rent} + \text{Interest} + \text{Profit}$

As we will see, both formulas prove useful for understanding business cycles and economic growth.

Economic data take time to collect and evaluate.

In April 1991, the NBER announced that a recession had started in July 1990. In 1992, the NBER announced that the recession had ended in March 1991, a few weeks before the recession was first recognized!

CHECK YOURSELF

> What are business fluctuations?
> Why is it sometimes difficult to determine if an economy is in a recession?

The National Spending Approach: $Y = C + I + G + NX$

Economists have found it useful, especially for the analysis of short-run economic fluctuations, to split GDP into consumption (C), investment (I), government purchases (G) and exports minus imports (NX). The latter two terms are often put together and written as net exports, NX. To understand why this is equivalent to thinking of GDP as the market value of all final goods and services produced within a country in a year, note that produced goods can be consumed, invested, or purchased by governments or foreigners. Finally, some consumed, invested, and government-purchased goods are imported. Imported goods are not part of U.S. GDP, so we subtract imports. Thus, GDP can also be written as:

$$\text{The national spending identity: } Y \equiv C + I + G + NX$$

Where:

Y = Nominal GDP (The market value all final goods and services)
C = The market value of consumption goods and services
I = The market value of investment goods also called capital goods
G = The market value of government purchases
NX = Net exports defined as the market value of exports minus the market value of imports

We explain each of these factors more in turn.

Consumption spending is private spending on final goods and services.

Consumption spending is private spending on final goods and services. Most consumption spending is made by households. Note that while economists think of education as an investment in "human capital," the Bureau of Economic Analysis includes education as a consumption spending alongside purchases of automobiles, MP3 players, and televisions. How would you classify your education spending? Are you here to consume (party!) or invest for the future (study hard!)?

Investment spending is private spending on tools, plant, and equipment used to produce future output.

Investment spending is private spending on tools, plant, and equipment that are used to produce future output. Most investment spending is made by businesses but an important exception is that consumer purchases of new homes are counted as investment. It's important to emphasize that by "investment," economists mean spending on tools, plant, and equipment (capital). When a farmer buys a tractor, that is investment. If your university builds new classrooms and labs, that is investment. Buying IBM stock, however, is not investment, as this is a mere change in ownership of some capital goods from one person to another.

Government purchases are spending by all levels of government on final goods and services. Transfers are not included in government purchases.

The third component of GDP is **government purchases**, or spending by all levels of government on final goods and services. Government purchases include spending on tanks, airplanes, office equipment, and roads, as well as spending on wages for government employees. This category includes both government consumption items (like toner cartridges for printers) and government investment items (like roads and levees) and is thus also called government consumption and investment purchases.

A large part of what government does is transfer money from one citizen to another citizen; about 21 percent of the spending of the federal government for example is for social security payments. Unemployment and disability insurance, various welfare programs, and Medicare are also large transfer programs. We do not include transfers in government purchases because if we did we would be double counting. When the senior citizen buys a television with his or her social security check, it is counted in the consumption portion of GDP. Thus, we do not also count the check as part of government purchases. Another way of thinking about this is that we count only government purchases of *final goods and services*. When the government sends a check to a senior citizen it is not purchasing a final good or service—it is transferring wealth.

Net exports is exports minus imports. If a nation sells more final goods and services abroad than it buys from other nations, net exports will be positive. A nation that imports more than it exports has negative net exports. The United States has had negative net exports for every quarter since the third quarter of 1980. Note that U.S. imports contribute to the GDP of other nations—the locations where that value was produced—and we don't want to count them twice, thus in GDP for the United States we include U.S. exports but subtract U.S. imports. Importing goods and services remains a valuable activity (French cheese is delicious!), but the purpose of the GDP measure is to evaluate production in the U.S. economy.

> **Net exports** are the value of exports minus the value of imports.

Figure 20.6 shows the four components of U.S. GDP in 2007. Consumption is by far the largest component, accounting for $9.7 trillion or 70.3 percent of U.S. GDP. Investment was $2.1 trillion or 15.2 percent of GDP, government purchases $2.7 trillion or 19.6 percent, and net exports −$0.7 trillion or −5.1 percent. If you look at the "long-term averages" part of Figure 20.6, you'll get an idea of the relative sizes of these numbers in recent times. Later on, in the chapters on aggregate demand and business cycles, you will see that changes in these categories represent one way of thinking about the causes or sources of short-run economic downturns and that is one reason why we have covered these particular categories.

The Factor Income Approach: The Other Side of the Spending Coin

When a consumer spends money, the money is received by workers (wages), landlords (rent), owners of capital (interest), and businesses (profit). Thus, we have yet another way of calculating GDP: we can add up all the spending or we can add up all the receiving. The first method is called the spending approach, while the second is called the factor income approach.

> The factor income approach:
> Y = Wages + Rent + Interest + Profit

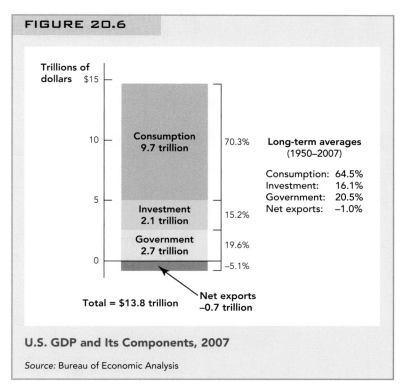

FIGURE 20.6

Trillions of dollars $15

Consumption 9.7 trillion — 70.3%

Investment 2.1 trillion — 15.2%

Government 2.7 trillion — 19.6%

−5.1%

Total = $13.8 trillion

Net exports −0.7 trillion

Long-term averages (1950–2007)

Consumption: 64.5%
Investment: 16.1%
Government: 20.5%
Net exports: −1.0%

U.S. GDP and Its Components, 2007

Source: Bureau of Economic Analysis

As usual, some corrections are necessary to get the accounting right. For example, not every dollar spent on goods and services is a dollar received in income. Sales taxes are one exception with which you can identify. Sales taxes create a difference between what consumers pay and what businesses and workers receive so if we calculate GDP using the income approach we need to add in sales taxes.[*]

For our purposes, the details are less important than the basic idea: every dollar spent is a dollar of income received so if we are careful in our accounting, we can measure GDP by summing up all the spending on final goods and services or by summing up everyone's income.

Why Split?

Each of the ways of splitting GDP throws a different light on the economy. Economists who study business fluctuations, for example, are often interested in splitting GDP according to the national spending identity because consumption, investment, government purchases, and net exports behave differently over time. Consumption spending, for example, tends to be much more stable than investment spending. Economists are interested in understanding why.

The factor income approach is useful if we are thinking about how economic growth is divided between wages, rent, interest, and profits. It turns out, for example, that the largest payment in GDP is to labor. Wages account for about 56 percent of GDP—more than most people expect and much larger than profits, which are less than 18 percent of GDP. The wage and profit shares of GDP are quite stable over time and even across countries. Economists are interested in understanding what drives the relative sizes of these shares.

It also helps to have more than one way of counting GDP because different methods are subject to different errors. Calculating GDP in more than one way lets us check our calculations.

No way of splitting GDP is better than another—it all depends on the questions being asked. Many other methods of splitting GDP are also possible and useful. We could look at the market value of food versus all other items, or durable versus nondurable goods, or we could break down GDP into finer geographic areas like regions or states (the latter is called gross state product). In principle, there are millions of ways of building a GDP measure by summing up its smaller parts. Economists continue to refine the idea of GDP, to improve the measurement of GDP, and to develop new ways of splitting GDP.

CHECK YOURSELF

> Which is the largest of the national spending components: C, I, G, or NX?

> Which is more stable, consumption spending or investment spending?

> Why does the income approach to GDP give the same answer (in theory!) as the spending approach? (In practice, the answers are close but differ due to accounting errors and data omissions.)

Problems with GDP as a Measure of Output and Welfare

GDP measures the market value of final goods and services. *But there are many goods and services for which we do not know the market value.* We don't know the market value, for example, of illegally produced goods and services because neither

---

[*] We also have to make some corrections for depreciation. Over time machines wear down, factories fall into disrepair, and homes age. Depreciated capital doesn't add to anyone's income but GDP measures production before depreciation so if we calculate GDP using the income approach we need to adjust for the depreciation of capital.

the buyers nor the sellers are willing to answer questions from government statisticians. An even more serious problem is that we don't know the market value of goods and service that are not bought and sold in markets. We don't know, for example, the market value of clean air because clean air is not bought and sold in a market.

Let's look in more detail at some examples of each of these problems.

GDP Does not Count the Underground Economy

Illegal or underground-market transactions are omitted from GDP. Sales of crack cocaine, for example, or sales of counterfeit DVDs are not reported and so do not show up in government statistics. Legal goods sold "under the table" to avoid taxes also do not show up in GDP.

Nations that have greater levels of corruption and higher tax rates usually have higher levels of underground transactions. In Haiti, the poorest country in the Western hemisphere, it takes an estimated 203 days of fighting the bureaucracy to start and register a legal business.[4] It is no wonder that so many Haitians keep their commercial activity outside the law. More generally, the size of the informal or "outside the law" sector in Latin America is estimated at 41 percent of officially measured GDP.[5]

Nations with a great deal of illegal and off-the-books activity are not as poor as they appear in the official GDP statistics. In the United States or Western Europe, the underground economy is likely between 10 and 20 percent of GDP; that percentage is small relative to the percentage in Haiti or most of Latin America but in absolute terms it is still quite large.

GDP Does not Count Nonmarket Production

Nonmarket production occurs when valuable goods and services are produced but no explicit payment is made. If a son mows his parent's lawn, the service will not be included in GDP. If a lawn care firm provided the identical work, it would be included in GDP. Yet either way the grass gets cut and economic output increases. Similarly, church workers deliver food to the elderly, volunteers pick up garbage in parks, and many blogs are written without pay as a hobby. Since there is no registered economic transaction, none of these activities are counted in GDP even though each adds to economic output.

The omission of nonmarket production introduces two biases into GDP statistics: biases over time and biases across nations.

In the United States, the portion of women who are in the official labor force has almost doubled since 1950, rising from 34 percent to about 60 percent today. As a result, mothers spend less time working at home than in 1950 but there are more nannies and house cleaners in the economy today. The mothers who worked at home in 1950 were not paid and their valuable services were not counted in GDP. Nannies and house cleaners today are paid and their services are counted in GDP (unless the nanny is hired "under the table" to avoid paying social security taxes, of course!). The result is that U.S. GDP in 1950 underestimates a little the real production of goods and services in 1950 relative to that of today.

Nonmarket production also affects GDP comparisons across countries. For example, many cultures discourage women from taking part in the official workforce.

Mr. Mom: Not increasing GDP

In India, women make up only 28 percent of the labor force, compared with 46 percent for the U.S.[6] The output of the other 72 percent of Indian women is not included in Indian GDP. Indian GDP statistics, therefore, underestimate the real production of goods and services in India.

Household production is especially important in poor countries and in rural areas. It is common to read of families, say in rural Mexico, which earn no more than $1,000 a year. Living off this sum sounds impossible to a contemporary American, but keep in mind that many of these families build their own homes (with help from relatives and friends), grow their own food, and sew their own clothes. Their lives are hard, but much of what they produce is not captured in GDP statistics.

GDP Does not Count Leisure

Leisure, or time spent not working, is also omitted from GDP statistics. People value leisure, just as they value food and transportation. But when people consume food and transportation, measured GDP increases. When people consume more leisure, however, measured GDP does not rise and in fact it will fall if we are not at work. Of course, for some forms of leisure we must make purchases like fishing rods and campers, which are counted in GDP, but it's difficult to measure the true value of leisure.

In the United States, the average workweek has fallen by 10 percent since 1964 (from 38 hours to about 34.5 hours per week). Moreover, work at home has also declined as washing machines, microwaves, and vacuum cleaners have made work at home easier and less time consuming. This growth in leisure time is an improvement in human well-being but is not reflected in GDP.

While the average workweek in the United States has fallen, it has dropped much farther in some other nations. Figure 20.7 shows the average number of hours worked per week in a selection of nations. While the workweek in the United States is down to about 34.5 hours, individuals in other developed nations such as France, Germany, and the United Kingdom work less. In the Netherlands, the average workweek is only 27 hours per week! Since leisure time is not added to GDP, the longer workweek will make the United States look better off compared to Europe than is actually the case. Note, however, that although the workweek in the United States is long compared to other developed countries the workweek is even longer in many poorer countries. In China, for example, the average workweek is about 42.5 hours.

GDP Does not Count Bads: Environmental Costs

GDP adds up the market value of final goods and services but does not subtract the value of bads. Pollution, for example, is a bad that is produced every year but this bad is not counted in the GDP statistics. GDP statistics also do not count the destruction of water aquifers, the accumulation of carbon dioxide in the atmosphere, or changing supplies of natural resources. Similarly, GDP statistics do not count the loss of animal or plant species as economic costs, unless those animals and plants had a direct commercial role in the economy. Other bads are also not counted in GDP. The bad of crime, for example, is not counted in the GDP statistics.

Since more pollution isn't counted as a bad, it's not surprising that less pollution is also not counted as a good. America has cleaner air and cleaner water than it did in 1960, but GDP statistics do not reflect this improvement.

FIGURE 20.7

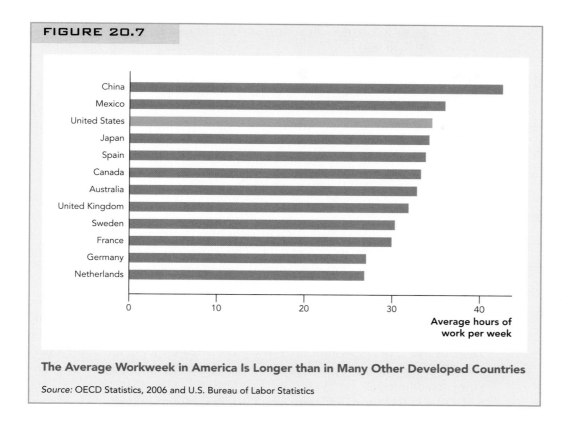

The Average Workweek in America Is Longer than in Many Other Developed Countries

Source: OECD Statistics, 2006 and U.S. Bureau of Labor Statistics

The movement for "green accounting" has tried to reform GDP statistics to cover the environment more explicitly. Most economists agree with the logic behind green accounting: GDP should measure the market value of all final goods and services even if those goods and services are not traded in markets. They also acknowledge other attempts to improve GDP statistics to take into account nonmarket production, leisure, crime, and so forth but most of these problems are very difficult to solve. Environmental amenities, for example, are difficult to value. How much, for instance, should be added to GDP because polar bears are present in Alaska? How much is a glacier worth? A coral reef? Estimates of the values of these resources may be computed for individual problems, but when it comes to the economy as a whole, the measurement task seems insurmountable. Rather than introduce so much uncertainty into the entire GDP concept, economists usually restrict green accounting (and other GDP modifications) to the analysis of particular problems.

GDP Does not Measure the Distribution of Income

GDP per capita is a rough measure of the standard of living in a country. But if GDP per capita grows by 10 percent this does not necessarily mean that *everyone's* income grows by 10 percent or even that the average person's income grows by 10 percent.

To see why, imagine that we have a country of four people, John, Paul, George, and Ringo, whose factor incomes in year 1 are 10, 20, 30, and 40. Using the factor income approach we know that GDP is 100 (10 + 20 + 30 + 40) and thus GDP per capita is 25 (100/4). GDP in year 1 and its distribution are shown in the first row of Table 20.3.

TABLE 20.3 Growth in GDP per Capita Can Be Distributed in Different Ways

	John	Paul	George	Ringo	GDP	GDP per Capita
Year 1	10	20	30	40	100	25
(a) Year 2	11	22	33	44	110	27.5
(b) Year 2	10	20	30	50	110	27.5
(c) Year 2	20	20	30	40	110	27.5

Now suppose that in year 2 GDP grows by 10 percent to 110 and thus GDP per capita grows to 27.5 (110/4). This growth in GDP, however, is consistent with any of the three outcomes shown in rows *a*, *b*, and *c* of Table 20.3. In row *a*, everyone's income grows by 10 percent—so John's income grows from 10 to 11, Paul's income grows from 20 to 22, and so forth. In row *b*, the growth in GDP is concentrated on Ringo, the richest person: his income grows by 25 percent (from 40 to 50) and everyone else's income stays the same. In row *c*, the growth in GDP is concentrated on John, the poorest person. His income grows by 100 percent (from 10 to 20) and everyone else's income stays the same.

GDP and GDP per capita grow by the same amount in each of these cases but in row *a* inequality stays the same, in row *b* inequality increases, and in row *c* inequality decreases.

In most countries most of the time, growth in GDP per capita is like row *a*: everyone's income grows by approximately the same amount.[7] Thus, growth in real GDP per capita usually does tell us roughly how the average person's standard of living is changing over time. In examining particular countries and periods, however, we might want to look more carefully at how growth in GDP is distributed. In other words, GDP figures are useful but they will always be imperfect.

☐ Takeaway

The primary topics of macroeconomics are economic growth and business fluctuations. But when we say that "the economy" is growing what do we mean? And what is it precisely that is fluctuating? If we want to understand growth and fluctuations, we need some concept that defines and measures growth and fluctuations.

The concept of gross domestic product was developed to quantify the ideas of economic growth and fluctuations. GDP, the market value of all final goods and services produced within a country in a year, is an estimate of the economic output of a nation over a year. When we say that an economy is growing we mean that GDP, or a closely related concept like GDP per capita, is growing. When we say that an economy is booming or contracting, we mean that growth in real GDP is above or below its long-run trend.

GDP can be measured and summed up in different ways, each of which casts a different light on the economy. The national spending identity, $Y = C + I + G +$

NX, splits GDP according to different classes of income spending. The factor income approach, *Y* = Wages + Interest + Rent + Profit, splits GDP into different classes of income receiving.

GDP per capita is a rough estimate of the standard of living in a nation. Real GDP is GDP per capita corrected for inflation by calculating GDP using the same set of prices in every year. Growth in real GDP per capita tells us roughly how the average person's standard of living is changing over time.

GDP statistics are imperfect. GDP does not include the value of leisure, or goods bought and sold in the underground economy, nor does it include the value of goods that are difficult to price, such as the value of having polar bears in Alaska. GDP and GDP per capita also do not tell us anything about how equally GDP is distributed. Economists and statisticians try to refine and improve the measurement of GDP over time. GDP measures are imperfect but they have proven they are useful in estimating the standard of living and the scope of economic activity.

□ CHAPTER REVIEW

KEY CONCEPTS

Gross domestic product (GDP), p. 407

GDP per capita, p. 407

Gross national product (GNP), p. 408

Nominal variables, p. 409

Real variables, p. 410

Recession, p. 412

Business fluctuations (business cycles), p. 412

Consumption, p. 414

Investment, p. 414

Government purchases, p. 414

Net exports, p. 415

FACTS AND TOOLS

1. According to Table 20.1, what country has the highest GDP? What country on the list has the highest GDP per person? What countries on the list have the *second* highest GDP and the *second* highest GDP per person?

2. What is included in GDP: all goods, all services, or both?

3. What happened to spending on medical services and recreational activities since 1950?

4. Police officer: "I pulled you over for speeding. You were going 80 miles per hour."

   Driver: "But that's impossible, officer! I've only been driving for 15 minutes!"

The government reports GDP numbers every quarter. How does this story illustrate the meaning of "GDP per year" when the GDP number gets reported every three months?

5. Calculate the annual growth rate of nominal GDP in the following examples:

   Nominal GDP in 1930: $97 billion. Nominal GDP in 1931: $84 billion.

   Nominal GDP in 1931: $84 billion. Nominal GDP in 1932: $68 billion.

   Nominal GDP in 2000: $9,744 billion. Nominal GDP in 2001: $10,151 billion.

   (*Source:* Historical Tables, Budget of the United States Government, Congressional Budget Office)

6. Are the following included in U.S. GDP? Briefly explain why or why not:

   a. Used textbooks sold at your college bookstore.

   b. Used books sold at a garage sale.

   c. Cars made in the United States at a Toyota factory.

   d. Cars made in Germany at a General Motors factory.

   e. The price paid by a German tourist when staying at a New York hotel.

   f. The price paid by an American tourist staying at a Berlin hotel.

   g. A ticket for a Yankees game.

7. By definition, is nominal GDP higher than real GDP?

8. In the last 20 years, have recessions been getting more frequent or less frequent than they used to be?

9. According to the National Bureau of Economic Research, which of the following are "normally" part of the definition of a recession?

   A fall in nominal income

   A fall in employment

   A fall in real income

   A fall in the price level

10. Looking back over the last 10,000 years of human history, which is more "normal": For GDP per capita to grow or for GDP per capita to stay about the same?

11. Attach the appropriate fractions to the "long-term averages" in Figure 20.6. (Some fractions will be left over.) These fractions may turn out to be more memorable than the exact percentages in the figure.

Long-Run Averages	Fraction of GDP
Consumption	$\frac{1}{3}$
	$\frac{1}{8}$
Investment	$\frac{1}{5}$
	$-\frac{1}{14}$
Government purchases	$\frac{1}{4}$
	$\frac{2}{3}$
Net exports	$\frac{9}{10}$

12. What is the national spending identity? This identity is very important in macroeconomics. It is as important as basic anatomy in medical school: You won't be able to cure a person until you know what's inside a person.

THINKING AND PROBLEM SOLVING

1. Calculate GDP in this simple economy:

   Consumer purchases: $100 per year

   Investment purchases: $50 per year

   Government purchases: $20 per year

   Total exports: $50 per year

   Total imports: $70 per year

2. Since World War II, who were the only three recession-free U.S. presidents? (We'll revisit the question of how presidents matter for the economy in later chapters.)

3. We noted that "government purchases" don't include all government spending. A big part of what the U.S. government does is transfer money from one person to another. Social security (payments to retirees), and Medicare and Medicaid (paying for medical care for the elderly and the poor) make up most of these "government transfers." We'll look into this in more detail in Chapter 30, but right now, let's see how big "government transfers" are and how fast they've grown in the federal government's budget. The figures in this table are all in noninflation-adjusted dollars. Complete the table.

Year	Total Federal Transfers	Total Federal Spending	Transfers as Percent of Spending
1950	$13.6 Billion	$42.5 Billion	_____
2000	$1,057 Billion	$1,788 Billion	_____
Growth Rate in %:	_____	_____	

Source: Budget of the United States Government: Historical Tables, Fiscal Year 2003. Washington, D.C.: U.S. Government Printing Office.

4. Let's see what fraction of the economic pie goes to workers in the form of wages, and let's see if it has changed over the years. The "wage share" seems like it should be easy to calculate, but there's a problem. That problem brings us back to the big idea of opportunity cost. The problem itself is straightforward: When a small business owner makes money, should we count that as "wages" or as "profit"? Usually, a small business owner is working at the business most days, doing the kinds of tasks that you could easily pay someone else to do: In other words, from the looking-in-the-window perspective, a business owner looks like a worker, and workers earn wages. But since the owner gets to keep all the profits that are left over after paying off the other workers and the bank, it looks like the money that he or she earns should count as profit.

   What to do? The *best* solution is to calculate the "opportunity cost" of the business owner's time: In other words, estimate roughly how much the business owner would get paid if he or she were working as an employee. It tells us how much of the business owner's income is truly wage income.

The *second* best solution, which we'll use in this question, is to just guess that one-third, one-half, or two-thirds of the business owner's income is really wages, and the rest is profit. As so often in economics, we make some assumptions; let's see if that changes our view of the economy. Using this measure, let's see what has happened to the slice of the pie going to workers:

Year	Wages (including salaries and bonuses)	Business Owner's Income
1959	62 percent of national income	11 percent of national income
2003	64 percent of national income	9 percent of national income

Source: *Survey of Current Business.* Bureau of Economic Analysis, March 2004.

Using the data above, complete the following table:

Year	Total Wages as percentage of national income		
	Including one-third of business income	Including one-half of business income	Including two-thirds of business income
1959			
2003			

So, now that you've calculated this, does it appear that "wage share" has risen by more than 5 percent, fallen by more than 5 percent, or stayed roughly the same over the decades? Does the one-third, one-half, or two-thirds business owner adjustment impact this conclusion?

5. Let's figure out GDP for Robinson Crusoe.

   a. Initially he is stuck on an island without the wisdom and local knowledge of Friday. Because Crusoe is a proper Englishman, he wants to keep his accounts. This year, he catches and eats 2,000 fish valued at one British pound (£) each, grows and eats 4,000 coconuts valued at 0.5 British pounds each, and makes 2 huts (housing) valued at 200 pounds each.

If government purchases are zero and there is no trade, what is C for Crusoe? What is I? What is Y? (We are going to start using those letters as if they mean something: See question 12 in the previous section.)

   b. One year, he learns of a tribe on a nearby island who are willing to trade with him: If he gives fish, they give clams. He produces just as much as before, but he trades 500 of the 2,000 fish and receives 10,000 clams valued at 5 clams per British pound. What is the British pound value of the exported fish? Of the imported clams? What are C, I, and X now? What is GDP now?

   c. The following year, Crusoe produces the same as in every other year, but a tribe on the other side of the island steals his two huts after he makes them, and gives him nothing in return. So he exports, but does not import at all. What are C, I, X, and Y now?

   d. In Crusoe's final year on the island, he produces the same as in every other year (he's a reliable worker), but a new shipwreck washes up on his island containing a clock worth £3, a new shirt worth £2, and a copy of Milton's *Paradise Lost* and Shakespeare's complete works, each worth £1. Treat these as imported consumer goods. What is GDP this year? (Note: Emphasize the "P" in GDP when considering your answer.) What are C, I, X, and Y this year? (Note: One of the four is bigger than usual, one is negative.)

   e. Is Crusoe probably happy about what happens in question 5c? Is he probably happy about what happens in question 5d? Keep these answers in mind for when we discuss the economics of trade later on.

6. Let's think about an economically sound way to measure the value of leisure. To keep this simple, we'll just think about the value of leisure to people who *could* work but who decide to stay home. Also, we won't think about how much *actual* workers value their free time, or how much children and retirees value their time.

In a standard supply and demand labor model, firms "demand" labor while workers "supply" labor. Let's think about a labor market that is in equilibrium, with a wage of $20 per hour (close to the U.S. average) and with 150 million Americans working out of a total of 225 million working-age Americans.

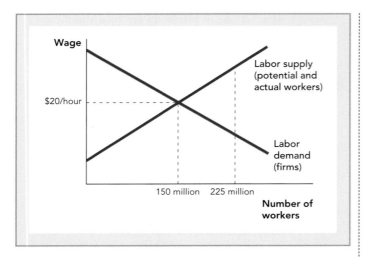

a. According to this simplified model of the U.S. economy, some workers *would* work if the wage were higher, but at the current wage, they'd rather stay home and watch re-runs of *Seinfeld* or (don't let this be you!) *Two and a Half Men*. For the workers who are right on the margin between working and not working, what would their wage be if wages rose ever so slightly and they went to work?

b. Let's use this wage as a shorthand for how much nonworkers value their time. After all, the "opportunity cost" of their free time must be at least this high, because otherwise they'd take a job. Now, let's calculate a GDP measure that adds in a rough estimate of the value enjoyed by these nonworkers. We'll use the following identity, and we'll round the value of nominal GDP to $14 trillion (close to the actual 2008 level).

Leisure-augmented GDP = Regular GDP + Total monetary value of leisure

If the average working person works 2,000 hours per year (that's a 40-hour week for 50 weeks a year), then what is the leisure-augmented value of U.S. GDP?

7. Consider the following two claims. The first would be a typical statement at the magazine *The Nation*, while the second would be a typical statement at the magazine *National Review*:

Europeans have strong labor unions, so their workers get a bigger share of the pie than American workers.

Since European businesses are highly regulated, they have little incentive to make big profits. Therefore, they get a much smaller share of national product than American workers.

It is true that Europeans have stronger labor unions than Americans, and it is true that European businesses face higher regulatory burdens than American businesses. But with that in mind, what is wrong with these two statements? What fact are they ignoring? And what does that fact tell us about what strong unions and high levels of government regulation *can't* do?

8. The underground economy and other nonmarket production make it hard to accurately measure the precise level of GDP. But GDP could still be very accurate for measuring changes in the economy. If Ben Bernanke, the Federal Reserve chairman, is trying to find out whether the U.S. economy has gone into a recession, are the difficulties of measuring nonmarket production likely to be important problems for his purposes? How is this like always wearing your shoes when you step on the bathroom scale?

9. a. U.S. GDP is approximately $14 trillion. If GDP were divided up equally among all 300 million Americans, what would each person get? If you and your nine best friends took almost all of the GDP for yourselves, but gave $1,000 per person for everyone else, how much would you get each year, just for yourself?

b. More seriously, currently 150,000 people in the United States earn over $1.5 million per year. If you could take their money and divide it up among the approximately 300 million other Americans, how much money could you give to each person every year? Note that $1.5 million is only the cutoff: On average, this group earns $3 million per year, so use that number in your calculations.

(*Source:* David Cay Johnston, "Richest Are Leaving Even the Rich Far Behind," *New York Times*, June 5, 2005, based on U.S. government data.)

10. Let's sum up some basic facts of U.S. economic history with numbers:

a. First, let's measure the size of the Great Depression:

Real GDP in 1929 (peak): $323 billion	Real GDP in 1933 (trough): $206 billion
Price level in 1929: 33	Price level in 1933: 24

Calculate the percent change in real GDP and the percent change in the price level from 1929 to 1933. First, calculate the total change, and then divide it by the number of years to get the more typical measure of "percent per year." (Note: this is four full years, not three or five.)

b. Second, let's measure how much the economy grew from the lowest depths of the Depression to the peak of World War II's economic boom:

Real GDP in 1933 (trough): $206 billion	Real GDP in 1945: $596 billion
Price level in 1933: 24	Price level in 1945: 38

Again, first calculate the total change, and then divide it by the number of years to get the more typical measure of "percent per year."

c. Finally, let's see if a growing economy must mean growing prices:

Real GDP in 1870: $36 billion	Real GDP in 1900: $124 billion
Price level in 1870: 22	Price level in 1900: 16

Calculate the total and annual growth rates as before. Note: The price level fell fairly smoothly across these three decades, a time when the economy grew rapidly and many great American novels were written about life in the growing cities.

(*Source:* Robert J. Gordon, ed., *The American Business Cycle: Continuity and Change.* Cambridge, MA, National Bureau of Economic Research, 1986.)

CHALLENGES

1. During World War II, the government did a good job measuring nominal GDP. But if the price level was calculated incorrectly, we might get a completely wrong idea about what happened with real GDP. During World War II, price ceilings were in place. That means that some things that would've been expensive were artificially cheap instead. Within a few years of the war's end, price controls finally ended, and the price level spiked up about 20 percent. If the true price level *during the war* was actually 20 percent higher than reported, would that mean that real GDP is higher than the official number in question 10b in the previous section, lower than that number, or is it still the same as that number?

2. If U.S. government statistics counted education spending as part of investment, which would rise, which would fall, and which would remain unchanged? (Note: You might use rise, fall, and unchanged more than once each or you might not.)

Consumption   Investment   Gross Domestic Product

3. If U.S. government statistics counted people who are receiving unemployment benefits as people who are "government employees" hired to "search for work," which of the following would rise, which would fall, and which would remain unchanged? (Note: You might use rise, fall, and unchanged more than once each or you might not.)

Consumption   Government Purchases   Gross Domestic Product

4. According to legend, some government employees do very little work. If this legend is true enough to be important, then we may be measuring GDP incorrectly. Officially, we say that these are "employed workers," but to a great extent these "employees" are really unemployed in any useful task; they are receiving transfer payments and watching YouTube for 40 hours per week. If instead government statistics counted these YouTube-watching government employees as simply retired or unemployed, which of the following would rise, which would fall, and which would remain unchanged? (Note: You might use rise, fall, and unchanged more than once each or you might not.)

Consumption   Government Purchases   Gross Domestic Product

21

The Wealth of Nations and Economic Growth

CHAPTER OUTLINE

Key Facts about the Wealth of Nations and Economic Growth

Understanding the Wealth of Nations

Incentives and Institutions

Takeaway

Appendix: The Magic of Compound Growth Using a Spreadsheet

In the United States, diarrhea is a pain, an annoyance, and of course an embarrassment. In much of the developing world, diarrhea is a killer, especially of children. Every year 1.8 million children die from diarrhea. To prevent the deaths of these children we do not need any scientific breakthroughs, nor do we need new drugs or fancy medical devices. What these children need most is one thing: economic growth.

Economic growth brings piped water and flush toilets, which together cut infant mortality from diarrhea by 70 percent or more. Malaria, measles, and infections also kill millions of children a year. Again, the lesson is clear, millions of children are dying who would live if there were more economic growth.

Figure 21.1 on the next page illustrates how health and wealth go together. The vertical axis shows GDP per capita and the horizontal axis shows how many children, out of every 1,000 births, survive to the age of 5. In the United States, one of the world's richest countries, 993 out of every 1,000 children born survive to the age of 5 (i.e., 7 out of every 1,000 die before the age of 5). In Liberia, one of the world's poorest countries, only about 765 children survive to age 5 (i.e., 235 of every 1,000 children die before seeing their fifth birthday). The graph illustrates a strong correlation between a country's GDP per capita and infant survival. The size of each country's data bubble is proportional to the population of that country; notice that India and China each have populations of over a billion people so economic growth in these countries has the potential to save millions of infants from an early death.

Infant health and wealth tend to move together; indeed, just about *any* standard indicator of societal well-being tends to increase with wealth. Infant survival rates, life expectancy, and nutrition (caloric intake levels), for example, all tend to be higher in wealthier nations. Educational opportunities, leisure, and

427

FIGURE 21.1

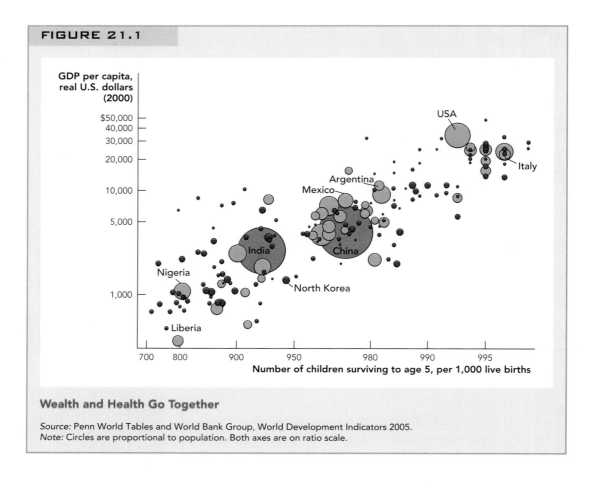

Wealth and Health Go Together

Source: Penn World Tables and World Bank Group, World Development Indicators 2005.
Note: Circles are proportional to population. Both axes are on ratio scale.

entertainment also tend to be higher in wealthier nations. Wealthier nations even have fewer conflicts such as civil wars and riots. And, of course, wealthier nations have more material goods such as televisions, iPods, and swimming pools.

Wealth is clearly important so we want answers to the following questions. Why are some nations wealthy while others are poor? Why are some nations getting wealthier faster than others? Can anything be done to help poor nations become wealthy? The answers to these questions are literally a matter of life and death. In this chapter and the next, we will try to answer these questions.

Key Facts about the Wealth of Nations and Economic Growth

Let's begin with some important facts about the wealth of nations and economic growth.

Fact One: GDP per Capita Today Varies Enormously among Nations

We already have some understanding of the enormous differences that exist in the wealth of nations and how these differences affect infant mortality and other measures of well-being. Figure 21.2 shows in more detail how GDP per capita differs around the world. To construct this figure we start on the left with the world's poorest country which happens to be the Democratic Republic of the Congo (DRC). The DRC (not labeled) accounts for just under 1% of the

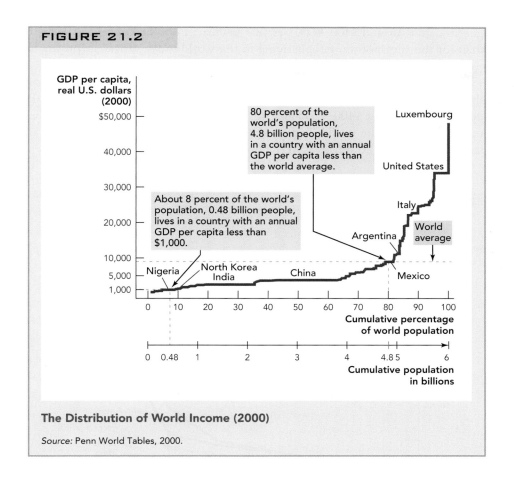

FIGURE 21.2

The Distribution of World Income (2000)

Source: Penn World Tables, 2000.

world's population. As we add successively richer countries and their popula- tions we move further to the right in population and upwards in GDP per capita. The graph tells us, for example, that about 8 percent of the world's population—or 0.48 billion people in 2000—live in a country with a GDP per capita of less than $1,000—about the level in Nigeria. Moving further to the right we see that just over 60 percent of the world's population lives in a coun- try with a GDP per capita equal to or less than $4,000, about the level in China. The red horizontal dashed line shows the world's average level of GDP per capita in 2000, $9,133, which is about the same as that of Mexico. Fully 80 per- cent of the world's population—or 4.8 billion people—live in a country with a GDP per capita less than average. In other words, most of the world's population is poor relative to the United States.

In thinking about poverty, remember that GDP per capita is simply an aver- age, and there is a distribution of income within each country. In India, GDP per capita is around $3,000 but many Indians have yearly incomes that are less than $3,000 and some have yearly incomes that are higher than the average income in the United States. Around the world, about a billion people have incomes of less than $2 per day.

Fact Two: Everyone Used to Be Poor

The distribution of world income tells us that poverty is normal. It's wealth that is unusual. Poverty is even more normal when we think about human history. What was GDP per capita like in the year 1? No one knows for sure, but a good guesstimate is around $400–$600 per year in current dollars, not much different than for the very poorest people living in the world today. What's surprising is not that people in the past were poor but that *everyone* in the past was poor.

Figure 21.3 shows some estimates of GDP per capita in different regions of the world in different periods from the year 1 to 2000 AD. In the year 1, GDP per capita was about $400–$600 and this was approximately the same in all the major regions of the world. Today GDP per capita is more than 50 times as large in the richest countries as in the poorest countries.

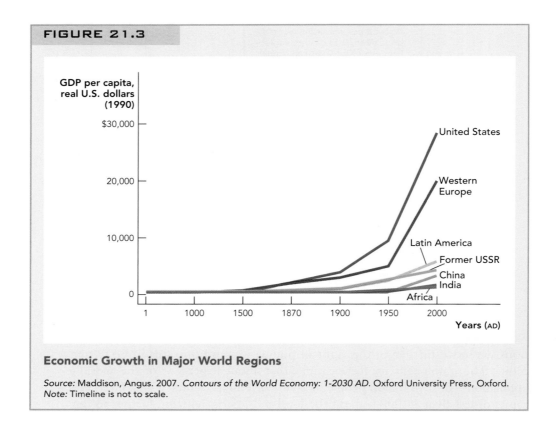

FIGURE 21.3

Economic Growth in Major World Regions

Source: Maddison, Angus. 2007. *Contours of the World Economy: 1-2030 AD.* Oxford University Press, Oxford. *Note:* Timeline is not to scale.

Figure 21.3 illustrates something else of interest: GDP per capita was about the same in year 1 as it would be 1,000 years later and indeed about the same as it had been 1,000 years earlier. For most of recorded human history there was *no long-run growth in real per capita GDP*. Countries might grow in particular good years, but soon enough a disaster would ensue and the gains would be given back. Only beginning in the nineteenth century does it become clear that some parts of the world began to grow at a rate unprecedented in human history.

Figure 21.3 tells us that economic growth is unusual. But once economic growth begins, it can make some parts of the world rich while other parts languish at levels of per capita GDP similar to that in the Dark Ages. To see more clearly how small changes in economic growth can have enormous effects on GDP per capita, we pause for a primer on economic growth rates.

A Primer on Growth Rates Recall from Chapter 20 on GDP that a growth rate is the percentage change in a variable over a given time period such as a year. When we refer to **economic growth** we mean the growth rate of real per capita GDP.

Economic growth is the growth rate of real GDP per capita.

$$g_t = \frac{Y_t - Y_{t-1}}{Y_{t-1}} \times 100$$

Where y_t is real per capita GDP in period t.

While computing growth rates is simple math, grasping the impact of growth rates on economic progress is critical. Keep in mind that even slow growth, if sustained over many years, produces large differences in real GDP per capita.

To appreciate the power of economic growth, let's consider a few cases. Suppose that the annual growth rate of real GDP per capita is 2 percent. How long will it take for real per capita GDP to double from $40,000 to $80,000? An average person on the street might answer "It will take 50 years to double your income at a 2 percent growth rate." But that is wrong because growth builds on top of growth. This is called "compounding" or "exponential growth."

We can better understand compounding by creating a simple table in a spreadsheet. In Table 21.1, per capita GDP is $40,000 at the beginning of year 1. Over the course of the year, we move across a row, and per capita GDP increases by 2 percent or $800 (note the formula for the increase in cell C2); thus at the end of one year per capita GDP is $40,800. In the second year, 2 percent growth yields $816 of new income (2 percent of $40,800), so at the end of two years, per capita GDP is $41,616. Two percent of this is $832.32. Each year (represented by moving down a row), the dollar increase in per capita GDP gets larger, as 2 percent of a growing number continues to grow.

TABLE 21.1 Excellent Growth

	C2	▼	f_x =B2*0.02	
	A	B	C	D
	Year	Beginning GDP	Increase in GDP	GDP at end of Year
1		(per capita)		
2	1	$40,000	$800	$40,800
3	2	$40,800	$816	$41,616
4	3	$41,616	$832	$42,448
36	35	$78,427	$1,569	$79,996

In fact, as Table 21.1 shows, at a 2 percent growth rate it takes only 35 years for GDP per capita to double.

There is a simple approximation, called the rule of 70, for determining the length of time necessary for a growing variable to double:

Rule of 70: If the annual growth rate of a variable is x percent, then the doubling time is $\frac{70}{x}$ years.

Table 21.2 illustrates the rule of 70 by showing how long it takes for GDP per capita to double given different growth rates. At a growth rate of 1 percent, GDP per capita will double approximately every 70 years (70/1 = 70). If growth increases to 2 percent, GDP per capita will double every 35 years (70/2 = 35). Consider the impact of a 4 percent growth rate. If this growth can be sustained, then GDP per capita doubles every 17.5 years (70/4 = 17.5). In 70 years, income doubles 4 times reaching a level 16 times its starting value!

TABLE 21.2 Years to Double Using the Rule of 70

Annual Growth Rate	Years to Double
0%	Never
1%	70
2%	35
3%	23.3
4%	17.5

The rule of 70 is just a mathematical approximation but it bears out the key concept that small differences in growth rates have large effects on economic progress.

Another way of seeing how small changes in the rate of economic growth can lead to big effects is to think about how rich people will be in the future. U.S. per capita GDP is about $46,000 (as of 2007). How many years will it take for real per capita GDP to increase to $1 million? If growth is 2 percent per year, which would be a little low by U.S. standards, average income will be $1 million per year in just 155 years. If GDP per capita grows at 3 percent per year, which is a little high by U.S. standards but certainly not impossible, then in just 105 years the average income will be approximately $1 million per year. You and I are unlikely to see this future, but if our grandchildren are lucky, they will see a world in which U.S. GDP per capita is a million dollars, more than 22 times higher than it is today.

Fact Three: There Are Growth Miracles and Growth Disasters

The United States is one of the wealthiest countries in the world because the United States has grown slowly but relatively consistently for over two hundred years. Can other countries catch up to the United States and if so will it take two hundred years? Fortunately other countries can catch up and amazingly quickly. Figure 21.4 shows two "growth miracles." Following World War II, Japan was one of the poorest countries in the world with a per capita GDP less than that of Mexico. From 1950 to 1970, however, Japan grew at an astonishing rate of 8.5 percent per year. Remember, at that rate, GDP per capita doubles in approximately 8 years (70/8.5 = 8.2)! Today, Japan is one of the richest countries in the world.

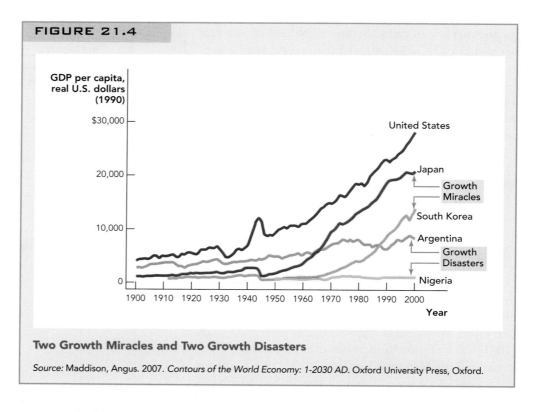

FIGURE 21.4

Two Growth Miracles and Two Growth Disasters

Source: Maddison, Angus. 2007. Contours of the World Economy: 1-2030 AD. Oxford University Press, Oxford.

In 1950, South Korea was even poorer than Japan with a GDP per capita about the same as that of Nigeria. South Korea's growth miracle began a little later than Japan's, but between 1970 and 1990, South Korea grew at a rate of 7.2 percent per year. Today, South Korea is a thriving, modern economy on par with many European economies.

Growth miracles are possible but so are growth disasters. Nigeria has barely grown since 1950 and was poorer in 2000 than in 1974 when high oil prices briefly bumped up its per capita GDP. More surprising is the case of Argentina. In 1900, Argentina was one of the richest countries in the world with a per capita GDP almost as large (75 percent) as that of the United States. By 1950, Argentina's per capita GDP had fallen to half that in the United States. In 1950, however, Argentina was still a relatively wealthy country with a per capita GDP more than twice as high as that of Japan and more than five times as high as that of South Korea. Argentina failed to grow much, however, and by 2000 Argentina's per capita GDP was less than a third of that of the United States; Japan and South Korea are now much wealthier than Argentina.

The gap between Argentina and many other countries is continuing to grow. China (not pictured) began its own growth miracle in the late 1970s. China is still a very poor nation with a per capita GDP that in 2007 is a little less than half that of Argentina. But China is growing rapidly—remember, if China continues to grow at 7 or 8 percent per year it will double its income in about 10 years. Even if Argentina grows modestly, China could pass Argentina in per capita GDP in less than 20 years.

Summarizing the Facts: Good and Bad News

The facts presented above imply both good and bad news. The bad news is that most of the world is poor and more than one billion people live on incomes of less than $2 per day. These people have greatly reduced prospects for health, happiness, and peace. The bad news, however, is old news. For most of human history, people were poor and there was no economic growth.

The good news is this: despite being a relatively recent phenomenon, economic growth has quickly transformed the world. It has raised the standard of living of most people in developed nations many times above the historical norm. Even though economic growth has yet to reach much of the world, there appears to be no reason why in principle economic growth cannot occur everywhere. Indeed, growth miracles tell us that it doesn't take 250 years to reach the level of wealth of the United States—South Korea was as poor as Nigeria in 1950 but today has a per capita GDP not that far behind Germany or the United Kingdom.

Progress, however, is not guaranteed. The growth disasters tell us that economic growth is not automatic. Some countries such as Nigeria show few signs that they have started along the growth path, while other countries such as Argentina seem to have fallen off the growth path. Understanding the wealth of nations and economic growth, therefore, is critical.

Understanding the Wealth of Nations

Let's begin with Figure 21.5 on the next page, a guide to the major factors behind the wealth of nations. At the bottom of the figure is what we would like to explain, GDP per capita. As we move up the figure we see some of the causes of the wealth of nations, beginning with the proximate or most direct causes and moving toward the ultimate or indirect causes.

The Factors of Production

The most proximate cause of the wealth of nations is this: countries with a high GDP per capita have a lot of physical and human capital per worker and that capital is organized using the best technological knowledge to be highly productive. Physical capital, human capital, and technological knowledge are called factors of production. Let's take a look at each factor of production.

By **physical capital** (or just "capital") economists mean tools in the broadest sense: pencils, desks, computers, hammers, shovels, tractors, cell phones, factories, roads, and bridges. More and better tools make workers more productive.

Farming is a good illustration of the role of capital. In much of the world, farmers are laborers pure and simple: they dig, seed, cut, and harvest using hard labor and a few simple tools like hoes and plows (often pulled by oxen). In the United States, farmers use a lot more capital—tractors, trucks, combines, and harvesters.

UNDERSTAND YOUR
world

CHECK YOURSELF

> According to Figure 21.2, approximately what percentage of the world's population lived in China in 2000?

> If you make 5 percent on your savings in a bank account, how many years will it take for your savings to double? How about if you make 8 percent?

> In Figure 21.4, approximately when did Japan's real GDP per capita cross the $10,000 barrier? The $20,000 barrier? What was Japan's growth rate in that time span?

UNDERSTAND YOUR
world

Physical capital is the stock of tools including machines, structures, and equipment.

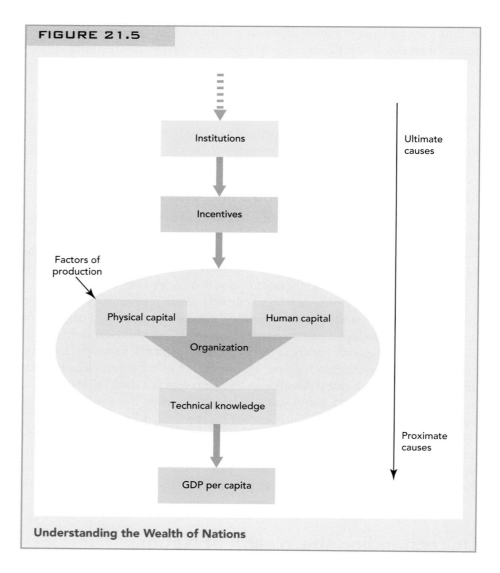

FIGURE 21.5

Institutions

Incentives

Factors of production

Physical capital   Human capital

Organization

Technical knowledge

GDP per capita

Ultimate causes

Proximate causes

Understanding the Wealth of Nations

Farmers practicing capitalism

Human capital is the productive knowledge and skills that workers acquire through education, training, and experience.

It's not just farmers that use a lot of capital. The typical worker in the United States works with over $100,000 worth of capital. A typical worker in India works with less than one-tenth as much capital.

It's also not just physical capital that makes U.S. farmers productive. A farmer in the United States riding his tractor uses a GPS (global positioning system) receiver to triangulate his exact location using signals from a series of satellites orbiting the earth some 16,500 miles high. The tractor's location is combined with data from other satellites and land-based sensors to precisely adjust the amount of seed, fertilizer, and water to be applied to the land. The fertilizer has been carefully designed, and the seeds almost certainly have been genetically engineered.

The high-tech nature of farming in the United States draws our attention to the importance of human capital and technological knowledge. **Human capital** is *tools of the mind*, or the stuff in people's heads that makes them productive. Human capital is not something we are born with—it is produced by an investment of time and other resources in education, training, and experience. Farmers in the United States, for example, have more human capital than farmers in most of the world, and it's this human capital that enables them to take advantage of tools like GPS receivers. The same is true in the larger economy—the typical person in the United States, for example, has about 12 years of schooling while in Pakistan the typical person has less than 5 years of schooling.

The greater quantities of physical and human capital per worker used in U.S. farming make U.S. farmers more productive. U.S. farmers produce more than three times as much corn per acre than do farmers in Pakistan, for example.

The third factor of production is technological knowledge. This factor includes, for instance, the genetics, chemistry, and physics that form the basis of the techniques used in U.S. agriculture. (Did you know that the clocks on GPS satellites must be adjusted to account for the effects of Einstein's theory of relativity?)

Technological knowledge and human capital are related but different. Human capital is the knowledge and skills that a farmer needs to understand and to make productive use of technology. **Technological knowledge** is knowledge about how the world works—the kind of knowledge that makes technology possible. We increase human capital with education. We increase technological knowledge with research and development. Technological knowledge is potentially boundless. We can learn more and more about how the world works even if human capital remains relatively constant.

Improved technological knowledge has made U.S. farmers more productive over time. U.S. farms today produce more than two and half times as much output as they did in 1950 and they do so using *less* land! More physical and human capital has helped to drive this increase in output, but better technological knowledge has been the primary factor.[1]

The final factor, a factor often taken for granted, is organization. Human capital, physical capital, and technological knowledge must be organized to produce valuable goods and services. Who does this organizing and why? To answer this question, we turn to the issue of incentives and institutions.

> **Technological knowledge** is knowledge about how the world works that is used to produce goods and services.

Incentives and Institutions

South Korea has a per capita GDP more than 10 times higher than North Korea. Why? In one sense, we have just given an answer: South Korea has more physical and human capital per worker than North Korea.* But this answer is incomplete and partial. The answer is incomplete because we still want to know: *Why* does South Korea have more physical and human capital than North Korea? The answer is partial because poor countries like North Korea not only have less physical and human capital than rich countries, they also fail to organize the capital that they do have in the most productive ways. To understand the wealth of nations more deeply, we need to take a look at some of the indirect or more ultimate causes.

The example of South and North Korea is useful because we can rule out some explanations for the huge differences in wealth between these two countries. The explanation, for example, cannot be differences in the people, culture, or geography. Before South and North Korea were divided at the end of World War II, they shared the same people and culture, in other words, the same human

CHECK YOURSELF

> Which country has more physical capital per worker: the United States or China? China or Nigeria?

> What are the three primary factors of production?

---

* What about technological knowledge? North Korea has access to most of the world's technological knowledge and is able, for example, to build sophisticated weapons—perhaps even a nuclear bomb—thus differences in technological knowledge probably only explain a small fraction of the differences in the wealth of nations.

Increases in technological knowledge, however, are clearly important for growth at the world level (as opposed to explaining differences in wealth across nations)—as we will discuss at greater length in the next chapter.

capital. South and North Korea also had similar levels of physical capital—natural resources were about the same in the South as the North, and if there were any advantages in man-made physical capital, they went to the North, which was at that time more industrialized than the South. When the two regions were split, therefore, South and North Korea were in all important respects the same, almost as if the split was designed as a giant social experiment.

South and North Korea differed in their economic institutions. Broadly speaking, South Korea had capitalism, and North Korea had communism. South Korea was never a pure capitalist economy, of course, but in South Korea the organizers of human capital, physical capital, and technological knowledge are private, profit-seeking firms and entrepreneurs to a much greater extent than in North Korea. In South Korea a worker earns more money if he provides goods and services of value to consumers or if he invents new ideas for more efficient production. Those same incentives do not exist in North Korea, where workers are rewarded for being loyal to the ruling communist party. In short, South Korea uses markets to organize its production much more than North Korea and so is able to take advantage of all the efficiency properties of markets that we discussed in Chapters 2 and 3.

Fifty years later the results of the "experiment" splitting North and South Korea are so clear they can be seen even from outer space, as seen in Figure 21.6.

FIGURE 21.6

Can You Tell Which Country Has Better Institutions?
South Korea and North Korea photographed at night from outer space.

Source: REUTERS/Jason Reed

The experiment splitting South and North Korea is especially dramatic. But wherever similar experiments have been tried, such as in East and West Germany, or Taiwan and China, the results have been similar.

We said earlier that countries with a high GDP per capita have a lot of physical and human capital that is organized using the best technological knowledge to be highly productive. But factors of production do not fall from the sky like manna from heaven. Factors of production must be produced. Similarly, factors of production do not organize themselves. Physical capital, human capital, and technology must be combined and organized purposely for it to be productive.

Do you remember Big Idea One and Big Idea Two from the introductory chapter? These ideas were that incentives matter and good institutions align self-interest with the social interest.

Thus, we can now deepen our understanding of the wealth of nations. Countries with a high GDP per capita have institutions that make it in people's self-interest to invest in physical capital, human capital, and technological knowledge and to efficiently organize these resources for production.

In short, the key to producing and organizing the factors of production are *institutions* that create appropriate *incentives*. Let's look at institutions and the incentives that they create in more detail.

Institutions

Institutions include laws and regulations but also customs, practices, organizations, and social mores—institutions are the "rules of the game" that shape human interaction and structure economic incentives within a society.

> **Institutions** are the "rules of the game" that structure economic incentives.

What kinds of institutions encourage investment and the efficient organization of the factors of production? Understanding institutions is an important area of research in economics, and there is considerable agreement that among the key institutions are property rights, honest government, political stability, a dependable legal system, and competitive and open markets.

Institutions of Economic Growth

> Property rights
> Honest government
> Political stability
> A dependable legal system
> Competitive and open markets

Entire books have been written about each of these institutions and their role in economic growth. Indeed, much of this book is about property rights and the benefits of open markets and rivalrous economic competition. Thus, we will give only a few examples here of how each of these institutions create appropriate incentives, incentives that align self-interest with the social interest.

Property Rights   When the communist revolutionaries took control of China, they abolished private property in land. In the "Little Leap Forward," they put farmers to work in collectives of 100–300 families. Communal property meant that the incentives to invest in the land and work hard were low. Imagine that a day's work can produce an extra bushel of corn. Thus, an extra day's work on a commune with 100 families earned the worker 1/100th of a bushel of corn. Would you work an extra day for a few earfuls of corn? Under communal property, working an extra day doesn't add much to a worker's take-home pay and working a day less doesn't subtract much. Thus, *under communal property, effort is divorced from payment*

A **free rider** is someone who consumes a resource without working or contributing to the resource's upkeep.

so there is little incentive to work—in fact, there is an incentive not to work and to **free ride** on the work of others. In the "Great Leap Forward," the incentive to free ride was made even stronger when communes were increased to 5,000 families. But if everyone free rides, the commune will starve. Communal property in agricultural land did not align a farmer's self-interest with the social interest. And, as a result of this and many similar errors on the part of the Chinese leadership, some 20–40 million Chinese farmers and workers starved during this period.

The Great Leap Forward was actually a great leap backward—agricultural land was less productive in 1978 than it had been in 1949 when the communists took over. In 1978, however, farmers in the village of Xiaogang held a secret meeting. The farmers agreed to divide the communal land and assign it to individuals—each farmer had to produce a quota for the government but anything he or she produced in excess of the quota they would keep. The agreement violated government policy and as a result the farmers also pledged that if any of them were to be jailed the others would raise their children.

The change from collective property rights to something closer to private property rights had an immediate effect: investment, work effort, and productivity increased. "You can't be lazy when you work for your family and yourself," said one of the farmers.

Word of the secret agreement leaked out and local bureaucrats cut off Xiaogang from fertilizer, seeds, and pesticides. But amazingly, before Xiaogang could be stopped, farmers in other villages also began to abandon collective property. In Beijing, Mao Zedong was dead and a new set of rulers, seeing the productivity improvements, decided to let the experiment proceed.

In the five short years between 1978 and 1983, when China's central government endorsed individual farming, food production increased by nearly 50 percent and 170 million people were lifted above the World Bank's lowest poverty line. Simply put, increases in agricultural productivity brought about by the switch to individual farming were the greatest antipoverty program in the history of the world. By 1984, the collective farms were gone and soon after that China's leader Deng Xiaoping announced a new government policy: "it is glorious to be rich."

Property rights in land greatly increased China's agricultural productivity. With fewer workers producing more food, more workers were available to produce other goods. To take advantage of its millions of workers, China opened up to foreign investment, making the label "Made in China" common throughout the world. With their secret pact, the farmers of Xiaogang had begun a second and more successful Chinese revolution.[2]

Property rights are important institutions for encouraging investment in physical and human capital, not just in agriculture but throughout the economy. It can take decades, for example, for an investment in a new apartment building or a factory to pay off. As we will discuss further in Chapter 23 savings are necessary to generate investment and thus growth. But why do people save and invest? Savers won't save and investors won't invest if they don't expect that their property will be secure and they will receive a return for their savings and investment. Property rights are also important for encouraging technological innovation. For instance, investments in new pharmaceuticals take decades to pay off and they are risky—years of research and development sometimes have to be abandoned when the guinea pigs start to die unexpectedly. Just like farmers, investors and workers throughout the economy need to know that they will reap what they sow.

Honest Government China under its former communist rulers was extreme in abolishing most forms of private property. In many other countries, private property rights exist on paper—but only on paper. In a country like Zimbabwe, for example, an individual might have a legal right to land or a factory but everyone knows that the government can take these goods at any moment. Zimbabwe lacks the rule of law.

More generally, corruption is like a heavy tax that bleeds resources away from productive entrepreneurs. Resources "invested" in bribing politicians and bureaucrats cannot be invested in machinery and equipment, thus reducing productivity. Corrupt government officials will also harass entrepreneurs, creating excessive rules and regulations that force entrepreneurs to pay them to stop making trouble.

Not all taxes are bad of course. A tax that funds investment in roads, universities, or law and order can increase the productivity of private investments. Corruption, therefore, is a doubly bad tax because corruption makes it less profitable to be an entrepreneur at the same time as it makes it more profitable to be a corrupt politician or bureaucrat. At some point, corruption can feed on itself creating a poverty trap: few people want to be entrepreneurs because they know that their wealth will be stolen and thus there is no wealth to steal.

Figure 21.7 on the next page graphs corruption on the horizontal axis. The most corrupt countries like Somalia, Liberia, and North Korea are on the right, scoring about 2 on a 5-point scale running from −2.5 (least corrupt) to 2.5 (most corrupt). The least corrupt countries like Singapore, Iceland, the United States, and Norway are on the left. Real GDP per capita is on the vertical axis. Countries that are more corrupt have much lower per capita GDP.

Top Ten Least Corrupt Countries (2000)	Top Ten Most Corrupt Countries (2000)
Country	Country
Finland	North Korea
Singapore	Afghanistan
Sweden	Somalia
Iceland	Liberia
Netherlands	Equatorial Guinea
Denmark	Congo, Democratic Republic
New Zealand	Angola
Norway	Iraq
United Kingdom	Haiti
Switzerland	Myanmar
Source: World Bank, World Governance Indicators	*Source:* World Bank, World Governance Indicators

Political Stability Investors have more to fear than government expropriation—sometimes the threat of anarchy can be even worse. Liberia, for example, has had little but conflict for the past 40 years. Prior to the election in 2006 of President Ellen Johnson-Sirleaf, the first elected female head of state in Africa, it had been 35 years since a Liberian president assumed office by means other than bloodshed. Both the previous two national leaders (Charles Taylor and Samuel Doe) consistently used the force of government to eradicate their opposition. Who wants to invest in the future when civil war threatens to wash away all plans?

More generally, in many nations, civil war, military dictatorship, and anarchy have destroyed the institutions necessary for economic growth.

A Dependable Legal System The problem of poorly protected property rights is not always a problem of too much government—sometimes property rights are poorly protected because there is too little government. The legal system in many countries, for example, is of such low quality that no one knows for certain who owns what. In India, residents who purchase land often have to do so two or three times (from different parties), as there exists no reliable record of true ownership. A lawsuit, if you even bother to bring one, can take 20 years or more to resolve. In a major urban area, it's very difficult to build something as simple as a supermarket because developers cannot acquire good

Not a good place to grow

Bullet casings cover a street in Monrovia, the capital of Liberia, in the summer of 2003.

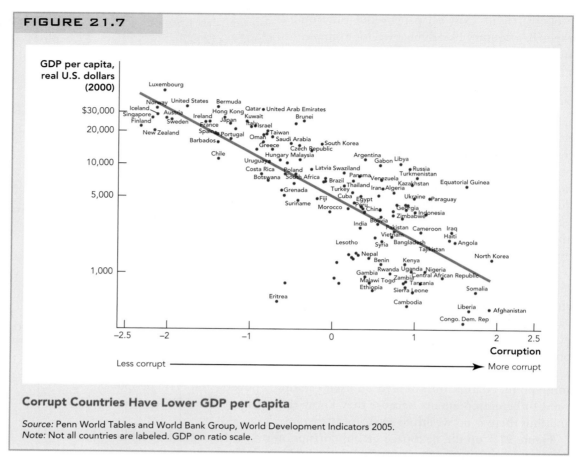

FIGURE 21.7

Corrupt Countries Have Lower GDP per Capita

Source: Penn World Tables and World Bank Group, World Development Indicators 2005.
Note: Not all countries are labeled. GDP on ratio scale.

title to a modestly sized piece of land. No one wants to build when they cannot protect their investment.

A good legal system facilitates contracts and protects private parties from expropriating one another. Few people think of the U.S. legal system as a paradigm of productivity but it is compared to the Indian legal system. In the United States, for example, it takes 17 procedures and 300 days to collect on a debt (say a bounced check). In India, it takes 56 procedures and 1,420 days to do the same thing. That's one reason why it is hard to borrow money in the first place: lenders know how hard it is to get their money back.

Competitive and Open Markets   The factors of production must not only be produced—they must also be organized. Detailed studies from a large number of countries suggest that the failure to organize capital efficiently has a huge effect on the wealth of nations. Poor countries are poor, in other words, not just because they lack capital but also because they use the capital that they do have inefficiently. Overall, about half the differences in per capita income across countries are explained by differences in the amount of physical and human capital (some of those differences in capital spring from deeper differences in institutions) and about half the differences are explained by a failure to use capital efficiently. One study, for example, estimates that if India used the physical and human capital that it does have as efficiently as the United States uses its capital, India would be four times richer than it is today.[3]

Why does India use its capital inefficiently? The reasons are numerous, but competitive and open markets are one of the best ways to encourage the efficient organization of resources. India, as well as other poor countries, has many inefficient and unnecessary regulations, which create monopolies or otherwise impede markets.

For instance, Indian shirts are usually made by hand in small shops of 3 or 4 tailors that design, measure, sew, and sell, all on the same premises. It sounds elegant but this is not Savile Row, the section of London where the finest tailors in the world create custom suits for the rich and powerful. Shirts would be cheaper and of higher quality if they were mass manufactured in small factories—the way shirts for Americans are produced. Why doesn't this happen in India? Shirts in India are produced inefficiently because, until recently, large-scale production was illegal.

India prohibited investment in shirt factories from exceeding about $200,000. This restriction meant that Indian shirt manufacturers could not take advantage of **economies of scale,** the decrease in the average cost of production that often occurs as the total quantity of production increases. India has been reforming its economy, which is one reason why economic growth in India has increased in recent years (as we discussed in Chapter 20). India recently lifted the ban on large garment factories, for example, but many, many regulations remain that reduce the productivity of the Indian economy.[4]

> **Economies of scale** are the advantages of large-scale production that reduce average cost as quantity increases.

Poor countries also suffer from expensive red tape. Economists at the World Bank have estimated the time and cost to do simple tasks such as starting a business or enforcing a contract in a court of law. In the United States, for example, it takes about 5 days to start a business and the total costs of the procedures are minor, less than 1 percent of the average income per capita. In Peru, starting a business takes 72 days and 32.5 percent of income per capita. In Haiti, it takes 203 days and the costs are 127 percent of income per capita. Thus, even before a business is begun, a Peruvian or Haitian entrepreneur must invest extensively in dealing with bureaucracies—that same physical and human capital is not being used to produce goods and services.

Institutions and Growth Miracles Revisited

When China changed its institutions from collective farming to individual farming, agricultural productivity increased dramatically and China began to grow. The example of China is enormously encouraging because it suggests that growth miracles could become common if more countries changed their institutions. But take a look again at Figure 21.5. Institutions have a large effect on increasing and organizing the factors of production and thus institutions have a large effect on economic growth. But where do institutions come from? Are institutions products of ideas? Culture? History? Geography? Luck? Try "all of the above" and then some.

If you consider the history of America, its constitution was written at a time when the ideas of John Locke and Adam Smith were popular and it inherited a tendency toward a market economy and democratic institutions from its colonizer, Great Britain. An open frontier meant cheap land and plenty of freedom to try new ideas and ways of living, perhaps influencing America's entrepreneurial culture even into modern times. And we are very lucky that George Washington had the virtue to stop at two Presidential terms, rather than trying to become the next king.

No one understands for certain all the influences that go into creating a nation's institutions which means that changing institutions isn't easy. When it comes to institutions, we know where we want to go but we don't always know how to get there. Understanding institutions, where they come from, and how they can be changed, is thus a key research question in economics.

□ Takeaway

It's hard to overstate the importance of economic growth. Once, everyone was poor. Today, GDP per capita is more than 50 times higher in the richest countries than in the poorest. Economic growth has raised billions of people out of near-starvation poverty but billions more remain in dire poverty with shocking consequences for their quality of life.

Fortunately, poor countries can catch up to rich countries and in a surprisingly short period of time. Growth "miracles" have brought Japan and South Korea up to European levels of wealth within the lifespan of a single generation. Since the agricultural reforms beginning in 1978, poverty in China has been reduced to an unprecedented degree and China continues to grow rapidly.

What makes a country rich? The most proximate cause is that countries with a high GDP per capita have lots of physical and human capital per worker and that capital is organized using the best technological knowledge to be highly productive.

How do countries get a lot of physical and human capital and how do they organize it using the best technological knowledge? Countries with a high GDP per capita have institutions that encourage investment in physical capital, human capital, technological innovation, and the efficient organization of resources. Among the most powerful institutions for increasing economic growth are property rights, honest government, political stability, a dependable legal system, and competitive and open markets.

□ CHAPTER REVIEW

KEY CONCEPTS

Economic growth, p. 430

Physical capital, p. 433

Human capital, p. 434

Technological knowledge, p. 435

Institutions, p. 437

Free rider, p. 438

Economies of scale, p. 441

FACTS AND TOOLS

1. Look at Figure 21.1. About how many babies die before the age of 5 in Nigeria versus Argentina? What is the difference in GDP per person in those two countries?

2. Look at Figure 21.2. About what fraction of the world's population lives in countries richer than Italy? What fraction lives in countries poorer than India?

3. The world's average (mean) GDP per capita is $9,133. There are roughly 6 billion people in the world.

   a. What is the world's total GDP?

   b. About 20 percent of the world's population produces 50 percent of the world's total GDP. (Notice the use of "produces," not "consumes." In popular discussion, you are more likely to hear about the people at the top "consuming" more than their share, not "producing" more than their share. But remember what the last letter of GDP stands for!) How much GDP does the top 20 percent produce?

c. What is the average GDP per capita of the most productive 20 percent of the world's population? (Hint: 20 percent of 6 billion people equals how many people?)

4. Now let's look at the productivity of the world's least productive 80 percent.

a. How much GDP do they produce? (Hint: You've already calculated this number in the previous question.)

b. What is the average GDP per capita of the least productive 80 percent of the world's population?

c. Now, the payoff: How productive is the average person in the top 20 percent compared to the average person in the bottom 80 percent of the planet? Answer this by dividing your answer to question 3c by your answer to question 4b. This chapter and the next are devoted to explaining why this ratio is so large.

5. According to Fact Two, what would your answer to question 4c have been if you calculated it two thousand years ago?

6. What are the factors of production? Name them and briefly describe them in plain English.

7. Using data from the Penn World Tables, calculate the annual growth rate of real GDP per person for China for the years in the table. The Penn World Tables, available free online, are a reliable source of international economic data, and they are very popular among economists.

Year	Real GDP per capita (in 1996 U.S. dollars)	Annual Growth Rate
2000	4,001	
2001	4,389	___
2002	4,847	___
2003	5,321	___
2004	5,771	___

8. Practice with the rule of 70: If you inherit $10,000 this year and you invest your money so that it grows 7 percent per year, how many years will it take for your investment to be worth

$20,000? $40,000? $160,000? (Note: Investments in stocks have grown at an average inflation-adjusted rate of 7 percent per year since the U.S. Civil War. We'll practice this some more in Chapter 22.)

Value today: $10,000. Growth Rate: 7 percent

Number of years until money doubles: ___

Number of years until money quadruples:

___

Number of years until your inheritance is 16X larger: ___

9. More practice with the rule of 70: Suppose that instead, you put your money into a savings account that grows at an inflation-adjusted return of 2 percent per year. How many years will it take to be worth $20,000? $40,000? $160,000? (Note: Bank deposits have grown at roughly this rate over the last 50 years in the United States.)

Value today: $10,000.   Growth Rate: 2 percent

Number of years until money doubles: ___

Number of years until money quadruples:

___

Number of years until your inheritance is 16X larger: ___

10. India and China come up a lot in this chapter. You might wonder why so much time is spent talking about just two countries out of over 180 on the planet. But what fraction of humans live in India and China together?

11. Let's convert Figure 21.5 into words.

Institutions create ___, which in turn affect the amount of ___, ___, and ___ in a country, which, combined with the right kind of ___ generates a level of ___ per person.

THINKING AND PROBLEM SOLVING

1. The average person in Argentina today is about as rich (in inflation-adjusted terms) as his or her parents. How can this be called a "growth disaster?"

2. Before the rise of affordable automobiles and subways, many people used trolleys—small trains on rails that ran along ordinary streets—to get around in urban areas. On trolleys, there is a literal "free rider problem": since the trains were right next to sidewalks, and since trolleys were wide open and never had doors, people could hop on and off very easily. How much money will a trolley lose if it is easy to ride for free? If

"free riders" are a big problem, what will happen to the supply of trolley rides? What are a few things the trolley industry could do to solve the problem of free riders?

The trolley: a literal "free-rider" problem.

3. During the Great Leap Forward, millions of Chinese starved to death because not enough food was produced by farmers. Why didn't farmers grow food? In particular, was it because there wasn't enough human capital or physical capital?

The text on the Great Leap Forward era flag reads, in part, "Long live the People's Commune!" Unfortunately, this patriotic appeal didn't work as well as good economic incentives and millions lost their lives. *(Source: Wikipedia, "Great Leap Forward")*

4. Laws that encourage businesses to stay small are often very popular. The laws governing Indian shirt tailors discussed in this chapter are just one example. What are some *noneconomic* (e.g., social, moral, ethical) reasons why voters might want businesses to stay small? What are some *economic* reasons they might want businesses to grow large?

5. Economists use the term "human capital" to refer to education and job skills. How is education like a piece of capital?

6. Many people say that natural resources like oil and minerals are the way to prosperity. Indeed, in an old cartoon by Matt Groening, creator of *The Simpsons*, a professor taught his students, "The nation that controls magnesium controls the universe!" But natural resources have been left out of this chapter completely. Is this a big mistake? (Source: Sala-i-Martin, X., G. Doppelhofer, and R. Miller, "Determinants of Long-Term Economic Growth," *American Economic Review,* September 2004.)

   a. Here are the ten countries in the world that have the highest amount of hydrocarbons (oil, natural gas, etc.) per person, in rank order:

     1. Kuwait

     2. United Arab Emirates (UAE)

     3. Saudi Arabia

     4. Iraq

     5. Norway

     6. Venezuela

     7. Oman

     8. Iran

     9. Trinidad & Tobago

     10. Gabon

Use the *CIA World Factbook,* a convenient online source of information, to see if most of these countries are prosperous. How many of these 10 countries have a GDP per person that is at least half of the U.S. level? How many are less than 10 percent of the U.S. level? Are any actually higher than the U.S. level?

   b. Now, let's look at the reverse: Let's see if the 10 richest countries in GDP per capita have a lot of hydrocarbon wealth:

     1. Luxembourg

     2. United States

     3. Singapore

     4. Hong Kong

     5. Norway

     6. Australia

     7. Sweden

     8. Canada

     9. Denmark

     10. Japan

The one country on both lists also makes another list in this chapter. Which one is it?

7. Economists often refer to the "natural resource curse," by which they mean that large amounts of natural resources tend to create bad politics because as long as the oil keeps flowing or the diamonds remain plentiful, political leaders don't need to care much about what goes on in the rest of the country.

   a. Which one of the three factors of production do you think matters most to a leader of a resource-rich country? Why? (Note: Does this help explain what you see happening in many resource-rich countries?)

   b. Which one of the five key institutions do you think matters most to a leader of a resource-rich republic? Why? (Note: Does this help explain what you see happening in many resource-rich countries?)

8. Let's figure out how long it will take for the average Indian to be as wealthy as the average Western European is today. Note that all numbers are *adjusted for inflation*, so we're measuring output in "piles of stuff," not "piles of money." India's GDP per capita is $3,000, and (somewhat optimistically) let's say that real output per person there grows at 5 percent per year. Using the rule of 70, how many years will it take for India to reach Italy's current level of GDP per capita, about $24,000 per year?

9. In the Soviet Union, especially in the early decades under Lenin and Stalin, the official doctrine was communism, and the use of incentives was considered a form of treason. One important exception was the military equipment sector, where bonuses were common for engineers who designed and manufactured jets, nuclear missiles, tanks, and rifles. Why was this an exception?

10. Free rider problems are everywhere. For example, some restaurants let every food server keep their own tips. Other restaurants require all of the food servers to put their tips into a tip pool, which then gets divided up equally among all of the servers. It's easy to adjust the tip pool so that people who work more hours or serve more tables get their "fair share," so that's not the issue we're concerned about here. Instead, let's think about how the tip pool changes the server's incentive to be nice to the customer.

   a. To keep it simple, let's assume that a server can be "nice" and earn $100 in tips per shift, or be "mean" and earn $40 in tips per shift. If an individual server goes from being "mean" to being "nice," how much more will he earn in a non-tip-pooling world? (Yes this is an easy question.)

   b. Now let's look at incentives in a tip pool. If all the servers are mean, how much will the average server earn? If all the servers are nice, how much will the average server earn? What's the change in tips per server if *all* of them switch from being mean to being nice?

   c. But in the real world, of course, each server makes her own decision to be mean or nice. Suppose that some servers are being nice and others are being mean, and you're trying to decide whether to be nice or mean. What's the payoff *to you* if you switch your behavior? Does your answer depend on how many other servers are being nice?

   d. So when are you most likely to be nice: When you're in a tip pool or when you keep your own tips? If the restaurant cares a lot about keeping its customers happy, which policy will it follow?

11. If "everyone used to be poor," then how could some ancient civilizations afford to create massive buildings like the pyramids of Egypt and the Buddhist statues of Afghanistan (sadly, the latter were recently destroyed by the Taliban)?

CHALLENGES

1. One way to learn about what makes some countries richer is to run statistical tests to see which factors are good at predicting a nation's level of productivity. Sometimes it turns out that a relationship is just a coincidence (like the fact that people in rich countries eat more ice cream), while other statistical tests really can tell you about the ultimate causes of productivity. A statistical test can't tell you everything, but it might help point you in the right direction. In courses on econometrics and statistics, you can learn about how to run sensible tests.

   Let's look at one well-known set of tests, to see if what you learned in this chapter matches the statistical evidence. Here are 17 variables that turned out to be very strong predictors of a nation's long-run economic performance in literally millions of statistical tests (Source: Sala-i-Martin, X., G. Doppelhofer, and R. Miller, "Determinants of Long-Term Economic Growth," *American Economic Review*, September 2004).

They are in rank order, and a "+" means more of that value was good for long-run productivity:

1. Whether a country is in East Asia (+)
2. Level of K-6 schooling (+)
3. Price of capital goods (−)
4. Fraction of land close to the coast (+)
5. Fraction of population close to the coast (+)
6. Malaria prevalence (−)
7. Life expectancy (+)
8. Fraction of population Confucian (+)
9. Whether a country is in Africa (−)
10. Whether a country is in Latin America (−)
11. Fraction of GDP in mining industries (+)
12. Whether a country was a Spanish colony (−)
13. Years open to relatively free trade (+)
14. Fraction of population Muslim (+)
15. Fraction of population Buddhist (+)
16. Number of languages widely spoken (−)
17. Fraction of GDP spent on government purchases (−)

   a. Which of these factors sound like the "three factors of production?" Which ones do they sound like?
   b. Which of these factors sound like the "five key institutions?" Which ones do they sound like?
   c. Which of these factors sound like geography?
   d. The western United States was a Spanish colony until 1849. On average, former Spanish colonies have had poor economic performance. Does the western United States fit that pattern? Why or why not?

2. What do *you* think creates the good institutions that exist in rich countries? Why don't these institutions—property rights, markets, a society where you can usually trust strangers—exist everywhere on the planet?

3. Why do you think expensive red tape is hard to get rid of in many poor countries? Yes, this is a miniature version of the previous question.

4. Communists thought that their system would be much more efficient than capitalism: They thought that competition between companies was wasteful. Why build three separate headquarters for carmakers (General Motors, Chrysler, and Ford), when you can just build one? Why have three advertising budgets? Why pay for three CEOs? Why not put all the factories together, so that the same engineers can fix problems at all of the plants? Doesn't one large firm maximize economies of scale? These are all good questions. So why do you think communism turned out to be such a disaster, when it sounded like it would be so efficient?

5. The chapter lists five key institutions of economic growth. But isn't there really just one: Good government? Support your argument with facts from this chapter.

The Magic of Compound Growth Using a Spreadsheet

The rule of 70 gives us a quick way to compute doubling times given a growth rate. We can also use a Microsoft Excel spreadsheet to easily answer more difficult questions. We know, for example, that if GDP per capita starts at $40,000 and if the growth rate is 2 percent then GDP per capita after one year will be $40,800 and after just 35 years it will double to $79,996. We showed this in the chapter using a simple spreadsheet as in Figure A21.1.

FIGURE A21.1

	C2	▼	f_x =B2*0.02	
	A	B	C	D
	Year	Beginning GDP (per capita)	Increase in GDP	GDP at end of Year
1				
2	1	$40,000	$800	$40,800
3	2	$40,800	$816	$41,616
4	3	$41,616	$832	$42,448
36	35	$78,427	$1,569	$79,996
37				

Compound Growth in a Spreadsheet: The Long Method

Once we understand the principles, however, we don't need to write each year on a separate line. Instead, we can simplify by using a little bit of mathematical notation.

If our Starting Value for GDP per capita is $40,000 and the growth rate is r percent, for example, 2 percent, and we grow for one year, then our Ending Value will be $40,000 \times (1 + r/100)$. If we grow for two years our Ending Value will be $40,000 \times (1 + r/100) \times (1 + r/100)$, which is the same thing as $40,000 \times \left(1 + \dfrac{r}{100}\right)^2$. More generally, if the growth rate is r percent and we grow for n years then:

$$\text{Ending Value} = \text{Starting Value} \times \left(1 + \frac{r}{100}\right)^n \qquad \textbf{(A1)}$$

We can use this formula to simplify our spreadsheet as in Figure A21.2.

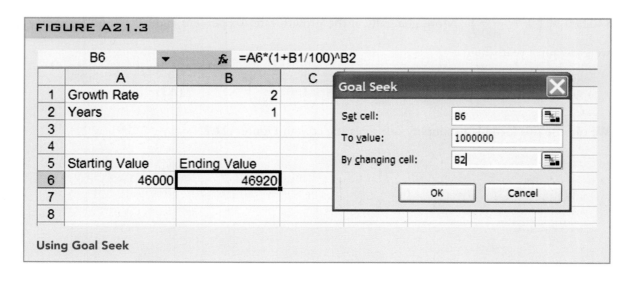

FIGURE A21.2

	A	B	C
		B6 ▼ ƒₓ =A6*(1+B1/100)^B2	
1	Growth Rate	2	
2	Years	1	
3			
4			
5	Starting Value	Ending Value	
6	40000	40800	
7			

Compound Growth in a Spreadsheet: The Shortcut

Notice that we put the starting level of GDP per capita, or whatever quantity we are interested in (this could also be the amount of money in a bank account, for example), in cell A6, the growth rate is in cell B1, the number of years we want to grow is in cell B2, and thus the formula in cell B6, "=A6★(1+B1/100)^B2", is exactly as in equation A1.

By adjusting the Starting Value, the Growth Rate, and the Number of Years, we can find out how much any amount will grow to given any interest rate over any number of years.

We can also use Excel's Goal Seek ability to work backward to find, say, the number of years it will take growing at 2 percent to reach a certain level of GDP per capita. Remember, for example, that we said in the chapter that starting at a GDP per capita of about $46,000 and growing at a growth rate of 2 percent a year GDP per capita will be $1,000,000 per year in just 155 years. Here's how you can easily find numbers like this. Go to the Tools menu and click Goal Seek (in Excel 2007 go to the Data menu and under the submenu What-If Analysis click on Goal Seek). A box will pop up asking you for three inputs: Set cell ___, To value ___, By changing cell ___. In our case we want to Set cell **B6**, the Ending Value, To value **1,000,000**, by Changing cell **B2**, the number of years. Figure A21.3 shows you what you should see and input. Notice that we also changed the Starting Value to $46,000.

FIGURE A21.3

	A	B	C
		B6 ▼ ƒₓ =A6*(1+B1/100)^B2	
1	Growth Rate	2	
2	Years	1	
3			
4			
5	Starting Value	Ending Value	
6	46000	46920	
7			
8			

Goal Seek

Set cell: B6

To value: 1000000

By changing cell: B2

OK   Cancel

Using Goal Seek

Clicking OK produces what you see in Figure A21.4.

FIGURE A21.4

	B6 ▼	f_x =A6*(1+B1/100)^B2	
	A	B	C
1	Growth Rate	2	
2	Years	155.4901699	
3			
4			
5	Starting Value	Ending Value	
6	46000	1000000	
7			
8			
9			

Goal Seek Status — Goal Seeking with Cell B6 found a solution. Target value: 1000000 Current value: 1000000

Goal Seek Solves the Problem

Goal Seek has solved the problem! If we start at a value of GDP per capita of $46,000 and we grow at 2 percent a year, then in 155.49 years we will reach a value of GDP per capita of $1,000,000.

By using Goal Seek and varying the inputs, you can find the answer to all kinds of questions. Can you find, for example, how high the growth rate would have to be to reach a level of GDP per capita of $1,000,000 in say 50 years?

CHAPTER APPENDIX QUESTIONS

Use Excel's Goal Seek ability to calculate the following:

1. If a country starts off as rich as the United States, with a GDP per capita of $46,000, and if GDP per capita grows 3 percent per year, then how many years will it take before GDP per capita is $1,000,000 per year?

2. If a country with a GDP per capita of $4,000 at its start grows at 8 percent per year how many years will it take before GDP per capita is $46,000?

3. If you wanted to double $1,000 in 10 years time, what average rate of return would you require on your investment?

22

Growth, Capital Accumulation, and the Economics of Ideas: Catching Up vs. the Cutting Edge

CHAPTER OUTLINE

The Solow Model and Catch-Up Growth

The Solow Model—Details and Further Lessons (Optional Section)

Growing on the Cutting Edge: The Economics of Ideas

The Future of Economic Growth

Takeaway

Appendix: Excellent Growth

The Chinese economy has been growing at an astonishing rate. In 2006, GDP per capita in China grew by 10 percent. In the same year, GDP per capita in the United States grew by just 2.3 percent. In its entire history, the U.S. economy has never grown as fast as the Chinese economy is growing today. If these rates continue, China will be richer than the United States in less than 25 years. How can this make sense? Is there something wrong with the U.S. economy? Do the Chinese have a magical potion for economic growth?

Remember, in the last chapter we explained that among the key institutions promoting economic growth were property rights, honest government, political stability, a dependable legal system, and competitive and open markets. But for each and every one of these institutions, the United States ranks higher than China, despite China's having made remarkable improvements in recent decades. So why is China growing so much more rapidly than the United States?

To answer this question, we must distinguish between two types of growth, catching up and cutting edge. Countries that are catching up have some enormous advantages. To become rich, a poor country does not have to invent new ideas, technologies, or methods of management. All it has to do is adopt the ideas already developed in the rich countries. As we will see, catch-up countries like China grow primarily through capital accumulation and the adoption of some simple ideas that massively improve productivity.

The United States is the world's leading economy—it is on the cutting edge. Growth on the cutting edge is primarily about developing new ideas. But developing new ideas is more difficult than adopting ideas already in existence. Calculus isn't easy but it doesn't take a genius to understand calculus; it does take a genius to invent calculus. Countries on the cutting edge grow primarily through idea generation.

451

In this chapter, we will do two things. First, we will develop a model of economic growth based on capital accumulation. The model will help us understand some puzzles such as why China is growing so much faster right now than the United States and why the countries that lost World War II, Germany and Japan, grew much faster in the postwar decades than did the winner, the United States. We will also discuss how poor and rich countries can converge in income over time.

Our model of economic growth based on capital accumulation does a good job of explaining catch-up growth but it doesn't help much to explain growth on the cutting edge. If we think about growth in the United States, for example, we probably do not think first about more tractors, buildings, and factories—the sorts of things that characterize growth in China. Instead, we think about iPhones, the Internet, and genetic engineering, that is, new products, new processes, and new ideas. Thus, in the second half of the chapter we turn to cutting-edge growth and the economics of ideas. The economics of ideas explains why growth in the United States is slower than in China, but also why growth in China will slow down. It also suggests, however, that U.S. and worldwide economic growth may become faster in the decades ahead than it has been in the past. To put it bluntly (but regretfully for us), many of you will see more progress in your lifetimes than we will have seen in ours.

The Solow Model and Catch-Up Growth

Let's begin with a model of the wealth of nations and economic growth called the Solow model (after Nobel Prize–winning economist Robert Solow). The Solow model begins with a production function. A production function expresses a relationship between output and the factors of production, namely the exact way in which more inputs will produce more outputs. For simplicity, we assume that there is only one output, Y, which we can think of as GDP, and the three factors of production that we discussed in the last chapter: physical capital written K; human capital, which we write as eL, and can understand as education, e, times Labor; and ideas that increase the productivity of capital and labor, which we write as A. Thus, we can write that output, Y, is a function, F, of the inputs A, K, and eL:

$$Y = F(A, K, eL) \tag{1}$$

That looks abstract but it represents a simple economic truth. If we look at a typical production process, say an automobile factory, output depends on capital (the machines, K), labor (the workers, L, adjusted for their level of skill, so eL), and the whole factory is based on ideas (A), namely the invention of the auto and all the machines that help make it.

We also can think of the entire economy as relying on capital, labor, and ideas on a larger scale. We will focus on the Solow production function as a description of an entire economy because we are looking at the causes and consequences of overall economic growth.

For our first look at the Solow model, we will temporarily ignore changes in ideas, education, and labor. If we assume that A, e, and L are constant, then we can simplify our expression for output as $Y = F(K)$. Notice that because L is constant an increase in K always implies an increase in the amount of capital per worker, K/L, and an increase in Y is also always an increase in output per worker, Y/L.

Capital, Production and Diminishing Returns

Let's make a quick sketch of what our production function, $F(K)$, should look like. More K should produce more Y but at a diminishing rate. On a farm, for example, the first tractor is very productive. The second tractor is still useful, but not as much as the first tractor. The third tractor is driven only when one of the other tractors breaks down (remember that the amount of labor is constant). What this means is that increases in capital, K, produce less output, Y, the more K you already have—so we should have a production function where output increases with more K but at a decreasing rate. Following this logic, Figure 22.1 graphs output, Y, on the vertical axis against capital, K, on the horizontal axis, holding L and the other inputs constant.

FIGURE 22.1

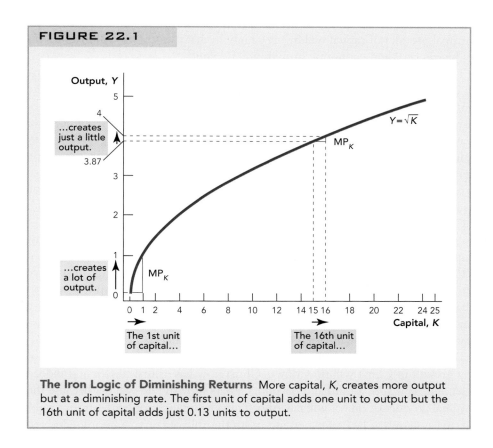

The Iron Logic of Diminishing Returns More capital, K, creates more output but at a diminishing rate. The first unit of capital adds one unit to output but the 16th unit of capital adds just 0.13 units to output.

Notice from Figure 22.1 that the first unit of capital increases output by one unit, but as more and more capital is added output increases by less and less—this is the "iron logic" of diminishing returns and it plays a key role in the Solow model. Economists call the increase in output when capital increases by one unit the **marginal product of capital**. The graph shows that the marginal product of capital is diminishing.

It can sometimes help to look at a specific production function. In Figure 22.1, we used the production function $Y = F(K) = \sqrt{K}$, which means that output is the square root of the capital input. To see how this works in more detail, plug in some numbers. If $K = 4$, then $Y = \sqrt{4} = 2$. If K increases to 16, then $Y = \sqrt{16} = 4$ and so forth.

The **marginal product of capital** is the increase in output caused by the addition of one more unit of capital. The marginal product of capital diminishes as more and more capital is added.

As we said, the reason the marginal product of capital diminishes is that the first unit of capital (the first tractor) is applied where it is most productive, the second unit is applied to slightly less productive tasks because the first unit is already performing the most productive tasks, the third unit is applied to even less productive tasks, and so on.

Growth in China and the United States   The iron logic of diminishing returns explains quite a bit about why China is now growing so much more rapidly than the United States. Imagine, for example, that a country labors under poor institutions—like a lack of competitive and open markets—so that the incentives to invest in capital are low. Now suppose that new institutions are put into place, perhaps new leaders with better ideas replace the old guard. The new institutions increase the incentives to invest and the capital stock grows. But in a country without a lot of capital but good (or much improved) institutions, the marginal product of capital will be very high. In that case, even small investments pay big rewards and economic growth will be rapid.

This process describes what has happened in China. For most of the twentieth century, China labored under very poor economic institutions. China in the 1950s and 1960s was a growth disaster with mass starvation as a common occurrence. Since the death of Chairman Mao in 1976 and the subsequent move away from communism and toward markets, China has been growing very rapidly. Chinese growth has been rapid because China began with very little capital, so the marginal product of capital was very high, and with the new reforms the investment rate increased dramatically. In addition, of course, China has benefited by opening up to trade and investment with the developed world.

China also grew rapidly because improved productivity in agriculture—brought about primarily by better institutions, as we discussed in the last chapter—meant that several hundred million Chinese rural peasants migrated to Chinese cities. Almost overnight these people went from being subsistence farmers, producing perhaps a few hundred dollars worth of output a year, to urban workers, producing perhaps a few thousand dollars worth of output a year in a factory. This is one of the largest economic migrations in human history and for the most part it has been a resounding success.

The iron logic explains why China is catching up to the United States but also why growth in China will slow down. China now has its first tractor and indeed its second. As it adds a third and beyond, China's growth rate will fall because the marginal product of capital will fall. Also, China has many problems—from a poor banking system to a lack of experience with the rule of law to a poorly educated population. At the moment, these problems are being swamped by the high productivity of capital. But as capital accumulates and the productivity of capital declines, China's problems will become more of a drag on Chinese growth.

Why Bombing a Country Can Raise Its Growth Rate   The iron logic also explains why bombing a country can increase its growth rate. Following World War II, for example, Germany and Japan both grew faster than the United States. It may seem odd at first that the losers of a war should grow faster than the winners, but the iron logic of diminishing returns predicts exactly this result. During World War II the capital stock of Germany and Japan—the factories, the roads, and the buildings—was nearly obliterated by Allied bombing. With so little capital remaining, any new capital was highly productive and meant that Germany and Japan had a strong incentive to put new capital into place. In other words, they grew rapidly as they were rebuilding their economies. It's also the case that Germany and Japan had reasonably good postwar institutions.

But don't make the mistake of envying Germany and Japan their high growth rates. Germany and Japan grew rapidly because they were catching up. Children who have been malnourished often grow rapidly when they are put on a proper diet but it's not good to be malnourished. Similarly, countries whose capital stock has been destroyed will grow rapidly, all else being equal, as they catch up but it is not good to have your capital stock destroyed. Note also that growth in Germany and Japan slowed down as their capital stocks grew and approached U.S. levels; by the 1980s they were growing at close to the U.S. rate. The growth rate in Germany and Japan fell not because they did anything wrong but, again, because the marginal product of capital declines the more capital a country has.

	Average Annual Growth Rate of GDP per Capita for Germany, Japan, and the United States	
	1950–1960	1980–1990
Germany	6.6%	1.9%
Japan	6.8%	3.4%
United States	1.2%	2.3%

Figure 22.1 explains that more capital means more output, albeit at a diminishing rate. But where does capital come from and where does it go? Capital is output that is saved and invested, but capital depreciates over time. In the next section, we show how these two aspects of capital—investment and depreciation—fit together. Understanding investment and depreciation will prove important for isolating the ultimate sources of economic growth.

Capital Growth Equals Investment Minus Depreciation

Capital is output that is saved and invested rather than consumed. Imagine, for example, that 10 units of output are produced. Of the 10 units of output, 7 units might be consumed and 3 units invested in new capital. We write the fraction of output that is invested in new capital as gamma (γ), and in the example just given, $\gamma = \frac{3}{10} = 0.3$.

Figure 22.2 shows how output is divided between consumption and investment when $\gamma = 0.3$. Notice that when $K = 100$, 10 units of output are

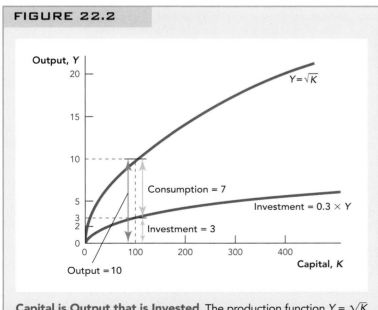

FIGURE 22.2

Capital is Output that is Invested The production function $Y = \sqrt{K}$ shows how much output is produced for every level of K, the capital stock. When $K = 100$, 10 units of output are produced. The investment rate is 0.3 so $0.3 \times 10 = 3$ units of output are devoted to investment. The remaining 7 units of output are consumed.

Rome did not replenish its capital stock.

produced and of these 10 units, 7 units are consumed and 3 units are invested in new capital.

Capital also depreciates—roads wear out, harbors become silted, and machines break down. Thus, if there are 100 units of capital in this period, for example, then 2 units might depreciate, leaving just 98 for use in the next period.

We write the fraction of capital that wears out or depreciates as delta (δ); in the example just given, $\delta = \frac{2}{100} = 0.02$. Figure 22.3 shows how much capital depreciates as a function of the capital stock. When the capital stock is 100, for example, then 2 units of capital will depreciate and when the capital stock is 200, 4 units will depreciate, and so on.

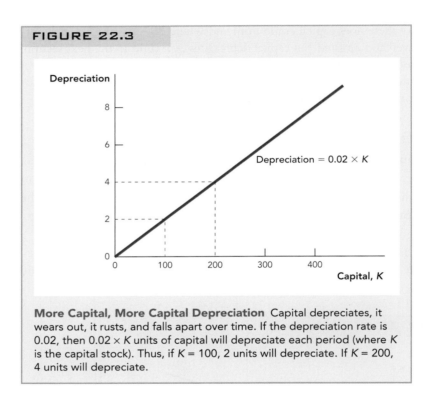

FIGURE 22.3

More Capital, More Capital Depreciation Capital depreciates, it wears out, it rusts, and falls apart over time. If the depreciation rate is 0.02, then 0.02 × K units of capital will depreciate each period (where K is the capital stock). Thus, if K = 100, 2 units will depreciate. If K = 200, 4 units will depreciate.

The greater the capital stock, the greater the depreciation, so a country with a lot of roads, harbors, and machines needs to devote a lot of resources to filling potholes, removing silt, and repairing and replacing. In other words, a successful economy must continually replenish its capital stock just to keep going. An economy that does not replenish its capital stock will quickly fall into ruin.

Again, Figure 22.3 shows that capital depreciation increases the greater the capital stock—this will turn out to place another constraint on economic growth.

Why Capital Alone Cannot Be the Key to Economic Growth

We now have everything we need to develop a second important insight from the Solow model. Capital depreciation increases, the greater the capital stock so at some point so much capital will be depreciating every period that *every* unit of investment will be needed just to keep the capital stock constant. When investment just covers capital depreciation, the capital stock stops growing, and when the capital stock stops growing, output stops growing as well. Thus, the iron logic of diminishing returns tells us that capital alone cannot be the key to economic growth. Let's explain this in more detail.

Figure 22.4 focuses attention on the two key functions, the investment function from Figure 22.2 and the depreciation function from Figure 22.3.

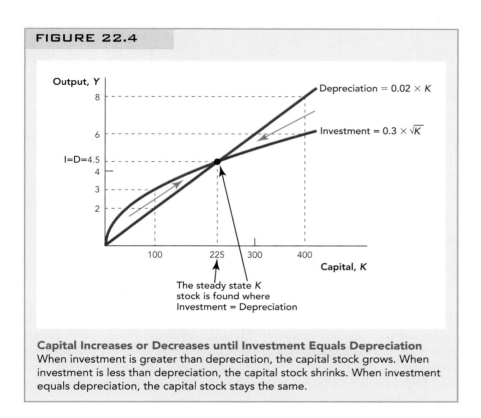

FIGURE 22.4

Capital Increases or Decreases until Investment Equals Depreciation
When investment is greater than depreciation, the capital stock grows. When investment is less than depreciation, the capital stock shrinks. When investment equals depreciation, the capital stock stays the same.

Consider first a case where the capital stock grows larger. For instance, when $K = 100$, 3 units of output are invested in new capital and 2 units of capital depreciate. Investment exceeds depreciation so in the next period both the capital stock and output will be larger. Thus, when investment is greater than depreciation (*Investment* > *Depreciation*) we have economic growth.

Investment increases as the capital stock gets larger, but because of the iron logic, investment increases at a diminishing rate. Depreciation, however, increases with the capital stock at a linear (constant) rate. Thus, at some point investment equals depreciation (*Investment* = *Depreciation*). At this point, every unit of investment is being used to replace depreciated capital, so the amount of net or new investment (investment after depreciation) is zero. We call this the **steady state** level of capital. At the steady state level of capital, there is no new (net) investment and economic growth stops. We can summarize as follows:

Investment > *Depreciation*—the capital stock grows and output next period
is bigger

Investment < *Depreciation*—the capital stock shrinks and output next period
is smaller

Investment = *Depreciation*—the capital stock and output are constant
(the steady state)

Check the Math
When K = 100, $Y = \sqrt{100} = 10$, of these 10 units $0.3 \times 10 = 3$ units are invested in new capital. Depreciation is $0.02 \times 100 = 2$ units so *Investment* (3) > *Depreciation* (2) and the capital stock and output grow.

At the **steady state** the capital stock is neither increasing nor decreasing.

Check the Math
As Figure 22.4 is drawn the steady state occurs when $K = 225$ because:
Investment $= 0.3 \times \sqrt{225} = 4.5$
Depreciation $= 0.02 \times 225 = 4.5$
thus when $K = 225$
Investment = *Depreciation*

FIGURE 22.5

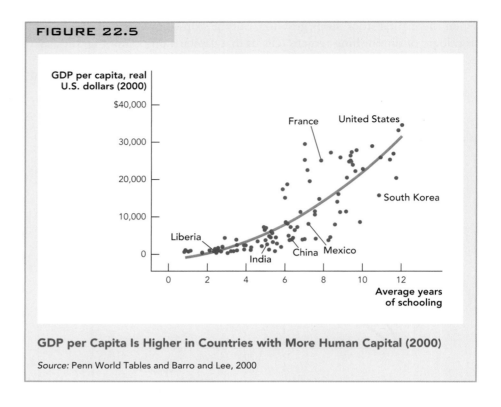

GDP per Capita Is Higher in Countries with More Human Capital (2000)

Source: Penn World Tables and Barro and Lee, 2000

We learn from our "capital only" model that long-run economic growth cannot be due to capital accumulation. The logic of diminishing returns means that eventually capital and output will cease growing. Economic growth, however, does not seem to be slowing. So what else could drive long-run economic growth? Let's return to the other factors of production that we discussed in Chapter 21—human capital and technological knowledge.

Can increases in human capital drive long-run economic growth? Human capital is an important contributor to the wealth of nations. Figure 22.5 shows that GDP per capita is higher in countries with more human capital, as measured by average years of schooling.

But human capital is just like physical capital in that it has diminishing returns and it depreciates. In other words, an economic principles class is probably the most important economics class that you will take and all the human capital in the world today will be gone in a hundred years. (Why will all the human capital in the world today be gone in a hundred years? Hint: Where will your human capital be in a hundred years?) Thus, within the Solow model, the logic of diminishing returns applies to human capital just as much as to physical capital and neither can drive long-run economic growth.

Better Ideas Drive Long-Run Economic Growth

Can better ideas maintain long-run economic growth? Better ideas let us produce more output from the same inputs of physical and human capital. A personal computer today has about the same amount of silicon and labor input as a computer produced 20 years ago but today's computer is much better—the difference is ideas. Recall our simple production function:

$$Y = \sqrt{K}$$

We can think of better ideas as a way of getting more output from the same input. So remembering that we let A stand for ideas that increase productivity, let's now write our production function as:

$$Y = A\sqrt{K}$$

Notice that an increase in better ideas or technological knowledge—as represented by A—increases output even while holding K constant, that is, an increase in A represents an increase in productivity. Figure 22.6 graphs two production functions. The first is when $A = 1$, the production function that we have been working with all along. The second is when $A = 2$. Notice that when $K = 16$, output is 4 when $A = 1$, but it's 8 when $A = 2$. Technological knowledge means that we can get more output from the same input.

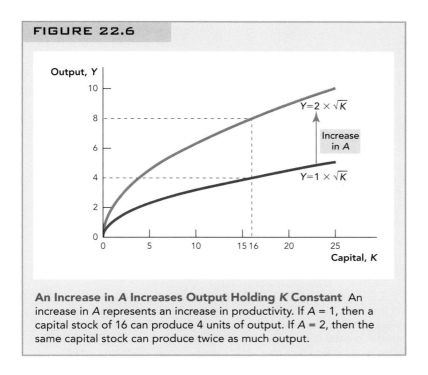

FIGURE 22.6

An Increase in *A* Increases Output Holding *K* Constant An increase in *A* represents an increase in productivity. If *A* = 1, then a capital stock of 16 can produce 4 units of output. If *A* = 2, then the same capital stock can produce twice as much output.

So long as we can develop better ideas that shift the production function upwards then economic growth will continue. In a way, it should be obvious that better ideas are the key to long-run economic growth. How much economic growth would there have been without the discovery of electricity or DNA or the development of the internal combustion engine, the computer chip, or the polymerase chain reaction? It's just not enough to throw more effort at a problem; we have to actually know what we are doing and that boils down to ideas.

Solow himself tried to estimate how much of U.S. economic prosperity was due to capital and labor and how much was due to ideas. He came up with the figure that better ideas are responsible for about three-fourths of the U.S. standard of living. Many economists have subsequently debated the exact number, but no one contests the central importance of ideas and technological progress for human well-being.

CHECK YOURSELF

> What happens to the marginal product of capital as more capital is added?

> Why does capital depreciate? What happens to the total amount of capital depreciation as the capital stock increases?

So to understand economic growth we must move from capital accumulation to take a closer look at the economics of ideas. To do that head to the section below titled "Growing on the Cutting Edge: The Economics of Ideas." Alternatively, more lessons can be learned from a closer inspection of the Solow model. We delve into these further lessons in the next (optional) section.

The Solow Model—Details and Further Lessons (Optional Section)

Let's return to Figure 22.4, which we also reprint here as Figure 22.7.

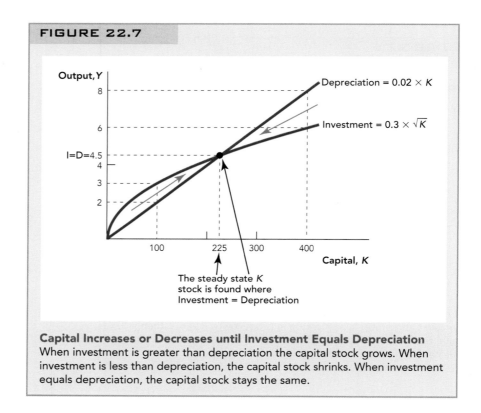

FIGURE 22.7

Capital Increases or Decreases until Investment Equals Depreciation
When investment is greater than depreciation the capital stock grows. When investment is less than depreciation, the capital stock shrinks. When investment equals depreciation, the capital stock stays the same.

We know that if *Investment* > *Depreciation* the capital stock increases and if *Investment* = *Depreciation* we are at the *steady state* level of capital, the level of capital such that the capital stock neither increases nor decreases. It's also true that if *Investment* < *Depreciation* then the capital stock and output shrink.

Remember that $Y = \sqrt{K}$, so if we know K we know Y. And if K is growing, then Y is growing. We can see this relationship a little better in Figure 22.8, which plots investment, depreciation, and output in the same graph.

That figure may look complicated, but don't get thrown off the basic idea, which is simply that the capital stock drives output, Y. For example, if K is at the steady state level ($K = 225$, in this case), then Y will also be at a steady state level of output, in this case 15. We take the 225 off the horizontal axis and bounce it off the $Y = \sqrt{K}$ curve to get to GDP = 15 on the vertical axis. Similarly, since K drives Y, whenever K is growing then so is Y. Thus, Figure 22.8

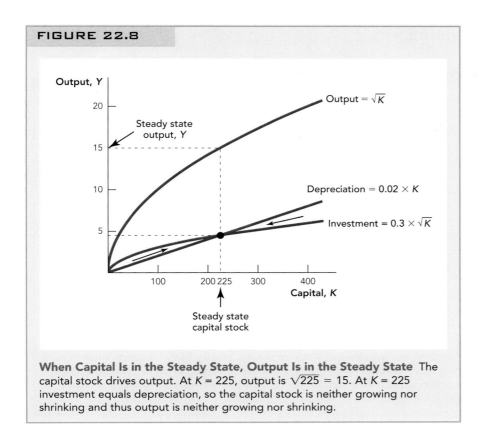

FIGURE 22.8

When Capital Is in the Steady State, Output Is in the Steady State The capital stock drives output. At $K = 225$, output is $\sqrt{225} = 15$. At $K = 225$ investment equals depreciation, so the capital stock is neither growing nor shrinking and thus output is neither growing nor shrinking.

demonstrates in a little more detail than we had before that our theory of capital growth is also a theory of economic growth.

The Solow Model and an Increase in the Investment Rate

What happens in the Solow model if γ, the fraction of output that is saved and invested, increases? It is simple: a greater investment rate means more capital, which means more output. An increase in the investment rate therefore increases a country's steady state level of GDP. The result just shows that investment increases the number of "tractors" per worker which raises GDP per worker.

In Figure 22.9 on the next page, we show this intuition in the graph by plotting two investment functions: *Investment* $= 0.3\sqrt{K}$, which means that 3 units of every 10 units of output are saved and invested ($\gamma = 0.3$, as it was in Figure 22.8), and also *Investment* $= 0.4\sqrt{K}$, which means that 4 units of every 10 units of output are saved and invested ($\gamma = 0.4$). Notice that when $\gamma = 0.4$, the new steady state capital stock increases to $K = 400$ and output increases to 20.

Thus, the Solow model predicts that countries with higher rates of investment will be wealthier. Is this prediction of the Solow model consistent with the evidence? Yes. Figure 22.10, also on the next page, shows that GDP per capita is higher in countries that have higher investment rates.

This makes intuitive sense. More savings mean that more capital goods can be produced and consumers can enjoy a higher standard of living. How wealthy would a country be if it spent all of its resources on partying?

The Solow model says that an increase in the investment rate will increase steady state output. But in the Solow model, the iron logic of diminishing returns cannot be forever avoided. When the investment rate increases we have

CHECK YOURSELF

In Figure 22.8

> What happens when the capital stock is 400?
> What is investment?
> What is depreciation?
> What happens to output?

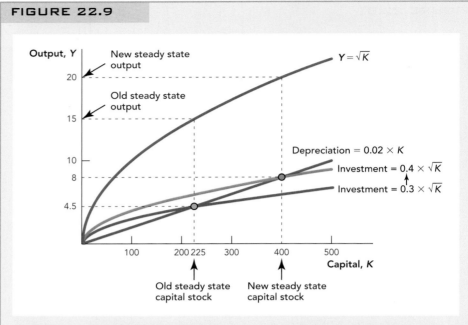

FIGURE 22.9

An Increase in the Investment Rate Increases Steady State Output When the investment rate increases from 0.3 to 0.4, the investment curve shifts up and the steady state capital stock increases from 225 to 400. Output increases along with the capital stock, rising from 15 to 20.

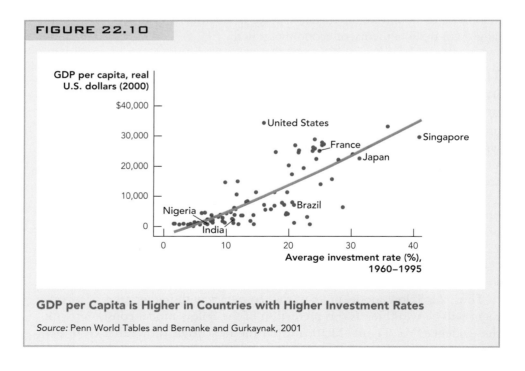

FIGURE 22.10

GDP per Capita is Higher in Countries with Higher Investment Rates

Source: Penn World Tables and Bernanke and Gurkaynak, 2001

Investment > Depreciation so the capital stock increases and the economy grows. But as more capital accumulates, the iron logic sets in and the economy eventually slows until at the new steady state it stops growing once again. So the level of the capital stock determines the output level but not its growth rate, at least not in the very long run.

For further confirmation of this idea, recall the growth miracle of South Korea from the last chapter. In 1950, South Korea was poorer than Nigeria, while today it is richer than some European nations. The evidence on South Korea's growth is consistent with the Solow model. In the 1950s, the investment rate in South Korea was less than 10 percent of GDP, but the rate more than doubled in the 1970s and increased to over 35 percent by the 1990s. Higher investment rates helped to increase South Korea's GDP, as the country opened many factories and exported cars and electronics to the rest of the world. As South Korea has caught up to western levels of GDP, however, its growth rate has slowed.

Of course, we should remember that investment rates are themselves caused by other factors such as incentives and institutions. No one wants to invest in an economy, for example, where their investments may be expropriated. One of the reasons the investment rate in South Korea increased is that capitalists believed that their investments would be protected.

In this chapter, we have referred to γ as the rate of savings *and* investment, implicitly assuming that savings equals investment. But savings must be efficiently collected and then transformed into investment. The Soviet Union had a high rate of saving but its savings were not invested well, and thus its effective investment rate was very low. In other words, a country that invests its savings poorly is like a country that doesn't invest much at all. A country could also have a low rate of saving but a high rate of investment if it imported savings from other countries. The next chapter will discuss in more detail how financial intermediaries efficiently collect savings, often from around the world, and then transform those savings into productive investments.

The Solow Model and Conditional Convergence

The Solow model also predicts that a country will grow more rapidly the farther its capital stock is below its steady state value. To understand this result, remember that when the capital stock is below its steady state value, investment will exceed depreciation. In other words, the capital stock will grow. Now look again at Figure 22.1—when the capital stock is low, it has a very high marginal product. Thus, when a country's capital stock is below its steady state value, the country will grow rapidly as it invests in capital that has a high marginal product. That's just restating our tractor parable. The tractor is most valuable on the farm that doesn't already have a tractor, as opposed to the farm that is already working with 13 tractors. (A more detailed explanation of this point can be found in the appendix to this chapter.)

We already used this result to explain why China is growing rapidly and why Germany and Japan grew rapidly after World War II. More generally, the Solow model predicts that if two countries have the same steady state level of output, the country that is poorer today will catch up because it will grow faster. We don't know for certain which countries have the same steady state level of output but we might guess, for example, that countries with similar institutions and history have similar steady states. Figure 22.11 on the next page tests this prediction using data from 18 of the 20 founding members of the OECD (Organisation for Economic Co-operation and Development).[1] The average annual growth rate between 1960 and 2000 is on the vertical axis, and real per capita GDP in 1960 is on the horizontal axis. The data clearly show that among the OECD countries the poorer countries grew faster. You can see that lower income in 1960 is associated with higher growth between 1960 and 2000.

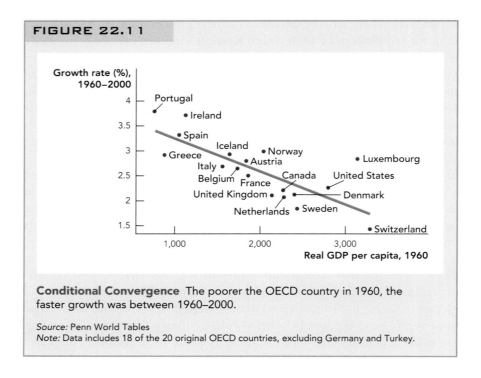

FIGURE 22.11

Growth rate (%), 1960–2000

Conditional Convergence The poorer the OECD country in 1960, the faster growth was between 1960–2000.

Source: Penn World Tables
Note: Data includes 18 of the 20 original OECD countries, excluding Germany and Turkey.

Conditional convergence is the tendency—among countries with similar steady state levels of output—for poorer countries to grow faster than richer countries and thus for poor and rich countries to converge in income.

Since the poorer countries grow faster, they eventually catch up to the richer countries. Thus, over time the OECD countries have converged to a similar level of GDP per capita. We say that the model and the data exhibit **conditional convergence** because we only see convergence among countries that plausibly have similar steady state levels of output. As we know from Chapter 21, we do not observe convergence among all countries—the existence of growth disasters such as Nigeria means that some countries are diverging from the rest of the world rather than catching up.

From Catching Up to Cutting Edge

Several predictions of the simple Solow model are consistent with the evidence—countries with higher investment rates have higher GDP per capita, and countries grow faster the farther their capital stock is from its steady state level. One prediction of the simplest form of the Solow model, however, is inconsistent with the evidence. The simplest form of the Solow model predicts zero economic growth in the long run. Remember, in the long run, the capital stock stops growing because *Investment = Depreciation* and if the capital stock isn't growing then neither is output. The United States, however, has been growing for over two hundred years, so we will need to look at a better developed version of the Solow model. In particular, is there any way to escape the iron logic? Yes, better ideas can keep the economy growing even in the long run.

Solow and the Economics of Ideas in One Diagram

Let's revisit the Solow model one last time and show how better ideas fit within that model. It's simple: better ideas let us produce more output from the same inputs of capital. But when we produce more output, it makes sense to increase consumption and *investment*. So better ideas also increase capital accumulation.

Figure 22.12 shows the process in a diagram. Okay, the diagram is not so simple. Let's take it in steps. Remember that A denotes ideas and a bigger A means that we are working with better ideas that increase output for the same level as capital. So imagine that we begin with A = ideas = 1. The economy is in the steady state and output = 15 (at point a'). Now suppose that A increases to A = 1.5. Better ideas produce more output from the same capital stock, so output immediately increases from 15 at point a' to 22.5 at point b'. But with greater output, investment also increases, moving from point a to point b. Since investment is now greater than depreciation, capital begins to accumulate. Capital accumulates and the economy grows until investment is once again equal to depreciation at point c at which point output is now 33.75 (at point c').

FIGURE 22.12

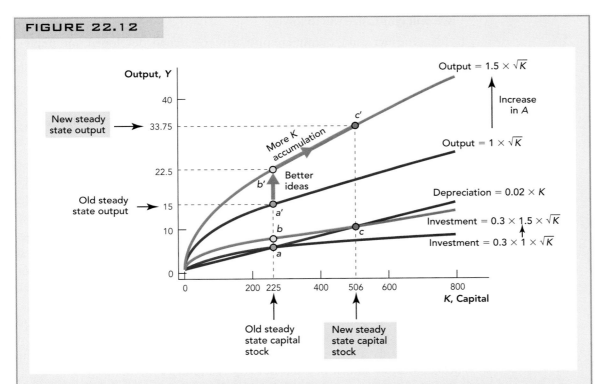

Better Ideas Generate More Output and More Capital Accumulation When A = 1, output = 15 (at point a'). Having better ideas (A = 1.5) means that more output is produced from the same capital stock so output immediately increases from a' to b'. Since investment = 0.3 × Output, more output also means more investment so investment increases from a to b. Since investment is now greater than depreciation, the economy begins to accumulate more capital and thus to grow. The economy grows until a new steady state is reached at point c with capital stock of 506 and output = 33.75 at point c'. Notice that better ideas increase output directly because of higher productivity and indirectly due to more capital accumulation.

Thus, Figure 22.12 shows how the Solow model and the economics of ideas fit together. Better ideas increase output directly and by so doing they increase capital accumulation indirectly. Of course, before we ever reach the new level of output, ideas may have gotten even better! And, thus, the process

CHECK YOURSELF

> What happens to investment and depreciation at the steady state level of capital?

> In Figure 22.9, how much is *consumed* in the old steady state? How much is *consumed* in the new steady state?

> Do countries grow faster if they are far below their steady state or if they are close?

> Do countries with higher investment rates have lower or higher GDP per capita?

of economic growth is a continuous two-step process of better ideas and more capital accumulation.

Growing on the Cutting Edge: The Economics of Ideas

We have learned from the Solow model that better ideas are the key to economic growth in the long run. Capital accumulation alone will not create much growth in the United States or the other developed economies such as Japan and Western Europe because these economies already have so much capital that investment is subject to a lot of depreciation. Instead, these countries are on the cutting edge; they must develop new ideas to increase the productivity of capital and labor. Thus, to better understand economic growth on the cutting edge we must turn to the economics of ideas.

We will emphasize the following:

1. Ideas for increasing output are primarily researched, developed, and implemented by profit-seeking firms.

2. Spillovers mean that ideas are underprovided.

3. Government has a role in improving the production of ideas.

4. The larger the market, the greater the incentive to research and develop new ideas.

Research and Development Is Investment for Profit

In Chapter 21, we emphasized that economic growth was not automatic, and we said that the factors of production do not fall from the sky like manna from heaven. In order to increase output, the factors of production must be produced and organized efficiently. All of this applies to ideas or technological knowledge just as much as to physical and human capital. Once again, incentives are the key. Economic growth requires institutions that encourage investment in physical capital, human capital, and *technological knowledge* (ideas).

In the United States, there are about 1.3 million scientists who research and develop new products, more than in any other country in the world, and most of these scientists and engineers, about 70 percent, work for private firms. (The ratios are broadly similar in other developed countries.)

Private firms invest in research and development when they expect to profit from their endeavors. Thus, the institutions we discussed in the last chapter—property rights, honest government, political stability, a dependable legal system, and competitive and open markets—also drive the generation of technological knowledge. When it comes to knowledge, other institutions are especially important. These institutions include a commercial setting that helps innovators to connect with capitalists, intellectual property rights such as copyright and patents, and a high-quality educational system (we will turn to these issues shortly).

It's not just the number of scientists and engineers that matters for economic growth, as many other people come up with new ideas on their jobs, at school, or at home in their garages. Mark Zuckerberg, for example, wrote the software for Facebook as a Harvard student. Just as important, the business culture and institutions of the United States are good at connecting innovators with business people and venture capitalists looking to fund or otherwise take a chance on new ideas. Ideas without backers are sterile. In the United States, potential innovators know that if they come up with a good idea, that idea has a good chance of making it to the market. The incentive to discover new ideas is correspondingly strong.

American culture also supports entrepreneurs. People like Apple CEO Steve Jobs, for example, are lauded in the popular media. Historically, however, entrepreneurs were often attacked as job destroyers, as the sidebar on eighteenth-century British entrepreneur John Kay illustrates.

Compared to most other countries, the United States has a very good cultural and commercial infrastructure for supporting new ideas and their conversion into usable commercial products.

Artistic innovation also requires many individuals with a diversity of viewpoints, many sources of support and employment, and businesspeople looking to profit from and support innovations. It's not surprising, therefore, that the United States is also a leader in artistic innovation. American movies, popular music, and dance have spread around the world. But the United States is not just good at popular culture: It is also a leader in abstract art, contemporary classical composition, avant-garde fiction and poetry, and modern dance, to name just a few fields. The lesson is that artistic, economic, and scientific innovations spring from similar sources.

A further significant part of the infrastructure for creativity is property rights. We now turn to one form of intellectual property rights, patents.

Patents Many ideas have peculiar properties that can make it difficult for private firms to recoup their investments in those ideas. In particular, new processes, products, and methods can be copied by competitors. The world's first MP3 player was the Eiger Labs' MPMan introduced in 1998. Ever heard of it? Probably not. Other firms quickly copied the idea and Eiger Labs lost out in the race to innovate. Imitators get the benefit of new ideas without having to pay the costs of development. Imitators, therefore, have lower costs so they tend to drive innovators out of the market unless some barrier prevents quick imitation.

Imitation often takes time and this does give innovators a chance to recoup their investments. The Apple iPhone design, for example, is already being copied by other firms, but until that happens, Apple can exploit monopoly power to sell millions of iPhones for high profits. That is what makes Apple willing to invest in research and development in the first place and that is why the iPhone exists. Firms often compete not by offering the same product at a lower price but by offering substantially new and better products.

Apple also relies on patents to protect its innovations. A patent is a government grant of temporary monopoly rights, typically 20 years from the date of filing. Patents delay imitation, thus allowing innovative firms a greater period of monopoly power. Apple, for example, has patented one of the most distinctive features of the iPhone, the multipoint touchscreen. Apple's patent, filed in 2004, gives Apple the right to prevent other firms from copying its technology until 2024. Still, we may well see other similar devices in the near future if Apple licenses its technology to other firms. Furthermore, competitors are finding ways to produce the same effect using different methods—a majority of patented innovations are imitated within five years.

Nevertheless, Apple's patent gives it some monopoly power, and as you know if you studied micro first, firms with monopoly power raise prices above competitive levels. Thus, patents increase the incentive to research and develop new

John Kay (1704–1780) invented the "flying shuttle" used in cotton weaving, the single most important invention launching the Industrial Revolution. Kay, however, was not rewarded for his efforts. His house was destroyed by "machine breakers," who were afraid that his invention would put them out of a job. Kay was forced to flee to France where he died a poor man.

"The patent system . . . added the fuel of interest to the fire of genius." **Abraham Lincoln (1859).** Lincoln is the only U.S. president to have been granted a patent.

▶▶**THE SEARCH ENGINE**
You can find Apple's patent on the iPhone's multipoint touchscreen (20,060,097,991) by searching at the U.S. Patent and Trademark Office.

Thomas Jefferson on the Economics of Ideas *"He who receives an idea from me, receives instruction himself without lessening mine; as he who lights his taper at mine, receives light without darkening me. That ideas should freely spread from one to another over the globe . . . seems to have been peculiarly and benevolently designed by nature, when she made them . . . incapable of confinement or exclusive appropriation."*

A good is **non-rivalrous** if two or more people can consume it at the same time. Ideas are non-rivalrous goods.

products, but also increase monopoly power once the products are created. The trade-off between creating incentives to research and develop new products while avoiding too much monopoly power is one of the trickiest in economic policy. [2]

Spillovers, and Why There Aren't Enough Good Ideas

Even when a firm has a patent on its technological innovation and other firms cannot imitate in a direct way, ideas tend to spill over and benefit other firms and consumers. A new pharmaceutical will be patented, for example, but the mechanism of action—how the pharmaceutical works—can be examined and broadly copied by other firms to develop their own pharmaceuticals.

Spillovers have good and bad aspects. The good aspect of imitation or spillovers is that ideas are **non-rivalrous**. If you consume an apple, then I cannot consume the same apple. When it comes to eating an apple, it's either you or me—we can't share what we each consume so economists say that apples are rivalrous. But ideas can be shared. You can use the Pythagorean theorem and I can use the very same theorem at the very same time. The Pythagorean theorem can be shared by all of humanity, which is why economists say that ideas are non-rivalrous.

Since many ideas can be shared at low cost, they *should* be shared—that's the way to maximize the benefit from an idea. The spillover or diffusion of ideas throughout the world is thus a good thing. For instance, the idea of breeding and growing corn originated in ancient Mexico but now people grow corn all over the world. Spillovers, however, mean that the originator of an idea doesn't get all the benefits. And if the originator doesn't get enough of the benefits, ideas will be underprovided. For this reason, while economists know that idea spillovers are good, they also know that spillovers mean that too few good ideas are produced in the first place.

To understand why spillovers mean that ideas will be underprovided, think about why firms explore for oil. Answer: to make money. So what would happen to the amount of exploration if whenever a firm struck oil, other firms jumped in and drilled wells right next door? Clearly, the incentive to explore would decline if firms didn't have property rights to oil *fields*. Firms explore for ideas just like they explore for oil and if other firms can set up right next door to exploit the same *field of ideas,* the incentive to explore will decline.

Figure 22.13 illustrates the argument in a diagram. A profit-maximizing firm invests in research and development (R&D) so long as the private marginal benefit is larger than the marginal cost. As a result private investment occurs until point *a* in Figure 22.13. Spillovers, however, mean that the social benefit of R&D exceeds the private benefit so the optimal social investment is found where the marginal social benefit just equals the marginal cost at point *b*. Since the private benefit to R&D is less than the social benefit, private investment in R&D is less than ideal.

Government's Role in the Production of New Ideas

Can anything be done to increase the production of new ideas? We have already mentioned one important government policy that affects the production of new ideas, namely patents. Patents reduce spillovers and thus increase the incentive to produce new ideas, but they can also slow down the spread of new ideas.

FIGURE 22.13

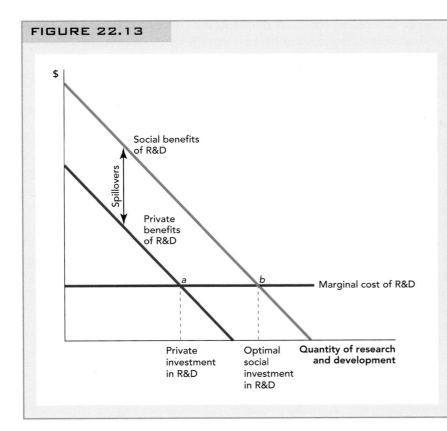

Spillovers Mean There Is Too Little Investment in R&D The profit-maximizing private investment in R&D is found where the private marginal benefits just equal the (private) marginal costs (point *a*). Some of the benefits of R&D spill over to people other than the producer. The social benefits of R&D are higher than the private benefits by the amount of the spillover. The optimal social investment in R&D is found where the social marginal benefits just equal the marginal cost (point *b*). Thus, when the private benefits of R&D are less than the social benefits, private investment in R&D will be less than the optimal social investment in R&D.

The government could also subsidize the production of new ideas. Returning to Figure 22.13, a subsidy or tax break to R&D expenditures, for example, will shift the (private) marginal cost of R&D curve down, thus increasing private investment.

The argument for government subsidies is strongest when the spillovers are largest. The modern world is founded on mathematics, physics, and molecular biology—basic ideas in these fields have many applications so spillovers can be large. But even if the social benefits to basic science are large, the private returns can be small. It's probably easier to make a million dollars producing pizza than it is to make a million dollars producing mathematical theorems. In fact, Thomas S. Monaghan made a billion dollars producing pizza (he's the founder of Domino's) while mathematicians Ron Rivest, Adi Shamir, and Leonard Adleman didn't make nearly so much on their RSA algorithm even though their algorithm is used to encrypt data sent over the Internet and thus forms the backbone for all Internet commerce.

The large spillovers to basic science suggest a role for government subsidies to universities, especially the parts of universities that produce innovations and the basic science behind innovations. Perhaps most importantly universities produce *scientists*. Most of the 1.3 million scientists who research and develop new products in the United States were trained in government-subsidized universities. Thus, subsidies to the hard sciences support the private development of new ideas and those initial subsidies are likely to pay for themselves many times over.

Market Size and Research and Development

Imagine that there are two diseases that if left untreated are equally deadly. One of the diseases is rare, the other one is common. If you had to choose, would you rather be afflicted with the rare disease or the common disease? Take a moment to think about this question because there is a right answer.

If you don't want to die, it's much better to have the common disease. The reason? The costs of developing drugs for rare and common diseases are about the same, but the revenues are greater, the more common the disease. Pharmaceutical companies concentrate on drugs for common diseases because larger markets mean more profits.

As a result, there are more drugs to treat common diseases than to treat rare diseases, and more drugs means greater life expectancy. Patients diagnosed with rare diseases—those ranked at the bottom quarter in terms of how frequently they are diagnosed—are 45 percent more likely to die before age 55 than are patients diagnosed with more common diseases.[3]

Larger markets mean increased incentives to invest in research and development, more new drugs, and greater life expectancy. So imagine this, if China and India were as wealthy as the United States, the market for cancer drugs would be eight times larger than it is today.

China and India are not yet wealthy countries but what this thought experiment tells us is that *people in the United States benefit tremendously when other countries grow rich.*

Like pharmaceuticals, new computer chips, software, and chemicals also require large R&D expenditures. As India, China, and other countries including the United States become wealthier, companies will increase their worldwide R&D investments.

CHECK YOURSELF

> What would happen to the incentive to produce new ideas if all countries imposed high tax rates on imports?

> What are spillovers and how do they affect the production of ideas?

> Some economists have proposed that the government offer large cash prizes for the discovery of cures for diseases like malaria that affect people in developing countries. What economic reasons might there be to support a prize for malaria research rather than, say, cancer research?

The Future of Economic Growth

Over the last 10,000 years, growth in per capita world GDP has been increasing. Growth in per capita GDP was approximately zero from the dawn of civilization to about 1500, increased to 0.08 percent a year between 1500 and 1760, doubled during the next hundred years, and increased even further during the nineteenth and twentieth centuries. Today, worldwide per capita GDP is growing at around 2.2 percent a year.

Could economic growth become even faster? Yes. Let's take a look again at our measure of technological progress, A. We can summarize what we have said about the factors causing A to increase in a simple equation:

$$A(\text{ideas}) = \text{Population} \times \text{Incentives} \times \text{Ideas per Hour}$$

In words, the number of new ideas is a function of the number of people, the incentives to innovate, and the number of ideas per hour that each person has. Of course, this equation is not meant to be exact—it's just a way of thinking about some of the key factors driving technological growth. So let's go through each of the factors and think about what they imply for the future of economic growth.

The number of people is increasing, which is good for idea generation. More important, the number of people whose job it is to produce new ideas is increasing. In all the world today, there are perhaps 6 million scientists and engineers of which 1.3 million come from the United States. These 1.3 million represent about one-half of one percent of the U.S. population, a surprisingly small percentage. Yet for the world as a whole, the ratio of scientists and engineers to population is much lower.

Today, because much of the world is poor, thousands of potentially great scientists will spend most of their lives doing backbreaking work on a farm. If the world as a whole were as wealthy as the United States and could devote the same share of population to research and development as does the U.S. today, there would be more than five times as many scientists and engineers. Thus, as the world gets richer more people will be producing ideas and because of spillovers, these ideas will benefit everyone.

The incentives to innovate also appear to be increasing. Consumers are richer and the world is becoming one giant integrated market due to trade; each of these factors boosts the incentives to innovate.

The incentives to innovate also increase when innovators can profit from their investments without fear of expropriation. The worldwide improvement in institutions—that is the movement toward property rights, honest government, political stability, and a dependable legal system—has been very positive for both innovation and economic growth.

It could be that someday we will run out of new ideas, or new ideas will experience diminishing returns so the number of ideas per hour falls. When the law of diminishing returns applies to ideas as well as to capital, then economic growth will end. There are at least two reasons, however, for thinking that this day of reckoning lies far in the future.

First, many ideas make creating other ideas easier. Sadly, the authors of this book can remember the day when answering even simple questions like who won the 1969 World Series could not be answered without going to a library, consulting a card catalog (don't ask), looking for the appropriate book in the stacks, and then (if the book hadn't been checked out) finding the answer. Today, you can probably find the answer using Google on your cell phone faster than you can read this paragraph. (By the way, it was the New York Mets in one of the greatest upsets of baseball history.) Since we still have many new ideas about creating even more ideas, it does not seem that ideas production has come close to diminishing returns.

The second reason to think that the number of ideas per hour is not yet strongly diminishing comes from one of the pioneers of the economics of ideas, Paul Romer. (Romer is not only a distinguished theorist of ideas, he is a first-class idea entrepreneur; he started Aplia, the online economics test bank and tutorial system that many of you use and which is a good example of an idea that makes learning new ideas easier.) Romer points out that ideas for production are like recipes and the number of potential recipes in the universe is unimaginably vast.

> The periodic table contains about a hundred different types of atoms, which means that the number of combinations made up of four different elements is about $100 \times 99 \times 98 \times 97 = 94,000,000$. A list of numbers like 6, 2, 1, 7 can represent the proportions for using the four elements in a recipe. To keep things simple, assume that the numbers in the list must lie between 1 and 10, that no fractions are allowed, and that the smallest number must always be 1. Then there are about 3,500 different sets of proportions for each choice of four elements, and $3,500 \times 94,000,000$ (or 330 billion) different recipes in total. If laboratories around the world evaluated 1,000 recipes each day, it would take nearly a million years to go through them all.[4]

True, many of the recipes are going to be like chicken liver ice cream (not that good), but the field of ideas that we can explore is so large that diminishing returns may not set in for a very long time.

Putting all this together, economic growth might be even faster in the future than it has been in the past. There are more scientists and engineers in the world today than ever before and their numbers are increasing both in absolute terms and as a percentage of the population. The incentives to invest in R&D are also increasing because markets are getting larger due to globalization and increased wealth in developing countries such as China and India. Better institutions and more secure property rights are spreading throughout the world.

UNDERSTAND YOUR **world**

We have reason to be optimistic about the future of economic growth but, of course, nothing is guaranteed. In the twentieth century, two world wars diverted the energy of two generations from production to destruction. When the wars ended, an iron curtain isolated billions of people from the rest of the world, reducing trade in goods and ideas—to everyone's detriment. World poverty meant that the United States and a few other countries shouldered the burden of advancing knowledge nearly alone. We must hope that this does not happen again.

☐ Takeaway

The Solow model is governed by the iron logic of diminishing returns. When the capital stock is low, the marginal product of capital is high and capital accumulates, leading to economic growth. But as capital accumulates, its marginal product declines until per period investment is just equal to depreciation, and growth stops.

Despite the simplicity of the Solow model, it tells us three important things about economic growth. First, countries that devote a larger share of output to investment will be wealthier. The Solow model doesn't tell us *why* some countries might devote a larger share of output to investment, but we know from Chapter 21 that wealthy countries have institutions that promote investment in physical capital, human capital, and technological knowledge. We will also say more about how financial intermediaries channel saving into investment in Chapter 23.

Second, growth will be faster the farther away a country's capital stock is from its steady state value. This explains why the German and Japanese economies were able to catch up to other advanced economies after World War II, why countries that reform their institutions often grow very rapidly (growth miracles), and why poor countries grow faster than rich countries with similar levels of steady state output.

Third, the Solow model tells us that capital accumulation cannot explain long-run economic growth. Holding other things constant, the marginal product of physical and human capital will eventually diminish, thereby leaving the economy in a zero-growth steady state. If we want to explain long-run economic growth, we must explain why other things are not held constant.

New ideas are the driving force behind long-run economic growth. Ideas, however, aren't like other goods: ideas can be easily copied and ideas are non-rivalrous. The fact that ideas can be easily copied means that the originator of a new idea won't receive all the benefits of that idea so the incentive to produce ideas will be too low. Governments can play a role in supporting the production of new ideas by protecting intellectual property and subsidizing the production of new ideas when spillovers are most likely to be present.

The non-rivalry of ideas, however, means that once an idea is created we want it to be shared, which is a nice way of saying copied, as much as possible. There is thus a trade-off between providing appropriate incentives to produce new ideas and providing appropriate incentives to share new ideas.

An important lesson from the economics of ideas is that the larger the market, whether in terms of people or wealth, the greater the incentive to invest in research and development. Similarly, having more people and wealthier countries increases the number of people devoted to the production of new ideas. Thus, the increased wealth of many developing nations, the move to freer trade in global markets, and the spread of better institutions throughout the world are all encouraging for the future of economic growth.

□ CHAPTER REVIEW

KEY CONCEPTS

Marginal product of capital, p. 453

Steady state, p. 457

Conditional convergence, p. 464

Non-rivalrous, p. 468

FACTS AND TOOLS

1. Which countries are likely to grow faster: Countries doing "cutting-edge" growth or those doing "catch-up" growth?

2. When will people work harder to invent new ideas: When they can sell them to a market of 10,000 people or when they can sell them to a market of 1 billion? Does your answer tell us anything about whether it's good or bad from the U.S. point of view for China and India to become rich countries?

3. Many people say that if people save too much, the economy will be hurt. They often refer to the fact that consumer spending is two-thirds of GDP to make this point. This is sometimes called the "paradox of thrift."

   a. In the Solow model, is there a paradox of thrift? In other words, is a high savings rate good or bad for a country's long-run economic performance?

   b. What about in the real world? According to the data in Figure 22.10, is there a paradox of thrift?

4. Many people say that "the rich grow richer and the poor grow poorer." Is this what Figure 22.11 says about the countries in that graph? Did the rich countries grow faster or slower than the poor countries?

5. Compared to its fast growth today, is China's economy likely to grow faster or slower in the future?

6. What is more important for explaining the standard of living in the rich countries: Capital or ideas?

7. According to Thomas Jefferson, how are ideas like flames?

8. What is a patent?

9. When will people work harder to invent new ideas: When they can patent those ideas for one year or when they can patent them for 10 years?

10. Which three countries on the list are good examples of "conditional convergence?"

    China

    Ireland

    Argentina

    North Korea

    Greece

11. Let's keep track of a nation's capital stock for five years. Mordor starts off with 1,000 machines, and every year, 5 percent of the machines depreciate or wear out. Fortunately, the people in this land produce 75 machines per year,

every year. The key equation for keeping track of capital is quite simple:

Next year's capital = This year's capital + Investment − Depreciation

Fill in the table.

Year	Capital	Depreciation	Investment
1	1,000	0.05 × 1,000	75
2	1,025		75
3			75
4			75
5			75

THINKING AND PROBLEM SOLVING

1. Consider the following three countries that produce GDP this way:

$$Y = 5\sqrt{K}$$

Ilia: $K = 100$ machines
Caplania: $K = 10,000$ machines
Hansonia: $K = 1,000,000$ machines

What will GDP (Y) be in these three countries? Hansonia has 10,000 times more machines than Ilia, so why isn't it 10,000 times more productive?

2. Consider the data in the previous question: If 10 percent of all machines become worthless every year (they depreciate, in other words), then how many machines will become worthless in these three countries this year? Are there any countries where the amount of depreciation is actually greater than GDP? (This question reminds you that "More machines mean more machines wearing out.")

3. Of course, no country makes *only* investment goods like machines, equipment, and computers. They also make consumer goods. Let's consider a case where the countries in question 1 devote 25 percent of GDP to making investment goods (so γ, gamma, = 0.25). What is the amount of savings in these three countries? In which countries is *Investment < Depreciation*? When is *Investment > Depreciation*?

4. A drug company has $1 billion to spend on research and development. It has to decide on one of two projects:

a. Spend the money on a project to fight deadly forms of influenza including bird flu.

b. Spend the money on a project to fight a condition of red, itchy skin known as eczema.

The company expects both projects to be equally profitable, all things considered: Yes, project A is riskier (since the rare flu may never come along), but if the disease hits, there will be a worldwide market willing to pay a lot of money to cure the flu.

Then one day, before deciding between A and B, the drug company's CEO reads in the newspaper that the European Union and the United States will not honor patents in the event of a major flu outbreak. Instead, these governments will "break the patent" and just make the drug available everywhere for $1 per pill. The company will only get $1 per pill instead of the $100 or $200 per pill they had expected.

Given this new information about the possibility that governments will "break the patent," which project is the company likely to spend its research and development money on? (Note: In the wake of the deadly anthrax attacks of 2001, the U.S. government threatened to do just this with the patent for Cipro, the one antibiotic proven to cure the symptoms of anthrax infection.)

5. After World War II, a lot of France's capital stock was destroyed, but it had educated workers and a market-oriented economy. Do you think the war's destruction increased or decreased the marginal product of capital?

6. In the Solow model, you've seen that as the total stock of capital equipment gets larger, the number of machines wearing out grows as well. Often, most investment ends up just replacing worn-out machines. This is actually true in the United States and other rich countries. According to the U.S. National Income and Product Accounts (the official U.S. GDP measures), about 12 percent of total GDP just goes toward replacing worn-out machines and computers and construction equipment.

a. In the Solow model, if the depreciation rate increases, what happens to the steady state capital level and output level? Answer in words and by using a diagram such as Figure 22.4. (Bonus: if the depreciation rate increases from 0.02 to 0.03 what is the new steady state level of capital and output?)

b. If the Solow model explains an important part of the real world, should countries hope for high depreciation rates or low depreciation rates? How does this square with the observation that when machines wear out, that "creates jobs" in the manufacturing industries?

7. The Solow model isn't useful for only thinking about entire countries: As long as the production function runs into diminishing returns and your total stock of inputs constantly wears out, then the Solow model applies. Consider a professor's knowledge of economics. The more she learns about economics, the more she will forget (depreciation), but the more she knows, the more knowledge she can create (production). So eventually in steady state, she will know only a fixed amount about economics, but what she knows might change over time; some decades she might know a lot about the Federal Reserve while other decades she might know a lot about the electricity market. In any case, knowledge fades away.

a. Apply the Solow model to a chef's skill at cooking.

b. Apply the Solow model to the size of a navy's fleet of ships.

c. Apply the Solow model to the speed of a cheetah, where the input is calories.

8. Many inventors decide that patents are a bad way to protect their intellectual property. Instead, they keep their ideas a secret. Trade secrets are actually quite common: The formula for Coca-Cola is a trade secret, as is Colonel Sander's secret recipe. What is one major strength of keeping a trade secret rather than applying for a patent? What is a major weakness inherent in going down the trade secret route?

9. Since ideas can sometimes be copied quite easily, many people think that we should put more effort into creating new ideas. Let's see if there are trade-offs to having more people creating new ideas. To keep things simple, let's assume that the growth rate of the economy depends on how many people search for ideas, whether in laboratories, or huddled over laptops in coffee shops, or while listening to "Stairway to Heaven" at three in the morning. People either produce stuff or produce ideas. Here's how this economy works:

$Y_t = (1 - R) \times A_t L$ (GDP production function)

$A_{t+1} = (1 + R) \times A_t$ (Technology production function)

There are a total of L people in the society, a fraction $(1 - R)$ of them work in factories and offices making stuff (remember, people working in offices help create output too!), while the remaining fraction R try to come up with good ideas all day long. To keep the story simple, there are no diminishing returns.

a. What's the trade-off here? If 100 percent of the people work to make new ideas ($R = 1$), won't that create a prosperous world?

b. In this society, if people are willing to wait a long time for a reward, should they choose a large R or a small R?

c. Plot out GDP in this society for 5 years if A starts off at 100, L starts off at 100, and R is 10 percent.

Year	A	Y	Y/L
1	100	9,000	90
2	110		
3			
4			
5			

d. Plot out GDP in this society if the society instead chose $R = 20$ percent.

10. In Facts and Tools question 2, we saw that big markets create a big *demand* for inventions. This is an example of what Adam Smith meant when he said that "the division of labor is limited by the extent of the market." Now let's look at how big markets impact the *supply* side of inventions. The big idea is quite simple: *More people means more ideas*.

a. In order to create new ideas, you need to have people trying to come up with new ideas. In 1800, there were approximately 300 million humans on the planet—roughly equal to today's U.S. population. If good ideas are "one in a million," that is, if one person per year out of a million comes up with a world-shaking idea like contact lenses or James Brown's song "The Payback" or the video game Grand Theft Auto, how many great new ideas will occur in the world of 1800? How many will occur in a world of 6 billion people?

b. More realistically, people in the rich countries are most likely to invent earth-shaking ideas and share them with others. There's nothing special about people in rich countries but they have the education and the laboratories and the Internet connections that will make it practical to invent and spread ideas. If only the top 20 percent of the earth's population is really in the running to create new ideas, how many new big ideas will come along each year in 1800 and today?

c. If half of the population of India and China become rich enough to create new ideas (to simplify assume populations of 1 billion each), and start coming up with big ideas at the same rate as the top 20 percent, how many big ideas will India and China alone create for the planet every year?

d. Many people think there are too many people on the planet. (As P. J. O'Rourke once wrote, many people's attitude toward global population is "Just enough of me, way too much of you.") Look at your answer from part b. If the world's population now gets cut in half from the current 6 billion, how many big ideas will come along each year?

11. According to economists Robert Barro and Xavier Sala-i-Martin, convergence isn't just for entire nations: It's also true for states and regions as well. They looked at state-level GDP per capita in the United States in 1880, and then calculated how fast each state grew over the next 120 years. They found that convergence held almost exactly.

a. With this in mind, draw arrows to connect the GDP per capita data on the left with the long-term growth rates on the right.

GDP per capita in 1880	Annual growth rate, 1880–2000
West: $8,500	1.6%
East: $6,300	1.7%
Midwest: $4,700	2.2%
South: $2,800	1.2%

b. Graph the data from part a in the figure below. Does this look like Figure 22.11's story about the OECD countries, or is it quite different?

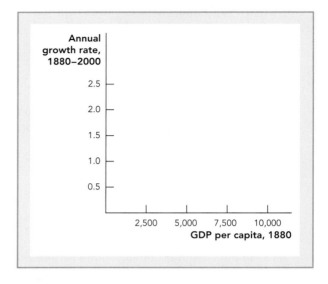

Note: Barro and Sala-i-Martin also found that convergence also held almost exactly for regions of Japan: The areas that were poorest in 1930 grew fastest over the next 70 years. Thus, it is difficult to find major evidence in favor of the commonsense idea that "the poor areas grow poorer."

12. Are we running out of ideas? Economist Paul Romer thinks not. To make things concrete, he notes that if we keep trying out different molecules to search for interesting compounds like new drugs, new plastics, etc., the universe may end from heat death before we finish our search. For example, if we try out 100 different atoms out of the 117+ (and rising!) elements in the periodic table, and only look at the 6-atom molecules, this is 100^6 different molecules. And, of course, many common molecules in our bodies consist of hundreds of atoms, so this only scratches the surface of interesting compounds.

a. If it takes a machine 1 minute to test out and fully analyze a new 6-atom molecule, how many years will it take for this one machine to test out all 100^6 molecules? (Note: Modern biochemists create computer simulations of molecules to analyze whether potential drugs are likely to work in the molecules that make up the human body, but this is only one narrow form of analysis.)

b. How many machines would it take to test out all of these molecules within 100 years?

c. What about all 10-atom molecules: How many years would it take for one machine to test all of these compounds at one per minute? If your computer can handle it, what about all 100-atom molecules, molecules vastly simpler than many proteins in your body?

CHALLENGES

1. Which country would you expect to have a higher rate of investment: A catch-up country or a cutting-edge country?

2. If the government of a poor catch-up country is trying to decide whether to encourage investment or encourage research and development, which of the two should it favor? (Note: in a world of trade-offs, you can't just say "Both are important!")

3. The Solow model makes it quite easy to figure out how rich a country will be in its steady state. We already know that you're in a steady state when investment equals depreciation. In math, that's:

$$\gamma Y = \delta K$$

Since $Y = \sqrt{K}$ in our simplest model, that means that $K = Y^2$:

$$\gamma Y = \delta Y^2$$

There are a lot of ways to solve this for Y— the easiest might just be to divide both sides by Y, and then put everything else on the other side. When you do this, you can learn how steady state GDP depends on the savings rate γ and the depreciation rate δ. Here are a few questions:

a. Many people say that if people save more, that's bad for the economy: They say that spending money on consumer goods keeps the money moving through the economy. Does this model say that?

b. Many people say that when machines and equipment get destroyed by bad weather or war, that makes the economy better off by encouraging businesses and families to spend money on new capital goods. Does this model say that?

4. Let's think about two countries, Frugal and Smart. In Frugal, people devote 50 percent of GDP to making new investment goods, so $\gamma = 0.5$, and their production function is $Y = \sqrt{K}$. In Smart, people devote 25 percent of GDP to making new investment goods, so $\gamma = 0.25$, and their production function is $Y = 2\sqrt{K}$. Both countries start off with $K = 100$.

a. What is the amount of investment in each country this year?

b. What is the amount of consumption (GDP − Investment, or $Y - I$) in each country this year?

c. Where would you rather be a citizen: Frugal or Smart?

5. Which of the following goods are non-rivalrous?

Sunshine

An apple

A national park

A Mozart symphony

The idea of penicillin

A dose of penicillin

6. According to economist Michael Kremer, as human populations have grown over the last million years, so has the human population growth *rate*. This was true until the 1800s. How does Thinking and Problem Solving question 10 help explain why human populations grew faster despite the fact that there were more mouths to feed?

CHAPTER **APPENDIX**

Excellent Growth

Using a spreadsheet, you can easily explore the Solow model and duplicate all the graphs in this chapter. First, label column A, "Capital, K" and put a 1 in cell A2. Second, you can create an increasing series by inputting the formula "=A2+1" in cell A3 and copying and pasting that formula into cells A4 to say A500. Your spreadsheet should look like Figure A22.1.

FIGURE A22.1

	A3	▼	f_x =A2+1	
	A	**B**	**C**	**D**
1	Capital, K			
2	1			
3	2			
4	3			
5	4			
6	5			
7	6			
8	7			
9	8			
10	9			
11	10			
12	11			
13	12			
14	13			
15	14			
16	15			
17	⋮			

In column B, create a series for Output. Remember that $Y = \sqrt{K}$, so in cell B2 input the formula "=SQRT(A2)" and then copy and paste that formula into B3 to B500, as in Figure A22.2.

Now create the headings Investment, Depreciation, Investment Share, and Depreciation Rate in columns C to F—like in Figure A22.3.

In cell E2, put the investment share, 0.3, used in the text and in cell F2 put the rate of depreciation that we used, 0.02.

In cell C2, which is highlighted, we want to input the formula for investment, which is γY, where γ is the investment share. We could input "=0.3*B2" into C2 but we would like to be able to easily adjust the investment share and see what happens, so we will input "=$E$2*B2". The $E$2 says take the investment share from cell E2 and when we copy and paste this formula it *always* uses cell E2 (not E3, E4, etc.). Copy and paste cell C2 into C3 to C500.

FIGURE A22.2

| B2 | ▼ | _fx_ =SQRT(A2) |

	A	B	C	D	
1	Capital, K	Output			
2	1	1.00			
3	2	1.41			
4	3	1.73			
5	4	2.00			
6	5	2.24			
7	6	2.45			
8	7	2.65			
9	8	2.83			
10	9	3.00			
11	10	3.16			
12	11	3.32			
13	12	3.46			
14	13	3.61			
15	14	3.74			
16	15	3.87			
17	⋮	⋮			

FIGURE A22.3

| C2 | ▼ | _fx_ =$E$2*B2 |

	A	B	C	D	E	F	
1	Capital, K	Output	Investment	Depreciation	Investment Share, γ	Depreciation Rate, δ	
2	1	1.00	0.30	0.02	0.3	0.02	
3	2	1.41	0.42	0.04			
4	3	1.73	0.52	0.06			
5	4	2.00	0.60	0.08			
6	5	2.24	0.67	0.10			
7	6	2.45	0.73	0.12			
8	7	2.65	0.79	0.14			
9	8	2.83	0.85	0.16			
10	9	3.00	0.90	0.18			
11	10	3.16	0.95	0.20			
12	11	3.32	0.99	0.22			
13	12	3.46	1.04	0.24			
14	13	3.61	1.08	0.26			
15	14	3.74	1.12	0.28			
16	15	3.87	1.16	0.30			
17	⋮	⋮	⋮	⋮			

Depreciation is just δK, where δ is the depreciation rate. As with investment, we might want to alter this parameter so into cell D2 we will input "=$F$2*A2".

That's it! To duplicate the graph in Figure 22.4, for example, just highlight columns A, B, C, and D, click the Chart icon (you can also click Chart in the Insert menu), choose XY (Scatter) and the highlighted sub-type, and then click on finish. (In Excel 2007 click Insert and then Scatter in the Chart submenu to do the same thing.) See Figure A22.4.

FIGURE A22.4

The result is as in Figure A22.5.

If you want to see what happens if the investment share increases to 0.4, as in Figure 22.9 in the chapter, just change cell E2 to 0.4 and the graph will change automatically. You can make other adjustments as well. One thing to watch for is that with parameters too different than the ones we have given, the equilibrium capital stock may be greater than 500. So if you want to see the full picture, you will need to extend the rows even further.

FIGURE A22.5

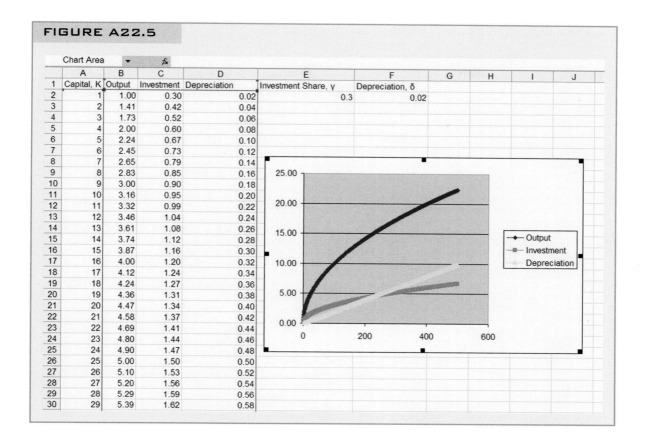

	A	B	C	D	E	F	G	H	I	J
1	Capital, K	Output	Investment	Depreciation	Investment Share, γ	Depreciation, δ				
2	1	1.00	0.30	0.02	0.3	0.02				
3	2	1.41	0.42	0.04						
4	3	1.73	0.52	0.06						
5	4	2.00	0.60	0.08						
6	5	2.24	0.67	0.10						
7	6	2.45	0.73	0.12						
8	7	2.65	0.79	0.14						
9	8	2.83	0.85	0.16						
10	9	3.00	0.90	0.18						
11	10	3.16	0.95	0.20						
12	11	3.32	0.99	0.22						
13	12	3.46	1.04	0.24						
14	13	3.61	1.08	0.26						
15	14	3.74	1.12	0.28						
16	15	3.87	1.16	0.30						
17	16	4.00	1.20	0.32						
18	17	4.12	1.24	0.34						
19	18	4.24	1.27	0.36						
20	19	4.36	1.31	0.38						
21	20	4.47	1.34	0.40						
22	21	4.58	1.37	0.42						
23	22	4.69	1.41	0.44						
24	23	4.80	1.44	0.46						
25	24	4.90	1.47	0.48						
26	25	5.00	1.50	0.50						
27	26	5.10	1.53	0.52						
28	27	5.20	1.56	0.54						
29	28	5.29	1.59	0.56						
30	29	5.39	1.62	0.58						

CHAPTER EXCEL APPENDIX QUESTION

1. Use the instructions in the appendix to set up the Solow model in Excel with the Investment Share, γ, equal to 0.3 and with the Depreciation Rate, δ, equal to 0.02. Both numbers are just what we used in the chapter. Now increase the Investment Share to 0.36.

   a. What is the new level of steady state capital? (Remember, the level of steady state capital is where Investment = Depreciation.)

   b. At the new steady level of capital what is the level of output, Y?

   Now change the Investment Share back to 0.3 and this time increase the Depreciation Rate to 0.025.

   c. What is the new level of steady state capital?

   d. At the steady state level of capital what is the level of output, Y?

   e. Fill in the blanks with your conclusions:

   An increase in the investment share _____ the steady state level of capital and output.

   An increase in the depreciation rate _____ the steady state level of capital and output.

23

Saving, Investment, and the Financial System

CHAPTER OUTLINE

The Supply of Savings

The Demand to Borrow

Equilibrium in the Market for Loanable Funds

The Role of Intermediaries: Banks, Bonds, and Stock Markets

What Happens When Intermediation Fails?

Takeaway

Appendix: Bond Pricing and Arbitrage

On a typical day in 2005, Chinese savers bought $600 million of American bonds, stocks and other financial assets. Americans used those funds to buy homes, to build factories, and to support government programs like Medicare and even the Department of Defense. Chairman Mao would be spinning in his grave because "communist" China is now a key participant in the worldwide market for capital, the very market that gives capitalism its name.

The global market for capital links Chinese savers and American borrowers and it makes both better off. Chinese savers earn a higher rate of return when they can lend to anyone in the world and not just to borrowers in their own village, city, or even country. Access to world capital markets also allows the Chinese to diversify their holdings and so the Chinese have been major investors in Africa as well as the United States.

Americans also benefit from global capital markets. Americans can borrow at lower interest rates, and therefore invest more, when they have access to savings from around the world. The movement of financial capital within a country and around the world is part of the broader process of creating value by moving resources to their most highly valued uses.

This chapter is about savers and borrowers and the institutions—banks, bond markets, and stock exchanges—that bridge the gap between savers and borrowers. These specialized institutions have evolved to lower the costs of connecting savers with borrowers. Figure 23.1 on the next page illustrates.

Recall from Chapters 21 and 22 that savings are necessary for capital accumulation and the more capital an economy has the greater its GDP per capita. So reducing the costs of connecting savers and borrowers is important: connecting savers and borrowers increases the gains from trade and smooths the process of economic growth.

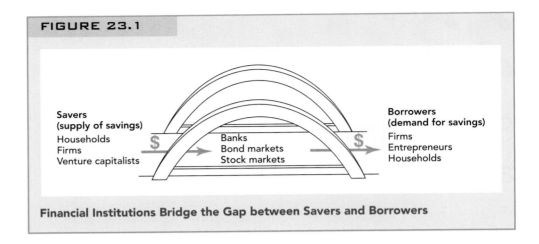

FIGURE 23.1

Savers
(supply of savings)

Households
Firms
Venture capitalists

$

Banks
Bond markets
Stock markets

$

Borrowers
(demand for savings)

Firms
Entrepreneurs
Households

Financial Institutions Bridge the Gap between Savers and Borrowers

Saving is income that is not spent on consumption goods.

Investment is the purchase of new capital goods.

Before proceeding, let's make it clear what we mean by the words **saving** and **investment**. Saving is income that is not spent on consumption goods. Investment is the purchase of new capital, things like tools, machinery, and factories. It's important to see that the way economists define investment is not the same as the way a stockbroker defines investment. If Starbucks buys new espresso machines for its stores, that's investment. If John buys stock in Starbucks, that is not investment in the economic sense but merely a transfer of ownership rights of already existing capital (see the next chapter for a treatment of how individuals should allocate their funds for their personal "investments"). Most of the trading on stock exchanges is thus not investment in the economic sense because it simply transfers ownership of a stock from one person to another. From an economic point of view, investment requires a net increase in the economy's ability to produce goods and services.

Okay, let's see how savings are mobilized and transformed into investment. We will be using the economist's tools in trade—supply and demand—and we'll start with the supply of savings.

The Supply of Savings

We begin with the left side of Figure 23.1, the supply of savings. Economists have a good but imperfect understanding of what determines the supply of savings. Here are four of the major factors: smoothing consumption, impatience, marketing and psychological factors, and interest rates.

Individuals Want to Smooth Consumption

If you consumed what you earned every year, your consumption over time might look like Path A in Figure 23.2. Along Path A, consumption is equal to income. Consumption is high during your working years, but after retirement consumption drops precipitously—as a result, once you retire and your income falls, you must sell the nice car and give up the fancy lifestyle just to scrape by. Most people would prefer consumption Path B. Along Path B consumption is less than income during the working years because you save for retirement. But when retirement comes, consumption is greater than income as you spend your savings or "dissave."

FIGURE 23.2

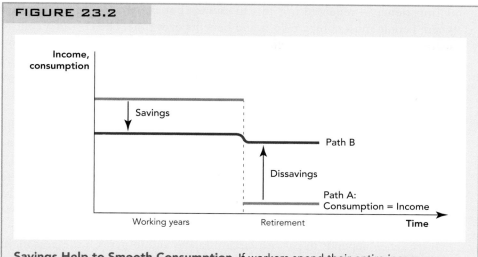

Savings Help to Smooth Consumption If workers spend their entire income every year, their consumption over time will follow Path A. Notice that along Path A consumption drops tremendously at retirement. By saving during the working years and dissaving during the retirement years, workers can smooth their consumption so that it looks more like Path B.

Economists say that Path B is "smoother" than Path A. The desire to smooth consumption over time is a reason to save and, as we will discuss shortly, also a reason to borrow.

The consumption-smoothing theory of saving can tell us something important about AIDS, Africa, and economic growth. Remember from previous chapters that savings are necessary to finance the capital accumulation that generates high standards of living. If there are no savings, investment dries up, economic growth declines, and the standard of living falls.

Now consider that AIDS has dramatically reduced life expectancy in Africa. What is your prediction about savings rates? Imagine that you expected to die in a few years—would you save much? Probably not. Similarly, many poorer Africans don't save much because, sadly, they expect to die young.[1] This gives rise to a vicious cycle. The decline in life expectancy caused by AIDS reduces saving rates, which in turn reduces economic growth and the standard of living and that makes it more difficult to combat diseases like AIDS.

Fluctuations in income are another reason why people save. Some workers, such as salespeople, writers, and home builders have incomes that fluctuate from year to year. Most workers could have unexpected health problems or they could find themselves unemployed and so they also fear that their income might fluctuate. By saving in the good years, workers can build a cushion of wealth to draw from in the bad years, thereby smoothing their consumption across all years.

UNDERSTAND YOUR **world**

Individuals Are Impatient

Another reason why people save, or fail to save, is their level of impatience. Most individuals prefer to consume now rather than later so saving is not always easy. Some people, however, are very impatient, others less so. This is what economists call **time preference.** Time preference reflects the fact that today feels more real than tomorrow. The more impatient a person, the more likely that person's savings rate will be low.

Time preference is the desire to have goods and services sooner rather than later (all else being equal).

Impatience is reflected not just in savings but in any economic situation where people must compare costs and benefits over time. The cost of a college degree, for example, comes well before the benefit. To get a college degree, you must pay for tuition and books and, most important, you must give up the income that you could earn from a job, all right now. The benefits of a college degree are large—in 1998 the average worker with a college degree earned almost $20,000 more per year than a worker with just a high school diploma—but all the benefits are in the future. An impatient person will weigh the upfront costs highly and discount the future benefits. Impatient people are unlikely to go to college.

Crime is another economic activity with immediate benefits and future costs so it's not surprising that criminals tend to be impatient people. Similarly, heroin addicts, alcoholics, and smokers all tend to discount the future more heavily than nonaddicts.

Impatience depends in part on circumstances and in part on the person. In one fascinating study, four-year-old children were asked whether they wanted one cookie now or two cookies in 20 minutes. Many years later, the children were evaluated again—the children who had waited were less impulsive and had higher grades than the children who had not waited.[2]

Marketing and Psychological Factors

Marketing matters, even for savings. Often individuals save more if saving is presented as the natural or default alternative. In one study, economists studied retirement savings plans. Some employers automatically enrolled all new employees in a retirement savings plan, leaving the employees the choice to opt out, whereas others required employees to request such an account, in effect asking them to opt in. In the businesses that used automatic enrollment, the savings plan participation rate was 25 percent higher than in the businesses where employees needed to request a retirement account.

The default also mattered for how much was saved. In one firm, the default savings rate was 3 percent of salary. More than a quarter of the workers chose that as their savings rate, despite an employer guarantee of a dollar-for-dollar match on contributions of up to 6 percent of salary. Later, the company switched to a 6 percent default savings rate; in that setting hardly any new workers chose the 3 percent savings contribution rate even though they could have switched with just a phone call.[3]

It's quite surprising how some simple psychological changes, combined with effective marketing and promotion, can change how much people save for their retirement. Behavioral economics, a new and growing field within economics, combines economics, psychology, and neurology to study how people make decisions and how they can be helped to overcome biases in decision making.

The Interest Rate

The quantity of savings also depends on the interest rate, namely how much savers are paid to save. If the interest rate is 5 percent per year, then $100 saved today returns $105 a year from now. If the interest rate is 10 percent per year, then $100 saved today returns $110 a year from now. All else being equal, higher interest rates usually call forth more savings.* Figure 23.3 shows the supply curve for savings. The vertical axis of Figure 23.3 measures the interest rate. The horizontal axis measures savings in dollars. In this example, an interest rate of 5 percent generates total savings of $200 billion and an interest rate of 10 percent generates total savings of $280 billion.

You might wonder why the supply curve for savings has the interest rate on the vertical axis while other supply curves have had price on the vertical axis. In fact, interest rates are just a convenient way of expressing the price of savings. An interest rate of 5 percent, for example, means that the saver will be paid $5 (in one year) for every $100 saved. Thus, we could say that when the price of lending is $5 per $100 saved, the quantity of savings is $200 billion. It's a bit easier, however, to think in terms of interest rates.

The bottom line is that the interest rate is a market price and it has the same properties of market prices that we discussed in the introductory chapters of this book.

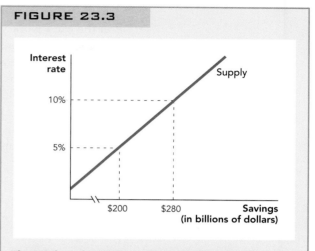

FIGURE 23.3

The Higher the Interest Rate the Greater the Quantity Saved At an interest rate of 5 percent, $200 billion is saved. At an interest rate of 10 percent, $280 billion is saved.

The Demand to Borrow

Why do people borrow? People borrow to smooth their consumption path and especially to finance large investments. Let's look at each of these reasons for borrowing.

Individuals Want to Smooth Consumption

Just as people save in order to smooth consumption, one reason people borrow is to smooth consumption. Many young people, for example, borrow so that they can invest in their education. If they had to pay their tuition expenses all at once, many students would have to sell their car or eat nothing but beans and oatmeal for a year. But if tuition payments can be made over many years, as borrowing makes possible, the sacrifices are spread out and become less painful. A student who can borrow can move some of the sacrifices into future periods when the (now former) student has a job and a regular income. Student borrowing is thus another example of how credit markets let people smooth their consumption over time.

The "lifecycle" theory of savings, pioneered by Nobel Laureate Franco Modigliani, puts the demand to borrow and save together. The lifecycle theory

CHECK YOURSELF

> Examining Figure 23.1, what is the crucial function that financial institutions perform?

> Financial advisors have warned that increased life expectancy means that many people have not saved enough for their retirement. If true, what will the consumption path of these people look like as they reach their retirement years? Will this consumption path be smooth?

> Can you think of other factors that might generate a demand to save? Hint: Other than retirement what other factors could cause income to be volatile?

---

* In principle, it is possible for the supply curve for savings to be negatively sloped. For instance, if an individual wanted exactly $100 in one year's time, then at an interest rate of 10 percent he or she would need to save $90.91, but at an interest rate of 20 percent he or she would need to save only $83.33. Thus, an increase in the interest rate could reduce savings. The evidence, however, indicates that individual savings rates typically respond positively to higher interest rates. In addition, higher U.S. interest rates also encourage lenders in other countries to move some of their savings to U.S. markets. Both forces mean that the supply curve for savings is upwardly sloped in most circumstances.

is illustrated in Figure 23.4. Income starts out low during the college years and in the early work years. To finance college and to buy a first home, people borrow so their consumption is higher than their income. As workers enter their prime earning years, they save to pay off their college debt and mortgage and they prepare for retirement—during this time period consumption is less than income. As people get older and retire, consumption is once again above income as dissaving (that is, using up savings) occurs. Overall, borrowing, saving, and dissaving help people to smooth out their consumption path over time—although few people would have a consumption path as smooth as the one we have drawn here!

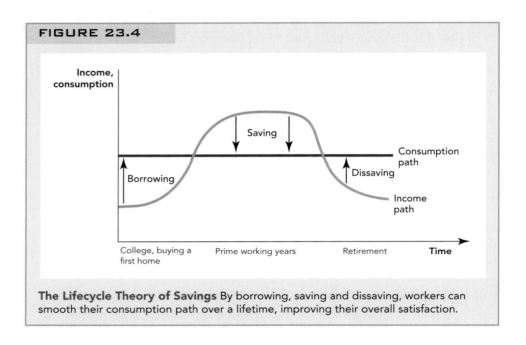

FIGURE 23.4

The Lifecycle Theory of Savings By borrowing, saving and dissaving, workers can smooth their consumption path over a lifetime, improving their overall satisfaction.

Governments also borrow for reasons much like consumers. Governments may borrow, for example, to finance unusually large expenditures such as are required to pay for a war, or to pay for large investments such as the interstate highway system. We discuss government taxes, spending, and borrowing at greater length in Chapter 30.

Borrowing Is Necessary to Finance Large Investments

Businesses also borrow extensively. Many new businesses can't get underway at all without borrowing. Often the people with the best business ideas are not the people with the most savings, so people with good ideas must borrow funds to start their careers as entrepreneurs.

Fred Smith, the legendary entrepreneur, first laid out the idea for FedEx in an undergraduate paper he had to write for an economics class. Smith's idea, overnight delivery of packages using a hub and spoke system, was great but the problem was that he couldn't start small. To be successful, Smith needed to cover a good part of the country from day one and he didn't have enough of his own money to build an entire network. Smith began FedEx with 16 planes covering 25 cities using money he borrowed and also by selling part ownership of FedEx to venture capitalists, investors willing to accept risk in return for a stake in future profits. FedEx, of course, has been a huge success—it changed the way America does business and made Smith a very wealthy man. By the way, Smith's grade on his paper: C!

More generally, businesses borrow to finance large projects. The costs of developing an apartment building are all upfront; the revenues don't start flowing until the building is completed and the tenants have moved in. In fact, it may take many years before the revenues fully cover all the upfront costs. If a developer like Donald Trump had to wait until he personally had enough funds to pay the upfront costs, he might be able to develop just one or two buildings in his lifetime. By borrowing, developers are able to invest now and develop many more buildings.

The examples of borrowing that we have given share a common theme. A student who can't borrow may not be able to get an education even though the education would be a good investment. A government that can't borrow may not be able to invest in an interstate highway system even though the highway system would pay for itself many times over. A builder who can't borrow may not be able to build an apartment building even though it would be a profitable investment. Thus borrowing plays an important role in the economy—the ability to borrow greatly increases the ability to invest and, as we showed in Chapters 21 and 22, higher investment increases the standard of living and the rate of economic growth.

In Shakespeare's *Hamlet*, Polonius advises "Neither a borrower nor a lender be." But people forget, Polonius was a fool.

The Interest Rate

Of course, the quantity of funds that people want to borrow also depends on the cost of the loan, or the interest rate. Businesses, for example, borrow when they expect that the return on their investment will be greater than the cost of the loan. Thus, if the interest rate is 10 percent, businesses will only borrow if they expect that their investment will return *greater* than 10 percent. If the interest rate is 5 percent, then businesses will only borrow if they expect that their investment will return *greater* than 5 percent. Since more investments will return greater than 5 percent than will return greater than 10 percent, the demand to borrow follows the law of demand: the lower the interest rate, the greater the quantity of funds demanded for investment as well as for other purposes.

In Figure 23.5, $190 billion is demanded when the interest rate is 10 percent and $300 billion is demanded when the interest rate is 5 percent.

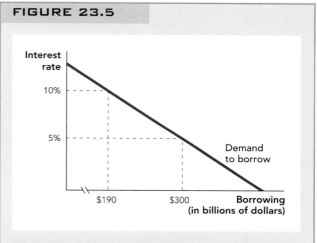

FIGURE 23.5

The Lower the Interest Rate the Greater the Quantity of Funds Demanded At an interest rate of 10 percent borrowers would like to borrow $190 billion. At an interest rate of 5 percent, borrowers would like to borrow more, $300 billion.

CHECK YOURSELF

> Under the lifecycle theory, when is an individual's savings likely to be at its peak?

> If interest rates fall from 7 percent to 5 percent (and all else is the same), what happens to the number of people buying homes? Starting businesses?

Equilibrium in the Market for Loanable Funds

Now that we have covered the supply of savings and the demand to borrow, we can put them together to find an equilibrium in what economists call the **market for loanable funds**. In Figure 23.6 on the next page, the equilibrium interest rate is 8 percent and the equilibrium quantity of savings is $250 billion. Notice that in equilibrium, the quantity of funds supplied equals the quantity of funds demanded.

The **market for loanable funds** is where suppliers of loanable funds (savers) trade with demanders of loanable funds (borrowers). Trading in the market for loanable funds determines the equilibrium interest rate.

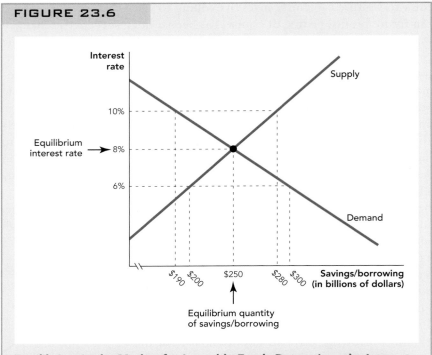

FIGURE 23.6

Equilibrium in the Market for Loanable Funds Determines the Interest Rate and the Quantity of Loanable Funds At an interest rate greater than 8 percent, there is a surplus of savings and the interest rate is bid down. At an interest rate less than 8 percent, there is a shortage of savings and the interest rate is bid up. At an interest rate of 8 percent, the quantity of savings supplied ($250 billion) is exactly equal to the quantity of savings demanded.

The interest rate adjusts to equalize savings and borrowing in the same way and for the same reasons that the price of oil adjusts to balance the supply and demand for oil. If the interest rate were higher than 8 percent, the quantity of savings supplied would exceed the quantity of savings demanded creating a surplus of savings. With a surplus of savings, suppliers will bid the interest rate down as they compete to lend. If the interest rate were lower than 8 percent, the quantity of savings demanded would exceed the quantity of savings supplied, a shortage. With a shortage of savings, demanders would bid the interest rate up as they compete to borrow. (See Chapter 3 for a review.)

Shifts in Supply and Demand

Changes in economic conditions will shift the supply or demand curve and change the equilibrium interest rate and quantity of savings. Consider an economy in which the citizens become less impatient, and more willing to save for the future. These shifts occurred in South Korea in the 1960s and 1970s, once many Korean citizens realized they could copy some aspects of the Japanese economic miracle. Across East Asia more generally, growing life spans and fewer children to support (and fewer children to be supported by, in old age) led to a regional savings boom. An increase in the supply of savings is shown by shifting the supply curve to the right and down (indicating more savings at any interest rate or equivalently a willingness to save any given amount in return for a lower interest rate).

In Figure 23.7, an increase in the supply of savings causes the equilibrium interest rate to fall from 8 percent to 6 percent and the quantity of savings to increase from $250 billion to $300 billion.

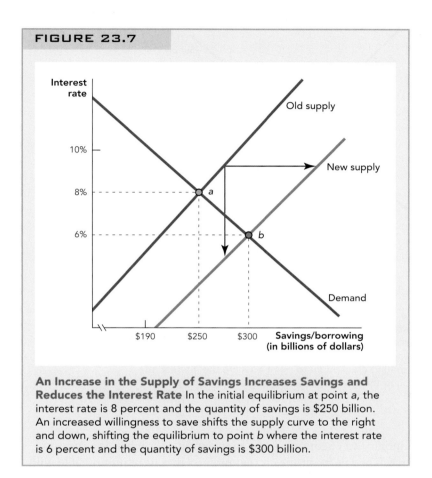

FIGURE 23.7

An Increase in the Supply of Savings Increases Savings and Reduces the Interest Rate In the initial equilibrium at point *a*, the interest rate is 8 percent and the quantity of savings is $250 billion. An increased willingness to save shifts the supply curve to the right and down, shifting the equilibrium to point *b* where the interest rate is 6 percent and the quantity of savings is $300 billion.

What did this shift in savings means for South Korea? In 1960, Korea was among the poorest countries in the world but today it is a fully developed nation. South Korea's increased savings were plowed into investment and as we know from our discussion of the Solow model in Chapter 22, one of the key drivers of economic growth is a high rate of investment and capital accumulation.

Of course, a decrease in the supply of savings is shown in the opposite manner, by shifting the supply curve to the left and up.

Sometimes investors become less optimistic, which decreases the demand to invest and borrow. For instance, during a recession many entrepreneurs get scared about the future and they are reluctant to invest. Projects that looked good to investors when the economy is booming may look unprofitable when the economy is in the doldrums. The decrease in investment demand can itself help to spread and prolong the recession, as we discuss at greater length in Chapter 27. In Figure 23.8 on the next page, a decrease in investment demand reduces the interest rate from 8 percent to 6 percent and the quantity of savings from $250 billion to $190 billion.

Sometimes, to counteract the decrease in investment demand during a recession, a government offers a temporary investment tax credit. An investment tax credit gives firms that invest in plants and equipment a tax break. The tax credit

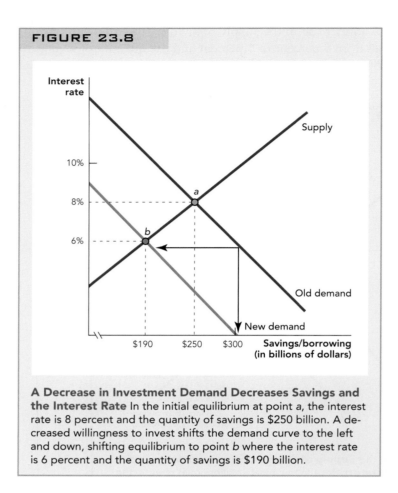

FIGURE 23.8

A Decrease in Investment Demand Decreases Savings and the Interest Rate In the initial equilibrium at point *a*, the interest rate is 8 percent and the quantity of savings is $250 billion. A decreased willingness to invest shifts the demand curve to the left and down, shifting equilibrium to point *b* where the interest rate is 6 percent and the quantity of savings is $190 billion.

is usually temporary to encourage firms to invest quickly, when the recession is still in full force. The tax credit means that projects that were unprofitable without the credit are profitable with the credit, so at any given interest rate firms are willing to invest more when a tax credit is available. In other words, the demand to borrow funds shifts to the right (and up) as shown in Figure 23.9.

The Role of Intermediaries: Banks, Bonds, and Stock Markets

Equilibrium in the market for loanable funds does not come about automatically. Savers move their capital, sometimes around the world, to find the highest returns. Entrepreneurs invest time and energy to find the right investments and the right loans. Equilibrium is brought about with the assistance of **financial institutions** such as banks, bond markets, and stock markets.

We will discuss banks, bond markets, and stock markets, but keep in mind the underlying common thread in the discussion. All of these institutions reduce the costs of moving savings from savers to borrowers and help mobilize savings toward productive uses. All of these institutions are middlemen, and they help to coordinate markets. At its core, a bank or a bond market is an institution that helps bring about the equilibrium in Figure 23.6 and helps bring resources to more highly valued uses.

CHECK YOURSELF

> How will greater patience shift the supply of savings and change the interest rate and quantity of savings?

> How will an increase in investment demand change the equilibrium interest rate and quantity of savings?

Financial institutions such as banks, bond markets, and stock markets reduce the costs of moving savings from savers to borrowers and investors.

FIGURE 23.9

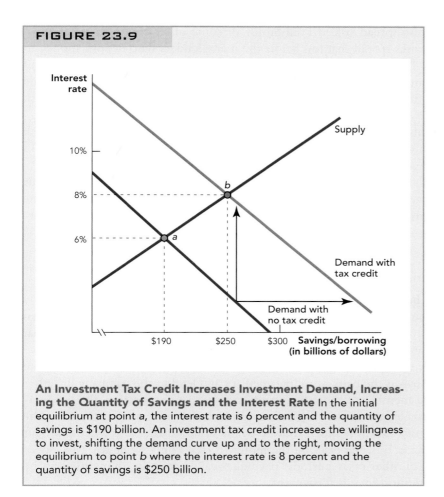

An Investment Tax Credit Increases Investment Demand, Increasing the Quantity of Savings and the Interest Rate In the initial equilibrium at point *a*, the interest rate is 6 percent and the quantity of savings is $190 billion. An investment tax credit increases the willingness to invest, shifting the demand curve up and to the right, moving the equilibrium to point *b* where the interest rate is 8 percent and the quantity of savings is $250 billion.

Banks

In their role as financial intermediary, banks receive savings from many individuals, pay them interest, and then loan these funds to borrowers or investors, charging them interest. Banks seek to earn profit by charging more for their loans than they pay for the savings. To earn this money, they must provide useful "middleman" services by evaluating investments and spreading risk.

Imagine that you, as a bank depositor, had to decide which companies were worth lending money to. Is this guy Fred Smith with his FedEx idea a genius or a kook? Banks don't always get it right, but by specializing in loan evaluation they have a better idea than most of us of which business ideas make sense. When banks specialize, individual savers don't have to evaluate which factories ought to be built or which businesses deserve to be supported.

Even if individuals could evaluate business ideas, it would be wasteful if every saver spent time evaluating the same business. Imagine that a business needs a million dollar loan. One thousand savers are each willing to lend the business $1,000. If each saver spent a day evaluating the quality of the business that would be 999 wasted days of effort. It makes more sense for the lenders to appoint a single person to evaluate the business on behalf of all of them. That's exactly what a bank does. Banks coordinate lenders and minimize information costs. Banks are thus an important example of the benefits of specialization and the division of labor.

Banks also spread risk. If Fred Smith, or some other borrower, defaults on his loan, banks spread that loss across the many lenders who deposit money in the bank. This avoids the risk that you have lent Fred Smith $50,000 and suddenly are out the entire sum. It's less risky and no less profitable to lend, one thousand firms $1 each than to lend one firm $1,000, so the spreading of risk encourages greater lending and investment.

Banks also play a role in the payments system. Money deposited in a bank can be drawn on with a check or debit card or via the ATM. We discuss banks and the payment system at greater length in Chapter 28.

Overall, banks make our lives simpler. We open our accounts, deposit our money, receive our interest payments, and write our checks; at the same time we are participating in the process of economic growth because the bank oversees a process by which our savings are turned into productive investments.

The Bond Market

Instead of borrowing from a bank, well-known corporations can borrow directly from the public. Your local pizza restaurant borrows from a bank, or perhaps even from relatives, because restaurants are a risky business and the finances of that company are hard for outside investors to evaluate. But when it comes to IBM or Toyota, investors can more easily find information about the firm and so they are willing to bypass the bank as an intermediary and lend to the company directly.

A **bond** is a sophisticated IOU that documents who owes how much and when payment must be made.

When a member of the public lends money to a corporation, the corporation acknowledges its debt by issuing a **bond**. *A bond is a corporate IOU.* The bond contract lists how much is owed to the bond's owner and when payment must be made. In some cases, all the money is owed on a single day (the day of maturity); in other cases, periodic payments, called coupon payments, must be made in addition to a final payment.

The New York Central and Hudson River Railroad Company borrowed money in 1897 for which they issued bonds, one of which is pictured on the left. The bond is an IOU that promises that the Central will pay the owner $1,000 in 1997. In addition, every six months until 1997, the Central promised to pay the owner $17.50. You can see from the picture why the periodic payments are called coupon payments: the coupons are on the right of the bond and can be clipped and sent to the issuer of the bond to receive payment.

A 100-year bond issued by the New York Central and Hudson River Railroad Company in 1897. The bond is an IOU that promised the owner $1,000 in 1997 and $17.50 every six months until that time.

Central's bond illustrates one of the advantages of bond finance—large sums of money can be raised now and invested in long-lived assets such as railroad track. The money can then be paid back over a long period of time, in the case of the Central over a 100-year period.

All bonds involve a risk that when the payments come due the borrower will not be able to pay; this is called default risk. The Central, for example, eventually defaulted when it went bankrupt, but it did pay its coupons until 1970. Major bond issues are graded by agencies like Moody's and Standard and Poor's. AAA, for example, is the highest grade issued by Standard and Poor's; that grade indicates, according to the rating agencies, that the bond is very likely to be paid. Grades range all the way from AAA to D when a firm is in default. Bonds rated less than BBB- are sometimes called "junk bonds." It's important to remember that risk can never be perfectly quantified and the rating agencies can be wrong—a point we will return to when we discuss the 2007–2008 financial crisis (see later in this chapter).

If a risky company wishes to borrow money, it has to promise a higher rate of interest because lenders will demand to be compensated for a greater risk of default. Why lend to a risky firm unless you have some prospect of earning higher returns?

Thus, the marketplace grades the risks of major investments and charges interest rates accordingly. As of 2007, Berkshire Hathaway, the firm managed by famed investor Warren Buffett, was evaluated by ratings agencies at AAA, the safest possible rating. Berkshire Hathaway was borrowing money at 4.48 percent while Ford Motor Company, which lost $12.6 billion in 2006, was rated only B and was having to pay 5.76 percent. At the time, mortgage rates were not much higher than 5.76 percent so the market was saying that in 2007 lending to the great Ford Motor Company involved about as much risk as lending to the average home buyer. Home loans are as cheap as they are, in part, because if the borrower defaults, the lender can seize the home and resell it; this is harder to do with a series of Ford automobile plants.

Similarly, can you think of one reason why interest rates on home loans are almost always lower than interest rates on vacation loans? The bank can repossess the house but not the vacation! The house is a form of **collateral,** something of value that by agreement becomes the property of the lender if the borrower defaults on the loan. Thus, the market for loanable funds is really a broad spectrum of markets; the interest rates differ depending on the borrower, repayment time, amount of the loan, type of collateral, and many other features of the loan.

> **Collateral** is something of value that by agreement becomes the property of the lender if the borrower defaults.

Greater risk can reduce the supply of funds to the market as a whole. If lenders expect a recession, for example, they may become concerned that many firms will go bankrupt and default on their debt. A lender who was willing to lend at 8 percent when he or she thought the risk was low will demand a higher return if the lender believes the risk of default has increased significantly.

Governments borrow money as well. In 2007 the U.S. government owed about $5 trillion dollars to private borrowers (individuals, firms, and governments other than the U.S. federal government). When the government borrows a lot of money, private consumption and investment can be **crowded out.** Imagine, for example, that the government borrows $100 billion to cover a budget deficit. In Figure 23.10 on the next page, the demand curve for loanable funds shifts to the right by $100 billion increasing the interest rate from 7 percent to 9 percent. The higher interest rate has two effects. First, it draws an additional $50 billion of savings into the market so total savings increase from $200 billion to $250 billion. Since greater savings mean less consumption, we can also say that consumption is reduced by $50 billion. Second, the higher interest rate means that some investments and other projects are no longer profitable so at a higher interest rate private borrowing falls. In Figure 23.10, we show private borrowing falling by $50 billion. Thus, the $100 billion necessary to cover the government's budget deficit comes from a combination of reduced consumption and reduced private investment and other private borrowing.

> **Crowding out** is the decrease in private consumption and investment that occurs when government borrows more.

We will return to the issues of crowding out, government debt, and deficits in Chapters 30 and 31.

When the U.S. government borrows, it issues a variety of different bonds. U.S. Treasury bonds or T-bonds are 30-year bonds that pay interest every 6 months. T-notes are bonds with maturities ranging from 2 to 10 years that also pay interest every 6 months. T-bills are bonds with maturities of a few days to 26 weeks that pay only at maturity. A bond that pays only at maturity is also called a zero-coupon bond or a discount bond since these bonds sell at a discount to their face value.

Treasury securities are desirable for many investors because they are easy to buy and sell and the U.S. government is unlikely to default on its payments. In

FIGURE 23.10

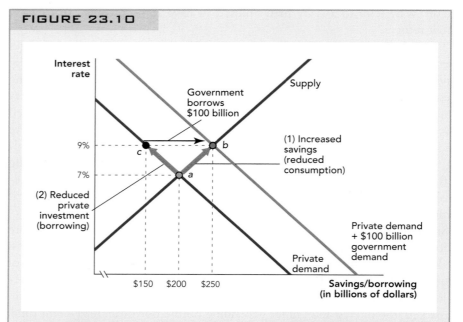

An Increase in Government Borrowing Crowds Out Private Consumption and Investment When the government borrows, it shifts the demand curve to the right moving the equilibrium from point *a* to point *b*. To reach the new equilibrium at point *b*, two things happen: (1) The higher interest rate draws forth more savings, which means that private consumption falls; and (2) the higher interest rate reduces the demand to borrow and invest. Thus, when the government borrows more, some of the increased borrowing is financed by reduced consumption and some by reduced investment.

general, short-term U.S. government securities tend to be the safest assets, and very short-term bonds, called commercial paper, issued by very large corporations tend to be safe as well. In addition, Treasury securities, especially T-bills, are important in monetary policy; the Federal Reserve buys and sells Treasury securities on a daily basis to influence the money supply (more on this in Chapter 29).

Bond Prices and Interest Rates It's often convenient to express the price of a bond in terms of an interest rate; this is easiest to do with a zero-coupon bond. Suppose, for example, that a bond with very little risk exists that will pay $1,000 in one year's time and that this bond is currently selling for $950. If you were to buy this bond today and hold it until maturity, you would earn $50, ($1,000 − $950), or a rate of return of $5.26\% = \dfrac{\$1000 - \$950}{\$950} \times 100$. Thus, every zero-coupon bond has an implied rate of return that can be calculated by subtracting the price from the value at maturity, often called the face value or FV, and then dividing by the price.

$$\text{Rate of return for a zero-coupon bond} = \frac{FV - \text{Price}}{\text{Price}} \times 100$$

Sellers of bonds must compete to attract lenders, who compare the implied rate of return on bonds with the rate of return on other assets. Imagine, for example, that the interest rate on say a savings account at a bank increases to 10 percent. Would you buy a bond that pays 5.26 percent? Would anyone?

Of course not. So if the interest rate rise to 10 percent, what must happen to the price of this bond? The price must fall. In fact, if the interest rate rises to 10 percent, the price of the bond must fall to $909. Why? Because at a price of $909, the rate of return on the bond is $10\% = \dfrac{\$1000 - \$909}{\$909} \times 100$. Thus, at a price of $909, sellers of bonds will be able to compete with banks, who are paying 10 percent on savings accounts, to attract funds, but at a higher price they won't find any buyers.

Our simple bond pricing example tells us two things of importance. First, equally risky assets must have the same rate of return. If they didn't, no one would buy the asset with the lower rate of return and the price of that asset would fall until the rate of return was competitive with other investments. This is called an **arbitrage** principle and we discuss it at greater length in the appendix to this chapter.

> **Arbitrage,** the buying and selling of equally risky assets, ensures that equally risky assets earn equal returns.

The second important lesson is that interest rates and bond prices move in opposite directions. When interest rates go up, bond prices fall. When interest rates go down, bond prices rise. We will be referring to this principle several times throughout the textbook so do study the principle and make a note of it:

> **> Interest rates and bond prices move in opposite directions.**

The inverse relationship between bond prices and interest rates tells us that in addition to default risk, people who buy bonds also face interest rate risk. For instance, perhaps a bond was issued in 2003 at an interest rate of 7 percent. If interest rates for comparable investments later rise to 9 percent, having bought a bond yielding 7 percent was in retrospect a mistake. If, instead, comparable interest rates were to fall to 3 percent, the bond purchase worked out for the better. The buyer locked in a 7 percent return when other rates of return were falling to 3 percent. In other words, bond buyers are making bets that interest rates will fall (bond prices will rise), or at least they are hoping that interest rates will fall. And similarly bond sellers are betting or hoping that interest rates will rise, which means bond prices will . . . do you remember? . . . fall. Again, for more on the relationship between bond prices and interest rates, see the chapter appendix.

The Stock Market

Just as businesses fund their activities by taking out bank loans and selling bonds, they also issue shares of stock. **Stocks** are shares of ownership in a corporation. Owners have a claim to the firm's profits, but remember that profit is revenue minus costs. In other words, profit is what is left over *after* everyone else—creditors, bond holders, suppliers, and employees—have been paid. If profits are high, shareholders benefit. They benefit directly if the firm pays out its profits in dividends or indirectly if the firm reinvests its profits in a way that increases the value of the stock. But if profits are low or negative, shareholders suffer losses.

> A **stock** or a share is a certificate of ownership in a corporation.

Stocks are traded on organized markets called stock exchanges. The New York Stock Exchange (NYSE) is the largest in the world. When new stocks are issued, that is called an **initial public offering** or an IPO. An IPO is the first time a stock is sold to the public.

> An **initial public offering (IPO)** is the first time a corporation sells stock to the public in order to raise capital.

You'll recall from the beginning of this chapter that simply buying and selling existing shares of stock does *not* increase net investment in the economy.

But when a firm sells *new* shares to the public, it typically uses the proceeds to fund investment, that is, to buy new capital goods. In addition, the possibility of offering equity or ownership in a firm opens the door to many business ventures that might never get off the ground, or might not be able to expand rapidly.

Consider Google. Google is today a household word but when the company began in September 1998 it was headquartered in a garage. Yet in August 2004, Google founders Sergei Brin and Larry Page sold $1.67 billion worth of stock in an IPO. The money helped Google to fund new investments and pay for research and development. In addition, Google's IPO turned the founders and the early investors into millionaires and billionaires. This big payoff was a reward for creating the company and making the early and risky investments that were necessary to get Google off the ground. Stock markets help people with great ideas become rich and that encourages innovation. It is no accident that the United States—one of the most innovative countries in the world—also has the best-developed stock and capital markets.

Selling part of Google to the public also let the founders diversify. If someday another search service bests Google, Brin and Page will not become paupers. This added safety also encourages innovation. People who come up with new ideas know that their wealth will not be locked into one firm.

We'll have a lot more to say about stock markets in Chapter 9, but for now what you need to know is that stock markets encourage investment and growth.

What Happens When Intermediation Fails?

Economic growth cannot occur without savings and those savings must be processed and intermediated through banks, bond markets, stock markets, and so on. Countries without these institutions have smaller markets for loans, use their savings less effectively, and make fewer good investments.[4] But why do some countries have poorly developed banking and financial systems?

The bridge between savers and borrowers can be broken in many ways, including insecure property rights, inflation and controls on interest rates, politicized lending, and massive bank failures and panics. These problems can break the bridge by (1) reducing the supply of savings, (2) raising the cost of intermediation, and (3) reducing the effectiveness of lending. Figure 23.11 illustrates the main ideas.

Insecure Property Rights

Consider, for example, the supply of savings. The expected return on savings depends on more than just the posted rate of interest at the bank. Some governments do not offer secure property rights to savers. That is, saved funds are not immune from later confiscation, freezes, or other restrictions.

During the financial crisis beginning in December 2001, for example, the Argentine government partially froze bank accounts for a year. Many of the banks subsequently went under, which meant that Argentine citizens lost their bank-based savings. This event was not a complete surprise. The Argentine government had a history of freezing bank accounts, such as during 1982 and 1989. Other countries in the region, such as Brazil in 1990, had also frozen bank accounts. Obviously this repeated pattern means that Argentines and Brazilians save less than they otherwise might wish to. Why save when those funds are simply being put up for grabs? Ana, a 40-year-old teacher from Argentina, kept her

UNDERSTAND YOUR world

FIGURE 23.11

Breaking the Bridge

savings in dollars in her house and then exchanged them for pesos to pay her bills. She said "You just can't put your money in banks here."[5] Ana is right, but unlike money in the bank, which can be lent out to fund investment, money under a mattress does not contribute to economic growth.

If individuals expect that contracts will be broken, they will be reluctant to invest in stock markets as well. For instance, the Russian government often does not respect the rights of minority shareholders and at times it has confiscated or restricted the value of their shareholdings, as in the case of the private energy company Yukos. The result is that many foreign investors are unwilling to put money into Russian ventures. They simply do not trust the Russian government, nor do they believe that Russian courts will enforce contracts impartially.

Law is one side of the equation, but custom and informal trust is another. In a healthy economy, shareholders expect that managers are interested in building their long-run reputations, rather than ripping off the company at every possible opportunity. When managers look only to short-run gains, it is hard to run a business enterprise, as investors will not entrust managers with the control of resources. Systems of monitoring and accounting, no matter how well developed, cannot overcome high levels of mistrust. This is a common problem in developing countries around the world but the Enron, WorldCom, and Madoff scandals demonstrate that the United States is also not immune to these problems. Trust is an important asset throughout the world.

Controls on Interest Rates and Inflation

Price controls on interest rates also cause the loanable funds market to malfunction. Consider a maximum ceiling on the interest rate that can be charged on a loan. Sometimes economists call these ceilings "usury laws"; usury laws date back to medieval times and earlier. Today most American states have usury laws, although often they have loopholes (they don't stop most credit card borrowing, for instance) or they are set at levels too high to influence most loan markets. Nonetheless, a binding and enforceable ceiling on interest rates would look like Figure 23.12 on the next page.

FIGURE 23.12

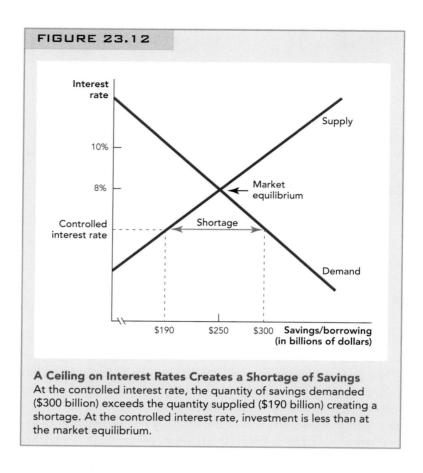

A Ceiling on Interest Rates Creates a Shortage of Savings
At the controlled interest rate, the quantity of savings demanded ($300 billion) exceeds the quantity supplied ($190 billion) creating a shortage. At the controlled interest rate, investment is less than at the market equilibrium.

The equilibrium is just like our analysis of price controls in Chapter 6. At the artificially low price, there is a shortage of credit, and many people who wish to borrow at the controlled interest rate cannot do so. Moreover, the control on interest rates reduces savings. In Figure 23.12 savings falls from $250 billion at the market equilibrium to just $190 billion at the controlled interest rate. Similarly, just as with price controls on oil, an interest rate control will cause a misallocation of savings and a loss of potential gains from exchange. Perhaps most important, investment, which is determined by the supply of savings, will fall below what it would be at the market equilibrium.

Inflation and controls on interest rates have often combined to destroy the incentive to save and thus to shrink the banking system. Imagine that interest rates are controlled at a nominal rate of 10 percent. Nominal just means the named rate, the rate on paper. At a nominal rate of 10 percent, $100 invested in the bank will return $110 in one year's time. Suppose, however, that inflation is running at 30 percent, which means that a basket of goods that cost $100 at the beginning of the year will cost $130 at the end of the year. Thus, a lender who lends $100 at the beginning of the year needs $130 at the end of the year just to keep even. If the lender only receives $110 at the end of the year, that's just like losing $20. Economists define the real rate of return as the nominal rate minus the inflation rate.

$$\text{Real interest rate} = \text{Nominal interest rate} - \text{Inflation rate}$$

In this case, the real interest rate is −20 percent (10 − 30 = −20). Thus, someone who lends at a nominal interest rate of 10 percent when the inflation rate is 30 percent is losing 20 percent per year. Inflation and interest rate controls turn savings accounts into wasting accounts. This is sometimes called "financial repression," and it is an extreme example of the situation illustrated in Figure 23.12.

When real interest rates turn negative, people take their money out of the banking system, using the cash to invest abroad (if they can), or to buy a real asset like land that is appreciating in value alongside inflation, or to simply consume more. In any of these cases, when many people pull their money out of the banking system, the supply of savings declines and financial intermediation becomes less efficient. Table 23.1 shows a number of examples of severely negative real interest rates. In every case, economic growth was also negative. Countries with negative real interest rates usually have many problems so we can't blame all of the poor economic

TABLE 23.1 Negative Interest Rates and Economic Growth

Country	Years	Real Interest Rate (percent)	Per Capita Growth (percent)
Argentina	1975–1976	−69	−2.2
Bolivia	1982–1984	−75	−5.2
Chile	1972–1974	−61	−3.6
Ghana	1976–1983	−35	−2.9
Peru	1976–1984	−19	−1.4
Poland	1981–1982	−33	−8.6
Sierra Leone	1984–1987	−44	−1.9
Turkey	1979–1980	−35	−3.1
Venezuela	1987–1989	−24	−2.7
Zaire	1976–1979	−34	−6.0
Zambia	1985–1988	−24	−1.9

Source: Easterly, W. 2002. *The Elusive Quest for Growth. Economists' Adventures and Misadventures in the Tropics.* MIT Press, Cambridge MA.

growth on inefficient financial intermediation. Nonetheless, studies show that even after controlling for other factors, negative real interest rates reduce financial intermediation and economic growth.

Politicized Lending and Government-Owned Banks

Japanese history from about 1990 to 2005 also illustrates the importance of banks in using a nation's savings effectively. During this period, the Japanese continued to save, but Japanese economic growth was zero or negative for most of these years. How can this have been? Many Japanese banks were bankrupt or propped up by the government. They were not allocating funds efficiently. Other banks were pressured to lend money to well-connected political allies, rather than to the most efficient new businesses. During this period, Japanese banks acted as storehouses for wealth, but they were not effective financial intermediaries. Japanese business innovation, and the Japanese standard of living, suffered accordingly.

In Japan, as in the United States, banks are privately owned so politicized lending, even when it occurs, is limited. But in many other countries most large banks are owned by the government. Government-owned banks are useful to authoritarian regimes that use the banks to direct capital to political supporters. While it might be politically wise for the ruler to support his uncle's firm, that uncle is probably not a superior entrepreneur. One important study by economists Rafael La Porta, Florencio Lopez-de-Silanes, and Andrei Shleifer finds that the larger the fraction of government-owned banks a country had in 1970, the slower was growth in per capita GDP and productivity over the next several decades.[6]

Bank Failures and Panics

Systematic problems in the banking system usually lead to large-scale economic crises. In the onset of America's Great Depression between 1929 and 1933, 11,000 banks—almost half of all U.S. banks—failed. The ripple effects were grim. Many people lost their life savings; they also had to curtail their spending, which meant that many businesses lost their customers and thus revenue. Many businesses were unable to get loans or daily working capital. Thus, bank failures were followed by a rash of small business failures. It took many years before the American banking system, and the American economy, recovered.

In their seminal work, *A Monetary History of the United States, 1867–1960*, Milton Friedman and Anna Schwartz argued that the Great Depression was brought about in part because the Federal Reserve—the U.S. central bank that is charged with overseeing the general health of the banking industry—failed in its job to prevent widespread bank failures.[7] (See Chapter 26 for further discussion of the Great Depression and Chapter 28 for more on the Federal Reserve.) Economist Ben Bernanke later showed that one of the reasons why bank failures were so crucial in the onset of the Great Depression was because banks provide loans to a particular class of borrowers and lenders.[8] According to Bernanke:

> As the real costs of intermediation increased, some borrowers (especially households, farmers, and small firms) found credit to be expensive and difficult to obtain. The effects of this credit squeeze . . . helped convert the severe but not unprecedented downturn of 1929–30 into a protracted depression.

By the way, if you recognize Bernanke's name, it is with good reason: he is now the chairman of the Federal Reserve. This study of American banking was one of Bernanke's most famous papers as an academic and helped give him the recognition to later be named head of the Federal Reserve.

Bernanke, as chairman of the Federal Reserve, had to face his own intermediation crisis during 2007 and 2008. Sometimes bank loans are "securitized," or bundled together and sold on the market as financial assets. Before the 2007–2008 financial crisis, many mortgage loans were bundled and sold as if they had very low risk. In reality, many of these securitized mortgages turned out to have much higher risk than had been advertised. In part some of the securitized bundles were sold on false terms, in part the credit rating agencies performed poorly, and in part people simply estimated risk incorrectly by assuming that house prices would continue rising more or less indefinitely.

When housing prices started to fall in 2006, many people defaulted on their mortgages and the U.S. economy suddenly ended up in a situation where many banks and other financial intermediaries were holding loans of questionable value. Yet because the mortgages had been bundled and sold many times over in different combinations and permutations, no one knew exactly whose loans were rotten or by how much. Investors suspected that some firms were going under (indeed Bear Stearns, the investment bank did crash, among others) but most investors had little advance notice on where the biggest problems would fall. As a result, no one wanted to lend or invest in banks and other intermediaries that might have significant quantities of mortgage assets on their books. Why lend or invest in a bank when the bank might be gone tomorrow? Investors also became wary of any institution that lent money to potentially troubled banks, even if that institution did not itself hold mortgage-backed assets. But when financial intermediaries can't get new funds, the bridge between savers and borrowers collapses. Indeed, credit markets froze up in parts of 2008 for precisely this reason. Bernanke, fearing a financial panic similar to that

UNDERSTAND YOUR **world**

which gripped the Great Depression, responded with some very aggressive and dramatic ways of getting credit markets back on their feet. We'll consider those remedies in more detail in Chapters 28 and 29.

CHECK YOURSELF

> How do usury laws (controls on interest rates) cause savings to decline?

> Besides decreasing the number of banks, how do bank failures hinder financial intermediation?

> How does awarding bank loans by political criteria or by cronyism (to your pals) affect the efficiency of the economy?

□ Takeaway

Individuals save to prepare for their retirement, to help fund large purchases, and to cushion swings in their income—most generally, savings help individuals, firms, and governments to smooth their consumption over time. Similarly, individuals, firms, and governments borrow to finance large purchases like a home, to invest in new capital, or in the case of governments to finance large expenditures such as are necessary for a war. Once again, borrowing helps agents to smooth their consumption streams. Financial institutions bridge the gap between savers and borrowers.

Financial institutions also collect savings, evaluate investments, and diversify risk. Banks, bonds, and stock markets help finance new and innovative ideas, such as Google and Federal Express. Financial intermediation is a central part of healthy economic growth.

Capital markets are becoming increasingly global, but globalization does not differ in kind from how markets work within a single country or region. Entrepreneurs seek out profitable trading opportunities to bring resources, including investment, to more highly valued economic uses. This happens both within borders and across borders.

Without effective financial intermediation, an economy will end up adrift. Insecure property rights, inflation, politicized lending, and bank failures all contribute to the breakdown of financial intermediation. Whenever possible, government policy should seek to avoid these outcomes.

□ CHAPTER REVIEW

KEY CONCEPTS

Saving, p. 484

Investment, p. 484

Time preference, p. 485

Market for loanable funds, p. 489

Financial institutions, p. 492

Bond, p. 494

Collateral, p. 495

Crowding out, p. 495

Arbitrage, p. 497

Stock, p. 497

Initial public offering (IPO), p. 497

FACTS AND TOOLS

1. If people want to smooth their consumption over time, what will they tend to do when they win the lottery: Spend most of it within a year or save most of it for later?

2. A large number of economic and psychological studies demonstrate that people who are impatient in one area of their life tend to be impatient in other areas as well. This isn't true in every single case, but of course that doesn't matter if we're trying to understand the "typical person." Based on your general knowledge and educated guessing:

   a. Who is more likely to smoke: A criminal or a law-abiding citizen?

b. Who is more likely to shoot heroin: A person who saves 20 percent of their income or a person who can't ever find a way to save?

c. Who is more likely to have a lot of credit card debt: A smoker or a nonsmoker?

3. The typical savings supply curve has a positive slope. If a nation's saving supply curve had a perfectly vertical slope, what would that mean?

a. People in this country save the same amount no matter what the interest rate is.

b. People in this country are extremely sensitive to interest rates when deciding how much to save.

4. Consider three countries: Jovenia (average age: 25), Mittelaltistan (average age: 45), and Decrepetia (average age: 75). Based on the lifecycle theory, which of these countries will probably have:

a. High savings rates?

b. High rates of borrowing?

c. High rates of dissaving? (That's spending your past savings.)

Note: The way for entire countries to save is to build up the stock of productive capital either at home (through high investment rates) or abroad (by exporting more than importing, that is, running a trade surplus, and using the proceeds to buy foreign investment goods and assets).

5. Sometimes, in supply and demand models, it's not clear who "supplies" and who "demands." For instance, in the labor market, it's individual workers (not firms) who supply labor. In the loanable funds market, who is usually the supplier and who is usually the demander? Choose the correct answer.

a. Entrepreneurs supply loanable funds and savers demand loanable funds.

b. Entrepreneurs supply loanable funds and savers also supply loanable funds.

c. Entrepreneurs demand loanable funds and savers demand loanable funds.

d. Entrepreneurs demand loanable funds and savers supply loanable funds.

6. In each of the following, answer either "bank account," "bonds," or "stocks."

a. Which investment is typically the riskiest?

b. Which is a corporate IOU?

c. Which one gives you an ownership "share" in a company?

d. Which one usually lets you "withdraw" part of your investment at any time, for any reason?

e. Which form of investment usually spreads your money over the largest number of investment projects?

f. Which is usually rated by private companies like Moody's or Standard and Poor's?

g. Which one is offered by the U.S. government as well as by private corporations?

7. If savers don't feel safe putting their money in banks or buying bonds, what's the best way to sum up what's happening in the market for loanable funds?

a. Supply of savings falls and the interest rate falls.

b. Supply of savings falls and the interest rate rises.

c. Demand for savings falls and the interest rate falls.

d. Demand for savings falls and the interest rate rises.

8. When governments outlaw high interest rates and the ceiling is binding, what probably happens to the total amount of money borrowed?

a. It rises because borrowers are protected from high interest rates.

b. It falls because savers aren't willing to lend as much money at this low interest rate.

c. Both a and b are usually true.

9. Calculate the real interest rate in the following five cases:

a. Nominal interest rate = 4 percent, inflation rate = 2 percent

b. Nominal interest rate = 6 percent, inflation rate = 3 percent

c. Nominal interest rate = 10 percent, inflation rate = 15 percent

d. Nominal interest rate = 0 percent, inflation rate = −2 percent (An example of the Friedman rule: see Challenge question 2 below on this case for further information)

e. Nominal interest rate = 1,000 percent, inflation rate = 1,100 percent (Not uncommon during hyperinflations, as we'll see later)

10. If financial intermediation breaks down, what category of GDP will probably fall the most: consumption, investment, government purchases, or net exports?

11. a. In a competitive banking system, what tends to happen to banks that make low-interest rate loans to the banker's friends: Do they tend to be more successful or less successful than other, more ruthless banks?

  b. Given your answer to the previous question, how do you suspect that politicized government-owned banks stay in business?

THINKING AND PROBLEM SOLVING

1. Let's work out a simple example where a person smoothes her consumption over time. Gwen is a real estate agent, and she knows that she will have some good years and some bad years. She figures that half the time she'll earn $90,000 per year, and half the time she'll earn $20,000 per year. These numbers are after taxes and after saving for retirement. These numbers are all she has to worry about.

  a. If we ignore interest costs just to keep things simple, how much should Gwen consume in the average year?

  b. How many dollars will she save during the good years?

  c. How many dollars will she borrow during the bad years? (Note: "Borrowing," in this context, is basically the same as "pulling money out of savings.")

2. Let's think about how the supply of savings might shift in two different cases.

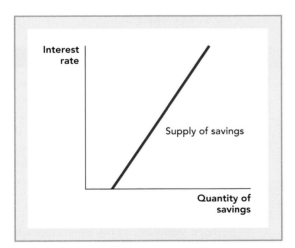

  a. Under current U.S. law, businesses are allowed to automatically enroll you in a savings plan that puts 5 percent of your salary in a retirement fund. Suppose Congress *abolishes*

this law: draw the appropriate shift in the supply curve, and label it "a."

  b. If Americans all go to see the classic Robin Williams/Ethan Hawke film *Dead Poets Society* and decide to *carpe diem,* or if they read the quotes of a famous Mediterranean preacher who said, "Take therefore no thought for the morrow," or if they watch the appalling 1970s sitcom *One Day at a Time,* what direction is the supply of savings likely to shift? Denote this with a new supply curve labeled "b."

3. In this chapter, we focus on three big functions that banks perform:

  I. They evaluate business ideas to see who's worth lending to.

  II. They spread an investment's risk among many different projects.

  III. They make it easier for people to make payments through checks, ATMs, and wire transfers.

  None of these functions are unique to banks. In the following anecdotes, is the person doing function I, function II, or function III?

  a. Emmanuel donates a little money to five different charities, in the hopes that at least one of them will do some good in the world.

  b. In Lorien's family, she's the one who specializes in deciding which bank everyone else in the family will use.

  c. Popeye always has a little cash on hand, so he is always able to lend a little money to Wimpy and Olive Oyl at lunchtime.

  d. George spends his time at the Carlyle Group deciding which companies are worth his investment partners' dollars.

  e. Scooter wants a good education, so he takes a variety of different classes: some history, some economics, some physics.

  f. Frances subscribes to *Consumer Reports* to decide which washing machine to buy.

4. In many poor countries, the banking system just isn't advanced enough to lend money for many large investments. Based on this single fact, where would you expect to see more entrepreneurs coming from rich families rather than poor families: In the rich countries or the poor countries? Why?

5. a. The financial analysts at Lexmark have evaluated five major projects. Each project, if it actually goes forward, will be financed by going to a bank to borrow the money. They've calculated a "break even interest rate": If they can borrow cash to pay for the project at less than that rate, the project will likely be a success; if the rate is higher, then it's not worth it.

	Cost	Break even interest rate
Project A	$100 million	8 percent
Project B	$50 million	12 percent
Project C	$200 million	50 percent
Project D	$25 million	4 percent
Project E	$150 million	10 percent

a. If the interest rate is 11 percent, which projects will Lexmark take on? If the market interest rate is 6 percent, which projects will it take on?

b. Let's turn the above information into a demand curve for loanable funds.

Organize this data to convert it into Lexmark's "loanable funds demand" curve. Note: It will look just like an ordinary demand curve, only with more breaks.

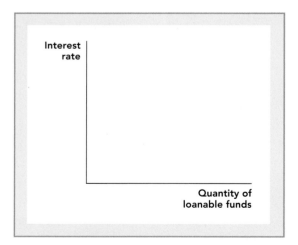

6. In each of the three cases, which bond will usually pay a higher interest rate?

a. A bond rated AAA, or a bond rated BBB?

b. A U.S. government bond, or a General Motors bond?

c. A Citibank bond that gets repaid in 30 years or a Citibank bond that gets repaid in 1 year?

7. Consider your answers to the previous question. When one bond pays a higher interest rate than another bond, is that mostly because savers are less willing to *supply* loanable funds to the higher-rate bond, or because businesses are more interested in *demanding* loanable funds for the higher-rate bond? Why is this so?

8. Consider Figure 23.10. Would a rise in government borrowing make it harder or easier for a new business to sell new stocks in an initial public offering (IPO)? In other words, are government bonds and corporate stocks substitutes for each other or complements to each other?

9. "If the government keeps real interest rates low (either by raising inflation or by decreeing low interest rates), then this encourages extra borrowing by businesses, which leads to more investment purchases, a larger stock of capital equipment, and higher productivity. Therefore, an interest rate ceiling is a good idea." What's wrong with this argument?

10. a. If a zero-coupon bond with a face value of $1,000 payable in 1 year sells for $925, what is the interest rate?

b. If another bond with the same face value and maturity sells for $900, what is the interest rate on this bond?

c. Which bond, that discussed in question a or question b, would you rather invest in? Are you sure? Think again!

CHALLENGES

1. The United States borrows a lot of money from other countries, as we noted at the start of this chapter. If you wanted to use the lifecycle theory to explain this, would you say that the United States is acting like a "young" country, an "old" country, or a "middle-aged" country? There's more than one correct way to answer this question.

2. a. It sure would be nice if the money in your purse or wallet could pay interest, wouldn't it? Nobel laureate Milton Friedman once pointed out that it's actually quite easy for money to pay interest—"real" interest, that is. Money in your wallet or purse (or most checking accounts) pays 0 percent nominal interest. But if the price level is falling, then the buying power of your money is constantly increasing, minute by minute. Let's see how this works.

Calculate the real rate in the following cases:

Real Rate	Nominal Rate	Inflation Rate
	0 percent	−1 percent
	0 percent	−2 percent
	0 percent	−3 percent

b. Using the rule of 70, how many years would it take for the buying power of $1 to double in each of the above three cases?

c. Friedman argued that since, in the United States, the real rate on safe assets tends to be about 2 percent, then the U.S. government should push for an inflation rate of −2 percent (a 2 percent deflation). At this rate of −2 percent, would people want to hold more money in their purses and checking accounts than they do now, less money than now, or would there be no change?

3. Lenders are more willing to lend if the borrower can put up collateral for the loan. Remember that collateral is something of value that by agreement becomes the property of the lender if the borrower defaults. In the United States, many small business owners borrow money for their business by using their houses or business assets as collateral. But in many developing countries, people don't have secure property rights or *title* to the land or house in which they live. In Bangalore, India, for example, it's nearly impossible to say who owns a piece of land and about 85 percent of the people in that city live on a piece of land for which they have no title. How difficult do you think it would be for a small business person in Bangalore to get a modest-sized loan?

CHAPTER **APPENDIX**

Bond Pricing and Arbitrage

Bond pricing may seem complicated but it can be understood with a few simple principles. Let's start with something more familiar than bonds. Suppose that you invest $100 in a savings account that pays a 10 percent rate of interest. How much money will you have in one year? That's easy; every dollar invested at 10 percent turns into $1.10 in one year so $100 invested at 10 percent turns into $110, which we can write as $100 × (1.10) = $110.

More generally, let's call the money that you invest the present value (PV), let's call the interest rate, r, and let's call the money that you will withdraw from the bank in one year the future value (FV). Then, the relationship between PV, r, and FV is simply:

$$PV \times (1 + r) = FV \tag{1}$$

For example, if you invested $100 in present value at an interest rate of 5 percent, how much money would you have in a year (FV)? Substituting in equation (1) we have $100 × (1.05) = $105.

Okay, now let's ask a slightly more difficult question. Suppose that the interest rate is 10 percent and that in one year you would like to have the future value of $100. How much do you need to put in the bank today? In other words, if the interest rate is 10 percent and you want a future value of $100, what present value do you need to put in the bank? Let's fill in what we know:

$$PV \times (1.10) = \$100$$

To solve for PV divide both sides by 1.10.

$$PV = \frac{\$100}{1.10} = \$90.91$$

Thus, if the interest rate is 10 percent and we want $100 in the bank in one year, we need to invest $90.91 today. More generally, we can rewrite equation (1) in any of the following three ways depending on whether we want to solve for FV, PV, or r:

$$PV \times (1 + r) = FV \tag{1}$$

$$PV = \frac{FV}{(1 + r)} \tag{2}$$

$$(1 + r) = \frac{FV}{PV} \tag{3}$$

We now have everything we need to explain bond pricing. Imagine that the interest rate is 10 percent and suppose that a bond exists that promises to pay $100 in one year's time. Thus, the future value of the bond—conveniently this is also called the face value—is $100, the interest rate, r, is 10 percent, and we want to know PV. We can use version (2) of our equation:

$$PV = \frac{\$100}{1.10} = \$90.91$$

In other words, when the interest rate is 10 percent, a bond promising to pay $100 in one year will sell for $90.91.

Students are often confused by the fact that interest rates and bond prices move in *opposite* directions: that is, when the interest rate rises, bond prices fall and when the interest rate falls, bond prices rise. But now we can explain this result easily. We know that at an interest rate of 10 percent a bond that has a future value of $100 will have a price or present value of $90.91. So what happens to the present value of the same bond when the interest rate falls to 5 percent?

$$PV = \frac{FV}{1 + r}$$

Substituting what we know, we have:

$$PV = \frac{\$100}{1.05} = \$95.24$$

Thus, when the interest rate falls from 10 percent to 5 percent, the price of the bond rises from $90.91 to $95.23.

We can see from version (2) of our formula that the price of a bond rises when the interest rate falls (and vice versa), but what is the economics behind this result? To understand the economics, we will use version (3) of our equation.

Let's suppose that the interest rate falls from 10 percent to 5 percent—in other words, the most that investors can earn on their loanable funds is a 5 percent rate of return. But imagine that instead of rising to $95.24 that the price of a bond paying $100 in one year's time stayed at $90.91. How much could investors earn by investing in this bond? The present value of the bond is $90.91, the future value is $100, so the return *on this bond* is:

$$(1 + r) = \frac{FV}{PV} = \frac{\$100}{\$90.91} = 1.10$$

Now what would you do if every other investment in the economy is earning a 5 percent rate of return but an equally safe bond exists that earns 10 percent? Correct, you would buy the bond paying 10 percent. And what happens when you—and everyone else—starts buying this extraordinary bond? Correct, the bond increases in price and as it increases in price, the return on the bond falls. In fact, the bond will increase in price and its rate of return will fall until it earns a rate of return roughly equal to that on similarly risky investments elsewhere in the economy.

Our last result can be stated more generally: *buying and selling will equalize the rate of return on equally risky assets.* The buying and selling of equally risky assets is called arbitrage. Arbitrage is a very important idea with many more implications than we can address here, but if you continue on in economics or finance you will study arbitrage in more detail.

We have shown how the simplest types of bonds are priced. Many bonds mature in more than one year and many bonds include coupon payments: periodic payments in addition to the final payment at maturity. The formula for determining the present value of a bond that matures in more than one year and that has coupon payments is more complicated than formula 2 but the ideas are exactly the same. We will give one quick example to illustrate.

Let's begin, once again, with a $100 investment in a savings account that pays a 10 percent rate of interest. But this time, let's suppose that we invest the money for two years—what is the future value of this investment? We can break our two-year investment into two one-year investments. We first invest $100 at 10 percent giving us $110 at the end of the first year. We then invest $110 at 10 percent for another year, which gives us $121 at the end of two years. In general terms we can write:

$$[PV \times (1 + r_1)] \times (1 + r_2) = FV \qquad \text{(A1)}$$

The term in the square brackets is how much we will have after the first year of investment; we then multiply this amount by $(1 + r_2)$, the rate of interest in year two, to give us the amount that we will have at the end of two years.

As we did before, we can divide both sides of equation A1 by $(1 + r_1)(1 + r_2)$ in order to rewrite A1 as:

$$PV = \frac{FV}{(1 + r_1)(1 + r_2)} \qquad \text{(A2)}$$

Let's use formula A2 to figure out the present value or selling price of a bond that pays $100 in two years when the interest rate in year one and year two is 10 percent. Substituting what we know, we have:

$$PV = \frac{\$100}{(1.10) \times (1.10)} = \$82.64$$

Thus, if the interest rate in year one and year two is 10 percent then a bond that pays $100 two years from now has a present value or selling price of $82.64.

Now here is the big payoff. What is the price of a bond that pays $100 at the end of year one and another $100 at the end of year two? We can easily price this bond because this bond is just a combination of two bonds, one of which pays $100 at the end of year one and one of which pays $100 at the end of year two. But we just calculated the value of these bonds! And, because of arbitrage, the combination bond must sell for the same price as the sum of the two bonds that we calculated earlier or $173.55 = $90.91 + $82.64.

We can also calculate the value of the combination bond directly. When the interest rate is 10 percent, the PV of a bond that pays $100 in one year and another $100 in two years is:

$$PV = \frac{\$100}{1.10} + \frac{\$100}{(1.10) \times (1.10)} = \$173.55$$

Following through on the same logic, we can now calculate the price of very complicated bonds. The present value of a bond that makes potentially different payments every year for n years is:

$$PV = \frac{Payment_1}{(1 + r)} + \frac{Payment_2}{(1 + r)^2} + \frac{Payment_3}{(1 + r)^3} + \ldots \frac{FinalPayment_n}{(1 + r)^n}$$

Bond Pricing with a Spreadsheet

We can calculate the price of bonds like this using a spreadsheet. Figure A23.1 shows a bond that pays $100 in each of the first nine years and then in the tenth year it pays $1,000. The present value of each payment is calculated in Column C. Note that the formula in cell C2=B2/(1+$D$2)^A2 is equivalent to $\frac{Payment_1}{(1 + r)}$. Copying this formula for the nine other payments gives us a column of present values, which we sum up in cell C14 to find the price of the bond, $1,324.70.

FIGURE A23.1

	C2		f_x =B2/(1+$D$2)^A2	
	A	B	C	D
1	Year	Payment	Present Value	Interest Rate
2	1	$100	$95.24	0.05
3	2	$100	$90.70	
4	3	$100	$86.38	
5	4	$100	$82.27	
6	5	$100	$78.35	
7	6	$100	$74.62	
8	7	$100	$71.07	
9	8	$100	$67.68	
10	9	$100	$64.46	
11	10	$1,000	$613.91	
12				
13		Sum PV		
14		or Price->	$1,324.70	

You can easily vary the interest rate to see what happens to the price of the bond. If the interest rate rises to 10 percent, for example, we have the result in Figure A23.2 on the next page.

FIGURE A23.2

	C14	▼	f_x =SUM(C2:C11)	
	A	B	C	D
1	Year	Payment	Present Value	Interest Rate
2	1	$100	$90.91	0.1
3	2	$100	$82.64	
4	3	$100	$75.13	
5	4	$100	$68.30	
6	5	$100	$62.09	
7	6	$100	$56.45	
8	7	$100	$51.32	
9	8	$100	$46.65	
10	9	$100	$42.41	
11	10	$1,000	$385.54	
12				
13		Sum PV		
14		or Price->	$961.45	
15				

And thus the price of the bond falls to $961.45. Note once again that a higher interest rate means a lower price for the bond. It's also interesting to see that a higher interest rate has a small effect on payments that come soon (compare the PV of the first payment in Figure A23.1 and Figure A23.2), but a very large effect on payments far into the future (compare the PV of the final payment in the two scenarios).

One final point of importance. Bond pricing might seem to be far away from your interests but the techniques in this appendix can be used to price and understand any kind of asset that has a payment stream over time. A mortgage, for example, is very similar to a bond except instead of receiving bond payments, you will typically be sending mortgage payments. If you want to compare two different mortgages, for example, a 20-year mortgage and a 30-year mortgage where the mortgages have different interest rates, you will want to compute the present value of each mortgage to find the one with the lowest PV. Online mortgage calculators help you to do this. What those calculators do is compute present values using the same types of techniques as found in this appendix.

24

Unemployment and Labor Force Participation

CHAPTER OUTLINE

Defining Unemployment

Frictional Unemployment

Structural Unemployment

Cyclical Unemployment

Labor Force Participation

Takeaway

Thirty-six thousand travel agents lost their jobs on November 10, 1999. Actually, it didn't happen quite that fast, but when Expedia.com went public there were 124,000 travel agents in the United States but by 2006 there were less than 88,000. Even though tourism is increasing, travel agents are disappearing as more people book their travel online.

The disappearance of the travel agent represents a recurring story in American history. Many jobs have disappeared—blacksmiths, chimney sweeps, and dark-room technicians, for example, are no longer in demand. Employment in other fields has greatly declined. For example, in 1910 there were 11.5 million farm workers in the United States; today there are less than a million. New jobs, however, have replaced old jobs. Typewriter repairmen are no longer in demand but the Geek Squad, an "elite tactical unit of highly trained Agents that focus solely on computer and other technology support," is hiring. Jobs are growing rapidly in high-tech areas like software engineering and the bio-sciences, but a wealthier society also means more and better-paying jobs in professions that have been around for a long time. Today, for example, there are over 212,000 professional athletes in the United States—more than in any other country or any other time in history.

A growing economy is a changing economy and *some* unemployment is a necessary consequence of economic growth. The unemployment rate in France, however, has hovered around 10 percent for several decades. High and long-lasting unemployment is unlikely to be caused by economic growth. Thus, there are different types of unemployment with different causes.

Figure 24.1 on the next page illustrates the organization of this chapter. We are going to start at the top with the issue that is most prominent in the economics and business news, namely whether or not workers are employed. We explain

LOGO COURTESY OF GEEK SQUAD

Typewriter repairmen are gone but the Geek Squad has hired thousands of Geeks in the last several years.

FIGURE 24.1

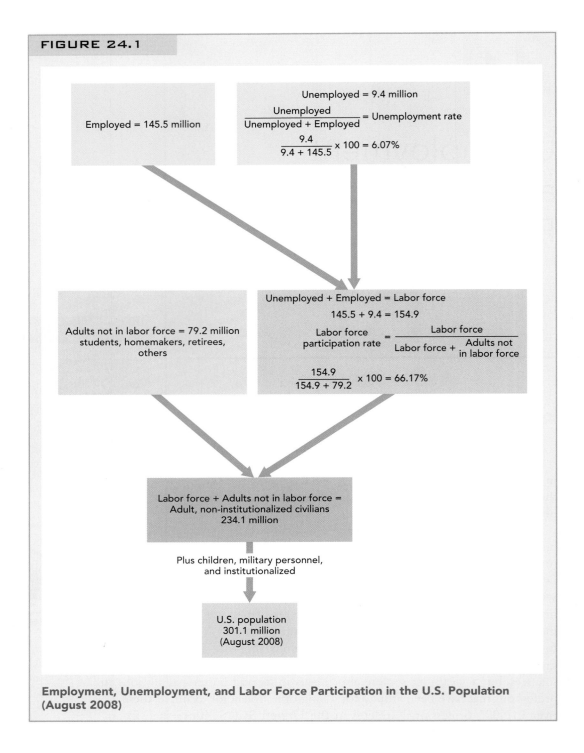

Employment, Unemployment, and Labor Force Participation in the U.S. Population (August 2008)

how unemployment is defined and then the different types of unemployment and their causes.

Don't forget, however, that many individuals neither have a job nor are looking for work—these individuals are not part of the labor force. As we move down the tree we will ask: Why do some people choose to be in the labor force while others do not? Why is it, for example, that most women are in the (paid) labor force today even though this was uncommon in the 1950s? And why is labor force participation for some workers much higher in some countries than in others? The topic of labor force participation makes up the second half of the chapter. And what about total population, at the very bottom of this structure? For that you must take a demography course, but you'll even find a brief discussion of birth control at the close of the chapter.

Defining Unemployment

Is a 6-year-old without a job unemployed? Is someone in prison unemployed? What about a retired 60-year-old? In all cases the answer is no. We want to count someone as **unemployed** only if they are *willing and able to work but cannot find a job*. In practice, this means to be counted as unemployed, a person must be an adult (16 years or older), not institutionalized (e.g., not in prison), a civilian, and, most important, they must be *looking for work*. Similarly, to be counted as employed, a person must be an adult, noninstitutionalized civilian with a job.

In August 2008, there were 9.4 million unemployed persons in the United States and 145.5 million employed persons. Together, the unemployed and the employed make up the **labor force** of 154.9 million (9.4 + 145.5).

The **unemployment rate** is the percentage of the labor force without a job.

Unemployed workers are adults who do not have a job but who are looking for work.

The **labor force** is all workers, employed plus unemployed.

The **unemployment rate** is the percentage of the labor force without a job.

$$\text{Unemployment rate} = \frac{\text{Unemployed}}{\text{Unemployed} + \text{Employed}} \times 100$$

$$= \frac{\text{Unemployed}}{\text{Labor force}} \times 100$$

Thus, in August 2008, the unemployment rate was 6.07 percent:

$$\frac{9.4 \text{ million}}{9.4 \text{ million} + 145.5 \text{ million}} \times 100 = \frac{9.4}{154.9} \times 100 = 6.07\%$$

Once we have examined the issue of unemployment, we will investigate some of the determinants of the **labor force participation rate,** the percentage of the adult, civilian, noninstitutionalized population (adults for short) in the labor force.

Figure 24.1 summarizes our discussion by showing how the U.S. population is divided among the employed, the unemployed, and those not in the labor force.

The **labor force participation rate** is the percentage of adults in the labor force.

How Good an Indicator Is the Unemployment Rate?

We are interested in the unemployment rate because unemployment, especially long-term unemployment, can be financially and psychologically devastating to the unemployed individuals and their families. Unemployment also means that the economy is underperforming—labor that could be used to produce valuable goods and services is being wasted. The unemployment rate is the single best indicator of how well the labor market is working in both of these senses, but it is an incomplete indicator.

Individuals without a job are not counted as unemployed if they are not actively looking for work. But some people who are unemployed for a long period of time may get discouraged and stop looking for work even though they want a job. It's difficult to know exactly how many **discouraged workers** there

Discouraged workers are workers who have given up looking for work but who would still like a job.

▶▶ SEARCH ENGINE
Statistics on unemployment and alternative measures of labor underutilization can be found at the Bureau of Labor Statistics.

are because the concept is not well defined. Many people who are happily retired would take a job if the wage were high enough, but should every retired person count as a discouraged worker? The Bureau of Labor Statistics (BLS) keeps statistics on one definition of discouraged workers, which it defines as workers who have not looked for a job in the past four weeks but who are available for work and who have looked for work in the past 12 months. Using this definition, the number of discouraged workers in the United States is small (approximately 0.3 percent of the labor force in 2008).

The unemployment rate also doesn't measure the quality of the jobs people take or how well workers are matched to their jobs. A taxi driver with a PhD in chemistry, for example, is counted as fully employed by the BLS. Similarly, a worker who has a part-time job but who wants a full-time job is counted as fully employed. If we counted these workers as partially unemployed, the unemployment rate would be higher, but defining and measuring partial employment isn't easy. If a taxi driver has a BA in English, should that be counted as almost fully employed? Nearly everyone wants a better job in some dimension (more hours, fewer hours, closer to home, higher wages, better benefits, etc.) so is everyone less than fully employed?

Given these imperfections, economists also look at other measures of labor underutilization and indicators of how well the labor market is performing, such as the labor force participation rate, the number of full-time jobs, and average wages. Fortunately, most of these other indicators (and probably many other job aspects that are more difficult to measure) correlate well with the official unemployment rate. (See Thinking and Problem Solving question #11 for more on this.) When the unemployment rate goes down, for example, wages and benefits usually go up.

Frictional Unemployment

Economists distinguish three types of unemployment: frictional, structural, and cyclical. We start with frictional.

What is the fastest way to sell a house? Lower the price! At a low enough price, any house will sell quickly. So selling houses is easy: It's finding a price that the seller is willing to accept and the buyer is willing to pay that is difficult. In the same way, it's always easy to find a job if you are willing to work for peanuts. Finding a job that you want at a wage that you will accept and the employer will pay, however, takes time and effort. The difficulty of matching employees to employers creates friction in the labor market, and the resulting temporary unemployment is called frictional unemployment. Thus, **frictional unemployment** is short-term unemployment caused by the ordinary difficulties of matching employee to employer.

Scarcity of information is one of the causes of frictional unemployment. Workers do not know all of the job opportunities available to them and employers do not know all the available candidates and their respective qualifications. The Internet has probably lowered the underlying rate of frictional unemployment by making it easier for workers to search for jobs and for firms to search for workers.

Frictional unemployment usually doesn't last very long. If the economy is not in a recession, it might take a few weeks to find a new job, or for specialized workers perhaps a few months but not much longer. Figure 24.2 shows the typical duration of unemployment in the United States. In 2005, a non-recession

CHECK YOURSELF
> Other than not working, what other factors are part of the definition of unemployment?
> Define the labor force.
> Is the labor force participation rate close to 100 percent? How is it defined?

Frictional unemployment is short-term unemployment caused by the ordinary difficulties of matching employee to employer.

ZDOROV KIRILL VLADIMIROVICH/SHUTTERSTOCK

year, 35.1 percent of the unemployed were jobless for less than five weeks. Another 30.4 percent were jobless for only 5 weeks to 14 weeks. The remaining one-third were jobless for more than 14 weeks with 11.7 percent jobless for more than a year. In the United States in a non-recession year, a significant fraction of unemployment is frictional.

Later, we will discuss long-term unemployment, especially in Germany, France, Italy, and Spain, and how it differs from unemployment in the United States. In these countries, a much larger fraction of the unemployed are unemployed for more than one year.

Frictional unemployment is a large share of total unemployment because the U.S. economy is so dynamic. Innovation and the relentless pressure of competition drive progress. Progress, however, is not simply creating new jobs and adding them to the old. Rather it's about creating new jobs and destroying old jobs. Webmasters are in; travel agents are out. We can see this process in more detail by looking at statistics on job creation and destruction.

In a typical month in 2005, for example, 230,000 jobs were added to the economy. The figure is impressive but it hides an underlying reality that is even more impressive. In 2005, there were an average of 4.77 million new hires *every month,* but there were also approximately 4.54 million new job separations (quits and layoffs) *every month.* The difference between the hires and the separations is the net number of new jobs (4.77 − 4.54 = 0.23 million or 230,000 new jobs per month). Thus, even in a year when net employment does not change, millions of jobs are created and millions of jobs are destroyed. "Creative destruction," a term coined by economist Joseph Schumpeter, describes this process well.

Creative destruction occurs at the level of the firm and the industry. Even in an industry with constant or increasing employment, the location of employment changes as uncompetitive firms disappear or shrink and new firms grow. K-Mart filed for bankruptcy in 2002 and laid off 34,000 workers, but in that same year its more productive rival, Wal-Mart, hired 139,000 workers.[1]

Creative destruction also occurs at the level of the industry. During the 1970s, for example, the real price of oil increased from about $10 a barrel to nearly $80 a barrel (see Chapter 3, Figure 3.9). The oil shocks required a fundamental reallocation of labor from industries that were heavily dependent on oil to industries less dependent on oil. But it takes more time (and thus more unemployment) for workers to move from one industry to another industry than to move from one firm to another firm in the same industry—this brings us to the topic of structural unemployment.

Structural Unemployment

Structural unemployment is persistent, long-term unemployment. Isn't it redundant to say that unemployment is persistent *and* long-term? Not quite. In France, Germany, Italy, and Spain, for example, approximately 40 to 50 percent of the unemployed have been unemployed for more than one year and this has been true for about 20 years.[2] Very few individuals, however, have been

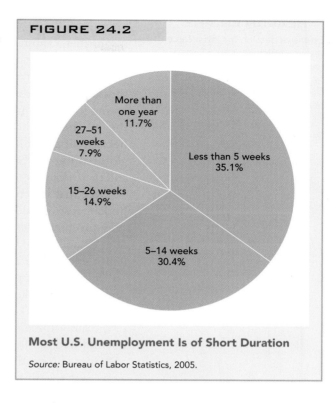

FIGURE 24.2

More than one year 11.7%
27–51 weeks 7.9%
15–26 weeks 14.9%
Less than 5 weeks 35.1%
5–14 weeks 30.4%

Most U.S. Unemployment Is of Short Duration

Source: Bureau of Labor Statistics, 2005.

Structural unemployment is persistent, long-term unemployment caused by long-lasting shocks or permanent features of an economy that make it more difficult for some workers to find jobs.

CHECK YOURSELF

> What is a key cause of frictional unemployment?

> To minimize frictional unemployment, unemployed workers would have to accept the first job they were offered no matter what the wage. Is frictional unemployment always a bad thing?

▶▶SEARCH ENGINE
Extensive data on the labor force and unemployment for a large sample of countries is collected by the Organization for Economic Co-operation and Development (search for OECD Statistics).

unemployed for 20 years. The phrase "persistent, long-term unemployment" means that a substantial fraction of the unemployed have been unemployed for more than one year and that this problem has lasted for a long time.

What causes structural unemployment? One cause is large, economy-wide shocks that occur relatively quickly. Adjusting to these shocks can create long-lasting unemployment as the economy takes time to restructure. In addition to the oil shocks, the U.S. economy has had to restructure in recent decades because of the shift from a manufacturing to a service economy, because of globalization and because of new information technologies such as the computer and the Internet.

Note that structural unemployment, if it lasts long enough, brings significant human costs in addition to the loss of economic output. Not only is the economy producing less but the unemployed suffer higher levels of stress, higher rates of suicide, and lower rates of measured happiness. Wanting a job—and not being able to find a good one—is a recipe for misery and social decay.

At some point unemployment can become chronic. It can be harder for an unemployed worker to find a job than for an employed worker to switch jobs. Unemployed workers face two problems. First, the longer a worker remains out of the labor force the more his or her skills atrophy. An administrative assistant unemployed in 1998, for example, would probably have no idea what it meant to "Google something," a critical skill for a job in 2002. Second, hiring managers may regard unemployment as a sign of laziness or other problems. Who would you rather hire: a worker who is looking to switch jobs or a worker who has been unemployed for five years? Unemployment can become a trap and is another reason why unemployment rates in Western Europe are taking so long to return to normal.

Labor Regulations and Structural Unemployment

The late 1970s oil shock (as well as the other shocks listed above) hit the United States as hard as Europe, but in the United States unemployment tends to increase with a shock and then decrease, while in Europe (especially in the big four continental economies: France, Germany, Italy, and Spain), unemployment has increased with shocks and then remained at high levels. Table 24.1 shows that unemployment in the big four European countries has hovered around 10 percent or higher for 20 years and a large fraction of this unemployment has

TABLE 24.1 Unemployment Rates in Europe Versus the United States, 1980–2004

Country	1980–1984	1985–1989	1990–1994	1995–1999	2000–2004	Fraction Unemployed for More Than One Year (2004)
France	7.3%	9.3%	9.6%	10.8%	8.4%	41.6%
Germany	5.9%	6.4%	6.7%	9.8%	8.8%	51.8%
Italy	8.8%	11.6%	10.9%	11.8%	9.3%	49.7%
Spain	15.9%	19.9%	19.6%	20.0%	11.7%	37.7%
United States	8.3%	6.2%	6.6%	4.9%	5.2%	12.7%

Source: OECD Statistics and OECD Employment Outlook, 2005.

been long term. Why have unemployment rates in the United States and Europe behaved so differently?

Structural unemployment has been a more serious problem in Europe than in the United States because of labor regulations. More specifically, unemployment benefits, minimum wages, unions, and employment protection laws benefit some workers, but these regulations can also increase unemployment rates. All of these regulations are more generous and wide-ranging in Europe than in the United States, and that helps explain why structural unemployment is a more serious problem in Europe than in the United States. Let's go through each labor market intervention in turn.

Unemployment Benefits Unemployment benefits are the most obvious labor regulation that can increase unemployment rates. Unemployment benefits include unemployment insurance, but also other benefits such as housing assistance that may be available in some countries. Table 24.2 shows how much of a worker's take-home pay was replaced by unemployment benefits in France, Germany, Spain, and the United States in 1994.[3] (We focus on 1994 because this is about midway through Europe's long spell of unemployment—there have been only modest changes since then.)

In the first year of unemployment in France, the unemployment benefit system replaced 80 percent of a worker's income. A worker who lost his or her job in France, in

TABLE 24.2 Unemployment Benefit Replacement Rates in Europe Versus the United States, 1994			
	First Year	Second and Third Year	Fourth and Fifth Year
France	80%	62%	60%
Germany	74%	72%	72%
Spain	70%	55%	39%
United States	38%	14%	14%

Note: The data cover a worker with a dependent spouse and are net rates after taking into account taxes and other benefits.

Source: Ljungqvist L., Sargent T. 1998. "The European Unemployment Dilemma." *Journal of Political Economy.* 106(3): 514–550.

Martin, John P. 1996. "Measures of Replacement Rates for the Purpose of International Comparisons: A Note." *OECD Economic Studies.* no. 26: 99–115.

other words, faced only a 20 percent cut in pay. In fact, if we look only at income, and not at the satisfaction that comes from having a job, a French worker who lost his or her job was probably better off—after all an unemployed worker had 80 percent of the income of an employed worker and much more leisure time ("unemployed workers" may also work for pay in the black market). In comparison, the unemployment benefit system in the United States replaced only 38 percent of a worker's pay so a worker who lost his or her job faced a 62 percent cut in pay.

Unemployment benefits also last much longer in Europe than in the United States. In the United States, for example, unemployment benefits fall by more than half after just one year. But in France, Germany, and Spain, unemployment benefits never decrease by so wide a margin.

Given these figures, it shouldn't be surprising that long-term unemployment is much more common in Europe than in the United States (see the last column in Table 24.1). In Europe, the price of unemployment is low, so more unemployment (leisure) is demanded. Or, if you like, workers in Europe can afford to remain unemployed for longer periods than workers in the United States.

In summary, unemployment benefits reduce the incentive for workers to search for and take new jobs. Now switching to look at the demand side of the labor market, minimum wage, unions, and employment protection laws reduce the incentive of firms to create and offer new jobs.

Minimum Wages and Unions   In the left panel of Figure 24.3, we analyze the minimum wage (see Chapter 7 for a more extensive discussion). The minimum wage raises the price of labor from the market wage to the minimum wage and as labor becomes more expensive firms reduce employment from market employment to minimum wage employment Q_d. At the minimum wage the number of workers looking for work, Q_s, exceeds the number of jobs, Q_d—thus, the minimum wage creates unemployment in the amount $Q_s - Q_d$.

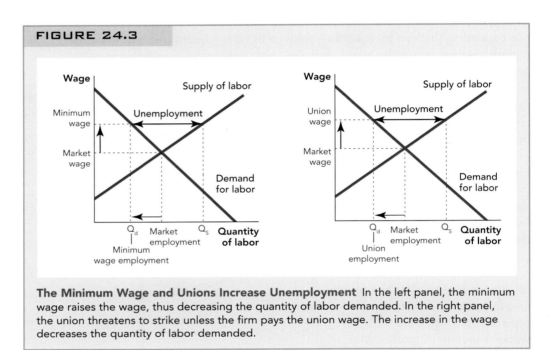

FIGURE 24.3

The Minimum Wage and Unions Increase Unemployment In the left panel, the minimum wage raises the wage, thus decreasing the quantity of labor demanded. In the right panel, the union threatens to strike unless the firm pays the union wage. The increase in the wage decreases the quantity of labor demanded.

The **median wage** is the wage such that one-half of all workers earn wages below the median and one-half of all workers earn wages above the median.

In Western Europe, minimum wages have been higher than in the United States. Between 2000 and 2007, for example, the minimum wage in France was about 40 percent higher than in the United States. Minimum wages in Western Europe have also been higher relative to the **median wage** than in the United States. (The median wage is defined so that half of all workers earn less than the median and half more.) In France, the minimum wage has been about 61 percent as large as the median wage. In the United States, the minimum wage has only been about 32 percent as large as the median wage.[4] What this means is that the minimum wage will affect more workers and create more unemployment in France than in the United States. As we discussed in Chapter 7, the minimum wage is more likely to create unemployment among young workers, who tend to be less productive, than among older workers. Thus, in both France and the United States, unemployment rates are higher among the young than the old but in France 23 percent of workers under the age of 25 are unemployed while in the United States 10 percent of these workers are unemployed.[5] The U.S. minimum wage, however, has been rising rapidly in recent years from $5.15 at the beginning of 2007 to $7.25 in 2009.

A **union** is an association of workers that bargains collectively with employers over wages, benefits, and working conditions.

Unions are also more powerful in Europe than in the United States. A union is an association of workers that bargains collectively with employers over wages, benefits, and working conditions. In the United States, most (87 percent) workers are not governed by a union contract; instead, they have an individual contract (written or unwritten) with employers. In many European countries, however, 80 percent of workers or more are governed by a union contract.

Unions can provide value for workers and employers alike, but excessively strong unions have a very similar effect to minimum wages. Unions demand higher wages by using their power to strike and to prevent the firm from hiring substitute labor. In the right panel of Figure 24.3, the union raises the price of labor from the market wage to the union wage. As labor becomes more expensive, firms reduce employment from market employment to union employment Q_d. At the union wage, the number of workers looking for work, Q_s, exceeds the number of jobs, Q_d—thus, unions increase unemployment by the amount $Q_s - Q_d$.

Employment Protection Laws In the United States, an employee may quit and an employer may fire at any time and for any reason. This is called the **employment at-will doctrine**. There are many exceptions to the at-will doctrine, the most important being that the doctrine can be changed by contract. Many workers, for example, have contractually guaranteed severance packages and tenured university professors cannot be fired at will. Employees can also be restricted by contract. Employees in some industries with a lot of trade secrets are often asked to sign a noncompete agreement when they are hired. If an employee who signs a noncompete agreement quits, he or she may be forbidden, for example, from working for a competitor for a set period. Public law also imposes certain restrictions; employers, for example, are forbidden from hiring or firing on the basis of race, religion, sex, sexual orientation, national origin, age, or handicap status. Despite many exceptions, the at-will doctrine can be thought of as the most basic U.S. labor law.

In most of Europe, labor law is quite different. Portugal's constitution, for example, forbids at-will employment and requires employers to notify the government whenever a worker is dismissed. Moreover, if a Portuguese firm needs to lay off a group of workers, it must get the government's permission. Nor can the firm choose which workers to lay off; instead, it must follow strict guidelines determining which workers will be laid off first (generally the most junior workers are fired first). In addition, laid-off workers must be given 60 days notice, severance pay, and other benefits. Throughout Western Europe, public law and collective bargaining, not contracts, govern things like the length of the workweek, overtime pay, paid leave, temporary employment, notice periods, severance pay, and more.

Hiring and firing costs make labor markets less flexible and dynamic. A European firm with an unexpected increase in orders, for example, will not simply hire more workers. If the firm hired more workers and orders then declined, it would be stuck with workers who it could not lay off without incurring great expense. Thus, hiring and firing costs make firms more cautious and slower to act.

Greater job security is valuable to workers with full-time jobs but the more expensive it is to hire and fire workers, the more difficult it will be for new workers and unemployed workers to find jobs. Imagine, for example, how difficult it would be to get a date if every date required marriage! In the same way, it's more difficult to find a job when every job requires a long-term commitment from the employer.

The World Bank calculates a "rigidity of employment index," which summarizes hiring and firing costs as well as how easy it is for firms to adjust hours

The **employment at-will doctrine** says an employee may quit and an employer may fire an employee at any time and for any reason. There are many exceptions to the at-will doctrine but it is the most basic U.S. employment law.

of work (e.g., whether there are restrictions on night or weekend hours). A higher index number means that it is more expensive to hire and fire workers and more difficult to adjust hours. Figure 24.4 plots the rigidity index against the percentage of unemployment that is long-term (lasting more than one year). The red line shows the trend in the data; greater rigidity in labor markets is clearly associated with greater long-term unemployment. Notice especially that France, Germany, Italy, and Spain all have high rigidity and high long-term unemployment while the United States has the least rigid labor markets and one of the lowest rates of long-term unemployment.

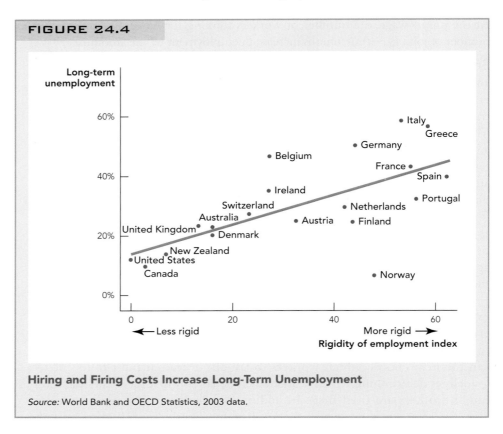

FIGURE 24.4

Hiring and Firing Costs Increase Long-Term Unemployment

Source: World Bank and OECD Statistics, 2003 data.

A Tale of Two Riots   The tale of two riots illustrates another effect of employment protection laws. Paris, the city of lights, was lit up by hundreds of burning vehicles in November 2005 as angry, predominantly immigrant youth rioted in the streets. The riots were triggered by accusations of police brutality, but poverty and unemployment were the larger underlying frustrations. Unemployment rates among the rioting youth were over 30 percent.

French firms were reluctant to hire young, minority workers—perhaps, in some instances, because of discrimination, but also because the more expensive it is to hire and fire, the more reluctant firms will be to hire workers without experience and workers for which there is any perceived uncertainty about quality. Once again, if every date required marriage, would you go on a blind date? A blind date might be worth some risk if you can dump a loser, but who will go on a blind date if a date means forever? Returning to firms, young workers are riskier than older workers. Workers without a job are riskier than workers with a job (recall our discussion of the unemployment trap).

And minority workers or workers who in some way differ from the "norm" may be regarded as more risky than typical workers by some employers. Thus, employment protection laws tend to have the most negative effects for young, already unemployed, and minority workers.

The French government was aware of these problems and in response to the riots it proposed to change labor law so that for workers under the age of 26 employment would be at-will for the first two years. The idea was to reassure firms that hiring a young, immigrant worker could be more like a blind date and less like marriage. Of course, this at-will employment is the norm in the United States. For elite French youth, however, the idea that they could be fired at will was upsetting and an infringement of what they considered to be their rights. Several hundred students barricaded themselves in the Sorbonne, the famous Paris university, and called on students everywhere to protest.

Now it was time for the insiders, the young elite, to riot and they proved every bit as adept at burning cars as had the impoverished youth of the year before. Not surprisingly, the elite riots were effective—the French government quickly backed down from the at-will employment doctrine. Unemployment in France, especially among young, immigrant workers remains high.

Summarizing, employment protection laws have the following effects. They:

> Create valuable insurance for workers with a full-time job.

> Make labor markets less flexible and dynamic.

> Increase the duration of unemployment.

> Increase unemployment rates among young, minority, or otherwise "riskier" workers.

UNDERSTAND YOUR **world**

Outsider riot
Paris suburbs, 2005

Insider riot
Central Paris, 2006

Labor Regulations to Reduce Structural Unemployment

In recent years, Europe has begun to change some of its labor regulations to try to reduce long-term unemployment. In Denmark, for example, unemployment benefits were limited to four years and after one year workers who wish to continue receiving benefits must either enroll in job search or job training programs or take public employment. Denmark also subsidizes employers who are willing to train unemployed workers. Denmark and other countries now also have work tests—requirements that unemployed workers who want benefits must prove that they are actively seeking work.[6] These types of laws are called **active labor market policies.**

The United States has been a leader in testing active labor market programs. One of the most successful programs is the simplest—pay workers to get a job! In several large-scale experiments, randomly chosen unemployed workers were told that they would be paid a bonus if they found work early. The workers who were told about the bonus got jobs significantly sooner than those not promised bonuses.

Europe has also been slowly moving toward more flexible labor markets by allowing some exceptions to collective bargaining agreements for certain categories of workers such as young workers, temporary workers, and part-time workers. Remember, however, the tale of the two riots. "Insiders" have been very reluctant to give up their benefits for the sake of the unemployed "outsiders."

Active labor market policies like work tests, job search assistance and job retraining programs focus on getting unemployed workers back to work.

Factors That Affect Structural Unemployment

Let's summarize the factors that can increase structural unemployment. These are:

> Large, long-lasting shocks that require the economy to restructure. For example:
>> Oil shocks
>> Shift from manufacturing to services
>> Globalization and global competition
>> Fundamental technology (computers and the Internet)

> Labor regulations:
>> Unemployment benefits
>> Minimum wages
>> Powerful unions
>> Employment protection laws

We also discussed some policies that can reduce structural unemployment. These are:

> Active labor market policies:
>> Job retraining
>> Job-search assistance
>> Work tests
>> Early employment bonuses

Cyclical unemployment is unemployment correlated with the business cycle.

Cyclical Unemployment

The final category of unemployment is **cyclical unemployment,** or unemployment correlated with the ups and downs of the business cycle. Figure 24.5 graphs the U.S. unemployment rate since 1948. The shaded areas are recessions. Notice that during every recession, unemployment increases dramatically.

Lower growth is usually accompanied with higher unemployment for two reasons. First, and most obviously, when GDP is falling, firms often lay off workers, which increases unemployment. The second reason is more subtle. Higher unemployment means that fewer workers are producing goods and services. When workers are sitting idle, it's likely that related capital is also sitting idle (e.g., factories are boarded up). An economy with idle labor and idle capital cannot be maximizing growth, and that will hurt the ability of that economy to create more jobs.

Figure 24.6 emphasizes the flip side of the idea that lower growth is correlated with increases in unemployment—faster growth is correlated with decreases in unemployment. Figure 24.6 plots changes in the U.S. unemployment rate on the y-axis against growth on the x-axis. As you can see, faster growth in real GDP decreases unemployment. In fact, unemployment tends to fall when growth is above average and it tends to rise when growth is below average. Consider 1982 when the economy was in a deep recession and the unemployment rate increased by 2.1 percent. On the other hand, just two years later, real GDP was growing rapidly at 7.2 percent a year, unemployment was falling, and, partly as a consequence, Ronald Reagan was reelected in a landslide.

FIGURE 24.5

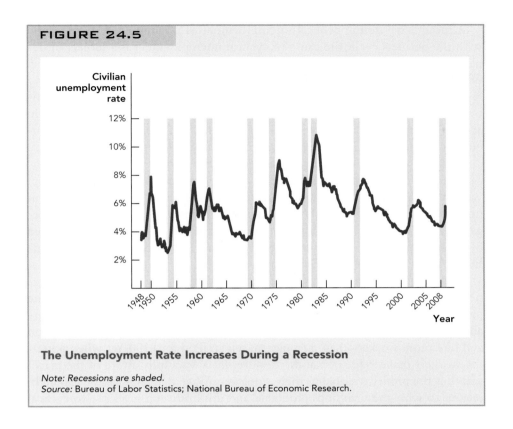

The Unemployment Rate Increases During a Recession

Note: Recessions are shaded.
Source: Bureau of Labor Statistics; National Bureau of Economic Research.

FIGURE 24.6

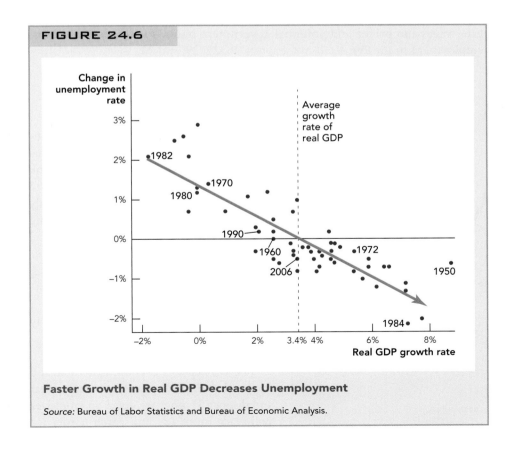

Faster Growth in Real GDP Decreases Unemployment

Source: Bureau of Labor Statistics and Bureau of Economic Analysis.

Although we define cyclical unemployment as unemployment correlated with the business cycle, the cause of cyclical unemployment is a subject of debate among economists, largely because the cause of business cycles is a subject of debate. Some economists think that business cycles are mostly a response to real shocks that require a reallocation of labor across industries. For these economists, a business cycle is nothing more than the economic growth process in action—growth is volatile not smooth. Thus, for these economists, cyclical unemployment is just another example of frictional and structural unemployment.

Other economists, typically of the "Keynesian" persuasion, think that cyclical unemployment is caused by deficiencies in aggregate demand. This concept will be explained in later chapters, but for the time being we can think of this notion of cyclical unemployment as caused by a mismatch between the aggregate level of wages in an economy and the level of prices. The wages demanded by workers are out of synch with the level of prices, so workers are too expensive to hire from the point of view of firms.

To give a simple example, whether a firm wants to hire another worker depends not only on the wage of that worker but on that wage relative to the price of the firm's product (and of course relative to other prices more generally). If Apple can sell an iPod for $200, it is more likely to step up production and hire more workers, than if Apple can sell an iPod for $100. Yet when potential workers make wage demands, they are not always fully aware of the prices and thus the profits available to their employers. Wage demands can be too high, relative to what the firm finds profitable, and this mismatch gives rise to cyclical unemployment. Yet if aggregate demand for goods and services were somehow higher, the higher wage demands perhaps could be justified and the workers could be hired.

The natural unemployment rate is the rate of structural plus frictional unemployment.

We will return to the concepts of real shocks, mismatches between aggregate wages and prices, and potential government policy to reduce cyclical unemployment in greater detail in Chapters 26, 27, 29, and 31.

The Natural Unemployment Rate

The **natural unemployment rate** is defined as the rate of structural plus frictional unemployment. Economists typically think of the underlying rates of frictional and structural unemployment as changing only slowly through time as major, long-lasting features of the economy change. Cyclical employment, however, can increase or decrease dramatically over a matter of months. Figure 24.7 plots one estimate of the natural rate against the actual unemployment rate. The natural rate changes only slowly through time and the actual rate of unemployment varies around the natural rate.

The concepts of cyclical, structural, and frictional unemployment are not always clear and distinct. If times are good, an employer will place more ads and search harder for

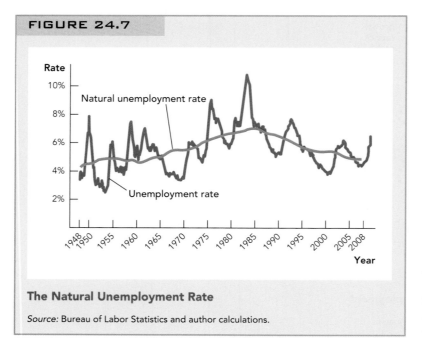

FIGURE 24.7

The Natural Unemployment Rate

Source: Bureau of Labor Statistics and author calculations.

workers. We might say that the frictional rate of unemployment has fallen, but we also might say that the cyclical rate of unemployment has fallen. Both descriptions of the improvement are true. Similarly, how well an economy absorbs, say, displaced auto workers (structural unemployment) will depend on the overall strength of economic conditions. One type of unemployment can even turn into another. Cyclical unemployment, for example, can turn into structural unemployment if workers remain on unemployment benefits for too long, thereby leading to a decline in skills and employment prospects.

Most economists view observed unemployment as a mix of structural, frictional, and cyclical characteristics. The three categories nonetheless give us some useful ideas for organizing the sources of unemployment.

CHECK YOURSELF

> What happens to cyclical unemployment during the business cycle?

> How are economic growth and unemployment related?

Labor Force Participation

So far we've focused on whether people can get a job if they want one, but it is also important to ask whether people *want* a job. We therefore turn from the unemployment rate to the labor force participation rate. Recall that the labor force participation rate is the percentage of the adult, noninstitutionalized, civilian population (adults for short) who are working or actively looking for work. In other words, the labor force participation rate is the percentage of adults who are in the labor force.

$$\text{Labor force participation rate} = \frac{\text{Unemployed} + \text{Employed}}{\text{Adult population}} \times 100$$

$$= \frac{\text{Labor force}}{\text{Adult population}} \times 100$$

In the United States, there are 154.9 million members of the labor force and 234.1 million adult, noninstitutionalized civilians, so the labor force participation rate is:

$$\frac{154.9 \text{ million}}{234.1 \text{ million}} \times 100 = 66.17\%.$$

What determines the labor force participation rate? We will discuss two factors.

1. Lifecycle effects and demographics
2. Incentives

Lifecycle Effects and Demographics

Table 24.3 shows how labor force participation rates vary with age. Only 44 percent of the population aged 16 to 19 are in the labor force. Not surprisingly, most people this age are full-time students not workers. Labor force participation peaks in the prime working years, ages 25–54, when 83 percent of adults are in the labor force. After age 65, most people retire and only 15 percent remain in the labor force.

TABLE 24.3 The Labor Force Participation Rate at Different Ages

Age Range (years)	Labor Force Participation Rate
16–19	44%
25–54	83%
65+	15%

Source: Bureau of Labor Statistics, 2006.

Baby boomers are the people born during the high-birth rate years, 1946–1964.

Lifecycle effects can interact with demographics to change national labor force participation rates. For example, as the **baby boomers** begin to retire in 2008, an increasingly large share of the population will become 65 years of age or older. In 2000, 12.4 percent of the population was 65 years or older, but by 2030 nearly 20 percent of the population will be 65 years or older. In fact, by 2030 it's estimated that 18.2 million people in the United States will be 85 years or older.[7] Since older people are less likely to participate in the labor force, the aging of the U.S. population will lower the labor force participation rate.

Many economists are concerned because falling labor force participation means lower tax receipts. Of greater concern, tax receipts will be falling just as the demands on Social Security and Medicare rise. The head of the U.S. Government Accountability Office, whose job it is to analyze the long-term financial health of the U.S. government, has said in this regard, "when those boomers start retiring en masse, then that will be a tsunami of spending that could swamp our ship of state if we don't get serious."[8] We take up these important issues at greater length in Chapter 30.

A natural response to rising life expectancies and better health at older ages is later retirement. The "normal" retirement age is partly a matter of culture and convention but it is also partly determined by economic incentives, especially taxes—a subject to which we now turn.

Incentives

Why do people join the labor force? A few artists (and some professors!) love to work, but most people work because work pays more than leisure. More specifically, the choice to work depends on the difference between what work pays and what leisure pays. The choice to work, therefore, can be influenced by taxes on workers and benefits paid to nonworkers. Taxes discourage work and benefits encourage nonwork. We can see both of these effects in action by looking at how retirement systems in different countries change the incentives that older people have to work.

Taxes and Benefits Figure 24.8 shows labor participation rates for men ages 55–64 in different countries in 1998. In Belgium, only one-third of men in this age range were working, while in the United States only one-third of men of this age range were retired! Why are there such large differences in labor force participation rates? It's not just cultural differences concerning the right age for retirement.

FIGURE 24.8

Country	Labor force participation rate
Belgium	33.9
France	41.3
Italy	43.5
Netherlands	46.9
Germany	55.4
Spain	58.2
Canada	58.8
United Kingdom	62.6
United States	68.1
Sweden	71.5
Japan	85.2

Labor Force Participation Rates of Older Workers Differ Significantly Across Countries (Males Aged 55–64, 1998)

Source: OECD Labor Statistics.

In the United States, a worker of retirement age who continues working is not penalized.* But many countries penalize workers who work past the normal or early retirement age because many countries do not allow a worker to work *and* receive the same government pension. For example, in the Netherlands in the 1990s, a worker who worked past the age of 60 lost one year of benefits. The lost benefits can be thought of as a tax on working. Workers who kept working also had to pay payroll taxes on their wages. The net result was that a worker who worked past the age of 60 in the Netherlands earned less money than a worker who retired! In other words, a worker who did not retire at age 60 had to pay to work. If you had to pay to work, how much work would you do?

Figure 24.9 graphs the labor force participation rate of older men against a measure of the penalty, the implicit tax, on working. Countries with a high implicit tax have a low labor force participation rate.

Early retirement is beneficial for workers if they want to retire early, but taxing older workers at significantly higher rates than younger workers (sometimes at rates above 100 percent!) does not benefit the older workers. Pushing older workers into retirement also imposes significant costs on younger workers who must pay higher taxes because older workers are not contributing to GDP.

Men aged 55–64 are a large share of the population, about 17 percent in most Western European countries, so the tax on working means that millions of men retire early and draw on their pensions instead of continuing to work and produce wealth. The graying of the population that we mentioned earlier is even more serious in Europe than in the United States—in part because the incentives created by European retirement programs greatly decrease the labor force participation rates of older workers.

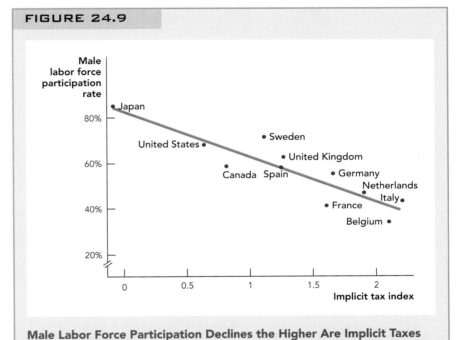

FIGURE 24.9

Male Labor Force Participation Declines the Higher Are Implicit Taxes (Males aged 55–64)

Source: OECD Labor Force Statistics, 2005.
Gruber, Jonathan and David A. Wise. 1999. "Introduction and Summary," In J. Gruber and D.A. Wise, (eds.), *Social Security Programs and Retirement Around the World,* University of Chicago Press, Chicago.

Incentives and the Increase in Female Labor Force Participation

Incentives have also played a role in the dramatic increase in the labor force participation rates of women. In 1948, only 35 percent of women aged 25–54 were in

---

* After age 65, Social Security payments are not reduced at all by earnings. Between the ages of 62 and 65, a worker's Social Security payment is reduced when the worker continues to work but payments beginning at age 65 are increased in rough proportion—thus, there is very little penalty to continuing work even at age 62. See Gruber, J. and P. Orszag. 2003. "Does the Social Security Earnings Test Affect Labor Supply and Benefits Receipt?", *National Tax Journal.* 56(4): 755–773.

the (paid) labor force. In 2008, 75 percent of these women are in the labor force. Figure 24.10 plots U.S. labor force participation rates for women since 1948. Notice that the 1970s brought especially large increases in labor force participation rates.

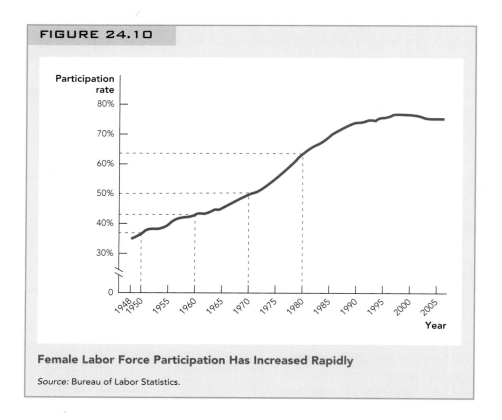

FIGURE 24.10

Female Labor Force Participation Has Increased Rapidly

Source: Bureau of Labor Statistics.

Cultural factors such as the rise of feminism and the growing acceptance of equality for women certainly played a role in rising female labor force participation. But cultural changes do not happen in a vacuum. Changes in the economy such as the move from a manufacturing to a service economy also brought more women to work. Even today, for example, there are almost three times as many male semiskilled factory and machine operators as female operators, but there are more female professionals (lawyers, professors, accountants, etc.) than there are male professionals.[9] As the manufacturing sector declined and the service sector rose, there was less demand for machine operators and more demand for professionals. This raised wages in sectors where females had a comparative advantage, thereby drawing more females into the labor force. In turn, the phenomenon of women in the workplace fueled the rise of feminism.

The growth in women working was especially dramatic in the professions. Figure 24.11 shows the percentage of the first-year students who were female in medical school, dentistry, law, and business programs from 1955 to 2005. From 1955 to about 1970, fewer than 10 percent of first-year students in the professions were females. Beginning around 1970, however, female participation shot up—more than doubling in all professions in just 10 years and continuing to increase until between 40 to 50 percent of all students in professional programs are female.

FIGURE 24.11

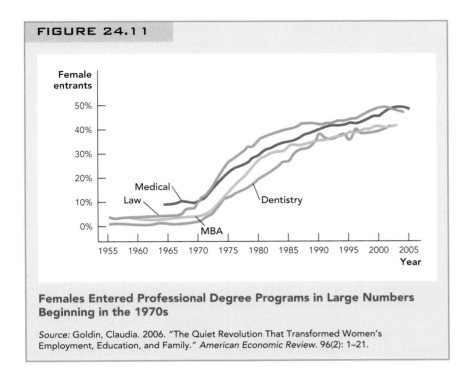

Females Entered Professional Degree Programs in Large Numbers Beginning in the 1970s

Source: Goldin, Claudia. 2006. "The Quiet Revolution That Transformed Women's Employment, Education, and Family." *American Economic Review.* 96(2): 1–21.

Why did females start entering professional schools in increasing numbers beginning around 1970? Economists Claudia Goldin and Lawrence Katz have an intriguing and controversial answer—the pill.[10]

How the Pill Increased Female Labor Force Participation

The pill has been called the greatest technological advance of the twentieth century. For the first time in history, the pill gave women a low-cost, reliable, and convenient method of controlling fertility. Condoms can also prevent unwanted pregnancy, but the pill is easier to use, less prone to error, and more reliable. Among typical users, the pill is seven times more reliable than condoms, and among those who always use the pill according to directions it is 60 times more reliable.

Economists Goldin and Katz argue that the pill lowered the costs of earning a professional degree by giving women greater certainty about the consequences of sex. It takes years of effort to earn a professional degree, and earning a degree while bearing or taking care of a baby is very difficult. Thus, women who wanted a professional degree before the advent of the pill had either to bear the costs of abstinence or risk pregnancy. The pill lowered these costs and increased the incentive of women to invest in a long-term education.

The availability of the pill and the increase in women entering college and professional degree programs do coincide. Although the pill was first sold for contraceptive use in 1960, at that time 30 states banned advertisements for birth control devices and some even banned the sale of contraceptives. It wasn't until 1965 in the landmark case *Griswold v. Connecticut* that the U.S. Supreme Court said states could not ban the sale of contraceptives to *married couples*. Single women could still be prohibited from buying contraceptives until 1972. As laws banning the sale of contraceptives fell, more women bought contraceptives and according to Goldin and Katz more women began to plan for long-term careers.

Goldin and Katz make a plausible argument for their hypothesis (and they provide more evidence than we discuss here); nevertheless, it would be interesting to know if similar effects happened in other countries as the pill became available. Questions like these are on the cutting edge of economics—perhaps some of you will help to answer them.

□ Takeaway

Perhaps the most important lesson of this chapter is that even in the best of times unemployment will exist and fluctuate. The economy is always changing and only through change is there growth. It is important to help workers who are buffeted by change, but there is a difference between helping workers to adjust and trying to prevent adjustment—ultimately, we can do the former but not the latter. As we discussed in this chapter, some labor market policies intended to protect workers have increased structural unemployment in Western Europe compared to the United States. Labor market policies that make it easier for workers to retrain and move to employment have had greater success in keeping long-term unemployment low.

After reading this chapter you should know how unemployment, the unemployment rate, and the labor force participation rate are defined. You should also be able to apply these definitions to data. For example, there are 10 people; 6 have jobs, 1 is looking for work, 1 is a child, 1 is in prison, and the last is retired. What is the labor force? What is the unemployment rate? What is the labor force participation rate?[11] You should also know something about frictional, structural, and cyclical unemployment, which includes defining each and giving examples of their causes.

Finally, it's important to know something about the factors that increase or decrease the labor force participation rate. Changing demographics such as aging baby boomers, technology like the pill, cultural attitudes toward women and work, and government policy such as taxes and pension benefits can all change the labor force participation rate. At the most basic and important level, the labor force participation rate responds to the incentive to work.

Changes in the labor force participation rate can have a large impact on an economy. In much of the world today, women have fewer opportunities to be educated and to fully participate in the paid workforce than men—this failure to fully utilize the talents of women is an enormous loss to these women and to the economy. The labor force participation rates of older workers will become a subject of increasing concern as more workers retire and place increasing demands on pension and health systems not just in the United States but around the developed world.

□ CHAPTER REVIEW

KEY CONCEPTS

Unemployed, p. 515

Labor force, p. 515

Unemployment rate, p. 515

Labor force participation rate, p. 515

Discouraged workers, p. 515

Frictional unemployment, p. 516

Structural unemployment, p. 517

Median wage, p. 520

Union, p. 520

Employment at-will doctrine, p. 521

Active labor market policies, p. 523

Cyclical unemployment, p. 524

Natural unemployment rate, p. 526

Baby boomers, p. 528

FACTS AND TOOLS

1. Which of the following people are counted as unemployed?

    A person out of work and actively searching for work

    A person in prison

    A person who wants to work but stopped searching six months ago

    A person who works part time but who wants full-time work

2. According to Figure 24.1, what percent of all Americans are employed? (This number is the "employment–population ratio.") What percent of the labor force is employed?

3. If we count "discouraged workers" as unemployed when calculating the unemployment rate, does the rate more than double, less than double, or remain unchanged?

4. Decide whether each of the following are frictional, structural, or cyclical unemployment.

    a. The economy gets worse, so General Motors shuts down a factory for four months, laying off workers.

    b. General Motors lays off 5,000 workers and replaces them with robots. The workers start looking for jobs outside the auto industry.

    c. About 10 workers per month at a General Motors plant quit their jobs because they

want to live in another town. They start searching for work in the new town.

5. Let's connect the minimum wage model back to the supply and demand model of Chapter 7. Is a minimum wage a price ceiling or a price floor? Does it create a surplus or a shortage in the labor market?

6. Who is more likely to ask politicians for stronger labor unions and laws making it harder to fire workers: insiders who have jobs or outsiders who don't have jobs?

7. Let's look at how the unemployment rate changes during and after a typical recession. In Figure 24.5, does the unemployment rate tend to reach its peak *during* the recession, or does it usually reach its peak *after* the recession?

8. According to Figure 24.7, during which decade was the natural unemployment rate the highest?

9. Take a look at Figure 24.9. About how big is the difference in labor force participation rates between countries with the highest implicit tax rate on older men compared to countries with the lowest implicit tax rate? Round to the nearest 10 percent.

10. Based on the ideas in this chapter, name three labor market policy changes that would be likely to decrease the rate of structural unemployment. There are many more than three possible answers.

THINKING AND PROBLEM SOLVING

1. When the following events happen, does that cause the unemployment rate to rise, fall, or stay the same?

    a. Workers are laid off and start looking for work

    b. People without jobs who are looking for work find work

    c. People without jobs and looking for work give up and stop looking

    d. People without jobs and not looking for work become encouraged and decide to start looking for work

    e. People without jobs and not looking for work take a job immediately

2. Let's see how many jobs have to be destroyed for one *net* job to be created. As noted in the text, millions of jobs are created and destroyed every month. Suppose that 5 millions jobs are destroyed every month and about 5.25 million jobs are created. What is total job destruction divided by net job creation? So how many total jobs are destroyed for every net job created?

3. Take a look at Table 24.2. If you have to pick a country to lose your job in, and you know you're going to be out of work for one year, which country offers the highest one-year average replacement rate? Which offers the highest two-year average replacement rate? If you're going to be out of work for three years, which country offers the highest average rate of wage replacement?

4. When a government raises the minimum wage by $2.00 per hour, where would we expect more jobs to be lost: in the fast food industry or in city government? Why?

5. Let's see how GDP per person can be affected by changes in the fraction of citizens who work. This fraction is better known as the employment–population ratio. To keep things simple, let's assume that every employed worker produces $50,000 worth of output. If the employment–population ratio rises from 50 percent to 55 percent, what happens to GDP per *person*?

6. Calculate the unemployment rate and the labor force participation rate in the following cases:

   a. Employed: 100 million. Population: 200 million. In labor force: 110 million.

   b. Unemployed: 10 million. Population: 200 million. Employed: 90 million.

   c. In labor force: 30 million. Population: 80 million. Unemployed: 3 million.

7. Goldin and Katz looked for the link between birth control and women's labor force participation by looking at the difference between states that acted early to make birth control legal and states that waited until later. Which states do you think had the biggest jump in women joining the labor force: states that legalized birth control earlier or those that legalized it later? (Note: Goldin and Katz provide evidence for the right answer in their paper.)

8. Here's a story economists tell each other: A Nobel prize-winning economist flew in to New York City for a conference. He got into a cab, and started talking with the cab driver. The cab driver said, "Oh, you're an economist? Let me tell you, this economy is terrible. I'm an unemployed architect." The economist immediately replied, "No you're not, you're an employed cab driver." According to the way the U.S. government measures unemployment, who is right?

9. Between 1984 and 2001, the U.S. government made it much easier to get disability payments and the number of disabled people more than doubled from 3.8 million to 7.7 million. Most of the people who try to qualify for disability payments have a tough time finding jobs, and spend a lot of time "out of work and actively searching for work." Once people start receiving disability payments, however, they rarely work again and continue to get the disability payments for decades: These citizens then count as "out of the labor force." What effect did reducing the requirements to get disability payments have on the unemployment rate?

10. It's been said that "once you reach the top of the ladder of opportunity, the first thing to do is pull up the ladder behind you." Let's consider the implications of this adage for labor market outcomes.

    a. When doctors, schoolteachers, and barbers encourage the government to make it harder for people to enter their industries, does this tend to lower or raise the supply of these professionals?

    b. If government requires higher educational and training standards for doctors, schoolteachers, and barbers, does this tend to raise or lower the demand for the services of these professionals?

    c. In equilibrium, taking into account your answers to parts a and b, what is the total effect of this lobbying on the wages of these professionals: Do wages rise, fall, or is the total effect ambiguous? Does the total number of people employed in these professions rise, fall, or is the total effect ambiguous?

11. "The unemployment rate also fails to capture all of the people who have given up looking for work," reports the *New York Times*. This is one of many complaints about how the U.S. government measures the unemployment rate.

But as hinted at in the chapter, the U.S. government actually *does* count these "discouraged workers," and it includes them in the "U-4" and "U-5" definitions of unemployment. The government also has a few other measures of the labor market: It just so happens that the media and economists typically ignore these measures. Let's look at these measures in 2007 and 2008 as the U.S. economy slowed and the official "unemployment rate" rose to see if we get a different story.

	September 2007	September 2008
Official unemployment rate	4.7%	6.1%
U-4 (includes discouraged workers)	4.9%	6.4%
U-5 (also counts a few part-time workers as unemployed)	5.5%	7.1%
U-6 (counts many part-time workers as unemployed)	8.4%	11.0%
Employment as percentage of population	62.9%	62.0%

(*Source:* Bureau of Labor Statistics, Table A-12. "Alternative measures of labor underutilization," http://www.bls.gov.)

Answer the following questions.

a. For each of the five measures calculate the rise in the unemployment rate (or, in one case, the fall in the employment rate.)

b. Do any of these alternate measures indicate that the rise in the unemployment rate was larger than the official measure would indicate? Which ones?

c. Do any of these alternate measures indicate that the rise in the unemployment rate was *twice as big* as the official measure? (That might serve as a rough measure of whether our official measure is off by a lot.) Which ones?

d. Which of these alternate measures indicate at first glance that the labor market is actually a little better than the official measure? What is it about the denominator of this value that makes this change smaller than the rest?

(*Source:* Patrick McGeehan, City's Unemployment Rate Falls to Its Lowest Level in 30 Years, *New York Times,* November 17, 2006.)

CHALLENGES

1. Long-term, structural unemployment is higher in Europe than in the United States, but some European countries have it worse than others. Take a look at Table 24.1. Spain has a lower fraction of long-term unemployment than the other European countries, but a higher rate of unemployment than the other European countries in that table. What can we conclude about the kind of unemployment taking place in Spain?

2. **a.** If European governments set rules for marriage the same way they set rules for employment—with tough, preset rules that make it hard to end the relationship—would you expect rates of divorce to rise, fall, or can't you tell with the information given?

   b. Would the length of marriages rise, fall, or can't you tell with the information given?

   c. Would married couples probably be happier (more productive) or less happy (less productive) than under more flexible marriage rules? The last of these three questions might have more than one right answer.

3. When are workers more likely to get a job: six weeks before their unemployment benefits run out, or a week before their unemployment benefits run out? (Note: The correct answer to this question is solidly backed up by U.S. job data.)

4. Take a look at Figure 24.3. In that figure, we're holding "job quality" or "working conditions" constant, and looking at how changes in *wages* impact the quantity of labor supplied and demanded. In many union negotiations, the union and its workers don't push for higher wages. Instead, they push for better working conditions: safer machines, better insurance coverage, or cleaner restrooms.

   So now let's model this: Let's hold *wages* constant, and look at how changes in *working conditions* impact the quantity supplied and quantity demanded of labor. Thus, set it up just like a real-life labor negotiation. Draw a conventional supply-and-demand chart, but on the vertical axis, just put "job quality—high or low" instead of "wage." Then, show what happens to the amount of unemployment created when a union successfully negotiates a higher-than-equilibrium job quality.

5. Even though most Americans who become unemployed are only unemployed for a short period of time, when you look at who is unemployed *at a given moment in time*, you'll find that most of the unemployed have been without a job for quite a while. Let's imagine a simple economy to see how to resolve this paradox. In this economy, there are two types of workers, type A workers take one month to find a new job and type B workers take 10 months to find a new job.

Each month, let's assume that *one* type A and *one* type B worker lose their jobs. Notice that *we're assuming that half of all people who lose their jobs today will find new jobs in a month*. But, as we shall see, this implies that most of the unemployed will have been unemployed for a long period of time.

a. In the long-run (or "steady state"), there will be 11 workers out of work in this simple society at any given point in time. Show that this is true by keeping track of the "pool" of unemployed workers in this society for two years. You can start off assuming that the pool is empty at time zero—that no one is unemployed—but you'd get the same steady-state answer regardless of your starting point. You can prove that 11 will be out of work just with pencil and paper or much more quickly with Excel. To help you out, here's an example of what the pool of unemployed will look like in month 7. Keep going with this calculation until you see that the number of workers in the pool no longer

changes month to month—this is called the "steady state."

The Unemployment Pool: Month 7	
Shallow End (Type A's)	Deep End (Type B's)
1 Type A worker enters pool (loses job)	1 Type B worker enters pool
1 Type A worker exits pool (find works)	6 Type B workers are already in the pool
	0 Type B workers exit the pool
Total: 1 Type A worker is in the pool (unemployed).	Total: 7 Type B workers are in the pool (unemployed).

b. In the steady state—that is when your pool starts having the same numbers every month—how many of the 11 workers in the unemployment pool have been unemployed for "one month"? How many of the 11 workers in the unemployment pool have been unemployed for more than one month?

c. If you see an economy where most *currently* unemployed workers have been out of work for a long time, does this mean that most *people* who have been unemployed in the last few years were unemployed for a long time? How does this example illustrate your answer?

25

Inflation and the Quantity Theory of Money

CHAPTER OUTLINE

Defining and Measuring Inflation

The Quantity Theory of Money

The Costs of Inflation

Takeaway

Appendix: Get Real! An Excellent Adventure

Robert Mugabe had a problem. The dictatorial president of Zimbabwe needed money. Unfortunately, Mugabe's policy of seizing commercial farms had driven productive farmers and entrepreneurs out of the country, frightened off foreign investors, and pushed Zimbabwe, once called the breadbasket of Africa, to the verge of mass starvation. Zimbabwe had almost nothing left to tax, but Mugabe still needed money to bribe his enemies and reward his supporters, especially the still loyal Zimbabwean army. Mugabe thus turned to the last refuge of needy governments, the printing press.

Governments and counterfeiters alone can pay their bills by printing money. Beginning in 2001, when inflation was already running at 50 percent per year, Mugabe pushed the printing presses to breakneck speed. Whenever a bill came due or soldiers needed paying it was no problem—just print more money. In May 2006, for example, the government announced plans to print 60 *trillion* Zimbabwean dollars to finance a 300 percent increase in pay for soldiers. Ironically, the payment was delayed because Zimbabwe didn't have enough U.S. dollars to buy ink and paper.[1]

When the ink and paper arrived, the government flooded the economy with more money. The economy, however, could not produce more goods. When more money chases the same goods, the consequences are easy to see: inflation. In Zimbabwe, the inflation rate quickly increased from 50 percent a year to 50 percent a month to more than 50 percent a day! The Zimbabwean economy was disintegrating.

In this chapter, we explain how inflation is defined and measured, the causes of inflation, the costs and benefits of inflation, and why governments sometimes resort to inflation.

537

Defining and Measuring Inflation

Inflation is an increase in the average level of prices.

The **inflation rate** is the percentage change in the average level of prices (as measured by a price index) over a period of time.

Inflation rate $= \dfrac{P_2 - P_1}{P_1}$

Inflation is an increase in the average level of prices. We measure the average level of prices with an index, the average price from a large and representative basket of goods and services. Thus, inflation is measured by changes in a price index and the **inflation rate** is the percentage change in a price index from one year to the next:

$$\text{Inflation rate} = \frac{P_2 - P_1}{P_1}$$

where P_2 is the index value in year 2 and P_1 is the index value in year 1. A 10 percent inflation rate means, quite simply, that goods and services are priced (on average) 10 percent higher than they were a year ago.

Shifts in supply and demand push prices up and down all the time, but inflation is an increase in the average level of prices. We can think of inflation as an elevator lifting all prices over time. In Figure 25.1, some prices in year 1 are going up and some are going down, but overall the average level of prices is 100. Inflation tends to lift all prices so by year 10 the average level of prices is 200.

FIGURE 25.1

The Inflation Elevator At any one point in time some prices are going up and some are going down. Inflation is an increase in the price level.

Price Indexes

Economists measure inflation using several different price indexes that are based on different bundles of goods:

1. **Consumer price index (CPI):** Measures the average price for a basket of goods bought by a typical American consumer. The index covers some 80,000 goods and is weighted so that an increase in the price of a major item such as housing counts for more than an increase in the price of a minor item like kitty litter.

2. **GDP deflator:** Similar to the CPI, includes all final goods and services, that is, the goods that make up GDP, not just goods bought by consumers. The GDP deflator is used to compute real GDP from nominal GDP.

3. **Producer price indexes (PPI):** Measure the average price received by producers. Unlike the CPI and GDP deflator, producer price indexes measure prices of intermediate as well as final goods. PPI for different industries are often used to calculate changes in the cost of inputs.

For most Americans, the CPI is the measure of inflation that corresponds most directly to their daily economic activity; for businesses and government, the other indexes take on greater relevance. We focus on the CPI unless otherwise indicated.

Inflation in the United States and Around the World

Figure 25.2 shows the annual inflation rate in the United States since 1950. The average inflation rate over this period was 3.9 percent, but in many periods, especially in the 1970s, inflation was significantly higher. Over the past 10 years (1997–2007), inflation in the United States has averaged about 2.6 percent.

FIGURE 25.2

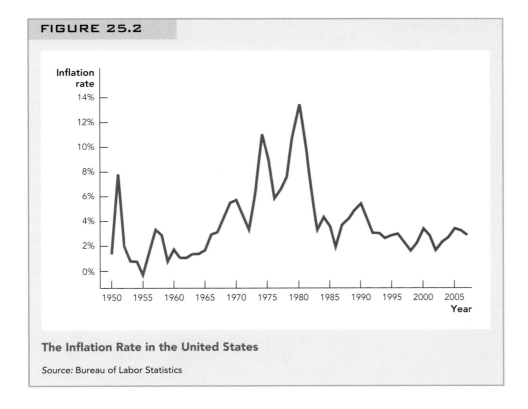

The Inflation Rate in the United States

Source: Bureau of Labor Statistics

Figure 25.3 on the next page illustrates the cumulative effect of inflation on a large basket of goods. A basket that cost about $10 in 1913 would have cost $36.70 in 1969, $100 in 1982, and $207 in 2007. The height of the line represents the level of the CPI during each year.

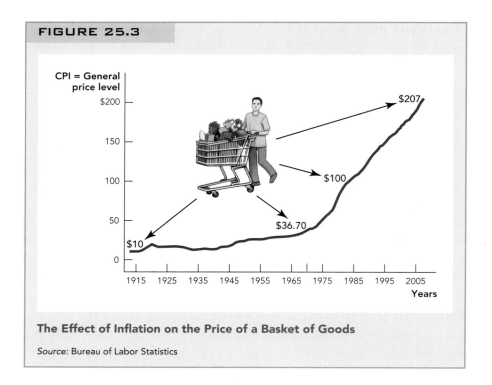

FIGURE 25.3

The Effect of Inflation on the Price of a Basket of Goods

Source: Bureau of Labor Statistics

A **real price** is a price that has been corrected for inflation. Real prices are used to compare the prices of goods over time.

TABLE 25.1 Average Annual Inflation Rates in Selected Countries (2002–2007)

Country	Inflation Rate (%)
Zimbabwe	735.6
Angola	33.8
Guinea	20.0
Myanmar	19.9
Eritrea	19.7
Russia	11.0
United States	3.0
China	2.1
United Kingdom	1.9
Brunei	0.8
Saudi Arabia	0.7
Hong Kong	0.5
Kiribati	0.4
Japan	0.03

Source: International Monetary Fund, World Economic Outlook Database.

Some 2007 figures estimated.

The CPI is often used to calculate "real prices." A **real price** is a price that has been corrected for inflation. Real prices are used to compare the prices of goods over time. Suppose, for example, that you are told that the average price of a gallon of gasoline was $1.25 in 1982 but double that, $2.50, in 2006. These prices are correct but should we conclude that gasoline was twice as expensive in 2006 than in 1982? No. The CPI was 100 in 1982 and 202 in 2006 so the price of most products doubled during this time period; wages rose as well. Thus, the price of gasoline did not increase over this time period relative to other goods so the real price of gasoline was about the same in 1982 as 2006. In the appendix to this chapter, "Get Real," we show in more detail how you can use data on the Internet to compute real prices over time.

Most prices go up over time, but there are exceptions. Pocket calculators now cost a few dollars; in 1972 they cost $395. In 1927, two-way radio phone service, America to London, cost $75 for five minutes. Today a five-minute phone call to England costs mere pennies with Skype. In some cases, technological progress is so rapid that for particular goods and services, it overcomes the general tendency of prices to rise.

Recent U.S. inflation experience is moderate compared to international inflation rates and the historical record. Table 25.1 displays selected international inflation rates over the five years from 2002 to 2007. Between 2002 and 2007 Zimbabwe had the highest inflation rate in the world at 735 percent a year. At that rate, prices were doubling about every five weeks but Zimbabwe was just beginning its inflation and in 2008 prices started to increase faster and faster and faster so that by the end of 2008 prices were increasing at a rate of 79,600,000,000 percent per month! On the other end of the spectrum, the countries with the lowest inflation rates had rates of less than 1 percent. Using the rule of 70, we can see that if Japan continues to have an average inflation rate of 0.03 percent the price level in Japan will double in about 2,333 years. From five weeks to 2,333 years, that is quite a difference.

UNDERSTAND YOUR **world**

The inflation rate in Zimbabwe is now approaching the worst case on record for an inflation. Table 25.2 presents some figures for major "hyperinflations." The numbers in Table 25.2 are so high they are hard to believe but they are true. In Germany, for example, what cost 1 reichsmark in 1919 cost half a trillion reichsmarks in 1923.

TABLE 25.2 Selected Episodes of Hyperinflation

Nation	Period	Cumulative Inflation Rate (%)	Maximum Inflation Rate on a Monthly Basis (%)
America	1777–1780	2,702	1,342
Bolivia	1984–1985	97,282	196
Peru	1987–1992	17,991,287	1,031
Yugoslavia	1993–1994	1.6×10^9	5×10^{15}
Nicaragua	1986–1991	1.2×10^{10}	261
Greece	1941–1944	1.60×10^{11}	8.5×10^9
Germany	1919–1923	0.5×10^{12}	3,250,000
Zimbabwe	2001–2008	8.53×10^{23}	7.96×10^{10}
Hungary	1945–1946	1.3×10^{24}	4.19×10^{16}

Source: Fisher, Stanley & Ratna Sahay & Carlos A. Vegh. 2002. "Modern Hyper- and High Inflations," *Journal of Economic Literature, American Economic Association,* vol. 40(3): 837–880.

Anderson, Robert B; William A. Bomberger; Gail E. Makinen. 1988. "The Demand for Money, the "Reform Effect," and the Money Supply Process in Hyperinflation: the Evidence from Greece and Hungary Reexamined." *Journal of Money, Credit and Banking,* Vol. 20: 653–672.

http://en.wikipedia.org/wiki/Hyperinflation, http://www.sjsu.edu/faculty/watkins/hyper.htm, http://www.cato.org/zimbabwe

NATIONAL BANK OF SERBIA

A 500,000,000,000 dinar bank note from a world hyperinflation leader, Yugoslavia circa 1993. At the time 500 billion dinars could buy about $5 worth of goods. Photo courtesy of National Bank of Serbia.

Hungary's postwar hyperinflation is the largest on record. The numbers are so high, they are difficult to describe. What cost 1 Hungarian pengo in 1945 cost 1.3 septillion pengos at the end of 1946. Seeing numbers like this, the physicist

> If the CPI was 120 this time last year and is 125 right now, what is the inflation rate?

> If the inflation rate goes from 1 percent to 4 percent to 7 percent over two years, what will happen to the prices of the great majority of goods: will they go up, stay the same, go down, or do you not have enough information to say?

> Why do we use real prices to compare the price of goods across time?

Richard Feynman said that really big numbers should not be called "astronomical" but "economical."

The Quantity Theory of Money

We already have a good idea about the causes of inflation from the opening discussion of Zimbabwe. We can now examine the inflationary mechanism in more detail by explaining the **quantity theory of money**. The quantity theory of money does two things: first, it sets out the general relationship between inflation, money, real output, and prices; second, it presents the critical role of the money supply in regulating the level of prices.

Imagine that every month you are paid \$4,000 and you spend \$4,000. In a year, you spend \$4,000 12 times so your total yearly spending is \$4,000 × 12 = \$48,000. Another way of figuring out your total yearly spending is to add up all the goods that you buy and multiply by their prices. We can write this identity (an equation that must hold true by definition) as:

$$M \times v = P \times Y_R$$

v, velocity of money, is the average number of times a dollar is spent on final goods and services in a year.

where M is the money you are paid, v is the number of times in a year that you spend M (we call v the "**velocity of money**," hence the v), P is prices, and Y_R is a measure of the real goods and services that you buy. A similar identity holds for the nation as a whole, where we interpret M as the supply of money, v as the average number of times in a year that a dollar is spent on final goods and services, P as the price level, and Y_R as real GDP.

Thus, for the nation as a whole we can write:

$$Mv = PY_R$$

M = Money supply	P = Price level
v = Velocity of money	Y_R = Real GDP

With some additional assumptions, the simple identity, $Mv = PY_R$, helps us think through how money affects output and prices. We proceed with two further assumptions, namely that both real GDP (Y_R) and velocity (v) are stable compared to the money supply (M).

Let's discuss why these assumptions are usually reasonable. Over the period we are interested in, real GDP is fixed by the real factors of production—capital, labor, and technology—exactly as we discussed in Chapters 21 and 22 on growth. We know that inflation can be 10 percent, 500 percent, 5,000 percent a year, or much higher. Real GDP, in contrast, never grows by more than say 10 percent a year (and that is extraordinary performance), so changes in real GDP don't seem like a plausible candidate for explaining large changes in prices.

Let's also assume that v, the velocity of money, is stable. The velocity of money is the average number of times a dollar is used to purchase final goods and services within a year. In the example above, v was 12 because you were paid monthly and you spent your entire monthly income of \$4,000 12 times in a year. In the U.S. economy today, v is about 8 and it is determined by the same kind of factors that might determine your personal v, factors such as whether workers are paid monthly or biweekly, by how long it takes to clear a check, and how easy it is to find and use an ATM. These factors change over time but only slowly. Other

The **Quantity Theory of Money** in a Nutshell

When v and Y are fixed, (indicated by a top bar) increases in M must cause increases in P.

$$M\bar{v} = P\bar{Y}_R$$

factors that we will discuss at greater length in the chapters on business fluctuations can change v more quickly but not by enough to account for large and sustained increases in prices. For these reasons, changes in v also do not seem like a plausible candidate for explaining large and sustained increases in prices.

The Cause of Inflation

If Y_R is fixed by the real factors of production and v is stable, then it follows immediately that the only thing that can cause increases in P are increases in M, the supply of money. In other words, inflation is caused by an increase in the supply of money.

How well does this theory hold up? The left panel of Figure 25.4 plots the price level (P) and the supply of money (M) in Peru during its hyperinflation. A product with a price of 1 Peruvian Intis in 1980 would have cost more than *10 million* Intis by 1995. (To reduce the number of zeroes, the Peruvian government changed the name of the currency twice during this period first from Intis to Soles de Oro and then to the Nuevo Sol.) As you can see, the supply of money also increased about 10 million times in lockstep with the increase in prices.

FIGURE 25.4

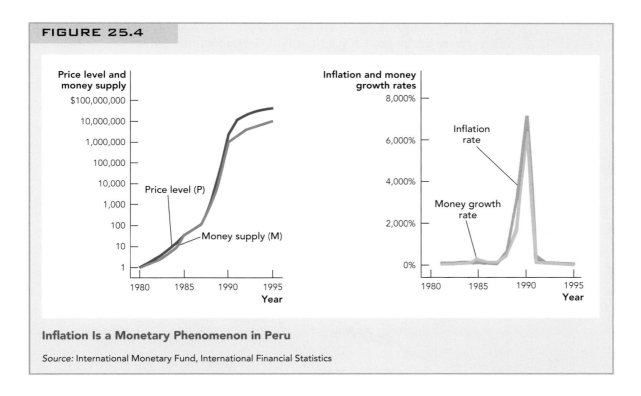

Inflation Is a Monetary Phenomenon in Peru

Source: International Monetary Fund, International Financial Statistics

The quantity theory of money can also be written in terms of growth rates. We denote the growth rate of any variable with a little arrow over the variable, so $\vec{M}$ is the growth rate of the money supply, $\vec{P}$ is the growth rate of prices, and so forth. If $Mv = PY_R$ then it is also true that[*]:

$$\vec{M} + \vec{v} \equiv \vec{P} + \vec{Y}_R$$

---

[*] To derive this equation, we have used a convenient mathematical fact that if $Y = A \times B$, then the growth rate of Y is approximately equal to the growth rate of A plus the growth rate of B.

We have a special word for the growth rate of prices, $\vec{P}$: inflation! If we assume that velocity isn't changing much, as we did above, then the growth rate of velocity, $\vec{v}$, will be zero or very low. We also know that the growth rate of real GDP, $\vec{Y}_R$, is relatively low, say between 2 percent and at most 10 percent. Thus, if we ignore these two factors, we see immediately that $\vec{M}$ ≈ *Inflation Rate*, where ≈ means approximately equal. In other words, the quantity theory of money says that the growth rate of the money supply will be approximately equal to the inflation rate.

The right panel of Figure 25.4 shows that during Peru's hyperinflation this was true: as the supply of money grew faster so did the inflation rate, peaking in 1990 at a rate of 7,500 percent per year.

What about other times and places? Figure 25.5 plots inflation rates on the vertical axis versus money growth rates on the horizontal axis for 110 nations between 1960 and 1990. Nations with rapidly growing money supplies had high inflation rates. Nations with slowly growing money supplies had low inflation rates. In fact, as the red line indicates, on average the relationship is almost perfectly linear with a 10 percentage point increase in the money growth rate leading to a 10 percentage point increase in the inflation rate.

If we are thinking about sustained inflation, a significant and continuing increase in the price level, then Nobel Prize winner Milton Friedman has it exactly right: "Inflation is always and everywhere a monetary phenomenon." This is one of the most important truths of macroeconomics.

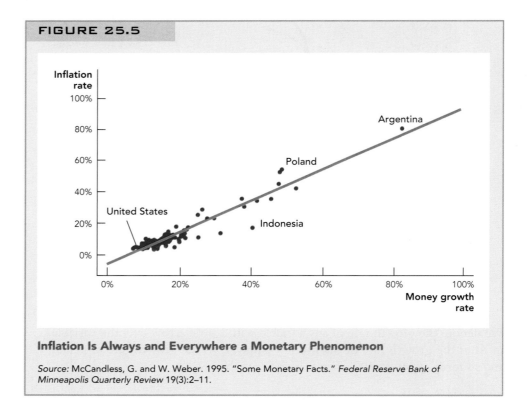

FIGURE 25.5

Inflation Is Always and Everywhere a Monetary Phenomenon

Source: McCandless, G. and W. Weber. 1995. "Some Monetary Facts." *Federal Reserve Bank of Minneapolis Quarterly Review* 19(3):2–11.

Even though large and sustained increases in prices stem from increases in the money supply, changes in v and Y_R can have modest influences on inflation rates. Suppose, for example, that M and v are fixed, then increases in Y_R (real

GDP) must lower prices. In the past, many countries have used a commodity such as gold or silver as money. The dollar, for example, was defined as 1/20th of an ounce of gold between 1834 and 1933. Since the supply of gold or silver usually increases slowly under commodity-money standards, prices typically decrease a bit every year as Y_R increases faster than M.

Finally, even taking the influence of M into account, changes in the velocity of money will affect prices. For instance, increases in the velocity of money can accelerate an already-existing inflation. At the height of the German hyperinflation in 1923, prices were increasing by the minute. Velocity increased in response to this extreme condition. Instead of being paid weekly, for example, workers would be paid as often as three times a day and they would hand off their earnings to their wives, who would rush to the stores to buy food, soap, clothes, *anything* before prices rose even further. Inflation itself caused an increase in velocity, which further fueled inflation.

The velocity of money can also decrease. In an economic panic, individuals may simply hold their money and be afraid to spend it. People might believe that keeping money under the mattress could be less risky than putting money in a bank. During the Great Depression, many people in the United States behaved in precisely this way and the decrease in monetary velocity helped to fuel a **deflation**, a decrease in prices, that worsened the depression. (We discuss the Great Depression at greater length in Chapter 26.) More moderate decreases in velocity or in the growth rate of the money supply would reduce the inflation rate, a **disinflation** rather than a deflation.

Deflation is a decrease in the average level of prices.

A **disinflation** is a reduction in the inflation rate.

The quantity theory also assumes that changes in M cannot change Y_R. In the long run, this makes sense because we know that real GDP is determined by capital, labor, and technology and changes in M won't change any of these factors. Thus, in the long run money is neutral. Imagine, for example, that we doubled the money supply. In the long run, the quantity theory says that prices will double and nothing else will change. We will return to the long-run neutrality of money again and again so let's make a special note of this principle.

In the long run, money is neutral.

Although money is neutral in the long run, it's possible that changes in M can change Y_R in the short run. In particular, under some circumstances increases in M can *temporarily increase* real GDP and decreases in M can *temporarily decrease* real GDP. To see how changes in M could cause changes in real GDP in the short run, let's look at an inflation parable that illustrates how new money works its way through an economy.

An Inflation Parable

Consider a mini-economy consisting of a baker, tailor, and carpenter who buy and sell products among themselves. Now consider what happens when a government like that in Zimbabwe starts paying its soldiers with newly printed money. At first, the baker is delighted when soldiers walk through his door with cash for bread. To satisfy his new customers, the baker works extra hours, bakes more bread, and is able to raise prices. "How wonderful," he thinks, "with the increase in the demand for bread I will be able to buy more clothes and cabinets." Meanwhile, the tailor and carpenter are thinking much the same thing as soldiers are also buying goods from them.

When the baker arrives at the tailor to buy shirts, however, he finds that he has been fooled. The soldiers have bought shirts for themselves and the price of shirts has now gone up. Similarly, the tailor and carpenter discover that the prices of the goods that they want to buy have also increased. Although they earned more dollars, their real wages, the amount of goods that the baker, tailor, and carpenter can buy with their dollars, have decreased.

When the government next wants to buy goods, it faces higher prices and must print even more money to buy just as many goods as before. Moreover, as the new money enters the economy the baker, for example, will now *race* to the tailor and carpenter to try to spend the money before prices rise. Unfortunately, the tailor and carpenter are likely to have had the same idea and the result is that prices increase even more quickly than the time before.

Eventually as the government continues to print money and buy goods, the baker, tailor, and carpenter will come to expect and prepare for inflation. Instead of working extra hours, the baker, tailor, and carpenter will realize that by the time they get to spend their new money, the prices of the goods that they want to buy will have risen in price. Knowing this, the baker, tailor, and carpenter will no longer be so happy to see the soldiers enter their shop waving fistfuls of dollars and they will no longer work extra hours baking more bread, sewing more clothes, or building more cabinets.

The inflation parable tells us that an unexpected increase in the money supply can boost the economy in the short run but as firms and workers come to expect and adjust to the new influx of money, output will not grow any faster than normal. The inflation parable serves us well for now, but the short-run relationship between unexpected inflation and output is a key idea in economics and one we will return to in much greater detail in Chapter 26.

The Costs of Inflation

To the person in the street, the costs of inflation are obvious—prices are going up, what could be worse? But most people rarely consider that inflation also raises their wages. (No doubt, we all have a tendency to think that bad events, like price increases, are the fault of others but good events, like higher wages, are due to our own virtues.) If all prices including wages are going up, then what is the problem with inflation?

If everyone knew whether the rate of inflation was 2 percent or 8 percent then everyone could prepare and the exact inflation rate would not matter very much. But instead of everyone knowing the rate it's more often the case that no one knows the rate of inflation! Take a look again at the right panel of Figure 25.4. Inflation in Peru went from 77 percent in 1986 to 7,500 percent in 1990 and then back down to 73 percent in 1992. Who can predict such changes? Even when inflation is more moderate, it can be difficult to predict. In the United States, inflation was 1.3 percent in 1964; the rate more than quadrupled to 5.7 percent in 1970 and increased to 11 percent per year by 1974. Inflation caught most people by surprise. And when inflation decreased from 13 percent in 1980 to 3 percent in 1983, most people were surprised again.

High rates of inflation do create some problems, as we discuss below, but volatile or uncertain inflation is even more costly. We now cover some specific problems or costs introduced by high and volatile inflation. Keep in mind the picture of inflation as a kind of insidious, slow-moving cancer. Inflation destroys the ability of market prices to send signals about the value of resources and opportunities.

Price Confusion and Money Illusion

Prices are signals and inflation makes price signals more difficult to interpret. In our inflation parable, for example, the baker initially thought that the increase in the demand for bread signaled that the real demand for bread had increased. In fact, since all prices were rising, the real demand for bread had not increased. Confusing a nominal signal with a real signal has real consequences. The baker thought that prices were telling him to work harder and produce more bread. When he later discovered that all prices had risen, he knew that he had made a costly mistake.

Now imagine that one day the real demand for bread *does increase,* only now the baker is so used to inflation he ignores the signal. Instead of working harder the baker continues to bake the same number of loaves of bread as before. Opportunities are missed because signals have become obscured.

In a modern economy, it might seem easy enough to figure out whether an increase in demand for bread reflects a real increase in demand or just an increase in the money supply. Just pick up the *Wall Street Journal* and read the articles about monetary policy. But it's not actually so easy. Sometimes the money supply is increasing and the real demand for bread is going up, both at the same time. It is difficult to sort out the relative strength of both influences. Or perhaps the baker never had principles of economics, or, unlike you (!), never had a really good economics textbook.

Human beings are not always perfectly rational, which makes reading signals even more difficult. Even when we should know better, we sometimes treat the higher wages and prices that result from inflation as higher wages and prices in real terms. If the price of a movie goes up 10 percent and other prices including wages go up by about the same amount, we ought to conclude that the real terms of trade have stayed more or less the same. But many people conclude, mistakenly, that movies have become "more expensive." They treat this as a change in relative price: they may see fewer movies or make other decisions based on this new price. Economists call this "money illusion." **Money illusion** is when people mistake changes in nominal prices for changes in real prices.

> **Money illusion** is when people mistake changes in nominal prices for changes in real prices.

In short, inflation usually confuses consumers, workers, firms, and entrepreneurs. When price signals are difficult to interpret, the market economy doesn't work as well—resources are wasted in activities that appear profitable but in fact are not, entrepreneurs are less quick to respond to real opportunities, and resources flow more slowly to profitable uses.

Inflation Redistributes Wealth

In our inflation parable, the government bought bread, shirts, and woodwork simply by printing paper. Where did these real goods come from? They came from the baker, tailor, and carpenter. Inflation transfers real resources from citizens to the government. Thus, *inflation is a type of tax.*

The inflation tax does not require tax collectors, a tax bureaucracy, or extensive record keeping. You can hide from most taxes by keeping your transactions secret and saving your money under the bed. But you can't hide from the inflation tax! Money under the bed is precisely what inflation does tax because as prices rise, the value of the dollars under the bed falls. It's not surprising, therefore, that money-strapped governments in danger of collapsing typically use massive inflation. Almost all the hyperinflations in Table 25.2 involved governments with massive debts or spending that could not be paid for with regular taxes.

Inflation does more than transfer wealth to the government—it also redistributes wealth among the public, especially between lenders and borrowers. To see why, suppose that a lender lends money at an interest rate of 10 percent but that over the course of the year the inflation rate is also 10 percent. On paper, the lender has earned a return of 10 percent—we call this the nominal return. But what is the lender's actual rate of return? The lender is paid 10 percent interest but she is paid in dollars that have become 10 percent less valuable. Thus, the lender's actual rate of return is 0 percent.

Thus, inflation can reduce the real return that lenders receive on their loans, in effect transferring wealth from lenders to borrowers. In the 1970s, for example, high inflation rates meant the real value of 30-year fixed-rate mortgages that were taken out in the 1960s declined tremendously, redistributing billions of dollars from lenders to borrowers. Borrowers benefited but many lenders went bankrupt.

In the late 1970s, however, many people began to expect that 10 percent inflation was here to stay so home buyers were willing to take out long-term mortgages with interest rates of 15 percent or higher. When inflation fell unexpectedly in the early 1980s, these borrowers found that their real payments were much higher than they had anticipated. Wealth was redistributed from borrowers to lenders.

We can explain the relationship between inflation and wealth redistribution more precisely by writing the relationship between the lender's actual rate of return, the nominal rate of return, and the inflation rate as follows:

$$r_{actual} = i - \pi \tag{1}$$

$$r_{actual} = \text{Actual rate of return, } i = \text{Nominal interest rate}$$
$$\pi = \text{Inflation rate}$$

In words, the actual rate of return is equal to the nominal rate of return minus the inflation rate.

Lenders, of course, will not lend money at a loss. Thus, when lenders *expect* inflation to increase, they will demand a higher nominal interest rate. For example, if lenders expect that the inflation rate will be 7 percent and the equilibrium real rate (determined in the market for loanable funds—see Chapter 23) is 5 percent, then lenders will ask for a nominal interest rate of approximately 12 percent (7 percent to break even given the expected rate of inflation plus the 5 percent equilibrium rate). If lenders expect that the inflation rate will be 10 percent, lenders will demand a nominal interest rate of approximately 15 percent (10 percent to break even given the expected rate of inflation plus the 5 percent equilibrium rate).

The tendency of nominal interest rates to increase with expected inflation rates is called the **Fisher effect** (after economist Irving Fisher, 1867–1947). As an approximation,* we can write the Fisher effect as:

$$i = E\pi + r_{equilibrium} \qquad (2)$$

i = Nominal interest rate, $E\pi$ = Expected inflation rate

$r_{equilibrium}$ = Equilibrium real rate of return

The **Fisher effect** is the tendency of nominal interest rates to rise with expected inflation rates.

The Fisher effect says that the nominal interest rate is equal to the expected inflation rate plus the equilibrium real interest rate. Most important, the Fisher effect says that the nominal rate will rise with expected inflation. We can see the Fisher effect in Figure 25.6, which graphs the inflation rate and short-term nominal interest rates in the United States from 1955 to 2007.

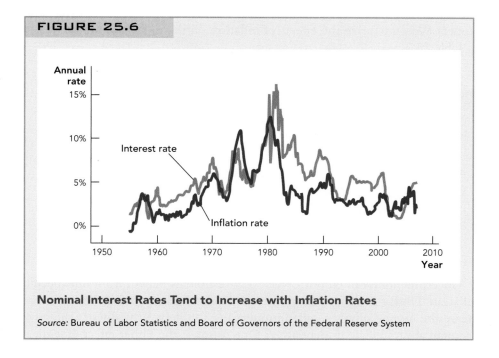

FIGURE 25.6

Nominal Interest Rates Tend to Increase with Inflation Rates

Source: Bureau of Labor Statistics and Board of Governors of the Federal Reserve System

Thus repeating equations (1) and (2) from above we have:

$$r_{actual} = i - \pi \qquad (1)$$

and

$$i = E\pi + r_{equilibrium} \qquad (2)$$

---

* The Fisher effect equation in the text is only approximate. The exact Fisher effect equation is $(1 + i) = (1 + r)(1 + \pi)$. If a lender wants a real rate of return of 5 percent ($r = 0.05$) and the inflation rate is 10 percent ($\pi = 0.1$), then the lender must charge a nominal rate of 1.155 (1.10×1.05) or 15.5%. When inflation rates are low, the approximation works well but not during hyperinflations.

If we substitute i from equation (2) into equation (1), we see that the actual rate of return will be determined in large part by the difference between expected inflation and actual inflation.

$$r_{actual} = (E\pi - \pi) + r_{equilibrium}$$

If $(E\pi < \pi)$, that is, if expected inflation is less than actual inflation, then the actual rate of return will be less than the equilibrium rate and will quite possibly be negative. Wealth will be redistributed from lenders to borrowers.

If $(E\pi > \pi)$, that is, if expected inflation is greater than actual inflation or equivalently if there is an unexpected "disinflation," then the actual rate of return will be higher than the equilibrium rate. Wealth will be redistributed from borrowers to lenders.

Only when $(E\pi = \pi)$, that is, when expected inflation is equal to actual inflation, will the actual return be equal to the equilibrium return. In this case, there will be no unexpected redistribution of wealth between borrowers and lenders. We summarize the effects of inflation on the redistribution of wealth in Table 25.3.

TABLE 25.3 The Redistribution of Wealth Caused by Inflation

Unexpected inflation ($E\pi < \pi$)	Unexpected disinflation ($E\pi > \pi$)	Expected inflation = Actual inflation ($E\pi = \pi$)
Actual rate less than equilibrium rate	Actual rate greater than equilibrium rate	Actual rate equal to equilibrium rate
Harms lenders Benefits borrowers	Benefits lenders Harms borrowers	No redistribution of wealth

Monetizing the debt is when the government pays off its debts by printing money.

Governments are often borrowers so governments benefit from unexpected inflation. Thus, a government with massive debts has a special incentive to increase the money supply—called **monetizing the debt**. Why doesn't the government always inflate its debt away? One reason is the Fisher effect. If lenders expect that the government will inflate its debt away, they will only lend at high nominal rates of interest. To avoid this outcome, the government may try to make a credible promise to keep the inflation rate low.

Another reason the government doesn't always inflate its debt away is that people who buy government bonds are typically voters who would be upset if their real returns were shrunk to zero or less. But what do you think would happen to inflation rates if a nation's debt was owed to foreigners? A government would probably have a stronger incentive to inflate away debt owed to foreigners than debt owed to voters. The U.S. debt is increasingly owed to foreigners, which makes some economists predict a return of inflation in the United States, especially if a future U.S. government finds it difficult to cover its debt with other taxes (see Chapter 30 on fiscal problems in the United States).

It's not only lenders and borrowers that need to forecast future inflation rates. Any contract involving future payments will be affected by inflation. Workers and firms, for example, often make wage agreements several years in advance, especially when unions or other forms of collective bargaining are in place. If the rate of inflation is high and volatile, they are more likely to set wages at the wrong level. Either wages will be too high, and the firm will be reluctant to use more overtime or hire more workers, or wages will be too low, in which case workers are underpaid, they will slack off, and some will quit the job altogether.

Hyperinflation and the Breakdown of Financial Intermediation   If inflation is moderate and stable, lenders and borrowers can probably forecast reasonably well and loans can be signed with rough certainty regarding the real value of the future payments. But when inflation is volatile and unpredictable, long-term loans become riskier and they may not be signed at all. Thus, the real problem of unexpected inflation is not simply that it redistributes wealth, but—even worse—that few long-term contracts will be signed when borrowers and lenders both fear that unexpected inflation or deflation *could* redistribute their wealth.

High and volatile inflation rates have decimated many developing nations. When Peru experienced hyperinflation between 1987 and 1992, private loans virtually disappeared. When firms cannot get loans, they cannot build for future expansion and growth. The price level in Peru is approximately 10 million times higher today than it was in 1997. Who could have predicted these rates of increase or built them into a contract?

The virtual elimination of inflation in Mexico shows how much capital markets can flourish in a stable environment. In the 1980s, the rate of Mexican inflation at times exceeded 100 percent. Long-term loans were very hard to come by. In the United States, it's relatively easy to borrow money for 10, 20, or 30 years or even longer. But as recently as 2002, 90 percent of the local currency debt in Mexico matured within one year.

In the 1990s, the inflation rate in Mexico came down to about 10 percent and more recently it has been 3 percent to 4 percent, close to the rate in the United States. Mexican capital markets have grown rapidly as inflation has been stabilized. In 2006, the Mexican government was able to introduce a 30-year bond, denominated in Mexican pesos; this would have been unheard of as recently as the mid-1990s.

The greater ease and predictability of long-term borrowing also has caused the Mexican mortgage market to take off. It is now relatively easy to obtain a long-term mortgage in Mexico—due largely to lower and less volatile inflation—and many more middle-class Mexicans have been able to afford homes.

Unexpected inflation redistributes wealth throughout society in arbitrary ways. When the inflation rate is high and volatile, unexpected inflation is difficult to avoid and society suffers as long-term contracting grinds to a halt.

Inflation Interacts with Other Taxes

Most tax systems define incomes, profits, and capital gains in nominal terms. In these systems, inflation, even expected inflation, will produce some tax burdens and tax liabilities that do not make economic sense.

To make this concrete, let's say you bought a stock share for $100, and over several years inflation alone pushed its price to $150. The U.S. tax system requires that you pay profits on the $50 gain even though the gain is illusory. Yes, you have more money in nominal terms but that money is worth less in terms of its ability to purchase real goods and services. In real terms, the share hasn't increased in price at all yet you must still pay tax on the phantom gain.

In this case, inflation leads to people paying capital gain taxes when they should not. The overall tax burden rises. The long-run effect is to discourage investment in the first place.

Depending on the details of particular tax systems, inflation can also push people into higher tax brackets or make corporations pay taxes on phantom business profits. In short, inflation increases the costs associated with tax systems.

Inflation Is Painful to Stop

Once inflation starts it's painful to stop—this is one of the biggest costs of inflation. Imagine that the inflation rate has been 10 percent in an economy for some time so that loans, wage agreements, and all kinds of business contracts are based on the expectation that inflation will continue at 10 percent. The government can reduce inflation by reducing the growth in the money supply but what will happen to the economy? When workers, firms, and consumers expect 10 percent inflation, a lower rate is a shock. At first, firms may interpret the lower rate as a reduction in real demand and thus they may reduce output and employment. Furthermore, contracts signed on the expectation of 10 percent inflation are now out of whack with actual inflation. Wage bargains that promised raises of 12 percent per year were modest when inflation was 10 percent, but are huge increases in real wages when the inflation rate is 3 percent. Workers may be thrown out of work as the unexpected increase in their real wage makes them unaffordable. Only in the long run, as expectations adjust, does the economy move to a point where both inflation and unemployment are low.

In the United States, for example, Ronald Reagan was elected to the presidency in 1980 after inflation in the United States hit 13.5 percent a year. By 1983, tough monetary policy had reduced the inflation rate to 3 percent, but the consequence was the worst recession since the Great Depression and an unemployment rate of just over 10 percent. Only in 1988 did unemployment return to near 5.5 percent.

Just Say No

Inflation has been likened to a drug addiction. At first the highs (a booming economy) are good. But soon bigger and bigger doses are needed to generate the same high as before (unexpected inflation turns to expected inflation). Eventually all that is left is the fear of withdrawal (disinflation).

CHECK YOURSELF

> Consider unexpected inflation and unexpected disinflation. How is wealth redistributed between borrowers and lenders under each case?

> What happens to nominal interest rates when expected inflation increases? What do we call this effect?

> What does unexpected inflation do to price signals?

☐ Takeaway

Inflation is an increase in the average level of prices as measured by a price index such as the consumer price index (CPI). A price index can be used to convert a nominal price into a real price, a price corrected for inflation.

Sustained inflation is always and everywhere a monetary phenomenon. In the long run, real GDP is determined by the real factors of production—capital, labor, and technology—so changes in the money supply cannot permanently increase real GDP. Thus, the quantity theory of money is a good guide to how prices respond to changes in the money supply in the long run. Although money is neutral in the long run, changes in the money supply can influence real GDP in the short run for a variety of reasons.

Inflation makes price signals more difficult to interpret, especially when people may suffer from money illusion. Inflation is a type of tax. Governments with few other sources of tax revenue often turn to inflation because the inflation tax is difficult to avoid.

Workers and firms will adjust to a predictable inflation by incorporating inflation rates into wage contracts and loan agreements. The tendency of the nominal interest rate to increase with expected inflation is called the Fisher effect. But inflation is often difficult to predict. When inflation is greater than expected, wealth is redistributed from lenders to borrowers. When inflation is less than expected, wealth is redistributed from borrowers to lenders. The possibility of arbitrary redistributions of wealth in either direction makes lending and borrowing more risky and thus breaks down financial intermediation.

Anything above a mild sustained rate of inflation is generally bad for an economy. Economists disagree, however, as to whether and how much small amounts of well-timed inflation can benefit an economy. In Chapters 26 and 29, we discuss at greater length how policymakers might use the short-run trade-off between inflation and output to smooth recessions and booms. This remains one of the most important and controversial "fault lines" in modern macroeconomics.

☐ CHAPTER REVIEW

KEY CONCEPTS

Inflation, p. 538

Inflation rate, p. 538

Real price, p. 540

v, velocity of money, p. 542

Quantity theory of money, p. 542

Deflation, p. 545

Disinflation, p. 545

Money illusion, p. 547

Fisher effect, p. 549

Monetizing the debt, p. 550

FACTS AND TOOLS

1. What is a "price level"? If the "price level" is higher in one country than another, what does that tell us, if anything, about the standard of living in that country?

2. What are some forces that could cause shocks to v, the velocity of money?

3. When is the inflation rate more likely to have a big change either up *or* down: when inflation is high or when it is low?

4. Who gets helped by a surprise inflation: people who owe money or people who lend money?

5. Who is more likely to lobby the government for fast money growth: people who have mortgages or people who own banks that lent money for those mortgages?

6. Consider the interaction between inflation and the tax system. Does high inflation encourage people to save more or discourage saving? If a government wants to raise more tax revenue in the short run, should it push for higher or lower inflation?

7. Which tells me more about how many more goods and services I can buy next year if I save my money today: the nominal interest rate or the real interest rate? Which interest rate gets talked about more in the media?

8. According to the Fisher effect, if everyone expects inflation to rise by 10 percent over the next few years, where will the biggest effect be: on nominal interest rates or on real interest rates?

THINKING AND PROBLEM SOLVING

1. Calculate inflation in the following cases:

Price Level Last Year	Price Level This Year	Inflation Rate
100	110	
250	300	
4,000	4,040	

2. What does the quantity theory of money predict will happen *in the long run* in these cases? According to the quantity theory, a rise in the money supply can't change v or Y in the long run, so it must affect P. Let's use that fact to see how changes in the money supply affect the price level. Fill in the following table.

M	v	P	Y
100	5		50
150	5		50
50	5		50

3. In the long run according to the quantity theory of money, if the money supply doubles, what happens to the price level? What happens to real GDP? In both cases, state the percentage change in either the price level or real GDP.

4. Much of the economic news we read about can be reinterpreted into our "$Mv = PY$" framework. Turn each of the following news headlines into a precise statement about M, v, P, or Y.

   a. "Deposits in U.S. banks fell in 2015."

   b. "American businesses are spending faster than ever."

   c. "Prices of most consumer goods rose 12 percent last year."

   d. "Workers produced 4 percent more output per hour last year."

   e. "Real GDP increased 32 percent in last decade."

   f. "Interest rates fall: consumers hold more cash."

5. It's time to take control of the Federal Reserve (which controls the U.S. money supply). In this chapter, we're thinking only about the "long run," so Y (real GDP) is out of the Fed's control, as is v. The Fed's only goal is to make sure that the price level is equal to 100 each and every year—that's just known as "price stability," one of the main goals of most governments.

   In question 2, you acted like an economic *forecaster*. You knew the values of M, v, and Y and had to guess what the long-run price level would be. In this question, you will act like an economic *policymaker*. You know the values of v and Y, and you know your goal for P. Your job

is to set the level of M so that you meet your price-level target.

In some years, there will be long-lasting shocks to v and Y, so your job as a policymaker is to offset those shocks by changing the supply of money in the economy. Some of these changes might not make you popular with the citizens, but they are part of keeping P equal to the price-level target. Fill in the following table.

Year	M	v	=	P	Y
1	25,000	2		100	500
2		4		100	500
3		4		100	400
4		4		100	200
5		2		100	400
6		1		100	600

6. Nobel laureate Milton Friedman often said that "inflation is the cruelest tax." Who is it a tax on? More than one may be correct:

   a. People who hold currency and coins in their wallet, purse, or at home

   b. Businesses that hold currency and coins in their cash registers

   c. People or businesses who keep deposits in a checking account that pays zero interest

   d. People or businesses who keep deposits in a savings account that pays an interest rate higher than the rate of inflation

   e. People or businesses who invest in gold, silver, platinum, or other metals

7. In countries with hyperinflation, the government prints money and uses it to pay government workers. How is this similar to counterfeiting? How is it different?

8. The Fisher effect says that nominal interest rates will equal expected inflation plus the real equilibrium rate of return:

$$i = E\pi + r_{equilibrium} \qquad (2)$$

i = Nominal interest rate,
$E\pi$ = Expected inflation rate,
$r_{equilibrium}$ = Equilibrium real rate of return

Economists and Wall Street experts often use the Fisher effect to learn about economic variables that are hard to measure because when the Fisher effect holds, if we know any two of the three items in the equation we can calculate the third. Sometimes, for example, economists are trying to estimate what investors *expect* inflation is going to be over the next few years, but they only have good estimates of nominal interest rates and the equilibrium real rate. Other times, they have good estimates of expected inflation and today's nominal interest rates, and want to learn about the equilibrium real rate. Let's use the Fisher effect just like the experts do: Use two *known* values to learn about the *unknown* third one.

i	$E\pi$	$r_{\text{equilibrium}}$
5%	2%	3%
5%	1%	
5%		8%
	10%	2%
6%		2%
0%	–2%	

Note: The last entry is an example of the "Friedman rule," something that we'll come back to in a later chapter.

CHALLENGES

1. If I get more money, does that typically make me richer? If society gets more money, does it make society richer? What's the contradiction?

2. Why is it so painful to get rid of inflation? Why can't the government just stop printing so much money?

3. Who gets hurt most in the following cases: banks, mortgage holders (i.e., homeowners), or neither?

$E\pi$	π	Who gets hurt?
4%	10%	
10%	4%	
–3%	0%	
3%	6%	
10%	10%	

4. Let's see just how much high expected inflation can hurt incentives to save for the long run. Let's assume the government takes about one-third of every extra dollar of nominal interest you earn (a reasonable approximation for recent college graduates in the United States). You must pay taxes on nominal interest—just like under current U.S. law—but if you're rational you'll care mostly about your real, after-tax interest rate when deciding how much to save.

To make the economic lesson clear, note that in every case, the real rate (before taxes) is an identical 3 percent. In each case, calculate the nominal after-tax rate of return and the real after-tax rate of return. Notice that as inflation rises, your after-tax rate of return plummets.

i	$E\pi = \pi$	$(2/3) \times i$	$(2/3) \times (i - \pi)$
Nominal interest rate	Inflation (no surprises)	Nominal after-tax return	Real after-tax return
15%	12%	10%	–2%
6%	3%		
12%	9%		
90%	87%		
900%	897%		

CHAPTER **APPENDIX**

Get Real! An Excellent Adventure

Suppose that you would like to convert a nominal data series into an inflation-corrected or *real* data series. How do you do it? Let's suppose that you have already imported the nominal data that you want to convert into a spreadsheet. At the U.S. Census Bureau, for example, we found monthly data showing the average price of new houses sold from 1975 to 2006.* We then imported these into a spreadsheet as shown in Figure A25.1. In 2006, the average house price was $304,400, but in 1975 it was only $39,500. Do you think the average new house was really more than seven times as expensive in 2006 as in 1975?

FIGURE A25.1

	A	B	C
	Year	Month	Avg. House Price
1	Year	Month	Avg. House Price
2	2006	8	304400
3	2006	7	314200
4	2006	6	305900
5	2006	5	293900
6	2006	4	310300
7	2006	3	298800
8	2006	2	307900
9	2006	1	301000
10	2005	12	290200
11	2005	11	294400
12	⋮		
13	1975	5	43200
14	1975	4	42000
15	1975	3	42100
16	1975	2	40600
17	1975	1	39500
18			

Inflation has increased all prices, including wages, since 1975 so some of the increase in house prices isn't real. To correct for inflation we need a price index, a measure of how much prices in general have changed. We found several monthly price indexes at the Bureau of Economic Analysis. The most commonly

* http://www.census.gov/const/www/newressalesindex.html

used index is the consumer price index or CPI.* Importing the CPI gives us a spreadsheet like Figure A25.2.

FIGURE A25.2

	A	B	C	D	
1	Year	Month	Avg. House Price	CPI	
2	2006	8	304400	203.7	
3	2006	7	314200	203.2	
4	2006	6	305900	202.3	
5	2006	5	293900	201.9	
6	2006	4	310300	201	
7	2006	3	298800	199.8	
8	2006	2	307900	199.1	
9	2006	1	301000	199	
10	2005	12	290200	197.7	
11	2005	11	294400	197.8	
12	2005	10	293600	199.1	
⋮					
375	1975	7	42300	54	
376	1975	6	42500	53.5	
377	1975	5	43200	53.1	
378	1975	4	42000	53	
379	1975	3	42100	52.8	
380	1975	2	40600	52.6	
381	1975	1	39500	52.3	
382					
383					

The CPI for August 2006 was 203.7 and for January 1975 it was 52.3. Prices in general were about 3.89 times higher (203.7/52.3 = 3.89) in 2006 than in 1975 so a substantial fraction of the increase in house prices wasn't real. We can be more precise by calculating for any year how much a house would have cost in that year if general prices had been at the same level as they were in August 2006. Another way of saying this is that we will convert all prices into "August 2006 dollars."

To convert into August 2006 dollars, we need two more steps. First, we divide every CPI number by the level of the CPI in the 8th month of 2006, 203.7. We call the new series the deflator. Figure A25.3 on the next page gives the picture—note that we copied the formula D2/203.7 into each cell in the Deflator column.

---

* Since housing makes up a large component of the CPI, we should technically use the CPI-Less Shelter, but in practice the two series are nearly identical.

FIGURE A25.3

	E2			f_x =D2/203.7	
	A	B	C	D	E
1	Year	Month	Avg. House Price	CPI	Deflator
2	2006	8	304400	203.7	1
3	2006	7	314200	203.2	0.9975
4	2006	6	305900	202.3	0.9931
5	2006	5	293900	201.9	0.9912
6	2006	4	310300	201	0.9867
7	2006	3	298800	199.8	0.9809
8	2006	2	307900	199.1	0.9774
9	2006	1	301000	199	0.9769
10	2005	12	290200	197.7	0.9705
11	2005	11	294400	197.8	0.971
12	2005	10	293600	199.1	0.9774
375	1975	7	42300	54	0.2651
376	1975	6	42500	53.5	0.2626
377	1975	5	43200	53.1	0.2607
378	1975	4	42000	53	0.2602
379	1975	3	42100	52.8	0.2592
380	1975	2	40600	52.6	0.2582
381	1975	1	39500	52.3	0.2568
382					

Finally, we divide the average house price by the deflator. Note that dividing the average price in August 2006, $304,400, by 1 doesn't change the price—that makes sense because we are converting all prices into August 2006 dollars! Figure A25.4 gives the final picture.

What we have now discovered is that if prices in general were as high in 1975 as they were in 2006, then house prices in 1975 would have been $153,846 instead of the 1975-dollar price of $39,500. Now that we have created a real-price series for housing, we can find the real *increase* in the price of housing. Holding prices constant at 2006 levels, house prices in 2006 were $304,400 and in 1975 they were $153,846, so over this time period houses have about doubled in price ($304,400/$153,846 = 1.98). A doubling is a substantial increase, but it's a lot less than a seven times increase!

FIGURE 25.4

	F2		▼		f_x	=C2/E2	

	A	B	C	D	E	F
1	Year	Month	Avg. House Price	CPI	Deflator	Avg House Price (Real, $2006)
2	2006	8	304400	203.7	1	304400
3	2006	7	314200	203.2	0.9975	314973
4	2006	6	305900	202.3	0.9931	308017
5	2006	5	293900	201.9	0.9912	296520
6	2006	4	310300	201	0.9867	314468
7	2006	3	298800	199.8	0.9809	304632
8	2006	2	307900	199.1	0.9774	315014
9	2006	1	301000	199	0.9769	308109
10	2005	12	290200	197.7	0.9705	299007
11	2005	11	294400	197.8	0.971	303181
12	2005	10	293600	199.1	0.9774	300383
⋮						
375	1975	7	42300	54	0.2651	159565
376	1975	6	42500	53.5	0.2626	161818
377	1975	5	43200	53.1	0.2607	165722
378	1975	4	42000	53	0.2602	161423
379	1975	3	42100	52.8	0.2592	162420
380	1975	2	40600	52.6	0.2582	157229
381	1975	1	39500	52.3	0.2568	153846

Can you think of a reason, other than inflation, why houses might be more expensive in 2006 than in 1975? Here's one—the average new house in 1975 was quite a bit smaller than the average new house in 2006. In 1975, for example, 25 percent of houses were less than 1,200 square feet in size! In 2006, only 4 percent of new houses were less than 1,200 feet in size.* So if we wanted to get an even more accurate picture of the true increase in the price of housing, we should calculate the price per square foot of housing. If we were to do that, we would find that the average price of housing has less than doubled. All of this demonstrates that getting real can be quite tricky, but it's worthwhile if we want to correctly understand how the economy has grown and changed over time.

* http://www.census.gov/const/www/charindex.html

26

Business Fluctuations and the Dynamic Aggregate Demand–Aggregate Supply Model

CHAPTER OUTLINE

A Skeleton Model

The Real Business Cycle Model: Real Shocks and the Solow Growth Curve

The New Keynesian Model

Shocks to Aggregate Demand in the New Keynesian Model

Understanding the Great Depression: Aggregate Demand Shocks and Real Shocks

Takeaway

Economic growth is not a smooth process. Real GDP in the United States has grown at an average rate of 3.3 percent per year over the past 50 years. But the economy didn't grow at this rate every day or every month or even every year. The economy advances and recedes, it rises and falls, it booms and busts.

In Chapters 21 and 22, we looked at why some countries are rich and others are poor. In answering that question, we could safely ignore booms and recessions and focus on average rates of growth over periods of many years. We now turn from average growth rates to focus on the deviations from average, namely the booms and the recessions.

Figure 26.1 on the next page illustrates the booms and recessions of the U.S. economy by quarter since 1948. The average rate of growth of real GDP is 3.3 percent per quarter (on an annual basis), as marked by the red line, but the economy rarely grew at an average rate. In a typical recession, the growth rate might drop to −5 percent in some quarters and in a boom the economy can grow at a rate of 7 percent to 8 percent or higher. We call the fluctuations of real GDP around its long-term trend or "normal" growth rate **business fluctuations** or business cycles. **Recessions,** which we defined in Chapter 21 as significant, widespread declines in real income and employment, are shaded.

Recessions are of special concern to policymakers and the public because unemployment increases during a recession. Notice in Figure 26.2 on the next page, for example, how unemployment increases dramatically within each of the shaded regions that are the periods of U.S. recessions.

More generally, a recession is a time when all kinds of resources, not just labor but also capital and land, are not fully employed. During a recession, factories close, stores are boarded up, and farmland is left fallow. We know that some unemployment is a natural or normal consequence of economic growth—in Chapter 24, we called this level of unemployment the natural unemployment

Business fluctuations are fluctuations in the growth rate of real GDP around its trend growth rate.

A **recession** is a significant, widespread decline in real income and employment.

561

FIGURE 26.1

Economic Growth Is Not Smooth

Source: Bureau of Economic Analysis.
Note: Quarterly growth rates calculated on an annual basis. Recessions are shaded.

FIGURE 26.2

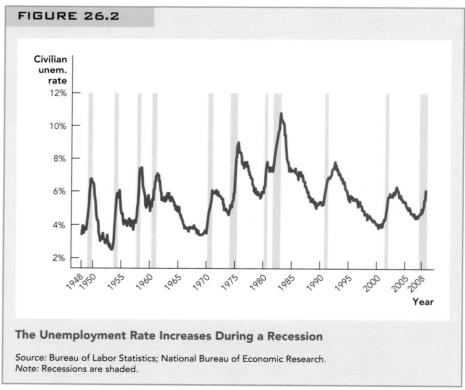

The Unemployment Rate Increases During a Recession

Source: Bureau of Labor Statistics; National Bureau of Economic Research.
Note: Recessions are shaded.

rate—but often unemployment exceeds the natural rate. More generally, when we see a lot of unemployed resources, it is a sign that resources are being wasted and the economy is operating below its potential. One of the goals of economic thinking is to better understand the causes of booms and recessions and perhaps learn how policy might help to smooth out these fluctuations. Recessions are the exception rather than the norm, but still we would all be richer and more secure if we could limit the frequency and severity of recessions.

A Skeleton Model

To understand booms and recessions we are going to develop a dynamic model of aggregate demand and aggregate supply. Our model will show how unexpected economic disturbances or "shocks" can temporarily increase or decrease the economy's rate of growth. We will focus on how an economy responds to two types of shocks, real shocks and aggregate demand shocks.

Models that explain how the economy responds to real shocks are often called Real Business Cycle models while those that focus on aggregate demand shocks are often called New Keynesian models. We think insights from both types of models are important so we will explain real shocks and aggregate demand shocks using the same dynamic AD-AS model.

In this chapter, we only present the model as a skeleton, giving the basics of the curves and how they shift. In the next few chapters, we add flesh to our skeleton by explaining the real-world mechanisms that generate and amplify fluctuations and by showing how monetary policy and fiscal policy might be used to smooth fluctuations.

Ultimately, our dynamic AD-AS model will have three curves: what we call the Solow growth curve, the dynamic aggregate demand curve, and the short-run aggregate supply curve. Let's begin with the Solow growth curve.

The Solow Growth Curve

We learned in Chapters 21 and 22 that economic growth depends on increases in the stocks of labor and capital and on increases in productivity (driven by new and better ideas and better institutions). Thus, the economy has a potential growth rate given by these fundamental or real factors of production. If markets are working well and prices are flexible, then an economy will grow at its potential rate. In other words, when prices are flexible, actual growth will be equal to potential growth. But, we will see later that all prices are not perfectly flexible; in the short run some prices, especially wages, can be "sticky" and because of this an economy need not always be growing at its potential.

We call it the Solow growth curve because Robert Solow, one of the giants of economics, created an important model of an economy's potential growth rate. In Chapter 22, we described Solow's model in more detail, but if you skipped that section don't worry; just think of the **Solow growth rate** as the rate of economic growth given flexible prices and the existing real factors of capital, labor, and ideas.

It's important to understand that the Solow growth rate does not depend on the rate of inflation. As we emphasized in Chapter 25, in the long run money is neutral.* Thus, when we put the inflation rate on the vertical axis of a graph and real growth (the growth rate of real GDP) on the horizontal axis,

The **Solow growth rate** is an economy's potential growth rate, the rate of economic growth that would occur given flexible prices and the existing real factors of production.

---

* Saying that potential growth does not depend on the rate of inflation is a strong form of the money neutrality result that we discussed in Chapter 25. Unexpected and variable inflation can reduce a country's potential growth rate and there are a variety of reasons why even an expected inflation rate might have a small influence on potential growth. Dealing with these issues, however, would complicate our model without leading to a better understanding of our current topic, business fluctuations.

FIGURE 26.3

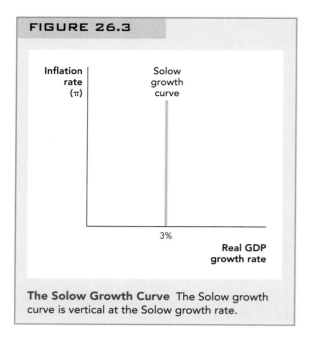

The Solow Growth Curve The Solow growth curve is vertical at the Solow growth rate.

FIGURE 26.4

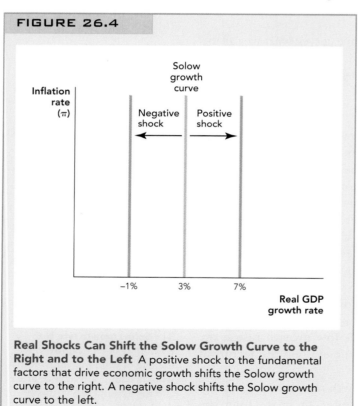

Real Shocks Can Shift the Solow Growth Curve to the Right and to the Left A positive shock to the fundamental factors that drive economic growth shifts the Solow growth curve to the right. A negative shock shifts the Solow growth curve to the left.

the Solow growth curve is very simple—it's a vertical line at the Solow growth rate. Figure 26.3 illustrates the Solow growth curve.

Notice that the Solow growth curve is a vertical line at the Solow growth rate. Once again, the potential growth rate of the economy depends on fundamental factors and not on the rate of inflation.

Shifts in the Solow Growth Curve   Take a look again at Figure 26.1, which shows the growth rate of U.S. GDP over time. Although the growth rate has averaged about 3 percent (at an annual rate) per quarter for many years, it has fluctuated around this average. Why?

One reason that the growth rate fluctuates is that economies are continually being hit by shocks, which shift potential growth and thus shift the Solow growth curve. As an example, consider an agricultural economy: Good weather can increase crop production—driving the growth rate up—while bad weather can decrease production, thereby driving the growth rate down.

All economies are subject to shocks not just from the weather but from wars, strikes, new technologies, and sudden changes in the supply of important inputs such as oil. Sometimes the shocks are big, such as a sudden decrease in the oil supply or a major technological advance. But many small shocks impinge on the economy all the time. When many of these small shocks are positive, the economy grows strongly and when many of these shocks are negative the economy slows down.

We call these shocks **real shocks** or productivity shocks because they increase or decrease an economy's fundamental ability to produce goods and services and, thus, they increase or decrease the Solow growth rate. In the next chapter, we say much more about real shocks and how transmission mechanisms spread and amplify shocks. For now, we emphasize that real shocks shift the Solow growth curve. A positive shock, shown in Figure 26.4, shifts the Solow growth curve to the right, increasing real growth. A negative shock shifts the Solow growth curve to the left, decreasing real growth.

The Dynamic Aggregate Demand Curve

A **real shock**, also called a productivity shock, is any shock that increases or decreases the potential growth rate.

Now let's introduce the dynamic aggregate demand curve, or AD curve. The **aggregate demand curve** tells us all the combinations of inflation and real growth that are consistent with a *specified* rate of spending growth. The easiest way to explain a dynamic AD curve is to derive it using the quantity theory of money from Chapter 25. Recall that we can write the quantity theory in dynamic form as:

$$\vec{M} + \vec{v} = \vec{P} + \vec{Y}_R \tag{1}$$

where $\vec{M}$ is the growth rate of the money supply; $\vec{v}$ is growth in velocity (how quickly money is turning over); $\vec{P}$ is the growth rate of prices, that is, the inflation rate; and $\vec{Y}_R$ is the growth rate of real GDP, which we simplify and call real growth. Thus, we can also write equation 1 as:

$$\vec{M} + \vec{v} = \text{Inflation} + \text{Real growth} \tag{2}$$

Now imagine that $\vec{M} = 5\%$, $\vec{v} = 0\%$, and real growth is 0%. What is the inflation rate? To answer that question, we substitute what we know into equation 2. Thus, 5% + 0% = Inflation + 0%, so Inflation = 5%. Intuitively, if the money supply is growing by 5 percent a year ($\vec{M} = 5\%$) and velocity is stable ($\vec{v} = 0\%$), then spending is growing by 5 percent a year. But if there are no additional goods to spend the money on, that is, if real growth is 0 percent, then prices must rise by 5 percent. In short, more spending plus the same goods equals higher prices.

An AD curve tells us *all* the combinations of inflation and real growth that are consistent with a specified rate of spending growth. We have just discovered *one* such combination; an inflation rate of 5 percent and a real growth rate of 0 percent are consistent with a spending growth rate of 5 percent. But what other combinations of inflation and real growth are consistent with a spending growth rate of 5 percent?

What would the inflation rate be if, just as before, $\vec{M} = 5\%$ and $\vec{v} = 0\%$ but now real growth = 3%? Once again, we substitute what we know into equation 2. Thus, we have 5% + 0% = Inflation + 3%, so Inflation = 2%. The intuition is quite simple. Inflation is caused when more money chases the same goods. So, if more money is chasing an increased quantity of goods, then, all else being equal, the inflation rate will be less than the increase in money growth.

Thus, we now have *two* combinations of inflation and real growth that are consistent with a spending growth rate of 5 percent. In Figure 26.5 on the next page, point *a* shows an inflation rate of 5 percent and a real growth rate of 0 percent and point *b* shows an inflation rate of 2 percent and a real growth rate of 3 percent. Both of these combinations are consistent with a spending growth rate of 5 percent, *so they belong on the same AD curve*. In fact, from equation 2 we know that all the combinations of inflation and real growth that are consistent with a spending growth rate of 5 percent must satisfy the equation, 5% = Inflation + Real growth. In other words, any combination of inflation and real growth that add up to 5 percent is on the same AD curve. Figure 26.5 shows the AD curve for a spending growth rate of 5 percent. Thus, all the points on this line add up to 5 percent.

Notice also that the AD curve is a straight line with a slope of −1.* This means that, given the rate of spending growth, a 1 percentage point increase in real growth reduces inflation by 1 percentage point.

The **aggregate demand curve** shows all the combinations of inflation and real growth that are consistent with a specified rate of spending growth.

Key Equation
$\vec{M} + \vec{v} = \text{Inflation}$
$\quad\quad\quad + \text{Real Growth}$

Check the Math

If the money supply is growing at 5% per year ($\vec{M} = 5\%$) and velocity is stable ($\vec{v} = 0\%$) then Inflation + Real Growth must equal 5%. If Real growth is 3% then Inflation must be 2%.

---

* We can easily show this by rewriting equation 2 in the familiar $Y = b + mX$ format, Inflation = $(\vec{M} + \vec{v}) - 1 \times$ Real growth. Notice that m, the slope of the curve, is −1.

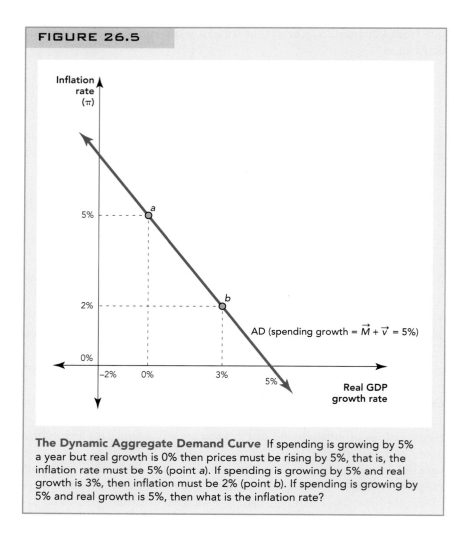

FIGURE 26.5

The Dynamic Aggregate Demand Curve If spending is growing by 5% a year but real growth is 0% then prices must be rising by 5%, that is, the inflation rate must be 5% (point *a*). If spending is growing by 5% and real growth is 3%, then inflation must be 2% (point *b*). If spending is growing by 5% and real growth is 5%, then what is the inflation rate?

Shifts in the Dynamic Aggregate Demand Curve The AD curve for a spending growth rate of 5 percent is all the combinations of inflation and real growth that add up to 5 percent. So, what is the AD curve for a spending growth rate of 7 percent? Right, all the combinations of inflation and real growth that add up to 7 percent. So, now that we know what an AD curve is, we also know how the AD curve shifts. In Figure 26.6, for example, notice that all the combinations of inflation and real growth along the AD curve denoted AD ($\vec{M} + \vec{v} = 5\%$) add up to 5 percent and all the combinations of inflation and real growth along the AD curve denoted AD ($\vec{M} + \vec{v} = 7\%$) add up to 7 percent. Thus, if spending growth increases to 7 percent, either because of an increase in $\vec{M}$ or an increase in $\vec{v}$, then the AD curve shifts up and to the right (outward). The intuition is that increased spending must flow into either a higher inflation rate or into a higher growth rate. Thus, an increase in spending growth shifts the AD curve outward, up and to the right, and, of course, a decrease in spending growth shifts the AD curve inward.

As we have said, an increase in spending growth can be caused by either an increase in $\vec{M}$ or $\vec{v}$. Later on in this chapter and in Chapters 29 and 31 on monetary and fiscal policy respectively, we explain exactly what this means in practice. For now, we just need to remember that increased spending growth shifts the dynamic AD curve outward and decreased spending growth shifts the dynamic AD curve inward.

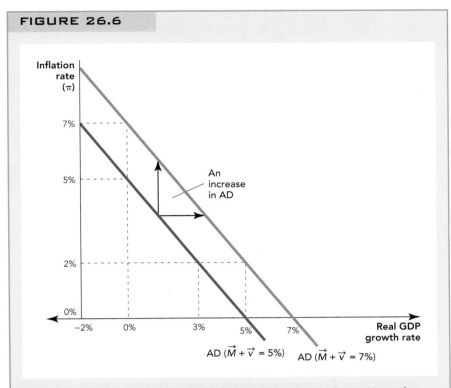

FIGURE 26.6

An Increase in Spending Growth Shifts the Dynamic AD Curve Up and to the Right (Outward) An increase in spending growth, $\vec{M} + \vec{v}$, increases AD, shifting the curve up and to the right (outward). Note that each curve is defined by a specified level of spending growth. For example, along the curve AD ($\vec{M} + \vec{v} = 5\%$) each combination of inflation and real growth must add to 5%. Along the curve AD ($\vec{M} + \vec{v} = 7\%$) each combination of inflation and real growth must add to 7%.

Now that we understand the Solow growth curve and the dynamic AD curve, we have enough to introduce the basics of our first model of business fluctuations, the real business cycle model.

The Real Business Cycle Model: Real Shocks and the Solow Growth Curve

Let's put the AD and Solow growth curve together. This will let us explain how business fluctuations can be caused by real shocks, a way of thinking about business fluctuations often called the real business cycle (RBC) model. Figure 26.7 on the next page shows an AD curve in which the growth rate of spending is 10 percent a year and a Solow growth curve with a growth rate of 3 percent. Since $\vec{M} + \vec{v}$ = Inflation + Real growth, and $\vec{M} + \vec{v}$ = 10%, and Real growth = 3%, we know that inflation is 7% a year. Thus, in this model, the equilibrium inflation rate and growth rate are determined by the intersection of the AD and Solow growth curve.

As we discussed above, the Solow growth rate can increase or decrease when the economy is hit by real shocks. In Figure 26.8 on the next page, we show the effect of a positive and a negative real shock.

A positive real shock shifts the Solow growth curve to the right, increasing real growth. The increase in the supply of goods brought about by a higher real growth rate reduces the inflation rate. During the late 1990s, for example,

CHECK YOURSELF

> If inflation is 2 percent and the Solow growth rate is 5 percent what, if anything, happens to the Solow growth rate when inflation increases to 5 percent?

> If we have a dynamic aggregate demand curve with $\vec{M}$ = 7 percent and $\vec{v}$ = 0 percent, what will inflation plus real growth equal? If we find out that real growth is 0 percent, what is inflation?

> Increased spending growth shifts the dynamic aggregate demand curve which way: inward or outward?

FIGURE 26.7

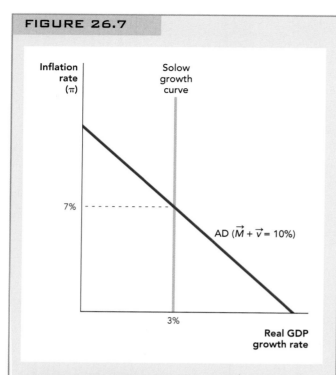

The AD and Solow Growth Curves If $\vec{M} + \vec{v}$ is 10% and real growth is given by the Solow growth rate at 3%, then the inflation rate will be 7%.

the Internet revolution, a positive real shock, increased the growth rate of the economy. Faster, more powerful computers at lower prices helped to keep inflation low.

A negative real shock shifts the Solow growth curve to the left, decreasing real growth. The slower growth rate means fewer new goods to spend money on so the inflation rate increases. In the 1970s, for example, a negative real shock—a sudden, sharp decrease in the relative supply of oil leading to several big jumps in the price of oil—reduced the growth rate and increased inflation.

Shocks to the Solow growth curve will change the growth rate and the inflation rate *temporarily* because the Solow growth curve is always shifting back and forth as new shocks hit the economy. Remember from Figure 26.1 that growth is not smooth. Thus, growth rates fluctuate from quarter to quarter as positive shocks increase growth temporarily and negative shocks reduce growth temporarily. In the United States, growth has fluctuated around approximately 3 percent for about a century. In different times and places, the average Solow growth rate could be higher or lower depending on growth in the fundamentals—

FIGURE 26.8

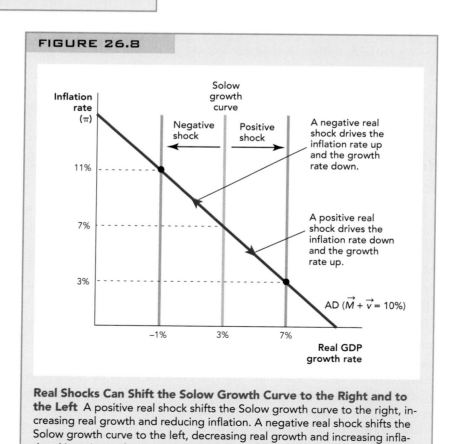

Real Shocks Can Shift the Solow Growth Curve to the Right and to the Left A positive real shock shifts the Solow growth curve to the right, increasing real growth and reducing inflation. A negative real shock shifts the Solow growth curve to the left, decreasing real growth and increasing inflation. Negative and positive real shocks are hitting the economy at all times.

capital, labor, ideas, and institutions—but every economy will always be subject to real shocks so growth will always fluctuate.

The RBC model is a natural extension of the Solow growth model. In the RBC framework, business fluctuations are simply changes in economic growth in the short run, driven by real shocks, changes in the productive capability of the economy. Let's look at how shocks to the dynamic aggregate demand curve work in the RBC model.

Shocks to Aggregate Demand in the Real Business Cycle Model

A shock to aggregate demand is shown by a shift in the AD curve. Aggregate demand shocks change how much people are willing to spend but since they do not change the potential capacity of an economy to grow, they do not change the Solow growth rate.

Let's work out how a shock to AD, brought about by changes in $\vec{M}$ or $\vec{v}$, influences real growth and inflation in the model that we have developed to this point. Imagine, for example, that $\vec{M}$, the growth rate of money, increases. This means more money in the economy, which increases spending growth, shifting the AD curve outward as we show in Figure 26.9. The outward shift in AD increases the inflation rate but has no effect on real growth. Similarly, a decrease in AD reduces the inflation rate but has no effect on real growth.

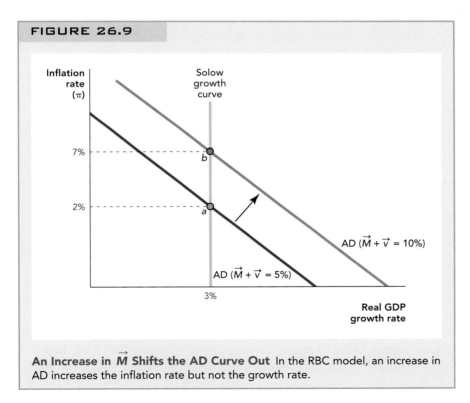

FIGURE 26.9

An Increase in $\vec{M}$ Shifts the AD Curve Out In the RBC model, an increase in AD increases the inflation rate but not the growth rate.

Shifts in AD do not influence real growth in the RBC model because real growth is fixed at the Solow rate by real factors such as the stocks and productivity of labor and capital. Returning again to equation 2, we have it that $\vec{M} + \vec{v} =$ Inflation + Real growth. *If the rate of real growth is fixed by real factors changes in $\vec{M}$ and $\vec{v}$ can only change the inflation rate.* Notice, for example, that an increase of 5 percentage points in $\vec{M}$ will increase the inflation rate by 5 percentage points. Thus, money is neutral. We know from Chapter 25 that this is a good prediction of what happens in the long run but is money neutral in the short run?

Most economists think that changes in the growth rate of money, especially unexpected changes, will have substantial effects on real growth in the short run. This is one reason why economists and politicians pay close attention to the policies of the Federal Reserve Bank, the institution that controls the supply of money in the American economy. But in the model we have developed so far, a basic RBC model, money is neutral in the short run as well as in the long run. So, if we want our dynamic AD-AS model of business fluctuations to be consistent with how we think the world works, we will need to add to the model.

A key assumption of the model so far, one that leads to the focus on factors like labor, capital, and productivity, is that prices are perfectly flexible. We now turn to what happens when prices are not perfectly flexible. This means adding a new curve to our model.

The New Keynesian Model

Models of the economy with "sticky" (not perfectly flexible) prices are often called New Keynesian models because they are based on ideas first developed by John Maynard Keynes in the 1930s. Since that time, these models have been elaborated by many people, hence the term "New" Keynesian. The key to New Keynesian models is that when some prices are sticky, the economy need not always be growing at its potential. In other words, when prices are sticky, the economy can grow slower or faster than the Solow rate of growth. Since real growth will no longer be determined solely by the Solow rate, we need to develop a new curve to describe the economy during the period in which prices are sticky.

The Short-Run Aggregate Supply Curve

Imagine that the growth rate of the money supply increases and as a result the inflation rate increases from 5 percent to 15 percent. In the long run, we know that wage growth will also increase by 10 percentage points but what would happen to firm profits if wages *do not* grow as fast as prices? If wages do not grow as fast as prices, then production will be very profitable (wages are most firms' biggest cost) and firms will want to hire more workers and expand output. Now, what would happen if inflation falls from 15 percent to 5 percent but wages *do not* fall as quickly? If wages do not fall as quickly as prices, then production will be very unprofitable and firms will want to fire workers and reduce output.

What we have shown in this simple example is that *if* wages are not as flexible as prices, then in the short run inflation and real growth will be positively related—an increase in inflation will increase real growth and a decrease in inflation will decrease real growth. We show such a relationship with a **short-run aggregate supply (SRAS) curve** like that shown in Figure 26.10. We have not yet given you reasons explaining *why* wages might not be as flexible as prices. As we explain these reasons, you will gain a better understanding of the short-run aggregate supply curve.

We will actually give you two reasons why there can be a positive relationship between the inflation rate and the growth rate in the short run. These are:

1. Sticky wages
2. Sticky prices

Let's look at each of these in turn.

In 1936, John Maynard Keynes published a revolutionary book, *The General Theory of Employment, Interest and Money. The General Theory* explained that when prices were not perfectly flexible, deficiencies in aggregate demand could generate recessions.

The **short-run aggregate supply (SRAS) curve** shows the positive relationship between inflation and real growth during the period when prices are sticky.

> **CHECK YOURSELF**
>
> > In what direction would a technological innovation such as the Internet or cheap fusion power shift the Solow growth curve?
>
> > In the real business cycle model, what effect does a large fall in aggregate demand have on real growth?

Sticky Wages When wages do not respond very quickly to changes in economic conditions, economists say that *wages are sticky*. One reason that wages are sticky is that they are not set every day or every month and sometimes wages are not even set every year. Labor contracts with unions, for example, often set wages for two to three years.

Workers and employers understand that inflation will reduce the value of money over time so when wages are set they will be set to grow in accordance with expectations of inflation. But expectations are not always correct. If inflation is greater than expected, then prices will be rising faster than wages so profits will increase and firms will expand output. If inflation is less than expected, then prices will be rising slower than wages so profits will decrease and firms will contract output.

The SRAS curve shows the positive relationship between inflation and real growth in the short run, that is, during the period when wages are sticky. We call it a short run curve because in the long run prices are flexible and thus growth will be at the Solow rate regard-

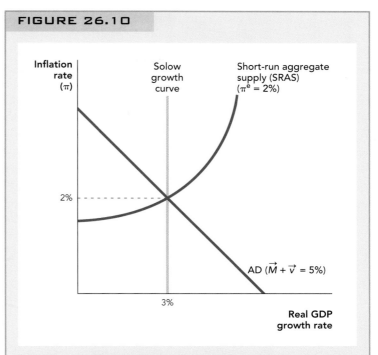

FIGURE 26.10

The Short-Run Aggregate Supply Curve In the New Keynesian model, inflation and real growth are positively related in the short run when prices are sticky. We illustrate this relationship with an upward-sloped, short-run aggregate supply curve.

less of the inflation rate. Notice that higher inflation *than expected* will increase output and lower inflation *than expected* will decrease output. Thus, every SRAS curve shows the relationship between inflation and output for a given expected inflation rate. The SRAS curve in Figure 26.10, for example, is the SRAS curve given that firms and workers expect an inflation rate of 2 percent. What would happen if workers and producers expected a different rate of inflation?

Shifting the SRAS Curve Figure 26.11 on the next page shows two SRAS curves, one when workers and producers expect an inflation rate of 2 percent, denoted SRAS (π^e = 2%), and the other when workers and producers expect an inflation rate of 4 percent, written SRAS (π^e = 4%). In both cases, the notation π^e means the expected inflation rate. Let's explain why the curves are positioned as they are.

Suppose we begin at point *a* when workers and producers expect inflation of 2 percent and actual inflation is 2 percent. Now imagine that there is an unexpected increase in the inflation rate to 4 percent a year, this moves the economy along SRAS (π^e = 2%) to point *b* where actual inflation is 4 percent and real growth has increased to 7 percent.

What would have happened if workers and producers had *expected* an inflation rate of 4 percent? Remember that *only unexpected inflation increases real growth*. If inflation is expected, it will be built into wages and prices and the growth rate will then be determined solely by real factors. So, if workers and producers expect inflation of 4 percent and actual inflation is 4 percent, then the economy will be at point *c*, a 4 percent rate of inflation and a 3 percent rate of real growth.

If workers and producers expect an inflation rate of 4 percent, then how high must actual inflation be to generate a real growth rate of 7 percent? If workers and producers expect an inflation rate of 4 percent, then actual

The rate of inflation that workers and producers expect is written π^e.

FIGURE 26.11

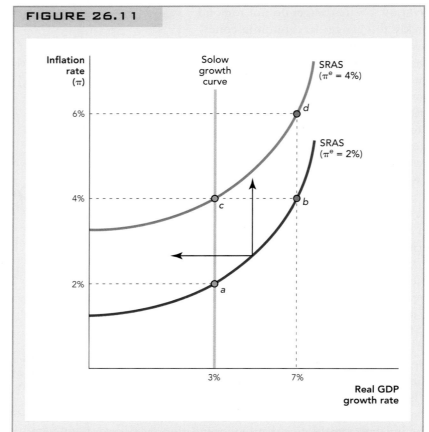

An Increase in the Expected Inflation Rate Shifts the SRAS Curve Up and to the Left If workers and producers expect an inflation rate of 2% and actual inflation is 2%, then the economy will be at point *a*. If the actual inflation rate increases unexpectedly to 4%, the economy will move along the SRAS (π^e = 2%) curve from point *a* to point *b*.

If workers and producers expect an inflation rate of 4% and actual inflation is 4%, there will be no increase in real growth and the economy will be at point *c*. To increase real growth to 7%, actual inflation needs to be 6% moving the economy along SRAS (π^e = 4%) to point *d*.

Notice that for each level of expected inflation, there is a different SRAS curve. An increase in the expected inflation rate from 2% to 4% moves the economy from SRAS (π^e = 2%) to SRAS (π^e = 4%) or equivalently an increase in the expected inflation rate shifts the SRAS up and to the left.

inflation will have to be higher, in this case 6 percent a year to increase real growth to 7 percent. Thus, an actual inflation rate of 6 percent will move the economy from point *c* along the curve labeled SRAS (π^e = 4 %) to point *d*.

Notice that for every rate of expected inflation, there is a *different* upward sloping SRAS curve. An increase in the expected rate of inflation from 2 percent to 4 percent, for example, moves the economy from SRAS (π^e = 2%) to SRAS (π^e = 4%). Alternatively, we can see from Figure 26.11 that higher rates of expected inflation "shift" the SRAS up and to the left.

The Parable of the Angry Professor We have drawn the SRAS curve to be flatter to the left of the Solow growth curve and steeper to the right of the Solow growth curve. Why?

Remember that one reason why the SRAS has an upward slope is that wages are sticky. And, importantly, wages are *especially* sticky in the downward direction. To see why downward stickiness in wages matters, imagine that expected inflation is 5 percent a year and workers are expecting wage increases of at least 5 percent a year. Now suppose inflation falls unexpectedly to 1 percent. If wage growth also fell to 1 percent, then there would be no problem: Real wages, real growth, and employment would all be constant. But how will workers feel when their salary increase is much less than expected? What will happen to morale and motivation?

One of the reasons that cutting wages or wage growth is so difficult is that everyone knows and understands their nominal wage, their wage in dollars. Every two weeks, most people get a paycheck showing them their nominal wage. Few people, however, know or understand much about their real wage, their nominal wage corrected for inflation or, in other words, the goods and services that their wage is able to purchase. Ultimately, what workers care about is their real wage, but since their nominal wage is so much easier to measure and understand most people pay more attention to their nominal wage, especially in the short run. Focusing on the nominal wage, however, can cause people to behave in peculiar ways. We illustrate this point with the parable of the angry professor.

One year a professor we know—yes, also an economist—received a pay cut. The professor rushed to the office of the department chair screaming bloody murder and threatening to leave or stop preparing for his classes. This professor was very angry. A few years later, the same professor received a pay increase of 3 percent but this was when inflation was running at 6 percent so this professor's real pay fell by 3 percent. Did the professor get angry and run to complain to the department chair? No, he was pretty happy. In real terms, he had received a pay cut but he still felt he got something, some form of recognition, plus it was a little more than what his friends down the hall got. The professor's immediate reaction was driven by the increase in the nominal wage even though a more careful calculation would show that he had received no greater command over goods and services.

Is this professor irrational? Maybe. Is this story for real? For sure. Is he the only person in the world like this? No way. And this guy is an economist who understands how things work. The lesson is that nominal variables can influence real economic choices.

The department chair learned a valuable lesson as well. Sometimes it is harder to cut nominal wages than real wages! The lesson applies to more than the angry professor. People don't like having things taken away from them, even when what is at stake is only symbolic. This is sometimes called an **endowment effect**. Once we possess something or feel we have a right to expect it, we consider it ours and are especially upset to give it up. The economist Truman Bewley interviewed employers and labor leaders, and concluded that the main reason employers don't like to cut wages is that if workers see smaller numbers on their paycheck, their morale declines and they often take their anger out on their employers. In contrast, layoffs get the misery out the door. One study examined pay records of a single large U.S. firm. From over 50,000 observations of wages, wage cuts were found fewer than 200 times, 0.4 percent of the total.

Thus, when inflation slows, growth in nominal wages should also slow but because of downward wage stickiness and confusion between nominal and real wages that process often results in painful declines in employment and real growth.

So why is the SRAS curve steeper above the Solow growth curve? First, wages are less sticky in the upward direction, or in other words not so many

An **endowment effect** is when people attach special importance to their starting point and have an especially strong dislike for losing that position.

people complain when their wages increase! Second, the SRAS curve must turn vertical at some point because there is a limit to how fast the economy can grow. The Solow growth rate can be thought of as the growth rate the economy can sustain in the long run given the growth rates in the fundamental factors of labor, capital, ideas, and institutions. The growth rate can be above the Solow rate if people work overtime and capital is pushed to its limit (e.g., by temporarily running equipment 24 hours a day), but at some point labor and capital are working around the clock and the economy just cannot grow any faster.

Sticky Prices   Wages are not the only prices that can be sticky. When a shock hits an economy, many prices do not move instantaneously to their new equilibrium levels. Why not? First, because it's costly to change prices and, second, because it's often not obvious whether a shock is temporary or permanent or nominal or real. That's a mouthful so let's explain.

Economists call the costs of changing prices **menu costs** because an obvious example is the costs of printing new menus when a restaurant changes its prices. Catalog companies like Lands' End and L.L. Bean face similar costs. Menu costs, however, are more than printing costs. Firms may want to keep prices steady to create trust—if prices are always changing, how do customers know they are getting a fair deal? Firms may also want to keep prices steady because if a firm raises its prices, it gives customers an incentive to search out other firms. Even if other firms are also raising prices, customers who leave may never come back.

Even small menu costs can discourage firms from changing prices when there is uncertainty about whether a shock is temporary or permanent. Imagine that the price of eggs increases. Does the restaurant change the price of an omelet? If the restaurant knew the price change was permanent, then maybe it would. But maybe the price of eggs will go down tomorrow. If the change in the price of eggs is temporary and the firm prints new menus today, it might also have to print new menus again tomorrow. Better to wait and see before printing the new menus. Thus, uncertainty creates incentives for firms to delay a price change until better information comes along.

Small menu costs can also create significant price stickiness when the nature of a shock is uncertain. Imagine that you are a baker—like the baker in Chapter 25's inflation parable—and suddenly you have more customers spending more money in your store than before. That's good news, right? Well, maybe it's not as good as it looks. It could be that more bread is being demanded or it could be that the nation's central bank is printing money at a faster rate and people are spending more on everything. If you knew for certain that people were spending more on bread simply because there were more dollars being printed you would raise prices immediately. But as a businessperson, how do you know whether the increase is a nominal increase or a real increase?

When a baker sees increased spending on bread, there is some chance that she interprets the greater spending as a signal that more people want to eat bread and thus instead of raising prices to completely offset the increased spending, she works longer hours or expands her bakery. Not all entrepreneurs or even most entrepreneurs will expand in this manner but probably some will, and that means that the growth rate increases. Thus, as with sticky wage theory, sticky prices generated by uncertainty over the nature of a shock (real versus

Menu costs are the costs of changing prices.

nominal) offer another reason why there is a positive relationship between un-expected inflation and real growth in the short run.

Shocks to Aggregate Demand in the New Keynesian Model

In the RBC model, shocks to AD had no effect on real growth but that was because the RBC model assumes prices are fully flexible. Let's now use our New Keynesian model with sticky prices to examine how shocks to aggregate demand can change real growth.

An Increase in $\vec{M}$ in the New Keynesian Model

In Panel A of Figure 26.12, we show an initial equilibrium at point a where in-flation is 2 percent, expected inflation is 2 percent, and the real growth rate is 3 percent.

CHECK YOURSELF

> Contrast wage and price flexibility in the real business cycle and new Keynesian models. Which model assumes significant price and wage stickiness?

> The Solow growth curve is vertical, the short-run aggregate supply curve is not. What explains the difference?

> What happens to the short-run aggregate supply curve when people expect inflation to increase from 2 percent to 3 percent?

FIGURE 26.12

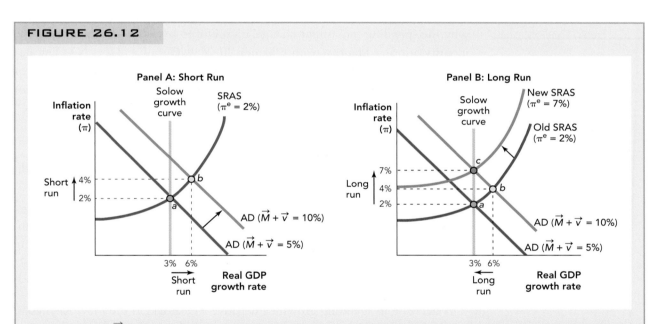

An Increase in $\vec{M}$ Shifts the AD Curve Out **Panel A:** In the New Keynesian model, an increase in AD increases real growth in the short run. The equilibrium moves from point a to the short-run equilibrium at point b. **Panel B:** In the long run the SRAS curve shifts upward as inflation expectations adjust and wages become unstuck. As a result, real growth will eventually return to the Solow rate and inflation will increase. In the long run, after all transitions are complete, the economy will end up at point c.

Now suppose that the growth rate of the money supply increases unexpect-edly from 5 percent to 10 percent. The injection of more money into the eco-nomic system creates a temporary boom at point b at which point the economy is growing at a 6 percent rate of real growth with inflation of 4 percent. Notice that $\vec{M}$ has increased by 5 percentage points. Some of that increase in spending is reflected in the inflation rate, which increases by 2 percentage points, and because of sticky wages and sticky prices, some of the increase in spending is reflected in real growth, which increases by 3 percentage points.

In Panel B of Figure 26.12, we show what happens in the long run. In the long run, *unexpected inflation always turns into expected inflation* and so the SRAS curve shifts up and to the left. As wages and prices become unstuck and expectations adjust more and more of the increase in $\vec{M}$ is reflected in the inflation rate and less is reflected in the real growth rate. In the long run, after all transitions are complete, all of the increase in $\vec{M}$ is reflected in the inflation rate—$\vec{M}$ increases by 5 percentage points and the inflation rate increases by 5 percentage points and the growth rate returns to the Solow level. Thus, the New Keynesian and RBC models have the same prediction for inflation and growth in the long run (compare Figure 26.9 with Panel B of Figure 26.12). But in the New Keynesian model, an increase in $\vec{M}$ increases real growth in the short run—during the period in which prices and wages are sticky.

Shocks to the Components of Aggregate Demand

Changes in $\vec{v}$ can be broken down into changes in $\vec{C}$, $\vec{I}$, $\vec{G}$, or $\vec{NX}$.

We have already looked at how changes in $\vec{M}$ shift the AD curve so the only other shifter is changes in $\vec{v}$. We can think of changes in $\vec{v}$ as increasing or decreasing the spending rate, holding the money supply constant. To understand why the spending rate might change, it's useful to recall, the national spending identity another identity from Chapter 20, $Y = C + I + G + NX$. The national spending identity reminds us that spending is spending on something. For example, if $\vec{v}$ increases that means that the growth rate of C, I, G, or NX must increase—that is, an increase in $\vec{v}$ must be apportioned among an increase in $\vec{C}$, $\vec{I}$, $\vec{G}$, or $\vec{NX}$.

It's often easier to think about changes in $\vec{v}$ working through changes in $\vec{C}$, $\vec{I}$, $\vec{G}$, or $\vec{NX}$ because each of these factors has somewhat different causes and consequences. Let's look at a change in $\vec{C}$. Why might $\vec{C}$ decrease?

A Decrease in $\vec{C}$ in the New Keynesian Model

Fear can cause $\vec{C}$ to decrease. Imagine that consumers suddenly become more pessimistic and fearful about the economy. Workers, for example, might be worried about becoming unemployed, so they build up their cash reserves by slowing down their consumption spending (a reduction in $\vec{v}$ working through a reduction in $\vec{C}$). Thus, fear causes consumers to reduce their spending. What happens?

A decrease in spending growth, a negative AD shock, in the New Keynesian model shifts the AD curve inward, reducing the real growth rate in the short run. Figure 26.13 illustrates. We begin at point *a* with an inflation rate of 7 percent, an expected inflation rate of 7 percent, and a real growth rate of 3 percent. A decrease in spending growth shifts the AD curve inward. With lower spending growth, wage growth should fall to match the reduction in price growth, but because wages are sticky, especially in the downward direction, wage growth remains high so firms are unprofitable, employment falls, and the economy slows.

Thus, in the short run, the economy moves from point *a* to point *b* where the inflation rate is lower and the real growth rate is also lower—in this example at point *b* growth is negative and the economy is in a recession.

★ For the purpose of making the models simple, we've focused on showing the initial short-run change and then the long-run results, after all the necessary transitions and adjustments have worked their way through the system. But if you're interested in better understanding the transition path to the long run for both real and aggregate demand shocks—and how this relates to some important economic issues about the length and nature of recessions—we cover this in detail in an online appendix to this chapter available at www.SeeTheInvisibleHand.com.

In the long run, fear recedes, wages adjust, and the spending growth rate returns to normal so the economy returns to long-run equilibrium at point *a*. Let's explain the shift back of the AD curve in the long run in greater detail.

Why Changes in $\vec{v}$ Tend to Be Temporary

Changes in $\vec{v}$ (that is, changes in the *growth rate* of C, I, G, or NX) differ from changes in $\vec{M}$ in one respect. $\vec{M}$ can be permanently set at any rate—5 percent, 17 percent, 103 percent—but changes in $\vec{v}$ tend to be temporary. How do we know this? Recall from Chapter 5 that the shares of GDP devoted to C, I, G, and NX have been quite stable over time. Over the past 50 years, for example, consumption expenditures in the United States have never been less than 60 percent of GDP nor have they ever been more than 71 percent of GDP. Investment expenditures vary more than consumption expenditures on a year-to-year basis, but over time these have also been remarkably stable, never less than 13 percent of GDP nor more than 20 percent of GDP. But if C, I, G, and NX are relatively stable as shares of GDP, it follows that changes in the growth rates of these variables, summarized by $\vec{v}$, must be temporary.

FIGURE 26.13

In the New Keynesian Model, a Temporary Decrease in AD Reduces the Inflation Rate and the Growth Rate in the Short Run At point *a*, spending is growing at a rate of 10% and real growth is 3% so inflation is 7%. If consumers become fearful and reduce their spending, $\vec{v}$ declines so the dynamic AD curve shifts inward. In the short run, wages are sticky so although spending growth declines, wage growth does not. As a result, real growth falls to −1% and the inflation rate falls to 6% at point *b*. In the long run as fear recedes and wages become unstuck, $\vec{v}$ returns to its normal rate, as does real growth.

Imagine what would happen if changes in $\vec{C}$, $\vec{I}$, $\vec{G}$, or $\vec{NX}$ were not temporary. Suppose, for example, that the government increases the growth rate of government spending, $\vec{G}$, perhaps in an effort to spend an economy out of a recession (this is called fiscal policy, which we study in Chapter 17). The government can do this in the short run, but if $\vec{G}$ were to grow at an unusually high rate year after year, then government purchases would soon dominate the economy. In fact, even if voters did not object, eventually $\vec{G}$ would have to fall because in the long run government spending cannot grow faster than the rate of economic growth (otherwise, government spending would eventually be more than GDP and that is not possible).

Thus, returning to Figure 26.13, we show that a decrease in $\vec{C}$ reduces AD and the rate of inflation in this period. In future periods, however, $\vec{C}$ will return to its normal rate and as it does AD and inflation will return to their previous rates. Notice that because the AD curve shifts back in the long run that *changes in $\vec{C}$, $\vec{I}$, $\vec{G}$, or $\vec{NX}$ do not change the rate of inflation in the long run*. In other words, sustained inflation requires ongoing increases in the money supply, a truth we've already outlined in Chapter 11.

Other Factors That Shift the AD Curve

We have already said that fear could decrease consumption spending (and, thus, confidence could increase consumption spending). What other factors could change $\vec{C}$, $\vec{I}$, $\vec{G}$, or $\vec{NX}$?

Fear and confidence play a similar role in investment spending as in consumption spending. If businesspeople fear that the economy is entering a recession, they may want to wait to make large investments. Similarly, confidence about the future will encourage businesspeople to make significant investments.

Wealth shocks can also increase or decrease AD. Imagine, for example, that the stock market or the housing market tumbles. Before the fall in prices consumers might have spent freely expecting that in their retirement years or in an emergency they could sell their stocks or their homes and live on the proceeds. When prices fall consumers suddenly realize that their wealth has fallen so they need to save more, thus they cut back on their spending. In 2008, for example, a simultaneous fall in stocks and housing prices caused a very large decrease in consumption spending. (A positive wealth shock works the opposite way. As the stock market rises, for example, consumers spend more today as their increasing wealth gives them confidence that they will also have plenty in the future.)

Taxes are another important shifter of $\vec{C}$ and $\vec{I}$. An increase in taxes can reduce consumption growth and a decrease in taxes can increase consumption growth. Taxes targeted at investment spending—such as an investment tax credit—can have a similar effect on investment growth. Changes in taxes are also a part of fiscal policy to be studied in Chapter 31.

Big increases in the growth rate of government spending will increase AD, and decreases in the growth rate of government spending will reduce AD. During a war, for example, government spending usually increases at a high rate, thereby shifting the AD curve outward. Government spending can also be timed to try to offset the business cycle (fiscal policy again—see Chapter 31).

The category called net exports consists of exports minus imports. We look at exports and imports more closely in Chapters 8 and 32, but for now the basic idea is simple. If other countries increase their spending on our goods (exports), that increases our AD. If we shift our spending away from domestic goods to foreign goods (imports), that reduces our AD.

Table 26.1 summarizes some of the factors that can shift the dynamic AD curve.

TABLE 26.1 Some Factors That Shift the Dynamic Aggregate Demand Curve

Increase AD (= Higher Growth Rate of Spending) (= Positive AD Shock)	Decrease AD (= Lower Growth Rate of Spending) (= Negative AD Shock)
A faster money growth rate	A slower money growth rate
Confidence	Fear
Increased wealth	Reduced wealth
Lower taxes	Higher taxes
Greater growth of government spending	Lower growth of government spending
Increased export growth	Decreased export growth
Decreased import growth	Increased import growth

Let's now apply the insights from the real business cycle model and the New Keynesian model to understanding the *Great Depression*, a watershed event in U.S. history.

Understanding the Great Depression: Aggregate Demand Shocks and Real Shocks

The Great Depression (1929–1940) was the most catastrophic economic event in the history of the United States; GDP plummeted by 30 percent, unemployment rates exceeded 20 percent, and the stock market fell to less than a third of its original value. Almost overnight America went from confidence to desperation. In fact, the Great Depression was a worldwide event, plaguing almost all the developed nations. In some cases, such as Germany, the economic downturn led to totalitarian regimes followed by war. The 1930s and 1940s were terrible years for the world and bad economic policy was partly at fault.

But the good news is this: We know how to prevent a great depression from happening again. The Great Depression became "great" because policymakers allowed aggregate demand to collapse.

Aggregate Demand Shocks and the Great Depression

The Great Depression occurred in the United States as follows. In 1929, the stock market crashed, creating a mood of pessimism among the American public. In part, this stock market crash had been brought on by tight monetary policy, aimed at limiting a stock market bubble. The fall in stock prices was a wealth shock that made many people feel poorer and so they limited their spending, causing $\vec{C}$ to fall. This, combined with the initial monetary contraction, that is, a reduction in $\vec{M}$, reduced aggregate demand, shifting the AD curve inward to the left.

But that is only the beginning of the story. In 1930, depositors lost confidence in their banks and as they withdrew their money, they created a wave of bank failures. These bank failures meant that people lost their money, again diminishing aggregate demand. Moreover, at the time there was no government deposit insurance so when the first banks failed, people became suspicious of every other bank and rushed to withdraw their money even from banks that were otherwise sound. From 1930 to 1932, there were four waves of banking panics; by 1933, more than 40 percent of all American banks had failed.

The fear and uncertainty created by bank failures, rising unemployment rates, falling consumer confidence, and inconsistent policy making in Washington also reduced investment spending. Between 1929 and 1933, for example, investment spending fell by nearly 75 percent. In many years, spending on new investment was not enough to replace the tools, machines, and buildings that had depreciated due to natural wear and tear. Astoundingly, the U.S. capital stock was lower in 1940 than it had been in 1930.[1]

Furthermore, in 1931, instead of increasing $\vec{M}$, the Federal Reserve allowed the money supply to contract even further. In the early 1930s, the U.S. money supply fell by about a third, *the largest negative shock to aggregate demand in American history*. At that time, the Fed should have been expanding the

CHECK YOURSELF

> What always happens to unexpected inflation in the long run?
> Show what happens to the dynamic aggregate demand curve if consumers fear a recession is coming and cut back on their expenditures.

UNDERSTAND YOUR world

money supply, to drive up output in an emergency situation and also to boost the reserves of failing banks (we analyze monetary policy further in Chapter 29). But, instead, the Fed allowed the money supply to contract and a disaster ensued. Bad decision making caused an additional monetary contraction during 1937–1938, which led to yet another wave of economic distress and it made the Great Depression much longer than it needed to be.

Figure 26.14 shows the story in a diagram. In the late 1920s, the economy was growing at a rate of about 4 percent per year with no inflation. Starting in 1929, a series of brutal shocks to aggregate demand reduced $\vec{C}$, $\vec{I}$, and $\vec{M}$ and by 1932 pushed real growth to a rate of −13 percent and inflation to −10 percent per year. Note that although drawn separately, all these shocks were intertwined as we discussed above.

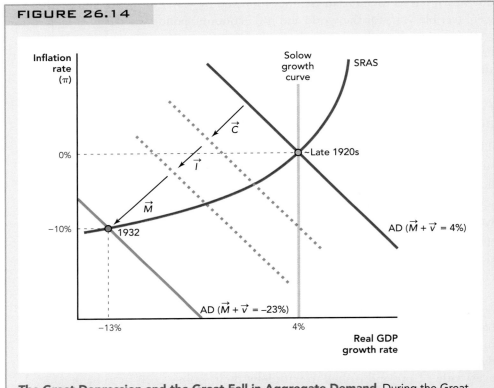

FIGURE 26.14

The Great Depression and the Great Fall in Aggregate Demand During the Great Depression, the growth rate of consumption, investment, and the money supply declined dramatically, creating deflation and an unprecedented decline in real growth.

Thus, the Great Depression was due primarily to the *great fall in aggregate demand*. Real shocks, however, also played a role in the Great Depression and in the failure of the economy to recover more quickly from the great fall. Let's take a look at how real factors contributed to the Great Depression.

Real Shocks and the Great Depression

We have already mentioned one real shock—the bank failures—and you can see why bank failures are a real shock by thinking back to Chapter 23 on financial intermediation. Bank failures reduced the money supply and spending (an aggregate demand shock), but they also reduced the efficiency of financial intermediation. As we discussed in Chapter 23, banks play a key role in bridging the gap between savers and investors and as banks failed this bridge collapsed. Some firms could rely on internally generated funds for investment and large firms could turn to the stock and bond markets for new funds. But many small businesses relied on loans from local banks who understood these businesses, and thus many small firms were especially harmed by bank failures.

To sum up the causal chain of events: A fall in $\overrightarrow{M}$ reduced aggregate demand, which led to bank failures, which led to a reduction in the productivity of financial intermediation, a real shock. As you would by now expect, the real shock reduced growth even further. One of the broader lessons of this episode—which is true more generally—is that shocks to AD and shocks to the Solow growth curve are linked in most recessions. In some cases, the shock to AD creates a real shock and in other cases a real shock creates a shock to AD; for instance, the fear and uncertainty created by a real shock can reduce AD by inducing people to cut back on spending and investment.

Some economic policy mistakes during the Great Depression also impeded recovery. As we have already mentioned, the Federal Reserve failed to use its power over the money supply to increase aggregate demand. In addition, there were other policy failures. The Smoot-Hawley Tariff of 1930, for example, raised tariffs (taxes) on tens of thousands of imported goods.[2] In principle a tariff, by taxing foreign goods, can boost demand for domestic goods, thereby increasing AD. (Notice from Table 26.1, our list of factors that can shift AD, that a decrease in imports can increase AD.) But, in reality, retaliations against the Smoot-Hawley Tariff by other countries created a spiraling decline in world trade. When other countries raised their tariffs, U.S. exports fell and remember that a reduction in exports reduces aggregate demand. Unfortunately, the large decline in world trade meant that the net effect of the tariff was to reduce aggregate demand.

A second negative effect of the tariff occurred because *a tariff is a negative productivity shock*. We get the most output from our capital and labor when we specialize in fields in which we have a comparative advantage and then trade for the goods that we produce at a comparative disadvantage (see Chapter 8 for more on comparative advantage). A tariff pushes capital and labor into lower productivity sectors, thereby reducing total output. Another way of seeing this point is to recognize that a tariff has exactly the same effects as an increase in transportation costs. Therefore, a tariff is like a negative productivity shock to the shipping industry, which ripples out to all the other industries dependent on shipping.

As if these shocks were not enough, the United States was beset during the early years of the Great Depression by a natural shock, namely the onset of the so-called Dust Bowl. A severe drought and decades of ecologically unsustainable farming practices turned millions of acres of farmland in Texas, Oklahoma, New Mexico, Colorado, and Kansas to dust. Dust storms blackened the sky, reducing visibility to a matter of feet. Hundreds of thousands of people were forced to leave their homes and millions of acres of farmland became useless.

The Dust Bowl was a real shock.
NOAA George E. Marsh Album

CHECK YOURSELF

> What happened to the U.S. money supply in the early 1930s? Did this primarily or initially affect aggregate demand or the Solow growth curve, and in which direction?

> If, as was said earlier in this chapter, real shocks hit the economy all of the time, should we ignore them in explaining the Great Depression?

In a good year, the real shocks of the Great Depression could have been absorbed without major difficulty, but in a bad year the shocks compounded one another and made a desperate situation even worse.

□ Takeaway

We've covered a lot in this chapter but the basic point is that we have used the model of dynamic aggregate demand and aggregate supply to analyze business fluctuations. A business fluctuation refers to the fact that the growth rate of GDP is volatile in the short run. A negative rate of growth is known as a recession. A recession is bad because it means that workers are unemployed and economies are not producing as many goods and services as they might.

Using our model we laid out how to analyze two types of shocks, real shocks and aggregate demand shocks. Real shocks are analyzed through shifts in the Solow growth curve. When we focus on real shocks and assume that prices are flexible we call our model of the economy a "real business cycle model." Aggregate demand shocks are analyzed using shifts in the AD curve. Aggregate demand shocks matter most when wages and prices are sticky and thus there is a positive relation between inflation rates and growth rates, which we summarize with a short run aggregate supply curve. When we focus on aggregate demand shocks and sticky wages and prices we call our model of the economy a "New Keynesian model." Some economists tend to emphasize real shocks and flexible prices (the RBC model) while others emphasize aggregate demand shocks and sticky prices (the New Keynesian model), but both types of shocks are important and business fluctuations are best understood when we put these models together.

When you combine the aggregate demand, Solow growth curve, and short-run aggregate supply curves into a single diagram, you can analyze a wide variety of economic scenarios and how they affect the growth rate of the economy. As you will see in future chapters, our model will also help us to explain when government policy can and cannot be used to successfully smooth business fluctuations.

For reasons outlined in the chapter, the aggregate demand curve slopes downward and the short-run aggregate supply curve slopes upward. We also showed how the aggregate demand curve can be broken down into changes in $\vec{M}$ and $\vec{v}$. In addition, changes in $\vec{v}$ can be broken down into changes in $\vec{C}$, $\vec{I}$, $\vec{G}$, or $\vec{NX}$. You should know and understand how menu costs, uncertainty, and confusion between nominal and real values make wages and prices sticky and how sticky wages and prices create an upward-sloped, short-run aggregate supply curve.

We outlined the history of America's Great Depression from the 1930s using our model. The Great Depression resulted from an unfortunate, concentrated, and interrelated series of aggregate demand and real shocks.

The material in this chapter is central to macroeconomics. If you understand where these curves come from, and how to shift them, you will have a basic toolbox for many macroeconomic questions. You are now ready to tackle many of the core topics of macroeconomics and business cycles.

□ C H A P T E R   R E V I E W

KEY CONCEPTS

Business fluctuations, p. 561

Recession, p. 561

Solow growth rate, p. 563

Real shock, p. 564

Aggregate demand curve, p. 565

Short-run aggregate supply curve, p. 570

Endowment effect, p. 573

Menu costs, p. 574

FACTS AND TOOLS

1. Sort the following shocks into real shocks or aggregate demand shocks. Remember that "shocks" include both good and bad events.

   A fall in the price of oil

   A rise in consumer optimism

   A hurricane that destroys factories in Florida

   Good weather that creates a bumper crop of California oranges

   A rise in sales taxes

   Foreigners watch fewer U.S.-made movies

   Fear

   New inventions occur at a faster pace

   A faster money growth rate

2. Look at Figure 26.2. Let's sum up some basic facts about the link between unemployment rates and recessions. Notice that the shaded bars indicate periods of recession, and wider bars mean longer recessions.

   a. How many recessions have there been since World War II?

   b. Since World War II, how many recessions had unemployment rates of over 10 percent?

   c. Often, the unemployment rate seems to hit its peak after the recession ends: The economy goes back to growing while the unemployment rate rises for a while. As the figure shows, the last two recessions have been clear examples of such "jobless recoveries." Approximately how many times did the unemployment rate peak after the recession ended?

3. Look at Figure 26.3. When inflation rises, does the Solow growth rate rise, fall, or remain unchanged?

4. Are "real shocks" negative shocks, by definition?

5. When negative real shocks hit, what typically happens to the Solow growth curve: Does it shift left, shift right, or stay in the same place?

6. In the real business cycle model, when negative real shocks hit, what typically happens to the aggregate demand curve? Does it shift left, shift right, or stay in the same place?

7. As Figure 26.1 implies, for the United States, the Solow growth curve has on average been approximately 3 percent real growth per year. If a negative real shock hits, shifting it by 2 percentage points what will happen to real growth: Will it be positive or negative? Would you call the resulting economic conditions a recession?

8. a. In the real business cycle model, what does a negative real shock do to inflation: Does it rise, fall, or remain unchanged?

   b. In the real business cycle model, what does a negative real shock do to spending growth: Does it rise, fall, or remain unchanged?

   c. In the real business cycle model, what does a fall in spending growth, that is, a shift inward of the AD curve, do to real growth: Does it rise, fall, or remain unchanged?

9. In the following cases, will real growth rise, fall, or remain unchanged according to the New Keynesian model?

   Expected inflation = 5 percent, Actual inflation = 7 percent

   Expected inflation = 3 percent, Actual inflation = 1 percent

   Expected inflation = 6 percent, Actual inflation = 6 percent

   Expected inflation = 7 percent, Actual inflation = −10 percent

   Expected inflation = −1 percent, Actual inflation = 0 percent

10. Consider the New Keynesian model below. In this relatively unsuccessful economy, the Solow growth rate is 1 percent per year:

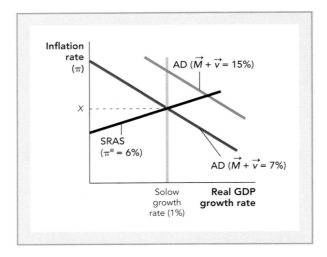

a. Calculate the inflation rate at X in this economy. (Hint: Use the quantity theory.)

b. If spending growth were 15 percent in this economy, what would the inflation rate be in the long run, assuming the Solow growth rate stays fixed?

11. a. The short-run aggregate supply (SRAS) curve is very predictable. When inflation is greater than people expect, SRAS eventually shifts (choose one: up, down) over the next year or so, and when inflation is less than people expect, SRAS eventually shifts (up, down) over the next year or so.

b. Here's another, equally valid way to look at the SRAS curve: When real GDP growth is above the Solow growth rate, SRAS eventually shifts (choose one: right, left) over the next year or so, and when real GDP growth is below the Solow growth rate, SRAS eventually shifts (choose one: right, left) over the next year or so.

c. Explain why the two ways of looking at the SRAS curve are equivalent.

THINKING AND PROBLEM SOLVING

1. Complete the following sentences:

According to the real business cycle model, when real growth is worse than usual, inflation is _____ than usual.

According to the New Keynesian model, when real growth is worse than usual, inflation is _____ than usual.

Since the two models *seem* to make clear-cut predictions about the link between short-term changes in growth and inflation, economists have spent some time trying to find out which of the two models gets more support from the data. In practice, economists find support for both points of view, which is another way of saying that there are real shocks and aggregate demand shocks.

2. a. In the 1970s, the United States had slow growth and high inflation. Which kind of shock and which model better fits these facts?

Real business cycle model: Negative real shock

Real business cycle model: Positive real shock

New Keynesian model: Negative aggregate demand shock

New Keynesian model: Positive aggregate demand shock

b. Using the same categories, explain the late 1990s, when the United States experienced fast growth and falling inflation.

c. Again using the four above categories, explain the early 2000s, when the United States experienced slow growth and falling inflation.

d. Which shock and which model best explains the 1981–1982 recession, when inflation fell quickly and unemployment rose quickly?

3. In the short run, it looks like many workers suffer from an "endowment effect" that makes wages sticky. Let's put this into a familiar supply-and-demand story. To keep things simple, we'll assume that in the long run, workers offer a fixed supply of labor: In other words, while they may be picky about jobs in the short run, in the long run they'll work regardless of the going wage.

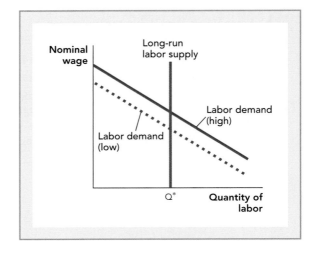

It's the businesses who *demand* labor and workers who *supply* labor. Currently, let's assume the economy starts off at long-run equilibrium, so that the normal number of workers, Q★, are working.

a. Suppose labor demand falls, shifting to the left, as in the figure on the previous page. What does the short-run supply curve for labor look like if workers refuse to take pay cuts even if it means losing their jobs (we can call this the "take this job and shove it" strategy after the famous country and western song). Indicate your answer by drawing a new line on the figure above, labeling it "short-run labor supply." You only need to focus on the area to the left of Q★.

b. Recalling your basic supply-and-demand model, does this fall in labor demand then create a "surplus" of workers or a "shortage" of workers?

c. According to the basic supply-and-demand model, what will happen to the price of labor over time as a result of this fall in labor demand?

4. a. If newspapers and magazines report a lot of good news about the economy, what is likely to happen to velocity?

b. If the Federal Reserve wants to keep aggregate demand (i.e., spending growth) stable, what will it do to the growth rate of the money supply when a lot of good news comes out about the economy: increase it, decrease it, or leave it unchanged? (Hint: In practice, central bankers often call this "leaning against the wind.")

5. In the New Keynesian model, after a monetary shock hits aggregate demand, which curve will shift to bring output growth back to the Solow growth rate: the short-run aggregate supply curve or the aggregate demand curve? (Hint: Which curve is more like a microeconomic story about prices adjusting in order to bring supply and demand into balance?)

6. Let's use the New Keynesian model to think about what happens when bad aggregate demand shocks hit the economy. Consider the following graph.

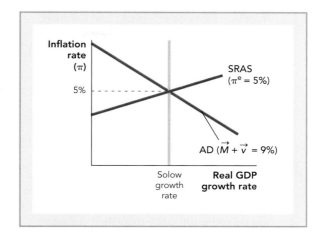

a. Before we get to the bad aggregate demand shock, let's find out what the Solow growth rate is in this economy. Use the quantity theory to find your answer.

b. Because of a fall in the growth of the money supply, spending growth falls to 4 percent per year. Draw the immediate result on aggregate demand in the graph above.

c. This fall in money growth lasts for many years. Eventually, in the long run, workers, business owners, and consumers all adjust their inflation expectations enough so that the economy returns to the Solow growth rate. Draw this new SRAS curve in the figure above.

d. In the long run, after spending growth falls to 4 percent per year, what will the Solow growth rate be? What will inflation be?

7. Real-world economies get hit with lots of shocks to aggregate demand and real shocks. Some shocks clearly fit into the first category, some into the second, and some include a generous mix of both. Let's categorize the following shocks. Only one is a clear case of "both."

Steelworkers go on strike, so less steel is produced

Businesses read about the glories of the Internet, so demand for high-tech investment purchases increase

U.S. senators read about the glories of the Internet, so demand for high-tech government purchases increase

A series of investment banks like Lehman Brothers and Bear Stearns go bankrupt

Around 2000, the glories of the Internet fade a bit so innovations increase at a somewhat slower rate for a few years

The U.S. government launches two costly wars almost simultaneously, so government purchases increase dramatically (referring to World War II, of course)

The U.S. government launches two costly wars almost simultaneously, using the draft to force many men to work much longer hours and supply more labor than they would otherwise

8. Let's have some practice with the dynamic aggregate demand curve. If you want to draw it in your familiar $y = b + mx$ format, you can think of it this way:

Inflation = (Growth in money + Growth in velocity) − Real growth

a. When you look at a fixed dynamic aggregate demand curve, like in Figure 26.5, what is being held constant? (choose one):

Spending growth (growth in M + growth in v)

Real GDP growth (growth in Y)

Inflation (growth in P)

b. When you look at a shifting dynamic aggregate demand curve, like in Figure 26.6, what *had* to change to make the curve shift? (choose one):

Spending growth (growth in M + growth in v)

Real GDP growth (growth in Y)

Inflation (growth in P)

c. According to the quantity theory, which of the following statements *must be* false, and why? More than one may be false.

"Last year, spending grew at 10 percent, real growth was 4 percent, and inflation was 6 percent."

"Last year, spending grew at 4 percent, real growth was −2 percent, and inflation was 6 percent."

"Last year, spending grew at 100 percent, real growth was 0 percent, and inflation was 20 percent."

"Last year, spending grew at 5 percent, real growth was 5 percent, and inflation was 2 percent."

"Last year, spending grew at 10 percent, real growth was 5 percent, and inflation was −5 percent."

9. In the New Keynesian model, what is "sticky?" More than one may be true: Wages, Real growth, Prices, Velocity, Money growth, Unemployment

10. During the Great Depression, which of the following were mostly aggregate demand shocks and which were mostly negative real shocks?

The fall in the growth rate of money

The fall in farm productivity

The Smoot-Hawley Tariff Act

CHALLENGES

1. Here is a puzzle. A country with a relatively small positive aggregate demand shock (a shift outward in the AD curve) may have a substantial economic boom, but sometimes countries that have massive increases in the AD curve (hyperinflation countries like Germany before World War II, for example) don't seem to have massive economic booms. Why does a small AD increase sometimes raise GDP much more than a giant AD increase?

2. Some companies raise their workers' pay by giving raises, but others prefer to give one-time bonuses instead.

a. How might bonuses help solve the problem of the "endowment effect?"

b. Think about two steel mills facing a big two-year drop in steel demand: In one steel mill, workers have received pay raises every year for five years. In the second mill, most of the pay increases have been through big bonuses at the end of each year. Which steel mill will probably keep more jobs during the two-year downturn? Why?

3. Reconsider your answer to Facts and Tools question 3. If you wanted to draw the Solow growth curve accurately, taking into account the idea that very high rates of inflation are likely to reduce real growth, how would you draw the Solow growth curve?

a. Would you draw a perfectly vertical curve, a curve with a positive slope, or a curve with a negative slope?

4. a. If the New Keynesian model's aggregate demand shocks are the most important drivers of business fluctuations, then should we expect real wages to be procyclical (rising when GDP growth is high) or countercyclical (rising when GDP growth is low)?

    b. If the real business cycle model's real shocks are the most important drivers of business fluctuations, then should we expect real wages to be procyclical or countercyclical?

    c. In Thinking and Problem Solving question 1, we noted that macroeconomists find mixed evidence on the link between business fluctuations and inflation. But there's more agreement on the link between business fluctuations and real wages: The real wage is procyclical, growing quickly during good times and growing slowly or falling during bad times. Which of the two theories is this most consistent with? (We'll revisit this question in the next chapter.)

5. Often, more than one kind of shock hits the economy at once. When this happens, the different shocks *could* push inflation (or real growth) in different directions in the short run, leaving the final short-run result ambiguous. What is most likely to happen to inflation and real output growth in the following cases: Will they rise, fall, or can't you tell with the information given? Note that you will often (maybe always) be able to definitely know the answer for one but not the other.

    a. A nation's scientists invent many new Internet search tools, raising current productivity and making investors optimistic about future inventions as well.

    b. A government raises taxes and its economy has a year of excellent weather for growing crops.

    c. Oil prices skyrocket and the central bank slows the rate of money growth.

27

The Real Business Cycle Model: Shocks and Transmission Mechanisms

CHAPTER OUTLINE

Shocks

How Transmission Mechanisms Amplify and Spread Shocks

Takeaway

Appendix: Business Fluctuations and the Solow Model

In the last chapter, we introduced the real business cycle model. In this chapter, we look in more detail at shocks and the economic forces, called **transmission mechanisms,** that can amplify the impact of shocks by spreading or transmitting them across time and sectors of the economy.

Let's begin with the idea of shocks. **Shocks** are rapid changes in economic conditions that increase or diminish the productivity of capital and labor, which in turn influences GDP and employment. To understand shocks and to see why they matter, we start with poorer economies, where shocks are easier to see and understand. Later in the chapter, we move to how shocks can create problems for the U.S. and other developed economies.

Transmission mechanisms are economic forces that can amplify shocks by transmitting them across time and sectors of the economy.

Shocks are rapid changes in economic conditions that have large effects on the productivity of capital and labor.

Shocks

There are several billion farmers in the world and for many countries agriculture remains the single-largest contributor to GDP. How much a farm produces depends on the quantity and quality of the inputs of capital and labor, but agricultural output also depends on the weather. When the weather fluctuates, so does output and therefore so does GDP, especially in agricultural economies.

Figure 27.1 on the next page shows how shocks to the weather influence India's agricultural output and GDP. The blue line is the percentage deviation in India's yearly rainfall from the average (1970–1990). Above average rainfall is good for the crops and below average rainfall is bad. In 1975, for example, rainfall was 10.8 percent above average and, in Panel A, we see that agricultural output in that year grew by a bountiful 12.8 percent. In 1979, however, rainfall was 11 percent below average and agricultural output fell by nearly 13 percent, compared to the year before.

FIGURE 27.1

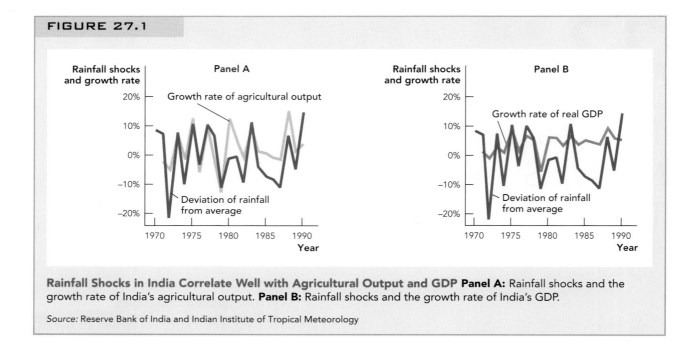

Rainfall Shocks in India Correlate Well with Agricultural Output and GDP **Panel A:** Rainfall shocks and the growth rate of India's agricultural output. **Panel B:** Rainfall shocks and the growth rate of India's GDP.

Source: Reserve Bank of India and Indian Institute of Tropical Meteorology

When India's agricultural output falls, so does India's GDP. It is not just that agriculture contributes to GDP directly but, if farmers struggle, many other sectors of the Indian economy suffer as well. For instance, the demand for tractors will go down and farmers will buy fewer items for their own consumption. Thus, the shock spreads to other sectors of the economy.

Agriculture was the largest contributor to India's GDP, so the shocks to agricultural output caused by the weather have had a big impact on GDP growth. In Panel B of Figure 27.1, the red line shows the growth rate of India's GDP. As expected, GDP boomed in 1975, growing by nearly 10 percent, and busted in 1979 with a decline of 5.2 percent. Note that the booms and busts in GDP are not as strong as the booms and busts in agricultural output because other sectors, less influenced by the weather, also contribute to GDP.

Take a close look at Panel B of Figure 27.1. Does it seem to you that shocks to rainfall are becoming less important to India's GDP since around 1980? Agriculture contributed 40 percent of India's GDP in 1970. Since then, the Indian economy has grown and diversified, and so agriculture contributed only 20 percent of India's GDP in 1990. Therefore, shocks to the weather are becoming less economically important in India over time. In the United States, agriculture contributes around 1 percent to GDP, so yearly variations in the weather don't have much of an effect on GDP. Other shocks, however, can rock the U.S. economy.

Oil Shocks

In an economy with a large manufacturing sector, a reduction in the oil supply is like a reduction in rainfall in an agricultural economy. Oil and machines are complementary, which means they work together, along with labor, to produce output. Thus, when the oil supply is reduced, capital and labor become less productive. Oil greases the wheels of industry, sometimes literally, and with less oil the wheels do not turn as well.

The first oil shock came in late 1973, when many of the oil-producing nations under the guise of OPEC (Organization of Petroleum Exporting

Countries) reduced the global oil supply to protest America's support of Israel in the Middle East. The result was that the price of oil more than tripled in just two years. This became a significant problem for the American economy.

The higher price of oil, for instance, also meant a much higher price for gasoline (oil is one input into gasoline). Higher gas prices reduced the demand for larger cars and increased the demand for smaller cars. The U.S. auto industry was specialized in the production of larger cars and had a difficult time adjusting. Factories cannot simply be switched from the production of one type of car to another—much of the physical capital in an auto factory is specialized. A machine that is used to bend steel is no longer useful when production switches to lightweight, fuel-saving plastic composites. Workers are specialized too in both knowledge and location. Thus, the oil shock meant that many auto plants producing larger cars shut down or were used at less than full capacity. Similarly, autoworkers became unemployed and many had to learn new skills and often they had to move to new jobs.

Not every part of the American economy was harmed. The demand for smaller cars increased, for example, but the U.S. auto industry could not immediately meet that demand. It can take a decade to design and build a new car so it took considerable time for capital and labor to reallocate to the production of smaller American cars. In the meantime, output and employment in the auto industry fell. Similarly, over time, the city of Houston (which services much of the American oil industry) became populated with many former residents of Detroit (which made large American cars) but the transition was costly and disruptive.

Since oil is an important input in many sectors of the economy, high oil prices—or oil shocks—hurt many American industries. Thus, sharp increases in the price of oil can disrupt the economy as a whole. Figure 27.2 shows the price of oil and the last six U.S. recessions. In each case, there was a large increase in the price of oil just prior to or coincident with the onset of recession (oil prices were still very high in the 1981–1982 recession, which was almost a continuation of the

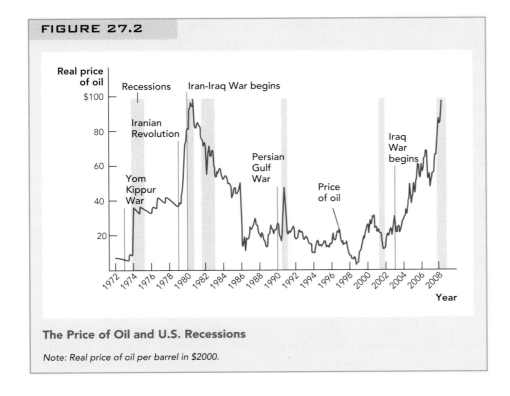

FIGURE 27.2

The Price of Oil and U.S. Recessions

Note: Real price of oil per barrel in $2000.

1980 recession). The pattern is especially clear with the first three recessions in the graph. In these cases, the onset of a war reduced the oil supply, driving up the price *unexpectedly*. Unexpected shocks are the most costly to deal with.

It's fairly easy to see the impact on the economy of a large increase in the price of oil, but it's harder to eyeball the effect of smaller shocks. Careful statistical analysis, however, can disentangle the effect of oil shocks from the many other shocks that keep on hitting the economy. In Figure 27.3, we show how the economy responds to an unexpected and permanent increase of 10 percent in the oil price.

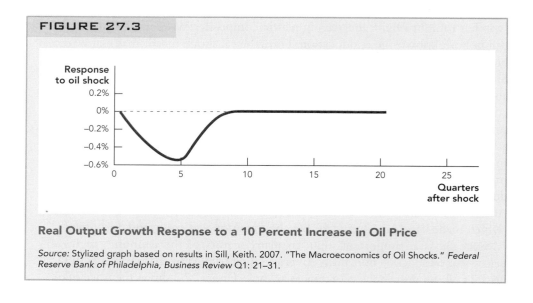

FIGURE 27.3

Real Output Growth Response to a 10 Percent Increase in Oil Price

Source: Stylized graph based on results in Sill, Keith. 2007. "The Macroeconomics of Oil Shocks." *Federal Reserve Bank of Philadelphia, Business Review* Q1: 21–31.

Starting from the normal or trend rate of growth (which is fixed at the 0 point on the vertical axis of the graph), Figure 27.3 shows that a 10 percent increase in the price of oil slows the economy down gradually with the biggest slowdown occurring about five quarters (a little over a year) after the onset of the increase in price. After five quarters, the growth rate begins to pick up again quite quickly and after 10 quarters (two and a half years), the economy has adjusted to the higher price and the growth rate returns to normal.

Thus, a 10 percent increase in the price of oil lowers the GDP growth rate from what it would have been without the price increase for just over two years. The total effect on GDP is a decrease of about 1.4 percent. In other words, if the price of oil had not increased, real GDP would have been about 1.4 percent higher.

Since 2002, the price of oil has increased dramatically and in 2008 peaked at a real price as high as at any time in American history. To be sure, this was not good for the U.S. economy, but the price increase did not cause an immediate recession. Why not? Several answers have been proposed. First, just as the Indian economy has become less dependent on agriculture, so has the American economy become less dependent on oil. Since the price of oil spiked in the 1970s, American producers have learned to protect themselves. The American economy uses energy and oil more efficiently today than it did in the 1970s. In 1970, it took about 1.3 barrels of oil to produce $1,000 of GDP, but in 2004 it took only 0.64 barrels of oil. Figure 27.4 shows that energy consumption per dollar of GDP, not just oil consumption, is today less than half of what it was in 1950. This means that oil price spikes do not hurt the American economy nearly as much as before.

Second, recent increases in the price of oil have been slower and driven by increases in demand due to a growing world economy rather than by sudden cuts in supply. If individuals and firms have time to adjust to a higher price and if the price is driven by a growing economy, it is less likely to cause disruptions.

Third, the U.S. economy may have been lucky because negative oil shocks have been offset in recent years by positive productivity shocks. Remember that shocks can be positive like good weather, as well as negative. In the case of the United States, in the early part of the twenty-first century, productivity grew at especially high rates, mostly because of advances in computers and information technology. Think about how much and how quickly the United States has been transformed by the Internet. Almost all American workplaces during this period became more efficient at processing and storing information. In this case, some positive shocks outweighed the costs of other negative shocks.

A final reason why oil shocks have been less damaging in recent years may be that the Federal Reserve has responded more appropriately to recent oil shocks than they did in the past. We discuss this explanation, which requires an explanation of aggregate demand and monetary policy, in a later chapter.

Even though oil shocks are less important to the U.S. economy than they used to be, sharp changes in the price of oil are still a major influence on the U.S. economy. A sharp increase in the price of oil, when combined with other shocks, can help to drive the economy into recession. As Figure 27.2 indicates, in late 2007 and early 2008 as the price of oil peaked the U.S. economy did in fact enter into a recession.

FIGURE 27.4

Energy Consumption per Dollar of GDP

Source: Energy Information Administration

Shocks, Shocks, Shocks

Oil and rainfall shocks are only two among many shocks that might hit an economy. Other possible shocks are wars, terrorist attacks, major new regulations, tax rate changes, mass strikes, new technologies such as the Internet, and significant changes in consumer preferences (for example, if consumers suddenly decided they needed to save a larger fraction of their incomes). Most generally, economies are continually hit by many small shocks. Some of the shocks are good, like a productive new technology, and some are bad, like a drought. In a typical year, the good shocks outweigh the bad and the economy grows. People build on previous knowledge and most of the time are able to do better and produce a bit more than in previous years. In a bad year, however, an economy may be hit with a big shock, like an oil shock, or more small shocks are negative than positive and it experiences a recession. It is a bit like playing poker. Every now and then you get a hand of cards that simply cannot be played well, no matter what else you do.

How Transmission Mechanisms Amplify and Spread Shocks

A negative shock reduces output directly—when rainfall is below average the same capital and labor inputs produce less output. But a series of indirect negative effects can amplify shocks and spread them throughout an economy in

CHECK YOURSELF

> Consider the ubiquity of cell phones throughout the world. How can this ubiquity be considered a positive shock? (Hint: compare with 10 years ago.)

> How would a large and sudden increase in taxes, for example a tax on energy, shift the Solow growth curve?

ways that lower output even further. We focus on five transmission mechanisms: intertemporal substitution, uncertainty and irreversible investments, labor adjustment costs, time bunching, and sticky wages and prices.

Intertemporal Substitution

Let's go back to our farm example. If rainfall is below average, farmers may work less hard and devote less capital to their fields.

Why would farmers choose to use less labor and capital in response to a negative shock? Think about it this way: When the crops are bountiful it makes sense to work from dawn till dusk because each hour of additional work pays a lot—remember the old saying, make hay when the sun shines? But when the crops are poor, the returns to an additional hour of work are low and so farmers may rationally decide to work less. The same is true for applications of capital. When planted crops will blossom, it may be worth paying the fuel costs to run the tractor an extra hour. When planted crops will in any case wither, why bother spending the money on fuel? Just leave the tractor in the shed.

Intertemporal substitution reflects how people choose to allocate consumption of goods, work, and leisure across time to maximize well-being.

Economists call this effect **intertemporal substitution**. That phrase means that a person or a business is most likely to work hard when working hard brings the greatest return. We work hard in some times and rest in others, and of course we pick and choose the spots when we try hardest. We are substituting effort across time and thus the phrase *intertemporal substitution*.

When you study for a test, do you practice intertemporal substitution or do you study an equal amount every day? As a test approaches, you probably study harder, turning down some opportunities for fun. Once the test is over, you study less and have more fun. Intertemporal substitution means that when you study, you study a lot and when you party, well, you know.

Intertemporal substitution, however, is not just about substituting between work and leisure. We pointed out in Chapter 1, for example, that when jobs are plentiful and wages are increasing there is a tendency for fewer people to enter university, but when jobs are scarce and wages are stagnant, more people decide to invest in an education. Students understand that the opportunity cost of getting an education falls when jobs are scarce.

During a boom, people are less likely to retire or take early retirement—why not stay another year or two and bank the high wages? Similarly, stay-at-home parents and other people who might otherwise not work outside the home will choose to enter the workforce during boom periods. During recessions, people are more likely to take early retirement or focus on homemaking. Figure 27.5 shows that when GDP is growing faster than trend, then the employment to population ratio also tends to grow faster than trend. The implication is that the supply of labor increases in a boom and falls during a recession.

Notice that intertemporal substitution magnifies negative economic shocks. When things go a bit bad, the return to work and investing falls and often people work less and invest less, which makes things go just a bit worse. The ripple effects of this process help turn an initial shock into a broader recession. Of course, on the upside, intertemporal substitution can feed an economic boom and make it more intense. If things are going well, many people will be inclined to work harder, which will in turn increase output and make things go even better. Figure 27.6 shows how intertemporal substitution amplifies shocks to the Solow growth curve, which we introduced in Chapter 26. Intertemporal substitution is hardly the only force behind employment decisions (see Chapter 24),

Intertemporal substitution at work during World War II.

FIGURE 27.5

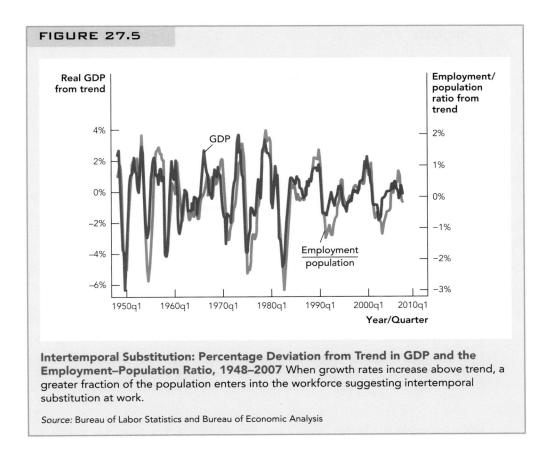

Intertemporal Substitution: Percentage Deviation from Trend in GDP and the Employment–Population Ratio, 1948–2007 When growth rates increase above trend, a greater fraction of the population enters into the workforce suggesting intertemporal substitution at work.

Source: Bureau of Labor Statistics and Bureau of Economic Analysis

but it does play a role in magnifying shocks, both on the upside and the downside.

Once we add intertemporal substitution to the RBC model, real shifts in aggregate demand (AD) can also change the growth rate of the economy. A large increase in government spending, $\vec{G}$, for example, can encourage workers to enter the workforce, temporarily increasing the supply of labor and raising the Solow growth rate. During World War II, for example, government spending increased dramatically and more workers, especially women, were drawn into the labor force. They faced, at least for a while, superior wage opportunities.

In Figure 27.7 on the next page, we show a long-run equilibrium at point *a*. From this starting point, a large increase in $\vec{G}$ shifts the AD curve outward. If intertemporal substitution is *not* important, then the inflation rate increases, but the Solow growth curve does not shift and thus there is no change in the growth rate, as we showed in the last chapter. But if intertemporal substitution is important, then workers respond to the increase in $\vec{G}$ by entering the

FIGURE 27.6

Intertemporal Substitution Amplifies Shocks

workforce or temporarily working longer hours. With an increase in labor, *L*, the Solow growth curve shifts out and the economy operates in the short run at

FIGURE 27.7

Inflation rate (π)

1. An increase in government purchases increases aggregate demand (AD).

2. Workers take advantage of higher aggregate demand by working more so the Solow growth curve shifts out.

3. The growth rate and the inflation rate increase in the short run...

4. ...but in the long run the aggregate demand curve returns to its normal level as does the Solow growth curve.

Solow growth curve

5%

2%

b

a

AD ($\vec{M} + \vec{v} = 10\%$)

AD ($\vec{M} + \vec{v} = 5\%$)

3% 5%

Real GDP growth rate

Intertemporal Substitution and Fiscal Policy An increase in $\vec{G}$ increases AD and with intertemporal substitution real growth increases temporarily.

point b, namely at a higher growth rate for real GDP. Over time, however, $\vec{G}$ returns to its normal rate and workers return to their normal effort levels so the economy returns to point a.

Economists disagree on the importance of intertemporal substitution as a way of generating real effects from fiscal policy. For very large shocks such as World War II, the intertemporal substitution story is plausible, but most economists think that the primary reason why an increase in AD has real effects in the short run is the sticky wages, sticky prices story of the New Keynesian model.

Let's turn to another transmission mechanism, uncertainty and irreversible investments.

Uncertainty and Irreversible Investments

Negative shocks also increase uncertainty, which is bad for business investment. Bad news usually also means uncertain news, as the arrival of the bad news causes people to rethink how the world works. For instance, when the 9/11 attacks hit the United States, uncertainty about the future increased. All of a sudden many people started worrying—rightly or wrongly—that subsequent terrorist attacks would be a big problem. The initial response was to hold off on business investment. Until it became clear that such attacks would not become regular occurrences, for instance, many investors were reluctant to fund new construction in New York City. When investors are uncertain, often they prefer to wait and sample more information, before committing themselves.

The key idea here is that many investments are **irreversible investments,** or very costly to reverse. That is, once a new office building has been constructed on Wall Street, it is hard to tear down that building and redeploy the steel and glass to other economic uses. So, before investors build a new skyscraper, they will

Irreversible investments have high value only under specific conditions—they cannot be easily moved, adjusted, or reversed if conditions change.

try to make sure that there will be a demand for the offices. Of course, investors sometime get this wrong, just as commercial real estate overexpanded in the mid- to late 1980s, or too many homes were built in the years preceding the real estate crash of 2007. But prior to expansion, investors want to see many strong signals that market conditions will validate their plans.

The more uncertain the world appears, the harder it is for investors to receive definite signals about where to invest their resources. Investors may see that the demand to watch television programs is shrinking, as it has been for years, but investors do not know which new sectors will be expanding. Will all those extra TV-watching hours be replaced by time spent on Facebook, on Second Life, or by time spent outdoors? When investors wait to see what happens, that means resources are sitting idle rather than being productive. That means lower GDP and it contributes to the economic slowdown.

To see the logic of irreversible investment, just consider the decision to marry. Marriage is a kind of investment and not just in the financial sense. It is making a commitment to the future and it is often for a very long period. Given the seriousness of this commitment, you ought to make (relatively) sure that your marriage is a good idea. If you receive some information causing you to doubt your potential partner (did someone hint he or she is a convicted felon?), maybe you should wait a while and discover the truth before proceeding. Of course, if you wait to decide on marriage, you may also wait to buy a house together, even if buying a house is a good idea. That's just common sense. The point is that the same logic applies to economic investments. Uncertainty usually slows investment and keeps resources in less productive uses.

One of the most irreversible investments of them all

Labor Adjustment Costs

Once a negative shock hits the economy, labor must adjust. Workers must look for new jobs, they must move to new areas, and sometimes they must change their wage expectations. Recall from Chapter 24 how search—looking for a new job—is one reason for unemployment. A negative shock to the economy, by remixing opportunities, induces more search and thus causes more search-related unemployment. **Labor adjustment costs** are the costs of shifting workers from declining sectors of the economy to growing sectors.

Labor adjustments to shocks are not always rational in the narrowly economic sense of that term. If an automobile worker is laid off the General Motors assembly line, and he loses his formerly unionized job, he may not be able to find the same wage elsewhere. Currently, the less unionized foreign automakers in the United States pay less than GM does per hour. Some automobile workers without a high school degree may make up to $100,000 per year. It may take a while for that person, if thrown out of work, to admit that he must settle for a lower wage. In the meantime, he is looking for a job and perhaps even rejecting offers that are as good as he will ever find.

The high cost of reversing job decisions can lead to unemployment, just as the costs of reversing investment can cause investors to wait. Again, consider the closure of a Detroit automobile plant and the fate of the former workers. These workers face at least three options: They can wait for the plant to reopen, they can seek another job in Detroit, or they can move to a more prosperous part of the country. Which course of action is best?

It's not always easy to say which choice is best, yet the choice involves a costly-to-reverse decision. Once the house is sold and the belongings are packed and

Labor adjustment costs are the costs of shifting workers from declining sectors of the economy to growing sectors.

moved to Houston, it is costly to go back to Detroit. The unemployed autoworker, rather than moving to Houston, might wait for a while to see what happens, even if he knows the probability of finding a job in Houston is higher than in Detroit. Or if that person opens up a pet shop, it will be hard to shift back into automobile manufacture. So, when faced with these uncertainties, many workers simply will bide their time until the future is clearer. Maybe they'll do some part-time or casual work (or maybe they'll put a new deck on the house), but they probably won't be employed at full productivity. The result is ongoing unemployment, or at least underemployment, and again the initial negative real shock is magnified.

In sum, changes to the world require people to adjust their jobs and their careers. People can't always make those adjustments right away, and in the mean time output and employment will be lower than normal.

Time Bunching

People often bunch their activities at common points in time. Most people work from 9 AM to 5 PM rather than from 10 PM to 6 AM. One reason is that these are daylight hours, but another reason is because everyone else is working during this time. If you and your coworker are in the office at the same time, it is easier to collaborate. Furthermore, it makes working more fun to be there with other people.

We also like to party at the same time and to see movies and concerts with other people. It's not just a question of fun—it is also economics. If you want to cook an elaborate meal, order some fancy bottles of wine, or clean up the house for a party, you want to make sure that enough people attend for those efforts to be worthwhile.

Most generally, many economic activities **bunch or cluster in time** because it pays to coordinate your economic actions with those of others. That just means that we want to be investing, producing, and selling at the same time that others are investing, producing, or selling.

Bunching occurs across different time frames. There is bunching across the course of a single day; most people don't do their food shopping at 4 AM, even if they live near 24-hour supermarkets. But there is also bunching across weeks, months, and even years. Economic activity tends to cluster together in time just as it clusters together in space. (What do we call a cluster of economic activity in space? A city.)

The clustering of economic activity in time makes buying and selling more efficient, but it also causes shocks to spread through the economy and to spread through time. Let's say that a negative economic shock arrives and the economy slows down in the current period. Many people are less keen to work, and they will save up their working for some point in the future (intertemporal substitution, as we discussed earlier). This effect will induce others to cut back on their work as well. If the Indian farmers mentioned above work less when the weather is bad, then tractor salespeople will probably work less as well. Similarly, if fewer people are showing up at the office, you might be less productive as well. You'll be more likely to stay home and more likely to make your big work effort in some other period, perhaps when you expect the office to be up and running at full speed. So if some people retreat from full-speed work, these decisions spill over onto others and cause them to cut back their effort as well.

The "seasonal business cycle" is one form of economic clustering in time. The fourth quarter of the year—October through December—brings more economic activity than any other time. Production is higher, sales are higher,

Time bunching is the tendency for economic activities to be coordinated at common points in time.

employment is higher, and GDP grows faster, relative to the other quarters of the year. After Christmas is over, however, the party ends and GDP in the next period is typically lower. Figure 27.8 shows GDP growth rates over recent years. Notice the clear spike downward in GDP in the first quarter of the year (the winter season after Christmas).

FIGURE 27.8

GDP Growth Rates Bunch by Season

Note: Seasonally unadjusted data in real GDP.
Source: BEA data on GDP 1985:1–1995:4

Based on seasonal averages over many more years, Figure 27.9 on the next page shows that GDP typically grows most during the Christmas boom, but slows dramatically in the post-Christmas bust. GDP also grows quickly in the spring season. Growth is positive but not nearly so high in the summer when many people go on vacation.

Most advanced economies have a seasonal business cycle of this nature, usually with the fourth quarter as the boom quarter. Indeed, most economic data is reported on a "seasonally adjusted" basis so if you read that GDP grew in the first quarter by 2 percent, it really means that GDP fell in this quarter less than expected given the season.

Of course, the seasonal cycle booms in the fourth quarter because of Christmas and other gift-giving holidays in December. People are simply spending a lot more money in the fourth quarter. But it is a mistake to think that the entire effect is driven by gift giving. After all, many people simply aren't that generous at Christmas time. But even Scrooge may be more likely to buy things for himself during the Christmas season when there is a superior selection of products and more new products on the shelves. Many people buy in the fourth quarter, due to the economies of clustering, even if they don't care about Christmas for its own sake.

Just as the fourth quarter is the most active, the first quarter—January through March—is the slowest. People just spent large sums of money at Christmas. Yes, many people do look for sales and specials in this period, but overall both production and retail activity simply aren't as intense.

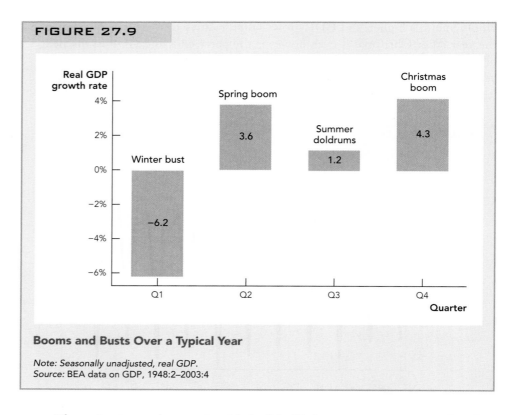

FIGURE 27.9

Real GDP growth rate

Spring boom

Christmas boom

Winter bust

Summer doldrums

3.6

1.2

4.3

−6.2

4%

2%

0%

−2%

−4%

−6%

Q1   Q2   Q3   Q4

Quarter

Booms and Busts Over a Typical Year

Note: Seasonally unadjusted, real GDP.
Source: BEA data on GDP, 1948:2–2003:4

The point is not that we should abolish Christmas or summer vacation, but rather that seasonal cycles help us understand some features of regular business cycles. Once some economic activity is moving in the upward or downward direction, other parts of economic activity tend to follow that momentum.

Sticky Wages and Prices

A final transmission mechanism comes from the New Keynesian theory of business fluctuations that we introduced in Chapter 26. Recall that the emphasis in New Keynesian theory is on how sticky wages and prices mean that shocks to aggregate demand can reduce real growth. It is also the case that sticky wages and prices can amplify real shocks. Let's focus on the sticky wages story and show how sticky wages make a negative real shock even worse.

We begin in Figure 27.10 at point *a* with an inflation rate of 2 percent, expected inflation of 2 percent, and real growth of 3 percent. A negative real shock reduces productivity and shifts the Solow growth curve to the left. If wages were perfectly flexible, then the SRAS curve would simply shift along with the Solow growth curve, placing the economy at point *b*. At point *b*, the economy is in a recession and there will be some increased frictional unemployment as workers adjust to the new situation. But if wages are sticky the situation can get much worse.

Here is the key point: *when the economy grows slowly, wages must grow slowly*. At point *b*, the growth rate of the economy is negative so wages must fall. But suppose that wages are sticky—workers don't like to see a reduction in the growth rate of their wages, let alone an actual fall in wages—thus, for all the reasons we discussed in the last chapter, it will be difficult for firms to lower wages. But if wages aren't falling at point *b*, then firms must cut output and hiring to remain profitable. In addition, to restore profitability, firms will try to raise prices even faster. Notice that the declines in output and hiring and the

FIGURE 27.10

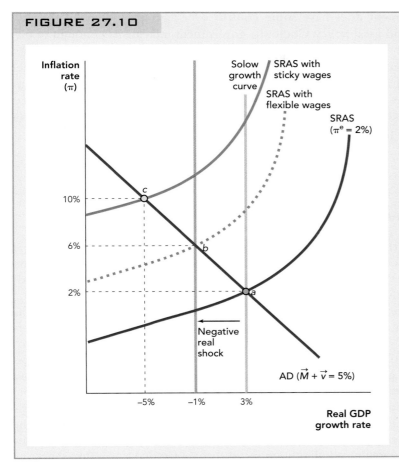

Sticky Wages Can Amplify a Real Shock Beginning at point *a*, a negative real shock shifts the Solow growth curve to the left. If prices and wages were perfectly flexible, the economy would move to a new equilibrium at point *b*. But at point *b* the economy is shrinking, so real wages need to fall. If wages are sticky, wage growth will be too high and firms will be unprofitable. Unprofitable firms reduce employment and thus the SRAS curve shifts even further to the left moving the economy to point *c* with an even lower growth rate and higher inflation rate.

increase in inflation mean that *with sticky wages the SRAS curve shifts farther to the left (and up) than did the Solow growth curve.* As the SRAS shifts to the left and up, the economy moves along the AD curve from point *b* to point *c*, thus the inflation rate increases and the real growth rate falls. At point *c*, the growth rate is –5 percent. Sticky wages have transformed a mild recession into a much more serious recession.

When wages are sticky, a negative productivity shock creates two problems. First, the productivity shocks mean output growth will be lower—that's just the meaning of a negative productivity shock and there's not much that can be done about this effect. The economy's capital is simply less productive. But when wages are sticky, the negative productivity shock also means that wages will be too high and some workers will lose their jobs, or lose hours of employment, thus cutting back aggregate supply even further.

Transmission Mechanisms: Summary

In sum, at least five factors magnify negative economic shocks and help bring business downturns. Those factors are labor supply and intertemporal substitution, uncertainty and irreversible investment, labor adjustment costs, the desire to bunch or cluster economic activity together in time, and sticky wages and prices. The core lesson is this: A medium-sized negative economic shock is capable of causing a disproportionately large downturn in economic production and employment.

We've also worked through these transmission mechanisms to set you up for some of the material to come. As shown in detail in the next few chapters, the government does have some control over aggregate demand through monetary and fiscal policy. Could the government increase AD enough to off-set some of these negative supply shocks and get the economy back to a higher Solow growth rate? Should the government do this and, if so, under what conditions? To answer this and related questions, in the next four chapters we look at the institutions and tools of monetary and fiscal policy. Real business cycles are a very important part of macroeconomic theory, but they are not the whole story.

CHECK YOURSELF

> Immediately after 9/11, most U.S. companies eliminated business travel temporarily. After a few weeks, business travel started to pick up again. Which transmission mechanism came in to play? Go through as many aspects of business travel as you can think of: air travel, transportation to and from airports, hotel stays, meals out and contact with people remaining back in the office. Explain how the unexpected almost-cessation in business travel amplified the original shock.

□ Takeaway

One reason that the economy fluctuates is because of real shocks, namely rapid changes in economic conditions that affect the productivity of capital and labor. Shocks to the weather are clearly evident in the fluctuations of GDP in agricultural economies. In wealthier economies, shocks to major inputs into production processes like oil can generate fluctuations in GDP, such as it has done in the United States and other developed economies. Other possible shocks are wars, terrorist attacks, major new regulations, tax rate changes, mass strikes, new technologies such as the Internet, and significant changes in consumer preferences. Most generally, we get a boom when we have a lucky series of positive shocks and a bust when we have an unlucky series of negative shocks.

Transmission mechanisms magnify shocks. There are five major factors that amplify economic shocks. "Make hay when the sun shines" is a saying that reflects the idea of intertemporal substitution. Work hard when working hard brings the greatest return. Intertemporal substitution means that we respond to negative shocks by working less and positive shocks by working more, thus magnifying the shock.

Shocks, especially negative shocks, often increase uncertainty, and when we are uncertain we, as businesspeople and workers, are less likely to make big decisions. Thus, a negative shock can reduce investment, especially when investments are hard to reverse. Uncertainty can also cause people to delay making big changes such as moving to a better job or selling a house.

Labor adjustment costs can also increase structural unemployment by raising the costs of moving labor from declining sectors of the economy to growing sectors of the economy.

Economic activity does not occur evenly across space or time. Every day there is a boom between 9 AM and 5 PM and a bust between 12 AM and 5 AM. Every year there is a boom around Christmas and a bust after New Year. Time bunching occurs because people work better together and it often makes sense to coordinate production processes. Thus, when one sector of the economy is booming, say because of a positive productivity shock, other sectors tend to follow. The same is true for busts. Thus bunching through time magnifies shocks.

Finally, sticky wages and prices can magnify real shocks. In this case, the growth rate falls because productivity is lower and also because sticky wages create a mismatch between aggregate demand and the Solow growth rate.

The productivity shocks that we have discussed in this chapter play an important role in some business fluctuations. The transmission mechanisms that we have described play an important role in virtually *all* business fluctuations. In the next four chapters, we look more closely at shocks to monetary and fiscal policy and also how monetary and fiscal policy might smooth out some real shocks or in some unfortunate situations possibly make them worse.

□ CHAPTER REVIEW

KEY CONCEPTS

Transmission mechanisms, p. 589

Shocks, p. 589

Intertemporal substitution, p. 594

Irreversible investments, p. 596

Labor adjustment costs, p. 597

Time bunching, p. 598

FACTS AND TOOLS

1. According to Figure 27.9, the U.S. economy typically grows faster in some quarters than in others.

   a. In which quarter is the gross domestic product actually falling?

   b. What major spending-related holiday occurs just before this big decline in GDP?

2. Take a look at Figure 27.2. In the last few decades, what has usually happened to the price of oil just before or during a recession?

3. When oil price shocks force people to switch jobs, how much GDP are they producing when they are out of work?

4. Do you know anyone who "intertemporally substitutes" their labor? In other words, what are some careers where someone might choose to work more during times when the wage is higher but less when the wage is lower? (Example: Someone with a lawn-mowing business.) Think of three examples of such careers. (Hint: Seasonal jobs provide a lot of easy examples.)

5. When an investment is irreversible, are you likely to make that decision in a hurry or wait until more information comes in?

6. When do you want to study for a test: when your friends are studying for the same test or when they are not? How can this help explain seasonal business fluctuations?

7. If the Solow growth curve increased because of a sudden fall in the price of oil, what would happen to inflation? Assume that spending growth (aggregate demand) does not change—only the growth curve shifts. Draw the shift in the following figure. (Note: In the real world, this happens fairly often. Big declines in the

price of oil happened in 1986 and again in 1998, and the price of oil fell by 50 percent in late 2008.)

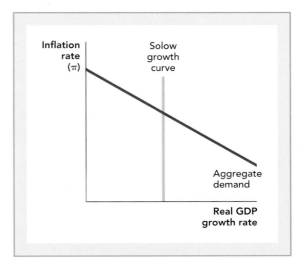

8. Office buildings have a boom-bust cycle every day. At what hours of the weekday do grocery stores have an economic boom? What days of the week do shopping malls have an economic boom?

THINKING AND PROBLEM SOLVING

1. In India, the economy grows faster when there's a lot of rain and grows more slowly when there is a drought. This creates big fluctuations in the economy. If the government wrote laws to smooth out these fluctuations, by paying people to work more in the dry years and by taxing people so that they would work less in the heavy-rain years, would that make the average Indian better off? Why or why not? (Keep your answer in mind during the next recession, when pundits and politicians recommend tax breaks to encourage more hiring.)

2. **a.** According to Figure 27.3, about how long does it take for an oil price shock to have its biggest impact on the economy? How long does it take before the oil shock's effects completely go away?

   b. What might be happening in the labor market that might explain why it takes so long for an oil shock to do its worst?

(Glance through the transmission mechanisms listed in the chapter for some ideas.)

3. When would a restaurant owner prefer to open a new restaurant: one year after an oil shock hits or two years after the oil shock hits?

4. How is marriage like a decision to build a new factory? Which decision is easier to reverse?

5. **a.** Who would you be more likely to hire at your company: someone who has stayed in the same career for years, or someone who tries an entirely new career every time they become unhappy with their job?

   b. How does this help explain why workers are reluctant to quickly move on to a new career when they get laid off?

6. People sometimes use the expression, "Kicking the can down the road." It refers to putting a big decision off until later—it's almost (but not quite!) a synonym for procrastinating, and it's usually used in a negative sense. "Fred graduated and decided to spend a year waiting tables in New York. Grad school? He's kicking the can down the road on that one." What economic idea is equivalent to "kicking the can down the road," and how can it be a good thing?

7. As we note in the chapter, an oil price shock will probably increase the size of an oil-centered city like Houston, Texas. During the time that people are moving to Houston, looking for jobs, and switching jobs to find the best job possible, do you think GDP will be lower than usual or higher than usual? (Try focusing on the *production* part of GDP in answering this question.)

8. In the chapter, we discussed how intertemporal substitution can amplify a boom by causing people to work more and by causing more people to work (while the reverse is true in a recession). Capital is also subject to intertemporal substitution. For example, it's possible to run a factory at close to capacity in one period while putting off maintenance to a later period. How do you think capacity utilization varies across the business cycle? Is capacity utilization procyclical (varies positively with GDP) or countercyclical (varies negatively with GDP)?

9. Can you think of some reasons why the following examples of time bunching and intertemporal substitution might be true? (Yes, you'll notice that there's a blurry line between the two.)

a. People who work outside work more when the weather is good.

b. People work when others are also working.

c. Even nonreligious people who don't give gifts shop more as Christmastime approaches.

d. Food servers at a restaurant prefer to work the dinner shift.

What do all of these examples have to do with the business cycle?

CHALLENGES

1. In 1971, Intel invented the first computer microprocessor. In early 1993, the National Center for Supercomputing Applications released the first web browser, Mosaic (which later became Netscape). Both inventions seem like good news, and both inventions created great uncertainty about which business models would succeed in the future: They were game changers. Would these uncertainty-creating inventions encourage businesses to make massive investments quickly, or would they encourage businesses to wait a few years to see how it all pans out?

   Boyan Jovanovic and his coauthors discuss this topic in several papers. For an introduction see Bart Hobijn & Boyan Jovanovic, 2001. The Information-Technology Revolution and the Stock Market: Evidence. *American Economic Review* 91(5): 1203–1220.

2. For the sake of the economy, should the government ban Christmas, and instead encourage people to give gifts throughout the year? Why or why not?

3. How is the previous question similar to this question: Should the government encourage people to move from the East and West coasts to the Midwest and Rocky Mountain states, where the population is less crowded?

4. Part of the real business cycle story is that workers *choose* to work more *because* wages are temporarily high and workers *choose* to work less *because* wages are temporarily low. This is key to the "intertemporal substitution" story of this chapter. The following chart shows how much wages change in the short run: Except in the 1970s, the moves are almost always in a 2 percent range, running from 1 percent higher than average to 1 percent lower than average.

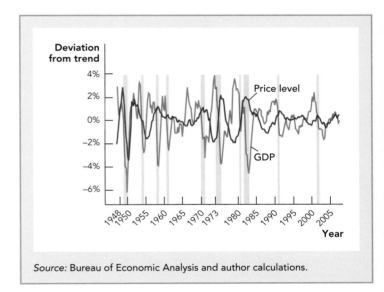

5. a. The real business cycle model says that Solow growth rate shocks are important, while the aggregate demand curve mostly stays fixed. If this is correct, then should prices be higher than usual or lower than usual during a recession?

  b. The following chart has historical U.S. data on the relationship between the price level and real GDP. The chart doesn't fit the RBC model perfectly—no economist would claim that the RBC model explains *all* economic fluctuations, after all. If you take a look at the big swings in the 1970s and early 1980s, especially during recessions, do the facts roughly fit the RBC model, or do they pretty much conflict with the RBC model?

Source: Bureau of Economic Analysis and author calculations.

So, when wages move up or down for a year or two, does the number of Americans working move in the same direction at the same time? Let's see. The economic simulation at the bottom of this column is based on actual U.S. data and shows how a 1 percent rise in wages usually impacts the number of Americans employed. Sometimes the effect is bigger than this, and sometimes smaller, but this is the average.

In practice, a 1 percent rise in wages apparently causes a 0.2 percent rise in the number of Americans with jobs. It takes nine months for this to happen.

How much would wages have to rise to raise employment by 1% or 2%, according to these estimates? [Note: This is roughly how much employment rises during a boom.] Is this "wage-channel" effect large enough to explain most of the job fluctuations we see during real-world business cycles?

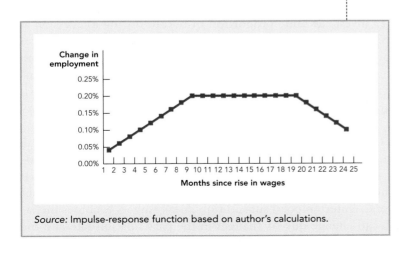

Source: Impulse-response function based on author's calculations.

Business Fluctuations and the Solow Model

A way of summarizing some of the lessons of this chapter is that at least some business fluctuations are just economic growth in the short run. Economic growth happens in fits and starts rather than smoothly. The economists Finn Kydland and Edward Prescott developed key aspects of the RBC model in the 1980s and were awarded the Nobel prize for their work in 2004. One advantage of thinking about business fluctuations in this way is that they can then be analyzed using a version of the Solow growth model, which is called the real business cycle model. A complete understanding of the real business cycle model requires quite a bit of advanced mathematics, but we can briefly describe the main ideas. Consider the following production function, which is just like that used in Chapter 22 but with the addition of labor as well as capital:

$$Y = A_t \times F(K, L)$$

To recap, output, Y, is a function of the inputs of capital, K, and labor, L. In Chapter 22, we talked about the A factor as an index of ideas. Better ideas mean a larger A, which means that more output can be produced from the same inputs of capital and labor. That is a good interpretation of A in the long run, but we can also think about A as representing *any* factor that influences the productivity of K and L. Thus, if Y is the output of corn then A could be deviations of rainfall from the average. Above average rainfall, say $A = 2$, means that the inputs of K and L produce a lot of corn. Below average rainfall, say $A = \frac{1}{2}$, means that the same inputs of K and L produce less corn.

When we are thinking about long-run economic growth, it doesn't hurt to simplify and think about A as increasing smoothly through time. To analyze business fluctuations, however, we need to recognize that A jumps around. Thus, in the business fluctuation model, A is a productivity shock variable.

The second complication we need to add to the Solow growth model to analyze business fluctuations is to give a more sophisticated account of investment and labor supply. In the Solow growth model investment is a simple function of output, Investment $= \gamma Y$, where the investment rate, γ, is a constant proportion like 0.3. That's not a very realistic assumption. Will savers and investors want to invest the same proportion of output during a recession as during a boom? Probably not, for the reasons we discussed in the chapter (uncertainty, for example). How do savers and investors decide how much and when to invest? This is a complicated decision, requiring savers and investors to forecast future events. Solving this problem is difficult, which is where the complicated mathematics come in, but we know that γ will vary over time.

Similarly, in the growth version of the Solow model, we assumed that L was population and that L was fixed. (It's also easy to think about L as increasing slowly and steadily.) But in the short run, we need to recognize that workers may choose to enter or exit the workforce and choose to take jobs or search for work—intertemporal substitution. As a result, L becomes the labor force and L can change due to changes in the participation rate and the unemployment rate. How do workers decide how much and when to work? Again, this is a complicated decision problem that requires workers to forecast the future and carefully optimize.

Adding shocks to the Solow model and giving a more sophisticated account of how savers, investors, and workers make decisions creates what is known as the real business cycle model or the standard "neoclassical" model of business cycles. The intuitive account of business fluctuations that we have given in this chapter is based on this model.[*]

Explaining a full RBC model is too advanced for this appendix but we recall that we showed how to simulate the Solow model using Excel in the appendix to Chapter 22. We can easily modify that model to include productivity shocks. Figure A27.1 shows our Excel model with a new column (column B) labeled A. Excel's RAND() formula creates a random number between 0 and 1. If we want a number between X and Y, we can write $= RAND()(Y-X) + X$. We will use our random number as a productivity shock, A_t, so we want a number that can be a little bigger than 1 or a little smaller than 1. Thus, when we get a random number that is greater than 1 that is a positive productivity shock (output increases) and when we get a random number that is less than 1 that is a negative productivity shock (output decreases). Thus, we input into cell B2 = RAND()(1/0.95−0.95) + 0.95 which create a random number between 1/0.95 and 0.95; over many draws this random number is designed so that it will average out to 1. We now modify our output formula in D2 so it reads = B2*C2^(1/2), in other words we multiply the contribution of capital (C2^1/2) by the productivity shock, A_t, which we generated in column B.

FIGURE A27.1

B2		f_x	=RAND()*(1/0.95-0.95)+0.95							
	A	B	C	D	E	F	G	H	I	J
1	Time	A	Capital, K	Output	Investment	Depreciation	Capital Growth	Y Growth	Investment Share, γ	Depreciation, δ
2	1	0.956905382	200	13.53	4.06	4.00	0.06		0.3	0.02
3	2	0.967909022	200.06	13.69	4.11	4.00	0.11	1.17		
4	3	0.983678593	200.17	13.92	4.18	4.00	0.17	1.66		
5	4	0.952410981	200.34	13.48	4.04	4.01	0.04	-3.14		
6	5	1.018061434	200.37	14.41	4.32	4.01	0.32	6.90		
7	6	1.036326744	200.69	14.68	4.40	4.01	0.39	1.87		
8	7	0.976878889	201.08	13.85	4.16	4.02	0.13	-5.64		
9	8	0.990237834	201.22	14.05	4.21	4.02	0.19	1.40		
10	9	0.963290803	201.41	13.67	4.10	4.03	0.07	-2.68		
11	10	0.994149412	201.48	14.11	4.23	4.03	0.20	3.22		
12	11	1.041301257	201.68	14.79	4.44	4.03	0.40	4.80		
13	12	1.028858954	202.08	14.63	4.39	4.04	0.35	-1.10		
14	13	0.995156067	202.43	14.16	4.25	4.05	0.20	-3.19		
15	14	0.953711687	202.63	13.58	4.07	4.05	0.02	-4.12		
16	15	0.984056799	202.65	14.01	4.20	4.05	0.15	3.19		
377	376	0.997989023	225.44	14.98	4.50	4.51	-0.01	3.46		
378	377	0.973955736	225.42	14.62	4.39	4.51	-0.12	-2.41		
379	378	1.032046001	225.30	15.49	4.65	4.51	0.14	5.94		
380	379	0.961868177	225.44	14.44	4.33	4.51	-0.18	-6.77		
381	380	0.982599886	225.27	14.75	4.42	4.51	-0.08	2.12		

[*] For a more complete but still accessible explanation of this model, see Plosser, Charles I. 1989. Understanding Real Business Cycles. *Journal of Economic Perspectives* 3, No. 3. (Summer, 1989), 51–77.

This model works very much like the Solow model in Chapter 7, but now the random shocks increase or decrease growth around the average Solow growth rate. Figure A27.2, for example, simulates 100 periods of the Solow model around the equilibrium output of 15. Notice how shocks can generate business fluctuations.

FIGURE A27.2

The Solow Model with Shocks

28

The Federal Reserve System and Open Market Operations

CHAPTER OUTLINE

What Is the Federal Reserve System?

The U.S. Money Supplies

Fractional Reserve Banking, the Reserve Ratio, and the Money Multiplier

How the Fed Controls the Money Supply

The Federal Reserve and Systemic Risk

Revisiting Aggregate Demand and Monetary Policy

Who Controls the Fed?

Takeaway

Appendix: The Money Multiplier Process in Detail

Imagine that you wanted to borrow $2 *trillion*. Whom would you ask? In 2008, the worldwide financial system was in a crisis and banks and other financial institutions wanted to borrow more than $2 trillion—they turned to the only person in the world capable of lending that kind of money, a mild-mannered, former professor of economics named Ben Bernanke. As chairman of the Federal Reserve System (the Fed), Bernanke is sometimes said to be the second most powerful person in the world, after the President of the United States. Bernanke was able to make the loans because he could draw on the awesome power of the Federal Reserve Bank to create money.

What is the Federal Reserve? How does it create money? What does it use its power for?

If you read this chapter, you'll come away with an understanding of the Federal Reserve and its powers. The quick and dirty answer is that through its control of the money supply the Federal Reserve usually has more influence over aggregate demand than any other institution and shifts in aggregate demand can greatly influence the economy in the short run (as we first showed in Chapter 26). So, let's take a look at the Federal Reserve System first, then examine what is meant by the money supply, and finally focus on the tools that the Fed uses to influence the money supply, aggregate demand, and the economy.

What Is the Federal Reserve System?

The Federal Reserve acquires its unique powers through its ability to issue money. Open your wallet or your purse and take a look at some bills. At the top, you will see the words "Federal Reserve Note." In the past, many banks issued their own bank notes, which were used as money. But today the money we use in the United States is provided by just one bank, the Federal Reserve. Thus, the Federal Reserve has the power to create money—an awesome power that forms the centerpiece of this chapter. The Fed doesn't have to literally print money. It can, as we shall see in more depth later in this chapter, also create money "by computer" by adding reserves to bank accounts held at the Fed. This new money can be given away or lent out in a way that increases aggregate demand.

If the Federal Reserve is a bank, who are its customers? The Fed is both the government's bank and the banker's bank. As the government's bank, the Fed maintains the bank account of the U.S. Treasury. When you write a check to the IRS to pay your taxes, the money ends up in the Treasury's account at the Fed. In addition to receiving money, the U.S. Treasury also borrows a lot of money and the Fed manages this borrowing—that is, the Fed manages the issuing, transferring, and redeeming of U.S. Treasury bonds, bills, and notes. Since the U.S. Treasury is by far the world's largest bank customer—it has more income and it also borrows more than any other bank customer—the Federal Reserve is a large and powerful bank.

In addition, the Fed is also the banker's bank. Large private banks keep their own accounts at the Fed—in part, because some banks are required to hold accounts with the Federal Reserve and in part because other banks and financial institutions want a safe and convenient place to hold their money. The Fed also regulates other banks and it lends money to other banks. Finally, the Fed manages the nation's payment system—the system of accounts that makes it possible to write checks from one bank to another—and it protects financial consumers with disclosure regulations. Many of these and other duties are shared with other state and federal agencies.

Now that we know what the Fed is, let's turn to its most important function: regulating the U.S. money supply. But first we have to understand what the money supply is.

The U.S. Money Supplies

Just about everyone expects to be paid in money. If you show up with money—at least in its appropriate form, hardly anyone will turn you away. In other words, **money** is a widely accepted means of payment.

Money is a widely accepted means of payment.

But money is more than cash. Cash, or currency, is paper bills and coins, which serve as a quick and efficient way of making small transactions. But currency is not so useful for larger transactions, especially between businesses. Often it is easier to pay by check or debit card (which can be thought of as an electronic check) or by credit card (and then pay your bill later by check). For larger purchases, you might transfer money from a savings account to a checking account and then pay by check or debit. All these means of payment are money but they are not currency.

The most important assets that serve as means of payment in the U.S. today are:

1. Currency—paper bills and coins
2. Total reserves held by banks at the Fed
3. Checkable deposits—your checking or debit account
4. Savings deposits, money market mutual funds, and small-time deposits

Figure 28.1 shows the magnitude and proportions of the major means of payment in the United States (there are also some smaller items, such as traveler's checks, that we have omitted):

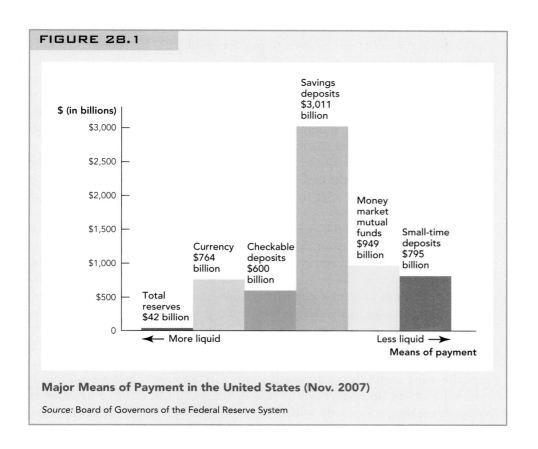

FIGURE 28.1

$ (in billions)

Savings deposits $3,011 billion

Money market mutual funds $949 billion

Small-time deposits $795 billion

Currency $764 billion

Checkable deposits $600 billion

Total reserves $42 billion

← More liquid   Less liquid →
                       Means of payment

Major Means of Payment in the United States (Nov. 2007)

Source: Board of Governors of the Federal Reserve System

Let's say a few words about each of these means of payment. "Total reserves" held by banks at the Fed is the means of payment you probably don't have personal experience with, but total reserves play a very important role in the financial system. All major banks have accounts at the Federal Reserve System— accounts that they use for trading with other major banks and for dealings with the Fed itself. It's not currency in these accounts but electronic claims that can be converted into currency if the bank wishes.

If you look at the total for currency (almost $800 billion) and divide it by the American population (about 300 million), that amounts to about $2,500 per person (and even more per adult). Who has this much cash on hand? Of course, some of the money is in ATMs and cash registers and some drug dealers do hold a lot of cash but the real explanation for why so much U.S. cash exists is that quite a bit is used in other countries. Panama, Ecuador, and El Salvador all use the U.S. dollar as their official currency as do some other small nations like the Turks and Caicos Islands. Dollars are also used unofficially in many other unstable countries as a means of preserving and protecting wealth. When Iraqi dictator Saddam Hussein was captured, he had $750,000 in U.S. hundred dollar bills in his hideaway.

Checkable deposits are just like they sound, namely deposits that you can write checks on or can access with a debit card. These are the sorts of deposits we use most often in making daily transactions. Often these are also called demand deposits because you can access this money "on demand."

The largest means of payment are savings accounts, money market mutual funds, and small-time deposits (also called certificates of deposit or CDs). Each of these components can be used to pay for goods and services but typically with a little bit of extra work or trouble. Payments from a savings account can be made, for example, by first transferring the money to a checkable account. A money market mutual fund is a mutual fund invested in relatively safe short-term debt and government securities. Money market mutual funds typically allow you to write some number of checks per year or you can always sell part of your fund and transfer the money to a checkable account. Small-time deposits cannot be withdrawn without penalty before a certain time period has elapsed, usually six months or a year.

A **liquid asset** is an asset that can be used for payments or, quickly and without loss of value, be converted into an asset that can be used for payments. The more liquid the asset, the more it can serve as money. Currency is usually the most liquid asset since currency can be spent almost everywhere. Checkable deposits and reserves are also very liquid, since they can also be spent easily and they can be turned into currency without loss. Money market mutual funds and time deposits are less liquid since sometimes it takes time and a little bit of trouble to turn these assets into currency or checkable deposits. It's possible to use even less liquid assets as means of payment (we will take your house in return for, say, a copy of this textbook), but it is inconvenient. Economists therefore have found that the above components are the most useful for analyzing the effect of "money" on the economy. It should be clear, however, that the money supply can be defined in different ways depending on exactly which kinds of liquid assets are included in the definition.

Economists have created many definitions of the money supply. The three most important are:

> The monetary base (MB): currency and total reserves held at the Fed

> M1: currency plus checkable deposits

> M2: M1 plus savings deposits, money market mutual funds, and small-time deposits

These definitions correspond to an inverted pyramid of ever-expanding size as shown in Figure 28.2.

The Fed has direct control only over the monetary base, the narrowest part of the pyramid. But it's the larger components of the money supply—M1 and M2—that have the most significant effects on aggregate demand; the monetary base simply isn't that big a part of the overall money supply.

The pyramid diagram therefore illustrates one difficulty of central banking. The central bank tries to use its control over MB to influence M1 and M2, but there are many other influences on M1 and M2 so each monetary aggregate can shrink or grow independent of the others. Finally, the Fed ultimately wants to steer aggregate demand, but once again its steering is sometimes wobbly because, although M1 and M2 influence aggregate demand, there are also other influences.

A **liquid asset** is an asset that can be used for payments or, quickly and without loss of value, be converted into an asset that can be used for payments.

FIGURE 28.2

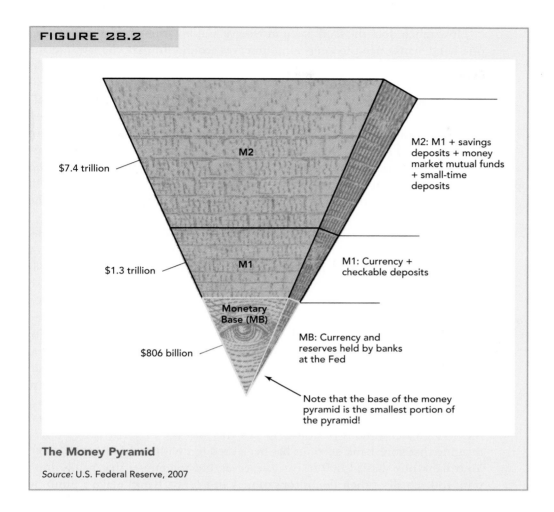

M2

$7.4 trillion

M1

$1.3 trillion

Monetary Base (MB)

$806 billion

M2: M1 + savings deposits + money market mutual funds + small-time deposits

M1: Currency + checkable deposits

MB: Currency and reserves held by banks at the Fed

Note that the base of the money pyramid is the smallest portion of the pyramid!

The Money Pyramid

Source: U.S. Federal Reserve, 2007

To understand how the Fed influences M1 and M2 but also why its influence is sometimes tenuous, we must introduce the concepts of fractional reserve banking, the reserve ratio, and the money multiplier.

Fractional Reserve Banking, the Reserve Ratio, and the Money Multiplier

When you open a bank account, the teller doesn't take your money and put it into a box labeled with your name. Instead the bank holds a *fraction* of your account balance in reserve—hence the term **fractional reserve banking**—and it uses the rest of your money to make loans.

Banks earn profit on these loans. So do you. Competition among banks to attract your funds means that if the bank lends out your money and charges 5 percent interest, the bank must share some of that return with you. The bank will pay you, say, 2 percent for providing the money that they lend. The bank doesn't just pay you interest, it also gives you useful services like check writing and check clearing, which are in part funded from bank profits on loans. Of course, you don't get the full 5 percent return because the bank is bearing risk on the loans, plus paying the costs of making the loans and monitoring the loan borrowers.

Under **fractional reserve banking,** banks hold only a fraction of deposits in reserve, lending the rest.

The **reserve ratio, RR,** is the ratio of reserves to deposits.

How much does the bank keep in reserve and how much does it lend? On one hand, banks need to keep some reserves around. In part, the law and the Federal Reserve require them to keep some reserves. More important, banks need those reserves to meet ordinary depositor demands for currency and payment services. Who would patronize a bank where the ATM machine was always empty? On the other hand, banks don't want to hold too many reserves. Currency sitting in the vault doesn't earn anything for the bank, plus they have to guard it and store it. Thus, there are opportunity costs to holding onto reserves. Banks balance these benefits and costs and thus they decide on the ratio between reserves and deposits. We define the **reserve ratio, RR,** as the ratio of reserves to deposits. If $1 in cash is held in reserve for every $10 of deposits, the reserve ratio is 1/10.

The reserve ratio is determined primarily by how liquid banks wish to be. When banks are worried that depositors might want to withdraw their cash or when loans don't seem so profitable anyway, they want a reserve ratio that is relatively high; when banks aren't worried about depositors demanding cash and when loans are profitable, they want to have a relatively low reserve ratio.

The **money multiplier, MM,** is the amount the money supply expands with each dollar increase in reserves. MM = 1/RR.

It's also useful to work with the inverse of the reserve ratio, called the **money multiplier, MM.** The money multiplier is the ratio of deposits to reserves, or in this case 10. Why is it called the money multiplier? Imagine that the Federal Reserve creates $1,000 of new money by crediting your bank account with an additional $1,000. Does that sound incredible? In fact, the Fed can create new money at will either by printing it or—the more modern method—by adding numbers to bank accounts held at the Fed. As we shall see below, the Federal Reserve creates billions of dollars in just this way on a regular basis. So let's imagine that your bank account has been credited with an additional $1,000. Your bank now has $1,000 in extra reserves, but remember that banks don't want to keep all of their depositor's money in reserve. Banks make a profit by lending so now that your bank has extra reserves, it will also feel comfortable making more loans. To restore its reserve ratio to 1/10, your bank will want to keep $100 in reserve and make additional loans of $900. So let's say it lends $900 to Sam.

Now here's where it gets tricky. You have an extra $1,000 in your account but in addition Sam now has an extra $900 in his bank account, which for convenience we will assume is held at another bank. Now Sam's bank has an extra $900, but it too doesn't want to hold all of its new money in reserves so it will keep $90 in reserve and make $810 in new loans—thus, the bank's reserve ratio stays at 1/10. The process does not stop there as Sam's bank now lends money to Tom and Tom's bank lends money to Dick and . . . well you get the idea. This process keeps going through a ripple effect as one bank increases its loans, leading to an increase in deposits in another bank, which in turn increases its loans, which leads to an increase in deposits in another bank, which increases its loans . . . and so forth.

What is the end result of the ripple process? There are two ways to see the end result, the long way and the shortcut. We are going to save the long way for the appendix. Here's the shortcut. If banks want a reserve ratio of 1/10, then when the Federal Reserve increases reserves by $1,000, deposits must ultimately increase by $10,000. Now remember that the money multiplier is the inverse of the reserve ratio, or 10. Did you notice that deposits eventually increase by the increase in reserves *multiplied* by the money multiplier? That's why it's called the money multiplier.

Let's summarize: The money multiplier tells us how much deposits expand with each dollar increase in reserves. If the money multiplier is 10, for example, then an increase in reserves of $1,000 will lead to an increase in deposits of $10,000. Since checkable deposits are part of the money supply (M1 and M2), we can also say that an increase in reserves of $1,000 increases the money supply by $10,000. Thus, we have:

$$\text{Change in money supply} = \text{Change in reserves} \times \text{Money multiplier}$$

or

$$\Delta MS = \Delta \text{Reserves} \times MM$$

CHECK YOURSELF

> If the reserve ratio is 1/20, what percent of deposits is kept as reserves?

> If the reserve ratio is 1/20, what is the money multiplier?

> If the Fed increases bank reserves by $10,000 and the banking system has a reserve ratio of 1/20, what is the change in the money supply?

How the Fed Controls the Money Supply

Now that we have seen what the money supply is and why the money multiplier multiplies a change in reserves, let's look at the three major tools the Fed uses to control the money supply. These are:

1. Open market operations—the buying and selling of U.S. government bonds on the open market

2. Discount rate lending and the term auction facility—Federal Reserve lending to banks and other financial institutions

3. Required reserves and payment of interest on reserves—changing the minimum ratio of reserves to deposits, which is legally required of banks and other depository institutions and paying interest on any reserves held by banks at the Fed

Let's look at each in turn.

Open Market Operations

Suppose that the Federal Reserve wants to increase the money supply. How does it do it? As we said earlier, if the Fed wants to create money, it can simply print money or add numbers to bank accounts. But how does the new money find its way into the economy? Imagine, for example, that the Fed added money to its own bank account and bought apples with the new money. At first, the money would flow to apple farmers and then the apple farmers would buy more tractors and television sets and vacations, and the money would flow out to other people who themselves would buy more goods. In this way, the Fed's increase in the money supply would spread throughout the economy. And if the Fed wanted to reduce the money supply, it could sell some of the apples that it had bought earlier.

The Fed, however, doesn't want to buy and sell apples. Apples are difficult to store, expensive to ship, and available in very large quantities during only part of the year. So instead of apples, the Fed buys and sells government bonds, usually short-term bonds called Treasury bills or T-bills (these are also often called Treasury securities or Treasuries). Government bonds can be stored and shipped electronically and the market for government bonds is liquid and deep, which means that the Fed can easily buy and sell billions of dollars worth of government bonds in a matter of minutes.

So, if the Fed wants to change the money supply, it usually does so by buying or selling government bonds. This is called an **open market operation.**

Open market operations occur when the Fed buys and sells government bonds.

To pay for the T-bills, the Fed electronically increases the reserves of the seller, usually a bank or a large dealer in Treasury securities. With more reserves on hand, that bank will respond by increasing its loans beginning the ripple process we described above. That is, banks will make additional loans, the loans will in turn be used to buy goods and pay wages, and people will deposit some of these payments into other banks. The new deposits will increase the reserves of these other banks, which will now also be able to make more loans. Thus, the purchase of bonds by the Federal Reserve leads to a ripple process of increasing deposits, loans, deposits, loans, deposits, more loans, and so forth.

We noted earlier that the change in the money supply is equal to the change in reserves multiplied by the money multiplier, $\Delta MS = \Delta \text{Reserves} \times MM$. It's important to remember, however, that the size of the money multiplier is not fixed. The multiplier is the inverse of the reserve ratio and the reserve ratio is determined by banks. When banks are confident and eager to lend, they will want to keep their reserves relatively low so the money multiplier will be large ($MM = 1/RR$). In this case, changes at the base of the money pyramid (Figure 28.2) have a relatively large effect on the entire pyramid.

But when banks are fearful and reluctant to lend—that is they wish to hold a high level of reserves, the money multiplier will be low and a change in the monetary base need not change the broader monetary aggregates much at all. In this case, changes at the base of the money pyramid have a relatively small effect on the entire pyramid.

Thus, even though the Fed controls the monetary base, the Fed may not know how much or how quickly changes in the base will change loans and the broader measures of the money supply.

Summarizing, (1) the Federal Reserve can increase or decrease reserves at banks by buying or selling government bonds, (2) the increase in reserves boosts the money supply through a multiplier process, and (3) the size of the multiplier is not fixed but depends on how much of their assets the banks want to hold as reserves.

Open Market Operations and Interest Rates   Conducting monetary policy by buying and selling government bonds rather than, say, apples has another advantage. You may recall from Chapter 23 that bond prices and interest rates are inversely related: When bond prices go up, that is another way of saying interest rates go down, and when bond prices go down, that means interest rates go up. Thus, when the Fed buys or sells bonds, it changes the monetary base and influences interest rates at the same time. Let's go through this in more detail.

When the Fed buys bonds, it increases the demand for bonds, which pushes up the price of bonds, thus lowering the interest rate. So, buying bonds stimulates the economy through two distinct mechanisms, namely higher money supplies and lower interest rates. In a sense, the increase in the money supply increases the supply of loans and the lower interest rates increase the quantity of loans demanded.

When you hear that "the Fed has lowered (or raised) interest rates," do not be confused. The Fed does not "set" interest rates in the same way that a 7-Eleven owner "sets" the price of milk in the store. Instead, interest rates are determined in a broad market through the supply and demand for loans as outlined in Chapter 23. The Fed works through supply and demand, and if the Fed wants short-term interest rates to fall, it has to buy more bonds, thereby influencing market prices.

The Fed Controls a Real Rate Only in the Short Run   Lending and borrowing decisions depend on the real interest rate, the interest rate after inflation has been taken into account (see Chapter 25). It's important to understand, therefore, that the Fed has influence on real interest rates only in the short run. Remember from Chapter 25 that money is neutral in the long run—that neutrality includes real interest rates. Similarly, remember from Chapter 26 that an increase in aggregate demand (AD) increases the real growth rate only in the short run. Thus, the long-run neutrality of money, the long-run neutrality of aggregate demand, and the long-run neutrality of Federal Reserve influence over real rates are all different sides of the same "coin."

The Fed has the most influence over a short-term interest rate called the Federal Funds rate. The **Federal Funds rate** is simply the *overnight* rate (that's really short term!) for a loan from one major bank to another. Banks lend not only to entrepreneurs and consumers and home buyers but also to other banks and financial institutions.

> The **Federal Funds rate** is the overnight lending rate from one major bank to another.

Since the Federal Reserve can easily change the reserves of major banks through open market operations, it can exercise especially tight control over the Federal Funds rate. In fact, monetary policy is usually conducted in terms of the Federal Funds rate. For example, instead of deciding to increase the money supply by $50 billion, the Fed might decide to reduce the Federal Funds rate by a quarter of a point—the Fed will then buy bonds until the Federal Funds rate drops by a quarter of a point. Similarly, if the Fed wants to increase the Federal Funds rate, it will sell bonds until the Federal Funds rate increases by the desired amount.

The Fed usually focuses on the Federal Funds rate because it is a convenient signal of monetary policy, it responds very quickly to actions by the Fed, and it can be monitored on a day-to-day basis. In contrast, the broader measures of the money supply, such as M1 and M2, are more difficult to measure and monitor because they require data from many different corners of the banking system. But don't forget that the Fed controls the Federal Funds rate through its control over the monetary base.

Discount Rate Lending and the Term Auction Facility

The second tool in the Fed's toolbox is lending. Remember the more than $2 trillion we discussed in the opening that banks and other financial institutions borrowed in 2008? Now we know why the Fed had the power to make these loans: The Fed can create money at will. Thus, the Fed is often said to be the **lender of last resort.** When all other institutions have run out of funds or fear to lend, banks and other financial institutions may still turn to the Fed. The Fed's ability to quickly lend enormous sums in a crisis is a very powerful tool. Let's see how it works in more detail.

> A **lender of last resort** loans money to banks and other financial institutions when no one else will.

The Fed has several methods of making loans. In normal times, the Fed offers to lend to banks at the **discount rate** and a bank that borrows from the Fed is often said to be borrowing from the discount window. If banks borrow from the Fed that increases the money supply. The Fed lends to banks by simply adding extra (electronic) dollars to their accounts at the Fed. These loans increase the monetary base directly, and indirectly they may encourage banks to lend more money, increasing M1 and M2. Of course, when banks pay back these loans, the monetary base shrinks once again. Discount window borrowing therefore tends to be used for short-run "tide-me-overs" rather than for long-run monetary policy decisions.

> **Discount rate** is the interest rate banks pay when they borrow directly from the Fed.

618 • PART 7 • Macroeconomic Policy and Institutions

Market traders read the discount rate as a signal of the Fed's attitude or "stance," namely the Fed's willingness to allow the money supply to increase. When the Fed lowers the discount rate, the market reads this as signaling an expansionary monetary policy. But of course, the lower discount rate doesn't directly affect the monetary base unless banks actually borrow more from the Fed.

Most of the time, most banks are not borrowing from the discount window. It is expected that if a bank is in good health, it will borrow most of its credit needs from other banks or financial institutions, not the Fed. The discount window is intended to help out banks in financial stress when they cannot borrow from the private sector. In fact, if a bank suddenly starts borrowing a lot of money from the discount window, usually it receives a rapid but discreet inquiry from the Fed, asking what exactly is wrong. Banks do not generally want to be in this position.

Nonetheless, all banks know that discount window borrowing is available if they get into financial trouble. For instance, if Citigroup lends money to Wells Fargo, Citigroup knows that Wells Fargo could borrow at the discount window to repay Citigroup, if need be. The very existence of the discount window makes private bank loans work more smoothly, even if the discount window isn't being used.

Note that the possibility of financial troubles at a bank stems from the very nature of fractional reserve banking. Loans are the main asset of fractional reserve banks, so the value of the bank depends on how willing and able borrowers are to repay their loans.

A **solvency crisis** occurs when banks become insolvent.

An **insolvent bank** has liabilities that are greater than its assets.

One potential problem—known as a **solvency crisis**—occurs when banks become **insolvent**: The value of a bank's loans falls so far that the bank can no longer pay back its depositors. Banks usually hold "capital" as a cushion against such losses but of course the scope of the losses may exceed the capital of the bank. In this context, the use of the word "capital" refers to a very specifically defined legal term, not just to the word "capital" in the general economic sense. The legal formula for bank capital is complex, but the core intuition is that banks are required to hold some of their assets in relatively safe forms in order to provide a protective cushion to shield depositors against potential losses. A bank with a lot of capital is in little danger of defaulting. Internationally coordinated regulations, supported by the Fed, impose capital requirements on U.S. banks.

In 2008, we saw an extraordinary development: The U.S. Treasury acted to "recapitalize" parts of the U.S. banking system. That is, the Treasury invested additional money into these banks to boost their future prospects, in return for the promise that banks would someday repay this investment. The fear was that many U.S. banks were insolvent, due to bad real estate loans and other investment mistakes. This recapitalization was under the authority of the U.S. Treasury, but it was very much an action in conjunction with the Federal Reserve. The goal of recapitalization is to get banks on their feet again and thus get them lending again. Whether or not this action counts as "monetary policy" in the formal sense of that term, it has many of the same effects as monetary policy, namely that it encourages bank lending and thus money supply growth.

A **liquidity crisis** occurs when banks are illiquid.

A second potential problem is called a **liquidity crisis.** Maybe the bank assets are good, but there is a potential problem if all the depositors want their money back at the same time. A bank might have a lot of good assets on its books, like long-term loans that are repaid over time, but the income from those loans is not available right away. But how do depositors know whether a bank's assets are good? Often they don't. As a result, fear can turn solvent banks into **illiquid banks** very quickly. During the Great Depression, for example, even a rumor that a bank might go under caused depositors to rush to their bank to get their money out before it was too late—thus, causing even good, solvent banks to go under!

To avoid bank runs such as occurred during the Great Depression, the Federal Deposit Insurance Corporation (FDIC) was created. The FDIC guarantees bank deposits up to $250,000 for each depositor name on an account (in practice, the guarantee is often even larger in value). Since depositors know their deposits are insured, they have less reason to run to the bank to withdraw their deposits even if they do hear rumors. Thus, the mere existence of the FDIC can reduce bank panics even if the FDIC never has to pay out.

If despite the FDIC guarantee many people do want to withdraw their funds, the Federal Reserve System can act as a lender of last resort to help banks meet their obligations. Ideally, the Fed uses the discount window to lend to illiquid (but solvent) institutions and waits for them to regain their liquidity and return to financial health. Of course, in practice, especially during an emergency, it is not always easy to tell which banks are insolvent and which are merely illiquid.

If the Fed knows a bank is insolvent, usually the best thing to do is to pay off depositors and close down that bank before it can incur any further losses. The 2008 Treasury recapitalization of U.S. banks was a break from this traditional practice; the judgment at the time was that too many banks might be insolvent for the economy to survive widespread bank closures, so the Treasury decided to offer aid to banks instead.

The Term Auction Facility   During the financial crisis of 2007–2008, sparked initially by problems in the subprime mortgage market (more on this in the next chapter and see also Chapter 23), the Fed went considerably beyond its traditional role in helping out financial institutions.

First, the Fed set up a Term Auction Facility. The Term Auction Facility is best understood in contrast to the discount rate. The discount rate sets an interest rate and then the Fed waits to see how many banks want to borrow. One problem with the discount rate is that banks may not borrow, for fear of admitting to the market that they are in a weak position. The Term Auction Facility had the Fed announce that it wanted to inject a certain quantity of reserves into banks; those funds were then auctioned until the rate was low enough that banks would borrow the money. Furthermore, the Fed loosened collateral requirements for its loans and stressed to banks that there would be no negative stigma from borrowing from the facility. In other words, the Term Auction Facility and related lending activities were designed to give the Fed more control over the money supply, to get around some of the problems discussed above.

The amount of extra lending done by the Fed during the period of the financial crisis was staggering. For instance between December 2007 and May 2008, the Fed lent approximately $475 billion to the U.S. banking system, mostly to restore liquidity to credit markets. Over the course of the year, the Fed lent over $2 trillion in total. To put that latter figure in perspective, it is over $6,000 for every person in the United States. Of course to the extent those banks end up as insolvent, the taxpayer will have to pick up the resulting losses.

An **illiquid bank** has short-term liabilities that are greater than its short-term assets but overall has assets that are greater than its liabilities.

Required Reserves and Payment of Interest on Reserves

Required reserves are the portion of their deposits that banks are required by law to hold as reserves.

Open market operations and lending are the Fed's most important tool in normal times, but the Fed has several other ways of influencing the money supply and thus aggregate demand. The Fed, for example, can change the ratio of **required reserves.** By force of law, the Fed tells banks that their deposits must be backed by a certain amount of reserves, either currency or reserves held at the Fed. As of spring 2009, the legally mandated reserve ratio is 0 percent for deposit liabilities under $10.3 million, 3 percent for liabilities under $44.4 million, and 10 percent for liabilities more than this sum. This is called the reserve requirement.

If the Fed lowers the required reserve ratio, this may boost the money supply. For instance, if the reserve ratio for some specified set of bank liabilities is cut from 10 percent to 5 percent, a dollar in reserves may lead to more loans.

The reserve requirement, however, is not the most important tool of monetary policy. With or without Fed regulations, banks need to hold reserves anyway, if only to reassure their customers and to conduct regular business, as we mentioned above. Ordinary business demands tend to be a more important determinant of the reserve ratio than the Fed. For instance, the Fed might lower the required reserve ratio but there is no guarantee banks will use that new freedom to make more loans. Not all loans are profitable for a bank, if only because not all potential borrowers are likely to repay.

The Fed may also eliminate required reserves altogether in the not too distant future because as of 2008, the Fed has another instrument at its disposal: It can vary the rate of interest that it pays banks on reserves held at the Fed. In previous times, banks received no interest payments on reserves. Not surprisingly, banks wished to minimize those holdings because they brought no profit. In trying to minimize reserves, however, banks sometimes worked at cross-purposes with the Fed, especially when the Fed wanted to make sure that the banking system had plenty of reserves on hand for payment purposes. But now the Fed is paying interest on those reserves, and the Fed consciously varies that interest rate to help achieve the goals of monetary policy.

> Underline the correct answers. The Fed wants to lower interest rates: It does so by (buying/ selling) bonds in an open market operation. By doing this, the Fed (adds/subtracts) reserves and through the multiplier process (increases/decreases) the money supply.

The Federal Reserve and Systemic Risk

We have covered the three major tools the Fed has to control the money supply: open market operations, lending, and required reserve regulation and the payment of interest on reserves. In times of crisis, the Fed can and has gone beyond these tools to address problems with the financial system that extend beyond banks.

In times of crisis, for example, the Fed has decided that its lender of last resort function is not restricted to traditional banks alone. In March 2008, the Fed made extensive loan guarantees to JP Morgan, which was in the midst of purchasing the failing company of Bear Stearns, a financial institution but not a bank in the traditional sense. In fact, Bear Stearns, which falls under the legal definition of "investment bank," is regulated by the Securities and Exchange Commission. The Fed's view was that Bear Stearns owed a lot of money to banks (true), so if Bear Stearns failed a lot of banks would fail too, thus causing the money supply to plummet. The Fed therefore thought that it needed to prevent Bear Stearns from shutting down to prevent much bigger problems. The Fed probably had a reasonable worry and they acted promptly to address that worry. Nonetheless, the market has since been wondering what exactly are the powers and duties of the Fed since it acted outside of its traditional legal mandate. The Fed also has loaned many billions of dollars to the insurance company American International Group (AIG), again under the rationale that AIG owed a lot of money to banks. The financial crisis of 2007–2008 has led to a true blurring of the functions of the Fed and it is widely recognized that a more comprehensive redefinition of the Fed's responsibilities is needed.

The general issue in the Bear Stearns case and also the AIG case is called **systemic risk.** Systemic risk simply means that the failure of one financial institution can bring down other institutions as well, just as if a chain of dominoes were collapsing. Do you know the old joke: "If you owe your banker a million dollars and can't pay, you have a problem. If you owe your banker a billion dollars and can't pay, your banker has a problem." Preventing the spread of systemic risk is one of the most important things the Fed does.

There is, however, a problem. Whenever the Fed acts to limit systemic risk, it insulates at least some banks from the financial consequences of their bad decisions. For instance, a bank that lent too much money to Bear Stearns now knows it doesn't have to worry so much the next time around because the Fed will probably step in to bail them out. When individuals or institutions are insured, they tend to take on too much risk—incentives matter—and economists call this the problem of **moral hazard.** A homeowner who is insured, for example, has a reduced incentive to install smoke alarms, which is one reason why insurance companies give discounts to those who do install alarms. In the case of banks, the longer-run consequence of moral hazard is that banks will be less careful about their financial commitments. Limiting systemic risk while checking moral hazard is the fundamental problem the Fed faces as a regulator of bank safety.

When it comes to the Fed's lender of last resort function, it can be said that we live in interesting times. A great deal has been changing in the last few years and those changes probably are not over. The general tendency has been for the Fed to become much more active and to assume greater powers in the case of emergency and perhaps during normal times as well.

Revisiting Aggregate Demand and Monetary Policy

Now that we have covered the major tools of the Federal Reserve, let's remember that what the Fed ultimately wants to do is to use its tools to influence aggregate demand (AD). Let's imagine, for example, that the Fed wants to increase aggregate demand and it chooses to do so by buying bonds in an open market operation. The bond purchase increases the monetary base and decreases short-term interest rates. The increase in the base increases deposits and loans through the multiplier process, and the decrease in interest rates stimulates investment (and consumption) borrowing. As a result—if all goes well, AD increases. The increase in AD then influences the economy as we discussed in Chapter 26 and is shown in Figure 28.3 on the next page. Beginning at point *a*, an increase in $\overrightarrow{M}$ shifts the aggregate demand curve outward moving the economy to point *b* where inflation and the real growth rate are higher. In the long run, after transition the economy will move to point *c* with a higher inflation rate (money neutrality again) but a growth rate given by the fundamentals at the long-run Solow level.

Systemic risk is the risk that the failure of one financial institution can bring down other institutions as well.

Moral hazard occurs when banks and other financial institutions take on too much risk, hoping that the Fed and regulators will later bail them out.

CHECK YOURSELF

> If a large bank makes some bad lending mistakes, will the Fed always let the bank bear the brunt of its mistakes and go under? If not, what justification will the Fed use?

> Consider the moral hazard that could arise if the Fed bailed out large banks. If you work at a large bank and lose a lot of money betting that oil prices would rise when they in fact fell, what incentive would you have to double your bet the next time?

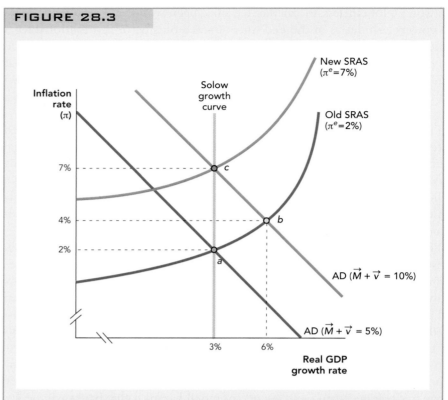

FIGURE 28.3

An Increase in $\vec{M}$ Increases Aggregate Demand, Increasing Real Growth in the Short Run An increase in aggregate demand moves the economy from point *a* to point *b* in the short run, increasing real growth and the inflation rate. In the long run, the economy will move to point *c* with a higher inflation rate but with long-run real growth equal to the Solow rate.

We now know that the process is not quite so simple. The Fed can buy bonds and increase the monetary base, but these actions do not increase aggregate demand by any guaranteed amount, since we don't know exactly how much M1 and M2 will go up in response to the higher monetary base. Nor do we know exactly how much the lower interest rates will stimulate investment spending, especially since the Fed has the most influence over *short-term* rates, while most investment spending will depend on longer-term rates. In addition, all of these processes take time and the lags from action to response are not fixed but may vary. If the Fed acts to reduce interest rates today, for example, it may take 6 to 18 months before aggregate demand and economic growth begin to respond significantly. In the meantime, economic conditions may change.

Thus, to estimate the effect of its actions on aggregate demand, the Fed must try to predict and monitor many variables determining the size and timing of the response to its actions. Some of the things the Fed must try to predict and monitor are:

> Will banks lend out all the new reserves or will they lend out only a portion, holding the rest as excess reserves?

> How quickly will increases in the monetary base translate into new bank loans and thus larger increases in M1 and M2?

> Do businesses want to borrow? How low do short-term interest rates have to go to stimulate more investment borrowing?

> If businesses do borrow, will they promptly hire labor and capital, or will they just hold the money as a precaution against bad times?

The Federal Reserve's power should not be underestimated but increasing or decreasing aggregate demand is not like turning a tap on and off. The Fed has a limited set of tools and it must constantly adapt those tools to new circumstances and conditions. We will be taking up the difficulties and dilemmas of monetary policy in the real world at greater length in the next chapter.

Who Controls the Fed?

The power to create money out of thin air and to lend trillions of dollars is an awesome power. How is this power controlled?

The Fed has a seven-member Board of Governors, who are appointed by the President and confirmed by the Senate. Governors are appointed for 14-year terms and cannot be reappointed—this means a single President will rarely appoint a majority of the board. Once appointed, members of the Board of Governors cannot be easily fired. The chairperson of the Fed is appointed by the President from among the members of Board of Governors and confirmed by the Senate for a term of four years.

Although we say "the Fed," the Fed is not just one bank but 12 Federal Reserve Banks each headquartered in a different region of the country.* The regional structure of the Fed explains another peculiarity: The Fed is a quasi-private, quasi-public institution. Each regional bank is a nonprofit bank with nine directors: six of these directors are elected by commercial banks from the region and three are elected by the Board of Governors. Six of the directors must be nonbankers and these are drawn from business, labor, academia, and other fields. In 2008, for example, the chairman of UPS was a director of the Atlanta Federal Reserve Bank, the president of Yarnell Ice Cream was a director of the St. Louis Federal Reserve Bank, and the head of the New York State AFL-CIO was a director of the New York Federal Reserve Bank. The directors of the regional banks appoint a regional bank president. Finally, the presidents of the regional banks participate, along with the Board of Governors, in the Federal Open Market Committee, the most important committee of the Federal Reserve and the one that controls open market operations.

Confused? Yes, it is confusing and we have spared you many of the details! Perhaps it will help to know that the confusing structure of the Federal Reserve system has a purpose. The Federal Reserve is powerful, so in keeping with the U.S. system of checks and balances, the power of the Fed is dispersed—no single President appoints all the governors of the Fed, the governors do not have complete control over Fed policy, the regional bank presidents come from all over the United States, and they are appointed by directors who are drawn not just from banking but from a wide variety of fields.

The bottom line is that the Federal Reserve is usually one of the most independent agencies in the U.S. government. It is relatively insulated from politics,

CHECK YOURSELF

> If money is neutral in the long run, why would the Fed want to increase the money supply in the short run?

> How will fear about the economy entering a recession affect the disposition of banks to lend? How will this affect the Fed's ability to shift aggregate demand in a recession?

*The headquarters of the 12 regional banks are located in Boston, New York, Philadelphia, Cleveland, Richmond, Atlanta, Chicago, St. Louis, Minneapolis, Kansas City, Dallas, and San Francisco.

party, and elections—perhaps only the Supreme Court is more independent. That said, in the financial crisis of 2008, the Fed had to work closely with the Treasury Department (for one thing, Treasury resources were required to re-capitalize banks) and in that sense it was much less independent than usual. In general, the independence of the Federal Reserve worries some people who would prefer that the Fed be more directly accountable to democratically elected politicians. Other people are concerned that if the Federal Reserve could be controlled directly by, say, the President this would give the President the power to order the Federal Reserve to expand the money supply and boost the economy just before an election.

Political pressures have been put on the Federal Reserve and some chairper-sons have been less independent than others. In 1972, President Nixon asked Arthur Burns, the chair of the Fed, to stimulate the economy before the elec-tion. Burns did stimulate the economy and Nixon won in a landslide, but the economic gains were temporary. Not surprisingly, inflation was too high for the rest of the 1970s. This was not a proud moment in the history of the Federal Reserve or the presidency.

Overall, an independent Federal Reserve is defended by most economists as part of the U.S. system of checks and balances.

□ Takeaway

To return to the opening of this chapter, we now have a sense why the Fed chair-person is (possibly) the second most powerful person in the world. The Federal Reserve is the government bank and the banker's bank and it has the power to cre-ate money. The ability to create money, regulate the money supply, and potentially lend trillions of dollars means that the Fed has significant powers to influence ag-gregate demand in the world's largest economy.

The concept of "the money supply" can refer to several different measures. It is important to know the major definitions of the money supply and how they differ. The Fed controls the money supply by buying and selling government bonds in what are called open market operations.

By buying and selling bonds, the Fed changes bank reserves. A change in re-serves changes the money supply through a multiplier process of rippling loans and deposits. The final result is that $\Delta MS = \Delta \text{Reserves} \times MM$. The money multiplier, however, changes over time, so the Fed's influence over aggregate demand is sub-ject to uncertainty in both impact and timing.

When the government buys securities, the interest rate decreases and that stim-ulates consumption and investment borrowing. When the government sells securi-ties, the interest rate increases, thereby reducing borrowing for either consumption or investment. For day-to-day operations, the Fed focuses its attention on the Federal Funds rate, the interest rate on overnight loans between major banks. The Fed has the most influence over real rates of interest in the short run. The Fed has little influence over long-run real rates of interest.

The Fed serves as a "lender of last resort" for banks and for major financial insti-tutions that find themselves in trouble. Preventing "systemic risk"—or the spread of financial problems from one institution to another—is one of the Fed's most im-portant jobs.

□ CHAPTER REVIEW

KEY CONCEPTS

Money, p. 610

Liquid asset, p. 612

Fractional reserve banking, p. 613

Reserve ratio, RR, p. 614

Money multiplier, MM, p. 614

Open market operations, p. 615

Federal Funds rate, p. 617

Lender of last resort, p. 617

Discount rate, p. 617

Solvency crisis, p. 618

Insolvent bank, p. 618

Liquidity crisis, p. 618

Illiquid bank, p. 619

Required reserves, p. 620

Systemic risk, p. 621

Moral hazard, p. 621

FACTS AND TOOLS

1. Let's find out what counts as money. In this chapter, we used a typical definition of money: "A widely accepted means of payment." Under this definition, are people using "money" in the following transactions? If not, why not?

   a. Lucy sells her Saab to Karen for $1,000 in cash

   b. Lucy sells her Saab to Karen for $1,000 worth of old Bob Dylan records

   c. Lucy sells her Saab to Karen for $1,000 in checking account balances (transferred by writing a check)

   d. Lucy sells her Saab to Karen by Karen promising $1,000 worth of auto-detailing services over the next year

   e. Lucy sells her Saab to Karen for $1,000 worth of Revolutionary War-era continental dollars

2. Define the following

   a. The monetary base, MB

   b. M1

   c. M2

3. a. Suppose that banks have decided they need to keep a reserve ratio of 10 percent—this

guarantees that they'll have enough cash in ATM machines to keep depositors happy, and enough electronic deposits at the Federal Reserve so that they can redeem checks presented by other banks. What is the money multiplier in this case?

   b. If depositors start visiting the ATM a lot more often, will banks want to have a higher reserve ratio or a lower reserve ratio? Will this increase the money multiplier or lower it?

4. If the Federal Reserve wants to lower interest rates via open market operations, should it buy bonds or should it sell bonds?

5. Practice with money multipliers. Think of the "money supply" (MS) as equal to either M1 or M2.

   a. RR = 5%, Change in reserves = $10 billion. MM = ?; Change in MS = ?

   b. RR = ?, Change in reserves = −$1,000, MM = 5; Change in MS = ?

   c. RR = 100%, Change in reserves = $10 billion. MM = ?; Change in MS = ?

6. In the previous question, one example assumed that banks kept a 100 percent reserve ratio. Some economists have recommended that *all* banks be required by law to keep 100 percent of their deposits in the bank vault, at the Federal Reserve, or invested in ultrasafe investments such as short-term U.S. Treasury bills.

   a. If this happened, what would the money multiplier be equal to?

   b. If this happened, would the interest rate on bank deposits probably go up or down?

   c. If this happened, would people be more likely or less likely to invest their savings in bank alternatives, such as bonds, mutual funds, or their cousin's lawn-mowing business?

7. The main interest rate that the Federal Reserve tries to control is the Federal Funds rate, the interest rate that banks charge on short-term (usually overnight) loans to other banks. Let's see how much interest a bank can earn if it lends money at the Federal Funds rate.

   Virginia Community Bank has $2,000,000 of extra cash sitting in its account at the Federal Reserve Bank of Richmond. It gets a call from Bank of America asking to borrow the whole

$2,000,000 for 24 hours. (This is typical: it's usually the smaller banks lending money overnight to the bigger banks.)

a. If the *annual* interest rate on federal funds is 4 percent, what (approximately) is the *one-day* interest rate on federal funds? (Note that interest rates, like GDP growth rates, are usually reported as "per year," just as speeds are reported as miles "per hour.")

b. How many dollars of interest will Virginia Community Bank earn for lending this money for one day?

c. If Virginia Community Bank lent this amount every day at the same rate for an entire year, how much interest would it earn?

8. Let's use the model of the supply and demand for bank reserves to explain how the Federal Reserve can change aggregate demand in the short run. Remember that the Federal Reserve controls the *supply* of bank reserves, but private banks create *demand* for bank reserves.

a. After a meeting, the Federal Reserve's Open Market Committee votes to cut interest rates from 2 percent to 1.5 percent. How will they make this happen: Will they increase the supply of reserves or decrease the supply?

b. As a result of your answer to part a, will banks usually lend more money in response, or will they lend less money? Will this tend to increase the nation's money supply, lower it, or will it have no net effect on the money supply?

c. Will this typically increase aggregate demand or lower it?

9. We mentioned that the central bank can influence a short-run real interest rate—this is because in the short run the inflation rate is relatively constant but the central bank can adjust the nominal rate on short-term loans. Recall that after investing in a T-bill, the real rate that investors receive is:

Real interest rate = Nominal interest rate − Inflation

a. If inflation is 3 percent and the Fed wants the real rate on short-term loans to be 2 percent, what should it set the nominal Fed Funds rate equal to?

b. If inflation is 3 percent, and the Fed wants to encourage borrowing by cutting the real rate on short-term loans to −1 percent, what should it set the nominal Fed Funds rate equal to?

c. If inflation is 6 percent, and the Fed wants to discourage borrowing by raising the real rate on short-term loans to 4 percent, what should it set the nominal Fed Funds rate equal to?

THINKING AND PROBLEM SOLVING

1. Whether an asset is "liquid" often depends on what situation you are in. For each of the pairs of assets below, which is more liquid in the particular setting?

You want to buy a sofa:

A savings account or currency

You want to trade for a bologna sandwich in elementary school:

A peanut butter and jelly sandwich or sushi

You want to buy a house:

Currency or a checking account

You live in a postapocalyptic wasteland:

Rice or currency

You are traveling across Europe during the Middle Ages:

Gold coins or works of art

You are an investment banker buying a corporation:

U.S. Treasury bonds or currency

2. a. Who is more likely to take bigger risks: a trapeze artist with a safety net beneath or a trapeze artist without a safety net?

b. Who is more likely to take bigger risks with his deposits: a bank CEO in a country where there is a lender of last resort or a bank CEO in a country where there is no lender of last resort?

c. Who is more likely to spend more time searching for a well-run, safe bank: a depositor living in a country with government-run deposit insurance or a depositor living in a country without government-run deposit insurance?

d. Do government-run central banks and deposit insurance both increase moral hazard problems, both decrease moral hazard problems, or do they push in different directions when it comes to moral hazard?

3. a. In the short run, if the Fed wants to cut short-term, nominal interest rates, what does it do: Does it increase the growth rate of money or decrease the growth rate of money? Why? Will this tend to lower the real rate or will it tend to lower inflation?

b. In the long run, if the Fed wants to cut short-term, nominal interest rates, what does it do: Does it increase the growth rate of money or decrease the growth rate of money? Why? Will this tend to lower the real rate or will it tend to lower inflation?

4. Let's watch a bank create money. Last Wednesday, the Bank of Numenor opened for business. The first customer, Edith, walked in the door with 100 pieces of silver to deposit in a new checking account. The second customer, Max, walks in the door a few minutes later, asking to borrow 50 pieces of silver for a week. The bank lends Max the silver. Just to keep things simple, assume these are the *only* financial transactions in Numenor. And just to be clear: silver pieces are either "currency" or "reserves": Silver in Max or Edith's hands is "currency," while silver in the bank is "reserves."

a. How much "money" is there in the Numenor economy before Edith walks into the bank?

Monetary base:

M1:

b. How much "money" is there in the Numenor economy after Edith makes her deposit, but before Max walks in for his loan?

Monetary base:

M1:

c. How much "money" is there in the Numenor economy after the Bank makes Max the loan?

Monetary base:

M1:

d. Which action created money: Edith's deposit or Max's loan?

5. You are a bank regulator working for the Federal Reserve. It is your job to see whether banks are solvent or insolvent, liquid or illiquid. Fit each bank below into one of the following four categories:

Liquid and solvent (best)

Illiquid but solvent (probably needs short-term loans from other banks or from the Fed)

Liquid but insolvent (should be shut down immediately: could fool people for a while if not for your good efforts)

Illiquid and insolvent (should be shut down immediately)

a. Bank of DelMarVa

Short-term assets	*Short-term liabilities*
$10 million	$6 million
Total assets	*Total liabilities*
$40 million	$50 million

b. Bank of Escondido

Short-term assets	*Short-term liabilities*
$6 million	$10 million
Total assets	*Total liabilities*
$50 million	$40 million

c. Bank of Previa

Short-term assets	*Short-term liabilities*
$12 million	$10 million
Total assets	*Total liabilities*
$50 million	$40 million

d. Bank of Cambia

Short-term assets	*Short-term liabilities*
$8 million	$10 million
Total assets	*Total liabilities*
$30 million	$40 million

e. Bank of Marshall

Short-term assets	*Short-term liabilities*
$120 million	$100 million
Total assets	*Total liabilities*
$500 million	$400 million

6. We mentioned that banks are reluctant to borrow from the Fed's discount window because it's looked down on by other banks: Other banks think that if a bank needs to use the discount window, it's probably not very healthy. So where you get your loans is a *signal* about what kind of bank you are. Which of the following would seem like bad signs? If you think one or more of the cases are ambiguous, explain.

a. Your friend borrows money from a federal student loan program.

b. Your friend borrows money from a payday loan store.

c. Your friend pays for ordinary living expenses by borrowing with her credit card.

d. Your friend borrows money from her parents.

e. Your friend borrows money from an illegal loan shark.

7. Does the House of Representatives get to vote on who becomes the chairperson of the Federal Reserve Board? If not, who *does* get to vote?

8. In the nation of San Ysidro, the central bank raises the required reserve ratio without changing the amount of reserves. (Note: The U.S. Federal Reserve actually did this in 1937–1938, while the U.S. economy was slowly emerging from the Great Depression.)

a. Will this tend to shift the aggregate demand curve to the left or to the right?

b. In the short run, what will this do to inflation and real growth? (The correct answer to this question is what actually happened to the United States in the 1937–1938 period.)

CHALLENGES

1. We mentioned how difficult it can be for the Federal Reserve to actually control aggregate demand: Its control over the broader money supply (M1 and M2) is weak and indirect, plus it can't control velocity very much at all. Let's translate the following bullet points from the chapter into an expanded aggregate demand equation. You know that increasing AD means increasing spending growth, $\vec{M} + \vec{v}$, but now you know that M (growth in M1 or M2, money measures that include checking accounts) depends on growth in the monetary base (MB) and on the money multiplier (MM). That means that an increase in AD requires an increase in $\vec{MB} + \vec{MM} + \vec{v}$.

Let's apply this fact to the following cases mentioned in the chapter. In all cases, the Federal Reserve is trying to boost AD by raising $\vec{MB}$. But if there's a fall in $\vec{MM}$ or a fall in $\vec{v}$ at the same time, the Fed's actions might do nothing to AD. In each case below, what are we concerned about: A fall in $\vec{MM}$ or a fall in $\vec{v}$?

a. Will banks lend out all the new reserves or will they lend out only a portion, holding the rest as excess reserves?

b. How quickly will increases in the monetary base translate into new bank loans and thus larger increases in M1 and M2?

c. If businesses do borrow will they promptly hire labor and capital, or will they just hold the money as a precaution against bad times?

2. In the past, the Federal Reserve didn't pay interest on reserves kept in Federal Reserve banks: For an ordinary U.S. bank, money kept at the Fed earned zero interest, just like money stored in a vault or in an ATM machine. In 2008, the Fed started paying interest on deposits kept at the Fed.

a. Once the Fed started paying interest, what would you predict would happen to demand for reserves by banks: Would they demand more reserves or fewer reserves from the Fed?

b. If a central bank starts paying interest on reserves, will private banks tend to make more loans or fewer loans, holding all else equal? (Hint: Does the opportunity cost of making a car loan rise or fall when the central bank starts paying interest on reserves?)

c. Let's put parts a and b together, keeping in mind the fact that bank loans create money. That means that your answer to part b also tells you about the money supply, not just about the loan supply. If a central bank starts paying interest on reserves, will the reserve ratio chosen by banks tend to rise or fall? And will the money multiplier tend to rise or fall?

d. Your answer to part c tells us that when the central bank starts paying interest on reserves, there's going to be a shift in M1 and M2, the broad forms of money supply that include money created through loans. But there are a lot of ways to affect the money supply, so if there's one force pushing the money supply in one direction, we can find another tool to push the money supply in the opposite direction. Therefore, if a central bank chooses to start paying interest on reserves, but it wants M2 to remain unchanged, what should the bank do to the supply of reserves: Should it increase the supply of reserves or decrease the supply of reserves?

3. Economist Bennett McCallum says that in order to push interest rates down in the long run, the central bank needs to raise interest rates in the short run. How can this be true?

CHAPTER **APPENDIX**

The Money Multiplier Process in Detail

Just to recap from the chapter, when the Federal Reserve conducts an open market operation, we said that the money supply changes by the change in reserves times the money multiplier, $\Delta MS = \Delta\text{Reserves} \times MM$. If the Fed buys government bonds, for example, this increases bank reserves, which increases the money supply by the increase in reserves times the money multiplier.

We've already mentioned the idea of a ripple effect: As one bank increases its loans, this leads to an increase in deposits in another bank, which in turn increases its loans, which leads to an increase in deposits in another bank, which increases its loans . . . and so forth.

Now it is time to look at this multiplier process in more detail.

It's helpful to examine a simple form of accounting statement called a T-account. On the left side of a T-account, we list the bank's assets, and on the right side, we list the bank's liabilities. An asset is simply something that represents wealth or value to the bank. In our simple T-accounts, the only assets a bank can have are its reserves and its portfolio of loans. A liability refers to a debt or something owed to someone else. In our simple T-accounts, the only liabilities a bank can have will be deposits (the bank owes the depositor the money in his or her account).

Now suppose that the Fed buys a government bond for $1,000 from a dealer in Treasury securities. The dealer has an account at the First National Bank and thus the Federal Reserve adds $1,000 to the dealer's account. As a result, the First National Bank's liabilities (its deposits) increase by $1,000, but the bank now also has an extra $1,000 in reserves. The First National Bank's T-account looks like this:

First National Bank	
Assets	**Liabilities**
Reserves: +$1,000	Deposits: +$1,000
Loans:	

But what will the First National Bank do with its reserves? The bank wants to make a profit so it will take a portion of its reserves and lend them out. Suppose that the bank keeps $100 in reserves and lends out $900. The bank's T-account now looks like this:

First National Bank	
Assets	**Liabilities**
Reserves: $100	Deposits: $1,000
Loans: +$900	

Notice that the ratio of the bank's reserves to deposits is \$100/\$1,000 or 0.1; thus, the reserve ratio = 0.1. Now the firm or person that borrowed the \$900 did so to purchase goods and services. Let's suppose that the borrower wrote a check for a cruise to Luxury Vacations Inc., which has an account at the Second National Bank. Luxury Vacations Inc. deposits the check into its account at the Second National Bank so the T-account of the Second National Bank now looks like this:

Second National Bank		
Assets	Liabilities	
Reserves: +\$900	Deposits: +\$900	
Loans:		

Notice that the Second National Bank's reserves have increased by \$900. What does the bank want to do with these reserves? Lend them! Suppose that the Second National Bank also wants a reserve ratio of 0.1 so the Second National Bank keeps \$90 in reserves and lends out \$810. Its T-account now looks like this:

Second National Bank		
Assets	Liabilities	
Reserves: \$90	Deposits: \$900	
Loans: +\$810		

Are you beginning to see the multiplier in action? Let's do one more. Suppose that the person or firm who borrowed money from the Second National Bank wanted the money to buy a computer. The borrower writes a check to Apple who deposits the money in their account at the Third National Bank. The T-account of the Third National Bank now looks like this:

Third National Bank		
Assets	Liabilities	
Reserves: +\$810	Deposits: +\$810	
Loans:		

The Third National Bank also wants to make a profit, so it lends out a portion of its reserves, leading to a T-account like this:

Third National Bank		
Assets	Liabilities	
Reserves: \$81	Deposits: \$810	
Loans: +\$729		

So let's summarize what we have so far:

The Banking System	Assets		Liabilities
	Reserves	Loans	Deposits
First National Bank	+$100	+$900	+$1,000
Second National Bank	+$90	+$810	+$900
Third National Bank	+$81	+$729	+$810
. . .	. . .	. . .	. . .

Notice that the process doesn't stop with the Third National Bank but continues onward. What is the final result of this process of expansion? Let's focus on what is happening to deposits and see if we can get to the answer a little quicker by figuring out the pattern.

At the First National Bank deposits increase by $1,000, at the Second Bank deposits increase by $900, or $0.9 \times \$1,000$, at the Third Bank deposits increase by $810 or $0.9^2 \times \$1,000$. If you guessed that at the Fourth Bank deposits would increase by $729 or $0.9^3 \times \$1,000$ you are correct so the total process looks like this:

$$\$1,000 \times (1 + 0.9 + 0.9^2 + 0.9^3 + \ldots (0.9)^n)$$

This is an example of an infinite geometric series and mathematics can show that $(1 + 0.9 + 0.9^2 + 0.9^3 + \ldots (0.9)^n)$ converges to $\dfrac{1}{1 - 0.9}$ so deposits will increase by:

$$\$1,000 \times \frac{1}{1 - 0.9} = \$1,000 \times \frac{1}{0.1} = \$1,000 \times 10$$

The last expression should look familiar. Remember that we assumed in our derivations that each bank wanted a reserve ratio of 0.1 so the money multiplier, MM = 1/RR = 10. Thus, the last statement says that deposits increase by the increase in reserves ($1,000) times the money multiplier, 10. The increase in the money supply can be measured by the increase in deposits. Thus, we have that $\Delta MS = \Delta \text{Reserves} \times MM$ exactly as we said in the chapter. Aren't you glad we saved the details for the appendix!

We can summarize by looking at how the initial increase in reserves created by the Fed open market purchase of bonds affects the entire banking system. A multiplier similar to that for deposits applies to reserves and loans so the final result looks like this:

| | The Banking System | | |
| | Assets | | Liabilities |
	Reserves	Loans	Deposits
First National Bank	+$100	+$900	+$1,000
Second National Bank	+$90	+$810	+$900
Third National Bank	+$81	+$729	+$810
. . .	. . .	. . .	. . .
Total	$1,000	$9,000	$10,000

Note that we can measure the increase in the money supply by either the increase in the banking system's assets, Reserves + Loans, or by the increase in the banking system's liabilities, namely deposits. Thus, either way the money supply increases by the $10,000, or more generally $\Delta MS = \Delta \text{Reserves} \times MM$ as we have said before.

Let's make one qualification. In the multiplier process we went through, we assumed that every borrower wrote a check for every dollar of their loan and kept none of the money in cash. Thus, if a loan was made for $900, then somewhere in the banking system deposits increased by $900. If any of the borrowers keep some of their loan in cash, however, then the multiplier process does not operate on the cash component. For example, if a borrower receives a loan for $900 and writes a check for $800, keeping $100 in cash, then the multiplier process works only on the $800. Thus, the public's demand for cash also influences the multiplier process and complicates the Fed's job because the demand for cash can change over time.

29

Monetary Policy

CHAPTER OUTLINE

Monetary Policy: The Best Case

The Negative Real Shock Dilemma

The Problem with Positive Shocks: The 1997–2006 Housing Boom and Bust

Takeaway

The Nobel Prize-winning economist Milton Friedman once likened monetary policy to throwing money from a helicopter. Thus, when *Business Week* asked in 2008, "Will 'Helicopter Ben' Ride to the Rescue?" they were asking whether Ben Bernanke, the chairman of the Federal Reserve, would be able to use monetary policy to jolt the economy out of a looming recession.

In reality, the Federal Reserve rarely uses helicopters in its rescue operations. As we discussed in Chapter 28, the Fed uses three primary tools to influence aggregate demand (AD), namely (1) open market operations in which the Fed buys bonds which increases the money supply and reduces interest rates, or the Fed sells bonds which decreases the money supply and increases interest rates; (2) lending to banks and other financial institutions; and (3) changes in reserve requirements and the interest rate paid on reserves. These are the essential methods through which the Fed affects the real economy.

In this chapter, we take for granted *how* the Fed influences AD and turn more directly to three key practical questions: When *should* the Fed try to influence AD, when *will* the Fed be able to influence AD, and when will the influence on AD *result* in higher GDP growth rates?

We start with the best case for monetary policy: where it is clear what the Fed should do in general terms, such as responding to negative monetary shocks, and when the Fed has a good chance of being successful. We then consider some reasons why even in the best case the Fed doesn't always know which detailed course of action is best. We next consider why some of the other cases—such as negative real shocks—are much harder for the Fed to respond to effectively. Finally, we learn that there are some cases, such as positive real shocks, where it's not clear what the best monetary policy is. We end with a look at the financial crisis that started in 2007.

Monetary Policy: The Best Case

Let's start with the most straightforward case, namely a negative shock to aggregate demand. Suppose, for example, that the rate of growth of the money supply or $\vec{M}$ falls. Imagine, for example, that entrepreneurs are suddenly more pessimistic about the future state of the economy. Entrepreneurs will wish to borrow less, banks will wish to lend less, and the growth rates of M1 and M2 will fall, causing a fall in aggregate demand.

In terms of our basic dynamic AD-AS diagram, the AD curve shifts down and to the left, moving the economy from point a to point b as shown in Figure 29.1. Of course, you're already familiar with that basic result from Chapter 26 on aggregate supply and aggregate demand. As you can see, the negative shock (if not counteracted by the Fed) means that the growth rate of output will decline. If the monetary contraction is severe enough, the rate of output growth can even turn negative, bringing the economy into a recession, just as we have discussed in Chapters 26 and 28.

Eventually, the economy will recover from the negative monetary shock. If the reduction in $\vec{M}$ is permanent, for example, wage growth will decline from 10 percent to 5 percent and the economy will move to point c. But as we pointed out in Chapter 26, wages are often sticky, especially in the downward direction,

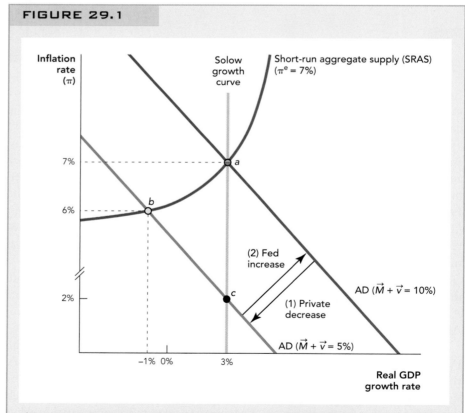

FIGURE 29.1

In the Best Case Scenario the Federal Reserve Can Offset a Negative Shock to AD with an Increase in $\vec{M}$ A decrease in AD (Step 1) shifts the AD curve inward, shifting the equilibrium from point a to point b. If the Federal Reserve acts quickly, an increase in $\vec{M}$ (Step 2) will move the economy back to point a without a prolonged recession.

so it may take time and considerable unemployment before the economy adjusts to the decline in $\vec{M}$.

But if the Fed can increase the rate of growth of the money supply, reducing interest rates and encouraging more bank lending and investor borrowing, then the AD curve shifts back up and to the right. Using the policy tools outlined in Chapter 28, the Federal Reserve is able to push the AD curve back to its original position so the economy will transition from point *a* to *b* thereby reducing the severity and length of the recession. In essence, instead of allowing the economy to adjust to a decrease in AD, which may require lower growth and higher unemployment, the Federal Reserve quickly restores AD to its previous level.

But Figure 29.1 makes monetary policy look too easy—what could be easier than shifting a curve? Two difficulties make it hard for the Fed to get this right all the time:

1. The Federal Reserve must operate in real time when much of the data about the state of the economy is unknown.

More specifically, it takes time for data to be gathered. Data are often released on a monthly or quarterly basis. Sometimes data are amended, after the fact. Then, it takes time for data to be interpreted and for problems to be recognized. Was the dip in employment last month a precursor of a recession or was it an exception? If the price of oil went up last month, does that indicate a longer-term trend or was it the result of some temporary shock? Is a decline in the stock market predicting a future recession or not? In the recent financial crisis, the first major signs of trouble in the subprime market came in August 2007, but most investors—and also the Fed—had no idea that so many banks and financial firms would fail, or be on the brink of failing, over the next year. In fact as late as the spring of 2008, GDP growth figures were still strongly positive and not everyone thought the United States was headed for a recession.

2. The Federal Reserve's control of the money supply is incomplete and subject to uncertain lags.

Recall from Chapter 28 that an increase in the money supply typically affects the economy with a lag that can vary in time from 6 to 18 months. And remember in atypical situations, if banks aren't willing to lend, then although the Fed may increase the monetary base, the larger monetary aggregates and thus aggregate demand won't increase very much in response. Thus, if banks are slow to lend, then the Fed can easily undershoot, generating a smaller shift in AD and a smaller increase in the rate of economic growth than is desirable. But a larger stimulus is not necessarily better because if the economy recovers before the money supply works its magic, the Fed can easily end up overshooting its goal—producing a higher rate of inflation than is desirable.

Figure 29.2 on the next page portrays the more realistic case for monetary policy in which too little stimulation pushes the economy only to point *c* where growth is still sluggish. But "Too much" monetary stimulation pushes the economy to point *d* with a higher than desirable inflation rate at 9 percent (and a growth rate that is high but unsustainable in the long run). Only with the "Just right" or Goldilocks amount of stimulation does the economy quickly return to its long-run balanced growth path at point *a*. We would like it if the Fed hit the Just right or Goldilocks amount of stimulation every time, but don't forget: Goldilocks is a fairy tale.

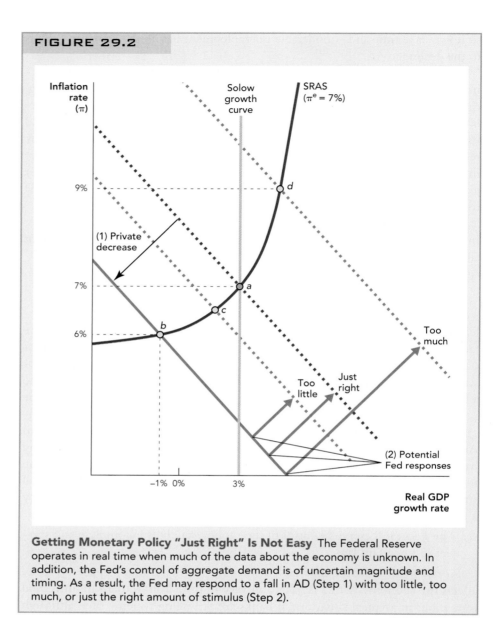

FIGURE 29.2

Getting Monetary Policy "Just Right" Is Not Easy The Federal Reserve operates in real time when much of the data about the economy is unknown. In addition, the Fed's control of aggregate demand is of uncertain magnitude and timing. As a result, the Fed may respond to a fall in AD (Step 1) with too little, too much, or just the right amount of stimulus (Step 2).

Rules vs. Discretion

The possibility of the "Too little" and "Too much" responses, or in other words the imperfections of monetary policy, has led to a debate over rules vs. discretion when it comes to monetary policy. Ideally, monetary policy tries to adjust for shocks aggregate demand, but it is often debated whether these adjustments are effective in reducing the volatility of output. If the Fed responds too often in the wrong direction or with the wrong strength, GDP volatility will increase rather than decrease.

Economists who think that the Fed is likely to make a lot of mistakes believe that apart from extreme cases, the Fed is best advised to follow a consistent policy and not try to adjust to every aggregate demand shock. A typical monetary rule would set target ranges for the monetary aggregates like M1 or M2 or for the rate of inflation. Nobel Prize winner Milton Friedman, for example, advocated a strict rule in which the money supply would grow by 3 percent a year every year; since the U.S. economy has a long-run growth rate near 3 percent, he thought this would provide for rough price stability over time. Other rules would allow for some adjustment in Fed policy depending on the state of the economy, but these adjustments would be stated in advance and the Fed would not be allowed to make policy "on the fly."

The advocates of discretion, in contrast, do not wish to tie the hands of the central bank in advance. They admit that central banks make many mistakes but still think that the Fed's adjustments on average push the economy in the right direction and thus lower volatility.

Reversing Course and Engineering a Decrease in AD

Suppose that the Federal Reserve does overstimulate, pushing the aggregate demand curve "Too much" in Figure 29.2. What then? Remember from our discussion in Chapter 25 that inflation makes price signals more difficult to interpret, creates arbitrary redistributions of wealth, and makes long-term planning and contracting more difficult, among other problems. Thus, we don't want inflation to be too high. But, we also know from Chapters 25 and 26 that bringing down the rate of inflation is costly because prices and wages are not fully flexible in the downward direction. That means economies sometimes get stuck between a rock and a hard place—between continuing a costly rate of inflation or reducing it at the risk of a recession.

Many economists think that the Federal Reserve did overstimulate the economy in the 1970s; and, as a result, by 1980, the inflation rate hit 13.5 percent a year. Ronald Reagan was elected to the presidency in part to change economic policies. By 1983, tough monetary policy under Reagan and cigar-chomping Federal Reserve Chairman Paul Volcker had reduced the inflation rate to 3 percent, but the consequence was a very severe recession with an unemployment rate of just over 10 percent.

The **disinflation** experiment was costly, but unlike the **deflation** of the Great Depression, when prices fell, it was a policy chosen on purpose. The 1980s disinflation broke the back of inflation and provided the foundation for the 25 or so years of successful economic growth—and mostly low unemployment—that the American economy enjoyed since that time.

Since World War II there have been six episodes when the Fed deliberately put the brakes on money growth, most prominently the shift beginning with the 1980 presidential election just mentioned. In every case, the tighter monetary policies were followed by declines in output. On average, industrial production, 33 months later, was 12 percent lower than otherwise would have been expected. But again, these contractions aren't always bad. Sometimes a contraction is necessary to bring down the rate of inflation. Of course, economists debate which of these contractions were needed and which were not.

Whether or not a particular contraction is a good idea, economists do agree on one point: A monetary contraction goes best when it is **credible,** namely when market participants expect the central bank to carry through its tough stance. This makes sense if you think through exactly why a disinflation is difficult for an economy. A sufficiently radical disinflation leads to unemployment because wages and prices are sticky, especially in the downward direction (as we explained in Chapter 26). If nominal wage growth is too high, some workers will end up being very expensive and employers will choose to lay them off. So, the key to a less painful disinflation is to increase nominal wage flexibility. Now imagine that a central bank has announced a disinflation but no one really believes it, or people believe it only halfheartedly. Nominal wages probably

UNDERSTAND YOUR
world

AP PHOTO/CHICK HARRITY

Paul Volcker, chairman of the Federal Reserve in 1980, had to choose between high inflation or high unemployment.

A **disinflation** is a significant reduction in the rate of inflation.

A **deflation** is a decrease in prices, that is, a negative inflation rate.

A monetary policy is **credible** when it is expected that a central bank will stick with its policy.

aren't going to grow more slowly and when the disinflation comes, if indeed it does come, the unemployment cost will be high. Alternatively, if the coming disinflation is widely expected, then workers will be prepared for slower wage growth and will quickly adjust to what they know is inevitable. Thus, a credible disinflation reduces the unemployment effects of disinflation. So, the lesson is this: If a central bank wishes to undertake a disinflation, it has to be ready to stay the course and it should announce and explain its policy very publicly. This is called making monetary policy credibile.

The Fed as Manager of Market Confidence

Fear and confidence are some of the most important shifters of aggregate demand. And one of the Federal Reserve's most powerful tools is not its influence over the money supply but its influence over expectations, namely its ability to boost **market confidence.** Recall from Chapter 27 that when investors are uncertain, they often prefer to wait, to delay, and to try to learn more information, before they commit themselves. In addition, remember that one reason we see a lot of time bunching or clustering of investments is that it pays to coordinate your economic actions with those of others—that is, you want to be investing, producing, and selling at the same time that others are investing, producing, or selling. Uncertainty, therefore, can create what economists call a *bandwagon effect* on investment—I am uncertain and so delay my investments, you follow suit not because of uncertainty alone but because your investment is less likely to work well if it doesn't happen at the same time as my investment (time bunching or coordination of investment). Moreover, the fact that you cut back investment verifies that my decision to cut back was a good idea so no one can be accused of behaving irrationally.

Market confidence: One of the Federal Reserve's most powerful tools is its influence over expectations, not its influence over the money supply.

Uncertainty drives people away from investment spending and toward assets like cash. Holding cash isn't very productive but cash and other similar assets are what you want when you are in "wait and see" mode. In terms of our model of aggregate demand, an increase in the demand for cash is indicated by a decrease in $\vec{v}$. At the same time, increased uncertainty will lead to a fall in $\vec{M}$, as both borrowers and lenders will cut back, and M1 and M2 will grow at lower rates. Both the $\vec{v}$ and the $\vec{M}$ changes work to shift the aggregate demand curve inward or to the left as in Figure 29.1 near the beginning of this chapter.

To cite an example, uncertainty increased after the terrorist attacks of September 11, 2001. Although the devastation in Manhattan was extreme, the economic cost of the attack was small relative to the size of the U.S. economy. Nevertheless, if enough people had taken the attack as a signal to reduce investment, the bandwagon effect could have created a severe recession. The Federal Reserve stepped in to try to prevent this from happening by lending billions of dollars to banks. In the week before September 11, for example, the Federal Reserve lent about $34 million to banks, a trivial amount. On September 12, the Federal Reserve lent $45.5 *billion* to banks.

The mere fact that the Federal Reserve sent a countersignal—we are going to massively maintain or increase AD if necessary—helped stabilize expectations, reduce fear, and raise confidence. The Federal Reserve can't always prevent an increase in uncertainty from reducing $\vec{v}$ and $\vec{M}$; sometimes uncertainty really does increase, such as when a war is imminent, and waiting is the appropriate response. But the Fed often can reduce the bandwagon effect and stabilize expectations toward a more positive outcome.

Monetary policy is often about changing expectations and perceptions, rather than just manipulating numbers and equations. That's one reason why central banking can be so difficult and why it is an art as well as a science.

The Negative Real Shock Dilemma

A very difficult case for monetary policy is when the economy is hit by a negative real shock such as a rapid oil price increase. As we saw in Chapters 26 and 27, a negative real shock shifts the Solow growth curve to the left (and the SRAS curve shifts by the same amount in the absence of sticky prices and wages). That means a higher rate of price inflation and a lower growth rate for GDP, again as we previously covered. How should monetary policy respond?

Unfortunately, monetary policy is much less effective at combating a real shock than an aggregate demand shock. In Figure 29.3, the economy is hit by a negative real shock and the Solow growth curve shifts to the left, moving the economy from point a to point b.

As before, the Federal Reserve can increase aggregate demand by increasing the money growth rate, but now the economy is less productive than before,

FIGURE 29.3

Monetary Policy Is Less Effective at Combating a Real Shock A real shock shifts the Solow growth curve to the left (Step 1), moving the economy from point a to a recession at point b. To combat the recession, the Federal Reserve increases $\vec{M}$ (Step 2). Due to the real shock the economy is now less productive than before and so the increase in aggregate demand shifts the economy to point c where the growth rate is a little bit higher but the inflation rate is much higher.

due to the real shock. As a result, an increase in $\overrightarrow{M}$ will not move the economy back to point *a*. Instead, most of the increase in $\overrightarrow{M}$ will show up in inflation rather than in real growth so the economy will shift from point *b* to point *c*, with a much higher inflation rate and a slightly higher growth rate.

Is it worthwhile responding to a real shock with an increase in AD? Maybe not. Although an increase in $\overrightarrow{M}$ may increase the growth rate a little, the inflation rate increases by a lot and, as we just saw in our discussion of the Volcker disinflation, higher inflation now can cause serious problems later. In particular, if the inflation rate gets too high, the Fed has to reduce inflation, thereby creating a lot of unemployment. In essence, with a real shock we have little choice but to take our lumps.

Alas, the situation is not quite so simple because real shocks are often accompanied by shocks to short-run aggregate supply and aggregate demand. In Chapter 27, for example, we discussed how sticky wages and prices can amplify a real shock, shifting the SRAS curve back to the left even further than the Solow growth curve. Moreover, we also showed how uncertainty and fear generated by a real shock can reduce consumption and investment, which shift the AD curve inward. The result is illustrated in Figure 29.4.

The real shock shifts the Solow growth curve to the left moving the economy from point *a* to point *b*. If prices were perfectly flexible, this would be the end of the story—real growth would fall but so would wages; and employment would fall only somewhat (due to adjustment factors as outlined in Chapter 27). But if wages are sticky and don't fall when real growth falls, then firms will be unprofitable and employment must decline considerably, driving real growth even lower. As in Chapter 27, we show this process by shifting the SRAS curve to the left (and up) even farther than the Solow growth curve initially shifted; this additional shift moves the economy to point *c*. The fear and uncertainty now reduce investment and consumption growth, which shifts the AD curve inward, therefore moving the economy to point *d*.

Confused? Don't worry, that is exactly how the economists at the Federal Reserve feel. Figure 29.4 looks imposing, but it is really putting together three things you already know well. A negative real shock shifts the Solow growth curve to the left; sticky wages and prices amplify the real shock by shifting the SRAS even more to the left (and up) than the Solow growth curve; and a negative shock to aggregate demand shifts the AD curve to the left and down. You have seen each of these curves shift alone: Figure 29.4 combines the three negative shifts in one diagram.

FIGURE 29.4

Real Shocks, SRAS Shocks, and AD Shocks Often Come Together
A real shock shifts the Solow growth curve to the left (Step 1), moving the equilibrium from point *a* to point *b*. If wages or other prices are sticky, the SRAS shifts to the left (Step 2) even further than the Solow growth curve, moving the equilibrium to point *c*. Fear and uncertainty can then reduce AD (Step 3), shifting the equilibrium to point *d*. Note that for clarity, we have suppressed the label for the new AD curve and also the old SRAS curve, which runs through point *a*.

We are also quite serious when we say that a combination of shocks like this can confuse economists at the Federal Reserve! Don't forget that in addition to the problems you face as students, the Federal Reserve is looking at real-time data, which as we have noted are often uncertain and subject to revision.

So what should be done in such a situation? One approach is to focus on the inflation rate, which has jumped from 2 percent to 7 percent. What is the recipe for reducing inflation? Correct—a *decrease* in $\vec{M}$. In the 1970s, for example, the Federal Reserve often responded to supply shocks, such as an oil shock, by decreasing $\vec{M}$ and *reducing* aggregate demand. That means taking the AD curve and shifting it even further back to the left through the use of monetary policy. In Figure 29.5, we show the new equilibrium at point *e*. The reduction in $\vec{M}$ reduces the inflation rate from 7 percent to 6 percent but also reduces economic growth and by more than the supply shock alone would have done.

Some economists have argued that the Federal Reserve's actions in trying to stem inflation were even

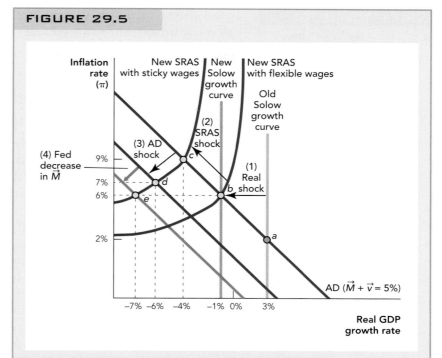

FIGURE 29.5

The Federal Reserve's Dilemma When Responding to a Real Shock
A real shock shifts the Solow growth curve to the left (Step 1), moving the equilibrium from point *a* to point *b*. If wages or other prices are sticky, the SRAS shifts to the left (Step 2) even further than the Solow growth curve, moving the equilibrium to point *c*. Fear and uncertainty can then reduce AD (Step 3), shifting the equilibrium to point *d*. At point *d*, the inflation rate is much higher than at point *a*, but reducing inflation with a cut in $\vec{M}$ (Step 4) reduces real growth even further, pushing the economy to point *e*. Note that for clarity we have suppressed the old SRAS curve which runs through point *a* and also the labels for the two new AD curves.

worse for the economy than the oil shocks. Interestingly, the most prominent critic of the Federal Reserve's actions in the 1970s was Ben Bernanke and consistent with his criticism, when he was Fed chairman and faced with rising oil prices in 2007–2008, he did not contract the growth rate of the money supply.[1]

Today central bankers are more likely to think that a central bank should respond to a negative real shock by holding the growth rate of the money supply steady or perhaps even expanding the growth rate a bit. If the central bank expands $\vec{M}$, it may be able to lessen or even reverse the AD shock so the economy would end up at point *c* in Figure 29.5 (or Figure 29.4).

As you can see, GDP takes less of a hit than in the previous case, but the new equilibrium involves a higher rate of inflation. Again, you may have wondered in the section above on engineering a disinflation, why the rate of inflation might have ended up too high in the first place. Now you know at least one way inflation can end up too high and that also helps us understand why the dilemmas of monetary policy arise so frequently.

The bottom line is that with a real shock the central bank faces a dilemma: It must choose between too low a rate of growth (with a high rate of unemployment) and too high a rate of inflation. The central bank in fact stands a

CHECK YOURSELF

> Looking at Figure 29.4, if the Fed wanted to restore some growth in the economy to deal with high unemployment, what would it do? What would be the problem of acting in this way?

> Suppose that the Fed reacts to a series of negative real shocks by increasing AD every time. What will happen to the inflation rate?

good chance of getting a mix of both problems. The lesson is this: if you are a central banker, hope that you don't face too many negative real shocks in your term!

The Problem with Positive Shocks: The 1997–2006 Housing Boom and Bust

If negative shocks are bad, then surely positive shocks are great! Who could be against fast growth, falling unemployment, and rising incomes? Unfortunately, for a central banker, even positive shocks can be worrisome, especially if they contain the seeds of their own destruction. Let's take a look at the housing boom that ended in 2006.

In 1997, inflation–adjusted house prices were close to their average levels over the previous half-century. Only four years later, the price of the average home nationwide exceeded anything ever seen before in the United States. Prices continued to rise for another five years, peaking in 2006 at nearly twice the average price in 1997. Figure 29.6 shows the extent of the boom in real house prices compared to historical trends.

As the price of real estate rose, so did the economy. High and rising house prices, for example, encouraged new home construction. During the boom, some builders were working 60 or 80 hours a week instead of 40. From 2002 to 2005, 6 million new houses were built. The boom in construction contributed to the boom in other sectors of the economy.

In addition, the boom increased aggregate demand: first, from the new employment and higher wages in the construction sector and, second, previous homeowners felt wealthier as they saw their homes rising in value each year. Homeowners who feel wealthier tend to spend more money and even borrow money on the hope or expectation that rising wealth will let them pay the money back in the future.

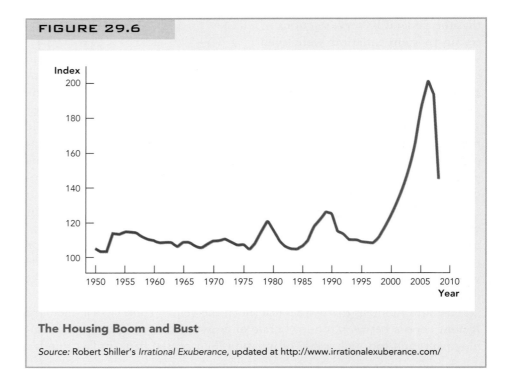

FIGURE 29.6

The Housing Boom and Bust

Source: Robert Shiller's *Irrational Exuberance*, updated at http://www.irrationalexuberance.com/

The problem, of course, came when the price of real estate started to fall in 2006. New home construction dropped very quickly. Homeowners felt poorer and started to spend less, reducing $\vec{C}$. In addition, the real estate crash contributed to a freezing up of financial intermediation as banks and other intermediaries took huge losses on poor investments in mortgage securities (as we discussed in Chapter 16). Since bank lending is a main generator of M1 and M2, this means lower rates of growth for the money supply. As a result, economic growth rates started to decline. By fall 2008, the growth rate was negative, meaning that the American economy was shrinking.

The negative shock of the bust can be analyzed using the dynamic AS-AD model just as we have outlined above. As we've already discussed in Chapter 28, the Fed took many patchwork actions after the bad news became fully evident in 2007. The key question we want to address in this section is this: What if anything could or should the Fed have done in advance of the crash, that is, when housing prices were booming? Or more generally, how should the Fed respond to positive economic shocks?

It seemed so much easier in the textbook.
Federal Reserve Chairman Ben Bernanke.

Many economists argue that the rise of real estate prices during this period was a "bubble," as that concept is defined in Chapter 16. That is, the increase in prices was due to shifts in market psychology and successive waves of irrational exuberance. These people argue that Alan Greenspan (the chairman of the Federal Reserve from 1987 to 2006) should have warned the market or tried to cool down the economy by raising interest rates.

If indeed the cycle was driven by a real estate bubble, the Fed might have been able to smooth out fluctuations in the economy by "popping the bubble" with tight monetary policy before housing prices rose too high. In that scenario, the economy would have had a more moderate boom but also a more moderate downturn; that probably would have been preferable if possible.

But monetary policy is, again, not so simple. First, it is not always easy to identify when a bubble is present, for reasons we discussed in Chapter 16. If everyone knew it was an unsustainable bubble, then everyone should have invested accordingly and bet against the bubble, thereby enriching themselves and also stopping the bubble in the first place. Of course, that isn't what happened and the bursting of the bubble was in large part a surprise to many people, including the Fed. Also, don't make the mistake of thinking that if prices rise a lot and then fall that must mean a bubble was present. Prices can rise and fall for reasons closely related to fundamentals and still cause macroeconomic problems.

Second, monetary policy is a crude means of "popping" a bubble. Monetary policy can influence *aggregate* demand, but monetary policy can't push the demand for housing down and keep the demand for everything else up. Thus, popping a bubble means reducing the growth rate of GDP for the broader economy as a whole. Is it worth the price, especially when we do not always know when we have an unsustainable bubble on our hands?

Note, however, that in addition to monetary policy, the Fed does have the power to regulate banks and it probably could have restrained some of the "subprime," no-questions asked mortgages that were sold during the boom and later went into default. That would have been the best way of limiting the bubble without taking down the broader economy.

Economists have not settled on what to do when asset prices like housing prices or stock prices boom. Booms are great while they last, but when the bust

> How can the Fed tell when increases in asset prices reach the bubble stage?

> If the Fed thinks there is a bubble in housing prices and contracts the growth in the money supply to pop it, what collateral damage can it cause?

comes the repercussions can be very costly. The bottom line is this: Monetary policy is difficult in the worst of times and it's not easy in the best of times.

□ Takeaway

Summarizing, we can point toward a few key lessons:

The Fed has some influence over the growth rate of GDP through its influence over the money supply and thus AD. An increase in $\vec{M}$ increases AD and a decrease in $\vec{M}$ decreases AD.

When faced with a negative shock to AD, the central bank can restore aggregate demand through an expansionary monetary policy. Monetary policy, however, is subject to uncertainties in impact and timing and getting it "Just right" is not guaranteed. Poor monetary policy can decrease the stability of GDP.

If in responding to a series of recessions the Fed increases $\vec{M}$ too much, it may find that it later has to contract $\vec{M}$ when inflation becomes too high. Usually this process—called a disinflation—is painful and it results in a recession. A disinflation goes best when the central bank has some degree of credibility in its attempt to set things right.

A central bank would like low unemployment and low inflation, but it is not always possible to achieve both goals. When a negative real shock comes, the Fed must choose between allowing low rates of growth, excessively high rates of inflation, or some combination of both. There is no easy way out of this dilemma.

Monetary policy is difficult in the worst of times and it's not easy in the best of times. Positive real shocks may generate booms that can become bubbles in asset prices like housing prices or stock prices. How to recognize and respond to asset price booms is not obvious and the economics of asset price booms is unsettled.

Real shocks and aggregate demand shocks are always mixed and not easy to disentangle. The data on which central bankers operate are often slow to arrive and subject to revision. As a result, central banking is as much art as science.

□ CHAPTER REVIEW

KEY CONCEPTS

Disinflation, p. 637

Deflation, p. 637

Credible, p. 637

Market confidence, p. 638

FACTS AND TOOLS

1. This chapter is concerned mostly with how monetary policy might be able to return an economy *quickly* to the Solow growth rate after a shock. But as we saw in Chapter 25's

discussion of the quantity theory of money, a market economy has a correction mechanism to return itself *slowly* to the Solow growth rate after a shock: flexible prices. Let's review the quantity theory, and remember that in the quantity theory, inflation does *all* of the adjusting.

Recall: $\vec{M} + \vec{v} = $ Inflation + Real growth

a. Consider the nation of Kydland. Before the shock to Kydland's economy, $\vec{M} = 10$ percent, $\vec{v} = 3$ percent, real growth = 4 percent. What is inflation?

b. In Kydland, $\vec{v}$ falls to 0 percent, but $\vec{M}$ stays the same. In the long run, what will inflation equal? What will real growth equal?

c. Consider the nation of Prescottia. Before the shock to Prescottia's economy, $\vec{M}$ = 2 percent, $\vec{v}$ = 4 percent, real growth = 2 percent. What is inflation?

d. In Prescottia, $\vec{v}$ rises to 8 percent. In the long run, what will inflation equal? What will real growth equal?

e. Consider the nation of Friedmania. Before the shock to Friedmania's economy, $\vec{M}$ = 3 percent, $\vec{v}$ = 0 percent, real growth = 3 percent. What is inflation?

f. In Friedmania, $\vec{M}$ falls to 1 percent. In the long run, what will inflation equal? What will real growth equal?

2. We've just reviewed the quantity theory of money, which is a theory that shows how the economy fixes itself in the long run. But as economist John Maynard Keynes famously said, "In the long run we are all dead." Let's bring SRAS back into the model, and play the role of a central banker reacting to a rise in velocity growth.

a. The diagram below shows the economy growing at the Solow growth rate with 10 percent inflation. Illustrate what happens if consumers and investors become more optimistic. Clearly label the new growth rate on the *x*-axis with the words "high-AD real growth," and label the new inflation rate on the *y*-axis with the words "high-AD inflation."

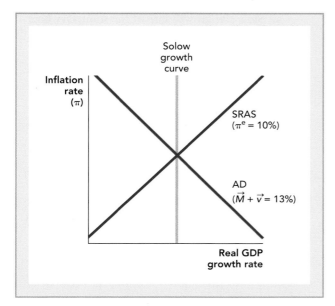

b. Once the central banker sees this rise in AD, she decides to fully reverse it with monetary policy. In the graph above, illustrate what happens if she does her job just right.

c. If she does her job just right, what will the inflation rate be? Provide an exact number.

3. Let's look at the Federal Reserve's dilemma when there's a positive shock to the Solow growth rate. We'll consider the reverse of Figure 29.3.

a. In the figure below, illustrate the effect of this positive Solow growth shock, ignoring the possible effect of sticky wages and prices.

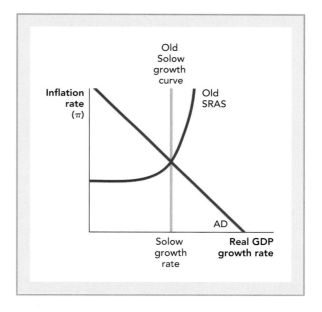

b. If the central bank kept AD fixed, would inflation be higher or lower after this positive real shock? Would real growth be higher or lower after this positive real shock?

c. If the central bank wants to return inflation to its old level, should it raise money growth or lower it?

d. If the central bank wants to return real growth to its old level, should it raise money growth or lower it?

e. Economists say that central bankers face a "cruel trade-off" between inflation and real growth when a Solow growth shock hits. Do your answers to parts c and d fit in with this theory?

4. All of the following are called "rules." Which of the following so-called rules are actually like "rules" and which are more like "discretion"? How can you tell the difference?

   a. Congress passes a law providing automatic cost of living increases to Social Security every year. (Note: This is current U.S. law.)

   b. Congress follows a rule to vote every few years on how much to increase Social Security payments—votes that usually occur just before an election. (This was the law before 1972.)

   c. The Federal Reserve follows the famous "Taylor rule" for setting the federal funds rate:

   Nominal rate = 2 percent + Inflation + 0.5 × (Real growth rate − Solow growth rate)

   d. The Federal Reserve follows a rule of "doing whatever seems right at the time."

   e. The police follow a rule of questioning anyone loitering outside of a bank who looks suspicious.

   f. The police follow a rule of questioning anyone loitering outside of a bank who is dressed in bulky clothing that could conceal a weapon.

5. Let's consider a case that has some similarities to Figure 29.2. We mentioned that it's difficult for the Fed to know what's really happening to the economy in real time. This is similar to the well-known "fog of war," where wartime news accounts often turn out to be exaggerations of the real story. In this question, the Federal Reserve thinks that consumer pessimism has pushed AD down by 10 percent, but in reality, the pessimism has only pushed AD down by 5 percent.

   a. In the following figure, illustrate two AD curves: "AD with false shock" (AD-F to save room) and "AD with true shock" (AD-T).

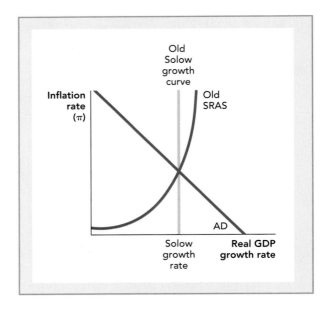

   b. If the central bank wants to use monetary policy to reverse a 10 percent shock to AD, it will have to raise money growth by 10 percent. Now draw two more AD curves on the figure above: "Fed reacts to false shock" (FR-F to keep it short) and "Fed reacts to true shock" (FR-T).

   c. After the central bank overreacts to the exaggerated news reports of economic calamity, what is the final result: Will real growth be higher or lower than before the shock hit? Will inflation be higher or lower than before the shock hit?

6. Which of the following would be methods that the Fed could use to "maintain market confidence" when a negative AD shock hits?

   a. Slow the growth rate of the monetary base.

   b. Raise the interest rate on "discount window" loans.

   c. Promise to increase the growth rate of money if the economy worsens further.

   d. Sell Treasury bills and buy bank reserves through open market operations.

   e. Raise the reserve requirements for banks.

7. When talking about the economy, people often make a distinction between policies that work "only in theory" compared to those that work "in practice." In theory, a fall in money growth slows down the economy in the short run. In the six episodes since World War II when, as we discussed, the Fed deliberately put the brakes on money growth, did this theory work "in practice" every single time, most of the time but not all of the time, or did this theory fail most of the time?

8. A monetary policy is said to be *credible* if the central bank will have an incentive to do tomorrow what it says today that it will do tomorrow. Other policies may be credible or noncredible. Which of the following policies are credible?

   a. A student promises to study for the final after going to the frat party.

   b. A long-established store offers "Guaranteed satisfaction or your money back."

   c. A government promises never to bail out banks that take on too much risk and go bankrupt.

9. a. When a financial bubble collapses, is that more like a fall in aggregate demand or a fall in the Solow growth rate?

   b. When a financial bubble collapses, what is more likely to happen as a result: A fall in inflation or a rise in inflation?

10. Central banks and voters alike usually want higher real growth and lower inflation. What kind of shock makes that happen? (Note: This is similar to the type of shock that causes higher quantity and lower price in a simple supply-and-demand model.)

THINKING AND PROBLEM SOLVING

1. Let's reenact a simplified version of the 1981–1982 Volcker disinflation. Expected inflation and actual inflation are both 10 percent, real growth is 3 percent, and to keep it simple assume that velocity growth is zero. (Historical note: In fact, velocity growth shifted quite a lot during this period, which made Volcker's job harder than in this problem. Otherwise, the numbers are close to the historical facts.) Thus, we have:

   AD: Money growth = Inflation + Real growth

   Let's define a simple SRAS curve:

   SRAS: Inflation = Expected inflation + 1 × (Real growth rate − Solow growth rate)

   Notice that this equation gives a positive relationship between inflation and real growth for a fixed Solow growth rate and expected inflation rate.

   a. First, let's calculate how fast the money supply grew back when inflation was 10 percent in 1980 and real growth was at the Solow rate of 3 percent. How fast did the money supply grow at this point, before Volcker started fighting inflation? (Hint: Use the AD equation.)

   b. Now, let's calculate how fast Volcker will let the money supply grow in the long run, after he pulls inflation down to 4 percent per year. Remember, he'll assume that in the long run, the economy will just grow at the Solow growth rate. (Hint: Use AD again.)

   c. In the short run, when Volcker cuts money growth to the rate you calculated in part b, the economy won't grow at the Solow rate. Instead, real output will grow at whatever rate the SRAS dictates. In terms of algebra, this means you have to combine SRAS and AD: it's a system of two equations and two unknowns (inflation and real growth: You know the values of money growth, expected inflation, and the Solow growth rate already). In the short run, what will real growth and inflation be?

2. Now, let's reenact the Volcker disinflation in an alternate universe where the central bank is more credible. In this world, workers are more likely to believe the Fed when it says it's going to fight inflation. So, when they see Volcker cut money growth in 1981, workers become much more willing to take slower-growing wages. (Notice how a credible Fed creates more flexible wages, as if the workers were "led by an invisible hand.") This will make the SRAS steeper, as we saw in our original discussion of short-run aggregate supply.

   Our model economy is thus as follows:

   SRAS: Inflation = Expected inflation + 2 × (Real growth rate − Solow growth rate)

   AD: Money growth = Inflation + Real growth

   a. Answer part c of the previous question again, now in this world with a more-credible Fed and a steeper SRAS.

   b. Let's see how far this can go: What if workers pay constant attention to the Fed's every move and will slow their wage demands the moment they see Volcker tightening the money supply? Answer the previous question with "100" in the place of "2" in the SRAS equation. Feel free to round your answers to the nearest percent.

c. If you were a central banker trying to cut inflation, and you want to keep real growth as close as possible to the Solow growth rate, what would you prefer: a steep SRAS (i.e., workers with flexible wages), or a flatter SRAS (i.e., workers with sticky wages)?

3. The Fed plays an important role in maintaining market confidence. As Chairman Greenspan put it in a 1997 address: "In [financial crises] the Federal Reserve *stands ready* to provide liquidity, if necessary. . . . The objectives of the central bank in crisis management are to . . . prevent a contagious loss of confidence." [emphasis added]

By *standing ready* to provide loans to banks in an emergency, the Fed can often prevent emergencies from happening in the first place. In each of the examples below, how does the fact that someone or something *stands ready* to cure the bad outcome help prevent the bad outcome from ever happening in the first place?

a. A security guard stands inside a bank.

b. Federal agents guard Fort Knox, where about one-half of the U.S. government's gold is stored.

c. The Federal Reserve promises to insure almost 100 percent of bank deposits.

d. Police, worried about possible riots during spring break in Palm Springs, California, bring in police from other cities.

4. In the United States, the government's data on real growth improve over time. For instance, we now know that in the early 1970s, the economy was actually growing 4 percent faster than people thought at the time. At the time, the Fed thought the economy was in a deep recession, so it mistakenly boosted money growth. The Fed's overreaction caused inflation. Real-time surveys in the early 1970s depicted an awful economy, but as economic historians have gone back to the data, they found that the economy wasn't as awful as they thought: Someone just put the thermometer in the fridge.

Economists at the Philadelphia Federal Reserve have collected data on how our view of the economy has changed over time. This "real-time data" is summarized by Croushore and Stark in a review article entitled "A Funny Thing Happened On the Way to the Data Bank: A Real-Time Data Set for Macroeconomists."

Let's use their summary of the data and a six-sided die to see just how inaccurate our real-time views of the economy actually are.

a. We're going to reenact the 1970s, and we'll start figuring out how error-filled the government's growth estimates will be. Croushore and Stark report that on average:

I. One-sixth of the time, measured growth is 2 percent better than actual growth.

II. One-third of the time, measured growth is 1 percent better than actual growth.

III. One-third of the time, measured growth is 1.5 percent worse than actual growth.

IV. One-sixth of the time, measured growth is 3 percent worse than actual growth.

Find a six-sided die (or use Excel to simulate same) and record your rolls below. If you've rolled a 1, count that in category I, if you roll a 2 or 3, place that in category II, a four or five goes in category III, and if you roll a six, place that in category IV. Then write down how much measurement error you'll have for that year.

Example: If your first roll was a 4, that places you in category III; so write down "–1.5 percent" as the amount of measurement error for 1971.

(Note: Psychologists and behavioral economists have found that people are pretty bad at generating truly random numbers on their own, so it's best to just roll the die.)

Year	Roll (value)	Category	Measurement Error (percent)
1971			
1972			
1973			
1974			
1975			
1976			
1977			
1978			
1979			
1980			

b. Let's see what values we get when we add together the true real growth rate (which economists will only know years later) with the measurement error in the previous table. For "true real growth," we use the most recent data in the table below—but of course even these estimates could change in the future. The sum is the actual government data that will wind up in the Federal Reserve chair's hands.

Example: If your first roll was a 4, that placed you in category III; so subtract 1.5 percent from the true 1971 growth rate to yield a real-time government report of 1.9 percent annual growth.

Year	True Real Growth	Government Data (percent)
1971	3.4%	
1972	5.3%	
1973	5.8%	
1974	–0.5%	
1975	–0.2%	
1976	5.3%	
1977	4.6%	
1978	5.6%	
1979	3.2%	
1980	–0.2%	

c. In your simulation, how many times was the government data off by 2 percent or more?

d. If the Solow growth rate in the 1970s was actually 3.6 percent (the average growth rate in the 1970s), then in how many years did your government data give values *below* 3.6 percent when true real growth was *above* 3.6 percent? How often did the reverse occur, with your government data *above* the Solow rate while true real growth was *below*?

e. Add together your two values from part d. This is the number of times that even a *very good* central banker would have wanted to push AD in the wrong direction: it's the number of times this weather vane was pointing in entirely the wrong direction.

(Note: You might be wondering whether the U.S. government tends to exaggerate extra-good economic news just before an election. As far as economists can tell, the answer is no, at least when it come to the official GDP number. U.S. GDP estimates contain mistakes before an election just as often as usual, but those mistakes don't tend to favor the political party in power. In Japan, though, GDP reports *do* tend to be extra-optimistic just before an election. For more, see Faust, Rogers, and Wright, "News and Noise in G-7 GDP Announcements," online at the Federal Reserve Board's website.)

5. We discussed how hard it is to keep AD stable or put it back "where it belongs" after a shock. Alan Blinder, a former vice-chairman of the Federal Reserve, noticed that this was a major problem. In his book *Central Banking in Theory and Practice,* he argued that this was a good reason for the Fed to take baby steps whenever it needed to make big shifts in AD. Sometimes you're better off taking two years to slowly and carefully undo an AD shock rather than shift it back quickly and inaccurately in one year.

To illustrate, let's see how things turn out if you, the central banker, take two years rather than one year to react to a negative velocity shock. You have better control over AD if you make small moves than if you make big moves, but big moves can get you back to the Solow growth rate more quickly: As so often in economics, you face a trade-off.

In this question, your ultimate goal is to get AD back to 5 percent per year; the Solow growth rate is 3 percent, and expected inflation is always 2 percent per year.

Starting point:

AD: 1 percent = Inflation + Real growth rate

SRAS: Inflation = Expected inflation + (Real growth rate − Solow growth rate)

a. Slow approach: Add 2 percent per year to AD for two years (through some mix of money growth and higher confidence). What will real growth equal each year?

	Start	End of Year 1	End of Year 2
Real Growth			

b. Fast approach: Assume that you tried to add 4 percent to AD in Year 1, but you mistakenly add 7 percent instead (through some mix of excess bank lending and irrational exuberance). In the second year, you tried to correct by cutting back by 3 percent, but you mistakenly cut back by 4 percent (through some mix of slower bank lending and investors' loss of confidence). What will real growth equal each year?

	Start	End of Year 1	End of Year 2
Real Growth			

c. You can see how the "best approach" is a matter of taste, but which method would you expect a central banker to prefer if Congress has to decide whether to reappoint the central banker to a new four-year term in a few months?

6. Milton Friedman and Anna Schwartz argued in the last chapter of their *Monetary History of the United States* that a shift in money growth will usually cause velocity to shift in the same direction: So higher money growth causes optimism, and slower growth causes pessimism. They believed that velocity had its own shocks, as well.

a. Let's run through some examples of how this might work, in a setting where the Fed wants to keep AD stable at 10 percent. To keep things simple, we'll just assume that the Fed can control money growth perfectly, and we'll assume that a 1 percent change in money growth causes a 0.5 percent shock to velocity growth in the same direction. Fill in the table below.

In each case, AD = Initial velocity shock + Money growth + Velocity shock caused by money growth

Year	Initial Velocity Shock	Money Growth	Velocity Shock Caused by Money Growth
1	4%	4%	4% × 0.5 = 2%
2	3%		
3	16%		
4	8%		
5	4%		
6	0%		

b. If velocity does tend to move in the direction of money growth, how does this change the Fed's response to economic shocks: Should it take bigger moves or smaller moves in money growth when a shock comes along?

7. We saw that real shocks and AD shocks often occur simultaneously. When this happens, unless we know the exact size of each shock, we can't be sure of the effect on both inflation *and* real growth: We'll only know one or the other for sure.

In each case below, we can be *sure* that *one* of the four events will happen:

A fall in inflation

A rise in inflation

A fall in real growth

A rise in real growth

In the cases below, which change can we confidently predict?

a. The banking system becomes less efficient at building bridges between savers and borrowers, and investor confidence declines: A negative real shock and a negative velocity shock occur simultaneously.

b. The banking system becomes less efficient at building bridges between savers and borrowers, and the Federal Reserve increases money growth: A negative real shock and a positive money shock occur simultaneously.

c. Biologists learn how to use computer simulations to rapidly search for molecules that would make promising medicines, and investors become optimistic about future profit opportunities: A positive real shock and a positive velocity shock occur simultaneously.

8. One argument for giving discretion to central bankers is that sometimes emergencies come along that a simple rule can't solve. Suppose there's a massive, permanent negative shock to velocity. Naturally, if the central bank has discretion, it will immediately respond by boosting money growth. But let's look at the alternative:

a. Suppose that the central bank follows a fixed 3 percent annual monetary growth rule, like Milton Friedman sometimes recommended. In the short run, what will the velocity shock do to real growth and to inflation?

b. In the long run, what will this velocity shock do to real growth and to inflation?

c. If voters are concerned only about real growth in the long run, will they favor rules, will they favor discretion, or will they be indifferent between the two?

d. If voters are impatient, and concerned only about real growth in the short run, will they favor rules, will they favor discretion, or will they be indifferent between the two?

e. Which kind of voters favor discretion: those with a long-run horizon or those with a short-run horizon?

CHALLENGES

This chapter has more Challenge questions than usual. Take this as a sign of how difficult monetary policy really is!

1. Practice with the best case: You are the central banker, and you have to decide how fast the money supply should grow. Your economy gets hit by the following AD shocks and your job is simply to neutralize them: just push money growth in the opposite direction of the shock.

In all of the cases below, assume that there's no change whatsoever to the Solow growth rate, and assume that before the shock, you're at your optimal inflation rate and optimal real growth rate. (Yes, this really is the best case!) These are all shocks, so think of each case study below as preceded by the word, "Suddenly . . . ." Given the shocks to $\vec{v}$, velocity, should the central bank react by raising money growth or by cutting money growth?

a. Investors become pessimistic about future profit opportunities.

b. State governments increase spending on schools, prisons, and health care.

c. The federal government passes a national sales tax.

d. The federal government increases military spending.

e. Foreigners buy fewer American-made airplanes and movies.

f. American consumers start buying fewer domestically made Hondas and more imported Hondas.

g. Domestically made computers, cars, and furniture all become much more durable and longer lasting.

2. Milton Friedman famously said that changes in money growth affect the economy with "long and variable lags." That means that if the government increases growth in the monetary base this month, the money multiplier takes a few months to turn this into growth in checking and savings deposits, and it takes a few months more before businesses and consumers actually spend this money to purchase goods and services. Let's see how this changes our views of the previous question.

In each case from the previous question, the Fed predicts how long the velocity shock itself will last: we call this "shock duration" in the table below. After that time, velocity growth will go back to its old level. Additionally, in each case, the Fed's staff of PhD economists estimates how many months it will take for a change in money supply to actually push AD in the desired direction: This is the "monetary lag."

The question is quite simple: If monetary lags are shorter than the shock duration—if the Fed has "fair warning"—then a shift in AD will be stabilizing. If not, then a shift in AD will be like mailing a birthday card to your mother the day before her birthday: Possibly destabilizing. So, in which cases below should the Federal Reserve change money growth?

Case	Monetary Lag (months)	Shock Duration (months)	Shift in Money Growth: Stabilizing or Destabilizing?
a.	14	8	
b.	18	12	
c.	20	Permanent	
d.	12	24	
e.	16	9	
f.	10	Permanent	
g.	18	Permanent	

3. One of the reasons it's hard to be a monetary policymaker is because it's so hard to tell what's actually going on in the economy. It's a lot like being a doctor in a world before X-rays, MRIs, and inexpensive blood tests: When the patient complains about a stomach ache, you don't know if it's caused by food poisoning or by a tumor the size of a grapefruit.

In each of the cases from the first question, consider the fact that your data are often quite unreliable (Fed Chair Alan Greenspan was famous for holding meetings with 100 staff economists, peppering them with questions about the quality of their data on the economy, and often knowing more than his own staff economists about the strengths and weaknesses of various surveys of the U.S. economy). To make matters more difficult, the Federal Reserve has to forecast the behavior of Congress, which is at least as difficult as predicting the behavior of businesses: Politicians often claim they are going to raise or cut spending or taxes, but then fail to do so.

If in cases a, b, and d above, the Fed chairman decides that the forecasted shocks really aren't very likely to happen, then taking into account your answers to questions 1 and 2, in which cases should the Fed actually do nothing whatsoever in response to news about the economy?

4. We explained how a central bank has an important role in maintaining confidence: "High confidence" keeps velocity growth and the money multiplier from falling. But as we've seen, sometimes one has to be cruel to be kind.

President Franklin Roosevelt followed this "tough love" approach during the Great Depression. Soon after taking office, he closed all banks for a four-day "bank holiday." During this holiday, he gave his first Fireside Chat, a radio address where he explained his policies to the American people in plain language. After the four-day holiday, he still kept one-third of all U.S. banks closed (mostly small farmer banks with one or two branches). Over the next few years, only half of this one-third eventually reopened.

Thus, FDR's bank holiday pushed the broad U.S. money supply (M1 or M2) down. Nevertheless, the economy grew quickly during FDR's first year, 1933. Why? Because FDR promised that the banks that reopened were the safest banks, and he promised that the federal government would keep these safer banks open through generous discount window lending. This boosted confidence and encouraged people to borrow from and lend to the remaining banks.

As Milton Friedman and Anna Schwartz put it in their classic book *A Monetary History of the United States*: "The emergency revival of the banking system contributed to recovery by restoring confidence in the monetary and economic system and thereby inducing the public ... to raise velocity ... rather than by producing a growth in the stock of money" (p. 433).

Let's see how an emotional concept like "confidence" shows up mathematically. To keep things simple, we'll look at AD in terms of growth in nominal GDP (growth in dollar sales) rather than growth in real GDP (growth in actual output). We'll compare the "before" and "after," so we'll skip over 1933, the year of the biggest banking crisis and of FDR's solution to the crisis:

Year	M2	v
1932	$35.3 billion	2.16
1934	$33.1 billion	2.36

a. What was the level of nominal GDP in 1932 and 1934?

b. What was the growth of M2 between these two years?

c. What was the growth of velocity between these two years?

d. What was the growth of nominal GDP between these two years?

e. If velocity growth had been zero during this period (perhaps due to low confidence), but money growth stayed the same, what would have happened to nominal GDP growth?

5. Central bankers often believe that their hands are tied by the public. Arthur Burns, the Fed chairman under President Nixon, reportedly said in the November 1970 Federal Reserve board meeting that "he did not believe the country was willing to accept for any long period an unemployment rate in the area of 6 percent." In other words, if AD shocks or Solow growth shocks came along that pushed the unemployment rate up, Burns believed he had to boost AD to help the economy: The voters wouldn't tolerate anything else.

a. In the early 1970s, the economy was hit with some negative Solow growth shocks, the most famous of which were the massive oil price increases caused by the OPEC oil embargo. Inflation started off at 4 percent, and Burns actually behaved according to his stated philosophy. What did Burns do to AD in the 1970s: Did he raise it or lower it?

b. If Burns had kept AD fixed instead of shifting it as he did, would inflation have been lower or higher than it actually turned out to be?

c. According to our model, did Burns' actions raise, lower, or have no impact on the Solow growth curve?

d. If in the 1970s the United States had been hit by negative AD shocks instead of negative Solow growth shocks, and Burns had followed his same philosophy, would inflation have been higher or lower than it actually turned out to be?

6. Central bankers are reluctant to try to pop alleged bubbles. Which topics covered in this chapter might explain why they are reluctant to do so?

7. We mentioned Milton Friedman's advice that central bankers should follow a "fixed money growth rule," where the broad money supply (M1 or M2) grows the same rate every year. Other economists have instead recommended that central bankers follow "nominal GDP targeting," which is similar to a fixed AD curve. Assume that the central bank really can control money growth and velocity growth within a reasonable period of time if it tries to do so.

a. What is the difference between a fixed money growth rule and nominal GDP targeting from the point of view of the AD equation?

b. If velocity shocks never occur, what's the best policy for keeping AD as stable as possible: fixed money growth, nominal GDP targeting, or are both equivalent?

c. If velocity shocks are common, what's the best policy for keeping AD as stable as possible: fixed money growth, nominal GDP targeting, or are both equivalent?

8. The previous question assumed that the central bank can really control money growth and velocity growth within a reasonable period of time. Instead, let's work with the more realistic assumption that it takes about a year for a change in monetary policy to actually influence money growth: Even though the central bank can increase bank reserves literally within *minutes* through open market operations or the term auction facility, it takes months for banks to find out who they should lend to. And as you know, most money is created through bank loans.

In this question, the central bank *tries* to follow nominal GDP targeting so that AD grows at 7 percent per year. In other words, the central banks tries to set the money growth rate so that velocity growth plus money growth equals 7 percent. Each year, it responds to *that year's* velocity growth, but the response won't actually kick in until next year (think of this as driving a car with loose steering: You steer to the right, but the car only starts moving to the right about two seconds later).

a. Fill in the table below. Notice that in each year, Actual AD = Velocity growth + Money growth. In the first year, the central bank observes velocity growth of 3 percent and thus targets money growth of 4 percent. The next year money grows at 4 percent as targeted, but velocity growth in that year is 1 percent so Actual AD grows at 5 percent. In Year 2, the central bank observes velocity growth of 1 percent and thus targets money growth of 6 percent. Keep going.

Year	Velocity Growth	Target Money Growth	Money Growth	Actual AD
1	3%	4%	n/a	n/a
2	1%	6%	4%	5%
3	9%	−2%	6%	15%
4	6%			
5	2%			
6	5%			
7	0%			
8	4%			
9	6%			
10	5%			

b. Every year, the central bank tries to keep AD = 7 percent, yet it never accomplishes its goal. How do "long lags" explain this failure?

c. How would this table look if you had followed Friedman's 3 percent money growth rule instead? Don't calculate any numbers, just answer verbally: Would the swings tend to be bigger than in the table or smaller?

9. a. Central bankers must manage expectations. Suppose that inflation is running at 10 percent and the central banker would like to lower inflation to 2 percent *without* reducing real growth. What should the central banker tell the public? And at what level should the central banker set money growth? Assume that velocity shocks are zero and that the Solow growth rate is 3 percent.

Draw the new SRAS and AD curves.

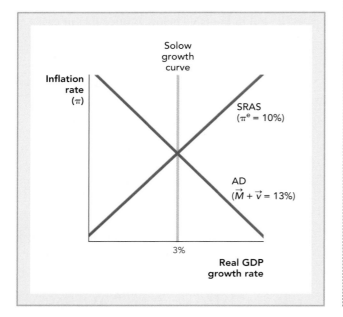

b. Suppose that the public does believe the central banker. What temptation might the central banker face? (Hint: Imagine that it is an election year and the central banker would like to see the current administration reelected.)

c. If the central banker is not believed what will happen? Use your answers to parts a and b to discuss the importance of independent central banks.

30

The Federal Budget: Taxes and Spending

CHAPTER OUTLINE

Tax Revenues

Spending

Will the U.S. Government Go Bankrupt?

Revenues and Spending Undercount the Role of Government in the Economy

Takeaway

Some people do better from the federal government than others. Take Ida May Fuller. In 1940, Ida May received Social Security check #00-000-001, the very first in the program's history. Ida May's working career had almost ended by the time Social Security began, so she had paid just $24.75 in Social Security taxes and she got almost all of that back with her first check, which was for $22.54. Moreover, Ida May lived to be 100, so by the time she died in 1975, she had received a total of $22,888.92 in benefits.

You can see why Ida May is smiling. But will you be smiling from federal taxes and spending? After all, you will pay Social Security taxes throughout your working life, and what about the benefits? You can be pretty sure that unlike Ida May, you won't receive almost a thousand times more than what you put in.

More generally, the federal government spends over 18 percent of GDP and it raises in taxes just under 17 percent of GDP. That's a lot of money, more than $2.5 trillion in spending. Where does all that money come from? Where does it all go? And for how long can the U.S. government keep spending more than it raises in taxes?

Tax Revenues

As of 2007, the federal government was taking in about $2.4 trillion a year, or about $8,000 for every person in the United States. The federal government takes in money in many ways, but three sources—the individual income tax, the Social Security and Medicare taxes, and the corporate income tax—account for more than 90 percent of the revenue. Figure 30.1 on the next page shows the major sources of revenue for the U.S. government.

Ida May Fuller received the very first Social Security check.

UNDERSTAND YOUR **world**

655

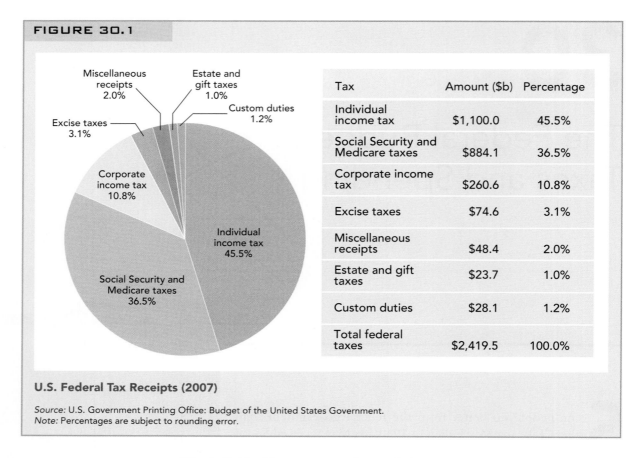

FIGURE 30.1

Tax	Amount ($b)	Percentage
Individual income tax	$1,100.0	45.5%
Social Security and Medicare taxes	$884.1	36.5%
Corporate income tax	$260.6	10.8%
Excise taxes	$74.6	3.1%
Miscellaneous receipts	$48.4	2.0%
Estate and gift taxes	$23.7	1.0%
Custom duties	$28.1	1.2%
Total federal taxes	$2,419.5	100.0%

U.S. Federal Tax Receipts (2007)

Source: U.S. Government Printing Office: Budget of the United States Government.
Note: Percentages are subject to rounding error.

The individual income tax is the single largest source of revenue for the federal government. The second category, Social Security and Medicare taxes (a few other smaller taxes are also included in this category), includes the "FICA tax" you have seen on your paycheck—these taxes are so named because unlike the income tax, the revenue from these taxes is tied to specific programs. Social Security and Medicare taxes have increased in recent decades and now bring in almost as much money as the income tax. Corporate income taxes are a distant third. The other sources are much smaller and they include excise taxes such as taxes on gasoline and alcohol, capital gains taxes, user fees, estate and gift taxes, and custom duties or tariffs. Let's take a closer look at the three largest sources of revenue.

The Individual Income Tax

Most Americans are required to file an income tax return with the federal government. On this form a person reports his income and the tax code determines how much money is due. The current schedule of marginal tax rates for a typical taxpayer, someone who is married filing jointly with their spouse, is shown in Figure 30.2.

The marginal tax rate is the tax rate that you must pay on an additional dollar of income. Figure 30.2 tells us that if you earn less than $15,650, then the marginal tax rate, the rate on an additional dollar of income, is 10 percent (some deductions are allowed—see below). If you earn between $15,650 and $63,700, the rate of tax on an additional dollar of income is 15 percent. If you earn between $63,700 and $128,500, you must pay 25 percent of any additional income to the federal government. Marginal tax rates increase in uneven steps

The **marginal tax rate** is the tax rate paid on an additional dollar of income.

FIGURE 30.2

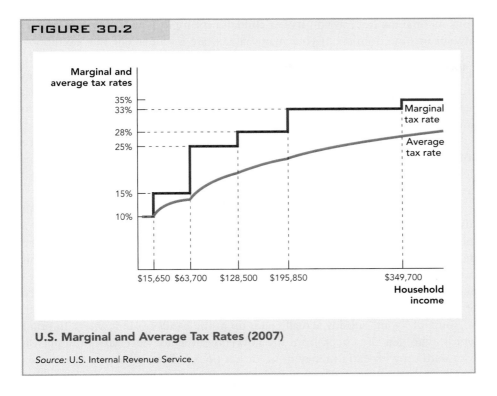

U.S. Marginal and Average Tax Rates (2007)

Source: U.S. Internal Revenue Service.

until the top marginal tax rate of 35 percent is reached on any income earned greater than $349,700.

We care about the marginal tax rate because, as usual in economics, it's the *marginal* rate that matters for determining things like the incentive to work additional hours. If you are considering doing an extra carpentry job for spare cash, you don't care what tax you are paying on the money you've already earned. You care about how much additional tax you will be paying on the extra money that you might earn if you choose to take the job.

Marginal tax rates today are lower and flatter than they have been in the past. In 1960, for example, the lowest marginal tax rate was 20 percent and the highest rate was 91 percent! Of course in the further past, rates were much lower than today. In 1913, when the income tax began, the top marginal rate was just 7 percent and that rate didn't take effect until annual income was over $10 million (in today's dollars).

Your **average tax rate** is simply your total tax payment divided by your total income. If your income is $50,000, for example, then your total income tax under the current system can be calculated as follows. You pay 10 percent on the first $15,650 or $1,565, then you pay 15 percent on the next $34,350 ($50,000 − $15,650) or $5,153, for a total tax of $6,718. Your average tax rate is then

$$\frac{\$6718}{\$50,000} \times 100 = 13.4\%$$

Unfortunately the tax system is not quite as simple as we have presented so far because not every dollar of income is taxed. Tax professionals say that some income is *exempt* from taxation. Each person, for example, generally gets one tax exemption for him or herself, one exemption for a spouse, and one exemption for each child or dependent. In 2006 each exemption let you have $3,300 of

The **average tax rate** is the total tax payment divided by total income.

your income tax free.[1] If you have a child, for example, you can exempt $3,300 of your income from tax. If your marginal tax rate is 25 percent, that exemption means that your taxes fall by about $825 a year ($0.25 \times \$3,300$). In other words, the federal government, using the tax system, makes it cheaper to have another child compared to spending your money on say a new car. This also means that people with the same income may pay different tax amounts. The exemption amount is indexed for inflation so it typically increases a bit every year.

The tax system also allows for deductions. Like exemptions, deductions reduce your taxable income, but only if you have specific expenses. The most important deductions are for home mortgage interest, donations to charity, state and local taxes, and very high medical expenses.

For instance, if you buy a house, the interest payments on your mortgage can (usually) be deducted from your taxable income. So, if you are paying $1,000 a month in mortgage interest and you are facing a 25 percent marginal tax rate, the mortgage interest deduction will save you about $250 a month in taxes. Does this make buying a house cheaper? Not by as much as you might think. The tax deduction means that more people want to buy houses and that drives up the price of houses, especially in places like Manhattan where the amount of land is fixed. So, some of "your" subsidy actually ends up in the hands of landowners. In other words, who gets the check from the government is not necessarily the person who ends up with extra money in his or her pocket. More generally, economists understand that who really pays a tax or a subsidy can be quite different from who must send the check to the government or how those taxes and subsidies are described to the public. That point will not be the focus of this chapter—see your microeconomics textbook for more—but do keep it in mind as you think about the different taxes in the American economy.

Taxes on Capital Gains and Interest and Dividends   The income tax is a tax on your labor income and also on any income you receive from your investments, namely your interest income, your dividends, and your capital gains. You receive interest income for instance on your savings and checking accounts, and this income usually is taxed as if it were labor income.

If you own shares of stock, you likely receive dividends, which are regular income payments paid out of corporate earnings. You must pay taxes on those dividends, and the current rate of taxation is 15 percent for most people, 5 percent for low-income individuals.

The taxation of capital gains is more complicated. You receive a capital gain, for instance, if you buy stock at $100 a share and later resell it at $200 a share. Your capital gain is the extra $100 you made from the rise in the value of the stock. You pay a tax on those profits and currently the standard capital gains rate is 15 percent if you hold the stock for over one year, with a 5 percent rate for low-income individuals. Capital gains taxes are paid only when the assets are actually sold and not in the mean time while the assets are simply being held.

As is often the case in our tax system, the real rates people pay are not the same as the rates written into the tax code. For instance, capital gains allow for "loss offsets." If you gain $100 selling one stock and lose $100 selling another, usually the two sums cancel each other out in the calculation of your tax liability. If you know how to group your winners and losers together at the right time, the true rate of capital gains taxation you face may be much lower than the published rate of 15 percent.

Republicans and Democrats often disagree about how much investment income should be taxed. Democrats often favor higher taxes on investment income, on the grounds that the rich invest quite a bit and thus taxing investment income means the rich will bear a larger share of the tax burden. Republicans are more likely to argue that lower taxes on investment spur investment and thus economic growth, creating jobs, raising wages, and contributing to general prosperity in the long run.

The Alternative Minimum Tax (AMT)   There is yet another complication to the American tax system, and that is the **alternative minimum tax,** or AMT. The AMT was started in 1969 after a televised congressional hearing revealed that 155 households with income over $200,000 (about $1.2 million in today's dollars) had paid no income tax. These families had done nothing illegal, but they had managed to take advantage of tax laws to avoid income taxes. Thus, the original goal of the AMT was to make sure that it would not be possible to avoid all income tax.

The AMT requires taxpayers to make two computations. First, they must compute what they owe under the standard tax code, then they must compute what they owe under the AMT, which is typically based on a flat rate of either 26 percent or 28 percent, with no deductions allowed. The taxpayer must then pay whichever number is higher.

The AMT was supposed to hit just a few hundred families among the super-rich but it was never adjusted for inflation, so every year more and more people became subject to the AMT. In 2006, around 3.5 million Americans paid the AMT and it's now often the case that families earning $100,000 a year or less are paying the AMT and thus paying more taxes than under the regular tax code. The number of Americans covered by the AMT will likely continue to rise by the millions. The increasing reach of the AMT is in fact the largest tax increase in recent times, although it is rarely explained or presented as such. Both Republicans and Democrats claim they are unhappy about the growing reach of the AMT, but the two parties cannot agree on how to change or replace it, or how to make up for the lost revenue, should the AMT be restricted in its application.

> **Alternative minimum tax (AMT)** is a separate income tax code that began in 1969 to prevent the rich from not paying income taxes. It was not indexed to inflation and is now an extra tax burden on many upper middle class families.

Even the simplified tax forms are complex.

Social Security and Medicare Taxes

Almost all workers in the United States pay the Federal Insurance Contributions Act tax, better known as the FICA tax for the acronym that you will see on your payroll check. The FICA tax is 6.2 percent of your wages on the first $106,800 of income. In addition, your employer also pays a 6.2 percent tax on the same earnings so the total FICA tax is 12.4 percent. The FICA taxes fund Social Security payments.

Many Americans believe "I pay half of this tax, my employer pays the other half," but this isn't quite right. As we've already mentioned, the person who appears to pay a tax isn't always the person who actually pays. In reality, economic research shows that the employer's payment is mostly taken out of the worker's prospective wage; in other words if your employer didn't have to pay the FICA tax your wages would be higher.* Much of the burden of the FICA tax falls on workers, not employers.

---

* In fact, exactly this situation occurred in Chile when it privatized its social security program in 1981. Beginning in 1981, employers no longer had to pay social security taxes for their employees. The fall in employer taxes, however, did not result in extra profits. Instead, wages rose as the payroll tax fell—exactly as predicted by tax incidence theory. Other studies in the United States show that when the government mandates that firms provide benefits to their employees such as health benefits, wages fall. Thus, employees rather than employers pay for mandated benefits. On Chile and for references to other studies, see Gruber, J, 1997. "The Incidence of Payroll Taxation: Evidence from Chile," *Journal of Labor Economics* 15(3), S72–S101.

Medicare is partly financed out of general revenues and partly financed out of special payroll taxes. For most workers, 1.45 percent is withheld from their paychecks in the form of a Medicare premium and the employer pays another 1.45 percent. Again, workers pay much of the employer's premium in the form of lower wages. Self-employed individuals pay the full 2.9 percent themselves.

The Corporate Income Tax

In the United States, the corporate income tax rate is generally 35 percent. This is one of the highest rates in the world. The rate of 35 percent, however, is applied to a legal measure of income, but the tax code is so constructed that a good accountant can often make corporate income come out very low, even for profitable corporations. In fact, some apparently profitable corporations manage to define their income and expenses in such a way that they often don't pay any corporate income tax at all. Maybe you've heard of Boeing, the large and profitable airplane manufacturer; over a recent period of five years the company has paid an average tax rate of 0.7 percent.[2] Other companies aren't so well situated to take advantage of such tax breaks and accounting maneuvers.

Who pays the corporate income tax? Not corporations, which in the final analysis are legal fictions. All taxes are eventually paid by human beings. The corporate income tax is paid initially by shareholders and bondholders of corporations who earn a lower rate of return on their investments. More generally, the rate of return will fall on all forms of capital and in the long run that will also mean somewhat lower wages for workers and higher prices for goods and services.

The Bottom Line on the Distribution of Federal Taxes

Once we add in deductions, exemptions, corporate taxes, payroll taxes, excise taxes, the AMT, and assumptions about tax incidence (who pays the tax), what is the final result? It's not an easy calculation but the best estimate of the distribution of federal taxes by income class is shown in Table 30.1.

TABLE 30.1 Who Pays Federal Taxes?

Income Category	Average Pretax Income	Effective Tax Rate on All Federal Taxes	Share of Total Federal Tax Revenue
Bottom 20 percent	$15,900	4.3%	0.8%
Second 20 percent	$37,400	9.9%	4.1%
Middle 20 percent	$58,500	14.2%	9.3%
Fourth 20 percent	$85,200	17.4%	16.9%
Top 20 percent	$231,300	25.5%	68.7%
Top 10 percent	$339,100	27.4%	54.7%
Top 5 percent	$520,200	28.9%	43.8%
Top 1 percent	$1,558,500	31.2%	27.6%

Source: Congressional Budget Office, 2005

Table 30.1 shows that if we divide households into categories according to how much they earn, then households with income in the bottom 20 percent, those with average incomes of $15,900, pay 4.3 percent of their income to the federal government. As income rises so does the effective tax rate so that households in the top 20 percent of income, with average incomes of $231,300, pay 25.5 percent of their income to the federal government. The effective tax rate continues to rise if we look at the "super-rich," households in the top 10 percent, 5 percent, and 1 percent of earnings. The effective tax rate for households in the top 1 percent of income, with average yearly incomes of $1,558,500, is 31.2 percent, higher than for any other income category.

It is sometimes said that the rich do not pay taxes in the United States. That is false. Whether they pay *enough* taxes depends on your point of view, but despite all the deductions, exemptions, loopholes, and so forth, the U.S. tax system is **progressive**—people with higher income pay a higher percentage of their income in tax to the federal government than people with lower income.

In contrast to a progressive tax is a **flat tax,** which has a constant tax rate applied to income at all levels of earning. If the tax code were radically simplified to eliminate almost all deductions including the deductions for mortgage interest and charitable giving, then by some calculations a flat rate of around 19 percent would raise approximately the same revenue as today.[3] A flat tax has a number of desirable properties. Simplification of the tax code would be appreciated by many taxpayers and elimination of deductions and loopholes would encourage people to make investment, consumption and work decisions for good economic reasons rather than merely to reduce tax payments.

The disadvantage of a flat tax is that moving to a flat tax would require lowering rates on the rich and raising rates on the middle class and poor. If you compare the effective tax rate paid by different income classes under the current tax code—shown in Table 30.1—with a flat rate of 19 percent, you can see that tax rates for the rich and poor could change quite dramatically under a flat tax. Proponents of a flat tax, including Republican Steve Forbes and Democrat Jerry Brown, argue that the efficiency advantages of a flat tax mean that even people who paid a higher tax rate would, with increased economic growth, pay less in total tax.

Even if a flat tax were significantly more efficient than our current tax code, it's hard to see how the United States could ever move to such a system. Do you remember what we said about the effect of the mortgage interest deduction on house prices? The mortgage interest deduction raises house prices, so eliminating the deduction would cause a fall in house prices. Is it any wonder that neither Jerry Brown's nor Steve Forbes's tax plans caught on when they ran for president? Other countries, including Russia, the Czech Republic, and Estonia have moved toward a flat tax recently, however, so it will be interesting to see how they fare.

Returning to the current U.S. tax code, the effective tax rate is higher on the rich and the rich have more money—put these two things together and we can calculate who pays for the federal government. The final column in Table 30.1 shows the share of the $2.4 trillion in federal tax revenues that is paid for by each income category. The finding is that the rich, and especially the very rich, bear by far the largest share of the federal tax liability. The top 10 percent of households by income, for example, pay more than half of federal taxes, and the top 1 percent alone pay over a quarter of all federal taxes.

A **progressive tax** has higher tax rates on people with higher incomes.

A **flat tax** has a constant tax rate.

A **regressive tax** has higher tax rates on people with lower incomes.

UNDERSTAND YOUR world

State and Local Taxes In addition to federal taxes, most people pay state and local taxes, so the federal tax burden is not the end of the story. Overall, state and local taxes are about half the level of federal taxes, just under 10 percent of GDP. Compared to the federal government, states raise more of their revenues, about 20 percent on average, from sales taxes. Since sales tax rates are the same for everyone, regardless of income, state and local taxation as a whole is less progressive than income taxation. Thus, state and local taxes probably make the overall tax system a little bit less progressive than the federal tax system but it does depend on the state.

Spending

Almost two-thirds of the U.S. federal budget is spent on just four programs: Social Security, defense, Medicare, and Medicaid. Combined, these four programs account for 64.3 percent of federal spending in 2007, as we illustrate in Figure 30.3. Interest on the national debt and various unemployment insurance programs and welfare programs are also large. Everything else—spending on roads, education, police, prisons, science and technology, agriculture, the environment, and more—accounts for just 17.2 percent of the budget. Let's take a closer look at the big items to see just where our tax money goes.

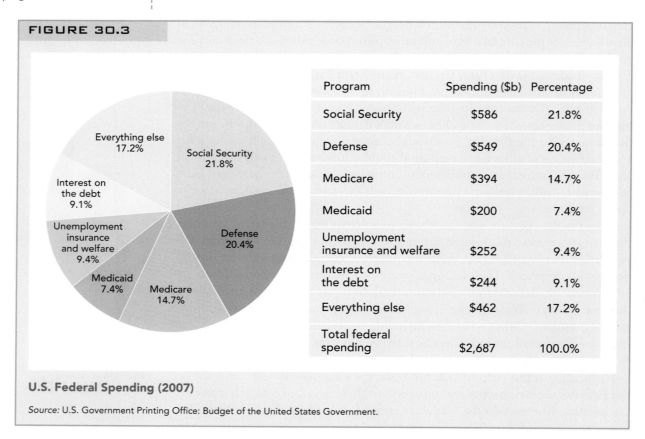

FIGURE 30.3

Program	Spending ($b)	Percentage
Social Security	$586	21.8%
Defense	$549	20.4%
Medicare	$394	14.7%
Medicaid	$200	7.4%
Unemployment insurance and welfare	$252	9.4%
Interest on the debt	$244	9.1%
Everything else	$462	17.2%
Total federal spending	$2,687	100.0%

U.S. Federal Spending (2007)

Source: U.S. Government Printing Office: Budget of the United States Government.

Social Security

If measured in terms of dollars paid out, Social Security is the single largest government program in the world. In 2007, $586 billion of benefits were paid to nearly 50 million beneficiaries.

We've already seen how the Social Security tax works. If you are wondering where that money goes, Social Security is run on a "pay as you go" basis. That means that when the government takes in your dollars, the money does not go into an account or trust with your name on it. The money is shipped out right away to the current elderly, who of course are receiving benefits. When you become old, you'll get your benefits from taxes on the young at that later point in time.

Every year the federal government sends Americans letters telling us how much money is in "our" personal social security accounts. Don't be misled. There is no money in "your account," there isn't a "your account" at all. Those letters are just the government's prediction of how much you'll get back some day. Of course, since you are in the meantime a voter, don't be surprised if those predictions turn out to be a little bit optimistic.

Social Security benefits are set at a basic minimum, but most people's benefits are defined by a complex formula depending on how long they worked, what their average earnings were over their working life, whether or not they are married, what year they retire, and at what age. In recent years, the average retiree has been paid $1,000 a month so one immediate lesson is that you shouldn't count on Social Security alone to support you in your old age.

The age at which workers can claim their full retirement benefits was 65 for many years but, because the Social Security program was getting very expensive, in 1983, the full retirement age was made to slowly increase depending on when the worker was born. You—assuming you were born after 1960—must wait until age 67 to claim your full retirement benefits. Some people advocate increasing the full retirement age again so you may want to keep an eye on the age at which you will be able to claim full benefits. A worker can start claiming some benefits as early as age 62 but people who opt for early retirement get a lower monthly payment. Benefits are indexed to the level of wages in the United States, so over time benefits rise automatically with general increases in prosperity.

Do you recall Ida May Fuller from the introduction? She paid $24.75 in Social Security taxes and received $22,888.92 in payments. Ida May's example is extreme but the basic idea is quite general. Workers who retired in the early years of Social Security received full benefits even though they paid Social Security taxes for only a portion of their working life. In addition, the Social Security tax rate increased over time, rising from 2 percent in 1940 to today's rate of 12.4 percent. The higher tax rate on today's workers funds larger benefits for *yesterday's* workers—even though yesterday's workers paid a lower tax rate on their earnings.

It's not surprising, therefore, that Social Security has become less generous over time. To see how generous Social Security is, we can add up all the taxes an individual can expect to pay into Social Security and then subtract all the benefits an individual can expect to receive from Social Security, being sure to adjust for the fact that taxes must be paid before benefits are received (a present value calculation; note that the concept of present value has been defined in the appendix to Chapter 23). Table 30.2 does just this for a single male worker with different average wages and retiring in different years.

Table 30.2 tells us that a single male with low lifetime earnings who retired in 1975

President Franklin D. Roosevelt signing the Social Security bill.

TABLE 30.2 Net Benefits of Social Security (Single male assuming various retirement years and average wages)

Average Wages	Retiree Turned 65 in 1975	Retiree Turns 65 in 2010	Retiree Turns 65 in 2030
Low	$46,807	$8,286	$3,062
Medium	$53,999	–$43,255	–$85,945
High	$52,284	–$95,212	–$193,874

Source: Steuerle and Carasso, 2004.
Low, medium, and high earnings are $30,000, $60,000, and $120,000 in inflation adjusted 2004 dollars.

received $46,807 more in Social Security benefits over his prospective lifetime than he paid in taxes. Now consider the same low-wage worker except that now he is scheduled to retire in 2010 instead of 1975—this worker can expect to receive only $8,286 more in benefits than he pays in taxes. If the same worker retires in 2030, he can expect to receive just $3,062 more in benefits than he pays in taxes. Thus, the Social Security program is becoming less generous over time, in large part because the program was very generous to workers who have already retired.

We can also see from Table 30.2 that Social Security redistributes wealth across income classes. A low-wage worker who retires in 2030 will receive $3,062 more in benefits than he pays in taxes, but for medium- and high-wage workers Social Security is a net cost. A medium-wage worker retiring in 2030 will pay $85,945 more in Social Security taxes than he will receive in benefits and a high-wage worker will pay $193,874 more in taxes than he will receive in benefits. Thus, Social Security is not just a retirement system—it's also a welfare system.

As usual, there are complications, only three of which we will mention here. Social Security pays more to married couples than to singles. A married man gets 50 percent more than a single man with the same earnings, even if his spouse has never worked. (The same is true for married females with nonworking spouses.) Thus, Social Security is more beneficial for married people than singles.

Social Security pays more the longer you live, so anyone with greater life expectancy gets a bigger benefit from Social Security (remember Ida May Fuller lived to 100!). Similarly, anyone with lower life expectancy doesn't get as good a deal from Social Security as they would otherwise. If you are 55, for example, and your doctor tells you that you have five years left to live, you don't get to make an early withdrawal from "your" Social Security account.

Because Social Security redistributes toward those with higher life expectancy, it's better for females than for males. In other words, a single woman with the same earnings as a single man will get more from Social Security because on average she will live longer. More generally, different individuals are treated differently by Social Security depending on their wealth, life expectancy, marriage status, and other factors.

Defense

In 2007, the official budget for the Department of Defense plus defense-related activities like nuclear weapons research was $549 billion. Even that figure did not include much of the expenses for the wars in Iraq and Afghanistan, which are funded outside the usual budgetary process and amounted to about $120 billion in 2007. Nor does the defense budget include spending on benefits to veterans, which falls under other spending.

The United States spends much more on its military than does any other country in the world. Table 30.3 presents some data on the top 10 countries by military expenditure. Do we get value for our money? Unfortunately, assessing how much we should spend on the military goes

TABLE 30.3 Top Ten Countries by Military Expenditure (Billions of U.S. Dollars)

Country	Military Expenditure (in billions)
United States	$549
China	$140
Russia	$79
India	$73
United Kingdom	$55
Saudi Arabia	$53
France	$48
Japan	$37
Germany	$33
Italy	$30

Source: Budget of the U.S. Government and Stockholm International Peace Research Institute.
Note: Military expenditures are as of 2007 and converted into 2005 U.S. dollars using purchasing power parity rates.

well beyond standard economics and into issues of foreign policy. That is an important question but it isn't a topic for this book.

Medicare and Medicaid

Medicare reimburses the elderly for much of their medical care spending, covering hospital stays, doctor bills, and prescription drugs. To be eligible for Medicare, an individual should be 65 or older and have worked for at least 10 years in a job paying Medicare premiums. Many of the disabled are covered as well, even if they have not held such jobs.

In fiscal year 2007, Medicare spending amounted to $394 billion. Social Security and Medicare, taken together, comprise 36.5 percent of the U.S. federal budget. Together these programs are by far the largest undertakings of the U.S. government, and both are programs that transfer money to the elderly.

Medicare does not pay all medical bills outright. Instead, beneficiaries are required to pay some percent of the charges, known as a copayment. A beneficiary also has to pay for relatively small charges, which is known as a deductible. Many of the elderly buy private insurance to pay for the gaps in their Medicare coverage.

In addition to Medicare, you may have heard of Medicaid. Whereas Medicare covers the elderly, Medicaid covers the poor and the disabled. Of course, some of the elderly are poor as well and these people are eligible for both programs. The federal government and state governments pay for Medicaid jointly, but the program itself is run through state governments at the state level. As of fiscal 2007, Medicaid expenditures were around $200 billion, which is just a little more than half the expenditures of Medicare.

Unemployment Insurance and Welfare Spending

It is a common myth that most of the money spent by our federal government goes to welfare programs. In reality, federal welfare payments (not including Medicaid) amount to about $252 billion per year or 9 percent of the federal budget.

Remember, other than defense, the largest spending programs are Social Security and Medicare, and these programs primarily transfer wealth to the elderly, not to the poor. Since we will all be elderly sooner or later (at least if we are lucky), these transfers eventually go to virtually all Americans. Of course, some of the people receiving Social Security and Medicare are poor and there is some redistribution to the poor within these programs but on average the elderly are a little bit wealthier than other Americans.

Most welfare payments fall into a few common categories. First, personal welfare payments are made to poor households with children. The largest of these is called Temporary Assistance for Needy Families. Since 1996, an individual cannot receive these benefits for more than five years in a lifetime. Housing vouchers under the Section 8 program give poor households a voucher that subsidizes a portion of their rent. Unemployment insurance makes payments to people who are out of work and is not restricted to the poor.

Especially important is the Earned Income Tax Credit (EITC), which is now the main form that antipoverty policy takes at the federal level. The EITC, quite simply, pays poor people cash through the tax system depending on how much they earn. So, for instance, if you are married, have a child, and earn $20,000 a year, you are below the poverty line and the EITC will supplement your income, giving you over $2,000 for the year. With more than one child, the credit goes up to almost $4,000. In 2007, over $35 billion was spent on the EITC and these federal programs are supplemented by a wide variety of state and local welfare programs for the poor.

Everything Else

Before discussing paying interest on the national debt, let's look at everything else. Everything else accounts for all the other spending programs of the federal government, which includes:

> Farm subsidies

> Spending on roads, bridges, and infrastructure

> The Disaster Relief Fund

> The Small Business Administration

> The Food and Drug Administration

> All federal courts

> Federal prisons

> The FBI

> Foreign aid

> Border security

> NASA

> The National Institutes of Health

> The National Science Foundation

> Financial assistance to students

> The wages of all federal employees

All of these programs add up to a large amount of money, about $462 billion in total, but none of these programs is large compared to Social Security, defense, or Medicare.

A common misconception about the budget involves foreign aid. When polled, 41 percent of Americans said that foreign aid is one of the two largest sources of federal expenditure. In reality, foreign aid is about 1 percent of the overall federal budget; the exact number depends on how that term is defined since sometimes "foreign aid" and "military assistance" are difficult to distinguish.

You may have heard about "earmarks" as one component of discretionary domestic spending. An earmark arises when a congressperson puts a favored expenditure for his or her district into a broader bill. For instance, Rep. James Clyburn earmarked $3 million for a golf program in a defense appropriations act. It is estimated that earmarks in fiscal 2006 amounted to $29 billion.

Many earmarked expenditures are wasteful, but if a politician claims that he or she will pay for new spending programs or tax cuts by cutting "waste"—beware! Our trip through the federal budget shows that cutting waste may sound good, but the reality is that most of the money is being spent in the big programs. And overhead expenses for Social Security and Medicare are quite low, so it is hard to cut spending on those programs without cutting actual benefits. There's no such thing as a free lunch. If we want more spending, taxes must rise. If we want lower taxes, spending must fall.

KEN REDDING/CORBIS

Is this defense spending?

The National Debt, Interest on the National Debt, and Deficits

The final category of spending we will discuss is interest on the national debt. If you Google the "U.S. national debt," you will probably find a number around $11 trillion, but quite a bit of this amount is held by other branches of the federal government. The Social Security Trust Fund, for example, holds billions of dollars in Treasury bonds, which simply represent an IOU on future Social Security payments. It is important to look not just at our current expenses, but also at the expenses we are committed to in the future, such as Social Security payments. Since we are committed to a lot more than Social Security payments, however, we will hold off on looking at our future commitments for a moment.

A better measure of our current debt is the **national debt held by the public,** which is all federal debt held by individuals, corporations, state or local governments, foreign governments, and other entities other than the federal government itself. The national debt held by the public is as of 2009 just over $7 trillion. From now on when we talk about the national debt, the federal debt, or just the debt we mean the national debt held by the public.

> The **national debt held by the public** is all federal debt held outside the United States government.

Seven trillion dollars is a very big number, but it has to be compared with another very big number, GDP, which is about $14 trillion. Thus, the United States has a debt-to-GDP ratio of 50 percent. Is this a big number? Mortgage lenders often require a debt-to-income ratio of less than 36 percent so few people would recommend that *you* carry that much debt. The U.S. government will live for a lot longer than you or we will so for the federal government this debt-to-GDP ratio is not excessive. Figure 30.4 shows the debt-to-GDP ratio since 1940. Today's debt-to-GDP ratio of 50 percent is large but not as large as the ratio has been in the past. More worrying is that in 2007 the debt was only five trillion dollars so the national debt is rising very quickly.

The highest debt-to-GDP ratio in U.S. history occurred in 1946 at 108 percent. As we discussed in Chapter 23, it makes sense for you to borrow to pay for large expenses, thereby smoothing your consumption, and the same thing is true for the U.S. government. The government borrowed heavily to finance emergency expenditures for World War II, but following the war the debt-to-GDP ratio slowly declined until the 1980s. In the 1980s, a combination of tax cuts and increases in defense spending increased the debt-to-GDP ratio. The ratio then fell as the economy expanded and the federal government briefly ran a series of budget surpluses under President Clinton in the 1990s. More recently, the debt-to-GDP ratio increased slightly due to further tax cuts and defense spending under former President George W. Bush and is now increasing sharply due to the recession that began in late 2007 and government spending designed to stimulate the economy under President Obama.

Every year, the government must pay interest to the people who lent it money, namely the bondholders. If your debt is $100 and the interest rate is 5 percent, then you owe the lender $5 a year in interest payments. It works the same way with the national debt. The national debt in 2007 was about $5 trillion and the average interest rate on U.S. debt in 2007 was 5 percent, so in 2007

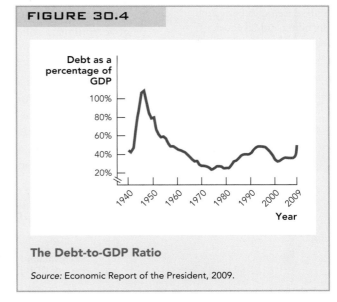

FIGURE 30.4

The Debt-to-GDP Ratio

Source: Economic Report of the President, 2009.

the federal government had to pay about $250 billion in interest payments to bondholders. (The exact number, which you can see in Figure 30.3, was $244 billion.) Interest on the debt is about 9.1 percent of the federal budget or about 2 percent of GDP and will increase as the debt-to-GDP ratio increases. As we discuss further below, we need to keep an eye on the national debt.

Sometimes television commentators suggest it makes a big difference if the debt of the U.S. government is held by foreigners or Americans. From a purely economic point of view, however, this distinction does not matter. The real decision is made when the money is spent on goods and services and what matters is how the money is spent. If, years later, interest payments go to foreigners, that is because the foreigners have invested in the United States. This is economically beneficial for the United States and the fact that foreigners also may become wealthy is an economic plus not a minus. You can make a moral or ethical judgment that Americans ought to be spending less and saving more (which would mean less borrowing from foreigners), but low savings would be an even greater problem without foreign investors.

The **deficit** is the annual difference between federal spending and revenues.

We now need to make a distinction between the national debt and the deficit. The debt is the total amount of money owed by the federal government at a point in time. It is a cumulative total of previous obligations. The **deficit** is the difference—this year—between what the government is spending and what the government is collecting in revenues. You can think of the deficit as the annual change in the national debt.

The top half of Figure 30.5 shows federal government spending (green) and revenues (blue) as a percentage of GDP from 1960 to 2009. When spending is greater than revenues, the government must borrow to make up the difference— the difference is the deficit, shown in the bottom half of Figure 30.5 also as a percentage of GDP (and as a negative value). In 1990, for example, the federal government spent almost 22 percent of GDP, but it collected only 18 percent of GDP in tax revenues. Since government spending was greater than revenues,

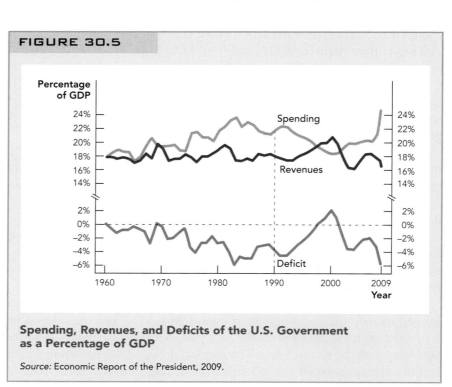

FIGURE 30.5

Spending, Revenues, and Deficits of the U.S. Government as a Percentage of GDP

Source: Economic Report of the President, 2009.

the government had to borrow the difference so in 1990 the deficit was about 4 percent of GDP (22 percent − 18 percent).

Will the U.S. Government Go Bankrupt?

We said earlier that the current debt-to-GDP ratio of 50 percent is large but not unprecedented. Nevertheless, many economists are worried about the future debt-to-GDP ratio. The Congressional Budget Office (CBO), for example, argues that "under any plausible scenario, the federal budget is on an unsustainable path—that is, the federal debt will grow much faster than the economy over the long run."[4] The Congressional Budget Office's projections for the debt-to-GDP ratio are shown in Figure 30.6. (Note that these projections were made in 2007 before the debt jumped by two trillion dollars—so the projections today would be even a little bit worse.) According to the CBO, if taxes and spending trends do not change significantly, the debt-to-GDP ratio will soar to rates well above any seen in U.S. history.

The main forces driving the CBO's projections are not recessions but demographics and increasing health care costs. The U.S. population is getting older. In 2008, about 12 percent of the population was aged 65 or older, but in 2030, 19 percent of the population will be 65 or older. The increase in the number of elderly people means higher Social Security and Medicare payments. As a fraction of GDP, for example, Social Security payments will have to increase by about 41 percent if benefits are to be maintained at promised levels. More elderly people also means we will see increases in Medicare payments, although in this case an even bigger problem than demographics is rising health care costs per person.

In recent decades, health care costs per person have been rising more than twice as fast as GDP per capita. If health care costs continue rising at their current rate, those costs will account for a larger and larger part of the economy. Because of Medicare and Medicaid, health care costs will consume a larger and larger share of the federal budget.

When we add together spending increases that we can expect to occur because of an older population and rising health care costs, the result is Figure 30.7 on the next page.

To understand Figure 30.7, first take a look at the solid red line: this is total spending on programs (i.e., not including interest on the national debt) over approximately the past 50 years and projected into the future. Notice that over the past 50 years spending on programs has fluctuated around 18 percent of GDP. Tax revenues, the solid black line, have been a little bit lower on average, leading to deficits in most years, but not very large deficits in percentage terms.

As we enter the future, however, an increasingly older population and higher health care costs are projected to increase spending far above past totals. The main cause of higher spending is a modest but significant increase in Social Security payments relative to GDP and a large increase in Medicare and Medicaid spending. Notice that the CBO projects all other government spending programs, including defense, shown by the purple line to *decline* as a percentage of GDP—if that scenario proves overly optimistic, spending could rise even more than is shown in these projections.

CHECK YOURSELF

> When you retire, you will receive Social Security benefits and most Americans will also receive Medicare benefits. Right now, what percentage of federal spending is represented by Social Security plus Medicare payments?

> Why is it important to consider the debt-to-GDP ratio rather than just the absolute amount of the national debt? What does this ratio tell us?

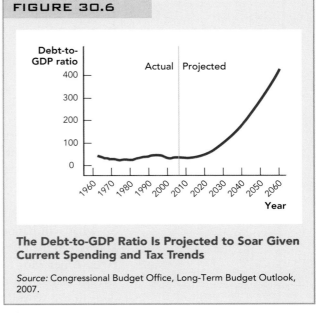

FIGURE 30.6

The Debt-to-GDP Ratio Is Projected to Soar Given Current Spending and Tax Trends

Source: Congressional Budget Office, Long-Term Budget Outlook, 2007.

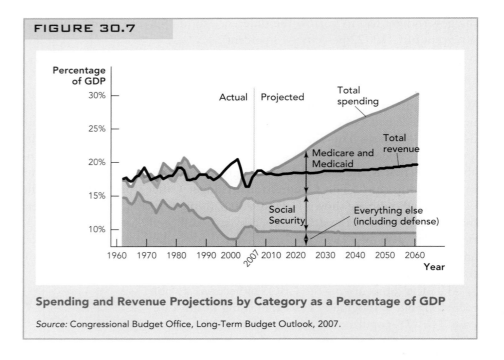

FIGURE 30.7

Spending and Revenue Projections by Category as a Percentage of GDP

Source: Congressional Budget Office, Long-Term Budget Outlook, 2007.

UNDERSTAND YOUR **world**

If spending increases rapidly and taxes rise only modestly, the result will be a soaring debt-to-GDP ratio, which is where the CBO's scary projection seen in Figure 30.6 comes from. But the CBO is not really predicting a soaring debt-to-GDP ratio. Instead, they are suggesting that *something else must change*—either government spending must decrease or taxes must increase or perhaps health care costs cannot continue on their current upward spiral.

The Future Is Hard to Predict

So what will happen? Will spending decrease or will taxes increase? No one knows. On the one hand, the United States does have a history of relatively low taxes. Americans fought the Revolutionary War, in part, as a protest against British taxes even though British Americans had one of the smallest tax burdens in the world! The modern income tax didn't begin until 1913 and that required a separate amendment to the Constitution. Even as late as 1916, the federal government accounted for less than 5 percent of GDP.

Taxes and federal spending increased dramatically during 1916–1919 and 1942–1945, corresponding to World War I and World War II, respectively. But since that time federal taxes and spending have been fairly stable—as we noted above, around 18 percent of GDP. When taxes have increased, there have often been backlashes, when Americans elect politicians who promise to cut taxes. So, will Americans accept much higher tax rates in the future than they ever have in the past? Will you?

If taxes and spending in the United States do increase, this would make the United States more like other developed countries. Figure 30.8 shows total government spending by country, including spending by federal, state, and local governments. Government in the United States today spends a smaller fraction of GDP than in most other developed countries. As a result, spending could increase substantially in the United States over the next several decades and the United States would still be spending at levels comparable to Germany, Italy, and the Netherlands today.

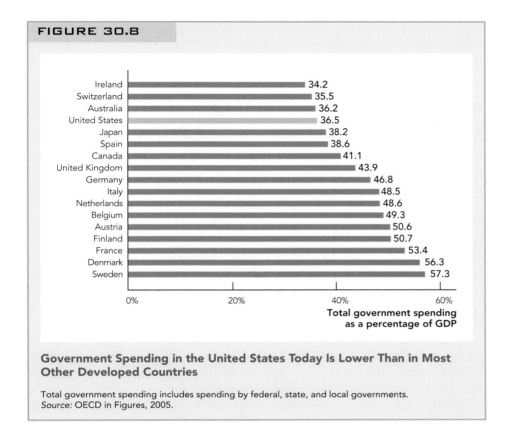

FIGURE 30.8

Country	Value
Ireland	34.2
Switzerland	35.5
Australia	36.2
United States	36.5
Japan	38.2
Spain	38.6
Canada	41.1
United Kingdom	43.9
Germany	46.8
Italy	48.5
Netherlands	48.6
Belgium	49.3
Austria	50.6
Finland	50.7
France	53.4
Denmark	56.3
Sweden	57.3

Total government spending
as a percentage of GDP

Government Spending in the United States Today Is Lower Than in Most Other Developed Countries

Total government spending includes spending by federal, state, and local governments.
Source: OECD in Figures, 2005.

Could spending be cut? We have already cut some projected Social Security spending by increasing the age of retirement. Perhaps we can cut spending even more—but don't expect the elderly to take this sitting down! And remember a large part of the growth in spending is due to rising health care costs. Many people talk about slowing the growth of health care costs but it isn't so easy. There is a lot of waste in health care markets, but also there are many wonderful innovations. Drugs known as statins lower our cholesterol and new surgical procedures save many lives; a triple bypass operation is now more or less standard procedure. It's not so easy to sort out the good medical procedures from the bad ones, and so by most accounts health care costs will continue to rise. Other countries do spend a smaller fraction of their GDP on health care costs, but the *growth* in health care costs is pretty similar throughout the developed world.

Don't forget that whatever happens, the news is actually quite good for the most part. Americans are living longer than ever before and many medical advances are paying off. Let's say you thought you would live to be 80 but then you learn you will live to be 100 instead. You might worry about how to finance your now-longer retirement and perhaps you might even despair that it seems impossible. But this is the kind of problem that we can live with!

Another scenario is that GDP will grow faster in the future than it has in the past. We outlined one case for optimism in Chapter 22. Nevertheless, although we hope for the best, it's probably wise to plan if not for the worst then at least for the most likely outcome, and that will require some painful tax increases or spending cuts.

One general lesson is that we cannot judge the fiscal health of the federal government simply by looking at today's budget or today's deficit. New government programs often grow over time and we ought to think about implicit

STOCKBYTE/GETTY IMAGES

The federal government has not planned for future expenses. Have you?

CHECK YOURSELF

> Projecting forward for the next 40 years, what categories of spending are likely to increase or decrease? What does this mean for overall government spending? Will it grow, fall, or stay the same?

> If the pace of idea generation quickens, as was discussed in Chapter 22, the Solow growth curve might shift permanently. If this happens, how would it affect the debt-to-GDP ratio? Explain what this means for our nation's ability to pay for increased benefits for retirees.

future spending commitments when evaluating these new programs. Politicians in the past made many promises to spend in the future and today we are dealing with the legacy of these promises.

Revenues and Spending Undercount the Role of Government in the Economy

This chapter has mostly been about federal revenues and expenditures. But our government does many things and imposes many costs, which do not show up on any formal budgetary accounts. The Environmental Protection Agency (EPA), for instance, has a budget of only about $8 billion yet its real reach, in terms of both costs and benefits, is much higher. The EPA has the power to regulate how business affects the environment and its mandates involve many billions of dollars of costs and benefits. Government spending is one measure of how government affects the economy, but it is not a complete or fully accurate measure.

Governments take many other actions that commandeer resources from the private sector but do not show up as full budgetary expenditures. For instance, until 1973 the United States ran a military draft. Drafted soldiers, of course, are relatively cheap if you just look at their paychecks, but the draft involves a very significant opportunity cost. Many people who were ill suited to be soldiers were removed from their jobs or their studies. The real cost of the draft—the opportunity cost—was pointed out by Milton Friedman, who advocated a move to a volunteer army. The United States had to pay soldiers more, so military costs appeared to go up. In reality, the volunteer army reduced the total cost to society of providing national defense by freeing up more productive labor, even if that efficiency was not reflected in the government's budget statements.

☐ Takeaway

An examination of the current federal budget reveals some key points. First and foremost is the simple point that the federal government takes in and spends a great deal of money. It is hard to imagine revenues and spending of over $2.5 *trillion*.

Next, it is useful to recognize where this money comes from. Contrary to what some people might think, the corporate income tax represents only a little over 10 percent of total tax revenues. The huge majority of tax revenues—over 82 percent—come from individuals in the form of individual income taxes and tax on wages linked to Social Security and Medicare.

For many people, it is surprising to learn what the federal government spends its money on. The obvious category of defense spending represents around 20 percent of spending. Over one-third (36.5 percent) of the federal budget goes for Social Security and Medicare payments. Comprehensive general transfers to the elderly represent far more money than do welfare expenditures per se.

What about the future? The U.S. tax system is very complicated and not always transparent in its effects. Nevertheless, we can estimate future expenditures and revenues as a way of understanding the fiscal strength or weakness of a nation. It is very likely that federal expenditures will rise in the future, most of all because of rising Medicare expenditures. One question is whether and how federal revenues will rise to keep the budget sufficiently close to balance.

☐ CHAPTER REVIEW

KEY CONCEPTS

Marginal tax rate, p. 656

Average tax rate, p. 657

Alternative minimum tax (AMT), p. 659

Progressive tax, p. 661

Flat tax, p. 661

Regressive tax, p. 661

National debt held by the public, p. 667

Deficit, p. 668

FACTS AND TOOLS

1. a. Consider Table 30.1. We can use these data to find out what percentage of federal taxes is paid from the "top down" by the top 40 percent, top 60 percent, or top 80 percent of income earners. Likewise, we can count from the "bottom up" by the bottom 40 percent, 60 percent, or 80 percent of income earners. Fill in the table below.

Share of Total Federal Tax Revenue		Share of Total Federal Tax Revenue	
Everyone	100%	Everyone	100%
Bottom 20%		Top 80%	
Bottom 40%	4.9%	Top 60%	
Bottom 60%		Top 40%	85.6%
Bottom 80%		Top 20%	

b. Given these data, which of the following are true?

   a) *The bottom 60% of taxpayers pay less than 25% of federal taxes.*

   b) *The top 80% of taxpayers pay over 98% of federal taxes.*

   c) *The top 40% of taxpayers pay less than 60% of federal taxes.*

2. In 2007, corporate income taxes were about 11 percent of total federal revenue. Use Figure 30.5 to help estimate what fraction of GDP represents corporate income taxes.

3. a. Let's explore the difference between the average income tax rate and the marginal income tax rate. In the simple land of Rabushka, there is only one tax rate, 20 percent, but workers don't have to pay tax on the first $10,000 of their income. For every dollar they earn above $10,000, they pay 20 cents on the dollar to the Lord High Mayor of Rabushka.

The easy way to calculate the tax bill is the same way that America's IRS does: Subtract $10,000 from each person's income and call the remainder "taxable income." Multiply taxable income by 0.20, and the result is "tax due." Fill in the table below.

Income	Taxable Income	Tax Due	Marginal Tax Rate	Average Income Tax Rate
$5,000	$0	0	0%	0%
$10,000	$0	0	0%	0%
$15,000	$5,000	$1,000	20%	6.7%
$20,000				
$50,000				
$100,000				
$1,000,000				

b. Is the marginal tax rate ever lower than the average tax rate?

c. As a worker's income rises and rises past $1,000,000, will the average tax rate ever be greater than 20 percent?

d. Just to make sure you know what these terms mean in plain English: For an accountant making $50,000 per year, what percentage of her income goes to the Lord High Mayor?

Note: This simple tax system is quite similar to the plan that economist Robert Hall and political scientist Alvin Rabushka spell out in their book, *The Flat Tax*, widely available for free online. Hall and Rabushka estimate that a system like this one would raise roughly the same amount of revenue as the current federal income tax.

4. a. Do most federal government transfers of cash go to the elderly or to the poor?

b. Do most federal government purchases of health care go to the elderly or to the poor?

5. a. According to Table 30.2, which generation gets the best deal from Social Security: The one turning 65 in 1975, in 2010, or in 2030?

b. Out of the nine categories in Table 30.2, which kind of worker gets the best deal overall from Social Security?

6. Based on the information in this chapter, let's see who gets a better deal, a greater net-benefit, from Social Security. In each pairing, choose one, or write "unclear."

Women or men?

Married couples or singles?

People born in 1910 or people born in 1965?

High-income earners or low-income earners?

7. There are a lot of ways to slice up the U.S. budget. With this in mind, which of the following statements are true, according to Figure 30.3?

a. Most of the federal budget is spent on welfare and foreign aid.

b. About half of the federal budget goes toward Medicare, Medicaid, and Social Security combined.

c. More than half of the federal budget goes toward Medicare, Medicaid, Social Security, and interest on the debt combined.

d. The federal government spends about $1,830 on the military per person in the United States.

8. Pundits and commentators often state (correctly) that entitlement spending (spending on Medicare, Medicaid, and Social Security) is going to explode in the future. But by lumping all three together, we obscure the source of the explosion. Review Figure 30.7.

a. Which of the three really won't be "exploding" all that much compared to the other two?

b. Which category of federal spending is projected to actually decline in future decades?

THINKING AND PROBLEM SOLVING

1. By U.S. law, your employer pays half of the payroll tax and you, the worker, pay the other half. We mentioned that according to the basics of supply and demand, the part of the tax paid by the employer is likely to cut the worker's take-home pay. Let's see why. We'll start off in a land without any payroll taxes and then see how adding payroll taxes (like FICA and Medicare) affects the worker's take-home pay.

a. Who is it that "supplies labor?" Is it workers or firms? And who demands labor? Workers or firms?

b. The chart below illustrates the pretax equilibrium. Mark the equilibrium wage and quantity of labor in this market. In part c, remember that this "wage" is the amount paid directly to workers.

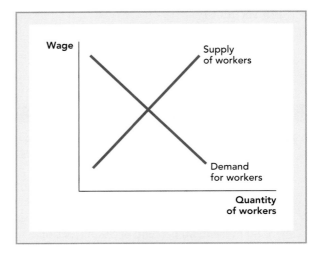

c. Suppose the government enacts a new payroll tax of 10 percent of worker wages, "paid" 100 percent by employers. What will happen to the typical firm's demand for labor? In other words, when firms learn that every time they hire a worker, they have to pay not only that worker's wage but they must also pay 10 percent of that worker's wage to the government, will that increase or decrease their willingness to hire workers? After you answer in words, also illustrate the shift in the graph above.

d. So, in the equilibrium with a new 100 percent-employer-paid payroll tax, will worker's take-home wages be higher or lower than beforehand?

e. Imagine that most workers want full-time jobs to support their families whether the wage is high or low. What does this imply about the shape of the supply curve? Redo the analysis with the new supply curve and discuss the exact effect on wages of the payroll tax.

2. It's easy to confuse the "federal deficit" with the "federal debt." We'll work out an example to make the differences clear. To keep the math simple, we'll falsely assume that in this land of Barrovia, the government can borrow from the public at an interest rate of 0 percent—so there is no interest on the debt. We will also assume that the government is unwilling to print money to finance its budget so the only way to finance a deficit is by borrowing. The debt inherited from 2011 is 4,000 credits (C4,000, in the local notation). Fill in the accompanying table.

Note: The relationship between deficits and debts is similar to the relationship between investment and the capital stock, which we investigated back in Chapters 21 and 22: The first is a "flow" while the second is a "stock"; the first is like a river while the second is like a lake.

Year	Revenue	Spending	Deficit	Debt
2012	C100	C120	C20	C4,020
2013	C80	C130	C50	
2014	C110	C140		
2015	C120	C150		
2016	C120	C160		

3. Social Security is primarily a pay-as-you-go program, which means that the government pays retirees their promised benefits by taxing today's workers. Imagine that Social Security moved to a fully funded program in which today's workers (or the government on their behalf) invested in assets, such as stock and bonds, to pay for their own retirement.

    a. Discuss some of the costs and benefits of a fully funded program.

    b. Discuss some of the difficulties of transitioning to the new system. Hint: If today's workers pay for their own future retirement, who will pay today's retirees?

4. Under current law, homeowners get a big tax break: The details of the tax break really don't matter as much as the mere fact that if you make mortgage payments on a home that you live in, your taxes will be lower than otherwise.

    a. Suppose that Congress eliminated the tax break for homeowners. What will this law do to the demand for homes: Raise, lower, or have no impact?

    b. What will be the net effect of eliminating the break on the price of houses?

    c. Given your answers to parts a and b comment on who gets the benefits of the tax break. Is it

people who buy homes? Sellers? (Be careful, sellers were buyers once!) Why could eliminating the tax break prove difficult?

5. Calculating taxes on capital gains takes a little work, but if you buy and sell stocks, bonds, works of art, or homes, you'll probably have to do this at some point. Let's practice. In a few cases below, the price will fall—just record that as a negative rise (a "capital loss," in tax jargon, and calculate the negative "tax due").

    a. Fill in the table below.

Item	Purchase price 2015	Sale Price 2020	Capital Gain	Tax Due at 15% rate
10 Shares of Microsoft Stock	$1,200	$1,250	$50	$7.50
1 Share of Berkshire Hathaway stock	$8,000	$11,000		
100 Shares of GM stock	$1,000	$500		
1 Picasso napkin sketch	$15,000	$14,000		
1 Mexican Amate folk painting	$2,000	$3,500		

    b. One nice thing about the capital gains tax is that you can choose what year to pay it by choosing what year to sell your investment. If you wanted to sell your single share of Berkshire stock and your Picasso in the same year, how much tax would you pay?

6. How big is the tax break from the $3,300 per child income tax deduction for:

    a. Families in the 10 percent tax bracket?

    b. Families in the 25 percent tax bracket? (Hint: This is worked out in the chapter.)

    c. Families in the 35 percent tax bracket?

7. a. If 1 percent of federal spending goes toward foreign aid, then what percent of U.S. GDP goes toward foreign aid? Figures 30.3 and 30.5 will help.

    b. If 20 percent of federal spending goes toward defense spending, then what percent of U.S. GDP goes toward defense spending?

c. If $30 billion of federal spending goes toward earmarked appropriations, what percent of federal spending goes toward earmarks?

8. Some people argue that a large national debt will make future generations poorer. One way to test this is to see what happened after the last time the United States had a large national debt: after World War II. As Figure 30.4 shows, the debt-to-GDP ratio was over 100 percent, more than double today's ratio. Let's compare this to Figure 20.3 and Figure 24.5, which shows the growth rate of GDP and the unemployment rate, respectively.

a. During the 1950s, was the growth rate lower than average? How about during the 1960s?

b. During the 1950s, was the unemployment rate higher than average? How about during the 1960s?

c. Overall, is it fair to say that the two decades after the massive World War II debt were worse than average?

Note that this single case doesn't count as conclusive proof: Perhaps the United States just got lucky, or the federal government did an unusually good job spending its World War II expenditures to build up its capital stock (a point emphasized in the excellent Francis Ford Coppola film *Tucker: The Man and His Dream*), or perhaps a massive short-term debt doesn't cause much economic trouble. You can learn more about these possible explanations in other economics courses.

9. Which of the following actual government programs show up as costs in the federal budget?

The Department of Labor mandates the minimum wage for workers.

The Environmental Protection Agency mandates that cars have equipment to keep pollution levels low.

The National Oceanic and Atmospheric Administration forecasts the weather.

The Coast Guard rescues sailors from a sinking yacht off the coast of Cape Cod.

The Border Patrol requires that all vehicles driving on highways out of San Diego be stopped to be inspected for the presence of illegal aliens.

CHALLENGES

1. In 1989, Senator Bob Packwood asked Congress's Joint Committee on Taxation how much extra revenue the government would raise if it just started taxing 100 percent of all income over $200,000 per year. The Joint Committee crunched some numbers and reported an answer: $204 billion per year.

a. What is wrong with this answer?

b. Under Packwood's proposal, what would the marginal tax rate be at $250,000 per year? At $500,000 per year?

Note: Packwood asked the Joint Committee this question not because he wanted to raise taxes that high, but to make a point. The tale of his efforts—and the efforts of Ronald Reagan, Dan Rostenkowski, Bill Bradley, and many others—to improve the U.S. tax code in the 1980s is compellingly told in Birnbaum and Murray's book *Showdown at Gucci Gulch: Lawmakers, Lobbyists, and the Unlikely Triumph of Tax Reform.*

2. Today, many government transfer programs are run through the tax code. The Earned Income Tax Credit (EITC), which we discussed in this chapter, is one important example. The federal government also has a variety of other "refundable tax credits," that is, spending programs run through the tax code. These blur the line between "tax breaks" and "government spending." This may explain their popularity: voters and politicians who like tax breaks can claim that these programs are tax breaks, while voters and politicians who like higher government spending can claim that these programs are government spending.

a. Your income is $20,000 per year. You pay your initial tax bill of $5,000 but the government sends you a $1,000 tax refund because you have a young child. What is your after-tax income, including the value of the government check?

b. Your income is $20,000 per year. You pay your initial tax bill of $5,000 and the government sends you a $1,000 check because you have a young child. What is your after-tax income, including the value of the government check?

c. Your income is $20,000 per year. You pay your initial tax bill of $500 but the government sends you a $1,000 tax refund because you have a young child. What is your after-tax income, including the value of the government check?

d. Your income is $20,000 per year. You pay your tax bill of $500 and the government sends you a $1,000 check because you have a young child. What is your after-tax income, including the value of the government check?

e. In which of these cases does the government check seem like "government spending" to you, and why? You may find more than one case applicable—this question borders on the philosophical.

3. a. If the debt-to-GDP ratio rose to 100 percent and the interest rate on the debt were 5 percent per year, what fraction of GDP would go toward paying interest on the debt?

b. If this happened, would interest on the debt be a bigger share of GDP than Social Security is today?

c. In your opinion, do you think that Americans would tolerate spending this much of the national income on interest payments for past spending? More important, do you think Americans would want their politicians to stop making the interest payments and just default on some or all of the federal debt? Why or why not?

4. Currently, the U.S. government offers "food stamps" to poor Americans. These "stamps" are pieces of paper that look like Monopoly money and can be spent just like money at many grocery stores. The government has a complex formula that determines how much each poor person gets each month in food stamps (or more often these days, government-provided debit cards).

Let's suppose that instead, the government decides to pay 95 percent of every poor person's food bill, as long as it is purchased at a typical grocery store: The poor person would make a "copayment" of 5 percent of the total bill, and the federal government would reimburse the grocery store for the remaining 95 percent. Just to keep things simple, let's assume that the government has a good way to make sure that poor people can't resell this food to others.

a. Which method would probably lead to more spending on food: the current method or the 5 percent copayment method? Why?

b. If food companies like Kellogg's and Quaker Oats start inventing new, more delicious dishes at a rapid rate, under which method will the federal government's food spending grow fastest: the current method or the 5 percent copayment method?

c. Which method is more like how most people pay for health care including the elderly and the poor under the federal government's Medicare and Medicaid programs: the current method or the 5 percent copayment method?

d. Recall that health care is a field of rapid innovation. How can your answer to parts b and c explain the rapid growth of medical spending?

5. When discussing the statements sent to you by the federal government that predict your future Social Security payments, we said, "don't be surprised if those predictions turn out to be a little bit optimistic." Consider why this might be *wrong*: Why might these predictions be too *pessimistic*, precisely because Social Security recipients are also voters? Hint: Senior citizens are more likely to vote than younger citizens.

31

Fiscal Policy

CHAPTER OUTLINE

Fiscal Policy: The Best Case

The Limits to Fiscal Policy

When Fiscal Policy Might Make Matters Worse

So When Is Fiscal Policy a Good Idea?

Takeaway

The U.S. economy was falling toward a severe recession. The S&P 500 stock index was plummeting. And in the third quarter of 2008 consumer spending dropped by 3.7 percent, the largest fall in 28 years. Consumer spending is about 70 percent of GDP (as you will recall from Chapter 20) so the sudden drop in spending pushed down the growth rate of GDP. To encourage more spending, President George W. Bush had authorized the Treasury to send checks to millions of U.S. taxpayers. Could the new money jump-start the economy? Not this time. Consumer confidence was ebbing. Even with a few extra bucks in their pocket, consumers weren't ready to spend. The economy continued to worsen and in 2009 President Barack Obama tried a different approach: hundreds of billions in new government spending on roads, bridges, education and other infrastructure. If the American consumer wouldn't spend, then the American government would.

Fighting a recession with tax cuts and fighting a recession with increased government spending are two forms of fiscal policy. **Fiscal policy** is federal government policy on taxes, spending, and borrowing that is designed to influence business fluctuations.

In this chapter, we use the dynamic aggregate demand and aggregate supply curves familiar to you from Chapter 26 to understand fiscal policy. We start with the situations in which fiscal policy is most effective, move to the cases where fiscal policy doesn't matter much at all for macroeconomic performance, and close by considering when an activist fiscal policy is downright harmful.

As we said, there are two general categories of fiscal policy used to fight a recession:

1. The government spends more money.

2. The government cuts taxes, giving people more money to spend.

Fiscal policy is federal government policy on taxes, spending, and borrowing that is designed to influence business fluctuations.

679

In both cases, the goal is more spending, although in the first case the new spending comes from government and in the second it comes from the private sector. We will start by focusing on expansionary fiscal policy done through increases in government spending because that is the most straightforward case of fiscal policy and the underlying issues are easiest to identify.

Fiscal Policy: The Best Case

An economic recession is underway and fear is in the air. Worried about their future, consumers cut back on consumption growth; that is, $\vec{C}$ falls. Consumers are spending less in order to build up their cash reserves so we can also say equivalently that $\vec{v}$ falls. Figure 31.1 shows the result: The fall in $\vec{C}$ shifts the AD curve to the left and down, moving the economy from a long-run equilibrium at point a to a short-run equilibrium at point b. At point b, the growth rate is negative and the economy is in a recession.

The problem at point b is that consumers want to hold more money and this means that the rate of inflation must decrease. Wages and prices, however, are sticky (see Chapter 26) so when spending growth declines, instead of just

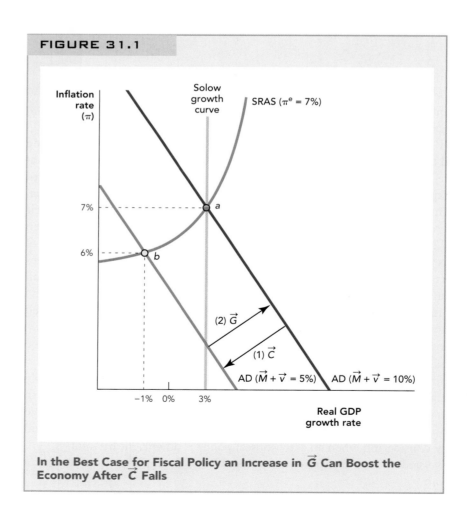

FIGURE 31.1

In the Best Case for Fiscal Policy an Increase in $\vec{G}$ Can Boost the Economy After $\vec{C}$ Falls a decrease in inflation, we get a decrease in real growth as well. In terms of our dynamic AD curve, we have $\vec{M} + \vec{v}$ = Inflation + Real growth. $\vec{M}$, by assumption, isn't changing and in the short run the decrease in $\vec{v}$ is split between a decrease in inflation and a decrease in real growth.

In the long run, prices and wages will become "unstuck," fear will pass, and $\vec{C}$ will return to its normal growth rate so the economy will transition until it returns to point a. But in John Maynard Keynes's famous phrase "in the long run, we are all dead." Can government do anything to make recovery a reality now? Quite possibly so.

Remember that the components of aggregate demand are $\vec{C}$, $\vec{I}$, $\vec{G}$, and $\vec{NX}$. The government has (some) control over $\vec{G}$ so if $\vec{C}$ falls, why not increase $\vec{G}$ to compensate? In Figure 31.1, we show how an increase in $\vec{G}$ can shift the AD curve to the right and up, thereby putting the economy on a transition path back to point a, reversing the decline in $\vec{C}$ and ending the recession.

An increase in $\vec{G}$ means the government is spending more money—and thus commanding more real resources—so where does the money come from? That's a very good question. The money must come from taxes or increased borrowing and, as we will see shortly, that will mean reduced aggregate demand from some quarters, thereby making the increase in $\vec{G}$ less effective. But, in the best case scenario, the increase in $\vec{G}$ is still effective because more spending creates more growth which supports the increased spending.

Can an economy really pull itself up by its bootstraps? Yes. Since John Maynard Keynes's *The General Theory of Employment, Interest and Money* (1936), economists have understood that in some situations spending can increase growth, or as economists like to say *demand can create its own supply*. More generally, the reason this is possible is that at point b the economy is operating *inefficiently*. Remember that the economy has the capital, the labor, and the technology to grow at the rate given by the Solow growth curve, so when the economy is operating at point b, it is growing at less than potential; it is growing more slowly than is possible given the fundamental factors of production. The increase in $\vec{G}$ puts the economy back on track and, if everything goes well, the increase more than pays for itself.

The Multiplier

To understand how an increase in government spending can generate growth, let's look a little more closely at what economists call the multiplier. In the best case scenario, the increase in $\vec{G}$ doesn't even have to be as large as the fall in $\vec{C}$ in order to restore the economy because as $\vec{G}$ increases so does $\vec{C}$. Let's explain how this can happen.

Imagine that Joe becomes worried about unemployment so he cuts back on his daily consumption of mocha Frappuccinos in an effort to hold more cash in reserve. But remember that Joe's spending is the coffee shop owner's income (as we discussed in Chapter 20). Thus, when Joe cuts back on his spending, the coffee shop owner may cut back on her spending by, for example, hiring fewer employees or not investing in that fancy new Clover coffee machine. Thus, the decrease in Joe's spending is added to the decrease in the coffee shop owner's spending, which is added to the decrease in the spending

FIGURE 31.2

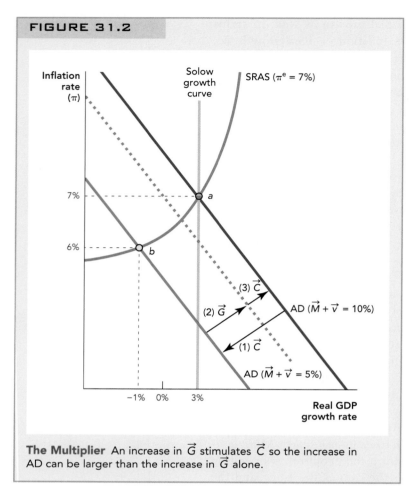

The Multiplier An increase in $\vec{G}$ stimulates $\vec{C}$ so the increase in AD can be larger than the increase in $\vec{G}$ alone.

The **multiplier effect** is the additional increase in AD caused when expansionary fiscal policy increases income and thus consumer spending.

CHECK YOURSELF

> What are the two types of expansionary fiscal policy?

of her employees and so forth. Now on an ordinary day, Joe is worried about unemployment, but Jennifer gets a new job so Joe's reduction in consumption is matched by Jennifer's increase and the net effect, even taking into account all the multiplier effects, is zero.

Trouble starts when a lot of people fear unemployment and reduce their spending at the same time. When many people reduce their spending, this reduces other people's income and these people then reduce their spending and so forth in a multiplier process. But now who will act as Jennifer to restore the economy to growth? In this situation, the government may take the place of Jennifer. By spending more to build a dam, for example, the government not only increases aggregate demand directly, it also increases the income of dam workers who spend more on haircuts, which increases the income of barbers, who spend more on restaurant meals and so forth. In Figure 31.2, we show that the increase in $\vec{G}$ stimulates an increase in income and thus an increase in $\vec{C}$ (we have drawn the figure so the net increase in AD is exactly the same as in Figure 31.1). Since the increase in $\vec{C}$ multiplies the effect of expansionary fiscal policy on AD, this effect is called the **multiplier effect**.

All of this sounds great. The government can offset decreases in AD with increases in $\vec{G}$ and because of the multiplier effect, it doesn't even have to spend that much. As you probably expected, however, the real world isn't quite so simple.

The Limits to Fiscal Policy

There are four major limits to fiscal policy. Three of these limits have to do with the difficulty of using fiscal policy to shift aggregate demand (AD).

1. **Crowding out:** If government spending crowds out or leads to less private spending, then the increase in AD is reduced or neutralized on net.

2. **A drop in the bucket:** The economy is so large that government can rarely increase spending enough to have a large impact.

3. **A matter of timing:** It can be difficult to time fiscal policy so that the AD curve shifts at just the right moments.

The fourth limit is that even if fiscal policy shifts AD that may not solve the problem. The best case for fiscal policy is when a recession is caused by a decrease in aggregate demand. But sometimes the problem isn't that people aren't spending enough, the problem is that people don't have enough to spend. In other words, some recessions are caused by real shocks of the type we analyzed in Chapter 27. As we will see, fiscal policy doesn't work well at combating real shocks. Thus, in addition to the difficulty of shifting AD we also have:

4. Real shocks: Shifting AD doesn't help much to combat real shocks.

Let's look at each of these limits in turn, noting that we are sticking with our basic scenario of an increase in government spending before we turn to the second type of expansionary fiscal policy, a decrease in taxes.

Crowding Out

When increased government spending comes at the expense of reduced private spending, we have the phenomenon of **crowding out.** Crowding out means that the initial shift in AD is less than the amount of the new government spending.

To consider an example, if the federal government builds a new interstate highway, that highway must be paid for. That means either higher taxes or more government borrowing (i.e., selling government bonds to the private sector). Both the taxes and the sale of bonds decrease aggregate demand, although perhaps with different timing. Let's now consider those two financing scenarios in more detail, namely raising taxes and borrowing by selling more government bonds.

Crowding out is the decrease in private spending that occurs when government increases spending.

Raising Taxes to Finance Fiscal Policy The simplest case for understanding crowding out is when the new government spending is financed by an increase in taxes. That means the government spends more money but of course higher taxes mean that private individuals have less money to spend.

More concretely, let's say that government increases taxes by $300 million, all of which it spends building a new highway. What would the private sector have done with that $300 million? Let's assume that the private sector would have spent $270 million of the $300 million and simply held on to the other $30 million. Because the $270 million would have been spent by the private sector anyway, in this case the initial increase in short-run aggregate demand is only $30 million, or one-tenth of what was spent in gross terms on the new highway. So, if the private sector is spending, say, 90 percent of real income, fiscal policy won't be very effective for stimulating aggregate demand. If government spends an extra dollar, 90 cents of that dollar would have been spent anyway. Only 10 percent of a given government expenditure will represent a net boost to aggregate demand.

At lower rates of private spending, more government spending does usually boost short-run aggregate demand. The government spends more money, whereas the private sector probably was not keen to have spent that entire amount right away. So fiscal policy will be most effective when people are otherwise afraid to spend their money. The latter scenario fits the story of the Great Depression that we discussed in Chapter 26 and also corresponds most closely to Figure 31.1 when the decrease in AD was caused by a decrease in $\vec{C}$.

Selling More Bonds to Finance Fiscal Policy Rather than raising taxes today, the government often pays its bills with borrowed money. It's like using a credit card: You don't have to pay the bill today, but you do have to pay the bill sooner or later. Let's look at what happens when the government borrows from the private sector to fund a spending increase.

Imagine that the government prints a bond and sells that bond to investors. The bond is an IOU, a promise to pay the investors in the future. The government sells the bond today and pockets the cash. With more cash in hand, the government can increase spending without increasing taxes. (Alternatively the government could keep its own spending the same but cut taxes—we analyze this case further below.)

If government and consumers are spending more and taxes are the same, is there no crowding out? Not so fast. Remember that someone bought the bonds that the government sold. Where did the money to buy bonds come from?

In the simplest case, people bought more bonds instead of buying other financial assets. So, people buy more government bonds but fewer private bonds. If the private bonds were used to finance factories, then growth in investment, $\vec{I}$, declines. This is another form of crowding out, and of course if crowding out is 100 percent of the initial change in fiscal policy, aggregate demand won't shift out at all. The economy is simply substituting one form of spending for another form of spending.

Remember also what happens to interest rates when the government sells bonds. Selling bonds pushes bond prices down, which pushes interest rates up. In other words, to sell more bonds, the government must offer a higher interest rate. A higher interest rate will encourage people to save more—you might think that is good but "saving more" is another way of saying "spending less." Thus, when the government sells bonds and uses the proceeds to increase spending, some of the money comes from reduced private spending. So, there are two sources of crowding out in this case: Selling more bonds reduces private investment and also reduces private consumption, as we first showed in Chapter 23.

Given the possibilities for crowding out, bond-financed expansionary fiscal policy is most likely to be effective when the private sector is, for some reason, reluctant to spend or invest. This is often the case in a depression or in times of great uncertainty or when people, for whatever reason, are simply holding onto their cash. In this case, the government investments do not displace comparable private investments, as the private investments would not have been forthcoming in any case.

This point introduces a recurring theme of this chapter: *The case for fiscal policy is strongest when the economy is in a recession because aggregate demand is too low.*

Now let's turn away from an increase in government spending and consider tax rebates and tax cuts, which are also designed to boost the flow of spending in the economy.

Tax Rebates and Tax Cuts as a Tool of Fiscal Policy
Instead of government spending increases, tax rebates and tax cuts are another form of expansionary fiscal policy. In early 2008, for example, the economy was weakening due to, among other factors, a slump in housing prices. The Bush administration tried to increase consumer spending by sending many taxpayers a check, called a tax rebate, for $300–$600 or about $78 billion in total.

If taxpayers spend the extra money from a rebate, aggregate demand shifts up and to the right, just as with increases in government spending. But taxpayers might also use their rebate to pay down debt. But if the government borrows money to fund a rebate and taxpayers turn around and use the same money to reduce their debt, there is no increase in spending at all!

In fact, something like this happened in 2008. Taxpayers used most of their rebate, about $62 billion of the $78 billion in total, to reduce their debt rather than to increase their spending. As a result, the net fiscal stimulus was not very large.

It makes sense for consumers to use tax rebates to pay off debt. Do you remember the idea of consumption smoothing from Chapter 23? As a rule, consumers want to avoid big ups and downs in consumption so when consumers are hit with a temporary negative shock like unemployment, they take on debt. When they are hit with a temporary positive shock, like an unexpected check from the government, they often pay down debt. As a result of consumption smoothing, a temporary tax rebate tends to create a small increase in spending over many years rather than a big increase in spending now; the latter, of course, is what the government wants to boost the economy.

If a temporary tax rebate doesn't increase spending very much, what if politicians promise to make the rebate permanent? Yes, if consumers believe the rebate is permanent, they will spend more of it. But will consumers believe that a rebate is permanent when they can see that the government is borrowing a lot of money? The debt must be paid sometime, right? If consumers know that the government has a lot of debt and the government reduces taxes today, what do you think consumers will expect to happen to taxes tomorrow? We will return to this important question below when we introduce the idea of Ricardian equivalence.

A tax rebate is different from a cut in marginal tax *rates*. A rebate means that taxpayers are handed a check—it's just as if your Uncle Sam gives you some cash for your birthday. A rebate does not increase the incentive to invest or work. To increase the incentive to invest or work, the government must cut marginal tax *rates,* the additional tax that must be paid on additional earned income (see Chapter 30 for more on marginal tax rates). Cuts in tax rates as opposed to rebates have *two* expansionary effects, the spending effect and an additional incentive effect from the increased incentive to invest and work.

Consider a temporary investment tax credit. An investment tax credit gives businesses a tax cut or payment if they make an investment in, say, plant or machinery. The tax credit increases the incentive to invest but more importantly it increases the incentive to invest *now,* when times are tough. In other words, a temporary tax credit can accelerate investments that would have happened anyway (intertemporal substitution as we discussed in Chapter 27). In a similar way, a temporary reduction in the payroll tax or in the sales tax can encourage employers to hire more workers and consumers to spend more now—before the tax rises again—in this way increasing aggregate demand. If times are tough, this may be worthwhile.

A Special Case of Crowding Out: Ricardian Equivalence   A tax cut opens the possibility of a special type of crowding out. If we hold government spending constant through time, then a tax cut today must be matched by a tax increase in the future. But if people recognize and understand that lower taxes today are *equivalent* to higher taxes tomorrow, then lower taxes today won't increase aggregate demand.

Imagine that people are patient and very forward-looking. When the government cuts taxes today, these people realize that this means higher taxes in the future. These far-sighted people will plan accordingly and save more today. Basically, they are saving more so that the future tax payments don't cause them to give up familiar habits or move into old-age poverty; this "consumption smoothing" was explained in Chapter 23.

Ricardian equivalence occurs when people see that lower taxes today means higher taxes in the future, so instead of spending their tax cut they save it to pay future taxes. When Ricardian equivalence holds, a tax cut doesn't increase aggregate demand even in the short run.

Is the Ricardian equivalence realistic?

"I got a tax cut this year, son. But that means that your taxes will be going up in the future so I'm going to save more."

If people save their tax cut instead of spending it, the aggregate demand curve does not shift to the right and there are no systematic macroeconomic effects. This scenario is sometimes called **Ricardian equivalence,** after the nineteenth-century British economist David Ricardo.

Most economists think it is unrealistic to stipulate that people understand their future tax burden and save accordingly to offset future tax burdens. Tyler *knows* that *he* doesn't behave this way (and he's a trained economist), but he does see some signs of this behavior from Alex. So Ricardian equivalence probably describes some people but not most people. In any case, to the extent that Ricardian equivalence reflects how people plan, bond-financed tax cuts are less effective in the short run than otherwise.

We've run through a few different cases. It is convenient to sum them up in the form of a diagram in Figure 31.3.

FIGURE 31.3

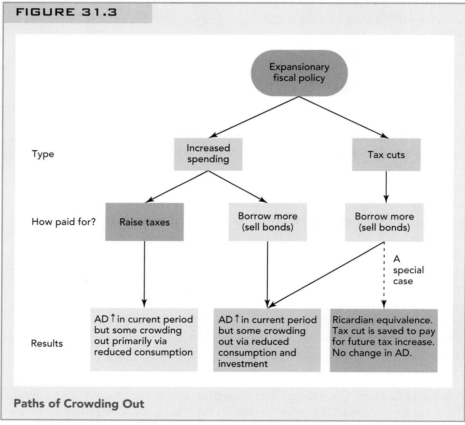

Paths of Crowding Out

Figure 31.3 reminds us that expansionary fiscal policy can consist of either increased spending or tax cuts and this policy can be paid for with either higher taxes or borrowing. Higher taxes reduce private spending, which means that some of the increased government spending has crowded out private spending. If the government borrows the money, some crowding out will still occur as private investment and private consumption fall. If Ricardian equivalence holds, then increased government borrowing to finance a tax cut will be matched by increased private saving and crowding out will be 100 percent.

A Drop in the Bucket: Can Government Spend Enough to Stimulate Aggregate Demand?

Surprisingly, one of the biggest problems with government spending as a boost to aggregate demand is simply that most changes in government spending are not very large in the short run. If changes to government spending are not large in the short run, the boost to aggregate demand won't be very large either.

In the contemporary United States, changes in fiscal policy, in percentage terms, simply aren't that large in a typical year. Most of the federal budget is determined well in advance and is remarkably stable. As we have seen in the previous chapter, among the largest budget categories are national defense, Social Security, Medicare, and interest on the debt. Those categories alone account for more than 60 percent of spending in a typical year and these programs are more or less on automatic pilot, with their yearly levels of spending set by automatic formulas or by previous agreements or commitments. Non-security federal discretionary spending is less than 20 percent of the federal budget and most of this is not seriously up for grabs in any given year. Government spending, in today's world, simply does not change very much in percentage terms on a year-to-year basis.

The fiscal stimulus plan passed under President Obama in 2009 is the largest fiscal stimulus since military spending rose tremendously during World War II. Even this $800–$900 billion dollar stimulus, however, is spread over 3–4 years so at its peak the stimulus is about 2% of annual GDP. Depending on the balance of the multiplier and crowding out effects, the net increase in spending could be somewhat larger or smaller than 2%. These are large numbers relative to previous stimulus plans but, although significant, they are still modest compared to the total size of the economy. As noted, typical post-World War II stimulus plans are much smaller than 2% of GDP so economists will be carefully evaluating the effects of this historic stimulus.

A Matter of Timing

Bad timing provides another reason why fiscal policy is often not very effective, even in the short run. The United States Constitution stipulates that both Congress and the president must approve all expenditures. There are two houses of Congress, and of course legislation must pass through various committees. Sometimes an emergency stimulus occurs quickly, as in the 2008 case discussed above, which Congress passed a mere two weeks after President Bush requested it. But often the proposed fiscal projects are complicated and the budget cycle takes place over many months or sometimes even years; it can take a long time for new bills to be conceived, written, debated, and passed. Specific expenditures often must be coordinated with state and local governments, or the projects must produce environmental impact statements, or they must survive legal challenges. Even once the money is in place, it takes time to spend it; for instance you can't build a large airport or dam all at once and it doesn't make sense to pay every contractor in advance.

In short, even a single government expenditure can take years to move from dream to reality. Yet fiscal policy is often intended to correct short-term problems in the business cycle. By the time the fiscal policy is in place, macroeconomic conditions often have changed entirely.

The list of relevant lags includes the following:

1. Recognition lag—The problem must be recognized.
2. Legislative lag—Congress must propose and pass a plan.
3. Implementation lag—Bureaucracies must implement the plan.
4. Effectiveness lag—The plan takes time to work.
5. Evaluation and adjustment lag—Did the plan work? Have conditions changed? (Return to lag 1!)

Tax cuts, the other major form of fiscal policy, also involve lags and uncertainties, at least with respect to their role in stimulating aggregate demand.

John F. Kennedy promoted some of the most famous tax cuts in American history, lowering tax rates from 91 percent to 70 percent at the top of the income distribution and from 20 percent to 14 percent at the bottom, with similar cuts applied to the rates in between. Most economists think these changes were a good idea for long-run economic growth, but it is not so clear that they served as effective fiscal policy. These were among the largest tax cuts in the post-World War II era, but even so they were only 1.9 percent of national income, and of course not all of that was spent.

This action was seen as highly decisive at the time, but the lags were significant. The Kennedy tax cuts were discussed in 1961, proposed in 1962, enacted in 1964, and probably had little effect on the economy until 1965–1967. That doesn't imply those tax cuts were a bad idea, but it does show just how slow fiscal policy can be.

President George W. Bush cut marginal tax rates in 2001, 2002, and 2003. The latter tax cuts came quite quickly after a recession loomed following 9/11 (in part because the tax cuts were mostly planned in advance for other reasons). But these tax cuts were not very effective as fiscal policy either. Each cut was less than 1 percent of national income, the economy was already recovering, plus most of the tax cuts went to relatively high-income groups, who tend to save their surplus funds. If we are thinking in terms of fiscal policy alone, tax cuts to the poor would probably result in more spending, except of course, that the poor don't pay that much in taxes.

Unemployment insurance benefits are often extended during a recession. This may be a good idea to help people through tough times, but we should not count on these measures to revive the economy because the total increase in spending relative to the size of the economy is just too small.

Monetary policy is also subject to lags, but these are generally shorter than for fiscal policy. Once the Federal Reserve recognizes a problem, it can act very quickly to implement changes to monetary policy. After 9/11, for example, the Federal Reserve stepped in the next *day* with massive infusions of cash to the banking system. The Federal Reserve can also evaluate and adjust their plan quickly as the economy responds or fails to respond. Fiscal policy, in contrast, is rarely adjusted in response to changes in economic conditions. The only place where fiscal policy might have an advantage over monetary policy is through the effectiveness lag. As we discussed in Chapters 28 and 29, the effectiveness of changes in monetary policy depends on matters like how willing banks are to lend and businesses are to borrow. A spending program, in contrast, typically has a direct impact on economic conditions, at least once the money is put into the economy.

Automatic Stabilizers   Some kinds of fiscal policy are built right into the tax and transfer system, and they do take effect without significant lags; these are called **automatic stabilizers.** Virtually all economists recognize the virtue of automatic stabilizers in keeping aggregate demand on a steady and regular course.

Fiscal policy automatically changes to keep private spending higher during bad economic times. For instance, when the economy is doing poorly, income, capital gains, and corporate profits are all down. As a result, most people and businesses will pay lower taxes and, given that the American tax system is progressive (see Chapter 30), possibly a lower tax rate as well. The lower tax burden makes aggregate demand more robust than it otherwise would be. The lower taxes don't offset the curse of hard times (lowering your taxes by lowering your income is not the preferred way to go) but they soften the blow. Pretax incomes are perhaps falling, but post-tax incomes are not falling by as much.

Welfare and transfer programs also provide automatic stabilizers. When the economy is declining, increasing numbers of people apply for welfare, food stamps, unemployment insurance, and other programs designed to help low-income groups. These groups receive more income, and because of their precarious economic situation, they tend to spend that money pretty quickly. That also helps maintain aggregate demand.

Of course, it is not just fiscal policy that provides automatic stabilizers. When people save during good times and use their savings to tide them over in bad times (consumption smoothing, as we discussed in Chapter 23), it's an automatic stabilizer. Private market innovations, most of all credit, have also contributed to stabilization. Even though the 2008 credit crisis pared back some kinds of borrowing, it is still easier today to take out a second mortgage on one's home than it was 30 years ago. If you need to send your kid to college, you can borrow more rather than cutting your spending ruthlessly. That way you can pay back the money over time, for a smoother adjustment. Credit cards, durable assets, and the increased availability of used goods (eBay), and discount outlets, all allow the economy to weather hard times more easily than before.

> **Automatic stabilizers** are changes in fiscal policy that stimulate AD in a recession without the need for explicit action by policymakers.

Government Spending versus Tax Cuts as Expansionary Fiscal Policy

Before turning to the last limit on fiscal policy, the fact that fiscal policy does not work well with real shocks, let's briefly examine the differences between the two types of fiscal policy we have discussed, namely government spending and tax cuts. The differences between these types of fiscal policy are political and also economic. Let's discuss the political differences first.

A tax cut or tax rebate puts more spending in the hands of the private sector while an increase in government spending puts more spending in the hands of the government. People who are skeptical about government spending typically prefer fiscal policy to work through tax rebates and tax cuts rather than through changes in government spending.

Consider the infamous "Bridge to Nowhere," a proposed bridge in Alaska that was to connect the town of Ketchikan (population 8,900) with its airport on the Island of Gravina (population 50) at a cost to federal taxpayers of $320 million. At present, a ferry service runs to the island, but some people in the

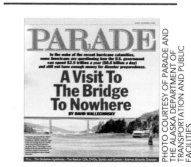

Fiscal policy that we don't want.

town complain that it costs too much ($6 per car). If the town's residents had to pay the $320 million cost of the bridge themselves—that's $35,754 each!—do you think they would want the bridge? Of course not, so if the bridge is ever built, it may raise measured GDP but the costs will still exceed the benefits. That is a type of fiscal policy that we don't want.

On the other hand, people who think that the U.S. government is not spending enough will tend to prefer that fiscal policy work through spending increases. The U.S. highway system is generally regarded as a highly productive investment of capital. If we can find equally productive public investments such as improvements to schools, science funding, and infrastructure ("bridges to somewhere"), then the case for public investment is strong and if we can time these spending increases to help offset a recession so much the better.

Do you recall our opening example? It's a useful illustration of the political differences over fiscal policy. George Bush and Barack Obama both used expansionary fiscal policy to fight a recession but Bush, a Republican, focused on tax cuts while Obama, a Democrat, focused on government spending.

What about the economic differences? A disadvantage of tax cuts that we have already mentioned is that tax cuts don't necessarily lead to new spending if consumers save their new money. In contrast, government spending is spending by definition and thus has a more certain influence. Tax cuts, however, can usually happen more quickly than new government spending since with a tax cut the government doesn't have to decide what to spend the money on. Government spending can sometimes also happen quickly, but when it happens too quickly, we have to worry that it may not be well spent.

Fiscal Policy Does Not Work Well to Combat Real Shocks

We have assumed so far that the problem fiscal policy needs to address is a deficiency in aggregate demand. But imagine, for example, that the recession is caused not by a fall in $\vec{C}$, but by a real shock that reduces the productivity of capital and labor, shifting the Solow growth curve to the left. In Figure 31.4, for example, a real shock shifts the Solow growth curve to the left, moving the economy from point a to point b.

As before, the economy is in a recession at point b. Now suppose that government responds by increasing $\vec{G}$. As usual, the aggregate demand curve shifts out, but now the economy is less productive than before, due to the real shock. As a result, an increase in $\vec{G}$ will not move the economy back to point a. Instead, most of the increase in $\vec{G}$ will show up in inflation rather than in real growth so the economy will shift from point b to point c with a much higher inflation rate and a slightly higher growth rate. As you may recall, the analysis is very similar to the analysis of monetary policy when facing a real shock.

In fact, the situation for fiscal policy is worse than Figure 31.4 indicates because when the problem an economy faces is a real shock, there is no inefficiency. Thus, unlike in Figure 31.1, the increase in $\vec{G}$ is unlikely to create much new growth and most of (perhaps even all of) $\vec{G}$ will *crowd out* other spending. (Another way of seeing this is to remember that the Solow growth curve shows the real rate of growth when the economy is operating at its full potential and neither fiscal nor monetary policy can increase the growth rate above the Solow

FIGURE 31.4

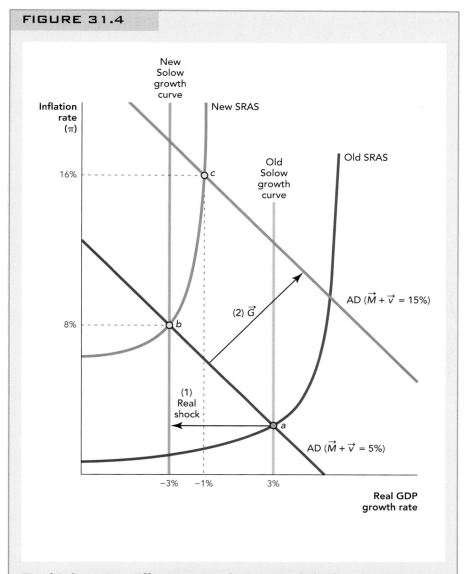

Fiscal Policy Is Less Effective at Combating a Real Shock A real shock shifts the Solow growth curve to the left (Step 1), moving the economy from point *a* to a recession at point *b*. To combat the recession, the government increases $\vec{G}$ (Step 2) but due to the real shock the economy is now less productive than before, and so the increase in aggregate demand shifts the economy to point *c* where the growth rate is a little bit higher but the inflation rate is much higher.

rate for very long.) As a result of crowding out, the situation is more likely to be like that in Figure 31.5 on the next page where an increase in $\vec{G}$ at best moves the economy from point *b* to point *d*, where the growth rate is only slightly higher than it would have been without fiscal policy.

The economy is subject to both aggregate demand shocks and real shocks. John Maynard Keynes, the economist who first hammered home the importance of fiscal policy in response to an aggregate demand shock, called his theory and book, *The General Theory*. Keynes was a brilliant, path-breaking economist, one of the greatest of all time, but after many decades of debate

FIGURE 31.5

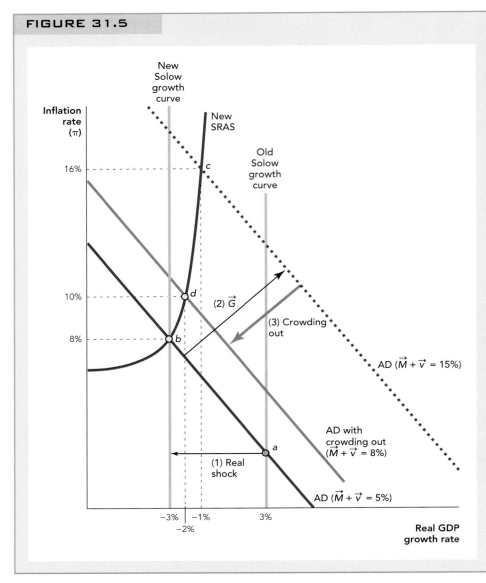

Crowding Out Reduces the Effectiveness of Fiscal Policy A real shock shifts the Solow growth curve to the left (Step 1), moving the economy from point *a* to a recession at point *b*. To combat the recession, the government increases $\vec{G}$ (Step 2). If there were no crowding out, the economy would shift to point *c* (as in the previous diagram). But since the economy is not operating inefficiently at point *b*, $\vec{G}$ is unlikely to increase growth rates and thus crowding out (Step 3) will be large. As a result, the AD curve shifts out only by a small amount and the economy moves only to point *d*. Note that for clarity we have suppressed the old SRAS curve in this figure.

most economists today think a better title for his book would have been *The Special Theory*. Since some recessions are driven by real shocks, fiscal policy will not always be an effective method of combating a recession.

When Fiscal Policy Might Make Matters Worse

If expansionary fiscal policy is paid for by borrowing, taxes will rise in the future. When taxes rise, people will have less money to spend and aggregate demand will fall. Ideal fiscal policy will increase AD in bad times and pay off the bill in good times. Unfortunately, governments often find it easier to increase spending in bad times than they do to increase taxes in good times. As a result, there are deficits in most years and the total debt grows larger, as we discussed in Chapter 30. When the debt is large, governments must spend a large fraction of their budget on interest payments alone. This usually means there is less room for expansionary fiscal policy when it is needed.

CHECK YOURSELF

> What happened to make the 2008 Bush tax rebate less powerful than anticipated?

> Explain why a permanent cut in income tax rates can create a larger fiscal stimulus than a temporary cut.

> Keeping your answer to the previous question in mind, why does a permanent investment tax credit create a *smaller* fiscal stimulus than a temporary investment tax credit?

In extreme situations, debt can be such a problem that *expansionary fiscal policy can reduce real growth.* Some countries are so heavily in debt that any more government borrowing runs the risk of total economic collapse. Take for instance Argentina, which had a major financial crisis in the 1999–2002 period; in those years, Argentine GDP fell by rates of −3.4 percent, −0.8 percent, −4.4 percent, and −10.9 percent, respectively.[1] That's not a good record. In the years leading up to this collapse, the Argentine government spent more and more, and did not pay off its bills. By 2002, Argentine government debt was 150 percent of GDP, a very high level. (For purposes of contrast, the U.S. federal government has net debt of about 50 percent of GDP although that level is rising.) The Argentine government could not pay off these debts and the final result was the largest default by a government in the history of the world.

In the years leading up to the collapse, many investors feared that the Argentine currency would lose most of its value and that the economy would fall apart. More government spending led to more anxiety, rather than economic stimulation.

So, in this setting, if the government increases spending, aggregate demand does not go up. Instead private spending and production fall by so much that real GDP falls (i.e., more than 100 percent crowding out!). Aggregate demand falls because in times of great uncertainty, people save or hoard their money in anticipation of hard times ahead. In the case of Argentina, people put their wealth into bank accounts in Miami or Switzerland, rather than investing it at home or spending it in the shops of Buenos Aires. Of course, that flight of capital only hastened the economic collapse.

We've mentioned Argentina, but similar scenarios (the details differ) have occurred in many other lesser developed nations, including Thailand, Indonesia, and Mexico. The lesson is this: Too high of a debt can drive a nation to ruin by undercutting the credibility of everything a government does and whether that government can meet its commitments. The United States isn't in that position at this time, but if you wish to understand global events, you need to realize that fiscal policy has an immediate negative effect in many economic situations, especially when the credibility of the government is low.

So When Is Fiscal Policy a Good Idea?

The macroeconomic case for government spending is strongest when the government faces some immediate emergency, such as a war, a worsening depression, or a natural disaster. Government spending is best for the macroeconomy when it is worth incurring some long-run costs to get a short-run economic boost.

It is also the case—as with monetary policy—that fiscal policy is most effective when the relevant shock is to aggregate demand and there are many unemployed resources. For these reasons, most economists look back on the Great Depression of the 1930s and see expansionary fiscal policy as a good idea in that setting. As we saw in Chapter 26, the Great Depression was primarily caused by a reduction in aggregate demand rather than by a productivity shock, so increasing aggregate demand was the right type of solution.

Furthermore, at the time, rates of unemployment were sometimes as high as 25 percent, which meant that the degree of crowding out was probably not very large. Let's say that the federal government hires some workers to build a dam. If the government is simply pulling already-employed workers from other

When unemployment is at 25% there is less private spending to crowd out.

jobs, we shouldn't expect this to help the economy much. But if those people otherwise would have been out of work, we should expect a greater economic stimulus in the short term. In other words, when it comes to these workers, the government investment is not crowding out alternative private investments. The government investment is creating economic activity in addition to private investments.

In addition, the increase in government spending during the Great Depression was relatively rapid and quite dramatic in percentage terms. Roosevelt, the architect of the New Deal, won the election in 1932. By 1936, federal government spending was more than twice what it had been in 1932.

Notice that today rates of unemployment range more often between 4 percent and 8 percent so increased government spending is likely to draw people from one job to another job rather than from unemployment to work. It would also be more difficult for the federal government to increase spending by as large a percentage as it did in the 1930s. So for these reasons, fiscal policy is less likely to be successful today than it was in the 1930s, and crowding out is more likely to happen.[2]

In spite of short-term gains, the aggregate demand effects of more government spending do not boost the long-term growth rate. Expansionary fiscal policy is best thought of as a way to deliver a short-term boost to an ailing economy.

So let's sum up when fiscal policy is most likely to matter:

1. When the economy needs a short-run boost, even at the expense of the long run.
2. When the problem is a deficiency in aggregate demand rather than a real shock.
3. When many resources are unemployed.

□ Takeaway

Fiscal policy is most effective in times of emergency, when there are unemployed resources due to a fall in aggregate demand, and when the economy needs an immediate short-term boost. In contrast, fiscal policy is not usually a good means of boosting long-term growth.

Even for macroeconomic purposes, fiscal policy sometimes doesn't work. "Crowding out"—the replacement of private spending by government spending—sometimes means that fiscal policy isn't very effective. Furthermore, if people worry a great deal about their future tax burdens, fiscal policy driven by tax cuts will not be very effective. Most important, most changes in government spending aren't big enough, or quick enough, to have significant and positive macroeconomic impact.

Other forms of fiscal policy are less visible. Automatic stabilizers, built into the tax and transfer systems, help to stabilize aggregate demand.

Some countries, especially some of the world's poorer countries, take fiscal policy too far. They accumulate very large levels of debt. The finances, currencies, and sometimes even the governments of those countries become unstable. Even if good fiscal policy doesn't always do a lot of good, bad fiscal policy can do a great deal of harm.

□ CHAPTER REVIEW

KEY CONCEPTS

Fiscal policy, p. 679

Multiplier effect, p. 682

Crowding out, p. 683

Ricardian equivalence, p. 686

Automatic stabilizers, p. 689

FACTS AND TOOLS

1. What shifts AD to the left: a rise in taxes or a cut in taxes? Does this push $\vec{v}$ up or push it down?

2. Let's see what the "three difficulties with using fiscal policy" look like in real life. Categorize each of the three stories below as either 1) Crowding out, 2) A drop in the bucket or 3) A matter of timing.

   a. During a recession, the State of New York hires 1,000 new trash collectors. The state legislature in Albany takes six months to pass a law to hire the new trash collectors, and because of government rules and paperwork, the government actually hires the workers 18 months after the recession has begun.

   b. During a recession, the State of New York hires 1,000 new trash collectors. Five hundred of the new trash collectors, however, were just people who quit their jobs as restaurant employees in order to take the better-paying trash collector jobs.

   c. During a recession, the State of New York hires 1,000 new trash collectors. However, during the course of the recession, 300,000 additional people in New York lose their jobs.

3. When people "buy government bonds," are they borrowing money or saving money?

4. Imagine you live in the land of Ricardia, where every citizen is a Ricardian and thus "Ricardian equivalence" is 100 percent true. Government spending never changes in Ricardia: It's a fixed amount every year. Thus, when the Ricardian government cuts taxes, it has to pay for the government spending by borrowing more money and raising future taxes to repay the debt.

   a. When Ricardian income taxes are cut, what will Ricardian citizens do with the extra money in their paycheck: Will they spend all of it, save all of it, or spend some and save the rest?

   b. Suppose that instead of a tax cut, the Ricardian government just sends citizens "rebate" checks. What will Ricardian citizens do with the extra money from these rebate checks: Will they spend all of it, save all of it, or spend some and save the rest?

5. It's often very difficult to get the timing of fiscal policy right. In this chapter, we listed five relevant lags.

   a. If each of the lags lasts three months, is the total lag longer or shorter than the typical recession since World War II? Data on the length of recessions is here: http://www.nber .org/cycles.html. Look at the bottom of the column titled "Contraction."

   b. Of the five lags, the last one only involves watching how things turned out. If there are only four important lags, and they last three months each, will the average recession last longer than the average fiscal policy lag?

6. You're flipping through the newspaper, reading about shocks that have hit the U.S. economy and reading what Congress is planning to do about the shocks. (Remember that "shocks" can be either good or bad.) Is Congress even getting the direction of its response right? And if it is getting the basic direction correct, is it fighting against a Solow growth shock, where a fiscal response may not be very effective? While these policy choices will each have effects on long-run growth and on income distribution, in this chapter you should only focus on the effect on aggregate demand. Fit each of the following cases into one of three categories:

   1. Wrong direction

   2. Correct direction for an AD shock

   3. Correct direction for a Solow growth shock, but expect a big change in inflation

   a. Many banks have failed, and the money supply has fallen. In response, Congress decides to raise income taxes to pay down the federal debt. (Historical note: This policy response was similar to FDR's campaign platform when he ran for president in 1932.)

b. Many banks have failed, and the money supply has fallen. In response, Congress decides to cut back on government purchases to save money.

c. A wave of investor euphoria ("irrational exuberance") about the Internet has increased spending growth. Congress raises income taxes on the richest Americans in response.

d. Oil prices double over the course of a year, from $2 per gallon to $4 per gallon. In response, Congress sends $300 checks to every American family so that people can better afford to pay for gas.

e. Oil prices double over the course of a year, from $2 per gallon to $4 per gallon. In response, Congress raises taxes on companies that refine and deliver petroleum products.

f. The Federal Reserve has followed a slow-money-growth policy, despite the wishes of Congress. In response, Congress cuts taxes and increases government purchases.

7. Which of the following is an "automatic stabilizer" in the U.S. economy? There may be more than one:

a. Consumers usually spend some of their savings and eat food from the pantry during recessions.

b. Business owners usually purchase more capital equipment whenever profits fall.

c. Governments automatically transfer cash to the unemployed when the economy is weak.

d. When Americans have less demand for U.S-manufactured products, foreigners might pick up some of the slack, buying these unsold U.S.-made goods.

8. Why was the Great Depression an especially appropriate time to use fiscal policy rather than just monetary policy alone?

9. U.S. net government debt is about 50 percent of GDP. If it rose to 100 percent of GDP, and the interest rate on the debt were 5 percent (not far from the truth at present), then what fraction of U.S. GDP would go toward paying interest on the debt? (Note: After World War II, U.S. debt was greater than 100 percent of GDP.)

10. Which kind of aggregate demand shift has fewer lags: changes in monetary policy or changes in fiscal policy?

1. a. In the chapter, we wrote that Tyler does not save and plan according to the theory of Ricardian equivalence but Alex is more of a "Ricardian." In light of this, who probably cuts back their spending the most when their taxes temporarily rise: someone like Tyler who is not "Ricardian" or someone like Alex who is?

b. If the U.S. government wants to use fiscal policy to shift AD around easily, which one would the U.S. government prefer to make more copies of: Tyler or Alex?

2. Using the figure below, suppose that a change in fiscal policy shifts AD from AD(1) to AD(2). Which response below would be most likely to cause that shift? Choose one of a, b, c, or d.

a. A rise in taxes OR a rise in government spending

b. A rise in taxes OR a fall in government spending

c. A fall in taxes OR a rise in government spending

d. A fall in taxes OR a fall in government spending

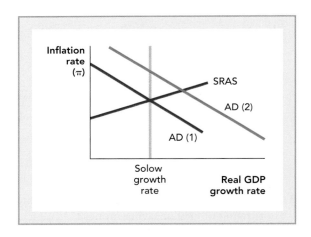

3. Consider the figure below. Suppose that there's a rise in $\vec{v}$ due to business optimism—what Keynes called the "animal spirits" of investors. This pushes us to AD(2). If the government's goal is to keep output close to the Solow growth rate, and if fiscal policy is the tool that the government wants to use, what should it do? Choose one of a, b, c, or d.

a. A rise in taxes OR a rise in government spending

b. A rise in taxes OR a fall in government spending

c. A fall in taxes OR a rise in government spending

d. A fall in taxes OR a fall in government spending

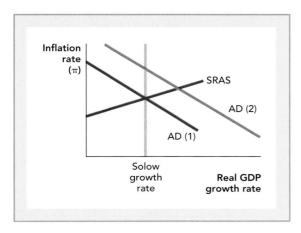

4. Consider the following imaginary newspaper quote, the type that you often read when Congress passes a tax rebate during a recession:

"Many Americans report that they will put the tax rebate straight into their savings accounts or use it to pay off credit cards that they maxed out during the recent economic boom."

If Congress is trying to shift AD to the right, are these kinds of quotes good news or bad news from Congress's point of view?

5. Which of the following government policies are "automatic stabilizers" for the economy?

Unemployment insurance

Temporary tax cuts that Congress passes when bad economic news hits

Temporary spending increases that Congress passes when bad economic news hits

6. a. Which policy is likely to shift aggregate demand more? In which direction will it shift?

A tax increase that occurs in the same year as a spending increase

A tax increase that occurs without a spending increase

b. Why is this so?

7. Ricardian equivalence is the idea that people might just use the extra money from their tax cuts to buy the very government bonds that pay for the tax cut. Let's think about the opposite situation: If Ricardian equivalence is true, and the government *raises* taxes (holding spending constant), how does the average person's behavior change? In other words, how do they react to a tax increase?

8. Again, think about the extreme case of crowding out known as Ricardian equivalence. In real life, few citizens buy or sell government bonds directly; instead, normal people put their money in a bank (or invest it in a mutual fund), and then their bank (or mutual fund) uses that money to buy government bonds.

a. So does a tax cut mean banks will get more deposits, fewer deposits, or can't you tell with the information given?

b. How will the average bank's behavior change as a result of this tax cut, taking your response to part a into account?

9. We discussed three situations where fiscal policy is most likely to matter (though fiscal policy is best when *all* three are true):

1. When the economy needs a short-run boost.

2. When the problem is low AD, not low Solow growth.

3. When many machines and workers are unemployed.

Let's fit each of the following news stories into one (or more) of the above categories.

a. World War II ends, and millions of U.S. soldiers return home. (Note: As a matter of history, returning WWII soldiers were overwhelmingly employed by the private sector.)

b. Consumption spending declines dramatically as people fear a recession.

c. Foreigners decide they are unwilling to buy U.S.-made airplanes because of rumors they read on the Internet.

10. Fiscal policy cannot cure all ills. Sometimes:

X. The economy needs a long-run boost.

Y. The problem isn't low AD, but low Solow growth.

Z. Almost all machines and workers are employed; they're just not very productive.

Sort the following cases into either "fiscal solution possible" or "productivity problem."

a. American wages have grown slowly for many years.

b. Peasants in the Middle Ages are using primitive tools to produce food.

c. Peasants in the Middle Ages suffer from a drought that hurts the season's crops.

d. American workers get laid off by the hundreds of thousands because of a rapid collapse in investment purchases.

e. Schools are doing a bad job teaching students, so students become ineffective employees.

f. High taxes on investment discourage people from saving and building up the capital stock for future workers to use.

g. High taxes on investment discourage businesses from purchasing investment goods.

CHALLENGES

1. When we discussed unemployment in Chapter 24, we noted that people will search a long time to find a good job. So it might only take you two weeks to find a minimum wage job, but it might take you six months to find a job paying five times the minimum wage. Let's investigate how this simple fact might cause expansionary fiscal policy to *increase* the unemployment rate, at least temporarily.

In the United States, federal contracts to build roads, bridges, or buildings must pay higher-than-average wages. The law requiring this is known as the Davis-Bacon Act, or the "prevailing wage law."

a. If the unemployment rate is 6 percent before a rise in government purchases, and if a rise in government purchases induces the typical unemployed person to search 10 percent longer in the hopes of finding a high-paying government job, what will the value of the unemployment rate be after the rise in government purchases? Only consider the impact of this waiting-for-a-good-job effect.

b. If the government wanted to get the good aggregate-demand stimulating effects of fiscal policy, but wanted to eliminate this extra waiting-for-a-good-job unemployment, how could it change current law to do so?

2. Nobel Laureate Amartya Sen has pointed out that one way to prevent starvation during droughts in the poorest countries is to just pay peasants to build roads, sewer lines, and other public goods during these droughts. In the poorest countries, these peasants have no savings accounts, and almost no way to borrow money. In rich countries by contrast, most people have savings accounts and credit cards.

a. Is the poor-country "multiplier" probably bigger or smaller than the rich-country multiplier, based on these facts?

b. All countries get hit by shocks, but not all countries have the same automatic stabilizers. Based on these facts, which countries probably have smoother GDP growth: Poor countries or rich countries? (Note: The answer that is true in theory is also true in practice, a point emphasized in a 1995 paper in the *American Economic Review* by Garey and Valerie Ramey, "Cross-Country Evidence on the Link between Volatility and Growth.")

3. If the U.S. government wanted to, it could just say that everyone who gets an unemployment insurance check is "employed in searching for a job," and the government could claim that these government employees are producing "job search services." Recall that in the official definition of GDP, government *purchases (G)*, do not include *transfer payments* like unemployment checks and Social Security.

a. Would this change in the definition of GDP increase GDP? Would it improve well-being?

b. If the government permanently defined unemployed people as "employed in job search," then over the course of a few decades as the economy fluctuated, would GDP look more volatile or less volatile than it does under the regular definition? (Hint: You might find it easier to answer if you consider GDP from the "factor income" perspective.)

4. We usually think about crowding out as a decrease in private consumption or investment in response to an increase in government purchases. But the idea works in reverse as well, an idea we might call "crowding in." Consider the economy below.

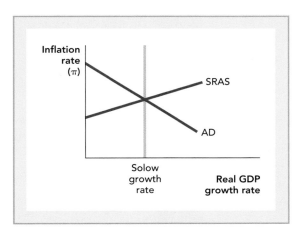

a. Starting from this initial position, the economy is hit by one shock: A large *decrease* in government purchases, perhaps caused by the end of a war. Holding the growth of *C*, *I*, and *NX* constant for a moment, illustrate this shock above, labeling the change "Fall in growth of *G*."

b. Now consider a possible side effect of the fall in the growth of *G*: the reversal of crowding out or crowding in. If there is 100 percent crowding in what happens to the AD shift you described in part a?

c. If there were 100 percent crowding out/in and no multiplier effect, what can we say about the effect of a change in the growth of *G* on aggregate demand?

d. Consider all of the laid-off government workers in this question: If there were 100 percent crowding out/in and no multiplier effect, where do these laid-off workers end up?

5. According to recent estimates by Susan Woodward and Robert Hall, an extra dollar of government purchases raises GDP by one dollar—so there is little evidence for a "multiplier effect" in the short run, but also little evidence for "crowding out" in the short run. (Perhaps both effects are at work, but they just happen to balance out in practice.) Let's use these estimates as a rule of thumb to solve the following economic puzzles:

a. U.S. GDP is about $14 trillion. In a typical recession, GDP is about 2 percent below the Solow growth rate. If Congress wants to return GDP to the Solow growth rate by increasing government purchases, how big a rise in government purchases should it enact? Give your answer in dollars.

b. Canadian GDP is about $1.2 trillion (U.S. dollars). If Canadian GDP is 3 percent above its Solow growth rate, and the Canadian Parliament wants to change government purchases to return to the Solow growth rate, what change in government purchases should it enact, measured in U.S. dollars?

c. How do your answers to parts a and b change if there's stronger crowding out, and the multiplier falls to 0.5? (In other words, a rise in G of $1 raises GDP by only $0.50.) Answer in U.S. dollars.

d. How do your answers to parts a and b change if there's a bigger multiplier effect on consumer spending, and the multiplier rises to 2? (In other words, a rise in G of $1 raises GDP by $2.) Answer in U.S. dollars.

32

International Finance

CHAPTER OUTLINE

The U.S. Trade Deficit and Your
Trade Deficit

The Balance of Payments

What Are Exchange Rates?

How Monetary and Fiscal Policy Affect
Exchange Rates and How Exchange Rates
Affect Aggregate Demand

Fixed vs. Floating Exchange Rates

What Are the IMF and the World Bank?

Takeaway

"Why are we spending our dollars in China and Japan rather than in Ohio and Michigan?"

"Why does America have such a large trade deficit?"

"We need to keep our money at home, not send it abroad!"

So run some common questions and complaints about globalization and international finance. The more connected the world economy becomes, the more these kinds of questions arise and increase in importance.

In chapter 8, we discussed how specialization and trade let us take advantage of the division of knowledge, economies of scale, and comparative advantage and thus raise the standard of living. Gains from trade occur when individuals within a nation trade and people in different countries trade.

It's important to keep these deep principles in mind when we discuss trade, but we also want to understand more about the kind of international financial events discussed on a daily basis on the financial blogs and in the newspapers. What does it mean when we are told that the dollar is "strong" or "weak"? What is a trade deficit and is it worse than a trade surplus? And why are the students in the picture protesting against the World Bank and the International Monetary Fund? What are these strange institutions?

As we will see, some knowledge of international finance is extremely practical. If you wish to do international business, make international investments, or understand how an exchange rate crisis can wreck an economy, you need to know some basic truths about international finance. Understanding international finance will also help you to pick the best place to take a good vacation. And you will even learn why many James Bond movies have a scene set in Switzerland.

Protesters clash with police in Washington, D.C., at the annual meeting of the IMF and World Bank, April 2000.

On the surface, international finance is one of the most intimidating fields of economics because the presence of different currencies can be confusing. So let's begin with some of the key principles behind this chapter:

1. Gains from trade occur when people trade across different countries with different currencies, just as gains from trade occur within a single nation with a single currency.

2. The rate of savings is a key variable in understanding international trade and finance.

3. Market equilibrium means that, at the margin, the gains from holding or spending one currency are equal to the gains from holding or spending some other currency. That sounds simple but we'll see that this principle will be a building block for understanding the market value of one currency relative to another.

The U.S. Trade Deficit and Your Trade Deficit

Let's start by looking at the trade deficit in more detail. In 2006, Americans exported (sold) to China $55.2 billion worth of goods and they imported (bought) from China $287.7 billion in goods. The difference between what Americans exported to China and what they imported from China, −$232.5 billion, is called the U.S. **trade deficit** with China.

> A **trade deficit** occurs when the value of a country's imports exceeds the value of its exports.

The U.S. trade deficit with China is controversial. In response to the trade deficit, some politicians, like America's first female Speaker of the House, Nancy Pelosi, called for a tariff on all imports of Chinese goods. To understand this debate, it will be useful to begin with some trade deficits closer to home, namely your trade deficit with your local supermarket.

Do you shop at Giant, Safeway, or the Piggly Wiggly? If you do, you run a trade deficit with those stores. That is, you buy more goods from them than they buy from you (unless of course you work at one of these stores or sell them goods from your farm). We too, the authors of this book, run a trade deficit with supermarkets. In fact, we have been running a trade deficit with Whole Foods for many years. Is our Whole Foods deficit a problem?

> A **trade surplus** occurs when the value of a country's exports exceeds the value of its imports.

Our deficit with Whole Foods isn't a problem because it's balanced with a **trade surplus** with someone else. Who? You, the students, whether we teach you or whether you have bought our book. You buy more goods from us than we buy from you. We export education to you, but we do not import your goods and services. In short, we run a trade deficit with Whole Foods but a trade surplus with our students. In fact, it is only because we run a trade surplus with you that we can run a trade deficit with Whole Foods. Thanks!

The lesson is simple. Trade deficits and surpluses are to be found everywhere.

The fact that the United States has a trade deficit with one country is not, taken alone, special cause for worry. Trade across countries is very much like trade across individuals. Not every person or every country can run a trade surplus all the time. Suddenly a trade deficit does not seem so troublesome, even though the word "deficit" makes it sound like a problem or an economic shortcoming.

What if the United States runs a trade deficit not just with China or Japan or Mexico but with the world as a whole, as indeed it does? Is that a bad thing?

This will require some deeper investigation. So far we have only looked at the flow of goods from the grocery store to you or from China to the United States, but for every flow of goods there is a corresponding and opposite flow of money or financial claims. When China sells us goods, we pay for those goods in dollars. At the present time, China (and other countries) is not using all of those dollars to buy U.S. goods and thus the United States is running a trade deficit on net. What is China doing with the dollars and is this cause for concern? We need some more tools and a few more terms to answer these questions.

The Balance of Payments

Let's start with the international balance of payments. The **balance of payments** is a yearly summary of all the economic transactions between residents of one country and residents of the rest of the world. The balance of payments records sales of goods and services and also transfers of financial claims including stocks, bonds, loans, and ownership rights. We can also speak of the balance of payments with a specific country such as the balance of payments with China.

That sounds a little forbidding, but let's go back to your trade deficit with the local supermarket. You spend money at the supermarket but earn money through your job. In the simplest case, when there is no borrowing or lending, a person's trade deficits must be matched with other trade surpluses. In other words, if you want to spend you must earn so your balance of payments does in fact balance (nets out to zero).

Now let's make this more realistic by adding borrowing and lending. Suppose you take out a student loan to pay for books, supplies, and housing. You have to pay back the loan someday, but in the mean time you are running a trade deficit. You are spending but you are not earning or "exporting" equivalent goods and services. In this case, your trade deficit is balanced with a loan, which we call a capital inflow or **capital surplus**. When we add up your trade deficit and the capital surplus, the balance of payments once again nets out to zero.

In the long run, unless you default on the loan, your trade deficit must disappear, and indeed it must turn into a trade surplus. That is, someday you will get a job and use your surplus earnings to pay back the bank loan. Paying back the loan limits your future consumption, that is, your ability to buy goods and services, but all things considered your earlier borrowing was still a good idea, at least if you invested the money well.

We have seen that you can finance a trade deficit with a job or a loan. How else could you finance a trade deficit? If you had assets from previous transactions, you could sell the assets and spend the proceeds. If you owned some land, for example, you could sell the land creating a capital surplus, which would offset your current deficit. Similarly, if you had reserves of cash from previous periods you could draw on your reserves to finance a deficit. The more assets or cash that you had from previous transactions, the longer you could live the partying lifestyle by spending more than you were earning in the current period. Notice that when we add up the trade deficit, the capital inflow, and the changes in reserves, the balance of payments still balances.

We can write down these relationships as an identity, an equality that is always true:

$$\text{Earning} - \text{Spending} = \text{Changes in debt} + \text{Changes in ownership of assets} + \text{Changes in your cash reserves}$$

If earnings are less than spending, then you are running a trade deficit. A trade deficit must be balanced by increases in debt (written as a negative number),

The **balance of payments** is a yearly summary of all the economic transactions between residents of one country and residents of the rest of the world.

A country runs a **capital surplus** when the inflow of foreign capital is greater than the outflow of domestic capital to other nations.

sales of assets, or reductions in cash reserves. The reverse holds as well: If earnings are greater than spending, then a trade surplus must be balanced by reductions in debt, purchases of assets, or increases in cash reserves.

If you can understand that equation—and indeed you live it every day—you can understand the basic categories of international finance. The terms simply become a little more complicated once we move to the bigger level of a nation.

The international balance of payments presents a comparable expression:

$$\text{Current account } = (-)\text{Capital account} + \text{Change in official reserves}$$

Now let's go through each term in detail.

The Current Account

> The **current account** is the sum of the balance of trade, net income on capital held abroad, and net transfer payments.

The **current account** is the sum of three items:

1. The balance of trade (exports minus imports of goods and services)
2. Net income on capital held abroad, including interest and dividends
3. Net transfer payments, such as foreign aid

What unites the items in the current account is that they all measure transactions that are fully completed or closed out in a *current* period; they do not require any further transfer of funds in the future. To relate these categories back to the example of a single individual, category (1) is like earnings minus spending; category (2) is like earning money on a savings bond that your grandmother gave you when you were 10 ("interest income from abroad"); and category (3) is like getting money from relatives ("foreign aid").

Now let's apply these concepts to the United States. The U.S. current account will be higher and positive to the extent that, for instance, (1) America exports a lot of tractors, (2) American-owned beer factories in Canada pay high dividends to Americans, and (3) America receives foreign aid (this latter example is not usually the case). To consider the alternative, the current account balance will be lower and negative to the extent that, for instance, (1) America buys imported grapes from Chile, (2) German investments in Florida pay high dividends to Germans, and (3) America sends foreign aid to Afghanistan.

Categories (2) and (3) in a country's current account tend to be stable over time. We can simplify by speaking as if the current account was just the balance of trade, exports minus imports. But keep in the back of your mind that terms (2) and (3) can be important for some countries. Foreign aid, for example, is important for smaller and poorer nations, when it can account for 10 percent or more of GDP. But when it comes to the United States, the balance of trade and the capital account are where we find most of the action.

The Capital Account, Sometimes Called the Financial Account

> The **capital account** measures changes in foreign ownership of domestic assets including financial assets likes stocks and bonds as well as physical assets.

The **capital account** measures changes in foreign ownership of domestic assets including financial assets likes stocks and bonds as well as physical assets. When the Chinese government buys American government bonds or when Japanese investors buy assets like Rockefeller Center in Manhattan, the capital account of the United States increases. More generally, when there is more investment going into a country than out, that country is running a capital account surplus. When investment is leaving a country that is called a capital account deficit; an example is when Zimbabwe residents send their money abroad rather than investing under their corrupt dictatorship. Less dramatically, many banks in New Zealand are owned by Australian companies and that represents a shift of capital from Australia to New Zealand.

Notice how the capital account differs from "net income held on foreign assets abroad," component (2) of the current account, mentioned above. When a Belgian buys a U.S. stock, the U.S. *capital account* increases (money flows into the United States). Three months later, when that same Belgian receives a dividend from the company, the U.S. *current account* decreases as "net income held on foreign assets abroad" suddenly is higher for Belgium. The capital account measures transactions like buying a stock that may result in future financial flows. The current account measures current financial flows.

The investments in the capital account are divided into the following categories:

Foreign direct investment (FDI)—When foreigners construct new business plants or set up other specific and tangible operations in the United States.

Portfolio investment—When foreigners buy U.S. stocks, bonds, and other asset claims. Unlike FDI, this switches the ownership of already existing investments and it does not immediately create new investment on net.

Other investment—This usually consists of movements of bank deposits. For instance, a wealthy French citizen might shift his or her bank account from Paris to New York.

The Official Reserves Account

This third category measures reserves or currency held by the government. This can include foreign currencies, gold reserves, and also International Monetary Fund (see below) claims known as special drawing rights (SDRs), but for simplicity we will focus on foreign currencies. Sometimes governments stockpile U.S. dollars or other currencies such as the euro. Right now the Chinese government and central bank have stockpiled more than $1 trillion worth of U.S. dollars and dollar-denominated assets.

How the Pieces Fit Together

To understand the balance of payments in its totality, consider more concretely how this accounting identity stays in balance. Say that Wal-Mart decides to buy more toys from China. Spending money on the toys increases the current account deficit of the United States. Toy makers in China receive the money and must do something with it. If they take the money and use it to buy American tractors, the current account is back in balance. If they take the money and invest it back in the United States, say by buying stocks, the American capital account surplus goes up by an equivalent amount. If they take the money and send it to a bank in New York, the capital account surplus goes up (this time in the "other investment" category). If they keep the money in a Chinese bank, there has been a change in reserves. No matter what they do with the money, the balance of payments will balance.

Two Sides, One Coin

Usually the major changes in the balance of payments come through the current account and the capital account, rather than through changes in official reserves. So, a country that is running a current account deficit, such as the United States, balances its payments by running a capital account surplus. Similarly, a country, such as China, that is running a current account surplus, is usually also running a capital account deficit.

Figure 32.1 shows the U.S. balance of payments from 1980 to 2005. Notice that the two accounts are close to mirror images—when the current account is in deficit (negative), the capital account is in surplus (positive), and vice versa.

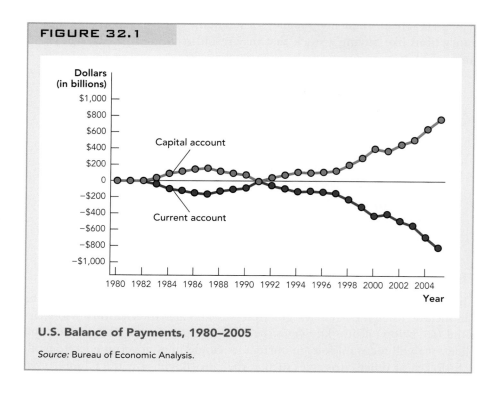

FIGURE 32.1

U.S. Balance of Payments, 1980–2005

Source: Bureau of Economic Analysis.

UNDERSTAND YOUR world

The current and capital account are two sides of the same coin. The media and politicians typically focus on the trade deficit, but it's equally correct to look at the other side of the coin, the capital account surplus.

Now that we know that a trade deficit is typically balanced by a capital account surplus, let's go back to our opening question and ask whether our trade deficit is a problem. First, note that this is the same thing as asking whether our capital account surplus is a problem. A surplus sounds better than a deficit so it is not surprising that many economists who think that trade deficits are not a problem focus on the flip side, the capital account surplus. We call the most optimistic view of those who focus on the capital account the "Great Place to Invest" view. We call the less optimistic view the "Foolishly Saving Too Little" view. Let's start with optimism.

"The United States Is a Great Place to Invest." In this view, the trade deficit is driven by the fact that foreigners want to invest in the United States, the world's wealthiest country and largest single, unified market. Instead of using dollars to buy U.S. cars, foreigners are using dollars to buy bonds and stocks and this inflow of investment is great for the United States. A capital account surplus will necessitate a current account deficit, but this is no problem. The investments in America will create more wealth and allow the United States to pay off future obligations without major problems. The fact that America is borrowing or selling assets is from this perspective like borrowing money or selling assets to pay for medical school—it isn't a problem because the investment will pay off with a high-wage job. Advocates of this view sometimes speak of the rest of the world as having a "savings glut," namely a lot of savings but no good place to put them, other than in the United States that is.

Not all economists who focus on the capital account are optimists, however. It's also possible to look at the inflow of capital and ask why are American savings so low? We'll call this the "Foolishly Saving Too Little" view.

"Americans Are Foolishly Saving Too Little." In this view, the reason that capital is flowing into the United States is that Americans are consuming too much and not saving enough. Proponents of this view often tie the trade deficit with the government's budget deficit. The U.S. government is spending more than it is taxing and the difference is being made up by borrowing from foreigners, creating a capital account surplus. In this view, a day of reckoning will come. Foreign investments in America represent a claim on American assets and someday the U.S. government will have to pay off those investment claims. This will lower American living standards and bring higher taxes, as well as the pain of significant economic adjustments. American borrowing from this perspective is like borrowing to buy a closet full of Manolo Blahnik shoes—fun while it lasts but not necessarily wise.

Happy feet for $3,145 a pair, but what happens when the bill comes due?

The Bottom Line on the Trade Deficit

The bottom line is this: Most economists think that the trade deficit per se is not a problem. As we discussed in Chapter 8, trade is beneficial for the United States and as we showed above there is nothing peculiar about running a trade deficit—we all run trade deficits in some areas (e.g., with Whole Foods) and for some periods of time (e.g., when we finance education with a student loan). Countries, in this respect, are no different than individuals.

The trade deficit, however, might indicate or *signal* a problem of low savings. If the United States has a problem with low savings, however, then it's better to address the savings problem directly—in which case the balance of trade will take care of itself—rather than blaming the Chinese or obsessing over the balance of trade numbers. Quotas, tariffs, and trade wars, for example, are unlikely to solve a savings problem. Indeed, if the United States is saving too little, then Americans are at least fortunate that they can borrow in international markets so that investment remains high even when U.S. savings rates are low.

To the extent that Americans are saving too little, there is a stronger case for reducing the government's budget deficit by a combination of tax hikes and spending cuts. In the "Foolishly Saving Too Little" view, the United States is spending too much and the government could do its share to limit this problem by saving more, which means moving closer to a balanced budget or perhaps even running a surplus. We discussed the government budget deficit at greater length in Chapter 30.

Let us now turn to exchange rates. Working with the concepts in the balance of payments identity, we can see how supplies and demands will determine the relative values of different currencies.

What Are Exchange Rates?

The most common means of payment in most (but not all!) foreign countries is a foreign currency and not the U.S. dollar. So, if you travel to a foreign country and you want to buy goods and services in that country, you will usually

An **exchange rate** is the price of one currency in another currency.

▶▶ SEARCH ENGINE

For current information on exchange rates search for the "Yahoo currency converter."

have to buy foreign currency with U.S. dollars. An **exchange rate** is the price of one currency in terms of another currency.

Yahoo! finance prints a table like Table 32.1 every day. Table 32.1 gives exchange rates that held on February 28, 2007.

TABLE 32.1 Major Currency Exchange Rates						
Currency	U.S. $	¥en	Euro	Can $	U.K. £	Swiss Franc
1 U.S. $	1	118.225	0.7571	1.1718	0.5103	1.2218
1 ¥en	0.008458	1	0.006404	0.009912	0.004317	0.010335
1 Euro	1.3208	156.1516	1	1.5477	0.674	1.6138
1 Can $	0.8534	100.8918	0.6461	1	0.4355	1.0427
1 U.K. £	1.9596	231.6679	1.4836	2.2962	1	2.3942
1 Swiss Franc	0.8185	96.763	0.6197	0.9591	0.4177	1

We can read this table in either the vertical or horizontal direction. Read vertically it tells us that the price of one yen is 0.008458 dollars, the price of one euro is 1.3208 dollars, the price of one Canadian dollar is 0.8534 U.S. dollars, and so forth. Read horizontally it tells us that the price of one dollar is 118.225 yen, 0.7571 euro, 1.1718 Canadian dollars, and so forth. Notice that there are always two ways of writing the price of a currency. We can say that one yen trades for 0.008458 dollars or that one dollar trades for 118.225 yen—this sometimes causes confusion so always make sure you know which rate is being quoted!

Exchange Rate Determination in the Short Run

Exchange rates, like other market prices, are determined by supply and demand. For each currency, there is a price in every other currency. At any given moment, the exchange rate for a currency is determined by the intersection of the supply and demand for that currency. Figure 32.2, for example, shows the supply and demand for yen and the exchange rate in dollars per yen.

Notice that we have written "Dollars per yen" ("$/yen" in many books) on the vertical axis. This is the price of one yen in dollars. If this price goes up—that is we move up along the vertical axis—it means that the Japanese yen is stronger, namely it takes more dollars to buy one yen. If this price goes down, the Japanese yen is weaker.

In this chapter when we are analyzing the supply and demand for yen we will always put

FIGURE 32.2

The Exchange Rate Is Determined by the Supply and Demand for Currencies The exchange rate, the number of dollars it takes to buy one yen, is determined by the supply and demand for yen. In this case, the equilibrium exchange rate is 0.0085 dollars for one yen.

the price of yen, "Dollars per yen," on the vertical axis. But if we analyze the supply and demand for dollars, we will put the *price of dollars* in, say, euros per dollar on the vertical axis.*

Let's now look at some factors that can shift the demand and supply curves.

Changes in Demand for a Currency The first principle is simple:

1. An increase (decrease) in the demand for a country's exports tends to increase (decrease) the value of its currency.

When Japanese cars become popular around the world, this strengthens the value of the yen. For instance, when U.S. car dealerships order more Toyotas from Japan, they must (ultimately) pay for the cars in yen. An increase in the demand for Japanese goods, therefore, shifts the demand curve for yen up and to the right, illustrated in Figure 32.3.

An **appreciation** is an increase in the price of one currency in terms of another currency.

As usual, an increase in demand increases the price. In this case, the price of one yen increases from 0.0085 dollars to 0.0090 dollars. An increase in the price of a currency is also called an **appreciation**.

Increasing exports are not the only way a currency can change in value. We also have a second principle:

2. The more desirable (undesirable) a country is for foreign investment, the higher (lower) the value of that nation's currency.

Ever since the signing of NAFTA (North American Free Trade Agreement) and the evolution of real democracy in Mexico, American investors have been keener to invest in that country. To invest in Mexico, an American business must convert dollars into pesos, thereby shifting the demand curve for pesos to the right and raising the value of the peso. In this context, note that a "stronger peso" means a "weaker dollar," or whatever other currency we are considering.

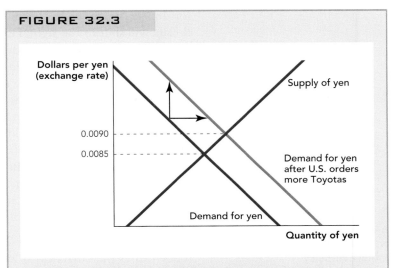

FIGURE 32.3

An Increase in the Demand for Yen Increases the Price of Yen
An increase in the demand for Toyotas increases the demand for yen, which shifts the demand curve for yen outward (up and to the right). The increase in the demand for yen increases the exchange rate from 0.0085 dollars per yen to 0.0090 dollars per yen.

Alternatively, many governments of sub-Saharan Africa have failed to secure the property rights of foreign investors. The demand to invest is correspondingly weak, shifting the demand curve for these countries' currencies to the left and lowering the value of these currencies.

High interest rates, all other factors held equal, is another factor that attracts investment, increasing the demand for and thus the value of a currency. For instance, if New Zealand "Kiwi bonds" are yielding 9 percent, and U.S. Treasury securities of comparable maturity are yielding 4 percent, this favors the strength of the New Zealand currency. (The New Zealand currency is also called the dollar; investors sometimes say "the Kiwi dollar" to avoid confusion with the U.S. dollar.) Investors will be more inclined to hold New Zealand securities, and

---

* Other textbooks or sources, however, might put "yen per dollar" (or yen/$) instead of "dollars per yen" on the price axis. Either way is correct so long as you remember which one you are working with.

of course to do so they must use the New Zealand currency, thereby shifting out demand.

There is yet another cause of stronger demand for a currency:

3. An increase in the demand to hold dollar reserves boosts the value of the dollar on international markets.

Many governments and central banks hold dollars as a "reserve currency." This means simply that dollars are a preferred means of saving and enjoying liquidity. Of all the currencies held in the world for these official reserves purposes, American dollars comprise two-thirds of the total.

The U.S. dollar is truly a global currency. If a Brazilian company buys a turbine engine from Turkey, they are probably billed in dollars and probably pay in dollars, not the currency of either Turkey or Brazil. If Colombian drug dealers bury some money in their backyard, it is probably dollars. When these demands for dollars rise, the dollar becomes more valuable. Again, the demand curve for dollars will shift to the right. However, if the Colombian government ever succeeds in stopping the drug trade, the demand for U.S. dollars would fall and the demand curve for dollars would shift back to the left.

The Swiss franc, by the way, is another global reserve currency. Even though Switzerland is a small country, it has a long tradition of peace and stability, and to some extent bank secrecy. The Swiss franc is viewed as a "safe haven" currency, even when the rest of the world is experiencing trouble. This is one reason why the Swiss franc tends to be relatively strong. Furthermore, the proverbial "bad guys" used to have secret Swiss bank accounts (since 9/11 and the growth of financial investigations, they're not so secret any more) and to invest some of their money in Swiss francs; that is one reason why so many James Bond movies have scenes there, and of course because the Alps are pretty on the big screen.

A **depreciation** is a decrease in the price of a currency in terms of another currency.

Changes in the Supply of a Currency

An increase in the supply of a currency causes the currency to lose some of its value, that is, fall in price. A fall in the price of a currency is also called a **depreciation**. Figure 32.4 shows the effects of an increase in supply, a shift of the supply curve down and to the right.

If the Federal Reserve increases the supply of U.S. money, this will reduce the value of the dollar relative to other currencies. The not-so-surprising result, as shown in Figure 32.4, is a lower value for the U.S. dollar on world markets.

You may recall from Chapter 25 that the government in Zimbabwe has been printing trillions of Zimbabwe dollars, causing a large increase in the Zimbabwean inflation rate. At the beginning of 2002, for example, one Zimbabwe dollar was worth about 0.018 of a U.S. dollar or just under 2 cents. With the massive increase in the supply of Zimbabwean dollars, the value of the Zimbabwean dollar fell, so that by 2006 one Zimbabwe dollar was worth less than 0.00001 of a U.S. dollar or about one thousandth of a U.S. penny.

FIGURE 32.4

An Increase in the Supply of a Currency Reduces Its Price An increase in the supply of a currency shifts the supply curve down and to the right, which reduces the exchange rate. In the figure, the Federal Reserve increases the supply of dollars and the price of dollars in euros per dollar decreases from 0.76 euros per dollar to 0.68 euros per dollar.

A tighter monetary policy, which means a decrease (or slower increase) in the supply of a currency, would shift the supply curve up and to the left and raise the value of the dollar as we show in Figure 32.5.

Exchange Rate Determination in the Long Run

These changes play themselves out in foreign exchange markets every day. But a full explanation outlines why the supply and demand curves lie where they do in the first place, and not just what happens when they shift.

To see the broader picture, consider that the value of a currency is derived, ultimately, from the value of what it can purchase. Money buys or is a potential claim on goods, services, and investments. Given this fact, equilibrium requires that the return to spending a dollar in Chicago, Berlin, or Paris—whether on goods, services, or investments—all yield the same expected return.

FIGURE 32.5

A Decrease in the Supply of a Currency Increases Its Price A decrease in the supply of a currency shifts the supply curve up and to the left. In the figure, the Federal Reserve decreases the supply of dollars and the price of dollars in euros increases from 0.76 euros per dollar to 0.81 euros per dollar.

Before we can explain this point fully and use it to give a more exact account of exchange rates, we must first outline the difference between real and nominal exchange rates.

We are already familiar with the distinction between real and nominal variables from earlier chapters. To recap, in a domestic setting how much a dollar is worth depends on the level of prices for goods and services. We now extend this same comparison to Cairo, Amsterdam, and Rio de Janeiro. How much a dollar is worth in Cairo depends on two things: the exchange rate between the dollar and the Egyptian pound, and the level of prices for goods and services in Egypt, measured in Egyptian pounds.

If you look at the financial news, you will see that one dollar buys more than one hundred Japanese yen, as of February 19, 2007, when the rate was 119.63 yen per dollar. At first glance, it might appear that the Japanese yen is a very weak currency. Why should it take so many yen to buy a dollar, if not for the weakness of the yen? But it is wrong to think that the stated rate of exchange reflects the relative weakness of the yen.

If one dollar buys 120 yen, we know only the **nominal exchange rate,** which is simply the rate at which you can exchange one currency for another; this is the rate you find quoted in the newspaper or on Yahoo! as we described above.

The **real exchange rate** is the rate at which you can exchange the goods and services of one country for the goods and services of another. To calculate the real exchange rate between the U.S. and Japan, for example, you need to know the nominal exchange rate plus the price of a similar basket of goods in both the United States and Japan. Notice that an exchange rate of one dollar to 120 yen means very different things, depending whether an order of sushi costs one yen, one million yen, or about 240 yen (the true price, roughly). If an order of sushi costs two dollars in the United States and 240 yen in Japan then the real exchange rate is about 1:1.

The **nominal exchange rate** is the rate at which you can exchange one currency for another.

The **real exchange rate** is the rate at which you can exchange the goods and services of one country for the goods and services of another.

The **purchasing power parity (PPP) theorem** says that the real purchasing power of a money should be the same, whether it is spent at home or converted into another currency and spent abroad.

The **law of one price** says that if trade were free, then identical goods should sell for about the same price throughout the world.

The Purchasing Power Parity Theorem   The purchasing power parity (PPP) theorem is the following:

> **The real purchasing power of a money should be about the same, whether it is spent at home or converted into another currency and spent abroad.**

Put in other words, the quantity of goods and services that can be obtained for a given currency should be about the same everywhere, adjusting for the costs of trading those goods and services. The core idea is that spending your dollars in Chicago, or converting them into yen and spending them in Osaka (which might include buying Japanese goods and shipping them back home for resale), should yield about the same benefits.

More concretely, the PPP theorem makes two predictions. First, Toyotas in Japan should cost about as much as Toyotas in California; the same should be true for other individual goods. Second, the cost of a general bundle of goods and services should be about the same everywhere.

Purchasing power parity is an application of the **law of one price**, the principle that if trade were free then identical goods should sell for about the same price throughout the world. If Toyotas were cheaper in Tokyo, it would make sense to buy Toyotas in Japan and ship them to the United States. Conversely, if Toyotas are cheaper in the United States, they will be shipped to Japan. Of course, shipping cars from one country to another is not the only way to gain from a difference across prices. Toyota might set up a new auto plant in Tennessee rather than in Osaka, thereby shifting supply into the North American market.

That example is only for cars but the principle can be extended to a broader set of possible transactions. The return to spending a dollar (or yen, or euro, etc.) at home or abroad must be roughly equal, and exchange rates and prices will adjust to equalize those returns. Those adjustments will determine the real exchange rate between any two currencies.

Recall from Chapter 25 that in the long run, money is neutral. We used that principle to explain why in the long run the money supply does not influence real GDP, real interest rates, or real prices. Exactly the same principle applies here, except that now we apply the principle to two monies! Since money is neutral in the United States and money is neutral in Japan, neither the supply of dollars nor the supply of yen can change the real exchange rate in the long run. In other words, governments or central banks set nominal exchange rates, but market forces set the real exchange rate. As usual, however, this applies only in the long run. In the short run, as we discuss further below, the government can influence the real exchange rate and this will be important for macroeconomic policy.

The Purchasing Power Parity Theorem Is only Approximately True   Purchasing power parity is limited by the costs of trading, transacting, and shuffling resources. That is one reason why purchasing power parity holds only approximately. At least three constraints on trade prevent prices from being fully equalized across borders:

1. **Transportation costs.** The price of cement might be much higher in Japan than California, but it still will not be profitable to put cement on a boat and ship it from California to Japan. Cement is very heavy and the shipping would cost a great deal. Purchasing power parity applies only to the extent that goods can be transported easily. Notice also that many

personal services—haircuts are the classic example—cannot easily be shipped, although sometimes the labor behind those services can migrate from one country to another. Thus, purchasing power parity is more likely to hold for goods that are cheap to ship, like oranges, than for cement or haircuts.

2. **Some goods cannot be shipped at all.** Sipping a coffee in Paris is different than going to a Starbucks in suburban Ohio, even if the coffee is the same. The coffee can be transported cheaply but Paris cannot be shipped.

Similarly, an apartment in London, Canada, costs less than a similar-sized apartment in London, England. Canada cannot easily cut off its land and ship it to England so prices of apartments will not equalize. More generally, the price of land and any good that uses a lot of land in its production will not equalize across countries.

3. **Tariffs and quotas.** To the extent that governments tax or otherwise restrict trade, prices will not equalize across countries. Tariffs or quotas will hinder market exchange and thus the arbitrage of differing prices.

Paris, Las Vegas. There is no parity here.

These restrictions show that purchasing power parity will hold approximately—rather than strictly—for a broad basket of goods and services. In other words, living in London, England, will remain more expensive than living in London, Canada.

Deviations from purchasing power parity are often large and long lasting for services. Goods are easy to transport and so tend to equalize in price more than services, which are difficult to transport. Services, therefore, are cheaper in poorer countries because immigration laws limit the extent to which labor can move from poor countries to rich countries. Wages on the American side of the border are much higher than wages on the Mexican side of the border. The result is that a haircut is much cheaper in Mexico than in the United States. One of the thriftier authors of this textbook often gets his hair cut during trips to Mexico for this reason! Servants are also much cheaper in poorer countries. Even a middle class family in Mexico, India, or Thailand will often employ many servants. The services of a physician, even a high-quality Western trained physician, are also cheaper in poorer countries; that explains why many people are going to India for plastic surgery or hip replacements—plus you can see the Taj Mahal after your surgery is over. Computers, iPods, automobiles, and other goods that can be easily shipped are not systematically cheaper in poorer countries.

UNDERSTAND YOUR world

How close the real world fits purchasing power parity depends on the nations involved and their ease of trading. As trading costs fall, purchasing power parity is more likely to hold closely. As trading costs rise, the bounds become looser. Purchasing power parity holds more exactly true between the United States and Canada—similar and adjacent countries—than between Japan and Mexico. Note that the concept of "tradeable" is a matter of degree, not an absolute, so how much purchasing power parity holds is a matter of degree as well.

Purchasing power parity also holds more tightly in the long run than in the short run. In the short run, trading costs might hinder entrepreneurs from erasing differences in prices. In the long run, it is more likely that entrepreneurs will find a way to bring prices closer together across international borders.

When it comes to the short run, and within the boundaries set by purchasing power parity, economists still debate the causes of daily exchange rate movements. About $1.9 *trillion* in foreign exchange transactions take place in a typical day. Most of those trades are speculative, done to earn a profit by trying to outguess the market. The short-run froth of daily price movements is set largely by psychology and expectations. Traders are guessing at the long run of where the market is headed, as shaped by supply and demand, but some of the short-run trading is just guessing at the short-run behavior of other traders. Sometimes the small, short-run movements in exchange rates are called "noise," which is the economist's polite way of saying we don't understand what causes them or what they mean.

How Monetary and Fiscal Policy Affect Exchange Rates and How Exchange Rates Affect Aggregate Demand

Monetary and fiscal policy will alter the exchange rate and trade balance (exports minus imports) of a country. To understand how, keep in mind that an approximate version of purchasing power parity (for tradable goods) holds in the long run, but that deviations from parity are possible in the short run.

Monetary Policy

Imagine that the Federal Reserve increases $\vec{M}$ through open market operations, a concept discussed in our chapters on the Federal Reserve and monetary policy. The increase in $\vec{M}$ shifts the supply curve for dollars down and to the right, which will result in a lower exchange rate (a depreciation). In the short run, dollar prices are sticky so as far as the rest of the world is concerned it's as if U.S. goods went on sale! Let's look at this in more detail.

Imagine that Caterpillar tractors sell for $50,000 and the exchange rate starts out at one euro per dollar so in Europe a Caterpillar tractor costs €50,000. Now suppose that as a result of Fed actions the exchange rate depreciates so that a European needs only 0.8 euros to buy a dollar. The dollar price is still $50,000 but because of the change in the exchange rate the price in euros has fallen from €50,000 to €40,000, which is in essence a 20 percent discount. Thus, a depreciation will increase U.S. exports. Recall from Chapter 26 that an increase in exports increases AD, which boosts the economy in the short run.

Figure 32.6 shows the process in a diagram. Keep in mind that this is exactly the same analysis of an increase in aggregate demand that we discussed in Chapter 26 and also in the chapters on monetary and fiscal policy. The only difference is that the *source* of the shift in AD is now a depreciation in the exchange rate; the mechanics are exactly as before.

The economy begins at point *a* in long run equilibrium. The increase in $\vec{M}$ causes a depreciation in the exchange rate, which in turn reduces the price of U.S. exports. As a result, exports increase, AD increases, and the growth rate of the economy increases, moving the economy in the short run to point *b*. But what about the long run?

In the long run, money is neutral, which means that domestic prices will rise to match the increase in $\vec{M}$. As a result, the nominal exchange rate will be lower but the real exchange rate—in the long run—won't have changed much, if at all. So, in the long run the real depreciation (the sale on U.S. exports) proves to be temporary and so the boost in exports is temporary as well. But if the increase in $\vec{M}$ is not reversed, the U.S. inflation rate increases. Thus, in the long run, the

FIGURE 32.6

A Depreciation Increases AD in the Short Run An increase in the growth rate of the money supply pushes the exchange rate down (a depreciation). As a result, exports increase, AD increases and the growth rate increases, moving the economy from point *a* to point *b*. In the long run, the domestic inflation rate increases enough to restore the real exchange rate so there is no longer a boost to exports and the economy moves to a new long-run equilibrium at point *c*.

economy moves from point *b* to point *c* and the boost to real output growth is not permanent.

We can, however, see one additional reason why politicians and central banks sometimes favor increases in the growth rate of money, $\vec{M}$. An increase in $\vec{M}$ usually will boost a nation's exports and thus employment. It will appear the economy is doing better, at least for a little while but, as usual, the boost to the economy is temporary and it raises the possibility of higher inflation rates.

Furthermore, although the depreciation makes exports cheaper, it makes imports more expensive. The diminished ability of the nation to invest abroad at good prices or buy imports at good prices—because of the lower real exchange rate—is a less visible but real cost of the lower real exchange rate. The lower real exchange rate nonetheless represents a political temptation, if only because the economy at least appears stronger when exports increase in the short run.

That's it for aggregate output. When it comes to the real exchange rate itself, the path of the market to equilibrium looks like the one portrayed in Figure 32.7 on the next page. Once a Fed action is announced, the dollar moves on international currency markets within seconds. Prices for most goods and services, even if they are relatively flexible, do not respond with this speed. So, at first the dollar has lower international value in real terms.

For a decrease in $\vec{M}$, the process is the reverse. In the short run, the real exchange rate will appreciate, causing U.S. exports to be more expensive on

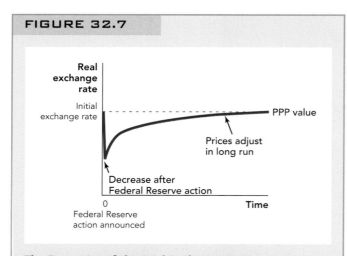

FIGURE 32.7

The Dynamics of the Real Exchange Rate An increase in $\vec{M}$ increases the supply of dollars, thus causing a depreciation in the nominal exchange rate. Domestic prices are sticky so at first the nominal depreciation is also a real depreciation. Over time, however, domestic prices rise, so in the long run the real exchange rate returns to its fundamental value as determined by approximate purchasing power parity.

world markets. In the long run, the real exchange rate will be reestablished at the approximate PPP value. Notice that we can see once again why nations with a high rate of inflation—nations that ought to lower $\vec{M}$—may be reluctant to do so. In the short run, a reduction in $\vec{M}$ reduces exports, reducing AD and reducing the real growth rate in the short run.

Fiscal Policy

Expansionary fiscal policy, or an increase in the budget deficit, will raise domestic interest rates. As explained in Chapters 23 and 31, when government borrows more money, the demand for loanable funds shifts outward and interest rates go up.

As a result, the higher interest rates will cause the nation—let's say the United States—to run a greater surplus on its capital account. That is, more foreigners will want to invest in the United States to enjoy those high interest rates. The greater demand to invest will cause an appreciation of the U.S. dollar. What does an appreciation of the dollar do to U.S. exports? An appreciation makes U.S. exports more expensive, thus reducing U.S. exports. Thus, a budget deficit can cause a trade deficit. These are sometimes called "the twin deficits."

We now see one more limitation of fiscal policy. The boost to domestic aggregate demand, resulting from the new government spending, will to some extent be offset by the greater difficulty of exporting at the new and higher real exchange rate. Total aggregate demand—domestic plus foreign—might not go up at all. In other words, the New Keynesian argument for fiscal policy that we discussed in Chapter 31 is less justified the more open the economy. This is yet another reason why monetary policy has typically become more important than fiscal policy as a tool of macroeconomic management.

A **floating exchange rate** is one determined primarily by market forces.

A **fixed or pegged exchange rate** means that a government or central bank has promised to convert its currency into another currency at a fixed rate.

Dollarization occurs when a foreign country uses the U.S. dollar as its currency.

Fixed vs. Floating Exchange Rates

So far we have treated the case of **floating exchange rates** with currency prices determined in open world markets. This is by far the most common scenario in the world today and indeed throughout history.

Still, in other cases the world has seen **fixed or pegged exchange rates,** where currencies do not fluctuate against one another on a daily basis. Fixed exchange rate systems can take three forms:

1. Simply adopting the money of another country

Panama, Ecuador, and El Salvador all use U.S. dollars as their currency; this is called **dollarization.** The central banks of these nations have no active role in managing their money supplies.

The disadvantage of this approach is that Ecuador must buy and save enough dollars to use that currency. The advantage is that, once in place, Ecuador receives the monetary policy of the United States. Once the transition is made, the common currency runs on automatic pilot. Overall, it is plausible that the U.S. Fed does a better job than would an Ecuadorian central bank. Indeed, at the time of dollarization in 2000, the rate of inflation in Ecuador was above 50 percent. Today, the rate of inflation in Ecuador roughly tracks that of the United States and of course this is much lower.

2. Setting up a currency union

Many European countries gave up their currencies and created the euro, a common currency under the supervision of the European Union and (as of early 2009) shared by 16 different EU countries. The wealthier European countries, such as Germany and France, saw the euro as a way to unify Europe economically. Some of the poorer countries, such as Greece, saw the euro as a way to obtain a more stable currency. In any case, all of these countries allow the European Central Bank to control their common monetary policy; the euro does not belong to any single country. The euro, however, is unique and no other comparable arrangement exists today.

3. Backing a currency with high levels of reserves and promising convertibility at a certain rate

A country could promise to convert its currency into U.S. dollars, or some other currency, at a specified rate. Holding sufficient reserves of the foreign currency to ensure conversion would make this promise more credible. Since 1983, Hong Kong has pledged that 7.80 Hong Kong dollars are equal to one U.S. dollar and required Hong Kong banks to have full American backing for any note issued. For many years, Austria pegged its currency to the value of the German mark, prior to adopting the euro.

Option 3 is, of course, a matter of degree. Economists refer to a "peg" to describe a relatively rigid commitment to a specified conversion rate. A **dirty or managed float** refers to a relatively loose commitment to a floating exchange rate. Under a dirty float, a currency will vary in value daily, although the central bank or treasury will intervene if that currency moves too far outside of a band of intended or pre-announced values.

Due to Hong Kong's currency peg, these 10 Hong Kong dollars could be exchanged for $1.29 U.S.

A **dirty or managed float** is a currency whose value is not pegged but governments will intervene extensively in the market to keep the value within a certain range.

The Problem with Pegs

The pegging option has become less popular over time. Many nations have attempted currency pegs, but usually they have failed. For instance, Thailand, Indonesia, Brazil, and Argentina, among others, all tried to peg their currencies to the U.S. dollar or to a weighted basket of currencies. In each case, the peg was broken by speculators, largely because these countries did not and could not match the monetary and fiscal policies of the United States. Why hold one Argentine peso—supposedly equal in value to a dollar throughout the late 1990s—when you can hold a U.S. dollar instead?

When Argentina pegged its currency to the U.S. dollar in 1991, it promised that one Argentine peso was equal in value to one U.S. dollar. For a while, markets believed this promise. The Argentine economy was doing well, foreign investment was flowing in, and the Argentine government instituted many desirable economic reforms.

But over time people began to doubt whether this peg could be maintained. Eventually the weaknesses of the Argentine economy became revealed more clearly. The government was unable to bring about true fiscal balance. Many foreign investors began to believe that the Argentine peg would break and that the one-to-one rate would go away. This would mean that one peso would become worth less than one U.S. dollar. Many people who had invested in pesos withdrew their money from the country or tried to convert their peso holdings into dollars before the one-to-one rate disappeared. Argentine citizens panicked as well, and many of them also sought to convert their pesos into U.S. dollars.

The resulting rush to convert pesos into dollars put great strain on the peso. The Argentine government did not have enough U.S. dollars to keep up the value of the peg. The result was that the peso fell from being worth a dollar (January 6, 2002) to being worth about 26 cents (June 28, 2002), across the course of only five and a one-half months. In other words, the Argentine government had to officially announce a new peg with a much lower value for the Argentine currency.

The rapid reduction in the official exchange rate ruined the economic reputation of the country and the withdrawal of money from the country led to a collapse of the banking system. This is sometimes called capital flight. Argentina probably would have been better off had it never pegged its currency in the first place.

Overall, the lesson is simple. Most countries should not attempt exchange rate pegs. An effective peg requires a very serious commitment to a high level of monetary and fiscal stability. If a country doesn't have as sound an economy as the United States, in the long run it cannot peg to the U.S. dollar.

CHECK YOURSELF

> When the value of a country's currency is determined by the forces of supply and demand, is this a floating exchange rate or a fixed exchange rate?

> Who controls the monetary policy of the European Union?

What Are the IMF and the World Bank?

To close this chapter let us look at two very controversial global institutions, the International Monetary Fund and the International Bank for Reconstruction and Development, more commonly known as the World Bank. These institutions have occasioned protests, the throwing of bricks, conspiracy theories, and political T-shirts. What is up? Are they noxious carriers of evil global forces, benevolent do-gooders, or something else altogether?

For the most part, these agencies are bureaucracies. They do some good, some bad, but they are not as important—for better or worse—as many people think.

International Monetary Fund

Today the International Monetary Fund (IMF) serves as an international lender of last resort. That is, when countries experience financial troubles, the IMF steps in to organize a rescue package, lend money, and monitor the economic situation. Often the loans are tied to a country's willingness to take the IMF's economic advice.

The IMF, created after the end of World War II, is located in Washington, D.C., but it is a "multilateral" institution. It is set up by the world's governments and is independent of any single government. It receives a monetary allocation from each government and also may earn income from its loans. Historically, the director of the IMF is a European. The director reports to a board, and board membership is roughly proportional to how much money a country puts into the institution. The United States, Western Europe, and Japan exercise a dominant influence in this regard, but the staff is drawn from around the world.

The IMF was very active in the Asian currency crises of the 1990s—in Indonesia, Thailand, and South Korea—and in the Argentine financial crisis starting in 2001. Critics of the IMF, such as Nobel Laureate Joseph Stiglitz, charge that it forces borrowing governments to cut government spending, tighten monetary policy, and raise interest rates. In other words, the claim is that the IMF has encouraged contractionary macroeconomic policies when (perhaps) expansionary policies were called for. Defenders of the IMF have argued that the advice is more subtle than is often portrayed, tough fiscal reforms are sometimes needed, or that borrowing countries do not in fact follow the advice, regardless of whether or not it is good advice.

The World Bank

The World Bank also dates from the immediate aftermath of World War II. It was designed to facilitate the flow of capital to poor countries, especially those parts of the world not being served by private capital markets. The full-time staff of about 10,000 employees is headquartered in Washington, D.C., right next to the IMF. The Bank is ruled by a board, whose members are drawn from supporting nations, and a president who has historically been an American.

Mostly the World Bank lends money for specific projects in developing countries. This includes loans for water projects, roads, dams, health care, and environmental projects, among other activities. World Bank loans are tied to the use of Bank expertise and the understanding that the borrowing country will work cooperatively with the Bank.

In 2006, the World Bank lent $21 billion to developing nation governments, and collected about $15 billion in loan repayments. Currently the Bank's largest borrower, by far, is China. Other top borrowers are India, Brazil, Mexico, and Turkey. This has led to debate over the Bank's proper mission. China receives at least $70 billion in foreign investment per year, while it is sitting on over $1 trillion in foreign currency reserves. So why is the World Bank lending to China? Private capital markets are today much more active than in the early days of the Bank, so it is no longer clear that the World Bank is filling a gap in a useful way. Defenders of the Bank note that much of China remains poor, and the Chinese loans turn a profit and help the Bank carry out its mission in poorer places like Africa.

The World Bank also gives away money, lends it out at very low rates of interest, or makes loans that it does not expect will be repaid. This is the aid side of the Bank, which is separate from the Bank's loans. To an increasing extent, the Bank's aid is flowing to sub-Saharan Africa.

Critics claim that the Bank does not pay enough attention to results. The commercial incentive is for the Bank to make many loans. The lent funds first go to governments and then they often are used to purchase goods and services from Western companies. For instance, a World Bank loan to Senegal might help finance a contract with a French company for the supply of urban water. This benefits commercial interests in the countries that control the Bank. Accountability is often low, since each year another round of loans will be made in any case. The World Bank makes money off its loans, so perhaps not enough attention is paid to whether those projects deliver their promised benefits. Defenders note that the Bank has responded to criticism in the past, improved its environmental record, and avoided many previous mistakes. Foreign aid is a difficult business to succeed at, and many people believe that the World Bank is overall a force for good.

The IMF and the World Bank attract so much attention because they are seen as icons of global capitalism. Furthermore, both groups hire many technocrats, and neither is subject to direct accountability through democratic rule. They seem to stand above national borders and make decisions, while reporting to no one. They encourage poor countries to borrow money and those debts cannot always be repaid. Such are the charges, but the reality is more prosaic. Both agencies are highly constrained in what they can accomplish, if only because their resources are limited and they deal frequently with contrary governments. At the margin, they make a difference, but they are not the driving forces behind global capitalism.

□ Takeaway

International currencies are a tricky business, but basic economic principles hold internationally as well as nationally. Contrary to the statements of many politicians, trade deficits are not necessarily a problem, unless a country is investing foolishly or not saving enough. In either case, the trade deficit is not the root of the relevant problem. Instead of complaining about America's current trade deficit with China, it is better to consider how the United States might save more. The trade balance is simply one side of the coin, with the capital account serving as the other side. If a lot of capital is flowing into a country, that country also will be running a trade deficit.

Exchange rates are set in active markets, changing by the second every day, and following the laws of supply and demand. Monetary policy can affect real exchange rates in the short run, but not in the long run. In the long run, exchanges rates are set according to purchasing power parity, so that profits cannot be made buying goods in one country and shipping them to another.

Both monetary and fiscal policies will affect a country's real exchange rate in the short run and these exchange rate effects will influence aggregate demand by affecting some mix of exports, imports, and the flow of capital from one country to another.

Most countries today have floating exchange rates with values determined in international currency markets. Fixed or pegged exchange rates are possible but in most circumstances they are difficult to maintain over the longer run. Thus, a combination of currency unions and floating exchange rates has increasingly become the global norm.

□ CHAPTER REVIEW

KEY CONCEPTS

Trade deficit, p. 702

Trade surplus, p. 702

Balance of payments, p. 703

Capital surplus, p. 703

Current account, p. 704

Capital account, p. 704

Exchange rate, p. 708

Appreciation, p. 709

Depreciation, p. 710

Nominal exchange rate, p. 711

Real exchange rate, p. 711

Purchasing power parity (PPP) theorem, p. 712

Law of one price, p. 712

Floating exchange rate, p. 716

Fixed or pegged exchange rate, p. 716

Dollarization, p. 716

Dirty or managed float, p. 717

FACTS AND TOOLS

1. Start with the facts about the trade deficit (also known as the "balance of trade"), the most widely discussed part of the balance of payments. Head to the database run by the Federal Reserve Bank of St. Louis, http://research.stlouisfed.org/fred2. In the search box, look for data on two series, "EXPGSCA" (real annual exports in year 2000 dollars) and IMPGSCA (real annual imports in year 2000 dollars). Below each graph, you should see the raw annual data for the last five years.

    a. What was the level of exports for each of the last five years? Did exports rise every year?

    b. What was the level of imports for each of the last five years? Did imports rise every year? If not, did exports and imports fall at the same time?

    c. How big was the trade deficit (or surplus) each year?

    d. Divide each year's number by real GDP for each year (GDPCA): What was the trade deficit (or surplus) as a percentage of GDP each year? In years where GDP fell from the previous year, did the trade deficit rise or fall?

2. Practice with the balance of payments:

    Current account + Capital account = Change in official reserves

    a. Current account = −$10, Capital account = +$15. What is the change in reserves?

    b. Current account = −$10, Change in reserves = −$3. What is the capital account?

    c. Your college expenses = $12,000, Income from your barista job = $4,000. What is your current account? If you haven't changed your reserves (i.e., cash savings) at all, what is the capital account (i.e., borrowing from parents or bank)?

3. a. Consider two headlines: "Money is pouring into the U.S. faster than ever" versus "Record U.S. trade deficit." How can both be true simultaneously?

    b. Consider two headlines: "Money is fleeing the U.S. faster than ever" versus "Record U.S. trade surplus." How can both be true simultaneously?

4. In the chapter, two stories about the deficit are told: "the great place to invest" story and the "foolishly saving too little" story. In the examples below, which is more like the "great place to invest" story and which is more like the "foolishly saving too little" story?

    a. Goofus uses his student loan money to buy a nice flat-screen TV and can't afford most of his textbooks. Gallant uses his student loan money to buy his textbooks and coffee that keeps him awake during study sessions.

    b. Charlie borrows money from his dad, Martin, to attend the right parties, make useful industry connections, and build his career. Emilio borrows money from his dad to attend fun parties, meet fun people, and, well, that's about it.

    c. America 1 borrows money to invest in her future. America 2 borrows money to pay for a spending binge.

5. a. According to Table 32.1, how many Japanese yen could you get for one dollar on February 28, 2007? Use the currency converter on Yahoo! Finance to find out how many yen you could buy for a dollar today.

    b. Given your answer to the previous question, did the buying power of the dollar rise or fall over this period? (Get this one right: It's crucial to understanding exchange rates.)

    c. Repeat parts a and b for one other currency in Table 32.1.

6. According to the purchasing power parity theorem, what must be approximately equal across countries: the nominal exchange rate or the real exchange rate?

7. a. According to purchasing power parity theory, a country with massive inflation should also experience a massive fall in the price of its currency compared to other currencies (a depreciation). Is this what happened in Zimbabwe, or did the opposite occur?

    b. Hyperinflation is defined as a rapid rise in the price of goods and services. According to purchasing power parity theory, does hyperinflation also cause a rapid rise in the price of foreign currencies?

8. Which international financial institution focuses on the long-run health of developing countries: The IMF or the World Bank? Which one

focuses on short-run financial crises in developing countries?

9. Let's translate between newspaper jargon about exchange rates and the economic reality of exchange rates.

   a. Last week, the currency of Frobia was trading one for one with the currency of Bozzum. This week, one unit of Frobian currency buys two units of Bozzumian currency. Which currency "rose?" Which currency became "stronger?" Which currency "appreciated?"

   b. The currency in the nation of Malvolio becomes "weaker." Now that it's weaker, can 10 U.S. dollars buy more of the Malvolian currency than before or less than before?

   c. A college student travels from the United States to Germany. Just before he leaves, he changes $400 into euros. He spends only half the money while in Germany, so on his return to the United States, he exchanges his euros back into dollars. However, while he was admiring Munich's historic Marienplatz, the dollar "weakened" considerably. Is this good news or bad news from the college student's point of view?

10. a. When the Japanese government slows the rate of money growth, will that tend to strengthen the yen against the dollar or weaken the yen against the dollar?

   b. When the Japanese government slows the rate of money growth, will the dollar tend to appreciate against the yen or will the dollar tend to depreciate against the yen?

   c. When Americans increase their demand for Japanese-made cars, will that tend to strengthen the yen against the dollar or weaken the yen against the dollar?

   d. When Americans increase their demand for Japanese-made cars, will the dollar tend to appreciate against the yen or will the dollar tend to depreciate against the yen?

THINKING AND PROBLEM SOLVING

1. Practice with the current account: Which of the following tend to raise the value of Country X's current account?

   a. Country X sends cash to aid war victims in Country Y.

   b. Investors living in Country X receive more dividend payments than usual from businesses operating in Country Y.

   c. Investors living in Country Y receive more interest payments than usual from businesses operating in Country X.

   d. Immigrants from Country Y who live and work in Country X send massive amounts of currency back to their families in Country Y.

   e. The government of Country X imports more jet fighters and missiles from Country Y.

2. Practice with the capital account: Which of the three categories of the capital account does each belong in? Which of the following tend to raise the value of Country X's capital account?

   a. A corporation in Country Y pays for a new factory to be built in Country X.

   b. A corporation in Country Y sells all of its stock in a corporation located in Country X to a citizen of Country X.

   c. A citizen of Country Y purchases 20 percent of the shares of a corporation in Country X from a citizen of Country X.

   d. A business owner in Country X pays for a new factory to be built in Country Y.

3. Let's translate "Americans are foolishly saving too little" into a simple GDP story. Recall that GDP = C + I + G + Net exports. GDP is fixed and equal to 100 throughout the story: After all, it's pinned down by the production function of Chapter 22. Thus, the size of the pie is fixed: The only question is how the pie is sliced into C, I, G, and net exports. To keep it simple, assume that I + G = 40 throughout.

   a. The "saving too little" story comes in two parts: In part one (now), the United States has high C and low (really, negative) net exports. If C = 70, what do net exports equal? Is this a trade deficit or a trade surplus?

   b. In part two (later), foreign countries are tired of sending so many goods to the United States, and want to start receiving goods from the United States. Net exports now become positive, rising to +5. What does C equal? If citizens value consumption, which period do they prefer: "now" or "later?"

4. Let's translate "The United States is a great place to invest" into a simple GDP story. Recall that GDP = C + I + G + Net exports. In this story, foreigners build up the U.S. capital stock by pushing investment (I) above its normal level. Thus, GDP equals 100 in the "now" period but equals 110 in the "later" period. To keep it simple, assume that C + G = 80 throughout.

   a. The "great place to invest" story comes in two parts: In part one (now), the United States has high I and low (really, negative) net exports. If I = 35, what do net exports equal? Is this a trade deficit or a trade surplus?

   b. In part two (later), foreign countries are tired of sending so many machines and pieces of equipment to the United States, and want to start receiving goods from the United States. Net exports now become positive, rising to +5. What does I equal?

5. The market for foreign currencies is a lot like the market for apples or cars or fish, so we can use the same intuition—as long as we keep reminding ourselves which way is "up" and which is "down." Consider the market for something called "euros" (maybe it's a new breakfast cereal) and measure the price in dollars. Discuss the following cases:

   a. The people who make "euros" decide to produce many more of them. Is this a shift in supply or in demand, and in which direction? What does this do to the price of euros?

   b. Consumers and businesses decide that they'd like to own a lot more euros than before. Is this a shift in supply or in demand, and in which direction? What does this do to the price of euros?

   c. There's a slowdown in the production of euros, initiated by the executives in charge of euro production. Is this a shift in supply or in demand, and in which direction? What does this do to the price of euros?

   d. Suppose that the price of apples rises. Using the same language as in questions a and b, would you describe this as a strengthening of the dollar or a weakening of the dollar?

6. Now that we've built up some intuition about exchange rates, let's apply the principles more thoroughly. In this question, we discuss the U.S.-China exchange rate. Officially, the Chinese government fixed this exchange rate for years at

a time, but in this question, we treat it as a market rate that can change every day.

   a. In the figure below, shift the appropriate curves to illustrate the effect of the following news story: Chinese factory sells poisonous dog food.

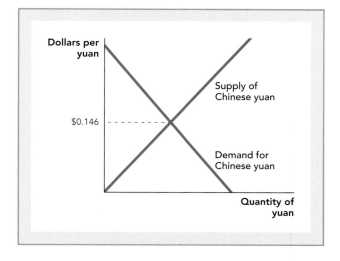

   b. Does this news story raise or lower the price of the yuan? Does this strengthen or weaken the Chinese currency? Does this strengthen or weaken the U.S. dollar?

7. Nobel Laureate Robert Solow once jokingly noted, "I have a chronic [trade] deficit with my barber, who doesn't buy a darned thing from me." Is this a problem? Why or why not? How does this relate to the U.S.-China, U.S.-Mexico, and U.S.-Japan trade deficits?

8. Corey, a young entrepreneur, notices that cigarette lighters sell for only $0.50 each in Utah but they sell for $1.00 each in Nevada.

   a. If Corey wants to make money by buying and selling lighters, where should he buy the lighters and where should he sell them?

   b. If many other people imitate Corey's behavior, what will happen to the supply of lighters in Utah (rise, fall, unchanged)? What will happen to the supply of lighters in Nevada (rise, fall, unchanged)?

   c. What will the behavior in part b do to the price of lighters in Utah? In Nevada?

   d. According to the law of one price, what can we say about the price of cigarette lighters in Nevada after all of this arbitrage? More than one of the following may be true:

Less than $1.00 each

More than $1.00 each

The same as the Utah price

9. At Christmas, five-year-old Gwen runs a massive trade deficit with her parents: She "exports" only a wrapped candy cane to her parents, but she "imports" a massive number of video games, dolls, and pairs of socks.

   a. Is this trade deficit a good thing for Gwen?

   b. When Gwen turns 25, her parents insist on being repaid for all those years of Christmas presents—that is, they require her to run a "trade surplus." Is this "trade surplus" good news for Gwen? Why or why not?

10. a. Suppose that the price level in the United States doubled, while the price level in the U.K. remained unchanged. According to purchasing power parity theory, would the dollar/pound nominal exchange rate double or would it fall in half?

   b. In practice, PPP tends to hold more true in the long run than in the short run, because many prices are sticky. So if the U.S. money supply increased dramatically—a big enough rise for the price level to double in the long run—would this be good news for British tourists headed to the United States or would it be good news for U.S. tourists headed to Britain? Incidentally, would this be good news or bad news (in the short run) for U.S. tourists staying in the United States?

CHALLENGES

1. In our basic model, a rise in money growth causes currency depreciation: We also know from Chapter 26 and Chapter 29 on monetary policy that a rise in money growth normally raises aggregate demand and boosts short-run real growth. But in the 2001 Argentine crisis and the 1997 Asian financial crisis, a currency depreciation seemed to cause a massive *fall* in short-run output.

   a. What type of shock could cause a currency depreciation to be associated with a fall in short-run output?

   b. In both the Argentine and the Asian crises, these countries' banking sectors were hit especially hard: They had made big promises to pay their debts in foreign currencies—often dollars—and the depreciation made it impossible for them to keep those promises. What became more "expensive" as a result of the depreciation: foreign currency (dollars, yen, pounds) or domestic currency?

   c. In these crises, depreciation created bankruptcies: These bankruptcies are what causes the shock discussed in part a. To avoid this outcome in the future, Berkeley economist Barry Eichengreen, an expert on exchange rate policy, recommended that businesses in developing countries should encourage foreigners to invest in stock that pays dividends rather than in debt. He believed this would make it easier for countries to endure surprise depreciations. Why would he recommend this?

2. In Panama, a dollarized country, a Big Mac is about 30 percent cheaper than in the United States. Why?

3. A supply-and-demand model can illustrate the difficulty of keeping a fixed exchange rate: It's much the same as any other price floor. Consider the fixed exchange rate below. Sparta uses a currency called the spartonian, Athenians use the aton, and the Spartans have chosen a fixed exchange rate of two atons per spartonian:

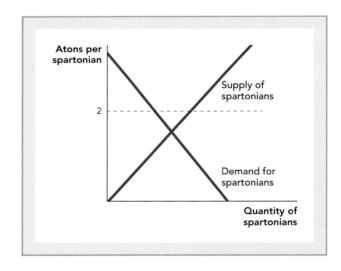

   a. In a typical supply-and-demand model, what would you call the gap that exists between quantity supplied and quantity demanded at this fixed exchange rate: a surplus or a shortage? Of which currency?

b. If the Spartan government wants to keep this exchange rate fixed, what will tend to happen to its official reserve account supply of atons: Will it rise, or will it tend to fall? (Hint: Remember that the suppliers of spartonians want to buy atons. How does this explain why governments of fixed exchange rate countries hold large amount of foreign currencies in their accounts?)

c. If demand for spartonians fell because of a weak Spartan economy, would this make it harder or easier for this government to maintain the exchange rate?

d. If the Spartan government wanted to bring quantity supplied and quantity demanded closer together, would it want to slow money growth or raise money growth? When real world countries have "overvalued" currencies, do you think they should fix it by slowing money growth or by raising money growth?

4. a. Ecuador is currently dollarized: Bank accounts are denominated in U.S. dollars, for example. If Ecuadoreans believe rumors that the country is going to go off the dollar and is going to convert all bank account deposits into a new unit of money called the "Ecuado" (similar to what Argentina actually did in 2001), what will this probably do to the Ecuadorean banking system?

b. "There is no such thing as a fixed exchange rate: Just pegs that haven't been changed . . . yet." Explain how this belief, by itself, can make it hard for a country to maintain a fixed exchange rate. Does this belief have a direct impact on the demand for a currency or on the supply of a currency?

5. We said that "an effective peg requires a very serious commitment to a high level of monetary and fiscal stability." As in our discussion of monetary policy, people's *beliefs* about what government *might* do in the future put limits on what governments should do *today*. Discuss how "commitment" can keep an exchange rate stable. Compare with how commitment can make it easier to keep inflation low. What can a government do in these situations to convince foreign investors and domestic citizens that it will keep its commitments? (Certainly, there is more than one good way to answer this question: The problem of creating commitment is an active area of research across the social sciences.)

Appendix A

Reading Graphs and Making Graphs

Economists use graphs to illustrate both ideas and data. In this appendix, we review commonly used graphs, explain how to read them, and give you a few tips on how you can make graphs using Microsoft Excel or similar software.

Graphs Express Ideas

In economics, graphs are used to express ideas. The most common graphs we use throughout this book plot two variables on a coordinate system. One variable is plotted on the vertical or y-axis, while the other variable is plotted on the horizontal or x-axis.

In Figure A.1, for example, we plot a very generic graph of variable Y against variable X. Starting on the vertical axis at Y = 100, you read across to the point at which you hit the graph and then down to find X = 800. Thus, when Y = 100, X = 800. In this case, you can also see that when X = 800, then Y = 100. Similarly, when Y = 60, you can read from the graph that X = 400, and vice versa. As you may recall, the slope of a straight line is defined as the rise over the run or rise/run. In this case, when Y rises from 60 to 100, a rise of 40, then X runs from 400 to 800, a run of 400, so the slope of the line is 40/400 = 0.1. The slope is positive, indicating that when Y increases so does X.

Let's now apply the idea of a graph to some economic concepts. In Chapter 2, we show how a demand curve can be constructed from hypothetical data on the price and quantity demanded of oil. We show this here as Figure A.2.

The table on the left of the figure shows that at a price of $55 per barrel buyers are willing and able to buy 5 million barrels of oil a day (MBD), or more simply at a price of $55, the quantity demanded is 5 MBD. You can read this information off the graph in the following way. Starting on the vertical axis, locate the price of $55. Then look to the right for the point where the

FIGURE A.1

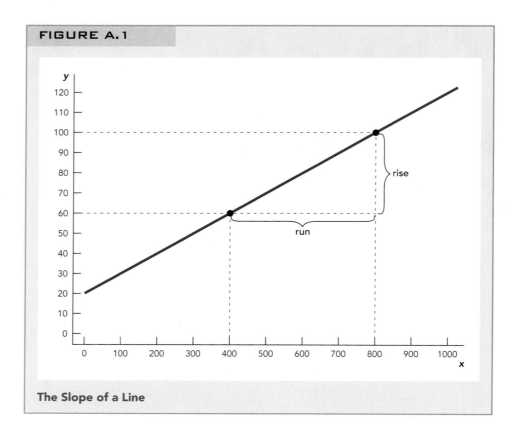

The Slope of a Line

FIGURE A.2

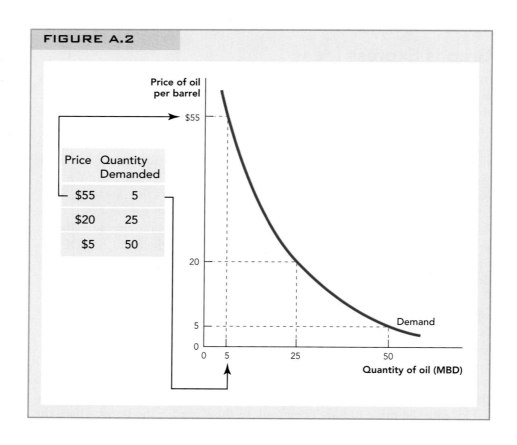

$55 price hits the demand curve: looking down from this point, you see that the quantity demanded is 5 million barrels of oil per day. How about at a lower price of $20 per day? Start at $20 on the vertical axis and read to the right until the price hits the demand curve, then read down. Can you see that the quantity demanded at this price of $20 per barrel is 25 million barrels of oil per day?

We said that graphs express ideas, so what is the idea being expressed here? The most important fact about a demand curve is that it has a negative slope, that is, it slopes downward. This tells us the important but simple idea that as the price of a good falls, the quantity demanded increases. This is key: as the price of a good such as oil falls, people demand more of it.

A demand curve is a description of what *would happen* to the quantity demanded as the price of a good changed *holding fixed all other influences on the quantity of oil demanded*. (In this sense, demand curves are hypothetical and we rarely observe them directly.)

The quantity of oil demanded, for example, depends not just on the price of oil but on many other factors such as income or the price of other goods like automobiles and population, to name just a few of many influences. Today's demand curve for oil, for example, depends on today's income, price of automobiles and population. Imagine, for example, that average income today is $10,000, the price of an average automobile is $25,000 and world population is 7 billion. The blue curve in Figure A.3 shows the demand curve for oil under these conditions. Note that there are also many other influences on the demand for oil that we don't list but that are also being held fixed. Most importantly, if any of these conditions changes then the demand curve for oil will shift.

FIGURE A.3

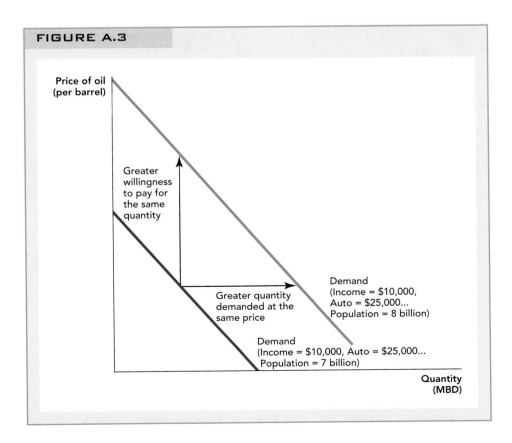

If world population increases to 8 billion, for example, there will be a new demand curve for oil. With a greater population, there will be more barrels of oil demanded at every specific price so the demand curve will shift to the right. Equivalently, as the population increases, there will be a greater willingness to pay for any given quantity of oil so the demand curve will shift up. Thus, we say that an increase in demand is a shift in the curve up and to the right shown by the red curve in Figure A.3. Chapter 2 explains in greater detail how a demand curve shifts in response to changes in factors other than price.

What is important to emphasize here is that a demand curve is drawn holding fixed every influence on the quantity demanded other than price. Changes in any factor that influences the demand for oil other than price will produce a new demand curve.

One more important feature of two variables graphed in a coordinate system is that these figures can be read in two different ways. For example, as we mention in Chapter 2, demand curves can be read both horizontally and vertically. Read "horizontally," you can see from Figure A.4 that at a price of $20 per barrel demanders are willing and able to buy 25 million barrels of oil per day. Read "vertically," you can see that the maximum price that demanders are willing to pay for 25 million barrels of oil a day is $20 per barrel. Thus, demand curves show the quantity demanded at any price or the maximum willingness to pay (per unit) for any quantity.

FIGURE A.4

It may seem difficult at first to interpret these graphs, but as you will see, graphs are amazingly useful for thinking about difficult economic problems. It's like learning to drive a car—at first it's not easy and you will make some mistakes but once you learn how to drive your ability to do things and go places increases enormously. The same thing is true with graphs!

Data Graphs

As well as expressing ideas, graphs can also be used to illustrate data. In Chapter 5, for example, we point out that GDP can be broken down according to the national spending identity into these components: Consumption, Investment, Government Purchases, and Net Exports (Exports minus Imports), that is, $GDP = Y = C + I + G + NX$. U.S. GDP for 2007 is shown in Table A.1.

TABLE A.1 U.S. GDP 2007 (in billions of dollars)	
Category	GDP
Consumption	9,710.2
Investment	2,130.4
Government	2,674.8
Net Exports	−707.8
GDP (Total)	13,807.6

Source: Bureau of Economic Analysis

If you type the components into Excel, as shown in Figure A.5, you can use the sum function to check that the components do add up to GDP.

Highlighting the data in columns A and B and clicking Insert > Column > Clustered Column and (with a few modifications to add axis titles and to make the graph look pretty), we have the graph on the left side of Figure A.6.

The graph on the right side of Figure A.6 shows exactly the same data only on the right side we chose Stacked Column (and we switched the rows and columns). Sometimes one visualization of the data is more revealing than another so it's a good idea to experiment a little bit with alternative ways of presenting the same data. But please don't get carried away with adding 3D effects or other chart junk. Always keep the focus on the data, not on the special effects.

FIGURE A.5

	B7		f_x	=SUM(B2:B5)	
	A	B	C	D	
1	Category	GDP			
2	Cons	9710.2			
3	Inv	2130.4			
4	Govt	2674.8			
5	NX	-707.8			
6					
7	GDP (Total)	13807.6			
8					

FIGURE A.6

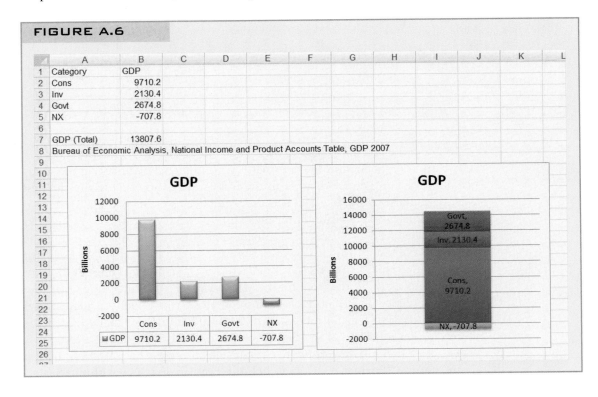

In Chapter 9, we explain the economics of stocks, bonds, and other invest-ments. A lot of financial data is available for free on the web. We used Yahoo! Finance, for example, to download data for the value of the S&P 500 Index on the first trading day of the month from 1950 to the end of 2000. The data is graphed in Figure A.7.

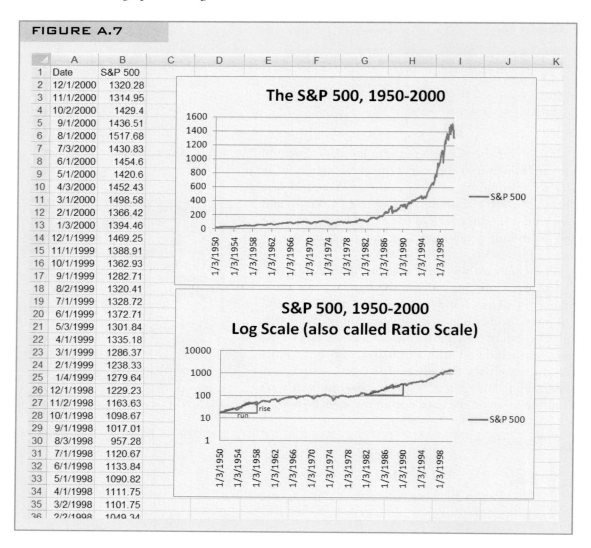

FIGURE A.7

To graph the S&P 500 data, we used a line graph. The top graph in Figure A.7 shows the data graphed in the "normal" way with equal distances on the verti-cal axis indicating equal changes in the index. That's not necessarily the best way to graph the data, however, because a quick look at the top figure suggests that stock prices were rising faster over time. In other words, the graph looks pretty flat between 1950 and approximately 1980, after which it shoots up. The appearance of faster growth, however, is mostly an illusion. The problem is that when the S&P 500 was at the level of 100, as it was around 1968, a 10 percent increase moves the index to 110, or an increase of 10 points. But when the index is at the level of 1,000, as it was around 1998, a 10 percent increase moves the index to 1,100, or an increase of 100 points. Thus, the same percentage increase looks much larger in 1998 than in 1968.

To get a different view of the data, right-click on the vertical axis of the top figure, choose "Format Axis" and click the box labeled "Logarithmic Scale," which produces the graph in the bottom of Figure A.7 (without the red triangles, which we will explain shortly).

Notice on the bottom figure that equal distances on the vertical axis now indicate equal percentage increases or ratios. The ratio 100/10, for example, is the same as the ratio 1,000/100. You can now see at a glance that if stock prices move the same vertical distance over the same length of time (as measured by the horizontal distance) then the percentage increase was the same. For example, we have superimposed two identical red triangles to show that the percentage increase in stock prices between 1950 and 1958 was about the same as between 1982 and 1990. The red triangles are identical so over the same 8-year period, given by the horizontal length of the triangle, the run, the S&P 500 rose by the same vertical distance, the rise. Recall that the slope of a line is given by the rise/run. Thus, we can also say that on a ratio graph, equal slopes mean equal percentage growth rates.

The log scale or ratio graph reveals more clearly than our earlier graph that stock prices increased from 1950 to the mid-1960s but were then flat throughout the 1970s and did not begin to rise again until after the recession in 1982. We use ratio graphs for a number of figures throughout this book to better identify patterns in the data.

Graphs are also very useful for suggesting possible relationships between two variables. In Chapter 10, for example, we present evidence that labor employment laws in much of Western Europe that make it difficult to fire workers also raise the costs of hiring workers. As a result, the percentage of unemployment that is long term in Europe tends to be very high. To show this relationship, we graphed an index called the "rigidity of employment index," produced by the World Bank. The rigidity of employment index summarizes hiring and firing costs as well as how easy it is for firms to adjust hours of work (e.g., whether there are restrictions on night or weekend hours). A higher index number means that it is more expensive to hire and fire workers and more difficult to adjust hours. We then graphed a country's rigidity of employment index against the share of a country's unemployment rate that is long term (lasting more than a year).

The data for this graph are shown in Figure A.8.

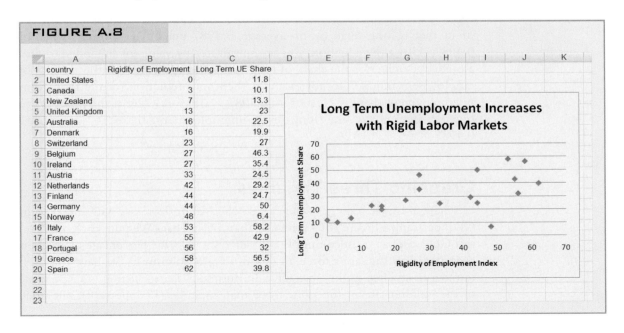

FIGURE A.8

	A	B	C
1	country	Rigidity of Employment	Long Term UE Share
2	United States	0	11.8
3	Canada	3	10.1
4	New Zealand	7	13.3
5	United Kingdom	13	23
6	Australia	16	22.5
7	Denmark	16	19.9
8	Switzerland	23	27
9	Belgium	27	46.3
10	Ireland	27	35.4
11	Austria	33	24.5
12	Netherlands	42	29.2
13	Finland	44	24.7
14	Germany	44	50
15	Norway	48	6.4
16	Italy	53	58.2
17	France	55	42.9
18	Portugal	56	32
19	Greece	58	56.5
20	Spain	62	39.8
21			
22			
23			

Long Term Unemployment Increases with Rigid Labor Markets

We can do something else of interest with this data. If you right-click on any of the data points in the figure, you will get the option to "Add Trendline." Clicking on this and then clicking the two boxes "Linear" and "Display Equation on Chart" produces Figure A.9 (absent the red arrow, which we added for clarity).

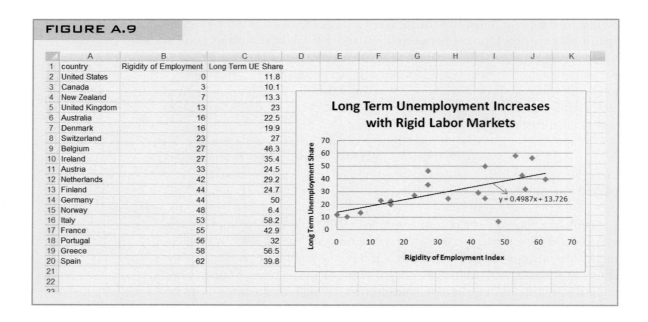

FIGURE A.9

	A	B	C	D	E	F	G	H	I	J	K
1	country	Rigidity of Employment	Long Term UE Share								
2	United States	0	11.8								
3	Canada	3	10.1								
4	New Zealand	7	13.3								
5	United Kingdom	13	23								
6	Australia	16	22.5								
7	Denmark	16	19.9								
8	Switzerland	23	27								
9	Belgium	27	46.3								
10	Ireland	27	35.4								
11	Austria	33	24.5								
12	Netherlands	42	29.2								
13	Finland	44	24.7								
14	Germany	44	50								
15	Norway	48	6.4								
16	Italy	53	58.2								
17	France	55	42.9								
18	Portugal	56	32								
19	Greece	58	56.5								
20	Spain	62	39.8								
21											
22											

The black line is the linear curve that "best fits" the data. (Best fit in this context is defined statistically; we won't go into the details here but if you take a statistics class you will learn about ordinary least squares.) Excel also produces for us the equation for the best-fit line, $Y = 0.4987 \times X + 13.726$. Do you remember from high school the formula for a straight line, $Y = m \times X + b$? In this case m, the slope of the line or the rise/run is 0.4987 and b, the intercept, is 13.726. The slope tells us that a 1 unit increase in the rigidity of employment index (a run of 1) increases the share of unemployment that is long term by, on average, 0.4987 percentage points (a rise of 0.4987). Using the equation, you can substitute any value for the index to find a predicted value for the share of long-term unemployment. If the rigidity of employment index is 15, for example, then our prediction for the long-term unemployment share is $21.2065 = 0.4987 \times 15 + 13.726$. If the index is 55, our prediction for the long-term unemployment share is $41.1545 = 0.4987 \times 55 + 13.726$.

Graphing Three Variables

In Chapter 18, we present evidence that child labor decreases with increases in GDP per capita. Figure A.10 shows a subset of that data. We put our X variable, real GDP per capita, in column B and our Y variable, the percentage of children ages 10–14 in the labor force, in column C. In column D, we have the total number of children in the labor force. In Burundi, a larger fraction (48.5 percent) of the children are in the labor force than in India (12.1 percent), but since

FIGURE A.10

	A	B	C	D	E
1	Country	Real GDP Per Capita	% Children in Work Force	Total Children in Work Force	
2	Burundi	523	48.5	439,623	
3	Ethiopia	635	41.1	3,472,114	
4	Bangladesh	1,684	27.7	4,592,758	
5	Thailand	6,857	12.2	666,602	
6	India	2,479	12.1	13,300,000	
7	Mexico	8,762	4.9	531,132	
8	Argentina	11,006	2.4	80,265	

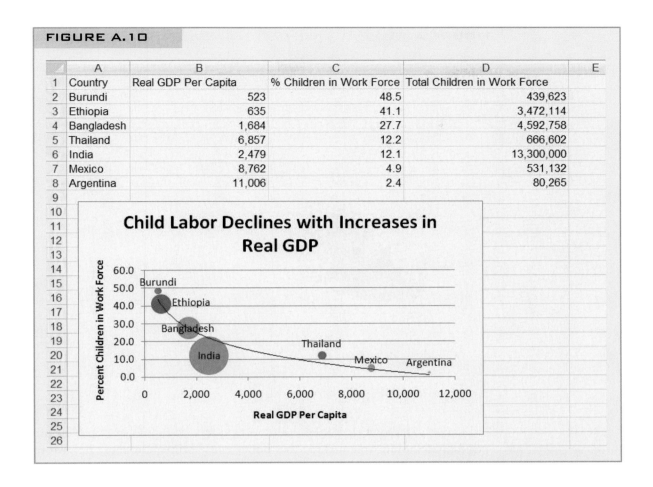

Burundi is a small country, the total number of children in the labor force is larger in India. To understand the problem of child labor, it's important to understand both types of information so we put both types of information on a graph.

Excel's bubble chart will take data arrayed in three columns and use the third column to set the area of the bubble or data point. In Figure A.10, for example, India has the largest number of children in the labor force and so has the bubble with the largest area. The area of the other bubbles is in relative proportion so Mexico's bubble is 1/25th the size of India's bubble because there are 1/25th as many children in the labor force in Mexico as in India. (Unfortunately, Excel doesn't label the bubbles automatically so we added these by hand.)

Cause and Effect

Do police reduce crime? If so, by how much? That's a key question that economists and criminologists are interested in understanding because local governments (and taxpayers) spend billions of dollars on police every year and would like to know whether they are getting their money's worth. Should they spend less on police or more? Unfortunately, it's surprisingly difficult to answer this question. To illustrate why, Figure A.11 shows the relationship between crime per capita and police per capita from across a large number of U.S. cities.

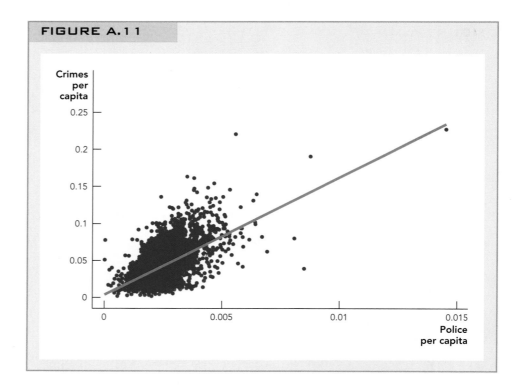

FIGURE A.11

Figure A.11 shows that cities with more police per capita have more crime per capita. Should we conclude that police cause crime? Probably not. More likely is "reverse causality," crime causes police—that is, greater crime rates lead to more hiring of police. We thus have two chains of potential cause and effect, more police reduce crime and more crime increases police. Unfortunately, you can't tell much about either of these two potential cause-and-effect relationships by looking at Figure A.11, which shows the correlation between police and crime but not the causation. But if you want to estimate the value of police, you need to know causation not just correlation. So what should you do?

The best way to estimate how much police reduce crime would be to take say 1,000 roughly similar cities and randomly flip a coin dividing the cities into two groups. In the first group of cities, double the police force and in the second group do nothing. Then compare crime rates over say the next year in cities with and without an increase in police. If the cities with an increase in police have lower rates of crime, then you can safely ascribe this difference to the effect of police on crime. What makes the correlation evidence in Figure A.11 difficult to interpret is that increases in crime sometimes cause increases in police. But if you increase the number of police randomly, you eliminate the possibility of this "reverse causality." Thus, if crime falls in the cities that have *random increases in police,* the cause is most plausibly the increase in police. Similarly, if crime were to increase in cities that have random decreases in police, the cause is most plausibly the decrease in police.

Unfortunately, randomized experiments have at least one big problem—they are very expensive. Occasionally, large randomized experiments are done in criminology and other social sciences but because they are so expensive we must usually look for alternative methods for assessing causality.

If you can't afford a randomized experiment, what else can you do? One possibility is to look for what economists call quasi-experiments or natural experiments. In 1969, for example, police in Montreal, Canada, went on strike and there were 50 times more bank robberies than normal.[1] If you can think of the strike as a random event, not tied in any direct way to increases or decreases in crime, then you can be reasonably certain that the increase in bank robberies was caused by the decrease in police.

The Montreal experiment tells you it's probably not a good idea to eliminate all police, but it doesn't tell you whether governments should increase or decrease police on the street by a more reasonable amount, say 10 percent to 20 percent. Jonathan Klick and Alex Tabarrok use another natural experiment to address this question.[2] Since shortly after 9/11, the United States has had a terror alert system run by the Department of Homeland Security. When the terror alert level rises from "elevated" (yellow) to "high" (orange) due to intelligence reports regarding the current threat posed by terrorist organizations, the Washington, D.C. Metropolitan Police Department reacts by increasing the number of hours each officer must work. Because the change in the terror alert system is not tied to any observed or expected changes in Washington crime patterns, this provides a useful quasi-experiment. In other words, whenever the terror alert system shifts from yellow to orange—a random decision with respect to crime in Washington—the effective police presence in Washington increases. Klick and Tabarrok find that during the high terror alert periods when more police are on the street, the amount of crime falls. Street crime such as stolen automobiles, thefts from automobiles, and burglaries decline especially sharply. Overall, Klick and Tabarrok estimate that a 10 percent increase in police reduces crime by about 3 percent. Using these numbers and figures on the cost of crime and of hiring more police, Klick and Tabarrok argue that more police would be very beneficial.

Economists have developed many techniques for assessing causality from data and we have only just brushed the surface. We can't go into details here. We want you to know, however, that in this textbook when we present data that suggests a causal relationship—such as when we argue in Chapter 18 that higher GDP leads to lower levels of child labor—that a significant amount of statistical research has gone into assessing causality, not just correlation. If you are interested in further details, we have provided you with the references to the original papers.

APPENDIX A QUESTIONS

1. We start with a simple idea from algebra: Which of the graphs at the top of the next page have a positive slope and which have a negative slope?

2. When social scientists talk about social and economic facts, they usually talk about a "positive relationship" or a "negative relationship" instead of "positive slope" or "negative slope." Based on your knowledge, which of the following pairs of variables tend to have a "positive relationship" (a positive slope when graphed), and which have a negative relationship? (Note: "Negative relationship" and "inverse relationship" mean the same thing. Also, in this question, we're only talking about correlation, not causation.)

   a. A professional baseball player's batting average and his annual salary.

   b. A professional golfer's average score and her average salary.

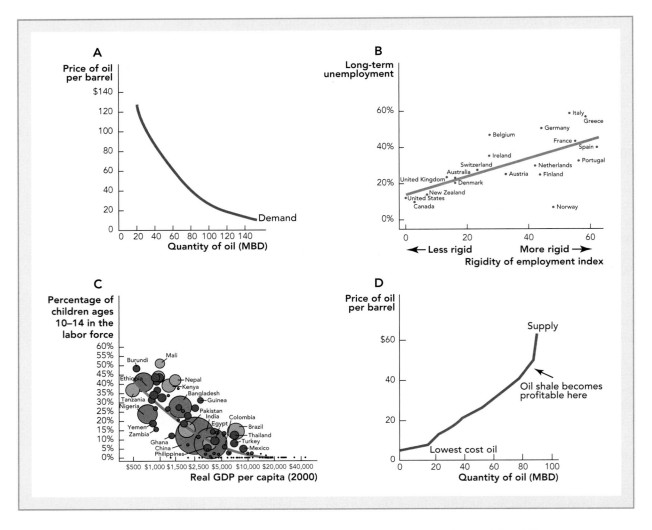

A

Price of oil per barrel

Demand

Quantity of oil (MBD)

B

Long-term unemployment

← Less rigid   More rigid →
Rigidity of employment index

C

Percentage of children ages 10–14 in the labor force

Real GDP per capita (2000)

D

Price of oil per barrel

Supply

Oil shale becomes profitable here

Lowest cost oil

Quantity of oil (MBD)

c. The number of cigarettes a person smokes and her life expectancy.

d. The size of the car you drive and your probability of surviving a serious accident.

e. A country's distance from the equator and how rich its citizens tend to be. (For the answer, see Robert Hall and Charles Jones. 1999. Why Do Some Countries Produce so Much More Output per Worker than Others? *Quarterly Journal of Economics.* 114: 83–116.)

3. Let's convert Klick and Tabarrok's research on crime into a simple algebra equation. We reported the result as the effect of a 10 percent increase in police on the crime rate in Washington, D.C. In the equation below, fill in the effect of a 1 percent increase in the police on the crime rate:

The percent change in crime = _____ ✕ The percent change in police officers

4. Let's read the child labor graph [A.10] horizontally and then vertically:

a. According to the trendline, in a typical country with 10 percent of the children in the labor force, what's the real GDP per person?

b. According to the trendline, when a country's GDP per person is $2,000, roughly what percentage of children are in the labor force?

5. Let's take another look at the ratio scale, and compare it to a normal scale.

    a. In Figure A.7, which one is presented in ratio scale and which in normal scale?

    b. In the top graph, every time the S&P 500 crosses a horizontal line, how many points did the S&P rise?

    c. In the bottom graph, every time the S&P 500 crosses a horizontal line, how many *times* higher is the S&P?

6. As a scientist, you have to plot the following data: The number of bacteria you have in a large petri dish, measured every hour over the course of a week. (Note: *E. coli* bacteria populations can double every 20 minutes) Should this data be plotted on a ratio scale and why?

7. Educated people are supposed to point out (correctly) that "correlation isn't proof of causation." This is an important fact—which explains why economists, medical doctors, and other researchers spend a lot of time trying to look for proof of causation. But sometimes, correlation is good enough. In the following examples, take the correlation as a true fact, and explain why the correlation is, all by itself, useful for the task presented in each question.

    a. Your task is to decide what brand of car to buy. You know that Brand H usually gets higher quality ratings than Brand C. You don't know what causes Brand H to get higher ratings—maybe Brand H hires better workers, maybe Brand H buys better raw materials. All you have is the correlation.

    b. Your task is to hire the job applicant who appears to be the smartest. Applicant M has a degree from MIT, and applicant S has a degree from a typical state university. You don't know what causes MIT graduates to be smarter than typical state university graduates—maybe they start off smarter before they get to MIT, maybe their professors teach them a lot, maybe having smart classmates for four years gives them constant brain exercise.

    c. Your task is to decide which city to move to, and you want to move to the city that is probably the safest. For some strange reason, the only fact you have to help you with your decision is the number of police per person.

8. If you haven't practiced in a while, let's calculate some slopes. In each case, we give two points, and you can use the "rise over run" formula to get the right answer.

    a. Point 1: $x = 0$, $y = 0$. Point 2: $x = 3$, $y = 6$

    b. Point 1: $x = 6$, $y = -9$. Point 2: $x = 3$, $y = 6$

    c. Point 1: $x = 4$, $y = 8$. Point 2: $x = 1$, $y = 12$

9. We mentioned that a demand curve is a hypothetical relationship: It answers a "what if" question: "What if today's price of oil rose (or fell), but the average consumer's income, beliefs about future oil prices, and the prices of everything else in the economy stayed the same?" When some of those other features change, then the demand curve isn't fixed any more: It shifts up (and right) or left (and down). In Figure A.3, we showed one shift graphically: Let's make some changes in algebra:

The economy of Perovia has the following demand for oil:

$$Price = B - M \times Quantity$$

When will B tend to be a larger number:

a. When population in Perovia is high or when it is low?

b. When the price of autos in Perovia is high or when it is low?

c. When Perovian income is high or when it is low?

10. Using the raw data from this chapter, use Excel to replicate simple versions of any two of our graphs. Figures A.6, A.7, A.9, and A.10 all provide the data you'll need. If you're adventurous, feel free to search out the newest GDP data and S&P 500 data on the Bureau of Economic Analysis (BEA) website and Yahoo! Finance, respectively.

Appendix B

Solutions to Check Yourself Questions

Here are suggested answers to the Check Yourself questions found within the chapters.

Chapter 2

Page 20

1. As the income of Indian workers rises, this will lead to an increase in the demand for automobiles. At first as income rises, workers may demand more charcoal bricks for heating, but charcoal bricks are a dangerous and unpleasant way to heat a home so as income increases beyond a certain level, workers will demand fewer charcoal bricks. Thus, a good can be a normal good over some levels of income and an inferior good over other (usually higher) levels of income.

2. As the price of oil rises, some people will substitute mopeds for automobiles so the demand for mopeds will increase.

Page 27

1. Improvements in chip-making technology have driven down the costs of this input so the supply of computers increases meaning that the supply curve for computers shifts to the right/down.

2. The ethanol subsidy lowers the cost of producing ethanol, therefore increasing the supply of ethanol (the supply curve for ethanol shifts to the right/down).

Chapter 3

Page 35

1. If the demand for large trucks and SUVs falls unexpectedly, auto companies will find that at the current price they have a surplus of trucks and SUVs. The quantity supplied is greater than the quantity demanded so they will lower prices in order to sell already-manufactured trucks and SUVs.

2. Sellers have produced too many clothes if they have them available at outlet malls where price discounts are the norm. Sellers are cutting their prices to reduce the surplus and move the clothes out the door.

Page 38

1. As the price of cars goes up, the least-valued wants will be the first to stop being satisfied. For example, parents may be more reluctant to buy their teenage sons and daughters a new automobile.

2. If telecommunication firms overinvest in fiber-optic cable, for example, they will have to lower the price of using fiber-optic lines. For example, a company such as Verizon will offer fiber-optic Internet and phone connections at discount prices. The ensuing losses from price cutting will dampen future investment in fiber-optic cable. More generally, firms invest in order to make a profit. If firms overinvest, they will take losses, which give them an incentive to invest carefully.

Page 42

1. If flooding destroys some of the corn and soybean crops, these crops will have a decrease in supply. This decrease in supply will lower the equilibrium quantity and increase the equilibrium price.

2. If resveratrol (from Japanese knotweed) increases life expectancy in fish, people might think it will have the same effect in humans, and so more people will demand it, increasing demand. This will increase the price of Japanese knotweed, and will lead to an increase in the quantity grown.

3. The demand for hybrid cars will increase as the price of gas increases, that is, the demand curve shifts to the right/up. We show this in Figure 3.7: think of the New demand as the demand for hybrids when the price of gas is high and the Old demand as the demand for hybrids when the price of gas is low. The price of hybrids will rise with an increase in demand, especially in the short run.

Page 46

1. The price of oil rose in 1991 primarily because of a supply shock, the Persian Gulf War. (It would also be okay to label this as a demand shock because the demand for oil increased when people expected that the war would reduce the future supply of oil.) Bonus points if you recognized both possibilities.

2. From 1981 to 1986, the price of oil fell steadily. The higher price in the preceding years encouraged exploration, which several years later led to increased supply especially from non-OPEC sources.

Chapter 4

Page 60

1. There are more substitutes for a brand than a general product category, so there are more substitutes for Dell computers than for computers. When there are more substitutes, demand is more elastic, so demand is more elastic for Dell computers than for computers.

2. An elasticity of demand of 0.1 is an inelastic demand. With inelastic demand, revenue and price move together. Thus, if the price of eggs increases, total revenue will increase. Bonus points if you said that with an elasticity of 0.1, when price goes up by 10%, quantity goes down by 1% so Revenues $(= P \times Q)$ increase by approximately 9%.

3. A fashionable clothing store might raise its prices by 25% if it thought there was inelastic demand for its products: the increase in price on everything would more than make up for the decrease in sales (quantity).

Page 68

1. Supply is usually not very elastic in the short run. In the case of computer chips, a factory can run 24 hours per day and pay overtime, but it takes years to build a new factory. In the long run, supply is more elastic because over time a computer chip firm can respond to increased demand by building new factories.

2. Manhattan is an island with very little land available for development so the supply of housing in Manhattan is very inelastic. In contrast, there is lots of unbuilt land available in the Des Moines area so the supply is more elastic. The same increase in demand will increase the price more when the supply is inelastic than elastic—thus the same increase in demand will increases prices more in Manhattan than in Des Moines.

Chapter 5

Page 81

1. If farmers receive a higher price for turning corn into ethanol, they will supply more of their corn for ethanol production. Thus, the (opportunity) cost of supplying corn for cornbread will increase and there will be a decrease in the supply of corn for cornbread. As a result, the price of cornbread will increase and customers will consume less, perhaps substituting towards cheaper items such as regular bread.

2. During the housing boom, the use of lumber skyrocketed as did the supply of a lumber byproduct, sawdust. The increase in the supply of sawdust caused a fall in the price of sawdust. Since a lot of sawdust is used in bedding milk cows, this reduced the cost of producing milk. When the housing boom collapsed, less lumber was produced so less sawdust was produced and the price of sawdust rose, which increased the cost of producing milk and thus the price of milk. Markets are linked in non-obvious ways. Who would have thought the housing and milk markets were linked so closely?

Page 84

1. We aren't peanut experts either but the highest value of peanuts is probably in its use as a food; furthermore there are fewer substitutes for peanuts in paint, varnish, and furniture polish, where the peanut has some unique properties, than in insecticides or soap or finally bird feed. So let's rank the use of peanuts from highest to least valued use as follows: food, paint, varnish, furniture polish, insecticides, soap and bird feed. Any ranking you have is fine—the point is that there is a ranking.

2. If there is a peanut crop failure in a large producer such as China, the price of peanuts and peanut products will rise and people will substitute away from peanuts in their least-value uses. Thus, we would expect fewer peanuts used in bird feed, soap, and insecticides, which will free up more peanuts for use in the higher-value categories. Thus, as the price of peanuts rises, there is a reallocation of peanuts from lower-valued to higher-valued uses. It's important to recognize that the best way of figuring out which uses are the higher-valued uses is to see what happens when the price rises.

Page 85

1. No central planner could possibly know or understand all of the links between products so the messaging system is unlikely to send the right information. But let's suppose that the *information problem* was solved. Even if the government sent the right messages there would still be an *incentive problem*. What incentives would producers and consumers have to obey the messages? In contrast, the price system sums up all of the links between products in one number, the price, and it provides an incentive to pay attention to the price. Thus, the price system solves the information problem and the incentive problem which is why we say that a price is a signal wrapped up in an incentive.

2. If firms do not have to face bankruptcy, they can continue with poor products, practices, and efforts. The fear of bankruptcy is a spur to innovate and grow, but the fear has to be backed up by the reality.

Page 88

1. In hindsight, it is clear that Lehman Brothers was engaged in wishful thinking. Speculators, with their money on the line, did not believe the Lehman forecasts. Companies can have a tendency to look at things in the best-possible way and to ignore reality, and speculators provide a market vote (a reality check).

Chapter 6

Page 106

1. Price ceilings set below equilibrium prices cause shortages. Price ceilings set above equilibrium prices have no effects.

2. A price control reduces the incentive to respond to shifts in demand, thus resources become misallocated according to essentially random factors.

For example, it costs much more to ship oil from Alaskan oil fields to refineries on the East Coast than on the West Coast. Price ceilings did not let that difference become factored in the price, and therefore reduced the incentive to ship oil to where it was most needed so shortages could be worse in some areas than in others.

Page 110

1. If landlords under rent control have an incentive to do only minimum upkeep, deteriorating buildings inevitably accompany rent control. Only major repairs are made. Tenants with dripping faucets may never get a response from landlords, and have to fix it themselves. At a minimum, they will have to wait, maybe until the drip becomes something larger and so has an effect on the landlord's water bill.

2. Vested interests will fight any attempt at rolling back rent control, and these vested interests become powerful over time. It's especially difficult to eliminate rent controls because tenants (people who already have an apartment) don't care much about the shortage—they do not have to find a new apartment every week. In contrast, buyers of gasoline have to deal with the shortage every time they need a fillup so it may be easier to get rid of price controls on oil than on apartments.

Page 112

1. Price ceilings cause shortages. Universal price controls cause shortages across the economy, with no obvious pattern. Sometimes one product is in abundance, at other times there are shortages. A rational response when there are products that face inexplicable shortages is to buy as much as possible when possible: buy as much toilet paper now because who knows when it will come available again? In other words, hoarding is a standard response to universal price controls. Hoarding is wasteful because it implies a misallocation of resources. Some people, for reasons of luck (or influence), may have a lot of toilet paper while others have none. If trade were allowed, people would experience gains from trade and products would gravitate to their highest value uses.

2. The Soviet Union also faced surpluses of goods as well as shortages because under universal price controls there was no incentive to get products to the places at the times that they had the highest value uses. As a result, goods would be misallocated and production and consumption would be chaotic. One week a farm might get enough oil to deliver its chickens to the city and in that week the city shops would get a lot of chickens as the farm dumped its accumulated stock. A few weeks later there might be no oil available and chickens would disappear from the shops.

Chapter 7

Page 125

1. A price floor set above the equilibrium price leads to surpluses. Because the European Union price floor for butter is above the equilibrium price, the EU has created a surplus of butter which the government must buy. The surplus has been so large that it has been called a butter mountain.

2. The U.S. price floor for milk, set above the equilibrium price, has led to a surplus of milk. The government has dealt with the surplus by buying the surplus and giving away milk and dairy products produced from milk (such as cheese) to schools. This accounts for the low or zero price you paid for milk at most schools.

Page 133

1. Because demand for insulin is highly inelastic, the users of insulin are likely ultimately to pay a government insulin tax. Producers of insulin have some ability to produce other products and so can escape the tax more readily.

2. The government would rather tax items that have relatively inelastic demands and supplies rather than elastic demands and supplies because the deadweight loss from taxation is lower when supply and demand are inelastic.

Page 137

1. Because of the ethanol subsidy, the quantity supplied of ethanol increases. The subsidy increases the price received by the ethanol producers (corn growers) and lowers the price paid by ethanol users. The relative amount received by producers versus that paid by buyers depends on the relative elasticities of demand and supply.

2. Government subsidies for college education increased the demand for education. The supply of education, however, is relatively inelastic, especially at elite colleges. Thus, the benefits of the subsidy flow to suppliers, i.e. the price paid to suppliers increases by more than the price paid by buyers falls. Much of the subsidy ends up raising the incomes of professors! Perhaps this is one reason that many professors argue for subsidies to education.

Chapter 8

Page 149

1. Specialization increases productivity because it increases knowledge and through economies of scale makes it more profitable to employ productive capital.

2. If people can't trade for other goods, they won't specialize in producing just one good. Thus, trade is necessary if people are to benefit from specialization.

3. Alex Rodriguez has a comparative advantage in playing baseball, but Harry has a comparative advantage in mowing Alex's lawn because Harry faces a much lower opportunity cost in mowing lawns than Alex Rodriguez does.

Page 155

1. Domestic producers gain from a tariff and domestic consumers lose.

2. Trade protectionism leads to wasted resources because it shifts production from the lowest cost producers to higher cost producers.

3. You hear more often about people who gain from trade restrictions than people who lose because the gains from trade restrictions are concentrated

on a few winners while the losses are diffused over many losers. Even though the total gains are smaller than the total losses the concentrated benefits mean that the winners have a greater incentive to argue for trade restriction than the losers do to argue against.

Page 159

1. The movement of the garment trade overseas has been a net benefit for the United States because clothing is now much cheaper for U.S. consumers and U.S. workers specialize in the fields in which they are most productive.

2. If the U.S. government subsidized the Silicon Valley computer industry, it would encourage more computer chip manufacturing, but at a higher cost (production would not be as efficient). This would be a waste of resources. Foreign competitors would be pushed out of the industry. Consumers of computer chips would benefit from the subsidy but they would benefit by less than the cost to U.S. taxpayers.

Chapter 9

Page 175

1. If the government overshoots and sets a Pigouvian tax that is too high, it will result in an equilibrium quantity that is lower than the efficient equilibrium. A tax that is too high will create a deadweight loss from too few trades. If the tax is much too high, it can be worse than leaving the externality alone.

2. If the government undershoots and provides a subsidy that is too low, the equilibrium quantity will be lower than the efficient equilibrium. In this case, there will be an undersupply.

Page 177

1. Using the Coase theorem, a solution to the prospect of elderly neighbors complaining about your party is to buy the elderly couple tickets to a movie or to a night away at a hotel. Transaction costs are low in this case: you can easily contact your neighbors and you might even pay for the gift by collecting contributions from the party-goers.

2. A solution to the polluting factory problem depends on the transactions costs. Are there many neighbors or only a few? Are the victims of the pollution located nearby or are they spread out? Is it clear whether the factory has the right to pollute, say because it was there first and everyone moved into the area knowing about the pollution? Transaction costs are key here, because even if the factory has the right to pollute, if you can negotiate with your neighbors, you may be able to pay off the factory if it has certain property rights.

Page 182

1. A falling price for tradable pollution allowances tells us that the value of the allowance has fallen. This means that the costs of eliminating pollution have fallen—perhaps because of technological developments in clean energy.

2. If a local government set tradable allowances for pollution in the neighborhood, some groups that would press for a large total quantity of allowances would be the big polluters: chemical factories, meat-processing plants, sometimes automobile repair shops. Some groups that would press for a smaller total quantity of allowances would be home owners, parents sending their children to local schools but who live outside of the immediate vicinity, the elderly. Unfortunately, there is no theorem that says that the rough-and-tumble of the political process will result in an efficient equilibrium. If the political process gets it approximately right and the externality is serious, the tradable allowance system will improve social welfare but this is not guaranteed.

Chapter 10

Page 190

1. In a competitive market, if a firm prices its product above the market price, no one will buy the firm's product. Why should anyone pay more for the same product? In a competitive market, if a firm prices its product below the market price, it will sell everything it produces, but why should it set price below the market price when it can sell the same amount *at* the market price?

2. Demand for a competitive firm's product is perfectly elastic, portrayed as a horizontal demand curve for the firm's product. It can sell all it wants at the competitive price.

3. If there is more than one firm in the industry, then the demand for a particular firm's product is always more elastic than the demand for the product itself. The demand for each stripper well's oil is very elastic even though the demand for oil is inelastic because there are very good substitutes for the oil from a particular firm, namely the oil from any other firm.

Page 193

1. When the firm in Figure 10.2 produces 4 barrels rather than 3, $33 in additional profit is made. Going from 7 to 8 barrels, no additional profit is made. Going from 8 to 9 barrels, profit falls to $-$40. Looking at the figure, MR = MC when the quantity produced is 8 barrels. At this quantity, marginal profit is $0.

Page 195

If Sandy's MC is higher than Pat's MC, total costs can be reduced by producing a little bit less on Sandy's farm and a little bit more on Pat's farm.

Page 198

1. Profit equals (price minus average cost) times quantity, $\pi = (P - AC) \times Q$. Another way of saying this is that profit per unit is price minus average cost (the cost for each unit), and profit per unit times the number of units sold gives you total profits.

Assuming that the firm produces the optimal quantity (found where P = MC) then at *any* price greater than average cost, the firm is making a profit and at *any* price less than average cost, the firm is taking a loss.

Page 200

1. Just because the price of a barrel of oil reaches $65 does not mean that the firm should undertake to spend $100 million to drill an oil well. The price easily could drop. The firm should project the price of oil over the life of the oil well to carefully determine revenues, and then see if it will make a lifetime profit considering its total costs. If lifetime profits are negative the firm should not enter. Even when lifetime profits are positive the firm should not necessarily invest right away—the firm may be better off waiting for a time to gather more information.

Page 202

1. In competitive markets, profits are a signal for new firms to enter. It is as if entrepreneurs see a sign flashing "Profits, Profits, Profits".

2. In competitive markets, because a firm has no control over price, its best opportunity for profits is to keep its costs low.

Page 208

1. In the early stages, an automobile manufacturing industry is a decreasing cost industry because as the industry expands it can draw upon economies of scale both in auto manufacturing and in steel, plastic, and other input industries. Economies of scale, however, don't increase forever so once the industry matures it becomes an increasing cost industry. Today, for example, the automobile industry is an increasing cost industry because greater demand for autos means an increased demand for steel and plastic, which will drive up the price of steel and plastic, thus increasing costs in the auto industry.

2. The U.S. film industry is clustered around Hollywood because the central location leads to lower costs. Perhaps only in Hollywood could a movie director easily arrange to interview four movie stars in a single afternoon.

Chapter 11

Page 225

1. As a firm with market power moves down its demand curve, the price it can charge on all units moves down as well.

2. A firm with market power prefers to face an inelastic demand curve because the more inelastic the demand curve, the more the firm with market power can raise its price above marginal cost. See Figure 11.4 for a display of this.

Page 226

1. A monopolist always prices its product above the price of an equal cost competitive firm.

2. A monopolist always produces less than an equal cost competitive firm because this way it produces more profit than a competitive firm.

Page 229

1. Apple has market power and plausibly it encourages innovation. Pharmaceutical companies have an incentive by the patent system to use market power to innovate. One can argue that many utilities have market power but do not seem to be great innovators. The Post Office has market power but does not seem to innovate much.

2. The prize for a new cancer drug should be calculated by taking the number of people expected to die of cancer over a long period of time, then multiplying this by the presumed willingness to pay of people with cancer for a cure, discounted for payments received over a long time period, minus the probable cost of research and the low marginal cost of producing the drug. The size of the prize is likely to be enormous.

Page 234

1. If regulators controlled the price at P = AC (and AC is at point *a*), the monopolist would produce where the AC curve crosses the demand curve. At this price the monopolist would make zero (normal) profits and the quantity would be greater than the monopoly quantity although still not as high as the efficient quantity.

2. Telephones used to be a natural monopoly because it was much cheaper for one firm to lay one set of lines and serve everyone than to have competing phone companies. Today, cell phones have broken the natural land-line monopoly because cell towers cost much less to create than telephone poles and wires so it makes sense to have multiple, competing operators. In this way, technology can quickly abolish what was once a natural monopoly.

Page 235

1. Major league baseball and professional football restrict the entry of competitors in local areas, thus supporting the market power of these local teams. With market power, teams raise prices, without the fear that competitors will see the higher prices as opportunities to enter. In this case, prospective teams face more than just barriers to entry in the form of high entry costs: the teams are prohibited from entering by the leagues.

2. Barriers to entry are strong when they are mandated and enforced: the U.S. Postal Service still has a monopoly on delivering first-class mail because by law other firms must charge three times as much as the U.S.P.S. if they wish to deliver a letter. Of course, the prevalence of email has made this monopoly less valuable. In contrast to this, when Congress took away the U.S. Postal Service's monopoly on the delivery of parcels, competitors such as UPS and FedEx jumped in and took over much of the market. People still send parcels through the Postal Service, but often not when delivery needs to be fast and guaranteed. NBA basketball restricts entry just as major league baseball does, and that looks to be fairly permanent for the near term, though the league may let additional teams in over time.

Chapter 12

Page 246

1. If a monopolist segments a market, it can price discriminate between the different segments and so raise its profits.

2. When demand is more inelastic, the price-discriminating firm would set higher prices. Remember that elasticity = escape. People with inelastic demand find it harder to escape and so will pay more.

3. Arbitrage is taking advantage of price differences for the same good in different markets by buying low in one market and selling high in another market. When the monopolist price discriminates by setting a low price in one market and a high price in another, it creates a potential arbitrage opportunity. In order to profitably price discriminate, the monopolist must prevent this arbitrage.

Page 250

1. The early bird special is a form of price discrimination if people who want to eat at a later time have a more inelastic demand curve. This could be true, for example, if people who want to eat at a later hour are wealthier (perhaps because they are working long hours!). An alternative explanation is that the restaurant's marginal costs increase as the restaurant becomes more crowded—thus restaurants charge more during peak hours. In the first case the markup of price over marginal cost increases in the later evening, in the second the firm's costs and price both increase in the later evening. It's not obvious which explanation is correct!

2. People who want to see movies right after the movies are released have a more inelastic demand for them than people who are willing to wait for the movies to be released as a DVD. Movie theaters know this and set their prices relatively high for those who cannot wait (have an inelastic demand). For the same reason, books are more expensive when they are first released (in hardback), than later when they are released (in paperback). The increased costs of producing a hardback are trivial compared to the difference in price.

Page 252

1. Price discrimination is likely to increase total surplus if output increases.

2. Price discrimination helps industries with high fixed costs because profits increase with market size. Simply, more market segments means that the price-discriminating firm can extract more consumer surplus. This leads to higher prices, which fund the high fixed costs. Universities have high fixed costs. The ability for a university to price discriminate means it can attract more paying students to its campus and so pay for its high fixed costs.

Page 255

1. Tying cell phones to service plans is a type of price discrimination whereby high demanders (long talkers) are charged more. If cell phone

companies were not allowed to tie cell phones with service plans, the price of cell phones likely would rise and the price of phone calls likely would fall. This would be good for people who want to talk a lot but bad for people who want to use their cell phone only occasionally. Profits for the cell phone companies would also fall so there would be fewer funds to pay for the fixed costs of building cell phone towers and infrastructure.

2. Bundling is likely to increase total surplus in high fixed cost, low marginal cost industries because without some form of price discrimination it's difficult to provide these goods at optimal levels.

Chapter 13

Page 275

1. When Great Britain found oil in the North Sea, it could obtain the benefits of OPEC (the cartel price) without any of the disadvantages of joining the cartel such as limiting production. Why join?

2. The surprising conclusion of the Prisoner's Dilemma is that there are situations when the pursuit of individual interest leads to a group outcome that is in the interest of no one. Think of three cases. First, the "invisible hand" is a metaphor for the idea that under the right circumstances the pursuit of self-interest can lead to the social interest. Second, theft is an intermediate case where the pursuit of self-interest benefits one's self but not the social interest. Third, the Prisoner's Dilemma reminds us that in some circumstances when everyone pursues their self-interest the result can be against the interest of everyone!

Page 281

1. A firm with an established network good such as Microsoft Office faces competition or potential competition for the market. Network monopolies can last for a long time but then evaporate very quickly.

2. It is useful to wait until standards are set because you don't want to be the person or firm who has chosen what turns out to be the loser: you will face diminished support and product offerings. Once standards are set, there is little risk of picking a loser and so sales should burst forward.

Chapter 14

Page 291

1. The marginal product of labor falls as more workers are hired because the first worker will focus on the most important tasks, and so the marginal product of labor will be high. The next worker will focus on the next important tasks, but these tasks will not be as important as the first worker tackled, so the marginal product of labor will not be as high as for the first worker. As more workers are hired, they do progressively less important tasks, so their marginal product falls relative to the first workers.

Page 293

1. An individual's labor supply curve might be backward bending because at some point, individuals might prefer more leisure to working more, even at a higher wage. In other words, one of the things that people may buy more of when their wage goes up is leisure.

Page 300

1. An increase in mine safety would lower the wages of miners because mine workers are paid extra to undertake their risky jobs. Making the job less risky would increase the number of people willing to be miners and thus would drive wages down.

2. Firms will pay for human capital improvements if the firm can reap the benefit. Training on a firm's specific inventory techniques will help the firm but this is a skill that it is hard to take to other firms so the firm need not pay a higher wage to individuals with specific training. In this sense, the firm reaps the benefit of this training exclusively. In contrast, an MBA provides skills that can be used by many firms so an individual with an MBA can earn a higher wage at other firms. In order to benefit from training an individual with general skills, the firm must keep the individual around at the lower wage long enough to recover its costs. Thus, the time requirement helps the firm recover a large portion of its investment in the worker.

Page 306

1. Employer discrimination is dumb or at least costly from a profit-making perspective because hiring equally good workers at a lower wage increases profit.

2. Market economies have had the most effect on eliminating discrimination by employers because the profit motive is a powerful incentive—notice that the more employers discriminate against minorities, the greater the profit from hiring a minority worker. Market economies have had some success in mitigating customer discrimination because market transactions bring different groups into regular contact with each other and thereby break down barriers. Market economies have had the toughest time eliminating employee discrimination because this type of discrimination can be self-reinforcing.

Chapter 15

Page 318

1. Workers sometimes fear that if they work harder under a piece rate system they will work themselves out of a job. Lincoln's policy of guaranteed employment reassures workers that productivity will always work to their advantage not to their detriment.

2. It is sometimes said that the word tips stands for "To Insure Prompt Service." Certainly the idea is that restaurant customers will give bigger tips the better the service, thus giving waiters an incentive to be attentive. Thus, we would predict that waiters would be less attentive in Europe

where the "tip" is typically automatic than in America where it usually is not.

Page 322

1. Professors have an incentive to be known as a hard grader because this reputation will keep away all but the serious students and maybe also all but the brightest students. Grading on a curve would encourage the usual diverse spectrum of students, from serious to indifferent and from smart to struggling.

2. In a tournament, one worker's gain is another's loss. Sometimes tournaments can encourage too much competition by discouraging cooperation. If a firm wants it sales staff to work together to land sales, for example, then it would not want a strong tournament scheme. Professors who want their students to work together on projects should not grade on a curve.

Page 324

1. A famous paper in economics calculated that on average $10 spent on gifts was worth only $8 to the gift receivers. In other words, when your Uncle gives you $10 in cash you get $10 worth of utility but when your Uncle gives you a $10 pair of socks on average you get only $8 worth of utility. Thus, according to the author of the study, Joel Waldfogel, Christmas wastes billions of dollars. Even though most people understand this idea when it is explained to them, we don't see a big shift to giving cash. Why not? Perhaps gift giving is valuable precisely because it is challenging. If you spend $10 giving something to someone that they value for $50 that shows how much you must really understand and care for them. Or perhaps we want the gift giver to buy something for us that we would not have bought for ourselves. Or perhaps people give gifts to signal something about themselves. Giving someone a CD of Bach sonatas says something about *you* that a gift of $15 does not. Understanding the answer to this question may tell us a lot about social life. The paper is Waldfogel, Joel. 1993. "The Deadweight Loss of Christmas". *The American Economic Review*, Vol. 83, No. 5 (Dec., 1993), pp. 1328–1336.

2. Maybe. Maybe not. If we pay for grades, some people worry that this will stifle the love of learning and perhaps send the message that getting good grades is like a job that the student is free to quit at any time. A number of experiments are currently underway testing these ideas.

Chapter 16

Page 335

1. According to the efficient markets hypothesis, one cannot consistently beat the market. Therefore, past performance is not a good guide to future success. On average, mutual funds that have performed well in the past are no more likely to perform well in the future than mutual funds that performed poorly in the past.

Page 341

1. Investing in the stocks of other countries helps to diversify your investments because the economies of other countries do not always rise and fall at the same time as the U.S. economy. If all economies tended to rise and fall together, there would not be any large benefits in diversifying across countries.

2. If many people dream of owning a football or baseball team, it is likely that the rewards to owning one go beyond monetary rewards. Thus, the monetary return on these assets is likely to be relatively low.

Page 343

1. This question is being hotly debated by many economists. It can be said that identifying and bursting bubbles is harder than it looks. How does the Federal Reserve know when there is a bubble? Increases in prices do not necessarily signify a bubble. Even if it can be said to be fairly certain that a bubble is present, how does the Federal Reserve burst the bubble while avoiding widespread collateral damage?

Chapter 17

Page 351

1. If government provides more of national defense than is efficient, it is pulling resources away from other, more valuable, goods and having taxpayers bear the burden. People with a very strong preference for national defense would benefit as well perhaps as those involved in providing national defense.

Page 352

1. Advertising could be used to pay for the upkeep of public parks. Advertising could be seen in obvious places such as signs by entryways to the park, on garbage cans, or on the sides of refreshment stands. If there is a music bandshell or a stage (in larger parks), advertising could be seen on the sides of these structures. Notice that under the Adopt-a-Highway program there is advertising on roads that supports road cleanup.

2. Airports charge for Wi-fi because they can make money from it by excluding non-payers. Since more Wi-fi users don't (usually) increase congestion by appreciable amounts, it would be more efficient to allow open-access.

Page 355

1. Small communities find it easier to deal with common resource problems than states or nations because they have an easier time enforcing norms (standards of behavior) that reduce free riding. Even so, the more unrelated people that have access to a common good, the harder it is to deal with common resource problems.

2. The establishment of property rights can help solve the tragedy of the commons because people who have property rights have no incentive to overuse a resource. The tragedy of the commons occurs because people

have an incentive to overuse common resources: to get theirs before someone else takes it.

Chapter 19

Page 383

1. National voters have a smaller chance of influencing the election than do local voters which suggests that people have a greater incentive to be informed about local issues. On the other hand, local issues are less important than national issues and there is less free information (e.g. from Jon Stewart) about local issues than about national issues, which suggests local voters would be even more rationally ignorant than national voters.

Page 387

1. Because of the benefits that special interest receive from current programs, they would fight against the setting up of a commission to examine federal waste. If the commission was set up, these special interest would then try to "capture" the commission: argue that their specific programs were needed, and exert political pressure to keep these programs. The bearers of the costs of these programs—the taxpayers—are too large and diverse a group to zero in on any particular program. The commission idea might be popular but the chance for it succeeding is low.

2. The beneficiaries of the local history collection at the library are the users of the collection. Ultimately, the taxpayers of the state pay for it. Benefits are concentrated on a small group, while the costs are spread over a large body of people (the taxpayers). Don't be surprised if the reading room is named after the state senator!

Page 389

1. If voters are myopic, politicians could prefer a policy with small gains now and big costs later (let's get reelected and maybe someone else will have to deal with the large costs down the road) than a policy with small costs now and large gains later (why jeopardize my chance to get reelected?). For these reasons, dealing with a large potential problem such as the fiscal sustainability of Medicare is often put off until the last minute when the solutions are much more difficult and costly.

Page 397

1. The free flow of ideas helps democracies function by getting alternatives out and on the table. Voters will always be rationally ignorant to some extent but the more information that is out there and available at low cost the more voters will be informed, at least about the big issues. Debate and dissent can improve the quality of ideas. The free flow of information reduces the possibility of corruption. New ideas help democracies adapt to changing conditions.

Chapter 20

Page 409

1. The purchase of wheat flour used to make bread is the purchase of an intermediate good. Thus, it is not counted in GDP: only final goods are counted in GDP.

2. Pokemon cards were counted in GDP when they were first produced. Selling used Pokemon cards on eBay does not contribute to GDP.

3. Because the worker from Colombia earns his money in New York, this is considered part of the GDP of the United States, not Colombia. GDP counts what is produced within a country, whether by its citizens or others.

Page 409

1. The growth rate is found by subtracting $5,803 billion from $5,995 billion, and then dividing that number by $5,803 billion:

   ($5,995 − $5,803)/$5,803 = $192/$5,803 = 0.033 or 3.3 percent

Page 412

1. China has a high GDP but a low GDP per capita.

2. Of the top 15 countries by GDP ranked in Table 5.1, Canada, Spain, and South Korea have GDP under $1 trillion but have considerable GDP per capita.

3. We convert nominal variables into real variables to account for price changes so that we can make comparisons over time.

Page 413

1. Business fluctuations are the short-run movements in real GDP around its long-term trend.

2. It is sometimes difficult to determine if an economy is in a recession because of simple data problems: it takes time to collect data, then the conclusions drawn from the data may be revised once additional data become available after additional time has passed.

Page 416

1. Consumption (C) is the largest component of national expenditure, averaging 64.5 percent.

2. Consumption expenditures are more stable than investment expenditures. It's usually easier to delay investment than consumption so consumption normally varies only slightly, but investment expenditure can vary dramatically, especially in an economic downturn, as businesses hold off on investment. For these reasons, the part of consumption that is most volatile is consumption of durable goods such as cars and major appliances because the purchase these goods can usually be easily delayed.

3. The income approach is the flip side of the spending approach: every dollar that someone earns in income is a dollar of income that someone else has spent.

Page 420

1. GDP measures things for which market values can be obtained. It does not measure things such as illegal activities or clean air because it is difficult to determine their market values.

2. Two countries that have the same level of GDP per capita do not necessarily have the same level of inequality. Let's take Country A and Country B, each of which has only two citizens. Country A's citizens earn $999 and $1, respectively, with GDP per capita of $500. Country B's citizens earn $500 and $500, respectively, with GDP per capita of $500 also. Note that the two countries have the same GDP per capita but they have different levels of inequality.

3. Because they do not account for everything, GDP statistics are not perfect. Nevertheless, they are useful in giving a good sense of how the value of what a nation produces changes over time.

Chapter 21

Page 433

1. According to Figure 6.2, approximately 30 percent of the world's population lived in China in 2000.

2. Using the rule of 70, if you make 5 percent on your savings, it will take 70/5 or 12 years for your savings to double. At 8 percent, it will take 70/8 or a little under 9 years to double.

3. According to Figure 6.4, Japan's real GDP per capita crossed the $10,000 barrier around 1970 and the $20,000 barrier around 1990. Using the rule of 70, we know that it took 20 years to double, or $70/x = 20$. Therefore, the growth rate was approximately 3.5 percent per year over this time span.

Page 435

1. The United States has much more physical capital—tools, machines, equipment—than China, but China has more than Nigeria.

2. Physical capital, human capital, and technological knowledge are the three primary factors of production.

Page 442

1. Five institutions that promote economic growth are property rights, honest government, political stability, a dependable legal system, and competitive and open markets.

2. The Wars of the Roses were a time of civil war. Economic growth tends to decline in such times. During Henry VII's unquestioned reign, economic growth picked up dramatically.

3. Under a system of collective farming where corn production was shared, increased individual effort would bring very little reward to the individual. Because individual incentives were poor, you would expect limited corn production, maybe even starvation.

Chapter 22

Page 460

1. As more capital is added, the marginal product of capital declines.

2. Capital depreciates because machines wear out over time and have to replaced, roads wear out and need to be repaired or replaced, bridges wear out. As the capital stock increases, the total amount of capital depreciation increases.

Page 461

1. In Figure 7.8, when the capital stock is 400, depreciation is higher than investment.

2. When capital is 400, investment is 6 units.

3. When capital is 400, depreciation is 8 units.

4. When depreciation is greater than investment, the capital stock shrinks.

Page 466

1. At the steady state level of capital, investment and depreciation are equal.

2. In Figure 7.9, output is 15 units available to be consumed in the old steady state, and 20 units in the new steady state.

3. The farther they are below their steady state level, the faster countries can grow.

4. Countries with higher investment rates have higher GDP per capita.

Page 470

1. High tax rates on imports would reduce trade and thus lower the incentive to produce new ideas.

2. Spillovers occur when ideas benefit other consumers and firms, besides the creator of the idea. If the creator of an idea cannot get the full benefit of the idea, this will reduce the incentive to generate new ideas.

3. The economic reason to support a prize for malaria research rather than cancer research is that the incentive to produce cancer drugs is already high because of a large and wealthy market. Malaria tends to be located in poorer countries where people have a lower ability to pay for drugs and thus the incentive to develop new drugs is lower.

Chapter 23

Page 487

1. Financial institutions build a bridge between savers and borrowers.

2. If people have saved enough for their retirement, they can have a smooth consumption path over their lives. If greater life expectancy

means that not enough has been saved for retirement, then consumption during the retirement years will have to be lower than currently planned. Thus, the consumption path throughout their lifetimes will not be smooth.

3. Other than retirement, numerous potential things can generate a demand to save because these things can cause income to be volatile: loss of a job, chronic illness, or accidents that cause some bodily harm. One saves for a rainy day.

Page 489

1. Under the lifecycle theory, individual savings are likely to be at their peak during an individual's prime earning years.

2. If interest rates fall from 7 percent to 5 percent, all else being equal, this is a fall in the price of borrowed funds. This fall in price will encourage more people to buy homes (they now may be able to afford something they could not afford before) or start businesses.

Page 492

1. Greater patience will shift the supply of savings curve to the right, leading to an increase in the quantity of savings and a decrease in the equilibrium interest rate.

2. An increase in investment demand shifts the demand curve to the right, leading to an increase in the equilibrium interest rate and an increase in the quantity of funds demanded and supplied.

Page 498

1. The primary role of financial intermediaries is to reduce the costs of moving savings from savers to borrowers and investors.

2. Interest rates and bond prices move in opposite directions. If you own a bond paying 6 percent in interest and the interest rate falls to 4 percent, the price of the bond must go up. If interest rates rise to 8 percent, the price of the 6 percent bond must fall.

3. An IPO is a first-time sale of a firm's stock to the market, and so usually increases net investment: the firm can take this new capital and use it to expand the business. Buying shares of stock from someone else, in contrast, is buying shares already issued and represents a transfer of ownership, not a net increase to investment: the firm does not get the purchase price of the stock.

Page 503

1. Usury laws are price ceilings. Remember from Chapter 4 that price ceilings cause shortages. If savers can get only the ceiling rate rather than the market rate for their savings, they will save less.

2. Bank failures can hinder financial intermediation in a variety of ways. If savers become reluctant to put their money in banks, for example, the supply of credit will decline and the cost of borrowing will rise. This can lead to a credit crisis as credit dries up.

3. Lending money to political cronies or pals lowers the efficiency of the economy because loans do not go to their highest-valued uses.

Chapter 24

Page 516

1. To be counted as unemployed in the United States, as well as not working, you have to be an adult (16 years or older), not institutionalized (not in jail), a civilian (not a soldier), and actively looking for work.

2. The labor force is defined as all workers, employed and unemployed.

3. The labor force participation rate varies slightly year to year but is approximately 66 percent (2008). It is defined as the labor force (consisting of employed and unemployed workers) divided by all adult non-institutionalized civilians.

Page 517

1. Frictional unemployment is caused by the ordinary difficulties of matching employee to employer. A reason for the difficulty of matching employer to employee is scarcity of information.

2. Some frictional unemployment is not bad if it means that prospective employers and prospective employees take the time to determine whether they are a good fit. Being forced to take the first job offered is not a good way to establish a good fit.

Page 524

1. Structural unemployment is persistent, long-term unemployment caused by long-lasting shocks or permanent features of an economy that make it more difficult for some workers to find jobs.

2. In the United States, "employment at will" fairly accurately describes the employment situation: employees may quit at any time and employers may fire an employee at any time and for any reason. In contrast, laws in Western European countries hinder the ability of employers to act at will. For example, in Portugal any business must get the government's permission to lay off workers, and even then the business must follow guidelines as to who can be laid off first.

Page 527

1. Cyclical unemployment is determined by the business cycle. It increases during a recession and decreases during a boom.

2. Lower growth is correlated with increasing unemployment; higher growth is correlated with decreasing unemployment.

Page 532

1. Lowering the marginal tax rate for married couples provided an incentive for more women to enter the labor force because they could now keep more of their pay rather than have it taxed away.

2. Raising the age that one can obtain Social Security benefits increases the incentive to stay in the labor force longer, thus increasing the labor force participation rate.

Chapter 25

Page 542

1. Using the formula on page 218, $(125 - 120)/120 = 4.16$ percent.
2. If the inflation rate goes from 1 percent to 4 percent to 7 percent over a period of two years, the prices of a great majority of goods are likely to go up.
3. Use real prices rather than nominal prices to compare the price of goods over time. Real prices subtract out the effect of inflation and thus give a better measure of whether a particular good is becoming more or less expensive over time compared to most other goods and services.

Page 546

1. In the long run, inflation is always and everywhere a monetary phenomenon: growth in the money supply causes inflation.
2. The quantity theory of money is $Mv = PY$.

Page 552

1. Under unexpected inflation, wealth is redistributed from lenders to borrowers. Under unexpected disinflation, wealth is redistributed from borrowers to lenders.
2. When the expected inflation rate increases, nominal interest rates rise to compensate. We call this the Fisher effect.
3. Unexpected inflation distorts price signals. They become more difficult to interpret. This leads to waste.

Chapter 26

Page 567

1. If inflation is 2 percent and climbs to 5 percent, this does not affect the Solow growth curve, the economy's fundamental ability to produce goods and services.
2. Because $\vec{M} + \vec{v} = \vec{P} + \vec{Y}_R$ in the dynamic AD/AS model, if $\vec{M}$ equals 7 percent and $\vec{v}$ equals 0 percent, by definition inflation plus real growth will equal 7 percent. If in this situation we find that real growth equal 0 percent, then inflation must be 7 percent.
3. Increased spending growth shifts the dynamic aggregate demand curve outward.

Page 570

1. A technological innovation such as the Internet shifts the Solow growth curve to the right.

2. In the real business cycle model, a large fall in aggregate demand has no effect on real growth.

Page 575

1. The New Keynesian model presumes significant wage and price stickiness. The real business cycle model is based on flexible prices and wages.

2. The Solow growth curve is vertical because price and wage stickiness do not affect the fundamental productive capacity of the economy over the long run. However, price and wage stickiness do affect aggregate supply in the short run, and this accounts for the fact that the SRAS curve is *not* vertical.

3. When people expect inflation to increase from 2 percent to 3 percent, the SRAS shifts up and to the left.

Page 579

1. In the long run, unexpected inflation always becomes expected inflation.

2. If consumers fear a recession and cut back on their expenditures, the dynamic aggregate demand curve will shift inward.

Page 582

1. The U.S. money supply fell in the early 1930s. This initially affected aggregate demand (the AD curve shifted inward—down/left), not the Solow growth curve. The decrease in aggregate demand resulted in bank failures that decreased the productivity of financial intermediation, which was a real shock, and so affected the Solow growth curve, shifting it to the left.

2. In an ordinary year, the real shocks of the 1930s might have been shrugged off but the combination of large shocks to AD and real shocks at the same time made the Great Depression great.

Chapter 27

Page 593

1. Putting down phone lines is very expensive, compared to the cost of putting up cell-phone towers. Cell phones have improved communications in all countries, but the change has been most dramatic in less-developed countries. This has been a positive shock throughout the world.

2. A large and sudden increase in taxes would suppress economic activity especially in the short run as consumers and firms reallocated from more energy intensive sectors of the economy to less energy intensive sectors. The reallocation would decrease the fundamental capacity of the economy to produce goods and services, which is a shift of the Solow growth curve to the left.

Page 602

1. The 9/11 attacks brought a high level of uncertainty into the economy. No one knew if more attacks were planned so no one wanted to be on an airplane. Cutting back on air travel hurt the airlines and all associated businesses: airports, airport services such as food vendors, companies that provide transportation to and from airports. When no one flew on airplanes to take business trips, some local business trips were still undertaken (by train or car), but longer trips (such as cross-country travel) came to a standstill. As travel declined, so did the need for hotel rooms and restaurant meals out. Hotels were hit hard: cutting the price of hotel rooms had little effect when uncertainty dried up business travel. The near-cessation in business travel amplified the economic effects of the attacks nationwide: attacks in New York had nationwide repercussions.

Chapter 28

Page 613

1. The monetary base is defined as currency plus reserves held by banks at the Fed.

2. In November 2007, there was $764 billion of currency in the United States compared to around $600 billion in checkable deposits. Thus, currency accounts for more than checkable deposits.

Page 615

1. If the reserve ratio is 1/20, then 5 percent of deposits are kept as reserves.

2. If the reserve ratio is 1/20, then the money multiplier is 20.

3. If the Fed increases bank reserves by $10,000 and the reserve ratio is 1/20, then the change in the money supply is $200,000.

Page 620

1. The Fed wants to lower interest rates. It does so by *buying* bonds in open market operations. By doing this, the Fed *adds* reserves and through the multiplier process, it *increases* the money supply.

Page 621

1. The Fed might not let a large bank fail if it fears systemic risk, the possibility that the failure will bring down other banks and financial institutions. In this case, the Fed will use its powers as the lender of last resort to support a bank that is "too big to fail."

2. Moral hazard increases my incentives to double my bet to make up for a large loss. If the Fed always bails out large banks, my actions will never lead to the bank's bankruptcy, so why not take the chance?

Page 623

1. Money is neutral in the long run but has a short-run effect on the economy. This explains the Fed's concerns with the money supply in the short run.

2. If banks are afraid of a recession, they will be more reluctant to lend. This will hamper the Fed's ability to shift aggregate demand in a recession. In this case, the Fed is sometimes said to be "pushing on a string."

Chapter 29

Page 639

1. Data problems affect the Fed's ability to set monetary policy that is "just right" because they make it difficult for the Fed to determine just what is

going on with the economy. If the Fed does not know exactly what is going on, it cannot prescribe the correct medicine.

2. Milton Friedman argued for a 3 percent money growth rate because the long-run growth rate for the U.S. economy trends around 3 percent. When money growth equals long-run growth in the economy, there will be a tendency for price stability.

Page 642

1. Looking at Figure 15.4, if the Fed wanted to restore some growth to the economy, it could work to increase aggregate demand. The problem is that increasing growth in this case comes at the expense of adding more inflation. This is the policy dilemma.

2. If the Fed increases AD every time in response to a series of negative real shocks, the inflation rate will climb. Eventually, the Fed will have to act to reduce inflation, possibly pushing the economy into a recession.

Page 644

1. The Fed can never be certain when asset prices reach the bubble stage. Bubbles are easier to identify with hindsight but even then identification is a judgment call.

2. Collateral damage to a contraction in the money supply could be reducing the growth rate for GDP for the broader economy as a whole.

Chapter 30

Page 662

1. Customs duties now account for only 1.2 percent of federal revenues.

2. Individual income taxes plus Social Security and other payroll taxes represent 82 percent of federal revenues.

3. A person in the fourth quintile pays an effective federal tax rate of 17.4 percent. On an income of $80,000, this would be $13,920 in tax. A person in the top quintile pays an effective rate of 25.5 percent on income of $160,000, thus a tax of $40,800. Because the person who made twice as much paid more than twice as much in tax, this gives evidence of progressivity in the tax system.

Page 669

1. Social Security and Medicare spending currently account for 36.5 percent of federal spending.

2. GDP gives us an idea of the capacity of the economy to pay debt so the debt-to-GDP ratio tells us what the debt is relative to the capacity to pay the debt.

Page 672

1. In the next 40 years, Social Security and especially Medicare and Medicaid are likely to increase relative to GDP. This means that the level of overall government spending relative to GDP is likely to increase.

2. If the pace of idea generation quickens, this will lead to a positive shift in the Solow growth curve. In other words, the economy will be able to

produce more goods and services. This would lead to a decrease in the debt-to-GDP ratio (all other things equal). This would increase the government's ability to pay for increased benefits for retirees.

Chapter 31

Page 682

1. The two types of expansionary fiscal policy are the government spends more money, or the government cuts taxes and thereby gives people more money to spend.

Page 692

1. The 2008 tax rebate was less powerful than expected because many people saved the rebate and paid down debt, rather than spending it.

2. A permanent cut in income tax rates can generate a larger fiscal stimulus than a temporary cut because people likely will save a large portion of a temporary tax cut, to pay for future taxes. But if the tax cut is permanent, they may choose to spend more. Of course, telling people that a tax cut is permanent is quite different from getting people to believe that it is permanent!

3. A permanent investment tax credit produces a smaller fiscal stimulus than a temporary investment tax credit because to get the temporary tax credit firms must spend money on equipment right away but a permanent investment tax credit gives firms the option of waiting to invest.

Chapter 32

Page 707

1. If an inhabitant of Nebraska buys a German sports car for $30,000, this lowers the U.S. current account balance by $30,000.

2. If a German sports car manufacturer opens a new plant in South Carolina, this investment is a capital account surplus for the United States.

3. The current and capital accounts are two sides of the same coin. When the capital account is in surplus, the current account will tend to mirror that in deficit, and vice versa.

Page 714

1. If the U.S. dollar is a safe haven currency, then in times of risk people will demand dollars, increasing their value.

2. If the Fed increases the money supply, this will reduce the value of the dollar compared to the euro.

3. If purchasing power parity holds and the nominal exchange rate is one pound for two dollars, a Big Mac should cost £2 in London if it costs $4.00 in New York.

4. A tariff will hinder market exchange and thus the arbitrage of differing prices. This limits purchasing power parity.

Page 716

1. In the short run, a Fed increase in the money supply will cause a depreciation in the exchange rate, leading to an increase in U.S. exports. In the long run, the temporary boost to exports will dissipate, and the increase in the money supply will lead to inflation.

2. In an open economy, monetary policy is more effective than fiscal policy. Expansionary monetary policy will tend to reduce interest rates, causing a currency depreciation and increased exports. In contrast, expansionary fiscal policy will tend to increase interest rates, causing an appreciation of the exchange rate and reduced exports.

Page 718

1. A floating exchange rate describes when the value of a country's currency is determined by the forces of supply and demand.

2. The European Central Bank controls the monetary policy of the European Union.

GLOSSARY

absolute advantage the ability to produce the same good using fewer inputs than another producer

active labor market policies policies that focus on getting unemployed workers back to work, such as job-search assistance, job-retraining programs, and work tests

alternative minimum tax (AMT) a separate income tax code, begun in 1969 to prevent the rich from not paying income taxes; not indexed to inflation and thus now an extra tax burden on many upper middle class families

antitrust laws laws that give the government the power to regulate or prohibit business practices that may be anti-competitive

appreciation an increase in the price of one currency in terms of another currency

arbitrage the practice of taking advantage of price differences for the same good in different markets by buying low in one market and selling high in another market

automatic stabilizers changes in fiscal policy that stimulate AD in a recession without the need for explicit action by policymakers; unemployment insurance is one example of an automatic stabilizer

average cost the cost per unit; the total cost of producing a given quantity divided by that quantity, AC=TC/Q

average tax rate the total tax payment divided by total income

baby boomers people born during the high–birth rate years of 1946–1964

balance of payments a yearly summary of all the economic transactions between residents of one country and residents of the rest of the world

barriers to entry factors that increase the cost to new firms of entering an industry

bond a sophisticated IOU that documents who owes how much and when payment must be made

bundling the requirement that products be bought together in a bundle or package

business fluctuations or **business cycles** the short-run movements in real GDP around its long-term trend

buy and hold the practice of buying stocks and then holding them for the long run, regardless of what prices do in the short run

capital account in the balance of payments, the account that measures changes in foreign ownership of domestic assets, including financial assets like stocks and bonds as well as physical assets

capital surplus the excess that exists when the inflow of foreign capital into a country is greater than the outflow of domestic capital to other nations

cartel a group of suppliers that tries to act *as if* they were a monopoly

Coase theorem the principle that if transactions costs are low and property rights are clearly defined, private bargains will ensure that the market equilibrium is efficient even when there are externalities

collateral something of value that by agreement becomes the property of the lender if the borrower defaults

common resources goods that are nonexcludable but rival

comparative advantage the ability to produce a good or service at a lower opportunity cost than another producer

compensating differential a difference in wages that offsets differences in working conditions for otherwise similar jobs

complements two goods for which a decrease in the price of one leads to an increase in the demand for the other, e.g. hamburgers and hamburger buns

conditional convergence the tendency—among countries with similar steady state levels of output—for poorer countries to grow faster than richer countries and thus for poor and rich countries to converge in income

constant cost industry an industry in which costs of production do not change with greater industry output; shown with a flat supply curve

consumer surplus the consumer's gain from exchange, or the difference between the maximum price a consumer is willing to pay for a certain quantity and the market price

consumer surplus (total) an amount measured by the area beneath the demand curve and above the price up to the quantity traded

consumption private spending on final goods and services

corporate culture the shared collection of values and norms that govern how people interact in an organization or firm

credible referring to a monetary policy when it is expected that a central bank will stick with that policy

crowding out the decrease in private consumption and investment that occurs when government borrows more; also, the decrease in private spending that occurs when government increases spending

current account in the balance of payments, the sum of the balance of trade, net income on capital held abroad, and net transfer payments

cyclical unemployment unemployment correlated with the business cycle

deadweight loss the total of lost consumer and producer surplus when not all mutually profitable gains from trade are exploited

decreasing cost industry an industry in which the costs of production decrease with an increase in industry output; shown with a downward sloping supply curve

deficit, fiscal the annual difference that results when federal government spending exceeds revenues

deficit, trade see trade deficit

deflation a decrease in the average level of prices; i.e., a negative inflation rate

demand curve a function that shows the quantity demanded at different prices.

depreciation a decrease in the price of a currency in terms of another currency

dirty or managed float a currency whose value is not fixed but for which governments will intervene extensively in the market to keep its value within a certain range

discount rate the interest rate banks pay when they borrow directly from the Fed at the discount window

discouraged workers jobless individuals who have given up looking for work but who would still like to find a job

disinflation a reduction in the inflation rate

dollarization a foreign country's use of the U.S. dollar as its currency

dominant strategy a strategy that has a higher payoff than any other strategy no matter the strategies of other players

economic growth the growth rate of real GDP per capita.

economies of scale the advantages of large-scale production that reduce average cost as quantity increases

efficient equilibrium the price and quantity that maximizes social surplus

efficient market hypothesis the claim that the prices of traded assets

reflect all publicly available information

efficient quantity the quantity that maximizes social surplus

$$\text{elasticity of demand} = \frac{\%\Delta Q_D}{\%\Delta P}$$

a measure of how responsive the quantity demanded is to a change in price

$$\text{elasticity of supply} = \frac{\%\Delta Q_S}{\%\Delta P}$$

a measure of how responsive the quantity supplied is to a change in price

elimination principle the principle that in a competitive market, above normal profits are eliminated by entry and below normal profits are eliminated by exit

employment at-will doctrine the policy that an employee may quit and an employer may fire an employee at any time and for any reason; the most basic U.S. employment law despite many exceptions to it

equilibrium price the price at which the quantity demanded is equal to the quantity supplied

equilibrium quantity the quantity at which the quantity demanded is equal to the quantity supplied

exchange rate the price of one currency in terms of another currency

external benefit a benefit received by people other than the consumers or producers trading in the market

external cost a cost borne by people other than the consumer or the producer trading in the market

externalities external costs or external benefits

federal funds rate the overnight lending rate from one major bank to another

financial intermediaries institutions such as banks, bond markets, and stock markets that reduce the costs of moving funds from savers to borrowers and investors

fiscal policy federal government policy on taxes, spending, and borrowing

that is designed to influence business fluctuations

Fisher effect the tendency of nominal interest rates to rise one to one with expected inflation rates

fixed costs costs that do not vary with output

fixed exchange rate (also known as a **pegged exchange rate**) an exchange rate based on the promise of a government or central bank to convert its currency into another currency at a fixed (set) rate.

flat tax a tax rate that is constant across income levels

floating exchange rate an exchange rate determined primarily by market forces

forced rider someone who pays a share of the costs of a public good but who does not enjoy the benefits

fractional reserve banking a system in which banks hold only a portion of deposits in reserve, lending the rest

free rider someone who consumes the benefits of a public good without paying a share of the costs

frictional unemployment short-term unemployment caused by the ordinary difficulties of matching employee to employer

futures a standardized contract to buy or sell specified quantities of a commodity or financial instrument at a specified price with delivery set at a specified time in the future

GDP (gross domestic product) per capita GDP divided by population

government purchases spending by all levels of government on final goods and services not including transfers

gross domestic product (GDP) the market value of all final goods and services produced within a country in a year

gross national product the market value of all final goods and services produced by a country's permanent residents, wherever located, in a year

human capital tools of the mind, the stuff in people's heads that makes them productive; the productive knowledge and skills that workers acquire through education, training, and experience

illiquid bank a bank whose short-term liabilities are greater than its short-term assets but overall has assets that are greater than its liabilities

incentives rewards and penalties that motivate behavior

increasing cost industry an industry in which the costs of production increase with greater output; shown with an upward sloped supply curve

inferior good a good for which demand decreases when income increases

inflation an increase in the general or average level of prices.

inflation rate the percentage increase in the average level of prices (as measured by a price index) over a period of time

initial public offering (IPO) the first instance of a corporation selling stock to the public in order to raise capital

insolvent bank a bank whose liabilities are greater in value than its assets

institutions the "rules of the game" that structure economic incentives

intertemporal substitution the allocation of consumption, work, and leisure across time to maximize well-being

investment expenditures private spending on tools, plant, and equipment used to produce future output; i.e., the purchase of new capital goods

invisible hand property #1 even though no actor in a market economy intends to do so, in a free market $P = MC_1 = MC_2 = \ldots = MC_N$ and as a result the total costs of production are minimized

invisible hand property #2 entry and exit decisions not only work to eliminate profits, they work to ensure that labor and capital move across industries to optimally balance production so that the greatest use is made of limited resources

irreversible investments investments that cannot be easily moved, adjusted, or reversed if conditions change

labor adjustment costs the costs of shifting workers from declining sectors of the economy to growing sectors

labor force all workers, employed plus unemployed

labor force participation rate the percentage of adults in the labor force

law of one price the principle that if trade were free, then identical goods should sell for about the same price throughout the world

lender of last resort a lender that loans money to banks and other financial institutions when no one else will, often a central bank or a country's Treasury or Finance department

liquid asset an asset that can be used for payments or, quickly and without loss of value, be converted into an asset that can be used for payments

liquidity crisis a situation that occurs when banks do not have enough liquid assets to meet their liability demands

long run the time it takes for substantial new investment and entry to occur

marginal cost $\frac{\Delta TC}{\Delta Q}$, the change in total cost from producing an additional unit

marginal product of labor (MPL) the increase in a firm's revenues created by hiring an additional laborer

marginal revenue $\frac{\Delta TR}{\Delta Q}$, the change in total revenue from selling an additional unit

marginal tax rate the tax rate paid on an additional dollar of income

market for loanable funds the market where suppliers of loanable funds (savers) trade with demanders of loanable funds (borrowers), thereby determining the equilibrium interest rate

market power the power to raise prices above marginal cost without fear that other firms will enter the market

median voter theorem the principle that when voters vote for the policy that is closest to their ideal point on a line, then the ideal point of the median voter will beat any other policy in a majority rule election

median wage the wage such that one-half of all workers earn wages below that amount and one-half of all workers earn wages above that amount

monetizing the debt the result of government paying off its debts by printing money

money a widely accepted means of payment

money illusion the false perception that occurs when people mistake changes in nominal prices for changes in real prices

money multiplier, MM the amount the money supply expands with each dollar increase in reserves; MM = 1/RR where RR is the reserve ratio

monopoly a firm with market power

moral hazard the situation that exists when people who are insulated from risk tend to take on more risk; in macroeconomics, occurs when banks and other financial institutions take on too much risk, expecting that the Fed and regulators will later bail them out

multiplier effect the additional increase in aggregate demand caused when expansionary fiscal policy increases income and thus consumption and investment spending

Nash equilibrium a situation in which no player has an incentive to change strategy unilaterally

national debt held by the public all federal debt held outside the U.S. government

natural monopoly a situation when a single firm can supply the entire market at a lower cost than two or more firms

natural rate of unemployment the rate of structural plus frictional unemployment

net exports the value of exports minus the value of imports

network good a good whose value to one consumer increases the more that other consumers use the good

nominal exchange rate the rate at which you can exchange one currency for another

nominal variables variables, such as nominal GDP, that have not been adjusted for changes in prices

nonexcludable when people who don't pay cannot easily be prevented from using the good the good is nonexcludable

nonrival (or nonrivalrous) goods when one person's use of the good does not reduce the ability of another person to use the same good the good is nonrival

nonrival private goods goods that are excludable but nonrival

normal good a good for which demand increases when income increases

normative economics recommendations or arguments about what economic policy should be

oligopoly a market dominated by a small number of firms

open market operations the buying and selling of government bonds by the Fed

opportunity cost the value of possibilities lost when a choice is made

perfect price discrimination (PPD) the situation that exists when each customer is charged his or her maximum willingness to pay

physical capital the stock of tools including machines, structures, and equipment

piece rate any payment system that pays workers directly for their output

Pigouvian subsidy a subsidy on a good with external benefits

Pigouvian tax a tax on a good with external costs

positive economics describing, explaining, or predicting without making recommendations

prediction market a speculative market designed so that prices can be interpreted as probabilities and used to make predictions

price ceiling a maximum price allowed by law

price discrimination the selling of the same product at different prices to different customers

price floor a minimum price allowed by law

prisoner's dilemma situations where the pursuit of individual interest leads to a group outcome that is in the interest of no one

private cost a cost paid by the consumer or the producer (as opposed to external cost)

private goods goods that are excludable and rival goods

producer surplus the producer's gain from exchange, or the difference between the market price and the minimum price at which a producer would be willing to sell a particular quantity

producer surplus (total) an amount measured by the area above the supply curve and below the price up to the quantity traded

progressive tax a type of tax that imposes higher tax rates on people with higher incomes

protectionism the economic policy of restraining trade through quotas, tariffs, or other regulations that burden foreign producers but not domestic producers

public goods goods that are nonexcludable and nonrival goods

purchasing power parity theorem the principle that the real purchasing power of money should be roughly the same, whether it is spent at home or converted into another currency and spent abroad

quantity demanded the quantity that buyers are willing and able to buy at a particular price

quantity supplied the quantity that sellers are willing and able to sell at a particular price

rational ignorance when the benefits of being informed are less than the costs of becoming informed a person may be rationally ignorant

real exchange rate the rate at which you can exchange the goods and services of one country for the goods and services of another

real price a price that has been corrected for inflation; used to compare the prices of goods over time

real variables variables such as real GDP, that have been adjusted for changes in prices by using the same set of prices in all time periods

recession a significant, widespread decline in real income and employment

regressive tax a type of tax that imposes higher tax rates on people with lower incomes

required reserves the minimum percentage of reserves a bank is required to hold, as dictated by the Fed

reserve ratio (RR) the ratio of reserves to deposits

Ricardian equivalence the theory according to which people understand that, for a given level of government spending, lower taxes today mean higher taxes in the future and therefore save the money from a tax cut to pay future taxes; when Ricardian equivalence holds, a tax cut doesn't increase aggregate demand even in the short run

risk-return trade-off higher returns come at the price of higher risk

saving income that is not spent on consumption goods

shocks rapid changes in economic conditions that affect the productivity of capital and labor

shortage a situation in which the quantity demanded is greater than the quantity supplied

short run the period before entry occurs

social cost the cost to everyone; the private cost plus the external cost

social surplus consumer surplus plus producer surplus plus everyone else's surplus

solvency crisis a situation that exists when many banks are insolvent; i.e., have liabilities greater in value than assets

speculation the attempt to profit from future price changes

statistical discrimination discrimination using information about group averages to make conclusions about individuals

steady state in a model of economic growth, a situation in which the capital stock is neither increasing nor decreasing

strategic decision making decision making in situations that are interactive

structural unemployment persistent, long-term unemployment caused by long-lasting shocks or permanent features of an economy that make it more difficult for some workers to find jobs

substitutes two goods for which a decrease in the price of one leads to a decrease in demand for the other

supply curve a function that shows the quantity supplied at different prices

surplus a situation in which the quantity supplied is greater than the quantity demanded

systemic risk the risk that the failure of one financial institution can bring down other institutions as well

tariff a tax on imports

technological knowledge knowledge about how the world works that is used to produce goods and services

time bunching the tendency for economic activities to be coordinated at common points in time

time preference the desire to have goods and services sooner rather than later (all else being equal)

total cost the cost of producing a given quantity of output

total revenue price times quantity sold: $TR = P \times Q$

tournament a compensation scheme in which payment is based on relative performance

trade deficit the annual difference that results when the value of a country's imports exceeds the value of its exports

trade quota a restriction on the quantity of goods that can be imported: imports greater than the quota amount are forbidden or heavily taxed

trade surplus the annual difference that results when the value of a country's exports exceeds the value of its imports

tragedy of the commons the tendency of any resource that is unowned and hence nonexcludable to be overused and undermaintained

transaction costs the costs necessary to reach an agreement

transmission mechanisms economic forces that can amplify shocks and transmit them across time and sectors of the economy

tying a form of price discrimination in which one good, called the base good, is tied to a second good called the variable good, e.g. printer and ink

unemployed workers adults who do not have a job but who are looking for work

unemployment rate the percentage of the labor force who are unemployed

union an association of workers that bargains collectively with employers over wages, benefits, and working conditions

variable costs costs that vary with output

velocity of money, v the average number of times a dollar is spent on final goods and services in a year

zero profits or normal profits the condition when $P = AC$; at this price the firm is covering all of its costs including enough to pay labor and capital their ordinary opportunity costs

REFERENCES

Chapter 1 Notes

1. Quoted in **Christopher, Emma**. 2007. " 'The Slave Trade is Merciful Compare to [this]': Slave Traders, Convict Transportation and the Abolitionists." In **Christopher, E., C. Pybus, & M. Rediker** (eds.). 2007. *Many Middle Passages*. Chapter 6: 109–128. Berkeley, CA: University of California Press.

2. **Chadwick, Edwin.** 1862. "Opening Address of the British Association for the Advancement of Science." *Journal of the Statistical Society of London*, 25(4): 502–524.

3. **Chadwick** op cit.

4. On the impact of new drugs, see **Lichtenberg, Frank**. 2007. "The Impact of New Drugs on U.S. Longevity and Medical Expenditure, 1990–2003." *American Economic Review*, 97(2): 438–443.

5. **Celis 3rd, William**. 1991. "Study Finds Enrollment is Up at Colleges Despite Recession." *The New York Times*, December 28.

Chapter 2 Notes

1. On changing U.S. demographics and their impact on the economy, see **Kotlikoff, Laurence J. & Scott Burns**. 2004. *The Coming Generational Storm*. Cambridge, MA: MIT Press.

2. *International Herald Tribune*, http://www.iht.com/articles/ap/2007/07/31/business/EU-FIN-MKT-Oil-Prices.php

3. Information Resources Inc. 2005. Times and Trends. September 16.

4. The Paleontological Research Institution, http://www.priweb.org/ed/pgws/history/spindletop/lucas_gusher.html.

5. Energy Information Institute, http://www.eia.doe.gov/emeu/perfpro/btab22.html

6. On the costs of oil production, see OPEC and the High Price of Oil, Joint Economic Committee, United States Congress, http://www.house.gov/jec/publications/109/11–17–05opec.pdf.

Chapter 3 Notes

1. **Smith, Vernon**. 1991. Experimental Economics at Purdue, in *Papers in Experimental Economics*, ed. **Smith, V.**, Cambridge, England: Cambridge University Press, originally appeared in *Essays in Contemporary Fields of Economics*, edited by **Horwich, G. & J. P. Quirk**, Purdue University Press, 1981.

2. **Conover, Ted**. 2006. "Capitalist Roaders." *New York Times Magazine*, July 2: 31–37, 50.

Chapter 4 Notes

1. See International Money Fund. 2005. World Economic Outlook—2005, Chapter 4. Washington, DC: IMF.

2. On the elasticity of demand for oil see **Cooper, John C. B.** 2003. Price Elasticity of Demand for Crude Oil: Estimates for 23 Countries. *OPEC Review* 27(1):1–8. On the elasticity of demand for Minute Maid orange juice, see **Capps, Oral Jr. and H. Alan Love**. 2002. Econometric Considerations in the Use of Electronic Scanner Data to Conduct Consumer Demand Analysis. *American Journal of Agricultural Economics* 84(3):807–816.

3. On the elasticity of demand for illegal drugs, see **Cicala, Steve J.** 2005. The Demand for Illicit Drugs: A Meta-analysis of Price Elasticities. Working paper, University of Chicago. On the elasticity of demand for cigarettes, see **Keeler T. E., T. W. Hu, P. G. Barnett, and W. G. Manning.** 1993. Taxation, Regulation, and Addiction: A Demand Function for Cigarettes Based on Time-Series Evidence." *Journal of Health Economics* Apr. 12(1):1–18.

4. On the elasticity of supply for cocoa, see **Burger, K.** 1996. *The European Chocolate Market and the Effects of the Proposed EU Directive*. Amsterdam: Economic and Social Institute, Free University and for the elasticity of supply of coffee, see **Akiyama, T. and P. Varangis.** 1990. The Impact of the International Coffee Agreement on Producing Countries. *World Bank Economic Review* 4(2):157–173.

5. For details on the national program, see the April 28, 2000 press release, President Clinton Announces Gun Buyback Partnership with the District of Columbia, from the Office of the Press Secretary, the White House, available online at http://clinton4.nara.gov/textonly/WH/New/html/2000042 8.html. Also from the Washington police, see http://mpdc.dc.gov/mpdc/cwp/view,a,1242,Q,546745,mpdcNav_GID,1 541,mpdcNav,%7C,.asp. HUD's gun buy back program was ended in 2001 although buybacks continue in many cities. In 2006, for example, the Boston Red Sox donated $25,000 to help Boston's buyback program. See Boston Red Sox press release, July 1, 2006, Red Sox Make $25,000 Donation to City's Gun Buyback Program, available online at http://boston.redsox.mlb.com/NASApp/mlb/news/press_re leases/press_release.jsp?ymd=20060701&content_id=153264 1&vkey=pr_bos&fext=.jsp&c_id=bos.

6. **Callahan, C., F. Rivara, and T. Koepsell.** 1994. Money for Guns: Evaluation of the Seattle Gun Buy-Back Program. *Public Health Reports* 109:472–477.

7. **Welch, William M.** 2008. Critics Take Aim at Gun Buybacks. *USA Today*, March 17.

8. See **Mullin, Wallace P.** 2001. Will Gun Buyback Programs Increase the Quantity of Guns? *International Review of Law and Economics* 21:87–102.

9. For a review of some of the evidence on a variety of crime fighting policies, see **Levitt, Steven D.** 2004. Understanding Why Crime Fell in the 1990s: Four Factors that Explain the Decline and Six that Do Not. *Journal of Economic Perspectives* (18)1:163–190.

10. For Williams's story, see **Gavel, Doug.** 2000. Sophomore Skips Orientation to Free 4,000 Slaves in Sudan. *Harvard University Gazette*. Sept. 28 and for Denver schoolchildren, *PBS OnlineNewsHour* transcript with Jim Lehrer on the Crisis in the Sudan, May 31, 1999, available online at http://www.pbs.org/newshour/bb/africa/jan-june99/sudan.html.

11. **Miniter, Richard.** 1999. The False Promise of Slave Redemption. *The Atlantic Monthly*. 284, 1 (July):63–71. Available online at http://www.theatlantic.com/issues/99jul/9907sudanslaves.htm. Note that although the Miniter article

contains some useful information, it has a confused account of economics. Miniter argues that a low price for slaves means the slave traffickers are being driven out of business and high prices means that slavery is profitable, but one has to ask why the price is low or high. High prices driven by increased demand from slave redeemers is a good sign because it means the slave redeemers are outbidding potential slave traffickers.

12. It is also possible to make predictions about quantities using two similar formulas.

13. The proof of these formulas is not difficult but a bit more advanced than is necessary for this textbook. For a proof, see **McAfee, Preston.** 2006. *Introduction to Economic Analysis.* Available online at http://www.introecon.com.

14. http://www.whitehouse.gov/news/releases/2005/11/20051103-10.html

15. The Klick and Tabarrok and Gruber articles use advanced statistical techniques to argue that the increase in police causes the decrease in crime and the increase in giving causes the decrease in attendance. For more details, see **Klick, J. and A. Tabarrok.** 2005. Using Terror Alert Levels to Estimate the Effect of Police on Crime. *Journal of Law and Economics* 48(1):267–280; **Gruber, Jonathan.** 2004. Pay or Pray? The Impact of Charitable Subsidies on Religious Attendance. *Journal of Public Economics*, 88(12):2635–2655.

Chapter 5 Notes

1. http://www.aboutflowers.com/press_b3b.html

2. Ecuador and Colombia also export millions of roses to the United States.

3. See **Hennock, Mary.** 2002. Kenya's flower farms flourish. *BBC News Online.* Available online at http://news.bbc.co.uk/1/hi/business/1820515.stm, last accessed July 7, 2006. For more on Kenya and the Dutch flower market, also see **McMillan, John.** 2002. *Reinventing the Bazaar.* New York: **W. W. Norton, and Wijnands, Jo.** 2005, Sustainable international networks in the flower industry: Bridging empirical findings and theoretical issues. *International Society for Horticultural Science,* The Hague.

4. See "Ethanol fuel in Brazil" on Wikipedia, http://en.wikipedia.org/wiki/Ethanol_fuel_in_Brazil, for more information.

5. See Ethanol is the new real estate, *New York Times,* Saturday, July 8, 2006, p. B5.

6. Oil Facts, American Petrochemical Institute, http://www.classroom-energy.org/teachers/oilfacts.pdf.

7. See **Williams, Scott.** 2006. Asphalt prices stalling budgets. *Milwaukee Journal Sentinel.* http://www.jsonline.com/story/index.aspx?id=434330.

8. **Smith, Vernon.** 1982. Microeconomic systems as an experimental science. *American Economic Review,* 72:923–955.

9. Federal Highway Administration. 1993. A study of the use of recycled paving material. FHWA-1993-RD-93–147.

10. **Roll, Richard.** 1984. Orange juice and weather. *American Economic Review* 74(5):861–880.

11. For much more on prediction markets and how they can be used to make decisions see **Hanson, Robin D.** 2002. Decision Markets. In Entrepreneurial Economics: Bright Ideas from the Dismal Science, ed. **Alexander Tabarrok,** 79-85. Oxford University Press. Also **Hanson, Robin.** forthcoming. Shall we Vote on Values, But Bet on Beliefs? Journal of Political Philosophy.

12. On polls versus prediction markets, see **Berg, J. E., R. Forsythe, F. D. Nelson, and T. A. Rietz.** 2001. Results from a dozen years of election futures markets research, forthcoming in C. A. Plott and V. Smith (eds.), *Handbook of Experimental Economic Results,* available online at http://www.biz.uiowa.edu/iem/archive/BFNR_2000.pdf and Berg, J. E., F. D. Nelson, and T. A. Rietz. 2003. Accuracy and forecast standard error of prediction markets, Working Paper, Tippie College of Business, available online at http://www.biz.uiowa.edu/iem/archive/forecasting.pdf.

Chapter 6 notes

1. See **Bradley, Robert L.** 1997. Oil, Gas and Government: The U.S. Experience: Volumes I and II. Rowman & Littlefield Inc. p. 477, 515.

2. As assessed in 1999. See Glaeser, E. 2002. "Does Rent Control Reduce Segregation?" NBER Working Paper.

3. Lindbeck, Assar. *The Political Economy of the New Left.* New York: Harper and Row, 1972, p. 39.

4. Quoted in **Block, Walter,** "Rent Control", *The Concise Encyclopedia of Economics.* Liberty Fund, Inc. Ed. David R. Henderson. Library of Economics and Liberty. 29 August 2006. <http://www.enonlib.org/library/Enc/RentControl.html>.

5. **Glaeser, Edward L. & Erzo F. P. Luttmer.** 2003. "The Misallocation of Housing Under Rent Control." *American Economic Review,* 93(4): 1027–1046.

6. For a recent discussion see Arnott, Richard. 1995. "Time for Revisionism on Rent Control?" *The Journal of Economic Perspectives* 9(1): 99–120.

7. On housing vouchers see Olsen, Ed. "Housing Programs for Low-Income Households" in *Means-Tested Transfer Programs in the U.S.,* ed., Robert Moffitt, National Bureau of Economic Research, Chicago: University of Chicago Press, forthcoming.

8. **Chandrasekaran, Rajiv.** 2003. "Fueling Anger in Iraq." *The Washington Post.* Tuesday, December 9, 2003; Page A01.

9. Ibid.

10. Drawn from Chapter 2, "Consumers: The Art of Queuing," in **Hedrick Smith.** 1976. *The Russians.* New York: Ballantine Books.

Chapter 7 Notes

1. C. Jackson Grayson. 1974. Let's End Controls—Completely. *Wall Street Journal,* Feb. 6, p. 14.

2. Data are from the Bureau of Labor Statistics, *Characteristics of Minimum Wage Workers: 2005,* available online at http://www.bls.gov/cps/minwage2005.htm.

3. See *50 Years of Research on the Minimum Wage,* U.S. Congress Joint Economic Committee, for a listing and abstract of many studies on the minimum wage. Recent studies include **Neumark, D. and W. Wascher.** 1992. "Employment Effects of Minimum and Subminimum Wages: Panel Data on State Minimum Wage Laws." *Industrial and Labor Relations Review* 46(1): 55–81, **Deere, D., K. M. Murphy and F. Welch.** 1995. "Employment and the 1990–1991 Minimum-Wage Hike." *American Economic Review.* 85(2): 232–237. Not all studies find a significant reduction in employment. See **Card, David, and Alan B.** 1994. "Minimum Wages and Employment: A Case Study of the Fast-Food Industry in New Jersey and Pennsylvania." *American Economic Review,* 84 (September): 772–793 for a well-designed study that challenges the conventional wisdom.

4. *Characteristics of Minimum Wage Workers: 2005*, available online at http://www.bls.gov/cps/minwage2005.htm.

5. On the minimum wage in **Puerto Rico** in 1938 see **Rottenberg, Simon**. 1981. *Minimum Wages in Puerto Rico.* In **Rottenberg** (ed.) *The Economics of Legal Minimum Wages.* Washington: American Enterprise Institute, 327–339 and **Rustici, Thomas**. 1985. "A Public Choice View of the Minimum Wage." *Cato Journal* 5(1): 103–131.

Beginning in 1974, the Puerto Rican minimum wage was raised in steps to the U.S. level, creating a repeat of the experiment of 1938. The results were the same. **Freeman and Freeman** (1991) estimate that the increase in the minimum wage reduced the number of jobs in Puerto Rico by 8 to 10 percent. See **Freeman, Alida Castillo and Richard B**. 1991. *Minimum Wages in Puerto Rico: Textbook Case of a Wage Floor?* National Bureau of Economic Research Working Paper No. 3759 (June).

6. On deregulation, see **Peltzman, Sam**. 1989. "The Economic Theory of Regulation After a Decade of Deregulation." *Brookings Papers on Economic Activity. Microeconomics*, 1989 (1989), pp. 1–59.

Chapter 8 Notes

1. On this point see **Sowell, Thomas**. 1980. *Knowledge and Decisions.* New York: Basic Books. And see also Chapter 4 of **Reisman, George**. 1996. *Capitalism: A Treatise on Economics.* Ottawa, IL: Jameson.

2. **Smith, Adam**. 2006. *An Inquiry into the Nature and Causes of the Wealth of Nations.* Methuen and Co., Ltd. 1904 [1776]. Ed. Edwin Cannan. Library of Economics and Liberty, Book IV, II. 2.11. 2 August. http://www.econlib.org/library/Smith/smWN13.html.

3. See **Schwabach, Aaron**. 2002. "How protectionism is destroying the Everglades." *National Wetlands Newsletter*, 24(1): 7–14 on the environmental cost of sugar production.

4. See **Bellamy, Carol**. 1997. *The state of the world's children—1997.* Unicef and Oxford University Press, 23. Available from http://www.unicef.org/sowc97/.

5. See **Edmonds, Eric V. & Nina Pavcnik**. 2006. "International trade and child labor: Cross-country evidence." *Journal of International Economics,* January: 115–140.

6. On the Food for Education program, see **Ahmed, A., & C. del Nino**. 2002. *The Food for Education Program in Bangladesh: An Evaluation of Its Impact on Educational Attainment and Food Security, FCND DP No. 138.* International Food Policy Research Institute and **Meng, Xin, and Jim Ryan.** 2003. *Evaluating the Food for Education Program in Bangladesh.* Working Paper from Australian National University, Australia South Asia Research Centre.

7. On the 1918 flu, see **Barry, John M**. 2005. *The Great Influenza: The Epic Story of the Deadliest Plague in History.* Penguin. New York. On policy for a future pandemic, see **Cowen, Tyler**. 2005. *Avian Flu: What Should Be Done.* Mercatus Center Working Paper. Available at http://www.mercatus.org/repository/docLib/20060726_Avian_Flu.pdf.

8. Quoted in **Norberg, Johan**. 2003. *In Defense of Global Capitalism.* Washington, D.C.: Cato Institute.

9. **Johnson, Bradford**. 2002. "Retail: The Wal-Mart Effect." *McKinsey Quarterly*, (1):40–43.

10. See **Paley, Amit R**. 2006. "Homework help, from a world away: Web joins students, cheap overseas tutors." *Washington Post*. Monday, May 15; A01. Available at http://www.washingtonpost.com/wp-dyn/content/article/2006/05/14/AR2006051401139_pf.html. See also **Bray, Hiawatha**. 2006. "Online tutoring pays off at home, abroad." *The Boston Globe*, March 28.

11. **Boudreaux, Donald J**. 2008. *Globalization.* Westport, CT: Greenwood Press.

Chapter 9 Notes

1. On the external cost of antibiotic use, see **Elbasha, Elamin H**. 2003. Deadweight loss of bacterial resistance due to overtreatment. *Health Economics* 12:125–138.

2. Meade's paper is **Meade, J. E**. 1952. External economies and diseconomies in a competitive situation. *Economic Journal* 62:54–67. On the market for pollination, see **Cheung, Steven N. S**. 1973. The fable of the bees: An economic investigation. *Journal of Law and Economics* 16:11–33, and for a recent description of the market in the United States see **Sumner, Daniel A. and Hayley Boriss.** 2006. Bee-conomics and the leap in pollination fees. *Agricultural and Resource Economics Update*, University of California, Davis (9) 3:9–11.

3. *Consumer Reports.* 2007. "Washers and dryers: Dirty laundry." June.

4. The elasticity of demand for electricity is about −0.5 so a 2 percent increase in the price would reduce consumption by about 1 percent.

5. For a good overview of the acid rain program, see the EPA's most recent *Acid Rain Program Progress Report,* available online at http://www.epa.gov/airmarkets/progress/progress-reports.html.

Chapter 10 Notes

1. See the U.S. Department of Energy website Marginal & Stripper Well Revitalization at http://www.fossil.energy.gov/programs/oilgas/marginalwells/#, last accessed October 7, 2006, for information on stripper wells.

2. **Schumpeter, Joseph**. 1975. *Capitalism, Socialism and Democracy,* New York: Harper [orig. pub. 1942]: 82–85.

3. Based on data from 1972 to 1992 in **Adams, William J**. 1993. TV Program Scheduling Strategies and Their Relationship to New Program Renewal Rates and Rating Changes. *Journal of Broadcasting and Electronic Media.* 37:465–475. The renewal rate is probably lower today as there are more television stations and viewers are harder to keep.

4. From **Bernstein, William J**. 2008. *A Splendid Exchange: How Trade Shaped the World.* New York: Atlantic Monthly Press: 62.

5. MPAA, http://www.mpaa.org/press_releases/2005%20tms%20report.pdf.

6. New Providence, http://www.redorbit.com/news/entertainment/499053/bookish_britain_overtakes_america_as_top_publisher/

Chapter 11 Notes

1. On deaths due to AIDS, see http://www.cdc.gov/hiv/graphics/mortalit.htm. On the efficacy of antiretrovirals, see **Weller I. V., I. G. Williams.** 2001. ABC of AIDS: Antiretroviral drugs. *British Medical Journal* 322(7299):1410–1412. And, in developing countries, **Severe, P** et al. 2005. Antiretroviral Therapy in a Thousand Patients with AIDS in Haiti. *New England Journal of Medicine.* 353(22):2325–2334. Also Lichtenberg, Frank. 2003. The Effect of New Drugs on HIV Mortality in the U.S., 1987–1998. *Economics and Human Biology* 1:259–266.

2. On the cost of AIDS drugs in the United States, see http://aids.about.com/od/hivmedicationfactsheets/a/drugcost.htm

3. On the number of people worldwide with AIDS, see the UNAIDS Report, 2006 Report on the global AIDS epidemic. Available online at http://www.unaids.org/en/HIV_data/2006GlobalReport/default.asp.

4. On the cost of Combivir, see http://money.cnn.com/magazines/fortune/fortune_archive/2006/09/18/8386170/index.htm?postversion=2006090806 and http://news.bbc.co.uk/1/hi/business/2981015.stm and further below on patents and differential pricing.

5. See **Pepper, Daniel.** 2006. Patently Unfair. *Fortune* (Sept. 18). Available online at http://money.cnn.com/magazines/fortune/fortune_archive/2006/09/18/8386170/index.htm?postversion=2006090806

6. American Airlines reservation website accessed on December 21, 2006.

7. **DiMasi, Joseph A., Ronald W. Hansen, Henry G. Grabowski.** 2003. The Price of Innovation: New Estimates of Drug Development Costs. *Journal of Health Economics* 22(2): 151–185.

8. One study suggests that a 10 percent decline in price will lead to at least a 5 percent decline in the number of new drugs (see footnote 1, Lichtenberg 2006). See also **Vernon, John.** 2005. Examining the Link Between Price Regulation and Pharmaceutical R&D Investment. *Health Economics* 14(1):1–17.

9. **North, Douglass C.** 1981. *Structure and Change in Economic History.* New York: Norton, p. 164.

10. **Kremer, M.** 1998. Patent Buyouts: A Mechanism for Encouraging Innovation. *Quarterly Journal of Economics* 113:1137–1167.

11. See **Hazlett, Thomas W. and Matthew L. Spitzer.** 1997. *Public Policy towards Cable Television: The Economics of Rate Controls.* AEI.

12. On the $3,900 price, see **Berthelsen, Christian.** 2001. Duke Admits Overcharging Utilities $3,880 Bill per Megawatt Hour. *San Francisco Chronicle.* (Saturday, June 2, 2001). Available online at: http://www.sfgate.com/cgi-bin/article.cgi%3Ffile%3D/chronicle/archive/2001/06/02/BU238492.DTL%20.

13. For good reviews of the California energy crisis, see **Borenstein, Severin.** 2002. The Trouble with Electricity Markets: Understanding California's Restructuring Disaster. *Journal of Economic Perspectives* 16(1):191–211. See also Congressional Budget Office. 2001. Causes and Lessons of the California Electricity Crisis. Available online at http://www.cbo.gov/ftpdocs/30xx/doc3062/CaliforniaEnergy.pdf and **Weare, Christopher.** 2003. The California Electricity Crisis: Causes and Policy Options. Public Policy Institute of California.

14. On Apple's market share, see **Sandisk Surprise.** *Business Week* (February 9, 2006) Available online at http://www.businessweek.com/technology/tech_stats/mp3s060209.htm.

Chapter 12 Notes

1. Information on the Combivir smuggling operation can be found in **Irving, Richard.** 2005. Aids drugs to Africa rebranded in drive to beat racket. The Times, Feb. 21, 2005 available online at http://business.timesonline.co.uk/tol/business/markets/africa/article516982.ece and on an earlier ring busted in 2002 at Syal, Rajeev. 2002. "Scandal of Africa's Aids drug re-sold to Britain," *Telegraph* 28/12/2002. available online at http://www.telegraph.co.uk/news/main.jhtml?xml=/news/2002/12/29/waids29.xml. See also **Morais, Richard C.** 2004. "Pssst...Wanna Buy Some Augmentin?" *Forbes.* Available online at http://www.forbes.com/free_forbes/2004/0412/112.html.

2. See **R. Preston McAfee.** 2002. *Competitive Solutions: The Strategist's Toolkit* (Princeton, NJ: Princeton University Press).

Chapter 13 Notes

1. Using http://www.nationmaster.com/graph/ene_oil_pro-energy-oil-production from CIA World Factbook 2007 and adding together production from African countries gets to about 9,062,000 and Saudi Arabian production is about 9,475,000.

2. **Carlton, Dennis W. and Jeffrey M. Perloff,** *Modern Industrial Organization,* pp.132–133.

3. See, for example, **Morgan, Dan, Sarah Cohen, and Gilbert M. Gaul.** 2006. Dairy Industry Crushed Innovator Who Bested Price-Control System. *Washington Post.* December 10, http://www.washingtonpost.com/wp-dyn/content/article/2006/12/09/AR2006120900925.html; also http://www.findarticles.com/p/articles/mi_m3778/is_1991_August/ai_12056311.

4. On police road barriers, see **Polgreen, Lydia.** 2005. As Nigeria Tries to Fight Graft, a New Sordid Tale. *New York Times,* November 29. On grade selling, see **Goldman, Antony.** 1997. Same Salary, Three Lifestyles: Corruption's Toll on Nigeria. *Christian Science Monitor.* As an example of cartelization, see **Omoh, Gabriel, Lukat Binniyat, Yemi Adeoye, and Victor Ahiuma-Young.** 2008. Nigeria: PPMC Cartel, Politicians Responsible for Soaring Diesel Price. Vanguard. Available online at http://allafrica.com/stories/200807140212.html.

5. http://www.match.com/help/aboutus.aspx

6. http://www.cc.gatech.edu/gvu/user_surveys/survey-10-1996/graphs/use/Browser_You_Expect_To_Use_In_12_Months.html. Exact estimates vary; see http://en.wikipedia.org/wiki/Usage_share_of_web_browsers.

7. **Watts, Duncan J., M. J., Salganik, and P. S. Dodds.** 2006. Experimental Study of Inequality and Unpredictability in an Artificial Cultural Market. *Science,* 311:854–856.

Chapter 14 Notes

1. On dangerous professions, see for instance http://www.forbes.com/2007/08/13/dangerous-jobs-fishing-lead-careers-cx_tvr_0813danger.html.

2. Here is one estimate of coal miner earnings: http://www.washingtonpost.com/wp-dyn/content/discussion/2006/01/04/DI2006010401171.html.

3. For one estimate of the union wage premium, see http://www.psi.org.uk/docs/2003/research/emp-union-wage-premium-us-uk.pdf.

4. Data from www.oecd.org for union members and employees.

Chapter 15 Notes

1. **Jacob, Brian A. and Steven D. Levitt.** 2003. Rotten Apples: An Investigation of the Prevalence and Predictors of Teacher Cheating. Quarterly Journal of Economics 118(3): 843–878.

2. **Wojciech Kopczuk & Joel Slemrod.** 2003. "Dying to Save Taxes: Evidence from Estate-Tax Returns on the Death Elasticity," *The Review of Economics and Statistics.* 85(2): 256–265.

3. **Figlio, David N. and Lawrence S. Getzler.** 2002. Accountability, Ability and Disability: Gaming the System. NBER Working Papers 9307, National Bureau of Economic Research, Inc.

4. For a calculation along these lines, see **Kane, T. and D. O. Staiger.** 2002. The Promise and Pitfalls of Using Imprecise School Accountability Measures. *Journal of Economic Perspectives* 16(4):91–114.

5. http://www.toyota101.com/No_Commission.aspx

6. For more on private prisons, see **Tabarrok, Alexander** (ed.). 2003. *Changing the Guard: Private Prisons and the Control of Crime.* Oakland, CA: The Independent Institute.

7. **Lazear, Edward P.** 2000. Performance Pay and Productivity. *AER* 90(5):1346–1361.

8. **Lemieux, T. W., Bentley MacLeod, and Daniel Parent.** 2007. Performance Pay and Wage Inequality. NBER Working Paper 13128.

9. **Bertrand, Marianne and Sendhil Mullainathan.** 2001. Are CEOs Rewarded for Luck? The Ones Without Principles Are. *Quarterly Journal of Economics* 116:901–932.

10. Ibid.

11. The Struggle to Measure Performance. *Business Week.* January 9, 2006.

12. On employee ownership of stock, see http://www.nceo. org/library/widespread.html, National Center for Employee Ownership.

13. On Kmart, see **Vance, Sandra S. and Roy V. Scott.** 1994. *Wal-Mart: A History of Sam Walton's Retail Phenomenon.* New York: Twayne, and on Kmart, see **Layton Turner, Marcia.** 2003. *K-Mart's Deadly Sins: How Incompetence Tainted an American Icon.* New York: John Wiley.

Chapter 16 Notes

1. For a comprehensive review of efficient markets and the performance of mutual fund managers see **Hebner, Mark T.** 2007. *Index Funds: The 12 Step Program for Active Investors.* Irvine, CA: IFA Publishing.

Chapter 17 Notes

1. Aristotle *Politics*, Book II, Chapter III, 1261b; translated by Benjamin Jowett as *The Politics of Aristotle: Translated into English with Introduction, Marginal Analysis, Essays, Notes and Indices* (Oxford: Clarendon, 1885), Vol. 1 of 2.

2. The system was later modified so the ITQs gave rights to a certain share of the total allowable catch.

3. See World Meteorological Organization. 2007. *Scientific Assessment of Ozone Depletion: 2006,* Global Ozone Research and Monitoring Project—Report No. 50, 572 pp., Geneva, Switzerland. Available online at http://www.esrl.noaa.gov/csd/assessments/2006/report.html.

4. http://www.greatchange.org/footnotes-overshoot-easter_island.html

5. **Demsetz, Harold.** 1967. *Towards a Theory of Property Rights.* AER 57:2.

Chapter 18 Notes

1. Working paper, personal communication from Robert Whaples.

2. **Meckler, Laura.** 2007. Kidney Shortage Inspires A Radical Idea: Organ Sales. *Wall Street Journal.* November 13, A1.

3. The commercial fishing mortality rate is from http://www.cdc.gov/niosh/fishfat.html, kidney donation mortality rate from **Matas A. J., S. T. Bartlett, A. B. Leichtman, F. L. Delmonico.** 2003. American Journal of Transplantation. Jul 3(7):830–834.

4. http://www.time.com/time/printout/0,8816,1686532,00.html

5. For one source, see http://www.whitehouse.gov/cea/cea_immigration_062007.html.

6. On measures of foreign aid, see for instance http://online.wsj.com/public/article/SB114964237227873311-9VLg4BPCPl76mawIeC92XypcO_E_20060706.html?mod=tff_main_tff_top.

Chapter 19 Notes

1. The Official Report, House of Commons (5th Series), 11 November 1947, vol. 444, cc. 206–207.

2. Kaiser/Harvard Program on the Public and Health/Social Policy Survey, January 1995.

3. See, for instance, **DeLorme, Charles D., Stacey Isom, and David R. Kamerschen.** 2005. Rent Seeking and Taxation in the Ancient Roman Empire., *Applied Economics,* April, 37:705–711, http://ideas.repec.org/a/taf/applec/v37y2005i6p705-711.html.

4. **Leeson, Peter T.** 2008. "Media Freedom, Political Knowledge, and Participation," Journal of Economic Perspectives, 22(2): 155–169.

5. **Djankov, S., C. McLiesh, T. Nenova, and A. Shleifer.** 2003. Who Owns the Media? *Journal of Law and Economics* 46(2):341–381.

6. See **Conquest, Robert.** 1987. *Harvest of Sorrow.* New York: Oxford University Press.

7. **Sen, Amartya.** 1990. Public Action to Remedy Hunger. Arturo Tanco Memorial Lecture given in London on 2 August 1990, http://www.thp.org/reports/sen/sen890.htm

8. **Besley, T. and R. Burgess.** 2002. The Political Economy of Government Responsiveness: Theory and Evidence from India. *Quarterly Journal of Economics.* 117(4): 1415–1452.

9. http://www.natso.com/AM/Template.cfm?Section=Top_NATSO_Issues&Template=/CM/ContentDisplay.cfm&ContentID=7700&FusePreview=True&WebsiteKey=e91dcade-9ead-43ab-b6bc-c608fd2a3c34

Chapter 20 Notes

1. Data on automobiles are from the Statistical Abstract of the United States. Prices from http://www.nada.org/Content/NavigationMenu/Newsroom/NADAData/20062/NADA_Data_2006.pdf. Data on computers are from Information Technology Industry Council, http://www.itic.org/statistics.php.

2. Bureau of Economic Analysis website (www.bea.gov), Table 2.3.3.

3. See Federal Reserve Board. 2009. "Flow of Funds Accounts of the United States: Flows and Outstandings, Fourth Quarter 2008." Available online at: http://www.federalreserve.gov/releases/z1/Current/z1.pdf

4. For data on business regulations worldwide see the World Bank's website, http://www.doingbusiness.org/.

5. http://rru.worldbank.org/Discussions/Topics/Topic18.aspx

6. http://www.gapminder.org/

7. See **Dollar, David & Aart Kraay**. 2004. "Trade, Growth, and Poverty." *Economic Journal*, 114(493): F22–F49.

Chapter 21 Notes

1. See United States Department of Agriculture, Economic Research Service. 2007. "Agricultural Productivity in the United States." http://www.ers.usda.gov/Data/Ag Productivity/.

2. This account draws upon **McMillan, John**. 2002. *Reinventing the Bazaar*. New York, NY: W.W. Norton and Company, and **Zhou, Kate Xiao**. 1997. *How Farmers Changed China*. Boulder, CO: Westview Press.

3. **Hall, Robert E**. & **Charles I. Jones**. 1999. "Why do some countries produce so much more output per worker than others?" *Quarterly Journal of Economics*: 83–116.

4. **Lewis, William W**. 2004. *The Power of Productivity*. Chicago, IL: University of Chicago Press.

Chapter 22 Notes

1. Germany is excluded for lack of data. Turkey is excluded because its history and institutions were quite different from the other founding members of the OECD.

2. Is there a way to reduce the trade-off between dynamic and static efficiency? Some ideas are suggested by **Tabarrok, Alexander**. 2002. "Patent Theory versus Patent Law." *Contributions to Economic Analysis & Policy*. 1(1), Article 9. http://www.bepress.com/bejeap/contributions/vol1/iss1/art9. And see also **Kremer, Michael**. 1998. "Patent Buyouts: A Mechanism for Encouraging Innovation." *Quarterly Journal of Economics*: 1137–1167.

3. Rare is defined as a disease at the bottom quarter of incidence in the United States in 1998; common is defined as a disease at the top quarter of incidence. See **Lichtenberg, Frank R**. & **Joel Waldfogel**. "*Does* Misery Love Company? Evidence from Pharmaceutical Markets Before and After the Orphan Drug Act" (June 2003). NBER Working Paper No. W9750. Available at SSRN: http://ssrn.com/abstract=414248.

4. **Romer, Paul**. 2007. "Economic Growth." *The Concise Encyclopedia of Economics*. David R. Henderson, ed. Liberty Fund, Indianapolis.

Chapter 23 Notes

1. **Bloom, David E., David Canning & Bryan S. Graham**. 2002. "Longevity and Life Cycle Savings." NBER Working Paper No. W8808. Available at SSRN: http://ssrn.com/abstract=302569

2. **Shoda, Y., W. Mischel, & P. Peake**. 1988. "Predicting Adolescent Cognitive and Self-Regulatory Competencies from Preschool Delay of Gratification: Identifying Diagnostic Conditions." *Developmental Psychology*, 26: 978–986.

3. **Beshears, John, James Choi, David Laibson, & Brigitte Madrian**. *The Importance of Default Options for Retirement Savings Outcomes: Evidence from the United States*. http://www.nber.org/aginghealth/summer06/w12009.html

4. **Levine, Ross & Zervos, Sara**. 1998. "Stock Markets, Banks, and Economic Growth," *American Economic Review*, vol. 88(3): 537–558.

5. **Blustein, Paul**. 2005. *And the Money Kept Rolling In (and Out): Wall Street, the IMF, and the Bankrupting of Argentina*. New York, NY: Public Affairs Press, 191.

6. See **La Porta, Rafael, Florencio Lopez-De-Silanes, & Andrei Shleifer**. 2002. "Government Ownership of Banks." *Journal of Finance, American Finance Association*, 57(1): 265–301.

7. **Friedman, Milton, & Anna J. Schwartz**. 1963. *A Monetary History of the United States, 1867–1960*. Princeton, NJ: Princeton University Press.

8. **Bernanke, Ben**. 1983. "Nonmonetary Effects of the Financial Crisis in the Propagation of the Great Depression." *The American Economic Review*, 73(3): 257–276.

Chapter 24 Notes

1. On K-Mart see http://en.wikipedia.org/wiki/Kmart; on Wal-Mart see the 2002 Annual Report, http://walmartstores.com/Files/annual_2002/page16.html.

2. Data on unemployment and its duration may be found in various issues of the OECD Employment Outlook and on the Web at http://www.oecd.org/statsportal/0,2639,en_2825_293564_1_1_1_1_1,00.html.

3. The Italian system is more difficult to describe than the systems in the other countries and it has changed considerably over time.

4. See OECD Statistics, http://stats.oecd.org/wbos/default.aspx, for minimum wages relative to median wages. For minimum wages relative to average wages, see **Lothar Funk & Hagen Lesch**. 2005. *Minimum Wages in Europe*. European Foundation for the Improvement of Living and Working Conditions. Available online at http://eurofound.europa.eu/eiro/2005/07/study/tn0507101s.html#contentpage.

5. **Salanie, Bernard & Guy Laroque**. 2002. "Labor Market Institutions and Employment in France." *Journal of Applied Econometrics*: 17, 25, 48. And **Ford, Peter**. 2005. "Deep Roots of Paris Riots." *Christian Science Monitor*. November 4, 2005. And for the United States, Bureau of Labor Statistics.

6. **Martin, John P**. 2000. "What works among active labour market policies: Evidence from OECD Countries' Experiences." *OECD Economic Studies*, No. 30: 79–113.

7. **Kotlikoff, Laurence & Scott Burns**. 2004. *The Coming Generation Storm*. Cambridge, MA: MIT Press.

8. U.S. Comptroller General David Walker speaking on *60 Minutes*, see http://www.cbsnews.com/stories/2007/03/01/60minutes/main2528226.shtml.

9. The U.S. Equal Employment Opportunity Commission collects statistics on job patterns by industry. See *Job Patterns For Minorities and Women in Private Industry* (EEO-1), available online at http://www.eeoc.gov/stats/jobpat/jobpat.html.

10. **Goldin, Claudia and Lawrence F. Katz**. 2002. "The Power of the Pill: Oral Contraceptives and Women's Career and Marriage Decisions." *Journal of Political Economy*, 110(4): 730–770.

11. There are 6 employed workers and 1 unemployed worker so there are 7 people in the labor force. Of the 7, 1 is unemployed so the unemployment rate is $1/7 = 14.3$ percent. The adult, civilian, noninstitutional population is 8, of these, 7 are in the labor force, so the labor force participation rate is 87.5 percent.

Chapter 25 Notes

1. See *Zimbabwe Has No Money to Print Currency*, November 3, 2006, http://www.newzimbabwe.com/pages/inflation66.14226.html.

Chapter 26 Notes

1. **Higgs, Robert**. 1997. "Regime Uncertainty: Why the Great Depression Lasted So Long and Why Prosperity Resumed after the War." *The Independent Review*, 1(4): 561–590.

2. For a good overview of the tariff and its effects, see **O'Brien, Anthony**. "Smoot-Hawley Tariff." *EH.Net Encyclopedia*, edited by **Robert Whaples**. August 15, 2001. http://eh.net/encyclopedia/article/obrien.hawley-smoot.tariff

3. Solon, Gary, Barsky, Robert, and Parker, Jonathan A. 1994. "Measuring the Cyclicality of Real Wages: How Important Is Composition Bias?" *Quarterly Journal of Economics,* 109 (February): 1–25.

Chapter 29 Notes

1. **Bernanke, Ben S., Mark Gertler, & Mark Watson**. 1997. "Systematic Monetary Policy and the Effects of Oil Price Shocks." *Brookings Papers on Economic Activity*, 1: 91–157.

Chapter 30 Notes

1. http://www.wwwebtax.com/miscellaneous/exemptions.htm

2. On Boeing, "The Taxman Barely Cometh." *Business Week*, December 3, 2007: 56–58.

3. **Hall, Robert E. & Alvin Rabushka**. 2007. *The Flat Tax— Revised and Expanded*. Stanford, CA: Hoover Institution.

4. Congressional Budget Office. 2007. *The Long Term Budget Outlook, 2007*. Available online at http://www.cbo.gov/ftpdocs/88xx/doc8877/12-13-LTBO.pdf, last accessed Nov. 20, 2008.

Chapter 31 Notes

1. **Hornbeck, J.F.** 2004. "Argentina's Sovereign Debt Restructuring." Congressional Research Service, RL 32637.

2. On New Deal fiscal policy, see **Hansen, Alvin**. 1963. "Was Fiscal Policy in the Thirties a Failure?" *Review of Economics and Statistics*, 45:320–323.

Appendix A Notes

1. **Clark, Gerald**. 1969. "What Happens When the Police Go On Strike." *New York Times Magazine*, November 16, sec. 6: 45, 176–185, 187, 194–195.

2. **Klick, Jonathan, & Alexander Tabarrok**. 2005. "Using Terror Alert Levels to Estimate the Effect of Police on Crime." *Journal of Law & Economics*, 48(1): 267–280.

INDEX

Note: Page numbers followed by f indicate figures; those followed by n indicate notes; those followed by t indicate tables.

A

Abdul Aziz Al Saud, Abdullah bin, 270
Ability risk, tournaments and, 320–321
Absolute advantage, 146
Acid rain, 177, 180
Active labor market policies, 523
Adleman, Leonard, 469
The Adventures of Pluto Nash (film), 90
Advertising, nonrival private goods and, 351–352
Afghanistan
    corruption in, 439t, 440
    real GDP per capita in, 440
Africa. *See also specific countries*
    deforestation in Sahel region of, 353
    economic growth of, 430f
    foreign investment in, 709
    government control of media in, 393
    individuals' attempt to smooth consumption and, 485
African Americans, labor market discrimination against, 303–304
Age
    aging of U.S. population and, 18, 528, 669
    labor force participation and, 527t, 527–529, 528f, 529f
Aggregate demand
    decreasing, 637–638
    monetary policy and, 621–623, 622f, 637–638
    stimulation by government spending, 687
Aggregate demand-aggregate supply model, 563–587
    dynamic aggregate demand curve and, 564–567, 566f
    New Keynesian model and. *See* New Keynesian model
    real business cycle model and, 567–570, 568f
    Solow growth curve and, 563–564, 564f
Aggregate demand curve, 564–567, 566f
    shifts in, 566–567, 567f
Aggregate demand shocks
    Great Depression and, 579–580, 580f
    in New Keynesian model, 575–579
    real business cycle model and, 569f, 569–570
Aggregate supply. *See* Aggregate demand-aggregate supply model; Short-run aggregate supply *(SRAS)* curve
Aging of U.S. population, 18, 528, 669
Agriculture
    collectivization of, 394
    elasticity of demand and, 58–59, 59f
    famine and, 393–395, 394f
    high-tech, 434–435

    price supports for, 385
    productivity increase in, prices and, 58–59, 59f
    subsidies and, 385
    water subsidies in, deadweight loss and, 135–136
Ahmed, A., R–3
AIDS (Acquired Immune Deficiency Syndrome)
    drugs for treatment of, 219, 220, 224, 227, 243–246, 251
    individuals' attempt to smooth consumption and, 485
AIG. *See* American International Group (AIG)
Air Jordans, 20
Airline industry
    price discrimination in, 246–247, 247f
    price setting by, 224–225
    regulation of, 123f, 123–124
Ajinomoto, 274
Alaska
    Arctic National Wildlife Refuge in, 68
    "Bridge to Nowhere" in, 385
Algeria
    corruption in, 440
    monopolies in, 227
    in OPEC, 45n
    real GDP per capita in, 440
Alternative minimum tax (AMT), 659
AMA. *See* American Medical Association (AMA)
American Airlines, fares set by, 224–225
American Crystal Sugar Political Action Committee, 384
American International Group (AIG), 621
American League, 302
American Medical Association (AMA), 300
American Pie (film), 90–91
American Sugarbeet Growers Association, 384
American Sugar Cane League, 384
Amish culture, 370
AMT. *See* Alternative minimum tax (AMT)
Anarchy, State, and Utopia (Nozick), 372
Andreas, Michael D., 274
Angola
    corruption in, 439t, 440
    economic freedom index and standard of living in, 392f
    inflation rate in, 540t
    in OPEC, 45n
    real GDP per capita in, 440
Ansari X Prize, 227, 228

Antibiotics, 169–170
Antiretroviral drugs, 219, 220, 224, 227, 243–246, 251
Antitrust laws, 274
ANWR. *See* Arctic National Wildlife Refuge (ANWR)
Apartheid, 304–305
Appiah, Kwame Anthony, 68n
Apple, 234–235, 467
Appreciation of currency, 709
Arbitrage, 245, 497, 509
    preventing, 245–246
Archer Daniels Midland, 274
Arctic National Wildlife Refuge (ANWR), 68
Argentina
    corruption in, 440
    economic growth of, 432f, 432–433
    financial crisis of 1999–2002 in, 498–499, 693, 718
    interest rate in, 501t
    pegging of currency of, 717–718
    real GDP and infant mortality in, 428f
    real GDP per capita in, 440
Armageddon (film), 347
Artistic innovation, 467
Asia. *See also specific countries*
    currency crises of 1990s in, 718
Atlanta Federal Reserve Bank, 623
Attractiveness, labor market discrimination and, 306
Australia
    government spending in, 671f
    hiring and firing costs in, 522f
    ownership of New Zealand banks by, 705
    workweek in, 419t
Austria
    conditional convergence and, 464f
    corruption in, 440
    government spending in, 671f
    hiring and firing costs in, 522f
    pegging of currency of, 717
    real GDP per capita in, 440
Automatic stabilizers, 689
Automobile dealers, incentives and, 315–316
Automobile industry
    Japanese voluntary import restraints and, 145
    oil prices and, 591
Average cost, 196
Average cost curve, profits and, 195–198, 196f, 198f
Average tax rate, 657, 657f

B

Baby boomers in labor force, 528
Balance of payments, 703–707
    capital (financial) account and, 704–705
    capital inflow and, 703

Balance of payments (cont.)
  current account and, 704
  official reserves account and, 705
  trade deficits and, 707
  two sides of, 705–707, 706f
Bandwagon effect, 638
Bangladesh
  child labor in, 156–157, 157f
  corruption in, 440
  famine in, 394, 394f
  real GDP per capita in, 440
Bank(s), 493–494
  Federal Reserve. See Federal Reserve
    System (Fed)
  fractional reserve banking and, 613–615
  government-owned, 501
  illiquid, 619
  in New Zealand, Australian ownership
    of, 705
  required reserves and, 620
Bank failures, 501–503
  Great Depression and, 501–502, 579,
    580–581
Barbados
  corruption in, 440
  real GDP per capita in, 440
Barriers to entry, 234
Barry, John M., R–3
Baucus, Max, 384t
Bear Stearns, 502, 620, 621
A Beautiful Mind (film), 277
Becker, Gary S., 60, 365–366
Beech, 105
Belgium
  conditional convergence and, 464f
  government spending in, 671f
  hiring and firing costs in, 522f
  labor force participation of older
    workers in, 528f
  taxes and labor force participation in,
    529f
Bellamy, Carol, R–3
Benefits, external, 173–175, 174f
Benin
  corruption in, 440
  real GDP per capita in, 440
Berkshire Hathaway, 495
Bermuda
  corruption in, 440
  real GDP per capita in, 440
Bernanke, Ben, 502–503, 609, 641, 643
Bertrand, Marianne, 305n
Beshears, John, 486, R–2
Besley, Timothy, 395
Bewley, Truman, 573
Big Ideas, 1–11
  alignment of self-interest with social
    interest and, 2–3
  central banks and, 9
  economic fluctuations and, 8
  incentives and, 2
  inflation and, 8–9
  institutions and, 7–8
  law of supply and demand and, 6

  study of economics and, 9–10
  thinking on the margin and, 5–6
  trade-offs and, 3–5
  wealth and economic growth and, 6–7
Blat, 111–112
Bloom, David, 485, R–2
BLS. See Bureau of Labor Statistics (BLS)
Blu-ray wars, 278f, 278–279
Blustein, Paul, 499, R–2
BMW, 298
Board of Governors, 623
Boeing, 660
Bolivia
  corruption in, 440
  inflation rate in, 541t
  interest rate in, 501t
  real GDP per capita in, 440
Bond(s), 494
  interest rates and, 496–497
  junk, 494
  prices of, 496–497, 508–512
  rating services for, 494
  selling to finance fiscal policy, 683–684
  U.S., 495–496
Bond market, 494–497, 496f
Book publishers, price discrimination by,
    247–248
Borrowing, 487–489
  to finance large investments, 488–489
  government. See Government
    borrowing
  from IMF, 718–719
  individuals' attempt to smooth
    consumption and, 487–488, 488f
  interest rate and, 489, 489f
  from World Bank, 719–720
Boston Celtics, 290
Botswana
  corruption in, 440
  real GDP per capita in, 440
Boudreaux, Donald J., R–3
Boutros-Ghali, Youssef, 158
Bradley, Robert Jr., 58, R–1
Bray, Hiawatha, R–3
Brazil
  child labor in, 157f
  corruption in, 440
  ethanol and sugar production of, 81
  financial crisis of 2001 in, 498
  pegging of currency of, 717
  real GDP per capita in, 406, 406t, 440
  as World Bank borrower, 719
Bribes, price controls and, 100, 109
Bridge to Nowhere, 689–690
Brin, Sergei, 498
Britain. See Great Britain; Ireland; United
    Kingdom
Brooklyn Dodgers, 302
Brown, Jerry, 661
Brown, Sherrod, 384t
Brunei
  corruption in, 440
  inflation rate in, 540t
  real GDP per capita in, 440

Budget deficits, 668
Budget surpluses, 667
Buffalo, 353
Buffett, Warren, 332, 333, 495
Bundling, 253–255, 254t
Bunzl, Martin, 68n
Bureau of Labor Statistics (BLS), 409, 517
Burgess, Robin, 395
Burns, Arthur, 624
Burns, Scott, 18, 528, R–1, R–2
Burundi, child labor in, 157, 157f
Bush, George W., 68, 667
  tax cuts under, 688, 690
  tax rebate under, 679, 684–685, 687
Business fluctuations (business cycles),
    412–413, 413f, 561–587, 562f. See
    also Great Depression; Recessions
  moderation of, 8
  New Keynesian model of. See New
    Keynesian model
  political, 387f, 387–389, 389f
  real business cycle model of, 563,
    567–570, 568f, 589–605. See also
    Real shocks; Shocks
  skeleton model of, 563–567
  Solow model and, 606–608, 607f, 608f
Buy and hold strategy, 336
Buyers, competition with other buyers, 35

C

CAB. See Civil Aeronautics Board (CAB)
Cable TV
  bundling and, 255
  regulation of subscription rates for,
    231–232
California, electricity prices in, 233f,
    233–234
Cambodia
  corruption in, 440
  real GDP per capita in, 440
Cameroon
  corruption in, 440
  real GDP per capita in, 440
Campanella, Roy, 302
Canada
  conditional convergence and, 464f
  drug prices in, 227
  government spending in, 671f
  hiring and firing costs in, 522f
  labor force participation of older
    workers in, 528f
  NAFTA and, 25–26, 26f
  oil production of, 22
  real GDP per capita in, 406t
  taxes and labor force participation in,
    529f
  workweek in, 419t
Canadian dollar, exchange rates and, 708,
    708t
Cantor Fitzgerald, 90
Canning, David, 485, R–2
Capital
  depreciation of, 456, 456f
  growth of, 455f, 455–456, 456f

human, 295f, 295–296, 434–435
insufficiency for economic growth, 456–458, 457f, 458f
marginal product of, 453
physical, 433–434
steady state level of, 457
Capital account, 704–705
investments in, 705
Capital gains taxes, 658
Capital inflow, 703
Capital surplus, 703
Capitol records, 98
Caplan, Bryan, 383n
Card, David, 59, R–1
Carlyle, Thomas, 375
Cartels, 265, 266f, 266–275, 267f. *See also* Organization of Petroleum Exporting Countries (OPEC)
breakdown of, 272–273
cheating on, 268t–270t, 268–272
government prosecution and regulation of, 274–275
sustainable, in market setting, 273
Carter, Jimmy, 265
Carter, John, 385–386
Casey, Robert, Jr., 384t
Catalog companies, 574
Cause and effect relationships, graphs of, and A–9—A–12, A.11f
CBO. *See* Congressional Budget Office (CBO)
CDs. *See* Certificates of deposit (CDs)
Celis, William, 3rd, 10, R–1
Central African Republic
corruption in, 440
real GDP per capita in, 440
Central bank of the United States. *See* Federal Reserve System (Fed)
Central planning, 82
Certificates of deposit (CDs), 612
Cessna, 105
Chadwick, Edwin, 1, 2, R–1
Chamberlain, Wilt, 373
Chambliss, Saxby, 384t
Chapman, Clark, 347n
Charles B. Rangel Center for Public Service, 386
Chavez, Hugo, 270
Cheating
on cartels, 268t–270t, 268–272
incentives for, 314
Checkable deposits, 612
Chernobyl accident, 334
Chicago Public Schools, 315
Child labor, international trade and, 156–158, 157f
Chile
corruption in, 440
interest rate in, 501t
real GDP per capita in, 440
taxes in, 659n
China
balance of payments of, 706
centrally planned economy of, 82

child labor in, 157f
corruption in, 440
economic growth of, 46, 430f, 433, 441, 451, 454
foreign investment of, 483
Great Leap Forward in, 438
inflation rate in, 540t
as largest World Bank borrower, 719
military expenditure of, 664t
property rights in, 437–438
real GDP per capita in, 406, 406t, 429, 429f, 440
stockpiling of U.S. dollars and dollar-denominated assets by, 705
U.S. trade deficit with, 702–703
workweek in, 419t
Choi, James, 486, R–2
Christian Freedom International, 65
Christian Solidarity International, 51, 65
Christopher, Emma, 1, R–1
Chrome, 279
Churchill, Winston, 381
Cigarette tax, 130–131
Civil Aeronautics Board (CAB), airline regulation and, 123f, 123–124
Clark, Gerald, A–11, R–3
Clean Air Act of 1990, 179–180, 180f
Cleveland Indians, 302
Clinton, Bill, 63
budget surpluses under, 667
recession beginning under, 413
Clyburn, James, 666
Coase, Ronald, 176
Coase theorem, 176–177, 180
Cochran, Thad, 384t
Coleman, Norm, 384t
Collateral, 495
College enrollment during recessions, 4–5, 5f
Colombia, child labor in, 157f
Combivir, 219, 220, 224, 227–246, 243, 251
Command and control method, 177–179
Commodity taxes, 125–133
on cigarettes, 130–131
elasticities of supply and demand and, 127–129
health insurance mandates and, 130
revenue increases and lost gains from trade due to, 131f, 131–133, 132f
ultimate payer of, 125–129, 126f, 127f
Common resources, 352
tragedy of the commons and, 352f, 352–355
Comparative advantage, 145–149, 146t–148t
wages and, 148–149
Compensating differentials, 296–299, 297f
Competition, 187–215
balance of industries and, 200–202
entry and exit from industries and, 198–200, 199t
industry supply curves and, 202f, 202–208

minimization of total costs of production and, 193f, 193–195, 194f
price setting and, 188–190, 189f
profits and average cost curve and, 195–198, 196f, 198f
quantity to produce and, 190–193, 191f, 192f
trade and, 145
Competitive markets, wealth and, 440–441
Competitors, 35
Complements, price of, demand and, 18–19
Compound growth, spreadsheet for calculating, 447–449, 447f–449f
Compound returns, 338t, 338–339
Computer keyboard design, 277–278
Conditional convergence, 463–464, 464f
Confidence, shifts in aggregate demand curve and, 577–578
Congo, Democratic Republic of. *See* Democratic Republic of the Congo (DRC)
Congressional Budget Office (CBO), 669
Conover, Ted, 46, R–1
Conrad, Kent, 384t
Constant cost industries, 202, 202f
industry supply curves for, 202–205, 204f
Consumer price index (CPI), 539
Consumer surplus, 16, 16f
Consumption
in GDP, 414, 415f
individuals' attempt to smooth, 484–485, 485f, 487–488, 488f
Contraceptive pill, female labor force participation and, 531–532
Coolidge, Calvin, 169
Coolidge, Calvin, Jr., 169
Cooperation, 79–80
Copper cartel, 273
Corporate culture, 323
Corporate finance, cheating and, 314
Corporate income tax, 656, 660
Corruption, 439. *See also* Bribes
monopoly and, 226–227
price controls and, 100
real GDP per capita and, 439, 440f
shortages and, 111–112
Cost(s)
average, 196
of drugs, 219, 220, 224, 227–228, 243–246, 251
environmental, GDP and, 418–419
external, 170, 171–173, 172f
fixed. *See* Fixed costs
of hiring and firing, international comparison of, 522f
of inflation, 546–552
labor adjustment, 597–598
marginal, 190, 192–193, 220–225, 221f–223f
menu, 574
of monopoly, 225–227, 226f
opportunity. *See* Opportunity cost
private, 170

Cost(s) *(cont.)*
  of protectionism, 152–155, 153f
  social, 170
  sunk. *See* Sunk costs
  total. *See* Total costs
  of trade, purchasing power parity and, 713
  transaction, 175
  variable, 190
Costa Rica
  corruption in, 440
  real GDP per capita in, 440
Cost curves
  of average costs, 195–198, 196f, 198f
  graphing using Excel, 216, 216f–218f, 218
Cowen, Tyler, R–3
CPI. *See* Consumer price index (CPI)
Craigslist, 276
Crapo, Mike, 384t
Creative destruction, 201–202, 517
Credibility, 637–638
Cross-price elasticity of demand, 76
Crowding out, 495, 496f
  fiscal policy and, 682, 683–687
  Ricardian equivalence and, 685–687, 686f
Crystal, Billy, 108
Cuba
  corruption in, 440
  real GDP per capita in, 440
Culture, government support of, 369–370
Currencies, 611. *See also specific currencies*
  appreciation of, 709
  changes in demand for, 709f, 709–710
  changes in supply of, 710f, 710–711, 711f
  dollarization of, 716–717
  reserve, global, 710
Current account, 704, 705
Customers, labor market discrimination by, 303–304
Cyclical unemployment, 524, 525f, 526–527
Czech Republic
  corruption in, 440
  real GDP per capita in, 440

D

Dalton, Georgia, 207
Dark Ages, 159
Data graphs, A.1t, A–4—A–8, A.5f—A.9f
David, Paul A., 278n
Deadweight loss, 101, 225–226, 226f
  commodity taxes and, 132
DeBeers cartel, 273
Debt, national, 550, 667f, 667–669, 668f
Decreasing cost industries, 202, 202f
  industry supply curves for, 207–208
Deere, Donald, 59, R–1
Default risk, 494
Defense
  government spending for, 662, 662f, 664t, 664–665
  political economy and, 383

Defense Department, 227, 228
Deficits
  budget, 668
  trade, 702–703, 707
Deflation, 545, 637
Deforestation, in African Sahel region, 353
Delmonico, Francis, 367
del Nino C., R–3
Delta, 225
Demand
  aggregate. *See* Aggregate demand; Aggregate demand-aggregate supply model; Aggregate demand curve
  for currency, changes in, 709f, 709–710
  for domain names, 202–204
  elastic, 55
  elasticity of. *See* Elasticity of demand
  factors shifting, 17–20
  inelastic, 55
  for labor, 289–291, 290t, 291f
  quantity demanded versus, 42–44, 43f
  shift in, change in price from, 68–69
  shifts in, savings and, 490–492, 491f–493f
  tariffs and, 150–152, 151f
  trade and, 149–152, 150f
  unit elastic, 55
Demand curve
  aggregate. *See* Aggregate demand curve
  definition of, 13
  factors shifting, 17, 17f
  for oil, 13–20, 14f, 15f
  shifts in, 40–42, 41f, 42f
Democracy, 389–397
  famine and, 393–395, 394f
  growth and, 395–397
  median voter theorem and, 390f, 390–392
  non-democracy and, 392f, 392–393
Democratic Republic of the Congo (DRC)
  corruption in, 439t, 440
  economic freedom index and standard of living in, 392f
  real GDP per capita in, 428–429, 429f, 440
Deng Xiaoping, 438
Denmark
  conditional convergence and, 464f
  corruption in, 439t
  government spending in, 671f
  hiring and firing costs in, 522f
  unemployment benefits in, 523
Department of Defense, 227, 228
Department of Housing and Urban Development, 63
Department of Labor, 409
Depreciation, 710f, 710–711, 711f
Depressions. *See* Great Depression
Destruction, creative, 201–202
Diamond cartel, 273
Diocletian, 6
Dirty float, 717

Disability insurance, GDP and, 415
Disabled persons, accessibility of mass transit to, 369
Discount rate, 617–618
Discouraged workers, 515–516
Disinflation, 545, 637
Dismal Science, 375n
Disney, 279
Diversification, 335–337
Dividends, taxes on, 658–659
DNS. *See* Domain Name System (DNS)
Doby, Larry, 302
Doe, Samuel, 439
Dollar. *See* Canadian dollar; New Zealand dollar; U.S. dollar
Dollar, David, 420, R–2
Dollarization, 716–717
Domain names, demand for, 202–204
Domain Name System (DNS), 203
Dominant strategy, 271
Domino's, 469
Dow Jones Industrial Average, 336
Dr. Atkins' New Diet Revolution, 19–20
DRC. *See* Democratic Republic of the Congo (DRC)
Drug(s). *See also* Pharmaceutical industry
  pricing of, 219, 220, 224, 227–228, 243–246, 251
  smuggling, 243
Drug lag, 3
Drug loss, 3, 4
DuPont, 252
Dust Bowl, 581
DVDs
  region codes and, 245
  standard for, 278f, 278–279
Dvorak, August, 278

E

Earned Income Tax Credit (EITC), 137, 665–666
East Asia. *See also specific countries*
  recession in, 46
Eastern Europe. *See specific countries*
easyJet, 125
eBay, 276
Economic fluctuations. *See* Business fluctuations (business cycles); Great Depression; Recessions
Economic freedom index, standard of living and, 392f, 392–393
Economic growth, 395–397, 429–431, 430f
  capital, production, and diminishing returns and, 453f, 453–455
  capital growth and, 455f, 455–458, 456f–458f
  economics of ideas and, 458–460, 459f
  future of, 470–472
  importance of, 6–7
  individuals' attempt to smooth consumption and, 485
  institutions of, 437–441
  miracles and disasters of, 432f, 432–433, 441–442

rates of, 430–431, 431t
Solow model of. *See* Solow growth curve; Solow model
spreadsheet for calculating compound growth and, 447–449, 447f–449f
Economics
  as exciting and important, 9–10
  of ideas. *See* Ideas, economics of
  normative, 366
  positive, 366
Economies of scale, 441
  regulation of monopoly and, 229–234, 230f, 231f
  trade and, 145
Ecuador
  in OPEC, 45n
  U.S. dollar as official currency of, 611, 716–717
Edison, Thomas, 156, 227
Edmonds, Eric V., R–3
Education
  college enrollment during recessions and, 4–5, 5f
  of workforce, 295f, 295–296
Effectiveness lag, 688
Efficient equilibrium, 171
Efficient markets hypothesis, 334
Efficient quantity, 171–173, 172f
Egypt
  child labor in, 157f
  corruption in, 440
  nationalization of Suez Canal by, 44
  real GDP per capita in, 440
  Suez Crisis and, 44
  Yom Kippur War and, 45
eHarmony, 276
Eiger Labs, 467
Einstein, Albert, 149
EITC. *See* Earned Income Tax Credit (EITC)
Elastic demand, 55
Elasticity of demand, 52f, 52–60
  applications of, 58–60
  calculation of, 54–56, 74f, 74–75, 75f
  change in price from shift in demand and, 68–69
  commodity taxes and, 127–129
  cross-price, 76
  determinants of, 53–54, 54f, 54t
  income, 76–77
  monopoly markup and, 223–225, 224f
  total revenues and, 56–58, 57f, 58t
Elasticity of supply, 60–68, 61f
  applications of, 63–68
  calculation of, 63, 74f, 74–75, 75f
  change in price from shift in supply and, 68–69
  commodity taxes and, 127–129
  determinants of, 61–63, 62f, 63t
Elasticity rule, 52
Electricity
  price of, 232–234, 233f
  reducing external cost of generating, 177–178

Elimination principle, 200
El Salvador
  dollarization in, 716
  U.S. dollar as official currency of, 611
Employees, labor market discrimination by, 304
Employers, labor market discrimination by, 302–303
Employment. *See also* Labor *entries;* Unemployment *entries*
  international trade and, 155–156
Employment-at-will doctrine, 521
Employment protection laws, 521–522, 522f
Endowment effect, 573
Energy Information Service (EIS), 68
Engemann, Kristie M., 306n
England. *See* Great Britain; United Kingdom
Enron, 314, 335, 499
Entourage (TV show), 232
Entrepreneurs, 467
Entry
  barriers to, 234
  into industries in competitive markets, 198–200, 199t
  of producers, supply and, 25–26, 26f
Environmental costs, GDP and, 418–419
Environment risk, tournaments and, 320
Ephron, Nora, 109
Equatorial Guinea
  corruption in, 439t, 440
  real GDP per capita in, 440
Equilibrium, 33–48
  adjustment process and, 33–35, 34f, 35f
  efficient, 171
  financial institutions and, 492–498
  gains from trade and, 35–38, 36f, 38f
  in market for loanable funds, 489–492, 490f
  Nash, 276–277
  oil prices and, 44–46, 45f
  in real world, 38–40, 39f
  shifting demand and supply curves and, 40–42, 41f, 42f
Equilibrium price, 34–35
  maximization of gains from trade at, 35–38, 36f, 38f
Equilibrium quantity
  definition of, 37
  maximization of gains from trade at, 35–38, 36f, 38f
Eritrea
  corruption in, 440
  inflation rate in, 540t
  real GDP per capita in, 440
Ethanol, Brazilian production of, 81
Ethics, 375n
Ethiopia
  child labor in, 157f
  corruption in, 440
  real GDP per capita in, 440
ETS. *See* Energy Information Service (EIS)
EU. *See* European Union (EU)

Euro, 717
  exchange rates and, 708, 708t
Europe. *See also specific countries*
  economic growth of, 430f
  labor law in, 521
  underground economy in, 417
  unemployment rate in, 520, 520f
  unions in, 520–521
  wages in, 520, 520f
European Central Bank, 717
European Renaissance, 159–160
European Union (EU), 145, 717
  HDTV subsidy in, 159
Evaluation and adjustment lag, 688
Excel, 279
Exchange rates, 707–718
  determination of, in long run, 711–714
  determination of, in short run, 708f, 708–711
  fiscal policy and, 716
  fixed vs. floating, 716–718
  monetary policy and, 714–716, 715f, 716f
  money supply and, 710f, 710–711, 711f, 714–716. 715f, 716f
  nominal, 711
  purchasing power parity and, 712–714
  real, 711
Excludable goods, 348, 349t
Executive compensation, 319–320
Exit
  from industries in competitive markets, 198–200, 199t
  of producers, supply and, 25–26, 26f
Expectations
  demand and, 19
  supply and, 25, 25f
Expected inflation, 548, 571–572, 572f
Exploitation, 367–368
Export(s). *See* International trade; Net exports
Exporting pollution, 366–367
External benefits, 173–175, 174f
External costs, 170, 171–173, 172f
Externalities, 169–186
  efficiency and, 170–175, 171f
  government solutions to problems of, 177–182
  private solutions to problems of, 175–177

F

Facebook, 275, 279, 466, 597
Factor income approach to GDP, 415–416
Factors of production, wealth and, 433–435
Fair and equal treatment, 369
Famine, 393–395, 394f
Fanjul, Jose and Alfonso, 384–385
Farming. *See* Agriculture
FDA. *See* Food and Drug Administration (FDA)
FDIC. *See* Federal Deposit Insurance Corporation (FDIC)

Fear, shifts in aggregate demand curve and, 577–578

Federal Deposit Insurance Corporation (FDIC), 619

Federal Funds rate, 617

Federal Insurance Contribution Act (FICA) tax, 655, 656, 659–660

Federal Reserve System (Fed), 8, 9, 609–628
  control of, 623–624
  control of money supply by, 615–620
  discount rate lending and, 617–618
  fractional reserve banking and, 613–615
  as lender of last resort, 617
  monetary policy and. *See* Monetary policy
  open market operations and, 615–617
  systemic risk and, 620–621
  U.S. money supplies and, 610–613, 611f, 613f

FedEx, 488–489

Fees, for investments and mutual funds, 337t, 337–338

Female labor force participation, 417
  incentives and, 529–531, 530f, 531f
  pill and, 531–532

Feynman, Richard, 542

FICA. *See* Federal Insurance Contribution Act (FICA) tax

Fiji
  corruption in, 440
  real GDP per capita in, 440

Final goods and services, 407

Financial account, 704–705

Financial institutions, 492–498
  banks as, 493–494. *See also* Bank(s); Bank failures
  bond market as, 494–497, 496f
  failure of intermediation and, 498–503, 499f
  stock market as, 497–498
  Treasury recapitalization of, 618, 619, 624

Finland
  corruption in, 439t, 440
  government spending in, 671f
  hiring and firing costs in, 522f
  real GDP per capita in, 440

Firefox, 279

Fiscal policy, 679–699, 680f. *See also* Government borrowing; Government spending; Tax(es)
  crowding out and, 682, 683–687
  effective use of, 693–694
  exchange rates and, 716
  expansionary, government spending versus tax cuts as, 689–690
  expansionary, making matters worse, 692–693
  lags and, 688
  multiplier and, 681–682, 682f
  raising taxes to finance, 683
  real shocks and, 683, 690–692, 691f, 692f
  sale of bonds to finance, 683–684

stimulating aggregate demand and, 682, 687
  timing of, 682, 687–689
  tools of, 8

Fisher, Irving, 549

Fisher effect, 549

Fixed costs, 190
  price discrimination and coverage of, 251–252

Fixed exchange rates, 716–718

Flat taxes, 661

Float, dirty (managed), 717

Floating exchange rates, 716

Florida Crystals Association, 384

Florida Sugar Cane League, 384

Flowers, Dutch market for, 80

Fogo De Chao, 20

Food and Drug Administration (FDA), 3

Forbes, Steve, 661

Forced riders, 350

Ford, Peter, 520, R–2

Ford Motor Company, 495

Foreign aid, 374–375, 383, 666

Foreign direct investment (FDI), 705

Fort Hood, 385–386

Forward contracts, 87n

Fractional reserve banking, 613–615

France
  conditional convergence and, 464f
  corruption in, 440
  euro and, 717
  government spending in, 671f
  government support of culture in, 369
  hiring and firing costs in, 522f
  labor force participation of older workers in, 528f
  military expenditure of, 664t
  Paris riots over unemployment in, 522–523
  real GDP per capita in, 406t, 440
  Suez Crisis and, 44
  taxes and labor force participation in, 529f
  unemployment benefits in, 519, 519t
  unemployment in, 517, 518, 518t, 520, 520f
  workweek in, 418, 419f

Freeman, Alida Castillo, 62, R–1

Freeman, Richard B., 62, R–1

Free riders, 349–350, 438

The French Laundry, 298

Frictional unemployment, 516–517, 517f

Friedman, Milton, 9, 372, 502, 544, 633, 636

Friendster, 279

Fryer, Roland G., Jr., 305

Fuller, Ida May, 655, 663, 664

Futures, 87
  prices of, as signals, 88

Futures markets, 87

G

Gabon
  corruption in, 440
  in OPEC, 45n
  real GDP per capita in, 440

Gains from trade, 701
  lost, commodity taxes and, 131f, 131–133, 132f
  lost, price ceilings and, 101f, 101–103, 109
  lost, price floors and, 121f, 121–122
  maximization at equilibrium price and quantity, 35–38, 36f, 38f

Gambia
  corruption in, 440
  real GDP per capita in, 440

Game theory, 265

Garfield, James A., 7

Garnett, Kevin, 290

Gates, Bill, 4

GDP. *See* Gross Domestic Product (GDP)

GDP deflator, 539

GDP per capita, 406
  corruption and, 439, 440f
  growth of, 410–412, 411f
  health and, 427–428, 428f
  largest countries ranked by, 406, 406t
  level of, 429–431, 430f, 431t
  population growth and, 411
  variation among nations, 428–429, 429f
  world, 470

General Electric, 321

General Steel, 227

The General Theory of Employment, Interest and Money (Keynes), 681, 691–692

General Tire, 227

General Wheat, 227

Georgia
  corruption in, 440
  real GDP per capita in, 440

Germany
  economic growth of, 454–455
  euro and, 717
  government spending in, 671f
  hiring and firing costs in, 522f
  inflation rate in, 541t
  labor force participation of older workers in, 528f
  military expenditure of, 664t
  real GDP per capita in, 406t
  taxes and labor force participation in, 529f
  unemployment benefits in, 519, 519t
  unemployment in, 517, 518, 518t
  workweek in, 418, 419f

Gertler, Mark, 641, R–3

GetRealNames.com, 203

Ghana
  child labor in, 157f
  interest rate in, 501t

Gingrich, Newt, 5

Glaeser, Edward, 109

GlaxoSmithKline, 220, 224, 227, 243–246, 251

Globalization. *See* International finance; International trade

Global reserve currencies, 710

GNP. *See* Gross national product (GNP)

GoDaddy.com, 203

Goldin, Claudia, 531–532
Goods
  excludable, 348, 349t
  final, 407
  in GDP, 407
  inferior, 18, 77
  network. *See* Network goods
  nonexcludable, 348, 349t
  nonrival, 348, 349t
  non-rivalrous, 468
  normal, 18, 77
  private, 349
  private, nonrival, 351–352
  public, 349–351
  rival, 348, 349t
Google, 279, 342–343, 351, 498
Google Docs, 276
Government
  control of media by, 393
  labor market discrimination by, 304–305
  prosecution of cartels by, 274
  role of, in production of new ideas,
    468–469
  solutions to externality problems and,
    177–182
  support of culture by, 369–370
  wealth and, 438–439, 440f
Government borrowing
  crowding out and, 495, 496f, 683–684
  to finance fiscal policy, 683–684
Government-controlled cartels, 274–275
Government revenues. *See also* Tax(es)
  undercounting of government's role in
    economy by, 672
Government spending, 662f, 662–669
  for defense, 662, 662f, 664t, 664–665
  in GDP, 414, 415f
  international comparison of, 671, 672f
  for Medicare and Medicaid, 662, 662f,
    665
  national debt and, 667f, 667–669, 668f
  shifts in aggregate demand curve and,
    578
  for Social Security, 662f, 662–664, 663t
  tax cuts versus, 689–690
  undercounting of government's role in
    economy by, 672
  for unemployment insurance, 662, 662f,
    665
  for welfare, 662, 662f, 665–666
Grades, tournaments and, 321–322
Graham, Lindsey, 384t
Grand Coulee Dam, 232
Grand Theft Auto IV, 227, 228
Grant, Ulysses S., 7
Graphs, A–1—A–14
  cause and effect relationships and,
    A–9—A–12, A.11f
  data, A.1t, A–4—A–8, A.5f—A.9f
  to express ideas, A–1—A–4, A.2f—A.4f
  of three variables, A–8—A–9, A.10f
Grassley, Charles, 384t
Grayson, C. Jackson, 99

Great Britain. *See also* United Kingdom
  child labor in, 157
  economic growth of, 441
  oil industry in Middle East and, 44
  unions in, 300
Great Depression, 8, 579–582
  aggregate demand shocks and, 579–580,
    580f
  bank failures and, 501–502, 579, 580–581
  fiscal policy and, 693, 694
  real shocks and, 580–582
  velocity of money and, 545
Great economic problem, 81–84, 83f
Great Leap Forward, 438
Greece
  conditional convergence and, 464f
  corruption in, 440
  euro and, 717
  hiring and firing costs in, 522f
  inflation rate in, 541t
  real GDP per capita in, 440
Green accounting, 419
Greenspan, Alan, 643
Grenada
  corruption in, 440
  real GDP per capita in, 440
Griswold v. Connecticut, 531
Gross domestic product (GDP), 405–425
  per capita. *See* GDP per capita
  cyclical and short-run changes in,
    412–413, 413f
  definition of, 406–409
  GDP deflator and, 539
  growth rates and, 409
  largest countries ranked by, 406, 406t
  as measure of output and welfare,
    problems with, 416–420
  methods for splitting, 413–416
  nominal, 409–410
  real. *See* Real GDP
Grossman, Michael, 60n
Gross national product (GNP), 408
GrowingStars.com, 159
Gruber, J., 529n, 659n
Guatemala, GDP growth in, 411
Guinea
  child labor in, 157f
  inflation rate in, 540t
Gun buyback programs, elasticity of supply
    and, 63–65, 64f

H

Haiti
  business startups in, 441
  corruption in, 439t, 440
  economic freedom index and standard
    of living in, 392f
  real GDP per capita in, 440
  underground economy in, 417
Hall, Robert E., 440, 661, R–2, R–3
Hall, Thomas E., 58, R–1
Halo, 227, 228
Hansen, Alvin, 693, R–3

Hardaway, Tim, 313
Harkin, Tom, 156, 384t
Harkin Grant Program, 386
Harry Potter books, 247–248, 373
Hart, Oliver, 315
Hayek, A. Friedrich, 83, 84
HBO, 351
HDTV, trade and, 159
Health, real GDP and, 427–428, 428f
Health insurance. *See also* Medicaid;
    Medicare
  taxes and, 130
Hebner, Mark T., R–2
Hechingers, 85
Height, labor market discrimination and,
    306
Hewlett-Packard (HP), 89, 252–253
Heyne, Paul, 88
Hobbes, Thomas, 350
Hollywood Stock Exchange, 90f, 90–91
Honey market, 175–176
Hong Kong
  corruption in, 440
  economic freedom index and standard
    of living in, 392f
  inflation rate in, 540t
  pegging of currency of, 717
  real GDP per capita in, 440
Hong Kong dollar, 717
Hoover Dam, 232
Horsemeat, 368
Horwich, G., 40, R–1
Household production, GDP and, 418
House Military Construction
    Appropriations Subcommittee,
    385–386
Housing and Urban Development
    Department, 63
Housing market
  bubble in, 643
  crisis in, during 2007-2008, 502–503
  prices in, 340–341, 341f
Housing vouchers, 110
  rent controls and, 106–110
HP. *See* Hewlett-Packard (HP)
H-Prize, 227, 228
Human capital, 295f, 295–296
  wealth and, 434–435
Hungary
  corruption in, 440
  inflation rate in, 541t, 541–542
  real GDP per capita in, 440
Hurricane Katrina, 19
Hussein, Saddam, 611
Hyperinflation, 541t, 541–542, 543, 543f,
    551

I

IBM, 248, 316–317
Iceland
  conditional convergence and, 464f
  corruption in, 439, 439t, 440
  real GDP per capita in, 440

Ideas, economics of, 458–460, 459f, 464–470, 465f, 471
  government's role and, 468–469
  market size and research and development and, 469–470
  research and development as investment and, 466–468
  spillovers and, 468, 469f
Illiquid banks, 619
IMF. *See* International Monetary Fund (IMF)
Immigration to United States, 298, 374
Implementation lag, 688
Imports. *See also* International trade
  of kidneys, 366–367
Incentives, 1, 2, 313–325
  elimination by price controls, 102
  for labor force participation, 528–532
  nonmonetary, 322–324
  pay for performance to reduce risk and, 318–322
  piece rates vs. hourly wages as, 316–318
  for research and development, 227–229
  significance of, 2
  strength of, 313–318
Income. *See also* Wages
  demand and, 18
  savings and, 485
Income distribution
  entitlement theory and, 372–373
  GDP and, 419–420, 420t
  maximin principle and, 370–371
  utilitarianism and, 371–372
Income elasticity of demand, 76–77
Income taxes
  corporate, 656, 660
  individual, 655, 656–659, 657f
Increasing cost industries, 202, 202f
  industry supply curves for, 205–207, 206f
India
  child labor in, 157, 157f
  corruption in, 440
  drug prices in, 227
  DVD region codes and, 245
  economic growth of, 46, 405, 406f, 430f
  labor market discrimination in, 304
  legal system in, 439
  military expenditure of, 664t
  online tutors in, 159
  poverty in, 405
  real GDP and infant mortality in, 428f
  real GDP per capita in, 405, 405f, 406, 406t, 440
  wages in, 293–295, 294f
  women in labor force in, 418
  as World Bank borrower, 719
Individual income tax, 655, 656–659, 657f
Individual transferable quotas (ITQs), 354, 355f
Indonesia
  corruption in, 440
  financial crisis in, 693, 718

  in OPEC, 45n
  pegging of currency of, 717
  real GDP per capita in, 406t, 440
  recession in, 46
Industries. *See also specific industries*
  balance of, 200–202
  clusters of, 207–208
  entering and exiting in competitive markets, 198–200, 199t
  key, trade and, 158–159
Industry supply curves, 202f, 202–208
  for constant cost industries, 202–205, 204f
  for decreasing cost industries, 207–208
  for increasing cost industries, 205–207, 206f
Inefficiency, monopoly and, 226–227
Inelastic demand, 55
Infant mortality, 7, 427, 428f
Inferior goods, 18, 77
Inflation, 8–9, 537–555, 538f
  cause of, 543f, 543–545, 544f
  controls on interest rates and, 499–501, 500f, 501t
  costs of, 546–552
  definition of, 538
  expected, 548, 571–572, 572f
  interaction with taxes, 551–552
  interest rates and, 549
  money illusion and, 547
  pain of stopping, 552
  price confusion and, 547
  price indexes and, 538–539
  quantity theory of money and, 542–546
  in United States, 539, 539f
  wealth redistribution by, 547–551, 549f, 550t
  in world, 539–542, 540f, 540t, 541t
Inflation rate, 538
Initial public offerings (IPOs), 497
Inputs, prices of, supply and, 24
Insolvency, 618
Institutions
  alignment of self-interest with social interest by, 2–3
  wealth and, 7–8, 435–441, 436f
Insurance
  deposit, 619
  disability, GDP and, 415
  health. *See* Medicaid; Medicare
  unemployment. *See* Unemployment insurance
Interest rates
  bond prices and, 496–497
  borrowing and, 489, 489f
  controls on, inflation and, 499–501, 500f, 501t
  discount rate, 617–619
  Federal Funds rate, 617
  inflation rates and, 549
  investment and, 709–710
  open market operations and, 616–617
  savings and, 486–487, 487f
Intergovernmental Council of Copper Exporting Countries, 273

Intermediation. *See also* Bank(s); Financial institutions
  breakdown of, inflation and, 551
  controls in interest rates and inflation and, 499–501, 500f, 501t
  politicized lending and, 501
  property rights and, 498–499
International finance, 701–720
  balance of payments and. *See* Balance of payments
  costs of, purchasing power parity and, 713
  exchange rates and. *See* Exchange rates
  International Monetary Fund and, 701, 718–719
  trade deficits and, 702–703
  World Bank and, 701, 719–720
International Monetary Fund (IMF), 701, 705, 718–719
International trade, 143–167, 159–160
  Adam Smith on, 149
  child labor and, 156–158, 157f
  comparative advantage and, 145–149, 146t–148t
  economies of scale and, 145
  globalization and, 159–160
  jobs and, 155–156
  key industries and, 158–159
  markets and, 79–80
  NAFTA and, 25–26, 26f
  national security and, 158
  protectionism and, 152–155, 159
  specialization and, 143–144
  supply and demand analysis of, 149–152, 150f
  winners and losers from, 154–155
Internet
  frictional unemployment and, 516
  Internet dating market and, 276
Internet Explorer, 279–280
Intertemporal substitution, 594–596, 595f, 596f
Investment(s)
  borrowing to finance large investments and, 488–489
  in capital account, 705
  definition of, 484
  foreign, in United States, 706–707
  foreign, of China, 483
  in GDP, 414, 415f
  increase in rate of, Solow model and, 461–463, 462f
  interest rates and, 709–710
  irreversible, 596–597
  marriage as, 597
  in Mexico, 709
  in stocks. *See* Stock *entries*
  taxes on dividends and, 658–659
Invisible hand, 3, 38, 84, 104, 148
Invisible hand property #1, 193f, 193–195, 194f
Invisible hand property #2, 200–202
Iowa Electronic Markets, 88–90
IP (Internet Protocol) addresses, 203

iPhone, 467
iPods, 234–235
IPOs. *See* Initial public offerings (IPOs)
Iran
    corruption in, 440
    nationalization of oil industry in, 44
    oil production of, 22, 46
    in OPEC, 45n
    real GDP per capita in, 440
Iraq
    corruption in, 439t, 440
    oil production of, 22
    in OPEC, 45n
    real GDP per capita in, 440
Ireland
    conditional convergence and, 464f
    corruption in, 440
    government spending in, 671f
    hiring and firing costs in, 522f
    real GDP per capita in, 440
Irreversible investments, 596–597
Israel
    corruption in, 440
    real GDP per capita in, 440
    Suez Crisis and, 44
    Yom Kippur War and, 45
Italy
    conditional convergence and, 464f
    corruption in, 440
    government spending in, 671f
    hiring and firing costs in, 522f
    labor force participation of older
        workers in, 528f
    military expenditure of, 664t
    real GDP and infant mortality in, 428f
    real GDP per capita in, 406t, 429f, 440
    taxes and labor force participation in, 529f
    unemployment in, 517, 518, 518t
ITQs. *See* Individual transferable quotas
    (ITQs)

J
Jackson, Andrew, 7
Jackson, C. Grayson, 105
Jacob, Brian, 314
Japan
    banks in, 501
    corruption in, 440
    economic growth of, 432, 432f, 433,
        454–455
    government spending in, 671f
    HDTV subsidy in, 159
    inflation rate in, 540t, 541
    influence on IMF, 718
    labor force participation of older
        workers in, 528f
    military expenditure of, 664t
    real GDP per capita in, 406t, 440
    taxes and labor force participation in, 529f
    voluntary import restraints and, 145
    workweek in, 419t
Japanese yen
    exchange rates and, 708, 708t
    strength of, 711

JDate.com, 276
Jefferson, Thomas, 468
JetBlue Airways, 125
Jim Crow policies, 304
Jobs, Steve, 467
Jobs, international trade and, 155–156
Johnson, Bradford, R–3
Johnson-Sirleaf, Ellen, 439
Jones, Charles I., 440, R–2
Jordan, Michael, 20
JP Morgan, 620
Junk bonds, 494

K
Katz, Lawrence, 531–532
Kay, John, 467
Kazakhstan
    corruption in, 440
    real GDP per capita in, 440
Kennedy, John F., tax cuts under, 688
Kenya
    child labor in, 157f
    corruption in, 440
    real GDP per capita in, 440
Kevlar prices, 252
Key industries, trade and, 158–159
Keynes, John Maynard, 570, 681, 691–692
Kidneys, importing, 366–367
Kiribati, inflation rate in, 540t
"Kiwi dollar," 709–710
Klick, Jonathan, A–11, R–3
Klobuchar, Amy, 384t
Kmart, 323, 517
Knowledge, division of, trade and,
    143–144
Koch, Ed, 369
Kotlikoff, Laurence J, 18, 528, R–1, R–2
Kraay, Aart, 420, R–2
Kremer, Michael, 228–229, 468, R–2
Krueger, Alan B., 59, R–1
Kuwait
    corruption in, 440
    in OPEC, 45n
    real GDP per capita in, 440
Kyowa Hakko Kogyo, 274

L
Labor
    child, international trade and, 156–158,
        157f
    demand for, 289–291, 290t, 291f
    marginal product of, 289–291, 290t,
        291f
    supply of, 291–293, 292f, 293f
Labor adjustment costs, 597–598
Labor Department, 409
Labor force, 515
Labor force participation, 527–532
    female, increase in, 529–532, 530f, 531f
    incentives and, 528–532
    lifecycle effects and demographics and,
        527t, 527–528
Labor force participation rate, 515

Labor market(s), 289–312
    demand for labor and, 289–291, 290t, 291f
    discrimination in. *See* Labor market
        discrimination
    human capital and, 295f, 295–296
    marginal product of labor and, 289–291,
        290t, 291f
    supply of labor and, 291–293, 292f, 293f
    wages and. *See* Wages
Labor market discrimination, 300–306
    identification of, 305–306
    preference-based, 301–305
    statistical, 301
Laibson, David, 486, R–2
Lands' End, 574
La Porta, Rafael, 501
Laroque, Guy, 520, R–2
Latin America. *See also specific countries*
    economic growth of, 430f
    underground economy in, 417
Latvia
    corruption in, 440
    real GDP per capita in, 440
Law. *See* Legal system
Law of one price, 712
Leahy, Patrick J., 384t
Lear, 105
Lee, Spike, 90
Legal system
    employment protection laws and,
        521–522, 522f
    European labor law and, 521
    wealth and, 439–440
Legislative lag, 688
Leisure, GDP and, 418, 419f
Lender of last resort, 617
Lesch, Hagen, 520, R–2
Lesotho
    corruption in, 440
    real GDP per capita in, 440
Levine, Ross, 498, R–2
Levitt, Steven D., 305, 314
Levy, David M., 375n
Lewis, William W., 441, R–2
Liberia
    corruption in, 439, 439t, 440
    infant mortality in, 7
    political instability in, 439
    real GDP and infant mortality in, 427,
        428f
    real GDP per capita in, 440
Libya
    corruption in, 440
    in OPEC, 45n
    real GDP per capita in, 440
Lichtenberg, Frank R., 3, 251n, 470, R–1,
    R–2
Liebowitz, Stan J., 278n
Lincoln, Abraham, 7, 467
Lincoln, Blanche, 384t
Lindbeck, Assar, 108
Lines, wasteful, price ceilings and, 99, 99f
Liquid assets, 612
Liquidity crisis, 618–619

Living standard, economic freedom index and, 392f, 392–393
L.L. Bean, 574
Loanable funds, market for, equilibrium in, 489–492, 490f
Local taxes, 662
Locke, John, 441
Long run, 205
Lopez-de-Silanes, Florencio, 501, R–2
Losses
  deadweight, 101, 132, 225–226, 226f
  drug, 3, 4
Lothar Funk, 520, R–2
Lotus 1-2-3, 279
Lugar, Richard G., 384t
Luttmer, Erzo, 109
Luxembourg
  conditional convergence and, 464f
  corruption in, 440
  economic freedom index and standard of living in, 392f
  real GDP per capita in, 429f, 440
Lysine market, 274

M

Macoun, Robert J., 59n
Madden NFL, 227, 228
Madoff scandal, 499
Madrian, Brigitte, 486, R–2
Major league sports. *See also specific teams and leagues*
  cartelization of, 273
  labor market discrimination by, 302–303, 305
  marginal product of labor and, 290
  work stoppages in, 300
Malaria, 6–7
Malawi
  corruption in, 440
  real GDP per capita in, 440
Malaysia
  corruption in, 440
  real GDP per capita in, 440
Mali, child labor in, 157f
Malkiel, Burton, 331
Managed float, 717
Mao Zedong, 438, 454, 483
Margin, thinking on, 5–6
Marginal costs, 190, 192–193, 220–225, 221f–223f
Marginal product of capital, 453
Marginal product of labor (MPL), 289–291, 290t, 291f
Marginal revenue, 190–191, 220–225, 221f–223f
Marginal tax rate, 656–657, 657f
Margolis, Stephen E., 278n
Market(s)
  alignment of self-interest with social interest by, 2–3
  bond, 494–497, 496f
  competitive, wealth and, 440–441
  efficient, 334

futures, 87
for honey, 175–176
international links and, 79–80
Internet dating, 276
labor. *See Labor market(s); Labor market discrimination*
links between, 80–81
for loanable funds, equilibrium in, 489–492, 490f
open, wealth and, 440–441
prediction, 88–91, 90f
real estate, prices in, 340–341, 341f
size of, research and development and, 469–470
stock. *See Stock entries*
Market confidence, 638–639
Marketing, savings and, 486
Market power, 220–225
  profit maximization and, 220–225, 221f–223f
Marriage as investment, 597
Martin, John P. 523, R–2
Martinez, Rivera, 122
Mass transit, accessibility to disabled persons, 369
Match.com, 275
Maximin principle, 370–371
MB. *See Monetary base (MB)*
McCain, John, 89
McConnell, Mitch, 384t
McDonald's, 290–291, 293
McMillan, John, 438, R–2
Meade, James, 175
Meany, George, 99
Meddlesome preferences, 368
Media. *See also specific media*
  government control of, 393
Median voter theorem, 390f, 390–392
Median wage, 520
Medicaid, government spending for, 662, 662f, 665
Medicare, 528, 660
  GDP and, 415
  government spending for, 662, 662f, 665
Medicare tax, 655, 656, 659–660
Mendez, Jose A., 80n
Menu costs, 574
Merck, 3
Mexico
  child labor in, 157f
  economic growth of, 432
  financial crisis in, 693
  immigrants from, 374
  inflation rate in, 551
  investment in, 709
  NAFTA and, 25–26, 26f
  oil production of, 46
  real GDP and infant mortality in, 428f
  real GDP per capita in, 406, 406t, 429, 429f
  wages in, 713
  workweek in, 419t
  as World Bank borrower, 719

Microsoft, 276, 279–280, 342–343
  bundling by, 253–255, 254f
Microsoft Windows, 279
Microsoft Word, 275, 279
Midpoint method
  for calculating elasticity of demand, 55–56
  for calculating elasticity of supply, 63
Milk cartels, 274
Mill, John Stuart, 375
Minimum wage, 520, 520f
  lost gains from trade and, 121f, 121–122
  surpluses and, 120f, 120–121
  unemployment and, 520, 520f
Miron, Jeffrey A., 59n
Mischel, W., 486, R–2
MM. *See Money multiplier (MM)*
M1 monetary aggregate, 612, 613f, 617
M2 monetary aggregate, 612, 613f, 617
MMR vaccine, 178n
Modigliani, Franco, 487
Mohair, national security and, 158
Monaghan, Thomas S., 469
Monetary base (MB), 612, 613f
A Monetary History of the United States, 1867–1960 (Friedman and Schwartz), 502
Monetary policy, 633–654
  aggregate demand and, 621–623, 622f, 637–638
  exchange rates and, 714–716, 715f, 716f
  lags and, 688
  market confidence and, 638–639
  negative real shocks and, 639f–641f, 639–642
  positive shocks and, 642f, 642–644
  rules versus discretion and, 636–637
  Term Auction Facility as, 617, 619
  tools of, 8
Monetizing the debt, 550
Money. *See also specific currencies*
  definition of, 610
  quantity theory of, 542–546
  velocity of, 542, 545
Money illusion, 547
Money market mutual funds, 612
Money multiplier (MM), 614, 629–632
Money supply, 610–613, 611f, 613f
  exchange rates and, 710f, 710–711, 711f, 714–716, 715f, 716f
  Fed's control of, 615–620. *See also Monetary policy*
  inflation and, 8–9
  shifts in aggregate demand curve and, 577
Monopoly, 219–241
  benefits of, 227–229
  costs of, 226–227
  deadweight loss and, 225–226, 226f
  economies of scale and regulation of, 229–234, 230f, 231f
  market power and, 220–225

natural, 229
network goods sold by, 276
Monroe, James, 7
Montreal Protocol, 355
Moody's, 494
Moral hazard, 621
Morocco
corruption in, 440
real GDP per capita in, 440
Morrison, David, 347n
Morrison, Steven A., 63, R–1
Mosaddeq, Mohammad, 44n
Mosquito control, 349–350
MPL. See Marginal product of labor (MPL)
MP3 players, 234, 467
MRSA. See Multidrug-resistant Staphylococcus aureus (MRSA)
Mullainathan, Sendil, 305n
Multidrug-resistant Staphylococcus aureus (MRSA), 169
Multiplier, money, 614, 629–632
Multiplier effect, 681–682, 682f
Murphy, Eddie, 90
Murphy, Kevin M., 59, R–1
Music as network good, 280–281
Mutual funds, fees for, 337t, 337–338
Myanmar
corruption in, 439t
inflation rate in, 540t
MySpace, 279

N
NAFTA. See North American Free Trade Agreement (NAFTA)
NASDAQ Composite Index, 336, 342, 343f
Nash, John, 276–277
Nash equilibrium, 276–277
National Bureau of Economic Research (NBER), 412, 413
National debt held by the public, 550, 667f, 667–669, 668f
monetizing, 550
National Endowment for the Arts, 370
National Horse Protection League, 368
National security, trade and, 158
National spending identity, 414–415, 415f
Natural monopoly, 229
Natural unemployment rate, 526f, 526–527
NBA, 273, 290, 300, 305
NBER. See National Bureau of Economic Research (NBER)
Negative productivity shocks, 581
Nelson, E. Benjamin, 384t
Nepal
child labor in, 157f
corruption in, 440
real GDP per capita in, 440
Net exports
in GDP, 415, 415f
shifts in aggregate demand curve and, 578

Netflix, 227, 228, 279
Netherlands
conditional convergence and, 464f
corruption in, 439t
flower market in, 80
government spending in, 671f
hiring and firing costs in, 522f
labor force participation of older workers in, 528f
marijuana shops in, 59
oil industry in Middle East and, 44
taxes and labor force participation in, 529f
workweek in, 419t
Netscape, 279, 280
Network goods, 275–281
competition "for the market" instead of "in the market" and, 279–280
music as, 280–281
sale by monopolies or oligopolies, 276
standard wars and, 278f, 278–279
winners in markets for, 276–278, 277f
Neumark, David, 59, R–1
Newcombe, Dan, 302
New Keynesian model, 563, 570–579
shocks to aggregate demand in, 575–579
short-run aggregate supply curve and, 570–575
New York Central and Hudson River Railroad Company, 494
New York City
accessibility of mass transit to disabled persons in, 369
rent control in, 108
New York Mercantile Exchange (NYMEX), 87
New York Stock Exchange (NYSE), 497
New Zealand
Australian ownership of banks in, 705
corruption in, 439t, 440
economic freedom index and standard of living in, 392f
hiring and firing costs in, 522f
Individual transferable quotas and, 354, 355f
investment in, 709–710
real GDP per capita in, 440
New Zealand dollar, 709–710
NFL, 300
Nicaragua, inflation rate in, 541t
Niger, economic freedom index and standard of living in, 392f
Nigeria
child labor in, 157f
corruption in, 440
economic growth of, 432, 432f
GDP growth in, 412
kidnapping of construction worker in, 19
oil production of, 22
in OPEC, 45n
real GDP and infant mortality in, 428f
real GDP per capita in, 412, 429, 429f, 440

Nike, 20, 253
Nitrogen oxide emissions, acid rain and, 177
Nixon, Richard M., 82
political economy and, 388, 624
wage and price controls under, 6, 97, 103–104, 105
Nominal data, conversion to real data, 556–559, 556f–559f
Nominal exchange rate, 711
Nominal GDP, 409–410
Nominal variables, 409
Nonexcludable goods, 348, 349t
Nonmarket production, GDP and, 417–418
Nonmonetary incentives, 322–324
Nonrival goods, 348, 349t
Nonrival private goods, 351–352
Non-rivalrous goods, 468
Norberg, Johan, R–3
Normal goods, 18, 77
Normative economics, 366
North, Douglass, 227, 228
North American Free Trade Agreement (NAFTA)
investment in Mexico and, 709
supply and, 25–26, 26f
North Korea
corruption in, 439, 439t, 440
real GDP and infant mortality in, 428f
real GDP per capita in, 429f, 440
South Korea compared with, 7, 435–437, 436f
North Sea, oil production of, 22
Northwest Airlines, 225
Norway
conditional convergence and, 464f
corruption in, 439, 439t, 440
hiring and firing costs in, 522f
real GDP per capita in, 440
Nozick, Robert, 370, 372
Nozick's entitlement theory of justice, 372–373
Nutmeg cartel, 272–273
NYMEX. See New York Mercantile Exchange (NYMEX)
NYSE. See New York Stock Exchange (NYSE)

O
Oakland, California, gun buyback program in, 64
Obama, Barack, 89, 365
stimulus package under, 667, 679, 687, 690
O'Brien, Anthony, 581, R–3
OECD. See Organization for Economic Cooperation and Development (OECD)
Oil
allocation in United States, blat and, 112
demand curve for, 13–20, 14f, 15f
lack of substitutes for, 15

Oil *(cont.)*
  misallocation of, 102f, 102–104
  OPEC and. *See* Organization of
      Petroleum Exporting Countries
      (OPEC)
  production of, in Iraq, 110–111
  reduction in supply of, 99
  supply curve for, 20, 21f, 22f, 22–27
  U.S. economy's dependence on, 592,
      593f
Oil crisis of 1973-1974, 82
Oil prices, 44–46, 45f
  automobile industry and, 591
  controls on, 105–106
  futures, 88
  increase in supply and, 68–69
  during 1960-2005, 266f, 266–268
  OPEC and. *See* Organization of
      Petroleum Exporting Countries
      (OPEC)
  shocks and, 590–593, 591f–593f
  strategic trade protectionism and, 159
  success of cartel and, 272
Oil shocks, 590–593, 591f–593f
Oligopoly, network goods sold by, 276
Oman
  corruption in, 440
  real GDP per capita in, 440
Ontario, Canada, rent control in, 107f,
      107–108
OPEC. *See* Organization of Petroleum
      Exporting Countries (OPEC)
Open market(s), wealth and, 440–441
Open market operations, 615–617
OpenOffice, 276
Opportunity cost, 4–5, 5f, 83
  supply and, 26–27, 27f
  trade and, 146–147
Organization, wealth and, 435
Organization for Economic Cooperation
      and Development (OECD),
      463–464, 464f
Organization of Petroleum Exporting
      Countries (OPEC), 299
  cheating on, 268t–270t, 268–272
  embargo of 1973 and, 99
  formation of, 45
  power of, 265
  success of, 272
The Original Kings of Comedy (film), 90
Orszag, P., 529n
Other investment, 705
Outback Steakhouse, 20
Output, GDP as measure of, 416–420
Overfishing, 352–353
  cartels and, 272
Owyanc, Michael T., 306n

P
Page, Larry, 498
Pakistan
  child labor in, 157f
  corruption in, 440

  educational level in, 435
  real GDP per capita in, 440
Paley, Amit R., R–3
Pan Am, 85
Panama
  corruption in, 440
  dollarization in, 716
  real GDP per capita in, 440
  U.S. dollar as official currency of, 611
Panera Bread, 351
Paraguay
  corruption in, 440
  real GDP per capita in, 440
Patents, 467–468
  buyouts of, 228–229
  drug prices and, 227, 228
Paternalism, 369–370
Pavcnik, Nina, R–3
Peake, P., 486, R–2
Peart, Sandra J., 375n
Pegged exchange rates, 716–718
Pelosi, Nancy, 382, 702
Peltzman, Sam, 63, R–1
Pemex, 272
Penicillin, 169
Per capita GDP. *See* GDP per capita
Perdue, Frank, 353
Perfect price discrimination (PPD),
      249–250
Persico, Nicola, 306n
Peru
  business startups in, 441
  corruption in, 440
  inflation rate in, 541t, 543, 543f, 546,
      551
  interest rate in, 501t
  real GDP per capita in, 440
Pharmaceutical industry. *See also* Drug(s)
  tradeoffs in, 3–4
Phelps, Edmund, 136–137
Philippines, child labor in, 157f
Physical capital. *See also* Capital
  wealth and, 433–434
Piece rates, 316–318
Pigou, Arthur C., 173, 174
Pigouvian subsidies, 174–175
Pigouvian taxes, 173, 175
  tradable allowances compared with,
      181f, 181–182
Pill, female labor force participation and,
      531–532
Poland
  corruption in, 440
  interest rate in, 501t
  real GDP per capita in, 440
Polaroid, 85
Political action committees, 384, 384t
Political economy, 381–398
  business cycles and, 387f, 387–389, 389f
  democracy and. *See* Democracy
  rational ignorance and, 382–383
  special interests and, 383–387, 384t
Political stability, wealth and, 439

Pollution, exporting, 366–367
Population, aging of, 18, 528, 669
Population growth
  GDP per capita and, 411
  idea generation and, 470–471
Portfolio investment, 705
Portugal
  conditional convergence and, 464f
  corruption in, 440
  hiring and firing costs in, 522f
  real GDP per capita in, 440
Positive economics, 366
Postlewaite, Andrew, 306n
Poverty
  maximin principle and, 370–371
  utilitarianism and, 371–372
PPD. *See* Perfect price discrimination
      (PPD)
PPIs. *See* Producer price indexes (PPIs)
Prediction markets, 88–91, 90f
Preference(s), meddlesome, 368
Preference-based discrimination, 301–305
  by customers, 303–304
  by employees, 304
  by employers, 302–303
  by government, 304–305
Presidential elections, economic conditions
      and, 387f, 387–389, 389f
Price(s)
  agricultural, productivity and, 58–59, 59f
  of bonds, 496–497, 508–512
  of cable TV, 231–232
  in competitive markets, 188–190, 189f
  of complements, demand and, 18–19
  confusion about, inflation and, 547
  equilibrium. *See* Equilibrium price
  freeze of, under Nixon, 97
  housing, 340–341, 341f
  inflation and. *See* Inflation
  of inputs, supply and, 24
  of Kevlar, 252
  law of one price and, 712
  money illusion and, 547
  of oil. *See* Oil prices
  real, 540
  as signals, 84–85, 88
  sticky, 574–575
  of substitutes, demand and, 18, 19f
  of video games, 227, 228
Price ceilings, 97–117
  arguments for, 110–111
  end of, 105–106
  lost gains from trade and, 101f, 101–103,
      109
  under Nixon, 6
  quality reduction and, 98–99, 108
  rent controls as, 106–110
  resource misallocation and, 102–105,
      102f–105f, 109
  search costs and, 99f, 99–100, 108–109
  shortages and, 98, 98f, 106f, 106–108,
      107f
  universal, 111–112

Price discrimination, 243–260, 244f
  bundling and, 253–255, 254t
  evaluation of, 250–252
  perfect, 249–250
  prevalence of, 246–250, 247f
  preventing arbitrage and, 245–246
  principles of, 245
  problem solving using Excel and, 261f–263f, 261–264
  tying and, 252–253
  universities and, 248–250, 249t, 250t
Price floors, 119–125
  lost gains from trade and, 121f, 121–122
  resource misallocation and, 124–125
  surpluses and, 120f, 120–121
  wasteful increases in quality and, 122–124, 123f
Price indexes, 538–539
Price supports, agricultural, 385
Prison(s), private, 315, 316
Prisoner's dilemma, 272
Private costs, 170
Private goods, 349
  nonrival, 351–352
Producer(s), entry of exit of, supply and, 25–26, 26f
Producer price indexes (PPIs), 539
Producer surplus, 23, 23f
Production
  factors of, wealth and, 433–435
  increase in, elasticity of supply and, 61–62, 62f
  minimization of total costs of, 193f, 193–195, 194f
  nonmarket, GDP and, 417–418
  resource misallocation and, 104–105
Productivity
  agricultural, prices and, 58–59, 59f
  agricultural, under Stalin, 394
  in Soviet Union, 317
  wage differences related to, 293–295, 294f
Productivity shocks, negative, 581
Profit(s)
  average cost curve and, 195–198, 196f, 198f
  zero, 198–199
Profit maximization, market power and, 220–225, 221f–223f
Progressive taxes, 661
Property rights
  insecure, 498–499
  wealth and, 437–438
Protectionism
  costs of, 152–155, 153f
  strategic, 159
  supply and demand and, 150–152, 151f
Psychological factors, savings and, 486
Public goods, 349–351
Publishers, price discrimination by, 247–248
Puerto Rico, minimum wage in, 122
Purchasing power parity (PPP) theorem, 712–714
Pybus, C., 1, R–1

Q
Qatar
  corruption in, 440
  in OPEC, 45n
  real GDP per capita in, 440
Quality
  price ceilings and, 98–99, 108
  wasteful increases in, price floors and, 122–124, 123f
Quantity
  equilibrium. *See* Equilibrium quantity
  to produce in competitive markets, 190–193, 191f, 192f
Quantity demanded, 14
  demand versus, 42–44, 43f
Quantity supplied, 20
  supply versus, 43f, 44
Quantity theory of money, 542–546
  cause of inflation and, 543f, 543–545, 544f
Quattro Pro, 279
Quirk, J. P., 40, R–1
Quotas, trade, 151
  purchasing power parity and, 713

R
Rabushka, Alvin, 661, R–3
Rain, acid, 177
Ramirez, Hanley, 305
A Random Walk Down Wall Street (Malkiel), 331
Rational ignorance, 382–383
Rawls, John, 370
RBC. *See* Real business cycle (RBC) model
R&D. *See* Research and development (R&D)
Reagan, Ronald, 106
  election of, 524, 552
  monetary policy under, 637
Real business cycle (RBC) model, 563, 567–570, 568f, 589–605
  shocks and. *See* Real shocks; Shocks
Real data, conversion of nominal data to, 556–559, 556f–559f
Real estate. *See* Housing *entries*
Real exchange rate, 711
Real GDP, 410
  growth per capita, 410–412, 411f
  for largest countries, 405–406, 406f, 406t
Real prices, 540
Real shocks, 564, 564f
  fiscal policy and, 690–692, 691f, 692f
  Great Depression and, 580–582
  negative, monetary policy and, 639f–641f, 639–642
  positive, monetary policy and, 642f, 642–644
  real business cycle model and, 567–570, 568f
Real variables, 410

Recessions, 412, 561. *See also* Business fluctuations (business cycles)
  college enrollment during, 4–5, 5f
  Fed and, 9
  U.S., of 2007-2008, 619, 679
Recognition lag, 688
Rediker, M., 1, R–1
Red tape, wealth and, 441
Regressive taxes, 661
Reisman, George, R–3
Remittances, 374
Renaissance, 159–160
Rent controls, 106–110
  shortages and, 106f, 106–108, 107f
Rent regulation, 109–110
Required reserves, 620
Research and development (R&D)
  government's role in, 468–469
  incentives for, 227–229
  as investment for profit, 466–468
  market size and, 469–470
  spillovers and, 468, 469f
Reserve(s)
  fixed exchange rates and, 717
  required, 620
Reserve ratio (RR), 614
Resource(s), common, tragedy of the commons and, 352f, 352–355
Resource misallocation
  price ceilings and, 102–105, 102f–105f, 109
  price floors and, 124–125
Returns
  compound, 338t, 338–339
  trade-off between risk and, 339f, 339–341, 341f
Reuter, Peter, 59n
Revenues
  commodity taxes and, 131f, 131–133, 132f
  marginal, 190–191, 220–225, 221f–223f
  total, 56–58, 57f, 58t, 190
  undercounting of government's role in economy by, 672
Rewarding Work (Phelps), 136
Reyes, Jose, 305
Reza Pahlavi, Mohammad, 44n
Ricardian equivalence, 685–687, 686f
Ricardo, David, 686
Rickey, Branch, 302, 303
Rigidity of employment index, 521f, 521–522
Risk
  arbitrage and, 497
  default, 494
  systemic, 620–621
  tournaments and, 320–321
  trade-off between returns and, 339f, 339–341, 341f
Rival goods, 348, 349t
Rivest, Ron, 469
Robert Nozick's entitlement theory of justice, 372–373

Roberts, Pat, 384t
Robinson, Jackie, 302, 303
Rodriguez, Alex, 305
Rohn and Haas, 246
Rolex, 234
Roll, Richard, 88
Romer, Paul, 471
Roosevelt, Franklin Delano, 663, 694
Rottenberg, Simon, 62, R–1
Rowling, J. K., 373
RR. *See* Reserve ratio (RR)
RSA algorithm, 469
Rule of 70, 338, 338t, 431, 431f
Russia
    Chernobyl accident in, 334
    corruption in, 440
    inflation rate in, 540t
    military expenditure of, 664t
    oil production of, 22
    real GDP per capita in, 406t, 440
Rustici, Thomas, 62, R–1
Rwanda
    corruption in, 440
    real GDP per capita in, 440

S
Safari, 279
Safelite Glass Corporation, 317
Safety, compensating differentials and, 297–298
St. Louis Federal Reserve Bank, 623
Salanie, Bernard, 520, R–2
Salazar, Ken, 384t
Saudi Arabia
    corruption in, 440
    inflation rate in, 540t
    military expenditure of, 664t
    oil production of, 20, 22
    in OPEC, 45n
    real GDP per capita in, 440
Saving, 484–487
    definition of, 484
    inadequate, in United States, 707
    individuals' attempt to smooth
        consumption, 484–485, 485f
    interest rate and, 486–487, 487f
    lifecycle theory of, 487–488, 488f
    marketing and psychological factors and, 486
    time preference and, 485–486
Schumpeter, Joseph, 201, 517
Schwabach, Aaron, R–3
Schwartz, Anna, 502, R–2
Scientists, 469
SDRs. *See* Special drawing rights (SDRs)
Search costs, price ceilings and, 99f, 99–100, 108–109
Second Life, 597
SeeTheInvisibleHand.com, 203
Self-interest, alignment with social interest, 2–3
Sellers, competition with other sellers, 35
Sen, Amartya, 394

Senate Agricultural Committee, 384
Senegal as World Bank borrower, 719
Services
    final, 407
    in GDP, 408, 408f
Sewon America Inc., 274
Shamir, Adi, 469
Sherman Antitrust Act of 1890, 274
Shleifer, Andrei, 315, 501, R–2
Shocks, 589–605, 590f
    to aggregate demand. *See* Aggregate
        demand shocks
    oil, 590–593, 591f–593f
    productivity, negative, 581
    real. *See* Real shocks
    transmission mechanisms and, 593–602
Shoda, Y., 486, R–2
Shortages, 34
    price ceilings and, 98, 98f, 106f, 106–108, 107f
    in Soviet Union, 111
Short run, 205
Short-run aggregate supply *(SRAS)* curve, 570–575
    shifting, 571–572, 572f
    sticky prices and, 574–575
    sticky wages and, 571, 571f
Sierra Leone
    corruption in, 440
    interest rate in, 501t
    real GDP per capita in, 440
Signals
    distortion by price controls, 102
    prices as, 84–85, 88
Silverman, Dan, 306n
The Sims, 227, 228
Singapore
    corruption in, 439, 439t, 440
    economic freedom index and standard
        of living in, 392f
    real GDP per capita in, 440
Slave redemption, elasticity of supply and, 65–68, 66f, 67f
Slovenia, economic freedom index and
    standard of living in, 392f
Smallpox, eradication of, 178
Small-time deposits, 612
Smith, Adam, 2, 3, 84, 149, 195, 441
Smith, Fred, 488–489
Smith, Hedrick, 111
Smith, Vernon, 39–40, 84, R–3
Smith Corona, 85
Smuggling of drugs, 243
Social costs, 170
Social interest, alignment of self-interest
    with, 2–3
Social Security, 528, 655
    government spending for, 662f, 662–664, 663t
    political economy and, 383, 388
Social Security tax, 655, 656, 659–660
Social surplus, 170
Solow, Robert, 563

Solow growth curve, 563–564, 564f
    intertemporal substitution and, 595–596, 595f
    real business cycle model and, 567–570, 568f
    shifts in, 564, 564f
Solow growth rate, 563
Solow model, 452–466
    business fluctuations and, 606–608, 607f, 608f
    catching up versus cutting edge and, 464
    conditional convergence and, 463–464, 464f
    economics of ideas and, 464–466, 465f
    increase in investment rate and, 461–463, 462f
    spreadsheet for exploring, 478–481, 478f–481f
Solvency crisis, 618
Somalia
    corruption in, 439, 439t, 440
    real GDP per capita in, 440
Sony, 278f, 278–279
The Sopranos (TV show), 232, 351
South Africa
    corruption in, 440
    labor market discrimination in, 304–305
    real GDP per capita in, 440
South Korea
    corruption in, 440
    currency crisis of, 718
    economic growth of, 432, 432f, 433, 463
    North Korea compared with, 7, 435–437, 436f
    real GDP per capita in, 406t, 440
    recession in, 46
    saving in, 490–491
Southwest Airlines, 124–125
Soviet Union
    centrally planned economy of, 82
    collectivization of agriculture in, 394
    former, economic growth of, 430f
    productivity in, 317
    shortages of goods in, 111
Sowell, Thomas, R–3
S&P. *See* Standard & Poor's 500 (S&P 500);
        Standard & Poor's (S&P)
SpaceShipOne, 227, 228
Spain
    conditional convergence and, 464f
    corruption in, 440
    government spending in, 671f
    hiring and firing costs in, 522f
    labor force participation of older
        workers in, 528f
    real GDP per capita in, 406t, 440
    taxes and labor force participation in, 529f
    unemployment benefits in, 519, 519t
    unemployment in, 517, 518, 518t
    workweek in, 419t
Spears, Britney, 280, 382
Special drawing rights (SDRs), 705
Specialization, trade and, 143–144
Speculation, 85, 86f, 87–88

Speculative bubbles, 342–343, 343f
Spillovers, 468, 469f
Spindletop, Texas oil well, 22
Sports. *See* Major league sports; *specific teams and leagues*
Spreadsheets
    bond pricing with, 511f, 511–512, 512f
    for calculating compound growth, 447–449, 447f–449f
    Solow model and, 478–481, 478f–481f
Springsteen, Bruce, 291–292
Stabenow, Debbie, 384t
Stalin, Joseph, 394
Standard of living, economic freedom index and, 392f, 392–393
Standard & Poor's (S&P), 494
Standard & Poor's 500 (S&P 500), 336
Standard wars, 278f, 278–279
Staphylococcus aureus, 169
Stata, 246
State taxes, 662
Statistical discrimination, 301
Steady state, 457
Stewart, Martha, 146
Sticky prices, 574–575
Sticky wages, 571, 571f
    as transmission mechanism, 600–601, 601f
Stiglitz, Joseph, 718–719
Stimulus package under Obama, 667, 679, 687, 690
Stock(s), 497
Stock indexes, 336
Stock markets, 331–345, 497–498
    benefits of, 341–342
    compound returns and, 338t, 338–339
    difficulty of beating, 333–335
    diversification and, 335–337
    fees and, 337t, 337–338
    passive vs. active investing in, 331–335, 332f, 333f
    risk and return and, 339f, 339–341, 341f
    speculative bubbles and, 342–343, 343f
Stossel, John, 331
Strategic decision-making, 265
Structural unemployment, 517–524
    employment protection laws and, 521–522, 522f
    factors affecting, 524
    minimum wages and, 520, 520f
    Paris riots and, 522–523
    regulations to reduce, 523
    unemployment benefits and, 519t, 519–520
    unions and, 520–521
Student aid, price discrimination and, 248–250, 249t, 250f
Subsidies, 133–137, 134f, 135f
    agricultural, 385
    Pigouvian, 174–175
    supply and, 24
    to universities, 469
    wage, 136f, 136–137
    water, deadweight loss of, 135–136

Substitutes
    elasticity of demand and, 53–54, 54f, 54t
    price of, demand and, 18, 19f
Substitution, intertemporal, 594–596, 595f, 596f
Sudan, slave redemption in, 65–68, 66f, 67f
Suez Canal, nationalization of, 44
Sugar
    Brazilian production of, 81
    tariff on, 152–153, 153f, 155
Sugar quota, 383–385, 384t
Suharto, Tommy, 226–227
Sulfur dioxide emissions, acid rain and, 177, 180
Summers, Larry, 365
Sunk costs, entry and exit from industries with, 199t, 199–200
Supply
    aggregate. *See* Aggregate demand-aggregate supply model; Short-run aggregate supply *(SRAS)* curve
    of currencies, change in, 710f, 710–711, 711f. *See also* Money supply
    elasticity of. *See* Elasticity of supply
    factors shifting, 23–27
    of labor, 291–293, 292f, 293f
    of money. *See* Money supply
    quantity supplied versus, 43f, 44
    of savings. *See* Saving
    shifts in, change in price from, 68–69
    shifts in, savings and, 490–492, 491f–493f
    tariffs and, 150–152, 151f
    trade and, 149–152, 150f
Supply and demand model. *See also* Equilibrium
    international trade analysis and, 149–152, 150f
    shifting demand and supply curves and, 40–42, 41f, 42f
    Smith's testing of, 39–40
Supply curve. *See also* Short-run aggregate supply *(SRAS)* curve
    definition of, 20
    factors shifting, 23, 24f
    industry. *See* Industry supply curves
    for oil, 20, 21f, 22f, 22–27
    shifts in, 40–42, 41f, 42f
Suriname
    corruption in, 440
    real GDP per capita in, 440
Surpluses, 34
    budget, 667
    capital, 703
    consumer, 16, 16f
    price floors and, 120f, 120–121
    producer, 23, 23f
    social, 170–171
    total, 225
    trade, 702
Sweden
    conditional convergence and, 464f
    corruption in, 440
    government spending in, 671f

labor force participation of older workers in, 528f
    real GDP per capita in, 440
    taxes and labor force participation in, 529f
    workweek in, 419t
Swiss franc
    exchange rates and, 708t
    as global reserve currency, 710
Switzerland
    conditional convergence and, 464f
    corruption in, 439t, 440
    government spending in, 671f
    hiring and firing costs in, 522f
    real GDP per capita in, 440
Syria
    corruption in, 440
    real GDP per capita in, 440
    Yom Kippur War and, 45
Systemic risk, 620–621

T
Tabarrok, Alexander, 468, A–11, R–2, R–3
Taiwan, GDP growth in, 412
Tajikistan
    corruption in, 440
    real GDP per capita in, 440
Tanzania, child labor in, 157f
Tariffs, 581
    Pelosi's call for, 702
    purchasing power parity and, 713
    on sugar, 152–153, 153f, 155
    supply and demand and, 150–152, 151f
TARP. *See* Troubled Asset Recovery Program (TARP)
Tastes, demand and, 19–20
Tax(es), 655–662, 656f
    alternative minimum tax, 659
    on capital gains, 658
    commodity. *See* Commodity taxes
    corporate income tax, 656, 660
    distribution of, 660t, 660–662
    on dividends, 658–659
    flat, 661
    individual income tax, 655, 656–659, 657f
    inflation as, 547–548
    interaction of inflation with, 551–552
    labor force participation and, 529, 529f
    local, 662
    Pigouvian, 173, 175, 181f, 181–182
    progressive, 661
    raising to finance fiscal policy, 683
    regressive, 661
    shifts in aggregate demand curve and, 578
    Social Security and Medicare, 655, 656, 659–660
    state, 662
    supply and, 24–25, 25f
    U.S., future predictions for, 671, 672f
Tax cuts, 685, 688
    government spending versus, 689–690

Tax rebates, 684–685
Taylor, Charles, 439
T-bills, 339, 495–496
T-bonds, 495–496
Technological innovations, supply and, 24
Technological knowledge. *See also* Ideas, economics of
   wealth and, 435
Tejada, Miguel, 305
Temporary Assistance for Needy Families, 665
Term Auction Facility, 617, 619
Thailand
   child labor in, 157f
   corruption in, 440
   currency crisis of, 718
   financial crisis in, 693
   pegging of currency of, 717
   real GDP per capita in, 440
   recession in, 46
Thatcher, Margaret, 300
A Theory of Justice (Rawls), 370
Think Free Office, 276
Thinking on the margin, 5–6
Thune, John, 384t
Time bunching, 598–600, 599f, 600f
Time preference, 485–486
Timex, 234
Togo
   corruption in, 440
   real GDP per capita in, 440
Toshiba, 278f, 278–279
Total consumer surplus, 16, 16f
Total costs, 190
   of production, minimization of, 193f, 193–195, 194f
Total producer surplus, 23, 23f
Total revenues, 190
   elasticity of demand and, 56–58, 57f, 58t
Total surplus, 225
Tournaments, 319
   grades and, 321–322
   risk and, 320–321
Tradable allowances, 179–180
   Pigouvian taxes compared with, 181f, 181–182
Trade. *See* Gains from trade; International trade
Trade deficits, 702–703, 707
Trade-offs, 3–5
   between return and risk, 339f, 339–341, 341f
Trade quotas, 151
   purchasing power parity and, 713
Trade surpluses, 702
Tragedy of the commons, 352f, 352–355
   solutions to, 354–355, 355f
   speed of, 362, 362f, 363f
Transaction costs, 175
Transfer payments, GDP and, 414–415, 415f
Transportation costs, purchasing power parity and, 712–713

Troubled Asset Recovery Program (TARP), 618, 619, 624
Trump, Donald, 489
Tuna fishing, 352
Turkey
   child labor in, 157f
   corruption in, 440
   interest rate in, 501t
   real GDP per capita in, 440
   as World Bank borrower, 719
Turkmenistan
   corruption in, 440
   real GDP per capita in, 440
Turks and Caicos Islands, U.S. dollar as official currency of, 611
20th Century Fox, 279
Tying, 252–253

U

Uganda
   corruption in, 440
   real GDP per capita in, 440
Ukraine
   corruption in, 440
   famine in, under Stalin, 394
   real GDP per capita in, 440
Uncertainty
   entry and exit from industries with, 199t, 199–200
   irreversible investments and, 596–597
Underground economy, GDP and, 417
Unemployment, 513–527
   cyclical, 524, 525f, 526–527
   definition of, 515–516
   frictional, 516–517, 517f
   during recessions, 561–562, 562f
   structural. *See* Structural unemployment
Unemployment insurance
   benefits paid by, 519t, 519–520
   extension of, during recessions, 688
   GDP and, 415
   government spending for, 662, 662f, 665
Unemployment rate, 515
   natural, 526f, 526–527
   value as indicator, 515–516
Unions
   unemployment and, 520–521
   wages and, 299f, 299–300
United Airlines, 225
United Arab Emirates in OPEC, 45n
United Kingdom. *See also* Great Britain
   conditional convergence and, 464f
   corruption in, 439t
   economic growth of, 406t
   government spending in, 671f
   hiring and firing costs in, 522f
   inflation rate in, 540t
   labor force participation of older workers in, 528f
   military expenditure of, 664t
   oil production of, 46
   Suez Crisis and, 44

   taxes and labor force participation in, 529f
   workweek in, 418, 419f
United Kingdom pound, exchange rates and, 708t
United States
   aging of population of, 18, 528, 669
   balance of payments of, 705–706, 706f
   beekeeping in, 175
   business startups in, 441
   child labor in, 157
   conditional convergence and, 464f
   corruption in, 439, 439t, 440
   economic freedom index and standard of living in, 392f
   economic growth of, 430f, 432, 432f, 441, 451, 454
   educational level in, 435
   financial crisis of 2007-2008 in, 619, 679
   foreign aid from, 374–375
   foreign investment in, 706–707
   future predictions for, 670–672, 671f
   GDP growth in, 411
   GDP per capita in, 451
   government borrowing in, 495–496
   government support of culture in, 370
   Great Depression in. *See* Great Depression
   HDTV and, 159
   hiring and firing costs in, 522f
   housing market in, 502–503
   immigration to, 298, 374
   inadequacy of savings in, 707
   infant mortality in, 7
   inflation rate in, 539, 539f, 540t, 541t
   influence on IMF, 718
   Japanese voluntary import restraints and, 145
   labor force participation of older workers in, 528f
   as leading economy of world, 451
   legal system in, 440
   military expenditure of, 664t, 664–665
   minimum wage in, 122
   NAFTA and, 25–26, 26f
   national debt of, 550, 667f, 667–669, 668f
   oil dependence of, 592, 593f
   oil industry in Middle East and, 44
   oil production of, 20, 22
   political business cycles in, 387f, 387–389, 389f
   potential for government bankruptcy in, 669f, 669–672, 670f
   real GDP and infant mortality in, 427, 428f
   real GDP per capita in, 406, 406t, 440
   recapitalization of financial institutions in, 618, 619, 624
   research and development in, 466–467
   taxes and labor force participation in, 529f
   trade deficit of, 702–703, 705–706, 707

underground economy in, 417
unemployment benefits in, 519, 519t
unemployment in, 518t, 520, 520f
wages in, 293–295, 294f, 713
workweek in, 418, 419f
Unit elastic demand, 55
Universal, 279
Universities
    government subsidies to, 469
    price discrimination by, 248–250, 249t, 250f
UPS, 623
Uruguay
    corruption in, 440
    economic freedom index and standard of living in, 392f
    real GDP per capita in, 440
U.S. Airways, 246–247, 248
USA Patriot Act, 383
U.S. Department of Defense, 227, 228
U.S. Department of Housing and Urban Development, 63
U.S. Department of Labor, 409
U.S. dollar
    China's stockpiling of, 705
    dollarization and, 716–717
    exchange rates and, 708t
    pegging of currencies to, 717–718
    as reserve currency, 710
U.S. presidents. See specific presidents' names
U.S. Sugar Beet Association, 384
U.S. Treasury bonds, 495–496
Utilitarianism, 371–372

V
Variable costs, 190
Velocity of money, 542, 545
Venezuela
    corruption in, 440
    economic freedom index and standard of living in, 392f
    interest rate in, 501t
    in OPEC, 45n
    real GDP per capita in, 440
Veronica Mars (TV show), 232
Video game prices, 227, 228
Vietnam
    corruption in, 440
    real GDP per capita in, 440
Vioxx, 3
Vishny, Robert, 315
Volcker, Paul, 637
Voluntary export restraints, 145
Voters. See Political economy

W
Wages
    comparative advantage and, 148–149
    compensating differentials and, 296–299, 297f
    executive compensation and, 319–320
    freeze of, under Nixon, 97
    international differences in, 293–295, 294f
    median, 520
    minimum. See Minimum wage
    pay for performance and, 318–322
    piece rates vs., 316–318
    sticky, 571, 571f, 600–601, 601f
    unions and, 299f, 299–300
    in United States and Mexico, 713
Wage subsidies, 136f, 136–137
Waldfogel, Joel, 251n, 470, R–2
Wal-Mart, 156, 159, 279, 323, 334, 336, 517
Walton, Sam, 323
Warner Brothers, 279
War on drugs, elasticity of demand and, 59–60, 60f
Wascher, William, 59, R–1
Washington, D.C., gun buyback program in, 63–65, 64f
Washington, George, 7, 441
Wasteful lines, price ceilings and, 99, 99f
Water subsidies, deadweight loss and, 135–316
Watson, Mark, 641, R–3
Watts, Duncan J., 280
Wayne's World (TV show), 232
Wealth, 433–435, 434f
    factors of production and, 433–435
    importance of, 6–7
    redistribution of, by inflation, 547–551, 549f, 550t
    Solow model of. See Solow model
The Wealth of Nations (Smith), 2, 195
Wealth shocks, shifts in aggregate demand curve and, 578
Wedge shortcut, 128f, 128–129, 129f
Welch, Finis, 59, R–1
Welch, Jack, 321
Welfare, GDP as measure of, 416–420
Welfare programs, GDP and, 415
Western Europe. See also Europe; specific countries
    influence of, on IMF, 718
WestJet, 125
West Nile virus, 349

Whaples, Robert, 366, 581, R–3
Wheat, futures prices for, 88
When Harry Met Sally (film), 108, 109
WHO. See World Health Organization (WHO)
Wi-Fi, 351–352
Williams, Jay, 51, 65
Williams College, price discrimination by, 248–250, 249t, 250f
Winston, Clifford, 63, R–1
Women. See Female labor force participation
Woods, Tiger, 320, 321–322
WordPerfect, 279
WordStar, 279
Workers compensation insurance, 299
World Bank, 701, 719–720
WorldCom, 499
World Health Organization (WHO), 178
Worldwatch Institute, 88

X
Xbox, 252

Y
Yahoo! Personals, 276
Yarnell Ice Cream, 623
Yemen, child labor in, 157f
Yen
    exchange rates and, 708, 708t
    strength of, 711
Yom Kippur War, 45
YouTube, 342
Yugoslavia, inflation rate in, 541, 541t

Z
Zaire, interest rate in, 501t
Zambia
    child labor in, 157f
    corruption in, 440
    interest rate in, 501t
    real GDP per capita in, 440
Zero profits, 198–199
Zervos, Sara, 498, R–2
Zimbabwe
    corruption in, 440, 704–705
    inflation in, 9, 540t, 541, 541t, 710
    real GDP per capita in, 440
    rule of law in, 439
Zuckerberg, Mark, 466

MACROECONOMICS ESSENTIALS

Basic Relationships and Magnitudes

Gross Domestic Product, GDP, is the market value of all final goods and services produced within a country in a year. (page 71)

GDP per capita is GDP divided by a country's population.

U.S. GDP is approximately $14 trillion and per capita GDP is approximately $47,000 (2009).

The **national spending identity:**

$$Y = C + I + G + NX$$

Y = nominal GDP, C = the market value of consumption goods and services, I = the market value of investment goods (also called capital goods), G = the market value of government purchases, NX = net exports defined as the market value of exports minus the market value of imports. (page 78)

Economic growth is the growth rate of real per capita GDP.

In an average year, U.S. GDP grows by about 3.2% and GDP per capita by about 2.1%. In a recession, GDP declines.

The **Rule of 70:** If the annual growth rate of a variable is x percent, then the doubling time is $\frac{70}{x}$ years.

The **labor force** is all workers, employed plus unemployed. (page 195)

Unemployed workers are adults who do not have a job but who are looking for work. (page 195)

The **unemployment rate** is the percentage of the labor force without a job. (page 195)

The **inflation rate** is the percentage increase in the average level of prices, as measured by a price index, over a period of time. (page 218)

The **Consumer Price Index, CPI,** measures the average price of a large basket of goods bought by a typical American consumer. (page 219)

A **real price** is a price that has been corrected for inflation. Real prices are used to compare the prices of goods over time. (pages 220, 236–239)

The **quantity theory of money:**

$$M \times v = P \times Y_R$$

M = Money supply P = Price level
v = velocity of money Y_R = Real GDP

When v and Y_R are relatively fixed then increases in the money stock, M, must cause increases in the price level, P. (page 222)

The **quantity theory in growth form:**

$$\vec{M} + \vec{v} = \vec{P} + \vec{Y_R}$$
$$\vec{M} + \vec{v} = \text{Inflation} + \text{Real growth}$$

An arrow indicates the growth rate of the indicated variable. For example, $\vec{P}$ is the growth rate of prices (the inflation rate). (page 223)

If $\vec{v}$ and Real growth are relatively fixed then an increase in the growth rate of the money supply, $\vec{M}$, must increase the Inflation rate.